The Literatures of Colonial America

"This is that rare thing, a landmark anthology. Susan Castillo and Ivy Schweitzer reconstruct our view of early American writing and, in the process, make a significant contribution to the rewriting of American literary history. Shifting the critical paradigms as it does, while providing a rich diversity of material, this anthology will undoubtedly be an indispensable resource for students of American literature and history. It will also prove invaluable for anyone wanting to know more about the Americas before the arrival of Europeans, the conflicts and legacy of the colonial period, and the founding of the American nation."

Richard Gray, Professor of Literature at the University of Essex, Editor of the *Journal of American Studies*, and Fellow of the British Academy.

BLACKWELL ANTHOLOGIES

EDITORIAL ADVISERS

Blackwell Anthologies are a series of extensive and comprehensive volumes designed to address the numerous issues raised by recent debates regarding the literary canon, value, text, context, gender, genre, and period. While providing the reader with key canonical writings in their entirety, the series is also ambitious in its coverage of hitherto marginalized texts, and flexible in the overall variety of its approaches to periods and movements. Each volume has been thoroughly researched to meet the current needs of teachers and students.

Victorian Women Poets: An Anthology
Edited by Angela Leighton and Margaret Reynolds

Romanticism: An Anthology. Second Edition
Edited by Duncan Wu

Romantic Women Poets: An Anthology
Edited by Duncan Wu

British Literature 1640–1789: An Anthology
Edited by Robert DeMaria, Jr

Chaucer to Spenser: An Anthology of English Writing 1375–1575
Edited by Derek Pearsall

Renaissance Drama: An Anthology of Plays and Entertainments
Edited by Arthur Kinney

Old and Middle English: An Anthology
Edited by Elaine Treharne

Restoration Drama: An Anthology
Edited by David Womersley

The Victorians: An Anthology of Poetry and Poetics
Edited by Valentine Cunningham

Medieval Drama: An Anthology
Edited by Greg Walker

Nineteenth-Century American Women Writers: An Anthology
Edited by Karen L Kilcup

Nineteenth-Century American Women Poets: An Anthology
Edited by Paula Bernat Bennett

American Gothic: An Anthology 1787–1916
Edited by Charles L. Crow

Native American Women Writers: An Anthology of Works c.1800–1924
Edited by Karen L. Kilcup

Children's Literature: An Anthology 1801–1902
Edited by Peter Hunt

Forthcoming

Renaissance Literature: An Anthology
Edited by Michael Payne and John Hunter

Gothic Novels: An Anthology
Edited by Nicola Trott

Modernism: An Anthology
Edited by Lawrence Rainey

Early African-American Literature: An Anthology
Edited by Phillip M. Richards

THE LITERATURES OF COLONIAL AMERICA

AN ANTHOLOGY

EDITED BY **SUSAN CASTILLO**
AND **IVY SCHWEITZER**

Copyright © Blackwell Publishers Ltd 2001
Introduction, notes, arrangement, and apparatus copyright © Susan Castillo and Ivy Schweitzer 2001

First published 2001

2 4 6 8 10 9 7 5 3 1

Blackwell Publishers Inc.
350 Main Street
Malden, Massachusetts 02148
USA

Blackwell Publishers Ltd
108 Cowley Road
Oxford OX4 1JF
UK

Library of Congress Cataloging-in-Publication Data

The literatures of colonial America : an anthology / edited by Susan Castillo and Ivy T. Schweitzer.
    p.   cm. — (Blackwell anthologies)
  Includes bibliographical references and index.
  ISBN 0-631-21124-1 (hbk. : alk. paper). — ISBN 0-631-21125-X (pbk. : alk. paper)
    1. American literature—Colonial oeriod, ca. 1600–1775. 2. United
States—History—Colonial period, ca. 1600–1775—Literary collections.   3. United
States—History—Colonial period, ca. 1600–1775—Sources.   4. United
States—Literatures—Translations into English.   I. Castillo, Susan P., 1948–   II. Schweitzer,
Ivy.   III. Series.

PS531 .L58   2001
810.8′001—dc21

00-042933

British Library Cataloguing in Publication Data

A CIP catalogue record for this book is available from the British Library.

Commissioning Editor: Andrew McNeillie
Development Editor: Alison Dunnett
Desk Editor: Paul Stringer
Picture Researcher: Leanda Shrimpton

Typeset in 10½ on 12 pt Garamond 3
by Ace Filmsetting Ltd, Frome, Somerset
Printed in Great Britain by T.J. International, Padstow, Cornwall

This book is printed on acid-free paper.

Contents

From *Chapter 88: Of the great and solemn Montezuma's great and solemn reception of Cortés and of all of us on our entrance into Mexico*

Early next day we left Iztapalapa with a large escort of those great Caciques, and followed the highway, which is eight paces in width and goes so straight to the city of Mexico that I do not think it curves at all. Broad though it was, it was so crowded with people that there was hardly room for them all, some going to Mexico and others coming away, besides those who had come out to see us, and we could hardly get through the crowds that were there. For the towers and the *cues*[5] were full, and they came in canoes from all parts of the lake. It was hardly to be wondered at, since they had never seen horses or men like us before!

Gazing on such wonderful sights, we did not know what to say, or whether what we saw before our eyes was real. On the land side there were great cities, and on the lake many more. The lake itself was crowded with canoes. At intervals along the highway there were many bridges, and before us was the great city of Mexico. As for us we were fewer than four hundred strong, and we well remembered the words and warnings given to us by the people of Huexotzinco and Tlaxcala and Tlamanalco, and the many other warnings we had received to beware of entering the city of Mexico, where they would kill us as soon as they had us inside. Let the curious reader consider whether there is not much to ponder over in this account of mine. What men in all the world have ever shown such daring? But let us go on.

We marched along our highway to a point where another small highway leading to another city called Coyoacan branches off, and there, beside some buildings like towers, which were their shrines, we were met by many more Caciques and dignitaries clad in very rich mantles. The different chieftains wore different brilliant liveries, and the highways were crowded with them. Montezuma had sent these great Caciques in advance to receive us, and as soon as they came before Cortés they told him in their language that we were welcome, and as a sign of peace, they touched the ground with their hands and kissed it.

There we halted for a good while while Cacamatzin, the lord of Texcoco, and the lords of Iztapalapa, Tacuba, and Coyoacan went ahead to meet the great Montezuma, who was approaching in a rich litter, accompanied by other great lords and feudal Caciques who owned vassals. When we came near to Mexico, at a place where there were some other small towers, the great Montezuma got down from his litter, and these other great Caciques supported him beneath a marvelously rich canopy of green feathers, decorated with gold work, silver, pearls, and *chalchihuites*[6] suspended from a sort of border. It was a marvelous sight. The great Montezuma was magnificently clad, according to their fashion, and wore a kind of sandals for which their name is *cotaras*, the soles of which are of gold and the upper parts adorned with precious stones. The four lords who supported him were also richly clad in garments which had apparently been kept ready for them on the road to enable them to accompany their prince. For they did not appear in such attire when they came out to receive us. There were four other great Caciques who carried the canopy above their heads, and many more lords who walked before the great Montezuma, sweeping the ground on which he was to tread, and spreading down cloaks so that his feet should not touch the earth. Not one of these chieftains dared to look him in the face, but kept their eyes lowered most reverently, except those four lords, his nephews, who were supporting him.

When Cortés saw, heard, and was told that the great Montezuma was approaching, he dismounted from his horse, and when he drew near to Montezuma each bowed deeply to the

---

[5]   Prayer-houses.   [6]   Jadeite stones.

Preface

In recent years, the field of American Studies has undergone a paradigm shift. In her Presidential Address to the American Studies Association in 1998, Janice Radway called for the recognition that American Studies has often been synonymous with the study of the United States, and urged members to reconceptualize the object of our discipline with respect to other nations and groups outside the territorial boundaries of the US that have created their own vision of what it means to be American. In Montreal in 1999, Mary Kelley in her Presidential Address to the same group, repeated this call. As teachers and scholars of the early period, we took these as a challenge to renovate our own work and our conception of the field. This anthology, a joint project, grew out of that commitment.

The controversy provoked by Radway's speech bears witness to the investment of many intellectuals in the myth of a unitary, exceptional "America." In an age of globalization, it has indeed become increasingly difficult to characterize the United States as culturally homogenous and impermeable to influences beyond its territorial boundaries. The reality and importance of such transculturation, however, is nothing new; for instance, it is possible but increasingly intellectually reductive to study the Arcadian imagery – and the underlying political agendas – of early English colonial writers without taking into account Spanish texts of the same period which preceded and materially shaped English colonial ambitions. In the rapidly expanding area of transnational studies, critics and readers are faced with the challenge of grasping the complex interrelationships between different groups and cultural practices, and conceptualizing the socially produced and constantly shifting hierarchies that resulted from the imperial expansion of the European powers. It is also important to bear in mind that the process of colonization was not a one-way street in which Europeans imposed their ideologies and social structures upon a passive continent, but rather, as Fernando Ortiz, Mary Louise Pratt and Michel de Certeau have suggested, an intricate series of interactions of power and resistance in which the individuals and groups concerned produced lasting effects upon one another.

When we began to prepare this anthology in 1997, it is fair to say that we did not have the slightest inkling of the magnitude of the task facing us. Although there are excellent collections of English colonial texts, such as Myra Jehlen and Michael Warner's *The English Literatures of America, 1500–1800*, which covers a similar period to this anthology, there was no single book that brought together texts from diverse linguistic and cultural traditions which could be used as a basis for transnational analysis. *The Heath Anthology of American Literature* has made an important effort to include non-canonical works by women and writers of color from the early period in North America. Continuing this effort, we have sought to include works from other parts of North America, such as New France, New Spain, New Netherland, the Chesapeake and West Indies, and other areas of the Americas. It has been a challenge, as every canonical intervention is, to include familiar, time-tested works and, at the same time, find room for unfamiliar writers from underrepresented areas of the Americas whose perspectives modify and enrich our understanding of colonial experiences and the multivocal trajectory of American identities across three centuries. We have tried, in our selections, to take Radway's and Kelley's exhortations to heart, and provide readers with opportunities to compare and contrast writing from across the vast land mass called the New World, from its putative "discovery," when the indigenous population became known as "native Americans," to the dawn of nationalism in the eighteenth century.

Editing *The Literatures of Colonial America: An Anthology* has been a transatlantic undertaking in the most literal sense, with e-mail enclosures/attachments flying back and forth in cyberspace between Glasgow and Vermont. Initially, we determined that the English language texts would be edited by Ivy Schweitzer, while the foreign-language texts would be edited and, in some cases, translated, by Susan Castillo. Nonetheless, there has been a constant interchange of ideas, questions, and suggestions, a true international intellectual exchange in the most positive and dynamic sense. Our major challenge has been selecting which texts to anthologize from the amazing wealth of material we gathered and unearthed. We decided not to include long works, such as five act plays and long prose texts that are available in inexpensive editions. We also felt that, except in a few cases, excerpts of novels were unsatisfactory, and better left out. We did not have room to include everything we thought fascinating or important, and because of limitations on space, in some cases we could not include full texts, and selected the most salient parts. For many of the more familiar writers, we chose to include personal narratives as opposed to their more public works, as particularly revealing of colonial subjectivity. We also had to decide about the presentation of texts, especially modernization of spelling, punctuation and capitalization. In general and where possible, the English texts appear in the original versions, as do early English translations of foreign texts, to give readers a sense of how these texts looked at the time of publication. However, because these features were quite erratic up to and including the eighteenth century, we sometimes modified texts for consistency or clarification. Works translated for the first time here are presented in modern English. The source for a selection is indicated in the list of "Primary Works." When the source we use differs from the first or major modern edition of a work, we indicate that in a footnote.

The organization of the anthology evolved out of our growing reluctance to impose categories on the selections. Even the division into centuries feels artificial, but is a convenient way of defining the broad issues that characterize different phases of colonial development: exploration, colonization, nationalism. Parts One and Three are organized chronologically by author to allow teachers to group writers and texts thematically or generically as it suits their needs. Selections in Part Two are grouped according to region in order to foreground the development of sectional identities that emerge in the seventeenth century as European powers stake their claims to different parts of the New World. In Part One, we have highlighted indigenous voices where possible, to leaven the heavy weight of exploration narratives written from European perspectives. In Part Two, we bring other colonial outposts into focus against the purely academic dominance of New England. In Part Three, we only had room to offer glimpses of later colonial voices, often characterized by a growing awareness of racial and

gender identities, and illuminated by a volatile discourse of natural rights, liberty, and equality – the discourse of Enlightenment-driven revolutions which exploded during this period in
several parts of the world. Introductions to each part situate the selections in historical and
cultural contexts. The introductory headnotes give biographical, critical, and contextual information for each writer, and suggest questions about the selections that readers can pursue
further.

Although one phase of our work on *The Literatures of Colonial America: An Anthology* is
complete, its publication will, we hope, contribute to the next phase in which an expanding
canon and shifting paradigm will bring the "New World" into clearer and fuller focus.

Acknowledgments

We would like to express our gratitude to the following individuals and institutions:

Colleagues at Glasgow University: Jean Anderson, Richard Cronin, Robert Cummings, Stuart Gillespie, Andrew Hook, Alice Jenkins, Vassiliki Kolotroni, Donald Mackenzie, Willy Maley, Rob Maslen, Elizabeth Moignard, Marina Moskowitz, Simon Newman, David Pascoe, Seamus Perry, Nicola Trott, and Vassiliki Kolocotroni. Special thanks go to Duncan Wu for his constant support and encouragement; the anthology would never have happened without his help.

Friends in other institutions: Janet Beer, Richard Gray, Jay Kleinberg, James Massender, Judie Newman, Michael McDonnell, Alan Velie.

To Father Charles Coffrey, SJ, for information about saints and their lives.

Thanks to the Arts Faculty and to the Department of English Literature of Glasgow University for Susan Castillo's term of research leave, and to Glasgow University Library.

Colleagues at Dartmouth College: Anne Brooks for giving an initial push, Bill Cook, Jonathan Crewe, Marty Favor, Marianne Hirsch, Alexis Jetter, Mary Kelley, Agnes Lugo-Ortiz, Tom Luxon, Annelise Orleck, Matthew Rowlinson, William Spengemann, Silvia Spitta, James Tatum, Melissa Zeiger. Special thanks go to Colin Calloway who unstintingly shared his expertise on Native America, and to Barbara Will, who put us in touch with each other in the first place.

Many thanks to the Dickey Center at Dartmouth College for generously funding Ivy Schweitzer's trip to Glasgow in July 1999 and to Susanne Zantop, Parents Distinguished Research Professor in the Humanities, for covering costs related to the use of images.

And to the indefatigable librarians at Baker Library, Special Collections and the Microtext Center at Dartmouth College, especially Patsy Carter at Interlibrary loan.

Other crucial, unofficial consultants whose expertise, encouragement and friendship were invaluable: Ralph Bauer, Paula Bennett, Michelle Burnham, Elizabeth Dillon, Jim Egan, Susan Imbarrato, Dana Nelson, David Shields, Frank Shuffleton, David Watters. And Richard Slotkin, who advised us wisely early in the project.

Last, but not least, the research assistants, who not only made most of this project possible by doing much of the basic work of photocopying and scanning, but whose dedication, enthusiasm and intelligence inspire us as teachers and scholars: Debra Brodsky, Kelly Keene, Greg Marx, Hilary Wolkoff, and the incomparable Kinohi Nishikawa.

Andrew McNeillie, Jennifer Lambert, Alison Dunnett of Blackwell Publishers who helped see the project through, and especially Andrew, whose enthusiasm and support carried us through the darkest hours.

Most especially, to our families.

The publishers gratefully acknowledge the following for permission to reproduce copyright material. Although every effort has been made to trace copyright holders, in some cases it has proved impossible. The publishers would be happy to hear from any copyright holder that has not been acknowledged.

Extract from "The Origin Myth of Acoma and Other Records" by Matthew Stirling from *Smithsonian Institution Bureau of American Ethnology Bulletin*, 135, 1942.

Extract from *Seneca Myths and Folk Tales*, edited by Arthur C. Parker, published by University of Nebraska Press 1989.

Extract from *The Trickster* by Paul Radin, published by Philosophical Library, New York 1969. Used with permission.

Extract from *Popol Vuh: The Sacred Book of the Ancient Quiché Maya* by Adrian Recinos, translated by Delia Goetz and Sylvanus G. Morely, published by University of Oklahoma Press. Used with permission.

Extract translated from *Historia de las Indias – Bartolomé de Las Casas* published in 1965 by Fondo de Cultura Economica. Used with permission.

Extract from *The Voyages of Giovanni da Verrazzano 1524–1528* published by Yale University Press. (Translation of the Cellere Codex by Susan Tarrow.) Reprinted with permission.

Extract from *The Broken Spears* by Miguel Leon-Portilla © 1962, 1990 by Miguel Leon-Portilla. Expanded and Updated Edition © 1992 by Miguel Leon-Portilla. Reprinted by permission of Beacon Press, Boston.

Extract from *A Picture of the Inca Civilisation*, edited by Chrisopher Dilke. Reprinted with permission of Mrs. A. M. Dilke.

Extract from *Historia de la Neuva Mexico, 1610* by Gaspar Pérez de Villagrá, translated and edited by Miguel Encinias, Alfred Rodriguez, and Joseph P. Sanchez, printed by University of New Mexico Press. Used with permission.

Extract from *Spanish-American Literature in Translation*, edited by Willis Knapp Jones, published by Ungar in 1963. Reprinted by permission of Continuum Publishing, New York.

Extracts from *Sor Juana Inés de la Cruz: Poems* (1985), translated by Margaret Sayers Peden, published by Bilingual Press, Arizona State University, Tempe, AZ. Reprinted with permission.

Extract from *Historical Documents relating to New Mexico, Nueva Vizcaya and Approaches Thereto, to 1773*, collected by Adolph and Fanny Bandelier; English translations, edited and annotated by Charles Wilson Hackett (1937); published by Carnegie Institution, Washington DC. Used with permission.

Extracts translated from *Anthologie de la Littérature Québécoise, Vol. 2, Écrits de la Nouvelle France*, edited by Leopold LeBlanc, Published by La Presse, Montreal. Reprinted with permission.

Extract from *The Complete Works of Captain John Smith, 1580–1631*, edited by Philip L. Barbour, with a foreword by Thad W. Tate. Copyright © 1986 by the University of North Carolina Press. Used by permission of the publisher.

Extract from *The Discoveries of John Lederer* (Charlottesville, University of Virginia Press, 1958), Tracy W. McGregor Library of American History, Special Collections Department, University of Virginia Library. Used with permission.

Extract from "The Poor Unhappy Transported Felon's Sorrowful Account of his Fourteen Years Transportation at Virginia America," edited by John Melville Jennings, from *Virginia Historical Magazine*, Vol. 56, No. 2, 1948. Reprinted with permission of Virginia Historical Society, Richmond, VA.

Extract from "A Modell of Christian Charity" taken from *The Winthrop Papers*, edited by A. Forbes, published by the Massachusetts Historical Society, Vol. 2, 1931. Reprinted with permission of Massachusetts Historical Society.

Extract from *The Correspondence of Roger Williams*, edited by Glen LaFantasie, Copyright © 1988, The Rhode Island Historical Society. Reprinted with permission of University Press of New England.

Extract from *The Autobiography of Thomas Shepard*, edited by Allyn B. Forbes, published by Colonial Society of Massachusetts, and used with permission.

Extracts from *Poems*, edited by Donald Stanford (poems of Edward Taylor), published by Yale University Press, 1960.

Extract of text from *Truth of a Hopi: Stories relating to the origin, myths, and clan histories of the Hopi*, Copyright © 1936, 1967, by Edmund Nequatewa, published by Northland Publishing in cooperation with the Museum of Northern Arizona. Used with permission.

Extract from *The Prose Works of William Byrd of Westover*, edited by Louis B. Wright (Cambridge, MA: The Belknap Press of Harvard University Press, Copyright © 1966 by the President and Fellows of Harvard College). Used with permission.

Extract from *Images of Divine Things, Vol. 11, The Works of Jonathan Edwards Typological Writings*, edited by Wallace Anderson and Mason Lowance Jr, published by Yale University Press.

Extract from *Journeys in New Worlds: Early American Women's Narratives*, edited by Daniel B. Shea, published by The University of Wisconsin Press, Wisconsin. © 1990. Reprinted with permission of The University of Wisconsin Press.

Extract from *El Lazarillo: A Guide for Inexperienced Travelers between Buenos Aires and Lima 1773*, translated by Walter D. Kline, published by Indiana University Press 1965. Used with permission.

Extract from *The Journal and Major Essays of John Woolman*, edited by Phillips P. Moulton, editor and copyright holder, published in 1971 by Oxford University Press. Reprinted by permission.

Extract from Bossu's *Travels in the Interior of North America, 1751–1762*, translated and edited by Seymour Feiler, published by University of Oklahoma Press. Used with permission of the University of Oklahoma Press.

Extract from *Adventure in the Wilderness: The American Journals of Louis Antoine de Bougainville, 1756–1760*, translated by Edward P. Hamilton, published by University of Oklahoma Press. Used with permission of the University of Oklahoma Press.

Extract from Rafael Landívar's *Rusticatio Mexicana*, on pages 155–306 of 11 *Philological and Documentary Studies*, Vol. 1, published by Middle American Research Institute. Reprinted courtesy of the Middle American Research Institute, Tulane University, New Orleans, Louisiana, USA.

Extract from *The Adams–Jefferson Letters: The Complete Correspondence of Thomas Jefferson and Abigail and John Adams*, edited by Lester Cappon. Copyright © 1959 by the University of North Carolina Press, renewed 1987 by S. B. Cappon. Used by permission of the publisher.

Extract from *The Papers of John Adams, Volume IV, February 1776 to August 1776*, edited by Robert J. Taylor, Gregg L. Lint, and Celeste Walker, published by Harvard University Press, Cambridge, MA. Copyright © 1979 by the Massachusetts Historical Society. Reprinted by permission of the publishers.

Extract from *Adams Family Correspondence, Volumes 1 and 2, December 1761—March 1778*, edited by L. H. Butterfield, Wendell D. Garrett, and Marjorie E. Sprague. Copyright © 1963 by the Massachusetts Historical Society. Extracts from *Adams Family Correspondence, Volumes 3 and 4, December 1761–March 1778*, edited by L. H. Butterfield and Marc Friedlander. Copyright © 1973 by the Massachusetts Historical Society. (Published by The Belknap Press, of Harvard University Press: Cambridge, MA.) Reprinted by permission of the publishers.

Extract from *The Complete Writings of Thomas Paine*, edited by Philip S. Foner, published in 1945 by Citadel Press. Reprinted by permission of Carol Publishing Group, Secaucus, NJ.

Extract from *Thomas Jefferson: Writings*, edited by Merrill D. Peterson, published by Library of America 1984.

Extracts from "Poems, 1773" in *Collected Works of Phillis Wheatley*, edited by Richard Newman, published by Oxford University Press, New York 1988.

Extract from *The Novels and Related Works of Charles Brockden Brown*, Bicentennial Edition, Vol. 6 *Alcuin* Part One (1771–1810), published by The Kent State University Press. Used with permission of the publishers.

Part One:
Exploration and Contact to 1600

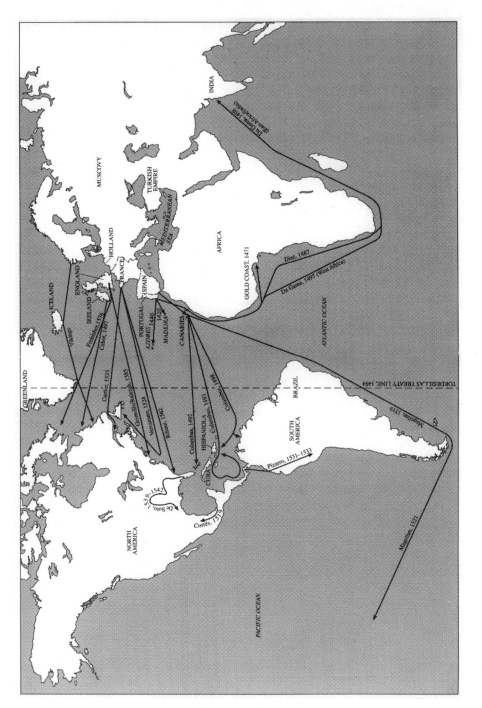

"The Age of Exploration." From Richard Middleton, *Colonial America*, 2nd edn (Oxford: Blackwell Publishers, 1997). (With permission of the author.)

Introduction

Although it was the famous voyage of Christopher Columbus in 1492 that opened the way for the European exploration of the Americas, many others had adventured to this "new world" before him. Leif Erickson and the Vikings explored up and down the northern coasts of North America, even establishing a short-lived settlement on the tip of Newfoundland around AD 1000. Hints in some accounts suggest the Chinese explored the southern coast of California, and recent evidence indicates that Africans may have traveled to the Americas a century before the Europeans. Columbus' expedition was actually one of many European attempts to find a sea route to Asia, a competition made imaginable by the travels of the Venetian merchant, Marco Polo, in China in the thirteenth century.

The competition was set off in 1415 by Portugal, which possessed considerable maritime expertise and was well situated geographically for ocean exploration. Portugal established its first colony in Ceuta, in Northern Africa, which gave it control of the western Mediterranean. From the 1420s, Prince Henry the Navigator sponsored many expeditions along the coast of Africa and the eastern Atlantic. In the 1440s Portugal established sugar plantations in the Azores, the first outside the Mediterranean to be worked by African slaves. In 1487, Bartholomew Diaz navigated past the Gold coast and rounded Africa's Cape of Good Hope. Vasco de Gama completed the route to the East in 1498 when he reached India, thus avoiding the Turks who held the eastern Mediterranean. Spain, newly united and strengthened by the marriage between Ferdinand and Isabella, wanted to gain control of the Atlantic. Seeking another route to Asia that bypassed Turkey, the Spanish crown sent out Columbus, an Italian explorer. Working under the completely speculative assumption that the world was round, not flat as the medieval world had thought, Columbus was trying to sail west to Asia when he stumbled upon the Americas. What would become the largest component of Europe's western expansion was, at first, just a barrier to the east.

It was also a disappointing barrier. Little if any gold, precious metals or exotic spices and silks were found among the native inhabitants, and little else seemed of interest. As a result, Columbus fell into disgrace and distraction, maintaining till the end that he had discovered India; hence, the name "Indians" from *los indios*, the name he gave the indigenous peoples. Still, the idea of the "discovery" – from a European perspective – of a New World caught the European imagination. Explorers like John Cabot and his sons, Giovanni da Verrazzano, Jacques Cartier, and Henry Hudson continued to search for a Northwest Passage to Asia, making unforeseen discoveries and bringing back stories that fascinated avid readers. It was another Italian, Amerigo Vespucci from Florence, whose account of his exploration of the South American coast in 1499 really sparked European interest, and so the lands he explored were named "America" in his honor. Fascination with geography and exploration, for both trade and conquest, increased. Spain took the lead in exploring and settling the Americas, repeating the success it had on the Mediterranean coast and Canary Islands of establishing ranching, sugar and tobacco production in the West Indies. Not to be outdone, and embracing the Spanish model – down to employing an adventurous Italian mariner – England's King Henry VII issued the following "letters patent" in 1497 to John Cabot which express succinctly the imperialistic Eurocentric attitude of the early explorations:

> Be it known that we have given and granted . . . to our well beloved John Cabot, citizen of Venice full and free authority, leave and power to sail to all parts, countries, and seas of the East, of the West, and of the North under our banners and ensigns . . . to seek out, discover and find whatsoever isles, countries, regions or provinces of the heathen and infidels whatsoever they be, and in what part of the world soever they be which before this time have been unknown to all Christians. We have granted to them . . . license to set up our banner and ensigns in every village, town, castle or mainland newly found by them which they can subdue, occupy and possess as our vassals and lieutenants, getting unto us the rule, title and jurisdiction of the same villages, towns, castles and firm land so found.

"Subdue, occupy and possess" they did. Spain's influence would spread all through South and Central America, and into Florida and southwestern North America, while England and France vied over eastern North America until the mid-eighteenth century, when English influence would eventually prevail.

When disputes began to brew over who controlled these far-flung lands, Pope Alexander VI intervened, and Spain and Portugal simply divided the non-Christian world between them. According to the Treaty of Tordesillas of 1494, everything west of an imaginary line in the Atlantic 370 leagues (about 1,000 miles) from the Cape Verde islands belonged to Spain and everything to the east to Portugal. The discovery of Brazil in 1500 by the fleet of Pedro Alvares Cabral, suggests that Portugal knew of its existence before the treaty, and negotiated the division of power accordingly. Initially, Portugal's territories in Africa and Asia were its main focus, while Spain only gradually realized the enormous possibilities of the New World. Spain continued occupying and subjugating islands in the Caribbean. Expeditions sent by Diego Velázquez, Governor of Cuba, made contact with the great Maya civilizations of Yucatán, and brought reports of the untold wealth of Aztec Mexico. In 1519 Hernán Cortés entered Mexico, and with the help of Native groups who were enemies of the Aztecs, overthrew Montezuma and conquered the extensive Aztec empire. By the 1520s the mines of Mexico and those of Bolivia two decades later were providing Spain with large quantities of gold and silver. Some years later, the reports of Alvar Núñez Cabeza de Vaca of golden cities to the north prompted expeditions to the southern part of what is now the United States, by Hernando de Soto and Francisco Vázquez Coronado. In the meantime, Francisco Pizarro and his stepbrothers Gonzalo and Hernando proceeded with the conquest of the Inca empire in 1531.

The consequences of contact with the European colonizers were little short of disastrous for the peoples of the New World. The population dwindled drastically, not only from direct violence and ill health resulting from economic exploitation, but also from European diseases such as smallpox and measles. In some areas, the population was reduced by almost 90 percent. Portugal made up for this drastic reduction of available labor with which to exploit the new territories by importing slaves from Africa, with a first shipment arriving in Hispaniola in 1510. Spain developed the *encomienda* system, in which Native groups were entrusted to Spanish proprietors charged with their physical and spiritual welfare, but who in practice often viewed them as a source of cheap and expendable labor. The *encomienda* system was the natural outgrowth of the belief, defended by Spanish theologians such as Ginés de Sepulveda and based on Aristotelian philosophy, that some peoples were naturally inferior and destined to be slaves. Other Spaniards such as Bartolomé de Las Casas, however, defended the rights of the Native peoples at considerable personal cost. Tragically, the Europeans' initial sense of wonder and strangeness on encountering Native peoples vanished quickly, giving way to a complex, hierarchical caste system based on racial difference and ethnic purity.

Although it is true that European explorers and priests were largely incapable of accepting the different worldviews of the Natives or the validity of their cultures, they were keen observers of the new lands and peoples they had encountered, and their accounts are characterized by the constant attempt to render the New World intelligible to their European readers. References abound to the act of naming islands, bays, regions and even groups of human beings, as though by doing so it was possible to lay claim to them and subjugate them by binding them within language. Other constant preoccupations are the permeability (or resistance) of the Native peoples to European ideology and the constant search of the Europeans for sources of material wealth.

Although France sent out some early explorers, their efforts only began to reap significant success in the seventeenth century. French explorers initially focused on the land around the St Lawrence River, Newfoundland, and Acadia or Nova Scotia, later expanding to much of the Great Lakes region and the West. The name Gallia Nova (New France) first appeared on a map prepared by a brother of Giovanni da Verrazzano, who had explored the coasts of North America on behalf of France in 1524. Ten years later, Jacques Cartier sailed up the Bay of St Lawrence and took possession of New France for King Francis I, later attempting to found a colony near what is now Quebec. Though this attempt ended in failure, it lay the foundations for the extensive French fur trade with the Indians of the St Lawrence area. For the rest of the sixteenth century, French energies were mostly directed to settlements in Brazil at Guanabara Bay, near Rio de Janeiro, and Florida, both ultimately unsuccessful. Jean Ribaut's attempts to found a colony in northern Florida as a refuge for French Protestants who were being threatened with persecution at home, merely encouraged Spain to redouble its efforts.

Like France, England was politically weak and so was also relatively late getting into the race for empire. In the early sixteenth century when Portugal and Spain were busy with their new territories in South America, the Protestant Reformation swept across northern Europe, temporarily stalling England's imperial activities. Queen Elizabeth's ascension to the throne at mid-century helped stabilize the country, and interest in exploration rekindled with Martin Frobisher's attempts to find a Northwest Passage in 1576. Two years later, the Queen granted a patent to Sir Humphrey Gilbert for the discovery and settlement of the vast tract of land called "Virginia" which stretched from Canada to Florida. Both of these attempts ended in failure, and after Gilbert drowned off the coast of Newfoundland in 1583, his half-brother Sir Walter Ralegh took up the patent, enlisted the help of several influential men, and began sending out expeditions. These first attempts tried to reduplicate the Spanish success: at the behest of the crown, groups of armed men came to unknown lands searching for precious metals or pearls, relying on limited food supplies or what they could get or cajole from the natives. The strong-arm tactics of Sir Richard Grenville and his successor Ralph Lane, the first "governors" of the English settlement – really a fortification – at Roanoke Island off the coast of what is now North Carolina, ended in a succession of failures, culminating with the mysterious disappearance of the second colony, which included the first child to be born to English parents in North America named, appropriately, Virginia Dare. Permanent English settlement in the New World did not begin until John Smith took over the command of the Jamestown settlement in 1608 and enforced a regimen of agricultural cultivation and hunting that would eventually make the colony self-sustaining. Central to the English endeavor was the work of Richard Hakluyt (1553–1616), a scholar and clergyman who as a boy became fascinated with maps and explorations and devoted his life to compiling and editing accounts of European voyages of discovery. In 1589 he published his major compilation, *Principal Navigations, Traffiques, Voyages, and Discoveries of the English Nation*, which was greatly enlarged in 1598–1600. All of the English selections in Part I come from this compilation, which also contained many translations, and stands as a register of what was known about world exploration by the end of the sixteenth century. Hakluyt not only made these narratives available to an eager public, but he also advanced a theory of "plantation," as opposed to naked military conquest, to influential explorers like Ralegh, and in so doing, energized and redirected the great exploring spirit of the Elizabethan age.

Exploration of the New World generated tremendous excitement among European readers hungry for glimpses of what they thought might be an earthly paradise or Arcadian idyll populated by gentle savages. Sponsors interested in continued support for their ostensibly fruitless and very expensive expeditions wanted to prolong that fascination, and so demanded optimistic accounts from the men they sent into the unknown. Some of the accounts in Part 1 were written specifically as promotional literature designed to boost public support and private interest and investment in the exploration and plantation ventures. Thus, it is sometimes hard to separate factual content from wish fulfillment, revealing as they do the ways in which Europeans attempted to affirm the superiority of European ideologies and cultures while at the same time justifying their eagerness to learn more about the landscape and peoples of the New World. Often, these writers come to the brink of the unspeakable: how to describe something completely outside of their realms of experience or knowledge, for which they have no words. Often, they fall back on the trope of comparison – the New described in sometimes incongruous terms of the Old – or on allusions to the ancient world and their myths, and certainly on hyperbole and apostrophe. "O brave new world," Shakespeare's Miranda exclaims rapturously in his "New World" drama *The Tempest*. She is meant to be the innocent struck with true wonder but, of course, she is only seeing ordinary, Old World men for the first time. Still, just the mention of the "New World" conjures up a sense of pristine vision and utter – here welcomed – difference.

The English poet John Donne also wittily turned the trope of New World exploration to reveal complex erotics beneath the rhetoric of imperial conquest used by his rival and the court favorite, Sir Walter Ralegh. Seeing his mistress before him in all her natural glory, he exclaims:

> Oh my America, my new founde lande.
> My kingdome, safeliest when with one man man'd,
> My myne of precious stones, my Empiree,
> How blest am I in this discovering thee.
>
> (from *Elegie* XIX)

Gendered descriptions of the New World had become conventional in this early literature of exploration, and perform a complicated ideological task. Columbus, for example, came to believe that the world "is not round as [Ptolmey and other geographers] describe it, but the shape of a pear; which is round everywhere except at the stalk, where it juts out a long way . . .

something like a woman's nipple." In his speaker's mimicry of Ralegh's proposed seduction of the New World, Donne employs sexual difference to imply the androcentric power hierarchy underlying this fantasy of conquest. The lover is compared to an explorer who discovers and possesses, while the beloved is depicted as the realm explored, an object of great interest and value but without agency. Her silence characterizes her as Europeans imagined and hoped the New World would be, unoccupied and unclaimed, passive and receptive, or desirous for "civilization." Furthermore, as the New World is likened to a new Eden, so the lover is metaphorically the new Adam. But since the beloved is the terrain of newness and pleasure, she is not a new Eve, and the Eden she provides becomes a paradise of one, where her nakedness suggests not sexual innocence but availability without protest and without guilt. This gendered fantasy of conquest reaches its most popular cultural form in the "myth" of Pocahontas from the settlement of Jamestown or the story of Inkle and Yarico from the West Indies, tales in which the romance between a native "princess" and white colonist underwrites Western imperial expansion.

What Columbus could not have known is that the most important product he could bring back from the New World was the knowledge and experience of newness, which provided a mirror for the old European self. Nonetheless, our view of the cultures on the other side of Columbus' mirror, our knowledge of Native oral literatures and cultures and even of the written texts of Central America, is at best diffuse, overlaid by layers of linguistic translation (for example, into Spanish, in the case of the Mayan *Chilam Balam*) and years of cultural accretions, or even more insidiously, distorted by the effort of the Europeans to translate the difference of native cultures into something intelligible for their readers. Indeed, both Europeans and Natives were often literally at a loss for words when they attempted to describe one another, and the texts which follow illustrate not only the interaction between diverse peoples and worldviews but also of language stretched to the limits by the vitality and radical uncertainty of human beings confronted by the opacity of difference.

Before Columbus:
Native American Cultures

The Pre-Columbian World

We still know relatively little about the New World before contact with European explorers. Although early writers thought that the indigenous people of what they called "America" were one of the Lost Tribes of Israel, or else survivors of the lost continent of Atlantis, most anthropologists agree that the groups we now call Native Americans in all probability arrived between 15,000 and 30,000 years ago from Asia across a land bridge that existed in the Ice Ages connecting Siberia to Alaska. They were nomadic tribes, and they migrated southward, looking for food sources and following bison and mammoths to more temperate regions. As the Ice Age ended, around 9000 BC, bands became less migratory and different language groups developed. When the Europeans arrived in the sixteenth century, more than two thousand languages were spoken.

An important development was the invention of agriculture, which began around 5000 BC in the Tehuacan Valley of central Mexico, and spread slowly north and south. With the cultivation of staple foods known as "the three sisters" maize (corn), beans and squash, more settled communities evolved into large market towns, and then into the great civilizations of Middle America. Most were patriarchal, with hierarchical political structures, and centered around communal markets where people exchanged food and engaged in extensive trading. The first great Mesoamerican civilization was the Olmecs, active between 1200 and

500 BC. They built large temple mounds faced with stone, devised irrigation systems, and carved huge heads from blocks of basalt. In the first century AD, the more sophisticated civilization of the Mayas arose in parts of Guatemala, Yucatán, and the Chiapas region of southern Mexico, with an important priestly caste and rich symbolic and religious systems. The Maya wove intricate cotton textiles, worked gold and silver to create elaborate jewelry, and built large stone structures which used the corbeled vault. Most notably, they developed a hieroglyphic alphabet, which they carved on stone and printed on paper, and invented a complex calendar revealing their advanced knowledge of astronomy and mathematics. The last great civilization to flourish before the European invasion was the Aztecs in the highlands of central Mexico. With a highly advanced military organization, the Aztecs conquered more advanced city-states and created an empire, at its height, of around six million people. The capital city, Tenochtitlan, built on an artificial island in the middle of a lake, had a population of over one hundred thousand people, and was laid out in squares with many stone buildings and temples, hillside terracing and extensive irrigation. Although this city astounded the Spanish when they arrived in 1519 and rivaled many capitals in Europe, they had little compunction about destroying it and subjugating its people.

The first migrations into what is now South America took place at some point after 10,000 BC.

The first immigrants settled in the areas of Tierra del Fuego, Argentina, southern Chile and portions of the central Andes, originally as nomadic hunters and later as highly developed agricultural societies. Their political organization was sophisticated and complex, especially in the case of the Inca, who had a hereditary royal class, nobles, craftsmen and peasants. Inca artistic production, particularly in sculpture and goldsmithing, was of an extraordinarily high quality. In comparison, development in North America was slower and never reached the heights achieved by the great civilizations of Mesoamerica. By the first century AD and onwards, the Hopewellian groups of the Mississippi Valley as well as the Anasazi of the Southwest began to develop sophisticated agriculture, bringing about many important cultural developments. Groups such as the Pueblo, in what is now New Mexico, developed techniques for building multi-storied houses of stone masonry and had a society not unlike peasant communities in the rest of the Euro-Asian world.

Larger populations required more social and religious organization. Complex religious traditions evolved that pervaded every aspect of daily life, with the underlying belief that human beings were part of an intricate ecosystem which could easily be unbalanced by selfishness or greed. In Eastern North America, early native cultures had some common features: they all built mounds for burial and religious purposes; they all had urban settlements and practiced horticulture; they all made pottery and used copper for some tools. The most advanced of these cultures were the Mississippi peoples, whose large mounds and buildings grouped around a central plaza linked them to Mesoamerican urban development, although they never used stone or developed advanced metallurgy. The largest of their cities was Cahokia, near present-day St Louis, which had mounds comprising four levels and may have had a population of as much as 30,000 people at its height, around AD 1200. The disappearance of these peoples and their culture is still puzzling to historians. By the sixteenth century, European explorers of North America found few traces of large cities or sophisticated mounds. Some speculate that even before the arrival of foreigners, the native population of the Americas was reduced by 90 percent in some areas by the introduction of pathogens carried by vermin from European sailing vessels. Thus, the Americas, with a pre-conquest population of between 80 and 100 million souls, as compared to

Europe's 60 million, was reduced to under 10 million, and must have seemed truly "uninhabited" in the eyes of the explorers.

Although it is difficult to reconstruct life in Native America before European contact, it is important to recognize that our understanding is colored by the preconceptions and misapprehension of European commentators. This included the idea, prevalent during the era of exploration and persisting into our time, that the "Indians," as Columbus called them, thinking he had found India, were a monolithic group characterized by a common "barbarity," "savagery" and "heathenism." Many of the accounts by explorers dispel the myth of native barbarity in their awestruck descriptions of the great Mesoamerican civilizations, which were as advanced in some areas of learning, engineering, and administration as the Europeans. Nor was Native America monolithic. The groups that inhabited the New World had enormous linguistic, cultural and ethnic diversity, preserved mainly in the oral tradition of native peoples, in accounts of Creation as well as in tales of Trickster, the liminal figure who symbolizes the healing power of laughter. As we read these tales, it is important to remember that they are nineteenth and twentieth century transcriptions of ancient songs and tales that have been passed down orally. Often, these tales and poems had a communal and performative quality that was spontaneous and improvised, depending on audience response and the different tellers of the tales, a quality that cannot be grasped in their written versions. Finally, it is important to note that native peoples were not merely victims of invasion and conquest or members of static cultures, but were agents whose strongly articulated societies had been changing and adapting for centuries. They responded strongly to the outsiders and thus shaped the course of European settlement in the New World.

FURTHER READING

Richard Adams, *Prehistoric Mesoamerica* (Boston: Little, Brown, 1977).

Philip Kopper, *The Smithsonian Book of North American Indians: Before the Coming of the Europeans* (Washington, DC: Smithsonian Books, 1986.)

Elizabeth Hill Boone and Walter D. Mignolo (eds), *Writing without Words: Alternative Literacies in Mesoamerica and the Andres* (Durham: Duke University Press, 1994).

Stephen Plog, *Ancient Peoples of the American Southwest* (New York: Thames and Hudson, 1997).

The Origin Myth of Acoma . . .

The village of Acoma, spectacularly located on a mesa in what is now western New Mexico, is said to be the oldest inhabited settlement in the United States. The following Acoma myth describes the creation of the world, with two female beings emerging from a subterranean realm and bringing forth the cosmos. As is common in Native American oral narratives, emphasis is placed on human beings existing in harmony with Nature.

PRIMARY WORK

Matthew Stirling, *The Origin Myth of Acoma and Other Records* (Washington: Smithsonian Institution Bureau of American Ethnology Bulletin 135, 1942).

In the beginning two female human beings were born. These two children were born underground at a place called *Shipapu*. As they grew up, they began to be aware of each other. There was no light and they could only feel each other. Being in the dark they grew slowly.

After they had grown considerably, a Spirit whom they afterward called *Tsichtinako* spoke to them, and they found that it would give them nourishment. After they had grown large enough to think for themselves, they spoke to the Spirit when it had come to them one day and asked it to make itself known to them and to say whether it was male or female, but it replied only that it was not allowed to meet with them. They then asked why they were living in the dark without knowing each other by name, but the Spirit answered that they were *nuk'timi*[1] but they were to be patient in waiting until everything was ready for them to go up into the light. So they waited a long time, and as they grew they learned their language from Tsichtinako.

When all was ready, they found a present from Tsichtinako, two baskets of seeds and little images of all the different animals (there were to be) in the world. The Spirit said they were sent by their father. They asked who was meant by their father, and Tsichtinako replied that his name was *Uch'tsiti*, and that he wished them to take their baskets out into the light, when the time came. Tsichtinako instructed them, "You will find the seeds of four kinds of pine trees, *la'khok, gei'etsu, wanuka*, and *la'nye* in your baskets. You are to plant these seeds and will use the trees to get up into the light." They could not see the things in their baskets but feeling each object in turn they asked, "Is this it?" until the seeds were found. They then planted the seeds as Tsichtinako instructed. All of the four seeds sprouted, but in the darkness the trees grew very slowly, and the two sisters became very anxious to reach the light as they waited this long time. They slept for many years as they had no use for eyes. Each time they awoke they would feel the trees to see how they were growing. The tree *lanye* grew faster than the others and after a very long time pushed a hole through the earth for them and let in a very little light. The others stopped growing, at various heights, when this happened.

The hole that the tree *lanye* made was not large enough for them to pass through, so Tsichtinako advised them to look again in their baskets where they would find the image of an animal called *dyu-p*[2] and tell it to become alive. They told it to live, and it did so as they spoke, exclaiming, "A'uha! Why have you given me life?" They told it not to be afraid nor to worry about coming to life. "We have brought you to life because you are to be useful." Tsichtinako spoke to them again, instructing them to tell Badger to climb the pine tree, to

---

[1]   Under the earth.

[2]   Badger.

bore a hole large enough for them to crawl up, cautioning him not to go out into the light, but to return when the hole was finished. Badger climbed the tree and, after he had dug a hole large enough, returned saying that he had done his work. They thanked him and said, "As a reward you will come up with us to the light and thereafter you will live happily. You will always know how to dig and your home will be in the ground where you will be neither too hot nor too cold."

Tsichtinako now spoke again, telling them to look in the basket for *Tawai'nu*[3], giving it life and asking it to smooth the hole by plastering. It, too, was to be cautioned to return. This they did and Locust smoothed the hole but, having finished, went out into the light. When it returned reporting that it had done its work, they asked it if it had gone out. Locust said no, and every time he was asked he replied no, until the fourth time when he admitted that he had gone out. They asked Locust what it was like outside. Locust replied that it was just *tsi'iti*[4]. They said, "From now on you will be known as *Tsi-k'a*. You will also come up with us, but you will be punished for disobedience by being allowed out only a short time. Your home will be in the ground and you will have to return when the weather is bad. You will soon die but you will be reborn each season."

The hole now let light into the place where the two sisters were, and Tsichtinako spoke to them, "Now is the time you are to go out. You are to take your baskets with you. In them you will find pollen and sacred corn meal. When you reach the top, you will wait for the sun to come up and that direction will be called *ha'nami*[5]. With the pollen and the sacred corn meal you will pray to the Sun. You will thank the Sun for bringing you to light, ask for a long life and happiness, and for success in the purpose for which you were created." Tsichtinako then taught them the prayers and the creation song, which they were to sing. This took a long while, but finally the sisters, followed by Badger and Locust, went out into the light, climbing the pine tree. Badger was very strong and skillful and helped them. On reaching the earth, they set down their baskets and saw for the first time what they had. The earth was soft and spongy under their feet as they walked, and they said, "This is not ripe." They stood waiting for the sun, not knowing where it would appear. Gradually it grew lighter and finally the sun came up. Before they began to pray, Tsichtinako told them they were facing east and that their right side, the side their best aim was on, would be known as *ku'a'me*[6] and the left *ti dyami*[7] while behind at their backs was the direction *puna'me*[8] where the sun would go down. They had already learned while underground the direction *nuk'um*[9] and later, when they asked where their father was, they were told *tyunami*.[10]

And as they waited to pray to the Sun, the girl on the right moved her best hand and was named *Iatiku*, which meant "bringing to life." Tsichtinako then told her to name her sister, but it took a long time. Finally Tsichtinako noticed that the other had more in her basket, so Tsichtinako told Iatiku to name her thus, and Iatiku called her *Nautsiti*, which meant "more of everything in the basket."

They now prayed to the Sun as they had been taught by Tsichtinako, and sang the creation song. Their eyes hurt for they were not accustomed to the strong light. For the first time they asked Tsichtinako why they were on earth and why they were created. Tsichtinako replied, "I did not make you. Your father, Uchtsiti, made you, and it is he who has made the world, the sun which you have seen, the sky, and many other things which you will see. But Uchtsiti says

---

[3] Locust.
[4] Laid out flat.
[5] East.
[6] South.

[7] North.
[8] West.
[9] Down, below.
[10] Four skies above.

the world is not yet completed, not yet satisfactory, as he wants it. This is the reason he has made you. You will rule and bring to life the rest of the things he has given you in the baskets." The sisters then asked how they themselves had come into being. Tsichtinako answered saying, "Uchtsiti first made the world. He threw a clot of his own blood into space and by his power it grew and grew until it became the earth. Then Uchtsiti planted you in this and by it you were nourished until you developed. Now that you have emerged from within the earth, you will have to provide nourishment for yourselves. I will instruct you in this." They then asked where their father lived and Tsichtinako replied, "You will never see your father, he lives four skies above, and has made you to live in this world. He has made you in the image of himself." So they asked why Tsichtinako did not become visible to them, but Tsichtinako replied, "I don't know how to live like a human being. I have been asked by Uchtsiti to look after you and to teach you. I will always guide you." And they asked again how they were to live, whether they could go down once more under the ground, for they were afraid of the winds and rains and their eyes were hurt by the light. Tsichtinako replied that Uchtsiti would take care of that and would furnish them means to keep warm and change the atmosphere so that they would get used to it.

. . . When they had completed their prayers to the sun, Tsichtinako said, "You have done everything well and now you are both to take up your baskets and you must look to the north, west, south, and east, for you are now to pray to the Earth to accept the things in the basket and to give them life. First you must pray to the north, at the same time lift up your baskets in that direction. You will then do the same to the west, then to the south and east." They did as they were told and did it well. And Tsichtinako said to them, "From now on you will rule in every direction, north, west, south and east."

They now questioned Tsichtinako again so that they would understand more clearly why they were given the baskets and their contents, and Tsichtinako replied, "Everything in the baskets is to be created by your word, for you are made in the image of Uchtsiti and your word will be as powerful as his word. He has created you to help him complete the world. You are to plant the seeds of the different plants to be used when anything is needed. I shall always be ready to point out to you the various plants and animals."

The sisters did not realize that they were not taking food and did not understand when Tsichtinako told them they were to plant seeds to give them nourishment. But they were always ready to do as Tsichtinako asked, and she told them to plant first that which would maintain life, grains of corn. "When this plant grows," said Tsichtinako, "it will produce a part which I will point out to you. This will be taken as food." Everything in the basket was in pairs and the sisters planted two of each kind of corn.

The corn grew very slowly so Tsichtinako told them to plant *isthe*[11] and to transmit its power of early ripening to the corn.

They were very interested in the corn and watched it every day as it grew. Tsichtinako showed them where the pollen came out and said, "That you will call *ku'ach'timu*; there the pollen will appear. When the pollen is plentiful, you will gather it, and with it and corn meal you will pray to the rising sun each morning." This they did always, but Nautsiti was sometimes a little lazy.

. . . After a long time, Tsichtinako spoke to them, "What we are going to do now concerns the earth. We are going to make the mountains." She told them to remember the words she was going to say. They were to say, "*Kaweshtima kot*[12], appear in the north, and we will always know you to be in that direction." Tsichtinako also pointed out an article in the basket that

---

[11]   Snowdrops.   [12]   North Mountain.

she named *ya'oni*[13] and instructed them to throw the stone to the north direction as they spoke the words. When they did so, a big mountain appeared in the north. After they had done this, Tsichtinako instructed them to do the same thing in the west, and in the south, and in the east.

Iatiku later asked Tsichtinako, "What remains in my basket?" and she was answered, "You have still many animals; these will be multiplied to populate the mountains." And as the two grew larger, they required more food. Tsichtinako saw this and told them that they were now to bring to life larger animals. She said they would find in their baskets cottontails, jack rabbits, antelope, and water deer. They were told to give life to these animals and to send them into the open plains. Everything was done as before, and when they killed the animals for food they were always careful to pray to their father as before. As they again asked Tsichtinako what remained in their baskets. Tsichtinako said, "You have images of the still bigger game. You will find deer, elk, mountain sheep, and bison." Iatiku asked where these animals were to be told to live and Tsichtinako told them that the elk and deer were to live in the lower mountains and the mountain sheep higher and in the rougher places. The bison, however, were to live on the plains. They followed the instructions and gave life to these animals and told them to go to these places to live and multiply. They again tried all these different animals for food. Their flesh was very good and always they prayed to Uchtsiti before tasting them.

In Nautsiti's basket there were many more things left than in Iatiku's. Nautsiti was selfish and hoarded her images, but Iatiku was ready to let her seeds and images be used. She was more interested in seeing things grow. They again asked what remained, and Tsichtinako replied, "You will find lion, wolf, wildcat and bear. These are strong beasts; they are going to use as food the same game that you also use. There is now game enough for them." When all these had been selected they were brought to life in the same manner as before.

The Winnebago Trickster Cycle

In Native American traditional narratives, Trickster is a comic figure who flouts social norms, a player of pranks whose jokes often rebound against himself. Among the Kiowa, he is known as Saynday, among the Anishinabe as Nanapush, among the Arapahoes as Wiho. Trickster tales are an affirmation of the healing power of laughter, particularly at oneself, and a rejection of tragic victimhood. The Trickster is invariably transgressive, ribald, anarchic, and faintly silly. One of the most notable collections of Trickster tales is related to the figure of Wakdjunkaga, the Winnebago (Siouan) Trickster.

PRIMARY WORK

Paul Radin, *The Trickster* (New York: Philosophical Library, 1969).

FURTHER READING

Lewis Hyde, *Trickster Makes This World: Mischief, Myth, and Art* (New York: Farrar, Strauss, and Giroux, 1998).

---

[13] Stone.

FROM THE WINNEBAGO TRICKSTER CYCLE

. . . As he, Trickster, walked along, suddenly, he came in sight of a knoll. As he approached it, he saw, to his surprise, an old buffalo near it. "My, my, what a pity! If only I hadn't thrown away that arrow bundle, I would now be able to kill and eat this animal," he exclaimed. Thereupon he took a knife, cut down the hay and fashioned it into figures of men. These he placed in a circle, leaving an opening at one end. The place was very muddy. Having constructed this enclosure, he went back to where he had seen the buffalo and shouted, "Oho! My younger brother, here he is! Here he is indeed eating without having anything to worry about. Indeed let nothing prey on his mind! I will keep watch for him against intruders." Thus he spoke to the buffalo who was feeding to his heart's content. Then he continued, "Listen, younger brother, this place is completely surrounded by people! Over there, however, is an opening through which you might escape." Just then the buffalo raised his head unsuspiciously and, to his surprise, he seemed really to be completely surrounded by people. Only at the place Trickster had designated did an opening appear. In that direction, therefore, the buffalo ran. Soon he sank in the mire and Trickster was immediately upon him with his knife and killed him. Then he dragged him over to a cluster of wood and skinned him. Throughout all these operations he used his right arm only.

. . . In the midst of these operations suddenly his left arm grabbed the buffalo. "Give that back to me, it is mine! Stop that or I will use my knife on you!" So spoke the right arm. "I will cut you to pieces, that is what I will do to you," continued the right arm. Thereupon the left arm released its hold. But, shortly after, the left arm again grabbed hold of the right arm. This time it grabbed hold of his wrist just at the moment that the right arm had commenced to skin the buffalo. Again and again this was repeated. In this manner did Trickster make both his arms quarrel. That quarrel soon turned into a vicious fight and the left arm was badly cut up. "Oh, oh! Why did I do this? Why have I done this? I have made myself suffer!" The left arm was indeed bleeding profusely.

Then he dressed the buffalo. When he was finished he started off again. As he walked along the birds would exclaim, "Look, look! There is Trickster!" Thus they would cry and fly away. "Ah, you naughty little birds! I wonder what they are saying?" This continued right along. Every bird he met would call out, "Look, look! There is Trickster! There he is walking about!"

. . . As he walked along, he came unexpectedly to a place where he saw a man with a club. "Hoho!" said Trickster, "my younger brother, he, too, is walking about! Younger brother, what are you doing?" But he received no answer. Suddenly this man spoke, "O, my poor children! They must be very hungry." Trickster plied him with many questions. Yet not once did he receive an answer. Trickster now saw the man do as follows. It so happened that he was near a knoll. He took his club, struck the knoll and, to Trickster's surprise, killed a large, old bear. After this he built a fire and singed the hair off the bear's body. Then he took a pail which he was carrying along with him and boiled the bear in it. As soon as it was cooked he served the meat and spoke again. "Hurry, children, hurry for you must indeed be very hungry!" Thereupon he took a wooden bowl, put some soup in it and cooled it. Finally he untied a bladder which he had attached to his belt. In it there were four tiny little children. To these it was that he had been speaking so lovingly.

Then Trickster said, "My, my, younger brother, what fine little children you have!" Thus spoke Trickster. The father of the children let them eat but he was careful not to let them eat very much. When they finished, he put them back again into the bladder and attached it to his belt. After this he broke off some branches, dished out the remaining contents of the kettle and, sitting down, began to eat himself. He ate all in the bowl. Then he drank all the soup that he had cooled in the pail.

Finally, when he was all through, and only then, did he speak to Trickster, "I was busy before, that is why I did not speak to you." Thereupon Trickster replied, "Truly, you have beautiful children, younger brother. Would you not care to entrust two of them to me?" "No, indeed, you would certainly kill them." "No indeed, younger brother, that is not so," said Trickster, "you exaggerate. I wish merely to have the children as companions. That is why I am asking you to let me have them. I will take care of them in the same manner you have been doing." Thus he continued and finally persuaded the man to let him have two of the children. The father gave him a club, a pail, a bowl and the bear he had killed. Then he took the bladder that was suspended from his belt and put two of the little children in it. "Now, Trickster, remember, if you kill any of these little children you will die. Remember if you kill these little children, no matter where you may be, I will pursue and kill you. Keep what I am giving you and feed these children once a month. Do not change this rule. If you change it in any respect, you will kill them. You have seen what I have done and do you do the same." Thus he spoke and Trickster replied, "My younger brother, you have spoken and I have heard. Just as you ordered so I will do." Then they separated, each one having a bladder suspended from his belt.

. . . Not long after they had separated, as Trickster was walking along, he suddenly exclaimed to himself, "My, my! My dear little children must be hungry by now. But why waste time talking about it? I will let them have something to eat immediately." He was quite near a knoll, so he took his club, struck it and in this manner killed a large old bear. Then he hurriedly built a fire and singed the hair off the bear. The body he cut open and boiled. As soon as it had begun to boil a little, he dished the meat out, cooled it and when it was cool opened the bladder and said, "My dear little children, I miss them a great deal!" Then he uncovered them and fed them. He filled the wooden bowl high and gave it to them. In spite of all that the man had told him he did many things strictly forbidden to him. After he had done all these prohibited things, he put the children back in the bladder and attached it dangling to his belt.

He had been gathering together pieces of broken wood as he walked along and now he was ready to sit down for his meal. He ate up everything that remained and drank all the soup that was in the pail. Then he proceeded on his journey. All the animals in the world mocked him and called out, "Trickster!"

After a little while he himself got hungry. "The little children were to eat once a month, I was told," he thought to himself. But now he himself was hungry. So again he said, "My, my! It is about time for my dear little children to be hungry again. I must get something for them to eat." He immediately searched for a knoll, struck it and killed a bear of enormous size. He then built a fire, singed the hairs off the bear; cut it up and put it on to boil. As soon as it was boiled he took the bladder attached to his belt and opened it. To his surprise the children were dead. "The dear little children! How unfortunate that they have died!"

. . . Just as he said this the father of the children appeared and said, "Well, Trickster, you will die for this! I will kill you, as I said I would if you killed my children." As he approached him, Trickster exclaimed appealingly, "Oh my younger brother!" However, the man rushed at him so menacingly that Trickster drew back at once and fled from him. He ran with all his speed with the other behind him throwing objects at him which barely missed him. There seemed to be no escape. Only by making sudden and unexpected turns did Trickster escape being struck.

Thus did the man pursue Trickster. In desperation he thought of seeking refuge up in the sky or under the ground, yet he felt that there, too, he would be followed. "Trickster, no matter where you flee, will you be able to save your life," shouted the man. "No matter where you go, I will pursue and kill you. So you might as well give it up now and be done with it. You are exhausted already as you see. You have nowhere to go. Indeed, you will not be able to find a refuge-place anywhere." Thus spoke the man.

He pursued Trickster everywhere. It was only by adroit dodging that he escaped being hit by objects thrown at him. Then, suddenly, Trickster got frightened. By this time he had run over the whole earth and he was now approaching the place where the sun rises, the end of the world. Toward a pointed piece of land that projected, in the form of a steep wall of rock into the ocean, toward this he ran. It was the edge of the ocean. He pressed up against it and finally jumped into the water. Right into the middle of the ocean he fell. "Ah, Trickster, you have saved yourself! You were indeed destined to die!" Then the man gave up the pursuit. Trickster uttered an exclamation of heartfelt relief and said to himself, "That such a thing should happen to Trickster, the warrior, I never imagined! Why, I almost came to grief!"...

The Origin of Stories (Seneca)

This Seneca folk tale reveals the Native American view of stories as not merely reflecting but actively shaping reality. In this worldview, nature is viewed as alive and articulate, in dialogue with human beings. One of the characteristics of oral literatures is their formulaic, repetitive character, with opening and closing declarations and with a refrain repeated by the audience to indicate attentiveness and participation in the tale.

PRIMARY WORK

Seneca Myths and Folk Tales, ed. Arthur C. Parker (Lincoln: University of Nebraska Press, 1989).

There was once a boy who had no home. His parents were dead and his uncles would not care for him. In order to live this boy, whose name was Gaqka, or Crow, made a bower of branches for an abiding place and hunted birds and squirrels for food.

He had almost no clothing but was very ragged and dirty. When the people from the village saw him they called him Filth-Covered-One, and laughed as they passed by, holding their noses. No one thought he would ever amount to anything, which made him feel heavy-hearted. He resolved to go away from his tormentors and become a great hunter.

One night Gaqka found a canoe. He had never seen this canoe before, so he took it. Stepping in he grasped the paddle, when the canoe immediately shot into the air, and he paddled above the clouds and under the moon. For a long time he went always southward. Finally the canoe dropped into a river and then Gaqka paddled for shore.

On the other side of the river was a great cliff that had a face that looked like a man. It was at the forks of the river where this cliff stood. The boy resolved to make his home on the top of the cliff and so climbed it and built a bark cabin.

The first night he sat on the edge of the cliff he heard a voice saying, "Give me some tobacco." Looking around the boy, seeing no one, replied, "Why should I give tobacco?"

There was no answer and the boy began to fix his arrows for the next day's hunt. After a while the voice spoke again, "Give me some tobacco."

Gaqka now took out some tobacco and threw it over the cliff. The voice spoke again: "Now I will tell you a story."

Feeling greatly awed the boy listened to a story that seemed to come directly out of the rock upon which he was sitting. Finally the voice paused, for the story had ended. Then it spoke again saying, "It shall be the custom hereafter to present me with a small gift for my stories." So the boy gave the rock a few bone beads. Then the rock said, "Hereafter when I speak, announcing that I shall tell a story you must say, 'Nio,' and as I speak you must say 'He,' that I may know that you are listening. You must never fall asleep but continue to listen until I say 'Da'neho nigag'is.' (So thus finished is the length of my story.) Then you shall give me presents and I shall be satisfied."

The next day the boy hunted and killed a great many birds. These he made into soup and roasts. He skinned the birds and saved the skins, keeping them in a bag.

That evening the boy sat on the rock again and looked westward at the sinking sun. He wondered if his friend would speak again. While waiting he chipped some new arrow-points, and made them very small so that he could use them in a blow gun. Suddenly, as he worked, he heard the voice again. "Give me some tobacco to smoke," it said. Gaqka threw a pinch of tobacco over the cliff and the voice said, "Hau'nio'," and commenced a story. Long into the night one wonderful tale after another flowed from a rock, until it called out, "So thus finished is the length of my story." Gaqka was sorry to have the stories ended but he gave the rock an awl made from a bird's leg and a pinch of tobacco.

The next day the boy hunted far to the east and there found a village. Nobody knew who he was but he soon found many friends. There were some hunters who offered to teach him how to kill big game, and these went with him to his own camp on the high rock. At night he allowed them to listen to the stories that came forth from the rock, but it would speak only when Gaqka was present. He therefore had many friends with whom to hunt.

Now after a time Gaqka made a new suit of clothing from deer skin and desired to obtain a decorated pouch. He therefore went to the village and found one house where there were two daughters living with an old mother. He asked that a pouch be made and the youngest daughter spoke up and said, "It is now finished. I have been waiting for you to come for it." So she gave him a handsome pouch.

Then the old mother spoke, saying, "I now perceive that my future son-in-law has passed through the door and is here." Soon thereafter, the younger woman brought Gaqka a basket of bread and said, "My mother greatly desires that you should marry me." Gaqka looked at the girl and was satisfied, and ate the bread. The older daughter was greatly displeased and frowned in an evil manner.

That night the bride said to her husband, "We must now go away. My older sister will kill you for she is jealous." So Gaqka arose and took his bride to his own lodge. Soon the rock spoke and began to relate wonder stories of things that happened in the old days. The bride was not surprised, but said, "This standing rock, indeed, is my grandfather. I will now present you with a pouch into which you must put a trophy for every tale related."

All winter long the young couple stayed in the lodge on the great rock and heard all the wonder tales of the old days. Gaqka's bag was full of stories and he knew all the lore of former times.

As springtime came the bride said, "We must now go north to your own people and you shall become a great man." But Gaqka was sad and said, "Alas, in my own country I am an outcast and called by an unpleasant name."

The bride only laughed, saying, "Nevertheless, we shall go north."

Taking their pelts and birdskins, the couple descended the cliff and seated themselves in the canoe. "This is my canoe," said the bride. "I sent it through the air to you."

The bride seated herself in the bow of the canoe and Gaqka in the stern. Grasping a paddle he swept it through the water, but soon the canoe arose and went through the air. Meanwhile the bride was singing all kinds of songs, which Gaqka learned as he paddled.

When they reached the north, the bride said, "Now I shall remove your clothing and take all the scars from your face and body." She then caused him to pass through a hollow log, and when Gaqka emerged from the other end he was dressed in the finest clothing and was a handsome man.

Together the two walked to the village where the people came out to see them. After a while Gaqka said, "I am the boy whom you once were accustomed to call 'Cia'do da.' I have now returned." That night the people of the village gathered around and listened to the tales he told, and he instructed them to give him small presents and tobacco. He would plunge his hand in his pouch and take out a trophy, saying, "Ho ho! So here is another one!" and then looking at his trophy would relate an ancient tale.

Everybody now thought Gaqka a great man and listened to his stories. He was the first man to find out all about the adventures of the old-time people. That is why there are so many legends now.

Pre-Columbian Literatures of the Quiché

At the time of the Spanish Conquest, various independent nations descending from the ancient Mayan civilization existed in Mexico and areas to the South in what is now Guatemala. The culture of these groups was remarkable for its artistic and intellectual achievements, particularly in the areas of astronomy and mathematics. Their mathematical system, based on the number 20, with the concept of zero and the use of place notations, enabled them to make the complex calculations necessary in establishing a 365-day calendar, more accurate than European systems of the period. As well, they were knowledgeable about the movements of the moon and the planet Venus, and their astronomer-priests could accurately predict lunar and solar eclipses. Mayan cosmology and mythology were rich and complex, and most deities were related to natural features such as the sun, moon, and rain. Their architecture was also of an advanced nature, most notably in the case of large pyramidical structures in sites such as Tulum and Chichen Itzá in Yucatán.

The existence of books (made from the bark of trees, smoothed and bleached with chalk) among the native peoples of Mexico has been noted by chroniclers ranging from Diáz del Castillo to Father Bartolomé de Las Casas. According to Las Casas, there were among the Indians chroniclers and historians who knew the origin of religious traditions, the founding of their cities, the heroic deeds of their kings and warriors, and their systems of government. As well, Las Casas states that the native peoples of Mexico had five books of figures and characters, with the first containing their history and information about their ways of calculating time, the second setting out the ceremonies and feast days of each year, the third describing dreams and omens, the fourth discussing rituals linked with the naming of children, and the fifth detailing marriage rites and ceremonies. Sadly, most of these manuscripts were destroyed by the Spanish missionaries, who viewed them as works of the devil.

Anonymous Quiché author (sixteenth century): *Popol Vuh*

One of the most powerful and advanced of the native peoples of Mexico, the Quiché, were later invaded and conquered in 1524 by Pedro de Alvarado, one of the captains who accompanied Hernán Cortés. It was shortly after the Conquest that an anonymous Quiché transcribed what he could recall of the text of the *Popol Vuh* (The Book of the People), the sacred book of the Maya, a saga containing information about the traditions of the Quiché, the history of their origins, and a chronology of their kings. The original book was in all likelihood destroyed in the flames of Utatlán, but the native author in his preamble explicitly states his intention of transcribing the traditional narrative so that the content of

the original book might not be completely lost. In the preamble to this work he also declares that he is writing after the introduction of Christianity, and indeed the influence of the Biblical account of creation can be noted in the following excerpt, a fascinating example of the ways in which the ideologies and traditions of colonizers and colonized coalesced to form an entirely new narrative.

PRIMARY WORK

Popol Vuh: The Sacred Book of the Ancient Quiché Maya, trans. Delia Goetz and Sylvanus Morley (Norman: University of Oklahoma Press, 1950).

FROM *POPOL VUH: THE SACRED BOOK OF THE ANCIENT QUICHÉ MAYA*

Chapter I

This is the account of how all was in suspense, all calm, in silence; all motionless, still, and the expanse of the sky was empty.

This is the first account, the first narrative. There was neither man, nor animal, birds, fishes, crabs, trees, stones, caves, ravines, grasses, nor forests; there was only the sky.

The surface of the earth had not appeared. There was only the calm sea and the great expanse of the sky.

There was nothing brought together, nothing which could make a noise, nor anything which might move, or tremble, or could make noise in the sky.

There was nothing standing; only the calm water, the placid sea, alone and tranquil. Nothing existed.

There was only immobility and silence in the darkness, in the night. Only the Creator, the Maker, Tepeu, Gucumatz[1], the Forefathers[2], were in the water surrounded with light. They were hidden under green and blue feathers, and were therefore called Gucumatz. By nature they were great sages and great thinkers. In this manner the sky existed and also the Heart of Heaven, which is the name of God and thus He is called.

Then came the word. Tepeu and Gucumatz came together in the darkness, in the night, and Tepeu and Gucumatz talked together. They talked then, discussing and deliberating; they agreed, they united their words and their thoughts.

Then while they meditated, it became clear to them that when dawn would break, man

---

[1]   The feathered serpent.

[2]   In the original text, E Alom, literally those who con-

ceive and give birth. The Quiché associated Gucumatz, the feathered serpent, with water.

must appear. Then they planned the creation, and the growth of the trees and the thickets and the birth of life and the creation of man. Thus it was arranged in the darkness and in the night by the Heart of Heaven who is called Huracán.

The first is called Caculhá Huracán. The second is Chipi-Caculhá. The third is Raxa-Caculhá.[3] And these three are the Heart of Heaven.

Then Tepeu and Gucumatz came together; then they conferred about life and light, what they would do so that there would be light and dawn, who it would be who would provide food and sustenance.

Thus let it be done! Let the emptiness be filled! Let the water recede and make a void, let the earth appear and become solid; let it be done. Thus they spoke. Let there be light, let there be dawn in the sky and on the earth! There shall be neither glory nor grandeur in our creation and formation until the human being is made, man is formed. So they spoke.

Then the earth was created by them. So it was, in truth, that they created the earth. Earth! they said, and instantly it was made.

Like the mist, like a cloud, and like a cloud of dust was the creation, when the mountains appeared from the water; and instantly the mountains grew.

Only by a miracle, only by magic art were the mountains and valleys formed; and instantly the groves of cypresses and pines put forth shoots together on the surface of the earth.

And thus Gucumatz was filled with joy, and exclaimed: "Your coming has been fruitful, Heart of Heaven; and you, Huracán, and you, Chipi-Caculhá, Raxa-Caculhá!"

"Our work, our creation shall be finished," they answered.

First the earth was formed, the mountains and the valleys; the currents of water were divided, the rivulets were running freely between the hills, and water was separated when the high mountains appeared.

Thus was the earth created, when it was formed by the Heart of Heaven, the Heart of Earth, as they are called who first made it fruitful, when the sky was in suspense, and the earth was submerged in the water.

So it was that they made perfect the work, when they did it after thinking and meditating upon it.

Excerpts from the Mayan *Chilam Balam*

The *Books of Chilam Balam*, the sacred books of the Maya, were named after their last and greatest prophet, who probably lived during the last decades of the fifteenth century and the first of the sixteenth century and was said to have forecast the coming of strangers who would establish a new religion. Among the Maya, predicting the future was the task of a special caste of priests called *chilans*, (meaning mouthpiece or interpreter), who were charged with transmitting the wishes of the gods. Most of these prophecies are classified in terms of time, with day-prophecies, year-prophecies, *katun*-prophecies (for twenty-year periods), and prophecies regarding the return of the god Kukulcan. Clearly, the *katun*-prophecies were of considerable interest to the Maya, given their belief that events occurring in a certain *katun* will inevitably return in a *katun* of the same name years later.

---

[3] *Huracán*, a leg; *Caculhá Huracán*, the flash of a leg or the lightning; *Chipi-Caculhá*, a small flash. The Caribs of the West Indies extended the use of the term to designate destructive natural phenomena such as hurricanes.

FROM *THE BOOK OF CHILAM BALAM OF CHUMAYEL*

From *An Incantation, XVII*

Strung end to end are the precious stones, the red precious stones, representing the substance of heaven, the moisture of heaven.

The form in which you created the sun, in which you created the earth! The form of the moisture of heaven, the substance of heaven, the yellow blossom of heaven! How did I create your sun? How did I create your moon? How did I create your precious stones? I created you. When you were sprinkled with water, you remembered the force of the sun. Then when the message was sent to you . . . under cover I created you, I set you where you are . . .

From *The Prophecies*

10 Kan[1] was the year-bearer when the seeker for a town passed. He was called Montejo, he who wrote down the towns. This was the year when the strangers in the land, the foreigners who ate annonas[2], passed. They were the first to distribute the towns. It was when the foreigners arrived that the "receivers"[3] received them. When they assembled at Campeche, when their ships came forth, then the nobles went to give gifts to them. There were thirteen "receivers of the foreigners." After that they came to Ichcaanizihoo.

. . . This is a record of the wisdom of the book in which is set down the course of the katun[4] . . . Thus it is written by the Holy Writer, the Evangelist, it is the word of the Lord of heaven and earth . . . it comes from on high. This was given to them at the beginning of the land, at the beginning of our humanity . . . These were the four lineages from heaven, the substance of heaven, the moisture of heaven, the head-chiefs, the rulers of the land: Azcaal Puc, Hooltun Balam, Hochtun Poot, Ah Mex-Cuc Chan.

Behold, within seven score years Christianity will be introduced amid the clamor of the rulers, those who violently seize land during the katun. Then suddenly appears the wise man; then there is the examination of the katun[5]. Miserable is the face of Chac Chuen Coyi. Then the Lord of the Church shall come. It is in the middle of the town of Tihoo. It shall come from the East, from the North, from the West, from the South; the word of Christianity shall be heard in the 17th tun in order that Christianity may truly arise. The Padres shall arrive; the Bishop shall arrive, the Holy Inquisition, the word of God. These things shall be accomplished. No one shall cause them to cease. Amen.

. . . The first: Katun 11 Ahau was the beginning of the katun-count, the first katun. The katun was established at Ichcaanzihoo when the foreigners arrived. Red were the beards of the children of the sun, the bearded ones from the east, when they arrived here in our land. The strangers to the land are white men, red men[6], . . . a beginning of carnal sin . . . Oh Itzá! . . . make ready. There cometh a white circle in the sky[7], the fair-skinned boy from heaven, the

---

[1] 1525.

[2] The fruit of the prickly pear.

[3] Presumably priests and chieftains.

[4] Twenty-year period.

[5] An interrogation of the chiefs every katun to prove that their claims to their positions were legitimate.

[6] A reference to the red beards of some of the Spaniards.

[7] This image, associated with drought in Maya prophecies, can also be interpreted as the halo around the head of the Christ Child.

white wooden standard that shall descend from heaven. A quarter of a league, a league away, it approaches. You shall see the dawn of a new day, you shall see the *mut*-bird[8]. Oh! How there shall be intercession for us when they come. There shall come multitudes who gather stone and wood, the worthless rabble of the town. Fire shall flame up at the tips of their hands. There shall be sufficient poison and also ropes to hang their fathers. Oh Itzá! Your worship is of no avail with the true God who has descended. It is false in word and teaching. Niggard is the katun; scanty are its rains. Who would be the priest, who would be the prophet who would understand it when he came to Tancah Maypan[9] or to Chichen Itzá? Prepare yourselves to endure the burden of misery which is to come among your villages . . . Your elder brothers, the men of Tantun, come. They shall ask of you an offering to God with them. Their priest was named Ah Miznilacpe. Their faces were like the puma, like the Antichrist, on that day which is to come, on that day which confronts you, alas, in much misery, my sons. This is the word of our Lord: "It shall burn on earth, there shall be a white circle in the sky, in that katun in time to come." It is the true word from the mouth of God the Father. Alas, very heavy is the burden of the katun that shall be established in Christianity[10]. When it comes there shall be slavish talk, slavish . . . servile men. When it comes, there shall be . . . you shall see . . .

. . . The katun is established at Ichcaanizhoo[11]. Then it was that the foreigners to the land received their tribute. Then it was that the fathers of our souls arrived. The scattered divisions of the towns under their local chieftains were gathered together. They began to teach the holy faith and baptise us. The foundations of the holy Cathedral were laid, the public house of God, the widely extended house of God the Father. Then the seven sacraments were established to take away our sins. There began to be much labor in the center of the town . . . the misery of the world. Then there was set up . . . the word of God, which shall also come from the mouth of God the Father. Then the fair complexioned boy arrives, he comes from heaven. The Virgin, as she is called, is the mother of the seven planets.

. . . Then begins the lewdness of the wise men, the beckoning of carnal sin, the beckoning of the katun. The katun begins to limp; it is all over the world. Carnal sin is its garment, carnal sin is its face . . . carnal sin is its sandal, carnal sin is its head, carnal sin is its gait. They twist their necks, they twist their mouths, they wink the eye, they slaver at the mouth, at men, women, chiefs, justices, presiding officers, clerks, choir-masters, everybody both great and small. There is no great teaching. Heaven and earth are truly lost to them; they have lost all shame. Then the head-chiefs of the towns, the rulers of the towns, the prophets of the towns, the priests of the Maya men are hanged. Understanding is lost; wisdom is lost. Prepare yourselves, oh Itzá! Your sons shall see the mirth of the katun, the jesting of the katun. Dissolute is the speech, dissolute the face of the rogue to the rulers, to the head-chiefs . . . Much hanging of men is the charge[12] of the katun.

---

[8]   In the Mayan language, *mut* is a term designating both "bird" and "news."

[9]   The man of Mayapán.

[10]   I.e. the twenty-year period in which Christianity was introduced to the Maya.

[11]   Mérida.

[12]   Essence.

New World Encounters

Christopher Columbus (1451–1506)

Though diverse accounts of the origins of Christopher Columbus exist, according to most scholars he was born near the port city Genoa in 1451. He became an accomplished seaman and navigator, sailing as far as England and the Gold Coast of Africa His lifelong obsession, however, was dual in nature: firstly, to find a new trade route to Asia by sailing west across the Atlantic; secondly, to spread the Catholic faith. Though many dismissed him as a dreamer or a lunatic, he finally succeeded in obtaining backing for his project from Ferdinand and Isabella, the Catholic monarchs of Spain, who had just won their last decisive battle against the Moors in Granada.

On his first voyage, Columbus and his crew finally sighted land on 12 October 1492. This was the island of San Salvador, which he named and claimed for Spain. Indeed, in his report to Ferdinand and Isabella, emphasis is placed on the importance of naming as an act of asserting political and ideological hegemony. Another feature of Columbus' text is his recourse to rhetorical figures, such as simile, in order to make his account intelligible to his royal European readers.

In all, Columbus made four voyages. The second (1493), to what is now Puerto Rico, Jamaica, Cuba, the Virgin Islands and the Lesser Antilles, was an unsuccessful endeavor to find gold and silver. The sense of wonder which is present in his first text gives way on subsequent voyages to accounts which reveal ideological rigidity and recount incidents of physical violence against the Native peoples of the New World, as in the punishment and enslavement of the Tainos. On his third voyage (1498), where he encountered the Orinoco river and the South American mainland, Columbus became increasingly obsessed with religion and with his search for an earthly Eden. The fourth and final voyage was marked by an extraordinary incident: suffering from malaria, Columbus claimed to have experienced a vision in which a voice from above told him that God would support him just as he had supported Old Testament heroes such as David and Moses, and that he should persist in his endeavors. His last years were ones of ill health and disillusionment, though he never abandoned his belief that he had discovered a terrestrial paradise.

Primary Work

The Letter of Columbus on the Discovery of America: A Facsimile of the Pictorial Edition, with a New and Literal Translation, and a Complete Reprint of the Oldest Four Editions in Latin. Anonymous translator (New York: Trustees of the Lenox Library, 1892).

Further Reading

Cecil Jane, Select Documents Illustrating the Four Voyages of Columbus (London: The Hakluyt Society, 1961).

FROM *THE LETTER OF COLUMBUS ON THE DISCOVERY OF AMERICA* . . .

Letter of Christopher Columbus, to whom our age owes much, concerning the islands recently discovered in the Indian sea.[1] For the search of which, eight months before, he was sent under the auspices and at the cost of the most invincible Ferdinand, king of Spain. Addressed to the magnificent lord Raphael Sanxis[2], treasurer of the same most illustrious king, and which the noble and learned man Leander de Cosco has translated from the Spanish language into Latin, on the third of the kalends of May[3] 1493, the first year of the pontificate of Alexander the Sixth.

Because my undertakings have attained success, I know that it will be pleasing to you: these I have determined to relate, so that you may be made acquainted with everything done and discovered in this our voyage. On the thirty-third day after I departed from Cadiz[4], I came to the Indian sea, where I found many islands inhabited by men without number, of all which I took possession for our most fortunate king, with proclaiming heralds and flying standards, no one objecting. To the first of these I gave the name of the blessed Saviour[5], on whose aid relying I had reached this as well as the other islands. But the Indians call it Guanahani. I also called each one of the others by a new name. For I ordered one island to be called Santa Maria of the Conception, another Femandina, another Isabella, another Juana[6], and so on with the rest. As soon as we had arrived at that island which I have just now said was called Juana, I proceeded along its coast towards the west for some distance; I found it so large and without perceptible end, that I believed it to be not an island, but the continental country of Cathay[7]; seeing, however, no towns or cities situated on the sea-coast, but only some villages and rude farms, with whose inhabitants I was unable to converse, because as soon as they saw us they took flight, I proceeded farther, thinking that I would discover some city or large residences.

. . . Now in the meantime I had learned from certain Indians, whom I had seized there, that this country was indeed an island, and therefore I proceeded towards the east, keeping all the time near the coast, for 322 miles, to the extreme ends of this island. From this place I saw another island to the east, distant from this Juana 54 miles, which I called forthwith Hispana[8] and I sailed to it; and I steered along the northern coast, as at Juana, towards the east, 564 miles. And the said Juana and the other islands there appear very fertile. This island is surrounded by many very safe and wide harbours, not excelled by any others that I have ever seen. Many great and salubrious rivers flow through it. There are also many very high mountains there. All these islands are very beautiful, and distinguished by various qualities; they are accessible, and full of a great variety of trees stretching up to the stars; the leaves of which I believe are never shed, for I saw them as green and flourishing as they are usually in Spain in the month of May; some of them were blossoming, some were bearing fruit, some were in other conditions; each one was thriving in its own way. The nightingale and various other birds without number were singing, in the month of November, when I was exploring them exceed belief, unless one has seen them.

[1]   In other editions this part of the sentence is as follows: "concerning the islands of India beyond the Ganges, recently discovered."

[2]   The correct name is Gabriel Sanchez.

[3]   29 April. A kalend or calend is the first day of each month in the ancient Roman calendar.

[4]   Here the Latin translator is in error. Columbus sailed from Palos de Moguer on 3 August 1492, reaching the Ca-

naries on 8 September. Thirty-three days later, on 11 October, he reached the Bahamas.

[5]   The island of San Salvador has been identified with Grand Turk, Cat, Watling, Mariguana, Samana and Acklin Islands.

[6]   The island of Cuba.

[7]   China.

[8]   Hispaniola, or Haiti.

. . . This Hispana, moreover, abounds in different kinds of spices, in gold, and in metals. On this island, indeed, and on all the others which I have seen, and of which I have knowledge, the inhabitants of both sexes go always naked, just as they came into the world, except some of the women, who use a covering of a leaf or some foliage, or a cotton cloth, which they make themselves for that purpose. All these people lack, as I said above, every kind of iron; they are also without weapons, which indeed are unknown; nor are they competent to use them, not on account of deformity of body, for they are well formed, but because they are timid and full of fear. They carry for weapons, however, reeds baked in the sun, on the lower ends of which they fasten some shafts of dried wood rubbed down to a point and indeed they do not venture to use these always; for it frequently happened when I sent two or three of my men to some of the villages, that they might speak with the natives, a compact troop of the Indians would march out, and as soon as they saw our men approaching, they would quickly take flight, children being pushed aside by their fathers, and fathers by their children. And this was not because any hurt or injury had been inflicted on any one of them, for to every one whom I visited and with whom I was able to converse, I distributed whatever I had, cloth and many other things, no return being made to me; but they are by nature fearful and timid. Yet when they perceive that they are safe, putting aside all fear, they are of simple manners and trustworthy, and very liberal with everything they have, refusing no one who asks for anything they may possess, and even themselves inviting us to ask for things. They show greater love for all others than for themselves; they give valuable things for trifles, being satisfied even with a very small return, or with nothing; however, I forbade that things so small and of no value should be given to them, such as pieces of plates, dishes and glass, likewise keys and shoe-straps; although if they were able to obtain these, it seemed to them like getting the most beautiful jewels in the world. . . . They also traded cotton and gold for pieces of bows, bottles, jugs and jars, like persons without reason, which I forbade because it was very wrong; and I gave to them many beautiful and pleasing things that I had brought with me, no value being taken in exchange, in order that I might the more easily make them friendly to me, that they might be made worshippers of Christ, and that they might be full of love towards our king, queen, and prince, and the whole Spanish nation; also that they might be zealous to search out and collect, and deliver to us those things of which they had plenty, and which we greatly needed. These people practice no kind of idolatry; on the contrary they firmly believe that all strength and power, and in fact all good things are in heaven, and that I had come down from thence with these ships and sailors; and in this belief I was received there after they had put aside fear. Nor are they slow or unskilled, but of excellent and acute understanding; and the men who have navigated that sea give an account of everything in an admirable manner; but they never saw people clothed, nor these kind of ships. As soon as I reached that sea, I seized by force several Indians on the first island, in order that they might learn from us, and in like manner tell us about those things in these lands of which they themselves had knowledge; and the plan succeeded, for in a short time we understood them and they us, sometimes by gestures and signs, sometimes by words; and it was a great advantage to us. They are coming with me now, yet always believing that I descended from heaven, although they have been living with us for a long time, and are living with us to-day. And these men were the first who announced it wherever we landed, continually proclaiming to the others in a loud voice, "Come, come, and you will see the celestial people." Whereupon both women and men, both children and adults, both young men and old men, laying aside the fear caused a little before, visited us eagerly, filling the road with a great crowd, some bringing food, and some drink, with great love and extraordinary goodwill.

. . . In all these islands there is no difference in the appearance of the people, nor in the manners and language, but all understand each other mutually; a fact that is very important for the end which I suppose to be earnestly desired by our most illustrious king, that is, their conversion to the holy religion of Christ, to which in truth, as far as I can perceive, they are very ready and favorably inclined.

. . . In all these islands, as I have understood, each man is content with only one wife, except the princes or kings, who are permitted to have twenty. The women appear to work more than the men. I was not able to find out surely whether they have individual property, for I saw that one man had the duty of distributing to the others, especially refreshments, food, and things of that kind. I found no monstrosities among them, as very many supposed, but men of great reverence, and friendly. Nor are they black like the Ethiopians. They have straight hair hanging down. They do not remain where the solar rays send out the heat, for the strength of the sun is very great here, because it is distant from the equinoctial line, as it seems, only twenty-six degrees. On the tops of the mountains too the cold is severe, but the Indians, however, moderate it, partly by being accustomed to the place, and partly by the help of very hot victuals, of which they eat frequently and immoderately. And so I did not see any monstrosity, nor did I have knowledge of them anywhere, excepting a certain island named Charis, which is the second in passing from Hispana to India. This island is inhabited by a certain people who are considered very warlike by their neighbors. These eat human flesh. The said people have many kinds of row-boats, in which they cross over to all the other Indian islands, and seize and carry away every thing that they can. They differ in no way from the others, only that they wear long hair like the women. They use bows and darts made of reeds, with sharpened shafts fastened to the larger end, as we have described. On this account they are considered warlike, wherefore the other Indians are afflicted with continual fear, but I regard them as of no more account than the others. These are the people who visit certain women, who alone inhabit the island Mateunin[9], which is the first in passing from Hispana to India. These women, moreover, perform no kind of work of their sex, for they use bows and darts, like those I have described of their husbands; they protect themselves with sheets of copper, of which there is great abundance among them. They tell me of another island greater than the aforesaid Hispana, whose inhabitants are without hair, and which abounds in gold above all the others. I am bringing with me men of this island and of the others that I have seen, who give proof of the things that I have described. Finally, that I may compress in few words the brief account of our departure and quick return, and the gain, I promise this, that if I am supported by our most invincible sovereigns with a little of their help, as much gold can be supplied as they will need, indeed as much of spices, of cotton, of chewing gum (which is found only in Chios), also as much of aloes wood, and as many slaves for the navy, as their majesties will wish to demand. Likewise rhubarb and other kinds of spices, which I suppose these men whom I left in the said fort have already found and will continue to find; since I remained in no place longer than the winds forced me, except in the town of the Nativity, while I provided for the building of the fort, and for the safety of all. Which things, although they are very great and remarkable, yet they would have been much greater, if I had been aided by as many ships as the occasion required. Truly great and wonderful is this, and not corresponding to our merits, but to the holy Christian religion, and to the piety and religion of our sovereigns, because what the human understanding could not attain, that the divine will has granted to human efforts. For God is wont to listen to his servants who love his precepts, even in impossibilities, as has happened to us on the present occasion, who have attained that which hitherto mortal

---

[9] Possibly Martinique.

men have never reached. For if any one has written or said any thing about these islands, it was all with obscurities and conjectures; no one claims that he had seen them; from which they seemed like fables. Therefore let the king and queen, the princes and their most fortunate kingdoms, and all other countries of Christendom give thanks to our Lord and Savior Jesus Christ, who has bestowed upon us so great a victory and gift. Let religious processions be solemnised; let sacred festivals be given; let the churches be covered with festive garlands. Let Christ rejoice on earth, as He rejoices in heaven, which He foresees coming to salvation so many souls of people hitherto lost. Let us be glad also, as well on account of the exaltation of our faith, as on account of the increase of our temporal affairs, of which not only Spain, but universal Christendom will be partaker. These things that have been done are thus briefly related. Farewell.

1493

Bartolomé de Las Casas (1474–1566)

Bartolomé de Las Casas has been described as the "authentic expression of the true Spanish conscience" and excoriated as a traitor to his country, the principal creator of the "Black Legend" of Spanish cruelty in the colonization of the New World. Born in Seville, he is said to have studied at the University of Salamanca before becoming a priest. He was an eyewitness to many of the key events in the conquest of New Spain, starting with the first voyage of Christopher Columbus. As well, he participated in the conquest of Cuba, receiving land as a reward. In 1514, however, he experienced a change of heart, and came to feel that the Native peoples of America had been unjustly treated. Las Casas soon became known as the champion of Native rights, successively as a reformer at the court in Spain, unsuccessful colonizer in Venezuela, friar in Hispaniola, defender of Indians in debates among ecclesiastics in Mexico, promoter of the plan to Christianize the Indians of Chiapa by peaceful means, agitator before the court of the Emperor Charles V[1] in favor of legislation favorable to Indians, and Bishop of Chiapas. After returning to Spain in 1547 at the age of seventy-three, he served as attorney-at-large for the Indians during the last years of his life.

Las Casas was one of the first Europeans to comprehend the implications of the discovery of the New World, and to praise Columbus for his perseverance in the face of adversity. However, after the initial sense of wonder felt by Spaniards and Indians at first contact began to subside, he soon realized that the European refusal to perceive the Native peoples of America as valid interlocutors would lead to the worst sort of oppression and direct violence on the part of the colonizers against the Native peoples of America. In his historical and juridical writings, Las Casas argues that ". . . the way to bring into the bosom of the Christian faith and religion men who are outside the church must be a method which persuades their understanding and which moves, exhorts and gently attracts their will." He denounces the atrocities committed in the course of Spanish colonization, and accumulates information on Indian culture in order to refute charges based on Aristotelian thought that Indians were natural slaves.

The *History of the Indies* is a detailed account of the discovery, exploration and settlement of the New World up to 1520 by Spain. Though Las Casas began it in 1527 and continued to work on it for the rest of his life, it was only published in 1875. It offers the reader an eyewitness account not only of the first voyage of Christopher Columbus but also of subsequent interactions between Spaniards and the Native peoples of the New World.

---

[1] King Charles I of Spain, the Emperor Charles V of the Hapsburg Empire (1500–1558).

Primary Work

The following excerpts are translated by Susan Castillo from the Spanish *Historia de las Indias* (Mexico City: Fondo de Cultura Economica, Biblioteca Americana, 1965).

Further Reading

Lewis Hanke, *The Spanish Struggle for Justice in the Conquest of America* (Boston: Little Brown, 1965).

History of the Indies

From Book I, Chapter XXXVII: On the Natural Law of God in His World, and the Difficulty of Greater Matters, mainly those of Faith, and the Reason for This. How the Men became Discouraged after such a Long Voyage without Sighting Land; How they murmured and cursed Christopher Columbus . . . How Christopher Columbus consoled them with Good Words, and great Modesty and Patience

Great deeds, and those which God holds in great esteem as those which must result in His own honor and glory and in the universal benefit of His Church and in the end promote the welfare of the number of His Elect, are only achieved (as we have said in some of the preceding chapters) with countless difficulties, contradictions, labor and dangers. Indeed, this is as it is duly ordained by divine Knowledge and Power as one of the inviolable laws placed in this world within everything which by its character and nature is good (temporal though these things may be) and even more within those which lead men to real life and eternal bounty, just as the great celebration is preceded by great fasting. . . . It is also the case that patience in adversity and affliction and delay in attaining what one desires cause the Elect to grow in merit, not least because gifts from such a mighty Donor, the more they are desired and the more difficulties and afflictions are encountered in obtaining them, the more esteemed and feared they are by all those who know them. For these reasons, God sent Christopher Columbus incomparable anguish and temptation (more intolerable than the rest), in order to test him. These tests did not come from the sea and the wind (though these too were reserved to him) but from the men and fellow voyagers who should have come to his assistance.

And it was thus, seeing that the men of the ships were not experts in such prolonged navigation but were accustomed to seeing land every day, or almost every day, since as we have said previously, the greatest space of sea which our people navigated was that of the Canaries[2], or the islands of the Azores[3], or that of the island of Madeira[4], or the islands of Cape Verde[5], in which one does not go without seeing land for more than 200 leagues. One of the many things they took as a pretext for faltering and thus for complaining that the voyage was so long and the reward and consolation so uncertain, was the prosperity God gave them in such good and favorable winds which always carried them so far. This was in a sea which seemed so flat that it was more like a lagoon of stagnant water than a sea, borne out by their not finding the water as salty as that they had left behind. They thus inferred that, as they always had a wind (as during most of the year there are northerly breezes in these seas), and the sea was always so

[2]   An archipelago of seven islands located in the Atlantic Ocean off the northwest coast of Africa.
[3]   The Azores archipelago, discovered by Goncalo Velho Cabral in 1431.
[4]   An island in the Atlantic, discovered by the Portuguese

explorers Joao Goncalves Zarco and Tristao Vaz Teixeira in 1418–19.
[5]   The Cape Verde islands were discovered by Alvise de Cadamosto in 1455.

calm, they must be in another world and in regions different, without a wind to enable them to turn around. And thus, one and all together took everything they saw and everything that happened to them in the worst way. The grumbling and cursing against their Captain General and those who had sent him[6] began to manifest itself, and they shamelessly said to his face that he had deceived them and was leading them to their deaths. They swore to this and that if he did not turn around, they would throw him first into the sea.

When the other ships arrived to speak with him, he heard many words which pierced his soul no less than the speech of those close to him who were rebelling. Christopher Columbus saw himself surrounded by a bitterness which caused his heart more anguish than finding himself among the waves of the sea. He was a foreigner among undisciplined, rudely spoken and occasionally insolent people (as is the case with most sailors). This notwithstanding, he ignored their feckless insubordination, and with great patience and prudence gave them encouragement with gentle and loving words and a gracious, cheerful countenance, and with authority. He begged them to remember how hard they had worked thus far, which was the most important thing, and how because of the little that remained they would not wish to lose what they had gained in the past; and that great things could only be attained by great labors and difficulties; and that he trusted in God who sooner than they thought would bring them joy and consolation. As well, they knew that the King and Queen who had sent him and those who sailed with him were telling the truth. With these and other words he did what he could, though it did not placate them, but caused them to flare up, as they were people of a disorderly and desperate nature. As God wished to confound their inconstancy and show favor to the humility of Christopher Columbus, and was about to manifest His truth, on Saturday, 22 September, they had contrary winds, gales, were tossed about and were blown 30 leagues off course, and on Sunday 23 September, the seas rose, so much so that they were afraid, as there are always winds and gales in this place. As the sea ahead was flat and tame, they thought they could not turn back and return to Spain, but trembled at so many contrary winds and at the roughness of the sea. . . . Christopher Columbus says of this that God dealt with him and with them just as He had dealt with Moses and the Jews when he delivered them from Egypt, giving signs which confused the Jews but which favored and aided Moses.[7] They saw that Sunday a turtledove on the ship, and later a gannet and a little river bird and other white fowl, and on the many plants floating on the water, they found small live crabs. On this day they traveled 22 leagues, though not in a straight line. The following Monday 24 September they traveled 14½ leagues on the right path. A gannet flew over the ship, as did many land birds which came from the West. As well, fish came toward the ship, and they shot some with harpoons (which are iron instruments like the fingers of the hand held out, but larger). The more God showed them manifest signs that it was impossible to be far from land, the more they raged against Columbus. All day and night, small groups formed, muttering to one another about how they could go back.

Thus they said it was madness and suicide to risk their lives to follow the madness of a foreign man who, in order to make himself a great lord, was determined to die. Placing them in an affliction as great as his own, and deceiving so many people, especially when his enterprise or dream had been contradicted and deemed vain or mad by so many great and erudite

---

[6]   I.e. Ferdinand and Isabella, the King and Queen of Spain. Columbus' crew is depicted not only as mutinous but as guilty of high treason.

[7] It should be noted that in the same year (1492) that Columbus reached America, the Jews were expelled from Spain by the Inquisition. Las Casas thus differentiates between the Jews, viewed as quarrelsome and factious, and Moses, their leader, who in his perspective enjoyed divine favor.

men was enough to justify any course of action; and they had gone further than anyone had dared sail, and they were under no obligation to sail to the end of the world, especially since if they went any further there would not be enough provisions for the return journey. Some even said that the best thing would be to cast him overboard one night, if he insisted on going ahead, and put about that he had fallen while reading the stars with his quadrant or astrolabe, adding that as he was a foreigner, few (or none) would call them to account, but that many would say that God had given him[8] his just desserts for his daring. In these and similar occupations they spent all their time, night and day, and were probably encouraged in this by the Pinzones[9], the captains and leaders of all the rest, who like the other sailors were from the town of Palos y Moguel[10]. Christopher Columbus complained greatly of these Pinzones and the pain they had given him. Whoever reads this can easily imagine what apprehension and fear Christopher Columbus must have felt that these people, free and reckless as most seafarers are, might do him harm. What sadness and anguish and bitterness must have accompanied him!

He constantly entrusted himself to God, prepared for any calamity or death that might come to him. He dissembled with them, cheering them by honouring the least of them as much as he could; he laughed with them while his heart was weeping, and sometimes reminded them of the severity with which the King and Queen might treat them if they turned back from a quest after seeing such unequivocal signs that they were so close, that nobody who heard of it would doubt this and that they would justly be blamed. To avoid this and other such consequences, he implored that as men of spirit and virtue, they suffer just a few days more, promising them by the faith he had in the Holy Trinity, they would soon see land, and would be gladdened with this sight.

Book I, Chapter XL: In Which is Described the Character of the Island which Lay Before Them, and its People

From this point on we must speak of Christopher Columbus in a different fashion, adding to his name the honorary title of Admiral and designation of His Grace, which the King and Queen so justly awarded him. Indeed, with so much sweat, danger and toil, both past and present as well as those still to be suffered, he had achieved for them far more than he had promised. At daylight (a moment desired by all), the three ships approached land and anchored, and they saw the beach full of naked people, so many that the sand and earth was completely out of sight. This land was and is an island 15 leagues in length, more or less, all very low, without any mountains, like an orchard full of fresh green trees, like all the other lands of the Lucayos in this area . . . In the middle of it was good fresh water, which they drank. It was populated by many people, so many that they could hardly fit on the island. As indeed later will be explained, all the lands in this part of the world are of gentle contours, especially the lands of the Lucayos (for it is thus that the peoples of these small islands call themselves), which means island dwellers, as *cayos* in their language are islands. Thus, as the Admiral and his men were eager to go ashore and see the people, just as the people were eager to see them land. Indeed, they were amazed to see those ships, which they must have thought were animals which had come by sea or emerged from it. (This was on Friday morning, Octo-

---

[8]   Columbus.

[9]   Martin Alonso Pinzon was commander of the second ship in the fleet, the *Pinta*, with his brother Francisco Martin as pilot. A third Pinzon brother, Vicente Yañez Pinzon, was

the captain of the *Niña*, the third ship.

[10]   A small fishing port on Spain's southwest Atlantic coast, from which Columbus and his expedition set sail.

ber 12.) He[11] went in an armed landing boat, with his weapons, and as many men who would fit in it. He also ordered that the captains Martin Alonso and Vicente Yañez[12] do the same. The Admiral brought out the royal flag, and the two captain's flags with the green cross which the Admiral carried on all the ships as his ensign and standard, with an F for King Ferdinand and an I for Queen Isabella, and above each letter their crowns, one at one end of the cross and one at the other.

When the Admiral and all the others leapt ashore, they knelt, many weeping, giving thanks to their Almighty God and Lord that He had brought them to safety and that He had shown them some of the fruits which they (especially Christopher Columbus) had desired and sighed for in such a long and unusual pilgrimage. . . . Who could ever express their rejoicing and jubilation, full of incomparable joy and inestimable glee, as well as the confusion of those who felt they were besieged because they had not believed him but rather resisted him and insulted him, the constant and patient Columbus? What would their bows mean to him? The forgiveness for which they begged him, with tears? The offers to serve him for the rest of his life? And lastly, the honours and gifts which they gave him, the obedience and subordination that they promised him? They outdid themselves to please him, placate him and make him joyful. He, in tears, embraced them, forgave them, urged them to remember that it all was due to God. All the men addressed him as Admiral, Viceroy and Governor appointed by the King and Queen of Castile, and they swore fealty to him and the royal persons he represented with so much rejoicing and gaiety that it would be best to leave the greatness of it all to the discretion of the prudent reader rather than attempt to express it in inadequate words.

Then the Admiral, before the two captains, Rodrigo de Escobedo, royal notary of all the fleet, Rodrigo Sanchez de Segovia, inspector general of the armament, and all the Christian men who had accompanied him, leapt ashore and declared that he took possession of said island, which he named San Salvador[13] for the King and Queen . . . The Indians who were present in great number, gazed in astonishment at the Christians, amazed at their beards, their whiteness and their clothing. They approached the bearded men, especially the Admiral, as though by the eminence and authority of his person and his scarlet clothing they had known he was the leader, and raised their hands to his beard in wonderment (for none of them have beards), scrutinizing the whiteness of the hands and feet of the Spaniards very carefully.

As the Admiral and the rest looked at the simplicity of the Indians, they endured this with pleasure and delight. Indeed, the Christians gazed at the Indians, no less than the Indians at them, amazed at the gentleness, innocence and trust of people whom they had never met, and whose appearance, if they deemed it ferocious, might have alarmed them and caused them to flee. They walked among them and drew close, with such nonchalance and ease, with all their shameful parts uncovered, as though the state of innocence was restored or had never been lost. . . . They had no weapons except for some *azagayas*, which are lances whose points have been burnt and sharpened, some with the tooth or bone of a fish, which they used more to catch fish than to kill men . . . We later perceived their natural kindness, their innocence, humility, tameness, peacefulness and virtuous inclinations, excellent wit, and readiness to receive our holy faith and to be imbued with Christian religion. Those of us who spoke with them on this island of Española often conversed about spiritual and divine things, transmitting Christian doctrine and administering all seven Holy Sacraments. We especially heard their confessions and gave them the Holy Sacrament of the Eucharist . . .

[11]   Columbus

[12]   The brothers Martin Alonso Pinzon and Vicente Yañez Pinzon, captains of the *Pinta* and the *Niña*.

[13] Literally, Holy Saviour.

From *Book III, Chapter LXXVIII: Of the Labors of the Indians in Cuba*

. . . At this time, of all these islands and indeed of all the Indies, the place most dreamed of and the one which inspired most hope was Cuba, which was said to have a great deal of gold and whose people were domesticated and peaceable. The Spaniards had arrived there to settle it two years ago under the leadership of Diego Velázquez . . . Diego Velázquez, who governed the island as the Admiral's lieutentant[14], chose five villages settled by Spaniards, as well as Baracoa. The Indians in the areas surrounding each village were divided among the Spaniards, each of whom, due to their avidity of gold and looseness of conscience, without taking into account that these people were made of flesh and bone, put them to work in the mines and indeed in everything else. This was so sudden and so merciless that in very few days the innumerable deaths among these people revealed the great inhumanity with which they were treated. They died more brutally and more quickly at this time than in other places, because as the Spaniards ranged about the island, pacifying it (as they said), the Spaniards took Indians from the villages to make use of them. Everyone was eating and no-one was sowing, and the people fled from them in confusion and fear in order not to be killed (as many had been). The land was thus left uncultivated and abandoned.

As the greed of the Spaniards, as I have already said, urged them on so that they did not sow in order to have bread but rather to gather the gold which they had not sown . . . they ordered the men and women (who did not eat enough to work, let alone to live) to work. And it is true, as I have said before, that in the presence of me and other witnesses one told us (as though it were something praiseworthy, a great feat) that with the Indians given to him they had plowed many fields and made mounds of earth, and that he had sent them every third day or every other day to the hills to eat whatever berries and fruits they could find there. After that he would make them work two or three days more at this task without giving them anything to eat, not a single bite. This labor involved digging all day long, and is much more arduous than digging in the vineyards and orchards of our Spain, because they have to make mounds three and four feet square and three or four feet high, not with hoes but with blackened sticks.

It was thus that, starving, with nothing to eat and working so hard, these people died more quickly and in greater number than in other places. And as they[15] took healthy men and women to the mines and to other labors, only the old and infirm were left in the villages, without anyone to look after them; they all died of anguish and disease, and raging hunger. On some occasions, as I was walking in those days around the island, I heard them cry out from inside the houses, and when I entered to see them, asking what was the matter, they answered, "Hunger, hunger." And, as not a single man, woman or child capable of standing on their own legs escaped from being taken to these labors, the milk of the childbearing women with small babies dried up due to the lack of food and the hard work, and these infants died; indeed, of this cause seven thousand babies, boys and girls, died in about three months. This was reported to the Catholic King[16] by a trustworthy person who had discovered it. At this time it also happened that an officer of the King, who had been given 300 Indians as his share, made them work so hard in the mines and at other tasks that in three months less than a tenth of them were still alive.

---

[14]   As the representative of Columbus.
[15]   The Spaniards.

[16]   Ferdinand of Spain.

Pero Vaz de Caminha (1467?–1520?)

Pero Vaz de Caminha was born to a family of land-owners in Northern Portugal, at a time when Portugal's maritime expansion had just begun. On 8 March 1500 he set off as scribe with the expedition of Pedro Alvares Cabral, consisting of a fleet of thirteen ships. Some weeks later, possibly due to a navigational error or to adverse winds, they encountered signs of land such as floating plants and land birds, and on 23 April first set foot on what is now Brazil, which they named the Land of the True Cross. After laying in a store of fresh water and firewood, they departed once again for Africa and India.

Pero Vaz de Caminha's letter to King Manuel I of Portugal is in many ways an extraordinary document. Though his style is not polished, Vaz de Caminha captures the initial sense of wonder with which the Portuguese and the Native Brazilians,

probably of the Tupinambá tribe, contemplated each other. Vaz de Caminha was an acute and pragmatic observer, however, and remarks that the Indians approach to watch a cross being erected not out of piety but because of their interest in the metal tools used by the Portuguese.

PRIMARY WORK

Translated by Susan Castillo from "Carta de Pero Vaz de Caminha ao Rei D. Manuel I," in W. Greenlee, ed., *A Viagem de Pedro Alvares Cabral ao Brasil e a India* (Porto: Livraria Civilizacao, s.d.).

FURTHER READING

C. R. Boxer, *The Portuguese Seaborne Empire, 1415–1825* (Manchester: Carcanet, 1991).

FROM THE LETTER OF PERO VAZ DE CAMINHA TO KING MANUEL I, MAY 1, 1500

My Lord,

As the Captain-Major of this fleet and the other captains have written to Your Highness the news of the finding of this new land on our present voyage, I too shall describe it to Your Highness as well as I may, though to depict it and speak of it well I am the least equipped of all. Still, Your Highness may view my ignorance as good will, in the knowledge that I shall neither prettify nor distort nor add anything to what I saw and to what appeared to me. Regarding navigation and occurrences of the voyage I shall not speak, as I would not know how to do so . . .

. . . They [the Tupinambá] are reddish-brown in colour, with goodly faces and well-made noses. They go about naked without any covering, nor care about covering or showing their private parts, and are as innocent about this as they are about showing their faces. Their bottom lips are pierced with a white bone the length of a hand and the thickness of a spindle, sharp as a needle at the ends. They put these through the inside of the lip and the part between the lips and the teeth resembles a rook used at chess. They carry it in such a way that it does not bother them and does not impede them from speaking or eating or drinking. Their hair is thick and shorn on top, cut over the ears, and one of them was wearing at the back of his neck a kind of wig made of the feathers of a yellow bird . . . One of them looked at the Captain's chain and began to gesture toward land and then to the chain, as though to say that there was gold there. They also saw a silver candlestick and nodded toward land and then toward the candlestick as though there were silver there as well. We showed them a grey parrot belonging to the Captain, and they held it and gestured toward land saying that they could be found there. They were shown a lamb and then a chicken, but they were almost afraid of the latter and did not want to touch it, and drew back in fright. They[1] gave them bread and cooked fish, cakes, honey, and figs, but they[2] ate almost nothing and spat most of it out. They brought them wine in a goblet, but they hardly tasted it and wanted no more. They brought them water in a jar, but they tasted it and spat it out. One of them saw some white rosary beads and nodded for them to be given to him. He played with them and put them around his neck and then took them off and wrapped them around his arm, and pointed to land and then to the beads and to the Captain's chain, as though saying they would give gold for them. We interpreted it thus because we wished it to be so, but if he meant that he would take the beads and the chain, we did not wish to understand because we had no intention of giving them to him. He then returned the beads to the man who had given them to him and they stretched out on the rug to sleep, without covering their private parts in any way.

. . . Going upriver, Diogo Dias of Sacavém, who was a charming, fun-loving man, took with him a piper of ours with his pipes and started dancing with them, taking them by the hands, and they frolicked and laughed and danced with him to the sound of the pipes. After they danced, he turned cartwheels and somersaults, which startled them, and they laughed and frolicked with him. Just when he thought he had gained their affection, they shied away like mountain goats and fled upland.

. . . Two of our carpenters made a great cross from wood which had been cut for this purpose the day before. Many of them approached the carpenters, and I think they did so more to see the iron tools they were using than to see the Cross, for they have nothing made of iron and cut their wood and sticks with stones like wedges between two sticks tied together . . . .

Giovanni da Verrazzano (1485–1528)

Born to an affluent Florentine family in 1485, Giovanni da Verrazzano set sail to the New World in January 1524 in search of a maritime route to the Orient. Clearly, however, he was aware that his first landfall would not be Asia. In his own words, ". . . I did not expect to find such an obstacle of new land as I have found; and if for some reason I did expect to find it, I estimated there would be some strait to get through to the Eastern Ocean[1]. This was the opinion of all the ancients, who certainly believed that our Western Ocean[2] was joined to the Eastern Ocean of India without any land in between. Aristotle supports this theory by arguments of various analogies, but this opinion is quite contrary to that of the moderns, and has been proven false by experience. Nevertheless, land has been found by modern man which was unknown to the ancients, another world with respect to the one they knew."

Verrazzano's 1524 voyage provided a basis for French claims to territories in the New World. Though he later made two further voyages, the last one, to the West Indies, ended in disaster in 1528, when the intrepid Florentine went ashore and was allegedly captured and eaten by cannibals.

PRIMARY WORK

Lawrence C. Wroth (ed.), *The Voyages of Giovanni da Verrazzano, 1524–1528*, translation of the Cèllere Codex by Susan Tarrow (New Haven: Yale University Press, 1970).

FURTHER READING

C. H. Johnson, *Famous Explorers and Discoverers of America* (Boston: Le Page & Co., 1941).

---

[1]   The Portuguese.
[2]   The Natives.

GIOVANNI DA VERRAZZANO
[1]   The Pacific.
[2]   The Atlantic.

FROM THE VOYAGE OF VERRAZZANO, FLORENTINE NOBLE IN THE SERVICE OF FRANÇOIS I, KING OF FRANCE, 1524

. . . we anchored off the coast and sent the small boat in to land. We had seen many people coming to the seashore, but they fled when they saw us approaching; several times they stopped and turned around to look at us in great wonderment. We reassured them with various signs, and some of them came up, showing great delight at seeing us and marveling at our clothes, appearance, and our whiteness; they showed us by various signs where we could most easily secure the boat, and offered us some of their food. We were on land, and I shall now tell Your Majesty briefly what we were able to learn of their life and customs.

They go completely naked except that around their loins they wear skins of small animals like martens[3], with a narrow belt of grass around the body, to which they tie various tails of other animals which hang down to the knees; the rest of the body is bare, and so is the head. Some of them wear garlands of birds' feathers. They are dark in color, not unlike the Ethiopians, with thick black hair, not very long, tied back behind the head like a small tail. As for the physique of these men, they are well proportioned, of medium height, a little taller than we are. They have broad chests, strong arms, and the legs and other parts of the body are well composed. There is nothing else, except that they tend to be rather broad in the face: but not all, for we saw many with angular faces. They have big black eyes, and an attentive and open look. They are not very strong, but they have a sharp cunning, and are agile and swift runners. From what we could tell from observation, in the last two respects they resemble the Orientals, particularly those from the farthest Sinarian[4] regions. We could not learn the details of the life and customs of these people because of the short time we spent on land, due to the fact that there were few men, and the ship was anchored on the high seas. Not far from these people, we found others on the shore whose way of life we think is similar. I will now tell Your Majesty about it, and describe the situation and nature of this land. The seashore is completely covered with fine sand 15 feet deep, which rises in the form of small hills about 50 paces wide. After climbing farther, we found other streams and inlets from the sea which come in by several mouths, and follow the ins and outs of the shoreline. Nearby we could see a stretch of country much higher than the sandy shore, with many beautiful fields and plains full of great forests, some sparse and some dense; and the trees have so many colors, and are so beautiful and delightful that they defy description. And do not think, Your Majesty, that these forests are like the Hyrcanian[5] Forest or the wild wastelands of Scythia[6] and the northern countries, full of common trees; they are adorned and clothed with palms, laurel, cypress, and other varieties of tree unknown in our Europe. And these trees emit a sweet fragrance over a large area, the nature of which we could not examine for the reason stated above, not because we found it difficult to get through the forests – indeed, they are nowhere so dense as to be impenetrable. We think that they belong to the Orient by virtue of the surroundings, and that they are not without some kind of narcotic or aromatic liquor. There are other riches, like gold, which ground of such a color usually denotes. There is an abun-

---

3 An animal related to the weasel.

4 Chinese.

5 Hyrcania, or Wolf's Land, an ancient region located southeast of the Caspian Sea.

6 A region north and northeast of the Black Sea.

dance of animals, stags, deer, hares; and also of lakes and pools of running water with various types of bird, perfect for all the delights and pleasures of the hunt.

. . . Due to the lack of [a common] language, we were unable to find out by signs or gestures how much religious faith these people we found possess. We think they have neither religion nor laws, that they do not know of a First Cause or Author[7], that they do not worship the sky, the stars, the sun, the moon, or other planets, nor do they even practice any kind of idolatry; we do not know whether they offer any sacrifices or other prayers, nor are there any temples or churches of prayer among their peoples. We consider that they have no religion and that they live in absolute freedom, and that everything they do proceeds from Ignorance; for they are very easily persuaded, and they imitated everything that they saw us Christians do with regard to divine worship, with the same fervor and enthusiasm that we had.

. . . I hope that with Your Majesty's help we shall have more certain knowledge of this; may God Almighty prosper you in everlasting glory, so that we may see the perfect end to our cosmography, and that the sacred word of the gospel may be fulfilled: "their sound has gone out into every land." In the ship "Dauphine" on the 8th day of July.

1524
Humble servant JANUS VERAZANUS.

Alvar Núñez Cabeza de Vaca (1490?–1556?)

When Alvar Núñez Cabeza de Vaca, a nobleman from Jerez de la Frontera, was appointed Treasurer for the Spanish Crown on the expedition of Panfilo de Narváez to Florida in 1527, it was clear that he was a young man of whom great things were expected. In the wake of the Conquest of Mexico, rivals of Hernán Cortés such as Panfilo de Narváez were eager to gain gold and glory for themselves, and Cabeza de Vaca's role on his expedition to Florida was to ensure that the Spanish Crown received its just share of any riches encountered. Narváez, however, was a remarkably incompetent leader. He had been jailed by Cortés for three years, was vain, proud and obsessed with gold and glory. As a result of a mixture of bad luck (two of his ships were lost in a hurricane) and ineptitude on the part of Narváez, only four men (out of six hundred) survived; the rest had either deserted, drowned, or been killed in encounters with hostile Indians.

Cabeza de Vaca was shipwrecked on Galveston Island in November 1528, along with two Span-iards (Andres Dorantes and Alonso del Castillo) and Estevanico the Moor, the black slave of Dorantes. After two years spent on the Gulf coast of what now is Texas as the slave and prisoner of the Karankawa Indians, he went toward the north and west, trading with other Native groups and exercising as a healer. In order to survive, he became an acute observer of (and active participant in) Native culture, to such a degree that he has been termed one of the first mestizo voices in North American literature. His texts offer the reader a view of the process of acculturation through which European colonizers, by interacting with Native culture, are themselves transformed.

After conflict with certain of his fellow Spaniards (which Cabeza de Vaca called, with perhaps unintentional oxymoronic irony, "Christian slavers") due to their mistreatment of the Natives of Western Mexico, he returned to Spain in 1537. There, Cabeza de Vaca completed his Relation, in an attempt to argue for further expeditions to the New World and for a more humane policy in re-

---

[7]   I.e. a divine Creator.

gard to Native peoples. Though he was appointed to an administrative post in the Rio de la Plata region of what is now Paraguay, his activities met with resistance from those who had most to gain from exploiting the local populations. He was arrested and sent back to Spain in chains in 1545. In 1551 he was not only exiled to the North of Africa but forbidden ever to return to the New World.

The following excerpts are taken from the Lenox Library edition (1907).

PRIMARY WORK

Alvar Núñez Cabeza de Vaca, *The Narrative of Alvar Núñez Cabeza de Vaca*, trans. Thomas Buckingham Smith, ed. Frederick Hodge (New York: Charles Scribners' Sons, 1907).

FURTHER READING

José Fernandez, *Alvar Núñez Cabeza de Vaca: The Forgotten Chronicler* (Miami: Ediciones Universal, 1975).
John Terrell, *Journey into Darkness: Cabeza de Vaca's Expedition Across North America, 1528–1536* (London: Jarrolds, 1964).

FROM CHAPTER 12: THE INDIANS BRING US FOOD

At sunrise the next day, the time the Indians appointed, they came according to their promise, and brought us a large quantity of fish with certain roots, some a little larger than walnuts, others a trifle smaller, the greater part got from under the water and with much labor. In the evening they returned and brought us more fish and roots. They sent their women and children to look at us, who went back rich with the hawk-bells and beads given them, and they came afterwards on other days, returning as before. Finding that we had provision, fish, roots, water, and other things we asked for, we determined to embark again and pursue our course. Having dug out our boat from the sand in which it was buried, it became necessary that we should strip, and go through great exertion to launch her, we being in such a state that things very much lighter sufficed to make us great labor.

Thus embarked, at the distance of two crossbow shots in the sea we shipped a wave that entirely wet us. As we were naked, and the cold was very great, the oars loosened in our hands, and the next blow the sea struck us, capsized the boat. The assessor and two others held fast to her for preservation, but it happened to be far otherwise; the boat carried them over, and they were drowned under her. As the surf near the shore was very high, a single roll of the sea threw the rest into the waves and half drowned upon the shore of the island, without our losing any more than those the boat took down. The survivors escaped naked as they were born, with the loss of all they had; and although the whole was of little value, at that time it was worth much, as we were then in November, the cold was severe, and our bodies were so emaciated the bones might be counted with little difficulty, having become the perfect figures of death. For myself I can say that from the month of May passed, I had eaten no other thing than maize, and sometimes I found myself obliged to eat it unparched; for although the beasts were slaughtered while the boats were building, I could never eat their flesh, and I did not eat fish ten times. I state this to avoid giving excuses, and that every one may judge in what condition we were. Besides all these misfortunes, came a north wind upon us, from which we were nearer to death than life. Thanks be to our Lord that, looking among the brands we had used there, we found sparks from which we made great fires. And thus were we asking mercy of Him and pardon for our transgressions, shedding many tears, and each regretting not his own fate alone, but that of his comrades about him.

At sunset, the Indians thinking that we had not gone, came to seek us and bring us food;

but when they saw us thus, in a plight so different from what it was before, and so extraordinary, they were alarmed and turned back. I went toward them and called, when they returned much frightened. I gave them to understand by signs that our boat had sunk and three of our number had been drowned. There, before them, they saw two of the departed, and we who remained were near joining them. The Indians, at sight of what had befallen us, and our state of suffering and melancholy destitution, sat down among us, and from the sorrow and pity they felt, they all began to lament so earnestly that they might have been heard at a distance, and continued so doing more than half an hour. It was strange to see these men, wild and untaught, howling like brutes over our misfortunes. It caused in me as in others, an increase of feeling and a livelier sense of our calamity.

The cries having ceased, I talked with the Christians, and said that if it appeared well to them, I would beg these Indians to take us to their houses. Some, who had been in New Spain, replied that we ought not to think of it; for if they should do so, they would sacrifice us to their idols. But seeing no better course, and that any other led to a nearer and more certain death, I disregarded what was said, and besought the Indians to take us to their dwellings. They signified that it would give them delight, and that we should tarry a little, that they might do what we asked. Presently thirty men loaded themselves with wood and started for their houses, which were far off, and we remained with the others until near night, when, holding us up, they carried us with all haste. Because of the extreme coldness of the weather, lest any one should die or fail by the way, they caused four or five very large fires to be placed at intervals, and at each they warmed us; and when they saw that we had regained some heat and strength, they took us to the next so swiftly that they hardly let us touch our feet to the ground. In this manner we went as far as their habitations, where we found that they had made a house for us with many fires in it. An hour after our arrival, they began to dance and hold great rejoicing, which lasted all night, although for us there was no joy, festivity nor sleep awaiting the hour they should make us victims. In the morning they again gave us fish and roots, showing us such hospitality that we were reassured, and lost somewhat the fear of sacrifice.

From Chapter 15: What Befell us Among the People of Malhado

On an island of which I have spoken, they wished to make us physicians without examination or inquiring for diplomas. They cure by blowing upon the sick, and with that breath and the imposing of hands they cast out infirmity. They ordered that we also should do this, and be of use to them in some way. We laughed at what they did, telling them it was folly, that we knew not how to heal. In consequence, they withheld food from us until we should practice what they required. Seeing our persistence, an Indian told me I knew not what I uttered, in saying that what he knew availed nothing; for stones and other matters growing about in the fields have virtue, and that passing a pebble along the stomach would take away pain and restore health, and certainly then we who were extraordinary men must possess power and efficacy over all other things. At last, finding ourselves in great want we were constrained to obey; but without fear lest we should be blamed for any failure or success.

Their custom is, on finding themselves sick to send for a physician, and after he has applied the cure, they give him not only all they have, but seek among their relatives for more to give. The practitioner scarifies over the seat of pain, and then sucks about the wound. They make cauteries with fire, a remedy among them in high repute, which I have tried on myself and found benefit from it. They afterwards blow on the spot, and having finished, the patient considers that he is relieved.

Our method was to bless the sick, breathing upon them, and recite a Pater-noster and an Ave-Maria, praying with all earnestness to God our Lord that he would give health and influence them to make us some good return. In his clemency he willed that all those for whom we supplicated, should tell the others that they were sound and in health, directly after we made the sign of the blessed cross over them. For this the Indians treated us kindly; they deprived themselves of food that they might give to us, and presented us with skins and some trifles.

FROM CHAPTER 22: THE COMING OF OTHER SICK TO US THE NEXT DAY

We remained with the Avavares eight months, reckoned by the number of moons. In all this time people came to seek us from many parts, and they said that most truly we were children of the sun.

. . . They said that a man wandered through the country whom they called Badthing; he was small of body and wore beard, and they never distinctly saw his features. When he came to the house where they lived, their hair stood up and they trembled. Presently a blazing torch shone at the door, when he entered and seized whom he chose, and giving him three great gashes in the side with a very sharp flint, the width of the hand and two palms in length, he put his hand through them, drawing forth the entrails, from one of which he would cut off a portion more or less, the length of a palm, and throw it on the embers. Then he would give three gashes to an arm, the second cut on the inside of an elbow, and would sever the limb. A little after this, he would begin to unite it, and putting his hands on the wounds, these would instantly become healed. They said that frequently in the dance he appeared among them, sometimes in the dress of a woman, at others in that of a man; that when it pleased him he would take a *buhio*[1], or house, and lifting it high, after a little he would come down with it in a heavy fall. They also stated that many times they offered him victuals, but that he never ate: they asked him whence he came and where was his abiding place, and he showed them a fissure in the earth and said that his house was there below. These things they told us of, we much laughed at and ridiculed; and they seeing our incredulity, brought to us many of those they said he had seized; and we saw the marks of the gashes made in the places according to the manner they had described. We told them he was an evil one, and in the best way we could, gave them to understand, that if they would believe in God our Lord, and become Christians like us, they need have no fear of him, nor would he dare to come and inflict those injuries, and they might be certain he would not venture to appear while we remained in the land. At this they were delighted and lost much of their dread.

---

[1]   An Arawak term for house, referring to a dwelling with an open shed attached.

Bernal Díaz del Castillo (1492–1581)

In his *History of the Conquest of New Spain*, written at the end of a long and eventful life, Bernal Díaz del Castillo offers the eyewitness perspective of one who fought alongside Hernán Cortés in Spanish conquest of the Aztec empire. His text was written in response to the accounts of contemporary historians Francisco López de Gomara and Gonzalo de Illescas, which Díaz del Castillo found distorted and, on occasion, false. Though he characterizes himself as lacking in eloquence, Díaz del Castillo's text offers the reader a fascinating insight into the mentality of a Spanish solider who took part in the conquest of Mexico. His style is vivid and realistic, evoking the personalities involved in the conflict (Cortés, his Indian mistress Doña Marina, Montezuma, and Guatemoc[1]), as well as the intrigues and conflicts within not only the group of Spanish soldiers but also among the different Native groups as well. In the following excerpts he portrays two groups of human beings confronted with a culture radically different from their own, and describes the ways in which they attempt to decode (or annihilate) each other's beliefs and symbolic systems. Díaz del Castillo offers us as well considerable insight into the political and military ability of Cortés, as well as his ruthlessness and intelligence.

In his *History*, Bernal Díaz del Castillo devotes an entire chapter to Doña Marina, an Indian woman sold by her family to another group, who then gave her to Cortés; indeed, Cortés came to be known to the Aztecs as Malinche, an abbreviated version of "Marina's Captain," and she herself was called La Malinche. In subsequent years, the figure of Doña Marina or La Malinche (also known depreciatively as La Chingada, loosely translatable as "She Who Is Violated") has come to symbolize the ambivalent role of the Native woman as mediator between two patriarchal cultures. Bernal Díaz speaks of her with considerable respect and points out that her linguistic ability and her services as a translator were essential to the success of the Conquest. As well, he describes in considerable detail Cortés and his captains' avidity for gold and eagerness to spread the Christian religion by whatever means necessary, including violence; the beauty and prosperity of the lake city of Mexico, capital of the Aztec empire, before the Conquest; the capture of Montezuma; the siege and destruction of the city, and the division of the spoils among Cortés and his men.

PRIMARY WORK

Translated by Susan Castillo from Bernal Díaz del Castillo, *Historia verdadera de la conquista de la Nueva España* , ed. Miguel León-Portilla, Vol. I and II (Madrid: Historia 16, 1984).

HISTORY OF THE CONQUEST OF NEW SPAIN

From *Chapter 37: Of how Doña Marina was a great lady and daughter of great lords, and mistress over towns and vassals, and how she was brought to Tabasco*

Before telling about the great Montezuma and of the famous city of Mexico and the Mexicans, I should like to give an account of Doña Marina, who since her childhood had been a great lady and a *Cacique*[2] over towns and vassals.

Her father and mother were lords and Caciques of a town called Paynala, which had other towns subject to it, and lay about twenty-four miles from the town of Coatzacoalcos. Her father died while she was still very young, and her mother married another Cacique, a young man, to whom she bore a son. It seems that the mother and father were very fond of this son, for they agreed that he should succeed to the Caciqueship when they were dead. To avoid any

---

[1]   Montezuma's nephew and son-in-law.   [2]   Chieftain.

difficulty, they gave Doña Marina to some Indians from Xicalango, and this they did by night in order to be unobserved. They then spread the report that the child had died; and as the daughter of one of their Indian slaves happened to die at this time, they gave it out that it was their daughter the heiress who was dead.

The Indians of Xicalango gave the child to the people of Tabasco, and the Tabascans gave her to Cortés. I myself knew her mother and her half-brother (her mother's son), who was already grown up and ruled the town jointly with his mother, since the old lady's second husband had died. After they became Christians, the mother was called Marta and the son Lazaro. I know all this very well, because in the year 1523, after the conquest of Mexico and the other provinces and at the time of Cristobal de Olid's revolt in Honduras, I passed through the place with Cortés, and the majority of its inhabitants accompanied him as well. As Doña Marina had proved such an excellent woman, and a good interpreter in all the wars of New Spain, Tlascala and Mexico – as I shall relate hereafter – Cortés always took her with him. During this expedition she married a gentleman called Juan Jaramillo at the town of Orizaba . . . Doña Marina was a person of the greatest importance, and was obeyed without question by all the Indians throughout New Spain. And while Cortés was in the town of Coatzacoalcos, he summoned all the Caciques of that province in order to address them on the subject of our holy religion, and the good way in which they had been treated; and Doña Marina's mother and her half brother Lazaro came, along with other Caciques. Doña Marina had told me some time before that she belonged to this province, and that she was the mistress of vassals, and that Cortés knew it well, as did the interpreter Aguilar. Thus it was that mother, son, and daughter came together, and they realised, due to the strong resemblance between them, that Doña Marina and the old lady were related. Both she and her son were very much afraid of Doña Marina; they feared that she had sent for them to have them put to death, and they wept.

When Doña Marina saw them in tears, she consoled them and told them to have no fear. She told her mother that when they had handed her over to the men from Xicalango, they had not known what they were doing. She pardoned the old woman, and gave them many golden jewels and some clothes. Then she sent them back to their town, saying that God had been very gracious to her in freeing her from the worship of idols and making her a Christian, and letting her bear a son by her lord and master Cortés, also in marrying her to such a gentleman as her husband Juan Jaramillo. Even if they made her *Cacica*[3] of all the provinces of New Spain, she said, she would refuse, for she would rather serve her husband and Cortés than anything else in the world. All that I have related here I know for certain and swear to. The whole story seems very much like that of Joseph and his brothers in Egypt, when the Egyptians came into his power over the wheat.[4]

Returning to the matter at hand, Doña Marina knew the language of Coatzacoalcos, which is that of Mexico, and she knew the Tabascan language also. This language is common to Tabasco and Yucatán, and Jeronimo de Aguilar spoke it also. These two understood one another well, and Aguilar translated into Castilian for Cortés.

This was the great beginning of our conquests and thus, thanks be to God, things prospered with us. I have made a point of telling this story, because without Doña Marina we could not have understood the language of New Spain and Mexico.

---

[3]   Female chieftain.

[4]   Cf. Chapters 37–43 of the Book of Genesis. Joseph, sold to the Egyptians by his brothers, interpreted a dream of the Pharoah as presaging seven years of abundance followed by seven years of famine. This enabled the Egyptians to store enough wheat to see them through the lean years. Joseph was then reunited with his family, who had come to buy food.

other. Montezuma welcomed our Captain, and Cortés, speaking through Doña Marina, answered by wishing him very good health. It seems to me that Cortés offered Montezuma his right hand, but Montezuma refused it and extended his own. Then Cortés brought out a necklace which he had been holding, made of those elaborately worked colored glass beads called margaritas, of which I have spoken, and was strung on a cord of gold and dipped in musk to give it a good odor. This he hung round the great Montezuma's neck, and as he did so attempted to embrace him. But the great princes who accompanied Montezuma grasped Cortés' arm to prevent him, for they considered it an indignity.

Then Cortés through Doña Marina told Montezuma that he rejoiced in his heart to have seen such a great prince, and that he took his coming in person to receive him and the repeated favors he had done him as a high honor. After this Montezuma made him another pleasant speech, and told two of his nephews who were supporting him, the Lord of Texcoco and the Lord of Coyoacan, to go with us and show us our quarters. Montezuma returned to the city with the other two kinsmen of his escort, the lords of Cuitlahuac and Tacuba; and all those grand companies of Caciques and dignitaries who had come with him returned also in his train. And as they accompanied their lord we observed them marching with their eyes lowered so that they should not see him, keeping close to the wall as they followed him with great reverence. Thus space was made for us to enter the streets of Mexico without being pressed by the crowd.

. . . They took us to our quarters, which were in some large houses capable of accommodating us all and had formerly belonged to the great Montezuma's father, who was called Axayaca. It was here that Montezuma now kept the great shrines of his idols, and a secret chamber containing gold bars and jewels. This was the treasure he had inherited from his father Axayaca, which he never touched. Their reason for lodging us here may have been that, since they called us *Teules*[7] and considered us as such, they wished to have us near their idols. In any case they took us to this place, where there were many great halls, and chambers canopied with the cloth of the country for our Captain, and matting beds with canopies over them for each of us; and no better bed is given, however great the chief may be. . . .

We entered the large court, where the great Montezuma was awaiting our Captain. Taking him by the hand, the prince led him to his apartment in the hall where he was to lodge, which was very richly furnished in their manner. Montezuma had ready for him a very rich necklace, made of golden crabs, a marvelous piece of work, which he himself hung round Cortés' neck. His captains were greatly astonished at this sign of honor. After this ceremony, for which Cortés thanked him through our interpreters, Montezuma said: "Malinche[8], you and your brothers are in your own house. Rest awhile." He then returned to his palace, which was not far off.

. . . So, with luck on our side, we boldly entered the city of Tenochtitlan or Mexico on 8 November in the year of our Lord 1519.

---

[7] Gods.

[8] As Doña Marina always accompanied Cortés, the Indians gave him the name of "Marina's Captain," later shortened to Malinche. Doña Marina was later known as La Malinche.

From *Chapter 89: Of how Montezuma came to our quarters with many chieftains, and the conversation he had with our Captain*

When the great Montezuma had dined and was told that our Captain and all of us had finished our meal some time ago, he came to our quarters in the greatest state with a large number of princes, all of them his kinsmen. On being told of his approach, Cortés came out to the middle of the hall to receive him, and Montezuma took him by the hand. They brought some chairs made in their fashion and very richly decorated in various designs with gold. Montezuma asked our Captain to be seated, and both of them sat down, each on his own chair.

Then Montezuma began a very good speech, saying that he rejoiced to have in his house and his kingdom such valiant gentlemen as Cortés and the rest of us. That two years ago they had brought him news of a Captain who had come to Champoton, and that last year as well he had received a report of another Captain who had come with four ships. Each time he had wished to see them, and now that he had us with him he was at our service and would share all that he possessed with us. He ended by saying that we must indeed be the men about whom his ancestors had long ago prophesied, saying that they would come from the direction of the rising sun to rule over these lands, and that the valor with which we had fought at Champoton and Tabasco and against the Tlascalans confirmed his belief, for lifelike pictures of these battles had been brought to him.

Cortés answered through our interpreters, who always accompanied him, that we did not know how to repay the great favors we received from him every day, and that indeed we did come from the direction where the sun rose, and were vassals and servants of a great Prince called the Emperor Charles[9], who was ruler over many great princes. Having heard news of Montezuma and what a great prince he was, the Emperor, he said, had sent us to this country to see him, and to beg them to become Christians, like our Emperor and all of us, so that his soul and those of all his vassals might be saved. Cortés promised that he would explain later how this could be, and how we worship the one true God, and who He is, as well as many other good things which he had already communicated to his ambassadors Tendile, Pitalpitoque, and Quintalbor.

After this conversation was over, the great Montezuma had at hand some fine gold jewels of varied shapes which he gave to Cortés. And to each of our captains he presented small objects made of gold and three loads of cloaks of rich feather work; and to each of the soldiers he gave two loads of cloaks each, all in a manner befitting a ruler. For in every way he seemed to be a great prince. After the presents had been distributed, he asked Cortés if we were all brothers and vassals of our great Emperor; and Cortés answered that we were brothers in love and friendship, persons of great distinction, and servants of our great King and lord. Further polite speeches passed between Montezuma and Cortés, and as this was the first time he had visited us and we did not want to tire him, the talks ended. Montezuma had ordered his stewards that, according to our own usage and customs, we should be given maize and grindstones, as well as women to make bread, and poultry and fruit, and abundant hay for the horses. Then Montezuma took leave of our Captain and all of us with the greatest courtesy, and we went out with him as far as the street. Cortés ordered us not to go far from our quarters until we knew more about the situation.

9　Charles V, Holy Roman Emperor (1519–56), King of
Spain (1516–56).

From *Chapter 90: Of how soon thereafter our Captain went to see the great
Montezuma, and of certain conversations they had*

The next day Cortés decided to go to Montezuma's palace, and he first sent to ascertain what
he intended doing and to let him know we were coming. He took with him four Captains . . .
When Montezuma was told of our coming, he advanced into the middle of the hall to receive
us, accompanied by many of his nephews, for no other chiefs were permitted to enter his palace
or communicate with him except upon important business. Cortés and Montezuma paid the
greatest reverence to each other, and clasped hands. Then Montezuma led Cortés to his own
dais, and indicating that he should sit to his right, called for more seats, on which he ordered
us all to sit as well.

Then Cortés began to make a speech through our interpreters Doña Marina and Aguilar,
saying that we had all now been put at ease, and that in coming to see and converse with such
a great prince we had fulfilled the purpose of our voyage and the orders of our lord the King.
The principal things he had come to say on behalf of our Lord God had already been brought to
Montezuma's notice through his three ambassadors Tendile, Patalpitoque, and Quintalbor, on
that occasion in the sand dunes when he did us the favor of sending us the golden moon and
sun. We had told him then that we were Christians and worshipped one God alone, named
Jesus Christ, who had suffered His death and passion in order to save us; and that what they
worshipped as gods were not gods but devils, which are evil things, and if they were ugly to
look at, their deeds were even uglier. He added that their gods were so evil and worthless, as
both the prince and his people would observe in the course of time, that where we had put up
crosses such as their ambassadors had seen, they had been too frightened to appear before them.

The favor he now begged of the great Montezuma was that he should listen carefully to the
words he now wished to speak. Then he very carefully set forth the creation of the world, how
we are all brothers, the children of one mother and father called Adam and Eve; and how such
a brother as our great Emperor, grieving for the perdition of so many souls as their idols were
leading to hell, where they burnt in living flame, had sent us to tell him this, so that he might
put a stop to it, and so that they might cease worshipping idols and make no more human
sacrifices – for all men are brothers – and commit no more robbery or sodomy. He also promised that in the course of time the King would send some men who lead very holy lives, much
better than our own, to explain this more fully, for we had only come to give them due warning. Therefore he begged Montezuma to do as he was asked and to carry it into effect.

As Montezuma seemed about to reply, Cortés broke off his speech, saying to those of us who
were with him: "Since this is only the first attempt, we have now done our duty."

"My lord Malinche," Montezuma replied, "I have comprehended these arguments of yours
long before now. I understand what you said to my ambassadors on the sand dunes about the
three gods and the Cross, and all those things that you preached in the various towns through
which you passed. We have not given you an answer, since we have worshipped our own gods
here from the beginning of time and know them to be good. No doubt yours are good also, but
do not trouble to speak to us any more about them at present. Regarding the creation of the
world, we have held the same belief for ages, and for this reason we take it for certain that you
are those who our ancestors predicted would come from the direction of the sunrise. As for
your great King, I am indebted to him and will give him of what I possess. For, as I have
already said, two years ago I had news of the Captains who came in ships from the direction in
which you came, and they said they were servants of this great King of yours. I should like to
know if you are all the same people."

Cortés answered that we were all brothers and servants of our Emperor, and that they had come to discover a route and explore the seas and ports, so as to know them well in order that we might follow, as we had done. Montezuma was referring to the expeditions of Francisco Hernandez de Cordoba and of Grijalva, the first voyages of discovery. He said that ever since that time he had wanted to invite some of these men to visit the cities of his kingdom, where he would receive them and do them honor, and that now his gods had fulfilled his desires, for we were in his home, which we might call our own. Here we might rest and enjoy ourselves, for we should be well treated. If on other occasions he had sent to say that we should not enter into his city, it was not of his own free will, but because his vassals were afraid. For they told him we shot our flashes of lightning, and killed many Indians with our horses, and that we were angry Teules, and other such childish stories. And now that he had seen us, he knew that we were of flesh and blood and of sound sense, as well as very brave. Therefore he had a far higher regard for us than these reports had given him, and would share with us what he had.

We all thanked him heartily for his signal good will, and Montezuma said laughing, because in his princely manner he spoke very gaily: "Malinche, I know that these people of Tlascala with whom you are so friendly have told you that I am a sort of god or Teule, and that everything in my houses is made of silver and gold and precious stones. But I know very well that you are too wise to believe this and will take it as a joke. See now, Malinche, my body is made of flesh and blood like yours and my houses and palaces are of stone, wood, and plaster. It is true that I am a great king, and have inherited the riches of my ancestors, but the nonsense and lies you have heard of us are not true. You must take them as jokes, as I take the story of your thunders and lightnings."

Cortés answered, also laughing that enemies always speak evil and tell lies about the people they hate, but he knew he could not hope to find a more magnificent prince in that land, and there was good reason why his fame should have reached our Emperor.

While this conversation was going on, Montezuma secretly sent one of his nephews, a great Cacique, to order his stewards to bring certain pieces of gold, which had apparently been set apart as a gift for Cortés, and ten loads of fine cloaks which he divided: the gold and cloaks between Cortés and the four captains, and for each of us soldiers two gold necklaces, each worth ten pesos, and two loads of cloaks. The gold that he gave us then was worth in all more than a thousand pesos and he gave it all cheerfully, like a great and valiant prince.

As it was now past midday, so as not to be importunate, Cortés said to Montezuma: "My lord, the favors you do us increase every day, load by load, and it is now the hour of your dinner. Montezuma replied that he thanked us for visiting him. We then took our leave with the greatest courtesy, and returned to our lodgings, talking as we went of the prince's fine breeding and good manners and deciding to show him the greatest respect in every way, and to remove our quilted caps in his presence. And this we always did.

Chapter 91: *Of the manner and appearance of Montezuma*

The great Montezuma was about forty years old, of good height and well-proportioned, spare and slight, and not very swarthy, though of the usual Indian complexion. He did not wear his hair long but so just as to cover his ears, and he had a short black beard, well-shaped and thin. His face was somewhat long, but cheerful. He had fine eyes and in his appearance and manner could express geniality or, when necessary, appropriate gravity. He was very neat and clean, and took a bath every afternoon. He had many women as his mistresses, the daughters of chieftains, but two legitimate wives who were themselves Caciques, and when he had intercourse with any of them it was so secret that only some of his servants knew of it. He was very free of sodomy. The mantles and clothes he wore one day he did not wear again till three or four days later. He had a guard of two hundred chieftains lodged in rooms next to his, but only some were permitted to speak to him. When they entered his presence they were compelled to take off their rich cloaks and put on others of lesser value. They had to be clean and walk barefoot, with their eyes lowered, for they were not allowed to look him directly in the face, and as they approached they had to make three obeisances[10], saying as they did so, "Lord, my Lord, my great Lord!" Then, when they had said what they had come to say, he would dismiss them with a few words: they did not turn their backs on him as they went out, but kept their faces towards him and their eyes lowered, only turning round when they had left the room. Another thing I noticed was that when other great chiefs came from distant lands about disputes or on business, they too before entering Montezuma's apartments had to take off their shoes and put on poor cloaks; and they were not allowed to enter the palace directly but had to linger for a while near the door, since to enter hurriedly was seen as disrespectful.

. . . Let us go on to another large house where they kept many idols whom they call their fierce gods, and with them many kinds of beasts of prey, tigers and two kinds of lion, and beasts somewhat like wolves which they call *adives*[11], and foxes and other small animals, all of them carnivores, and most of them bred there. They feed them on deer, fowls, small dogs, and other creatures which they hunt and also on the bodies of the Indians who have been sacrificed, as I was told.

I have already described the manner of their sacrifices. They strike open the wretched Indian's chest with flint knives and quickly tear out the palpitating heart and blood, which they present to the idols in whose name the sacrifice has been performed. Then they cut off the arms, thighs, and head, eating the arms and thighs at their ceremonial feasts. The head is hung up on a beam, and the body of the man sacrificed is not eaten but given to the beasts of prey. They also have many vipers in this accursed house, and poisonous snakes which have something that sounds like a bell on their tails. These, which are the deadliest snakes of all, they kept in jars and great pottery vessels full of feathers, and there they lay their eggs and rear their young. They are fed on the bodies of sacrificed Indians and the flesh of the dogs that they breed. We know for certain, too, that when they drove us out of Mexico and killed over eight hundred and fifty of our soldiers, they fed those beasts and snakes on their bodies for many days, as I shall relate in due course. These snakes and wild beasts were dedicated to their fierce idols, and kept them company. As for the infernal noise when the lions and tigers roared, and the jackals and foxes howled, and the serpents hissed, it was so hideous that one seemed to be in hell.

. . . Now to speak of the great number of performers kept by Montezuma for his amusement. There were dancers and stilt-walkers, and some who seemed to leap flying through the air, and men like jesters to make him laugh. There was a whole district full of these people who had no other occupation. He had as many workmen as he needed, too, stone cutters, masons, and carpenters, to maintain his houses in good repair.

We must not forget the gardens with their many varieties of flowers and sweet-scented trees planted in orderly fashion, and their ponds and tanks of fresh water where the water flowed in at one end and out at the other, and the baths he had there, and the variety of small birds that nested in the branches, and the medicinal and useful herbs that grew there in the

---

[10] Bows.

[11] *Adives*, the Arabic word for jackal, used in Spain in the fifteenth century.

gardens. They were a wonderful sight, and required many gardeners to take care of them. Everything was built of stone and plastered; baths and walks and closets and rooms like summer houses where they danced and sang. There was so much to see in these gardens, as there was everywhere else, that we could not tire of contemplating his great power and the large number of craftsmen employed in the many skills they practiced.

. . . Let us begin with the dealers in gold, silver, precious stones, feathers, mantles, and embroidered goods, and slaves both male and female who are also sold there. They bring as many slaves to be sold in that market as the Portuguese bring Negroes from Guinea. Some are brought there, attached to long poles with collars round their necks to keep them from escaping, but others are left loose. Next there were those who sold coarser cloth, and other articles made of twisted thread, and there were chocolate sellers with their chocolate. In this way you could see every kind of merchandise to be found in the whole of New Spain, laid out in the same way as goods are laid out in my own district of Medina del Campo, a market town where each line of stalls has its own particular sort. So it was in this great market there were those who sold sisal cloth[12] and ropes and the sandals they wear on their feet, which are made from the same plant. All these were kept in one part of the market, in the place assigned to them. In another part were skins of tigers and lions, otters and jackals, deer, badgers, mountain cats, and other wild animals, some tanned and some untanned, and other classes of merchandise.

There were sellers of beans and sage and other vegetables and herbs in another part, and in yet another they had for sale fowls, and birds with great wattles[13], also rabbits, hares, deer, young ducks, small dogs, and other such creatures. There were also the fruiterers; and the women who sold cooked food, flour and honey cake, and tripe, had their own part of the market. Then came pottery of all kinds, from big water-jars to little jugs, displayed in a place of its own, also honey, honey-paste, and other sweets like nougat[14]. As well, they sold lumber too, boards, cradles, beams, blocks, and benches, all in a quarter of their own.

Then there were the sellers of pitch pine for torches, and other things of that kind, and I must also mention, with all apologies, that they sold many canoe-loads of human filth, which they kept in the creeks near the market. This was for the curing of skins, which they say cannot be done without it. I know that many will laugh at this, but I assure them it is true. I might add that on all the roads they have shelters made of reeds or straw or grass so that they can retire when they wish to do so, and purge their bowels out of sight of passers-by, in order that their excrement shall not be lost.

But why waste so many words in recounting what they sell in their great market? If I describe everything in detail I shall never be finished. Paper, which in Mexico they call *amal*, and some reeds scented of liquidamber[15], and full of tobacco, and yellow ointments and things of that sort, are sold in a separate part. Much cochineal[16] is sold too under the arcades of that market, and there are many vendors of herbs and other such things. They have a building there also in which three magistrates sit, and there are officials like constables who inspect the merchandise. I am forgetting the sellers of salt and the makers of flint knives, and how they split them off the stone itself, and the fisherwomen and others who sell small cakes made from a sort of weed which they get out of the great lake, which curdles and from which they make a kind of bread which tastes somewhat like cheese. They sell axes too, made of bronze and copper and tin, and gourds and gaily painted wooden jars.

---

[12]   Woven from hemp.
[13]   Turkeys.
[14]   A sweet usually filled with almonds or pistachio nuts.

[15]   A native tree, whose name is derived from its brilliant yellow foliage.
[16]   Scarlet dye.

. . . We then went to the great *cue*[17], and as we approached its wide courts, before leaving the market-place itself, we saw many more merchants who, so I was told, brought gold for sale in grains or nuggets, just as they extract it from the mines. This gold is placed in the thin quills of the large geese of that country, which are so white as to be transparent. According to the length and thickness of these little quills, they used to reckon their accounts with one another, how much so many gourds of chocolate or so many slaves or mantles were worth, or anything else they were bartering. Now let us leave the market without looking back, and come to the courts and enclosures in which their great cue stood. Before reaching it you passed through a series of large courts, larger it seems to me than the Plaza[18] at Salamanca. These courts were surrounded by a double masonry wall and paved, like the whole place, with very smooth large white flag-stones. Where there were no stones, everything was whitened and polished; indeed it was all so clean that there was not a straw or a grain of dust to be found there.

When we arrived near the great temple and before we had climbed a single step of it, the great Montezuma sent down from above, where he was making his sacrifices, six *priests*[19] and two chieftains to escort our Captain; and as he climbed the steps, of which there were one hundred and fourteen in number, they tried to take him by the arms to help him ascend in the same way as they helped Montezuma, thinking he might be tired, but he would not let them near him.

The top of the great cue formed an open square on which stood something like a platform, with some large stones atop it, on which they placed the poor Indians for sacrifice. Here also was a massive image like a dragon, and other hideous figures, and a great deal of blood that had been shed that very day. Emerging in the company of two *priests* from the sanctuary which houses his accursed images Montezuma made a deep bow to us and said: "My lord Malinche, you must be tired after climbing our great cue." And Cortés replied through our interpreters that none of us was ever tired by anything. Then Montezuma took him by the hand, and told him to look at his great city and at the other cities standing in the water, and the many other towns on the land round the lake: and he said that if Cortés had not had a good view of the great market-place he could see it better from where he now was. So we stood there looking because that huge accursed temple stood so high that it dominated everything. We saw the three highways that led into Mexico: the highway of Itzapalapa by which we had entered four days before, and that of Tacuba along which we were afterwards to flee on the night of our great defeat, when the new prince Cuitlahuac drove us out of the city (as I shall tell in due course), and that of Tepeaquilla[20]. As well, we saw the fresh water coming from Chapultepec which supplies the city, and the bridges that were constructed at intervals on the highways so that the water could flow in and out from one part of the lake to another. We saw a great multitude of canoes, some coming with provisions and others returning with cargo and merchandise; and we saw too that one could not pass from one house to another of that great city and the other cities that were built on the water except over drawbridges made of wood or by canoe. We saw cues and shrines in these cities that looked like gleaming white towers and castles: it was a marvelous sight. All the houses had flat roofs, and on the highways were other small towers and shrines built like fortresses.

After having examined and considered all that we had seen, we turned back to the great market and the crowds of people buying and selling. The mere murmur of their voices was loud enough to be heard more than three miles away. Some of our soldiers who had been in many parts of the world, in Constantinople, all over Italy, and in Rome, said that they had never seen a market so well laid out, so large, so orderly, and so full of people.

---

[17] A tower-like religious temple.
[18] Central city square.

[19] Priests.
[20] Guadalupe.

But returning to our Captain, he said to Father Bartolomé de Olmedo, whom I have often mentioned and who happened to be standing near him: "It would be a good thing I think, Father, if we were to approach Montezuma as to whether he would let us build our church here." Father Bartolomé answered that it would be a good thing if it were successful, but he did not think this a suitable time to speak of it, for Montezuma did not look as if he would allow such a thing.

Cortés, nonetheless, addressed Montezuma through Doña Marina: "Your Highness is a great prince and worthy of even greater things. We have enjoyed the sight of your cities, and since we are now here in your temple, I beg of you to show us your gods and *Teules*[21]." Montezuma answered that first he would consult his chief *priests*[22]; and when he had spoken to them he said that we might enter a small tower, a sort of hall in which there were two altars with very rich wooden carvings over the roof. On each altar was a giant figure, very tall and very fat. They said that the one on the right was the figure of Huichilobos, their god of war. He had a very broad face and monstrous terrible eyes. And there were so many precious stones, so much gold, so many pearls and seed pearls stuck to him with a paste which the natives made from a sort of root, that he was covered with them from head to foot. He was girdled with great snakes made of gold and precious stones, and in one hand he held a bow, in the other some arrows. Another smaller idol beside him, which they said was his page, carried a short lance and a shield richly decorated with gold and precious stones. Around Huichilobos' neck hung some Indian faces and other objects in the shape of hearts, the former made of gold and the latter of silver, with many precious blue stones.

There were some smoking braziers, with their incense, which they call *copal*, in which they were burning the hearts of three Indians whom they had sacrificed that day, and all the walls of that shrine were so splashed and encrusted with blood that they and the floor as well were black. Indeed, the whole place stank abominably. We then looked to the left and saw another great image of the same height as Huichilobos, with a face like a bear and eyes that glittered, being made of their mirrors, which they call *tezcat.* Its body, like that of Huichilobos, was covered in precious stones, for they said that the two were brothers. This Texcatlipoca, the god of hell, had charge of the souls of Mexicans, and his body was surrounded by figures of little devils with snakes' tails. The walls of this shrine also were so caked with blood and the floor so bathed in it that the stench was worse than that of any slaughterhouse in Spain. They had offered this idol five hearts from the day's sacrifices.

At the very top of the cue there was another recess with very finely carved woodwork, and here there was another image, half man and half lizard, encrusted with precious stones, with half its body covered in a cloak. They said that the body of this figure contained all the seeds in the world, and that he was the god of seedtime and harvest. I do not remember his name[23]. Here too everything was covered with blood, both walls and altar, and the stench was such that we could hardly wait to get out. They kept a very large drum there, and when they beat it the din was most dismal, like some music from the infernal regions, as you might say, and it could be heard six miles away. This drum was said to be covered with the skins of great snakes. In that small platform there were many more diabolical things, trumpets great and small, and large knives, and many hearts that had been burnt with incense before their idols; and everything was caked with blood, so much that I curse it all. The stench here too was like a slaughterhouse, and we could scarcely stay in the place.

Our Captain said to Montezuma, through our interpreters, half laughing: "Lord Montezuma,

---

[21] Sacred beings.

[22] Priests.

[23] Probably Tlaltecuhtli.

I cannot imagine how a prince as great and wise as you are can have failed to realise that these idols of yours are not gods but evil things, the proper name for which is devils. But so that I may prove this to you, and make it clear to all your priests, grant me one favor. Allow us to erect a cross here on the top of this tower, and let us divide off a part of this sanctuary where your Huichilobos and Texcatlipoca stand, as a place where we can set up an image of Our Lady" – which Montezuma had already seen – "and then you will see, by the fear that your idols have of her, how grievously they have deceived you."

Montezuma, however, replied heatedly (and the two priests beside him showed real anger): "Lord Malinche, if I had known that you were going to utter these insults I should not have shown you my gods. We consider them to be very good, for they give us health and rain and crops and weather, and all the victories we desire. So we are bound to worship them and sacrifice to them, and I ask you to say nothing more against them."

On hearing this and seeing Montezuma's fury, our Captain said no more on the subject but observed in a cheerful manner: "It is time for your Majesty and ourselves to depart." Montezuma replied that this was so, but that he had to pray and offer certain sacrifices on account of the great *tatacul* – that is to say sin – which he had committed in allowing us to ascend his great cue and in being instrumental in letting us see his gods and in the dishonor we had done them by speaking evil of them. Therefore before he left he must pray and worship.

Cortés answered, "I ask your pardon if that is so, my lord." And we went down the steps, of which there were a hundred and fourteen in number, as I said. As some of our soldiers were suffering from abscesses or running sores, their thighs pained them as they went down.

. . . Let me go on to describe the great and splendid courts in front of Huichilobos, on the site where that church now stands, which was called Tlatelolco at that time. I have already said that there were two walls of masonry before the entrance to the temple, and the court was paved with white stones like flagstones, and all was whitened, burnished, and clean. A little apart from the great cue stood another small tower which was also an idol-house or true hell, for one of its doors was in the shape of a terrible mouth, such as they paint to depict the jaws of hell. This mouth was open, with great fangs to devour souls. Beside this door were groups of devils and the bodies of serpents, and a little way off was a place of sacrifice, all caked in blood and black with smoke. There were many great pots and jars and pitchers in this house, full of water. For it was here that they cooked the flesh of the unfortunate Indians who were sacrificed and eaten by the priests. There were also near this place of sacrifice many large knives and chopping blocks like those on which men cut up meat in the slaughterhouse: and behind that cursed house, some distance away, were great piles of firewood, beside which was a tank of water that was filled and emptied through a pipe from the covered channel that comes into the city from Chapultepec. I always called that building the Infernal Regions.

Crossing the court you came to another cue, where the great Mexican princes were buried and where there were many idols. All was full of blood and smoke. It too had doorways with hellish figures; and beside that cue was another, full of skulls and large bones arranged in an orderly pattern, and so numerous that you could not count them however long you looked. The skulls were in one place and the bones in separate piles. Here there were other idols, and in every building or cue or shrine were priests in long black cloth robes and long hoods . . .

To proceed, there were other cues, a short distance away from that of the skulls, which contained other idols and places of sacrifice decorated with horrible paintings. These idols were said to preside over the marriages of men. But I will waste no more time on telling about idols. I will only add that all round that great court there were many low houses, used and occupied by the priests and other Indians who were in charge of them. On one side of the great cue there was another, much larger pond or tank of very clean water which was solely devoted to the service of Huichilobos and Texcatlipoca, and the water for this tank was also supplied by covered pipes that came from Chapultepec. Near to this were the large buildings of a kind of nunnery where many of the daughters of the inhabitants of Mexico dwelt in retirement until the time of their marriage. Here there were two huge female idols who presided over the marriages of women, and to which they offered sacrifices and feasts in order that they should get good husbands.

. . . When we were all tired of walking about and seeing such a diversity of idols and their sacrifices, we returned to our quarters, always accompanied by the many Caciques and dignitaries whom Montezuma had sent with us.

From *Chapter 93: Of how we made our Church and altar in our quarters, and a cross outside our quarters, and other events, and of how we found the antechamber and chamber where Montezuma's father's treasure is kept, and how it was agreed that Montezuma should be detained*

When our Captain and the Mercedarian friar realised that Montezuma would neither permit us to set up a cross at Huichilobos' cue nor build a church there, it was decided that we should ask his stewards for masons so that we could put up a church in our own quarters. For since entering the city of Mexico every time we had said mass we had had to erect an altar on tables and dismantle it again.

The stewards said they would tell Montezuma of our wishes, and Cortés also sent our interpreters to ask him in person. Montezuma gave his permission and ordered that we should be supplied with all the necessary material. We had our church finished in two days, and a cross erected in front of our lodgings and mass was said there each day until there was no more wine. For as Cortés and some other captains and a friar had been ill during the Tlascalan campaign, there had been a run on the wine that we kept for mass. Still, though it was finished, we still went to church every day and prayed on our knees before the altar and images. This was firstly because it was our obligation as Christians and a good habit, and secondly so that Montezuma and all his captains should observe us and, seeing us worshipping on our knees before the cross – especially when we intoned the Ave Maria – might be inclined to imitate our actions.

As it was our habit to examine and inquire into everything, when we were all assembled in our lodging and considering which was the best place for an altar, two of our men, one of whom was a carpenter named Alonso Yañez, called attention to some marks on one of the walls which showed that there had once been a door, though it had been well plastered up and painted. Now as we had heard a rumor that Montezuma kept his father's treasure in this building, we immediately suspected that it must be in this room, which had been closed up only a few days earlier. Yañez made the suggestion to Juan Velázquez de León and Francisco de Lugo, both relatives of mine, to whom he had attached himself as a servant; and those Captains mentioned the matter to Cortés. So the door was secretly opened, and Cortés went in first with certain captains. When they saw the quantity of jewels and golden objects – plates and ingots – which lay in that chamber they were quite carried away and did not know what to think of such riches. The news soon spread to the other captains and soldiers, and very secretly we all went in to see. The sight of all that wealth amazed me. As I was only a youth at the time and had never seen such riches before, I felt certain that there could not be another such store in the whole world. We unanimously decided that we could not think of touching a particle of it, and that the stones should immediately be replaced in the doorway, which should be blocked again and cemented just as we had found it. We resolved also that not a word should be said about this until times altered, fearing Montezuma might hear of our discovery.

Let us leave this subject of the treasure and tell how four of our most courageous captains took Cortés aside in the church, along with a dozen soldiers who were in his trust and confidence, myself among them, and asked him to consider the net and trap in which we were held, to look at the great strength of the city and observe the highways and bridges, and to think about the warnings we had received in every town we had passed through that Huichilobos had counseled Montezuma to let us into the city and kill us there. We reminded him that the hearts of men are very changeable, especially among the Indians, and begged him not to trust the good will and affection that Montezuma was showing us, because from one hour to another it might change. If he should take it into his head to attack us, we said, cutting off our supplies of food and water, or raising of any of the bridges would render us helpless. Then, considering the vast army of warriors he possessed, it would be impossible for us to attack or defend ourselves. And since all the houses stood in the water, how could our Tlascalan allies come in to help us? We asked him to think over all that we had said, for if we wanted to save our lives we must seize Montezuma immediately, without even a day's delay. We pointed out that all the gold Montezuma had given us, and that we had seen in the treasury of his father Axayacatl, and all the food we ate was turning to poison in our bodies, for we could neither sleep by night or day nor take any rest while these thoughts were in our minds. If any of our soldiers gave him less drastic advice, we concluded, they would be senseless beasts dazzled by the gold and incapable of looking death in the face.

When he had heard our opinion, Cortés answered: "Do not imagine, gentlemen, that I am asleep or that I do not share your anxiety. You must have seen that I do. But what possibility is there for us to take so bold a course as to seize this great lord in his own palace, surrounded as he is by guards and warriors? What scheme or trick can we devise to prevent him from ordering his soldiers to attack us at once ?"

Our captains (Juan Velázquez de León, Diego de Ordaz, Gonzalo de Sandoval, and Pedro de Alvarado) replied that Montezuma must be with smooth speeches got out of his palace and brought to our quarters. Once there, he must be told that he must remain as a prisoner, and that if he cried out or made any disturbance he would pay for it with his life. If Cortés was unwilling to take this course at once, he should give them permission to do it themselves. With two great dangers facing us, the better and more advantageous thing, they said, would be to seize Montezuma rather than wait for him to attack, for once he did so, what chance would we have? Some of us soldiers also remarked that Montezuma's stewards who brought us our food were becoming insolent, and did not serve us as politely as they had during the first days. Two of our Tlascalan allies had, moreover, secretly observed to Jerónimo de Aguilar, our interpreter, that for the last two days the Mexicans had appeared less well disposed to us. We spent a good hour discussing whether or not to take Montezuma prisoner, and how it was to be done. But our final advice, that in any case we should take him prisoner, was approved by our Captain, and we then left the matter till next day. All night we were praying to God that our plan might be in the interests of His holy service . . .

From *Chapter 95: Montezuma's arrest*

Having determined on the previous day that we would seize Montezuma, we prayed to God all night that it would turn out in a manner benefitting His holy service, and next morning we settled on a course of action.

Cortés took with him five captains, Pedro de Alvarado, Gonzalo de Sandoval, Juan Velázquez de León, Francisco de Lugo, Alonso de Avila, and myself, along with our interpreters Doña Marina and Aguilar. He warned us all to stay very alert, and the horsemen to have their mounts saddled and bridled. I need not say that we were armed, since we went about armed by day and night, with our sandals always on our feet – for at that time we always wore sandals – and Montezuma was used to seeing us armed in that way whenever we went to speak with him. He was neither surprised nor disconcerted, therefore, when Cortés and the captains who had come to seize him approached him fully armed.

When we were all ready, our captains sent to inform the prince that we were coming to his palace. This had always been our practice, and we did not wish to frighten him by arriving suddenly. Montezuma guessed that the reason for Cortés' visit was his indignation about the attack on Escalante. But although apprehensive, he sent him a message of welcome.

On entering, Cortés made his usual salutations, and said to Montezuma through our interpreters: "Lord Montezuma, I am greatly astonished that you, a valiant prince who has proclaimed yourself our friend, should have ordered your captains on the coast near Tuxpan to take up arms against my Spaniards. I am astonished also at their having dared to rob towns which are in the keeping and under the protection of our King and master, and demanding of them Indian men and women for sacrifice, and at their having killed a Spaniard, who was my brother, and a horse.". . . Cortés went on to say: "Being so much your friend, I ordered my captains to help and serve you in every possible way. But Your Majesty has done exactly the contrary. In the affair at Cholula your captains and a large force of your warriors received your express commands to kill us. Because of my great regard for you I overlooked this at the time. But now your captains and vassals have once more become insolent and are secretly debating whether you do not wish to have us killed. I have no desire to begin a war on this account, or to destroy this city. Everything will be forgiven, if you will now come quietly with us to our quarters without protest. You will be as well served and attended there as in your own palace. But if you cry out, or make any disturbance, you will immediately be killed by these captains of mine, whom I have brought for this sole purpose."

This speech dumbfounded Montezuma. He replied that he had never ordered his people to take up arms against us, and that he would at once send to summon his captains so that the truth should be known and they be punished. Then he immediately took the sign and seal of Huichilobos from his wrist, which he never did except when giving some weighty command that had to be carried out at once. As to being taken prisoner and leaving his palace against his will, he said that he was not a person to whom such orders could be given, and that he would not go. Cortés answered him with excellent arguments, and Montezuma countered with even better, to the effect that he refused to leave his palace. More than half an hour was spent in these discussions. But when Juan Velázquez de León and the other captains saw that time was being wasted, they became impatient to remove Montezuma from his palace and take him prisoner. Turning to Cortés, Velázquez said somewhat angrily: "What is the use of all these words? Either we take him or we knife him. If we do not save ourselves now we shall be dead men."

Juan Velázquez spoke, as usual, in a loud and terrifying voice; and Montezuma, seeing that our captains were angry, asked Doña Marina what they were saying so loudly, and she, being very clever, replied: "Lord Montezuma, I counsel you to accompany them immediately to their quarters and make no protest. I know they will treat you very honorably as the great prince you are. Otherwise, if you stay here, you will be a dead man. In their quarters the truth will be discovered."

Then Montezuma said to Cortés: "Lord Malinche, I see what is in your mind. But I have a son and two legitimate daughters. Take them as hostages and spare me this affront. What will my chieftains say if they see me carried off a prisoner?"

Cortés replied that he must come with us himself and there was no alternative; and after a good deal of argument Montezuma agreed to go. Then Cortés and our captains spoke to him most ingratiatingly, saying that they begged him humbly not to be angry, and to tell his captains and his guard that he went of his own free will, since on consulting his idol Huichilobos and the priests who served him he had learned that for the sake of his health and the safety of his life he must stay with us. Then his rich litter, in which he used to go out attended by all his captains, was brought and he was taken to our quarters, where guards and a watch were placed over him.

Cortés and the rest of us did our best to afford him all possible attentions and amusements, and he was put under no personal restraint. Soon all the principal Mexican chieftains and his nephews visited him to inquire the reasons for his imprisonment, and to ask whether he wished them to make war on us. Montezuma replied that he was spending some days with us of his own free will and not by force, that he was happy and would tell them when he wanted anything of them. He told them not to disturb either themselves or the city, and not to be distressed, since his visit was agreeable to Huichilobos, as he had learned from certain priests who had consulted that idol.

. . . Those readers of this history must wonder at the great deeds we did in those days: first in destroying our own[24] ships; then in daring to enter that strong city in spite of many warnings that they would kill us once they had us inside; then in having the temerity to seize the great Montezuma, king of that country, in his own city and inside his very palace, and to throw him in chains while justice was carried out. Now that I am old, I often pause to consider the heroic actions of that time. I seem to see them present before my eyes; and I believe that we performed them not of our own volition but that God was our guide. For what breed of men has there ever been, numbering only four hundred and fifty – or even fewer – would have dared to enter a city as strong as Mexico, which is larger than Venice and more, 1,500 leagues[25] from our own Castile and, having seized so great a prince, execute his captains before his eyes? There is much there to ponder on, and not in the matter-of-fact way in which I presented it.

From *Chapter 97: Of how when Montezuma was held prisoner, Cortés and all our soldiers treated him with affection, and even allowed him to go to his temples*

. . . Our Captain was very diligent in every way. Fearing that Montezuma might be made melancholy by his imprisonment, he endeavored every day after prayers – for we had no wine for mass – to go to pay him court. He went accompanied by four captains, and usually Pedro de Alvarado, Juan Velázquez de León, and Diego de Ordaz were of that number. They would ask Montezuma most deferentially how he was, and ask him to issue orders, which would be carried out, and beg him not to be distressed by his captivity. He would reply that, on the contrary, he was glad to be a prisoner, since either our gods gave us power to confine him or Huichilobos allowed it. In one conversation after another they offered him a fuller explanation of the beliefs of our holy faith and of the great power of our lord the Emperor.

Sometimes Montezuma would play with Cortés at *totoloque*, a game with small, very smooth gold pellets specially made for it. They would throw these pellets a considerable distance, and some little pieces as well which were also made of gold, and in five throws they either gained or lost certain pieces of gold or rich jewels that they had staked. I remember that Pedro de

---

[24]   So as not to be tempted to retreat.   [25]   Four thousand five hundred miles.

Alvarado was once keeping score for Cortés, and one of Montezuma's nephews, a great chief, was doing the same for Montezuma; and Pedro de Alvarado was always marking one point more than Cortés had really gained. Montezuma saw this and observed with a courteous smile that he did not like Tonatio – which was what they called Pedro de Alvarado – marking for Cortés, because he made too much *ixoxal* in the score, which meant in their language that he cheated by always adding an extra point. We who were on guard at the time could not help laughing at Montezuma's remark, nor indeed could Cortés himself. You may ask why we found the remark so amusing. It was because Pedro de Alvarado, though handsome and polite, had the bad habit of talking too much. Knowing his character so well we burst out laughing. But to return to the game. If Cortés won he gave the jewels to those nephews and favorites of Montezuma who attended him, and if Montezuma won he divided them among us, the soldiers of the guard. In addition to what we gained from the game, he always gave presents of gold and cloth every day to us and to the captain on guard, at that time Juan Velázquez de León, who in every way showed himself Montezuma's true friend and servant.

From *Chapter 107: Of Cortés and Montezuma*

. . . The great Montezuma always showed his accustomed good will towards us, but never ceased his daily sacrifices of human beings. Cortés tried to dissuade him from this but with no success. He therefore consulted his captains as to what we should do in the matter, since he did not dare to put a stop to this practice for fear of arousing the city and the priests of Huichilobos. The advice he received was that he should announce his intention of overthrowing the great images of the idols. Then if we saw they were prepared to defend them or rise in revolt, he should merely ask permission to set up an altar in one part of the high tower with a crucifix and an image of Our Lady. When this plan was agreed upon Cortés went to the palace where Montezuma was imprisoned, taking seven captains and soldiers with him, and said: "My lord, I have often asked you to give up sacrificing human beings to your gods, who are false gods, but you have never done so. Now I must tell you that all my companions, and these captains who have come with me, ask that you give permission to remove the gods from your temple and put Our Lady and a cross in their place. But if you refuse they will go and remove them just the same, and I should not like them to kill any priests."

When Montezuma heard these words and saw that the captains were somewhat excited, he said: "Malinche, how can you wish to destroy our whole city? Our gods would be furious at us, and I do not know that they would even spare your lives. I pray you to be patient for the present, and I will summon all the priests and see what they reply."

On hearing this, Cortés made a sign to Montezuma that he wished to speak with him in private, without the presence of the captains he had brought with him, and ordered them to depart and leave him alone. When they were left alone he told the prince that, to prevent this matter from becoming known and causing a disturbance, and so as not to offend the priests by overthrowing their idols, he would persuade our people to refrain from doing so, provided they were given a room in the great cue where they could set up an altar on which they could put an image of Our Lady and a cross. Then, in the fullness of time, his people would see how good and beneficial it was for their souls, and for their health, prosperity, and good harvests. Heaving a deep sigh and with a very sorrowful face, Montezuma promised to consult his priests; and after a good deal of discussion our Altar was set up some distance from their accursed idols, with great reverence and thanks to God from all of us. Then mass was sung. Cortés chose an old soldier to remain there as a guard, and begged Montezuma to order his priests not to touch the altar, but only to keep it swept and burn incense, and burn wax candles, night and day, and decorate the place with branches and flowers.

From *Chapter 150: The Siege of Mexico*

. . . When night fell we heard loud shouts from the lake. The Mexicans were insulting us with the taunt that we were not men enough to come out and fight. They had many canoes full of warriors, and the highways were crowded with fighting men, and the purpose of their mockery was to provoke us to come out and fight them that night. But as we had gained experience from our battle on the roads and the bridges, we refused to come out till next day, which was Sunday (May 26). After Father Juan Diaz had said mass and we had commended ourselves to God, we decided that both divisions should go to cut off the city's water supply at Chapultepec, which was about half a league from Tacuba.

As we were marching to break the pipes we came upon many warriors waiting for us on the road, for they were well aware that this would be the first damage we could inflict on them. When they met us, near some difficult terrain, they began to shoot arrows and spears and to throw stones, so that three of our men were wounded. But we rapidly put them to flight, and our Tlascalan allies pursued them so successfully that they killed twenty and took seven or eight prisoners. Once these bands were dispersed we broke the conduits which supplied the city, and water did not flow into Mexico again until the war ended. When we had accomplished this, our captains agreed that we should immediately reconnoitre, push forward along the highway from Tacuba, and try to seize a bridge. But when we reached the highway, there were so many armed canoes on the lake and so many warriors on the highway itself, that we were filled with dismay; and they fired so many darts, spears, and stones at us that more than fifty of us were wounded at the first encounter. This notwithstanding, we advanced along the highway towards the bridge, and they retreated before us, as I understand, in order to trap us on the other side. For when we had crossed, such a swarm of warriors fell upon us that we could not hold out against them. The highway was only eight yards in breadth. So what could we do, against a force that assailed us from both sides and shot at us as a sitting target? Although our crossbowmen and musketeers kept firing at their canoes, they did them scarcely any damage, for they were very well protected by bulwarks made of wood. When we attacked the bands that were fighting on the highway itself, they immediately leapt into the water; and they were so numerous that we could do nothing against them. Our horsemen were useless, for the Indians wounded their horses from both sides, throwing spears from the water, into which, as I have already said, they jumped when pursued.

We fought them on the highway for about an hour, and they pressed us so hard that we could hold no longer. Finally we saw approaching from another direction a great fleet of canoes attempting to cut off our lines of retreat. When we saw this, realizing that our Tlascalan allies were obstructing the highway and that if they leapt off they could not fight in the water, we decided, both captains and soldiers, not to try to push further and to retire in good order.

When we reached dry land, hard pressed by the Mexicans and pursued by their jeers, shouts, and whistles, we thanked God for our escape from the fight. For eight of our soldiers had been killed and more than fifty wounded.

From *Chapter 152: Of how the Indians took seventy-two live prisoners to be sacrificed*

. . . When we had retreated almost to our quarters, across a great opening full of water, we were out of reach of their arrows, spears, and stones. Sandoval, Francisco de Lugo, and Andres de Tapia were standing with Pedro de Alvarado, each one telling his story and discussing Cortés' orders, when the dismal drum of Huichilobos sounded again accompanied by conches, horns, and instruments like trumpets. It was a terrifying sound, and when we looked at the tall tower where it was coming from we saw our comrades who had been captured in Cortés' defeat being dragged up the steps to be sacrificed. When they had hauled them up to a small platform in front of the shrine where their accursed idols were kept, we saw them put feathers on the heads of many of them; and then they forced them to dance with a kind of fan in front of Huichilobos. After they had danced the priests laid them down on their backs on some narrow stones of sacrifice and, cutting open their chests, drew out their still beating hearts, which they offered to the idols. They then kicked the bodies down the steps, and the Indian butchers who were waiting below cut off their arms and legs and flayed their faces, which they then prepared like glove leather, with their beards still on, and kept them for their drunken orgies. After this, they ate their flesh with *chilmole*[26]. They sacrificed all our men in this way, eating their legs and arms, offering their hearts and blood to their idols, as I have already said, and throwing their bodies and entrails to the lions and tigers and serpents and snakes that they kept in the wild-beast houses I have described earlier.

On seeing these cruelties, all of us in our camp said to one another: "Thank God they did not carry me off to be sacrificed!" Those who read this must remember that though we were not far away we could do nothing to help, and could only pray God to guard us from such a death. At the very moment of the sacrifice, great bands of Mexicans suddenly attacked us and kept us busy on all sides. We could find no way of holding out against them. They shouted to us, "Look! This is the way you will all die, as our gods have many times promised," and the threats they shouted at our Tlascalan allies were so cruel and so terrifying that they lost their spirit. The Mexicans threw them roasted legs of Indians and the arms of our soldiers with cries of: "Eat the flesh of these Teules[27] and of your brothers, for we are glutted with it and you can stuff yourselves on what is left over. Now see these houses you have destroyed. We shall force you to build them again, much finer, with white stone and fine masonry. So go on helping the Teules. You will see them all sacrificed."

Guatemoc[28] did something more after his victory. He sent the hands and feet of our soldiers, and their flayed faces with the beards, and the heads of the horses that had been killed, to all the towns of our allies and friends and their relations, along with the message that since more than half of us were dead and he would soon finish off the rest, they had better abandon their alliance with us and come to Mexico, because if they did not desert us quickly he would come and destroy them.

. . . To return to our conquest of the day. To be brief, Cortés decided with his captains and soldiers that we should advance until we reached Tlatelolco, the great square where there were seven lofty towers and shrines, and our three companies pushed each from its own side, capturing bridges and barricades. Cortés got as far as a small square in which there were some other shrines and small towers, and in one of the houses there were some beams from which the heads of many of our Spaniards whom they had killed and sacrificed during the recent battles

[26]   A sauce made of tomatoes and peppers.
[27]   Gods, obviously used ironically.

[28]   The nephew of Montezuma, who replaced him as leader.

had been hung. Their hair and beards had grown much longer than in life, which I would never have believed if I had not seen it with my own eyes. I recognized three of my fellow soldiers, and it made tears come to our eyes to see them in this condition. We left them where they were for the moment, but they were taken down twelve days later, when we took away those and other heads that had been offered to the idols and buried them in a church that we built, which is called the Martyrs, near the bridge named Alvarado's Leap.

. . . While we were in Tlatelolco, Cortés sent to Guatemoc asking him to surrender and not to be afraid. He made solemn promises that the prince's person would be respected and honored, and that he would continue to rule Mexico and all its lands and cities just as before; and Cortés sent him a gift of food – maize-cakes, poultry, prickly-pears, and chocolate – for he had nothing else at hand. Guatemoc consulted his captains, and they advised him to say that he desired peace but would wait three days before giving an answer. When this time had elapsed, Guatemoc and Cortés would then meet to discuss terms, but in the meantime he would have the opportunity to learn more fully the wishes of his god Huichilobos in this matter, as well as to repair bridges, make openings in the highway, prepare arrows, spears and stones, and build barricades.

Guatemoc sent four Mexican chieftains with his answer, and we believed that his desire for peace was sincere. Cortés ordered that these messengers should be given plenty to eat and drink, and sent them back to Guatemoc with more food of the same kind. Then Guatemoc sent other messengers with a gift of two fine mantles, and they said the prince would come himself when everything was ready. To make a long story short, Guatemoc never intended to come, as his counselors had advised him not to trust Cortés, and had reminded him of the fate of his uncle the great Montezuma and his relations, and of the destruction of all the Mexican nobility. They suggested to him that he plead illness, and then send out all his warriors in the hope that his gods would be pleased to grant them the victory they had so often promised.

We waited for Guatemoc in vain. No sooner had we realized his deceit than many battalions of Mexicans came out under their distinguishing signs heading toward our camp and Sandoval's. They seemed to have started the battle all over again. As we were somewhat taken by surprise, believing that they had already settled for peace, many of our men were wounded, three of them mortally. They also wounded two horses, but did not get away with much advantage, for we gave as good as we got. After this onslaught Cortés ordered us to attack again and push forward into those parts of the city where they had taken refuge.

From *Chapter 156: Guatemoc's arrest*

. . . When Guatemoc's people saw the launches getting in among the houses, they embarked in their fifty canoes, which were carrying Guatemoc's property, gold, and jewels, and all his family and women. Then he himself embarked and shot out into the lake ahead, accompanied by many captains. At the same time many more canoes set out and soon the lake was full of them. The moment that he received the news that Guatemoc was attempting to escape, Sandoval ordered all his launches to stop destroying the houses and fortifications and follow the flight of the canoes. He told them to keep track of where Guatemoc was going, and not to molest him or do him any harm, but simply to try to capture him.

Sandoval instructed a certain García Holguín, a friend of Sandoval's who was captain of a very fast launch with good sails and good oarsmen to follow him in the direction in which they said Guatemoc and his pirogues were heading, and capture him if he could overtake him. Sandoval himself went in another direction with a number of other launches. It was our Lord

God's will that García Holguín should overtake Guatemoc's fleet which due to its rich ornamentation, its canopies and royal seat he recognized as the craft in which the Lord of Mexico
was traveling. Holguín made signals to them to stop, but they refused to do so, so he made as
though he were going to shoot at them with muskets and crossbows. This alarmed Guatemoc,
who cried out: "Do not shoot. I am the king of this city. Guatemoc is my name. Please do not
disturb the things I am taking with me or molest my wife or relatives, but take me at once to
Malinche." When Holguín heard him, he was jubilant, and embraced Guatemoc respectfully.
He placed him in the launch with his wife and about thirty chieftains, seating him in the poop
on some cloth and mats, giving them some of his own food to eat, and touching nothing in the
canoes that carried Guatemoc's property, but bringing them along with the launch.

By this time Gonzalo de Sandoval had ordered all the launches to come back, because he had
heard that Holguín had captured Guatemoc and was taking him to Cortés. On receiving the
news he ordered the oarsmen in his own launch to make all possible speed and, overtaking
Holguín, claimed the prisoner. Holguín would not give him up, saying that he and not Sandoval
had made the capture. Sandoval answered that this was the case, but that he was commander of
the launches and García Holguín sailed under his orders, and that it was for reasons of friendship and because Holguín's launch was the fastest that he had ordered him to follow and take
Guatemoc, who must now be surrendered to him. Holguín, however, persisted in his refusal.
At that moment another launch went at high speed to Cortés to ask for a reward for this good
news. Cortés was still nearby at Tlatelolco, watching Sandoval's advance from the top of the
cue. When he was informed of the dispute between Holguín and Sandoval he ordered that
Sandoval and Holgúin bring Guatemoc and his wife and family to him at once, with all due
respect, saying that he himself would settle the matter of whose prisoner Guatemoc was and to
whom was due the honor of his capture . . . On appearing before him, Guatemoc treated our
Captain with great respect, and Cortés, embracing him with delight, treated him and his
captains with a great show of affection. "Lord Malinche," said Guatemoc, "I have assuredly
done my duty in defence of my city and my vassals, and I can do no more. I am brought by
force as a prisoner into your presence and into your power. Take the dagger that you have in
your belt, and kill me with it at once." He sobbed as he spoke and wept bitter tears, and the
other great lords whom he brought with him were weeping as well. Cortés answered him very
kindly through our interpreters Doña Marina and Aguilar that he admired him greatly for
having had the courage to defend his city, and did not blame him at all. On the contrary, he
thought well rather than ill of him for having done so. He only wished, however, that he had
sued for peace of his own accord when his defeat was certain, thus preventing so much of his
city from being destroyed, and so many of his Mexicans from losing their lives. But now that
all this had happened, there was no help for it and nothing could be mended; let his spirit and
the spirit of his captains be at rest. For he should rule over Mexico and his princes as before.

. . . It rained and thundered that evening, with flashes of lightning flashed, and until midnight rain fell more heavily than usual. After Guatemoc's capture all of us soldiers became as
deaf as though we had been on top of a belfry with all of the bells ringing and suddenly falling
silent. I say this because during the whole ninety-three days of our siege of the city, Mexican
captains were yelling and shouting night and day, summoning the bands of warriors who were
to fight on the highway, and calling to the men in the canoes to attack the launches and fight
with us on the bridges and build barricades, or to those who were driving in palisades and
deepening and widening the channels and bridges, and building breastworks, or to those who
were making spears and arrows, or to the women shaping rounded stones for them to shoot
from their slings. There was as well the unceasing sound of their accursed drums and trumpets, and their grim big drums in the shrines and temples. The din was so great both day and

night that we could hardly hear one another speak. But after Guatemoc's capture, all the shouting and the other noise ceased. It is for this reason that I have said that it was like being atop a belfry. But on to other matters.

Guatemoc was very well-favored, both in body and in features. His face was long but pleasant, and when his eyes dwelt on you they were grave and gentle, and did not look away. He was twenty-three or twenty-four, and his complexion was lighter than the dark skin of most of these Indians. They said he was a nephew of Montezuma, the son of one of his sisters; and he was married to one of Montezuma's daughters, who was a beautiful young woman. . . . Now let us speak of the dead bodies and heads in the houses where Guatemoc had taken shelter. I swear by all that is holy that all the houses and stockades in the lake were full of heads and corpses. I hardly know how to describe it but it was the same in the streets and courtyards of Tlatelolco. We could not walk without treading on the bodies and heads of dead Indians. I have read about the destruction of Jerusalem, but I doubt that the mortality was lesser there than here in Mexico, where most of the warriors who had crowded in from all the provinces and subject towns had lost their lives. As I have said, the dry land and the lagoon and the stockades were piled high with the bodies of the dead. The stench was so strong that no one could endure it, and for that reason each of us captains returned to his camp after Guatemoc's capture: even Cortés was ill from the smells which assailed his nostrils during those days in Tlatelolco.

. . . When Cortés went into the city, he encountered the houses full of dead Indians, and some poor Mexicans still in them who were unable to move away. Their excrement was the sort of filth that scrawny pigs pass which have been fed only on grass. The whole city looked as if it had been ploughed up. The roots of any edible greenery had been dug out, boiled and eaten; even the bark of some of the trees had been eaten as well. No fresh water could be found; all that was left was brackish. I must say as well that the Mexicans did not eat the flesh of their own people, but only that of our men and our Tlascalan allies whom they had captured. There has never been a generation in the world who has suffered so much from hunger and thirst and continual fighting.

. . . Now that our daily and nightly battles with the Mexicans are in the distant past, for which I give heartfelt thanks to God who delivered me from them, there is one thing that I wish to say, which happened to me after witnessing the death by sacrifice of the sixty-two soldiers who were carried off alive. What I am going to say may seem to some to arise from my lack of warlike spirit. However, on the contrary, anyone will see on reflection that it was due to the great daring with which I had to risk my life in the worst of the fighting. For at that time great courage was expected of a soldier. I must confess that when I saw my comrades dragged up each day to the altar, and their chests cut open and their hearts torn out still beating, and when I saw the arms and legs of these sixty-two men cut off and eaten, I feared that one day or another they would do the same to me. Twice already they had laid hands on me to drag me off, but it pleased God that I should escape. When I remembered their hideous deaths, and the proverb that the little pitcher goes many times to the fountain and so on[29], I came to fear death more than ever in the past. Before I went into battle, a sort of foreboding and gloom would seize my heart and I would make water[30] once or twice and commend my spirit to God and the blessed Mother. This always happened before battle, but my fear soon left me. It must seem very strange that I should have experienced this unusual feeling of terror.

[29]   In Spanish, "Cantarillo que va muchas vezes a la fuente   [30]   Urinate.
se acaba por romper:" that is, the jug that often goes to the
fountain to be filled ends up being broken.

For I can recall taking part in many battles, from the time when I made the voyage of discovery with Francisco Hernandez de Cordoba till the defeat of our army on the highway under Alvarado. But until time when I saw the cruel deaths inflicted on our comrades right before our very eyes, I never felt such fear as I did in these last battles . . . Let those who are experienced in military life, who have been themselves in great peril of death, say whether my fear should be attributed to faintheartedness or to bravery. As I have said, my own opinion is that having to thrust myself into such dangerous positions in the thick of the fighting I was bound to fear death more at that time than at others, and for that reason my heart beat hard and I was afraid of dying. As well, I was often ill and was badly wounded on several occasions, and for this reason was not able to go on all the expeditions. Both before and after the capture of Mexico, I often found myself in difficulties and deadly peril.

. . . When the news spread throughout all the provinces that Mexico had been destroyed, their chieftains and lords could not believe it. They nonetheless sent their leaders to congratulate Cortés on his victories and to offer themselves as vassals to His Majesty, and to see if the city of Mexico, which they had so greatly feared, had really been razed to the ground. They all carried great presents to Cortés, and even brought their little children to show them Mexico, pointing it out to them just as we might say, "Here stood Troy.". . .

1568

Native Views of the Conquest of Mexico

As one might expect, indigenous people had a different perspective on the events described by Bernal Díaz. Nahuatl accounts describe in vivid terms the Conquest of Tenochtitlan by the forces of Cortés, and offer a moving portrayal of the devastation the Spaniards left in their wake

Primary Work

The Broken Spears: The Aztec Account of the Conquest of Mexico, ed. Leon Portilla, trans. Lysander Kemp (London: Beacon Press, 1962). The following excerpts are taken from this collection. An original source is indicated in parentheses.

The Omens Described by Muñoz Camargo (1520)[1]

(From Diego Muñoz Camargo, Historia de Tlaxcala)

Ten years before the Spaniards came to this land, the people saw a strange wonder and took it to be an evil sign and portent. This wonder was a great column of flame which burned in the night, shooting out such brilliant sparks and flashes that it seemed to rain fire on the earth and to blaze like daybreak. It seemed to be fastened against the sky in the shape of a pyramid, its base set against the ground, where it was of vast width, and its bulk narrowing to a peak that reached up and touched the heavens. It appeared at midnight and could still be seen at dawn, but in the daytime it was quelled by the force and brilliance of the sun. This portent burned

---

[1]   According to Leon Portilla, this text is based on the accounts of Sahagun's informants.

for a year, beginning in the year which the natives called 12-House[2] – that is, 1517 in our Spanish reckoning.

When this sign and portent was first seen, the natives were overcome with terror, weeping and shouting and crying out, and beating the palms of their hands against their mouths, as is their custom. These shouts and cries were accompanied by sacrifices of blood and of human beings, for this was their practice whenever they thought they were endangered by some calamity.

This great marvel caused so much dread and wonder that they spoke of it constantly, trying to imagine what such a strange novelty could signify. They begged the seers and magicians to interpret its meaning, because no such thing had ever been seen or reported anywhere in the world. It should be noted that these signs began to appear ten years before the coming of the Spaniards, but that the year called 12-House in their reckoning was the year 1517, two years before the Spaniards reached this land.

The second wonder, sign or omen which the natives beheld was this: the temple of the demon Huitzilopochtli, in the sector named Tlacateco, caught fire and burned, though no one had set it afire. The blaze was so great and sudden that wings of flame rushed out of the doors and seemed to touch the sky. When this occurred, there was great confusion and much loud shouting and wailing. The people cried: "Mexicanos! Come as quickly as you can! Bring your water jars to put it out!" Everyone within hearing ran to help, but when they threw water on the fire, it leaped up with even greater violence, and thus the whole temple burned down.

The third wonder and sign was this: a lightning-bolt fell on a temple of idolatry whose roof was made of straw. The name of this temple was Tzonmolco, and it was dedicated to their idol Xiuhtecuhtli .The bolt fell on the temple with neither flash nor thunder, when there was only a light rain, like a dew. It was taken as an omen and miracle which boded evil and all burned down.

The fourth wonder was this: comets flashed through the sky in the daytime while the sun was shining. They raced by threes from the west to the east with great haste and violence, shooting off bright coals and sparks of fire, and trailing such long tails that their splendour filled the sky. When these portents were seen, the people were terrified, wailing, and crying aloud.

The fifth wonder was this: the Lake of Mexico rose when there was no wind. It boiled, and boiled again, and foamed until it reached a great height, until it washed against half the houses in the city. House after house collapsed and was destroyed by the waters.

The sixth wonder was this: the people heard in the night the voice of a weeping woman, who sobbed and sighed and drowned herself in her tears. This woman cried: "O my sons, we are lost . . .!" Or she cried: "O my sons, where can I hide you . . .?"

The seventh wonder was this: the men whose work is in the Lake of Mexico – the fishermen and other boatmen, or the fowlers in their canoes – trapped a dark-feathered bird resembling a crane and took it to Montezuma so that he might see it. He was in the palace of the Black Hall; the sun was already in the west. This bird was so unique and marvelous that no one could exaggerate its strangeness or describe it well. A round diadem was set in its head in the form of a clear and transparent mirror, in which could be seen the heavens, the three stars in Taurus and the stars in the sign of the Gemini. When Montezuma saw this, he was filled with dread and wonder, for he believed it was a bad omen to see the stars of heaven in the diadem of that bird.

When Montezuma looked into the mirror a second time, he saw a host of people, all armed

---

[2]   The Aztecs, like other Mesoamerican groups, had two principal types of calendars. The *xiupohaualli*, or "year-count," based on the astronomical year, consisting of eighteen twenty-day months and a remaining five-day period called nemontemi, which was considered highly unlucky. The other form was the *tonalpohualli*, with twenty thirteen-day months.

like warriors, coming forward in well-ordered ranks. They skirmished and fought with each other, and were accompanied by strange deer and other creatures.

Therefore, he called for his magicians and fortune-tellers, whose wisdom he trusted, and asked them what these unnatural visions meant: "My dear and learned friends, I have witnessed great signs in the diadem of a bird, which was brought to me as something new and marvelous that had never been seen before. What I witnessed in that diadem, which is pellucid like a mirror, was a strange host of people rushing toward me across a plain. Now look yourselves, and see what I have seen."

But when they wished to advise their lord on what seemed to them so wondrous a thing, and to give him their judgments, divinations and predictions, the bird suddenly disappeared; and thus they could not offer him any sure opinion.

The eighth wonder and sign that appeared in Mexico: the natives saw two men merged into one body – these they called *tlacantzolli*[3] – and others who had two heads but only one body. They were brought to the palace of the Black Hall to be shown to the great Montezuma, but they vanished as soon as he had seen them, and all these signs and others became invisible. To the natives, these marvels augured their death and ruin, signifying that the end of the world was coming and that other peoples would be created to inhabit the earth. They were so frightened and grief-stricken that they could form no judgment about these things, so new and strange and never before seen or reported.

A Macehual[4] *Arrives from the Gulf Coast*

A few days later a *macehual* came to the city from Mictlancuanhtla. No one had sent him, none of the officials; he came of his own accord. He went directly to the palace of Montezuma and said to him: "Our lord and king, forgive my boldness. I am from Mictlancuanhtla. When I went to the shores of the great sea, there was a mountain range or small mountain floating in the midst of the water, and moving here and there without touching the shore. My lord, we have never seen the like of this, although we guard the coast and are always on watch."

Montezuma thanked him and said: "You may rest now." The man who brought this news had no ears, for they had been cut off, and no toes, for they had also been cut off.

Montezuma said to his *petlacalcatl*: "Take him to the prison, and guard him well." Then he called for a *teuctlamacasqui*[5] and appointed him his grand emissary. He said to him: "Go to Cuetlaxtlan, and tell the official in charge of the village that it is true, strange things have appeared on the great sea. Tell him to investigate these things himself, so as to learn what they may signify. Tell him to do this as quickly as he can, and take the ambassador Cuitlalpitoc with you."

When they arrived in Cuetlaxtlan, the envoys spoke with the official in charge there, a man named Pinotl. He listened to them with great attention and then said: "My lords, rest here with me, and send your attendants out to the shore." The attendants went out and came back in great haste to report that it was true: they had seen two towers or small mountains floating on the waves of the sea. The grand emissary said to Pinotl: "I wish to see these things in person, in order to learn what they are, for I must testify to our lord as an eyewitness. I will be satisfied with this and will report to him exactly what I see." Therefore he went out to the shore with Cuitlalpitoc, and they saw what was floating there, beyond the edge of the water. They also saw that seven or eight of the strangers had left it in a small boat and were fishing with hooks and lines.

---

3   Men-squeezed-together.   5   Priest.
4   Common man, peasant.

The grand emissary and Cuitlalpitoc climbed up into a broad-limbed tree. From there they saw how the strangers were catching fish and how, when they were done, they returned to the ship in their small boat. The grand emissary said: "Come, Cuitlalpitoc." They climbed down from the tree and went back to the village, where they took hasty leave of Pinotl. They returned as swiftly as possible to the great city of Tenochtitlan, to report to Montezuma what they had observed.

When they reached the city, they went directly to the king's palace and spoke to him with all due reverence and humility: "Our lord and king, it is true that strange people have come to the shores of the great sea. They were fishing from a small boat, some with rods and others with a net. They fished until late and then they went back to their two great towers and climbed up into them. There were about fifteen of these people, some with blue jackets, others with red, others with black or green, and still others with jackets of a soiled color, very ugly, like our *ichtilmatli*[6]. There were also a few without jackets. On their heads they wore red kerchiefs, or bonnets of a fine scarlet color, and some wore large round hats like small *comales*[7], which must have been sunshades. They have very light skin, much lighter than ours. They all have long beards, and their hair comes only to their ears."

Montezuma was downcast when he heard this report, and did not speak a word. . . .

THE STORY OF THE CONQUEST AS TOLD BY THE ANONYMOUS AUTHORS OF TLATELOLCO

This indigenous account offers a succinct description of all the major incidents of the Conquest, but it also contains a considerable amount of material that cannot be found in other documents. It was written in Nahuatl in 1528 by anonymous authors in Tlatelolco, and recorded by a Spanish Franciscan called Bernardino de Sahagún. Like other texts by Sahagún's native informants, it reflects the pride of the Tlatelolcas in their home quarter of the city. The original document is now in the National Library in Paris, where it forms part of *Unos anales históricos de la nación mexicana*. As well, three *icnocuicatl* (poetic laments or songs of sorrow) are included.

The Arrival of Cortés (1519–1521)

Year 13-Rabbit. The Spaniards were sighted off the coast.

Year 1-Canestalk. The Spaniards came to the palace at Tlayacac. When the Captain[1] arrived at the palace, Montezuma sent the Cuetlaxteca[2] to greet him and to bring him two suns as gifts. One of these suns was made of the yellow metal, the other of the white[3]. The Cuetlaxteca also brought him a mirror to be hung on his person, a gold collar, a great gold pitcher, fans and ornaments of quetzal feathers and a shield inlaid with mother-of-pearl.

The envoys made sacrifices in front of the Captain. At this, he grew very angry. When they offered him blood in an "eagle dish," he shouted at the man who offered it and struck him with his sword. The envoys departed at once.

---

6   Cloak fastened at the shoulder.
7   Flat dishes.

THE ARRIVAL OF CORTÉS
  1   Cortés.
  2   An allied tribe.
  3   Gold and silver.

All the gifts which the Cuetlaxteca brought to the Captain were sent by Montezuma. That is why the Cuetlaxteca went to meet the Captain at Tlayacac: he[4] was only performing his duties as a royal envoy. Then the Captain marched to Tenochtitlan. He arrived here during the month called Bird[5], under the sign of the day 8-Wind. When he entered the city, we gave him chickens, eggs, corn, tortillas and drink. We also gave him firewood, and fodder for his "deer."[6] Some of these gifts were sent by the lord of Tenochtitlan, the rest by the lord of Tlatelolco.

Later the Captain marched back to the coast, leaving Don Pedro de Alvarado[7] – The Sun – in command.

The Massacre in the Main Temple

During this time, the people asked Montezuma how they should celebrate their god's fiesta. He said: "Dress him in all his finery, in all his sacred ornaments."

During this same time, The Sun commanded that Montezuma and Itzcohuatzin, the military chief of Tlatelolco, be made prisoners. The Spaniards hanged a chief from Acolhuacan named Nezahualquentzin. They also murdered the king of Nauhtla, Cohualpopocatzin, by wounding him with arrows and then burning him alive.

For this reason, our warriors were on guard at the Eagle Gate. The sentries from Tenochtitlan stood at one side of the gate, and the sentries from Tlatelolco at the other. But messengers came to tell them to dress the figure of Huitzilopochtli. They left their posts and went to dress him in his sacred finery: his ornaments and his paper clothing.

When this had been done, the celebrants began to sing their songs. That is how they celebrated the first day of the fiesta. On the second day they began to sing again, but without warning they were all put to death. The dancers and singers were completely unarmed. They brought only their embroidered cloaks, their turquoises, their lip plugs, their necklaces, their clusters of heron feathers, their trinkets made of deer hooves. Those who played the drums, the old men, had brought their gourds of snuff and their timbrels.

The Spaniards attacked the musicians first, slashing at their hands and faces until they had killed all of them. The singers – and even the spectators – were also killed. This slaughter in the Sacred Patio went on for three hours. Then the Spaniards burst into the rooms of the temple to kill the others: those who were carrying water, or bringing fodder for the horses, or grinding meal, or sweeping, or standing watch over this work.

The king Montezuma, who was accompanied by Itzcohuatzin and by those who had brought food for the Spaniards, protested: "Our lords, that is enough! What are you doing? These people are not carrying shields or clubs. Our lords, they are completely unarmed!"

The Sun treacherously murdered our people on the twentieth day after the Captain left for the coast. We allowed the Captain to return to the city in peace. But on the following day we attacked him with all our might, and that was the beginning of the war.

The Night of Sorrows

The Spaniards attempted to slip out of the city at night, but we attacked furiously at the Canal of the Toltecs, and many of them died. This took place during the fiesta of

---

4   Their leader.
5   The fourteenth month, 20 October to 8 November.
6   Horses.
7   One of the captains accompanying Cortés.

Tecuilhuitl. The survivors gathered first at Mazatzintamalco and waited for the stragglers to come up.

Year 2-Flint. This was the year in which Montezuma died. Itzcohuatzin of Tlatelolco died at the same time.

The Spaniards took refuge in Acueco, but they were driven out by our warriors. They fled to Tenhcalhueyacan and from there to Zoltepec. Then they marched through Citlaltepec and camped in Temazcalapan, where the people gave them hens, eggs and corn. They rested for a short while and marched on to Tlaxcala.

Soon after, an epidemic broke out in Tenochtitlan. Almost the whole population suffered from racking coughs and painful, burning sores.[8]

The Spaniards Return

When the epidemic had subsided a little, the Spaniards marched out of Tlaxcala. The first place they attacked and conquered was Tepeyacac. They departed from there during the fiesta of Tlahuano, and they arrived in Tlapechhuan during the fiesta of Izcalli. Twenty days later they marched to Tezcoco, where they remained for forty days. Then they reached Tlacopan and established themselves in the palace.

There was no fighting of any kind while they were in Tlacopan. At the end of a week they all marched back to Tezcoco.

Eighty days later they went to Huaxtepec and Cuauhnahuac[9], and from there they attacked Xochimilco. A great many Tlatelolcas died in that battle. Then the Spaniards returned to Tezcoco again.

Year 3-House. The Aztecs began to fight among themselves. The princes Tzihuacpopocatzin and Cicpatzin Tecuecuenotzin were put to death, as were Axayaca and Xoxopehualoc, the sons of Montezuma. These princes were killed because they tried to persuade the people to bring corn, hens and eggs to the Spaniards. They were killed by the priests, captains and elder brothers.

But the great chiefs were angry at these executions. They said to the murderers: "Have we ourselves become assassins? Only sixty days ago, our people were slaughtered at the fiesta of Toxcatl!"

The Tlatelolcas Are Invited to Make a Treaty

A Spaniard named Castaneda approached us in Yanhtenco. He was accompanied by a group of Tlaxcaltecas, who shouted at the guards on the watchtower near the breakwater. These guards were Itzpalanqui, the captain of Chapultepec; two captains from Tlapala; and Cuexacaltzin. Castaneda shouted to them: "Come here!"

"What do you want?" they asked him. "We will come closer." They got into a boat and approached to within speaking distance. "Now, what have you to say to us?"

---

[8]   Many deaths among the Native populations of America were due to diseases (such as smallpox) brought by the Europeans.

[9]   Present-day Cuernavaca.

The Tlaxcaltecas asked: "Where are you from?" 'And when they learned that the guards were from Tlatelolco, they said: "Good, you are the men we are looking for. Come with us. The 'god' has sent for you."

The guards went with Castaneda to Nonahualco. The Captain[10] was in the House of the Mist there, along with La Malinche[11], The Sun (Alvarado), and Sandoval. A number of the native lords were also present and they told the Captain: "The Tlatelolcas have arrived. We sent for them to come here."

La Malinche said to the guards: "Come forward! The Captain wants to know: what can the chiefs of Tenochtitlan be thinking of? Is Cuauhtemoc a stupid, willful little boy? Has he no mercy on the women and children of his city? Must even the old men perish? See, the kings of Tlaxcala, Huexotzinco, Cholula, Chalco, Acolhuacan, Cuauhnahuac, Xochimilco, Mizquic, Cuitlahuac and Culhuacan are all here with me."

One of the kings said: "Do the people of Tenochtitlan think they are playing a game? Already their hearts are grieving for the city in which they were born. If they will not surrender, we should abandon them and let them perish by themselves. Why should the Tlatelolcas feel sorry when the people of Tenochtitlan bring a senseless destruction on themselves?"

The guards from Tlatelolco said: "Our lords, it may be as you say."

The "god" said: "Tell Cuanhtemoc that the other kings have all abandoned him. I will go to Teocalhueyacan, where his forces are gathered, and I will send the ships to Coyoacan."

The guards returned to speak with the followers of Cuauhtemoc. They shouted the message to them from their boats. But the Tlatelolcas would not abandon the people of Tenochtitlan.

The Fighting is Renewed

The Spaniards made ready to attack us, and the war broke out again. They assembled their forces in Cuepopan and Cozcacuahco. A vast number of our warriors were killed by their metal darts. Their ships sailed to Texopan, and the battle there lasted three days. When they had forced us to retreat, they entered the Sacred Patio, where there was a four-day battle. Then they reached Yacacolco.

The Tlatelolcas set up three racks of heads in three different places. The first rack was in the Sacred Patio of Tlilancalco (Black House), where we strung up the heads of our lords the Spaniards. The second was in Acacolco, where we strung up Spanish heads and the heads of two of their horses.

The third was in Zacatla, in front of the temple of the earth-goddess Cihuacoatl, where we strung up the heads of Tlaxcaltecas.

The women of Tlatelolco joined in the fighting. They struck at the enemy and shot arrows at them; they tucked up their skirts and dressed in the regalia of war.

The Spaniards forced us to retreat. Then they occupied the market-place. The Tlatelolca – the Jaguar Knights, the Eagle Knights, the great warriors – were defeated, and this was the end of the battle. It had lasted five days, and two thousand Tlatelolcas were killed in action. During the battle, the Spaniards set up a canopy for the Captain in the market-place. They also mounted a catapult on the temple platform.

---

[10]   Cortés.   [11]   Doña Marina.

Epic Description of the Besieged City

And all these misfortunes befell us. We saw them and wondered at them; we suffered this unhappy fate.

Broken spears lie in the roads; we have torn our hair in our grief. The houses are roofless now, and their walls are red with blood.

Worms are swarming in the streets and plazas, and the walls are splattered with gore. The water has turned red, as if it were dyed, and when we drink it, it has the taste of brine.

We have pounded our hands in despair against the adobe walls, for our inheritance, our city, is lost and dead. The shields of our warriors were its defence, but they could not save it.

We have chewed dry twigs and salt grasses; we have filled our mouths with dust and bits of adobe; we have eaten lizards, rats and worms. . . .

When we had meat, we ate it almost raw. It was scarcely on the fire before we snatched it and gobbled it down.

They set a price on all of us: on the young men, the priests, the boys and girls. The price of a poor man was only two handfuls of corn, or ten cakes made from mosses or twenty cakes of salty couch-grass. Gold, jade, rich cloths, quetzal feathers – everything that once was precious was now considered worthless.

The captains delivered several prisoners of war to Cuanhtemoc to be sacrificed. He performed the sacrifices in person, cutting them open with a stone knife.

The Message from Cortés

Soon after this, the Spaniards brought Xochitl, the Acolnahuacatl[12] whose house was in Tenochtitlan, to the market-place in Tlatelolco. They gripped him by both arms as they brought him there. They kept him with them for twenty days and then let him go. They also brought in a cannon, which they set up in the place where incense was sold.

The Tlatelolcas ran forward to surround Xochitl. They were led by the captain from Huitznahuac, who was a Huasteco[13]. Xochitl was placed under guard in the Temple of the Woman[14] in Axacotzinco.

As soon as the Spaniards had set Xochitl loose in the market-place, they stopped attacking us. There was no more fighting, and no prisoners were taken.

Three of the great chiefs said to Cuanhtemoc[15]: "Our prince, the Spaniards have sent us one of the magistrates, Xochitl the Acolnahuacatl. It is said that he has a message for you."

Cuanhtemoc asked them, "What is your advice?"

The chiefs all began to shout at once: "Let the message be brought here! We have made auguries with paper and with incense! The captain who seized Xochitl should bring us the message!"

The captain was sent to question Xochitl in the Temple of the Woman. Xochitl said: "The 'god'and La Malinche send word to Cuanhtemoc and the other princes that there is no hope for them. Have they no pity on the little children, the old men, the old women? What more can they do? Everything is settled.

"You are to deliver women with light skins, corn, chickens, eggs and tortillas. This is your

---

[12]   High priest.

[13]   From eastern Mexico.

[14]   The earth-goddess Cihuacoatl.

[15]   Guatemoc.

last chance. The people of Tenochtitlan must choose whether to surrender or be destroyed."

The captain reported this message to Cuanhtemoc and the lords of Tlatelolco. The lords deliberated among themselves: "What do you think about this? What are we to do?"

The City Falls

Cuanhtemoc said to the fortune tellers: "Please come forward. What do you see in your books?"

One of the priests replied: "My prince, hear the truth that we tell you. In only four days we shall have completed the period of eighty days. It may be the will of Huitzilopochtli that nothing further shall happen to us. Let us wait until these four days have passed."

But then the fighting broke out again. The captain of Huitznahuac – the same Huasteco who had brought in Xochitl – renewed the struggle. The enemy forced us to retreat to Amaxac. When they also attacked us there, the general flight began. The lake was full of people, and the roads leading to the mainland were all crowded.

Thus the people of Tenochtitlan and Tlatelolco gave up the struggle and abandoned the city. We all gathered in Amaxac. We had no shields and no *macanas*[16]; we had nothing to eat and no shelter. And it rained all night.

The People Flee the City

Cuanhtemoc was taken to Cortés along with three other princes. The Captain was accompanied by Pedro de Alvarado and La Malinche.

When the princes were made captives, the people began to leave, searching for a place to stay. Everyone was in tatters, and the women's thighs were almost naked. The Christians searched all the refugees. They even opened the women's skirts and blouses and felt everywhere: their ears, their breasts, their hair. Our people scattered in all directions. They went to neighboring villages and huddled in corners in the houses of strangers.

The city was conquered in the year 3-House. The date on which we departed was the day 1-Serpent in the ninth month.

The lords of Tlatelolco went to Cuanhtitlan. Even the greatest captains and warriors left in tatters. The women had only old rags to cover their heads, and they had patched together their blouses out of many-colored scraps. The chiefs were grief-stricken and mourned to one another: "We have been defeated a second time!"[17]

The Fall of Tenochtitlan

Our cries of grief rise up and our tears rain down, for Tlatelolco is lost. The Aztecs are fleeing across the lake; they are running away like women.

How can we save our homes, my people? The Aztecs are deserting the city: the city is in flames, and all is darkness and destruction.

Motelchiuhtzin the Huiznahuacatl, Tlacotzin the Tlailotlacatl, Oquitzin the Tlacatecuhtli are greeted with tears.

---

[16] Clubs.   [17]   The first time by Tenochtitlan.

Weep, my people: know that with these disasters we have lost the Mexican nation. The
water has turned bitter, our food is bitter! These are the acts of the Giver of Life.
The Aztecs are besieged in the city; the Tlatelolcas are besieged in the city!
The walls are black, the air is black with smoke, the guns flash in the darkness. They have
captured Cuanhtemoc; they have captured the princes of Mexico.
The Aztecs are besieged in the city; the Tlatelolcas are besieged in the city!
After nine days, they were taken to Coyoacan: Cuauhtemoc, Coanacoch,
Tetlepanquetzaltzin. The kings are prisoners now.
Tlacotzin consoled them: "Oh my nephews, take heart! The kings are prisoners now; they
are bound with chains."
The king Cuanhtemoc replied: "Oh my nephew, you are a prisoner; they have bound you in
irons.
"But who is that at the side of the Captain-General? Ah, it is Dona Isabel, my little niece!
Ah, it is true: the kings are prisoners now!
"You will be a slave and belong to another: the collar will be fashioned in Coyoacan, where
the quetzal feathers will be woven.
"Who is that at the side of the Captain-General? Ah, it is Dona Isabel, my little niece! Ah,
it is true: the kings are prisoners now!"

Flowers and Songs of Sorrow

Nothing but flowers and songs of sorrow are left in Mexico and Tlatelolco, where once we
saw warriors and wise men.
We know it is we that must perish, for we are mortal men. You, the Giver of Life, you have
ordained it.
We wander here and there in our desolate poverty. We are mortal men. We have seen
bloodshed and pain where once we saw beauty and valor.
We are crushed to the ground; we lie in ruins. There is nothing but grief and suffering in
Mexico and Tlatelolco, where once we saw beauty and valor.
Have you grown weary of your servants? Are you angry with your servants, O Giver of Life?

Diego de Landa (1524?–1579)

Born into a noble family, Diego de Landa was sent
to the New World as a Franciscan missionary. Once
in Mexico, he attempted to protect the Native peoples from the worst abuses of colonial authorities,
and became the Franciscan provincial of Yucatán
in 1561. Landa was an acute observer of Mayan
culture, and his text on the life and religion of the
Maya, *Relación de las cosas de Yucatán*, remains the
classical text on Mayan civilization. Despite this,
however, he reacted with loathing to certain Mayan
ritual practices such as human sacrifice; on discovering traces of human sacrifice in a cave containing Mayan sacred objects, Landa ordered all the
existing religious images as well as all Mayan documents (pictograms set down on paper made of
pounded bark, joined together to create books) to
be burned as "works of the devil" in the town square
of Mani. His career illustrates in graphic form that
knowledge of a different culture does not necessarily lead one to value or even to respect it.

Though Landa's own book was not printed until 1864, it provided a phonetic alphabet which enabled scholars to decipher about one-third of the Mayan hieroglyphs.

PRIMARY WORK

Diego de Landa, *Account of Things in Yucatán*, in *Spanish-American Literature in Translation*, vol. I, ed. Willis Knapp Jones (New York: Frederick Ungar, 1966).

FROM *ACCOUNT OF THINGS IN YUCATÁN*

XV: *Cruelties of the Spaniards Toward the Indians*

The Indians received rebelliously the Spanish yoke of servitude, but the Spaniards had well distributed the towns covering the territory. Still there were among the natives a few who stirred them up, on which account they[1] inflicted very severe punishments that caused a diminution in the population. They burned alive several chief men of the Province of Cupul and hanged others. Charges were brought against the inhabitants of Yobain, a town of the Cheles, and the chief citizens were seized and put in stocks in one building that was then set on fire, burning them alive with the greatest inhumanity in the world. And Diego de Landa hereby says that he saw a gigantic tree in whose branches a captain hanged many Indian women with their children at their feet. And in the same village and in one two leagues away, called Verey, they hanged two Indian women, one a young girl and the other recently married whose only crime was that they were beautiful and might upset the Spanish soldiers. This act was to make the Indians realize that the Spaniards were not interested in their women; and the memory of these two has endured a long time among both Indians and Spaniards because of their extreme beauty and the cruel way in which they were killed . . .

The Spaniards gave as excuse the fact that, being so few in number, they would have been unable to control so many people without frightening them by terrible punishments, and they offer as an example the history of the Hebrews in The Promised Land, where because of God's commands they committed extreme cruelties. On the other hand, the Indians were right in defending their liberty and trusting to the most valiant among them, and they thought they would be brave against the Spaniards . . .

XLI: *Cycle of the Mayas. Their writing*

Not only did the Indians keep account of the year and the months, as I recorded previously, but they had a way of counting time and affairs by epochs composed of twenty year periods, reckoning thirteen twenties, named with one of the twenty letters of their days that they call Ahau, not in order, but reckoned backward as can be seen in my illustration.

In their language they call these periods Katunes, and by means of them it is remarkably easy to keep track of their epochs, and so it was not difficult for the old man whom I mentioned in the first chapter to speak of events that had happened three hundred years earlier.

I do not know who devised this count by Katunes. If it was the Demon, he did what honours him, and if it was a man, he must have been a great idolater because he added all the deceits, omens, and trickery with which these people walked in their misery, completely de-

---

[1] The Spaniards.

ceived; and so this was the science to which they gave most belief and most greatly esteemed and which even the priests could not completely figure out. The way they had of reckoning their affairs and making their divinations was that in their temples they had two idols dedicated to two of these characters. To the first one, according to the cross above my circular plan, they offered their worship and sacrifices to escape plagues during a twenty year epoch. But after the first ten of the twenty had passed, they did nothing but burn incense and revere it. And when the twenty years of the first idol was completed, they began to follow the fortunes of the second, and sacrifice to it, and they would get rid of the first idol and set up the second to be worshipped for ten years . . .

LII: Conclusion

The Indians have not lost, but rather have gained with the coming of the Spaniards, even in small matters; but it is no wonder, because in spite of the fact that at first the changes were forced upon them, they have begun to enjoy and make use of them. Now they have many fine horses and mules and machos[2]. Asses do not thrive and I believe it is wrong to provide them, because they are bad-tempered and destructive. There are many fine cows, pigs, sheep, goats, and such dogs as are useful, and these are the things that can be counted among the beneficial contributions to the Indies. Cats are useful and necessary, and the Indians are fond of them. Chickens and doves, oranges, limes, citrons, grapes, pomegranates, and many vegetables. But only the melons and calabashes provide more seeds; for the rest, seed from Mexico is necessary. Silk of very good quality is also produced.

The Indians also have iron tools and the use of mechanical devices that have profited them. The use of money and many other things from Spain, things without which the Indians previously got along all right, allow them to live more like human beings, helped in their physical activities and in their growth according to the precepts of philosophy, art, and nature.

Not only has God given them through the Spanish nation this increase in material things so necessary to man, so that whatever they give in repayment to the Spaniards is little, but there have also come to them what cannot be bought or deserved: justice and Christianity and the peace in which they live, which makes them still further indebted to Spain and the Spaniards, and especially to the very Catholic Monarchs[3] who with continued care and lofty Christianity have provided and continue to provide these two benefits – much more than their original founders, those evil parents who begat them in sin and as children of wrath, while Christianity creates them in grace for the enjoyment of eternal life . . .

Hans Staden (*fl.* 1550s)

Little is known about the life of Hans Staden other than the story of his voyages and captivity among the Tupi Indians of Brazil. Born in Homberg, he left for Lisbon in 1547 in the hope of finding employment on one of the Portuguese ships sailing for the New World. There was a sizable German colony in sixteenth-century Lisbon, and it was not uncommon for Germans to be recruited to serve as gunners in Portuguese ships. Staden obtained employment on a ship with a cargo of convicts which

---

[2]   Donkeys.

[3]   Ferdinand and Isabella.

set sail for Brazil in 1547, reaching Pernambuco in January 1548. The first five chapters of Staden's book describe the voyage, Staden's adventures near Pernambuco, and his return to Europe. The remainder of the book is concerned with his second voyage, his captivity, and his final escape. The volume was published in Marburg in 1557, with woodcuts apparently executed under the author's personal supervision. Little is known about Staden's subsequent life.

Staden's narrative is written in a succinct, unadorned style in which the author reveals himself to be a shrewd observer of Tupi religion, trade, and warfare. Clearly, his Lutheran faith enabled him to survive his ordeal, and he discerns divine will at every turn. His eyewitness description of episodes of ritual cannibalism is a fascinating account by any standard.

PRIMARY WORK

Hans Staden, *The True History of His Captivity, 1557*, trans. and ed. Malcolm Letts (New York: Robert McBride & Company, 1929).

FURTHER READING

W. Arens, *The Man-Eating Myth: Anthropology and Anthropophagy* (Oxford: Oxford University Press, 1980).

FROM *THE TRUE HISTORY OF HIS CAPTIVITY, 1557*

From Part I: The True History and Description of a Country of Savages, a Naked and Terrible People, Eaters of Men's Flesh, Who Dwell in the New World Called America, Being Wholly Unknown in Hesse Both Before and After Christ's Birth until Two Years Ago, When Hans Staden of Homberg in Hesse took Personal Knowledge of Them and Now Presents His Story in Print

Dedicated to the Serene and Highborn Lord, Lord Philip Landgrave of Hesse.

Chapter I

I, Hans Staden of Homberg in Hesse proposed, if God willed, to see the Indies, and with this intention I traveled from Bremen to Holland, where at Kampen I lighted upon a boat which was sailing for Portugal to take in salt. I embarked accordingly, and on the 29th day of April of the year 1547 we arrived at a town called Sanct Tuval[1], the voyage having taken four weeks. Thence I reached Lisbon which is distant from St. Tuval five miles. At Lisbon I lodged at an inn owned by a man known as the younger Leuhr, a German, with whom I stayed some time. I spoke with the host, my countryman, and told him that if it were possible I desired to see the Indies. He informed me that I had delayed too long, since the King's ships bound for the Indies had departed. I asked him therefore, since he knew the language, to help me to find another ship, and told him that if he could do so I should be much in his debt.

Thereupon he took me to a boat where I obtained employment as a gunner. The captain's name was Pintiado, and he was bound for Brazil on a trading voyage, but he had leave to attack certain ships which were trafficking off the coast of Barbary[2] with the White Moors, and to seize as prizes any French ships which he might find in Brazil trading with the savages. He carried with him also certain prisoners who had been convicted and sentenced to death, but who had been spared with the object of colonizing the New World.

---

[1]   Setúbal.

[2]   The northwest coast of Africa.

Our ship was well found and fitted with every kind of warlike contrivance which could be used at sea. There were three Germans on board, Hans von Bruchhausen, Heinrich Brant of Bremen and I.

From *Chapter XVIII*

. . . The day previously I had sent my slave into the forest to hunt for game, intending to go on the following day to fetch it so that we might have food, for in that country there is little to be had except what comes out of the wilderness.

As I was going through the forest I heard loud yells on either side of me, such as savages are accustomed to utter, and immediately a company of savages came running towards me, surrounding me on every side and shooting at me with their bows and arrows. Then I cried out: "Now may God preserve my soul." Scarcely had I uttered the words when they threw me to the ground and shot and stabbed at me. God be praised they only wounded me in the leg, but they tore my clothes from my body, one the jerkin, another the hat, a third the shirt, and so forth. Then they commenced to quarrel over me. One said he was the first to overtake me, another protested that it was he that caught me, while the rest smote me with their bows. At last two of them seized me and lifted me up, naked as I was, and taking me by the arms, some running in front and some behind, they carried me along with them through the forest at a great pace towards the sea where they had their canoes. As we approached the sea I saw the canoes about a stone's-throw away, which they had dragged out of the water and hidden behind the shrubs, and with the canoes were great multitudes of savages, all decked out with feathers according to their custom. When they saw me they rushed towards me, biting their arms and threatening me, and making gestures as if they would eat me. Then a king approached me carrying the club with which they kill their captives, who spoke saying that having captured me from the Perot, that is to say the Portuguese, they would now take vengeance on me for the death of their friends, and so carrying me to the canoes they beat me with their fists. Then they made haste to launch their canoes, for they feared that an alarm might be raised at Brikioka, as indeed was the case.

Before launching the canoes they bound my hands together, but since they were not all from the same place and no one wanted to go home empty-handed, they began to dispute with my two captors, saying that they had all been just as near to me when I was taken, and each one demanding a piece of me and clamoring to have me killed on the spot.

Then I stood and prayed, expecting every moment to be struck down. But at last the king, who desired to keep me, gave orders to carry me back alive so that their women might see me and make merry with me. For they intended to kill me "Kawewi Pepicke:" that is, to prepare a drink and gather together for a feast at which they would eat me. At these words they desisted, but they bound four ropes round my neck, and I was forced to climb into a canoe, while they made fast the ends of the ropes to the boats and then pushed off and commenced the homeward journey.

Chapter XXII

At this time I knew less of their customs than I knew later, and I thought to myself: now they are preparing to kill me. In a little time the two men who had captured me, namely Jeppipo Wasu and his brother, Alkindar Miri, came near and told me that they had presented me in friendship to their father's brother, Ipperu Wasu, who would keep me until I was ready to be eaten, when he would kill me and thus acquire a new name.

This Ipperu Wasu had captured a slave a year before, and had presented him in friendship to Alkindar Miri, who had slain him and gained a new name. This Alkindar Miri had then promised to present Ipperu Wasu with the first prisoner he caught. And I was that prisoner.

My two captors told me further that the women would lead me out Aprasse. This word I did not then understand, but it signifies a dance. Thus was I dragged from the huts by the rope which was still about my neck to the dancing place. All the women came running from the seven huts, and seized me while the men withdrew, some by the arms, some by the rope about my throat, which they pulled so tight that I could hardly breathe. So they carried me with them, for what purpose I knew not, and I could think only of our Saviour Jesus Christ, and of his innocent sufferings at the hands of the Jews, whereat I was comforted and grew more patient. They brought me to the hut of their king, who was called Vratinge Wasu, which means the great white bird. In front of this hut was a heap of fresh earth, and they brought me to it and sat me there, holding me fast. I could not but think that they would slay me forthwith and began to look about me for the club Iwera Pemme which they use to kill their prisoners, and I asked whether I was now to die, but they told me "not yet." Upon this a woman approached carrying a piece of crystal fastened to a kind of ring and with it she scraped off my eyebrows and tried to scrape off my beard also, but I resisted, saying that I would die with my beard. Then they answered that they were not ready to kill me yet and left me my beard. But a few days later they cut it off with some scissors which the Frenchmen had given them.

Chapter XXIII

After this they carried me from the place where they had cut off my eyebrows to the huts where they kept their idols, Tammerka. Here they made a ring round me, I being with two women in the center, and tied my leg with strings of objects which rattled. They bound me also with sheaves of feathers arranged in a square, which they fastened behind at my neck so that they stood up above my head. This ornament is called in their language Arasoya. Then the women commenced to sing all together, and I had to keep time with the rattles on my leg by stamping as they sang. But my wounded leg was so painful that I could hardly stand upright, for the wound had not been dressed.

Chapter XXIV

When the dance was ended I was handed over to Ipperu Wasu who guarded me closely. He told me that I had some time to live. And the people brought the idols from the huts and set them up around me, saying that these had prophesied that they would capture a Portuguese. Then I replied that the idols were powerless and could not speak, and that even so they lied, since I was no Portuguese, but a kinsman and friend to the French, and that my native land was called Allemania[3]. They made answer that it was I who lied, for if I was truly the Frenchmen's friend, how came it that I was among the Portuguese? For they knew well that the French were as much the enemies of the Portuguese as they were, and that they came every year in their boats, bringing knives, axes, mirrors, combs, and scissors, and taking in exchange Brazilian wood, cotton, and other goods, such as feathers and pepper. These men were their good friends which the Portuguese were not. For the Portuguese, when they came to their country, desiring to trade with them, and when they had gone down in all friendship and

---

[3] Germany.

entered the ships, as they are to this day accustomed to do with the Frenchmen, the Portuguese had waited until sufficient numbers were on board, and had then seized and bound them, carrying them away to their enemies who had killed and eaten them. Others the Portuguese had slain with their guns, committing also many further acts of aggression, and even joining with their enemies and waging frequent war, with intent to capture them.

Chapter XXVII

It fell out during my misery, just as men say, that troubles never come singly, for one of my teeth commenced to ache so violently that by reason of the pain I could not eat and lost flesh. Whereat my master enquired of me why I ate so little, and I replied that I had toothache. Then he came with an instrument made of wood, and wanted to pull out the tooth. I told him that it had ceased to trouble me, but nevertheless he tried to pull it out with force, and I resisted so vigorously that he gave up the attempt. Then he threatened that if I did not eat and grow fat again they would kill me before the appointed day. God knows how earnestly, from my heart, I desired, if it was His will, to die in peace without the savages perceiving it and before they could work their will on me.

From Chapter XLII

The capture had taken place at sea, two full miles from land, and we hurried back as quickly as we could in order to encamp in the place where we had spent the previous night. When we reached the land called Meyenbipe it was evening and the sun was setting, and each man took his prisoner to his hut. Those that had been badly wounded they carried to the land, where they were killed at once and cut up and roasted. Among those who were roasted that night were two of the mamelukes[4] who were Christians; one was a Portuguese named George Ferrero, the son of a captain by a native woman. The other was called Hieronymus. He had been captured by a native belonging to my hut, whose name was Parwaa, and this man spent the whole night roasting Hieronymus, scarcely a step from the spot where I lay. This same Hieronymus (God have his soul) was blood relation to Diego de Praga.

That night, when we were encamped, I went into the hut where the two brothers were to talk with them, for they had been my good friends at Brikioka where I was captured. They enquired of me whether they would also be eaten, but I told them that they must trust in our Heavenly Father and in his Son Jesus Christ, who was crucified for our sins, and in whose name we were baptized. I said also: "This is my belief. God has watched over me so long here among the savages, and what God decrees must satisfy us."

The two brothers enquired also concerning their cousin Hieronymus, and I told them that he lay by the fire roasting, and that I had seen a piece of Ferrero's son being eaten. Then they commenced to weep, and I comforted them, telling them that I had been eight months or thereabouts among the savages, and that God had been my protector. "So also," I said, "will He protect you, if you trust in Him." I told them also that it was harder for me than for them, for I had come from foreign countries, knowing nothing of the dreadful practices of the savages, but, as for them, they had been born in the country and bred there. They replied, however, that I had been hardened by misery and should therefore take less account of it . . .

---

4   Of mixed European and Native parentage.

From *Chapter XLIII*

On the day following we reached a place not far from the country of my captors, called Occarasu, a great mountain. There we camped for the night, and I went to the hut of Konyan Bebe, the chief king, and asked what he intended to do with the two mamelukes. He replied that they would be eaten, and forbade me to speak with them, saying that they should have stayed at home instead of going to fight with his enemies. I begged him to spare their lives and sell them back again to their friends, but he was resolved that they should be eaten.

This same Konyan Bebe had then a great vessel full of human flesh in front of him and was eating a leg which he held to my mouth, asking me to taste it. I replied that even beasts which were without understanding did not eat their own species, and should a man devour his fellow creatures? But he took a bite saying *Jau ware sehe*: "I am a tiger, it tastes well," and with that I left him . . .

From *Part II: A True and Brief Account of all that I learnt Concerning the Trade and Manners of the Tuppin Inbas, whose Captive I Was*

Chapter XXIII: How They Turn the Women into Soothsayers

They go first to a hut and take all the women, one after another, and fumigate them. After this the women have to jump and yell and run about until they become so exhausted that they fall down as if they were dead. Then the soothsayer says: "See now, she is dead; but I will bring her to life again." After the woman has come to herself they say that she is able to foretell future things, and when the men go out to war the women have to prophesy concerning it.

At one time the wife of the king to whom I had been presented to be killed began to prophesy and told her husband that a spirit had come to her from far away enquiring concerning me, when I was to be killed, and as to the club with which I was to be knocked on the head, and where it was. The king replied that it would not be long and that all was prepared, only he was afraid I was not a Portuguese, but a Frenchman. Afterwards I asked the woman why she desired my death, seeing that I was no enemy, and whether she was not afraid that my God would punish her? She replied that I must not be troubled since they were only strange spirits seeking news of me. They have many ceremonies of this nature.

From *Chapter XXV: Why One Enemy Eats Another*

. . . This they do, not from hunger, but from great hate and jealousy, and when they are fighting with each other one, filled with hate, will call out to his opponent: *Dete Immeraya, Schermiuramme, heiwoe*: "Cursed be you my meat:" *De kange Jueve eypota kurine*: "Today I will cut off your head:" *Sche Innamme pepicke Reseagu*: "Now am I come to take vengeance on you for the death of my friends:" *Yande soo, sche mocken Sera Quora Ossorime Rire*, etc.: "This day before sunset your flesh shall be my roast meat." All this they do from their great hatred.

Chapter XXVIII: Of Their Manner of Killing and Eating Their Enemies. Of the Instrument with which They Kill Them, and the Rites which Follow

When they first bring home a captive the women and children set upon him and beat him. Then they decorate him with grey feathers and shave off his eyebrows, and dance around him, having first bound him securely so that he cannot escape. They give him a woman who attends to him and has intercourse with him. If the woman conceives, the child is maintained until it is fully grown. Then, when the mood seizes them, they kill and eat it.

They feed the prisoner well and keep him for a time while they prepare the pots which are to contain their drink. They bake also special pots in which to prepare the mixture with which they paint him, and they make tassels to tie to the club with which he is to be killed, as well as a long cord, called Mussurana, to bind him when the time comes. When all is ready they fix the day of his death and invite the savages from the neighbouring villages to be present. The drinking vessels are filled a few days in advance, and before the women make the drink, they bring forth the prisoner once or twice to the place where he is to die and dance round him.

When the guests have assembled, the chief of the huts bids them welcome and desires that they shall help them to eat their enemy. The day before they commence to drink, the cord Mussurana is tied about the victim's neck and on this day also they paint the club called Iwera Pemme with which they intend to kill him . . .

It is about 6 feet (a fathom) long, and they cover it with a sticky mess, after which they take the eggs of a bird called Mackukawa, which they break up to powder and spread upon the club. Then a woman sits down and scratches figures in the powder, while the other women dance and sing around her. When the club Iwera Pemme is ready decked with tassels and other things, they hang it in an empty hut upon a pole, and sing in front of it all night.

In the same manner they paint the face of the victim, the women singing while another woman paints, and when they begin to drink they take their captive with them and talk to him while he drinks with them. After the drinking bout is over they rest the next day and build a hut on the place of execution, in which the prisoner spends the night under close guard. Then, a good while before daybreak on the day following, they commence to dance and sing before the club, and so they continue until day breaks. After this they take the prisoner from his hut, which they break to pieces and clear away. Then they remove the Mussurana from the prisoner's neck, and tying it round his body they draw it tight on either side so that he stands there bound in the midst of them, while numbers of them hold the two ends of the cord. So they leave him for a time, but they place stones beside him which he throws at the women, who run about mocking him and boasting that they will eat him. These women are painted, and are ready to take his four quarters when he is cut up, and run with them round the huts, a proceeding which causes great amusement to the others.

Then they make a fire about two paces from the prisoner which he has to tend. After this a woman brings the club Iwera Pemme, waving the tassels in the air, shrieking with joy, and running to and fro before the prisoner so that he may see it. Then a man takes the club and standing before the prisoner he shows it to him. Meanwhile he who is going to do the deed withdraws with fourteen or fifteen others, and they all paint their bodies grey with ashes. Then the slayer returns with his companions, and the man who holds the club before the prisoner hands it to the slayer. At this stage the king of the huts approaches, and taking the club he thrusts it once between the slayer's legs, which is a sign of great honor. Then the slayer seizes it and thus addresses the victim: "I am he that will kill you, since you and yours have slain and eaten many of my friends." To which the prisoner replies: "When I am dead I shall still have many to avenge my death." Then the slayer strikes from behind and beats out his brains.

The women seize the body at once and carry it to the fire where they scrape off the skin, making the flesh quite white, and stopping up the fundament[5] with a piece of wood so that

---

[5] Anus.

nothing may be lost. Then a man cuts up the body, removing the legs above the knee and the arms at the trunk, whereupon the four women seize the four limbs and run with them round the huts, making a joyful cry. After this they divide the trunk among themselves, and devour everything that can be eaten.

When this is finished they all depart, each one carrying a piece with him. The slayer takes a fresh name, and the king of the huts scratches him in the upper part of the arm with the tooth of a wild beast. When the wound is healed the scar remains visible, which is a great honor. He must lie all that day in his hammock, but they give him a small bow and an arrow, so that he can amuse himself by shooting into wax, lest his arm should become feeble from the shock of the death-blow. I was present and have seen all this with my own eyes.

From *The Concluding Address*

Hans Staden wishes the reader mercy and peace in God's name.

Kind reader. I have now described my voyage and journey with all brevity, in order to relate how I fell into the hands of barbarous people, and the manner in which our Savior, the lord God, delivered me out of their power when I was without hope. This I have done that all may know that Almighty God can still stretch forth his hand to save and direct his people among the heathen, as he was wont to do in times past, and that all may bless his name and rest upon him in their necessity. For he himself has said: "Call thou upon me in the time of trouble. I will save thee and thou shalt glorify me."

Some might say that if I had described all my trials and experiences I might have made a bigger book. That is true, for I could indeed have told much more. But that was not my intention. I have shown here and there what reasons led me to write this book. My mind is to show only how much we owe to God who is with us always to protect us from the day of our birth onwards.

I perceive also that the contents of my book will seem strange to many. This cannot be helped. Nevertheless I was not the first, nor shall I be the last, to undertake voyages and see strange lands and peoples. Those who have had similar experiences will not laugh at my relation, but will take it to heart. But that he who has been face to face with death should have the same mind as those who stay at home and listen to what is told them is not to be expected, and this everybody knows well. Moreover, if all who sailed to America were to fall into the hands of the savages, no one would set out to distant parts.

And this I know, that there are many honest men in Castile, Portugal, and France, and some even in Antwerp, in Brabant, who having been in America, can testify that all that I have written is true. For the benefit of those to whom such matters are unknown I call upon these witnesses, but above all I call upon God.

. . . If there is a young man among you, to whom this writing and these witnesses are still insufficient, then, lest he should live in doubt, let him, with God's help, undertake the voyage himself. I have given him information enough; let him follow my tracks, for the world is closed to none whom God assists.

Now to Almighty God, who is all in all, be praise, honor and glory for ever and ever. Amen.

At Marburg at the Clover-leaf, in the house of Andres Kolben, on Shrove Tuesday 1557.

Manuel da Nóbrega (1517–1570)

Born in the North of Portugal and educated at the University of Coimbra, the Jesuit priest Manuel da Nóbrega led the first Portuguese missionary expedition to Brazil in 1549. Though Nóbrega viewed the conversion of the Native peoples of Brazil to Catholicism as his main objective, he was also active in the founding of schools in Salvador da Baia, São Vicente, and Rio de Janeiro, where he died in 1570.

Nóbrega's *Dialogue for the Conversion of the Indians*, written between 1556 and 1557, takes the form of a conversation between a missionary priest, Gonçalo Alvarez, and a blacksmith, Matheus Nogueira. The two discuss issues related to the obstacles to the conversion of the Indians to Catholicism: the question of whether or not they possess souls, their alleged lack of a religion or social structure, the education of Indian children and the use of Native languages as tools for ideological expansion, and the flagging zeal of some of their fellow priests.

PRIMARY WORK

Translated by Susan Castillo from the original, Manuel da Nóbrega, *Dialogo sobre a Conversão do Gentio*, in *Cartas dos Primeiros Jesuitas do Brasil, 1538–1553*, vol. I, ed. Serafim Leite (São Paulo: Comissão do IV Centenário da Cidade de São Paulo, 1956).

DIALOGUE FOR THE CONVERSION OF THE INDIANS

As I have time to extend myself, I want to speak to my Brothers of that which my spirit feels, and I shall take as interlocutors my Brother Gonçalo Alvarez, whom God gave grace and talent to trumpet his Word in the port of Spiritu Sancto, and my Brother Matheus Nogueira, blacksmith of Jesus Christ, who, as he does not preach with the Word, does so with works and hammer blows.

Enter Brother Gonçalo Alvarez, tempted by the Gato Indians and all the others. Half despairing of their conversion, he says:

> *Gonçalo Alvarez*: I have worked too hard with these people; they are so bestial, that nothing about God can enter into their hearts. They are so inflamed with killing and eating each other that they wish for no other boon. To preach to them is to preach to stones in the desert.
>
> *Matheus Nogueira*: If they had a King, one could convert them, or if they worshipped something; but as they know neither what it is to believe nor what it is to worship, they cannot comprehend the preaching of the Gospel, for it is founded on believing and worshipping one God, and serving only Him. As these people worship nothing, and believe in nothing, everything you tell them comes to naught.
>
> *Gonçalo Alvarez*: How right you are about how far they are from being converted, 5,000 in one day and 3,000 in another after only one sermon by the Apostles[1], and from converting whole kingdoms, cities, as happened in the past, because they were people of sense.
>
> *Matheus Nogueira*: One thing about them is worst of all: when they come to my tent, with one fish-hook which I give them, I convert them all, and with other fish-

---

[1] Acts 2:41 and 4:4.

hooks I dis-convert them, as they are inconstant, and the real Faith does not enter into their hearts. I once heard the Gospel read by my priests, where Christ said: "Give not that which is holy unto the dogs, neither cast ye your pearls before swine."[2] If there is a generation in the world about whom Christ Our Lord said this, it must be this one, for we see they are dogs in eating and killing one another, and they are swine in their vices and the way they treat one another. This must be the reason for the cooling ardor of some priests who came from the Kingdom[3], because they came expecting to convert all of Brazil in one hour and now see that they cannot convert a single one because of their rudeness and bestiality.

Gonçalo Alvarez: That must be true, because I do not remember which one I over-heard, when they were coming over on the ship, imagining himself as Saint John the Baptist by the River Jordan baptising all comers.

Matheus Nogueira: If they were fish from the Piraiqué[4], it could be . . .

Gonçalo Alvarez: There is no man in this entire land who knows these people who says differently. I had an Indian, whom I brought up from a small child; I took care to raise him as a good Christian, and he escaped back to his people. If that one could not be good, I do not know who can. It is not this one who makes me doubt that they are capable of baptism, because it was not only I who raised this raven[5]; I do not even know if I should call him a raven, for we can see that ravens, taken from their nests, can be raised and tamed and taught; but these, more forgetful of their upbringing than brute animals, and more ungrateful than the sons of vipers who devour their own mothers, have no respect for the love and care given to them.

Matheus Nogueira: Which reasons make you doubt that our Priests, who were sent by the Lord to show them the Faith, will not bear fruit in these people? Heavens!

Gonçalo Alvarez: You describe them well. Do you know the greatest difficulty I en-counter? That it is so easy for them to say "yes" or "pa," or whatever else, to every-thing; they approve of everything, and with the same facility with which they say "pa," they say "aani."[6] And if, when they are called, they say "neim tia,"[7] you should not waste breath on them but show them the task, for if it is not with the cane[8] they will not get up; to get a drink they are never drowsy. This facility of theirs[9] for agreeing with everything, accompanied by the experience for no fruit from so much "pa," has broken the hearts of many. One of our Brothers said that these people were the son who said in the Gospel to his father that he was going, and did not.[10]

Matheus Nogueira: Well, what is the use, shall we struggle in vain? My forge rings day and night, and will my work serve for naught among them, so that I can place it before Christ when he comes to judge us, in order that some of my other sins may be redeemed?[11]

Gonçalo Alvarez: You may be sure, Brother, that none of this will be lost; if Christ promises the Kingdom of Heaven for a cup of cold water given in the name of His love, how could it be possible that so many hammer blows, so much sweat, so

---

[2]   Matthew 7:6.
[3]   I.e. Portugal.
[4]   The mouth of a river known for abundant schools of fish.
[5]   Ungrateful child. This is a reference to the popular say-ing, "Raise ravens and they will peck your eyes out."
[6]   No.

[7]   Yes, I'm coming.
[8]   I.e. if they are not threatened with caning.
[9]   The Indians.
[10]   Matthew 21:28–30.
[11]   The verb is missing in the original manuscript.

much alertness, and so many tools as you have made, be wasted? Your sickles and axes are very good to clear the stubble of sin, and for this the Holy Spirit will plant many graces and gifts of His, if you work for love of Him.

Matheus Nogueira: Ay! Ay!

Gonçalo Alvarez: Why are you crying out!

Matheus Nogueira: Why are you insisting on this, "if you work for love of Him?"

Gonçalo Alvarez: Why are you concerned? You can be sure that if this is not the case you will lose everything you have done.

Matheus Nogueira: Well, I can tell you, my Brother, that you are confusing me. How can I know that I work for love of Him, with those who neither love Him nor know Him?

Gonçalo Alvarez: You know the Lord, who will make you wish to make Him known, loved, and served by all these and by the whole world.

Matheus Nogueira: This is the right wish, and I always beg of Him that He be worshipped, known, and loved by all, for it is right that the creature know its Creator, who gave him all his Being and perfection. The rational creature loves Him and honors Him above all else; for this all things were created and made, and are obliged to be the voice of all to praise God for such a boon, of making him Lord of all.

Gonçalo Alvarez: Well, my Brother, it seems to me that it is enough for God to be pleased with your service or sacrifice; I call it this because your task makes it look as though you are performing the sacrifice which in the Old Law was called the holocaust[12], when all was burnt and nothing was given to anybody.

Matheus Nogueira: Brother, for the love of God do not say this. It is not good that a sinner such as I hear this about the imperfect service he renders God; and as well, I have heard that this is a figure of speech for the great love with which the Son of God burned in the fire of charity for us on the Cross.

Gonçalo Alvarez: That is right. Forgive me, Brother, for humility does not suffer praise well, and I forgot myself.

Matheus Nogueira: Now you have loved me well! You call overweening pride humility! Do not be like the Father or Brother who Father Leonardo Nuñez, who is now in glory, used to tell us, would get stuck like a fly in honey to justify himself.

Gonçalo Alvarez: I only wish I were like him, for I would be a saint. But let us return to the question at hand. Brother Nogueira, for the love of Our Lord, may you freely and according to what you understand before Our Lord say: what do you think of these people according to the experience you have of them in the years you have been conversing with them?

Matheus Nogueira: What use is it to converse, if I do not understand them? Even though it seems to me that in order to convert them and make them Christians great intelligence is not needed, for our works show how few signs they have given of being able to do so.

Gonçalo Alvarez: Then what use to me is my tongue?

Matheus Nogueira: Ha! Ha! Ha! . . . Do you know what I am laughing at? Of your asking me what your tongue is good for, because I ask you: what good is my forge?

---

[12]   Cf. Leviticus 1:17: ". . . the priest shall burn it upon the altar, upon the wood that is upon the fire; it is a burnt sacrifice, an offering made by fire." The same Biblical passage is quoted by William Bradford in his description of the destruction of a Pequot village.

Gonçalo Alvarez: I have already answered this question.

Matheus Nogueira: Take the same answer.

Gonçalo Alvarez: No, our tasks are different, for mine is to speak, and yours is to do.

Matheus Nogueira: Their end is not different, then, because each of us should carry out his own.

Gonçalo Alvarez: And what is this end?

Matheus Nogueira: Charity or the love of God and of one's neighbor.

Gonçalo Alvarez: And you, Brother, are you already a theologian?

Matheus Nogueira: I must have caught some of it from my fellow priests, just as the embers of coal from the forge catch it from me. May the Lord grant that my bad example not be catching, even though they[13] are spiritual and experienced in suffering the weak in spirit.

Gonçalo Alvarez: Tell me, Brother Nogueira, are these Indians our neighbors?

Matheus Nogueira: It seems to me that they are.

Gonçalo Alvarez: For what reason?

Matheus Nogueira: For I always find myself among them, and among their axes and sickles.

Gonçalo Alvarez: And for this reason you call them your neighbors?

Matheus Nogueira: Yes, because to be neighbors means to be close, and they always come near for me to do whatever they need, and I do it for them as neighbors, taking care to fulfill the precept of loving my neighbor as myself, doing what I would wish for them to do to me, if I were in the same necessity.

Gonçalo Alvarez: I have heard very wise persons say that they were not our neighbors. They insist repeatedly on this, and even say that they are not men like us.

Matheus Nogueira: Well! If they are not men, they are not neighbors, for all men, both bad and good, are neighbors. Each man has one same nature, and each may know God and save his soul, and I have heard that this man is our neighbor. This is proven in the Gospel of the Samaritan[14], where Christ our Lord says that our neighbor is the man who shows us mercy.

Gonçalo Alvarez: You must have a good memory, for you remember well what you hear. Have you heard disputes among the Brothers about this, about what we practice in our conversion of these Indians?

Matheus Nogueira: Often, almost always, among my Brothers this is spoken of, as well you know. Each one speaks of his task, and as they have no other but searching for this lost sheep, they always talk about the obstacles that prevent them from bringing it home.

Gonçalo Alvarez: And what do they conclude, or what do they determine, those who are carrying out this task, of the possibilities they find in these Indians to come to our holy faith?

Matheus Nogueira: They[15] all leave it up to God, and are determined to die in this quest, for they are obliged to do what obedience dictates and because they wish nothing to be left undone for these people. Some have no great hope, observing their crudity and the fact that matters of faith are delicate ones. They say that there is a great possibility for one[16] to become a Christian if he is of the sound reason (which, although it alone is not enough to understand matters of faith, helps to

---

13 Nogueira's fellow priests.
14 Cf. Luke 10:30–37.

15 The priests.
16 An Indian.

understand that there is nothing in it that goes against natural reason) that they do not possess. They also say that in the times of the Apostles, when men were wiser and led orderly lives, it was easier for them to know the truth, and martyrs struggled against the bad customs of tyrants rather than the objections which no tyrant could offer to their preaching. Because these Indians have no reason[17] and have many vices, the door to faith is naturally closed to them unless God in his mercy opens it.

Gonçalo Alvarez: These seem to be good reasons, the memory of matters of God. Tell me, Brother, for the love of Our Lord, is there not among my Brothers and fellow priests, anyone who is on the side of these Indians?

Matheus Nogueira: Everyone, for everyone wants to convert them and are determined to die in the attempt, as I said.

Gonçalo Alvarez: I do not doubt that they all share this wish, but what I need is one who would give reasons for us to light the fire; and to speak to you in your own terms, we would like some bellows to fan the flames that are burning out.

Matheus Nogueira: This isn't necessary. Our Fathers can make enough fireworks to burn all of us who are dedicated to this business. As they have it in their spirits, all they do is destroy reasons and give others, and this does not satisfy even cold ones like myself.

Gonçalo Alvarez: Why?

Matheus Nogueira: Because of all the reasons, the most important one is that we must work with much fervor with these people, which is good for all of us, for according to the charity with which we labor in the vineyard of the Lord, He will pay us when he calls the workers to receive their wages, which as you will have heard will be not according to their work and time but to the fervor, love, and diligence they apply to the task.[18]

Gonçalo Alvarez: We are not speaking like a blacksmith.

Matheus Nogueira: I do not know how I speak, I speak whatever pops into my mouth. If it is badly expressed, forgive me, for no one can be forced to give more than he has and knows.

Gonçalo Alvarez: Let us leave this matter! I am so careless that I forgot that you are known for giving off sparks like a thread of hot metal when it is struck! I shall abstain from giving you more hammer-blows, in order not to burn myself. For the love of God, tell me some of the reasons that the Fathers give regarding the capacity of these Indians to become Christians. Some have said we are working in vain, at least until these people are subjugated, and are frightened into faith.

Matheus Nogueira: And what good would it do if they were Christians by force, and Indians in their lives and customs and will?

Gonçalo Alvarez: To the parents, those who hold this opinion feel it would do little good; the children, grandchildren and so forth could become Christians, and it seems they are right.

Matheus Nogueira: It always seemed to me that this was the best path, if God made it so, than others. Let us not speak of secrets and power and wisdom, for counselors are not necessary. But humanly, speaking like men, this seems the best and straightest way.

---

[17] In the original Portuguese text, this can be interpreted in two ways: that the Indians are wrong or that they are irrational.

[18] Matthew 20:1–6.

Gonçalo Alvarez: But you will recall that I want to hear the reasons of the Fathers, for I do not know how they will argue against the reasons I mentioned at first.

Matheus Nogueira: You see, Brother, charity undoes and melts everything, just as fire softens hard iron and turns it into a mass.

Gonçalo Alvarez: In this it seems that you are not right, for charity cannot take away truth, and more so since reason belongs to understanding and charity to will, which are different things. Just as the fire only removes the impurities, and does not consume the pure clean iron, if the reasons are good ones charity can do nothing against them, for it would be against truth, and thus would not be charity but pertinacity.

Matheus Nogueira: It seems that is right that where there is excessive zeal, at times one must break away from reasons or use them seldom, which happens when we are very attached to something.

Gonçalo Alvarez: And is this not a bad thing?

Matheus Nogueira: I don't know now how bad it is! I seem to have heard it said that St. Paul did not approve of everything done with good zeal; and to some it was allowed to witness this zeal (though it was good) to see if it was in accordance with the will of God, for this is the rule by which all works are measured, and all are good and straight when they are accordance with it, and they veer away from goodness when they veer away from it.

Gonçalo Alvarez: It seems likely that this is true. In accordance with this, it was not good for King Manuel to force the Jews to convert to Christianity after the massacre[19], even though most of them said they would, but he took them with their doors full of blood shed by the ministers of the Devil who had wounded them, incited by two Dominican friars who died in Oporto at the orders of said King. Thus one evil was paid for by another, as usually happens in the world, allowed and permitted by Our Lord until He manifests all our works to everyone. Sisebuto, King of Aragon[20], is not condemned in the sacred canons for the zeal with which, against the will of their Jewish parents, he had their children baptized in his kingdom, but his goal is not praised either. Thus, not everything that seems good should be done, but only that which is really good.

Matheus Nogueira: And how can a man always do the right thing, when he is ignorant and weak, if even kings with their counselors are wrong?

Gonçalo Alvarez: By taking advice with God and with dispassionate men of good conscience.

Matheus Nogueira: And where can these be found? At times only cold creatures like me can be found, who in order to spare themselves do not wish to leave their nests, forgetting how much these souls are costing Christ. It seems that such men cannot advise one well in such matters.

Gonçalo Alvarez: Lacking the others, who have zeal and wisdom, I would still take advice with these, because the Holy Spirit has spoken and advised a prophet who was not very virtuous, for good of the people He loved. And if He wants to do them good, as I believe he does, He hates nothing of what He does, as what we do is advised by Him. But I would like to hear from you the reasons that you have heard from the Fathers to encourage us to work with them[21], and their objections to what we have said at the beginning.

---

[19]   The massacre referred to by Nóbrega took place in Lisbon in 1506, during the reign of King Manuel I.

[20]   A Visigoth king of the seventh century AD.

[21]   The Indians.

Matheus Nogueira: As you insist, and you seem to desire to know the truth of this matter (and I believe I have exhausted you), I shall tell you that often, as I hammer on that hard iron I am remembering what I have heard from my fellow priests. It seems that Christ, who is listening to us, could say: Oh fools, and slow of heart to believe![22] I am imagining the souls of men as human, all made of the same metal, made in the image and likeness of God, and all capable of Glory and created for it, and the soul of the Pope is worth as much in the sight of God as that of your slave Papaná.

Gonçalo Alvarez: Have they a soul like ours?

Matheus Nogueira: This is obvious, as the soul has three potentialities, understanding, memory, and will, which they all have. I thought you were a master of Israel[23], and you don't know this! I was right that the theologies (sic) you were repeating before were borrowed from Father Brás Lourenço[24], and not your own. I am going to disappoint you, my Brother Gonçalo Alvarez: your comprehension of what I wanted to say to you is as crude as that of these Indians in understanding matters relating to our faith.

Gonçalo Alvarez: You are right, for I wade in the water along with *peixes-boi*, and deal with brazil-wood in the jungle[25], and do not value coldness, while you are always among the flames, which is why you flare up. But do go on, for one of the works of mercy is to teach the ignorant.

Matheus Nogueira: Then pay attention. After our Father Adam sinned, as the psalmist says, without knowing the honor he had, was made similar to the beasts, so that all, from the Portuguese to the Castilians to the Tamoios[26], to the Aimurés[27], were made to be like animals because of our corrupt nature. And in this we are all equal, for nature has not endowed one generation more than another, or given better understanding to one than to another. Iron is all the same, cold and without virtue, but in the forge, fire makes it more like fire than like iron. Thus all the souls without grace and the charity of God are worthless cold iron, but the more they are heated in the fire, the more you can do whatever you wish with them. And this can be seen in one who is in mortal sin, beyond the grace of God, for whom the things of God are worthless, who cannot pray, cannot be in Church, for whom spiritual things are tedious, who has no wish to do good. If he does good out of fear or obedience or shame, it is done so morosely or lazily that it is worth nothing, for it is written that God loveth a cheerful giver.[28]

Gonçalo Alvarez: This I can understand well, for I saw it in myself before I married. I was a sinner and now, thank God, do not sin so often.

Matheus Nogueira: Then what shall I say, for I have grown old in sin, and speak as a man who has been wounded!

Gonçalo Alvarez: Well, if this is so, if we all have a soul and a natural bestiality, and without grace are all one, why is it that I see these Indians as such bestial creatures, and all the other nations[29], like the Romans, and the Greeks, and the Jews, of such good sense?

---

[22]   Luke 24:25.

[23]   John 3:10.

[24]   A Portuguese Jesuit missionary, contemporary of Nóbrega.

[25]   *Peixes-boi*: literally, ox-fish, a type of Amazonian fish. Brazil-wood: a term used to refer to the Natives.

[26]   A tribe of the Tupi, who inhabited what is now the area of Rio de Janeiro.

[27]   A tribe living near the coast, around what are now the cities of Porto Seguro, Ilheús, and Baia.

[28]   II Corinthians 9:7.

[29]   In the original text, "gerações."

Matheus Nogueira: This is a good question, but the answer is clear. All these nations had their own bestialities: they worshipped stones and sticks, made gods of men, believed in the Devil's witchcraft. Others worshipped oxen and cows, while still others worshipped as gods rats and other filth; and the Jews, who were the most rational people in the world, and who were esteemed by God, and have had the Scriptures since the beginning of the world, worshipped a golden calf. Could not God have kept them from worshipping idols and sacrificing their own sons to them, not regarding the many marvels God had done for them, releasing them from captivity in Egypt? Are not the Moors as bestial as the Indians, for after becoming Christians they were converted by Mafamede to his vile sect? If you want to compare one thing to another, sect to sect, blindness to blindness, bestiality to bestiality, you will find they are all of the same kind, all proceeding from the same blindness. The Moors believe in Mafamede, vicious and clumsy, and they find bliss in the delights of the flesh and the vices; the Indians believe in a wizard who promises bliss in vengeance against their enemies and in having many women. The Romans, the Greeks and all the other peoples, have as a god an idol, a cow, a cockerel; the Indians say there is a God and say that he is the thunder, because it is the thing that they find most terrible, and in this they are more correct than those who worship frogs or cockerels. So, if you compare error with error, blindness with blindness, you will find lies, proceeding from the father of lies, a liar since the beginning of the world.

Gonçalo Alvarez: I agree with this. But how is it that the others[30] are all more polished, know how to read and write, keep themselves clean, knew philosophy, invented the sciences that now exist, while the Indians have only learned to go naked and make arrows? It is clear that this denotes unequal intelligence between the two groups.

Matheus Nogueira: This is not the reasoning of a man who is harvesting brazil-wood in the jungle[31], but listen carefully and you will understand. The fact that the Romans and other peoples are more polished does not come from greater intelligence, but from a better upbringing and from having been brought up in a more polite fashion. And I do believe that you will see this clearly, for you deal with them and see that in things related to their needs and which they deal with, they are every bit as subtle, with inventions just as good, and words as discreet as anyone's. The Fathers experience this every day with the Indian children, the intelligence of many of whom they find outstrips that of the Christians.

Gonçalo Alvarez: How is it that they had a worse upbringing than the others, and Nature did not give them the same polish as it did to the others?

Matheus Nogueira: They can tell you directly, speaking the truth, that it came to them due to the curse of their grandparents, for we believe them to be descendants of Ham, son of Noah[32], who uncovered the nakedness of his drunken father, and God therefore, as a curse, condemned them[33] to go naked and to suffer more greatly. The other peoples, as they were the descendants of Seth and Japheth, had reason, for they were the sons of blessing, and had greater advantages. However, all of these peoples, ones and others, in the way they are created, have the same soul and the same understanding, and this is proven in the Scriptures, for of the first two

---

[30]   I.e. the Romans, Greeks, Jews, etc.

[31]   I.e. converting the Natives of Brazil.

[32]   Genesis 9:18–27.

[33]   The Indians.

brothers in the world[34], one followed certain customs and the other different ones. Isaac and Ishmael were brothers, but Isaac was more polished than Ishmael, who lived in the forest. One man has two sons of equal intelligence, one brought up in the village and another in the city; the one in the village uses his intelligence to make a plow or other things pertaining to the village, while the one in the city uses his to be a courtier and politician. It is true that they have different upbringings, but both have a natural intelligence, exercised according to their upbringing. And what you say about the sciences, discovered by the philosophers, denotes great intelligence, but it was a special God-given grace, neither to all the Romans nor to all the Indians, but to one or two, or few, for the benefit and beauty of the whole universe. But neither you nor all the reasons cited before will persuade me that the Indians, lacking in this polish, have less intelligence to receive the faith from others who possess it. On the contrary, I shall prove that this polish benefits on the one hand but hinders on the other, and the simplicity of these people, though it is an obstacle on the one hand, helps on the other. May God see this and judge it; may it also be judged by whoever hears the experience of the Church since it began, and you will see that more has been lost due to an excess of proud intelligence than due to simplicity and lack of knowledge. It is easier to convert an ignorant person than one who is malicious and proud. The greatest struggle of the Church was with excessive understanding, for from it came the heretics and those who were hardest and most contumacious; from it came the pertinacy of the Jews, who not even believing in their own Scriptures ever wished to surrender to faith; from it came St. Paul saying, "We preach Christ crucified, unto the Jews a stumbling-block and unto the Greeks a foolishness."[35] Tell me, Brother, what is it easier to do? To make one of these believe what is so easy to believe, that our Lord died, or to convert a Jew who awaited the powerful Messiah and Lord of all the earth?

Gonçalo Alvarez: A Jew would be more difficult, but once he realized the truth he would be more constant, as were many who gave their lives for it.

Matheus Nogueira: I too say to you that if these Indians realized the truth, they too would do the same. You will agree that if faith enters their hearts, one is the same as another, and regarding the time and work and diligence necessary to convince a Jew or a philosopher, if you spend the same time teaching one of these Indians, his heartfelt conversion will be easier, with God giving equal grace to one and the other. And the reason is clear, for as the most essential matters of our faith, such as the Holy Trinity and God making himself Man and the mysteries of the sacraments, cannot be proven by demonstrative reason, and are indeed beyond all human reason, it is evident that it is far more difficult to believe a philosopher, in whom all is based on subtleties of reason, rather than one who believes in simpler things.

Gonçalo Alvarez: This is true, for if you cast a deadly curse upon them, they believe that you can kill them, and they die of imagination, due to their great and excessive belief. And they believe they must carry their basket to the scything, and do other similar things their wizards suggest to them. But even this is not enough, for I have been in this land for a long time and have spoken a great deal of God at the request of the priests, and I have never seen any priest who had so much faith that it seemed to me that he would die for it if necessary.

---

[34]   Cain and Abel.   [35]   I Corinthians 1:23.

Matheus Nogueira: If you allow me, I'll tell you.

Gonçalo Alvarez: Tell me, my Brother, and I shall forgive you.

Matheus Nogueira: It seems to me that however easy it is to convert them, they will not be converted by the way you and the Fathers speak to them, so pay attention. You know that the task of converting souls is the greatest of all tasks on Earth, and for this reason it requires a higher state of perfection than any other.

Gonçalo Alvarez: Does it? Isn't it enough to be a linguist and know how to say things well?

Matheus Nogueira: Much more than this is necessary. Look at the Apostles of Christ who converted the world and guide yourselves accordingly. First of all, they had a great deal of spirit, so much so that they burned inwardly with the fire of the Holy Spirit, for otherwise how could they light a divine fire in the hearts of people without one in their own heart? They must have great faith, trusting in God and mistrusting themselves greatly; they must have the grace of speaking the language[36] well; they must have sufficient virtue to work miracles when necessary, and other many graces possessed by those who converted people; without this, I have not heard of anyone who has been converted. And do you want to convert them without any of this, and to make them holy at once? This would be the greatest miracle in the world; and even if you are a linguist and know well how to speak to them, you will not deny that if one of them does not say what you want him to say, you lose patience and say he will never be any good. Nor is there any reason to give credit to your words, for yesterday you asked them for their child as a slave, and the day before you tried to deceive them. And they are right to fear that you wish to deceive them, for this is what bad Christians commonly do to them.

Gonçalo Alvarez: This is true, but the priests who speak to them so lovingly, why don't the Indians believe them?

Matheus Nogueira: Because until now the Indians have not seen the difference between the priests and the other Christians. The conclusion is: when St. James, traveling throughout Spain and speaking the language well, and being great in charity, could convert no more than nine disciples, you believe that the priests, without performing miracles, without knowing the Indians' language, nor understanding them, by presuming to be an apostle and lacking confidence and faith in God and charity, will make of them good Christians? Still, to oblige you, I shall tell you that I've seen Indians of this land with very clear signs of true faith in their hearts, demonstrated by their works, not only the children we have brought up, but also adults with whom we have only recently spoken. Who saw, in the Port of São Vicente, where there have been more dealings with the Indians than anywhere else in Brazil, the glorious death of Pero Lopes?[37] Who saw his tears, his loving embraces of the friars and priests? Let those who saw it proclaim the virtue of his wife, so far from the customs which once she lived, now a widow who lives in honest fashion, to such an extent that all deemed her worthy of receiving the Holy Sacrament? And what can I say of his daughters, two of them, of whom it is hard to tell who is the most fervent Christian? What I can say about the grand old Cayobi[38],

---

[36]   The Indian languages.

[37]   Purportedly an Indian of Maniçoba who died for his faith.

[38]   An Indian who was one of the first converts of Father Ancieta, an early Jesuit missionary.

who left behind his village and his fields and came to die of starvation in Piratininga for love of us, whose life and customs demonstrate the faith in his heart! And many others of the village, who, though some have not abandoned their lives of vice due to the example of certain bad Christians, even they have faith, for they have ceased to commit the greatest sin and that which is hardest for them not to commit, which is killing on the field of battle and eating human flesh. Who is not aware that, when going to war and capturing enemies, they now kill them and bury them? And to cheer you up still more, I shall tell you as well that in Maniçoba, where some Carijó Indians were killing one another, still another Indian, who was with the priests, offered with great fervor and tears to die for the faith, in order that the former might die as Christians. And there are many other specific cases which happen every day, which would take too long to tell. Among so few, to gather such fruit, and with such inferior workmen, how could it be possible, if Our Lord sends good workmen to his vineyard with the necessary requisites, not to harvest a great deal of fruit? I am sure that if you found yourself in the time of the Martyrs, and saw the slaughter of those infidels, who were not softened even by miracles and marvels, nor by good sermons nor prayers, you and I would say: they will never be any good! In conclusion, I say: in the end, prayers! The matter of conversion is mainly up to God, and no-one brings to the knowledge of Jesus Christ anyone other than those brought by His Father. When He wishes, He can raise up Sons of Israel from stones[39], just as no one can be saved nor obtain grace without Him.

Gonçalo Alvarez: This is on God's part, but on the part of the Indians there must also be the disposition necessary, for I have heard that St. Augustine said that God, who made me without my help, will not save me without my help.

Matheus Nogueira: Regarding the Indians, I say that they are all cold iron, and when God places them in the forge they will be converted; and if in the forge of God they are prepared to go into the last fire, the real fire, Lord of iron, who is to know why, but they have just as much disposition as all the other nations.

Gonçalo Alvarez: I would like to know this more clearly.

Matheus Nogueira: The more impediments one of them has to conversion, the less disposition he will have, and the less evil God has to remove from them, the more disposed they are.

Gonçalo Alvarez: Go on, prove it.

Matheus Nogueira: Tell me about the evil of one of these and of a Roman philosopher. For these Indians, who are very bestial, their happiness is killing and having names, and this is their glory whatever else they do. They do not even obey natural law because they eat one another; they are lustful, given to lying, find nothing evil, and nothing good; they believe their wizards. This says it all. A very wise but very proud philosopher finds his happiness in fame or fleshy delights, or in victories over his enemies; in his malice, he hides the truth God taught him, as St. Paul has said. Philosophers do not obey natural law, for though they understand it, many commit the vice against nature[40]; they are very tyrannical and enjoy showing off; they are envious and fear losing what they have; they worship idols, sacrifice human blood to them, and commit every kind of wickedness. Regarding the Indians, according to the priests who hear their confessions, with two or three

---

[39] Matthew 3:9.

[40] Homosexuality.

commandments they are done.[41] Among themselves, they live in friendly fashion. Which boulder seems to you the harder to break down?

Gonçalo Alvarez: It is hard to choose between bad cattle, but I still would like for you to answer the above reasons more clearly.

Matheus Nogueira: The answer is clear in what has already been said.

Thomas Harriot (1560–1621)

A graduate of Oxford, distinguished mathematician and true Renaissance man, Harriot (also spelled Hariot or Heriot) was first engaged by Sir Walter Ralegh as a household tutor. He also studied astronomy and surveying, experimented with lenses, wrote a treatise on navigation, and probably trained members of Ralegh's first Roanoke expedition in navigational skills. Only twenty-five years old, Harriot joined the second voyage to Virginia in 1585, where he collaborated with the artist John White in studying the flora and fauna of the Chesapeake area and surveying its natural resources and economic possibilities. He also learned the Algonquian language and spent a good deal of time with the local inhabitants, giving force to the claims he makes in his report of in-depth, first-hand knowledge of the region. However, there was considerable turmoil in the fledgling colony established by Ralegh and situated on Roanoke, an island off what is now the North Carolina coast. Ralegh appointed as commander his cousin, Sir Richard Grenville, a volatile character who used violence against the Native Americans and lost the confidence of his men. When he departed for resupplying in England, his successor, Ralph Lane, used even more brutal tactics despite the initial generosity and amiability of Chief Wingina's tribe in their dealings with the English. Frustrated with Lane's harsh policies, Wingina began to withhold food supplies, and when other Native Americans intimated that this was the beginning of a plot to destroy the colonists, Lane's men surprised the sleeping village of Dasemunkepeuc on the mainland, killed many people, hounded Wingina into the woods, tracked him down and beheaded him. Despite – or because of – these strong-arm tactics,

this first attempt at colonization ended badly. Sir Francis Drake rescued a group of survivors during a storm in June 1586, leaving the compound abandoned until Grenville returned with reinforcements and supplies later that summer. Of the fifteen men he left there, some died and others departed in a boat, never to be heard of again.

Although Harriot alludes to the English treatment of the Natives in his account, *A briefe and true report of the new found land of Virginia*, he downplays it. Writing at Ralegh's behest, he is more concerned with countering the "slanderous" and "malicious" reports circulating at the time that painted Virginia as a harsh and wild land – an unsound investment both on the national and personal levels. This accounts for the defensive tone of his opening remarks and for the hopeful optimism of his conclusion about the riches and plenty yet to be discovered in Virginia. His report was important because, at the time, Ralegh was preparing to establish a new colony under the command of John White. However, events conspired to make his buoyant tone highly ironic. His account first appeared as a small volume in 1588; the larger edition, with many remarkable engravings by Theodor de Bry based on the paintings and drawings of John White, did not appear until 1590. By 1588, however, John White had brought another group of colonists to Roanoke, but was unable to return with supplies because of the war between England and Spain. By the time he arrived in August 1590, all of the members of this second colony had mysteriously disappeared; historians have still not adequately accounted for their fate.

---

[41] I.e. the Indians have broken only two or three commandments.

PRIMARY WORK

A briefe and true report of the new found land of Virginia: of the commodities there found, and to be raised, as well merchantable as others: Written by Thomas Heriot, servant of Sir Walter Ralegh, a member of the Colony, and there imployed in discovering a full twelvemoneth (London, 1588).

FURTHER READING

Everett Emerson, "Thomas Hariot, John White and Ould Virginia," in *Essays in Early Virginia Literature Honoring Richard Beale Davis*, ed. J. A. Leo Lemay (New York: Franklin, 1977).

Vivian Salmon, "Thomas Harriot and the English Origins of Algonkian Linguistics," *Historiographia Linguistica*, 19, 1 (1992) pp. 25–56.

William Hamlin, "Imagined Apotheoses: Drake, Harriot, and Ralegh in the Americas," *Journal of the History of Ideas*, July, 57, 3 (1996) pp. 405–28.

FROM *A BRIEFE AND TRUE REPORT OF THE NEW FOUND LAND OF VIRGINIA*[1]

From *The first part of Merchantable Commodities*

There is an herbe which is sowed apart by it selfe, and is called by the inhabitants Uppowoc: in the West Indies it hath divers names, according to the severall places and countreys where it groweth and is used: the Spanyards generally call it Tabacco. The leaves thereof being dried and brought into pouder, they use to take the fume or smoake thereof, by sucking it thorow pipes made of clay, into their stomacke and head; from whence it purgeth superfluous fleame[2] and other grosse humours, and openeth all the pores and passages of the body: by which meanes the use thereof not only preserveth the body from obstructions, but also (if any be, so that they have not bene of too long continuance) in short time breaketh them: whereby their bodies are notably preseverd in health, and know not many grievous diseases, wherewithall we in England are often time afflicted.

This Uppowoc is of so precious estimation amongst them, that they thinke their gods are marvellously delighted therewith: whereupon sometime they make hallowed fires, and cast some of the pouder therin for a sacrifice: being in a storme upon the waters, to pacifie their gods, they cast some up into the aire and into the water: so a weare[3] for fish being newly set up, they cast some therein and into the aire: also after an escape of danger, they cast some into the aire likewise: but all done with strange gestures, stamping, sometime dancing, clapping of hands, holding up of hands, and staring up into the heavens, uttering therewithall, and chattering strange words and noises.

Of the Nature and Maners[4] of the People

It resteth I speake a word or two of the naturall inhabitants, their natures and maners, leaving large discourse thereof until time more convenient hereafter: nowe onely so farre forth, as that you may know, how that they in respect of troubling our inhabiting and planting, are not

---

[1] The text, with slight modification, is from Richard Hakluyt, *The Principall Navigations, Voyages, Traffiques, & Discoveries of the English Nation*, vol. 8 (Glasgow: James MacLehose and Sons, 1904).

[2] Phlegm.

[3] Weir, net.

[4] Customs or practices.

to be feared, but that they shall have cause both to feare and love us, that shall inhabite with them.

They are a people clothed with loose mantles made of deere skinnes, and aprons of the same round about their middles, all els naked, of such a difference of statures onely as wee in England[5], having no edge tooles or weapons of yron or steele to offend us withall, neither knowe they how to make any: those weapons that they have, are onely bowes made of Witch-hazle, and arrowes of reedes, flat edged truncheons[6] also of wood about a yard long, neither have they any thing to defend themselves but targets[7] made of barkes, and some armours made of sticks wickered[8] together with thread.

Their townes are but small, and neere the Sea coast but fewe, some contayning but tenne or twelve houses; some 20. the greatest that we have seene hath bene but of 30. houses: if they bee walled, it is onely done with barkes of trees made fast to stakes, or els with poles onely fixed upright, and close one by another.

Their houses are made of small poles, made fast at the tops in round forme after the maner as is used in many arbories[9] in our gardens of England, in most townes covered with barkes, and in some with artificiall mats made of long rushes, from the tops of the houses downe to the ground. The length of them is commonly double to the breadth, in some places they are but 12. and 16. yards long, and in other some we have seene of foure and twentie.

In some places of the Countrey, one onely towne belongeth to the government of a Wiroans or chiefe Lord, in other some two or three, in some sixe, eight, and more: the greatest Wiroans that yet wee had dealing with, had but eighteene townes in his government, and able to make not above seven or eight hundreth fighting men at the most. The language of every government is different from any other, and the further they are distant, the greater is the difference.

Their maner of warres amongst themselves is either by sudden surprising one an other most commonly about the dawning of the day, or moone-light, or els by ambushes, or some subtile devises. Set battels are very rare, except it fall out where there are many trees, where either part may have some hope of defence, after the delivery of every arrow, in leaping behind some or other.

If there fall out any warres betweene us and them, what their fight is likely to bee, wee having advantages against them so many maner of wayes, as by our discipline, our strange weapons and devises else, especially Ordinance great and small, it may easily bee imagined: by the experience wee have had in some places, the turning up of their heeles against us in running away was their best defence.[10]

In respect of us they are a people poore, and for want of skill and judgement in the knowledge and use of our things, doe esteeme our trifles before things of greater value. Notwithstanding, in their proper maner[11] (considering the want of such meanes as we have), they seeme very ingenious. For although they have no such tooles, nor any such crafts, Sciences and Artes as wee, yet in those things they doe, they shew excellencie of wit. And by how much they upon due consideration shall finde our maner of knowledges and crafts to exceede theirs in perfection, and speede for doing or execution, by so much the more is it probable that they should desire our friendship and love, and have the greater respect for pleasing and obeying us.

---

5 With variations in height similar to the English.
6 Heavy clubs.
7 Small shields.
8 Woven.
9 Arbors, small, open shelters.
10 A disingenuous reference to Chief Wingina, mentioned below, who in 1586 was surprised by Roanoke governor Ralph Lane in his village of Dasemunkepeuc on the rumor of a plot against the fledgling English colony. Wingina ran away but was tracked, captured, shot in the back and beheaded.
11 Within the bounds of their own culture.

"The Town of Secota." Engraving by Theodor de Bry from a watercolor by John White, who accompanied Harriot on the voyage to Virginia. (Courtesy of the John Carter Brown Library at Brown University.)

"Those of their towns which are not fenced in are usually more beautiful, as can be seen in this picture of the town of Secota. The houses are farther apart and have gardens (marked E), in which they grow tobacco, called by the Natives *uppówoc*. They also have groves of trees where they hunt deer, and fields where they sow their corn. In the cornfields they set up a little hut on a scaffold, where a watchman is stationed (F). He makes a continual noise to keep off birds and beasts which would otherwise soon devour all the corn. They sow their corn a certain distance apart (H), so that one stalk should not choke the next. For the leaves are large like great reed leaves (G).

"They also have a large plot (C) where they meet with neighbors to celebrate solemn feasts, and a place (D) where they make merry when the feast is ended. In the round plot (B) they assemble to pray. The large building (A) holds the tombs of their kings and princes. In the garden on the right (I) they sow pumpkins. There is also a place (K) where they build a fire at feast time, and just outside the town is the river (L) from which they get their water.

"These people live happily together without envy or greed. They hold feasts at night, when they make large fires to light them and show their joy."

Whereby may bee hoped, if meanes of good government be used, that they may in short time bee brought to civilitie, and the imbracing of true Religion.

Some religion they have already, which although it be farre from the trueth, yet being as it is, there is hope it may be the easier and sooner reformed.

They beleeve that there are many gods, which they call Mantoac, but of different sorts & degrees, one onely chiefe and great God, which hath bene from all eternitie. Who, as they affirme, when hee purposed to make the world, made first other gods of a principall order, to be as meanes and instruments to be used in the creation and government to follow, and after the Sunne, moone, and starres as pettie gods, and the instruments of the other order more principal. First (they say) were made waters, out of which by the gods was made all diversitie of creatures that are visible or invisible.

For mankinde they say a woman was made first, which by the working of one of the gods, conceived and brought foorth children: And in such sort they say they had their beginning. But how many yeeres or ages have passed since, they say they can make no relation, having no letters nor other such meanes as we to keepe Records of the particularities of times past, but onely tradition from father to sonne.

They thinke that all the gods are of humane shape, and therefore they represent them by images in the formes of men, which they call Kewasowok, one alone is called Kewas: them they place in houses appropriate or temples, which they call Machicomuck, where they worship, pray, sing, and make many times offring unto them. In some Machicomuck we have seene but one Kewas, in some two, and in other some three. The common sort thinke them to be also gods.[12]

They beleeve also the immortalitie of the soule, that after this life as soone as the soule is departed from the body, according to the workes it hath done, it is either caried to heaven the habitacle[13] of gods, there to enjoy perpetuall blisse and happinesse, or els to a great pitte or hole, which they thinke to be in the furthest parts of their part of the world toward the Sunne set, there to burne continually: the place they call Popogusso.

For the confirmation of this opinion, they tolde me two stories of two men that had bene lately dead and revived againe, the one happened but few yeeres before our comming into the Countrey of a wicked man, which having bene dead and buried, the next day the earth of the grave being seene to move, was taken up againe, who made declaration where his soule had bene, that is to say, very neere entring into Popogusso, had not one of the gods saved him, and gave him leave to returne againe, and teach his friends what they should do to avoyd that terrible place of torment. The other happened in the same yeere we were there, but in a towne that was 60. miles from us, and it was told me for strange newes, that one being dead, buried, and taken up againe as the first, shewed that although his body had lien dead in the grave, yet his soule was alive, & had travailed farre in a long broad way, on both sides whereof grew most delicate and pleasant trees, bearing more rare and excellent fruits, then ever hee had seene before, or was able to expresse, and at length came to most brave and faire houses, neere which he met his father that had bene dead before, who gave him great charge to goe backe againe, and shew his friendes what good they were to doe to enjoy the pleasures of that place, which when he had done he should after come againe.

What subtiltie soever be in the Wiroances and priestes, this opinion worketh so much in

---

[12]   Arthur Barlowe in his account, *The First Voyage Made to the Coasts of America* (1584), makes a similar observation about "savage" confusion of material image and spiritual essence, which would have been particularly relevant to Protestant readers, given the strong iconoclastic, anti-Catholic, attitude in English religious thinking.

[13]   Habitation.

many of the common and simple sort of people, that it maketh them have great respect to their Governours, and also great care what they doe, to avoyd torment after death, and to enjoy blisse, although notwithstanding there is punishment ordeined for malefactours, as stealers, whoremongers, and other sorts of wicked doers, some punished with death, some with forfeitures, some with beating, according to the greatnesse of the facts.

And this is the summe of their Religion, which I learned by having speciall familiaritie with some of their priests. Wherein they were not so sure grounded, nor gave such credite to their traditions and stories, but through conversing with us they were brought into great doubts of their owne, and no small admiration of ours, with earnest desire in many, to learne more then wee had meanes for want of perfect utterance in their language to expresse.

Most things they sawe with us, as Mathematicall instruments, sea Compasses, the vertue of the load-stone in drawing yron, a perspective glasse whereby was shewed many strange sights, burning glasses, wilde fireworkes, gunnes, hookes, writing and reading, springclockes that seeme to goe of themselves[14] and many other things that wee had were so strange unto them, and so farre exceeded their capacities to comprehend the reason and meanes how they should be made and done, that they thought they were rather the workes of gods then of men, or at the leastwise they had bene given and taught us of the gods. Which made many of them to have such opinion of us, as that if they knew not the trueth of God and Religion already, it was rather to bee had from us whom God so specially loved, then from a people that were so simple, as they found themselves to be in comparison of us. Whereupon greater credite was given unto that wee spake of, concerning such matters.

Many times and in every towne where I came, according as I was able, I made declaration of the contents of the Bible, that therein was set foorth the true and onely God, and his mightie workes, that therein was conteined the true doctrine of salvation through Christ, with many particularities of Miracles and chiefe points of Religion, as I was able then to utter, and thought fit for the time. And although I told them the booke materially and of it selfe was not of any such vertue, as I thought they did conceive, but onely the doctrine therein conteined: yet would many be glad to touch it, to embrace it, to kisse it, to holde it to their breastes and heads, and stroke over all their body with it, to shew their hungry desire of that knowledge which was spoken of.

The Wiroans with whom we dwelt called Wingina, and many of his people would bee glad many times to be with us at our Prayers, and many times call upon us both in his owne towne, as also in others whither hee sometimes accompanied us, to pray and sing Psalmes, hoping thereby to be partaker of the same effects which we by that meanes also expected.

Twise this Wiroans was so grievously sicke that he was like to die, and as he lay languishing, doubting of any helpe by his owne priestes, and thinking hee was in such danger for offending us and thereby our God, sent for some of us to pray and bee a meanes to our God that it would please him either that he might live, or after death dwell with him in blisse, so likewise were the requests of many others in the like case.

On a time also when their corne began to wither by reason of a drought which happened extraordinarily[15], fearing that it had come to passe by reason that in some thing they had displeased us, many would come to us and desire us to pray to our God of England, that he would preserve their Corne, promising that when it was ripe we also should be partakers of the fruit.

There could at no time happen any strange sicknesse, losses, hurts, or any other crosse[16]

---

[14] Load-stone: magnet. Perspective glass: telescope or magnifying glass.

[15] The drought was extraordinarily severe.

[16] Troubles, afflictions.

unto them, but that they, would impute to us the cause or meanes thereof, for offending or not pleasing us. One other rare and strange accident, leaving others, wil I mention before I end, which moved the whole Countrey that either knew or heard of us, to have us in wonderfull admiration.

There was no towne where wee had any subtile devise practised against us, wee leaving it unpunished or not revenged (because we sought by all meanes possible to win them by gentlenesse) but that within a few dayes after our departure from every such Towne, the people began to die very fast, and many in short space, in some Townes about twentie, in some fourtie, and in one sixe score, which in trueth was very many in respect of their numbers. This happened in no place that we could learne, but where we had bin, where they used some practise against us, & after such time. The disease also was so strange, that they neither knewe what it was, nor how to cure it, the like by report of the oldest men in the Countrey never happened before, time out of minde. A thing specially observed by us, as also by the naturall inhabitants themselves. Insomuch that when some of the inhabitants which were our friends, and especially the Wiroans Wingina, had observed such effects in foure or five Townes to followe their wicked practises, they were perswaded that it was the worke of our God through our meanes, and that we by him might kill and slay whom we would without weapons, and not come neere them. And thereupon when it had happened that they had understanding that any of their enemies had abused us in our journeys, hearing that we had wrought no revenge with our weapons, and fearing upon some cause the matter should so rest: did come and intreate us that we would be a meanes to our God that they as others that had dealt ill with us might in like sort die, alleadging how much it would bee for our credite and profite, as also theirs, and hoping furthermore that we would doe so much at their requests in respect of the friendship we professed them.[17]

Whose entreaties although wee shewed that they were ungodly, affirming that our God would not subject himselfe to any such prayers and requests of men: that indeede all things have bene and were to be done according to his good pleasure as he had ordeined: and that we to shewe our selves his true servants ought rather to make petition for the contrary, that they with them might live together with us, be made partakers of his trueth, and serve him in righteousnesse, but notwithstanding in such sort, that wee referre that, as all other things, to bee done according to his divine will and pleasure, and as by his wisedome he had ordeined to be best.

Yet because the effect fell out so suddenly and shortly after according to their desires[18], they thought neverthelesse it came to passe by our meanes, & that we in using such speeches unto them, did but dissemble the matter, and therefore came unto us to give us thankes in their maner, that although we satisfied them not in promise, yet in deedes and effect we had fulfilled their desires.

This marvellous accident in all the Countrey wrought so strange opinions of us, that some people could not tell whether to thinke us gods or men, and the rather because that all the space of their sicknes, there was no man of ours knowen to die, or that was specially sicke: they noted also that we had no women amongst us, neither that we did care for any of theirs.

Some therefore were of opinion that we were not borne of women, and therefore not mortal,

---

[17] Throughout the New World, contact between Europeans and Native Americans touched off epidemics that decimated native populations. The "pattern of revenge" Harriot describes probably resulted when more intimate contact between parties caused disagreements as well as the spread of pathogens. Because Harriot does not give symptoms, historians have speculated that the infection may have been the common cold.

[18] That is, the enemies whom Wingina wished the English to visit their sickness on did, in fact, fall ill.

but that we were men of an old generation many yeeres past, then risen againe to immortalitie.

Some would likewise seeme to prophecie that there were more of our generation yet to come to kill theirs and take their places, as some thought the purpose was, by that which was already done. Those that were immediatly to come after us they imagined to be in the aire, yet invisible and without bodies, and that they by our intreatie and for the love of us, did make the people to die in that sort as they did, by shooting invisible bullets into them.

To confirme this opinion, their Phisitions (to excuse their ignorance in curing the disease) would not be ashamed to say, but earnestly make the simple people beleeve, that the strings of blood that they sucked out of the sicke bodies, were the strings wherewithall the invisible bullets were tied and cast. Some also thought that wee shot them our selves out of our pieces, from the place where wee dwelt, and killed the people in any Towne that had offended us, as wee listed, howe farre distant from us soever it were. And other some said, that it was the speciall worke of God for our sakes, as we our selves have cause in some sort to thinke no lesse, whatsoever some doe, or may imagine to the contrary, specially some Astrologers, knowing of the Eclipse of the Sunne which we saw the same yeere before in our voyage thitherward, which unto them appeared very terrible. And also of a Comet, which began to appeare but a fewe dayes before the beginning of the saide sicknesse. But to exclude them from being the speciall causes of so speciall an accident, there are further reasons then I thinke fit at this present to be alleadged. These their opinions I have set downe the more at large, that it may appeare unto you that there is good hope they may be brought through discreete dealing and government to the imbracing of the trueth, and consequently to honour, obey, feare and love us.

And although some of our company towards the end of the yeere, shewed themselves too fierce in slaying some of the people in some Townes, upon causes that on our part might easily ynough have bene borne withall: yet notwithstanding, because it was on their part justly deserved, the alteration of their opinions generally and for the most part concerning us is the lesse to be doubted. And whatsoever els they may be, by carefulnesse of our selves neede nothing at all to be feared.[19]

1587   1588, 1590

Samuel de Champlain (1570?–1635)

Champlain's first contact with North America was as Royal Geographer on a 1603 expedition following the route of Jacques Cartier. In 1604 he led a group of settlers from the St. Lawrence region to Acadia to establish a trading post at Port Royal. The rugged landscape of the Nova Scotian peninsula made it impossible, however, to enforce the monopoly of the fur trade. As a result, de Monts and Champlain returned to the St. Lawrence in 1608, and at "the place where the river narrowed," also known as Quebec, founded a trading center.

In later years, he collaborated with the Hurons in their war against the Iroquois. In the following excerpt from his account of his travels, Champlain sets forth the reasons for the settlement of New France within the larger context of European exploration and describes the difficulties and disease endured by the first settlers as well as their complex interactions with the Native peoples of Canada.

Champlain dedicated the final years of his life to rebuilding and improving the fort and build-

---

[19]   Harriot's second allusion to the brutal practices of Roanoke governor Ralph Lane.

ings of Quebec, and of forming alliances with Indian tribes against the Iroquois. He died on Christmas Day, 1635.

FURTHER READING

Marcel Trudeau, *The Beginnings of New France, 1524–
1663*, trans. Patricia Claxton (Toronto: McClelland
and Stewart, 1973).

PRIMARY WORK

Voyages of Samuel de Champlain, 1604–1618, ed. W. L.
Grant (New York: Charles Scribners' Sons, 1907).

FROM *VOYAGES OF SAMUEL DE CHAMPLAIN, 1604–1618*

The Voyages of 1604–7

Chapter 1: The benefits of commerce have induced several princes to seek an easier
route for traffic with the people of the East. Several unsuccessful voyages.
Determination of the French for this purpose. Undertaking of Sieur de Monts[1]: his
commission and its revocation. New commission to Sieur de Monts to enable him to
continue his undertaking.

The inclinations of men differ according to their varied dispositions; and each one in his
calling has his particular end in view. Some aim at gain, some at glory, some at the public
weal[2]. The greater number are engaged in trade, and especially that which is transacted on the
sea. Hence arise the principal support of the people, the opulence and honor of states. This is
what raised ancient Rome to the sovereignty and mastery over the entire world, and the
Venetians to a grandeur equal to that of powerful kings. It has in all times caused maritime
towns to abound in riches, among which Alexandria and Tyre are distinguished, and numerous others, which fill up the regions of the interior with the objects of beauty and rarity
obtained from foreign nations. For this reason, many princes have striven to find a northerly
route to China, in order to facilitate commerce with the Orientals, in the belief that this route
would be shorter and less dangerous.

In the year 1496, the king of England commissioned John Cabot and his son Sebastian[3] to
engage in this search. About the same time, Don Emanuel[4], king of Portugal, despatched on
the same errand Gaspar Corte-Real[5], who returned without attaining his object. Resuming his
journeys the year after, he died in the undertaking; as did also his brother Michel, who was
prosecuting it perseveringly. In the years 1534 and 1535, Jacques Cartier[6] received a like
commission from King Francis I, but was arrested in his course. Six years after, Sieur de
Roberval[7], having renewed it, sent Jean Alfonse of Saintonge farther northward along the
coast of Labrador; but he returned as wise as the others. In the years 1576, 1577, and 1578, Sir

---

[1]   Pierre de Guast, a Huguenot nobleman appointed Lieutenant-General of Acadia by the French king.
[2]   Well-being.
[3]   John Cabot was an explorer and navigator who by his
voyages in 1497 and 1498 helped lay the groundwork for
the later British claim to Canada. His son Sebastian was a
navigator and cartographer employed at various times by
the English and Spanish crowns.

[4]   King Manuel I, who reigned from 1495 to 1521.
[5]   Portuguese explorer, discoverer of Newfoundland in
1500.
[6]   The French mariner whose explorations of the North
America coast and the St. Lawrence River (1534, 1535,
1541–2) laid the basis for later French claims to Canada.
[7]   The Sieur de Roberval (1500–61), a French colonizer
chosen by Francis I to create a settlement in North America.

Martin Frobisher, an Englishman, made three voyages along the northern coasts.[8] Seven years later, Humphrey Gilbert, also an Englishman, set out with five ships, but suffered shipwreck on Sable Island, where three of his vessels were lost.[9]

In the same and two following years, John Davis, an Englishman, made three voyages for the same object; penetrating to the 72d degree, as far as a strait which is called at the present day by his name.[10] After him, Captain Georges[11] made also a voyage in 1590, but in consequence of the ice was compelled to return without having made any discovery. The Hollanders, on their part, had no more precise knowledge in the direction of Nova Zembla.

So many voyages and discoveries without result, and attended with so much hardship and expense, have caused us French in late years to attempt a permanent settlement in those lands which we call New France, in the hope of thus realizing more easily this object; since the voyage in search of the desired passage commences on the other side of the ocean, and is made along the coast of this region. These considerations had induced the Marquis de la Roche, in 1598, to take a commission from the king for making a settlement in the above region. With this object, he landed men and supplies on Sable Island; but, as the conditions which had been accorded to him by his Majesty were not fulfilled, he was obliged to abandon his undertaking, and leave his men there.[12] A year after, Captain Chauvin accepted another commission to transport settlers to the same region; but, as this was shortly after revoked, he prosecuted the matter no farther.

After the above, notwithstanding all these accidents and disappointments, Sieur de Monts desired to attempt what had been given up in despair, and requested a commission for this purpose of his Majesty, being satisfied that the previous enterprises had failed because the undertakers of them had not received assistance, who had not succeeded, in one nor even two years' time, in making the acquaintance of the regions and people there, nor in finding harbors adapted for a settlement. He proposed to his Majesty a means for covering these expenses, without drawing any thing from the royal revenues; viz., by granting to him the monopoly of the fur-trade in this land. This having been granted to him, he made great and excessive outlays, and carried out with him a large number of men of various vocations. Upon his arrival, he caused the necessary number of habitations for his followers to be constructed. This expenditure he continued for three consecutive years, after which, in consequence of the jealousy and annoyance of certain Basque merchants, together with some from Brittany, the monopoly which had been granted to him was revoked by the Council to the great injury and loss of Sieur de Monts, who, in consequence of this revocation, was compelled to abandon his entire undertaking, sacrificing his labors and the outfit for his settlement.

But since a report had been made to the king on the fertility of the soil by him, and by me on the feasibility of discovering the passage to China, without the inconveniences of the ice of the north or the heats of the torrid zone, through which our sailors pass twice in going and twice in returning, with inconceivable hardships and risks, his Majesty directed Sieur de Monts to make a new outfit, and send men to continue what he had commenced. This he did. And, in view of the uncertainty of his commission, he chose a new spot for his settlement, in order to deprive jealous persons of any such distrust as they had previously conceived. He was also influenced by the hope of greater advantages in case of settling in the interior, where the

---

8   Sir Martin Frobisher (1535–94), English navigator and early explorer of Canada's northeast coast.
9   Sir Humphrey Gilbert (1539–83), English soldier and navigator responsible for the annexation of Newfoundland.
10   John Davis (1550–1605), English navigator who attempted to find the Northwest Passage.

11   Possibly a reference to the voyage of Captain George Waymouth, undertaken in 1602 for the East India Company.
12   The Marquis de la Roche transported some forty convicts to Sable Island in order to establish a colony in 1598.

people are civilized, and where it is easier to plant the Christian faith and establish such order as is necessary for the protection of a country, than along the seashore, where the savages generally dwell. From this course, he believed the king would derive an inestimable profit; for it is easy to suppose that Europeans will seek out this advantage rather than those of a jealous and intractable disposition to be found on the shores, and the barbarous tribes. . .

Part Two: New World Identities: Exploration and Settlement to 1700

Introduction

By the beginning of the seventeenth century, Europe's ferocious conquest of the New World during the previous century had abated and was replaced by the slower-paced work of exploration and settlement. Settlers granted land could accumulate substantial wealth by exploiting cheap labor sources and producing staple crops and raw materials for Europe like tobacco, cotton, sugar, and furs. But the colonies also held out the seductive promise of starting over, of regained innocence and radical self-invention. Some immigrants gave up security and position in their homelands to administer colonial holdings or to found plantations in the wilderness. Others craved adventure, escape from debts or the possibilities of lucrative investment. Some fled religious persecution – the persecutors and persecuted exchanging roles several times over the course of the century – and sought to establish refuges and utopias. Others came forcibly as convicted felons, indentured servants, or enslaved labor. By the seventeenth century, several generations of settlers – the children of European colonists, called "creoles" – had been born in the New World, and so were Native and European simultaneously. Despite attempts on the part of these later generations to avoid what Cotton Mather called "creolian degeneracy," a new culture began to emerge which was anxiously related to but necessarily different from the cultures of the imperial metropolitan centers. This new culture began to reflect a definable "New World" identity, which was, from the beginning, hybrid, multiracial and multicultural, a mixture of the fantasies of the old world and the realities of the new.

Economic arrangements also strongly shaped the colonial world and the character of its inhabitants. In the late eighteenth century, Scottish philosopher Adam Smith coined the term "mercantilism," a theory advocating governmental regulation of economies in order to expand national interests at the expense of rival countries. According to this theory, the main indicator of a nation's wealth was the amount of gold and silver it possessed. Long before the term emerged, however, European colonial powers had put an incipient mercantilism into practice in the New World. Colonies existed for the benefit of the mother country as sources of raw materials and as profitable markets for manufactured goods. Because mother countries outlawed manufacturing in colonies, and held a monopoly on trade with their possessions, the relationship was far more beneficial to the colonizers than to the colonized. The resulting injustices sowed the seeds of political dissent and revolutionary fervor in the New World that flowered in the next century and had strong repercussions in Europe as well.

The Spanish empire was a case in point. By the mid-sixteenth century, Spain had established a network of settlements in the West to rival the vast empires of the ancient world. The missionary activities of Spanish priests formed the ideological arm of this territorial expansion. However, the enormous wealth produced by Spain's extensive holdings quickly undermined its economy. Spain's main preoccupation during and after the Conquest had been to extract as much bullion as possible from its overseas colonies. In fact, Spanish conquistadores indiscriminately melted down much intricately worked gold and silver artifacts into bars for shipment to Europe, erasing substantial evidence of the advanced level of Native arts and crafts. Spain's American trade consisted of two annual fleets that circulated between Mexico, the Caribbean, and Seville, and carried exported goods to the colonies and imported cargoes of gold and silver. Spain, however, was unable to supply manufactured goods on the scale required by the colonies, and the influx of precious metals caused rampant inflation. After the defeat of the Spanish Armada in 1588 by the English navy, Spain lost its long-held colonial monopoly in North America, giving way to incursions by the French in Florida, the Mississippi delta, and Canada, and the English on the eastern seaboard. The seventeenth century was a period of economic stagnation and political decline for Spain. Settlement continued in South and Central America and expanded into southwestern North America. Multiple pressures on the indigenous people, however, caused by the appropriation of land, exploitation of laborers, and repression of Native religions produced pockets of local resistance that soured Spain's imperial dreams. At mid-century, Chile experienced continuous social unrest, and in 1680 the Pueblo people of New Mexico revolted and forced the colonists to retreat south. The Spanish managed to restore their authority in the region through Diego de Vargas' reconquest in 1692, and his brutal suppression of another Pueblo rebellion in 1696.

Because the Native population proved to be an unreliable source of exploitable labor, at the beginning of the sixteenth century, Spain began importing Africans as slaves to work the gold and silver mines of their American colonies. When these gave out, Spain began to develop the production of staple crops which required a large and cheap labor force. The passage in 1542 of a Spanish law proscribing the enslavement of Native people forced Spain to rely even more heavily upon imported African slave labor. By mid-century, thousands of Africans were brought to the New World annually to supply the large sugar plantations that spread throughout the Caribbean Islands and the coffee plantations in Brazil. After a century and a half of slave trade, in some areas of Central and South America, and especially in the Caribbean where indigenous populations had been almost completely wiped out by disease, people of African descent comprised from a third to two-thirds of the total population. The interactions and intermarriage of the three main groups – Native Indian, Spanish, and African – formed the racially mixed or mestizo character of the population and culture of Latin America that is reflected in its literature to this day.

Despite frequent outbursts of religious and racial persecution, Spanish colonial society stabilized during the seventeenth century. More people, mostly of European extraction, had the leisure and means to pursue cultural and intellectual activities, but scholars are also discovering a literature of the oppressed. Around 1539, the first printing press in the Americas was established in Mexico City, and another began in Lima in 1584. Whereas both of these cities were granted university charters in 1551, no universities or presses were established in Brazil until after the end of the colonial period. By 1600, Spanish colonial culture, which had strong ties with its homeland, developed a literature with particular thematic concerns, such as ambiguity about national allegiance, shifting cultural identities and the emergence of new gender norms. Although it continued to reflect trends in Spain and Europe, this culture also incorporated Indian and African influences, traces of which can be found in the most cultivated of writers.

Initially, France cultivated a commercial presence in the New World, but colonial expansion gained new impetus with the decline of Spanish power in Europe and with King Henry IV's Edict of Nantes (1598) granting religious freedom to the French Protestants known as Huguenots. The King also chartered the *Compagnie d'Occident* (the Western Company), leading to further exploration and to the eventual settlement of Acadia, present-day Nova Scotia. In their attempts to find a Northwest Passage to Asia, French explorers opened up the St Lawrence River. Champlain founded Quebec in 1608, paving the way for the establishment of extensive trading posts in northeastern America. As the French expanded westward exploring the territory around Lake Huron, the exploits of the *coureurs de bois* (fur traders) became the stuff of legend. This expansion also opened the way for strategic missionizing of the Native population by the Jesuit and Récollect (Franciscan) orders. Avoiding the Spanish and English extremes of enslaving and exploiting or exterminating the Indians, the French sought to convert and make strong allies of them. Their success created loyalties and mutual interests, which would come into play as the European imperial powers vied for domination of North America in the latter part of the century. At the same time, French commercial interests materially affected Native activities, channeling their efforts from subsistence hunting and farming to trapping, which fed the seemingly insatiable European appetite for furs. In the French West Indies, sugar became the main crop, and African slaves were imported to work in the fields. A stratified class system began to emerge, with contract laborers (*engagés*) and slaves at the bottom, small farmers and merchants (*petits blancs*) in the middle, and officials and large planters (*gros blancs*) at the top.

Because the settlement at Quebec did not initially attract settlers, in 1627 Cardinal Richelieu, chief minister of France, created the Company of New France, popularly known as the Company of the Hundred Associates. He granted the Company a complete monopoly of the fur trade for the next fifteen years, in exchange for settling 200 to 300 people a year in New France. Later, Jean-Baptiste Colbert dominated French colonial policy during the reign of Louis XIV, and was a fervent supporter of mercantile economic theory. As a result, and despite the fact that the French colonies were for the most part lacking in precious metals, Colbert viewed French overseas possessions as potential sources of raw materials. But war with England, and the temporary surrender of Quebec to the English, who returned it in 1632, diminished the effectiveness of the Company, and in 1663 King Louis XIV canceled its charter and transformed the territory into a royal province with its own governor, military commander, and regiment. More incentives to settle were provided, such as *seigneuries*, proprietory grants of land which were allotted to small farmers. More than 3,000 settlers, including young women of marriageable age, embarked for New France in the 1660s. France continued to explore new territories with Marquette and Jolliet's expedition to the Mississippi River in 1682 and La Salle's journey down the Mississippi to the Gulf of Mexico which provided the basis for France's later claim to the Louisiana territory. Competition with the British for land and trade became intense and reached a head in King William's War (1689–97), when Sir William Phipps seized Nova Scotia for the English and the Count de Frontenac carried out daring border raids on New England. At war's end, the French held the Hudson Bay territories and all of their former possessions, except Newfoundland. Toward the end of the century, the French turned their attention to the Louisiana territory, with D'Iberville's expedition setting off in 1699. The literature of New France in this period, like that of New Spain, reflects the concerns of a developing provincial society: fascination with, on the one hand, the landscape and indigenous peoples of Canada, and the emergence of a distinct French Canadian identity on the other.

Not to be outdone by its rival Spain, England sent out several exploratory expeditions to the eastern coast of North America in the 1580s to survey the commercial potential of the vast tract of land known as "Virginia." All of these attempts proved unsuccessful, until John Smith took control of the tiny settlement at Jamestown in 1608 and forced the demoralized and recalcitrant group of gentlemen colonists and soldiers to farm and hunt, instead of searching for exotic sources of wealth, relying upon the bounty of the Native Americans, or waiting for supplies from the homeland. By contrast, after a few years of hardship and struggle, the "Pilgrims," Puritan separatists who came by way of Holland in 1620, established themselves in Plymouth. A decade later, the Congregationalists arrived armed with a royal charter from Charles I and began settling the Massachusetts Bay area. Unlike the southern colonies, which began primarily as commercial ventures, the New England plantations from the start included women and children, artisans and mechanics, and were fueled by religious zeal and united by a common social ideal. Smith recognized this, and although he extolled the New England method in his "Advertisements" to prospective colonists, he became indelibly linked with early Jamestown and the myth of Pocahontas, whose supposed intervention on his behalf constituted an implicit acceptance by the indigenous population of English imperial designs.

After a disastrous beginning, the Jamestown settlement turned from Spanish methods and myths of Edenic sustenance to the establishment of agricultural production and trade with the Native population, and soon had a monopoly on tobacco trade and planting. Unlike New England, which early on developed a regional identity based on religious solidarity, "the South," settled by more diverse and secular interests, was not identified as a discrete region until the American Revolution, and was not defined as a cultural entity until the Civil War, when its "integrity" began to be nostalgically imagined and projected backwards. Rather, the "staple colonies," so called for their individual production of a different staple commodity (like tobacco, sugar, cotton, or silk) not native to the region, included settlements from Maryland to Florida and the West Indies. These colonies were essentially provincial outposts connected by trading routes to an imperial center and shared a similar economic structure – large plantations owned by immigrant gentry and worked by indentured servants, transported convicts, and African slaves who first arrived in Virginia in 1619. This particular structure of staple agriculture was engineered by Charles II and his son James II, who feared the autonomy of the colonial settlements and sought to consolidate royal control over their interests in the west. In the latter half of the century, these monarchs founded the Carolinas, reorganized the labor system for island sugar production in the West Indies described by Richard Ligon, and supported the plantation aristocracy in Virginia challenged by Nathaniel Bacon in the rebellion of 1676 that bears his name.

But staple monoculture was labor intensive, and by the 1670s, as demand for raw materials grew, plantation owners began relying more heavily on imported slaves from Africa and the West Indies. Since the mid-sixteenth century, the extensive use of slave labor had been firmly entrenched in the Spanish colonies. The use of slaves as domestic servants and farm workers, and the enslavement in the West Indies of rebellious Native Americans captured in the colonial wars, were also widespread practices in New England by the seventeenth century. But slavery was never an economic necessity in New England as it was in the staple colonies, which depended on this form of labor. The practice also shaped the developing colonial cultures. As the black population grew, white owners demanded the passage of harsh slave codes to regulate interaction among races, prohibiting interracial marriage and contact between black men and white women. The most significant of these, first enacted in Virginia in 1662, declared that the legal status of children followed the condition of the mother. Not only did this make slave women fair game for unchecked sexual coercion and exclude their offspring from civil rights, but it buttressed the slave system and the attitudes about racial differences it reflected.

The practice and ramifications of slavery continued to raise issues that would become more divisive as reliance upon and opposition to the practice increased over the century. The plantation culture that flourished across the region, and was made possible by slave labor, was very much tied to English cultural patterns and religious upheavals, as the intriguing work of George Alsop demonstrates. Whether writing exploration accounts, tracts to promote immigration, official reports for the Crown on trading voyages, religious polemic, personal narrative, or popular ballads, writers of the Chesapeake and West Indies struggled to express the newness of the New World and the otherness of its indigenous inhabitants, and make sense of the effects of both upon exiled and displaced English sensibility.

Many of the settlers of New England came to the New World as religious refugees, but economic concerns motivated all. Since the mid-sixteenth century, England's economy had faltered because its production of consumable goods could not keep pace with an ever-increasing population. As inflation rose and real wages dropped, many people, including the well-off and landed gentry, began to experience financial hardship. Economic tensions were exacerbated by religious and political upheavals. The Protestant Reformation began in 1517 when Martin Luther, a German monk, nailed his ninety-five theses critical of the Roman Catholic Church to the door of Wittenberg Cathedral, and quickly spread across Europe and the low countries to England. In 1533, King Henry VIII broke with the Pope, who refused to grant him a divorce, and declared himself the head of the Church of England, later called the Anglican Church. This proved to be largely a change in name and leadership. The influence of continental reformers like Luther and the French theologian John Calvin, who fled his homeland and established himself in Geneva, encouraged English "dissenters" or "non-conformists" as they were called, to push for more radical reform of church structure and ritual. Following Calvin's teachings, English Protestants rejected the hierarchical structure of the church, advocating the creation of small, independent congregations of believers united by a covenant to which all subscribed. Many suffered active persecution under the reign of Mary, Henry's eldest daughter, who was a Catholic, and fared only a bit better under her Anglican half-sister Elizabeth. It was during this time that many congregations fled to Europe, separating themselves from the Church of England because they believed ecclesiastical reform was impossible. A group of separatists, dubbed "Pilgrims" by their chronicler William Bradford, settled in Plymouth in 1620. A larger group later known as "Puritans," who believed the church could be reformed from within, settled in Massachusetts Bay.

Although not every emigrant to New England was a Puritan, the political settlement and communal culture of the Puritans dominated the region and strongly influenced what would emerge in the eighteenth century as a post-colonial, United States national identity. It was a culture in which religion pervaded all aspects of public and private life. The New England Puritans adhered to Calvinist theology, which taught that at the creation of the world, God "predestined" everyone to either salvation or damnation. Although this rendered believers utterly helpless to influence their fate and totally dependent upon faith in divine mercy, God created "signs" by which they could "read" divine favor or disfavor in their lives and actions. As a result, the diary, journal, personal narrative, and poetry or prose meditation became popular genres. The accurate determination of one's spiritual state was crucial, because until the Halfway Covenant of 1662, church membership was limited to those who could prove, through a narration of their experience of conversion, that they had a reasonable assurance of election. Both gnawing doubt and its opposite, arrogant self-righteousness, were conspicuous in public and private life. While this imposed a heavy burden of self-regulation, self-discipline, and vigilance on individuals and communities, it also promoted universal literacy and an individualism that was kept in check by a strong sense of collective identity and a belief in the sacredness of having been chosen by God for this special mission. The sermon, historical narrative, and jeremiad, literary genres in which Puritan writers excelled, expressed and reiterated this mission.

Protestant religious doctrine also shaped the aesthetics that prevailed in most of New England for at least a century. A theology so focused on the next world was necessarily suspicious of the power of the senses, and rejected sensory aspects of Catholic worship like instrumental music and chanting, incense, elaborate vestments, cathedral architecture, and ornamentation. A good visual correlative is the adamant Puritan rejection of stained glass windows set high in cathedral walls letting in only filtered light, in favor of the large clear glass windows they put at eye level in their small, simple wooden meeting houses, flooding the interiors with a light they likened to divine illumination. They even thought the symbol of the cross encouraged "idolatry" – the worship of an idol or representation of the divine which Yahweh of the Old Testament expressly forbade. Puritans believed art should be a "handmaiden" or servant of religious truth, that it should edify and teach. Beauty was not a priority, but derived from the fitness of the form to the content. Wary of the power of the imagination when not held in check by reason, Puritans adopted what has been called a "plain style" which valued order and logic above all, clarity of idea and expression, and a judicious use of rhetorical figures. Verbal eloquence was highly valued, being considered the most important "means" to grace – and had a definite performative quality; hence, the written prose of many highly esteemed Puritan preachers seems dry and dusty to us, longwinded exercises in logic chopping. Ultimately, the New World Puritans believed that God was the consummate artist, and that his design could be discerned throughout the creation and within all human creations. Much of their writing sought to illustrate known truths, but sometimes the private, representative voice seeking its way to those truths achieved a unique artistry.

The Puritan commonwealth, as it evolved in Massachusetts Bay under the leadership of John Winthrop, was strongly theocratic and patriarchal. Although all people were "equal" before God, fallen human society was necessarily stratified, with the educated and powerful elite ruling the less privileged mass of merchants, artisans, farmers, and goodwives – by "consent." Although ministers did not hold offices, they wielded enormous power in the civic sphere, requiring that everyone attend public religious worship, and keeping a tight rein on dissent and immorality. Men headed up families and women ran them; children and servants were from early ages instilled with the central values of hard work, perseverance, self-discipline, and mutual support.

From the very beginning, however, the Puritan vision was rent by conflicts. Early on, Roger Williams, a promising young minister, arrived and began preaching against Puritan self-righteousness and intolerance of other religious practices, the blurring of church and state power, and the unjust appropriation of land from Native Americans. He was swiftly exiled and in 1635 established Providence Plantation, which became a haven for dissidents and tolerationists like himself. Soon after, Anne Hutchinson's preaching on the unmediated nature of divine grace nearly tore the small colony apart, and her excommunication and exile in 1637 closed down the small access to visibility – the public narrative of conversion experiences – that Puritan women had. At the same time, the expansion of British settlements along the Connecticut River valley through royal grants sparked conflicts with the powerful Pequot tribe native to that area, and ignited the first genocidal war between the English colonies and Native Americans. In 1641, a group of eminent Puritans produced the Massachusetts Bay "Body of Liberties" which made slave-holding legal, and ships from the region became active in the slave trade. Although missionizing the Native populations had been given lip service in the chartering of the New England colonies, it only began in earnest later in the century. By the beginning of Metacom's War in 1676, the second major conflict with the New England Native Americans, which the settlers called "King Philip's War," there were many converted Indians living in "praying towns." That bloody and destructive conflict, which subdued the powerful Wampanoags and Narragansetts, insured British dominance in New England but also set the region's development back several decades.

As the zealous first generation began dying off, the second and third generations seemed to fall short of the original ideal, giving rise to the persistent jeremiads of the latter half of the century. As New England's economy expanded, so its white inhabitants became increasingly affluent, dispersed and secular. The Halfway Covenant in 1662 was the first dilution of orthodox Congregationalism, allowing the children of church members admission to baptism and worship without evidence of conversion. The Salem witch trials in the early 1690s, in which over two hundred people were accused and twenty people were executed for witchcraft, dealt another blow to the ideology that produced the mass hysteria. As Puritan cultural authority unraveled, in 1682, Massachusetts' royal charter was revoked, and when James II became king, he began to centralize control of England's North American possessions. Plymouth became part of Massachusetts, and both were united with New Hampshire and Maine into one colony called the Dominion of New England, administered by a royal governor in chief, Sir Edmund Andros. Although Massachusetts won back some of its independence in the bloodless revolution of 1689 that ousted Andros, the dream of a Puritan commonwealth was over. The orthodox Puritan elite was forced to share power with adherents to other religious beliefs (though toleration did not extend to Catholics) and progressive forces infiltrated key institutions. Motivating the Bostonian Puritans was the ousting in England of James II, who was Catholic, by his Protestant son-in-law, William of Orange, in what is known as the Glorious Revolution of 1689. The events in Massachusetts sparked similar revolts in New York and Maryland, ignited by a fear of Catholicism, vulnerability to attacks by Native Americans, and a demand for rights as English subjects. Although the events of 1689 and the regranting of charters created more protection for property and against corruption in colonial administration, England still regarded the colonies as dependents which existed for the benefit of the mother country. This attitude would bear poisonous fruit in the next century. Meanwhile, New England closed out the century embroiled in a series of conflicts with New France and its Native allies, by-products of the ongoing wars among England, France and Spain in Europe, which were part of a wider struggle for imperial domination in North America.

Although culturally heterogeneous and regionally specific, colonial literature in the seventeenth century shared certain themes. Many of the writers were concerned with translation of various sorts, such as Gaspar Pérez de Villagrá's use of the genre of Renaissance epic poetry to narrate the Conquest of New Mexico, or Roger Williams' more literal, but highly allegorical, translations of the Narragansett language into English. Unlike the Conquest, travel, and exploration accounts of the sixteenth century, which created Edenic myths of the New World and focused on "otherness," seventeeth century literature reflects the anxious process of creolization, which differed across the Americas. These writers were not just eyewitnesses of "American" experience, they were also participants in it as well as shapers of its future. For American born and bred English and Europeans, the frontier became a zone of intercultural contact where they struggled both to apprehend the New World and keep a safe distance from it. The scanty writings of Native Americans from this period, gleaned from treaties, official letters, and negotiations over land, express many tribes' desire both to interact with the colonists and make clear their distinctive, unassimilated identities. Colonists like John Smith, Louis Hennepin, and Thomas Morton felt impelled to describe, categorize, and judge Native culture by European standards, which did not always come up short in the comparison. Others like Jerome Lalement and Samuel Sewall read the natural world and its calamitous events (earthquakes, storms, droughts, famines) almost as if they were decoding signs. Historiography served both to narrate the various colonialist missions, and to find natural and supernatural justifications for them. But, while Cotton Mather constructed an impregnable wall of Puritan history around the sacred garden of his New England, Garcilaso de la Vega demonstrated a curious fluidity, moving between his maternal Inca identity and his conquistadore paternity. The most "American" of genres, the captivity narrative, forerunner as some argue of the English novel, flourished in this century, and revealed most thoroughly the construction of hybrid cultural identities at various imperial peripheries. For Puritans, captivity by "savages" in the "wilderness" threatened their religious ideology as well as "civilized" European identity and superiority. By contrast, Francisco Núñez Pineda y Bascuñán, the "happy captive," was ambivalent about his Indianization. As Enlightenment ideas spread to the New World in the next century, questions of identity, allegiance, and power shaped a burgeoning revolutionary spirit and emerging post-colonial nationalisms.

New Spain

El Inca Garcilaso de la Vega (1539–1616)

The Inca Garcilaso de la Vega was the first major Native historian of America. Born in Cuzco, Peru, the illegitimate son of a Spanish conquistador and of Isabel Suarez Chimpu Ocllo, granddaughter of the Inca emperor Tupac Yupanqui, Garcilaso later took his father's name but always referred to himself with pride as "El Inca." As a young man, Garcilaso championed Incas and Spaniards with equal fervor during the Peruvian civil wars. In 1560 he traveled to Spain and fought alongside Don Juan de Austria in the wars of the Alpujarras. After the fighting was over, he retired to Cordoba, where he dedicated himself to religion and to literature. He took religious vows before his death in 1616.

Garcilaso el Inca's writings include a translation of a work in Tuscan by Leon Hebreo, *Los tres dialogos de amor* (1590), *The Florida of the Inca* (1605), a record of De Soto's conquests in North America, and two volumes on Inca culture and civilization. He used three main sources in compiling *The Florida of the Inca*. An eyewitness account was provided by Alonso de Carmona, supplemented by an account by Juan Coles, found by Garcilaso in the establishment of a printer in Cordoba. Most of his account, however, came from an unnamed noble Spaniard, probably Gonzalo Silvestre, known for his daring and for his equestrian prowess.

Given the circumstances surrounding his birth, Garcilaso el Inca was uniquely positioned to view the story of the De Soto expedition from diverse perspectives: that of the Spaniard searching for gold, wishing to extend the Catholic faith to the pagan populations of the New World; that of the Native inhabitant of the New World, confronted with men whose ideology and customs differed radically from his own; and finally that of the scholar and historian who attempts to mediate between two cultures.

Primary Work

Though *La Florida del Inca* was published in 1605, the following excerpts have been translated by Susan Castillo from the 1723 Madrid text. Other English translations include that of John and Jeanette Varner, *The Florida of the Inca: a history of the Adelantado, Hernando de Soto, Governor and Captain General of the kingdom of Florida and of other heroic Spanish and Indian Cavaliers* (Austin: University of Texas Press, 1951).

Further Reading

Donald Castellano, *El Inca Garcilaso de la Vega* (New York: Twayne, 1969).

FROM *THE FLORIDA OF THE INCA*

The Inca's Dedication

To the Very Excellent Señor Don Theodosio of Portugal, Duke of Braganza and of Barcelos, etc.

During my childhood, Most Serene Prince, both my father and his kinsmen told me of the heroic virtues and magnanimous deeds of the kings and princes of glorious memory who were Your Excellency's forebears, and of the military prowess of the nobility of this celebrated kingdom of Portugal. Then later in the course of my life I read of the accomplishments of the Lusitanians[1], not only in Spain but in Africa and in the great India to the east; of the long and amazing voyages and hardships which these men suffered both in their conquests and in the dissemination of the Holy Gospel; and of the magnificent provision that their kings and princes made for carrying out these various undertakings. In consequence, I always felt a desire to serve the people and the sovereigns of your realm. This desire later developed into a feeling of obligation, for on coming to Spain from my native Peru, the first places I visited were the Portuguese islands of Fayal and Tecera[2], and the imperial city of Lisbon. The royal ministers and inhabitants of that city as well as the people of the islands were most kind and charitable, offering me the finest reception and welcoming me as if I had been a native son. But not wishing to tire Your Excellency, I shall refrain from telling of the particular favors bestowed upon me by these people, other than to say that one of them eventually was to save me from death.

Being then on the one hand so indebted and on the other so consumed with admiration, I have been ignorant as to how I might repay my obligation and show my esteem unless it were by committing the audacity of offering and dedicating my history to Your Excellency. For an Indian this is a presumption, but a presumption which has been inspired no little by the deeds related in my account of the native Portuguese cavaliers who went on the conquest of the great Florida; for it is right that the acts of these men be appropriately and worthily used and dedicated, so that under the protection of Your Excellency they may be remembered, esteemed, and honored as they deserve.

I beseech Your Excellency, therefore, to deign to accept this small service with the affability and approbation consistent with your royal blood, and to look favorably upon the desire I have always had and still have of seeing my name placed among those of the subjects of Your Excellency's royal household. Should you grant me this favor, as I trust you will, I shall be more than humored in my fondness, and I shall at the same time be able to repay an obligation to the natives of this most Christian kingdom, for through Your Excellency's generosity I shall become as one of them. May Our Lord preserve Your Excellency for many happy years as a refuge and protection to the poor and needy. Amen.

El Inca Garcilaso de la Vega

The Inca's Preface

Conversing over a long period of time and in different places with a great and noble friend of mine who accompanied this expedition to Florida, and hearing him recount the numerous

---

[1]   The Portuguese.   [2]   Faial and Terceira, islands in the Azores archipelago.

very illustrious deeds that both Spaniards and Indians performed in the process of the conquest, I became convinced that when such heroic actions as these had been performed in this
world, it was unworthy and regrettable that they should remain in perpetual oblivion. Feeling
myself therefore under obligation to two races, since I am the son of a Spanish father and an
Indian mother, I many times urged this cavalier to record the details of the expedition, using
me as his amanuensis. And although it was the desire of us both to accomplish the task, we
were prevented from doing so by such circumstances as that of my going to war and the long
absences which occurred between us. Thus more than twenty years elapsed. But as time passed,
my desire to preserve this story increased, and I began to fear more and more that if something
should happen to either of us, our whole project would vanish. For were I to die, this man
would have no one to encourage him or serve as his scribe; and on the other hand, were I to lose
him, I should be ignorant as to whom I might turn for the facts that he was able to provide. I
determined therefore to overcome the obstacles and delays then existing by simply abandon-
ing the position and advantages I enjoyed in the town where I was living and moving to where
he resided. Here we devoted ourselves most carefully and industriously to recording all that
had happened from the beginning to the end of the expedition. And this we did, not alone for
the honor and renown of the Spanish nation, which has accomplished such great things in the
New World, but no less for that of the Indians who are revealed within our story, for they too
appear worthy of the same praise.

In addition to the brave deeds performed and the hardships suffered by the Christians both
individually and generally, and the notable things discovered among the Indians, we present
in this history a description of the many extensive provinces found throughout the great kingdom of Florida by the Governor Hernando de Soto[3] and the numerous other cavaliers who
hailed from Extremadura, Portugal, Andalusia, Castile, and all the rest of the lands of Spain.
Our purpose in offering this description has been to encourage Spain to make an effort to
acquire and populate this kingdom (now that its unsavory reputation for being sterile and
swampy, as it is along the coast, has been erased) even if, without the principal idea of aug-
menting the Holy Catholic Faith, she should carry forward the project for the sole purpose of
establishing colonies to which she might send her sons to reside just as the ancient Romans
did when there was no longer space in their native land. For Florida is fertile and abundant in
all things necessary to human life, and with the seed and livestock that can be sent there from
Spain and other places it can be made much more productive than it is in its natural state. As
will be seen in the course of our history, it is a region well adapted to such things. In recording
the details of this history I have taken the greatest care to present them chronologically and
accurately. And since my principal purpose is to bring about the acquisition of Florida through
the statements I make concerning it, I have attempted to elicit from the person who provided
me with this record all that he saw on the expedition. He was a noble hidalgo and as such
prided himself on speaking the truth in all matters. Many times I saw the royal Council of the
Indies call upon him as a man worthy of confidence to verify acts that had occurred in the
expedition to Florida as well as in other expeditions in which he had served. He was a very fine
soldier, performing frequently as a leader; and since he participated in each of the events of the
conquest, he was able to supply me with complete details of the history as they occurred.
There are people who would brand as cowards and liars those men who give a good description
of specific deeds that have occurred in battles in which they themselves have participated.
These people customarily inquire as to how it is that such men could have seen everything in

---

3   Hernando de Soto (1500–1542), Spanish conquistador
who explored in 1539–41 the southeastern portion of what
is now the southeastern US and discovered the Mississippi
River.

a battle if they were fighting in it, or how they could have fought if they were occupied in watching, since two such activities as watching and fighting cannot well be carried on simultaneously. And if someone should now ask such a question, my answer is that it was a common custom among these soldiers, as it is in all of the conflicts of the world, to relate the most notable events of a battle afterward in the presence of the general and the other officers. And often when some captain or soldier told of a very brave deed which was difficult to believe, those who heard him went out to see what actually had been done and to verify the report with their own eyes. It was in this manner that my author was able to obtain all of the information that he gave me to write down; and the many questions which I put to him repeatedly concerning the details and qualities of that land helped him no little to recall these facts to mind.

. . . I do not record fictions, and indeed it would be unlawful to me to do so since my history must be presented to the entire Spanish republic, which would have reason to be provoked with me should I give a dishonest and false report. Neither would I fail to displease gravely the Eternal Majesty (who is the one we should fear most), if with the idea of inciting and persuading Spaniards by my history to acquire the land of Florida for the augmentation of Our Holy Catholic Faith, I should deceive with fictions and falsehoods those of them who might wish to employ their property and life in such an undertaking. For indeed, to tell the whole truth, I have been moved to labor and to record this history solely by a desire to see Christianity extended to that land which is so broad and so long; and I neither aspire nor hope for temporal favors in recompense for my lengthy toil since I long ago lost faith in aspirations and despaired of hopes because of the inconsistency of my fate.

Yet examining my lot dispassionately, I ought to be very grateful to Fortune for having treated me so ill; for had it shared its wealth and its favors with me copiously, perhaps I would have gone down other roads and paths that would have led me to worse precipices or destroyed me altogether on that great sea with its waves and storms, as almost always it is accustomed to destroy those whom it has favored and elevated into the lofty positions of the world. But since I have experienced the disfavors and the persecutions of Fortune, I have been forced to retire from this world and to conceal myself in the haven and shelter of the disillusioned, which are the corners of solitude and poverty. Here consoled and content with the paucity of my scanty possessions, I live a quiet and peaceful life (thanks to the King of Kings and Lord of Lords) more envied by the rich than envious of them.

In this serene existence, to avoid an idleness more wearisome than labor and to obtain greater peace of mind than wealth can bring, I have engaged in other projects and ambitions, for instance the translating of the three *Dialogues of Love* by Leon Hebreo[4]. After publishing this translation, I occupied myself with writing this present history; and with the same pleasure I am fabricating, forging, and polishing a history of Peru, wherein I shall tell of the origin of the Inca kings, their ancient customs, their idolatry and conquests, and their laws and order of government both in peace and war. And now with God's help, I have almost reached the end of all this. There have been obstacles and not small ones, but still I value my labor more highly than the gifts Fortune might have bestowed upon me, even though it had treated me most favorably and propitiously; for I aspire to attain another and better end, and I trust in God that my words will bring me more honor and greater renown than I would have gained from the entailed estate that Lady Fortune might have bequeathed me from her store of worldly goods. Thus I am rather a debtor than a creditor of Fortune, and as such I give her many thanks; for in spite of herself she is now forced by divine clemency to permit me to offer this history to the world.

---

4   Garcilaso's translation was published in Madrid in 1590.

. . . I plead now that this account be received in the same spirit as I present it, and that I be pardoned its errors because I am an Indian. For since we Indians are a people who are ignorant and uninstructed in the arts and sciences, it seems ungenerous to judge our deeds and utterances strictly in accordance with the precepts of those subjects which we have not learned. We should be accepted as we are. And although I may not deserve such esteem, it would be a noble and magnanimous idea to carry this merciful consideration still further and to honor in me all of the mestizo Indians and the creoles of Peru, so that seeing a novice of their own race receive the favor and grace of the wise and learned, they would be encouraged to make advancements with similar ideas drawn from their own uncultivated mental resources. I trust therefore that the noble in understanding and the liberal in spirit will offer their favor most generously and approvingly to both my people and myself, for my desire and willingness to serve them (as my poor works, both past and present reveal, and as my future works will show) well deserve their consideration.

Felipe Guamán Poma de Ayala (1525?–1615?)

Felipe Guamán Poma de Ayala was born into an aristocratic Inca family of Peru. According to his own account, his mother, Curi Ochllo Coya, was the daughter of the Peruvian ruler Tupac Inca Yupanqui; his father, Guamán Mallqui, served as Viceroy to the Inca Huascar, and was active in suppressing battles and revolts against the Spanish Crown. In one of these conflicts, Guamán Mallqui was in the service of a Spanish captain named Luis de Avalos de Ayala, whose life he saved. As a result, Avalos de Ayala declared that Guamán Mallqui deserved a grant of land; in return, Guamán Mallqui adopted the name don Martin de Ayala in his honor. As well, Guamán Mallqui, now Ayala, adopted the captain's mestizo son. This young man, who later became a priest, taught his brothers to read and write; presumably, he taught them Spanish as well.

As a result, Guamán Poma de Ayala not only possessed a remarkable perspective on Inca culture and the Spanish conquest of Peru, but also was able to record his observations in writing. The result of this was an extraordinary document, with 800 pages of text and 400 captioned line drawings. This manuscript, rediscovered in the Danish Royal Archives of Copenhagen by the Peruvianist Richard Pietschmann in 1908, is dated in Cuzco in the year 1613 when its author was nearly ninety years old, some forty years after the Conquest. Written in a mixture of Quechua and ungrammatical Spanish, it begins with a history of Christendom including the Native peoples of America, followed by a revisionist account of the Conquest, with painstaking documentation of Spanish exploitation and violence. It concludes with an imagined dialogue between the author and King Philip III of Spain suggesting ways in which colonial administration could be made more equitable and just through cooperation between the Peruvian and Spanish ruling classes. It is not known how this text came to Denmark, nor indeed if anyone had taken the time to read it. It is clear, however, that if it had been read by the monarch, Philip III might well have reacted with outrage, not only due to the descriptions of the injustices perpetrated by his Spanish countrymen but also by Guamán Poma's radical assumption that the voices of the colonized deserved to be heard.

PRIMARY WORK

Felipe Guamán Poma de Ayala, *Letter to a King: A Picture-History of the Inca Civilisation*, ed. Christopher Dilke (London: George Allen & Unwin, 1978).

FURTHER READING

Mary Louise Pratt, *Imperial Eyes: Travel Writing and Transculturation* (London: Routledge, 1992).

Steve Stern, *Peru's Indian Peoples and the Challenge of Spanish Conquest* (Madison: University of Wisconsin Press, 1993).

FROM *LETTER TO A KING* (1613)

Royal Administrators

The so-called *corregidores* or royal administrators can usually count upon making 30,000 pesos in cash out of their term of office, and also upon retiring with an estate worth more than 50,000 pesos. It is their practice to collect Indians into groups and send them to forced labour without wages, while they themselves receive the payment for the work. During their term of office the royal administrators make all sorts of contracts and deals, embezzle public funds and even lay their hands on the royal fifth[1]. They also raise loans from church funds. The Indian chiefs do not protest because they are accomplices in many of the malpractices. They are praised and commended by the administrators, who go about saying, 'What a good chief so-and-so is'. The chiefs sometimes prefer to keep quiet because they are afraid, or have no intention of losing their position in the community. They are well aware of how easily they could be dismissed on a trumped-up charge.

The royal administrators and the other Spaniards lord it over the Indians with absolute power. They can commit crimes with impunity because of the support which they can count on from higher authority. All complaint against them is stifled by fear of the consequences.

Of course, administrators exist who commit no crimes and make no enemies, but even these virtuous ones invariably leave office with a well-filled purse. Their good record comes in useful to get them promotion.

There is an opposite case of those who run into debt and are dunned by their creditors. Their expenses become impossible to meet and writs, petitions and complaints rain down upon them until they have to flee from office as poor and naked as on the day they were born. Their plight is due to being uncontrollable gamblers or womanisers, or squandering money on banquets for their Spanish friends.

In order to obtain the post of a royal administrator, ambitious candidates are often prepared to risk their entire fortune. Sometimes they succeed and sometimes not. The appointment is often made in accordance with the merit and record of the candidate, rather than what he has spent in currying favour. Once appointed, all their efforts to obtain the post are forgotten and they accordingly set about maltreating and robbing the Indians. Some of them have already pledged their future to the last peso. In order to become solvent, they have to depopulate their region by hiring out gangs of workers.

One trick which they practise is that of lending money at interest in the name of some other Spaniard. Then, under the pretence of safeguarding the other Spaniard's investment, they initiate legal action to confiscate the debtor's property and keep it for themselves.

The excuse which royal administrators always give for failing to carry out any benevolent instructions from above is that they themselves are poor men and need more money. They take the precaution of explaining their non-compliance with orders by a string of letters to the Royal Audience, the Viceroy and even the King, in which they pass on false information and conceal the true state of affairs.

Legal actions brought against them seldom succeed and in this way they avoid paying debts to the Indians for goods, property and services. Either influence is brought to bear on the

---

[1]   The so-called *quinta real*, one-fifth of revenue, reverted directly to the monarch.

judge, or the judge himself is aiming at a similar post and intends to commit precisely the same abuses when he takes over. There is an unwritten pact of silence and hypocrisy between the officials. Whenever they find themselves in financial difficulty they get together and award each other lucrative posts and commissions.

When taxes are being collected, the royal administrators demand more than is actually due, or they confiscate cattle under the pretext of taxation. Meanwhile their underlings simply take whatever they want by force. All such officials are understandably hostile to clever Indians, who have learnt how to read and write and, even worse from the officials' point of view, know how to formulate complaints to higher authority. Indians of this sort are capable of appearing in court and demanding an account of the wrongs and sufferings of their people.

One Indian who dared to oppose the Spanish rulers of his province was Cristobal de Leon of the Omapacha tribe of Lucanas. He was one of several Christian pupils of mine who turned out to be clever as well as compassionate towards their fellow-Indians. Except for a certain tendency towards drunkenness, he was capable of matching his wits against any Spaniard. For some time he was able to defend himself against persecution and false accusations made against him. He refused to supply Indians for the transportation of wine from the plains to Cuzco or for making clothes for the Spaniards. Meanwhile other Indian chiefs were allowing their men to be treated like horses or donkeys, while the wives and daughters were kept busy spinning, twisting and weaving, or else debauched[2].

Cristobal de Leon made up his mind to demand justice and set out on the road to Lima, taking his detailed complaints with him. But Father Peralta, a priest whose conduct with girls he had criticised, was warned of his departure and went in pursuit of him with two men. They arrested him and took away his papers. Then Father Peralta had him brought before the royal administrator, a fellow of his own sort, to whom he had lent 2,000 pesos. Between the two of them, they tortured Leon and fabricated evidence against him. He was put in the stocks and his property sold.

Even when a new royal administrator took over, Cristobal de Leon was still kept in the stocks behind the house and denied any company, even that of his wife and family. His friends among the chiefs did not dare to come forward and defend him because of their fear of the consequences. As a last stroke, his house was burnt down. Finding himself stripped of his possessions and virtually naked, Cristobal de Leon gave notice of an appeal. The result was that he was murdered by beheading in 1612.

A protector of Indian rights ought to be appointed by Your Majesty to be present whenever judgement is being passed or administrative decisions of importance being discussed. Such a protector should be immune from any fear of Spanish officials, being solely responsible to the Crown.

In general, Indians and Spaniards ought to lead separate lives, not just in the country but in the cities. At present the Spanish administrators and Indians of noble family sit at the same table, eat and drink and gamble with every sort of buffoon[3], thief and drunkard. Jews and half-breeds are allowed to join in as well; and of course they pretend to be just as good as the rest. Some of the guests only come as a formality; some want to drink; and others are motivated by fear or the desire to ingratiate themselves, in case they need support on some future occasion.

My own opinion is that people ought to have more sense of their own dignity. The high officials should invite each other to their tables; and the church dignitaries should do the same. Our Indian chiefs should hold gatherings of their own sort; and the Indians of lower rank likewise.

---

[2] Seduced.　　　　　　　　　　　　　　[3] Fool, clown.

"Indian Kicked at an Inn," one of many drawings depicting abuse by conquistadores, priests, and landowners, by Poma de Ayala from his *Letter to a King*. (With permission of the Royal Library, Copenhagen, Denmark.) The caption reads: "Chapter Denouncing Spanish Travelers and Mixed-Blood Male Creoles and Mulattos and Mixed-Blood Female Creoles and Christian Spaniards from Castile."

It is proper that one person of quality should entertain another, but this custom should not be confused with charity, which is a demonstration of love for a neighbour. It is an honour for a poor man to entertain his master or employer. And this same consideration applies when a woman of humble birth gives herself to a person of quality without insisting on marriage. Even if she has a bastard son, it is still an honour for her.

Why should there be any disrespect for people of quality? If you happen to be one, you can recommend yourself to God and his saints and angels, live a quiet family life and end up as a royal administrator with a valuable property in the country.

The good administrator is one who does not surround himself with deputies and officials. He is content with a fat hen for lunch and a chicken for dinner; keeps two horses, two Indian servants and a boy; eats by himself and does not play[4] for money.

At Wayside Inns

Spaniards, including priests, who travel on the royal highways, are apt to arrive at the inns in a bad humour. They box the ears of the Indian servants, their tastes are finicky and they expect an infinite variety of foods and comforts.

The Spaniards impose excessive burdens on their animals, which often die on the road as a result. Then they demand replacements and ride off into the blue; or alternatively they load up five or ten Indians, who have to make do as animals.

The innkeepers are usually Spaniards, even if they have no legal right to possession of the inns. They sometimes employ as many as 20 Indians, who receive no pay whatever. It is quite usual for them to keep half a dozen whores on the premises, under the pretence that they are the wives of the Indian servants. In reality, of course, they are hired out to travellers who spend the night there. These women get no regular pay, but they are reasonably happy as long as they can spend their time dressing themselves up and painting their faces. Often they are put into the trade by their own mothers, while their husbands are sent off to the labour gangs and in most cases never return. Indians travelling on the highways sometimes have the experience that their wives, sisters or daughters are forcibly taken away from them and used for the pleasure of Spaniards.

I myself decided to stay for four days in a typical inn and observe the behaviour of both Spaniards and Indians. Because of its convenience I selected a place known as the 'burnt inn'. My attention was caught by the unscrupulous way in which even the priests among the customers behaved. As soon as a Spaniard enters the door he starts brandishing his stick at the nearest Indian, who for all he knows may be a chief or the local mayor. The customer demands service, food, firewood and other little trifles. He himself is the last person to keep any account of what he has had and is likely to go cheerfully on his way the next morning without enquiring about the cost. He probably carries off with him any blankets, mats or dishes which have taken his fancy.

Having observed a good number of the men and women who come to the inns for lodging, I believe there should be a stricter control on the use of titles such as Don and Doña, Maestro and Doctor[5]. These titles have some meaning, whether they have been obtained by examination or by inheritance. It is precisely the class of people without any right to them which

---

4   Gamble.
5   In Spain, these titles were supposed to indicate a degree
of breeding and formal education.

claims these titles and causes the worst damage and offence to Indians under Your Majesty's protection. Ordinary hawkers, tailors, cobblers and grocers promote themselves and their wives to the rank of Don and Doña and then half-castes and Indians of small consequence follow their example.

Spaniards

A large number of Spanish tramps and vagabonds are continually on the move along our highways and in and out of our inns and villages. Their refrain is always 'Give me a servant' and 'Give me a present.' The richest of them own no more than a negro servant, a boy, a beast to carry their own carcass and another for their mattress, a set of clothes for the road and another for wearing in the town. Every day of their lives they eat about twelve pesos' worth of food and ride off without paying, but still give themselves the airs of gentlemen. Although they are fit and healthy, they never condescend to bend their backs or do the hard work which they were used to in Castile.

All Spaniards travelling on honest business ought to carry passports, showing their rank and social standing. If they fail to produce these credentials on demand, they should be liable to confiscation of their belongings. But those carrying the proper papers and paying their debts at the inns would be allowed to pass without any hindrance.

As matters stand, there are more thieves in Peru than even in Castile; and the difference is that here they are provided with free meals and women.

The fat ones are perhaps the worst, but ironically it is they who eat most of the food and who drink the very best wines and spirits. They are slack[6], cowardly and lacking in judgement. Their stomachs are so distended[7] that they can hardly walk and are useless for soldiering. In my experience a fat face or a big head is an infallible sign of ignorance, laziness and greed, whether in men or in women.

Those who are broad in shoulder and hip are inclined to be more active. The little ones in this category, particularly, are as agile as monkeys. They have strong bones and a blow from their fists is like a sledge-hammer. You need to beware, too, of the dark-skinned, curly-haired ones with untrustworthy eyes.

Spaniards with honest eyes and well-proportioned bodies can usually be counted upon as friends. After all, if they are the rulers of a great part of the world, it is because they are in the main hard-working, able and decent. The men of this type are neatly barbered, with short beards. Their women have large eyes, small mouths and waists like ants; and they plant their feet firmly on the ground when they walk. It is fair to add that even the straightforward type of Spaniard makes a bad enemy and is quite capable of knocking you down if he gets annoyed.

Another type consists of the tall, desiccated[8] men and the women with no calves to their legs, who are usually the lecherous ones and extremely jealous into the bargain.

But the people with most influence in the Christian world are often light in body, thin and narrow-chested. These are the ones who become learned doctors or men of great wealth and position, because of their energy. They are at the opposite end of the scale from the wastrels, liars, boasters, drunkards and lechers who can be trusted with nothing and seldom deserve even charity.

Spanish couples who are blessed with big families spend all their days and nights dreaming

6   Idle.
7   Bloated.

8   Thin.

about the gold and silver which their children are going to earn. The husband says to the wife: 'You can't imagine how concerned I am, my dear, about our children's education. To give them a good start in life, we must put them into the Church.'

The wife answers: 'Well said, darling. Our son Iago can become a priest and little Francisco can do the same. Then they'll earn enough to let us have servants and give us lots of presents like partridges, chickens, eggs, fruit and vegetables. Later on, little Alonso can be an Augustinian, little Martin can be a Dominican and little Gonzalo can join the Order of Mercy.'[9]

When some outstanding service is rendered to the Crown, Your Majesty feels under an obligation to provide lucrative posts not only for the person concerned but for his sons and grandsons and other relations, even if they happen to be babes-in-arms or bedridden old men, or women. But important and indeed essential posts, like that of royal administrator, ought to be given to the people who deserve them and the fact of race should not come into the choice. If a baby or an old man has a claim on the appointment, at least the actual job should be given to somebody of intelligence and goodwill who would represent the beneficiary and watch over his interests.

To sum up what I have to say, the Spaniards in Peru should be made to refrain from arrogance and brutality towards the Indians. Just imagine that our people were to arrive in Spain and start confiscating property, sleeping with the women and girls, chastising the men and treating everybody like pigs! What would the Spaniards do then? Even if they tried to endure their lot with resignation, they would still be liable to be arrested, tied to a pillar and flogged[10]. And if they rebelled and attempted to kill their persecutors, they would certainly go to their death on the gallows.

One exception to the general rule of injustice in Peru was the case of a Spanish gentleman, who was hanged by the Viceroy, the Marquis de Canete, for ordering the death of a poor Indian. The Viceroy would not eat a morsel of food until he had seen justice done.

There is still time for the others to mend their ways.

Proprietors

Your majesty has granted large estates, including the right to employ Indian labour, to a number of individuals of whom some are good Christians and the remainder are very bad ones. These *encomenderos*, as they are termed, may boast about their high position, but in reality they are harmful both to the labour force and to the surviving Indian nobility. I therefore propose to set down the details of their life and conduct.

They exude an air of success as they go from their card-games to their dinners in fine silk clothes. Their money is squandered on these luxuries, as well it may, since it costs them no work or sweat whatever. Although the Indians ultimately pay the bill, no concern is ever felt for them or even for Your Majesty or God himself. Several of these big proprietors have been guilty of treason in their own person. Others had fathers or grandfathers who fought against the Crown under the elder or the younger Almagro, Gonzalo Pizarro or Girón[11]. What has happened so many times before can certainly happen again.

Official posts like those of royal administrator and judge ought not to be given to big employers or mine-owners or their obnoxious sons, because these people have enough to live on already. The appointments ought to go to Christian gentlemen of small means, who have rendered some service to the Crown and are educated and humane, not just greedy.

---

9   The Augustinians, Dominicans, and Mercedarians were three wealthy and influential religious orders.

10   Beaten.

11   Leaders of insurrections against royal authority.

Anybody with rights over Indian labour sees to it that his own household is well supplied with servant girls and indoor and outdoor staff. When collecting dues and taxes, it is usual to impose penalties and detain Indians against their will. There is no redress since, if any complaint is made, the law always favours the employer.

The collection of tribute is delegated to stewards, who make a practice of adding something on for themselves. They too consider themselves entitled to free service and obligatory presents, and they end up as bad as their masters. All of them, and their wives as well, regard themselves as entitled to eat at the Indians' expense.

The Indians are seldom paid the few reales[12] a day which are owed to them, but they are hired out for the porterage[13] of wine and making rope or clothing. Little rest is possible either by day or night and they are usually unable to sleep at home.

It is impossible for servant girls, or even married women, to remain chaste. They are bound to be corrupted and prostituted, because employers do not feel any scruple about threatening them with flogging, execution or burial alive if they refuse to satisfy their masters' desires.

The Spanish grandees and their wives have borrowed from the Inca the custom of having themselves conveyed about in litters like the images of saints in processions. These Spaniards are absolute lords without fear of either God or retribution. In their own eyes they are judges over our people, whom they can reserve for their personal service or their pleasure, to the detriment of the community.

Great positions are achieved by favour from above, by wealth or by having relations at Court in Castile. With some notable exceptions, the beneficiaries act without any consideration for those under their control. . . .

The Fathers

The priesthood began with Jesus Christ and his Apostles, but their successors in the various religious orders established in Peru do not follow this holy example. On the contrary, they show an unholy greed for worldly wealth and the sins of the flesh and a good example would be set to everyone if they were punished by the Holy Inquisition.

These priests are irascible and arrogant. They wield considerable power and usually act with great severity towards their parishioners, as if they had forgotten that Our Lord was poor and humble and the friend of sinners. Their own intimate circle is restricted to their relations and dependents, who are either Spanish or half-caste.

They readily engage in business, either on their own or other people's account, and employ a great deal of labour without adequate payment. Often they say that the work is for ecclesiastical vestments[14], when really it is for the sale of ordinary clothing. Managers are taken on, but seldom get themselves properly rewarded. And the native chiefs are blamed if they do not arrange the immediate purchase of the goods.

The usual practice is for a priest to have a man and two girls in the kitchen, a groom, a gardener, a porter, and others to carry wood and look after the animals.

Sometimes there are as many as ten mules in the stables, not counting the beasts belonging to neighbours, and they all have to be sustained at the Indians' expense. Herds of 1,000 cattle, goats, pigs or sheep are a commonplace and there are often hundreds of capons[15], chickens and rabbits, all requiring their own special arrangements, as well as market gardens. If a single

---

[12]   Coins.   [14]   Priestly robes.
[13]   Carrying.   [15]   Castrated roosters.

animal is lost, the Indian held responsible has to pay for it in full. Since the servants are not even properly fed, it is no wonder that they avoid work. But there are always pretty girls attached to the household, who have been corrupted by the priests and bear them children. This kind of showy establishment is of course enormously costly.

A favourite source of income of the priesthood consists in organising the porterage[16] of wine, chillies, coca[17] and maize. These wares are carried on the backs of Indians and llamas and in some cases need to be brought down from high altitudes. The descent often results in death for the Indians, who catch a fever when they arrive in a warm climate. Any damage to their loads during the journey has to be made good at their own expense.

. . . A priest named Juan Bautista Alvadan, who was in charge of the parish of Pampachire, acted in so gross and cruel a manner that it is difficult to find words for what he did. A local Indian named Diego Caruas had refused to hand over some mutton[18] to him, whereupon the priest had the man tied naked to a cross. He took a burning brand and thrust it into the Indian's body and private parts. He smeared one torch after another with pitch, set it alight and opened the man's body with his hands in order to push them in. And other atrocities were committed by this priest, which only God knows the whole truth about.

Their misbehaviour with girls, particularly, forfeits any claim which the priests might make to obedience and respect. Because they are obvious sinners, they are unable to give the sacrament of confession to their own mistresses or their mistresses' relations. Nor can they honestly claim their salary for absolving girls with whom they are committing mortal sin. The present practice is for them to get their fellow-priests to confess their Indian mistresses.

Negroes

The black men imported from Guinea are modest and decent-living. Once they become Christians they are faithful and obedient. Being affectionate in nature, they get on well with their neighbours and make excellent slaves. Their King in Africa is a strong ruler who defeated the Grand Turk but submitted to Your Majesty, bringing gifts of arms and provisions. San Juan Buenaventura[19] was himself a Guinean. Admittedly, the Spaniards insist that all imported negroes are worthless, but they are mistaken. A little religion and education makes a Guinean worth two Creole half-castes and in an extreme case he is capable of sainthood.

All the negroes ought to be married, both for moral reasons and for the financial benefit of their masters. I say this because in many cases they are actually prevented from marrying. In others, married negroes are sold and separated from their wives. The negroes, man and wife, ought preferably to live together in one house. If this cannot be arranged, they should at least be brought together at night.

Also the sons and daughters of negro homes ought not to be sold or separated from their mothers, with the result that there is nobody to look after them in life or grieve for them in death. The children should be treated fairly. If they are needed for work on the farms, they are entitled in return to be taught to read and write and become good Christians.

On one occasion some slaves who had been put in irons entered into conversation and began quarrelling. One of them said to another 'You're carrying that load of fetters[20] because you're

---

[16]   Transport.
[17]   A plant with stimulating narcotic effects, cultivated at the time in parts of South America and the West Indies.
[18]   Sheep meat.

[19]   Possibly St John Bonaventure, who succeeded St Francis as head of the Franciscan Order.
[20]   Chains.

a drunkard'; and the other answered: 'You're carrying yours because you're nothing but a thief.' When slaves go to the bad, the best way of dealing with them is indeed to put them in irons. Beating or smearing with tar is unnecessary, because the iron alone subdues them. Threatening them is unprofitable, because they simply take to the mountains. The best cure is good hard iron.

But the decent negroes, living in Christian marriage, show admirable patience in the service of their Spanish masters and mistresses. They have to work from morning until noon without eating, for they are fed only once a day. A man who is working hard needs to breakfast and lunch and dine, but these poor Christians are made by the mistresses to do without meat or treats of any kind. Yet they are only made of flesh and blood.

When mulattos – a mixture of negro and Indian – produce quadroon children[21], these children lose all physical trace of their negro origin except for the ear, which still gives them away by its shape and size.

Wherever there is a negro community of ten persons in any city, village, mine or farm, it should have the right to appoint a mayor, a magistrate and a clerk of its own race. If the community is still larger it will require constables, a lawyer and a town crier. These persons should be allowed to carry defensive weapons such as swords, halberds[22] and coats of mail. Similarly the negro slaves of people of importance should be entitled to carry arms, but only when at their masters' sides or on active duty. Otherwise they should not even be given a knife or there is bound to be trouble. Once a negro mayor has been elected to office, he should be given two days' leave of absence a week from his other work, in the interests of good administration. He should attend at council on Wednesdays and Thursdays. The masters and mistresses of negroes ought to be prevented from punishing their slaves for any crime, even if their guilt is established, and should certainly never be allowed to punish the families. All accusations ought to be made through the proper negro official and in accordance with justice. The master and mistress should be consulted about the value of any goods stolen and if this is considerable the punishment should be exemplary.

The King's Questions

Your Majesty may wish to ask the author of this book some questions with the object of discovering the true state of affairs in Peru, so that the country can be properly and justly governed and the lot of the poor improved. I, the author, will listen attentively to Your Majesty's questions and do my best to answer them for the edification of my readers and Your Majesty's greater glory. This is an important service which I am able to render, for Your Majesty hears many lies as well as truths, and much of what is reported is simply a means of obtaining preferment for the writer in Church and State.

In my capacity as a grandson of the Inca of Peru I would like to speak to Your Majesty face to face, but I cannot achieve this because I am now 80 years old and in frail health. I cannot take the risk of the long journey to Spain. However, I am ready to pass on the observations which I have made in the last 30 years, since I left my home and family to live the life of a poor traveller on the roads of my country. We can communicate with one another by letter, with Your Majesty asking for information and myself replying, as follows:

---

[21]   Children who are one-fourth Negro.
[22]   A weapon consisting of an ax mounted on the end of a pole.

'Tell me, author, how is it that the Indians were able to prosper and increase in numbers before the coming of the Incas?'

'Your Majesty, in those days there was only one King. He was well served by his nobles, who superintended the mining of gold and silver, the work on the farms and the herding of the Peruvian sheep. Although the population was considerable, enough was produced to provision the fortresses as well as feed the women and children at home. The smallest settlement possessed 1,000 soldiers and some could put an army into the field.'

'Tell me then, don Felipe de Ayala, how was the population maintained after the Incas came?'

'Your Majesty, the Inca himself was a supreme ruler although there were nobles of different ranks, similar to your Dukes, Marquesses and Counts, under his sovereignty. But all these nobles were tireless in their obedience to the Inca's laws and commands. So the people as a whole remained prosperous and never went short of food.'

'Tell me, author, what is wrong nowadays? Why is the population declining and why are the Indians getting poorer and poorer?'

'I'll explain to Your Majesty. The best of our girls and women are all carried off by your priests and the other Spanish officials. Hence the large number of half-castes in the country. Usually the priests give the excuse that they want to stop our women living in sin, but their next step is to appropriate them for themselves. As a result, many of our people give up hope and want to hang themselves, following the example of a group of Chanca Indians who collected on a hill-top at Andaguaylas and decided to finish with their miserable lives for once and all.'

'Tell me, author, how can the population be made to increase again?'

'I have already written, Your Majesty, that priests and others ought to try living a decent Christian life for a change. Indians ought to be allowed to enjoy their married lives and bring up their daughters in peace. Above all, the number of would-be Kings ruling over us ought to be reduced to one, namely Your Majesty.'

'And how can the prosperity of the ordinary Indian be raised?'

'Well, Your Majesty, a lot depends on the community, the sapci, which is responsible for growing maize, wheat, potatoes, chillies, coca, fruit and cotton. There are also the mines to be worked. Young girls and widows can be put to spinning and weaving, with ten of them engaged on a single garment. Castilian cattle and Peruvian sheep are another source of wealth to the community, but individuals need to have their own livestock as well. Usually the sapci keeps one third of all produce. Another seventh can go to the local administrator and of course Your Majesty is entitled to one fifth at any time. Within these arrangements the community ought to prosper.'

'And tell me, author, how can the Indians who have fled from their homes be persuaded to return?'

'The young ones can be tempted back to the abandoned villages if they are provided with fields and pastures with clearly marked boundaries. They should pay taxes, but the collection should be the responsibility of one salaried official only, and any money left over should go to the Crown. This official could well be the Indian chief. For it is a fact that we chiefs have never joined in rebellions and have proved ourselves to be remarkably loyal subjects. We handed over ourselves and our vassals to Your Majesty, together with the silver mines of Potosi, the gold-mines of Carabaya and the mercury mines of Huancavelica. For all this Your Majesty ought to show us some mark of gratitude. It ought to be recalled, too, that twelve learned men and four clerks of your own Council, as well as issuing a pronouncement against slavery, forbade the payment of taxes to the clergy. Thus the parish priests are no longer entitled to earn money as tax-collectors. They must live on the contributions which are left at the foot of their altars. These usually amount to between 1,000 and 2,000 pesos a year. They are made up of payments for Masses, voluntary offerings, responsories for the dead, presents, Christmas-boxes and alms. The quantity is adequate to provide them with enough to live on, dress and feed themselves decently. To go beyond this and arrogate to themselves the rights of landowners and employers is an offence against their calling. They ought to be content with our people's offerings and what they get from the Spaniards.'

'But tell me, author, why are you so much opposed to parish priests getting proper salaries?'

'Your Majesty, the first priest of our religion was Jesus Christ, who lived on earth as a poor man, and his Apostles did the same. None of those holy men asked for salaries, but they were content to live by the charity of others. By the same token parish priests can manage quite well without collecting taxes or setting themselves up as men of property. If they do not care for such a way of life, Your Majesty should consult with the Pope in order to admit Indians to the priesthood. Being good Christians our people will not require any salary and the savings which Your Majesty will make can be used for the general good of the Church.'

'Tell me this, author. What can be done to prevent so much death, suffocation and hardship in the mines?'

'The first point, Your Majesty, is that a stop should be put to the practice of hanging miners up by the feet and whipping them with their private parts openly displayed. Also the miners are forced to work day and night and paid only half of what is owed to them. Finally they are sent off to the high plateau where they die of exposure. The remedy would be to be more selective in the choice of labour and to allow any particular locality a six months' rest in between recruiting visits. It would also help if experts could be appointed and paid, who know how to cure the condition cause by poisonous fumes. That would alleviate much of the present hardship. Your Majesty should give orders that a store of provisions and water should be kept on the premises at every mine. In the case of the miners being trapped by a collapse of the roof it would be a godsend to have food and drink available whilst day-and-night operations were in progress to free the trapped men.'

'And tell me, author, how can we discover all the hidden mines in Peru?'

'Very well, I'll tell Your Majesty. In these times, whenever an Indian reports the discovery of gold, silver, mercury, lead, copper, tin or even pigment, the Spaniards at once take over and the Indian is maltreated. So naturally enough no Indian is keen to make any such report to the authorities. But if Your Majesty were to enter into personal relations with the discoverer in each case, and treat him well, all the best mines would soon be brought to light. The result would be that Your Majesty would indeed be the richest and most important King in the world, and this would benefit Peru. As matters stand at present, the Indians are in the process of dying out. In twenty years' time there will be none of them left to defend the Crown and the Catholic Faith. The Emperor, who is now in glory, was great because of his possession of the Indies and the same was true of Your Majesty's father. I dare to say that it is also true of Your Majesty, and yet it is possible that Peru will lose all its value and your Indian subjects will no longer exist. Where once there were 1,000 souls, now there are hardly 100 left. Those who remain are many of them old and incapable of having children. The young men cannot find young brides to bear them sons. The girls and women, whether single or married, are all removed into the Spaniards' homes. It is impossible to remedy this state of affairs because the Spaniards support one another in all circumstances. They not only treat the Indians as slaves or servants, but dispossess them of their land and property. Even to set these facts down on paper is enough to make me weep tears. And the worst of it is that nobody dares to tell Your Majesty what is going on. If I were asked to put a price on the Peruvian Indian, I would put the figure very high and I would draw the conclusion that he or she ought to be treated with care and kindness, in the interests of the country. If by any chance one of our girls bears a child to an Indian man, the parish priest and the other authorities treat her like a criminal. Then the priest takes her into his kitchen so that he can sleep with her whenever he likes. She starts to bear him children and finds this style of life much to her taste. Other Indian girls, too, notice the privileges which she enjoys and want to share them. As I say, the real indignation is aroused when an Indian woman bears children to an Indian man. It is as if the sky had fallen on the earth. The father is tied to a pillar and flogged, and the mother has her hair cut off. If I ever started telling the story of such cases in any detail, I would never stop.'

'Tell me, author Ayala, now that you have recounted all these sad things, tell me how it is that the Indians are being exterminated, their women taken from them and their property stolen, when I never intended my judges and officials to do any wrong or damage. On the contrary, I expect them to treat the Indian chiefs with honour and allow the common people to lead useful and productive lives. Tell me, my good Ayala, what can be done to put things right?'

'All I can say, Your Majesty, is that the Spaniards ought to live like Christians. They should marry and be content with ladies of their own race and class, and allow the Indians to keep their own women and property. Anyone who has used his power to steal property from others should be made to give it back, and should also pay for what he has enjoyed. These penalties should be imposed summarily, without room for delay.'

'Tell me, author, how should I deal with the problem of Indian labourers who fail to report for duty?'

'Your Majesty should have a list kept, in which their names are all inscribed. Then the chiefs should be given the order to have them tracked down and discovered, wherever they may be. The cost of pursuing and arresting these Indians can be diminished if the inns provide free board and if the authorities put horses at the disposal of the agents employed in the task.'

'Tell me more, author, about these fugitives.'

'Your Majesty, they can be divided into three categories. First there are the runaways who leave their villages to become thieves and highwaymen. The second category consists of strangers within any particular community, who feel themselves to be outcasts, abused and ill-treated by everybody, without any living soul to whom they can turn in their trouble. They are so poor, too, that they are unable to pay their taxes. In the third category, finally, are the unfortunates who are employed as servants in the households of the landowners and administrators and who wish to escape. If things continue as they are now, Your Majesty, you are likely to lose all your Indian subjects, indeed to lose everything you possess.'

'Go on, author. Tell me what you mean by these remarks of yours.'

'I say with frankness that the Indians provide much of Your Majesty's revenue. I am an Indian chief and I stand up for their interests. If they are allowed to perish, the land will become barren and inhospitable. That is the reason why Your Majesty ought to impose heavy penalties for any interference with the rights of the chiefs and also of the ordinary Indians.'

'And what other measures do you propose, author?'

'If the Indian birthrate is to be kept up, Your Majesty, it is essential that parish priests should be made to pay a sum of money as a guarantee when they enter upon their duties, whether it is for the first or second time and even if their term of office is only for a single day. The reason is that these priests are in the process of destroying the whole country.'

'Tell me this, author. Don't I send my Bishops to every large city with the mission of defending the oppressed and seeing that justice is done? And don't the Bishops send out Visitors with power to punish offending priests and remove them from their parishes? Why don't you Indians go to them or write your complaints to them, or else complain to the civil authorities?'

'Let me explain the truth of this matter to Your Majesty. It's perfectly correct that Your Majesty send all sorts of eminent persons with instructions to show special favour to our Indians. No doubt these people let you have reports on all the favour they have shown and the justice they have done. But the fact is that from the moment when they disembark in the harbour they forget your instructions and change into different beings. From then on, their only object is to keep on good terms with the richest of the Spaniards.'

'Tell me, author, how would you define service to God and the Crown, which I wear?'

'I will explain to Your Majesty. A servant of God is someone who obeys His laws and cares for the poor. But such a person is also rendering service to your Crown, because he is protecting the Indians who are a valuable possession acquired by your grandfather.'

'Tell me this, author. Since you are the grandson of Tupac Inca Yupanqui and the son of the former second person in the State, why can't you do more in my name to favour the cause of the poor Indians and look after their interests?'

'That is the purpose of my presenting myself now before Your Catholic Majesty. My conclusion is that Your Majesty ought to appoint a Visitor-General with power to remove unjust prelates from their posts and return them to Spain, if this becomes necessary. This Visitor-General should have his seat in Lima and send out his visitors to all parts of the country. Possibly his appointment could be agreed with the Pope, who would choose a Cardinal for the purpose. In particular, this Cardinal would supervise the various chapters, orders and monasteries and attend by this means to the wants of the Indians. Honest judges ought also to be appointed in the big cities for a period of five years at a time, at a fixed salary, to give their attention to wills and bequests of property, whether in the form of silver, clothing, livestock, farms or dowries. The judges should watch over the appreciation of property from year to year and make sure that the rights of minors in regard to legacies are upheld. In this way an advance in their living standards can be achieved for the poorest people.'

'Are there any other measures, author, which you can propose in the interests of good order and for the relief of suffering?'

'Yes, Your Majesty. The authority of the genuine Indian chiefs ought to be upheld. It has unfortunately become usual for petty overseers to assume the title of *Apo* or important chief. On payment of a small consideration, they can ensure that they are addressed in this fashion. To avoid any such trickery in the future, it is important that all petitions to higher authority should pass through the hands of an important chief. On payment of a small consideration, they can ensure that they are addressed in this fashion. To avoid any such trickery in the future, it is important that all petitions to higher authority should pass through the hands of an important chief who is able to give evidence about the petitioners' true standing. In this way cases can be avoided like the one which occurred in a place called Sancos, when an ordinary Indian declared himself to be a chief and proceeded to exempt the entire local population from work of any kind. The real chief of the place was not even consulted.'

'And how can such deceit be avoided, author?'

'The proper procedure is for me, as a writer and a prince of the Indian race, to give evidence of all claims to titles and send it to Your Majesty, duly signed. When I am gone, my descendants would be empowered to continue in the same office for all time to come.'

'What do you regard as the prime objective of policy?'

'The restoration of the Indian population, Your Majesty, and the ending of the flight of the Indians from their settlements. This would be easy and inexpensive to achieve if Your Majesty were determined to punish without appeal anybody who obstructs the necessary measures.

The principal one of these is that no officials, or their wives, should continue to have Indian boys or girls by force in their power, or be allowed to detain them for even a single hour by force or against their will, or have the right to force them to work for nothing. No category of Indians ought to escape the liability to pay taxes and render services to the Crown. For this purpose a census ought to be taken of the whole population. It would also be a wise precaution to prevent any Spaniard or half-caste of any sort from living in a purely Indian settlement. Your Majesty would do better not to employ half-castes at all, since they only cause uproar, dissension, crime and scandal. They are the sworn enemies of their own uncles, the Spaniards. Moreover, those who have been ordained as priests are the worst of all and should never have been approved by Your Majesty, if you have any concern for the success of your rule in Peru.'

'And how should I rule, in your opinion, author?'

'Only by virtue of your power and authority as monarch of the world. No other person should intervene between you and your people, except for your Viceroy and Council of the Realm, who should have the right to appoint the necessary officers such as mayors, judges, constables and clerks. No power of appointment whatsoever should be vested in your royal administrators, who are in the habit of retaining ten deputies, twice as many mayors and a number of judges to conduct their private business for them. Either they should be fined and suspended from office or they should be made to work on their own without any deputies or assistants. And the same procedure ought to be adopted in the case of the Church. The Pope, Your Majesty, the Cardinal and the Bishops ought to be the only authorities capable of appointing vicars in the capital cities of the various provinces. Those who are selected, and confirmed by Your Majesty, need to be learned Doctors who have reached a respectable age. At the present time there are as many as ten vicars in each province, many of whom are still boys, like chicks which have just emerged from the eggshell. Others are lecherous fools on the lookout for pretty girls to seduce. If all the girls are rounded up and kept in the priests' houses on the pretext of religious instruction, children are bound to follow. Now ask me, Your Majesty, what the remedy is for this state of affairs.'

'Tell me, then, author, what is the remedy for this state of affairs?'

'There is no remedy, I can assure Your Majesty, other than compliance with the following principles. First, no priest should also be a proprietor. Secondly, he should put down a guarantee in money for his good conduct. Thirdly, the young girls should have their religious instruction at home and only the young boys should be taught in church. Fourthly, no Indian, great or small, should be forced to work for nothing for the Spaniards, since the service which he owes is to the community.'

'Is there any other improvement, author, which you have in mind?'

'Yes, Your Majesty. Your most excellent Viceroys should be granted a term of office of twenty years at a time, or twelve years at least, so that they can impose an equitable and righteous form of government and come to know who are the bad people in the country and who are the good ones. This is the proper way to level out inequalities and bring to justice those who ill-treat your Indian vassals. If necessary, the Viceroys must punish and even banish the priests for the greater glory of your Crown.'

'What is your final conclusion, author Ayala?'

'My conclusion is that you, King Philip III, should bear our wretchedness in mind and cease to send us so many punishments, misfortunes and disasters as in the past. Do not allow us to be exterminated, Your Majesty. Send us your Visitor and after he has departed let the Indian chief and the other authorities join together in a tour of inspection of each town and village in the region, so that they can discover exactly what the Visitor has done or left undone. Did the Visitor ask the priest for money? Was he rude, irascible and insulting in his manner? If he deprived the priest of his living, was this punishment deserved? And if the priest was actually a good Christian, ought he not to be restored to the living? On all these questions Your Majesty and the Bishop can be informed, so that the right solution can be found and Your Majesty's conscience set at rest. The Visitors need to be visited and the judges judged, if good government is to be installed in your Kingdom of Peru.'

Gaspar Pérez de Villagrá (1555–1620)

Born at Puebla de los Angeles in New Spain to Spanish parents, Pérez de Villagrá studied at the University of Salamanca, where he presumably came into contact with the texts of Virgil and Lucan, as well as the writing of the Spanish *Siglo de Oro*. In 1596, he joined the expedition of Juan de Oñate to New Mexico as captain and legal officer, and was made ecclesiastical counsel of the expedition in 1598. Oñate's party was made up not only of adventurers looking for precious minerals but also of settlers wishing to establish farms and cattle ranches. Though the Native Americans of Ácoma Pueblo had received Oñate peacefully, thirteen Spanish soldiers who had allegedly caused trouble were killed. A punitive force under Vicente de Saldivar was sent against the Ácoma, and after a prolonged artillery attack against the city, situated strategically atop a mesa overlooking the surrounding fields, more than 800 Ácoma were killed. Pérez de Villagrá's epic poem, *Historia de Nueva Mexico*, dedicated to King Philip III and recounting the adventures of Oñate's expedition and the siege of Ácoma, was published in 1610. Patterned on

Virgil's *Aeneid*, it consists of thirty-four cantos in blank verse, with a rhyming couplet at the end of each Canto. The juxtaposition of elegant imagery, Classical allusions, and historical descriptions of instances of extreme violence is indeed arresting.

Little is known of subsequent events in Pérez de Villagrá's life. In 1614, after a long court battle, he was found guilty in absentia of the deaths of two deserters from Oñate's expedition. He nonetheless went on successfully to petition the Crown for a new position, and died en route to Guatemala in 1620.

PRIMARY WORK

Historia de la Nueva Mexico, trans. and ed. M. Eincinias, A. Rodríguez, and J. Sánchez (Albuquerque: University of New Mexico Press, 1992).

FURTHER READING

Joe Sando, *The Pueblo Indians* (San Francisco: The Indian Historian Press, 1976).

HISTORY OF NEW MEXICO, 1610

From *Canto I: Which sets forth the outline of the history and the location of New Mexico, and the reports had of it in the traditions of the Indians, and of the true origin and descent of the Mexicans*

I sing of arms and the heroic man[1],
The being, courage, care, and high emprise[2]
   Of him whose unconquered patience
   Though cast upon a sea of cares

In spite of envy slanderous,
In raising to new heights the feats,
   The deeds, of those brave Spaniards who,
   In the far India of the West[3]

---

[1]   Cf. the opening line of Virgil's *Aeneid*.
[2]   An enterprise or adventure of a chivalric nature.

[3]   The New World.

Discovering in the world that which was hid,
"Plus ultra"[4] go bravely saying
   By force of valor and strong arms
   In war and suffering as experienced
As celebrated now by pen unskilled
   I beg of thee, most Christian Philip[5]
Being the Phoenix[6] of New Mexico
Now newly brought forth from the flames
Of fire and new produced from ashes
   Of the most ardent faith, in whose hot
      coals
Sublime your sainted Father and our lord
We saw all burned and quite undone,
Suspend a moment from your back
The great and heavy weight which bears you
   down
Of this enormous globe which, in all right,
Is by your arm alone upheld,
   And lending, O great King, attentive ear
Thou here shalt see the load of toil,
Of calumny, affliction, under which

Did plant the evangel holy and the Faith of
   Christ
That Christian Achilles[7] whom you wished
To be employed in such heroic work
And if in fortune good I may succeed
In having you, my Monarch, listener,
Who doubts that, with a wondering fear,
The whole round world shall listen too
To that which holds so high a King intent.
For, being favored thus by you,
It being no less to write of deeds worthy
Of being elevated by the pen
Than to undertake those which are no less
Worthy of being written by this same pen,
'Tis only needed that those same brave men
For whom this task I undertook
Should nourish with their great, heroic valor
The daring flight of this my pen,
Because I think that this time we shall see
The words well equaled by the deeds.
Hear me, great King, for I am witness
Of all that here, my Lord, I say to you . . .

Canto XXI: How Zutacapán called an assembly of the Acoma Indians and the discord there was among them, and of the treason they made

Oh human glory, to whose peak
Swollen pretension and vile pride
Doth always wish to mount and to attain!
Tell me, infamous pride, how do you square
The powerful scepter and the Royal crown
With such a base, ruined barbarian,
Begotten of other vile barbarians?
Say what the lofty throne may have to do
With barbarous riffraff and confusion?
Of blind conceit, oh empty pomp,
By high and middle, low and crestfallen,
Without distinction, reason, reckoning,
Sought equally and so solicited!
Let that furious barbarian say,

Brought forth from such a humble strain,
Who, like to Lucifer, did wish to rise
And to obtain all government.
So, no leaving off his intention,
He ordered all should be in council joined,
And, all being joined in a plaza
As such cruel, unmeasured haughtiness
Continually, always erupts,
Not hesitating, he did then stand up,
Burning and glowing in himself,
And, gazing out over the folk,
All unashamed, bold, and brazen,
Thus he began and thus he spoke:
"Ye valiant and gallant men,

---

4   This "further on" became the watchword and motto of those who had broken the geographical limits of the ancient world, forming part of the Castilian coat of arms.

5   King Philip III of Spain.

6   The Phoenix's rebirth from its own ashes was common to most medieval and Renaissance bestiaries, with their com-

mon origin in Pliny's *Historia Naturalis*. Villagrá parallels that rebirth from fire with the renewed faith of Philip II's Counter-Reformation Catholicism.

7   The identification of the epic hero's Christian mission with the Homeric hero, Achilles, is characteristic of the New World epic.

The last of our trials and our dangers
Give a free entry, leave an open field,
For each man to declare the thing
That pains, presses and hurts him most.
Say what more infamous and vile affront
Can come upon all of this fort
Than to permit so harsh a servitude
As giving food to strangers is,
We all being as free as they?
I swear by all the gods at once,
From whom we all receive our lives,
There cannot be a man on earth
Who would imagine such baseness."
Seeing that they were taking arms,
Not letting him finish, there then spoke out
His son Zutancalpo, enraged
And gazing at his father angrily:
"The surest good that man can grasp
Is to be willing to give in to all
That may seem well on reason's road.
It is not my opinion we should show
Any enmity to these Castilians,
For it is rashness to insult
One who has never injured you.
To keep them carefully as friends
Is more sane counsel and less dangerous.
The other course is patent foolishness
And, not to be accused of this,
I counsel that we keep obedience
Since we have all professed the same.
And, since occasion gives us rein,
That we repress indiscreet wrath,
For peace is the most discreet course
That can ward off the evil expected
From him who is in danger of its fall."
With this the noble youth did cease,
And a confused murmur commenced
From all those people gathered there.
And, approving his words as good,
Never did word run through gauntlet
More respected, more free, or more exempt
Nor more obeyed nor carried out
Than that accord expressed, for then
They all obeyed and did lay down
The powerful arms they took up.
At this, old Chumpo, fearful lest
The peace and truce should be broken,
Burdened with age and with trials,

With words discreet and severed, too,
Raised up his tired voice, saying:
"Behold, my children, the advice is good,
And 'tis what always gains the victory
In perilous wars we have known.
And since Zutancalpo, in his young years,
Has told already what is best for you,
Since we see dying is no more than an
     instant
And our glory consists in dying well,
A proper time to die let us achieve,
A season and occasion well chosen,
And forego such great inconvenience
As talking furiously and movingly
Of things so great, grave, and weighty
As these we now have 'neath our hands."
Here, now, there flew about the words
And wicked and swaggering threats
Of those foolish conspirators,
Calling old Chumpo one deranged,
Senile, infamous, crazy, a wizard.
Hearing this, and being all enraged,
Zutacapán, furious, attacked,
Putting the old man in such peril
That, had Cotumbo not quickly detained
The force of the mace that he swung,
He would have crushed his whole back in.
Seeing himself, then, charged with words
Of great insult that he said, too,
As if upon him mountains high and valiant
Then all had fallen and been cast,
He did allow his feelings to be seen,
But as though he were center and the base
To bear up such a heavy weight,
He did dissimulate all that he could,
Bearing the anger poured on him
And giving a free reign to temperance.
Being thus composed, he spoke to all the
     folk:
"Never have I seen myself so inclined
To satisfy my honor, now gone by
As I am this day at such impudence
As you have seen was shown to me,
And if I have the juvenile ardor
That in my past age I did have,
Which is what this vile traitor counts upon,
His vain presumption would already have
     received

Its correction and deserved punishment.
But what can I do to avenge myself
If I am so burdened with age
And old age in its course afflicts me?
The insult is not made to my person,
But made to you, being children
Of those whose fathers I brought up."
Leaping, then, to the middle of the square,
Like a famous musket which is
Full charged with fine powder, waiting,
Its wadding and great ball, and is at peace
So long as fire does not move it,
And, when it comes, with a great noise,
It springs to life, bursts forth and cracks
Like lightning spat out by the clouds,
E'en so, not waiting and without delay,
Zutancalpo took up his cause for him
And whirling in air his mighty club
Went wildly toward his own father.
The father quickly seized his mighty mace[8]
And to meet him Purguapo went out.
Pilco there, too did go forward.
Otompo, then Melco and Guanambo, too.
Mulco and many other Acomans,
Each one supporting his party.
Throwing their blankets off from their
    shoulders,
They all did wish to prove their persons
    there,
But their approach was hindered
By the many there gathered.
With this the rabble did break up,
And each one went to his own house.
O vanity, tasty vile poison,
Subject to cruel envy, bitter death,
What seas of blood we see are shed
By the vain, haughty, aspiring to you!
How fixed on it is royal blood, noble,
Plebeian, barbarian, or highland
Being descended from that one father
Is all of one material and one source,
Of one colour and one source,
For in each one the cruel, haughty pride,
We know, is nourished and is treasured up
And like the hungry, dangerous moth
Or thirsty cancer that, eating

At its pleasure at one's veins and entrails
Destroys, breaks down, and ruins what it
    will
And thus, this vile, bloody idolater,
Borne on by a frenzy of pride,
Then did determine they should break
The peace and truce which they had made,
And destroy all Castilians
So that no living soul might still remain.
Better to accomplish their intent
All determined that, on entrance
Of Spanish folk into their towns,
Each one should take upon himself
To scatter all 'mongst the houses,
And, being well-scattered and spread,
They would attack together, in such wise
That not a hair of them should 'scape.
All being thus agreed upon
Zutancalpo with all his friends
And Chumpo with his did then depart
From the pueblo, that they might not be
    seen
In such an infamous and shameful scheme.
From this Zutacapán drew much content,
For thus they left to him the whole pueblo
Almost without a force that could
Oppose the thing he had ordered.
At this critical point arrived
That Army Master who had been betrayed
Already by those traitors there,
And, to accomplish their cause in a shorter
    order,
They all went out to receive him.
That poor gentleman, off his guard
For that strange snare and deception
Embraced them all with great content,
And, after he had caressed them,
He asked them to give him in barter
Such provisions as they might have.
At this, they all rejoicing, said
That he should pitch his camp and the next
    day
They would have everything prepared.
At this he went on back, and the next day,
Finally, by the order of rude fate,
He went to the pueblo, as he should not,

---

[8] Club.

That man who, lacking suspicion,
Went approaching the deception.
For double-dealing always does
Make feel secure poor innocents.
God free us from the evil waiting us
And with signs of good secure us,
For put into so difficult a test
There is no discretion, warning, or skill,
Arms, virtue, truth, or resistance
That can oppose its might violence.
The unfortunate youth set forth
As soon as he came to the fort
A pleasing and friendly discourse
That the barbarians might give

The provisions that he had asked.
They, with great easiness, replied
That they should go to their houses to seek
What all would give to him with great
   pleasure.
The Army Master, then, without suspicion,
That this thing might be sooner done,
Better to say, his own short life,
Remaining with but six soldiers,
Ordered that all should go to the houses
And gather up all the provisions.
If we are to tell of this treachery
I wish, lord, to rest to write it.

From *Canto XXXII: How Zutancalpo was found by his four sisters and of the end and death of Gicombo and Luzcoija*

What lofty rock or towering cliff
Can by the wrathful, haughty sea
Be battered harder, more atrociously,
Than our own sad and miserable life,
If we but note it, most mortals
Whom cruel pride, exaggerated,
And vile ambition, raving, furious
Could never satisfy: the great scepter,
The royal crown, and its brave throne,
The poorest commoner of lowliest estate?
Oh sad condition of our human life,
Subjected, prostrate, to such thirsty beasts,
From whom most greedy fountain, vile and
   infamous
Never contented of their thirst inordinate,
Each one pretends to take satisfaction!
What did it serve noble Zutancalpo
To have opposed with such great strength
The furious designs of his father
Which had ended so many human lives
And had consumed so many goodly men,
And burned down so many noble homes?
Cruel Zutacapán, why did you choose
To go against the current that did bear
The peaceful people who are now ruined
And that brave youth whom you begot!
What profited the threats and bravado
With which you did perturb so many
   innocents,

And what the harsh, wild pride you showed
In wishing the Castilians might come
In arms against your little strength?
What profited to have broken the truce,
Your word, and oath that you had given for
   the peace?
By what vile fury were you dragged along?
That you with such lofty ideas
Did move an unjust war so carelessly?
O pride, for since you have more than
   enough
'Twere well that you were named so!
And thus, as excess, you do rise
Soaring always to ever greater heights
The baser the subject who thus aspires.
It regrets not, that brute, the ambition
Of that insane and lost barbarian,
The pitiable loss and misfortune
Which, caused by it alone, has come
Upon the unhappy, ill-fated town
Whose public squares and lofty walls we see
Mere rivulets and puddles, aye, and lakes
All overflowing with fresh human blood,
And a great store of the bodies of the dead,
From whose deep, terror striking wounds
Terrible clots of blood emerged,
Congealed and liquid blood unheard of, too,
And bits of undigested food, as well,
From whence also had way been made

Through which their poor souls had es-
  caped.
And in this dreadful slaughter, yet unmissed,
Was noble Zutancalpo, for whom came,
That they might seek for him, from out their
  house
Four maiden sisters who he had,
Given up to most deadly anxiety
And uttering in vain at his absence,
From the innermost of their weary souls,
The most heartrending sighs and moans,
Turning over the bloodless bodies there
To see if among them they might perceive
Their dearly loved brother, because there
  had
Now passed a long time when he had not
  been
Seen or observed by any of his friends.
Mocauli, the oldest of them all,
Did six times examine one corpse
And, as 'tis certain that blood calls to blood
Once more she chose to take it and turn it,
And seeing that it was that great treasure
By which they always reckoned themselves
  rich,
Though she could not discover whose had
  been
The strength of that most deadly sword
Which by such deep, measureless mouths
Had made him give up his brave soul,
With prompt and with most piercing cries,
With open palm and with tightly clenched
  fist
She did begin to wound her beauteous face.
And as we see haste unto the barking
Of some quick eager-nosed hound
The rest, all of them, eager for the chase,
Speeding on with astounding leaps
And many a rapid burst of swift running,
So the three other sisters, overcome,
Set out in haste and, half out of their wits,
With speed incalculable, to the spot
Where she was tearing her fair flesh
Above her dear brother, now all bloodless.
And there the four together did tear out
In handfuls the long, beauteous hair
From their poor, sad, innocent heads,
Striking upon their rosy cheeks

With one hand and the other, lifted high.
And after they had wept for him right well
They then laid him upon a heavy plank
And carried him upon their shoulders
With funeral grief, all sad and downcast,
Unto his former home, now burnt to earth.
And when the unfortunate mother
Beheld before her own sad eyes
The horrible spectacle which she saw,
Tearing her face without the least mercy,
The poor creature began thus to lament:
"Ye gods, if in his tender flower ye wished
To take away from this unhappy wretch
The son, untimely dead, whom you gave
  her,
Tell me, if I have now reached such a point
And come now into such a ruined state,
What other evil you may yet reserve?
It remained only that this last trial,
This final sorrow, should have come to me
In my old age, poor, sad, and afflicted."
And shedding a great rain of tears,
Through bitter sorrow and through fiery
  love
Being deeply moved by her tragic distress,
She gave a hundred thousand grieving sighs
From out the depths of her anguish-wrung
  breast.
And as the madness of desperation
Is the most cruel executioner
Of him who suffers from such an evil,
So, desperate and utterly heedless,
She cast herself backward into the flames.
And after her the four grieving sisters
Did also choose to be consumed there,
Together with their dead, beloved brother.
Thus they, with him, did hurl themselves
In, next their mother, who burned there.
And like to the most monstrous snakes
Or poisonous, deadly vipers,
Who with each other intertwine
In clinging knots and twist about,
So these poor wretches were entwined
Among those ashes and embers
Which, crumbling and soft, seething
Fiercely, did burst out in a thousand spots,
And they, struggling up on the glowing
  coals,

With shoulders, hands, and feet, jointly
Attempted to get out. But all in vain,
For as we see sink neath the waves
Those who are overcome upon the deep,
Who, uselessly, with arms and legs
But shorten the sad thread of life,
And in a time unfortunate, short, brief,
Their souls, immortal yet oppressed,

Escape from their mortal prisons,
So these did make untimely end.
Yet giving in that last farewell
Their last embraces mid the coals,
And thus, leaving their fatherland beloved,
They gave a long farewell to its ashes
Mid which they all had willed to die.

Francisco Núñez de Pineda y Bascuñán
(1607–1682)

Núñez de Pineda, son of the conquistador don Álvaro, was taken hostage by the Araucanian chief Maulicán in the battle of Cangrejeras (1629), when he was twenty-two years old. During the seven months of his captivity, he became acquainted with Indian customs and culture, and was exhibited in several towns and villages. After he was ransomed, he went on to become governor of Valvidia in 1673. The account of his captivity was written twenty years after his release, but was only published in 1863.

PRIMARY WORK

El cautiverio feliz y razón de las guerras dilatadas de Chile (*The Happy Captivity and the Reason for the Long-Lasting Wars of Chile*), 1863. (London: The Folio Society, 1977.)

FURTHER READING

Ralph Bauer, "Imperial History, Captivity, and Creole Identity in Francisco Núñez de Pineda y Bascuñán's Cautiverio feliz," *Colonial Latin American Review*, June, 7, 1 (1998) pp. 59–82
Dennis Pollard, "The King's Justice in Pineda y Bascuñán's Cautiverio feliz," *Dispositio: Revista Americana de Estudios Comparados y Culturales/American Journal of Comparative and Cultural Studies*, 11, 28–29 (1986) pp. 113–35.

THE HAPPY CAPTIVITY . . .

From *Book I, Chapter IX: The Beginning of the Captivity*

In the midst of these tribulations and anguish, I found myself three or four times unsaddled and without my horse. I raised my hands and soul to heaven with trust, and when I least expected it, I once more found myself on the horse and firm in the saddle. The force of the current was so swift and strong that I will never know by what luck my horse got to the other bank of the Biobío River. The rest, who were with us, were carried more than 1000 feet down the river from where my companion, the other soldier, and I scrambled out, along with another Indian who was riding a spirited horse.

When I found myself safe from that terrible danger (for even in the bloody battle I had not worried about nor feared death) I did not cease to give infinite thanks to God for having rescued me from the rapid current. Although the Indians had been brought up along its water, two of the men drowned and the rest were swept from their horses.

When the soldier, my companion, estimated that the Indians were more than 1000 feet down the river, he had me lead his horse by the bridle from a great ravine which walled in the banks of the river. He said to me in a determined voice: "Captain, this is a good time for us to escape and avoid greater risks. And since the opportunity has presented itself, there's no reason why we shouldn't take it. These enemies cannot quickly escape from dangers and risks in which they find themselves, so in the meantime we can outdistance them. And even though we have only a small advantage, they will not dare to follow our footsteps, for the fear that our army might come in pursuit of them, right down to these banks; since this is still our land."

After we talked for a quarter of an hour, we saw an Indian coming out of the water, like the rest, without his horse, that had drowned. We asked him about our captors on the chance they had been seen to escape from the river. He told us that he thought my captor (Chief Maulicán) must have drowned, because he saw two dead Indians floating down the current. I was worried by his words, thinking there might be arguments now about who was my master, and in the midst of their quarrel I might be killed as the best way to end any bad feeling between either side. With these considerations, we went walking down stream looking for our masters. We met another Indian who assured us that some had crawled out and that my captor had taken shelter on a small island, where he was preparing his horse to swim with him to the mainland. With this information we started on and soon we sighted him on the island with other companions who had escaped to the island. Having driven their horses ahead of them, they were swimming along behind. As soon as I recognized my captor's horse, with my last bit of strength I hurried to seize it, and I took it by the bridle, and my companion had caught his chief's horse in the same way. When my captor saw me holding his horse by the bridle, he began to embrace me. He said to me very joyfully: "Captain, I thought you had already returned to your land. I am happy to see you since you have returned my soul to my body. Come, embrace me again and be very sure that if so far I had desired fervently to save you and look after your life, this act that you have now performed for me has so won me over that I will see myself dead rather than allow misfortune to come to you. And I give you my word of honor that you may return to your land and look again joyfully on your father and your friends."

Book III, Chapter XXXI: A Feast

That night was given over to dancing and festivities with which they are accustomed to follow their plowing and their planting, and since the sun had set my companion remained with us. The chief, Quintalebo, who was giving the feast, celebrated his arrival with more than usual ceremony, because he was truly ostentatious and gallant in his actions. After we had feasted splendidly, the old chiefs, the one from Villarrica, and I went to the fire where the dance had already begun. The chiefs begged me to dance with them, and I did so to please them. In the midst of this entertainment, Quintalebo, my new friend, brought his daughter to me, who was among those dancing. He brought her and some of the other girls to where we were watching and told her to take my hand and dance with me because he had given her to me as my wife. The rest of the chiefs chose among those girls who had accompanied Quintalebo's daughter and began dancing hand in hand with them. At the persuasion of her father and the rest of the ancient chiefs, I did the same thing after the girls toasted us. That is what the unmarried girls are accustomed to doing when they want the unmarried men to dance with them, or when they wish to flatter the old chiefs. And in this way they frequently find husbands at these feasts and dances, which they call "gnapitun."

On this occasion the girl's mother came to where we were standing, and engaged in conversation. She offered me a jar of clear, sweet corn liquor from the earthen jugs that Chief Lepumante had sent for me. She treated me as her son-in-law, signifying that she was happy that her husband, Quilalebo, had given her daughter to me. She was one of the principal ladies of Valdivia, and said her child was the granddaughter of one of the ancient conquistadores. At that time she told me his name, but since it did not matter to me that she had been involved with one of those barbarians, I did not try to remember the name. I took advantage of the occasion to tell her about the obstacles which prevented my marrying her daughter. I gave her polite and agreeable reasons, repeating what I had previously told the girl. Since she was an understanding woman, even though primitive in language, dress, and customs, she told me that my reasons seemed just, but nevertheless, her husband had wanted me to entertain and dance hand in hand with his daughter. The old lady took one of her daughter's hands and one of mine, and between the two of them, showing my excitement and happiness, I did what the rest of the people were doing. And although I was present in body, because I could not help it, in the midst of these dancers, my spirit and heart remained in God's presence as I sought His help and guidance which He bestows mercifully to those who fear and love Him. For this is the doctrine of St Paul.

Carlos de Siguenza y Góngora (1645–1700)

Carlos de Siguenza y Góngora, a relative of the Spanish Baroque poet Góngora, as well as a poet, philosopher and historian, has been called the foremost humanist of colonial New Spain. Influenced by the Spanish picaresque tradition, he wrote in 1690 what he called a genuine account of the adventures of a young Puerto Rican in Mexico, *The Misadventures of Alonso Ramírez*. This fictionalized history is notable for its vivid descriptions of seventeenth-century Mexican life and for its colorful account of the hero's encounter with man-eating English pirates.

FURTHER READING

Magda Graniela-Rodriguez, "Of Listeners, Narrative Voices, Readers and Narratees: The Structural Interlock Infortunios de Alonso Ramírez by Carlos de Siguenza y Góngora," *Readerly/Writerly Texts: Essays on Literature, Literary/Textual Criticism, and Pedagogy*, Spring–Summer, 1, 2 (1994) pp. 127–38.

Kimberle Lopez, "Identity and Alterity in the Emergence of a Creole Discourse: Siguenza y Góngora's Infortunios de Alonso Ramírez," *Colonial Latin American Review*, Dec., 5, 2 (1996) pp. 253–76.

PRIMARY WORK

The Misadventures of Alonso Ramírez, trans. Edwin H. Pleasants (Mexico City: Imprenta Mexicana, 1962).

THE MISADVENTURES OF ALONSO RAMÍREZ

From *Chapter I: The Motives He Had for Leaving His Country. Work and Travel through New Spain; His Presence in Mexico until Leaving for the Philippines*

I hope that the curious who read this book may entertain themselves for a few hours with the incidents which caused me mortal anguish for many years. And although we are concerned only with events which subsisted in the mind of a man who invented them, maxims and aphorisms may be deduced which together with the pleasures of the narrative may cultivate the reason of those persons who occupy themselves here. However, this will not be my main intention but rather to arouse sympathy, even though long after my ordeals, which will make their memory tolerable, thus coupling the reader's feelings with those which vexed me at that time. Not for the reason that I am so close to my pain would I fall into the error of vacillation and thus omit details which from a less unfortunate person would be the cause of many complaints. I will say first what seems most notable in this series of events.

My name is Alonso Ramírez and my homeland the city of San Juan in Puerto Rico, the capital of the island, known by this name now as in olden times it was called Borriquen and which lies between the Mexican mainland and the Atlantic Seas. It has become famous as a delightful watering place for those who for long times past suffered thirst in navigating to New Spain; for the beauty of her bay and the invincible Morro Castle which defends her; and the walls and bulwarks crowned by artillery assuring her safety. Thus she is protected from the hostilities of pirates as are other lands in the Indies, her defenses supporting the spirit which the genius of that land of plenty gives to its sons.

The natives are now hard pressed in their fidelity and honour since the wealthy gold veins which gave the island its name are no longer worked because the original inhabitants who provided the labor have died off. Also the vehemence of fearful hurricanes whipped the cacao trees that provided for their owners a substitute for gold. As a result the rest of the islanders became poor.

Among those who suffered from this situation were my parents who had it forced on them since their way of life deserved something better; but now it is an annoyance in the Indies that life is so hard. My father's name was Lucas de Villanueva, and although I do not know the place of his birth it is clear to me from what people heard him say that he was Andalucian[1], and I know very well that my mother was born in the same city of Puerto Rico and her name is Ana Ramírez, to whose Christianity I owed in my childhood the only thing which the poor can give their children: advice which inclines them toward virtue.

My father was a ship-carpenter who, when my age permitted, put me to work at his vocation, but recognizing that construction work was irregular and realizing that I would not live forever, for that reason, together with the inconveniences they forced on me even as a child, I determined to flee from my native land to seek out more convenient localities in other climes.

I took advantage of the opportunity which Captain Juan del Corcho's barque[2] offered me to become a page and to leave that port for Havana. It was the year 1675 and I was thirteen years old. The position did not seem laborious to me considering myself free and without the obligation of cutting wood; but I confess that perhaps foreseeing the future I doubted if it could promise me anything worthwhile, having begun my fortune at sea. But who can deny that my doubts were well-founded noting the events that followed that beginning? From the port of Havana (famous among those which the Windward Islands enjoy, both for the favour of nature and the fortresses which art and work provided for its protection), we went on to that of San Juan de Ulua, on the mainland of New Spain where I left my ship's master and went up to the city of Puebla de los Angeles, not without much discomfort along the way due to the rough paths that run from Jalapa to Perrote and also because of the cold which seemed intense to a person unaccustomed to it.

Those that inhabit this city declare it to be next to Mexico City in size, in the width of her

---

[1]   From southern Spain.   [2]   Ship.

streets, in the magnificence of her temples, and in every other way which makes her comparable to the capital. So it occurred to me (not having seen until then a larger one) that in such a large city it would be easy for me to find a more favourable life. I determined, without more thought than this, to remain there earning a living in the service of a carpenter until I should discover some other way to become rich.

During the period of six months which I lost there I experienced more hunger than in Puerto Rico. Despising the indiscreet resolution to abandon my country for a land where one does not always receive a welcome for generous liberality, increasing the number of muleteers[3], I reached Mexico City without considerable trouble.

It is a great pity that the greatness and magnificence of such a superb city should not spread through the world engraved by a glazier's diamond on plates of gold. What I had learned about the size of Puebla was erased from my memory from the moment I tread the causeway over the great lagoon which is open to strangers at the southern approach.

And since one of the greatest compliments due this metropolis is the magnanimity of those that inhabit it, aided as it is by the abundance of everything needed to spend a restful life, I attribute to the fatality of my star the necessity of having to exercise my vocation in order to sustain myself. Cristóbal de Medina, a master in building and architecture, employed me at a competent salary in what work he set forth, and I was to spend at this position about a year.

The reason I had for leaving Mexico City for Oaxaca was the news that don Luis Ramírez lived there, a relative of my mother, with the honorable title and duties of an alderman. I felt sure that I would find a helping hand there even if not an ascent disproportionate to what the situation seemed to represent.

After a trip of eighty leagues he denied the relationship in unpleasant language and I was obliged to turn to strangers so as not to suffer the world's asperity which was all the more painful being unexpected.

Thus I came to serve a merchant carrier by the name of Juan López. The latter bartered with the Mixes, the Contales, and the Cuicatecas[4] merchandise from Castile which they lacked, for the products of their lands which consist of cotton, blankets, cacao and cochineal[5]. To secure these items one passes over rough mountains fearful at every moment of falling off cliffs lining the paths, of deep ravines, annoyed by continuous rain and many swamps, and to which are added small humid valleys full of mosquitoes and everywhere vermin abominable to every living creature because of their poison.

My longing for wealth stumbled over all of this. I went along accompanied by my master, persuaded that the recompense would be in proportion to the effort required. We made a trip to Chiapas and from there to different places in the provinces of Soconusco and Guatemala, but as it is the lot of mankind to mingle with a joyful and prosperous day a sad and tasteless night, on our return to Oaxaca, my master became ill in the town of Talistaca to such an extreme that they administered the last sacrament for the dying.

I regretted his suffering and equally my own, passing the time thinking up ways of living less laboriously, but when Juan López had a turn for the better my depression disappeared to be followed by a tranquility which proved to be temporary since in the following journey he had the same attack in the village of Cuicatlán. No remedy could help him and he passed away.

I collected from his heirs what they were willing to give me for my presence and despising myself and my fortune, I returned to Mexico City. Wanting to enter this city with a few reales,

---

3   I.e. as a muleteer himself.

4   Native groups.

5   A material used in dyestuff.

I sought work in Puebla without finding any master at all who welcomed me. Fearful of experiencing the same hunger as when I was there before, I hurried on my way.

Due to my application at work when I was with master Cristóbal de Medina for a year, those who knew me tried to find me a location[6] in Mexico City. I managed this through marriage with Francisca Xavier, a young girl who was the daughter of the widow doña Maria de Poblete, sister of the venerable doctor Juan de Poblete, dean of the cathedral, who had renounced the miter[7] of Archbishop of Manila in order to die as a paragon in his native abode. He lived as an example to all who might aspire to eternal memory by the rectitude of their ways.

. . . In my wife I found much virtue and affection but such good fortune was as if in a dream since it lasted but eleven months when she died in childbirth. Left without her after such an unexpected and sensitive blow, I decided to distract my mind by returning to Puebla.

Entering the employ of Estevan Gutiérrez, a master carpenter, who sustained himself by extreme frugality, you can imagine how things would go with his assistant.

I despaired then of ever being anything and finding myself in the tribunal of my own conscience, not only accused but useless, I planned to sentence myself for this deed[8] as they do in Mexico City for delinquents by sending them into exile to the Philippines. Therefore I went there in the galley Santa Rosa, which (under orders of General Antonio Nieto whose pilot was Admiral Leandro Coello) left the port of Acapulco for that of Cavite in the year 1682. . . .

From *Chapter II: His Departure from Acapulco for the Philippines; the Route of this Voyage and How He Passed the Time until Captured by the English*

. . . By orders of General don Gabriel de Guzalaequi, who governed the islands, a one-deck frigate was dispatched to the province of Ilocos to bring supplies to the prison at Cavite as had been done before.

Those who embarked were all men of the sea and I was placed in charge of the ship and its twenty-five seamen. Four lances and two muskets were taken from the royal storehouse and given to me to defend the vessel, it being necessary to be instantly on guard since the twenty-four pounders were out of commission. They also gave me a few bullets and five pounds of powder.

With this supply of arms and munitions but without artillery or even a stone mortar (in spite of the fact that we had portholes for six pieces), I set sail. It took six days to reach Ilocos and about nine or ten were spent in the barter and loading of supplies. On the fifth day we were on our way back plying to the windward in order to enter the mouth of Marivelez and the port when, at four in the afternoon, two ships were discovered toward land. Presuming, not only myself, but those that were with me, that they were ships in charge of captains Juan Bautista and Juan Carvallo which had gone to Pangasinan and Panay to get rice and other things needed in the prison at Cavite and other nearby places, I proceeded (although to the leeward) without any suspicions because there was no reason for them.

Then, within a short while, two canoes came toward me at full speed and I became disturbed. My surprise was extreme when I recognized close up that they were enemies.

Prepared for the defence as best I would be with my two muskets and four lances, they rained shots upon us but without boarding us. The muskets responded striking one of the

---

[6] A situation; work.

[7] A type of headdress worn by certain Church dignataries.

[8] It is unclear here whether the author is referring to his

marrying for money or to his lack of professional success, presumably punishment for his sins.

canoes and setting fire to the other. Meanwhile we split the balls with a knife to double the ammunition so that with more shots we might continue for a longer time our ridiculous resistance.

The two large ships from which we had seen the canoes leave, bore down on us immediately. Taking in the main-topsail, asking quarter[9], and being boarded by fifty Englishmen with cutlasses in their hands was all a matter of a moment.

They seized the round-house, drove us into the bow and mocked us with loud laughter at the sight of the arms we had and even more when they discovered that the frigate belonged to the king and that the arms had been taken out of the royal storehouse. It was then six o'clock in the afternoon of Tuesday the fourth of March in the year 1687.

From *Chapter III: A Brief Summary of the Thievery and Cruelty of these Pirates on Land and Sea until Arriving in America*

Knowing that the ship had been in my charge, I was placed on one of the larger pirate vessels where the captain received me with false hospitality. He immediately promised me my freedom in return for news about which of the islands were more wealthy and if one could expect much resistance from them. I answered that I had left Cavite only to visit Ilocos and so could not satisfy his desire for information. He insisted on asking me if the island of Caponiz which at a distance of fourteen leagues is northwest southeast with respect to Marivelez would be safe for his ships and if there would be obstacles to face there. I told him that there was no village there at all and that I knew of a bay where he could easily secure what he needed. It was my intention, if he should go there, that he should be seized unexpectedly not only by the natives but by the Spanish who serve on the prison staff of that island. At about ten in the evening they anchored where they thought best and between this question and others the night passed.

Before setting sail they put my twenty-five men on board the flagship. It was commanded by an Englishman called master Bel. It had eighty men, twenty-four pieces of artillery and eight stone mortars all bronze. Captain Donkin was master of the second ship and he had seventy men, twenty pieces of artillery and eight stone mortars. In both there were a great many pieces of artillery and eight stone mortars. In both, there were many shot-guns, cutlasses, axes, grenades, and pots full of various foul-smelling ingredients beside grappling-irons.

. . . Turning the frigates toward Capniz with mine in tow, they began with pistols and cutlasses to examine me again and even to torture me. They tied me and a companion of mine to the main mast and as we did not answer their questions to their liking about where to find gold and silver, they laid hands on Francisco de la Cruz, a half-breed Chinese trader and companion of mine, and whipped him until he fainted on the deck almost lifeless.

They put me and my companions in the hold where we could hear above much shouting and the report of a blunderbuss[10]. I noticed the blood on the deck after they let us out and showing it to me they said it was that of one of my men who had died and that the same thing would happen to me if I did not respond properly to questioning. I told them humbly that they could do what they wanted with me because I had nothing to add to what I had already said.

Careful then to find out which of my companions had died, I checked and found the number the same as before, which puzzled me. I found out much later that what I had seen was the

---

[9]   Surrendering.   [10]   A short-barreled muzzle-loading gun.

blood of a dog and that the whole episode had been feigned.

Not satisfied with what I had said, they began asking questions again in a solicitous manner of my boatswain, who being Indian could not be expected to do things properly, and they discovered from him that there was a village and prison on the island of Caponiz which I had stated previously to be uninhabited.

With this news and more that they discovered for themselves such as the sight of two horsemen along the shore to which they added the lie that I had never left Cavite except for Ilocos, they fell upon me with cutlasses unsheathed and much shouting.

Never had I feared death more than at that moment; but they commuted it with kicks and blows on the neck until they left me unable to move for many days.

They anchored off land from a direction where they expected no trouble from the islanders and leaving on shore the Indians who were the owners of a junk which they had seized the previous day, they headed for Pulicondon, an island populated by Cochin Chinese on the coast of Cambodia. There they found a port and transferred to their two frigates everything they found in mine and set it on fire.

Arming the canoes with sufficient men they made for land and found the inhabitants friendly. They told the islanders they only wished a safe harbour for the ships so as to add provisions and fruit which they lacked.

Either through fear or for other motives which I did not learn about, the poor barbarians agreed to this. They received clothes which had been stolen in return for pitch, fat, salted turtle meat and other items.

Due to a lack of clothing on that island or to the pent-up emotions of the pirates, nakedness and curiosity forced them to commit the most shameful disgrace which I ever saw.

The mothers brought the daughters and even the husbands their wives and delivered them to the English with the recommendation that they were beautiful, for the vilest price of a blanket or some such trifle.

Such an ugly convenience made their stay of four months at the island tolerable, but since they felt they were not living if they were not stealing and since their ships were ready to navigate they placed on board all the supplies they could in order to depart.

Consulting over the price they should give the islanders for their hospitality, they settled it the same day they set sail by attacking at dawn those who were sleeping without precautions, and putting everyone to the knife, even the women they had left pregnant. Setting fire to the village, and then hoisting colours they boarded their ships with great rejoicing.

I was not present at this base cruelty but fearing that some day the same thing could come to pass in my case, I watched from the flagship where I was kept and saw the flames and heard the shots.

If they had carried out this abominable victory after consuming quantities of the brandy they use, it would not be important to keep silent about this deed; but having intervened the incidents which I saw, how could I fail to mention them without suffering pangs of conscience at remaining silent?

Among the things which they brought from the village which they had given in payment of the women and the supplies was a human arm from one of the victims of the fire. From this each one cut a small slice and praising the quality and flavour amid repeated toasts they finished it off.

I was watching them dismayed and scandalized at such bestial conduct when one of them approached me with a piece and insisted that I should eat it. When I rejected it he said, "Being Spanish it follows you are a prude and a coward unequal to men of valour." He insisted no further in order to respond to a toast.

Sor Juana Inés de la Cruz (1648–1695)

Sor Juana Inés de la Cruz is justly considered the greatest lyrical poet of colonial Mexico, and was known to her contemporaries as "the Phoenix of Mexico" and "the Tenth Muse." The illegitimate daughter of a Basque landowner and a creole mother, she was a favorite at the viceregal court, where she was popular due to her literary ability as well as to her undoubted beauty and charm. Though she wished to enter the University, this was not possible for women at the time, and she was forced to continue her studies privately. At the age of twenty-one, she entered a convent, where she assembled a sizable library and devoted herself to study and writing. She was not afraid to speak her mind, and did not hesitate to enter into a polemic with the Portuguese Jesuit Father Antonio Vieira, an able and lucid rhetorician, regarding the Biblical episode in which Jesus washes the feet of his disciples; according to Vieira, Christ had washed the feet of his disciples for the sake of love itself, while Sor Juana alleged that this act was proof of his love for humanity. Her dissent was viewed by the ecclesiastical authorities as insolent, and the Bishop of Puebla wrote her a letter demanding that she dedicate herself to her religious duties and give up her intellectual concerns. Commenting on the pressures she faced, she retorted, "Women feel that men surpass them, and that I seem to place myself on a level with men; some wish that I did not know so much; others say

that I ought to know more to merit such applause; elderly women do not wish that other women know more than they; young women, that others present a good appearance; and one and all wish me to conform to the rules of their judgement; so that from all sides comes such a singular martyrdom as I deem none other has ever experienced." Finally, however, she sold her library, donating the money to the poor, and devoted herself to spiritual concerns. She died after nursing her sister nuns during an epidemic in Mexico City on April 17, 1695. In her poetry, amid the elegant baroque play of light and shadow, reality and illusion, she articulates issues related to gender, race, and colonial/national identity.

Primary Work

Sor Juana Inés de la Cruz, *Poems, Protest and a Dream,* trans. Dorothy Sayers Peden (Harmondsworth: Penguin, 1997).

Further Reading

Electra Arenal and Stacey Schau (eds) *Untold Sisters: Hispanic Nuns in Their Own Works,* trans. Amanda Powell (Albuquerque: University of New Mexico Press, 1989).

Jean Franco, *Plotting Women: Gender and Representation in Mexico* (New York: Columbia University Press, 1989).

Number 48: In Reply to a Gentleman from Peru, Who Sent Her Clay Vessels While Suggesting She Would Better Be a Man

Kind Sir, while wishing to reply,
my Muses[1] all have taken leave,
and none, even for charity,
will aid me now I wish to speak;

and though we know these Sisters nine[2]
good mothers are of wit and jest,

not one, once having heard your verse,
will dare to jest at my behest.

The God Apollo[3] listens, rapt,
and races on, so high aloft
that those who guide his Chariot
must raise their voices to a shout.

[1]   The nine goddesses who presided over poetry, music, dancing, and all the liberal arts: Clio, Euterpe, Thalia, Melpomene, Terpsichore, Erato, Polyhymnia, Calliope, and Urania.

[2]   The Muses.
[3]   Apollo, Greek god of Poetry and the Sun, was often depicted flanked by the Muses.

To hear your lines, fleet Pegasus[4]
his lusty breathing will retain,
that no one fear his thunderous neigh
as your verses are declaimed.

Checking, against nature's order,
altering crystalline watercourse,
Helicon[5] stays its gurgling water,
Agannipe[6], her murmuring source:

for, having heard your murmuring,
the Nine Daughters all concede,
beside your verses they are wanting,
unfit to study at your feet.

Apollo sets aside the wand
that he employs to mark the beat,
because, on seeing you, he knows
he cannot justly take the lead.

And thus, acknowledge it I must,
I cannot scribe the verses owed
unless, perhaps, compassionate,
keen inspiration you bestow.

Be my Apollo, and behold
(as your light illumines me)
how my lyre will then be heard
the length and breadth of land and sea.

Though humble, oh, how powerful
my invocation's consequence,
I find new valor in my breast,
new spirit given utterance!

Ignited with unfamiliar fervor,
my pen bursting into flame,
while giving due to famed Apollo
I honor Navarrete's[7] name.

Traveling where none has trod,
expression rises to new heights,
and, revering in new invention,
finds in itself supreme delight.

Stammering with such abundance
my clumsy tongue is tied with pain:
much is seen, but little spoken,
some is known, but none explained.

You will think that I make mock;
no, nothing further from the truth,
to prophesy, my guiding spirit
is lacking but a fine hair's breadth.

But if I am so little able
to offer you sufficient praise,
to form the kind of compliment
that only your apt pen may phrase,

what serve me then to undertake it?
to venture it, what good will serve?
if mine be pens that write in water,
recording lessons unobserved.

That they themselves elucidate,
I now leave your eulogies:
as none to their measure correspond,
none can match them in degree,

and I turn to giving thanks
for your fair gifts, most subtly made;
Art lifts a toast to appetite
in lovely Vessels of fragrant clay.

Earthenware, so exquisite
that Chile properly is proud,
though it is not gold or silver
that gives your gift its wide renown

but, rather, from such lowly matter
forms emerge that put to shame
the brimming Goblets made of gold
from which Gods their nectar drained.

Kiss, I beg, the hands that made them,
though judging by the Vessels' charm
– such grace can surely leave no doubt –
yours were the hands that gave them form.

---

4   The winged horse of poetry, sprung from the head of
Medusa.
5   Mountain near the Gulf of Corinth, sacred to Apollo.

6   The fountain at the foot of Mount Helicon.
7   Surname of the gentleman from Peru (of the poem's
title).

As for the counsel that you offer,
I promise you, I will attend
with all my strength, although I judge no
    strength
on earth can en-Tarquin[8]:

for here we have no Salmacis[9],
whose crystal water, so they tell,
to nurture masculinity
possesses powers unexcelled.

I have no knowledge of these things,
except that I came to this place
so that, if true that I am female,
none substantiate that state.

I know, too, that they were wont
to call wife, or woman, in the Latin
uxor, only those who wed,
though wife or woman might be virgin.

So in my case, it is not seemly
that I be viewed as feminine,
as I will never be a woman
who may as woman serve a man.[10]

I know only that my body,
not to either state inclined,
is neuter, abstract, guardian
of only what my Soul consigns.

Let us renounce this argument,
let others, if they will, debate;
some matters better left unknown
no reason can illuminate.

Generous gentleman from Peru,
proclaiming such unhappiness,
did you leave Lima any art,
given the art you brought to us?

You must know that law of Athens
by which Aristides[11] was expelled:
it seems that, even if for good,
it is forbidden to excel.

He was expelled for being good,
and other famous men as well;
because to tower over all
is truly unforgivable.

He who always leads his peers
will by necessity invite
malicious envy, as his fame
will rob all others of the light.

To the degree that one is chosen
as the target for acclaim,
to that same measure, envy trails
in close pursuit, with perfect aim.

Now you are banished from Peru
and welcomed in my Native Land,
we see the Heavens grant to us
the blessing that Peru declined.

But it is well that such great talent
live in many different zones,
for those who are with greatness born
should live not for themselves alone.

Number 92: A Philosophical Satire

She proves the inconsistency of the caprice and criticism of men who accuse women of what
they cause.

---

[8] Tarquinius Superbus was said to have been deposed because his son Sextus raped Lucretia. Margaret Peden suggests in a footnote to her translation that the verb invented by Sor Juana Inés broadly means "to turn a woman into a man." Another reading is that she is asserting the inviolate nature of her own ideas.

[9] Here Sor Juana Inés refers ironically to the fountain of Salmacis, which rendered effeminate all those who drank of its waters, such as Hermaphroditas.

[10] Either due to her state as a nun or to her refusal to accept subordinate status.

[11] An Athenian, also called The Just, known for his temperance and virtue.

Misguided men, who will chastise
a woman when no blame is due,
oblivious that it is you
who prompted what you criticize;

if your passions are so strong
that you elicit their disdain,
how can you wish that they refrain
when you incite them to their wrong?

You strive to topple their defense,
and then, with utmost gravity,
you credit sensuality
for what was won with diligence.

Your daring must be qualified,
your sense is no less senseless
than the child who calls the bogeyman,
then weeps when he is terrified.

Your mad presumption knows no bounds,
though for a wife you want Lucrece[1],
in lovers you prefer Thais[2],
thus seeking blessings to compound.

If knowingly one clouds a mirror
– was ever humor so absurd
or good counsel so obscured? –
can he lament that it's not clearer?

From either favor or disdain
the selfsame purpose you achieve,
if they love, they are deceived,
if they love not, hear you complain.

There is no woman suits your taste,
though circumspection be her virtue:
ungrateful, she who does not love you,
yet she who does, you judge unchaste.

You men are such a foolish breed,
appraising with a faulty rule,

the first you charge with being cruel,
the second, easy, you decree.

So how can she be temperate,
the one who would her love expend?
if not willing, she offends,
but willing, she infuriates.

Amid the anger and torment
your whimsy causes you to bear,
one may be found who does not care:
how quickly then is grievance vent.

So lovingly you inflict pain
that inhibitions fly away;
how, after leading them astray,
can you wish them without stain?

Who does the greater guilt incur
when a passion is misleading?
She who errs and heeds his pleading,
or he who pleads with her to err?

Whose is the greater guilt therein
when either's conduct may dismay:
she who sins and takes the pay,
or he who pays her for the sin?

Why, for sins you're guilty of,
do you, amazed, your blame debate?
Either love what you create
or else create what you can love.

Were not it better to forbear,
and thus, with finer motivation,
obtain the unforced admiration
of her you plotted to ensnare?

But no, I deem you still will revel
in your arms and arrogance,
and in promise and persistence
adjoin flesh and world and devil.

---

[1]   Lucretia, a Roman exemplar of female virtue and chastity, who committed suicide when raped by the son of Tarquin Soberbus.

[2]   The Athenian mistress of Alexander the Great.

Number 94: Which Reveals the Honorable Ancestry of a High-Born Drunkard

Alfeo claims he comes from kings,
he boasts of blood of royal hue,
he speaks of queens with *diamond* rings,
whose *hearts* pump only royal blue.

The truth is, his line brandished *clubs*,
his House is the House of Topers[1],
but have no doubt, when in his cups,
he's king – in *spades* – the King of Jokers.

Number 145: She Attempts to Minimize the Praise Occasioned by a Portrait of Herself Inscribed by Truth – Which She Calls Ardor

This that you gaze on, colorful deceit,
that so immodestly displays art's favors,
with its fallacious arguments of colors
is to the senses cunning counterfeit,
this on which kindness practiced to delete
from cruel years accumulated horrors,
constraining time to mitigate its rigors,

and thus oblivion and age defeat,
is but an artifice, a sop to vanity,
is but a flower by the breezes bowed,
is but a ploy to counter destiny,
is but a foolish labor, ill-employed,
is but a fancy, and, as all may see,
is but cadaver, ashes, shadow, void.

Number 146: She Laments Her Fortune, She Hints of Her Aversion to All Vice, and Justifies Her Diversion with the Muses

In my pursuit, World, why such diligence?
What my offence, when I am thus inclined,
insuring elegance affect my mind,
not that my mind affect an elegance?
I have no love of riches or finance,
and thus do I most happily, I find,
expend finances to enrich my mind

and not mind expend upon finance.
I worship beauty not, but vilify
that spoil of time that mocks eternity,
nor less, deceitful treasures glorify,
but hold foremost, with greatest constancy,
consuming all the vanity in life,
and not consuming life in vanity.

Number 317: Villancico VI, from "Santa Catarina," 1691

Refrain
Victor! Victor! Catherine[1],
who with enlightenment divine
persuaded all the learned men,
she who with triumph overcame
– with knowledge truly sovereign –

the pride and arrogance profane
of those who challenged her, in vain
Victor! Victor! Victor!

Verses
There in Egypt, all the sages

94: THE HONORABLE ANCESTRY OF A HIGH-BORN DRUNKARD
[1]   Drunkards.

317: FROM "SANTA CATARINA"
[1]   St Catherine of Alexandria, a young noblewoman known for her erudition and religious ardor. The Emperor Maximinus, persecutor of Christians, was said to have as-

sembled the greatest philosophers to confound her. When Catherine refuted their arguments, they were burnt alive. Later, an attempt was made to break her on a spiked wheel, but it fell to pieces and she was unhurt. The analogies with the situation of Sor Juana Inés and her theological disputes with Father Antonio Vieira and with Bishop Sahagun are evident.

by a woman were convinced
that gender is not of the essence
in matters of intelligence.
Victor! Victor!

A victory, a miracle;
though more prodigious than the feat
of conquering, was surely that
the men themselves declared defeat.
Victor! Victor!

How wise they were, these Prudent Men,
acknowledging they were outdone,
for one conquers when one yields
to wisdom greater than one's own.
Victor! Victor!

Illumination shed by truth
will never by mere shouts be drowned;
persistently, its echo rings,
above all obstacles resounds.
Victor! Victor!

None of these Wise Men was ashamed
when he found himself convinced,
because, in being Wise, he knew
his knowledge was not infinite.
Victor! Victor!

It is of service to the Church
that women argue, tutor, learn,
for He who granted women reason
would not have them uninformed.
Victor! Victor!

How haughtily they must have come,
the men that Maximin[2] convened,
though at their advent arrogant,
they left with wonder and esteem.
Victor! Victor!

Persuaded, all of them, with her,
gave up their lives unto the knife:
how much good might have been lost,
were Catherine less erudite!
Victor! Victor!

No man, whatever his renown,
accomplished such a victory,
and we know that God, through her,
honored femininity.
Victor! Victor!

Too brief, the flowering of her years,
but ten and eight, the sun's rotations,
but when measuring her knowledge,
who could sum the countless ages?
Victor! Victor!

Now all her learned arguments
are lost to us (how great the grief).
But with her blood, if not with ink,
she wrote the lesson of her life.
Victor! Victor!

Tutelar and holy Patron,
Catherine, the Shrine of Arts;
long may she illumine Wise Men,
she who Wise to Saints converts.
Victor! Victor!

Number 367: Loa[1] *for the Auto sacramental* The Divine Narcissus *through allegories*

Cast of Characters

Occident	Religion
America	Musicians
Zeal	Soldiers

---

[2] Maximinus, Emperor of Rome in the third century BC, notorious for his intolerance.

THE DIVINE NARCISSUS
[1] A brief theatrical work which could be performed in isolation, but more frequently introduced a religious play (*auto*).

Scene I

Enter OCCIDENT, a stately Indian wearing a crown, and AMERICA beside him, a noble Indian woman, in the *mantas*[2] and *huipiles*[3] worn when singing a *tocotin*[4]. They sit in two chairs; several Indian men and women dance holding feathers and rattles in their hands, as is traditional during this celebration; as they dance, MUSIC sings:

MUSIC
Most noble Mexicans,
whose ancient origin
is found in the brilliant rays
cast like arrows by the Sun[5],
mark well the time of year,
this day is given to laud[6]
and honour in our way
the highest of our gods.
Come clad in ornaments
of your station the sign,
and to your piety
let happiness be joined:
with festive pageantry
worship the all-powerful God of Seeds![7]

MUSIC
The riches of our lands
in copious plenteousness
are owing to the one
who makes them bounteous.
So bring your fervent thanks,
and at the harvest time,
give unto Him his due,
the first fruit of the vine.
Let flow the purest blood,
give from your own veins,
to blend with many bloods
and thus His cult sustain.
　　With festive pageantry worship
　　the all-powerful God of Seeds!

(OCCIDENT *and* AMERICA *sit, as* MUSIC *ceases*.)

OCCIDENT
So great in number are the Gods
that our religion sanctifies,
so many in this place alone
the many rites we solemnise,
that this our Royal City is
the scene of cruelest sacrifice:
two thousand gods are satisfied,
but human blood must be the price;
now see the entrails that still throb,
now see hearts that redly beat,
and though the gods are myriad,
our gods so many (I repeat),
the greatest God among them all
is our Great God, the God of Seeds!

AMERICA
And rightly so, for He alone
has long sustained our Monarchy,
for all the riches of the field
we owe to Him our fealty,
and as the greatest benefice,
in which all others are contained,
is that abundance of the land,
our life and breath by it maintained,
we name Him greatest of the Gods.
What matters all the glittering gold
in which America abounds,

[2]　Shawls.
[3]　Women's blouses
[4]　Nahuatl ballad.
[5]　Friar Andres de Olmos reports that according to Native legend, the Sun cast down an arrow which made a hole from which human beings emerged.
[6]　Praise.

[7]　This probably refers to Huitzilopochtli, one of the gods of Tenochtitlan. According to Mendez Plancarte, a man-sized statue of this god was created each year with ground grains and seeds, bound with the blood of children. The ritual killing of the god was then carried out, in order to partake of his body.

what value precious ores untold,
if their excrescences befoul
and sterilise a fertile earth,
if no fruits ripen, no maize grows,
and no tender buds spring forth?
But the protection of this God
is broader than continuance,
with the provision of our food,
of our daily sustenance.
He makes a paste of His own flesh,
and we partake with veneration

(though first the paste is purified
of bodily contamination),
and so our Soul he purifies
of all its blemishes and stains.
And thus in homage to His cult,
may everyone with me proclaim:

ALL *and* MUSIC
     In festive pageantry,
     worship the all-powerful God of Seeds!

Scene II

(*They exit, dancing, and then enter Christian* RELIGION, *as a Spanish Lady, and* ZEAL, *as a Captain General, armed; behind them, Spanish* SOLDIERS.)

RELIGION
How is it, then, as you are Zeal,
your Christian wrath can tolerate
that here with blind conformity
they bow before Idolatry,
and, superstitious, elevate
an Idol, with effrontery,
above our Christianity?

ZEAL
Religion, do not be dismayed:
my compassion you upbraid,
my tolerance you disavow,
but see, I stand before you now
with arm upraised, unsheathed my blade,
which I address to your revenge.
And now, retire, your cares allayed,
as their transgressions I avenge.

(*Enter, dancing,* OCCIDENT *and* AMERICA, *and from the other side,* MUSIC, *with accompaniment.*)

MUSIC
And with festive pageantry,
worship the all-powerful God of Seeds!

ZEAL
They are here. I will approach.

RELIGION
And I as well, with all compassion,
for I would go with tones of peace
(before unleashing your aggression)
to urge them to accept my word,
and in the faith be sanctified.

ZEAL
Then let us go, for even now
they practice their revolting rite.

MUSIC
And with festive pageantry,
worship the great God of Seeds!

(ZEAL *and* RELIGION *approach.*)

RELIGION
Hear me, mighty Occident,
America, so beautiful,
your lives are led in misery
though your land is bountiful.
Abandon this unholy cult
which the Devil doth incite.
Open your eyes. Accept my word
and follow in the Path of Light,
fully persuaded by my love.

OCCIDENT
These unknown persons, who are they
who now before my presence stand?
Oh gods, who ventures thus to stay
the festive moment's rightful course?

AMERICA
What Nations these, which none has seen?
Do they come here to interfere,
my ancient power contravene?

OCCIDENT
Oh, Lovely Beauty, who are you,
fair Pilgrim from another nation?
I ask you now, why have you come
to interrupt my celebration?

RELIGION
Christian Religion is my name,
and I propose that all will bend
before the power of my word.

OCCIDENT
A great endeavour you intend!

AMERICA
A great madness you display!

OCCIDENT
The inconceivable you scheme!

AMERICA
She must be mad, ignore her now,
let them continue with our theme!

ALL *and* MUSIC
With festive pageantry,
worship the all-powerful God of Seeds!

ZEAL
How, barbaric Occident,
and you, oh blind Idolatry,
can you presume to scorn my Wife,
beloved Christianity?

For brimming to the vessel's lip
we see your sinful degradation;
the Lord our God will not allow
That you continue in transgression,
and He sends me to punish you.

OCCIDENT
And who are you, who terrorise
all those who gaze upon your face?

ZEAL
I am Zeal. Whence your surprise?
For when Religion you would scorn
with practices of vile excess,
then Zeal must enter on the scene
to castigate your wickedness.
I am a Minister from God
Who, witnessing your tyranny,
the error of these many years
of lives lived in barbarity,
has reached the limits of His grace
and sends His punishment through me.
And thus these armed and mighty Hosts
whose gleaming blades of steel you see
are His ministers of wrath,
the instruments of Holy rage.

OCCIDENT
What god, what error, what offence,
what punishment do you presage?
I do not understand your words,
nor does your argument persuade;
I know you not, who, brazenly,
would thus our rituals invade
and with such zeal that you prevent
that in just worship people say:

MUSIC
With festive pageantry,
worship the great God of Seeds!

AMERICA
Oh, mad, blind, barbaric man,[8]
disturbing our serenity,
you bring confusing arguments

---

[8]   Here Sor Juana Inés inverts the ideological rhetoric of
the colonizers, calling *them* barbaric.

to counter our tranquility;
you must immediately cease,
unless it is your wish to find
all here assembled turned to ash
with no trace even on the wind!
And you, Husband, and your vassals,

(*To* OCCIDENT)

you must close your ears and eyes,
do not heed their fantasies,
do not listen to their lies;
proceed, continue with your rites!
Our rituals shall not be banned
by these Nations, still unknown,
so newly come unto our land.

MUSIC
And with festive pageantry,
worship the great God of Seeds!

ZEAL
As our first offering of peace
you have so haughtily disdained,
accept the second, that of war,
from war we will not be restrained!
War! War! To arms! To arms!

(*Sound of drums and trumpets*)

OCCIDENT
What is this wrath the gods devise?
What are the weapons here displayed
that so confound my awestruck eyes?
Ho, my Soldiers, ho there, Guards!
Those arrows that you hold prepared
now send against the enemy!

AMERICA
Why have the gods their lightning bared
to strike me down? What are these spheres
that fall like fiery leaden hail?
What are these Centaurs, man and horse,
that now my followers assail?[9]

(*Off*)

To arms! To arms! We are at war!

(*Drums and trumpets*)

Long live Spain! Her King we hail!

(*The battle is struck;* INDIANS *enter and flee
across the stage, pursued by the* SPANISH;
OCCIDENT *and* AMERICA *begin to retreat
before* RELIGION *and* ZEAL.)

Scene III

RELIGION
Surrender, haughty Occident!

OCCIDENT
Your declarations I defy
and only to your power yield.

ZEAL
Now bold America must die!

RELIGION
Hold, Zeal, do not strike them dead,
keep America alive!

ZEAL
What, you defend America
when she has your faith reviled?

RELIGION
There is no doubt that her defeat
is owing to your bravery,
but now allowing her to live
is witness to my clemency;
it was your duty, with your force,
to conquer her; but now with reason
I, too, work to vanquish her,
but I shall win with soft persuasion.

9   Both firearms and horses were introduced into the New
World by the Spaniards.

ZEAL
But their perversion you have seen,
how they abhor and scorn your Word;
they are blind, is it not better
that they die?

RELIGION
Put up your sword.
Forebear, Zeal, do not attack,
it is my nature to forgive,
I do not want their immolation[10],
but conversion, let them live.

AMERICA
If in petitioning for my life,
and in exhibiting compassion,
it is your hope that I will yield,
that you will thus divert my passion,
employing arguments of words

as once before you employed arms,
then you will find yourself deceived,
for though my person come to harm,
and though I weep for liberty,
my liberty of will, will grow,
and I shall still adore my Gods!

OCCIDENT
I have told you, and all know,
that I have bowed before your might,
but this caution you must heed,
that there is no strength or might
that ever can my will impede
from *its just* course, free of control;
though captive I may moan in pain,
your will can never conquer mine,
and in my heart I will proclaim:
I worship the great God of Seeds!

Scene IV[11]

RELIGION
But wait, for what we offer here
is not might, but gentleness.
What God is this that you adore?

OCCIDENT
The Great Lord of fruitfulness.
He makes fertile all the fields
all the heavens bow to Him,
it is He the rain obeys, and finally, of all our
    sin
He cleanses us, then of His being
makes a feast to nurture us
Tell me whether there can be
in a God so bounteous
any greater benefice
than I give in this summary?
none other, who corroborates
in benefices all His works?

RELIGION
Then I shall be like Paul, and speak
from holy doctrine; for when he
had come to preach among the Greeks,
he found in Athens the strict law
that he who sought to introduce
an unfamiliar god, would die,
but as he knew they had the use
of faithful worship in a place
devoted to THE UNKNOWN GOD,
he said: this God I give to you
is not unknown, but One you laud,
you ignorantly worship Him,
now Him declare I unto you.
And thus do I. . . . Hear, Occident,
Idolatry, attend me, too,
for if you listen to my words
you will find salvation there.
Those many wonders you recount,

---

[10]   Destruction.
[11]   This scene is notable for its evocation of common elements in Christian and Native religious traditions.

the miracles to which you swear,
the shimmering light, the flashing gleam
you glimpsed through Superstition's veil,
the prodigies, the prophecies,
the portents we heard you detail,
attributing their consequence
to your mendacious deities,
are but the work of One True God,
His wisdom and His sovereignty.
For if the flowering meadows bloom
and gardens yield their rich supply,
if the fields are fertilised,
and if their fruits do multiply,
if the plants from seedlings grow,
and if the clouds their rain distil,
all must come from His right hand,
and never will the arm that tills,
nor the rains that feed the earth,
nor the warmth that wakes the seeds
have the power to make plants live
if Providence has not decreed
that they have life: all nature's green,
her verdant soul, is His design.

AMERICA
And if all this is as you say,
is He, tell me, so benign,
this God of yours, your Deity,
so kind that he will tolerate
that I touch Him with my hands,
like the Idol I create
from many seeds and from the blood
of innocents, blood that is shed
for this alone, this one intent?

RELIGION
Although in Essence the Godhead
is both invisible and vast,
as that Essence is combined
and with our Being bound so fast,
thus He is like to Humankind,
and His benevolence allows
that undeserving though they be,
He may be touched by hands of Priests.

AMERICA
In this much, then, we are agreed.
For of my God the same is true,

and none may touch our Deity
except for those who as His priests
to serve Him have authority;
not only may He not be touched,
but neither may they enter in
His Chapel who are not ordained.

ZEAL
What reverence, whose origin
were better found in Our True God!

OCCIDENT
Then tell me, though much more you swear:
is this God formed of elements
that are as exquisite, as rare,
as that of blood shed valiantly
and offered up as sacrifice,
as well as seeds, our sustenance?

RELIGION
His Majesty, I say this twice,
is infinite and without form,
but His divine Humanity,
found in the Sacrament of Mass,
with mercy, not with cruelty,
assuming the white innocence
that in the seeds of wheat resides,
becomes incarnate in these seeds,
in Flesh and Blood is deified;
here in this Chalice is His Blood,
the Blood He sacrificed for us,
that on the Altar of the Cross,
unsullied, pure, in righteousness,
was the Redemption of the World.

AMERICA
I stand in awe of all you say,
and hearing, I want to believe;
but could this God that you portray
be so loving that as food
He would give Himself to me,
like the God that I adore?

RELIGION
Yes, for in His Wisdom, He
came down with only this in view,
to live on earth among mankind.

AMERICA
So, may I not see this God,
that true persuasion I may find?

OCCIDENT
And I as well, thus will it be
that my obsession be forgot?

RELIGION
Oh, you will see, once you are washed
in the crystalline, holy font of Baptism.

OCCIDENT
Yes, this I know
before aspiring to come near
the fruitful table, I must bathe;
that ancient rite is practiced here.

ZEAL
That bathing for your rituals
will not cleanse you of your stains.

OCCIDENT
What bathing will?

RELIGION
The Sacrament,
which in pure waters like the rains
will cleanse you of your every sin.

AMERICA
The magnitude of this you bring
as notices[12], as yet I cannot
comprehend, of everything
I would know more, and in detail,
for I am moved by powers divine,
inspired to know all you can tell.

OCCIDENT
An even greater thirst is mine,
I would know of the Life and Death
of this great God found in the Bread.

RELIGION
That we shall do. I shall give you
a metaphor, an idea clad
in rhetoric of many colours
and fully visible to view,
this shall I show you, now I know
that you are given to imbue
with meaning what is visible;
it is now clear you value less
what Faith conveys unto your ears,
thus it is better you assess
what you can see, and with your eyes
accept the lessons She conveys.

OCCIDENT
Yes, it is so, for I would see,
and not rely on what you say.

Scene V

RELIGION
Let us begin.

ZEAL
Religion, speak,
to represent the Mysteries,
what form do you plan to employ?

RELIGION
An allegory it will be,
the better to instruct the two,
an *Auto*[13] that will clearly show

America and Occident
all that they now beg to know.

ZEAL
This Allegory as *Auto,*
what title for it do you plan?

RELIGION
Divine Narcissus, for although
America, unhappy land,
adored an Idol symbolised
by signs of such complexity

---

[12]   News.

[13]   Religious play.

that through that Idol Satan tried
to feign the highest Mystery,
that of the Sacred Eucharist,
there was, as well, intelligence
among the Gentiles[14] of this land
of other marvellous events.

ZEAL
And where will they enact your play?

RELIGION
In Madrid, the Royal Town,
the Centre of our Holy Faith,
the Jewel in the Royal Crown,
the Seat of Catholic Kings and Queens
through whom the Indies have been sent
the blessing of Evangel Light
that shines throughout the Occident.

ZEAL
But does it not seem ill-advised
that what you write in Mexico
be represented in Madrid?

RELIGION
Oh, tell me, did you never know
an object fashioned in one place
and subsequently employed elsewhere?
As for the act of writing it,
you find no whim or fancy there,
but only due obedience
attempting the impossible.
Therefore this work, though it may be
inelegant, its lustre dull,
is owing to obedience,
and not born of effrontery.

ZEAL
Religion, tell me, as the play
is your responsibility,
how do you counter the complaint
that in the Indies was begun
what you would carry to Madrid?

RELIGION
The drama's purpose is but one,

to celebrate the Mystery,
as to the persons introduced,
they are but abstraction,
symbolic figures who educe
the implication of the work,
and no part need be qualified
though it be taken to Madrid;
for men of reason realise
there is no distance that deters,
nor seas that interchange efface.

ZEAL
Prostrate, at the Royal Feet
that regally Two Worlds embrace,
we seek permission to proceed,

RELIGION
and of the Queen, our Sovereign,

AMERICA
at whose feet the Indies kneel
to pledge obeisance once again,

ZEAL
and of her Supreme Councillors,

RELIGION
and Ladies, who illuminate the
   Hemisphere;

AMERICA
and the Erudite
whom I most humbly supplicate
to pardon the poor lack of wit
in wishing with these clumsy lines
to treat so great a Mystery.

OCCIDENT
My agony is exquisite,
come, show me how in bread and wine
this God gives of Himself to me.

(AMERICA, OCCIDENT, *and* ZEAL *sing.*)

Now are the Indies all agreed,
there is but One True God of Seeds!

14   Native peoples.

With tender tears
by joy distilled,
raise voices high
with gladness filled:

ALL
Blessed the day
I came to know the great God of the Seeds!

(*All exit, dancing and singing.*)

The Miraculous Apparition of the Beloved Virgin Mary, Our Lady of Guadalupe, at Tepeyacac, near Mexico City (1649)

The original text of the narrative here given is in the Nahuatl language of the Aztecs, and was first published by Luis Lazo de la Vega in 1649; it is generally considered to be the work of Antonio Valeriano, a contemporary of the Indian Juan Diego and Bishop Zumárraga. It was later translated to Spanish in the eighteenth century by Lorenzo Boturini.

PRIMARY WORK

Donald Demarest and Coley Taylor (eds) *The Dark Virgin: The Book of Our Lady of Guadalupe* (New York: Academy Guild Press, 1956).

FURTHER READING

Jacques Lafaye, *Quetzacoatl and Guadalupe: The Formation of Mexican National Consciousness 1531–1813* (Chicago: University of Chicago Press, 1974).

HISTORY OF THE MIRACULOUS APPARITION

Herein is told, in all truth, how by a great miracle the illustrious Virgin, Blessed Mary, Mother of God, Our Lady, appeared anew, in the place known as Tepeyacac.

She appeared first to an Indian named Juan Diego; and later her divine Image appeared in the presence of the first Bishop of Mexico, Don Fray Juan de Zumárraga; also there are told various miracles which have been done. It was ten years after the beginning of bringing water from the mountain of Mexico, when the arrow and the shield had been put away, when in all parts of the country there was tranquillity which was beginning to show its light, and faith and knowledge of Him was being taught through Whose favor we have our being, Who is the only true God.

In the year 1531, early in the month of December, it happened that an humble Indian, called Juan Diego, whose dwelling, it is said, was in Quahutítlan, although for divine worship he pertained to Tlatilulco, one Saturday very early in the morning, while he was on his way to divine worship according to his custom, when he had arrived near the top of the hill called Tepeyacac, as it was near dawn, he heard above the hill a singing like that when many choice birds sing together, their voices resounding as if echoing throughout the hills; he was greatly rejoiced; their song gave him rapture exceeding that of the bell-bird and other rare birds of song.

Juan Diego stopped to wonder and said to himself: *Is it I who have this good fortune to hear what I hear? Or am I perhaps only dreaming? Where am I? Perhaps this is the place the ancients, our forefathers, used to tell about – our grandfathers – the flowery land, the fruitful land? Is it perchance the earthly paradise?*

And while he was looking towards the hilltop, facing the east, from which came the celestial song, suddenly the singing stopped and he heard someone calling as if from the top of the hill, saying: *Juan.*

Juan Diego did not dare to go there where he was being called; he did not move, perhaps in some way marvelling; yet he was filled with a great joy and delight, and then, presently, he began to climb to the summit where he was called.

And, when he was nearing it, on the top of the peak he saw a lady who was standing there who had called him from a distance, and having come into her presence, he was struck with wonder at the radiance of her exceeding great beauty, her garments shining like the sun; and the stones of the hill, and the caves, reflecting the brightness of her light were like precious gold; and he saw how the rainbow clothed the land so that the cactus and other things that grew there seemed like celestial plants, their leaves and thorns shining like gold in her presence. He made obeisance and heard her voice, her words, which rejoiced him utterly when she asked, very tenderly, as if she loved him: *Listen, xocoyote[1] mio, Juan, where are you going?*

And he replied: *My Holy One, my Lady, my Damsel, I am on my way to your house at Mexico-Tlatilolco; I go in pursuit of the holy things which our priests teach us.*

Whereupon She told him, and made him aware of her divine will, saying: *You must know, and be very certain in your heart, my son, that I am truly the eternal Virgin, holy Mother of the True God, through Whose favor we live, the Creator, Lord of Heaven, and the Lord of the Earth. I very much desire that they build me a church here, so that in it I may show and may make known and give all my love, my mercy and my help and my protection – I am in truth your merciful mother – to you and to all the other people dear to me who call upon me, who search for me, who confide in me; here I will hear their sorrow, their words, so that I may make perfect and cure their illnesses, their labors, and their calamities. And so that my intention may be made known, and my mercy, go now to the episcopal palace of the Bishop of Mexico and tell him that I send you to tell him how much I desire to have a church built here, and tell him very well all that you have seen and all that you have heard; and be sure in your heart that I will pay you with glory and you will deserve much that I will repay you for your weariness, your work, which you will bear diligently doing what I send you to do. Now hear my words, my dear son, and go and do everything carefully and quickly.*

Then he humbled himself before her and said: *My Holy One, my Lady, I will go now and fulfill your commandment.*

And straightway he went down to accomplish that with which he was charged, and took the road that leads straight to Mexico.

And when he had arrived within the city, he went at once to the episcopal palace of the Lord Bishop, who was the first (Bishop) to come, whose name was Don Fray Juan de Zumárraga, a religious of St Francis. And having arrived there, he made haste to ask to see the Lord Bishop, asking his servants to give notice of him. After a good while they came to call him, and the Bishop advised them that he should come in; and when he had come into his presence, he knelt and made obeisance, and then after this he related the words of the Queen of Heaven, and told besides all that he had seen and all that he had heard. And (the Bishop) having heard all his words and the commandment as if he were not perfectly persuaded, said in response: *My son, come again another time when we can be more leisurely; and I will hear more from you about the origin of this; I will look into this about which you have come, your will, your desire.*

---

[1]   Xocoyote, a Nahuatl word, meaning "son."

And he departed with much sorrow because he had not been able to convince him of the truth of his mission.

Thereupon he returned that same day and went straightaway to the hill where he had seen the Queen of Heaven, who was even then standing there where he had first seen Her, waiting for him, and he, having seen Her, made obeisance, kneeling upon the ground, and said: *My Holy One, most noble of persons, my Lady, my Xocoyota[2], my Damsel, I went there where You sent me; although it was most difficult to enter the house of the Lord Bishop, I saw him at last, and in his presence I gave him your message in the way You instructed me; he received me very courteously, and listened with attention; but he answered as if he could not be certain and did not believe; he told me: Come again another time when we can be at leisure, and I will hear you from beginning to end; I will look into that about which you come, what it is you want and ask me for. He seemed to me, when he answered, to be thinking perhaps that the church You desire to have made here was perchance not Your will, but a fancy of mine. I pray You, my Holy One, my Lady, my Daughter, that any one of the noble lords who are well known, reverenced and respected be the one to undertake this so that Your words will be believed. For it is true that I am only a poor man; I am not worthy of being there where You send me; pardon me, my Xocoyota, I do not wish to make your noble heart sad; I do not want to fall into your displeasure.*

Then the always noble Virgin answered him, saying: *Hear me, my son, it is true that I do not lack for servants or ambassadors to whom I could entrust my message so that my will could be verified, but it is important that you speak for me in this matter, weary as you are; in your hands you have the means of verifying, of making plain my desire, my will; I pray you, my xocoyote, and advise you with much care, that you go again tomorrow to see the Bishop and represent me; give him an understanding of my desire, my will, that he build the church that I ask; and tell him once again that it is the eternal Virgin, Holy Mary, the Mother of God, who sends you to him.*

And Juan Diego answered her, saying: *Queen of Heaven, my Holy One, my Damsel, do not trouble your heart, for I will go with all my heart and make plain Your voice, Your words. It is not because I did not want to go, or because the road is stony, but only because perhaps I would not be heard, and if I were heard I would not be believed. I will go and do your bidding and tomorrow in the afternoon about sunset I will return to give the answer to your words the Lord Bishop will make; and now I leave You, my Xocoyota, my Damsel, my Lady; meanwhile, rest You.*

With this, he went to his house to rest. The next day being Sunday, he left his house in the morning and went straightway to Tlatilolco, to attend Mass and the sermon. Then, being determined to see the Bishop, when Mass and the sermon were finished, at ten o'clock, with all the other Indians he came out of the church; but Juan Diego left them and went to the palace of the Lord Bishop. And having arrived there, he spared no effort in order to see him and when, after great difficulty, he did see him again, he fell to his knees and implored him to the point of weeping, much moved, in an effort to make plain the words of the Queen of Heaven, and that the message and the will of the most resplendent Virgin would be believed; that the church be built as She asked, where She wished it.

But the Lord Bishop asked Juan Diego many things, to know for certain what had taken place, questioning him: Where did he see Her? What did the Lady look like whom he saw? And he told the Lord Bishop all that he had seen. But although he told him everything exactly, so that it seemed in all likelihood that She was the Immaculate Virgin, Mary most pure, the beloved Mother of Our Lord Jesus Christ, the Bishop said he could not be certain. He said: *It is not only with her words that we have to do, but also to obtain that for which she asks. It is very necessary to have some sign by which we may believe that it is really the Queen of Heaven who sends you.*

And Juan Diego, having heard him, said to the Lord Bishop: *My Lord, wait for whatever sign*

---

[2]   This can be loosely translated as "My beloved one."

it is that you ask for, and I will go at once to ask the Queen of Heaven, who sent me. And the Lord Bishop, seeing that he had agreed, and so that he should not be confused or worried, in any way, urged him to go; and then, calling some of his servants in whom he had much confidence, he asked them to follow and to watch where he went and see whomsoever it was that he went to see, and with whom he might speak. And this was done accordingly, and when Juan Diego reached the place where a bridge over the river, near the hill, met the royal highway, they lost him, and although they searched for him everywhere they could not find him in any part of that land. And so they returned, and not only were they weary, but extremely annoyed with him, over all that had happened, for they did not believe in him; they said that he had been deceiving himself, and had imagined all that he had come to relate, or perhaps he had dreamed it, and they agreed and said that if he should come again they would seize him and chastise him severely so that he would not lie another time.

The next day, Monday, when Juan Diego was to bring some sign by which he might be believed, he did not return, since, when he arrived at his house, an uncle of his who was staying there, named Juan Bernardino, was very ill of a burning fever; Juan Diego went at once to bring a doctor and then he procured medicine; but there still was not time because the man was very ill. Early in the morning his uncle begged him to go out to bring one of the priests from Tlatilolco so that he might be confessed, for he was very certain that his time had come to die, now that he was too weak to rise, and could not get well.

And on Tuesday, very early in the morning, Juan Diego left his house to go to Tlatilulco to call a priest, and as he was nearing the hill on the road which lies at the foot of the hill toward the west, which was his usual way, he said to himself: *If I go straight on, without doubt I will see Our Lady and She will persuade me to take the sign to the Lord Bishop; let us first do our duty; I will go first to call the priest for my poor uncle; will he not be waiting for him?*

With this he turned to another road at the foot of the slope and was coming down the other side towards the east to take a short cut to Mexico; he thought that by turning that way the Queen of Heaven would not see him, but She was watching for him, and he saw Her on the hilltop where he had always seen Her before, coming down that side of the slope, by the shortest way, and She said to him: *Xoycoyote mio, where are you going? What road is this you are taking?*

And he was frightened; it is not known whether he was disgusted with himself, or was ashamed, or perhaps he was struck with wonder; he prostrated himself before Her and greeted Her, saying: *My Daughter, my Xocoyota, God keep You, Lady. How did You waken? And is your most pure body well, perchance? My Holy One, I will bring pain to your heart — for I must tell You, my Virgin, that an uncle of mine, who is Your servant, is very sick, with an illness so strong that without doubt he will die of it; I am hastening to Your house in Mexico to call one of Our Lord's dear ones, our priests, to come to confess him, and when I have done that, then I will come back to carry out Your commandment. My Virgin, my Lady, forgive me, be patient with me until I do my duty, and then tomorrow I will come back to You.*

And having heard Juan Diego's explanation, the most holy and immaculate Virgin replied to him: *Listen, and be sure, my dear son, that I will protect you; do not be frightened or grieve, or let your heart be dismayed; however great the illness may be that you speak of, am I not here, I who am your mother, and is not my help a refuge? Am I not of your kind? Do not be concerned about your uncle's illness, for he is not now going to die; be assured that he is now already well. Is there anything else needful?* (And in that same hour his uncle was healed, as later he learned.)

And Juan Diego, having heard the words of the Queen of Heaven, greatly rejoiced and was convinced, and besought Her that She would send him again to see the Lord Bishop, to carry him some sign by which he could believe, as he had asked.

Whereupon the Queen of Heaven commanded him to climb up to the top of the hill where he had always seen her, saying: *Climb up to the top of the hill, my xocoyote, where you have seen me stand, and there you will find many flowers; pluck them and gather them together, and then bring them down here in my presence.*

Then Juan Diego climbed up the hill and when he had reached the top he marvelled to see blooming there many kinds of beautiful flowers of Castile, for it was then very cold, and he marvelled at their fragrance and odor. Then he began to pluck them, and gathered them together carefully, and wrapped them in his mantle, and when he had finished he descended and carried to the Queen of Heaven all the flowers he had plucked. She, when she had seen them, took them into her immaculate hands, gathered them together again, and laid them in his cloak once more and said to him: *My xoycoyote, all these flowers are the sign that you must take to the Bishop; in my name tell him that with this he will see and recognize my will and that he must do what I ask; and you who are my ambassador worthy of confidence, I counsel you to take every care that you open your mantle only in the presence of the Bishop, and you must make it known to him what it is that you carry, and tell him how I asked you to climb the hill to gather the flowers. Tell him also all that you have seen, so that you will persuade the Lord Bishop and he will see that the church is built for which I ask.*

And the Queen of Heaven having acquainted him with this, he departed, following the royal highway which leads directly to Mexico; he traveled content, because he was persuaded that now he would succeed; he walked carefully, taking great pains not to injure what he was carrying in his mantle; he went glorying in the fragrance of the beautiful flowers. When he arrived at the Bishop's palace, he encountered his majordomo[3] and other servants and asked them to tell the Bishop that he would like to see him; but none of them would, perhaps because it was still very early in the morning or, perhaps recognizing him, they were vexed or, because they knew how others of their household had lost him on the road when they were following him. They kept him waiting there a long time; he waited very humbly to see if they would call him, and when it was getting very late, they came to him to see what it was he was carrying as a proof of what he had related. And Juan Diego, seeing that he could not hide from them what he was carrying, when they had tormented him and jostled him and knocked him about, let them glimpse that he had roses, to deliver himself from them; and they, when they saw that they were roses of Castile, very fragrant and fresh, and not at all in their season, marvelled and wanted to take some of them. Three times they made bold to take them, but they could not because, when they tried to take them, they were not roses that they touched, but were as if painted or embroidered. Upon this, they went to the Lord Bishop to tell him what they had seen, and that the Indian who was there often before had come again and wanted to see him, and that they had kept him waiting there a long time.

The Lord Bishop, having heard this, knew that now this was the sign that should persuade him whether what the Indian had told him was true. He straightway asked that he be brought in to see him.

Having come into his presence, Juan Diego fell to his knees (as he had always done) and again related fully all that he had seen, and full of satisfaction and wonder he said: *My Lord, I have done that which you asked me; I went to tell my Holy One, the Queen of Heaven, the beloved Virgin Mary, Mother of God, how you asked me for some sign that you might believe that it was She who desired you to build Her the church for which She asked. And also I told Her how I had given my word that I would bring you some sign so that you could believe in what She had put in my care, and She heard with pleasure your suggestion and found it good, and just now, early this morning, She told me to come again*

3   Steward.

to see you and I asked Her for the sign that I had asked her to give me, and then She sent me to the hilltop where I have always seen Her, to pluck the flowers that I should see there. And when I had plucked them, I took them to the foot of the mountain where She had remained, and she gathered them into her immaculate hands and then put them again into my mantle for me to bring them to you. Although I knew very well that the hilltop was not a place for flowers, since it is a place of thorns, cactuses, caves and mezquites, I was not confused and did not doubt Her. When I reached the summit I saw flowers which are found in Castile; I took them and carried them to the Queen of Heaven and She told me that I must bring them to you, and now I have done it, so that you may see the sign that you ask for in order to do Her bidding, and so that you will see that my word is true. And here they are.

Whereupon he opened his white cloak, in which he was carrying the flowers, and as the roses of Castile dropped out to the floor, suddenly there appeared the most pure image of the most noble Virgin Mary, Mother of God, just exactly as it is, even now, in Her holy house, in Her church which is named Guadalupe; and the Lord Bishop, having seen this, and all those who were with him, knelt down and gazed with wonder, and then they grew sad, and were sorrowful, and were aghast, and the Lord Bishop with tenderness and weeping begged Her forgiveness for not having done Her bidding at once. And when he had finished, he untied from Juan Diego's neck the cloak on which was printed the figure of the Queen of Heaven. And then he carried it into his chapel; and Juan Diego remained all that day in the house of the Bishop, who did not want him to go. And the following day the Bishop said to him: *Come, show us where it is the Queen of Heaven wishes us to build Her church.* And when he had shown them where it was, he told them that he wanted to go to his house to see his uncle Juan Bernardino who had been very ill and he had set out for Tlatilolco to get a priest to confess him, but the Queen of Heaven had told him that he was already cured.

They did not let him go alone, but went with him to his house, and when they arrived there, they saw that his uncle was well and that nothing was now the matter with him; and the uncle wondered much when he saw such a company with his nephew, and all treating him with great courtesy, and he asked him: *How is it they treat you this way? And why do they reverence you so much?*

And Juan Diego told him that when he had gone from the house to call a confessor for him, he saw the Queen of Heaven on the hill called Tepeyacac and She had sent him to Mexico to see the Lord Bishop to have a church built for Her. And that she had also told him not to worry about his uncle, that he was now well.

Whereupon his uncle showed great joy and told him that it was true that at that very hour he had been healed, and that he himself had seen exactly that same Person, and that She had told him how She had sent him to Mexico to see the Bishop, and also that when he saw him again, to tell him all that he had seen also, and how, miraculously, he had been restored to health, and that the most holy Image of the Immaculate Virgin should be called Santa María de Guadalupe.

And after this they brought Juan Bernardino into the Lord Bishop's presence so that he might tell him under oath all that he had just related; and the Bishop kept the two men (that is, Juan Diego and Juan Bernardino) as his guests in his own house several days until the church for the Queen of Heaven was built where Juan Diego had shown them. And the Lord Bishop moved the sacred Image of the Queen of Heaven, which he had in his chapel, to the cathedral so that all the people could see it.

All the city was in a turmoil upon seeing Her most holy portrait; they saw that it had appeared miraculously, that no one in the world had painted it on Juan Diego's mantle; for this, on which the miraculous Image of the Queen of Heaven appeared was *ayate*, a coarse fabric made of cactus fibre, rather like homespun, and well woven, for at that time all the

Indian people covered themselves with *ayate*, except the nobles, the gentlemen and the captains of war, who dressed themselves in cloaks of cotton, or in cloaks made of wool.

The esteemed *ayate* upon which the Immaculate Virgin, Our Sovereign Queen, appeared unexpectedly is made of two pieces sewn together with threads of cotton; the height of Her sacred Image from the sole of Her foot to the top of Her head measures six hands, and one woman's hand. Her sacred face is very beautiful, grave, and somewhat dark; her precious body, according to this, small; her hands are held at her breast; the girdle at her waist is violet; her right foot only shows, a very little, and her slipper is earthen in color; her robe is rose-colored; in the shadows it appears deeper red, and it is embroidered with various flowers outlined in gold; pendant at her throat is a little gold circlet which is outlined with a black line around it; in the middle it has a cross; and one discovers glimpses or another, inner vestment of white cotton, daintily gathered at her wrists . . .

A Nahuatl Song to Holy Mary

This song, translated from the Nahuatl by Daniel Brinton, is attributed to the Archbishop Juan de Zumárraga.

Tico toco toco tiquiti quiti quiti quito; where it is to turn back again.

1. Resting amid parti-coloured flowers I rejoiced;
   the many shining flowers came forth, blossomed, burst
   forth in honour of our mother, Holy Mary.
2. They sang as the beauteous season grew, that
   I am but a creature of the one only God, a work of
   his hands that he has made.
3. Mayst thy soul walk in the light, mayst
   thou sing in the great book, mayst thou join the
   dance of the great rulers as our father the bishop speaks
   in the great temple.
4. God created thee, he caused thee to be born
   in a flowery place, and this new song to
   Holy Mary the bishop wrote for thee.

Records of the Spanish Inquisition, New Mexico, 1664

The most powerful and dreaded of all the colonial ecclesiastical tribunals was that of the Holy Office of the Inquisition. The Holy Office had been established in Spain shortly before the discovery of America for the purpose of rooting out heresy and dissent, and was one of the first Spanish institutions to be transplanted to the New World. In 1569, tribunals of the Holy Office were established in Lima and Mexico City, and another was created in Cartagena in 1611. They consisted of a board of inquisitors, consultants on theology and canon law, attorneys, jailers, paid informers, servants, and others. Causes for prosecution included lack of respect for ecclesiastical persons and institutions, sorcery and demonology, heresy, superstition, and bigamy.

PRIMARY WORK

Historical Documents relating to New Mexico, Nueva Vizcaya and Approaches Thereto, to 1773, collected by Adolph and Fanny Bandelier, English Translations. Edited and annotated by Charles Wilson Hackett (Washington: Carnegie Institution, 1937).

FURTHER READING

M. Perry and A. Cruz (eds) *Cultural Encounters: The Impact of the Inquisition in Spain and the New World* (Berkeley: University of California Press, 1991).

Joe S. Sando, *The Pueblo Indians* (San Francisco: The Indian Historian Press, 1976).

EXCERPTS FROM THE TRIAL OF BERNARDO DE MENDIZABAL

One of the persons to be tried by the Inquisition was Don Bernardo de Mendizabal, who was Governor of New Mexico from 1659 to 1661. The following excerpts from the records of his trial provide an insight into Spanish colonial perceptions of Pueblo Indian culture and rituals as well as attitudes regarding ecclesiastical orthodoxy and norms of sexual behavior. Though Mendizabal was ultimately acquitted, he died in prison in 1664 and was buried in unconsecrated ground.

He (the accused) relates a case of a mestizo named Ramirez, who took lands away from the Indians of Isleta[1], a matter of small importance, but the mestizo was insolent. This mestizo was in the escort in Los Hemes[2], where he had trouble with Fray[3] Blas de Flerrera. . . . He does not remember whether he gave permission to the Indians of Isleta and Tesuque to dance the *catsinas*[4] . . . He says that the dance contains nothing of superstition, and the *doctrineros*[5], whenever they have need of an entire pueblo for the tasks connected with their gainful occupations, have the Indians dance it. In the *residencia*[6] of the accused this charge was brought against him, and he was acquitted of it by the royal *audiencia*[7], and it was ordered that in future the *doctrineros* should report what there was bad about this dance. Thus he replies.

The accused said that he never knew that this dance was prohibited because it was bad, nor for any other reason, and that the Indians of those parts customarily ask permission to dance it: they are ordered to dance it in public where they may be seen, and not in their *estufas*[8] so that they may not observe any superstitious practices. The accused knew, as he has said, that the ministers had this dance performed whenever it suited their own convenience. . . . The command to report if there was anything evil in the dance was tantamount to saying that it should not be prohibited without this having been done; for he knows that often the *doctrineros* in those parts, even the just and honest ones, attempt to forbid the Indians, whom they regard as slaves, to do certain things. The accused has already said that he knew neither that this dance was bad nor that it was prohibited, but he did know that it had been danced before and that even the Spaniards danced it in the time when Don Luis de Rocas was governor, in the plaza of

---

[1]   Isleta, Jemez, and Tesuque are communities existing among the Pueblo Indians of New Mexico.

[2]   Probably Jemez.

[3]   Father.

[4]   The cat'sina (also spelled Kat'sina or Kachina) groups perform sacred ceremonial dances at certain times of year, featuring masked dancers and clowns. The purpose of these dances was (and is) to ensure rain for the crops and to promote community integration and welfare.

[5]   Missionaries charged with teaching the Catholic catechism; literally, the indoctrinators.

[6]   Residence.

[7]   Tribunal.

[8]   The kivas or ceremonial chambers where traditional Pueblo rituals were (and still are) performed.

the villa[9] of Santa Fe; and that afterwards when he was accused of having permitted the dance, he did not forbid it nor could he, because he was not [then] governor; nor would he have raised the question in any case, but on the contrary he would have prohibited any person from saying that this dance was bad or could be bad. . . . He says that the statements made about the dance he knows to be false because of what he has already said, namely that the religious cause them to be danced, and if there had been anything to the contrary the accused would have known it . . . nor was his attention called, as is said, by the guardian of Sandia, to this or to any other impropriety. On the other hand, when the accused was in this pueblo and had dined with Father Miguel de Guebara, the *doctrinero*, the accused said to him: "Father, what is there bad about this dance of the *catsinas* for I have seen it, and it is only an evidence of a lightsome disposition?" The father responded: "It may be bad. Sir." To which the accused replied: "Well, why has your reverence permitted it to be danced?" He denied this, whereupon the accused called some Indians of the pueblo, and they told him through the interpreter of the said religious that it was true, and they had named custodians and religious before whom and by whose orders they had danced it . . . (He always says that he has seen nothing bad in the *catsinas*. He did not see the dances which were performed in secret.) He said that when the governor arrives at a pueblo and conducts his visitation, the Indians ask through an interpreter for permission to dance; the accused used to tell them to dance, provided it was in the public plaza and not within their council chambers, lest they might engage in some evil practice or dance therein. He added that permission is general, not for a specific dance, for he does not know the dances which they dance . . .

The accused does not know the particular features of the dance of the *catsinas*; he does not know because the license was asked for in the pueblo named, and he judges that it must be the most popular dance of the Indians, because it is so noisy. Not only do the Indians participate in it, but others who are not Indians endeavor to win prizes. . . . He was told that, inasmuch as this was the favorite dance of the Indians, they should not be refused general permission to dance it, but should be allowed to perform it as well as other dances. What he asks is why did they request special permission to perform this dance? For, if it was included in the general permission, they already had it; and if it was not included, some note should be taken of the reason why it was not.

He said that the Indians of those provinces are of most diverse nations and tongues, and each one dances according to his custom; they do not all dance the *catsinas* generally. He has already said that he did not know why his permission should have been asked especially for the pueblo of Tesuque unless it was for the dance of the *catsinas*, because this was the dance of that pueblo, which the accused had not visited before or since. . . .

. . . He said that it is false that the accused summoned the Indians of all the pueblos of his territory or of a single pueblo; as he has said, the Indians of the pueblo of Tesuque came to the villa of Santa Fe and, as he remembers, with them came their *encomendero*[10] Francisco Gomez, and Juan Griego as interpreter. Among other things they asked permission to dance the *catsinas*. The accused asked what dance this was. The *encomendero* having replied, as he recalls, as well as the interpreter and others present, concerning the nature of the dance, stating that it was simply an exhibition of agility, the accused wanted to see it desiring also that the guardian of the villa, Father Diego Rodriguez, who administered the Indians, should see it. In order that

[9]   Town.

[10]   The encomienda system was a feudal arrangement under which the Pueblo Indians were expected not only to pay tithes to the Church but also to "donate" proceeds from their farming activities, such as wheat, corn, and livestock, to the Spanish authorities. The encomendero was the official in charge of collecting these tributes.

he might do so, the accused sent Toribio de la Huerta to call him. The latter returned, saying that the friar, Diego Rodriguez, was finishing his prayers, or some other employment. The accused, seeing that it was late and that the Indians had to return to their pueblo, told them to dance. They did so after this fashion: Ten or twelve Indians dressed themselves in the ordinary clothes which they commonly wear and put on masks painted with human figures of men; then half of them, with timbrels[11], such as are commonly used in New Spain, in their hands, went out to the plaza. The others carried thongs, or whips, in their hands. They placed in the middle of the plaza four or six watermelons; the accused does not remember whether they brought them, or whether they took them from those which they had brought to him and which he had there in the living-room of his house. After putting the watermelons in the middle of the plaza, those who were dancing, continued to do so noisily, sounding the timbrels crazily, as they are accustomed to do, and saying "Hu, hu, hu." In this fashion they circled around the plaza and the other Indians with the thongs went along, leaping, watching the watermelons, or prizes, from a distance, and allowing opportunity for other youths and boys, Indians or others, to slip in and snatch the watermelons. The one who did so they chased, and if they caught him they gave him many blows with the thongs, but if they did not catch him, he, being more fleet of foot, carried off the watermelon without receiving any lashes. When several had thus run away the dance stopped, and it contained no other feature. The accused asked them, having noticed that the response, or echo, given by the Indians who were dancing contained no distinguishable word, whether any of it signified or meant anything. The interpreter and the others who knew the language of these Indians said that it meant nothing. To the accused it seemed mere foolishness on the part of the Indians, and an entertainment which proved their fleetness of foot. When they had finished dancing as has been described, and it was very short, Fray Diego Rodriguez came in great haste, saying, " Lord," and beginning to pray; then: "Let us see this dance." The accused said to him: "You must have been idling, father; the dance is over, and the Indians have gone back to their pueblo." This is what happened. . . .

It seemed to the accused a pleasurable entertainment, on account of the races and the lashings, to be sure . . . He only remembers one Indian of the pueblo of Sandia, whose little house, which he had built near his pueblo in spite of the command mentioned, the *doctrinero* of the pueblo, Fray Miguel de Guebara, burned with his own hands . . . What he remembers is that this Indian, when he left off staying with the *doctrinero* of Taxique, went to live about a league away, more or less, between the pueblos of Taxique and Cuarac, in the house of Joseph Nieto, a man who administers ordinary justice there. The accused remembers that the *doctrinero* of Cuarac, Father Somebody de Freitas, wrote to this man that neither he nor his family went to mass. The accused called Joseph Nieto to him and chided him, and he proved that the friar was wrong.

. . . The accused slept with his wife in a room apart from the household; he has always done this, as was proper. . . . The women servants slept in a room a little farther in, with the door open, and, being women, they came in and out as they liked, when necessary, even when the accused and his wife were in the bed. The men-servants were ordered that upon coming to the room, they should speak from the doorway and not come in, for the wife might be undressed in bed or risen and in her underclothing; this was simply out of regard for modesty and decency. . . .

. . . The accused never had any religious ceremonies in his house, and only two representations of the Christ. One of these was on an altar in his wife's drawing-room, under a canopy so

---

[11] Tambourines.

high that a ladder was required to reach up to clean it. The other statue was under a canopy at the head of his bed, where it was more accessible . . . (Speaking of a picture of St Michael, he asserts that) as a matter of special devotion he had an Indian paint it and ordered Manuel de Noriega to assist him. As there was no copy available, and [no guide save] the idea of the Indian, it was possible that, as the work of such a hand, and on such material as a piece of leather, the figure should come out rather imperfect, and the accused may have said as much, but not by way of derision or jest, as is attributed to him. . . . He said that he had always praised the chapels, or churches, which are in that country, which, in fact, are not remarkable, nor did he see any particular painting or figure or image which especially attracted his attention. . . . He confesses having had carnal intercourse with Ana Rodriguez, and Geronima, the wife of Francisco de Anaya.

The accused said that it is true that he once knew carnally the mestiza Teresa, but this was not a crime, nor cause for judicial trial; nor was it necessary for a mestiza or an Indian woman to appeal to a judge. It is also true that he knew carnally Petrona de Gamboa four or five times, and that she herself gave occasion for it.

The hearing was ended in March, 1664, Mendizabal then being very ill. He died in the prison on September 16, 1664. . . . He was absolved. On April 16, 1671, the Inquisitors said that they agreed, and that it was their vote and opinion that the memory of Don Bernardo Lopez de Mendizabal should be absolved from the odium of the judgement, and that it should be declared and ordered that his body be exhumed and his bones taken from the place in which they are and given ecclesiastical burial.

Don Antonio de Otermín (*fl.* 1680)

When he was appointed Governor of New Mexico in 1678, don Antonio de Otermín took over a territory with a complex and difficult historical legacy. For more than a century, the neo-feudal *encomienda* system had extracted goods and labor from the local Native Pueblo groups. Each year taxes in the form of produce were enforced by the civil authorities and hauled by oxcarts to Santa Fe. As well, the local ecosystem was altered by the use of land for Spanish cattle; overgrazing and the consequent soil erosion caused water shortages and economic hardship. Another cause of friction was the suppression of Pueblo spiritual traditions and rituals and the forced imposition of Catholicism.

Matters came to a head in 1680, when the Native communities of New Mexico rose in revolt. Led by Pope, a Tewa religious leader, Pueblo forces attacked Santa Fe, killing 21 Franciscan priests and effectively gaining control of northern New Mexico. Otermín's defeat at the hands of the Pueblo rebels was a major setback for the Spanish crown, given the fear that it could spark off similar insurrections elsewhere. Otermín's letter thus attempts to justify the ignominious rout of Spanish forces at the hands of presumably inferior Native groups. In order to do so, he invokes the "wickedness and treason" of the Natives in order to appeal for a major campaign to reconquer the lost territory.

PRIMARY WORK

C. W. Hackett (ed.) *Historical Documents Relating to New Mexico, Nueva Vizcaya, and Approaches Thereto, to 1773*, 3 vols (Washington: The Carnegie Institution, 1926).

FURTHER READING

Joe Sando, *The Pueblo Indians* (San Francisco: The Indian Historical Press, 1976).

LETTER ON THE PUEBLO REVOLT OF 1680

My very reverend father, Sir, and friend, most beloved Fray Francisco de Ayeta: The time has come when, with tears in my eyes and deep sorrow in my heart, I commence to give an account of the lamentable tragedy, such as has never before happened in the world, which has occurred in this miserable kingdom and holy *custodia*[1].

His Divine Majesty having thus permitted it because of my grievous sins. Before beginning my narration I desire, as one obligated and grateful, to give your reverence the thanks due for the demonstrations of affection and kindness which you have given in your solicitude in ascertaining and inquiring for definite notices about both my life and those of the rest in this miserable kingdom, in the midst of persistent reports which had been circulated of the deaths of myself and the others, and for sparing neither any kind of effort nor large expenditures. For this only Heaven can reward your reverence, though I do not doubt that his Majesty (may God keep him) will do so.

After I sent my last letter to your reverence by the *maese de campo*[2], Pedro de Leyba, while the necessary things were being made ready alike for the escort and in the way of provisions, for the most expeditious despatch of the returning carts and their guards, as your reverence had enjoined me, I received information that a plot for a general uprising of the Christian Indians was being formed and was spreading rapidly. This was wholly contrary to the existing peace and tranquillity in this miserable kingdom, not only among the Spaniards and natives, but even on the part of the heathen enemy, for it had been a long time since they had done us any considerable damage. It was my misfortune that I learned of it on the eve of the day set for the beginning of the said uprising, and though I immediately, at that instant, notified the lieutenant-general on the lower river and all the other *alcaldes mayores*[3] – so that they could take every care and precaution against whatever might occur, and so that they could make every effort to guard and protect the religious ministers and the temples, the cunning and cleverness of the rebels were such, and so great, that my efforts were of little avail. To this was added a certain degree of negligence by reason of the [report of the] uprising not having been given entire credence, as is apparent from the ease with which they captured and killed both those who were escorting some of the religious, as well as some citizens in their houses, and, particularly, in the efforts that they made to prevent my orders to the lieutenant-general passing through. This was the place where most of the forces of the kingdom were, and from which I could expect some help, but of three orders which I sent to the said lieutenant-general, not one reached his hands. The first messenger was killed and the others did not pass beyond Santo Domingo, because of their having encountered on the road the certain notice of the deaths of the religious[4] who were in that convent, and of the *alcalde mayor*, some other guards, and six more Spaniards whom they captured on that road. Added to this is the situation of this kingdom which, as your reverence is aware, makes it so easy for the said [Indian] *alcaldes* to carry out their devil designs, for it is entirely composed of *estancias*[5], quite distant from one another.

On the eve [of the day] of the glorious San Lorenzo[6], having received notice of the said rebellion from the governors of Pecos and Tanos, [who said] that two Indians had left the

---

[1] Guardianship.

[2] Military official.

[3] Municipal authorities.

[4] Missionary priests and friars, who were seen as threaten-

ing the traditional religious beliefs of Native American groups in the area.

[5] Farms.

[6] St Laurence, martyred on the gridiron.

Theguas, and particularly the pueblo of Thesuque[7], to which they belonged, to notify them to come and join the revolt, and that they [the governors] came to tell me of it and of how they were unwilling to participate in such wickedness and treason, saying that they now regarded the Spaniards as their brothers, I thanked them for their kindness in giving the notice, and told them to go to their pueblos and remain quiet. I busied myself immediately in giving the said orders which I mentioned to your reverence, and on the following morning as I was about to go to mass there arrived Pedro Hidalgo, who had gone to the pueblo of Thesuque, accompanying Father Fray Juan Pio, who went there to say mass. He told me that the Indians of the said pueblo had killed the said Father Fray Pio and that he himself had escaped miraculously. [He told me also] that the said Indians had retreated to the sierra with all the cattle and horses belonging to the convent, and with their own.

The receipt of this news left us all in the state that may be imagined. I immediately and instantly sent the *maese de campo*, Francisco Gomez, with a squadron of soldiers sufficient to investigate this case and also to attempt to extinguish the flame of the ruin already begun. He returned here on the same day, telling me that [the report] of the death of the said Fray Juan Pio was true. He said also that there had been killed that same morning Father Fray Tomas de Torres, *guardián* of Nambe, and his brother, with the latter's wife and a child, and another resident of Thaos, and also Father Fray Luis de Morales, *guardián* of San Ildefonso, and the family of Francisco de Anaya; and in Poxuaque Don Joseph de Goitia, Francisco Ximenez, his wife and family, and Dona Petronila de Salas with ten sons and daughters; and that they had robbed and profaned the convents and [had robbed] all the haciendas of those murdered and also all the horses and cattle of that jurisdiction and La Canada.

Upon receiving this news I immediately notified the *alcalde mayor* of that district to assemble all the people in his house in a body, and told him to advise at once the *alcalde mayor* of Los Taos to do the same. On this same day I received notice that two members of a convoy had been killed in the pueblo of Santa Clara, six others having escaped by flight. Also at the same time the *sargento mayor*[8], Bernabe Márquez, sent to ask me for assistance, saying that he was surrounded and hard pressed by the Indians of the Queres and Tanos nations. Having sent the aid for which he asked me, and an order for those families of Los Cerrillos to come to the villa, I instantly arranged for all the people in it and its environs to retire to the *casas reales*[9]. Believing that the uprising of the Tanos and Pecos might endanger the person of the reverend father custodian, I wrote him to set out at once for the villa, not feeling reassured even with the escort which the lieutenant took, at my orders, but when they arrived with the letter they found that the Indians had already killed the said father custodian; Father Fray Domingo de Vera; Father Fray Manuel Tinoco, the minister *guardián* of San Marcos, who was there; and Father Fray Fernando de Velasco, *guardián* of Los Pecos, near the pueblo of Galisteo, he having escaped that far from the fury of the Pecos. The latter killed in that pueblo Fray Juan de la Pedrosa, two Spanish women, and three children. There died also at the hands of the said enemies in Galisteo Joseph Nieto, two sons of *Maestre de Campo* Leiba, Francisco de Anaya, the younger, who was with the escort, and the wives of *Maestre de Campo* Leiba and Joseph Nieto, with all their daughters and families. I also learned definitely on this day that there had died in the pueblo of Santo Domingo fathers Fray Juan de Talaban, Fray Francisco Antonio Lorenzana, and Fray Joseph de Montesdoca, and the *alcalde mayor*, Andres de Peralta, together with the rest of the men who went as escort.

Seeing myself with notices of so many and such untimely deaths, and that not having

---

7   Pueblo Indian villages located between Santa Fe and Taoe.   9   Governor's palace.

8   Sergeant-major.

received any word from the lieutenant-general was probably due to the fact that he was in the same exigency and confusion, or that the Indians had killed most of those on the lower river, and considering also that in the pueblo of Los Taos the fathers *guardiánes* of that place and of the pueblo of Pecuries might be in danger, as well as the *alcalde mayor* and the residents of that valley, and that at all events it was the only place from which I could obtain any horses and cattle – for all these reasons I endeavored to send a relief of soldiers. Marching out for that purpose, they learned that in La Canada, as in Los Taos and Pecuries, the Indians had risen in rebellion, joining the Apaches of the Achos nation.[10] In Pecuries they had killed Francisco Blanco de la Vega, a *mulata*[11] belonging to the *maese de campo*, Francisco Xavier, and a son of the said *mulata*. Shortly thereafter I learned that they also killed in the pueblo of Taos the father *guardián*, Fray Francisco de Mora, and Father Fray Mathias Rendon, the *guardián* of Pecuries, and Fray Antonio de Pro, and the *alcalde mayor*, as well as another fourteen or fifteen soldiers, along with all the families of the inhabitants of that valley, all of whom were together in the convent. Thereupon I sent an order to the *alcalde mayor*, Luis de Quintana, to come at once to the villa with all the people whom he had assembled in his house, so that, joined with those of us who were in the *casa reales*, we might endeavor to defend ourselves against the enemy's invasions. It was necessarily supposed that they would join all their forces to take our lives, as was seen later by experience.

On Tuesday, the thirteenth of the said month, at about nine o'clock in the morning, there came in sight of us in the suburb of Analco, in the cultivated field of the hermitage of San Miguel, and on the other side of the river of the villa, all the Indians of the Tanos and Pecos nations and the Querez of San Marcos, armed and giving war-whoops. As I learned that one of the Indians who was leading them was from the villa and had gone to join them shortly before, I sent some soldiers to summon him and tell him on my behalf that he could come to see me in entire safety, so that I might ascertain from him the purpose for which they were coming. Upon receiving this message he came to where I was, and, since he was known, as I say, I asked him how it was that he had gone crazy too – being an Indian who spoke our language, was so intelligent, and had lived all his life in the villa among the Spaniards, where I had placed such confidence in him – and was now coming as a leader of the Indian rebels. He replied to me that they had elected him as their captain, and that they were carrying two banners, one white and the other red, and that the white one signified peace and the red one war. Thus if we wished to choose the white it must be [upon our agreeing] to leave the country, and if we chose the red, we must perish, because the rebels were numerous and we were very few; there was no alternative, inasmuch as they had killed so many religious and Spaniards.

On hearing his reply, I spoke to him very persuasively, to the effect that he and the rest of his followers were Catholic Christians, [asking] how they expected to live without the religious; and said that even though they had committed so many atrocities, still there was a remedy, for if they would return to the obedience of his Majesty they would be pardoned; and that thus he should go back to his people and tell them in my name all that had been said to him, and persuade them to [agree to] it and to withdraw from where they were; and that he was to advise me of what they might reply. He came back from there after a short time, saying that his people asked that all classes of Indians who were in our power be given up to them, both those in the service of the Spaniards and those of the Mexican nation of that suburb of Analco. He demanded also that his wife and children be given up to him, and likewise that all

---

[10]   The Spaniards must have found this highly alarming, given the traditional enmity between the Apaches and the Pueblo Indians.

[11]   Of mixed racial background.

the Apache men and women whom the Spaniards had captured in war [be turned over to them], inasmuch as some Apaches who were among them were asking for them. If these things were not done they would declare war immediately, and they were unwilling to leave the place where they were because they were awaiting the Taos, Pecuries, and Theguas nations, with whose aid they would destroy us.

Seeing his determination, and what they demanded of us, and especially the fact that it was untrue that there were any Apaches among them, because they were at war with all of them, and that these parleys were intended solely to obtain his wife and children and to gain time for the arrival of the other rebellious nations to join them and besiege us, and that during this time they were robbing and sacking what was in the said hermitage and the houses of the Mexicans, I told him (having given him all the preceding admonitions as a Christian and a Catholic) to return to his people and say to them that unless they immediately desisted from sacking the houses and dispersed, I would send to drive them away from there. Whereupon he went back, and his people received him with peals of bells and trumpets, giving loud shouts in sign of war.

With this, seeing after a short time that they not only did not cease the pillage but were advancing toward the villa with shamelessness and mockery, I ordered all the soldiers to go out and attack them until they succeeded in dislodging them from that place. Advancing for this purpose, they joined battle, killing some at the first encounter. Finding themselves repulsed, they took shelter and fortified themselves in the said hermitage and the houses of the Mexicans, from which they defended themselves a part of the day with the firearms that they had and with arrows. Having set fire to some of the houses in which they were, thus having them surrounded and at the point of perishing, there appeared on the road from Thesuque a band of the people whom they were awaiting, who were all the Teguas. Thus it was necessary to go to prevent these latter from passing on to the villa, because the *casas reales* were poorly defended; whereupon the said Tanos and Pecos fled to the mountains and the two parties joined together, sleeping that night in the sierra of the villa. Many of the rebels remained dead and wounded, and our men retired to the *casas reales* with one soldier killed and some fourteen or fifteen soldiers wounded, to attend them and entrench and fortify ourselves as best we could.

On the morning of the following day, Wednesday, I saw the enemy come down all together from the sierra where they had slept, toward the villa. Mounting my horse, I went out with the few forces that I had to meet them, above the convent. The enemy saw me and halted, making ready to resist the attack. They took up a better position, gaining the eminence of some ravines and thick timber, and began to give war-whoops, as if daring me to attack them.

I paused thus for a short time, in battle formation, and the enemy turned aside from the eminence and went nearer the sierras[12], to gain the one which comes down behind the house of the *maese de campo*, Francisco Gomez. There they took up their position, and this day passed without our having any further engagements or skirmishes than had already occurred, we taking care that they should not throw themselves upon us and burn the church and the houses of the villa.

The next day, Thursday, the enemy obliged us to take the same step as on the day before of mounting on horseback in fighting formation. There were only some light skirmishes to prevent their burning and sacking some of the houses which were at a distance from the main part of the villa. I knew well enough that these dilatory[13] tactics were to give time for the people of the other nations who were missing to join them in order to besiege and attempt to destroy us,

<hr />

[12]   Mountains.

[13]   Delaying.

but the height of the places in which they were, so favorable to them and on the contrary so unfavorable to us, made it impossible for us to go and drive them out before they should all be joined together.

On the next day, Friday, the nations of the Taos, Pecuries, Hemes, and Querez having assembled during the past night, when dawn came more than 2,500 Indians fell upon us in the villa, fortifying and entrenching themselves in all its houses and at the entrances of all the streets, and cutting off our water, which comes through the *arroyo*[14] and the irrigation canal in front of the *casas reales*. They burned the holy temple and many houses in the villa. We had several skirmishes over possession of the water, but seeing that it was impossible to hold even this against them, and almost all the soldiers of the post being already wounded, I endeavored to fortify myself in the *casas reales* and to make a defense without leaving their walls. [The Indians were] so dexterous and so bold that they came to set fire to the doors of the fortified tower of Nuestra Señora de las Casas Reales, and, seeing such audacity, and the manifest risk that we ran of having the *casas reales* set on fire, I resolved to make a sally[15] into the plaza of the said *casas reales* with all my available force of soldiers, without any protection, to attempt to prevent the fire which the enemy was trying to set. With this endeavor we fought the whole afternoon, and, since the enemy, as I said above, had fortified themselves and made embrasures[16] in all the houses, and had plenty of arquebuses[17], powder, and balls. They did us much damage. Night overtook us thus and God was pleased that they should desist somewhat from shooting us with arquebuses and arrows. We passed this night, like the rest, with much care and watchfulness, and suffered greatly from thirst because of the scarcity of water.

On the next day, Saturday, they began at dawn to press us harder and more closely with gunshots, arrows, and stones, saying to us that now we should not escape them, and that besides their own numbers, they were expecting help from the Apaches whom they had already summoned. They fatigued us greatly on this day, because all was fighting, and above all we suffered from thirst, as we were already oppressed by it. At nightfall, because of the evident peril in which we found ourselves by their gaining the two stations where cannon were mounted, which we had at the doors of the *casas reales*, aimed at the entrances of the streets, in order to bring them inside it was necessary to assemble all the forces that I had with me, because we realized that this was their [the Indians'] intention. Instantly all the said Indian rebels began a chant of victory and raised war-whoops, burning all the houses of the villa, and they kept us in this position the entire night, which I assure your reverence was the most horrible that could be thought of or imagined, because the whole villa was a torch and everywhere were war chants and shouts. What grieved us most were the dreadful flames from the church and the scoffing and ridicule which the wretched and miserable Indian rebels made of the sacred things, intoning the *alabado*[18] and the other prayers of the church with jeers.

Finding myself in this state, with the church and the villa burned, and with the few horses, sheep, goats, and cattle which we had without feed or water for so long that many had already died, and the rest were about to do so, and with such a multitude of people, most of them children and women, so that our numbers in all came to about a thousand persons, perishing with thirst – for we had nothing to drink during these two days except what had been kept in some jars and pitchers that were in the *casas reales* – surrounded by such a wailing of women and children, with confusion everywhere, I determined to take the resolution of going out in the morning to fight with the enemy until dying or conquering. Considering that the best

---

[14] Small stream.
[15] To rush out suddenly.
[16] Openings through which cannon can be discharged.

[17] An early type of gun, with matchlock and trigger.
[18] Hymn related with the sacrament of the Eucharist.

strength and armor were prayers to appease the Divine wrath, though on the preceding days the poor women had made them with fervor, that night I charged them to do so increasingly, and told the father *guardián* and the other two religious to say mass for us at dawn, and exhort all alike to repentance for their sins and to conformance with the Divine will, and to absolve us from guilt and punishment. These things being done, all of us who could mounted our horses, and the rest [went] on foot with their arquebuses, and some Indians who were in our service with their bows and arrows, and in the best order possible we directed our course toward the house of the *maese de campo*, Francisco Xavier, which was the place where (apparently) there were the most people and where they had been most active and boldest. On coming out of the entrance to the street it was seen that there was a great number of Indians. They were attacked in force, and though they resisted the first charge bravely, finally they were put to flight, many of them being overtaken and killed. Then turning at once upon those who were in the streets leading to the convent, they also were put to flight with little resistance. The houses in the direction of the house of the said *maese de campo*, Francisco Xavier, being still full of Indians who had taken refuge in them, and seeing that the enemy with the punishment and deaths that we had inflicted upon them in the first and second assaults were withdrawing toward the hills, giving us a little room, we laid siege to those who remained fortified in the said houses. Though they endeavored to defend themselves, and did so, seeing that they were being set afire and that they would be burned to death, those who remained alive surrendered and much was made of them. The deaths of both parties in this and the other encounters exceeded three hundred Indians.

Finding myself a little relieved by this miraculous event, though I had lost much blood from two arrow wounds which I had received in the face and from a remarkable gunshot wound in the chest on the day before, I immediately had water given to the cattle, the horses, and the people. Because we now found ourselves with very few provisions for so many people, and without hope of human aid, considering that our not having heard in so many days from the people on the lower river would be because of their all having been killed, like the others in the kingdom, or at least of their being or having been in dire straits, with the view of aiding them and joining with them into one body, so as to make the decisions most conducive to his Majesty's service, on the morning of the next day, Monday, I set out for La Isleta, where I judged the said comrades on the lower river would be. I trusted in Divine Providence, for I left without a crust of bread or a grain of wheat or maize, and with no other provisions for the convoy of so many people except four hundred animals and two carts belonging to private persons, and, for food, a few sheep, goats, and cows.

In this manner, and with this fine provision, besides a few small ears of maize that we found in the fields, we went as far as the pueblo of La Alameda, where we learned from an old Indian whom we found in a maize-field that the lieutenant-general with all the residents of his jurisdictions had left some fourteen or fifteen days before to return to El Paso to meet the carts. This news made me very uneasy, alike because I could not be persuaded that he would have left without having news of me as well as of all the others in the kingdom, and because I feared that from his absence there would necessarily follow the abandonment of this kingdom. On hearing this news I acted at once, sending four soldiers to overtake the said lieutenant-general and the others who were following him, with orders that they were to halt wherever they should come up with them. Going in pursuit of them, they overtook them at the place of Fray Cristobal. The lieutenant-general, Alonso Garcia, overtook me at the place of Las Nutrias, and a few days' march thereafter I encountered the *maese de campo*, Pedro de Leiba, with all the people under his command, who were escorting these carts and who came to ascertain whether or not we were dead, as your reverence had charged him to do, and to find me, ahead of the supply train. I was so short of provisions and of everything else that at best I should have had a little maize for six days or so.

Thus, after God, the only succor and relief that we have rests with your reverence and in your diligence: Wherefore, and in order that your reverence may come immediately; because of the great importance to the service of God and the king of your reverence's presence here, I am sending the said *maese de campo*, Pedro de Leyba, with the rest of the men whom he brought so that he may come as escort for your reverence and the carts or mule-train in which we hope you will bring us some assistance of provisions. Because of the haste which the case demands I do not write at more length, and for the same reason I cannot make a report at present concerning the above to the señor viceroy, because the *autos*[19] are not verified and there has been no opportunity to conclude them. I shall leave it until your reverence's arrival here. For the rest I refer to the account which will be given to your reverence by the father secretary, Fray Buene Ventura de Berganza. I am slowly overtaking the other party, which is sixteen leagues from here, with the view of joining them and discussing whether or not this miserable kingdom can be recovered. For this purpose I shall not spare any means in the service of God and of his Majesty, losing a thousand lives if I had them, as I have lost my estate and part of my health, and shedding my blood for God. May He protect me and permit me to see your reverence in this place at the head of the relief. September 8, 1680. Your servant, countryman, and friend kisses your reverence's hand. DON ANTONIO DE OTERMÍN.

[19]   Official reports.

New France

Jerome Lalemant (1593–1673)

Jerome Lalemant, a Jesuit priest, went to Canada in 1638, and was named Superior of the mission to the Hurons. There, he carried out a census of the tribe (thirty-two villages, 12,000 people in 1639), and wrote the *Relations des Hurons*. The following excerpt describes an earthquake which took place in 1663, and the ways in which it was interpreted both by French settlers and the local Native peoples.

PRIMARY WORK

Translated by Susan Castillo from Jerome Lalament, "Le tremble-terre," in *Anthologie de la Littérature Québécoise, vol. I, Écrites de la Nouvelle France 1534–1760*, ed. Léopold LeBlanc (Montreal: La Presse, 1978).

FURTHER READING

J. F. Bosher, *Business and religion in the age of New France (1600–1760)* (Toronto: Canadian Scholars' Press, 1994).
Laurent Mailhot, *La littérature Québécoise: depuis ses origines* (Montreal: Typo, 1997).

THE EARTHQUAKE

Heaven and Earth have spoken to us often for the last year. It was a pleasant, unknown language, which cast us into fear and admiration at the same time. The Heavens began with beautiful phenomena, and the Earth followed them with furious heavings which made us think that these voices of the air, mute and brilliant, were words borne on air, as they presaged the convulsions which would make us tremble in making the Earth itself tremble.

Last autumn we saw serpents embracing, entwined about each other forming a caduceus[1], and flying through the air on wings of fire. We saw over Quebec a great flaming globe, which turned the night into day, though the sparks which it cast everywhere caused the pleasure given by looking at it to be mixed with fear. This same meteor appeared above Montreal; but

---

[1]   Double spiral.

it seemed to emerge from the bosom of the Moon, with a noise like that of cannons or thunder, and after arching for three leagues into the air, was lost from sight behind the large mountain which gives this island its name.

But what seemed most extraordinary to us was the appearance of three suns. It was a beautiful day last winter, and at eight o'clock in the morning, a slight vapour rose from our great river, and when struck by the rays of the sun, became transparent, though nonetheless with enough consistency two images which this Star[2] painted below. These three suns were in a nearly straight line, a short distance one from the others. According to appearances, the real one was in the middle, and was flanked by the two others. All three were crowned by a rainbow, where the colours were not fixed, seeming at one moment varied and the next a luminous white, as if above them there were an exceedingly strong light.

This spectacle lasted nearly two hours the first time it occurred, on 7th January 1663; and the second time, which was on the 14th of the same month, it did not last so long, but only until the colours of the rainbow began to fade little by little, just as the two suns were eclipsed as well, leaving the one in the middle as victor.

We could include here the eclipse of the Sun which occurred in Quebec the first day of September 1663, which according to very exact observations, turned the forests pale, sombre and melancholy. Its beginning was at one hour twenty-four minutes forty-two seconds after noon, and its end at three fifty-two, forty-four seconds.

It was on the 5th of February 1663, around five-thirty in the evening, that a great noise was heard all over Canada. This noise, which seemed as though there was fire within the houses, made everyone run out fleeing from such an unexpected blaze; but instead of seeing smoke and flames, they were astonished to see the walls rocking back and forth and the stones moving about as though they were loose; the roofs seemed to buckle in one direction, then in another; the Bells rang by themselves; the beams, the joists and the floorboards cracked; the land leapt about, making the palisades dance in a way that could hardly be believed if we had not seen it ourselves in several places.

Everyone ran outside, the animals fled, the children were crying in the streets, the men and women were gripped with terror and did not know where to take refuge, thinking they would be crushed under the ruins of the houses or swallowed up in an abyss that would open under their feet. Some knelt on the snow, crying for mercy; others spent the rest of the night in prayers, because the earthquake continued with a certain rumble, very much like that of ships on the sea, so much so that the people felt their blood run cold just as it had at sea. Disorder was even greater in the forests: it seemed that there had been a combat among the trees, who struck one another; it was not just their branches, but one might even think that their trunks had emerged from their places to leap upon one another, with a noise and chaos which made our Savages say that the entire forest was drunk.

There seemed to be war among the mountains as well, where some uprooted themselves to fall upon the others, leaving great abysses in the places from which they had leapt. The trees they bore were turned upside down, some with the branches below in the place of the roots, leaving a forest of upturned trunks.

Amid this general debris, ice five and six feet thick was shattered into small pieces. When the ice opened in several places, from it came clouds of smoke, or jets of mud and sand which rose high into the air. Our fountains went dry, or had only water tasting of sulphur. The rivers were either lost or tainted, with the water of some becoming yellow, some red; and our great St Lawrence River seemed whitish as far as Tadoussac, a strange thing which will surprise and

2   The sun.

astonish those who know the quality of the waters of this great river which flows around the Isle d'Orleans and how difficult it would be to make them seem white.

. . . Indeed, three circumstances make this earthquake remarkable. The first is the time it lasted, continuing until the month of August, that is to say, six months. It is true that not all the quakes were equally severe. In certain places, like the mountains in back of us, the din and the tremors were incessant for a long time; in others, like toward Tadoussac, there were two or three severe tremors a day, and we noticed that in the higher places, the movement was less than it was on the flatlands. The second circumstance is the extent of this earthquake, which we thought was universal in all of New France, for we heard that it was felt at Isle Percée and Gaspé, at the mouth of our river, and beyond Montreal, as well as in New England, Acadia, and other distant places. Thus, as far as we know, we feel that the earthquake occurred over a territory two hundred leagues long and a hundred leagues wide, that is, twenty thousand leagues of land whose surface all trembled at once, on the same day and at the same moment.

The third circumstance is related to the particular protection of God of our dwellings, for we saw near ourselves great openings and a large area of country that was lost, without losing a single child, not even a hair of someone's head. We were surrounded by chaos and ruin, and yet we had only a few chimneys demolished, while the mountains around us fell into the abyss.

We should be even more grateful to Heaven for this kind protection, because a person of probity and irreproachable life who had had premonitions of what has happened, had a vision on the night the earthquake began of four fearful spectres who occupied the four directions surrounding Quebec and shook them fiercely as though they wished to turn them inside out. This they would without doubt have done, if a Higher Power of venerable majesty who gives impulse and movement to all things, had not opposed their efforts, and had not prevented them from harming those whom God wished to frighten for their own good but did not wish to lose.

The Savages had premonitions just as the French had of this horrible earthquake. A young Algonquin savage girl aged sixteen or seventeen called Catherine, who has always lived in great innocence and who thanks to her extraordinary trust in the Cross of the Son of God was almost miraculously cured of a lassitude she had suffered all winter, has said in all sincerity that the night before the earthquake she saw herself, with two other girls of her age and of her Nation, climbing a stairway, at whose top there stood a beautiful Church where the Holy Virgin with her Son appeared, preaching to them that the earth would tremble soon, that the trees would crash against one another, that the rocks would be shattered amid everybody's general astonishment. This poor girl, surprised at this news and fearing that it was from the Devil, decided to tell it all to the Priest who cared for the Algonquin church. On the night of the same day, just before the earthquake began, she cried out as though in the grip of strong emotion, saying to her parents, "It will be soon, it will be soon." She had the same premonitions each time the earth shook.

Here is yet another even more detailed testimony which we obtained from another young Algonquin savage woman, aged twenty-six, very innocent, simple and sincere, who when interrogated by two of our priests about what had happened to her, responded ingenuously, and her reply has been confirmed by her husband, her father and her mother, who saw with their own eyes and heard with their own ears what follows. Here is her testimony:

The night of 4 February 1663, entirely awake and in possession of my faculties, sitting in my chair, I heard a distinct and intelligible voice which said: "Strange things will happen today; the earth will tremble." I was gripped with fear, for I saw no-one whom this voice could be coming from. Full of fear, I tried with difficulty to go to sleep. When day arrived, I said softly to my husband, Joseph Onnentakité, what had happened to me, but he scolded me, saying that I was lying and that I wanted to awaken him, and I said no more. Around nine or ten o'clock of the same day, going to the woods, I had hardly entered the forest when the same voice was heard, saying the same thing in the same way as the night before. My fear was even greater, as I was all alone, and I looked around to see if I could see someone, but nothing appeared. With a load of firewood in my arms, I saw my sister, who had come to help me, and I told her what had occurred. Returning home with me, she told my mother and father what had happened to me, but as it was all so extraordinary, they listened without saying anything. This state of things lasted until five or six in the evening of the same day, when, with the first tremors of the earthquake, they recognised by experience that which they had heard before noon was only too true.

When God speaks, He makes Himself heard, especially when he speaks in the voice of the thunder or of earthquakes, which shake even the hardest hearts as well as the largest rocks, and has moved consciences far more than He moved the forests and the mountains.

This earthquake began on Monday before Carnival, at half past five in the evening. From this moment, which usually precedes the debauchery of the following day, everyone was concerned with their own health, and each one looked within himself, seeing himself at the bank of the abyss, about to appear before God to receive eternal judgement, a terrible thing for even the saintliest souls. Thus, Mardi Gras was happily changed to Good Friday and to an Easter Day. To us it was like Good Friday, with modesty, humility, and the tears of a perfect penitence. Never were more heartfelt confessions made, by spirits truly frightened of God's judgements. This same day was also like Easter for us, due to the number of Communions, which most people thought were the last of their life. The holy season of Lent has never been spent in such a holy fashion, as the continuing earth-tremors made the spirit of contrition and penance continue as well.

Louis Hennepin (1626–after 1701)

Born in Spanish-occupied Flanders in 1626, Louis Hennepin entered the Recollect order at the age of sixteen and led the life of a mendicant friar for more than three decades. Sent as a missionary to Canada in 1675, he was designated some time later along with two other monks of his order to accompany La Salle's expedition to explore the course of the Mississippi River. Returning to France in the autumn of 1681, he published his *Description of Louisiana* two years later, and later went to live once more in Flanders. In 1696 he offered his services as an explorer to King William III of England. In 1697, he published a second book titled *The New Discovery of a Very Great Country* (*Nouvelle Découverte d'un très grand pays*), and, less than one year later, *New Travels in a Country Larger than Europe* (*Nouveau Voyage d'un pays plus grand que l'Europe*). After a series of polemics in Utrecht, Hennepin wandered, lonely and embittered, between Rome and his native Flanders. His date of death is not known.

The *Description of Louisiana* begins with a letter to King Louis XIV, followed by the journal of Hennepin's journey from Quebec to the upper Mississippi valley, in which he describes the landscapes and peoples he observes, as well as his brief captivity among the Issati Sioux. Concluding the *Description of Louisiana* is a lengthy appendix titled "Manners of the Indians."

PRIMARY WORK

Father Louis Hennepin, *Description of Louisiana, Recently Discovered Southwest of New France, by Order of His Majesty, with a Map of the Country; The Manners and Mode of Life of the Indians,* trans. John Gilmary Shea (Paris: The Widow of Sebastian Huré, 1683).

FURTHER READING

Rhoda Gilman, "Reversing the Telescope: Louis Hennepin and Three Hundred Years of Historical Perspective," no. 18 (Minneapolis: Associates of the James Ford Bell Library, University of Minnesota, 1981).

Bruce Greenfield, "The Oral in the Written: The Irony of Representation in Louis Hennepin's Description de la Louisiane," *Historical Reflections/Reflexions Historiques*, Spring, 21, 2 (1995) pp. 243–59.

FROM DESCRIPTION OF LOUISIANA, RECENTLY DISCOVERED SOUTHWEST OF NEW FRANCE, BY ORDER OF HIS MAJESTY

Letter to King Louis XIV

Sire:

I never should have ventured to take the liberty of offering to your Majesty the Relation of a new Discovery which the Sieur de la Salle, Governor of Fort Frontenac, my companions and myself, have just made southwest of New France, had it not been undertaken by your orders, and had not the glory of obeying so glorious a Monarch, in an employment having in view the conversion of the heathen, led me into this enterprise.

It is in this thought, Sire, that I undertook so long and so painful a voyage, without fearing the greatest dangers. I even venture to assure your Majesty, that the bloody death of one of my Recollect companions, massacred by those savages, a captivity of eight months in which I have seen my life cruelly exposed, could not weaken my courage, having always made it a consolation amid my hardships, to labour for a God, whom I wished to see known and adored by these nations, and for a King whose glory and whose virtues are unbounded.

It is clear, Sire, that as soon as we have been able to tame them and win their friendship, the partial account we have given them of your Most Christian Majesty's heroic virtues, your surprising actions in your conquests, the happiness and love of your subjects, has inclined them to receive more readily the principles of Gospel truths and to reverence the cross which we have carved on trees above your Arms, as a mark of the continual protection which you give the Christian religion, and to make them remember the principles which we have happily taught them.

We have given the name of Louisiana[1] to this great Discovery, being persuaded that your Majesty would not disapprove that a part of the earth watered by a river more than eight hundred leagues in length, and much greater than Europe, which we may call the Delight of America and which is capable of forming a great Empire, should henceforth be known under the august name of Louis, that it may thereby have some show of right to aspire to the honour of your protection, and hope for the advantage of belonging to you.

It seems, Sire, that God had destined you to be its Master, by the happy correspondence that there is between your glorious name and the Sun, which they call Louis in their language, and to which in token of their respect and adoration, they extend their pipe before smoking, with these words: Tchendiouba Louis, that is to say "Smoke O Sun." Thus your Majesty's name is every moment on their lips, as they do nothing till they have rendered homage to the Sun under this name of Louis[2].

---

[1] The term Louisiana had been used before, in La Salle's grant of an island to François Daupin, Sieur de la Forest.

[2] According to Riggs' Dakota Dictionary, *wi* (similar to the French pronunciation of Louis) means sun or moon. Louis XIV was known throughout Europe as the Sun King.

After that, Sire, no one will doubt that it is a secret mystery of Providence which has reserved to your care and your piety, the glory of causing the Light of Faith to be borne to these blind ones, and of drawing them from the darkness in which they would always have lived, had not your Majesty, more devoted to the service of God and religion than to the government of your States, honoured us with this pious task, while you labour successfully for the destruction of heresy.

I implore of heaven, Sire, that the happiness which attends the justice of your actions, may crown such noble, grand and holy undertakings. These are the prayers and vows which all the Recollects of your kingdom offer to God at the foot of the Altars, and especially myself, who only desire to have the happiness of continuing to render your Majesty the service which I vowed to you at the time of the Campaigns in Holland, where I had the happiness of following your sacred person as a missionary, my greatest passion being to worship my God, to serve my King and to give him marks of the zeal and the most profound respect with which I am, Sire,

Your Majesty's most humble, most obedient and most faithful subject and servant

F. Louis Hennepin

Recollect Missionary

. . . It is some years since the Sieur Robert Cavelier de la Salle was convinced from the information which he had derived from several Indians of various nations that important establishments might be made in a southwesterly direction, beyond the great lakes, and that even by means of a great river which the Iroquois call Hohio[3], which empties into Meschasipi[4], which in the language of the Islinois[5] means great river, one could penetrate even to the sea.

With this design he purchased a house on the Island of Montreal at the spot called la Chine where they embark to ascend higher up along the great river St Lawrence; he subsequently imparted his idea to Monsieur de Courcelles, Governor of New France who found it well grounded, and who for this reason encouraged him to carry it out; he made several voyages, sometimes with Frenchmen, sometimes with Indians, and even for a distance of a hundred leagues, to the end of Lake Frontenac with Messrs Holier and Galinée, priests of St Sulpice, in the year 1669, but a violent fever compelled the latter to leave them as they entered Lake de Comty, and the former sometime afterwards were compiled by other unforeseen accidents to lay up among the Onttaouactz[6] and to return to Canada without their having ever since dreamed of carrying out their first design, the Providence of God having thus permitted it end reserved it to the religions of our order.

The Sieur de Courcelles and the Sieur Talon, the very vigilant Intendant of New France, wrote urging him to continue his discoveries, and a favourable opportunity offered.

After the Sieur Tracy sent by the King to Canada in 1665, had forced the Iroquois to sue for peace, he deemed it necessary in order to keep in check these savages, to erect some forts in the places by which the Iroquois had been accustomed to pass, in order to come and attack our settlements. With this view, Forts Sorel and Chambly were built on Richelieu river, which empties into the Saint Lawrence; and some years later Fort Frontenac was erected one hundred and twenty leagues further South near the outlet of Lake Frontenac or Ontario which means beautiful Lake.[7]

This fort was sodded and surrounded by palisade and four bastions by the care of the Count

---

3 Ohio.
4 Mississippi.
5 Illinois.

6 Ottawa.
7 Ontara, lake; ontario, beautiful lake.

de Frontenac[8], governor general of the country, to resist the Iroquois and this gallant noble-man for the ten years of his administration has made himself beloved, by the awe with which he inspired these savages, by planting Fort Frontenac which is situated within their country, and by this fortress he has revived in America the name of his ancestors, who were the favour-ites of one of our greatest kings, Henry IV, and governors of the castle of St Germain en Laye, and without disparaging the Governors General who preceded him, this one has been the father of the poor, the protector of the oppressed, and a perfect model of piety and religion. Those who come after us in Canada will regret him[9] and admire his wise administration and his zeal for the King's service in his perilous canoe voyages, on which this illustrious governor has often risked his life for the good and defence of the country.

The command of Fort Frontenac falling vacant, the Sieur de la Salle, who had experienced great difficulties in ascending the frightful hills and rapids, which are encountered for more than thirty leagues between Montreal and Fort Frontenac, resolved to come to France to solicit this post from the King.

He arrived at Rochelle in 1675 and offered to complete this fort at his own expense, and to maintain a sufficient garrison and as the Count de Frontenac had advanced more than 5000 livres[10] in establishing the fort and maintaining the garrison, he offered besides to reimburse him, provided the Court would grant him, the governorship and ownership of the fort. His proposals were accepted by M. Colbert[11], who caused the grants to be issued to him, through the influence of M. de Belizani, who greatly aided this noble enterprise, and the establish-ments that will be formed hereafter will owe him this obligation.

As soon as he had returned to Canada, the Count de Frontenac proceeded to the spot, to aid him in demolishing the first fort, which was enclosed only by stout palisades and turf. He erected another three hundred and sixty fathoms in circumference, revested[12] with four bas-tions of cut stone. They worked so diligently on it that it was brought to completion at the end of two years, although the Sieur de la Salle was not obliged to make so great an outlay.

This fort stands on the north side and near the outlet of Lake Frontenac on a peninsula, the isthmus of which he has dug through, the other three sides being surrounded by the lake and by a large harbour, where vessels of all kinds can anchor in safety. Lake Frontenac is eighty leagues long and twenty-five or thirty wide; it abounds in fish, is deep and navigable in all parts. The five cantons of the Iroquois live mainly south of this same lake, and some of them on the north.

The Count de Frontenac, having gone several years in succession to the fort escorted by soldiers and by forty canoes, managed[13] by men of great resolution in action, his presence has impressed fear and respect for the whole French nation on the mind of the haughtiest of these savages. He annually convened the most influential of the Iroquois in council, explaining to them the means they should adopt in order to embrace Christianity, exhorting them to hear the voice of the missionaries, giving them the bias[14] that they should take to entertain friendly relations with him, and to maintain trade with the French, whom after the mode of expression of the Indians, he called his nephews, and the Iroquois his children. It is by these methods that this wise governor has preserved peace as long as he has been in Canada, making presents to the Indians in favour of the Missionaries.

---

8   Louis de Buade, Count Frontenac (1621–98), Governor-General of Canada.

9   I.e. will remember him with nostalgia.

10   A French gold coin.

11   Jean-Baptiste Colbert (1619–83), Controller-General

of Finance and Secretary of the Navy under King Louis XIV of France.

12   Reinforced.

13   Manned.

14   I.e. explaining how they should proceed.

The situation of this fort is so advantageous, that by means of it, it is easy to cut off the Iroquois on their raids or their return, or to carry the war into their country in twenty-four hours, during the time that they are out on war parties, by means of barks[15] from Fort Frontenac; the Sieur de la Salle having built three, full decked, on the lake, has trained his men so well to manage canoes in the most frightful rapids, that they are now the most skilful canoemen in America.

As the land bordering on the lake is very fertile, he has cultivated several acres, where wheat, pulse and potherbs have succeeded very well, although the wheat was at first injured by grasshoppers, as generally happens in new clearings in Canada on account of the great humidity of the earth. He has raised poultry and horned cattle, of which he has now thirty-five head; and as there are very fine trees there fit for house and ship building, and the winter is nearly three months shorter than in Canada, there is reason to believe that a considerable colony will be formed, there being already thirteen or fourteen families and a mission house which I built with our dear Recollect Father, Lake Buisset, with the help of Sieur de LaSalle, whereby we have attracted a pretty large village of Iroquois, whose children we teach to read with our little French children, and they teach each other their language in turn. This maintains a good understanding with the Iroquois, who clear the land in order to plant Indian corn so as to subsist all the year except the hunting season.

While the Sieur de la Salle was engaged in building his fort, men envious of him, judging by this fine beginning what he might be able to do in the sequel, with our Recollect missionaries, who by their disinterested life[16], were attracting several families which came to settle at the Fort, put forward the Sieur Joliet to anticipate him in his discoveries. He went by the Bay of the Pump to the river Meschasipi, on which he descended to the Illinois, and returned by the Lakes to Canada, without having then or afterwards attempted to form any port or made any report to the Court.

At the end of the year 1678 the Sieur de la Salle came to France to report to Monsieur Colbert, what he had done to execute his orders; he then represented to him that this Fort Frontenac gave him great advantages for making discoveries with our Recollects, that his main object in building that fort had been to continue these discoveries in rich, fertile and temperate countries, where the trade merely in the skins and wool of the wild cattle, which the Spaniards call Cibola[17], might establish a great commerce, and support powerful colonies; that nevertheless, as it would be difficult to bring these cattle skins in canoes, he petitioned Monsieur Colbert to grant him a commission to go and discover the mouth of the great river Meschasipi, on which ships could be built to come to France; and that in view of the great expense that he had incurred chiefly for building and keeping up Fort Frontenac, he would deign to grant him the privilege of carrying on exclusively the trade in buffalo skins, of which he had brought one as a sample This was granted him.

He set out from France in the month of July in the year 1678 with the Sieurs la Motte and Tonty as pilot, sailors and several others, to the number of about thirty persons, anchors and rigging for the bark[18] which he intended to build, and the necessary arms and goods. At the close of September he reached Quebec, whence he sent on his men to transport the goods and provisions to Fort Frontenac. . . . .

. . . On the seventh we ascended two leagues up the river in a bark canoe, to seek a place

---

[15] Ships.

[16] I.e. due to their apparent lack of ulterior motives.

[17] Hennepin's error. Cibola was the Spanish name for the mythical Seven Cities of Gold.

[18] Ship.

suitable for building and being unable to go any higher up in a canoe, nor to surmount some very violent rapids, we proceeded to explore on land three leagues further, and finding no earth fit to cultivate, we slept near a river which flows from the west, one league above the great fall of Niagara. There was a foot of snow, which we removed to build a fire, and the next day we retraced our steps. On our way we saw a great number of deer, and flocks of wild turkeys; and after the first mass that had ever been celebrated in those places the carpenters with other men were employed under the direction of the Sieur de la Motte, who was never able to endure the rigour of such a life of hardship. He was compelled to give up some time afterwards and return to Fort Frontenac.

. . . The great river St Lawrence takes its rise from several large lakes, among which there are five of extraordinary size and which are all badly portrayed on the printed maps. These lakes are, first, Lake Conde or Tracy; second, Lake Dauphin or Islinois; third, Lake Orleans or of the Hurons; fourth, Lake Conty or Erie, and fifth Lake Ontario, called Frontenac. They are all of fresh water very good to drink, abound in fish, surrounded by fertile lands except the first. They are of easy navigation, even for large vessels, but difficult in winter on account of the high winds which prevail there.

Lake Orleans empties a long, very beautiful and navigable channel into Lake Conty, so that at these two latter lakes, are about equal to Lake Dauphin and are not separated from each other by any inconvenient rapid, you can sail by bark from the extremity of Lake Dauphin for a distance of four hundred leagues to the end of Lake Conty, where navigation is interrupted by the great Fall of Niagara. . . . Four leagues from Lake Frontenac there is an incredible Cataract or Waterfall, which has no equal. The Niagara river near this place is only the eighth of a league wide, but it is very deep in places, and so rapid above the great fall, that it hurries down all the animals which try to cross it, without a single one being able to withstand its current. They[19] plunge down a height of more than five hundred feet, and its fall is composed of two sheets of water and a cascade, with an island sloping down. In the middle these waters foam and boil in a fearful manner. They thunder continually and when the wind blows in a southerly direction, the noise which they make is heard for from more than fifteen leagues . . .

. . . The great Fall of the River Niagara, compelled him also to build his bark two leagues above it, and six leagues from the mouth of this river. But before beginning it, the Sieur de la Motte had orders to take his precautions and go to the great village of the Tsonnontouans Iroquois, to endeavour to dispel the umbrage which these envious men had already impressed on their minds, in regard to all our proceedings, and as I was labouring to build a cabin of the bark of trees which was to serve me as a house and chapel, to say the same thing to our people. The Sieur de la Motte begged me to accompany him to the Iroquois, and during the whole time of his embassy; I begged him to leave me with the greatest number of our men. He answered me that he was taking seven with him, that I knew something of the language, and of the customs of the Iroquois, that these Indians had seen me at Fort Frontenac at the council which the Governor of the country had held with them; that the King's service required it, and the Sieur de la Salle's especially, that he could not trust those whom he was taking. All them reasons compelled me to follow him through the wood, on a march of thirty-two leagues, over ground covered with snow. We all carried our blankets with our little equipage[20], often passing the night in the open air, and we had only some little bags of roast Indian corn. We met on the way Iroquois hunters who gave us some venison and fifteen or sixteen black squirrels very good to eat. After five days march we arrived at Tegarondies, a great village of the Tsonnontouans Iroquois, and as our Frenchmen were then well supplied with arms and fine

---

[19]   The Falls.   [20]   Baggage.

clothes, the Indians led us to the cabin of the great chief where all the women and children came to look at us, and after the cries made in the village by a sachem[21], according to the maxim of the Indians, the next day after the mass and sermon of New Year's Day, 1679, forty-two Iroquois old men appeared in the council with us, and although these Indians who are almost all large men, were merely wrapped in robes of beaver or wolf skin, and some in black squirrel skins, often with a pipe in the mouth, no senator of Venice ever assumed a graver countenance or spoke with more weight than the Iroquois sachems in their assemblies.

One of our men named Anthony Brassart, who served as interpreter, told them that we came to visit them in the name of Onnontio (which is the name that all the Indians give the Governors of the French), and to smoke their calumets[22] on their mat; that the Sieur de la Salle, their friend, was going to build a great wooden canoe, to go and seek goods in Europe by a shorter way than that by the rapids of the St Lawrence, in order to supply them with them at a cheaper rate. He added several other reasons to facilitate our enterprise and we gave them in the name of the whole nation, about four hundred livres[23] worth of goods according to the usage of this country, where the best reasons are never listened to, if they are not accompanied by presents.

. . . We set out the first of October, and after making twelve leagues fasting, arrived near another village of the Poutouatamies. These Indians all flocked to the lake shore to receive us and to haul us in from the waves which rose to an extraordinary height. The Sieur de la Salle, fearing that his men would desert, and that some of them would carelessly waste some of the goods, pushed on and we were obliged to follow him three leagues beyond the village of the Indians, notwithstanding the evident peril, and he saw no other alternative to take in order to land in safety than to leap into the water with his three canoemen, and all together take hold of the canoe and its load and drag it ashore in spite of the waves which sometimes covered them over their heads.

He then came to meet the canoe, which I guided with this man who had no experience in this work, and jumping waist high into the water, we carried our little craft all at once, and went to receive the other two canoes in the same manner as the former. And as the waves breaking on the shore formed a kind of undertow, which drags out into the lake those who think they are safe, I made a powerful effort and took on my shoulders our good old Recollect who accompanied us, and this amiable missionary of Saint Francis, seeing himself out of danger, all drenched as he was with water never failed to display an extraordinary cheerfulness.

As we had no acquaintance with the Indians of this village, the Commandant first ordered all the arms to be got ready, and posted himself on an eminence where it was difficult to surprise us, and whence he could with a small force defend himself against a greater number. He then sent three of his men to buy provisions in the village, under the protection of the calumet of peace[24] which the Poutouatamis of the Island had given the Sieur de la Salle, and which they had previously accompanied with their dances and ceremonies which they use in their feasts and public solemnities.

This calumet is a kind of large pipe for smoking, the head of which is of a fine red stone well polished, and the stem two feet and a half long is a pretty stout cane adorned with feathers of all sorts of colours, very neatly mingled and arranged, with several tresses of woman's hair, braided in various ways, with two wings, such as are usually represented on the Caduceus of Mercury[25], each nation embellishing it according to its especial usage. A calumet of this kind

---

[21] Shaman or person of religious authority.

[22] Pipes.

[23] Gold coins.

[24] Pipe with potent symbolic meaning.

[25] In classical mythology, the staff of Mercury, usually with two serpents entwined about it and surmounted by wings.

is a sure passport among all the allies of those who have given it; and they are convinced that great misfortunes would befall them, if they violated the faith of the calumet. And all their enterprises in war and peace and most important ceremonies are sealed and attested by the calumet which they make all smoke with whom they conclude any matter of consequence.

From *The Manners of the Indians*

On the Fertility of the Indian Country

Before entering here into details as to the manners of the Indians, it is well to say a word as to the fertility, of their country; it can but be judged how easy it is to found great colonies there. There are indeed many forests to clear, but these uncultivated parts are none the less advantageous. There are scarcely any in the world more fertile. Nothing is wanting that is necessary for life; every thing is in abundance, the lands there are very well adapted for sowing. In the vast countries of Louisiana, beautiful prairies are discovered as far as the eye can see, and to enter a little into detail as to things which grow among the Indians, there are many grape vines, very much like those we have in Europe, which bear grapes, somewhat sour, but the wine goes very well with ours, it even prevents it from spoiling. In Louisiana and the southern county, the grape is as good as in France but the seeds are larger. In both parts are found hops, plums, cherries, citrons[26], apples, pears, nuts, filberts[27], gooseberries of all kinds and a thousand other fruits of that nature delicious in taste. In both parts grow Indian corn, French wheat, turnips, very fine melons, enormous squashes, cabbages and a host of other vegetables, of which I do not here recall the names. In the forests there are great numbers of wolves, monstrous bears, deer, stags, and all kinds of animals of which I do not know the names, among others wild cats, beavers, otters, porcupines, turkey, and all these animals are of extraordinary size there. They catch there sturgeon, salmon, salmon trout; pike, carp, eels, armed fish, gold fish, bass, catfish, and all kinds of other fish. There is plenty of exercise too for our French sportsmen. There you can kill partridges, ducks of all kinds, wild pigeons, cranes, herons, swans, wild geese, and other game in abundance. In Louisiana, besides all these animals there are also wild cattle which the inhabitants of the country have never been able to exterminate entirely, on account of the great number of these animals which change their country according to the season. Several medicinal herbs are found there which are not in Europe, which have an infallible effect, according to the experience of the Indians, who use them daily to heal all kind of wounds, for quartain and tertian fevers[28], to purge and to allay pains in the kidney and other like troubles. There are also many poisons which these people employ for self destruction. Snakes are common, particularly the adders, asps and another kind of serpent, which has a kind of rattler on its tail, and is called on that account *rattlesnake*. They are of prodigious length and bulk. They bite passers-by dangerously; but wherever they are, there are found also sovereign remedies against their bites. Frogs are seen there too of strange size, whose bellowing is as loud as the lowing of cows . . .

Origins of the Indians

I am no longer surprised at the avowal of our historians, that they cannot tell how the Indian country has been populated, since the inhabitants, who ought to be the best informed, know

---

[26]   Lemons.

[27]   Hazelnuts.

[28]   Malarial fevers.

nothing about it themselves. Besides which, if in Europe, we were like them deprived of writing, and if we had not the use of that ingenious art, which brings the dead back to life, and recalls past times and which preserves for us an eternal memory of all things, we should not be less ignorant than they. It is true that they recount some things about their origin; but when you ask whether what they say about it is true, they answer that they know nothing about it, that they would not assure us of it, and that they believe them to be stories of their old men, to which they do not give much credit. If all North America had been discovered, we might perhaps learn the spot where these persons came over to it, which would contribute not a little to throw light on some points of ancient history

A rather curious story is related among them. They say that a woman descended from heaven and remained sometime fluttering in the air, unable to find a spot to rest her foot. The fish of the sea, having taken compassion on her, held a council to deliberate which of them should receive her; the Tortoise presented himself and offered his back above the water. This woman came there to rest and made her abode there. The unclean matter of the sea being gathered around this tortoise, a great extent of land had formed in time, which now constitutes America. But as solitude did not at all please this woman, who grew weary of having no one to converse with, in order to spend her days a little more agreeably than she was doing, a spirit descended from on high, who found her asleep from sorrow. He approached her imperceptibly, and begot by her two sons, who came out of her side. These two children could never, as time went on, agree, because one was a better hunter than the other, every day they had some quarrel with each other, and they came to such a pitch that they could not at all bear one another; especially one who was of an extremely fierce temper, conceived a deadly envy of his brother, whose disposition was completely mild. This one, unable to endure the ill treatment which he continually received, was at last obliged to depart from him and retire to heaven, whence as a mark of his just resentment, he from time to time makes the thunder roar over the head of his unhappy brother. Sometime after the spirit descended again to this woman and had by her a daughter, from whom have come the mighty nation which now occupies one of the biggest parts of the world. There are some other circumstances, which I do not remember, but fabulous as this story is, you can not fail to discern in it some truths. The woman's sleep has some analogy with that of Adam; the estrangement of the two brothers bears some resemblance to the irreconcilable hatred which Cain had for Abel, and the thunder pealing from heaven, shows us very clearly the curse which God pronounced upon that merciless fratricide. One might even doubt whether they are not of Jewish origin, because they have many things in common with them. They make their cabins in the form of a tent like the Jews. The anoint themselves with oil, they are superstitiously attached to dreams, they bewail the dead with lamentations and horrible howlings, women wear mourning for their near relatives for over a year, abstain from dances and feasts, and wear a kind of hood on their head. Usually the father of the deceased takes care of the widow. It seems too that the curse of God has fallen on them, as on the Jews, for they are brutal and extremely stubborn. They have no fixed and settled abode.

Physical Condition of the Indians

The Indians are very robust, men, women and even children are extremely rigorous; for this reason they are rarely sick, they know nothing about treating themselves delicately, hence they are not subject to a thousand ailments which too great effeminacy draws down on us. They are not gouty or dropsical[29], gravel[30] or fever-vexed, they are always in movement, and

---

[29] Having a tendency to retain fluids.   [30] Colic caused by kidney-stones or gallstones.

take so little rest, that they escape maladies which beset most of our Europeans for want of exercise; appetite scarcely ever fails them, even when they are advanced in years; they are as a rule so given to eating, that they rise in the night to eat unless they have meat or sagamity[31] near them, for then they eat like dogs without getting up. Yet on the other hand they undergo great abstinence which would beyond doubt be unsupportable to us. They go two or three days without eating, when such an occasion befalls them, without on that account discontinuing their work, whether they are engaged in hunting, fishing or war. Their children are so inured to cold, that in mid winter they run bare naked on the snow, and roll in it like little pigs, without being in any way injured, and in summer when the air is full of mosquitoes, they also go naked, and play without feeling the stings of these little insects. I admit that the fresh air to which they are constantly exposed contributes somewhat to harden their skin to fatigue, but this great insensibility must also come from an extremely robust constitution, in as much as our hands and face are always exposed to the air, without being for all that less sensitive to cold. When men are hunting, especially in the spring time, they are almost always in water, although it is very cold, and they return from it cheerfully to their cabins without complaining. When they go to war, they sometimes remain three or four days behind a tree, eating almost nothing. They are unwearied in their hunts; they run very fast and for a very long time. The nations of Louisiana run faster than the Iroquois, so that there is not a buffalo that they cannot run down. They sleep on the snow in a scanty blanket, without a fire and without cabins. The women act as porters, and have so much vigour, that there are few men in Europe who have as much as they. They carry burdens that two or three of us would find it difficult to raise. The warriors undertake journeys of three or four hundred leagues, as though it was only to go from Paris to Orleans. The women bear children without great pain, some of them leave the cabin and withdraw into the wood apart, and afterwards return with their children in their blanket. Others if labour comes on in the night, bring forth the children on their mats, without making the least noise, and in the morning rise and work as usual, inside and outside the cabin, as if nothing ailed them. Remark[32] also that while they are pregnant, they do not cease to be active, to carry very heavy loads, to plant Indian corn, and squashes, to go and come, and what is a wonder, their children are very well formed, humpbacks are very rare among them. To conclude, they have no natural bodily defects, which leads us to believe that their mind would easily adapt itself to this external disposition, if they were civilised and had much intercourse with the French.

When they are weary they enter a vapour bath to strengthen their limbs, and if their legs or arms pain, they take a well sharpened knife and make incisions in the part where the pain is. When the blood flows they scrape it with their knives or a stick till it ceases to flow. Then they cleanse the wound and rub it with oil or the fat of some animals. This is a sovereign remedy. They do the same when they have a pain in the head or arms. To cure tertian and quartan fevers, they make a medicine with a bark which they boil and give to drink immediately after the fever. They know roots and herbs with which they cure all kinds of diseases. They have sure remedies against the poison of toads, snakes and other animals, but have none against the smallpox. There are charlatans whom they call jugglers. There are certain old men who live at other people's expense by counterfeiting physicians in a superstitious manner. They do not use remedies, but when one of them is called to a sick man, he makes them entreat him, as if it were for some affair of great importance and very difficult. After many solicitations he comes, he approaches the patient, touches him all over the body, and after he has well considered and handled him, he tells him that he has a spell in such or such a part, for example, in the head,

---

[31]   Porridge made of Indian corn.   [32]   Note.

leg or stomach, which must be removed, but that this can be done only with great difficulty, and many things must be done previously. This spell is very malicious, he says; but it must be made to come out at any cost. All the sick man's friends who fall into the trap, say, "T. Chagon, T. Chagon, courage, courage;" "do what you can, spare nothing." The juggler sits down, deliberates for a time on the remedies which he wishes to employ, then rises as if coming out of a deep sleep, and cries out, "See the thing is done! Listen, such a one, your wife or child's life is at stake, so spare nothing, you must give a feast, today," "give such or such a thing" or do something else of the kind. At the same time that the orders of this juggler are carried out, the men enter the vapour bath and sing at the top of their voice, rattling tortoise shells or gourds full of Indian corn, to the sound of which the men and women dance. Sometimes even they all get intoxicated, so that they make fearful orgies. While all are thus engaged, this superstitious old man is near the patient, whom he torments, holding his feet or legs, or pressing his chest, according to the spot where he has said the spell is, he makes him undergo pain sufficient to kill him. He often makes the blood issue from the tips of his fingers or toes. At last after making a hundred grimaces, he takes a piece of skin or a lock of hair or something of the kind, making them believe it to be the spell which he has drawn from the patient's body, which is however, only a pure trick.

I one day baptised a little child which seemed to be in danger of death, but the next day, it was cured. Some days after its mother related to the others, in my presence, how I had cured her child. She took me for a juggler, saying that I was wonderful, that I knew how to cure all sorts of diseases by putting water on the forehead. They often have recourse to our medicines because they find them very good, but when we do not succeed, they ascribe the cause to the medicine and not to the wretched state of the patient . . .

Marriages of the Indians

The marriage of the Indians is not a civil contract because they have no intention of binding themselves but they cohabit, till they disagree with one another. Girls are married at the age of nine or ten years, not for marriage, because they know that they are incapable, but because the parents of this girl expect some profit from their son in law. In fact when he comes in from the hunt the girl's father has the disposal of the fur and the meat, but on the other hand the girl carries the sagamity or porridge made of Indian corn, for all her husband's meals although she does not live with him. Some act thus five or six years. On the day when they marry they give feasts with pomp and rejoicing. Sometimes the whole village goes there, and every one makes good cheer. After the meal they sing and dance. Very frequently they marry without any noise and for this only a word is needed, for the Indian who has no wife goes in search of a woman who has no husband and says to her: "Will you come with me? You shall be my wife." She makes no answer at first, but thinks for some time holding her head in her two hands. While she is thus thinking the man holds his head in the same posture without uttering a word. When she has deliberated some time she lifts up her head and says: "*Niau*[33], I am willing;" the man rises at once, and says to her, "*One*, that is settled." In the evening the woman takes her hatchet, and goes to cut a load of fire wood; on reaching the door of her husband's cabin she throws the wood on the ground, goes in and sits down near the Indian, who gives her no caress. When they have been thus long together without speaking, the man says to her: "*Sentaony*, lie down," and a little while after this man lies down near her.

You see very few who make love like Europeans, laughing and flirting.

[33] Yes.

They leave each other very easily and without any publicity, for they have only to say, "I leave you" and the thing is done. Then they regard each other no more than if they had never met.

They sometimes fight with each other before separating, but this occurs very rarely. Some have two wives, but it is not for a long time. When they separate the woman sometimes carries off all the goods, and all the furs; sometimes nothing at all but the short piece of cloth that forms her petticoat, and her blanket. They generally divide the children if they have had any together, so that some follow the father and some the mother. Some leave them all to their wives, saying that they do not believe they belong to them. In fact they very often say the truth, because there are very few who are proof against a coat and any other present that may be offered. If these children are of a French father, you can detect it in the face and eyes. Those of the Indians are entirely black, and they can see further than Europeans, and they have a more piercing eye. If the Indian women were capable of contracting marriage, we might marry as many as we would to our Frenchmen, but they have not the necessary dispositions, they have not the faith necessary for that, nor the will never to separate from their husband, as experience teaches us, and the conversations they hold on the point, show us clearly. When a man who has no wife passes through a village he hires one for a night or for two according to his fancy, and the parents find nothing to censure in this; very far from that, they are very glad to have their daughter earn some clothing or some furs. Among them there are men of all kinds of dispositions as in Europe; some love their wives a great deal, others entirely despise them, some beat them and ill treat them; but this does not last, as the wives leave them. There are some too who are jealous. I saw one who had beaten his wife, for having gone to the dance with other men.

Those who are good hunters choose the handsomest; the other have only the ugly ones, and the cast-off. When they are old, they never abandon each other except in rare cases, and for grave reasons. There are some, although very few, who remain from twenty to thirty years with their wives. The women grow desperate when the man who is a good hunter leaves them; they even poison themselves sometimes, as I saw one whose life I saved with treacle. When these Indians go beaver hunting in the spring, they often leave their wives in the village to plant Indian corn, and squashes, and hire another to go with them: when they return home they give her a beaver or two, and send her home in that way and go back to the first wife. If however the last pleases them better, they change the first without any ado. They are surprised that the Frenchmen do not act like them.

One day while the husband of one of our French women settlers had gone off twenty or thirty leagues the Indian women went to see this woman and said to her: "You have no sense, take another man for the present, and when your husband comes leave this one." This great inconstancy and changing of wives is a great opposition to the maxims of Christianity which we wish to impart to the Indians and one of the most considerable obstacles to the faith.

It is not the same with the southern nations among whom polygamy reigns for in all the lands of Louisiana, there are Indians who have as many as ten or eleven wives, and are often married to three sisters, alleging as a reason that they agree better among themselves.

When a man makes presents to the father and mother of a girl she belongs to him as his own for her whole life if he wishes; sometimes the parents take back children from their son-in-law restoring the presents which they have received from him but this is very rare. If a woman should be unfaithful her husband would cut off her nose, ear or would give her a slash in the face with a stone knife, and if he should kill her, he would clear himself by making a present to the dead woman's kindred to dry up their tears. I have seen several badly marked on the face who had nevertheless children by some scurvy fellow. The men in the warm countries are more jealous of their wives than those of the north. The former are so sensitive in matters of this kind, that they wound and sometimes kill one another, through some love madness. The young warriors do not often approach women till they reach the age of thirty years because they say that intercourse with women prevents their running. The men there go entirely naked but the women are partly covered with very neat skins especially at the dances and ceremonies. The girls curl their hair and the women wear theirs after the gypsy fashion. . . .

I have seen a boy seventeen or eighteen years old who had dreamed that he was a girl. He gave such credit to it, that he believed himself to be one. He dressed like the girls and did all the same works as women . . .

The Obstacles to the Conversion of the Indians

There are several, both on the part of the Indians and on that of the Dutch, the English and the Missionaries. On the part of the Indians their first obstacle to the faith is the indifference which they feel for everything. When we relate to them the history of our Creation, and the mysteries of the Christian religion, they tell us that we are right and then they relate their fables and when we reply that what they say is not true they retort that they agreed to what we said and that it is not showing sense to interrupt a man when he is speaking and to tell him that he lies. "This is all very well," they say, "for your countrymen; for them it is as you say, but not for us who belong to another nation." The second consists in their superstitions. The third is that they are not sedentary. The obstacle to the faith caused by the Dutch and English is that they reverse all our maxims and in general do before the Indians the very opposite of what they say making no scruple at lying to them at every moment from the spirit of lucre[34]. They endeavour maliciously to turn on us the hatred of these tribes in order that they may give no credit to the truths which we preach them.

The obstacle found to the faith on the part of the missionaries, is first, the difficulty they have in learning the language of the Indians. The second consists in the different opinions concerning the method of instructing them and teaching them the catechism. The third obstacle which might also hinder the progress of the faith, would be the temporal traffic, which would render the missionaries suspected by the Indians, when they wish to carry it on against the law of the church.

Indifference of the Indians

They have so great an indifference for all things that there is nothing like it under heaven. They take great complacency in hearing all that is said to them seriously, and in all that they are made to do. If we say to them: "Pray to God, brother, with me," they pray and they repeat word for word all the prayers you teach them. "Kneel down," they kneel. "Take off your hat," they take it off. "Be silent," they cease to speak. "Do not smoke," they stop smoking. If one says to them: "Listen to me," they listen calmly. When we give them pictures, a crucifix or beads, they use them as adornments just as if they were jewellery and array themselves in them, as though they were wampum. If I should say to them: "To-morrow is the day of prayer," they say, "Niaova." "See, that is right." If I said to them: "Do not get drunk," they answered: "There, that is right, I am willing." Yet the moment they receive drink from the French or Dutch, these latter never refusing them liquor for furs, they inevitably get drunk. When I ask them whether they believe, they say "Yes," and almost all the Indian women whom some missionaries have baptised and married to Frenchmen according to the rites of the church leave and often change their husbands because they are not subjected to the ordinances of our

---

[34]   I.e. in order to gain profit.

Christian laws, and that they have all liberty to change. These tribes must absolutely first be civilised to make them embrace Christianity for so long as Christians are not absolutely their masters we shall see little success, without a most special grace of God, without a miracle which he does not work in regard to all nations. These are my sentiments from the experience which I have had with our Recollects in America and the simple statement which I have made without intending to offend any one whatever being bound to write the truth.

Those who come after us will know in time the progress of our new discovery; since this year 1682 they write me from America that the Sieur de la Salle with our Recollects has been to the mouth of the river Colbert[35] as far as the South Sea[36]. They have found the Akansa, Taensa, Keroas and the Ouamats civilised tractable nations, who have laws, a king who commands as a sovereign with equitable, liberal and settled officers. These nations live on the banks of the River Colbert which is more than 800 leagues in length, 500 to our knowledge which we have acquired by ascending it, and 300 which the Sieur de la Salle has made descending. . . . It is as warm as July. The corn ripens there in fifty days. The soil bears two crops a year. There are found there palm trees, canes, laurels, forests of mulberry trees, a quantity of wild animals and other like things of which we shall give the public some account more amply hereafter.

I pray God to give his blessing to our new discovery of Louisiana and that the King may derive all possible benefit from it.

Chretian Le Clercq (*fl.* 1641–1695)

The Recollect priest and historiographer Chretian Le Clercq was sent to Canada in 1675 as a missionary to the Micmac Indians, returning to France in 1686. There, he wrote his *Nouvelle Relation de la Gaspésie*, a detailed description of the life and culture of the Micmac, and his *Primer Établissement de la Foy dans la Nouvelle France,* both published in 1691.

FURTHER READING

Harald Prins, *The Mi'kmaq: Resistance, Accommodation, and Cultural Survival* (Fort Worth : Harcourt Brace, 1996).
Marie-Christine Pioffet, "Relations de missions et intertextualite: Les Voies de Paul Lejeune et de Chrestien Leclercq," *Papers on French Seventeenth Century Literature*, 25, 49 (1998) pp. 497–509.

PRIMARY WORK

Translated from *Nouvelle Relation de la Gaspésie*, in *Anthologie de la Littérature Québécoise, Vol I, Écrits de la Nouvelle France, 1534–1760,* ed. Léopold LeBlanc (Montreal: La Presse, 1978).

FROM *NEW RELATION OF GASPESIA*

The Sun Wept in Grief

The origin of these peoples, and the way in which the New World came to be inhabited by an almost infinite multitude of different Peoples and Nations, seems so obscure to us that after

---

[35]   The Mississippi.   [36]   The Gulf of Mexico.

the most curious and exact investigation to date, we are all forced to confess that it is impossible to have correct and true knowledge on this matter.

It seems that this secret should be reserved only to the Savages, and that only from them could one learn the whole truth; for indeed there was a time among us when no-one knew that North America existed. Not even the wisest men could accommodate it in their imaginary space, and yet the first discoveries took place less than two hundred years ago. Our Gaspesians[1], however, could tell us nothing on this matter, perhaps because they had no knowledge of great literature which could give them knowledge about their ancestors and their origin. They do have, if you will, a vague fantastic idea about the creation of the Earth and of the Flood; they say that when the Sun, which they recognise and worship as a god, created all of this great Universe, he divided the land into several parts, separated from one another by great lakes. In each part he caused a man and a woman to be born, who multiplied and lived long lives; but as they began to treat their children cruelly, and killed one another, the Sun wept in grief, and rain fell from heaven in such abundance that the waters rose to the top of the rocks and of the tallest mountains. This flood, which, they say, occurred all over the world, forced them to embark in their bark canoes to save themselves from the gulf of this general deluge, but this was in vain, for they all unluckily died because of an impetuous gust of wind that made them capsize and fall into this horrible abyss, except for some old men and a few women, who had been the most virtuous and the best of all the Savages. God came to them then, to console them for the death of their relatives and friends, after which He allowed them to live on the earth, in happy tranquillity. He gave them as well the intelligence and industry necessary to trap the beavers and moose necessary for their subsistence.

"I am astonished that the French have so little wit"

(Here is what the Gaspesians) related one day to some of our gentlemen of Isle Percée, who had asked me to serve them as interpreter on a visit they wished to make to these Savages to make them realise that it would be to their benefit to live like us and to build houses like ours. They were taken aback when the chief, who had listened very patiently to everything I had said on behalf of these gentlemen, answered in these terms:

I am astonished that the French have so little wit, as it seems in what you have just told me, as to try to persuade us to change our tent-poles, our bark and our cabins into houses of stone and wood that are, according to what they say, as tall as trees! I would thus infer that for men five to six feet tall, houses of sixty or eighty (feet) would be necessary . . .

. . . You reproach us wrongly, that our country is a little hell in comparison to France, which you compare to the Earthly Paradise, even though our country supplies you with all sorts of provisions in abundance. You tell us as well that we are the most miserable and unhappy of all men, living without religion, without civility, without honour, without society, and in a world without rules, like beasts of the woods and the forests, denied bread, wine and a thousand other sweet things that you have in excess in Europe. But, my brother, if you do not know the real feelings of the Savages for your country and for all your nation, it is right that I should inform you today. I beseech you to believe that, however miserable we may appear to your eyes, we know ourselves to be far happier than you, in that we are far more content with the little we have. We believe as well that you are very wrong, if you intend to

---

[1]   The Micmac Indians.

persuade us that your country is better than ours, for if France, as you say, is a little Earthly Paradise, why did you leave it? and why did you leave behind wives, children relatives and friends? Why do you risk your life and your fortune every year, and gamble with luck in any season with the storms and the tempests at sea, to come to a foreign and barbarous country, which you feel to be the poorest and unhappiest on earth? Besides, as we are entirely convinced of the contrary, we make no effort to go to France, because we rightly realise that there we would find no satisfaction, seeing from our own experience that those who come from there leave home every year to come get rich from our land. We believe as well that you are incomparably poorer than we are, and that you are mere companions, mere valets, mere servants or slaves, however much you may seem to be great Captains. You laugh at our old rags, and our clothing of beaver skins, which are no good for you. You find yourselves among us because you fish for cod in our waters, to redeem the poverty and misery which overwhelm you, while we find all our wealth and all our comforts in our own land, without difficulty, without exposing our lives to the dangers you experience every day, in long voyages. We feel compassion for you, from the sweetness of our rest, on observing your worries and cares as you load your ship. We see that all your people live on nothing but the cod you fish here: continually Cod in the morning, Cod at noon, Cod in the evening, and nothing but Cod, to the point that when you want to have something good to eat, it is at our cost. You are forced to recur to the Savages, whom you despise so much, to beg them to go hunting in order to regale you. Now tell me, if you have the wit to do so, which of the two is wiser and happier: he who works without ceasing, and who only is able to amass enough to live with great difficulty, or he who rests pleasantly, and who finds all he needs in the pleasure of hunting and fishing? It is true that we still do not use bread and wine, which your France produces. But, before the arrival of the French, did not the Gaspesians live longer than at present? And if among us there were old men of one hundred thirty to one hundred forty years of age, it is not because we took on your way of living. Experience has taught us that those who live to an old age among us scorn your bread, your wine, and your brandy, contenting themselves with their natural nourishment of beaver, moose, small game and fish, according to the custom of our ancestors and of all the Gaspesian nation. Learn, then, my brother, once and for all, for I must open my heart to you, that there is not a Savage who does not feel himself to be infinitely happier and more powerful than the French.

Middle Atlantic:
The Chesapeake and the Indies

John Smith (1580–1631)

Now a bone fide Disney legend, John Smith's early life and adventurous career in the New World were indeed the stuff of legend. He was born into a farming family in Lincolnshire and apprenticed at fifteen to a local merchant. However, in 1596, shortly after his father's death, Smith volunteered to fight for the Dutch in their war of independence from Spain. After his tour of duty, Smith served in the Mediterranean on a privateer, and then joined the Austrian army, which was engaged in an extended war against the Turks. After being wounded in battle, Smith was taken prisoner and sold into slavery, which he escaped by murdering his Turkish master and fleeing back to England through Russia and Poland.

Selected by the Virginia Company, a group of private investors, to join an expedition to the New World, Smith quickly ran afoul of the high born members who, taking inspiration from the Spanish method of conquest, wanted to reap profits by the discovery of gold and other valuable substances. Unlike the Puritan colonists in New England who were united in a common purpose and religion, their competing interests, loyalties, and ambitions produced a contentiousness that plagued the Jamestown colony all through its disastrous first years. Smith was arrested during the voyage over as the fleet moored in the Canary Islands in February, 1607, on charges of fomenting mutiny. When they reached Cape Henry a month later, and opened the

Company's secret orders appointing the local council, Edward Maria Wingfield, who was elected first president (essentially governor of the colony), refused to accept Smith's appointment or take his oath of office. In May, after protests by members of the company, Smith was released from restraint, and sworn in. He was put in charge of the colony's stores, and in 1608 was elected president, the position he occupied until his departure in October 1609.

Smith organized the fractious colonists into building and fortifying the small settlement, and negotiated with the local tribes for the food. Recent research suggests that an unusually severe drought during the years 1609–12 substantially reduced Native foodstocks and rendered inconsequential any planting the English might have done. Furthermore, the drought increased the salt content of the drinking water, which also may have contributed to salt poisoning, a condition unknown to Europeans. Although Smith realized the importance of establishing trade with the Native Americans, he adopted a harsh policy towards them, using violence to subdue and control the "subtill" Natives whom he considered inferiors. His attitude can be glimpsed in the most famous episode in *The Generall Historie*, Smith's capture and rescue by Powhatan's daughter, Pocahontas. This incident, like several other memorable episodes in the Third Book, did not appear in the first accounts of Smith's experiences, *A True Relation of Such Occurrences and Accidents of Note as Hath Happened in Virginia* (1608), or the group effort penned by several hands including Smith's and published in 1612 as *A Map of Virginia, with a Description of the Country . . .* [and] *The Proceedings of those Colonies*, leading some historians to regard them as fabrications. Nevertheless, Pocahontas' intervention on Smith's behalf has achieved mythic status in the national imagination. Not only does this incident depict Native acceptance of the superiority of white civilization, implying a justification of the West's imperial ambitions, but it also inscribes gendered structures of power and domination at the heart of that project. It was, in part, Smith's unbending policy towards the Natives and the inability of the colony to turn a profit, that precipitated the replacement of his government by the Virginia Company. Injured in a gunpowder accident, he departed Jamestown in 1609 in failure, never to return.

Finding all his offers of further service to the Virginia colony rebuffed, Smith turned his attention to "North Virginia", voyaging to New England in 1614, a region which he, in fact, named. Seeing the vast potential in this area, Smith offered himself as a guide to the Pilgrims who undertook their famous journey to New England in 1620, but they wisely declined. Nevertheless, for Smith, the New England colonies exemplified the best approach to colonization. After this, Smith's explorations occurred mainly in print as rehearsals

of his great adventures. His later writing expresses his unwavering devotion to the honorable occupation of exploration and his lingering sense that his accomplishments were not fully appreciated.

PRIMARY WORKS

A True Relation of . . . Virginia, 1608.
A Description of New England, 1616.
The Generall Historie of Virginia, New England, and the Summer Isles, 1624.
The True Travels, Adventures, and Observations of Captaine John Smith, 1630.
Advertisements for the Unexperienced Planters of New England or Anywhere, 1631.
The Complete Works of Captain John Smith (1580–1631), 3 vols, ed. P. L. Barbour (Chapel Hill: University of North Carolina Press, 1986).

FURTHER READING

Philip L. Barbour, *The Three Worlds of Captain John Smith* (Boston: Houghton Mifflin, 1964).
J. A. Leo Lemay, *The American Dream of Captain John Smith* (Charlottesville, University Press of Virginia, 1991) and *Did Pocahontas Save Captain John Smith?* (Athens: University of Georgia Press, 1993).
Everett H. Emerson, *Captain John Smith* (New York: Twayne, 1971, rev. 1993).
Myra Jehlen, "History Before the Fact, or John Smith's Unfinished History," *Critical Inquiry*, Summer, 19, 4 (1993) pp. 677–92.

THE GENERALL HISTORIE OF VIRGINIA, NEW ENGLAND, AND THE SUMMER ISLES[1]

From *The Third Book, The Proceedings and Accidents of the English Colony in Virginia*

From *Chapter II: What happened till the first supply*

[The building of Jamestown and beginning of trade.]
The new President and Martin[2], being little beloved, of weake judgement in dangers, and

---

[1]   All texts, with slight modifications, are from *The Complete Works of Captain John Smith*, ed. Philip Barbour. The "Summer Isles" are the Bermuda Islands. The Third Book derives from an account entitled *A Map of Virginia, with a Description of the Country . . .* [and] *The Proceedings of those Colonies*, written by several of the colonists and published in

1612. Years later, Smith added sections by other writers and expanded his own contributions to produce *The Generall Historie*, which is also much grander in geographical scope and colonial ambition.

[2]   John Martin, a gentleman and member of the council. The "President is Edward Maria Wingfield. Smith refers to himself in the third person throughout the account.

lesse industrie in peace, committed the managing of all things abroad to Captaine Smith: who by his owne example, good words, and faire promises, set some to mow, others to binde thatch, some to build houses, others to thatch them, himselfe alwayes bearing the greatest taske for his owne share, so that in short time, he provided most of them lodgings, neglecting any for himselfe. This done, seeing the Salvages superfluitie beginne to decrease (with some of his workemen) shipped himselfe in the Shallop to search the Country for trade. The want of the language, knowledge to mannage his boat without sailes, the want of a sufficient power, (knowing the multitude of the Salvages) apparell for his men, and other necessaries, were infinite impediments, yet no discouragement. Being but six or seven in company he went downe the river to Kecoughtan[3], where at first they scorned him, as a famished man, and would in derision offer him a handfull of Corne, a peece of bread, for their swords and muskets, and such like proportions also for their apparell. But seeing by trade and courtesie there was nothing to be had, he made bold to try such conclusions as necessitie inforced, though contrary to his Commission: Let fly his muskets, ran his boat on shore, whereat they all fled into the woods. So marching towards their houses, they might see great heapes of corne: much adoe he had to restraine his hungry souldiers from present taking of it, expecting as it hapned that the Salvages would assault them, as not long after they did with a most hydeous noyse. Sixtie or seaventie of them, some blacke, some red, some white, some party-coloured, came in a square order, singing and dauncing out of the woods, with their *Okee* (which was an Idoll made of skinnes, stuffed with mosse, all painted and hung with chaines and copper) borne before them: and in this manner being well armed, with Clubs, Targets, Bowes and Arrowes, they charged the English, that so kindly received them with their muskets loaden with Pistoll shot, that downe fell their God, and divers lay sprauling on the ground; the rest fled againe to the woods, and ere long sent one of their *Quiyoughkasoucks*[4] to offer peace, and redeeme their *Okee.* Smith told them, if onely six of them would come unarmed and loade his boat, he would not only be their friend, but restore them their *Okee,* and give them Beads, Copper, and Hatchets besides: which on both sides was to their contents performed: and then they brought him Venison, Turkies, wild foule, bread, and what they had, singing and dauncing in signe of friendship till they departed. In his returne he discovered the Towne and Country of Warraskoyack[5].

> *Thus God unboundlesse by his power,*
> *Made them thus kind, would us devour.*

[On an exploration, Smith is taken prisoner by the Powhatans.]
The Salvages having drawne from George Cassen[6] whether Captaine Smith was gone, prosecuting that oportunity they followed him with 300. bowmen, conducted by the King of Pamaunkee[7], who in divisions searching the turnings of the river, found Robinson and Emry by the fire side, those they shot full of arrowes and slew. Then finding the Captaine, as is said, that used the Salvage that was his guide as his sheld (three of them being slaine and divers other so gauld[8]) all the rest would not come neere him. Thinking thus to have returned to his boat, regarding them, as he marched, more then his way, slipped up to the middle in an oasie[9]

---

[3] A village near the mouth of the James River.

[4] Priests, or "petty gods."

[5] A village near the mouth of the Pagan River.

[6] Cassen, like Robinson and Emry, were Englishmen killed while accompanying Smith on the exploration of the Chickahamania River.

[7] Opechankanough, Powhatan's younger half-brother, who led the Indian Confederacy in their attack on the colonists in 1622.

[8] Galled or filled with shot.

[9] Oozy or boggy.

creeke and his Salvage with him, yet durst they not come to him till being neere dead with cold, he threw away his armes. Then according to their composition[10] they drew him forth and led him to the fire, where his men were slaine. Diligently they chafed his benummed limbs. He demanding for their Captaine, they shewed him Opechankanough, King of Pamaunkee, to whom he gave a round Ivory double compass Dyall. Much they marvailed at the playing of the Fly and Needle, which they could see so plainely, and yet not touch it, because of the glasse that covered them. But when he demonstrated by that Globe-like Jewell, the roundnesse of the earth, and skies, the spheare of the Sunne, Moone, and Starres, and how the Sunne did chase the night round about the world continually; the greatnesse of the Land and Sea, the diversitie of Nations, varietie of complexions, and how we were to them Antipodes, and many other such like matters, they all stood as amazed with admiration. Notwithstanding, within an houre after they tyed him to a tree, and as many as could stand about him prepared to shoot him, but the King holding up the Compass in his hand, they all laid downe their Bowes and Arrowes, and in a triumphant manner led him to Orapaks[11], where he was after their manner kindly feasted, and well used.

. . . At last they brought him to Meronocomoco[12] where was Powhatan their Emperor. Here more then two hundred of those grim Courtiers stood wondering at him, as he had beene a monster; till Powhatan and his trayne had put themselves in their greatest braveries[13]. Before a fire upon a seat like a bedsted, he sat covered with a great robe, made of Rarowcun[14] skinnes, and all the tayles hanging by. On either hand did sit a young wench of 16 or 18 yeares, and along on each side the house, two rowes of men, and behind them as many women, with all their heads and shoulders painted red; many of their heads bedecked with the white downe of Birds; but every one with something: and a great chayne of white beads about their necks. At his entrance before the King, all the people gave a great shout. The Queene of Appamatuck[15] was appointed to bring him water to wash his hands, and another brought him a bunch of feathers, in stead of a Towell to dry them: having feasted him after their best barbarous manner they could, a long consultation was held, but the conclusion was, two great stones were brought before Powhatan: then as many as could layd hands on him, dragged him to them, and thereon laid his head, and being ready with their clubs, to beate out his braines, Pocahontas the Kings dearest daughter, when no intreaty could prevaile, got his head in her armes, and laid her owne upon his to save him from death: whereat the Emperour was contented he should live to make him hatchets, and her bells, beads, and copper; for they thought him as well of all occupations as themselves. For the King himselfe will make his owne robes, shooes, bowes, arrowes, pots; plant, hunt, or doe any thing so well as the rest.[16]

> They say he bore a pleasant shew,
> But sure his heart was sad.
> For who can pleasant be, and rest,
> That lives in feare and dread:
> And having life suspected, doth
> It still suspected lead.[17]

---

[10]   The agreement based on Smith's surrender.

[11]   A temporary hunting village located further inland.

[12]   Located on the York River, north of Jamestown.

[13]   Finest attire.

[14]   Raccoon.

[15]   Opossunoquonwke, the weroansqua, or leader, of the Appamatucks, who had entertained the English on other

occasions, but was killed in 1610 in retaliation for the deaths of several settlers.

[16]   This well-known passage, including the following scene with Powhatan and the earlier episode with Opechankanough, were later additions. In earlier accounts, Smith says he won his own liberty, and Pocahontas played only a symbolic or dramatic part.

Two dayes after, Powhatan having disguised himselfe in the most fearefullest manner he could, caused Captaine Smith to be brought forth to a great house in the woods, and there upon a mat by the fire to be left alone. Not long after from behinde a mat that divided the house, was made the most dolefullest noyse he ever heard; then Powhatan more like a devill then a man with some two hundred more as blacke as himselfe, came unto him and told him now they were friends, and presently he should goe to James towne, to send him two great gunnes, and a gryndstone, for which he would give him the Country of Capahowosick, and for ever esteeme him as his sonne Nantaquoud.[18] So to James towne with 12 guides Powhatan sent him. That night they quarterd in the woods, he still expecting (as he had done all this long time of his imprisonment) every houre to be put to one death or other: for all their feasting. But almightie God (by his divine providence) had mollified the hearts of those sterne Barbarians with compassion. The next morning betimes they came to the Fort, where Smith having used the Salvages with what kindnesse he could, he shewed Rawhunt, Powhatans trusty servant two demi-Culverins[19] and a millstone to carry to Powhatan: they found them somewhat too heavie; but when they did see him discharge them, being loaded with stones, among the boughs of a great tree loaded with Isickles, the yce and branches came so tumbling downe, that the poore Salvages ran away halfe dead with feare. But at last we regained some conference with them, and gave them such toyes, and sent to Powhatan, his women, and children such presents, as gave them in generall full content. Now in James Towne they were all in combustion, the strongest preparing once more to run away with the Pinnace; which with the hazzard of his life, with Sakre falcon[20] and musket shot, Smith forced now the third time to stay or sinke. Some no better then they should be, had plotted with the President, the next day to have put him to death by the Leviticall law, for the lives of Robinson and Emry,[21] pretending the fault was his that had led them to their ends: but he quickly tooke such order with such Lawyers, that he layd them by the heeles till he sent some of them prisoners for England. Now ever once in foure or five dayes, Pocahontas with her attendants, brought him so much provision, that saved many of their lives, that els for all this had starved with hunger.

> *Thus from numbe death our good God sent reliefe,*
> *The sweete asswager of all other griefe.*[22]

His relation of the plenty he had seene, especially at Werawocomoco, and of the state and bountie of Powhatan, (which till that time was unknowne) so revived their dead spirits (especially the love of Pocahontas[23]) as all mens feare was abandoned. Thus you may see what difficulties still crossed any good endevour: and the good successe of the businesse being thus oft brought to the very period of destruction; yet you see by what strange means God hath still delivered it. As for the insufficiency of them admitted in Commission, that error could not be

---

[17] From Martin Fotherby's translation of Euripides. Fotherby, Bishop of Sarum, was the author of *Atheomastix: clearing foure truthes against atheists and infidels* . . . (London, 1622), the source of most of the poetic quotations in the *Generall Historie*.

[18] Capahowosick was located a few miles downstream on the York River.

[19] Small cannons.

[20] Saker Falcons, birds of prey originally from the Middle East, trained by the English royalty and aristocracy for hunting and sport.

[21] Two of the men who had accompanied Smith on his exploration of the river and were killed in their sleep by the Powhatans. See Leviticus 24:17: "And he that killeth any man shall surely be put to death."

[22] The first line is Smith's; the second line is from Fotherby, from a sentence of Euripides quoted by Plutarch.

[23] Pocahontas married the tobacco planter, John Rolfe in 1613, an alliance that Smith contends produced peaceful trade between the settlers and the Powhatans.

prevented by the Electors; there being no other choise, and all strangers to each others education, qualities, or disposition. And if any deeme it a shame to our Nation to have any mention made of those inormities, let them peruse the Histories of the Spanyards Discoveries and Plantations, where they may see how many mutinies, disorders, and dissensions have accompanied them, and crossed their attempts: which being knowne to be particular mens offences; doth take away the generall scorne and contempt, which malice, presumption, covetousnesse, or ignorance might produce; to the scandall and reproach of those, whose actions and valiant resolutions deserve a more worthy respect.

Now whether it had beene better for Captaine Smith, to have concluded with any of those severall projects, to have abandoned the Country, with some ten or twelve of them, who were called the better sort, and have left Master Hunt our Preacher, Master Anthony Gosnoll, a most honest, worthy, and industrious Gentleman, Master Thomas Wotton, and some 27 others of his Countrymen to the fury of the Salvages, famine, and all manner of mischiefes, and inconveniences, (for they were but fortie in all to keepe possession of this large Country;) or starve himselfe with them for company, for want of lodging: or but adventuring abroad to make them provision, or by his opposition to preserve the action, and save all their lives; I leave to the censure of all honest men to consider. But

> We men imagine in our Jolitie,
> That 'tis all one, or good or bad to be.
> But then anone wee alter this againe,
> If happily wee feele the sence of paine;
> For then we're turn'd into a mourning vaine.[24]

From *Chapter III: The Arrivall of the first supply, with their Proceedings, and the Ships returne*

[Captain Newport, accompanied by Smith, visits Powhatan.]

But finding all things well, by two or three hundred Salvages they were kindly conducted to their towne. Where Powhatan strained himselfe to the utmost of his greatnesse to entertaine them, with great shouts of joy, Orations of protestations; and with the most plenty of victualls he could provide to feast them. Sitting upon his bed of mats, his pillow of leather imbrodered (after their rude manner with pearle and white Beads) his attyre a faire robe of skinnes as large as an Irish mantell: at his head and feete a handsome young woman: on each side his house sat twentie of his Concubines, their heads and shoulders painted red, with a great chaine of white beads about each of their neckes. Before those sat his chiefest men in like order in his arbour-like house, and more then fortie platters of fine bread stood as a guard in two fyles on each side the doore. Foure or five hundred people made a guard behinde them for our passage; and Proclamation was made, none upon paine of death to presume to doe us any wrong or discourtesie. With many pretty Discourses to renew their old acquaintance, this great King and our Captaine spent the time, till the ebbe left our Barge aground. Then renewing their feasts with feates, dauncing and singing, and such like mirth, we quartered that night with Powhatan. The next day Newport came a shore and received as much content as those people could give him: a boy named Thomas Salvage was then given unto Powhatan, whom Newport called his sonne; for whom Powhatan gave him Namontack his trustie servant, and one of a shrewd, subtill capacitie. Three or foure dayes more we spent in feasting, dauncing, and trad-

---

[24]   From Fotherby's translation of Solon.

ing, wherein Powhatan carried himselfe so proudly, yet discreetly (in his salvage manner) as made us all admire his naturall gifts, considering his education.

1624

FROM *A DESCRIPTION OF NEW ENGLAND*

. . . Who can desire more content that hath small meanes, or but onely his merit to advance his fortunes, then to tread and plant that ground he hath purchased by the hazard of his life; if hee have but the taste of vertue and magnanimity, what to such a minde can bee more pleasant then planting and building a foundation for his posterity, got from the rude earth by Gods blessing and his owne industry without prejudice to any, if hee have any graine of faith or zeale in Religion, what can he doe lesse hurtfull to any, or more agreeable to God, then to seeke to convert those poore Salvages to know Christ and humanity, whose labours with discretion will triple requite thy charge and paine; what so truly sutes with honour and honesty, as the discovering things unknowne, erecting Townes, peopling Countries, informing the ignorant, reforming things unjust, teaching vertue and gaine to our native mother Country; a Kingdome to attend her, finde imploiment for those that are idle, because they know not what to doe: so farre from wronging any, as to cause posterity to remember thee, and remembring thee, ever honour that remembrance with praise. Consider what were the beginnings and endings of the Monarchies of the Chaldeans, the Syrians, the Grecians and Romans, but this one rule; what was it they would not doe for the good of their common weale, or their mother City? For example: Rome, what made her such a Monarchesse, but onely the adventures of her youth, not in riots at home, but in dangers abroad, and the justice and judgement out of their experiences when they grew aged; what was their wine and hurt but this, the excesse of idlenesse, the fondnesse of parents, the want of experience in Majestrates, the admiration of their undeserved honours, the contempt of true merit, their unjust jealousies, their politike incredulities, their hypocriticall seeming goodnesse and their deeds of secret lewdnesse; finally in fine, growing onely formall temporists, all that their Predecessors got in many yeeres they lost in a few daies: those by their paines and vertues became Lords of the world, they by their ease and vices became slaves to their servants; this is the difference betwixt the use of armes in the field, and on the monuments of stones, the golden age and the leaden age, prosperity and misery, justice and corruption, substance and shadowes, words and deeds, experience and imagination, making common weales, and marring common weales, the fruits of vertue, and the conclusions of vice.

. . . but if an Angell should tell you any place yet unknowne can affoord such fortunes, you would not beleeve it, no more then Columbus was beleeved there was any such land, as is now the well knowne abounding America, much lesse such large Regions as are yet unknowne, as well in America, as in Africa and Asia, and Terra incognita[1].

I have not beene so ill bred but I have tasted of plenty and pleasure, as well as want and misery; nor do'th necessity yet, or occasion of discontent force me to these endevours, nor am I ignorant what small thankes I shall have for my paines, or that many would have the world imagine them to bee of great judgement, that can but blemish these my designes, by their witty objections and detractions, yet (I hope) my reasons with my deeds will so prevaile with some, that I shall not want imploiment in these affaires, to make the most blinde see his owne

---

[1]   Unknown earth (Latin).

senselesnesse and incredulity, hoping that gaine will make them affect that which Religion, Charity and the common good cannot. It were but a poore device in mee to deceive my selfe, much more the King and State, my Friends and Country with these inducements, which seeing his Majesty hath given permission, I wish all sorts of worthy honest industrious spirits would understand, and if they desire any further satisfaction, I will doe my best to give it, not to perswade them to goe onely, but goe with them; not leave them there, but live with them there: I will not say but by ill providing and undue managing, such courses may bee taken may make us miserable enough: but if I may have the execution of what I have projected, if they want to eat, let them eat or never digest mee; If I performe what I say, I desire but that reward out of the gaines may sute my paines, quality and condition, and if I abuse you with my tongue, take my head for satisfaction. If any dislike at the yeeres end, defraying their charge, by my consent they should freely returne; I feare not want of company sufficient, were it but knowne what I know of these Countries, and by the proofe of that wealth I hope yeerely to returne, if God please to blesse me from such accidents as are beyond my power in reason to prevent; for I am not so simple to thinke that ever any other motive then wealth will ever erect there a common wealth, or draw company from their ease and humors at home, to stay in New England to effect my purposes. . . .

My purpose is not to perswade children from their parents, men from their wives, nor servants from their masters; onely such as with free consent may bee spared: but that each Parish, or Village, in Citie, or Country, that will but apparell their fatherlesse children of thirteene or foureteene yeeres of age, or young maried people that have small wealth to live on, here by their labour may live exceeding well. Provided alwaies, that first there be a sufficient power to command them, houses to receive them, meanes to defend them, and meet provisions for them, for any place may be over-laine: and it is most necessary to have a fortresse (ere this grow to practice) and sufficient masters, of all necessarie, mecanicall qualities, to take ten or twelve of them for Apprentises; the Master by this may quickly grow rich, these may learne their trades themselves to doe the like, to a generall and an incredible benefit for King and Country, Master and Servant.

. . . Religion above all things should move us, especially the Clergie, if we are religious, to shew our faith by our works, in converting those poore Salvages to the knowledge of God, seeing what paines the Spaniards takes to bring them to their adultered[2] faith. Honour might move the Gentry, the valiant, and industrious, and the hope and assurance of wealth, all, if we were that we would seeme, and be accounted; or be we so farre inferior to other Nations, or our spirits so farre dejected from our ancient predecessors, or our mindes so upon spoile, piracy, and such villany, as to serve the Portugall, Spaniard, Dutch, French, or Turke, (as to the cost of Europe too many doe) rather then our God, our King, our Country, and our selves; excusing our idlenesse and our base complaints by want of imploiment, when here is such choice of all sorts, and for all degrees, in the planting and discovering these North parts of America.

1616

---

[2]   Adulterated.

Richard Ligon (1585?–1662)

The little we know about Richard Ligon comes from his single publication, *A True and Exact History of the Island of Barbadoes*. Apparently, through a series of unwise alliances, he found himself, as he says in his introductory remarks, "a stranger in my own Country, and therefore resolv'd to lay hold on the first opportunity that might convey me to any other part of the World, how far distant soever, rather than abide here." Like many of his fellow countrymen, he determined to start over in the New World and shipped out for the West Indies on June 16, 1647. After only about two years' residence, he fell seriously ill and was forced to return to England in much the same financial straits, and was immediately thrown into debtors' prison at Newgate. There, in the hopes of raising money for his release, he composed his detailed account of the life and customs of the island of Barbadoes, including descriptions of its burgeoning sugar refineries and slave culture, complete with diagrams, maps, and illustrations. This account, which first appeared in 1657, was widely successful and was reprinted in 1673. Ligon shares many attitudes with other imperial observers, but his eye for details and his relish of technical languages, from women's fancy dress, to the process of sugar refining, rises to the level of metaphor. He can, at once, revel in the unparalleled beauty of a Cape Verdean governor's "black Mistress," while analyzing acutely the "marked" and servile status of Africans in the colonial caste system. He is continually drawn to the mysterious tropical landscape, but lays out in hard-headed business terms the costs of starting and maintaining a plantation. In his eloquent and revealing rehearsal of the comparative charms of England and Barbadoes, he begins to imagine what the new hybrid – the man who creates himself anew, the "American" – might be.

PRIMARY WORK

A True and Exact History of the Island of Barbadoes, 1657.

FURTHER READING

Myra Jehlen, "History beside the Fact: What We Learn from *A True and Exact History of Barbadoes*," *The Politics of Research*, eds Ann E. Kaplan and George Levine (New Jersey: Rutgers University Press, 1997).

FROM *A TRUE AND EXACT HISTORY OF THE ISLAND OF BARBADOES*[1]

{Entertainment at the Cape Verde Islands}

Dinner being ended, and the Padre well neere wearie of his wayting, we rose, and made roome for better Companie; for now the Padre, and his blacke mistresse were to take their turnes; A *Negro* of the greatest beautie and majestie together that ever I saw in one woman. Her stature large, and excellently shap't, well favour'd, full eye'd, and admirably grac't; she wore on her head a roll of green taffatie, strip't with white and Philiamort[2], made up in the manner of a Turban; and over that a sleight vayle, which she tooke off at pleasure. On her bodie next her linen, a Peticoate of Orange Tawny and Skye Colour; not done with Straite stripes, but wav'd; and upon that a mantle of purple silke, ingrayld[3] with straw Colour. This Mantle was large, and tyed with a knot of verie broad black Ribbon, with a rich Jewell on her right shoulder, which came under her left arme, and so hung loose and carelessly, almost to the ground. On

---

[1]   The text, with slight modifications, is from the reprint of the first edition published in London in 1673.

[2]   A corruption of "feuille morte" or dead leaf, thus the color of dead or faded leaves.

[3]   Obsolete form of engrail, to ornament the edge in an indented pattern of curved notches, or to adorn with mixed colors.

her Legs, she wore buskins of wetched[4] Silke, deckt wth Silver lace, and Fringe; Her shooes, of white Leather, lac't with skie colour; and pinkt between those laces. In her eares, she wore Large Pendants, about her neck; and on her armes, fayre Pearles. But her eyes were her richest Jewells: for they were the largest, and most orientall, that I have ever seene.

Seing all these perfections in her onely at passage, but not yet heard her Speake; I was resolv'd after dinner, to make an Essay what a present of rich silver silke and gold Ribbon would doe, to perswade her to open her lips: Partly out of a Curiositie, to see whether her teeth were exactly white, and cleane, as I hop'd they were; for 'tis a generall opinion, that all *Negroes* have white teeth; but that is a Common error, for the black and white, being so neere together, they set off one another with the greater advantage. But looke neerer to them, and you shall find those teeth, which at a distance appear'd rarely white, are yellow and foul. This knowledge wrought this Curiositie in me, but it was not the mayne end of my enquirie; for there was now, but one thing more, to set her off in my opinion, the rarest black swanne that I had ever seen, and that was her language, and gracefull delivery of that, which was to unite and confirme a perfection in all the rest. And to that end I took a Gentleman that spoke good Spanish with me, and awaited her coming out, which was with far greater majesty, and gracefulness, then I have seen Queen *Anne*[5], descend from the Chaire of State, to dance the Measures with a Baron of *England*, at a Maske in the Banquetting house. And truly, had her followers and friends, with other perquisits (that ought to be the attendants on such a state and beautie) wayted on her, I had made a stop, and gone no farther. But finding her but slightly attended and considering she was but the Padres Mistres, and therefore the more accessible, I made my addresses to her, by my interpreter; and told her, I had some Trifles made by the people of *England*, which their value were not worthy her acceptance, yet for their Novelty, they might be of some esteem, such having bin worn by the great Queens of *Europe*, and intreated her to vouchsafe to receive them. She with much gravity, and reeserv'dness, opened the paper; but when she lookt on them, the Colours pleased her so, as she put her gravity into the loveliest smile that I have ever seen. And then shewed her rowes of pearls, so clean, white, Orient, and well shaped, as *Neptunes*[6] Court was never pav'd with such as these; and to shew whether was whiter, or more Orient, those or the whites of her eyes, she turn'd them up, and gave me such a look, as was a sufficient return for a far greater present, and withall wisht, I would think of somewhat wherein she might pleasure me, and I should find her both ready and willing. And so with a graceful bow of her neck, she took her way towards her own house; which was not above a stones cast from the *Padres*. Other addresses were not to be made without the dislike of the *Padre*, for they are there as jealous of their Mistrisses, as the *Italians* of their wives.

{The number and nature of the Inhabitants of Barbadoes}

The Island is divided into three sorts of men, *viz.* Masters, Servants, and Slaves. The slaves and their posterity, being subject to their Masters for ever, are kept and preserv'd with greater care than the servants, who are theirs but for five years, according to the law of the Island. So that for the time, the servants have the worser lives, for they are put to very hard labour, ill lodging, and their dyet very sleight. When we came first on the Island, some Planters themselves did not eat bone meat, above twice a week: the rest of the seven dayes, Potatoes, Loblolly, and

---

4 Obsolete form of watchet, a light blue color.

5 Anne of Denmark (1574–1619) married James Stuart, (James VI of Scotland and James I of England) and was crowned Queen of England in 1603.

6 Roman god of the sea.

Bonavist.[7] But the servants no bone meat at all, unless an Oxe dyed: and then they were feasted, as long as that lasted. And till they had planted good store of Plantines, the Negroes were fed with this kind of food; but most of it Bonavist, and Loblolly, with some ears of Mayes toasted, which food (especially Loblolly,) gave them much discontent: But when they had Plantines enough to serve them, they were heard no more to complain; for 'tis a food they take great delight in, and their manner of dressing, and eating it, is this: 'tis gathered for them (somewhat before it be ripe, for so they desire to have it,) upon *Saturday*, by the keeper of the Plantine grove; who is an able *Negro*, and knowes well the number of those that are to be fed with this fruit; and as he gathers, layes them all together, till they fetch them away, which is about five a clock in the afternoon, for that day they break off work sooner by an hour: partly for this purpose, and partly for that the fire in the furnaces is to be put out, and the Ingenio[8] and the rooms made clean; besides they are to wash, shave and trim themselves against *Sunday*. But 'tis a lovely sight to see a hundred handsom *Negroes*, men and women, with every one a grasse-green bunch of these fruits on their heads, every bunch twice as big as their heads, all coming in a train one after another, the black and green so well becoming one another. Having brought this fruit home to their own houses, and pilling off the skin of so much as they will use, they boyl it in water, making it into balls, and so they eat it. One bunch a week is a Negroe's allowance. To this, no bread nor drink, but water. Their lodging at night a board, with nothing under, nor any thing a top of them. They are happy people, whom so little contents. Very good servants, if they be not spoyled by the *English*. But more of them hereafter.

As for the usage of the Servants, it is much as the Master is, merciful or cruel; Those that are merciful, treat their Servants well, both in their meat, drink, and lodging, and given them such work, as is not unfit for Christians to do. But if the Masters be cruel, the Servants have very wearisome and miserable lives. Upon the arrival of any ship, that brings servants to the Island, the Planters go aboard; and having bought such of them as they like, send them with a guide to his Plantation; and being come, commands them instantly to make their Cabins, which they not knowing how to do, are to be advised by other of their servants, that are their Seniors; but, if they be churlish, and will not shew them, or if materials be wanting, to make them Cabins, then they are to lye on the ground that night. These Cabins are to be made of sticks, withs[9], and Plantine leaves, under some little shade that may keep the rain off; Their suppers being a few Potatoes for meat, and water or Mobbie[10] for drink. The next day they are rung out with a Bell to work, at six a clock in the morning, with a severe Overseer to command them, till the Bell ring again, which is at eleven a clock; and then they return, and are set to dinner, either with a mess of Loblolly, Bonavist, or Potatoes. At one a clock, they are rung out again to the field, there to work till six, and then come again, to a supper of the same. And if it chance to rain, and wet them through, they have no shift, but must lye so all night. If they put off their cloaths, the cold of the night will strike into them; and if they be not strong men, this ill lodging will put them into a sickness: if they complain, they are beaten by the Overseer; if they resist, their time is doubled, I have seen an Overseer beat a Servant with a cane about the head, till the blood has followed, for a fault that is not worth the speaking of; and yet he must have patience, or worse will follow. Truly, I have seen such cruelty there done to Servants, as I did not think one Christian could have done to another. But, as discreeter and better natur'd men have come to rule there, the servants lie in Hamocks, and in warm rooms,

---

[7]   Bonavist: a species of kidney beans. Loblolly: a rustic dish of thick gruel or spoon-meat.

[8]   Sugar mill.

[9]   Withes, a tough, flexible twig or branch used for binding, tying, or plaiting.

[10]   A spiritous liquor made from sweet potatoes.

and when they come in wet, have shift of shirts and drawers, which is all the cloths they wear, and are fed with *bone meat* twice or thrice a week. Collonel *Walrond* seeing his servants when they came home, toyled with their labour, and wet through with their sweating, thought that shifting of their linnen not sufficient refreshing, nor warmth for their bodies, their pores being much opened by their sweating; and therefore resolved to send into England for rug Gowns, such as poor people wear in Hospitals, that so when they had shifted themselves, they might put on those Gowns, and lye down and rest them in their Hamocks: For the Hamocks being but thin, and they having nothing on but Shirts and Drawers, when they awak'd out of their sleeps, they found themselves very cold; and a cold taken there, is harder to be recovered, than in *England*, by how much the body is infeebled by the great toyl, and the Sun's heat, which cannot but very much exhaust the spirits of bodies unaccustomed to it. But this care and charity of Collonel *Walrond's*, lost him nothing in the conclusion; for, he got such love of his servants, as they thought all too little they could do for him; and the love of the servants there, is of much concernment to the Masters, not only in their diligent and painful labour, but in fore-seeing and preventing mischiefs that often happen, by the carelessness and slothfulness of retchless servants; sometimes by laying fire so negligently, as whole lands of Canes and Houses too, are burnt down and consumed, to the utter ruine and undoing of their Masters . . .

It has been accounted a strange thing, that the *Negroes*, being more than double the numbers of the Christians that are there, and they accounted a bloody people, where they think they have power or advantages; and the more bloody, by how much they are more fearful than others: that these should not commit some horrid massacre upon the Christians, thereby to enfranchise themselves, and become Masters of the Island. But there are three reasons that take away this wonder; the one is, They are not suffered to touch or handle any weapons: The other, That they are held in such awe and slavery, as they are fearful to appear in any daring act; and seeing the mustering of our men, and hearing their Gun-shot, (than which nothing is more terrible to them) their spirits are subjugated to so low a condition, as they dare not look up to any bold attempt. Besides these, there is a third reason, which stops all designs of that kind, and that is, They are fetch'd from several parts of *Africa*, who speak several languages, and by that means, one of them understands not another: For, some of them are fetch'd from *Guinny* and *Binny*, some from *Cutchew*, some from *Angola*, and some from the River of *Gambia*.[11] And in some of these places where petty Kingdomes are, they sell their Subjects, and such as they take in Battle, whom they make slaves; and some mean men sell their Servants, their Children, and sometimes their Wives; and think all good traffick, for such commodities as our Merchants send them.

When they are brought to us, the Planters buy them out of the Ship, where they find them stark naked, and therefore cannot be deceived in any outward infirmity. They choose them as they do Horses in a Market; the strongest, youthfullest, and most beautiful, yield the greatest prices. Thirty pound sterling is a price for the best man *Negroe*; and twenty five, twenty six, or twenty seven pound for a Woman; the Children are at easier rates. And we buy them so, as the sexes may be equal, . . . the most of them are as near beasts as may be, setting their souls aside. Religion they know none; yet most of them acknowledge a God, as appears by their motions and gestures: For, if one of them do another wrong, and he cannot revenge himself, he looks up to Heaven for vengeance, and holds up both his hands, as if the power must come from thence, that must do him right. Chast they are as any people under the Sun; for, when the men and women are together naked, they never cast their eyes towards the parts that ought to be cov-

---

[11]   All places on the west coast of Africa which provided slaves for trading.

ered; and those amongst us, that have Breeches and Petticoats, I never saw so much as a kiss, or embrace, or a wanton glance with their eyes between them. Jealous they are of their Wives, and hold it up for a great injury and scorn, if another man make the least courtship to his Wife. And if any of their Wives have two Children at birth, they conclude her false to his Bed, and so no more adoe but hang her. . . .

At the time the wife is to be brought a bed, her Husband removes his board, (which is his bed) to another room (for many several divisions they have, in their little houses,) and none above six foot square. And leaves his wife to God, and her good fortune, in the room, and upon the board alone, and calls a neighbour to come to her, who gives little help to her delivery, but when the child is born, (which she calls her Pickaninny) she helps to make a little fire near her feet, and that serves instead of Possets, Broaths, and Caudles.[12] In a fortnight, this woman is at work with her Pickaninny at her back, as merry a soul as any is there. If the Overseer be discreet, she is suffer'd to rest her self a little more than ordinary; but if not, she is compelled to do as others do. Times they have of suckling their Children in the fields, and refreshing themselves; and good reason, for they carry burthens on their backs; and yet work too. Some women, whose Pickaninnies are three years old, will, as they work at weeding, which is a stooping work, suffer the hee Pickaninny, to sit a stride upon their backs, like *St George* a Horse-back; and there Spur his mother with his heels, and sings and crows on her back, clapping his hands, as if he meant to flye; which the mother is so pleas'd with, as she continues her painful stooping posture, longer than she would do, rather than discompose her Jovial Pickaninny of his pleasure, so glad she is to see him merry. The work which the women do, is most of it weeding, a stooping and painful work; at noon and night they are call'd home by the ring of a Bell, where they have two hours time for their repast at noon; and at night, they rest from six, till six a Clock next morning.

On *Sunday*, they rest, and have the whole day at their pleasure; and the most of them use it as a day of rest and pleasure; but some of them who will make benefit of that dayes liberty, go where the Mangrave trees grow, and gather the bark, of which they make ropes, which they truck away[13] for other Commodities, as Shirts and Drawers.

In the afternoons on *Sundayes*, they have their Musick, which is of kettle drums, and those of several sizes; upon the smallest the best Musitian playes, and the other come in a Chorasses: the drum all men know, has but one tone; and therefore variety of tunes have little to do in this musick; and yet so strangely they varie their time, as 'tis a pleasure to the most curious ears, and it was to me one of the strangest noises that ever I heard made of one tone; and if they had the variety of tune, which gives the greater scope in Musick, as they have of time, they would do wonders in that Art. And if I had not fal'n sick before my coming away, at least seven months in one sickness, I had given them some hints of tunes, which being understood, would have serv'd as a great addition to their hamony; for time without tune, is not an eighth part of the Science of Musick. . . .

Another, of another kind of speculation I found . . . and this man with three or four more, were to attend me into the woods, to cut Church wayes[14], for I was employed sometimes upon publick works; and those men were excellent Axe-men, and because there were many gullies in the way, which were impassable, and by that means I was compell'd to make traverses, up and down in the wood; and was by that in danger to miss of the point, to which I was to make my passage to the Church, and therefore was fain to take a Compass with me, which was a

---

[12]   Possets: a soothing drink of hot milk and liquor.
Caudles: a warm drink of thin gruel mixed with liquor.
[13]   Trade.

[14]   Wooden planks laid over gullies to make passage to Church possible.

Circumferenter[15], to make my traverses the more exact, and indeed without which, it could not be done, setting up the Circumferenter, and observing the Needle: This Negre *Sambo* comes to me, and seeing the needle wag, desired to know the reason of its stirring, and whether it were alive: I told him no, but it stood upon a point, and for a while it would stir, but by and by stand still, which he observ'd and found it to be true.

The next questions was, why it stood one way, and would not remove to any other point, I told him that it would stand no way but North and South, and upon that shew'd him the four Cardinal points of the compass, East, West, North, South, which he presently learnt by heart, and promis'd me never to forget it. His last question was, why it would stand North, I have this reason, because of the huge Rocks of Loadstone that were in the North part of the world, which had a quality to draw Iron to it; and this Needle being of Iron, and touch'd with a Loadstone, it would always stand that way.

This point of Philosophy was a little too hard for him, and so he stood in a strange muse; which to put him out of, I bad him reach his axe and put it near to the Compass, and remove it about; and as he did so, the Needle turned with it, which put him in the greatest admiration that ever I saw a man, and so quite gave over his questions, and desired me, that he might be made a Christian; for, he thought to be a Christian, was to be endued with all those knowledges he wanted.

I promised to do my best endeavour; and when I came home, spoke to the Master of the Plantation, and told him, that poor *Sambo* desired much to be a Christian. But his answer was, That the people of that Island were governed by the Lawes of *England*, and by those Lawes, we could not make Christian a Slave. I told him, my request was far different from that, for I desired him to make a Slave a Christian. His answer was, That it was true, there was a great difference in that: But, being once a Christian, he could no more account him a Slave, and so lose the hold they had of them as Slaves, by making them Christians; and by that means should open such a gap, as all the Planters in the Island would curse him. So I was struck mute, and poor *Sambo* kept out of the Church; as ingenious, as honest, and as good natur'd poor soul, as ever wore black, or eat green. . . .

Though there be a mark set upon these people, which will hardly ever be wip'd off, as of their cruelties when they have advantages, and of their fearfulness and falseness; yet no rule so general but hath his acception: for I believe, and I have strong motives to cause me to be of that perswasion, that there are as honest, faithful, and conscionable people amongst them, as amongst those of *Europe*, or any other part of the world. . . .

As for the *Indians*, we have but few, and those fetcht from other Countries; some from the neighbouring Islands, some from the Main, which we make slaves: the women who are better vers'd in ordering the Cassavie[16] and making bread, then the *Negroes*, we imploy for that purpose, as also for making Mobbie: the men we use for footmen, and killing of fish, which they are good at; with their own bowes and arrows they will go out; and in a dayes time, kill as much fish, as will serve a family of a dozen persons, two or three dayes, if you can keep the fish so long. They are very active men, and apt to learn any thing, sooner than the *Negroes*; and as different from them in shape, almost as in colour; the men very broad shoulder'd, deep breasted, with large heads, and their faces almost three square, broad about the eyes and temples, and sharp at the chin, their skins some of them brown, some a bright Bay[17], they are

[15] An instrument used for surveying, consisting of a flat brass bar with sights at the ends and a circular brass box in the middle, containing a magnetic needle that plays over a graduated circle.

[16] Cassava, a plant extensively cultivated in the West Indies, tropical America and Africa for its nutritious roots which was an important part of the native and slave diet.

[17] Reddish-brown color, generally used of horses.

much craftier, and subtiler than the *Negroes*; and in their nature falser; but in their bodies more active: their women have very small breasts, and have more of the shape of the *Europeans* than the *Negroes*, their hair black and long, a great part whereof hangs down upon their backs, as low as their haunches, with a large lock hanging over either breast, which seldom or never curles: cloaths they scorn to wear, especially if they be well shap'd; a girdle they use of tape, covered with little smooth shels of fishes, white, and from their flank of one side, to their flank on the other side, a fringe of blew *Bugle*[18], which hangs so low as to cover their privities. We had an *Indian* woman, a slave in the house, who was of excellent shape and colour, for it was a pure bright bay; small breasts, with the niples of a porphyrie[19] colour, this woman would not be woo'd by any means to wear Cloaths. She chanc'd to be with Child, by a Christian servant, and lodging in the *Indian* house, amongst other women of her own Country, where the Christian servants, both men and women came; and being very great, and that her time was come to be delivered, loath to fall in labour before the men, walk'd down to a Wood, in which was a Pond of water, and there by the side of the Pond, brought her self a bed; and presently washing her Child in some of the water of the Pond, lap'd it up in such rags, as she had begg'd of the Christians; and in three hours time came home, with her Child in her arms, a lusty Boy, frolick and lively.

This *Indian* dwelling near the Sea-coast, upon the Main, an *English* ship put in to a Bay, and sent some of her men ashoar, to try what victuals or water they could find, for in some distress they were: But the *Indians* perceiving them to go up so far into the Country, as they were sure they could not make a safe retreat, intercepted them in their return, and fell upon them, chasing them into a Wood, and being dispersed there, some were taken, and some kill'd: but a young man amongst them stragling from the rest, was met by this *Indian* Maid, who upon the first sight fell in love with him, and hid him close from her Countrymen (the *Indians*) in a Cave, and there fed him, till they could safely go down to the shoar, where the ship lay at anchor, expecting the return of their friends. But at last, seeing them upon the shoar, sent the long-Boat for them, took them aboard, and brought them away. But the youth, when he came ashoar in the *Barbadoes*, forgot the kindness of the poor maid, that had ventured her life for his safety, and sold her for a slave, who was as free born as he: And so poor *Tarico* for her love, lost her liberty.[20]

Now for the Masters, I have yet said but little, nor am able to say half of what they deserve. They are men of great abilities and parts, otherwise they could not go through, with such great works as they undertake; the managing of one of their Plantations, being a work of such a latitude, as will require a very good head-peece, to put in order, and continue it so. . . .

Now let us consider how many things there are to be thought on, that go to the actuating this great work, and how many cares to prevent the mischances, that are incident to the retarding, if not the frustrating of the whole work; and you will find them wise and provident men, that go on and prosper in a work, that depends upon so many contingents.

This I say, to stop those mens mouths, that lye here at home, and expect great profit in their adventures, and never consider, through what difficulty, industry and pains it is acquired. And thus much I thought good to say, of the abilities of the Planters.

---

[18]   A tube shaped glass bead, usually black, used to ornament clothing.
[19]   A shell of the genus Murex from which a deep purple dye was obtained.

[20]   This famous anecdote, a kind of epitome of the West's fantasy of colonization, was retold by Richard Steele in *The Spectator*, as the story of Inkle (slang for "English") and Yarico.

{Compares the Pleasures of England and Barbadoes}

And for the pleasures of England, let us consider what they are, that we may be the better able to judge how far they are consistent with the Climate of Barbadoes, and what gainers or losers they will be by the exchange, that makes the adventure; and by the knowledge and well weighting of that, invite or deter those, that are the great lovers and admirers of those delights, to come there, or stay away. . . .

Now for the beauty of the Heavens, they are as far transcending all we ever saw in England, or elsewhere 40 Degrees without the Line, on either side, as the land objects of the Barbadoes are short of ours in Europe. So he that can content himself with the beauties of the Heavens, may there be sufficiently satisfied. But we Mortals, that Till and love the earth, because our selves are made up of the same mold, take pleasure sometimes to look downward, upon the fruits and effects of our own labours; and when we find them thrive by the blessings of the great Creator, we look up to give thanks, where we find so great a glory, as to put us into astonishment and admiration. . . .

For the sense of feeling, it can be applied but two wayes, either in doing or suffering; the poor Negroes and Christian servants find it perfectly upon their heads and shoulders, by the hands of their severe Overseers; so that little pleasure is given the sense, by this coercive kind of feeling, more than a plaister for a broken Pate;[21] but, this is but a passive kind of feeling: But take it in the highest, and most active way it can be applied, which is upon the skins of women, and they are so sweaty and clammy, as the hand cannot passe over, without being glued and cemented in the passage or motion; and by that means, little pleasure is given to, or received by the agent or the patient: and therefore if this sense be neither pleased in doing nor suffering, we may decline it as useless in a Country, where down of Swans, or wool of Beaver is wanting.

Now for the sense of Tasting, I do confess, it receives a more home satisfaction, than all the rest, by reason of the fruits that grow there; so that the Epicure cannot be deceived, if he take a long journy to please his palate, finding all excellent tastes the world has, comprehended in one single fruit, the Pine. And would not any Prince be content to reduce his base coyne, into Ingots of pure gold? And so much shall serve touching the Barbadoes. . . .

The voluptuous man, who thinks the day not long enough for him to take his pleasure. Nor the sleepie man, who thinks the longest night too short for him to dream out his delights, are not fit to repose and solace themselves upon this Island; for in the whole compass of the Zodiack, they shall neither find St Barnabies day, or St Lucies night,[22] the sun running an even course, is there an indifferent Arbiter of the differences which are between those two Saints, and like a just and cleer sighted Judge, reconciles those extreams to a Medium of 12 and 12 hours, which equality of time is utterly inconsistent to the humours and dispositions of these men.

But I speak this, to such as have their fancies so Aereal, and refin'd as not to be pleased with ordinary delight, but think to build and settle a felicity here: above the ordinary level of mankind. Such Spirits, are too volatile to fix on business; and therefore I will leave them out, as useless in this Common-wealth. But such as are made of middle earth, and can be content to wave those pleasures, which stand as Blocks, and Portcullisses[23], in their way; and are indeed

---

[21]   Plaster: a curative application placed on a wound. Pate: head.

[22]   Saints whose feast days are on the longest and shortest days of the year respectively. St Lucy, a virgin martyr, and one of the first saints to achieve popularity, is venerated on December 13. John Donne composed a "Nocturnal Upon St Lucy's Day, Being the Shortest Day."

[23]   Portcullis: a heavy grating on the gateway of a fortress that can be quickly pulled up or down.

the main Remora's[24] in their passage to their profits. Such may here find moderate delights, with moderate labour, and those taken moderately will conduce much to their healths, and they that have industry, to imploy that well, may make it the Ladder to climb to a high degree of Wealth and opulencie, in this sweet Negotiation of Sugar, provided they have a competent stock to begin with; such I mean as may settle them in a Sugar-work, and less than 14,000 £. sterling, will not do that: in a Plantation of 500 acres of land, with a proportionable stock of Servants, Slaves, Horses, Camels, Cattle, Assinigoes, with an Ingenio, and all other houseing, thereunto belonging; such as I have formerly nam'd.

But one will say, why should any man that has 14,000£. in his purse need to run so long a Risco, as from hence to the Barbadoes: when he may live with ease and plenty at home; to such a one I answer, that every drone can sit and eat the Honey of his own Hive: But he that can by his own Industry, and activity, (having youth and strength to friends,) raise his fortune, from a small beginning to a very great one, and in his passage to that, do good to the publique, and be charitable to the poor, and this to be accomplished in a few years, deserves much more commendation and applause. And shall find his bread, gotten by his painful and honest labour and industry, eat sweeter by much, than his that onely minds his ease, and his belly.

1657

George Alsop (1636?–1673?)

Probably born in Westminster, London, in 1636, George Alsop was the older son of Rose and Peter Alsop. His father was a tailor by trade, and Alsop served a two-year apprenticeship in handicraft. But in 1658, fearful that he would suffer political recriminations from Oliver Cromwell's government because of his support for the restoration of the English monarchy, he emigrated to Maryland as an indentured servant. For the next four years, he worked for Thomas Stockett, a planter living on the frontier near the Susquehanna Indians. Exploiting his literacy, Alsop acted as secretary and accountant and perhaps also as an agent in trade with the Native Americans. After his indenture was over in 1662, Alsop remained in Maryland. When he returned to England late in 1663 or 1664, supporters of Lord Baltimore, the Maryland Proprietor, asked him to expand the letters he had written to his friends and parents during his sojourn, which formed the four chapters of his only book, *A Character of the Province of Mary-land*, along with his account of the Susquehanna Indians. The events of Alsop's life after this are shadowy; we only know that his name appears in his father's will of 1672.

Witty, satirical, and bawdy, Alsop's *A Character of the Province of Mary-land* promotes emigration, even as an indentured servant, to the colony it praises as the "only Emblem of Tranquility" in a world of regicide and revolution. But Alsop's promotion only thinly veils his fierce Royalist support and anti-Puritan, anti-democratic invective. His argument in Chapter Three for the necessity of servitude recapitulates his commitment to hierarchical social order. And though he argues that Maryland is a place of religious toleration, he reveals his own intolerance of cultural differences by his allegations that the Susquehanna Indians were cannibals, torturers, and practiced child sacrifice. Still, Alsop's prose and verse demonstrate what Maryland could, as he put it, "bring into England," thereby offering a fundamentally different basis for English identity, which he represented as necessary to the survival of the monarchy and all that was "truly English."

PRIMARY WORK

A Character of the Province of Mary-land, 1666.

---

[24]   Remora: obstacle, hindrance, or impediment; from a   sucking fish believed by the ancients to be able to stop ships.

FURTHER READING

J. A. Leo Lemay, *Men of Letters in Colonial Maryland* (Knoxville: University of Tennessee, 1972).

Ted-Larry Pebworth, "The 'Character' of George Alsop's

Mary-land," *Seventeenth-Century-News*, 34 (1976) pp. 64–6.

Darin E. Fields, "George Alsop's Indentured Servant in 'A Character of the Province of Maryland'," *Maryland Historical Magazine*, Fall, 85, 3 (1990) pp. 221–35.

FROM *A CHARACTER OF THE PROVINCE OF MARY-LAND*[1]

The Author to his Book

When first Apollo got my brain with Childe,[2]
He made large promise never to beguile,
But like an honest Father, he would keep
Whatever Issue from my Brain did creep:
With that I gave consent, and up he threw
Me on a Bench, and strangely he did do;
Then every week he daily came to see
How his new Physick still did work with me.
And when he did perceive he'd don the feat.
Like an unworthy man he made retreat,
Left me in desolation, and where none
Compassionated when they heard me groan.
What could he judge the Parish then would think,
To see me fair, his Brat as black as Ink?
If they had eyes, they'd swear I were no Nun,
But got with Child by some black Africk Son,
And so condemn me for my Fornication,
To beat them Hemp to stifle half the Nation.
Well, since 'tis so, I'le alter this base Fate,
And lay his Bastard at some Noble's Gate;
Withdraw my self from Beadles, and from such,
Who would give twelve pence I were in their clutch
Then, who can tell? this Child which I do hide,
May be in time a Small-beer Col'nel Pride.[3]
But while I talk, my business it is dumb,
I must lay double-clothes unto thy Bum,
Then lap thee warm, and to the world commit
The Bastard Off-spring of a New-born wit.
Farewel, poor Brat, thou in a monstrous World,

---

[1]   The selections, with modifications, are from the original edition of 1666, reprinted and edited by Newton D. Mereness (Cleveland: The Burrows Brothers Company, 1902).

[2]   Apollo is the son of Jupiter and patron god of the classical arts. During this period, literary inspiration was often figured as pregnancy which led to the birth of a "brainchild." See Bradstreet's "The Author to her Book."

[3]   During the contentious debate over the restoration of the monarchy, Parliament was largely dominated by supporters of Oliver Cromwell. Colonel Pride managed to prevent a hundred or more members of the House of Commons who favored the restoration of King Charles from entering the chamber. This incident, illustrating the strong-arm tactics of the Puritan regime, became known as "Pride's purge." Small-beer is weak or of inferior quality.

In swadling bands, thus up and down art hurl'd;
There to receive what Destiny doth contrive,
Either to perish, or be sav'd alive.
Good Fate protect thee from a Criticks power,
For If he comes, thou 'rt gon in half an hour,
Stifl'd and blasted, 'tis their usual way,
To make that Night, which is as bright as Day.
For if they once but wring, and skrew their mouth,
Cock up their Hats, and set the point Du-South,
Armes all a kimbo, and with belly strut,
As if they had Parnassus in their gut:[4]
These are the Symtomes of the murthering fall
Of my poor Infant, and his burial.
Say he should miss thee, and some ign'rant Asse
Should find thee out, as he along doth pass,
It were all one, he'd look into thy Tayle,
To see if thou wert Feminine or Male;
When he'd half starv'd thee, for to satisfie
His peeping Ign'rance, he'd then let thee lie;
And vow by's wit he ne're could understand,
The Heathen dresses of another Land:
Well, 'tis no matter, wherever such as he
Knows one grain, more than his simplicity.
Now, how the pulses of my Senses beat,
To think the rigid Fortune thou wilt meet;
Asses and captious Fools, not six in ten
Of thy Spectators will be real men,
To Umpire up the badness of the Cause,
And screen my weakness from the rav'nous Laws,
Of those that will undoubted sit to see
How they might blast this new-born Infancy:
If they should burn him, they'd conclude hereafter,
'Twere too good death for him to dye a Martyr;[5]
And if they let him live, they think it will
Be but a means for to encourage ill,
And bring in time some strange Antipod'ans,
A thousand Leagues beyond Philippians,[6]
To storm our Wits; therefore he must not rest,
But shall be hang'd, for all he has been prest:
Thus they conclude. – My Genius comforts give,
In Resurrection he will surely live.

---

4   Parnassus is a barren mountain in central Greece venerated by the ancient Greeks and Romans as the home of Apollo
and the Muses. Poets considered the mountain's fountain of
Castalia a source of inspiration.
5   During the first half of the seventeenth century, Anglican monarchs martyred Puritan rebels, while both sides
burned books they considered heretical or seditious.

6   People from the "antipodes," or the other side of the earth.
The Philippians were a fledgling Christian community in
eastern Macedonia, to whom St Paul wrote an epistle, the
eleventh book of the New Testament.

From *Chapter 2: Of the Government and Natural Disposition of the People*

. . . One great part of the inhabitants of this Province are desiredly Zealous, great pretenders to Holiness; and where any thing appears that carries on the Frontispiece of its Effigies the stamp Of Religion, though fundamentally never so imperfect, they are suddenly taken with it, and out of an eager desire to any thing that's new, not weighing the sure matter in the Ballance of Reason, are very apt to be catcht. Quakerism is the only Opinion that bears the Bell away: The Anabaptists have little to say here, as well as in other places, since the Ghost of John of Leyden haunts their Conventicles. The Adamite, Ranter, and Fifth-Monarchy men, Mary-Land cannot, nay will not digest within her liberal stomach such corroding morsels:[7] So that this Province is an utter Enemy to blasphemous and zealous Imprecations, drain'd from the Lymbeck[8] of hellish and damnable Spirits, as well as profuse prophaness, that issues from the prodigality of none but cract-brain Sots.

> 'Tis said the Gods lower down that Chain above,
> That tyes both Prince and Subject up in Love;
> And if this Fiction of the Gods be true,
> Few, Mary-Land, in this can boast but you:
> Live ever blest, and let those Clouds that do
> Eclipse most States, be alwayes Lights to you;
> And dwelling so, you may for ever be
> The only Emblem of Tranquility.

From *Chapter 3: The Necessariness of Servitude Proved, with the Common Usage of Servants in Mary-Land, Together with their Priviledges*

As there can be no Monarchy without the Supremacy of a King and Crown, nor no King without Subjects, nor any Parents without it be by the fruitful off-spring of Children; neither can there be any Masters, unless it be by the inferior Servitude of those that dwell under them, by a commanding enjoyment: And since it is ordained from the original and superabounding wisdom of all things, That there should be Degrees and Diversities amongst the Sons of men, in acknowledging of a Superiority from Inferiors to Superiors; the Servant with a reverent and befitting Obedience is as liable to this duty in a measurable performance to him whom he serves, as the loyalest of Subjects to his Prince. Then since it is a common and ordained Fate, that there must be Servants as well as Masters, and that good Servitudes are those Colledges of Sobriety that checks in the giddy and wild-headed youth from his profuse and uneven course of life, by a limited constrainment, as well as it otherwise agrees with the moderate and discreet Servant: Why should there be such an exclusive Obstacle in the minds and unreasonable

---

[7]   The Quakers were members of the Society of Friends, a Protestant sect founded by George Fox, who sought religious freedom in the American colonies. To "bear the bell away" means to take the prize or take first place. Anabaptists were Protestants who believed in the restoration of the primitive Church and practiced adult baptism as described in the Bible. Named after a leader in Bohemia who styled himself "Adam, son of God," the Adamites were a sect who believed they could attain primitive innocence by rejecting marriage and clothing. The Ranters were an amorphous group representing the extreme radical fringe of Protestant sectarianism. The Fifth Monarchists were a religious sect active during the Commonwealth period. Their name alludes to their belief in the need to establish a "fifth monarchy," one to succeed the monarchies of the ancient world (Assyrian, Persian, Grecian, and Roman) and led by Jesus Christ and his saints, who would reign for a thousand years.

[8]   Alembic, an apparatus used for distilling and purifying.

dispositions of many people, against the limited time of convenient and necessary Servitude, when it is a thing so requisite, that the best of Kingdoms would be unhing'd from their quiet and well setled Government without it. Which levelling doctrine we here of England in this latter age (whose womb was truss'd out with nothing but confused Rebellion) have too much experienced, and was daily wrung into the ears of the tumultuous Vulgar by the Bell weather Sectaries[9] of the Times. But (blessed be God) those Clouds are blown over, and the Government of the Kingdom coucht under a more stable form.[10]

There is no truer Emblem of confusion either in Monarchy or Domestick Governments, then when either the Subject, or the Servant, strives for the upper hand of his Prince, or Master, and to be equal with him, from whom he receives his present subsistance: Why then, if Servitude be so necessary that no place can be governed in order, nor people live without it, this may serve to tell those which prick up their ears and bray against it, That they are none but Asses, and deserve the Bridle of a strict commanding power to reine them in: For I'me certainly confident, that there are several Thousands in most Kingdoms of Christendom, that could not at all live and subsist, unless they had served some prefixed time, to learn either some Trade, Art, or Science, and by either of them to extract their present livelihood.

Then methinks this may stop the mouths of those that will undiscreetly compassionate them that dwell under necessary Servitudes; for let but Parents of an indifferent capacity in Estates, when their Childrens age by computation speak them seventeen or eighteen years old, turn them loose to the wide world, without a seven yeare working Apprenticeship (being just brought up to the bare formality of a little reading and writing) and you shall immediately see how weak and shiftless they'le be towards the maintaining and supporting of themselves; and (without either stealing or begging) their bodies like a Sentinel must continually wait to see when their Souls will be frighted away by the pale Ghost of a starving want.

Then let such, where Providence hath ordained to live as Servants, either in England or beyond Sea, endure the prefixed yoak of their limited time with patience, and then in a small computation of years, by an industrious endeavour, they may become Masters and Mistresses of Families themselves. And let this be spoke to the deserved praise of Mary-land, That the four years I served there were not to me so slavish, as a two years Servitude of a Handicraft Apprenticeship was here in London. *Volenti enim nil difficile*[11]: Not that I write this to seduce or delude any, or to draw them from their native soyle, but out of a love to my Countrymen, whom in the general I wish well to, and that the lowest of them may live in such a capacity of Estate, as that the bare interest of their Livelihoods might not altogether depend upon persons of the greatest extendments.

From Chapter 4: Upon Trafique, and what Merchandizing Commodities this Province Affords, also how Tobacco is Planted and made fit for Commerce

> Trafique is Earth's great Atlas, that supports
> The pay of Armies, and the height of Courts,
> And makes Mechanicks live, that else would die
> Meer starving Martyrs to their penury:
> None but the Merchant of this thing can boast,
> He, like the Bee, comes loaden from each Coast,

---

[9]   "Bell-wether" or predominant; from the leading sheep of the flock that wears a bell on its neck.

[10]   After the Commonwealth in which Oliver Cromwell and, at his death, his son acted as Lord Protector (1642–60), Charles II was restored to the throne in January 1661.

[11]   "Not wishing to cause anyone trouble" (Latin).

> And to all Kingdoms, as within a Hive,
> Stows up those Riches, that doth make them thrive:
> Be thrifty, Mary-Land, keep what thou hast in store,
> And each years Trafique to thy self get more.

FROM "A RELATION OF THE CUSTOMS, MANNERS, ABSURDITIES, AND RELIGION OF THE SUSQUEHANOCK INDIANS IN AND NEAR MARY-LAND"

. . . That it would be a most intricate and laborious trouble, to run (with a description) through the several Nations of Indians here in America, considering the innumerableness and diversities of them that dwell on this vast and unmeasured Continent: But rather then I'le be altogether silent, I shall do like the Painter in the Comedy, who being to limne out the Pourtraiture of the Furies, as they severally appeared, set himself behind a Pillar, and between fright and amazement, drew them by guess.[1] Those Indians that I have convers'd withall here in this Province of Mary-Land, and have had any occular experimental view of either of their Customs, Manners, Religions, and Absurdities, are called by the name of Susquehanocks, being a people lookt upon by the Christian Inhabitants, as the most Noble and Heroick Nation of Indians that dwell upon the confines of America; also are so allowed and lookt upon by the rest of the Indians, by a submissive and tributary acknowledgement; being a people cast into the mould of a most large and Warlike deportment, the men being for the most part seven foot high in latitude, and in magnitude and bulk suitable to so high a pitch; their voyce large and hollow, as ascending out of a Cave, their gate and behavior strait, stately and majestick, treading on the Earth with as much pride, contempt, and disdain to so sordid a Center, as can be imagined from a creature derived from the same mould and Earth.

Their bodies are cloth'd with no other Armour to defend them from the nipping frosts of a benumbing Winter, or the penetrating and scorching influence of the Sun in a hot Summer, then what Nature gave them when they parted with the dark receptacle of their mothers womb. They go Men, Women and Children, all naked, only where shame leads them by a natural instinct to be reservedly modest, there they become cover'd. The formality of Jezabels artificial Glory[2] is much courted and followed by these Indians, only in matter of colours (I conceive) they differ.

The Indians paint upon their faces one stroke of red, another of green, another of white, and another of black, so that when they have accomplished the Equipage of their Countenance in this trim, they are the only Hieroglyphicks and Representatives of the Furies[3]. Their skins are naturally white, but altered from their originals by the several dyings of Roots and Barks, that they prepare and make useful to metamorphize their hydes into a dark Cinamon brown. The hair of their head is black, long and harsh, but where Nature hath appointed the situation of it

---

[1] An obscure reference which is meant, perhaps, to disguise with humor Alsop's admission of his lack of knowledge of the Native inhabitants.

[2] Jezebel (d. c.843 BC) was a Phoenician princess and wife of Ahab, a king of ancient Israel. According to 1 Kings 18 and 19, she fostered the worship of the Phoenician god Baal and was opposed by the prophet Elijah. She was killed by the order of King Jehu, and her body was eaten by dogs, as Elijah had prophesied. A "painted jezebel" is a term for a bold and powerful woman who uses "artifices" such as face make-up to enhance her charms.

[3] The "Furies" or Erinyes of Greek mythology, were snaky-haired women who sprang from the blood of Uranus when he was castrated by his son Cronos. They lived in the underworld, from which they issued to pursue and drive mad those who had committed heinous crimes such as patricide. They represent the insistence on the ancient law of blood for blood.

any where else, they divert it (by an antient custom) from its growth, by pulling it up hair by hair by the root in its primitive appearance. Several of them wear divers impressions on their breasts and armes, as the picture of the Devil, Bears, Tigers, and Panthers, which are imprinted on their several lineaments with much difficulty and pain, with an irrevocable determination of its abiding there: And this they count a badge of Heroick Valour, and the only Ornament due to their Heroes.

These Susquehanock Indians are for the most part great Warriours, and seldom sleep one Summer in the quiet armes of a peaceable Rest, but keep (by their present Power, as well as by their former Conquest) the several Nations of Indians round about them, in a forceable obedience and subjection.

Their Government is wrapt up in so various and intricate a Laborynth, that the speculativ'st Artist in the whole World, with his artificial and natural Opticks, cannot see into the rule or sway of these Indians, to distinguish what name of Government to call them by; though Purchas in his Peregrinations between London and Essex, (which he calls the whole World) will undertake (forsooth) to make a Monarchy of them, but if he had said Anarchy, his word would have pass'd with a better belief.[4] All that ever I could observe in them as to this matter is, that he that is most cruelly Valorous, is accounted the most Noble: Here is very seldom any creeping from a Country Farm, into a Courtly Gallantry, by a sum of money; nor feeing the Heralds to put Daggers and Pistols into their Armes, to make the ignorant believe that they are lineally descended from the house of the Wars and conquests; he that fights best carries it here.

When they determine to go upon some Design that will and doth require a consideration, some six of them get into a corner, and sit in Juncto; and if thought fit, their business is made popular, and immediately put into action; if not, they make a full stop to it, and are silently reserv'd.

The Warlike Equipage they put themselves in when they prepare for Belona's March[5], is with their faces, armes, and breasts confusedly painted, their hair greazed with Bears oyl, and stuck thick with Swans feathers, with a wreath or Diadem of black arid white Beads upon their heads, a small Hatchet, instead of a Cymetre, stuck in their girts behind them, and either with Guns, or Bows and Arrows. In this posture and dress they march out from their Fort, or dwelling, to the number of Forty in a Troop, singing (or rather howling out) the Decades or Warlike exploits of their Ancestors, ranging the wide Woods untill their fury has met with an Enemy worthy of their Revenge. What Prisoners fall into their hands by the destiny of War, they treat them very civilly while they remain with them abroad, but when they once return homewards, they then begin to dress them in the habit for death, putting on their heads and armes wreaths of Beads, greazing their hair with fat, some going before, and the rest behind, at equal distance from their Prisoners, bellowing in a strange and confused manner, which is a true presage and forerunner of destruction to their then conquered Enemy.

In this manner of march they continue till they have brought them to their Barken City, where they deliver them up to those that in cruelty will execute them, without either the legal Judgement of a Council of War, or the benefit of their Clergy at the Common Law. The common and usual deaths they put their Prisonere to, is to bind them to stakes, making a fire

---

4   Samuel Purchas (1575?–1626), was an English author and clergyman known for his editions of Elizabethan travel literature. He describes Native American culture in Books Eight and Nine of his popular book, *Purchas his pilgrimage, or Relations of the world and the religions observed in all ages and places discovered, from the creation unto this present* (1613). Alsop implies that his inaccuracies about Native American systems of government stem from his lack of direct observations.

5   In Roman mythology, Bellona was the goddess of war and either wife or sister of Mars.

some distance from them; then one or other of them, whose Genius delights in the art of Paganish dissection, with a sharp knife or flint cuts the Cutis or outermost skin of the brow so deep, untill their nails, or rather Talons, can fasten themselves firm and secure in, then (with a most rigid jerk) disrobeth the head of skin and hair at one pull, leaving the skull almost as bare as those Monumental Skelitons at Chyrurgions-Hall[6]; but for fear they should get cold by leaving so warm and customary a Cap off, they immediately apply to the Skull a Cataplasm[7] of hot Embers to keep their Pericranium warm. While they are thus acting this cruelty on their heads, several others are preparing pieces of Iron, and barrels of old Guns, which they make red hot, to sear each part and lineament of their bodies, which they perform and act in a most cruel and barbarous manner: And while they are thus in the midst of their torments and execrable usage, some tearing their skin and hair of their head off by violence, others searing their bodies with hot irons, some are cutting their flesh off, and eating it before their eyes raw while they are alive; yet all this and much more never makes them lower the Top-gallant sail of their Heroick courage, to beg with a submissive Repentance any indulgent favour from their perse-cuting Enemies; but with an undaunted contempt to their cruelty, eye it with so slight and mean a respect, as if it were below them to value what they did, they courageously (while breath doth libertize them) sing the summary of their Warlike Atchievements.

Now after this cruelty has brought their tormented lives to a period, they immediately fall to butchering of them into parts, distributing the several pieces amongst the Sons of War, to intomb the ruines of their deceased Conquest in no other Sepulchre then their unsanctified maws; which they with more appetite and desire do eat and digest, then if the best of foods should court their stomachs to participate of the most restorative banquet. Yet though they now and then feed upon the Carkesses of their Enemies, this is not a common dyet, but only a particular dish for the better sort; for there is not a Beast that runs in the Woods of America, but if they can by any means come at him, without any scruple of Conscience they'le fall too (without saying Grace) with a devouring greediness.

As for their Religion, together with their Rites and Ceremonies, they are so absurd and ridiculous, that its almost a sin to name them. They own no other Deity then the Devil, (solid or profound) but with a kind of a wilde imaginary conjecture, they suppose from their ground-less conceits, that the World had a Maker, but where he is that made it, or whether he be living to this day, they know not. The Devil, as I said before, is all the God they own or worship; and that more out of a slavish fear then any real Reverence to his Infernal or Diaboli-cal greatness, he forcing them to their Obedience by his rough and rigid dealing with them, often appearing visibly among them to their terrour, bastinadoing[8] them (with cruel menaces) even unto death, and burning their Fields of Corn and houses, that the relation thereof makes them tremble themselves when they tell it.

Once in four years they Sacrifice a Childe to him, in an acknowledgement of their firm obedience to all his Devillish powers, and Hellish commands. The Priests to whom they apply themselves in matters of importance and greatest distress, are like those that attended upon the Oracle at Delphos[9], who by their Magic-spells could command a pro or con from the Devil when they pleas'd. These Indians oft-times raise great Tempests when they have any weighty matter or design in hand, and by blustering storms inquire of their Infernal God (the Devil) How matters shall go with them either in publick or private.

---

[6]   Hall where surgery was practiced and taught.
[7]   Poultice.
[8]   Beating with a stick.
[9]   An ancient oracle at Delphi, on the southern slope of

Mount Parnassus, where the Pythia, or priestess, made oracu-lar utterances that were regarded as the final authority in religious matters.

When any among them depart this life, they give him no other intombment, then to set him upright upon his breech in a hole dug in the Earth some five foot long, and three foot deep, covered over with the Bark of Trees Arch-wise, with his face Du-West, only leaving a hole half a foot square open. They dress him in the same Equipage and Gallantry that he used to be trim'd in when he was alive, and so bury him (if a Soldier) with his Bows, Arrows, and Target[10], together with all the rest of his implements and weapons of War, with a Kettle of Broth, and Corn standing before him, lest he should meet With bad quarters in his way. His Kindred and Relations follow him to the Grave, sheath'd in Bear skins for close mourning, with the tayl droyling on the ground, in imitation of our English Solemners, that think there's nothing like a tayl a Degree in length, to follow the dead Corpse to the Grave with. Here if that snuffling Prolocutor, that waits upon the dead Monuments of the Tombs at Wesminster,[11] with his white Rod were there, he might walk from Tomb to Tomb with his, Here lies the Duke of Ferrara and his Dutchess, and never find any decaying vacation, unless it were in the moldering Consumption of his own Lungs. They bury all within the wall or Pallisado'd impalement of their City, or Connadago as they call it. Their houses are low and long, built with the Bark of Trees Arch-wise, standing thick and confusedly together. They are situated a hundred and odd miles distant from the Christian Plantations of Mary-Land, at the head of a River that runs into the Bay of Chesapike, called by their own name The Susquehanock River, where they remain and inhabit most part of the Summer time, and seldom remove far from it, unless it be to subdue any Forreign Rebellion.

About November the best Hunters draw off to several remote places of the Woods, where they know the Deer, Bear, and Elke useth; there they build them several Cottages, which they call their Winter-quarter, where they remain for the space of three months, untill they have killed up a sufficiency of Provisions to supply their Families with in the Summer.

The Women are the Butchers, Cooks, and Tillers of the ground, the Men think it below the honour of a Masculine, to stoop to any thing but that which their Gun, or Bow and Arrows can command. The Men kill the several Beasts which they meet withall in the Woods, and the Women are the Pack horses to fetch it in upon their backs, fleying and dressing the hydes, (as well as the flesh for provision) to make them fit for Trading, and which are brought down to the English at several seasons in the year, to truck and dispose of them for course Blankets, Guns, Powder and Lead, Beads, small Looking-glasses, Knives, and Razors.

I never observed all the while I was amongst these naked Indians that ever the Women wore the Breeches, or dared either in look or action predominate over the Men. They are very constant to their Wives; and let this be spoken to their Heathenish praise, that did they not alter their bodies by their dyings, paintings, and cutting themselves, marring those Excellencies that Nature bestowed upon them in their original conceptions and birth, there would be as amiable beauties amongst them, as any Alexandria could afford, when Mark Anthony and Cleopatra dwelt there together. Their Marriages are short and authentique; for after 'tis resolv'd upon by both parties, the Woman sends her intended Husband a Kettle of boyl'd Venison, or Bear; and he returns in lieu thereof Beaver or Otters Skins, and so their Nuptial Rites are concluded without other Ceremony.

Before I bring my Heathenish Story to a period, I have one thing worthy your observation:

---

[10]   Shield.

[11]   A prolocutor is a presiding officer in the convocation of the Anglican church, and also a presiding officer and announcer in the Houses of Parliament. "Westminster" refers to the medieval abbey in London in which English royalty are crowned and buried, along with other notable English figures. It also may suggest Westminster Palace, the correct name for the building commonly called the Houses of Parliament.

For as our Grammar Rules have it, *Non decet quenquam mingere currentem aut mandantem*: It doth not become any man to piss running or eating. These Pagan men naturally observe the same Rule; for they are so far from running, that like a Hare, they squat to the ground as low as they can, while the Women stand bolt upright with their armes a Kimbo, performing the same action, in so confident and obscene a posture, as if they had taken their Degrees of Entrance at Venice and commenced Bawds of Art at Legorne.[12]

1662–3?   1666

John Lederer (1644–after 1672)

John Lederer, a scholar and student of medicine from Hamburg, Germany, was deeply interested in the Indians, in Indian trade, and in the natural resources of the New World. He was one of the first Europeans to explore the Piedmont and Blue Ridge Mountains and to leave a written record of his discoveries.

In 1670, though Governor William Berkeley had a strong interest in exploring the areas lying to the South beyond the Tidewater settlements, explorers were not easy to come by due to the expense and potential dangers of such an expedition. Lederer, however, took up the challenge of finding a path through the Appalachians and observing what lay beyond them, and the narratives of his three journeys of exploration shaped the perceptions of European geographers and ethnographers for many years. He was instrumental in opening the great Indian Trading path toward the southwest for Virginia fur traders, and left detailed accounts of the Native groups encountered in his travels.

Lederer was, however, the object of envy and intrigue on the part of English-speaking Virginians. His translator, Sir William Talbot, remarks, "That a stranger should presume (though with Sir William Berkeley's Commission) to go into those Parts of the American Continent where Englishmen never had been, and whither some refused to accompany him, was in Virginia looked on as so great an insolence, that our Traveller at his Return, instead of Welcome and Applause, met nothing but Affronts and Reproaches; for indeed it was their part, that forsook him in the Expedition to procure him discredit that was a witness to Theirs: Therefore no industry was wanting to prepare Men with a prejudice against him . . ." After his last expedition, he went briefly to Maryland, and returned to Germany in 1672, promising his friends that he would return. No record of his return has been found.

Primary Work

John Lederer, *The Discoveries of John Lederer*, trans. Sir William Talbot (Charlottesville: University of Virginia Press, 1958).

Further Reading

Douglas L. Rights and William P. Cumming (eds) *The Discoveries of John Lederer, with unpublished letters by and about Lederer to Governor John Winthrop, Jr, and an essay on the Indians of Lederer's Discoveries by Douglas L. Rights* (Charlottesville: University of Virginia Press, 1958).

---

[12]   Venice, the city in northeastern Italy famous for its canals. Leghorn (in Italian, Livorno) in the central Tuscany region, is a commercial city and one of Italy's main ports. In English and European literature, Italian cities are synonymous with sexual promiscuity. See, for example, Thomas Mann's "Death in Venice."

Instructions to Such as Shall March upon Discoveries into the North American Continent

Two breaches there are in the Apalataeen[1] Mountains, opening a passage into the Western parts of the Continent. One, as I am informed by Indians, at a place called Zynodoa[2], to the Norward[3]; the other at Sara, where I have been myself: but the way thither being through a vast forest, where you seldom fall into any road or path, you must shape your course by a compass; though some, for want of one, have taken their direction from the north side of the trees, which is distinguished from the rest by quantities of thick moss growing there. You will not meet with any hindrances on horseback in your passage to the Mountains, but where your course is interrupted by the branches of the great Rivers, which in many places are not fordable; and therefore if you be unprovided of means or strength to make a bridge by felling tress across, you may be forced to go a great way about: in this respect company is necessary, but in half a dozen, or ten at the most, to travel together; and of these, the major part Indians: for the Nations in your way are prone to jealousy and mischief towards Christians in a considerable body, and as courteous and hearty to a few, from whom they apprehend no danger.

When you pass through an even level country, where you can take no particular remarks from hill or waters to guide yourself by when you come back, you must not forget to notch the trees as you go along with your small hatchet, that in your return you may know when you fall into the same way which you went. By this means you will be certain of the place you are in, and may govern your course homeward accordingly.

Instead of bread, I used the meal of parched *mays*, i.e. Indian wheat; which, when I eat, I seasoned with a little salt. This is both more portable and strengthening than biscuit, and will suffer no mouldiness by any weather. For other provisions, you may securely trust to your gun, the woods being full of fallow, and Savanae of red deer[4], besides great variety of excellent fowl, as wild turkeys, pigeons, partridges, pheasants, etc. But you must not forget to dry or barbecue some of these before you come to the mountains: for upon them you will meet with no game, except a few bears.

Such as cannot lie on the ground, must be provided with light hammocks, which hung in the trees, are more cool and pleasant than any bed whatsoever.

The order and discipline to be observed in this expedition is, that an Indian Scout or two march as far before the rest of the company as they can in sight, both for the finding out provision, and discovery of ambushes, if any should be laid by enemies. Let your other Indians keep on the right and left hands, armed not only with guns, but bills and hatchets, to build small arbours or cottages of boughs and bark of trees, to shelter and defend you from the injuries of the weather. At nights it is necessary to make great fires round about the place where you take up your lodging, as well to scare wild beasts away, as to purify the air. Neither must you fail to go the round at the close of the evening: for then, and betimes in the morning, the Indians put all their designs in execution: in the night they never attempt anything.

When in the remote parts you draw near to an Indian town, you must by your Scouts inform yourself whether they hold any correspondence with the Sasquesahanaughs[5]: for to such you must give notice of your approach by a gun; which amongst other Indians is to be avoided,

---

[1] Appalachian.
[2] Probably Shenandoah.
[3] North.

[4] I.e. fallow (small) deer can be found in the woods and red deer in the swamps.
[5] Susquehanna Indians.

because being ignorant of their use, it would affright them and dispose them to some treacherous practice against you.

Being arrived at a town, enter no house until you are invited; and then seem not afraid to be led in pinioned[6] like a prisoner: for that is a ceremony they use to friend and enemies without distinction.

You must accept of an invitation from the Seniors[7], before that of young men; and refuse nothing that is offered or set afore you: for they are very jealous, and sensible of the least slighting or neglect from strangers, and mindful of Revenge.

Touching Trade with Indians

If you barely design a home-trade with neighbour-Indians, for skins of deer, beaver, otter, wildcat, fox, raccoon, etc. your best truck[8] is a sort of coarse trading cloth, of which a yard and a half makes a matchcoat or mantle fit for their wear; as also axes, hoes, knives, scissors, and all sorts of edged tools. Guns, powder and shot, etc. are commodities they will greedily barter for: but to supply the Indians with arms and ammunition, is prohibited in all English Governments.

In dealing with the Indians, you must be positive and at a word: for if they persuade you to fall anything in your price, they will spend time in higgling for further abatements[9] and seldom conclude any bargain. Sometimes you may with brandy or strong liquor dispose them to an humour of giving you ten times the value of your commodity; and at other times they are so hidebound, that they will not offer half the market price, especially if they be aware that you have a design to circumvent them with drink, or that they think you have a desire to their goods, which you must seem to slight and disparage.

To the remoter Indians you must carry other kinds of truck, as small looking-glasses, Pictures, beads and bracelets of glass, knives, scissors, and all manners of gaudy toys and knacks for children, which are light and portable. For they are apt to admire such trinkets, and will purchase them at any rate, either with their current coin of small shells, which they call *Roanoack* or *Peack*, or perhaps with pearl, vermilion[10], pieces of crystal; and towards *Ushery*, some odd pieces of plate or buillon[11], which they sometimes receive in truck from the Oestacks.

Could I have foreseen when I set out, the advantages to be made by a trade with these remote Indians, I had gone better provided; though perhaps I might have run a great hazard of my life, had I purchased considerably amongst them, by carrying wealth unguarded through so many different Nations of barbarous people: therefore it is vain for any man to propose to himself, or undertake a Trade at that distance, unless he goes with strength to defend, as well as an Adventure to purchase such Commodities: for in such a design many ought to join and go in company.

Some pieces of silver unwrought I purchased myself of the Usheries, for no other end than to justify this account of my second expedition, which had not determined[12].

1672

---

[6] Bound.
[7] Elders.
[8] Commodity to be exchanged in trade.
[9] I.e. bargaining for further price reductions.

[10] A red pigment.
[11] A showy ornament, such as a buckle, button, or clasp.
[12] Ended, terminated.

Nathaniel Bacon (1647–1676)

Bacon is known as the leader of the first popular uprising in colonial North America which took place in Virginia, England's oldest and most loyal colony. From a well-to-do family, Bacon decided to emigrate to America when his wife was disinherited on account of her father's opposition to the marriage. With financial support from his father, Bacon bought two estates along the James River, and within a year of his arrival was appointed to the council of Virginia's Governor William Berkeley, his cousin by marriage. But Bacon was a relative late-comer to booming Virginian society. By 1670, the population had grown to about thirty thousand, a high proportion of which was male indentured servants or ex-servants whose lives were hard and whose prospects, once they completed their service, were dim. Only about six percent of former servants became successful planters; the rest remained tenant farmers, foremen, or laborers.

Their discontent was echoed by the middle class of small planters who felt excluded by the high-handed rule of Governor William Berkeley. Although he had been popular during his first stint in office (1641–52) for his swift handling of the Indian war (1644–6) and his subsequent removal of all the indigenous populations from the Jamestown Peninsula, when he returned in 1660, Berkeley's popularity quickly faded. First, he failed to call new elections for the House of Burgesses that ruled the colony, and sat continuously for fourteen years. He taxed the inhabitants harshly and appointed favorites from the aristocratic class to important positions, an exclusivity reinforced by the Franchise Act of 1670 which restricted the vote to property owners. Furthermore, England had passed several navigation laws that reduced the market for tobacco, Virginia's only staple crop, and excluded cheaper goods offered by the Dutch, with whom England was at war. The economy had slumped so much that in 1666, Virginia, Maryland, and North Carolina agreed not to plant a tobacco crop that year. Still, Berkeley's pleas to develop other staple crops were ineffectual.

The best prospects for marginal settlers were to be found inland on the frontier, but there they met resistance from Native American tribes, like the Doeg, Oaneechee, Nottaway, Meherin, and the formidable Susquehanna, who were caught between English imperial expansion and aggression by the Five Nations of the Iroquois, whose League of Peace and Power would dominate the interior of northeastern America for the next century. The rebellion was set off when Doeg Indians killed an overseer on one of Bacon's estates in a dispute over some missing hogs, which had probably gotten into a Doeg corn patch. Berkeley hesitated to launch a retaliatory expedition because, according to Bacon's view, he did not want to interfere with the lucrative Indian fur trade; but he also may have recognized that the Indians were not fully to blame, and was aware of the ferocious war (Metacom's War) that had just broken out between Indians and settlers in New England. When angry farmers of those counties met, they quickly agreed to a launch their own expedition against the Indians in defiance of Berkeley, and elected the young, well-spoken, and well-connected Bacon as their leader.

Bacon rejected the Governor's policy of accommodation and maintenance of the frontier. In the attack he led against the Susquehannas, whom the militia confused with the offending Doegs, he allied with the Ocaneechees, but boasted that "In the heat of the Fight we . . . destroyed them all," justifying his actions by saying that the Native Americans were "all our enemies." Susquehanna revenge was particularly vicious and decimated the Chesapeake frontiers. Infuriated and humiliated, Berkeley declared his young relation and councilmember a traitor, but Bacon's defiance of colonial rule had roused popular sentiment; at its height, the rebellion involved hundreds of rebels who burned down Jamestown, captured a ship on the James River, and controlled most of the colony, forcing Berkeley to flee to the eastern shore. At the end of July, 1676, Bacon issued a manifesto "in the Name of the People of Virginia," calling for Berkeley's immediate surrender. Riding an enormous wave of popularity, it is unclear how far Bacon would have gotten if he hadn't fallen ill from malaria and died in October.

Bacon's rebellion is usually represented as a demand for more democratic political representation and more equitable taxation. It is often regarded as a precursor of the spirit of the American Revolution in its reliance, for the first time, on the sovereignty of the people for its justification. However, it must also be noted that Bacon's rebellion is one of the first popular movements that successfully rallied white settlers in their common antipathy for Native Americans.

Primary Works

"Proclamations of Nathaniel Bacon," published in *Virginia Historical Magazine*, 1 (1893) pp. 55–63.

Further Reading

Wilcomb Washburn, *The Governor and the Rebel; a History of Bacon's Rebellion in Virginia* (Chapel Hill: University of North Carolina Press, 1957).

John Frantz (ed.) *Bacon's Rebellion; Prologue to the Revolution?* (Lexington, Massachusetts: Heath, 1969).

Stephen Webb, *1676, The End of American Independence* (New York: Knopf, 1985).

Theodore Allen, *The Invention of the White Race* (London: Verso, vol. 1, 1994, vol. 2, 1997).

NATHANIEL BACON ESQ'R HIS MANIFESTO CONCERNING THE PRESENT TROUBLES IN VIRGINIA[1]

If vertue be a sin, if Piety be guilt, all the Principles of morality goodness and Justice be perverted, Wee must confesse That those who are now called Rebells may be in danger of those high imputations, Those loud and severall Bulls would affright Innocents and render the defence of our Brethren and the enquiry into our sad and heavy oppressions, Treason. But if there bee as sure there is, a just God to appeal too, if Religion and Justice be a sanctuary here, If to plead youre cause of the oppressed, If sincerely to aime at his Majesties[2] Honour and the Publick good without any reservation or by Interest, If to stand in the Gap after soe much blood of our dear Brethren bought and sold, If after the losse of a great part of his Majesties Colony deserted and dispeopled,[3] freely with our lives and estates to indeavor to save the remaynders bee Treason God Almighty Judge and lett guilty dye. But since wee cannot in our hearts find one single spott of Rebellion or Treason or that wee have in any manner aimed at the subverting youre setled Government or attempting of the Person of any either magistrate or private man not with standing the severall Reproaches and Threats of some who for sinister ends were disaffected to us and censured our ino[cent] and honest designes, and since all people in all places where wee have yet bin can attest our civill quiet peaseable behaviour farre different from that of Rebellion and tumultuous persons let Trueth be bold and all the world know the real Foundations of pretended guilt. Wee appeale to the Country itselfe what and of what nature their Oppressions have bin or by what Caball[4] and mistery the designes of many of those whom wee call great men have bin transacted and caryed on, but let us trace these men in Authority and Favour to whose hands the dispensation of the Countries wealth has been commited; let us observe the sudden Rise of their Estates composed with the Quality in which they first entered this Country Or the Reputation they have held here amongst wise and discerning men, And lett us see wither their extractions and Education have not bin vile, And

---

[1] The text, with some modifications, is from "Proclamations of Nathaniel Bacon," *Virginia Historical Magazine*, 1 (1893).

[2] King Charles II, who was restored to the throne in 1660 after the interval of the English Commonwealth.

[3] Bacon refers to the general displacement of white settlers caught in the cross-fire of the war between the tribes of the Fall Line and the aggressive Iroquois and their allies occurring along the Virginia frontier, and Governor Berkeley's failure to prevent it. Important to note is that, from Bacon's perspective, land occupied or used by Native Americans is "deserted and dispeopled."

[4] Intrigue, conspiracy.

by what pretence of learning and vertue they could soe soon into Imployments of so great Trust and consequence, let us consider wither any Publick work for our safety and defence or for the Advancement and propogation of Trade, liberall Arts or sciences is here Extant in any [way] adaquate to our vast chardg, now let us compare these things togit[her] and see what spounges have suckt up the Publique Treasure and wither it hath not bin privately contrived away by unworthy Favourites and juggling Parasites whose tottering tunes have bin repaired and supported at the Publique chard'g. Now if it be so Judg what greater guilt can bee then to offer to pry into these and to unriddle the misterious wiles of a powerfull Cabal let all people Judge what can be of more dangerous Import then to suspect the soe long Safe proceedings of Some of our Grandees and wither People may with safety open their Eyes in soe nice a Concerne.

Another main article of our Guilt is our open and manifest aversion of all, not onely the Foreign but the protected and Darling Indians, this wee are informed is Rebellion of a deep dye For that both the Governour and Councell are by Colonell Coales Assertion bound to defend the Queen and the Appamatocks with their blood.[5] Now whereas we doe declare and can prove that they have bin for these Many years enemies to the King and Country, Robbers and Theeves and Invaders of his Majesties Right and our Interest and Estates, but yet have by persons in Authority bin defended and protected even against his Majesties loyall Subjects and that in soe high a Nature that even the Complaints and oaths of his Majesties Most loyall Subjects in a lawfull Manner proffered by them against those barborous Outlawes have bin by youre right honourable Governour rejected and youre Delinquents from his presence dismissed not only with pardon and indemnitye but with all incouragement and favour, Their Fire Arms soe destructfull to us and by our lawes prohibited, Commanded to be restored them, and open Declaration before Witness made That they must have Ammunition although directly contrary to our law. Now what greater guilt can be then to oppose and indeavour the destruction of these Honest quiet neighbours of ours.

Another main article of our Guilt is our Design not only to ruine and extirpate all Indians in Generall but all Manner of Trade and Commerce with them, Judge who can be innocent that strike at this tender Eye of Interest; Since the Right honourable the Governour hath bin pleased by his Commission to warrant this Trade who dare oppose it, or opposing it can be innocent. Although Plantations be deserted, the blood of our dear Brethren Spilt, on all Sides our complaints, continually Murder upon Murder renewed upon us, who may or dare think of the generall Subversion of all Mannor of Trade and Commerce with our enemies who can or dare impeach any of Traders at the Heades of the Rivers if contrary to the wholesome provision made by lawes for the countries safety, they dare continue their illegall practises and dare asperse[6] ye right honourable Governours wisdome and Justice soe highly to pretend to have his warrant to break that law which himself made. Who dare say That these Men at the Heades of the Rivers buy and sell our blood, and doe still notwithstanding the late Act made to

5   The governor at the time was Sir William Berkeley (1606–77) who was first appointed in 1641 and served almost continuously until his death, except for the years of the English Commonwealth (1652–9), when he retired to his Virginia plantation. Colonel William Cole was a favorite of Berkeley's and a member of his Council. He and Nathaniel Bacon, Senior, had publicly told the settlers of New Kent County that the Pamunkey and Appomattox Indians, allies of the English who used them as spies and buffers against

more powerful Native enemies, were "our friends, and that we ought to defend them with our blood." The "Queen" is a reference to the squaw-sachem of the Pamunkeys, whose husband Tottopottooi and many warriors had been killed fighting as English allies. She had been called before the committee on Indian affairs of the House of Burgesses and asked to lend even more men as guides.

6   To spread false and injurious charges against.

the contrary,[7] admit Indians painted and continue to Commerce, although these things can be proved yet who dare bee soe guilty as to doe it.

Another Article of our Guilt is To Assert all those neighbour Indians as well as others to be outlawed, wholly unqualifyed for the benefitt and Protection of the law, For that the law does reciprocally protect and punish, and that all people offending must either in person or Estate make equivalent satisfaction or Restitution according to the manner and merit of youre Offences Debts or Trespasses; Now since the Indians cannot according to the tenure and forme of any law to us known be prosecuted, Seised or Complained against, Their Persons being difficulty distinguished or known, Their many nations languages, and their subterfuges such as makes them incapeable to make us Restitution or satisfaction would it not be very guilty to say They have bin unjustly defended and protected these many years.

If it should be said that the very foundation of all these disasters the Grant of the Beaver trade to the Right Honourable Governour was illegall and not granteable by any power here present as being a monopoly, were not this to deserve the name of Rebell and Traytor.

Judge therefore all wise and unprejudiced men who may or can faithfully or truly with an honest heart attempt youre country's good, their vindication and libertie without the aspersion of Traitor and Rebell, since as soe doing they must of necessity gall such tender and dear concernes, But to manifest Sincerity and loyalty to the World, and how much wee abhorre those bitter names, may all the world know that we doe unanimously desire to represent our sad and heavy grievances to his most sacred Majestie as our Refuge and Sanctuary, where wee doe well know that all our Causes will be impartially heard and Equall Justice administered to all men.

The Declaration of the People[8]

For having upon specious pretences of Publick works raised unjust Taxes upon the Commonalty for the advancement of private Favourits and other sinnister ends but noe visible effects in any measure adequate.

For not having dureing the long time of his Government in any measure advanced this hopefull Colony either by Fortification, Townes or Trade.

For having abused and rendered Contemptible the Majesty of Justice, of advancing to places of judicature scandalous and Ignorant favourits.

For having wronged his Majesties Prerogative and Interest by assuming the monopoley of the Beaver Trade.

By having in that unjust gaine Bartered and sould his Majesties Country and the lives of his Loyal Subjects to the Barbarous Heathen.

For having protected favoured and Imboldened the Indians against his Majesties most Loyall

---

[7] On Sunday, June 25, 1676, the House of Burgesses (referred to as "Bacon's Assembly") met and passed two bills, known as "Bacon's Laws." The first declared war "against the barbarous Indians" and referred to Bacon as "generall and commander in chiefe of the forces raised" by this authority (his "commission"). The second responded to the rebels' charge that it was the governor's monopoly of the fur trade with the Indians that led him to defend them, by eliminating his control. They repealed an earlier act that "permitted five persons in each county to trade with the Indians" and forbade all commerce with enemy aliens ("Indians painted" for the warpath).

[8] Issued on July 30, soon after Berkeley's counter-revolutionary attempt to embroil the colony in civil war through the "Gloucester Petition" described below. Although it was signed "by the consent of the people," in which most historians see a significant precursor of Jeffersonian democracy, the "Declaration" was not a product of the Middle Plantation Convention, described below, but was composed before the meeting without anyone else's consent or knowledge.

subjects never contriveing requireing or appointing any due or proper means of satisfaction for their many Invasions Murthers and Robberies Committed upon us.

For having when the Army of the English was Just upon the Track of the Indians, which now in all places Burne Spoyle and Murder, and when wee might with ease have destroyed them who then were in open Hostility for having expresly Countermanded and sent back our Army by passing his word for the peaceable demeanour of the said Indians, who imediately prosecuted their evill Intentions Committing horrid Murders and Robberies in all places being protected by the said Engagement and word pass'd of him the said S'r William Berkley having ruined and made desolate a great part of his Majesties Country, have now drawne themselves into such obscure and remote places and are by their successes soe imboldened and confirmed and by their Confederacy soe strengthened that the cryes of Bloud are in all places and the Terrour and consternation of the People soe great, that they are now become not only a difficult, but a very formidable Enemy who might with ease have been destroyed &c. When upon the Lord Outcries of blood the Assembly had with all care raised and framed an Army for the prevention of future Mischiefs and safeguard of his Majesties Colony.

For having with only the privacy of some few favourits without acquainting the People, only by the Alteration of a Figure forged a Commission by wee know not what hand, not only without but against the Consent of the People, for raising and effecting of Civill Warrs, and distractions, which being happily and without Bloodshedd prevented.[9]

For having the second tyme attempted the same thereby, calling downe our Forces from the defence of the Frontiers, and most weake Exposed Places, for the prevention of civill Mischief and Ruine amongst ourselves, whilst the barbarous Enemy in all places did Invade murder and spoyle us his Majesties most faithful subjects.

Of these the aforesaid Articles wee accuse S'r William Berkely, as guilty of each and every one of the same, and as one who hath Traiterously attempted, violated and Injured his Majesties Interest here, by the losse of a great Part of his Colony, and many of his Faithfull and Loyall subjects by him betrayed, and in such a barbarous and shamefull manner exposed to the Incursions and murthers of the Heathen.

And we further declare these the Ensueing Persons in this List, to have been his wicked, and pernitious Councellors, Aiders and Assisters against the Commonality in these our Cruell Commotions.

Sir Henry Chicherly, Knt.,	Jos. Bridger,
Col. Charles Wormley,	William Clabourne,
Phil. Dalowell,	Thos. Hawkins, Juni'r,
Robert Beverly,	William Sherwood,
Robert Lee,	Jos. Page, Clerk,

---

[9]   At the end of July 1676, "The Army of Virginia against the Indians" of about 2,300 infantry and cavalry, led by Bacon and Captain Giles Brent, marched out of Gloucester to begin their racist campaign. As soon as they left, a small group of Berkeley supporters presented the Governor with the so-called "Gloucester petition" purportedly signed by many people, protesting Bacon's political and economic aggression, carried out under pretence of raising forces and supplies. Thinking to recoup his power, Berkeley immediately rode out to Gloucester County, denied that he had granted Bacon a commission and called up the militias of Middlesex and Gloucester counties to fight the Indians. When some twelve hundred had mustered, he suggested they follow and suppress "that Rebel Bacon." Visibly unsettled, the men began muttering "Bacon, Bacon, Bacon," turned their backs and walked away. Berkeley, on horseback, apparently fainted from embarrassment on the field. When Bacon heard of this failed counterrevolutionary plot, he sent cavalry patrols to every county to take pledges of allegiance from local leaders, capture the leading Berkeley supporters (listed below) as traitors and confiscate their property. This sparked the "social revolution" of 1676.

Thos. Ballard,	Jo. Cliffe, Clerk
William Cole,	Hubberd Farrell,
Richard Whitacre,	John West,
Nicholas Spencer,	Thos. Reade.
Mathew Kemp.	

And wee doe further demand, That the said S'r William Berkley, with all the Persons in this List, be forthwith delivered upp, or surrender themselves, within foure dayes, after the notice hereof, or otherwise wee declare, as followeth. That in whatsoever place, or shipp, any of the said Persons shall reside, be hide, or protected, Wee doe declare, that the Owners, masters, or Inhabitants of the said places, to be Confederates, and Traitors to the People, and the Estates of them, as alsoe of all the aforesaid Persons to be Confiscated, This wee the Commons of Virginia doe declare desiring a prime Union among ourselves, that wee may Joyntly, and with one Accord defend ourselves against the Common Enemye. And Let not the Faults of the guilty, be the Reproach of the Innocent, or the Faults or Crimes of ye Oppressors divide and separate us, who have suffered by theire oppressions.

These are therefore in his Majesties name, to Command you forthwith to seize, the Persons above mentioned, as Traytors to ye King and Countrey, and them to bring to Middle Plantation[10], and there to secure them, till further Order, and in Case of opposition, if you want any other Assistance, you are forthwith to demand it in the Name of the People of all the Counties of Virginia

1676   1676

James Revel (after 1640s–?)

There is some evidence that James Revel was not only a convicted felon, but also a complete fabrication, perhaps dreamed up by an enterprising writer hoping to cash in on Daniel Defoe's success with the lurid adventures of Moll Flanders and Colonel Jack, the most notorious felons, fictional or otherwise, to be transported to colonial Virginia. Still, John Melville Jennings, who unearthed and first reprinted Revel's sad story, believes that the motif of enforced transportation was a feature of English folk literature well before Defoe hit upon it, and that there is evidence to suggest the credibility of Revel's tale. The known printed versions of Revel's account probably appeared in the mid-eighteenth century as undated chapbooks, a usually anonymous genre of popular literature roughly equivalent to modern-day picture books or comic books. However, as Jennings argues, the history of forced transportation, along with several allusions in Revel's account, place the events much earlier. During the seventeenth century in England, there were over three hundred crimes that warranted capital punishment. However, for youthful criminals, transportation to the colonies was often substituted, a practice encouraged by the colonies' need for labor. By 1671, however, the number of transports to Virginia was so great that the General Court prohibited the practice, but it was reinstated in 1717 by Parliament, despite vigorous protests. According to this history, Revel could have arrived before 1671 or after 1717, but internal evidence helps us narrow the range even further. He describes

---

[10]   Afterwards Williamsburg, the military focus of Virginia since 1634 and the center of rebel activity. On August 3, at what is called "the Middle Plantation Convention," Bacon and four other members of the colonial council of state summoned an unprecedented convention there to form a new civil government, taking an oath of allegiance called "the Middle Plantation oath."

working for a cruel master in Rappahannock County, which was not organized until 1656, and disappeared in 1692 when it was divided into Richmond and Essex counties. Jennings concludes that Revel's arrival, if his account is at all authentic, falls in the period between 1656 and 1671. He also concludes that in spite of its "doggerel verse," Revel is not overly sensational, as chapbooks were wont to be, but presents a "realistic picture" of the experience of a transported felon put to hard labor hoeing tobacco alongside Negro slaves in colonial Virginia. The first known published copies of the ballad date from the mid-1700s, but it probably appeared at least a half century before.

PRIMARY WORK

"The Poor Unhappy Transported Felon's Sorrowful Account of his Fourteen Years Transportation at Virginia in America," published (ed. John Melville Jennings) in *Virginia Historical Magazine* (1948) pp. 180–94.

FURTHER READING

The Other Print Tradition: Essays on Chapbooks, Broadsides, and Related Ephemera, eds. Cathy Lynn Preston and Michael Preston (New York: Garland, 1995).

"THE UNHAPPY TRANSPORTED FELON"[1]

Tune of, Death and the Lady[2]

My loving Countrymen pray lend an Ear,
  To this Relation which I bring you here,
My sufferings at large I will unfold,
Which tho' 'tis strange, 'tis true as e'er was
    told,
  Of honest parents I did come (tho' poor,)
Who besides me had never Children more;
Near Temple Bar was born their darling
    son,
And for some years in virtue's path did run.
  My parents in me took great delight,
And brought me up at School to read and
    write,
And cast accompts likewise, as it appears,
Until that I was aged thirteen years.
  Then to a Tin-man I was Prentice bound,
My master and mistress good I found,
They lik'd me well, my business I did mind,
From me my parents comfort hop'd to find.
  My master near unto Moorfields did
    dwell,
Where into wicked company I fell;
To wickedness I quickly was inclin'd,

Thus soon is tainted any youthful mind.
  I from my master then did run away,
And rov'd about the streets both night and
    day:
Did with a gang of rogues a thieving go,
Which filled my parents heart with grief
    and woe.
  At length my master got me home again,
And used me well, in hopes I might re-
    claim,
My father tenderly to me did say,
My dearest child, what made you run away?
  If you had any cause at all for grief,
Why came you not to me to seek relief?
I well do know you did for nothing lack,
Food for your belly and cloaths to your back.
  My mother cry'd, dear son I do implore,
That you will from your master go no more,
Your business mind, your master ne'er
    forsake,
Lest you again to wicked courses take.
  I promis'd fair, but yet could not refrain,
But to my vile companions went again:

[1] The text, slightly modified, is from "The Poor Unhappy Transported Felon's Sorrowful Account of his Fourteen Years Transportation at Virginia in America," ed. John Melville Jennings, *Virginia Historical Magazine* (1948) pp. 180–94.

[2] A well-known folk song. Printed ballads were often coupled with the music of earlier folksongs.

For vice when once, alas! it taints the mind,
Is not soon rooted out again we find.
　With them again I did a thieving go,
But little did my tender parents know,
I follow'd courses that could be so vile,
My absence griev'd them, being their only
　　child[,]
　A wretched life I liv'd, I must confess,
In fear and dread and great uneasiness;
Which does attend such actions that's
　unjust,
For thieves can never one another trust.
　Strong liquor banish'd all the thoughts of
　fear,
But Justice stops us in our full career:
One night was taken up one of our gang,
Who five impeach'd & three of these were
　hang'd.
　I was one of the five was try'd and cast,
Yet transportation I did get at last;
A just reward for my vile actions past,
Thus justice overtook me at the last.
　My Father griev'd, my mother she took
　on,
And cry'd, Alas! alas! my only Son:
My Father cry'd, It cuts me to the heart,
　To think on such a cause as this we part.
To see them grieve thus pierc'd my very
　soul,
My wretched case I sadly did condole;
With grief and shame my eyes did overflow,
And had much rather chuse to die than go.
　In vain I griev'd, in vain my parents
　weep,
For I was quickly sent on board the Ship:
With melting kisses and a heavy heart,
I from my dearest parents then did part.

PART II

In a few Days we left the river quite,
　And in short time of land we lost the
　sight,
The Captain and the sailors us'd us well,
But kept us under lest we should rebel.
　We were in number much about three-
　score,
A wicked lowsey crew as e'er went o'er;

Oaths and Tobacco with us plenty were,
For most did smoak, and all did curse and
　swear.
　Five of our number in our passage died,
Which were thrown into the Ocean wide:
And after sailing seven Weeks and more,
We at Virginia all were put on shore.
　Where, to refresh us, we were wash'd and
　cleaned
That to our buyers we might the better
　seem;[3]
Our things were gave to each they did
　belong,
And they that had clean linnen put it on.
　Our faces shav'd, comb'd out our wigs
　and hair,
That we in decent order might appear,
Against the planters did come down to
　view,
How well they lik'd this fresh transported
　crew.
　The Women s[e]parated from us stand,
As well as we, by them for to be view'd;
And in short time some men up to us came,
Some ask'd our trades, and others ask'd our
　names.
　Some view'd our limbs, and other's turn'd
　us round
Examening like Horses, if we're sound,
What trade are you, my Lad, says one to me,
A Tin-man, Sir, that will not do, says he[.]
　Some felt our hands and view'd our legs
　and feet,
And made us walk, to see we were compleat;
Some view'd our teeth, to see if they were
　good,
Or fit to chew our hard and homely Food.
　If any like our look, our limbs, our trade,
The Captain then a good advantage made:
For they a difference made it did appear,
'Twixt those for seven and for fourteen year.
　Another difference there is alow'd,
They who have money have most favour
　show'd;
For if no cloaths nor money they have got,
Hard is their fate, and hard will be their lot.
　At length a grim old Man unto me came,

3　Employers "bought" the indentures of the felons for either seven or fourteen years, from the ship captains who transported them, but the similarity to a slave market is undeniable.

He ask'd my trade, and likewise ask'd my
    Name:
I told him I a Tin-man was by trade,
And not quite eighteen years of age I said.
    Likewise the cause I told that brought me
        there,
That I for fourteen years transported were,
And when he this from me did understand,
He bought me of the Captain out of hand.

PART III

Down to the harbour I was took again,
    On board of a sloop, and loaded with a
        chain;
Which I was forc'd to wear both night and
    day,
For fear I from the Sloop should get away.
    My master was a man but of ill fame,
Who first of all a Transport thither came;
In Reppahannock county we did dwell,
Up Reppahannock river known full well,
    And when the Sloop with loading home
        was sent
An hundred mile we up the river went
The weather cold and very hard my fare,
My lodging on the deck both hard and bare,
    At last to my new master's house I came,
At the town of Wicocc[o]moco⁴ call'd by
    name,
Where my Europian clothes were took from
    me,
Which never after I again could see.
    A canvas shirt and trowsers then they gave,
With a hop-sack frock in which I was to
    slave:
No shoes nor stockings had I for to wear,
Nor hat, nor cap, both head and feet were
    bare.
    Thus dress'd into the Field I nex[t] must
        go,
Amongst tobacco plants all day to hoe,
At day break in the morn our work begun,
And so held to the setting of the Sun.
    My fellow slaves were just five Transports
        more,

With eighteen Negroes, which is twenty
    four:
Besides four transport women in the house,
To wait upon his daughter and his Spouse,
    We and the Negroes both alike did fare,
Of work and food we had an equal share;
But in a piece of ground we call our own,
The food we eat first by ourselves were
    sown,
    No other time to us they would allow,
But on a Sunday we the same must do:
Six days we slave for our master's good,
The seventh day is to produce our food.
    Sometimes when that a hard days work
        we've done,
Away unto the mill we must be gone;
Till twelve or one o'clock a grinding corn,
And must be up by daylight in the morn.
    And if you run in debt with any one,
It must be paid before from thence you
    come;
For in publick places they'll put up your
    name,
That every one their just demands may
    claim,
    And if we offer for to run away,
For every hour we must serve a day;
For every day a Week, They're so severe,
For every week a month, for every month a
    year
    But if they murder, rob or steal when
        there,
Then straightway hang'd, the Laws are so
    severe;
For by the Rigour of that very law
They're much kept under and to stand in
    awe.

PART IV

At length, it pleased God I sick did fall
But I no favour could receive at all,
For I was Forced to work while I could
    stand,
Or hold the hoe within my feeble hands.

⁴ Wicomico, a town in seventeenth century Virginia
which, however, was not in Rappahannock county, but in
the adjoining county of Northumberland.

Much hardships then in deed I did
   endure,
No dog was ever nursed so I'm sure,
More pity the poor Negroe slaves bestowed
Than my inhuman brutal master showed.
   Oft on my knees the Lord I did implore,
To let me see my native land once more;
For through God's grace my life I would
   amend
And be a comfort to my dearest friends.
   Helpless and sick and being left alone,
I by myself did use to make my moan;
And think upon my former wicked ways,
How they had brought me to this wretched
   case.
   The Lord above who saw my Grief and
   smart,
Heard my complaint and knew my contrite
   heart,
His gracious Mercy did to me afford,
My health again was unto me restor'd.
   It pleas'd the Lord to grant me so much
   Grace,
That tho' I was in such a barbarous place,
I serv'd the Lord with fervency and zeal,
By which I did much inward comfort feel.
   Thus twelve long tedious years did pass
   away,
And but two more by law I had to stay:
When Death did for my cruel Master call,
But that was no relief to us at all.
   The Widow would not the Plantation
   hold,
So we and that were both for to be sold,
A lawyer rich who at James-Town did
   dwell,
Came down to view it and lik'd it very well.
   He bought the Negroes who for life were
   slaves,
But no transported Fellons would he have,
So we were put like Sheep into a fold,
There unto the best bidder to be sold.

PART V
A Gentleman who seemed something grave,
Unto me said, how long are you to slave;
Not two years quite, I unto him reply'd,
That is but very short indeed he cry'd.

He ask'd my Name, my trade, and
   whence I came
And what vile Fate had brought me to that
   shame?
I told him all at which he shook his head,
I hope you have seen your folly now, he said,
   I told him yes and truly did repent,
But that which made me most of all relent
That I should to my parents prove so vile,
I being their darling and their only child.
   He said no more but from me short did
   turn,
While from my Eyes the tears did trinkling
   run,
To see him to my overseer go,
But what he said to him I do not know.
   He straightway came to me again,
And said no longer here you must remain,
For I have bought you of that Man said he,
Therefore prepare yourself to come with me.
   I with him went with heart oppressed
   with woe,
Not knowing him, or where I was to go;
But was surprised very much to find,
He used me so tenderly and kind.
   He said he would not use me as a slave,
But as a servant if I well behav'd;
And if I pleased him when my time expir'd,
He'd send me home again if I required.
   My kind new master did at James Town
   dwell;
By trade a Cooper, and liv'd very well:
I was his servant on him to attend,
Thus God, unlook'd for raised me up a
   friend.

PART VI
Thus did I live in plenty and at ease,
   Having none but my master for to
   please,
And if at any time he did ride out,
I with him rode the country round about.
   And in my heart I often cry'd to see,
So many transport fellons there to be;
Some who in England had lived fine and
   brave,
Were like old Horses forced to drudge and
   slave.

At length my fourteen years expired
quite,
Which fill'd my very soul with fond de-
light;
To think I should no longer there remain,
But to old England once return again.
   My master for me did express much love,
And as good as his promise to me prov'd:
He got me ship'd and I came home again
With joy and comfort tho' I went asham'd,
   My Father and my Mother wel[l] I found,
Who to see me, with Joy did much abound:
My Mother over me did weep for Joy,
My Father cry'd once more to see my Boy;
   Whom I thought dead, but does alive
remain,
And is resumed to me once again;
I hope God has so wrought upon your mind,
No more wickedness you'll be inclined,
   I told them all the dangers I went thro'
Likewise my sickness and my hardships too;
Which fill'd their tender hearts with sad
surprise,

While tears ran trinkling from their aged
eyes.
   I begg'd them from all grief to refrain,
Since God had brought me to them home
again,
The Lord unto me so much grace will give,
For to work for you both while I live,
   My country men take warning e'er too
late,
Lest you should share my hard unhappy fate;
Altho' but little crimes you here have done,
Consider seven or fourteen years to come,
   Forc'd from your friends and country for
to go,
Among the Negroes to work at the hoe;
In distant countries void of all relief,
Sold for a slave because you prov'd a thief.
   Now young men with speed your lives
amend,
Take my advice as one that is your friend:
For tho' so slight you make of it while here,
Hard is your lot when once the[y] get you
there.

*c.*1680s   after 1750s

New England

Thomas Morton (1579?–1647?)

One of the most colorful antagonists of the Puritan errand in the New World, Thomas Morton was fairly obscure before his first trip to New England in 1622. He practiced law, acting as an attorney based in London for the Council for New England, and moved in circles of influential people in the court of Charles I who were hostile to separatists and "schismatics." In 1625, dogged by the shadow of personal and business scandals, he returned to New England with a group led by Captain Wollaston, who established a settlement at Passonagessit very close to Plymouth Plantation. When Wollaston left after the first winter, Morton took over. He renamed the site Merry Mount and established a trading post there, doing a brisk business with the surrounding Nauset Indians exchanging guns and liquor for valuable beaver furs.

This trade disturbed the Puritans at Plymouth and Massachusetts Bay – spiritually as well as economically; they disparaged Morton's settlement as a haven for decadents, anarchists, and malcontents, and wanted a monopoly on the fur trade. When, in the spring of 1627, Morton erected a large Maypole to celebrate the rites of spring, the Plymouth colony decided to act and sent Myles Standish, their military leader, to arrest him. Morton was deported to England in 1628 on charges that he armed the Indians against the Puritan colonies. To the Puritans' utter surprise, he was acquitted, and returned to New England in 1629. In 1630, Morton was

arrested again, his property was destroyed and he was banished for a second time to England, where he began a campaign to undermine the Puritan mission by characterizing it as disloyal to King and Church. His only book, *New English Canaan*, was written during this period. Although he was unsuccessful, he did embroil the Puritan colonies in complicated and time-consuming legal battles over title to property which stopped only when Oliver Cromwell came to power. Not to be deterred but without power or financial support, Morton returned to New England one last time in 1643, and was imprisoned in Boston on charges of slander. A sad and broken figure by this time, he was released in 1645, and settled in the district of Maine where he died two years later.

Morton believed his Puritan adversaries were concealing the natural beauty of their refuge, and wrote his book, *New English Canaan,* to promote the region to prospective settlers. Its descriptions reveal his genuine pleasure in this wild and uncharted place. Through the use of anecdotes and classical allusions, Morton characterizes himself as the only cultured and reasonable man in a wilderness of zealots, and satirizes the "precise Separatists" as fanatics and spoilsports who disguise their material self-interest behind a veil of spiritual purity. By deliberate contrast, he presents the Native Americans as natural, humane, and contented, anticipating the critiques of Roger Williams, another victim of Puritan intolerance who wrote a decade later. Although Morton's accounts of early Puritan history are often garbled, distorted and unreliable, *New English Canaan* presents an important and witty counterpoint to the self-righteous representation of the Puritans contained in the histories of Bradford and Winthrop.

PRIMARY WORK

New English Canaan, 1637.

FURTHER READING

Donald F. Connors, *Thomas Morton* (New York: Twayne, 1969).

Robert Arner, "Pastoral Celebration and Satire in Thomas Morton's *New English Canaan*," *Criticism*, 16 (1974) pp. 217–31.

Wayne Franklin, *Discoverers, Explorers, Settlers: The Diligent Writers of Early America* (Chicago: University of Chicago Press, 1979).

Richard Drinnon, "The Maypole of Merrymount: Thomas Morton and the Puritan Patriarchs," *Massachusetts Review*, 21 (1980) pp. 382–410.

NEW ENGLISH CANAAN[1]

From *Book I: Containing the originall of the Natives, their manners & Customes, with their tractable nature and love towards the English*

Chapter VII: Of their Child-bearing, and delivery, and what manner of persons they are

The women of this Country are not suffered to be used for procreation untill the ripenesse of their age, at which time they weare a read cap made of lether, in forme like to our flat caps, and this they weare for the space of 12 moneths, for all men to take notice of them that have any minde to a wife; and then it is the custome of some of their Sachems or Lords of the territories, to have the first say or maidenhead of the females. Very apt they are to be with childe, and very laborious when they beare children; yea, when they are as great as they can be: yet in that case they neither forbeare labour, nor travaile; I have seen them in that plight with burthens at their backs enough to load a horse; yet do they not miscarry, but have a fair delivery, and a quick: their woman are very good midwives, and the women very lusty after delivery, and in a day or two will travell or trudge about. Their infants are borne with haire on their heads, and are of complexion white as our nation; but their mothers in their infancy make a bath of Wallnut leaves, hulhkes of Walnuts, and such things as will staine their skinne for ever, wherein they dip and washe them to make them tawny;[2] the colour of their haire is black, and their eyes black. These infants are carried at their mothers backs by the help of a cradle made of a board forket at both ends, whereon the childe is fast bound and wrapped in furres; his knees thrust up towards his bellie, because they may be the more usefull for them when he sitteth, which is as a dogge does on his bumme: and this cradle surely preserves them better then the cradles of our nation, for as, much as we finde them well proportioned, not any of them crooked backed or wry legged: and to give their charracter in a worde, they are as proper men and women for feature and limbes as, can be found, for flesh and bloud as active: longe handed they are, (I never sawe a clunchfisted Salvadg amonsgt them all in my time.) The colour of their eies being so generally black made a Salvage, that had a younge infant whose

---

[1]   The selections, with slight modifications, are from *New English Canaan*, ed. Charles Francis Adams (Boston: John Wilson & Sons, 1883). The title refers to the promised land of the Hebrews. In his description of the physical location of New England, Morton concludes "that it is nothing inferior to Canaan of Israel, but a kind of parallel to it in all points."

[2]   This was a common belief of English settlers in the seventeenth century, echoed by writers like John Smith and George Alsop.

eies were gray, shewed him to us, and said they were English mens eies; I tould the Father that his sonne was *nan weeteo*, which is a bastard; hee replied *titta Cheshetue Squaa*, which is, hee could not tell, his wife might play the whore; and this childe the father desired might have an English name, because of the liteness of his eies, which his father had in admiration because of novelty amongst their nation.

Chapter XVI: Of their acknowledgment of the Creation, and immortality of the Soule

Although these Salvages are found to be without Religion, Law, and King (as Sir William Alexander[3] hath well observed,) yet are they not altogether without the knowledge of God (historically); for they have it amongst them by tradition that God made one man and one woman, and bade them live together and get children, kill deare, beasts, birds, fish and fowle, and what they would at their pleasure; and that their posterity was full of evill, and made God so angry that hee let in the Sea upon them, and drowned the greatest part of them, that were naughty men, (the Lord destroyed so;) and they went to Sanaconquam, who feeds upon them (pointing to the Center of the Earth, where they imagine is the habitation of the Devill:) the other, (which were not destroyed,) increased the world, and when they died (because they were good) went to the howse of Kytan, pointing to the setting of the sonne;[4] where they eate all manner of dainties, and never take paines (as now) to provide it.

Kytan makes provision (they sey) and saves them that laboure; and there they shall live with him forever, voyd of care. And they are perswaded that Kytan is hee that makes corne growe, trees growe, and all manner of fruits.

And that wee that use the booke of Common prayer[5] doo it to declare to them, that cannot reade, what Kytan has commaunded us, and that wee doe pray to him with the helpe of that booke; and doe make so much accompt of it, that a Salvage (who had lived in my howse before hee had taken a wife, by whome hee had children) made this request to mee, (knowing that I allwayes used him with much more respect than others,) that I would let his sonne be brought up in my howse, that hee might be taught to reade in that booke: which request of his I granted; and hee was a very joyfull man to thinke that his sonne should thereby (as hee said) become an Englishman; and then hee would be a good man.

I asked him who was a good man; his answere was, hee that would not lye, nor steale.

These, with them, are all the capitall crimes that can be imagined; all other are nothing in respect of those; and hee that is free from these must live with Kytan for ever, in all manner of pleasure.

Chapter XX: That the Salvages live a contented life

A Gentleman and a traveller, that had bin in the parts of New England for a time, when hee retorned againe, in his discourse of the Country, wondered, (as hee said,) that the natives of the land lived so poorely in so rich a Country, like to our Beggers in England. Surely that Gentleman had not time or leasure whiles hee was there truely to informe himselfe of the state of that Country, and the happy life the Salvages would leade weare they once brought to Christianity.

I must confesse they want the use and benefit of Navigation, (which is the very sinnus[6] of a

---

3   Sir William Alexander (1567?–1640), a Scottish poet and statesman who colonized Nova Scotia in the 1620s.

4   Kytan is the name of the most powerful "manito" or god and means "greatest" or "preeminent."

5   The prayer book adopted by the Church of England.

6   Sinews; what holds it together.

flourishing Commonwealth,) yet are they supplied with all manner of needefull things for the maintenance of life and lifelyhood. Foode and rayment are the cheife of all that we make true use of; and of these they finde no want, but have, and may have, them in a most plentifull manner.

If our beggers of England should, with so much ease as they, furnish themselves with foode at all seasons, there would not be so many starved in the streets, neither would so many gaoles be stuffed, or gallouses furnished with poore wretches, as I have seene them. . . .

Now since it is but foode and rayment that men that live needeth, (though not all alike,) why should not the Natives of New England be sayd to live richly, having no want of either? Cloaths are the badge of sinne; and the more variety of fashions is but the greater abuse of the Creature: the bears of the forrest there doe serve to furnish them at any time when they please: fish and flesh they have in greate abundance, which they both roast and boyle.

They are indeed not served in dishes of plate with variety of Sauces to procure appetite; that needs not there. The rarity of the aire, begot by the medicinable quality of the sweete herbes of the Country, always procures good stomakes to the inhabitants.

I must needs commend them in this particular, that, though they buy many commodities of our Nation, yet they keepe but fewe, and those of speciall use.

They love not to bee cumbered with many utensilles, and although every proprietor knowes his owne, yet all things, (so long as they will last), are used in common amongst them: A bisket cake given to one, that one breakes it equally into so many parts as there be persons in his company, and distributes it. Platoes Commonwealth is so much prac'tifed by these peo-ple.[7]

According to humane reason, guided onely by the light of nature, these people leades the more happy and freer; life, being voyde of care, which torments the mindes of so many Christians: They are not delighted in baubles, but in usefull things.

Their naturall drinke is of the Cristall fountaine, and this they take up in their hands, by joyning them close together. They take up a great quantity at a time, and drinke at the wrists. It was the sight of such a feate which made Diogenes hurle away his dishe, and, like one that would have this principall confirmed, *Natura paucis contentat*, used a dish no more.[8]

I have observed that they will not be troubled with superfluous commodities. Such things as they finde they are taught by necessity to make use of, they will make choise of, and seeke to purchase with industry. So that, in respect that their life is so voyd of care, and they are so loving also that they make use of those things they enjoy, (the wife onely excepted,) as common goods, and are therein so compassionate that, rather than one should starve through want, they would starve all. Thus doe they passe awaye the time merrily, not regarding our pompe, (which they see dayly before their faces,) but are better content with their owne, which some men esteeme so meanely of.

They may be rather accompted to live richly, wanting nothing that is needefull; and to be commended for leading a contented life, the younger being ruled by the Elder, and the Elder ruled by the Powahs[9], and the Powahs are ruled by the Devill; and then you may imagin what good rule is like to be amongst them.

---

[7] Plato (429?–347 BC) the Greek philosopher, describes a communal society in his *Republic*.

[8] Diogenes (412?–323 BC), Greek philosopher and founder of the movement of Cynics. His principle is "Nature is satisfied with little" (Latin).

[9] Powahs were religious leaders.

From *Book II: A Description of the Beauty of the Country*

From Chapter I: The General Survey of the Country

In the month of June, *Anno Salutis*[10] 1622, it was my chance to arrive in the parts of New England with 30 servants and provision of all sorts fit for a plantation; and while our houses were building, I did endeavor to take a survey of the country. The more I looked, the more I liked it. And when I had more seriously considered of the beauty of the place, withall her fair endowments, I did not think that in all the known world it could be paralleled for so many goodly groves of trees, dainty fine round rising hillocks, delicate fair large plains, sweet crystal fountains, and clear running streams that twine in fine meanders through the meads[11], making so sweet a murmuring noise to hear as would even lull the senses with delight asleep, so pleasantly do they glide upon the pebble stones, jetting most jocundly where they do meet, and hand in hand run down to Neptune's[12] court, to pay the yearly tribute which they owe to him as sovereign lord of all the springs. Contained within the volume of the land, [are] fowls in abundance, [and] fish in multitude. And [I] discovered, besides, millions of turtledoves on the green boughs, which sat pecking of the full ripe pleasant grapes that were supported by the lusty trees, whose fruitful load did cause the arms to bend: [among] which here and there dispersed, you might see lillies and . . . the Daphnean-tree, which made the land to me seem paradise.[13] For in mine eye t'was Nature's masterpiece, her chiefest magazine[14] of all where lives her store. If this land be not rich, then is the whole world poor. . . .

From *Book III: Containing a description of the People that are planted there, what remarkable Accidents have happened there since they were setled, what Tenents they hould, together with the practise of their Church*

Chapter XIV: Of the Revells of New Canaan

The Inhabitants of Pasonagessit, (having translated the name of their habitation from that ancient Salvage name to Ma-re Mount[15], and being resolved to have the new name confirmed for a memorial to after ages,) did devise amongst themselves to have it performed in a solemne manner, with Revels and merriment after the old English custome; [they] prepared to sett up a Maypole upon the festivall day of Philip and Jacob,[16] and therefore brewed a barrell of excellent beare and provided a case of bottles, to be spent, with other good cheare, for all commers of that day. And because they would have it in a compleat forme, they had prepared a song fitting to the time and present occasion. And upon Mayday they brought the Maypole to the place appointed, with drumes, gunnes, pistols and other fitting instruments, for that

---

10   In the year of our prosperity (Latin).

11   Meadows.

12   The Roman god of the sea.

13   Lusty means vigorous and productive. In Greek mythology, Daphne was the daughter of a river-god loved by Apollo. To escape his amorous pursuit, she was transformed into a laurel.

14   Place for storage; "store" is plenty.

15   In Algonquin, meaning "a place near the little point," part of modern day Quincy, Massachusetts, south of Bos-

ton. It was first known as Mt Wollaston, after Captain Wollaston who led the group there, but who left after the first winter for Virginia. Morton renamed the settlement "Merry Mount," the name he plays on in his use of "Ma-re Mount" which means, a mountain by the sea.

16   Saints Philip and James (which in Latin is Jacob), whose feast days were celebrated by the Church of England on May 1. Maypoles were a feature of secular holiday rites descended from ancient Roman festivals celebrating the renewal of spring.

purpose; and there erected it with the help of Salvages, that came thether of purpose to see the manner of our Revels. A goodly pine tree of 80. foote longe was reared up, with a peare of buckshorns nayled on somewhat neare unto the top of it: where it stood, as a faire see marke for directions how to finde out the way to mine Hoste of Ma-re Mount[17]. . . .

The setting up of this Maypole was a lamentable spec'tacle to the precise Seperatists, that lived at new Plimmouth. They termed it an Idoll; yea, they called it the Calfe of Horeb, and stood at defiance with the place, naming it Mount Dagon; threatning to make it a woefull mount and not a merry mount.[18] . . .

There was likewise a merry song made, which, (to make their Revells more fashionable,) was sung with a Corus, every man bearing his part; which they performed in a daunce, hand in hand about the maypole, whiles one of the Company sung and filled out the good liquor, like gammedes and Jupiter.[19]

THE SONGE.

Cor,

Drinke and be merry, merry, merry boyes;
Let all your delight be in the Hymens joyes;[20]
Io[21] to Hymen, now the day is come,
About the merry Maypole take a Roome.

　　Make greene garlons, bring boottles out
　　And fill sweet Nectar freely about.
　　Uncover thy head and feare no harme,
　　For hers good liquor to keepe it warme.

Then drinke and be merry, &c.
Io to Hymen, &c.

　　Nectar is a thing assgn'd
　　By the Deities owne minde
　　To cure the hart opprest with greife,
　　And of good liquors is the cheife.

Then drinke, &c.
Io to Hymen, &c.

　　Give to the Mellancolly man
　　A cup or two of't now and than;
　　This physck will soone revive his bloud,
　　And make him be of a merrier moode.

Then drinke, &c.
Io to Hymen, &c.

　　Give to the Nymphe thats free from scorne
　　No Irish stuff nor Scotch over worne.[22]

---

[17]　Morton's way of referring to himself.

[18]　The term "precise Separatists" was another derogatory name for "Puritans," who emigrated in order to purify their worship and separate in deed, if not in word, from the Anglican Church. The Calf of Horeb was a golden idol in the shape of a calf made by the Israelites in Moses' absence, which he destroyed when he descended with the ten commandments; see Exodus 32. Dagon was the idol worshiped by the Philistines; see 1 Samuel 5. Morton is punning on place

names: Mt Wollaston (a woefull mount) and Merry Mount, its present name and site of merriment.

[19]　Ganymede, a young boy, is the cup-bearer of Jupiter, the king of the gods of Roman mythology.

[20]　Hymen is the Roman god of marriage; his "joys" are the celebration of marriage rites.

[21]　A word from the Latin meaning "hail" or "hurrah" and used in marriage celebrations.

[22]　Worn out Irish or Scottish cloth.

> *Lasses in beaver coats come away,*
> *Yee shall be welcome to us night and day.*
> *To drinke and be merry &c.*
> *Io to Hymen, &c.*

This harmeless mirth made by younge men, (that lived in hope to have wifes brought over to them, that would save them a laboure to make a voyage to fetch any over,) was much distasted of the precise Seperatists, that keepe much a doe about the tyth of Mint and Cummin,[23] troubling their braines more then reason would require about things that are indifferent[24]: and from that time sought occasion against my honest Host of Ma-re Mount, to overthrow his undertakings and to destroy his plantation quite cleane. . . . Some of them affirmed that the first institution [of the Maypole] was in memory of a whore; not knowing that it was a Trophe erected at first in honor of Maia, the Lady of learning which they despise, vilifying the two universities with uncivile termes, accounting what is there obtained by studdy is but unnecessary learning; not considering that learninge does inable mens mindes to converse with eliments of a higher nature then is to be found within the habitation of the Mole.[25]

Chapter XVI: How the 9. worthies put mine Host of Ma-re Mount in to the inchaunted Castle at Plimmouth, and terrified him with the Monster Briareus[26]

The nine worthies[27] of New Canaan having now the Law in their owne hands, (there being no generall Governour in the Land; nor none of the Seperations that regarded the dutey they owe their Soveraigne, whose naturall borne Subjects they were, though translated out of Holland, from whence they had learned to worke all to their own ends, and make a great shewe of Religion, but no humanity,) for they were not to sit in a Counsell on the cause.

And much it stood mine honest Host upon to be very circumspect, and to take Eacus[28] to taske; for that his voyce was more allowed of than both the other: and had not mine Host confounded all the arguments that Eacus could make in their defence, and confuted him that swaied the rest, they would have made him unable to drinke in such manner of merriment any more. So that following this private counsell, given him by one that knew who rules the rost, the Hiracano ceased that els would split his pinace.[29]

A conclusion was made and sentence given that mine host should be sent to England a prisoner. But when hee was brought to the shipps for that purpose, no man durst be so foole hardy as to undertake carry him. So these Worthies set mine Host upon an Island, without

[23] In Matthew 23:23, Jesus condemns the hypocrisy of the Jewish religious leaders, saying, "Woe unto you, scribes and Pharisees, hypocrites! for ye pay tithe of mint and anise and cummin and have omitted the weightier matters of the law, judgement, mercy, and faith."

[24] Unimportant.

[25] According to William Bradford's account, the Plymouth pilgrims thought the Maypole celebrated Flora, a Roman goddess whose cult worship involved licentious dancing and farces, while Morton contends that Maia, the goddess of the spring, was its object. Morton implies that this confusion indicates the Puritans' rejection of the wisdom of Athena, the "Lady of Learning," and that their disdain for the classical studies pursued at Oxford and Cambridge, the major centers of learning in England, suggests their blindness (thus

his comparison of them with moles) to the importance of higher learning.

[26] In Roman mythology, a hundred-armed monster that fought the Titans, a race of giants, and guarded the underworld.

[27] A group of prominent men, heroes, and kings, who epitomized the ideal of conduct for the Medieval world.

[28] In Greek mythology, one of the three judges of the underworld. Later, Morton identifies him as Samuel Fuller, and names William Bradford and Myles Standish as the other two judges.

[29] The hurricane ended that would damage his pinnace, a small boat, a figure for the verbal abuse heaped on Morton by the judges.

gunne, powther, or shot or dogge or so much as knife to get any thing to feede upon, or any other cloathes to shelter him with at winter then a thinne suite which hee had on at that time. Home hee could not get to Ma-re Mount. Upon this island hee stayed a moneth at least, and was releeved by Salvages that tooke notice that mine Host was a Sachem of Passonagessit, and would bringe bottles of strong liquor to him, and unite themselves into a league of brother hood with mine Host; so full of humanity are these infidels before those Christians.

From this place for England sailed mine Host in a Plimmouth shipp, (that came into the Land to fish upon the Coast,) that landed him safe in England at Plimmouth: and hee stayed in England untill the ordinary time for shipping to set forth for these parts, and then retorned: Noe man being able to taxe him of any things.[30]

But the Worthies, (in the mean time,) hoped they had bin ridd of him.

1637

John Winthrop (1588–1649)

The Massachusetts Bay was first settled in 1623 at Cape Anne by fishermen engaged by the New England Company. By 1629, the Company obtained a new grant from King Charles, changed its name to the Massachusetts Bay Company, and began to execute an ambitious plan to transform their mainly commercial venture into an asylum for persecuted non-conformists. John Winthrop, a wealthy landowner, lawyer, and ardent Puritan, was a crucial figure in this enterprise. Born into a well-off family of landed gentry on a prosperous estate in Groton, England, Winthrop attended Trinity College, Cambridge for two years, but left at age seventeen to marry the first of his four wives. In the next year, he became a justice of the peace and steward for Groton manor, an important position that, along with his training in law, gave him the administrative skills he would put to use in New England. After what he described in his spiritual autobiography as a "wild and dissolute" boyhood, he was seized by "an insatiable thirst" to know God. But his piety, which characterized his public as well as private life, did not lead him to Separatism, like Bradford's Pilgrims. Rather, he took the more moderate position that the established English church could be reformed from within.

The 1620s were an ominous time for England and for Puritans. Severe economic conditions caused

unemployment, deepened poverty and brought unfair taxation; even the eminent Winthrop lost his attorneyship. Furthermore, King Charles, who came to the throne in 1625, was sympathetic to Roman Catholicism and hostile to Puritanism and Protestant church reform. Although Winthrop did not personally suffer persecution, he, like many other Puritans who did, was profoundly discouraged about the future of religious life in what he called "this sinful land." In March 1629, a group of Puritan merchants managed to obtain a charter to settle in New England. In October, he was chosen governor under the unique charter which did not specify where the governing body of the Company would meet, thus allowing it to be established in New England, far from the persecutions of the monarchy. This arrangement was a crucial factor; only six days after the charter was granted, King Charles dissolved Parliament and did not recall it until 1640. By 1637 the Privy Council issued an order prohibiting the emigration of known dissenters. Winthrop, who supervised the move, and a sizable group of followers left Southampton in March 1630 and arrived in the port of Naumkeag, or Salem, on June 12, 1630.

For the next nineteen years of his life, Winthrop was governor or deputy governor of the Massachusetts Bay Colony, its leading citizen and guiding

---

[30]   Charge him with crimes. Morton was successful in having the charges brought against him by the Puritans dismissed.

light. A dignified, aristocratic, and – considering the company – moderate man, Winthrop tried to shape the colony after the idealized vision he outlined in the lay sermon he delivered during the crossing on board the fleet's flagship, the *Arbella*. In "A Modell of Christian Charity," Winthrop speaks in the words of Moses, leading his latter-day chosen people out of bondage to a new promised land. Through such comparisons, Winthrop not only set the high tone of the Puritan "errand," but he bound the Puritans into a radically new conception of providential history as its contemporary fulfillment. Winthrop envisioned a "commonwealth" in which the general good would always take priority over private interests. But as Winthrop's *Journal* records in escalating detail, this idealized vision never materialized. Begun in 1630 at Southampton aboard the *Arbella* and kept up until his death, his *Journal* is related to the private diary of spiritual experiences kept by many Puritans. However, instead of showing the hand of God working personally, Winthrop recounts major and minor events of the colony, hoping to glimpse therein God's pleasure or displeasure with New England. As the centrifugal forces within the colony multiplied, the entries grow longer, more adversarial, and less tolerant of the accommodations of the spirit to material reality. In the two decades of Winthrop's public service, the colony faced challenges from the charismatic Roger Williams, and from Anne Hutchinson, labeled by Winthrop "the American Jezabel," whose "infectious" doctrines of free grace almost split the colony in half. Both were banished, but similar challenges to Puritan authority continued, underscoring the Bay colony's legalism, absolutism, and patriarchalism. At the same time, the Puritans pursued a genocidal policy towards the powerful Pequot tribe. Appearing at times to be defending his own decisions, Winthrop was forced to do just that in 1645 when he was charged with overstepping his official powers. Though acquitted, he delivered a speech to the General Court that perfectly expresses the paradoxical Puritan notion of liberty. He distinguished civil liberty, the freedom to do what is "good, just and honest," from natural liberty which was sheer license to good or evil, and argued that civil liberty required subjection to authority. Given this understanding, it is not surprising that Winthrop feared and resisted "mere democracy" and religious toleration, though under his leadership, Massachusetts developed representative government and a bicameral legislature.

PRIMARY WORKS

Winthrop's Journal: History of New England, 1630–1649.
Winthrop's Journal, ed. James Hosmer (New York: Scribner's, 1908).

FURTHER READING

Edmund Morgan, *The Puritan Dilemma* (Boston: Little Brown, 1958).
Darret Rutman, *Winthrop's Boston: Portrait of a Puritan Town* (Chapel Hill: University of North Carolina Press, 1965).
Richard Dunn, "John Winthrop Writes his Journal," *William and Mary Quarterly*, 41, 2 (1984) pp. 185–212.
Amy Lang, *Prophetic Woman: Anne Hutchinson and the Problem of Dissent in the Literature of New England* (Berkeley: University of California Press, 1987).
Lee Schweninger, *John Winthrop* (Boston: Twayne, 1990).
Hugh Dawson, "'Christian Charitie' as Colonial Discourse: Rereading Winthrop's Sermon in Its English Context," *Early American Literature*, 33, 2 (1998) pp. 117–48.

"A MODELL OF CHRISTIAN CHARITY"[1]

Christian Charitie: A Modell Hereof

God Almightie in his most holy and wise providence hath soe disposed of the Condicion of mankinde, as in all times some must be rich some poore, some highe and eminent in power and dignitie; others meane and in subjeccion. . . .

[1]   Winthrop preached this lay sermon aboard the *Arbella* during the crossing to New England in 1630, and the manuscript was widely circulated thereafter. The text, with slight modifications, is from *The Winthrop Papers*, ed. A. Forbes, vol. 2 (Boston: The Massachusetts Historical Society, 1931).

Massachusetts Bay Colony Seal. This original seal promoted the colony's missionary intentions in its depiction of an Indian crying: "Come over and help us." (By permission of the Massachusetts State Archives, Boston, MA.)

The diffinition which the Scripture gives us of love is this Love is the bond of perfection.[2] First, it is a bond, or ligament. 2ly, it makes the worke perfect. There is noe body but consistes of partes and that which knitts these partes together gives the body its perfeccion, because it makes eache parte soe contiguous to other as thereby they doe mutually participate with eache other, both in strengthe and infirmity in pleasure and paine, to instance in the most perfect of all bodies, Christ and his church make one body: the severall partes of this body considered aparte before they were united were as disproportionate and as much disordering as soe many contrary quallities or elements but when Christ comes and by his spirit and love knitts all these partes to himselfe and each to other, it is become the most perfect and best proportioned

[2]   A paraphrase of the Geneva Bible, which was commonly used by the Puritans, Colossians 3:14: "love, which is the bond of perfectnesse." Most modern citations are from the King James version.

body in the world Eph: 4. 16. "Christ by whome all the body being knitt together by every joynt for the furniture thereof according to the effectuall power which is in the measure of every perfeccion of partes a glorious body without spots or wrinckle the ligaments hereof being Christ or his love for Christ is love 1 John: 4. 8. Soe this definition is right Love is the bond of perfeccion.

From hence wee may frame these Conclusions.

1 first all true Christians are of one body in Christ 1. Cor. 1. 12. 13. 17. [27.] Ye are the body of Christ and members of [your] parte.

2ly. The ligamentes of this body which knitt together are love.

3ly. Noe body can be perfect which wants its propper ligamentes.

4ly. All the partes of this body being thus united are made soe contiguous in a speciall relacion as they must needes partake of each others strength and infirmity, joy, and sorrowe, weale and woe. 1 Cor: 12. 26. If one member suffers all suffer with it, if one be in honour, all reioyce with it.

5ly. This sensiblenes and Sympathy of each others Condicions will necessarily infuse into each parte a native desire and endeavour, to strengthen defend preserve and comfort the other. . . .

The next Consideracion is how this love comes to be wrought; Adam in his first estate[3] was a perfect modell of mankinde in all theire generacions, and in him this love was perfected in regard of the habit, but Adam Rent in himselfe from his Creator, rent all his posterity allsoe one from another, whence it comes that every man is borne with this principle in him, to love and seeke himselfe onely and thus a man continueth till Christ comes and takes possession of the soule, and infuseth another principle love to God and our brother. And this latter haveing continuall supply from Christ, as the head and roote by which hee is united get the predominancy in the soule, soe by little and little expells the former 1 John 4. 7. love cometh of god and every one that loveth is borne of god, soe that this love is the fruite of the new birthe, and none can have it but the new Creature[4], now when this quallity is thus formed in the soules of men it workes like the Spirit upon the drie bones Ezek. 37. [7] bone came to bone, it gathers together the scattered bones or perfect old man Adam and knitts them into one body againe in Christ whereby a man is become againe a liveing soule.

The third Consideracion is concerning the exercise of this love, which is twofold, inward or outward, the outward hath beene handled in the former preface of this discourse, for unfolding the other wee must take in our way that maxime of philosophy, Simile simili gaudet or like will to like; for as it is things which are carved with disafeccion to eache other, the ground of it is from a dissimilitude or [blank] ariseing from the contrary or different nature of the things themselves, soe the ground of love is an apprehension of some resemblance in the things loved to that which affectes it, this is the cause why the Lord loves the Creature, soe farre as it hath any of his Image in it, he loves his elect[5] because they are like himselfe, he beholds them in his beloved sonne: soe a mother loves her childe, because shee throughly conceives a resemblance of herselfe in it. Thus it is betweene the members of Christ, each discernes by the worke of the spirit his owne Image and resemblance in another, and therefore cannot but love him as he loves himselfe: Now when the soule which is of a sociable nature findes any thing like to it selfe, it is like Adam when Eve was brought to him, shee must have it one with herselfe this is fleshe of my fleshe (saith shee) and bone of my bone shee conceives a greate delighte in it, therefore shee desires nearenes and familiarity with it: shee hath a greate propensity to doe it good and receives such content in it, as feareing the miscarriage of her beloved shee bestowes

---

3   His innocence, his prelapsarian state.
4   The reborn and regenerated soul.

5   Those predestined or "elected" by God before the Creation to be saved.

it in the inmost closett of her heart, shee will not endure that it shall want any good which shee can give it, if by occasion shee be withdrawne from the Company of it, shee is still lookeing towardes the place where shee left her beloved, if shee heare it groane shee is with it presently, if shee finde it sadd and disconsolate shee sighes and mournes with it, shee hath noe such joy, as to see her beloved merry and thriveing, if shee see it wronged, shee cannot beare it without passion, shee setts noe boundes of her affeccions, nor hath any thought of reward, shee findes recompence enoughe in the exercise of her love towardes it, wee may see this Acted to life in Jonathan and David.[6] Jonathan a valiant man endued with the spirit of Christ, soe soone as hee Discovers the same spirit in David had presently his hearte knitt to him by this linement of love, soe that it is said he loved him as his owne soule, he takes soe great pleasure in him that hee stripps himselfe to adorne his beloved, his fathers kingdome was not soe precious to him as his beloved David, David shall have it with all his hearte, himselfe desires noe more but that hee may be neare to him to rejoyce in his good he chooseth to converse with him in the wildernesse even to the hazzard of his owne life, rather then with the greate Courtiers in his fathers Pallace; when hee sees danger towards him, hee spares neither care paines, nor perill to divert it, when Injury was offered his beloved David, hee could not beare it, though from his owne father, and when they must parte for a Season onely, they thought theire heartes would have broake for sorrowe, had not theire affeccions found vent by aboundance of Teares: other instances might be brought to shewe the nature of this affeccion as of Ruthe and Naomi and many others,[7] but this truthe is cleared enough. If any shall object that it is not possible that love should be bred or upheld without hope of requitall, it is graunted but that is not our cause, for this love is allwayes under reward it never gives, but it allwayes receives with advantage: first, in regard that among the members of the same body, love and affection are reciprocall in a most equall and sweete kinde of Commerce. 2ly [3ly], in regard of the pleasure and content that the exercise of love carries with it as wee may see in the naturall body the mouth is at all the paines to receive, and mince the foode which serves for the nourishment of all the other partes of the body, yet it hath noe cause to complaine; for first, the other partes send backe by secret passages a due proporcion of the same nourishment in a better forme for the strengthening and comforteing the mouthe. 2ly the labour of the mouthe is accompanied with such pleasure and content as farre exceedes the paines it takes: soe is it in all the labour of love, among christians, the partie loveing, reapes love againe as was shewed before, which the soule covetts more then all the wealthe in the world. 2ly [4ly]. noething yeildes more pleasure and content to the soule then when it findes that which it may love fervently, for to love and live beloved is the soules paradice, both heare and in heaven: In the State of Wedlock there be many comfortes to beare out the troubles of that Condicion; but let such as have tryed the most, say if there be any sweetnes in that Condicion comparable to the exercise of mutuall love.

From the former Consideracions ariseth these Conclusions.

1 First, This love among Christians is a reall thing not Imaginarie.

2ly. This love is as absolutely necessary to the being of the body of Christ, as the sinewes and other ligaments of a naturall body are to the being of that body.

3ly. This love is a divine spirituall nature free, active strong Couragious permanent under valueing all things beneathe its propper object, and of all the graces this makes us nearer to resemble the virtues of our heavenly father.

---

[6] Young warriors who, despite the active hostility of Jonathan's father Saul, became fast friends and were held up as a model of love "surpassing the love of women;" see 1 Samuel 18ff.

[7] Ruth, Naomi's daughter-in-law, refused to leave her mother-in-law after they were both widowed; see the Book of Ruth.

4ly, It restes in the love and wellfare of its beloved, for the full and certaine knowledge of these truthes concerning the nature use, [and] excellency of this grace, that which the holy ghost hath left recorded 1. Cor. 13. may give full satisfaccion which is needfull for every true member of this lovely body of the Lord Jesus, to worke upon theire heartes, by prayer meditacion continuall exercise at least of the speciall [power] of this grace till Christ be formed in them and they in him all in eache other knitt together by this bond of love.

It rests now to make some applicacion of this discourse by the present designe which gave the occasion of writeing of it. Herein are 4 things to be propounded: first the persons, 2ly, the worke, 3ly, the end, 4ly the meanes.

1. For the persons, wee are a Company professing our selves fellow members of Christ, In which respect onely though wee were absent from eache other many miles, and had our imploymentes as farre distant, yet wee ought to account our selves knitt together by this bond of love, and live in the excercise of it, if wee would have comforte of our being in Christ, this was notorious in the practice of the Christians in former times, as is testified of the Waldenses from the mouth of one of the adversaries Aeneas Sylvius,[8] mutuo [solent amare] pene antequam norint, they use to love any of theire owne religion even before they were acquainted with them.

2ly. for the worke wee have in hand, it is by a mutuall consent through a speciall overruleing providence, and a more then an ordinary approbation of the Churches of Christ to seeke out a place of Cohabitation and Consorteshipp under a due forme of Goverment both civill and ecclesiasticall. In such cases as this the care of the publique must oversway all private respects, by which not onely conscience, but meare Civill pollicy doth binde us; for it is a true rule that perticuler estates cannott subsist in the ruine of the publique.

3ly. The end is to improve our lives to doe more service to the Lord the comforte and encrease of the body of christe whereof wee are members that our selves and posterity may be the better preserved from the Common corrupcions of this evill world to serve the Lord and worke out our Salvacion under the power and purity of his holy Ordinances.

4ly for the meanes whereby this must bee effected, they are 2fold, a Conformity with the worke and end wee aime at, these wee see are extraordinary, therefore wee must not content our selves with usuall ordinary meanes whatsoever wee did or ought to have done when wee lived in England, the same must wee doe and more allsoe where wee goe: That which the most in theire Churches maineteine as a truthe in profession onely, wee must bring into familiar and constant practice, as in this duty of love wee must love brotherly without dissimulation, wee must love one another with a pure hearte fervently wee must beare one anothers burthens, wee must not looke onely on our owne things, but allsoe on the things of our brethren, neither must wee think that the lord will beare with such faileings at our hands as hee dothe from those among whome wee have lived, and that for 3 Reasons.

1. In regard of the more neare bond of mariage, betweene him and us, wherein he hath taken us to be his after a most strickt and peculiar manner which will make him the more Jealous of our love and obedience soe he tells the people of Israell, you onely have I knowne of all the families of the Earthe therefore will I punishe you for your Transgressions.

2ly, because the lord will be sanctified in them that come neare him. Wee know that there were many that corrupted the service of the Lord some setting upp Alters before his owne, others offering both strange fire and strange Sacrifices allsoe; yet there came noe fire from

---

[8]   The Waldenses were followers of Pater Valdes, an early French reformer of the Church. Aeneas Sylvius Piccolomini (1405–64), Pope Pius II, a historian and scholar.

heaven, or other sudden Judgement upon them as did upon Nadab and Abihu whoe yet wee may thinke did not sinne presumptuously.[9]

3ly When God gives a speciall Commission he lookes to have it strickly observed in every Article, when hee gave Saule a Commission to destroy Amaleck hee indented with him upon certaine Articles and because hee failed in one of the least, and that upon a faire presence, it lost him the kingdome, which should have beene his reward, if hee had observed his Commission:[10] Thus stands the cause betweene God and us, wee are entered into Covenant[11] with him for this worke, wee have taken out a Commission, the Lord hath given us leave to drawe our owne Articles wee have professed to enterprise these Accions upon these and these ends, wee have hereupon besought him of favour and blessing: Now if the Lord shall please to heare us, and bring us in peace to the place wee desire, then hath hee ratified this Covenant and sealed our Commission, [and] will expect a strickt performance of the Articles contained in it, but if wee shall neglect the observacion of these Articles which are the ends wee have propounded, and dissembling with our God, shall fall to embrace this present world and prosecute our carnall intencions, seekeing great things for our selves and our posterity, the Lord will surely breake out in wrathe against us be revenged of such a perjured people and make us knowe the price of the breache of such a Covenant.

Now the onely way to avoyde this shipwracke and to provide for our posterity is to followe the Counsell of Micah, to doe Justly, to love mercy, to walke humbly with our God,[12] for this end, wee must be knitt together in this worke as one man, wee must entertaine each other in brotherly Affeccion, wee must be willing to abridge our selves of our superfluities, for the supply of others necessities, wee must uphold a familiar Commerce together in all meekenes, gentlenes, patience and liberallity, wee must delight in eache other, make others Condicions our owne rejoyce together, mourne together, labour, and suffer together, allwayes haveing before our eyes our Commission and Community in the worke, our Community as members of the same body, soe shall wee keepe the unitie of the spirit in the bond of peace, the Lord will be our God and delight to dwell among us, as his owne people and will commaund a blessing upon us in all our wayes, soe that wee shall see much more of his wisdome power goodnes and truthe then formerly wee have beene acquainted with, wee shall finde that the God of Israell is among us, when tenn of us shall be able to resist a thousand of our enemies, when hee shall make us a prayse and glory, that men shall say of succeeding plantacions: the lord make it like that of New England: for wee must Consider that wee shall be as a Citty upon a Hill, the eies of all people are uppon us;[13] soe that if wee shall deale falsely with our god in this worke wee

---

[9]   Nadab and Abihu were the sons of Aaron, high priest of the Hebrews, who "took either of them his censer, and put fire therein, and put incense thereon, and offered strange fire before the Lord, which he commanded them not. And there went out fire from the Lord, and devoured them, and they died before the Lord" (Leviticus 10:1–2). Winthrop implies, from this example, that the sins of the chosen people – the Puritans – will be more severely punished than the less "presumptuous" sins of others.

[10]   Saul was told to destroy the Amalekites and all their possessions, but in sparing their sheep and oxen he did not fulfill his promise to God and thus lost his bid to be king; see 1 Samuel 15:1–34.

[11]   A covenant is a legal contract that defines the terms, or articles, of an agreement and binds both parties to them. Thus, God promised to protect and preserve the Israelites,

if they promised to keep faith and follow his commandments. The Puritans believed that God had entered a covenant of works with Adam and Eve, in which salvation was achieved by active pursuit of good. When that was broken by the Fall, it was renewed as a covenant of grace by Christ, in which believers were predestined or elected for salvation before creation, and no amount of good or bad actions could change that decree.

[12]   Micah was an eighth-century prophet who emphasized the judgment of God on his people and the need for salvation; see Micah.

[13]   "Ye are the light of the world. A city that is set on a hill cannot be hid. Neither do men light a candle, and put it under a bushel, but on a candlestick; and it giveth light unto all that are in the house" (Matthew 5:14–15).

have undertaken and soe cause him to withdrawe his present help from us, wee shall be made a story and a by-word through the world, wee shall open the mouthes of enemies to speake evill of the wayes of god and all professours for Gods sake; wee shall shame the faces of many of gods worthy servants, and cause theire prayers to be turned into Cursses upon us till wee be consumed out of the good land whether wee are goeing: And to shuts upp this discourse with that exhortacion of Moses that faithfull servant of the Lord in his last farewell to Israell Deut. 30[14]. Beloved there is now sett before us life, and good, deathe and evill in that wee are Commaunded this day to love the Lord our God, and to love one another to walke in his wayes and to keepe his Commaundements and his Ordinance, and his lawes, and the Articles of our Covenant with him that wee may live and be multiplyed, and that the Lord our God may blesse us in the land whether wee goe to possesse it: But if our heartes shall turne away soe that wee will not obey, but shall be seduced and worshipp other Gods our pleasures, and proffitts, and serve them; it is propounded unto us this day, wee shall surely perishe out of the good Land whether wee passe over this vast Sea to possesse it; . . .

1630   1838

FROM *WINTHROP'S JOURNAL*[1]

June 8, 1630] . . . We had now fair sunshine weather, and so pleasant a sweet air as did much refresh us, and there came a smell off the shore like the smell of a garden.

Saturday, June 12, 1630] About four in the morning we were near our port . . .

Thursday, August 8, 1630] We kept a day of thanksgiving in all the plantations. Monday we kept a court[2].

April 17, 1631] A general court at Boston. The former governor was chosen again, and all the freemen of the commons were sworn to this government.[3]

July 5, 1632] At Watertown there was (in the view of divers witnesses) a great combat between a mouse and a snake; and after a long fight, the mouse prevailed and killed the snake. The pastor of Boston, Mr Wilson, a very sincere, holy man, hearing of it, gave this interpretation: That the snake was the devil; the mouse was a poor contemptible people, which God had brought hither, which should overcome Satan here, and dispossess him of his kingdom. Upon the same occasion, he told the governor, that, before he was resolved to come into this country, he dreamed he was here, and that he saw a church arise out of the earth, which grew up and became a marvelous goodly church.

---

[14]   "And it shall come to pass, when all these things are come upon thee, the blessing and the curse, which I have set before thee, and thou shalt call them to mind among all the nations, whither the Lord thy God hath driven thee, and shalt return unto the Lord thy God, and shalt obey his voice according to all that I command thee this day, thou and thy children, with all thine heart, and with all thy soul; that then the Lord thy God will turn thy captivity, and have compassion upon thee, and will return and gather thee from all the nations, whither the Lord thy God hath scattered thee;" (Deuteronomy 30:1–2).

JOURNAL
[1]   The text, with modifications, is from *Winthrop's Journal*, ed. James Hosmer (New York: Scribner's, 1908).
[2]   A court referred to a general meeting of the company. This was the first Court of Assistants held on August 23, 1630 at Charlestown.
[3]   By this point, Winthrop and the original seven assistants (who were also the only original freemen, or members of the Company and thus members of the General Court) had expanded "freeman" to include all of the adult males, excluding servants, in the colony who were members of covenanted churches, and who voted for the assistants who elected the governor. It was the very limited beginning of a popular franchise.

October 21, 1636] One Mrs Hutchinson[4], a member of the church of Boston, a woman of a ready wit and bold spirit, brought over with her two dangerous errors: 1. That the person of the Holy Ghost dwells in a justified person. 2. That no sanctification can help to evidence to us our justification[5]. – From these two grew many branches; as, 1. Our union with the Holy Ghost, so as a Christian remains dead to every spiritual action, and hath no gifts nor graces, other than such as are in hypocrites, nor any other sanctification but the Holy Ghost himself.

There joined with her in these opinions a brother of hers, one Mr Wheelwright, a silenced minister sometimes in England.[6]

May 25, 1637] Our English from Connecticut, with their Indians, and many of the Narragansetts, marched in the night to a fort of the Pequods at Mistick, and, besetting the same about break of the day, after two hours' fight they took it, (by firing it,) and slew therein two chief sachems, and one hundred and fifty fighting men, and about one hundred and fifty old men, women, and children, with the loss of two English, whereof but one was killed by the enemy. Divers of the Indian friends were hurt by the English, because they had not some mark to distinguish them from the Pequods, as some of them had.

November 1, 1637] . . . The court also sent for Mrs Hutchinson, and charged her with divers matters, as her keeping two public lectures every week in her house, whereto sixty or eighty persons did usually resort, and for reproaching most of the ministers (viz., all except Mr Cotton) for not preaching a covenant of free grace, and that they had not the seal of the spirit, nor were able ministers of the New Testament; which were clearly proved against her, though she sought to shift it off. And, after many speeches to and fro, at last she was so full as she could not contain, but vented her revelations; amongst which this was one, that she had it revealed to her, that she should come into New England, and should be here persecuted, and that God would ruin us and our posterity, and the whole state for the same. So the court proceeded and banished her; but because it was winter, they committed her to a private home, where she was well provided, and her own friends and other elders permitted to go to her, but none else.

February 12, 1638] About this time the Indians, which were in our families, were much frightened with Hobbamock (as they call the devil) appearing to them in divers shapes, and persuading them to forsake the English, and not to come at the assemblies, nor to learn to read, etc.

February 26, 1638] Mr Peirce, in the Salem ship, the *Desire,* returned from the West Indies after seven months. He had been at Providence[7], and brought some cotton, and tobacco, and negroes[8], etc., from thence, and salt from Tertugos.

---

4   Anne Hutchinson (1591–1643) was at the center of what was later called the Antinomian controversy that rent the colony and hardened its anti-tolerationist policies. Hutchinson followed her minister John Cotton from Lincolnshire to New England, and began preaching first to women, then to mixed audiences in her home, gaining a large following. She and her adherents were called "Antinomians" because they argued, from Cotton's own ideas, that saving grace was awarded only to the faithful, and once in possession of this grace, the recipient was above earthly law (hence, anti-nomian, meaning above the law), including the rule of ministers. This not only went to the heart of the ongoing and bitter ecclesiastical dispute over justification by faith or justification by works, and whether piety and worldly success were marks of God's favor, but it challenged the absolute authority of ministers and patriarchy, thus appearing to undermine civic order.

5   Justification meant election to salvation. Hutchinson argued that the elect were directly inhabited by the spirit and did not need the mediation of ministers. Sanctification was piety; for Hutchinson, outward actions were not evidence of the inward spiritual state.

6   John Wheelwright (1592?–1679) had been a vicar in Alford near Old Boston and married a sister of Anne Hutchinson. He was removed from his ministry there because he refused to sign the oath of loyalty to the Church of England. His appointment as teacher to the First Church of Boston was blocked by Winthrop and Wilson. Exiled by the Puritans of Massachusetts Bay in 1637 for a fast-day sermon upholding the covenant of grace, he went to New Hampshire where he founded Exeter and Hampton. His banishment was later lifted, when he recanted his beliefs.

7   In the Caribbean.

8   This is evidence of an early trade in slaves.

March 22, 1638] Mrs Hutchinson appeared again; (she had been licensed by the court, in regard she had given hope of her repentance, to be at Mr Cotton's house, that both he and Mr Davenport[9] might have the more opportunity to deal with her;) and the articles being again read to her, and her answer required, she delivered it in writing, wherein she made a retraction of near all, but with such explanations and circumstances as gave no satisfaction to the church; so as she was required to speak further to them. Then she declared, that it was just with God to leave her to herself, as he had done, for her slighting his ordinances, both magistracy and ministry; and confessed that what she had spoken against the magistrates at the court (by way of revelation) was rash and ungrounded; and desired the church to pray for her. This gave the church good hope of her repentance; but when she was examined about some particulars, as that she had denied inherent righteousness, etc., she affirmed that it was never her judgment; and though it was proved by many testimonies, that she had been of that judgment, and so had persisted, and maintained it by argument against divers, yet she impudently persisted in her affirmation, to the astonishment of all the assembly. So that, after much time and many arguments had been spent to bring her to see her sin, but all in vain, the church, with one consent, cast her out. . . .

September 1638] . . . Mrs Hutchinson, being removed to the Isle of Aquiday[10] in the Narragansetts Bay, after her time was fulfilled that she expected deliverance of a child, was delivered of a monstrous birth, which, being diversely related in the country, (and, in the open assembly at Boston, upon a lecture day, [was] declared by Mr Cotton to be twenty-seven several lumps of man's seed, without any alteration or mixture of anything from the woman, and thereupon gathered that it might signify her error in denying inherent righteousness, but that all was Christ in us, and nothing of ours in our faith, love, etc.). Hereupon the governor wrote to Mr Clarke, a physician and preacher to those of the island, to know the certainty thereof, who returned him this answer: Mrs Hutchinson, six weeks before her delivery, perceived her body to be greately distempered and her spirits failing and in that regard doubtful of life, she sent to me etc., and not long after (in *immoderato fluore uterino*[11]) it was brought to light and I was called to see it, where I beheld innumerable distinct bodies in the form of a globe, not much unlike the swims of some fish, so confusedly knit together by so many several strings (which I conceive were the beginning of veins and nerves) so that it was impossible either to number the small round pieces in every lump, much less to discern from whence every string did fetch its original, they were so snarled one within another. The small globes I likewise opened, and perceived the matter of them (setting aside the membrane in which it was involved) to be partly wind and partly water. The governor, not satisfied with this relation, spake after with the said Mr Clarke, who thus cleared all the doubts . . .[12]

December 6, 1638] Dorothy Talbye was hanged at Boston for murdering her own daughter, a child of three years old. She had been a member of the church of Salem, and of good esteem for godliness, etc.; but, falling at difference with her husband, through melancholy or spiritual delusions, she sometimes attempted to kill him, and her children, and herself, by refusing meat, saying it was so revealed to her, etc. After much patience, and divers admoni-

---

9   John Davenport (1597–1670), along with John Cotton and Thomas Hooker was one of the most powerful Puritan ministers in New England. He led his followers to New Haven and established a church there. Called to the First Church of Boston in 1668, his acceptance split the congregation.

10   Aquidneck Island, Rhode Island.

11   A heavy discharge from the womb (Latin).

12   The medical name for this condition is a "hydatidiform mole," an abnormal growth of the outermost vascular membrane that in a normal pregnancy would enclose the embryo which is either absent or dead. The mole, a collection of sacs containing a jelly-like substance resembling clusters of grapes, can attain a great size and is usually expelled in about the twentieth week of pregnancy.

tions not prevailing, the church cast her out. Whereupon she grew worse; so as the magistrate caused her to be whipped. Whereupon she was reformed for a time, and carried herself more dutifully to her husband, etc.; but soon after she was so possessed with Satan, that he persuaded her (by his delusions, which she listened to as revelations from God) to break the neck of her own child, that she might free it from future misery. This she confessed upon her apprehension; yet, at her arraignment, she stood mute a good space, till the governor told her she should be pressed to death, and then she confessed the indictment. When she was to receive judgment she would not uncover her face, nor stand up, but as she was forced, nor give any testimony of her repentance, either then or at her execution. The cloth, which should have covered her face, she plucked off and put between the rope and her neck. She desired to have been beheaded, giving this reason, that it was less painful and less shameful. After a swing or two, she catched at the ladder. Mr Peter, her late pastor, and Mr Wilson, went with her to the place of execution, but could do no good with her. Mr Peter gave an exhortation to the people to take heed of revelations, etc., and of despising the ordinance of excommunication as she had done; for when it was to have been denounced against her, she turned her back, and would have gone forth, if she had not been stayed by force.

December 15, 1640] About this time there fell out a thing worthy of observation. Mr Winthrop the younger, one of the magistrates, having many books in a chamber where there was corn of divers sorts, had among them one wherein the Greek testament, the psalms and the common prayer[13], were bound together. He found the common prayer eaten with mice, every leaf of it, and not any of the two other touched, nor any other of his books, though there were above a thousand.

July 5, 1643] There arose a sudden gust at N.W. so violent for half an hour, as it blew down multitudes of trees. It lifted up their meetinghouse at Newbury, the people being in it. It darkened the air with dust, yet through God's great mercy it did no hurt, but only killed one Indian with the fall of a tree.

April 13, 1645] Mr Hopkins, the governor of Hartford upon Connecticut, came to Boston, and brought his wife with him, (a godly young woman, and of special parts,) who was fallen into a sad infirmity, the loss of her understanding and reason, which had been growing upon her divers years, by occasion of her giving herself wholly to reading and writing, and had written many books. Her husband, being very loving and tender of her, was loath to grieve her; but he saw his error, when it was too late. For if she had attended her household affairs, and such things as belong to women, and not gone out of her way and calling to meddle in such things as are proper for men, whose minds are stronger, etc., she had kept her wits, and might have improved them usefully and honorably in the place God had set her. He brought her to Boston, and left her with her brother, one Mr Yale, a merchant, to try what means might be had here for her. But no help could be had.[14]

July 3, 1645] According to this agreement[15], presently after the lecture the magistrates and deputies took their places in the meeting house, and the people being come together, and the

---

[13]   The Book of Common Prayer, the prayer book of the Church of England. Many Puritans, especially Separatists, disdained the use of set prayers.

[14]   Mrs Hopkins was the aunt of Elihu Yale, the founder of Yale University. None of her writings survived.

[15]   An agreement to finally resolve an ordinary case of differences among residents of the town of Hingham that escalated and kept the Court in session from May 13 to July 3 with only one week's break. This case revealed the rift within

the commonwealth regarding the authority of the magistrates which was thought to abrogate some civil and church liberties. Thomas Dudley was governor, and Winthrop was deputy Governor at the time. He was accused of misusing his power by unfairly reporting "words spoken against the General Court" by several Hingham residents, who hoped to impeach him. He was acquitted. The speech he delivered to the General Court is a succinct expression of Puritan political theory.

deputy governor placing himself within the bar, as at the time of the hearing, etc., the governor read the sentence of the court, without speaking any more, for the deputies had (by importunity) obtained a promise of silence from the magistrates. Then was the deputy governor desired by the court to go up and take his place again upon the bench, which he did accordingly, and the court being about to arise, he desired leave for a little speech, which was to this effect.

I suppose something may be expected from me, upon this charge. It is befallen me, which moves me to speak now to you; yet I intend not to intermeddle in the proceedings of the court, or with any of the persons concerned therein. Only I bless God, that I see an issue of this troublesome business. I also acknowledge the justice of the court, and, for mine own part, I am well satisfied, I was publicly charged, and I am publicly and legally acquitted, which is all I did expect or desire. And though this be sufficient for my justification before men, yet not so before God, who hath seen so much amiss in my dispensations (and even in this affair) as calls me to be humble. For to be publicly and criminally charged in this court, is matter of humiliation, (and I desire to make a right use of it,) notwithstanding I be thus acquitted. If her father had spit in her face, (saith the Lord concerning Miriam,) should she not have been ashamed seven days?[16] Shame had lien upon her, whatever the occasion had been. I am unwilling to stay you from your urgent affairs, yet give me leave (upon this special occasion) to speak a little more to this assembly. It may be of some good use, to inform and rectify the judgments of some of the people, and may prevent such distempers as have arisen amongst us. The great questions that have troubled the country are about the authority of the magistrates and the liberty of the people. It is yourselves who have called us to this office, and being called by you, we have our authority from God, in way of an ordinance, such as hath the image of God eminently stamped upon it, the contempt and violation whereof hath been vindicated with examples of divine vengeance. I entreat you to consider, that when you choose magistrates, you take them from among yourselves, men subject to like passions as you are. Therefore when you see infirmities in us, you should reflect upon your own, and that would make you bear the more with us, and not be severe censurers of the failings of your magistrates, when you have continual experience of the like infirmities in yourselves and others. We account him a good servant, who breaks not his covenant. The covenant between you and us is the oath you have taken of us, which is to this purpose, that we shall govern you and judge your causes by the rules of God's laws and our own, according to our best skill. When you agree with a workman to build you a ship or house, etc., he undertakes as well for his skill as for his faithfulness, for it is his profession, and you pay him for both. But when you call one to be a magistrate, he doth not profess nor undertake to have sufficient skill for that office, nor can you furnish him with gifts, etc., therefore you must run the hazard of his skill and, ability. But if he fail in faithfulness, which by his oath he is bound unto, that he must answer for. If it fall out that the case be clear to common apprehension, and the rule clear also, if he transgress here, the error is not in the skill, but in the evil of the will: it must be required of him. But if the case be doubtful, or the rule doubtful, to men of such understanding and parts as your magistrates are, if your magistrates should err here, yourselves must bear it.

For the other point concerning liberty, I observe a great mistake in the country about that. There is a twofold liberty, natural (I mean as our nature is now corrupt) and civil or federal. The first is common to man with beasts and other creatures. By this, man, as he stands in relation to man simply, hath liberty to do what he lists; it is a liberty to evil as well as to good. This liberty is incompatible and inconsistent with authority, and cannot endure the least

---

[16]   Numbers 12:14; Miriam is Moses and Aaron's sister.

restraint of the most just authority. The exercise and maintaining of this liberty makes men grow more evil, and in time to be worse than brute beasts: *omnes sumus licentia deteriores*[17]. This is that great enemy of truth and peace, that wild beast, which all the ordinances of God are bent against, to restrain and subdue it. The other kind of liberty I call civil or federal, it may also be termed oral, in reference to the covenant between God and man, in the moral law, and the politic covenants and constitutions, amongst men themselves. This liberty is the proper end and object of authority, and cannot subsist without it; and it is a liberty to that only which is good, just, and honest. This liberty you are to stand for, with the hazard (not only of your goods, but) of your lives, if need be. Whatsoever crosseth this, is not authority, but a distemper thereof. This liberty is maintained and exercised in a way of subjection to authority; it is of the same kind of liberty wherewith Christ hath made us free.[18] The woman's own choice makes such a man her husband; yet being so chosen, he is her lord, and she is to be subject to him, yet in a way of liberty, not of bondage; and a true wife accounts her subjection her honor and freedom, and would not think her condition safe and free, but in her subjection to her husband's authority. Such is the liberty of the church under the authority of Christ, her king and husband; his yoke is so easy and sweet to her as a bride's ornaments;[19] and if through forwardness or wantonness, etc., she shake it off, at any time, she is at no rest in her spirit, until she take it up again; and whether her lord smiles upon her, and embraceth her in his arms, or whether he frowns, or rebukes, or smites her, she apprehends the sweetness of his love in all, and is refreshed, supported, and instructed by every such dispensation of his authority over her. On the other side, ye know who they are that complain of this yoke and say, let us break their bands, etc., we will not have this man to rule over us. Even so, brethren, it will be between you and your magistrates. If you stand for your natural corrupt liberties, and will do what is good in your own eyes, you will not endure the least weight of authority, but will murmur, and oppose, and be always striving to shake off that yoke; but if you will be satisfied to enjoy such civil and lawful liberties, such as Christ allows you, then will you quietly and cheerfully submit unto that authority which is set over you, in all the administrations of it, for your good. Wherein, if we fail at any time, we hope we shall be willing (by God's assistance) to hearken to good advice from any of you, or in any other way of God; so shall your liberties be preserved, in upholding the honor and power of authority amongst you.

The deputy governor having ended his speech the court arose, and the magistrates and deputies retired to attend their other affairs. . . .

March 1647] Mention was made before of some beginning to instruct Indians, etc. Mr John Eliot, teacher of the church of Roxbury, found such encouragement, as he took great pains to get their language, and in a few months could speak of the things of God to their understanding; and God prospered his endeavors, so as he kept a constant lecture to them in two places, one week at the wigwam of one Wabon, a new sachem near Watertown mill, and the other the next week in the wigwam of Cutshamekin near Dorchester mill. And for the furtherance of the work of God, divers of the English resorted to his lecture, and the governor and other of the magistrates and elders sometimes; and the Indians began to repair thither from other parts. His manner of proceeding was thus; he would persuade one of the other elders or some magistrate to begin the exercise with prayer in English; then he took a text, and read it first in the Indian language, and after in English; then he preached to them in Indian about an hour; (but

---

[17]   "We are all the worse for license," from the Roman author Terence (190?–159 BC), *Heauton Timorumenos* (*The Self-Tormentor*), 3:1, 74.

[18]   Galatians 5:1: "Stand fast therefore in the liberty where-

with Christ hath made us free, and be not entangled again with the yoke of bondage."

[19]   Matthew 11:30: "For my yoke is easy, and my burden is light."

first I should have spoke of the catechising their children, who were soon brought to answer him some short questions, whereupon he gave each of them an apple or a cake) then he demanded of some of the chiefs, if they understood him; if they answered, yea, then he asked of them if they had any questions to propound. And they had usually two or three or more questions, which he did resolve. . . . A second question was, what was the reason, that when all Englishmen did know God, yet some of them were poor. His answer was 1. that God knows it is better for his children to be good than to be rich; he knows withal, that if some of them had riches, they would abuse them, and wax proud and wanton, etc., therefore he gives them no more riches than may be needful for them, that they may be kept from pride, etc., to depend upon him, 2. he would hereby have men know, that he hath better blessings to bestow upon good men than riches, etc., and that their best portion is in heaven, etc. One [blank] of Windsor arraigned and executed at Hartford for a witch.[20]

1630–49   1826

William Bradford (1590–1657)

William Bradford's history of the "Pilgrims" is the first sustained literary work of the New England experience. It not only gave a distinctive shape to that experience which has, somewhat erroneously, become synonymous with the "American" experience, but it defined a distinctly "American" historiography whose purpose was to show the workings of divine Providence in the lives of the chosen few. Bradford's own life epitomized the Pilgrims' struggles and determination. He was born in Yorkshire into a modestly well-off farming family, but was orphaned at an early age and was raised by uncles who intended him to be a farmer. A frail and lonely youth, he was swept up at age twelve by the inspirational preaching of Richard Clyfton, minister of a neighboring parish preaching non-conformity – that is, resistance to the established Church of England with its hierarchical structure of bishops and "popish" rituals. Called "Separatists," these believers, unlike the majority of Puritans (so called for their desire to "purify" the church), saw no possibility of reforming the English Church from within. Instead, they formed small, self-governing

congregations (from which the label "Congregationalism" derived) around inspired preachers based upon the ancient model described in the Bible. Each member entered into a formal covenant that bound him or her individually to God.

Despite family protest, in 1606 Bradford left home to join the congregation organized by Clyfton in the nearby village of Scrooby. Harassed and persecuted for their beliefs, the group fled to Holland in 1608, spending the next twelve difficult years in Leyden where Bradford joined them in 1609, making his living as a weaver. Fearing war and further religious persecution when the truce between Holland and Catholic Spain expired, the Scrooby congregation decided to move to the New World. They secured a grant to settle in the Virginia territory, and with financial backing from private groups in London, a band of thirty, along with assorted other passengers, embarked from Southampton on the *Mayflower* in 1620. Hampered by storms, they were forced to land further north on Cape Cod, and in freezing December weather, finally landed on the site they called "New Plymouth." Brad-

---

[20]   The first mention of witchcraft in New England.

ford was a leader in this migration, and was elected governor of Plymouth colony when John Carver, the first governor, died in 1621. He was re-elected to that position thirty times, giving him extensive power over the colony's affairs, and served almost continuously until his death in 1657.

Bradford was self-educated, but had extensive knowledge of theological literature and the Geneva Bible, the version favored by the Puritans because of its annotations based on the commentaries of the famous Reformation theologian, John Calvin. At the outset, he announced his employment of a "plain style;" however, his profuse quotation of the Bible allows him to stitch the history of his small band of saints almost seamlessly into Biblical history as its latest manifestation. Some historians believe he began writing *Of Plymouth Plantation* in 1630 in response to the establishment in that year of the larger colony at Massachusetts Bay, to preserve Plymouth's distinctive history and identity. He put the manuscript aside for several years, then picked it up again in 1644 and finished it in 1650, with an account of the colony up to the year 1646. Part of Bradford's intention was not only to record, but to justify the Pilgrims' flight to the New World, especially after the deposing of Charles I in 1642 and the establishment of the Puritan Commonwealth of Oliver Cromwell which accomplished the Protestant reformation in England. However, the major theme that emerges from this work is Plymouth Plantation's failure to fulfill its initial promise as a self-sacrificing community of God's chosen people, and so Bradford exhorts the second generation to heed the example of their elders and take up their mission, despite the fragmenting effects of success and prosperity. Although early historians knew Bradford's history, and the first book through Chapter IX had been copied into the Plymouth church records, the manuscript which also contained Book Two disappeared from Boston, probably looted by the British during the American Revolution. Discovered in the house of the Bishop of London and published for the first time in 1856, the manuscript was returned to the State House in Boston in 1897.

PRIMARY WORKS

Mourt's Relation, with Edward Winslow, 1622.
Of Plymoth Plantation, in *Of Plymouth Plantation*, ed. S. E. Morison (New York: Knopf, 1952).

FURTHER READING

Perry Westbrook, *William Bradford* (Boston: Twayne, 1978).
Walter P. Wenska, "Bradford's Two Histories," *Early American Literature*, 13 (1978) pp. 151–64.
David Read, "Silent Partners: Historical Representation in William Bradford's *Of Plymouth Plantation*," *Early American Literature*, 33, 3 (1998) pp. 291–314.

OF PLYMOUTH PLANTATION[1]

From *Book I, Chapter IX: Of their Voyage, and how they Passed the Sea; and of their Safe Arrival at Cape Cod*

September 6. These troubles being blown over, and now all being compact together in one ship,[2] they put to sea again with a prosperous wind, which continued divers days together, which was some encouragement unto them; yet, according to the usual manner, many were

---

[1] The selections, with slight modifications, are from *Of Plymouth Plantation*, ed. S. E. Morison (New York: Knopf, 1952).
[2] The Leyden group had difficulty getting financial back-ing, and although King James promised not to interfere with them if they acted peacefully, he did not grant them toleration. One of their ships, the *Speedwell*, developed a leak and was forced to turn back; its passengers joined the *Mayflower*.

afflicted with seasickness. And I may not omit here a special work of God's providence. There was a proud and very profane young man, one of the seamen, of a lusty, able body, which made him the more haughty; he would always be contemning the poor people in their sickness and cursing them daily with grievous execrations; and did not let to tell them that he hoped to help to cast half of them overboard before they came to their journey's end, and to make merry with what they had; and if he were by any gently reproved, he would curse and swear most bitterly. But it pleased God before they came half seas over, to smite this young man with a grievous disease, of which he died in a desperate manner, and so was himself the first that was thrown overboard. Thus his curses light on his own head, and it was an astonishment to all his fellows for they noted it to be the just hand of God upon him. . . .

In sundry of these storms [that beset the ship] the winds were so fierce and the seas so high, as they could not bear a knot of sail, but were forced to hull[3] for divers days together. And in one of them, as they thus lay at hull in a mighty storm, a lusty young man called John Howland, coming upon some occasion above the gratings was, with a seele[4] of the ship, thrown into sea; but it pleased God that he caught hold of the topsail halyards which hung overboard and ran out at length. Yet he held his hold (though he was sundry fathoms under water) till he was hauled up by the same rope to the brim of the water, and then with a boat hook and other means got into the ship again and his life saved. And though he was something ill with it, yet he lived many years after and became a profitable member both in church and commonwealth. In all this voyage there died but one of the passengers, which was William Butten, a youth, servant to Samuel Fuller, when they drew near the coast.

But to omit other things (that I may be brief) after long beating at sea they fell with that land which is called Cape Cod; the which being made and certainly known to be it, they were not a little joyful. After some deliberation had amongst themselves and with the master of the ship, they tacked about and resolved to stand for the southward (the wind and weather being fair) to find some place about Hudson's River for their habitation.[5] But after they had sailed that course about half the day, they fell amongst dangerous shoals and roaring breakers, and they were so far entangled therewith as they conceived themselves in great danger; and the wind shrinking upon them withal, they resolved to bear up again for the Cape and thought themselves happy to get out of those dangers before night overtook them, as by God's good providence they did. And the next day they got into the Cape Harbor where they hid in safety.[6] . . .

But here I cannot but stay and make a pause, and stand half amazed at this poor people's present condition; and so I think will the reader, too, when he well considers the same. Being thus passed the vast ocean, and a sea of troubles before in their preparation (as may be remembered by that which went before), they had now no friends to welcome them nor inns to entertain or refresh their weatherbeaten bodies; no houses or much less towns to repair to, to seek for succour. It is recorded in Scripture 4 as a mercy to the Apostle and his shipwrecked company, that the barbarians showed them no small kindness in refreshing them,[7] but these savage barbarians, when they met with them (as after will appear) were readier to fill their sides full of arrows than otherwise. And for the season it was winter, and they that know the winter of that country know them to be sharp and violent and subject to cruel and fierce

---

3   To trim the sails and drift with the wind.
4   Roll or pitch.
5   This was the original destination of the Pilgrims, who carried with them the Peirce Patent from the Virginia Company, which granted them the right to colonize up to the latitude of Manhattan Island. Although the Dutch claimed

the region since Henry Hudson's voyage there in 1609, the English did not recognize their claim.
6   Modern day Provincetown Harbor; the date was November 11 (or 21st in the New Style of dating), 1620. Both dates will be given hereafter.
7   Acts 28:2.

storms, dangerous to travel to known places, much more to search an unknown coast. Besides, what could they see but a hideous and desolate wilderness, full of wild beasts and wild men – and what multitudes there might be of them they knew not. Neither could they, as it were, go up to the top of Pisgah to view from this wilderness a more goodly country to feed their hopes;[8] for which way soever they turned their eyes (save upward to the heavens) they could have little solace or content in respect of any outward objects. For summer being done, all things stand upon them with a weatherbeaten face, and the whole country, full of woods and thickets, represented a wild and savage hue. If they looked behind them, there was the mighty ocean which they had passed and was now as a main bar and gulf to separate them from all the civil parts of the world. If it be said they had a ship to succour them, it is true; but what heard they daily from the master and company? But that with speed they should look out a place (with their shallop) where they would be, at some near distance; for the season was such as he would not stir from thence till a safe harbor was discovered by them, where they would be, and he might go without danger; and that victuals consumed apace but he must and would keep sufficient for themselves and their return. Yea, it was muttered by some that if they got not a place in time, they would turn them and their goods ashore and leave them. Let it also be considered what weak hopes of supply and succour they left behind them, that might bear up their minds in this sad condition and trials they were under; and they could not but be very small. It is true, indeed, the affections and love of their brethren at Leyden was cordial and entire towards them, but they had little power to help them or themselves; and how the case stood between them and the merchants at their coming away hath already been declared.

What could now sustain them but the Spirit of God and His grace? May not and ought not the children of these fathers rightly say: "Our fathers were Englishmen which came over this great ocean, and were ready to perish in this wilderness; but they cried unto the Lord, and He heard their voice and looked on their adversity," etc.[9] "Let them therefore praise the Lord, because He is good: and His mercies endure forever." "Yea, let them which have been redeemed of the Lord, shew how He hath delivered them from the hand of the oppressor. When they wandered in the desert wilderness out of the way, and found no city to dwell in, both hungry and thirsty, their soul was overwhelmed in them. Let them confess before the Lord His loving kindness and His wonderful works before the sons of men.[10]

From *Book I, Chapter X: Showing How they Sought out a place of Habitation; and What Befell them Thereabout*

. . . They[11] set forth the 15th of November; and . . . they directed their course to come to the other shore, for they knew it was a neck of land they were to cross over, and so at length got to the seaside and marched to this supposed river, and by the way found a pond of clear, fresh water, and shortly after a good quantity of clear ground where the Indians had formerly set corn, and some of their graves. And proceeding further they saw new stubble where corn had been set the same year; also they found where lately a house had been, where some planks and a great kettle was remaining, and heaps of sand newly paddled with their hands. Which, they

---

8   As did Moses, who ascended Mt Pisgah to view the Promised Land to which he led the Hebrews after forty years of wandering in the desert, but which he could not enter. See Numbers 23:14; Deuteronomy 3:27.

9   Bradford's paraphrase of Deuteronomy 26:5, 7, the He-

brews' prayer to the Lord to be brought out of bondage in Egypt.

10   Psalm 107: 1–5, 8.

11   A small, exploratory party led by Miles Standish.

digging up, found in them divers fair Indian baskets filled with corn, and some in ears, fair and good, of divers colours, which seemed to them a very goodly sight (having never seen any such before). This was near the place of that supposed river they came to seek unto which they went and found it to open itself into two arms with a high cliff of sand in the entrance but more like to be creeks of salt water than any fresh, for aught they saw; and that there was good harborage for their shallop, leaving it further to be discovered by their shallop, when she was ready.[12] So, their time limited them being expired, they returned to the ship lest they should be in fear of their safety; and took with them part of the corn and buried up the rest. And so, like the men from Eshcol, carried with them of the fruits of the land and showed their brethren;[13] of which, and their return, they were marvelously glad and their hearts encouraged.

After this, the shallop being got ready, they set out again for the better discovery of this place, and the master of the ship desired to go himself. So there went some thirty men but found it to be no harbor for ships but only for boats.[14] There was also found two of their houses covered with mats, and sundry of their implements in them, but the people were run away and could not be seen.[15] Also there was found more of their corn and of their beans of various colours; the corn and beans they brought away, purposing to give them full satisfaction when they should meet with any of them as, about some six months afterward they did, to their good content.

And here is to be noted a special providence of God, and a great mercy to this poor people, that here they got seed to plant them corn the next year, or else they might have starved, for they had none nor any likelihood to get any till the season had been past, as the sequel did manifest. Neither is it likely they had had this, if the first voyage had not been made, for the ground was now all covered with snow and hard frozen; but the Lord is never wanting unto His in their greatest needs; let His holy name have all the praise.

From *Book II, Chapter XI: The Remainder of Anno 1620*

{The Mayflower Compact}

I shall a little return back, and begin with a combination made by them before they came ashore; being the first foundation of their government in this place. Occasioned partly by the discontented and mutinous speeches that some of the strangers amongst them[16] had let fall from them in the ship: That when they came ashore they would use their own liberty, for none had power to command them, the patent they had being for Virginia and not for New England, which belonged to another government, with which the Virginia Company had nothing to do. And partly that such an act by them done, this their condition considered, might be as firm as any patent, and in some respects more sure.

The form was as followeth:
IN THE NAME OF GOD, AMEN.

---

[12]   The river is the Pamet River, a salt creek. The place where the Pilgrims found the corn is known as Corn Hill, along the Bay side of the Cape, north of Little Pamet River.
[13]   Moses, searching for the Promised Land, sent out scouts who brought back giant clusters of grapes from near a brook they called "Eschol." See Numbers 13:23–26.

[14]   Cold Harbor on the mouth of the Pamet river.
[15]   The Nauset tribe.
[16]   A reference to those outside the Puritan church; only about a third of the one hundred passengers on the *Mayflower* were Puritans.

We whose names are underwritten, the loyal subjects of our dread Sovereign Lord King James, by the Grace of God of Great Britain, France, and Ireland King, Defender of the Faith, etc.

Having undertaken, for the Glory of God and advancement of the Christian Faith and Honour of our King and Country, a Voyage to plant the First Colony in the Northern Parts of Virginia, do by these presents solemnly and mutually in the presence of God and one of another, Covenant and Combine ourselves together into a Civil Body Politic, for our better ordering and preservation and furtherance of the ends aforesaid; and by virtue hereof to enact, constitute and frame such just and equal Laws, Ordinances, Acts, Constitutions and Offices, from time to time, as shall be thought most meet and convenient for the general good of the Colony, unto which we promise all due submission and obedience. In witness whereof we have hereunder subscribed our names at Cape Cod, the 11th [21st] of November, in the year of the reign of our Sovereign Lord King James, of England, France and Ireland the eighteenth, and of Scotland the fifty-fourth. Anno Domini 1620.

After this they chose, or rather confirmed, Mr John Carver (a man godly and well approved amongst them) their Governor for that year.[17] And after they had provided a place for their goods, or common store (which were long in unlading for want of boats, foulness of the winter weather and sickness of divers) and begun some small cottages for their habitation; as time would admit, they met and consulted of laws and orders, both for their civil and military government as the necessity of their condition did require, still adding thereunto as urgent occasion in several times, and as cases did require.

In these hard and difficult beginnings they found some discontents and murmurings arise amongst some, and mutinous speeches and carriages in other; but they were soon quelled and overcome by the wisdom, patience, and just and equal carriage of things, by the Governor and better part, which clave[18] faithfully together in the main.

{The Starving Time}

But that which was most sad and lamentable was, that in two or three months' time half of their company died, especially in January and February, being the depth of winter, and wanting houses and other comforts; being infected with the scurvy and other diseases which this long voyage and their inaccommodate condition had brought upon them. So as there died some times two or three of a day in the foresaid time, that of 100 and odd persons, scarce fifty remained. And of these, in the time of most distress, there was but six or seven sound persons who to their great commendations, be it spoken, spared no pains night nor day, but with abundance of toil and hazard of their own health, fetched them wood, made them fires, dressed them meat, made their beds, washed their loathsome clothes, clothed and unclothed them. In a word, did all the homely and necessary offices for them which dainty and queasy stomachs cannot endure to hear named; and all this willingly and cheerfully, without any grudging in the least, showing herein their true love unto their friends and brethren; a rare example and worthy to be remembered. Two of these seven were Mr William Brewster, their reverend Elder, and Myles Standish, their Captain and military commander, unto whom myself and many others were much beholden in our low and sick condition. And yet the Lord so upheld these persons as in this general calamity they were not at all infected either with sickness or

---

17   John Carver (1576?–1621), was, like Bradford, a member of the Scrooby congregation in Leyden; Bradford was elected governor after his death.

18   Held; past tense of "cleave."

lameness. And what I have said of these I may say of many others who died in this general visitation, and others yet living; that whilst they had health, yea, or any strength continuing, they were not wanting to any that had need of them. And I doubt not but their recompense is with the Lord.

But I may not here pass by another remarkable passage not to be forgotten. As this calamity fell among the passengers that were to be left here to plant, and were hasted ashore and made to drink water that the seamen might have the more beer, and one[19] in his sickness desiring but a small can of beer, it was answered that if he were their own father he should have none. The disease began to fall amongst them also, so as almost half of their company died before they went away, and many of their officers and lustiest men, as the boatswain, gunner, three quartermasters, the cook and others. At which the Master was something strucken and sent to the sick ashore and told the Governor he should send for beer for them that had need of it, though he drunk water homeward bound.

But now amongst his company there was far another kind of carriage in this misery than amongst the passengers. For they that before had been boon companions in drinking and jollity in the time of their health and welfare, began now to desert one another in this calamity, saying they would not hazard their lives for them, they should be infected by coming to help them in their cabins; and so, after they came to lie by it, would do little or nothing for them but, "if they died, let them die." But such of the passengers as were yet aboard showed them what mercy they could, which made some of their hearts relent, as the boatswain (and some others) who was a proud young man and would often curse and scoff at the passengers. But when he grew weak, they had compassion on him and helped him; then he confessed he did not deserve it at their hands, he had abused them in word and deed. "Oh!" (saith he) "you, I now see, show your love like Christians indeed one to another, but we let one another lie and die like dogs." Another lay cursing his wife, saying if it had not been for her he had never come this unlucky voyage, and anon cursing his fellows, saying he had done this and that for some of them; he had spent so much and so much amongst them, and they were now weary of him and did not help him, having need. Another gave his companion all he had, if he died, to help him in his weakness; he went and got a little spice and made him a mess of meat once or twice. And because he died not so soon as he expected, he went amongst his fellows and swore the rogue would cozen[20] him, he would see him choked before he made him any more meat; and yet the poor fellow died before morning.

{Indian Relations}

All this while the Indians came skulking about them, and would sometimes show themselves aloof off, but when any approached near them, they would run away; and once they stole away their tools where they had been at work and were gone to dinner. But about the 16th of March a certain Indian came boldly amongst them and spoke to them in broken English, which they could well understand but marveled at it. At length they understood by discourse with him, that he was not of these parts, but belonged to the eastern parts where some English ships came to fish, with whom he was acquainted and could name sundry of them by their names, amongst whom he had got his language. He became profitable to them in acquainting them with many things concerning the state of the country in the east parts where he lived, which was afterwards profitable unto them; as also of the people here, of their names, number and strength, of their situation and distance from this place, and who was chief amongst them. His

---

[19]   "Which was the author himself" [Bradford's note].   ·   [20]   Cheat; take advantage of.

name was Samoset. He told them also of another Indian whose name was Squanto, a native of this place, who had been in England and could speak better English than himself.[21]

Being, after some time of entertainment and gifts dismissed, a while after he came again, and five more with him, and they brought again all the tools that were stolen away before, and made way for the coming of their great Sachem, called Massasoit. Who, about four or five days after, came with the chief of his friends and other attendance, with the aforesaid Squanto. With whom, after friendly entertainment and some gifts given him, they made a peace with him (which hath now continued this 24 years)[22] in these terms:

1. That neither he nor any of his should injure or do hurt to any of their people.
2. That if any of his did hurt to any of theirs, he should send the offender, that they might punish him.
3. That if anything were taken away from any of theirs, he should cause it to be restored; and they should do the like to his.
4. If any did unjustly war against him, they would aid him; if any did war against them, he should aid them.
5. He should send to his neighbours confederates to certify them of this, that they might not wrong them, but might be likewise comprised in the conditions of peace.
6. That when their men came to them, they should leave their bows and arrows behind them.

After these things he returned to his place called Sowams, some 40 miles from this place, but Squanto continued with them and was their interpreter and was a special instrument sent of God for their good beyond their expectation. He directed them how to set their corn, where to take fish, and to procure other commodities, and was also their pilot to bring them to unknown places for their profit, and never left them till he died. He was a native of this place, and scarce any left alive besides himself.

From *Book II, Chapter XIV: Anno Domini 1623*

{End of the "Common Course and Condition"}

All this while no supply was heard of, neither knew they when they might expect any. So they began to think how they might raise as much corn as they could, and obtain a better crop than they had done, that they might not still thus languish in misery. At length, after much debate of things, the Governor (with the advice of the chiefest amongst them) gave way that they should set corn every man for his own particular, and in that regard trust to themselves; in all other things to go on in the general way as before. And so assigned to every family a parcel of land, according to the proportion of their number, for that end, only for present use (but made no division for inheritance) and ranged all boys and youth under some family. This had very good success, for it made all hands very industrious, so as much more corn was planted than otherwise would have been by any means the Governor or any other could use, and saved him a great deal of trouble, and gave far better content. The women now went willingly into the field, and took their little ones with them to set corn; which before would allege weakness and

---

[21] Samoset was a Pemaquid from Maine; Squanto was a Nauset or Patuxet from Plymouth.

[22] Massasoit was chief of the Wampanoag (also called Pokanoket), located at Sowams in what is now Barrington, Rhode Island. This treaty lasted until 1676, when conflict arose with Massasoit's son, Metacom, renamed King Philip by the settlers.

inability; whom to have compelled would have been thought great tyranny and oppression.

The experience that was had in this common course and condition, tried sundry years and that amongst godly and sober men, may well evince the vanity of that conceit of Plato's and other ancients applauded by some of later times;[23] that the taking away of property and bringing in community into a commonwealth would make them happy and flourishing; as if they were wiser than God. For this community (so far as it was) was found to breed much confusion and discontent and retard much employment that would have been to their benefit and comfort. For the young men, that were most able and fit for labour and service, did repine that they should spend their time and strength to work for other men's wives and children without any recompense. The strong, or man of parts, had no more in division of victuals and clothes than he that was weak and not able to do a quarter the other could; this was thought injustice. The aged and graver men to be ranked and equalized in labours and victuals, clothes, etc., with the meaner and younger sort, thought it some indignity and disrespect unto them. And for men's wives to be commanded to do service for other men, as dressing their meat, washing their clothes, etc., they deemed it a kind of slavery, neither could many husbands well brook it. Upon the point all being to have alike, and all to do alike, they thought themselves in the like condition, and one as good as another; and so, if it did not cut off those relations that God hath set amongst men, yet it did at least much diminish and take off the mutual respects that should be preserved amongst them. And would have been worse if they had been men of another condition. Let none object this is men's corruption, and nothing to the course itself. I answer, seeing all men have this corruption in them, God in His wisdom saw another course fitter for them. . . .

From *Book II, Chapter XXVIII: Anno Domini 1637*

{*The Pequot War*}[24]

In the fore part of this year, the Pequots fell openly upon the English at Connecticut, in the lower parts of the river, and slew sundry of them as they were at work in the fields, both men and women, to the great terrour of the rest, and went away in great pride and triumph, with many high threats.

In the meantime, the Pequots, especially in the winter before, sought to make peace with the Narragansetts, and used very pernicious arguments to move them thereunto: . . . But again, when they considered how much wrong they had received from the Pequots, and what an opportunity they now had by the help of the English to right themselves; revenge was so sweet unto them as it prevailed above all the rest, so as they resolved to join with the English against them, and did. . . .

I shall not take upon me exactly to describe their proceedings in these things, because I expect it will be fully done by themselves who best know the carriage and circumstances of things. I shall therefore but touch them in general. From Connecticut, who were most sensible of the hurt sustained and the present danger, they set out a party of men, and another party

---

[23] A reference to Plato's recommendation of a communal society in his work, *The Republic*.

[24] The origin of hostilities began in 1634 when several English traders were killed, supposedly by the Pequots, who fell out with both the Dutch, with whom they traded, and the Narragansetts, who were allied with the English settlers. Contemporary historians contend that the Narragansett committed the murders, but they were used as excuses to attack the powerful Pequot and expunge their influence in the Connecticut region.

met them from the Bay, at Narragansetts', who were to join with them. The Narragansetts were earnest to be gone before the English were well rested and refreshed, especially some of them which came last. It should seem their desire was to come upon the enemy suddenly and undiscovered. There was a bark of this place, newly put in there, which was come from Connecticut, who did encourage them to lay hold of the Indians' forwardness, and to show as great forwardness as they, for it would encourage them, and expedition might prove to their great advantage. So they went on, and so ordered their march as the Indians brought them to a fort of the enemy's (in which most of their chief men were) before day.[25] They approached the same with great silence and surrounded it both with English and Indians, that they might not break out; and so assaulted them with great courage, shooting amongst them, and entered the fort with all speed. And those that first entered found sharp resistance from the enemy who both shot at and grappled with them; others ran into their houses and brought out fire and set them on fire, which soon took in their mat; and standing close together, with the wind all was quickly on a flame, and thereby more were burnt to death than was otherwise slain; It burnt their bowstrings and made them unserviceable; those that escaped the fire were slain with the sword, some hewed to pieces, others run through with their rapiers, so as they were quickly dispatched and very few escaped. It was conceived they thus destroyed about 400 at this time. It was a fearful sight to see them thus frying in the fire and the streams of blood quenching the same, and horrible was the stink and scent thereof; but the victory seemed a sweet sacrifice, and they gave the praise thereof to God, who had wrought so wonderfully for them, thus to enclose their enemies in their hands and give them so speedy a victory over so proud and insulting an enemy.

The Narragansett Indians all this while stood round about, but aloof from all danger and left the whole execution to the English, except it were the stopping of any that broke away. Insulting over their enemies in this their ruin and misery, when they saw them dancing in the flames, calling them by a word in their own language, signifying "O brave Pequots!" which they used familiarly among themselves in their own praise in songs of triumph after their victories. . . .

From *Book II, Chapter XXXII: Anno Domini 1642*

{A Horrible Case of Bestiality}

And after the time of the writing of these things befell a very sad accident of the like foul nature in this government, this very year, which I shall now relate. There was a youth whose name was Thomas Granger. He was servant to an honest man of Duxbury, being about 16 or 17 years of age. (His father and mother lived at the same time at Scituate.) He was this year detected of buggery, and indicted for the same, with a mare, a cow, two goats, five sheep, two calves and a turkey. Horrible it is to mention, but the truth of the history requires it. He was first discovered by one that accidentally saw his lewd practice towards the mare. (I forbear particulars.) Being upon it examined and committed, in the end he not only confessed the fact with that beast at that time, but sundry times before and at several times with all the rest of the forenamed in his indictment. And this his free confession was not only in private to the magistrates (though at first he strived to deny it) but to sundry, both ministers and others; and afterwards, upon his indictment, to the whole Court and jury; and confirmed it at his execu-

---

[25]   Mystic Fort, near the mouth of the Mystic River.

tion. And whereas some of the sheep could not so well be known by his description of them, others with them were brought before him and he declared which were they and which were not. And accordingly he was cast by the jury and condemned, and after executed about the 8th of September, 1642. A very sad spectacle it was. For first the mare and then the cow and the rest of the lesser cattle were killed before his face, according to the law, Leviticus xx.15[26]; and then he himself was executed. The cattle were all cast into a great and large pit that was digged of purpose for them, and no use made of any part of them.

Upon the examination of this person and also of a former that had made some sodomitical attempts upon another, it being demanded of them how they came first to the knowledge and practice of such wickedness, the one confessed he had long used it in old England; and this youth last spoken of said he was taught it by another that had heard of such things from some in England when he was there, and they kept cattle together. By which it appears how one wicked person may infect many, and what care all ought to have what servants they bring into their families.

But it may be demanded how came it to pass that so many wicked persons and profane people should so quickly come over into this land and mix themselves amongst them? Seeing it was religious men that began the work and they came for religion's sake? I confess this may be marveled at, at least in time to come, when the reasons thereof should not be known; and the more because here was so many hardships and wants met withal. I shall therefore endeavour to give some answer hereunto.

1. And first, according to that in the gospel, it is ever to be remembered that where the Lord begins to sow good seed, there the envious man will endeavour to sow tares[27].

2. Men being to come over into a wilderness, in which much labour and service was to be done about building and planting, etc., such as wanted help in that respect, when they could not have such as they would, were glad to take such as they could; and so, many untoward servants, sundry of them proved, that were thus brought over, both men and womenkind who, when their times were expired, became families of themselves, which gave increase hereunto.

3. Another and a main reason hereof was that men, finding so any godly disposed persons willing to come into these parts, some began to make a trade of it, to transport passengers and their goods, and hired ships for that end. And then, to make up their freight and advance their profit, cared not who the persons were, so they had money to pay them. And by this means the country came pestered with many unworthy persons who, being come over, crept into one place or other.

4. Again, the Lord's blessing usually following His people as well in outward as spiritual things (though afflictions be mixed withal) do make many to adhere to the People of God, as many followed Christ for the loaves' sake (John vi.26) and a "mixed multitude" came into the wilderness with the People of God out of Egypt of old (Exodus xii.38). So also there were sent by their friends, some under hope that they would be made better; others that they might be eased of such burthens, and they kept from shame at home, that would necessarily follow their dissolute courses. And thus, by one means or other, in 20 years' time it is a question whether the greater part be not grown the worser?

1630, 1644, 1649–50   1856

---

[26] "And if a man lie with beast, he shall surely be put to death; and ye shall slay the beast."

[27] Tares are weeds that choke out the planted crops. In a parable, Jesus says, "But while men slept, his enemy came and sowed tares among the wheat, and went his way," (Matthew 13:25).

Roger Williams (1603?–1683)

Just as the Massachusetts Bay colony was struggling into existence, Roger Williams arrived and, most unexpectedly, interrogated its fundamental ideology, challenging the right of the church to demand religious conformity and the right of the state to enforce it. John Winthrop, a life-long friend, described him on his arrival in 1631 as "a godly minister," and supported the invitation of the First Boston Church that Williams, only twenty-eight years old, take over as minister in John Wilson's absence. Williams shocked the community by refusing, and informed them, adding insult to injury, that "he durst not officiate to an unseparated people." Accused of subversion, he went first to Salem, but objected to the unseparated church there. He moved to Plymouth where he began his studies of native language, but after a year returned to Salem, where he continued to preach "dangerous" opinions that unsettled both separatists and non-separatists alike. He argued that civil magistrates had no right to enforce religious doctrine or practice, like keeping the Sabbath, and that non-members of churches could not be forced to attend worship or to take religious oaths in a court of law. He infuriated the magistrates by asserting that the Bay's charter was invalid because King Charles had no right to grant possession of Indian lands, which he believed had to be purchased, and he continued to insist that the Bay churches separate from the Church of England and repent of their former connections, a move that would endanger their already vulnerable royal charter. Given several opportunities to "reform" his positions, Williams refused, and was banished from the commonwealth in October 1635.

Williams shared with the New England ministers the privileges of calling, class, and education, privileges which he ultimately rejected. Son of a merchant tailor, he grew up in Smithfield, a district of London brimming with Separatist activity. At a young age, he attracted the patronage of Sir Edward Coke who enrolled him at Pembroke College, Cambridge in 1623. He completed his BA and began an MA, but left in 1629 to become chaplain to Sir William Masham in Essex County. By December, 1630, he and his wife Mary had joined the Great Migration. The wildness of the New World fertilized his millennial epistemology;

and he came to believe that the entire world was in a "wilderness" condition which called not for the maintenance of the status quo, but for a ministry like Christ's, among the poor and unconverted. Once outside the Bay's jurisdiction, he purchased land from the Narragansett and established Providence as a haven for refugees of Puritan intolerance. Separatists, Antinomians like Anne Hutchinson, Baptists, Seekers, Quakers, Jews – even rogues like Thomas Morton – passed through. Still fearing interference from the Bay, Williams journeyed to England in 1643 to incorporate the towns of his plantation under a charter that would separate church and state. When this charter was invalidated by the death of Charles I in 1649, Williams returned to London in 1651 and by 1654 had negotiated a new patent. In 1663, Charles II awarded Rhode Island a royal charter that guaranteed freedom of conscience, a principle that has become basic to the very idea of "America" and is preserved in the Bill of Rights. As president of the General Assembly, governor of Rhode Island, and in the many offices he held during his long public career, Williams worked tirelessly to uphold this principle, which he, unlike other Puritan proselytizers, extended to Native peoples. Always on friendly terms with them, he tried in vain to keep the Narragansett out of the second Puritan conquest of the Natives (Metacom's War), but they allied with the Pequots, and burned Providence nearly to the ground. Williams remained throughout his life unaffiliated with any organized church or creed, calling himself a "seeker," one who perpetually searches for God's truth, but never expects to find it in this world.

Most of Williams' signal ideas can be found in his first book, *A Key into the Language of America*. Ostensibly a grammar of the Narragansett dialect that Williams composed at sea in 1643 as an aid to his own memory, *A Key* contains a blistering critique of the so-called civilized and Christian morality of the Puritan brethren who demonized the Indians and made Williams a pariah. However, Williams' anti-Puritan polemic is complicated by divided loyalties, as were his actions towards the Indians – in his lifetime, he served as ally, ambassador and spy for the Puritans who banished him. These complications are evident in the heterogeneous structure and allegorical quality of *A Key*. It contains thirty-two chapters, each describing an aspect of Native life and culture, which are divided into three interrelated parts: parallel lists of vocabulary, observations from Williams' personal experiences related to the vocabulary which lead to a "general observation" of a spiritual nature that draws a moral lesson, and a short, emblematic poem. While the chapters contain detailed descriptions of Narragansett life, they can also be read allegorically, so that the literal, figurative, and spiritual levels operate simultaneously. In his day, Williams was better known as the author of a series of densely argued tracts denouncing John Cotton's orthodox theory of the limitations of freedom of conscience. The first and most important of these, *The Bloody Tenent*, was published anonymously, and copies were burned by order of Parliament because of its radical democratic sentiments. Williams believed that Biblical events signified atemporal states of the soul, that spirituality was individual, and that everyone should be free to work out his or her salvation. But as he made clear in his letter to the town of Providence, that belief in religious freedom did not amount to an advocacy of anarchy. Ever true to this principle, when he debated the Quakers very late in his life, he fiercely denounced their doctrines and leader, but never once disputed their right to their beliefs or to live in peace.

Primary Works

A Key into the Language of America, 1643.
The Bloody Tenent of Persecution for Cause of Conscience, Discussed in a Conference betweene Truth and Peace, 1644.
Mr Cottons Letter lately Printed, Examined, and Answered, 1644.
Queries of the Highest Consideration, 1644.
Christenings Make Not Christians, 1645.
The Bloody Tenent Yet More Bloody by Mr Cottons Endeavour to Wash it White in the Blood of the Lambe, 1652.
Experiments of Spiritual Life and Health, 1652.
The Fourth Paper Presented by Major Butler, 1652.
The Hireling Ministry None of Christs, 1652.
George Fox Digg'd Out of His Burrowes, 1676.
The Complete Writings of Roger Williams, 6 vols, ed. J. Hammond Trumbell, 1866–1874; rpt. with an additional volume by Perry Miller, 1963.
The Correspondence of Roger Williams, 2 vols, ed. Glenn LaFantasie, 1988.

Further Reading

Perry Miller, *Roger Williams: His Contribution to the American Tradition* (Indianapolis: Bobbs-Merrill, 1953).
Edmund S. Morgan, *Roger Williams: The Church and the State* (New York: Harcourt, Brace and World, 1967).
Henry Chupack, *Roger Williams* (New York: Twayne, 1969).
W. Clark Gilpin, *The Millenarian Piety of Roger Williams* (Chicago: University of Chicago Press, 1979).
Hugh Spurgin, *Roger Williams and Puritan Radicalism in the English Separatist Tradition* (Lewiston: E. Mellen Press, 1989).
Timothy Hall, *Separating Church and State: Roger Williams and Religious Liberty* (Chicago: University of Illinois Press, 1998).

A Key into the Language of America[1]

To my Deare and Welbeloved Friends and Countrey-men, in old and new England
I Present you with a *Key*; I have not heard of the like, yet framed, since it pleased God to bring that mighty *Continent* of *America* to light: Others of my Country-men have often, and excellently, and lately written of the *Countrey* (and none that I know beyond the goodnesse and worth of it.)

This *Key*, respects the *Native Language* of it, and happily may unlocke some *Rarities* concerning the *Natives* themselves, not yet discovered.

---

[1]　First published in London in 1643 and subtitled *An help to the Language of the Natives in that part of America, called New-England*. The text, slightly modified, is from *A Key to* the *Language of America*, eds John J. Teunissen and Evelyn J. Hinz (Detroit: Wayne State University Press, 1973).

I drew the *Materialls* in a rude lumpe at Sea,[2] as a private *helpe* to my owne memory, that I might not by my present absence *lightly lose* what I had so *dearely bought* in some few yeares *hardship*, and *charges* among the *Barbarians*; yet being reminded by some, what pitie it were to bury those *Materialls* in my *Grave* at land or Sea; and withall, remembring how oft I have been importun'd by *worthy friends*, of all sorts, to afford them some helps this way.

I resolved (by the assistance of *the most High*) to cast those *Materialls* into this *Key*, *pleasant* and *profitable* for *All*, but specially for my *friends* residing in those parts:

A little *Key* may open a *Box*, where lies a *bunch* of *Keyes*.

With this I have entred into the secrets of those *Countries*, where ever *English* dwel about two hundred miles, betweene the *French* and *Dutch* Plantations; for want of this, I know what grosse *mis-takes* my selfe and others have run into.

There is a mixture of this *Language North* and *South*, from the place of my abode, about six hundred miles; yet within the two hundred miles (aforementioned) their *Dialects* doe exceedingly differ;[3] yet not so, but (within that compasse) a man may, by this *helpe*, converse with *thousands* of *Natives* all over the *Countrey*: and by such converse it may please the *Father* of *Mercies* to spread *civilitie*, (and in his owne most holy season) *Christianitie*; for *one Candle* will light *ten thousand*, and it may please *God* to blesse a *little Leaven* to season the *mightie Lump* of those *Peoples* and *Territories*.[4]

It is expected, that having had so much converse with these *Natives*, I should write some litle of them.

. . . to that great Point of their *Conversion* so much to bee longed for, and by all *New-English* so much pretended,[5] and I hope in Truth.

For my selfe I have uprightly laboured to suite my endeavours to my pretences: and of later times (out of desire to attaine their Language) I have run through varieties of *Intercourses*[6] with them Day and Night, Summer and Winter, by Land and Sea; particular passages tending to this, I have related divers, in the Chapter of their Religion.

Many solemne discourses I have had with all *sorts* of *Nations* of them, from one end of the Countrey to another (so farre as opportunity, and the little Language I have could reach.)

I know there is no small *preparation* in the hearts of Multitudes of them. I know their many solemne *Confessions* to my self, and one to another of their lost *wandring Conditions*.

I know strong *Convictions* upon the *Consciences* of many of them, and their desires uttered that way.

I know not with how little *Knowledge* and *Grace* of Christ, the Lord may save, and therefore neither will *despaire*, nor *report* much.

But since it hath pleased some of my Worthy *Countrymen* to mention (of late in print) *Wequash*, the *Pequt Captaine*,[7] I shall be bold so farre to second their *Relations*, as to relate mine owne Hopes of Him (though I dare not be so confident as others.)

Two dayes before his Death, as I past up to *Qunníhticut*[8] River, it pleased my worthy friend Mr *Fenwick* (whom I visited at his house in *Say-Brook* Fort at the mouth of that River) to tell me that my old friend *Wequash* lay very sick: I desired to see him, and Himselfe was pleased to be my Guide two miles where *Wequash* lay.

---

[2]   Williams was returning to England to obtain a patent for Providence Plantation during which time he composed *A Key*.

[3]   Williams refers to the Algonkian language, of which Narragansett was the dialect spoken by the natives in Williams' immediate area.

[4]   Matthew 13:33.

[5]   Proffered and promised.

[6]   Discourses, conversations.

[7]   The Puritan minister, Thomas Shepard, described Wequash's conversion in his tract, *New England's First Fruits* (1643).

[8]   Connecticut.

Amongst other discourse concerning his *sicknesse* and *Death* (in which hee freely bequeathed his son to Mr *Fenwick*) I closed with him concerning his *Soule*: Hee told me that some two or three yeare before, he had lodged at my House, where I acquainted him with the *Condition* of *all mankind*, & his *Own* in particular, how *God* created *Man* and *All things*: how *Man* fell from *God*, and of his present *Enmity* against *God*, and the *wrath* of *God* against *Him* untill *Repentance*: said he *your words were never out of my heart to this present*; and said hee *me much pray to Jesus Christ*: I told him so did many *English*, *French*, and *Dutch*, who had never turned to *God*, nor loved Him: He replyed in broken English: *Me so big naughty Heart, me heart all one stone!* Savory *expressions* using to breath *from compunct and broken Hearts*, and a sence of *inward hardnesse* and *unbrokennesse*. I had many discourses with him in his Life, but this was the summe of our last parting untill our generall meeting[9].

Now because this is the great Inquiry of all men what *Indians* have been converted? what have the *English* done in those parts? what hopes of the *Indians* receiving the Knowledge of Christ!

And because to this Question, some put an edge from the boast of the Jesuits in *Canada* and *Maryland*, and especially from the wonderfull conversions made by the Spaniards and Portugalls in the *West-Indies*; besides what I have here written, as also, beside what I have observed in the Chapter of their Religion! I shall further present you with a briefe Additionall discourse concerning this Great Point, being comfortably perswaded that that Father of Spirits, who was graciously pleased to perswade *Japhet* (the Gentiles) to dwell in the Tents of *Shem* (the Jewes)[10] will in his holy season (I hope approaching) perswade these Gentiles of *America* to partake of the mercies of *Europe*, and then shall bee fulfilled what is written, by the Prophet *Malachi*[11], from the rising of the Sunne (in *Europe*) to the going down of the same (in *America*) my Name shall [be] great among the Gentiles. So I desire to hope and pray,

Your unworthy Country-man
ROGER WILLIAMS.

Directions for the use of the Language

1. A Dictionary *or* Grammer *way I had consideration of, but purposely avoided, as not so accommo-date to the Benefit of all, as I hope this Forme is.*
2. A Dialogue *also I had thoughts of, but avoided for brevities sake, and yet (with no small paines) I have so framed every Chapter and the matter of it, as I may call it an Implicite Dialogue.*
3. *It is framed chiefly after the* Narroganset *Dialect, because most spoken in the Countrey, and yet (with attending to the variation of peoples and Dialects) it will be of great use in all parts of the Countrey.*
4. *Whatever your occasion bee either of Travell, Discourse, Trading &c. turne to the Table which will direct you to the Proper Chapter.*
5. *Because the Life of all Language is in the Pronunciation, I have been at paines and charges to Cause the Accents, Tones, or sounds to be affixed, (which some understand according to the* Greeke *Lan-*

9   On Judgement day.

10   After the great flood, all the peoples of the earth descended from Noah and his three sons. Japheth, Noah's second son, was said to give rise to the Indo-European peoples, "the Gentiles." Shem, Noah's eldest son, was ancestor of the Semitic people. Ham, the third son, was the "father of Canaan," and because he saw his father's nakedness, Noah

cursed him and made Canaan slaves, and blessed Shem, saying: "May God make space for Japheth and let him live in the tents of Shem: and let Canaan be his slave." (Genesis 9:18ff).

11   Malachi 1:11; Williams applied this prophecy to Europe and America.

guage) *Acutes, Graves, Circumflexes: for example, in the second leafe in the word* Ewò He: *the sound or Tone must not be put on* E, *but* wò *where the grave Accent is.*

In the same leafe, in the word Ascowequássin, *the Sound must not be on any of the Syllables, but on* quáss, *where the Acute or sharp sound is.*

In the same leafe, in the word Anspaumpmaûntam, *the sound must not be on many of the Syllables, but* Maûn, *where the* Circumflex *or long sounding Accent is.*

6. *The* English *for every* Indian *word or phrase stands in a straight line directly against the* Indian: *yet sometimes there are two words for the same thing (for their Language is exceeding copious, and they have five or six words sometimes for one thing) and then the* English *stands against them both: for example in the second leafe,*

Cowáunckamish &	*I pray your Favour.*
Cuckquénamish	

From *Chapter I: Of* Salutation

Observation.

The Natives are of two sorts, (as the English are.) Some more Rude and Clownish, who are not so apt to Salute, but upon *Salutation* resalute lovingly. Others, and the generall, are *sober* and *grave*, and yet chearfull in a meane, and as ready to begin a Salutation as to Resalute, which yet the English generally begin, out of desire to Civilize them.

What cheare Nétop? *is the generall salutation of all English toward them.* Nétop *is friend.*

Netompaûog.	*Friends.*

They are exceedingly delighted with Salutations in their own Language.

Neèn, Keèn, Ewò.	*I, you, he.*
Keén ka neen.	*You and I.*
Asco wequássin,	
Asco wequassunnúmmis.	*Good morrow.*
Askuttaaquompsìn?	*How doe you?*
Asupaumpmaûntam.	*I am very well.*
Taubot paumpmaúntaman.	*I am glad you are well.*
Cowaúnckamish.	*My service to you. . . .*

Observation.

Obscure and meane persons amongst them have no Names: *Nullius numeri, &c.* as the Lord Jesus foretells his followers, that their Names should be cast out, Luk. 6. 22 as not worthy to be named, *&c.* Againe, because they abhorre to name the dead (Death being the King of Terrours to all naturall men: and though the Natives hold the Soule to live ever, yet not holding a Resurrection, they die, and mourn without Hope.) In that respect I say, if any of their Sachims or neighbours die who were of their names, they lay down those Names as dead.

Nowánnehick nowésuonck.	*I have forgot my Name. . . .*

Observation.

In this respect they are remarkably free and courteous, to invite all Strangers in; and if any come to them upon any occasion, they request them to *come in*, if they come not in of themselves.

Awássish.	*Warme you.*
Máttapsh yóteg.	*Sit by the fire.*
Tocketúnnawem?	*What say you?*
Keén nétop?	*Is it you friend?*
Peeyàush nétop.	*Come hither friend.*
Pétitees.	*Come in.*
Kunnúnni?	*Have you seen me?*
Kunnúnnous.	*I have seen you.*
Taubot mequaunnamêan.	*I thank you for your kind remembrance.*
Taûbot neanawáyean.	*I thank you.*
Taûbot neaunanamêan.	*I thank you for your love.*

Observation.

I have acknowledged amongst them an heart sensible of kindnesses, and have reaped kindnesse again from many, seaven yeares after, when I my selfe had forgotten, *&c.* hence the Lord Jesus exhorts his followers to doe good for evill; for otherwise, sinners will do good for good, kindnesse for kindnesse, &c.[12] . . .

From these courteous *Salutations* Observe in generall: There is a savour of *civility* and *courtesie* even amongst these wild *Americans*, both amongst *themselves* and towards *strangers*.

More particular:

1. *The Courteous* Pagan *shall condemne*
   Uncourteous Englishmen,
   Who live like Foxes, Beares and Wolves,
   Or Lyon in his Den.

2. *Let none sing* blessings *to their soules,*
   For that they Courteous are:
   The wild Barbarians *with no more*
   Then Nature, goe so farre:

3. *If Natures Sons both* wild *and* tame,
   Humane and Courteous be:
   How ill becomes it Sonnes of God ,
   To want Humanity?

[12] Matthew 7:22.

From *Chapter VIII: Of* Discourse *and* Newes *{Canonicus' speech}*

. . . Wunnaumwaúonck,	
Wunnaumwáyean.	*If he say true.*

Obs. Canounicus, the old high *Sachim* of the *Nariganset Bay* (a wise and peaceable Prince) once in a solemne Oration to my self, in a solemne assembly, using this word, said, I have never suffered any wrong to be offered to the *English* since they landed; nor never will: he often repeated this word, *Wunnaumwáyean, Englishman*; if the *Englishman* speake true, if hee meane truly, then shall I goe to my grave in peace, and hope that the *English* and my posteritie shall live in love and peace together. I replied, that he had no cause (as I hoped) to question *Englishman's Wunnaumwaúonck*, that is, faithfulnesse, he having had long experience of their friendlinesse and trustinesse. He tooke a sticke, and broke it into ten pieces, and related ten instances (laying downe a sticke to every instance) which gave him cause thus to feare and say; I satisfied him in some presently, and presented the rest to the Governours of the *English*, who, I hope, will be far from giving just cause to have *Barbarians* to question their *Wunnaumwâuonck*, or faithfulnesse.

From *Chapter XI: Of* Travel

Máyi.	*A way.*
Mayúo?	*Is there a way?*
Mat mayanúnno.	*There is no way.*
Peemáyagat.	*A little way.*
Mishimmáyagat.	*A great path.*
Machípscat.	*A stone path.*

Obs. It is admirable to see, what paths their naked hardned feet have made in the wildernesse in most stony and rockie places.

Nnatotemúckaun.	*I will aske the way.*
Kunnatótemous.	*I will inquire of you.*
Kunnatotemi?	*Doe you aske me?*
Tou nishin méyi?	*Where lies the way?*
Kokotemíinnea méyi.	*Shew me the way.*
Yo áinshick méyi.	*There the way lies.*
Kukkakótemous.	*I will shew you.*
Yo cummittamáyon.	*There is the way you must goe.*
Yo chippachâusin.	*There the way divides.*
Maúchatea.	*A guide.*
Máuchase.	*Be my guide.*

Obs. The wildernesse being so vast, it is a mercy, that for a hire a man shall never want guides, who will carry provisions, and such as hire them over the Rivers and Brookes, and find out often times hunting-houses, or other lodgings at night.

Anóce wénawash.	*Hire him.*
Kuttánnoonsh.	*I will hire you.*
Kuttaúnckquittaunch.	*I will pay you.*
Kummuchickónckquatous.	*I will pay you well.*
Tocketaonckquittíinnea?	*What will you give me?*
Cummáuchanish.	*I will conduct you.*
Yò aûnta.	*Let us goe that way.*
Yò cuttâunan.	*Go that way.*
Yò mtúnnock.	*The right hand.*
Yò nmúnnatch.	*The left hand.*
Cowéchaush.	*I will goe with you.*
Wétash.	*Goe along.*
Cowéchaw ewò.	*He will goe with you.*
Cowechauatímmin.	*I will goe with you.*
Wechauatíttea.	*Let us accompany.*
Taûbot wétáyean.	*I thanke you for your company.*

Obs. I have heard of many *English* lost, and have oft been lost my selfe, and my selfe and others have often been found, and succoured by the *Indians*.

Pitchcowáwwon.	*You will lose your way.*
Meshnowáwwon.	*I lost my way.*
Nummauchèmin, Ntanniteímmin.	*I will be going.*
Mammauchêtuck.	*Let us be going.*
Ânakiteunck.	*He is gone.*

Memauchêwi ánittui,
    Memauchegushánnick,
    Anakagushánnick.
	They are gone.

Tunnockuttòme, Tunnockkuttoyeâim?	*Whither goe you?*
Tunnockkuttínshem, Nnegónshem.	*I will goe before you?*
Cuppompáish.	*I will stay for you.*
Negónshesh.	*Goe before.*
Mittummayaûcup.	*The way you went before.*
Cummáittanish.	*I will follow you.*
Cuppahímmin.	*Stay for me.*
Tawhich quaunqua quêan?	*Why doe you run so?*
Nowecóntum púmmishem.	*I have a mind to travel.*
Konkenuphshâuta.	*Let us goe apace.*
Konkenúppe.	*Goe apace.*
Michéme nquanunquaquémin.	*I have run alwayes.*
Yo ntoyamaushem.	*I goe this pace.*

Obs. They are generally quick on foot, brought up from the breasts to running: their legs being also from the wombe stretcht and bound up in a strange way on their Cradle backward, as also annointed; yet have they some that excell: so that I have knowne many of them run betweene fourescoure or an hundred miles in a Summers day, and back within two dayes: they doe also practice running of *Races*; and commonly in the Summer, they delight to goe without shoes, although they have them hanging at their backs: they are so exquisitely skilled in all the body and bowels of the Countrey (by reason of their huntings) that I have often been guided twentie, thirtie, sometimes fortie miles through the woods, a streight course, out of any path. . . .

Aspumméwi.	*He is not gone by.*
Aspumméwock.	*They are not gone by.*
Awánick payánchick?	*Who comes there?*
Awánick negonsháchick?	*Who are these before us?*
Yo cuppummesicómmin.	*Crosse over into the way there.*
Cuppì-machàug.	*Thick wood: a Swamp.*

Obs. These thick Woods and Swamps (like the Boggs to the *Irish*) are the Refuges for Women and children in Warre, whilst the men fight. As the Country is wondrous full of Brookes and Rivers, so doth it also abound with fresh ponds, some of many miles compasse.

Níps-nipsash.	*Pond: Ponds.*
Wèta: wétedg.	*The Woods on fire.*
Wussaumpátammin.	*To view or looke about.*
Wussaum patámoonck.	*A Prospect.*
Wuttocékémin.	*To wade.*
Tocekétuck.	*Let us wade.*
Tou wuttáuqussin?	*How deepe?*
Yò ntaúqussin.	*Thus deep.*
Kunnfish.	*I will carry you.*
Kuckqússuckqun.	*You are heavy.*
Kunnâukon.	*You are light.*
Pasúckquish.	*Rise*
Anakish: maúchish.	*Goe.*
Quaquìsh.	*Runne.*
Nokus káuatees.	*Meet him.*
Nockuskauatítea.	*Let us meet him.*
Neenmeshnóckuskaw.	*I did meet him.*

Obs. They are joyfull in meeting of any in travell, and will strike fire either with stones or sticks, to take Tobacco, and discourse a little together.

Mesh Kunnockqus kanatímmin?	*Did you meet? &c.*
Yò Kuttauntapímmin.	*Let us rest here.*
Kussackquêtuck.	*Let us sit downe.*
Yo appíttuck.	*Let us sit here.*
Nissówanis, Nissowànishkaûmen.	*I am weary.*
Nickqússaqus.	*I am lame.*
Ntouagonnausinnúmmin.	*We are distrest undone,* or *in misery.*

Obs. They use this word properly in wandring toward Winter night, in which case I have been many a night with them, and many times also alone, yet alwayes mercifully preserved.

Teâno wonck nippéeam.	*I will be here by and by againe.*
Mat Kunníckansh.	*I will not leave you.*
Aquie Kunnickatshash.	*Doe not leave me.*
Tawhítch nickatshiêan?	*Why doe you forsake me?*
Wuttánho.	*A staffe.*
Yò íish Wuttánho.	*Use this staffe.*

Obs. Sometimes a man shall meet a lame man or an old man with a Staffe: but generally a Staffe is a rare sight in the hand of the eldest, their Constitution is so strong. I have upon occasion travelled many a score, yea many a hundreth mile amongst them, without need of stick or staffe, for any appearance of danger amongst them: yet it is a rule amongst them, that it is not good for a man to travell without a Weapon nor alone. . . .

Generall Observations of their Travell.

As the same Sun shines on the Wildernesse that doth on a Garden! so the same faithfull and all sufficient God, can comfort, feede and safely guide even through a desolate howling Wildernesse.

More particular.

1. *God makes a Path, provides a Guide,*
   And feeds in Wildernesse!
   His glorious Name while breath remaines,
   O that I may confesse.

2. *Lost many a time, I have had no Guide,*
   No House, but hollow Tree!
   In stormy Winter night no Fire,
   No Food, no Company:

3. *In him I have found a House, a Bed,*
   A Table, Company:
   No Cup so bitter, buts made sweet,
   When God shall Sweet'ning be.

1643   1643

LETTER: TO THE TOWN OF PROVIDENCE[1]

Loving Friends and Neighbours,
It pleaseth GOD, yet to continue this great Liberty of our Town-Meetings, for which, we ought to be humbly thankful, and to improve these Liberties to the Praise of the Giver, and to the Peace and Welfare of the Town and Colony, without our own private Ends. – I thought it

[1] Undated, but probably written around January 1654–5 after Williams returned from England. The community was divided over issues of religious freedom and civil obedience. The text is from *The Correspondence of Roger Williams*, ed. LaFantasie (Hanover: Brown University Press/University Press of New England, 1988).

my Duty, to present you with this my impartial Testimony, and Answer to a Paper sent you the other Day from my Brother, – *That it is Blood-Guiltiness and against the Rule of the Gospel, to execute Judgment upon Transgressors, against the private or public Weal.*[2] – That ever I should speak or write a Tittle[3] that tends to such an infinite Liberty of Conscience, is a Mistake; and which I have ever disclaimed and abhorred. To prevent such Mistakes, I at present shall only propose this Case. – There goes many a Ship to Sea, with many a Hundred Souls in one Ship, whose Weal and Woe is common; and is a true Picture of a Common-Wealth, or an human Combination, or Society. It hath fallen out sometimes, that both *Papists* and *Protestants, Jews,* and *Turks,* may be embarqued into one Ship. Upon which Supposal, I do affirm, that all the Liberty of Conscience that ever I pleaded for, turns upon these two Hinges, that none of the *Papists, Protestants, Jews,* or *Turks,* be forced to come to the Ships Prayers or Worship; nor, secondly, compelled from their own particular Prayers or Worship, if they practice any. I further add, that I never denied that notwithstanding this Liberty, the Commander of this Ship ought to command the Ships Course; yea, and also to command that Justice, Peace, and Sobriety, be kept and practised, both among the Seaman and all the Passengers. If any Seamen refuse to perform their Service, or Passengers to pay their Freight; – if any refuse to help in Person or Purse, towards the Common Charges, or Defence; if any refuse to obey the common Laws and Orders of the Ship, concerning their common Peace and Preservation; – if any shall mutiny and rise up against their Commanders, and Officers; – if any shall preach or write, that there ought to be no Commanders, nor Officers, because all are equal in CHRIST, therefore no Masters, nor Officers, no Laws, nor Orders, no Corrections nor Punishments – I say, I never denied, but in such Cases, whatever is pretended, the Commander or Commanders may judge, resist, compel, and punish such Transgressors, according to their Deserts and Merits. This, if seriously and honestly minded, may, if so please the Father of Lights, let in some Light, to such as willingly shut not their Eyes – I – remain, studious of our common Peace and Liberty,–

Roger Williams

1654–5   1874

Thomas Shepard (1605–1649)

Despite the unsettled nature of his early life and his continual doubts about his own spiritual state, Thomas Shepard became one of the towering figures of the first generations of Puritan ministers. From a small village in Essex, the son of a grocer, and his mother's favorite, he was orphaned as a young child. He entered Emmanuel College, Cambridge where he struggled with his religious faith and was finally converted by the eminent minister John Preston. His own preaching was infused by his early experiences of sin and backsliding, and was so powerful in the cause of Puritanism that Bishop Laud, enforcing Anglican uniformity, silenced him in 1630. Barred from ministerial practice, he served as tutor and chaplain to the family of Sir Richard Darley, of Yorkshire, while also preaching fiery sermons across England and staying just ahead of the pursuivants. During this pe-

---

[2]   This paper did not survive, nor is its author known, but the same argument was made by Puritans like John Winthrop who in his *Journal* reported that Williams and his followers "would have no magistrates." They also misread Williams' position in *The Bloody Tenent*, and accused him of arguing that citizens could not be prosecuted for resisting civil law if that law violated their individual conscience, a position Williams explicitly rejects here.

[3]   One dot or least bit.

riod he married, but his first wife died in 1636, and he remarried Joanna Hooker, daughter of another leading New England minister, Thomas Hooker. Always fearing persecution and discouraged by the economic depression in England, Shepard decided to emigrate and sailed for New England in 1634. Deterred by a fierce storm, he had to remain in hiding in England until the following spring, when he finally reached New England. One of the youngest ministers to arrive in the new colony, he was chosen minister at Cambridge, and became a religious leader known for his forceful suppression of Antinomians like Anne Hutchinson, and his ravishing sermonizing. Edward Johnson, a prominent setter and author of *Wonder-Working Providence of Sions Savior in New England* (1654), recounts how he arrived in Boston in 1636 during the Antinomian crisis and was thrown into despair over the "errors" he heard circulating so freely. He found his way to Cambridge, and after a two hour sermon by Thomas Shepard, he "was metamorphosed, and was faine to hang down the head often, least his watry eyes should blab abroad the secret conjunctions of his affections, his heart crying loud to the Lords ecchoing answer, to his blessed spirit, that caused the Speech of a poore weake pale complectioned man to take such impression in his soule."

Shepard's published sermons were extremely popular as well. One collection, entitled *The Sincere Convert*, went through twenty editions between its publication in 1640 and 1812. With John Allin he coauthored an important defense of the New England experiment, in which they argued that leaving England was the only way they could continue preaching and "pursue the Word," the heart of Puritan spiritual practice. Shepard's eloquence and effectiveness derives in part from his sense of the endless struggle of the soul with its sin and with the requirements of God. His autobiography, which he wrote for his oldest son, Thomas Shepard, Jr, "that so he may learn to know and love the great and most high God, the God of his father," is one of the best expressions of the first generation Puritan spirit.

PRIMARY WORKS

The Sincere Convert, 1640.
New-Englands Lamentation for old Englands Present Errours, 1645.
The Sound Beleever: A Treatise of Evangelical Conversion, 1645.
The Autobiography (1646), 1832. *A Defense of the Answer made unto the Nine Questions or Positions sent from New England*, with John Allin, 1648.
Theses Sabbaticæ. Or, the Doctrine of the Sabbath, 1649.
Subjection to Christ in all his Ordinances and Appointments, 1654.
Parable of the Ten Virgins, 1660.

FURTHER READING

Thomas Werge, *Thomas Shepard* (Boston: Hall, 1987).
Mary Cappello, "The Authority of Self-Definition in Thomas Shepard's Autobiography and Journal," *Early American Literature*, 24, 1 (1989) pp. 35–51.
Michael McGiffert (ed.) *God's Plot: Puritan Spirituality in Thomas Shepard's Cambridge* (Amherst: University of Massachusetts Press, 1994).

FROM *THE AUTOBIOGRAPHY OF THOMAS SHEPARD*[1]

The first two yeares I spent in Cambridge was in studying & in my neglect of god & private prayer which I had sometime used. & I did not regard the Lord at all unless it were at some fits; the 3rd yeare wherin I was Sophister[2] I began to be foolish & proud & to shew my selfe in the publike Schooles; & there to be a disputer about things which now I see I did not know then at all but only prated about them; & toward the end of this yeare when I was most vile (after I hade bin next unto the gates of Death by the [small] Pox the yeare before) the Lord began to call me home to the fellowship of his grace; which was in this manner.

1. I doe remember that I had many good affections (but blind & unconstant) oft cast into me

[1]   The text, with slight modifications, is from The Autobiography of Thomas Shepard, ed. Allyn B. Forbes, *Publications of the Colonial Society of Massachusetts*, XXVII (1932).

[2]   At Cambridge College, a student in his second or third year.

since my fathers sickenes by the spirit of god wrastling with me, & hence I would pray in secret & hence when I was at Cambridge I heard old Doctor Chadderton[3] the master of the Colledge when I came & the first yeare I was there to heare him upon a Sacrament day my hart was much affected but I did breake loose from the Lord agayne & halfe a yeare after I heard m[r] Dickinson common place in the chappell upon those woords I will not destroy it for tens sake. Gen: 19[4]. & then agayne was much affected, but I shooke this off also & fell from god to loose & lewd company to lust & pride & gaming & bowling & drinking; & yet the Lord left me not but a godly Scholler walking with me, fell to discourse about the misery of every man out of Christ vis: that what ever they did was sin; & this did much affect me; & at another time when I did light in godly company I heard them discourse about the wrath of god, & the terrour of it & how intollerable it was which they did present by fire how intollerable the torment of that was for a time what then would æternaity be; & this did much awaken me; & I began to pray agayne; but then by loose company I came to dispute in the Schooles & there to joyne to loose schollers of other colledges & was fearfully left of god & fell to drinke with them; & I dranke so much one day that I was dead drunke & that upon a Saturday night & so was carryed from the place I had drinke at & did feast at, unto a Schollers chamber on Basset of Christs Colledge; & knew not where I was untill I awakened late on that sabboth & sick with my beastly carriage; & when I awakened I went from him in shame & confusion, & went out into the feelds & there spent that sabboth lying hid in the corne feelds where the Lord who might justly have cut me off in the midst of my sin; did meet me with much sadnes of hart & troubled my soule for this & other my sins which then I had cause & laysure to thinke of; & now when I was woorst he began to be best unto me & made me resolve to set upon a course of dayly meditation about the evill of sin & my own wayes, yet although I was troubled for this sin I did not know my sinfull nature all this while. . . .

At this time I cannot omit the goodnes of god as to my selfe so to all the cuntry in delivering us from the Pekoat furies;[5] these Indians were the stoutest proudest & most successful in there wars of all the Indians; there cheefe Sachem was Sasakus, a proud cruell unhapy & headstrong prince, who not willing to be guided by the perswasions of this fellow an aged Sachem Momanattuck nor fearing the revenge of the English, having first suckt the blood of captaine Stone & m[r] Oldham found it so sweet & his proceedings for one the whole winter so successfull that having beseeged & kild about 4 men that kept Seabrook fort he adventured to fall upon the English up the river at Wethersfeeld where he slew 9 or 10. Men women & children at unawares, & took two maids prisoners carrying them away captive to the Pekoat cuntry hereupon those upon the river first gathered about 70 men & sent them into Pekoat cuntry, to make that the seat of war, & revenge the death of those innocents whom they barbarously & most unnaturally slew; these men marched two dayes & nights from the way of the Naraganset unto Pekoat; being guided by those Indians then the ancient enemies of the Pekoats they intended to assault Sasakus Fort but falling short of it the second night the providence of god guided them to another nearer, full of stout men & their best souldiers being as it were coopt up there to the number of 3 or 400 in all for the divine slaughter by the hand of the English;

---

3   Laurence Chaderton (1536–1640), Master of Emmanuel College, teacher and preacher, and important influence upon all seventeenth century English Puritans.
4   Actually, Genesis 18:32. God warns Abraham that he will destroy the wicked cities of Sodom and Gomorrah, and Abraham begs him not to destroy the righteous, however few, with the wicked.
5   Shepard describes the Puritan conflict with the power-

ful Pequot tribe, 1636–7, which the Puritans claimed began when Pequots murdered the traders Stone and Oldham. There is evidence that it was actually Narragansetts who killed these traders to provoke the English to move against the Pequots, who were their rivals in the region. A large English force destroyed the Pequot fort at Mystic, slaughtering many including women and children.

these therefore being all night making merry & singing the death of the English the next day, toward breake of the day being very heavy with sleepe the English drew neare within the sight of the fort, very weary with travayle & want of sleepe, at which time 500 Naragansets fled for feare & only 2 of the company stood to it to conduct them to the fort & the dore & entrance thereof; the English being come to it awakened the fort with a peale of muskets directed into the midst of there wigwams; & after this some undertaking to compasse the fort without some adventured into the fort upon the very faces of the enemy standing ready with there arrowes ready bent to shoot who ever should adventure; but the English casting by there peeces tooke their swords in there hands (the Lord doubling there strength & courage) & fell upon the Indians where a hot fight continued about the space of an houre, at last by the direction of one Captayne Mason[6] there wigwams were set on fire which being dry & contiguous one to another was most dreadfull to the Indians, some burning some bleeding to death by the sword some resisting till they were cut off some flying were beat down by the men without untill the Lord had utterly consumed the whole company except 4 or 5. girles they tooke prisoners & dealt with them at Seabrooke as they dealt with ours at Wethersfeeld,[7] & tis verily thought scarce one man escaped unless one or two to carry foorth tydings of the lamentable end of there fellowes; & of the English not one man was kild but one by the musket of an Englishman (as was conceived) some were wounded much but all recovered & restored agayne. . . .

But the Lord hath not bin woont to let me live long without some affliction or other, & yet ever mixt with some mercy, & therefore Aprill the 2^d: 1646. As he gave me another son, John. So he tooke away my most deare precious meeke & loving wife, in childbed, after 3 weekes lying in, having left behind her two hopefull branches my deare children, Samuell, & John; this affliction was very heavy to me, for in it the Lord seemd to withdraw his tender care for me & mine, which he graciously manifested by my deare wife; also refused to heare prayer, when I did thinke he would have harkned & let me see his bewty in the land of the living, in restoring of her to health agayne; also in taking her away in the prime time of her life when shee might have lived to have glorifyed the Lord long. Also in threatning me to proceed in rooting out my family, & that he would not stop having begun here as in Ely[8] for my being zealous enough against the sins of his son; & I saw that if I had profited by former afflictions of this nature I should not have had this scourge; but I am the Lords, & he may doe with me what he will, he did teach me to prize a little grace gained by a crosse as a sufficient recompense for all outward losses; but this losse was very great; shee was a woman of incomparable meekens of spirit, toward my selfe especially & very loving; of great prudence to take care for & order my family affayres being neither too lavish nor sordid in any thing so that I knew not what was under her hands; shee had an excellency to reproove for sin & discerned the evills of men; shee loved gods people dearly & studious to profit by there fellowship, & therefore loved there company shee loved gods woord exceedingly & hence was glad shee could read my notes which shee had to muse on every weeke; shee had a spirit of prayer beyond ordinary of her time & experience shee was fit to dy long before shee did dy, even after the death of her first borne which was a great affliction to her, but her woorke not being done then shee lived almost 9. yeares with me & was the comfort of my life to me & the last Sacrament before her lying in seemd to be full of Christ & thereby fitted to heaven; shee did oft say shee should not outlive

---

[6] John Mason (1600?–72), soldier and colonial magistrate in Connecticut, who led the attack on the Pequots at Mystic.

[7] The Pequot allowed the two English girls to return to their homes; the Pequot captives remained prisoners of the Puritans.

[8] Eli was a high priest from a family which had been appointed priests by God when the Israelites were in bondage in Egypt. But because his sons took advantage of their position, God punished the family, saying "and all the increase of thine house shall die in the flower of their age.". See 1 Samuel 1–2.

this child; & when her fever first began (by taking some cold) shee told me soe, that we should love exceedingly together because we should not live long together; her fever tooke way her sleepe, want of sleepe wrought much distemper in her head, & filled it with fantasies & distractions but without raging; the night before shee dyed, shee had about 6 houres unquiet sleepe; but that so coold & setled in her head, that when she knew none else so as to speake to them, yet she knew Jesus Christ & could speake to him, & therefore as soone as shee awakened out of sleepe shee brake out into a most heavenly hartbreaking prayer after Christ her deare redeemer for the sparing of life; & so continued praying untill the last houre of her death: Lord tho I unwoorthy Lord on woord on woord &c. & so gave up the ghost; thus god hath visited & scourged me for my sins & sought to weane me from this woorld, but I have ever found it a difficult thing to profit ever but a little by the sorest & sharpest afflictions.

1646   1832

Anne Bradstreet (1612?–1672)

On the first of July, 1650, a volume of poems by Anne Bradstreet was entered in *The Stationer's Register* in London. This was the first volume of poetry by a single author to come out of the New World, and it was written by a modest Puritan goodwife and mother of eight. Of course, Bradstreet was no ordinary goodwife. She was the daughter of Dorothy Yorke, a gentlewoman of considerable means, and Thomas Dudley, a rigorous Puritan second only to Winthrop in influence and power during the early years of the Massachusetts Bay Colony. In England, Dudley had been steward to the Earl of Lincoln at Sempringham, where he was able to give his favorite daughter access to the Earl's considerable library and an unusually substantial education through private tutors. At sixteen, Anne Dudley married Simon Bradstreet, a recent Cambridge graduate and associate of her father. Both men were centrally involved with the Non-conformist group planning emigration to New England, and in 1630 the Dudleys and Bradstreets sailed with the Winthrops on the flagship *Arbella.* Simon quickly embarked on a long public career, serving like his father-in-law as governor of the Bay colony, and as an important member of the Puritan diplomatic mission. He soon moved the family from Boston to Newtown (modern-day Cambridge) and then to Ipswich in the north and finally, after 1644, to North Andover, a frontier settlement on the Merrimack River where Bradstreet lived until her death. Despite her advantages, life on the frontier was extremely diffi-

cult, and made more so by Bradstreet's frailty, a result of the rheumatic fever she suffered as a child which caused debilitating periods of fatigue and lameness throughout her life

As a young girl and even after her marriage, Bradstreet had written poetry that circulated among her family and friends. In 1649, her brother-in-law, John Wheelwright journeyed to London, and without Bradstreet's knowledge or consent, published her manuscript of poems under the pretentious title, *The Tenth Muse Lately Sprung up in America.* The volume received much acclaim, although Bradstreet's reactions on seeing her unfinished poems in print, recorded in "The Author to Her Book," was decidedly negative. Although the Puritans were adamant that women remain out of the public eye, this did not deny them education or intellectual attainments. On the contrary, the introspective piety of Puritanism required that women as well as men read, comprehend, and pass on the basic doctrines of scripture to their children. But since the debacle in 1637–8 with Anne Hutchinson, who through her preaching emboldened the goodwives of Boston, and many of their husbands, to challenge the authority of the powerful magistrates and clergy, women were banned from speaking in church and were kept under a tighter rein. Against the background of pamphlet wars raging in England on "the woman question," the spirit of Hutchinson seemed to rise again in Bradstreet's younger sister Sarah Keayne, who returned from London in 1647 without her husband

and began "prophesying" in public and speaking "out of place." Dudley, who was elected governor in 1649 on Winthrop's death, wanted to recoup his family's reputation, and the publication of his "good" daughter's highly laudable poems may have served his purposes well.

The poems in *The Tenth Muse* were, on the surface, extremely edifying, and made more acceptable by Wheelwright's strategic preface which assured readers that not only was this the work of a woman, but a "woman, honored, and esteemed where she lives, for her gracious demeanor, her eminent parts, her pious conversation, her courteous disposition, her exact diligence in her place, and discreet managing of her family occasions, and more than so, these poems are the fruit but of some few hours, curtailed from her sleep and other refreshments." In other words, she was not a threat to the patriarchal theocratic order. In this volume, Bradstreet took as her literary models eminent writers like Guilliame du Bartas, a French Protestant poet much favored by the Puritans, Joshua Sylvester, his translator, Quarles, Spencer, and Sidney. In imitation of the Renaissance masters, Bradstreet produced thousands of lines of historical and didactic verse – a distinctly unfeminine endeavor during an age in which, if women did compose poetry, they were confined to religious verse, epitaphs, and translation. Often regarded as conventional and imitative, these early poems are undeniably ambitious and challenge, albeit subtly and indirectly, the classical discourses of gendered power relations. After the publication of *The Tenth Muse*, Bradstreet continued to write and revised her early poems for a second edition, but this appeared only posthumously in Boston in 1678, and retained only its descriptive subtitle: *Several Poems, compiled with great Variety of Wit and Learning, full of delight.* The poetry also changed considerably. In her remaining twenty years, Bradstreet composed pri-

marily lyric poems and spiritual meditations on subjects garnered from her personal experiences with children, marriage, the burning of her house, and especially her spiritual struggles, in a voice more private, less ambitious, yet irreducibly gendered – the voice of wife, mother, and grandmother. Many readers argue that in these mature poems Bradstreet finds her own voice, modulating her Puritan didacticism with her individual experiences and her raptures in nature. However, she also manages, from within the subordinate *place* imposed upon her, to reconnect femininity and creativity long severed by androcentric culture. From her pioneering achievement extends the dominant lyric line of American poetry.

PRIMARY WORKS

The Tenth Muse Lately Sprung Up in America, 1650.
Several Poems Compiled with Great Variety of Wit and Learning, 1678; rpt. 1758.
The Works of Anne Bradstreet in Prose and Verse, ed. John Harvard Ellis, 1867.
The Works of Anne Bradstreet, ed. Jeannine Hensley, 1967.
The Complete Works of Anne Bradstreet, eds Joseph R. McElrath, Jr and Allan P. Robb, 1981.

FURTHER READING

Ann Stanford, *Anne Bradstreet: The Worldly Puritan* (Boston: G. K. Hall, 1974).
Pattie Cowell and Ann Stanford, eds, *Critical Essays on Anne Bradstreet* (Boston: G. K. Hall, 1983).
Wendy Martin, *An American Triptych: Anne Bradstreet, Emily Dickinson, Adrienne Rich* (Chapel Hill: University of North Carolina Press, 1984).
Timothy Sweet, "Gender, Genre and Subjectivity in Anne Bradstreet's Early Elegies," *Early American Literature,* 23, 2 (1988) pp. 152–74.
Rosamond Rosenmeier, *Anne Bradstreet Revisited* (Boston: Twayne, 1991).

FROM *SEVERAL POEMS*[1]

The Prologue[2]

1

To sing of wars, of captains, and of kings,
Of cities founded, commonwealths begun,
For my mean[3] pen are too superior things:
Or how they all, or each their dates have run
Let poets and historians set these forth,
My obscure lines shall not so dim their
    worth.

2

But when my wond'ring eyes and envious
    heart
Great Bartas' sugared lines do but read o'er,[4]
Fool I do grudge the Muses[5] did not part
'Twixt him and me that overfluent store;
A Bartas can do what a Bartas will
But simple I according to my skill.

3

From schoolboy's tongue no rhet'ric we
    expect,
Nor yet a sweet consort from broken strings,
Nor perfect beauty where's a main defect.
My foolish, broken, blemished Muse so
    sings,
And this to mend, alas, no art is able,
'Cause nature made it so irreparable.

4

Nor can I, like that fluent sweet tongued
    Greek,[6]
Who lisped at first, in future times speak
    plain.

By art he gladly found what he did seek,
A full requital of his striving pain.
Art can do much, but this maxim's most
    sure:
A weak or wounded brain admits no cure.

5

I am obnoxious to each carping tongue
Who says my hand a needle better fits,
A poet's pen all scorn I should thus wrong,
For such despite they cast on female wits:
If what I do prove well, it won't advance,
They'll say it's stol'n, or else it was by
    chance.

6

But sure the antique Greeks were far more
    mild
Else of our sex, why feigned they those nine
And poesy made Calliope's own child;[7]
So 'mongst the rest they placed the arts
    divine:
But this weak knot they will full soon untie,
The Greeks did nought, but play the fools
    and lie.

7

Let Greeks be Greeks, and women what
    they are
Men have precedency and still excel,
It is but vain unjustly to wage war;
Men can do best, and women know it well.
Preeminence in all and each is yours;

---

[1]   The selections are from *The Works of Anne Bradstreet*, ed. Jeannine Hensley (Cambridge: Belknap Press of Harvard University Press, 1967).

[2]   From internal reference, this was probably the prologue for Bradstreet's long poem in four parts, "Quaternions," but in *The Tenth Muse* (1650) it introduced the volume.

[3]   Low, humble.

[4]   Guillaume de Salluste du Bartas (1544–90), a French Protestant poet popular with English Puritans and one of Bradstreet's literary models. His most famous work, *The*

Divine Weeks, was an epic poem about Christian history translated by Joshua Sylvester in 1605.

[5]   The Muses, in Greek mythology, were nine female goddesses of the arts and sciences. Poets frequently addressed a personal muse as the source of their inspiration.

[6]   The Greek orator Demosthenes (383?–322 BC) was born with a speech defect which he overcame by filling his mouth with pebbles and shouting orations to the wind and sea.

[7]   Calliope, the muse, thus mother, of epic poetry.

Yet grant some small acknowledgement of
   ours.

8

And oh ye high flown quills[8] that soar the
   skies,
And ever with your prey still catch your
   praise,

If e'er you deign these lowly lines your eyes,
Give thyme or parsley wreath, I ask no
   bays;[9]
This mean and unrefined ore of mine
Will make your glist'ring gold but more to
   shine.

1650

In Honour of that High and Mighty Princess Queen Elizabeth of Happy Memory[1]

The Proem[2]
Although, great Queen, thou now in silence
   lie
Yet thy loud herald Fame doth to the sky
Thy wondrous worth proclaim in every
   clime,
And so hath vowed while there is world or
   time.
So great's thy glory and thine excellence,
The sound thereof rapts[3] every human sense,
That men account it no impiety,
To say thou wert a fleshly deity.
Thousands bring offerings (though out of
   date)
Thy world of honours to accumulate;
'Mongst hundred hecatombs[4] of roaring
   verse,
Mine bleating stands before thy royal herse[5].
Thou never didst nor canst thou now
   disdain
T' accept the tribute of a loyal brain.
Thy clemency did erst esteem as much
The acclamations of the poor as rich,

Which makes me deem my rudeness is no
   wrong,
Though I resound thy praises 'mongst the
   throng.

The Poem
No Phoenix pen, nor Spenser's poetry,
No Speed's nor Camden's learned history,[6]
Eliza's works wars, praise, can e'er compact;
The world's the theatre where she did act.
No memories nor volumes can contain
The 'leven Olympiads of her happy reign.[7]
Who was so good, so just, so learn'd, so
   wise,
From all the kings on earth she won the
   prize.
Nor say I more than duly is her due,
Millions will testify that this is true.
She hath wiped off th' aspersion of her sex,
That women wisdom lack to play the rex[8].
Spain's monarch, says not so, nor yet his
   host;

---

[8] Quills, or feathers, were sharpened and used as pens; a figure for writers or critics.
[9] Garlands of leaves from the bay or laurel tree were given by the Greeks as crowns of honor. Parsley and thyme were common, household herbs.

QUEEN ELIZABETH
[1] Elizabeth 1 (1533–1603) became queen of England in 1558 and reigned until her death.
[2] Prelude.
[3] Enraptures.
[4] One hundred beasts sacrificed as offerings to the gods in ancient Greek worship.
[5] A large framework constructed over the tombs of roy-

alty to which mourners attached poems and epitaphs.
[6] The phoenix is a mythological bird that dies in flames and is reborn from its own ashes, much like authors who, according to Bradstreet's elegy for Sir Philip Sidney, die young and are reborn in their works. Edmund Spenser (1552?–99) wrote *The Faerie Queene* (1590) and dedicated it to Queen Elizabeth. John Speed (1552?–1629) was the author of *Historie of Great Britain* (1611). William Camden (1551–1623) wrote *Annales*, translated in 1630 as *The History of the Most Renowned and Victorious Princess Elizabeth.*
[7] The four-year intervals between the Olympic games by which the ancient Greeks reckoned dates. Elizabeth reigned for forty-four years.
[8] King (Latin).

She taught them better manners, to their
  cost.[9]
The Salic law[10], in force now had not been,
If France had ever hoped for such a queen.
But can you, doctors[11], now this point
  dispute,
She's argument enough to make you mute.
Since first the Sun did run his ne'er run
  race,[12]
And earth had, once a year, a new old face,
Since time was time, and man unmanly
  man,
Come show me such a Phoenix if you can.
Was ever people better ruled than hers?
Was ever land more happy freed from
  stirs[13]?
Did ever wealth in England more abound?
Her victories in foreign coasts resound;
Ships more invincible than Spain's, her foe,
She wracked, she sacked, she sunk his
  Armado;
Her stately troops advanced to Lisbon's wall,
Don Anthony in's right there to install.[14]
She frankly helped Frank's brave distressed
  king;[15]
The states united now her fame do sing.[16]
She their protectrix was; they well do know

Unto our dread virago[17], what they owe.
Her nobles sacrificed their noble blood,
Nor men nor coin she spared to do them
  good.
The rude untamed Irish, she did quell,
Before her picture the proud Tyrone fell.[18]
Had ever prince such counsellors as she?
Herself Minerva[19] caused them so to be.
Such captains and such soldiers never seen,
As were the subjects of our Pallas queen.
Her seamen through all straits the world did
  round;
Terra incognita[20] might know the sound.
Her Drake came laden home with Spanish
  gold;[21]
Her Essex took Cadiz, their Herculean
  hold.[22]
But time would fail me, so my tongue
  would too,
To tell of half she did, or she could do.
Semiramis[23] to her is but obscure,
More infamy than fame she did procure.
She built her glory but on Babel's walls,[24]
World's wonder for a while, but yet it falls.
Fierce Tomris (Cyrus' headsman) Scythians'
  queen,[25]
Had put her harness off, had she but seen

---

9   Phillip II (1527–98), king of Spain with imperial ambitions; Elizabeth's navy defeated his "host" of ships, the Spanish Armada, in 1588.
10   A law observed in France established by the Salian Franks that prevented women from succeeding to the throne.
11   Learned men.
12   Never completed race.
13   Disturbances; disputes.
14   Don Antonio of Crato (1531–95), whom England helped in his claim to the throne of Portugal.
15   Henry IV (1533–1610), the Protestant king of France, a largely Catholic country.
16   A reference to the Netherlands, united under a national assembly called the States General. Elizabeth came to their aid during their long war with Spain.
17   Term for a female warrior.
18   Ulster chieftain Hugh O'Neill (1540?–1616), second earl of Tyrone, led the last stand of Ireland's old Gaelic social order against English rule and was defeated and forced to submit in 1603. When in 1607, he and other tribal chiefs left for the Continent, the crown confiscated their vast landholdings for Protestant settlement.

19   Roman goddess of war, wisdom, the arts, and chastity, who oversaw justice. In Greek mythology, Pallas Athena.
20   Unknown land (Latin).
21   Sir Francis Drake (1540?–1596) explored South America and brought back Spanish gold from Chile and Peru to England.
22   Robert Devereux (1566–1601), second earl of Essex, and favorite of Queen Elizabeth, captured the well-defended Spanish port of Cadiz in 1596.
23   Assyrian queen of the late ninth century who reigned after her husband, Ninus', death for forty-two years, and is said to have built the beautiful city of Babylon.
24   The tower of Babel was built by the descendants of Noah's sons in an attempt to reach the heavens and "make a name for ourselves." God came down and confused their language, thus scattering the people (Genesis 11).
25   Tomyris, queen of the Massagetæ, a Scythian tribe, defeated Cyrus the Great of Persia who invaded her kingdom in 529 BC Dante, in his *Purgatory*, reports that she killed him and threw his head into a vessel of blood, crying "It was blood you thirsted for; now take your fill."

Our Amazon in th' Camp of Tilbury,[26]
Judging all valour and all majesty
Within that princess to have residence,
And prostrate yielded to her excellence.
Dido[27], first foundress of proud Carthage
   walls
(Who living consummates her funerals),
A great Eliza, but compared with ours,
How vanisheth her glory, wealth, and
   powers.
Profuse, proud Cleopatra[28], whose wrong
   name,
Instead of glory, proved her country's
   shame,
Of her what worth in stories to be seen,
But that she was a rich Egyptian queen.
Zenobya, potent empress of the East,[29]
And of all these without compare the best,
Whom none but great Aurelius could quell;
Yet for our Queen is no fit parallel.
She was a Phoenix queen, so shall she be,
Her ashes not revived, more Phoenix she.
Her personal perfections, who would tell
Must dip his pen in th' Heleconian well,[30]
Which I may not, my pride doth but aspire
To read what others write and so admire.
Now say, have women worth? or have they
   none?
Or had they some, but with our Queen is't
   gone?
Nay masculines, you have thus taxed us
   long,

But she, though dead, will vindicate our
   wrong.
Let such as say our sex is void of reason,
Know 'tis a slander now but once was
   treason.
But happy England which had such a queen;
Yea happy, happy, had those days still been.
But happiness lies in a higher sphere,
Then wonder not Eliza moves not here.
Full fraught with honour, riches and with
   days
She set, she set, like Titan in his rays.[31]
No more shall rise or set so glorious sun
Until the heaven's great revolution;[32]
If then new things their old forms shall
   retain,
Eliza shall rule Albion[33] once again.

Her Epitaph

Here sleeps the queen, this is the royal bed
Of th' damask rose, sprung from the white
   and red,[34]
Whose sweet perfume fills the all-filling air.
This rose is withered, once so lovely fair.
On neither tree did grow such rose before,
The greater was our gain, our loss the more.

Another

Here lies the pride of queens, pattern of
   kings,
So blaze it, Fame, here's feathers for thy
   wings.

---

[26]   The site on the banks of the Thames where, according to some reports, in 1588 Elizabeth, dressed in a silver breast-plate like the fierce female warriors known as Amazons, led the English troops who were mustering in anticipation of an invasion from Spain.

[27]   Queen of Carthage. The Roman poet Virgil (70–19 BC) in Book IV of his *Aeneid* tells of the tragic love between Dido and Aeneas, the Trojan hero who survives the fall of Troy. When he sailed away on the instructions of Jupiter to found Rome, Dido killed herself.

[28]   Renowned queen of Egypt (69–30 BC) driven from her throne by her brother, but reestablished by Julius Ceasar, her powerful lover. After his death, she and Mark Anthony tried to win back Egypt but were defeated at the battle of Actium. After Antony's death, Cleopatra killed herself with an asp. In Greek "Cleopatra" means "glory to the father," which Bradstreet extends to mean "fatherland" or country.

[29]   Queen of Palmyra in Syria, who claimed the title "Queen

of the East," was defeated by the Roman emperor Aurelian and taken prisoner in AD 273.

[30]   A spring on Mount Helicon in Bœotia, sacred to the Muses and thus a source of poetic inspiration.

[31]   Titan was called the sun or Helios by Latin poets.

[32]   The coming of the new world described in the Book of Revelation: "And I saw a new heaven and a new earth: for the first heaven and the first earth were passed away" (Revelation 21:1).

[33]   Ancient name for England.

[34]   A reference to Elizabeth's genealogy. Her father, Henry VIII (1491–1547), was a descendant of the House of Lancaster, symbolized by the red rose. Her mother, Anne Boleyn (1507?–36), was from the House of York, symbolized by the white rose. The two houses fought for many years, but are brought together, Bradstreet suggests, in the damask rose, a combination of the white and red.

Here lies the envied, yet unparalleled
   prince,
Whose living virtues speak (though dead
   long since).

If many worlds, as that fantastic framed,
In every one be her great glory famed.

1650

The Author to her Book[1]

Thou ill-formed offspring of my feeble brain,
Who after birth didst by my side remain,
Till snatched from thence by friends, less wise than true,
Who thee abroad, exposed to public view,
Made thee in rags, halting to th' press to trudge,
Where errors were not lessened (all may judge).
At thy return my blushing was not small,
My rambling brat (in print) should mother call,
I cast thee by as one unfit for light,
Thy visage was so irksome in my sight;
Yet being mine own, at length affection would
Thy blemishes amend, if so I could:
I washed thy face, but more defects I saw,
And rubbing off a spot still made a flaw.
I stretched they joints to make thee even feet,[2]
Yet still thou run'st more hobbling than is meet;
In better dress to trim thee was my mind,
But nought save homespun cloth i' th' house I find.
In this array 'mongst vulgars[3] may'st thou roam.
In critic's hands beware thou dost not come,
And take thy way where yet thou art not known;
If for thy father asked, say thou hadst none;
And for thy mother, she alas is poor,
Which caused her thus to send thee out of door.

1678

The Flesh and the Spirit

In secret place where once I stood
Close by the banks of Lacrim[1] flood,
I heard two sisters reason on
Things that are past and things to come;

One Flesh was called, who had her eye
On worldly wealth and vanity;
The other spirit, who did rear
Her thoughts unto a higher sphere:

---

[1] Bradstreet's poems were taken to London by her brother-in-law and published there in 1650 without her knowledge. This poem was written around 1666 when she was considering a second edition of *The Tenth Muse.*

[2] A pun on the metrical feet of poetry; her attempt to regularize the lines.

[3] Common people.

FLESH AND SPIRIT
[1] *Lacrima* is Latin for "tear."

Sister, quoth Flesh, what liv'st thou on,
Nothing but meditation?
Doth contemplation feed thee so
Regardlessly to let earth go?
Can speculation satisfy
Notion[2] without reality?
Dost dream of things beyond the moon,
And dost thou hope to dwell there soon?
Hast treasures there laid up in store
That all in th' world thou count'st but poor?
Art fancy sick, or turned a sot[3]
To catch at shadows which are not?
Come, come, I'll show unto thy sense
Industry hath its recompense.
What canst desire, but thou may'st see
True substance in variety?
Dost honour like? Acquire the same
As some to their immortal fame
And trophies to thy name erect
Which wearing time shall ne'er deject
For riches doth thou long full sore?
Behold enough of precious store.
Earth hath more silver, pearls, and gold,
Than eyes can see or hands can hold.
Affect's thou pleasure? Take thy fill,
Earth hath enough of what you will.
Then let not go, what thou may'st find
For things unknown, only in mind.

Spirit. Be still thou unregenerate[4] part,
Disturb no more my settled heart,
For I have vowed (and so will do)
Thee as a foe still to pursue.
And combat with thee will and must,
Until I see thee laid in th' dust.
Sisters we are, yea, twins we be,
Yet deadly feud 'twixt thee and me;
For from one father are we not,
Thou by old Adam wast begot,
But my arise is from above,
Whence my dear Father I do love

Thou speak'st me fair, but hat'st me sore,
Thy flatt'ring shows I'll trust no more.
How oft thy slave, hast thou me made,
When I believed what thou hast said,
And never had more cause of woe
Than when I did what thou bad'st do.
I'll stop mine ears at these thy charms,
And count them for my deadly harms.
Thy sinful pleasures I do hate,
Thy riches are to me no bait,
Thine honours do, nor will I love;
For my ambition lies above.
My greatest honour it shall be
When I am victor over thee,
And triumph shall with laurel head,[5]
When thou my captive shall be led,
How I do live, thou need'st not scoff,
For I have meat thou know'st not of;[6]
The hidden manna[7] I do eat,
The word of life it is my meat.
My thoughts do yield me more content
Than can thy hours in pleasure spent.
Nor are they shadows which I catch,
Nor fancies vain at which I snatch,
But reach at things that are so high,
Beyond thy dull capacity;
Eternal substance I do see,
With which enriched I would be.
Mine eye doth pierce the heavens and see
What is invisible to thee.
My garments are not silk nor gold,
Nor such trash which earth doth hold,
But royal robes I shall have on,
More glorious than the glist'ring sun;
My crown not diamonds, pearls, and gold,
But such as angels' heads enfold.
The city where I hope to dwell,[8]
There's none on earth can parallel;
The stately walls both high and strong,
Are made of precious jasper stone;
The gates of pearl, both rich and clear,

---

[2]   Knowledge, from the Latin *notio.*
[3]   Fool.
[4]   Unrepentant, unsaved.
[5]   A crown of laurel, which in ancient Greece was a sign of honor for poets, athletes, and heroes.
[6]   See John 4:32.
[7]   Food sent by God to the Hebrews who had escaped bond-

age in Egypt and wandered forty years in the desert (Exodus 16:15). Spiritual "hidden manna" is promised to the redeemed (Revelation 2:17).
[8]   The next twenty-one lines paraphrase the description of the heavenly city of the New Jerusalem in Revelation 21:10–27, 22:1–5.

And angels are for porters there;
The streets thereof transparent gold,
Such as no eye did e'er behold;
A crystal river there doth run,
Which doth proceed from the Lamb's
    throne.
Of life, there are the waters sure,
Which shall remain forever pure,
Nor sun, nor moon, they have no need,
For glory doth from God proceed.

No candle there, nor yet torchlight,
For there shall be no darksome night.
From sickness and infirmity
For evermore they shall be free;
Nor withering age shall e're come there,
But beauty shall be bright and clear;
This city pure is not for thee,
For things unclean there shall not be.
If I of heaven may have my fill,
Take thou the world and all that will.

                                    1678

To My Dear and Loving Husband

If ever two were one, then surely we.
If ever man were loved by wife, then thee;
If ever wife was happy in a man,
Compare with me, ye women, if you can.
I prize thy love more than whole mines of gold
Or all the riches that the East doth hold.
My love is such that rivers cannot quench,
Nor ought but love from thee, give recompense.
Thy love is such I can no way repay,
The heavens reward thee manifold, I pray.
Then while we live, in love let's so persevere
That when we live no more, we may live ever.

                                    1678

In Memory of My Dear Grandchild Elizabeth Bradstreet, Who Deceased August, 1665, Being a Year and a Half Old

Farewell dear babe, my heart's too much content,
Farewell sweet babe, the pleasure of mine eye,
Farewell fair flower that for a space was lent,
Then ta'en away unto eternity.
Blest babe, why should I once bewail thy fate,
Or sigh thy days so soon were terminate,
Sith[1] thou art settled in an everlasting state.

2

By nature trees do rot when they are grown,
And plums and apples thoroughly ripe do fall,
And corn and grass are in their season mown,

---

[1] Since.

And time brings down what is both strong and tall.
But plants new set to be eradicate,
And buds new blown to have so short a date,
Is by His hand alone that guides nature and fate.

1678

Upon the Burning of Our House, July 10th, 1666

[Copied out of a Loose Paper]

In silent night when rest I took
For sorrow near I did not look
I wakened was with thund'ring noise
And piteous shrieks of dreadful voice.
That fearful sound of "Fire" and "Fire!"
Let no man know is my desire.
I, starting up, the light did spy,
And to my God my heart did cry
To strengthen me in my distress
And not to leave me succourless.
Then, coming out, beheld a space
The flame consume my dwelling place.
And when I could no longer look,
I blest His name that gave and took,[1]
That laid my goods now in the dust.
Yea, so it was, and so 'twas just.
It was His own, it was not mine,
Far be it that I should repine;
He might of all justly bereft
But yet sufficient for us left.
When by the ruins oft I past
My sorrowing eyes aside did cast,
And here and there the places spy
Where oft I sat and long did lie:
Here stood that trunk, and there that chest.
There lay that store I counted best.
My pleasant things in ashes lie,
And them behold no more shall I.

Under thy roof no guest shall sit,
Nor at thy table eat a bit.
No pleasant tale shall e'er be told,
Nor things recounted done of old.
No candle e'er shall shine in thee,
Nor bridegroom's voice e'er heard shall be.
In silence ever shall thou lie,
Adieu, Adieu, all's vanity.
Then straight I 'gin my heart to chide,
And did thy wealth on earth abide?
Didst fix thy hope on mould'ring dust?
The arm of flesh didst make thy trust?
Raise up thy thoughts above the sky
That dunghill mists away may fly.
Thou hast an house on high erect,
Framed by that mighty Architect,
With glory richly furnished,
Stands permanent though this be fled.
It's purchased and paid for too
By Him who hath enough to do.
A price so vast as is unknown
Yet by His gift is made thine own;
There's wealth enough, I need no more,
Farewell, my pelf,[2] farewell my store.
The world no longer let me love,
My hope and treasure lies above.

1666

1867

To My Dear Children

My dear children,
I, knowing by experience that the exhortations of parents take most effect when the speakers

---

[1] "The Lord gave, and the Lord hath taken away; blessed be the name of the Lord" (Job 1:21).

[2] Possessions, illicitly gained.

leave to speak,[1] and those especially sink deepest which are spoke latest, and being ignorant whether on my death bed I shall have opportunity to speak to any of you, much less to all, thought it the best, whilst I was able, to compose some short matters (for what else to call them I know not) and bequeath to you, that when I am no more with you, yet I may be daily in your remembrance (although that is the least in my aim in what I now do), but that you may gain some spiritual advantage by my experience. I have not studied in this you read to show my skill, but to declare the truth, not to set forth myself, but the glory of God. If I had minded the former, it had been perhaps better pleasing to you, but seeing the last is the best, let it be best pleasing to you.

The method I will observe shall be this: I will begin with God's dealing with me from my childhood to this day.

In my young years, about 6 or 7 as I take it, I began to make conscience of my ways, and what I knew was sinful, as lying, disobedience to parents, etc., I avoided it. If at any time I was overtaken with the like evils, it was as a great trouble, and I could not be at rest till by prayer I had confessed it unto God. I was also troubled at the neglect of private duties though too often tardy that way. I also found much comfort in reading the Scriptures, especially those places I thought most concerned my condition, and as I grew to have more understanding, so the more solace I took in them.

In a long fit of sickness which I had on my bed I often communed with my heart and made my supplication to the most High who set me free from that affliction.

But as I grew up to be about 14 or 15, I found my heart more carnal[2], and sitting loose from God, vanity and the follies of youth take hold of me.

About 16, the Lord laid His hand sore upon me and smote me with the smallpox. When I was in my affliction, I besought the Lord and confessed my pride and vanity, and He was entreated of me and again restored me. But I rendered not to Him according to the benefit received.

After a short time I changed my condition and was married, and came into this country, where I found a new world and new manners, at which my heart rose. But after I was convinced it was the way of God, I submitted to it and joined to the church at Boston.

After some time I fell into a lingering sickness like a consumption together with a lameness, which correction I saw the Lord sent to humble and try me and do me good, and it was not altogether ineffectual.

It pleased God to keep me a long time without a child, which was a great grief to me and cost me many prayers and tears before I obtained one, and after him gave me many more of whom I now take the care, that as I have brought you into the world, and with great pains, weakness, cares, and fears brought you to this, I now travail[3] in birth again of you till Christ be formed in you.

Among all my experiences of God's gracious dealings with me, I have constantly observed this, that He hath never suffered me long to sit loose from Him, but by one affliction or other hath made me look home, and search what was amiss; so usually thus it hath been with me that I have no sooner felt my heart out of order, but I have expected correction for it, which most commonly hath been upon my own person in sickness, weakness, pains, sometimes on my soul, in doubts and fears of God's displeasure and my sincerity towards Him; sometimes He hath smote a child with a sickness, sometimes chastened by losses in estate[4], and these times (through His great mercy) have been the times of my greatest getting and advantage;

---

[1]   Stop speaking, leave off.
[2]   Interested in worldly, material things.

[3]   Labor, now in the spiritual sense.
[4]   Wealth.

yea, I have found them the times when the Lord hath manifested the most love to me. Then have I gone to searching and have said with David, "Lord, search me and try me, see what ways of wickedness are in me, and lead me in the way everlasting,"[5] and seldom or never but I have found either some sin I lay under which God would have reformed, or some duty neglected which He would have performed, and by His help I have laid vows and bonds upon my soul to perform His righteous commands.

If at any time you are chastened of God, take it as thankfully and joyfully as in greatest mercies, for if ye be His, ye shall reap the greatest benefit by it. It hath been no small support to me in times of darkness when the Almighty hath hid His face from me that yet I have had abundance of sweetness and refreshment after affliction and more circumspection in my walking after I have been afflicted. I have been with God like an untoward child, that no longer than the rod has been on my back (or at least in sight) but I have been apt to forget Him and myself, too. Before I was afflicted, I went astray, but now I keep Thy statutes.[6]

I have had great experience of God's hearing my prayers and returning comfortable answers to me, either in granting the thing I prayed for, or else in satisfying my mind without it, and I have been confident it hath been from Him, because I have found my heart through His goodness enlarged in thankfulness to Him.

I have often been perplexed that I have not found that constant joy in my pilgrimage and refreshing which I supposed most of the servants of God have, although He hath not left me altogether without the witness of His holy spirit, who hath oft given me His word and set to His seal that it shall be well with me. I have sometimes tasted of that hidden manna that the world knows not,[7] and have set up my Ebenezer[8], and have resolved with myself that against such a promise, such tastes of sweetness, the gates of hell shall never prevail; yet have I many times sinkings and droopings, and not enjoyed that felicity that sometimes I have done. But when I have been in darkness and seen no light, yet have I desired to stay myself upon the Lord, and when I have been in sickness and pain, I have thought if the Lord would but lift up the light of His countenance upon me, although He ground me to powder, it would be but light to me; yea, oft have I thought were I in hell itself and could there find the love of God toward me, it would be a heaven. And could I have been in heaven without the love of God, it would have been a hell to me, for in truth it is the absence and presence of God that makes heaven or hell.

Many times hath Satan troubled me concerning the verity of the Scriptures, many times by atheism how I could know whether there was a God; I never saw any miracles to confirm me, and those which I read of, how did I know but they were feigned? That there is a God my reason would soon tell me by the wondrous works that I see, the vast frame of the heaven and the earth, the order of all things, night and day, summer and winter, spring and autumn, the daily providing for this great household upon the earth, the preserving and directing of all to its proper end. The consideration of these things would with amazement certainly resolve me that there is an Eternal Being. But how should I know He is such a God as I worship in Trinity, and such a Saviour as I rely upon? Though this hath thousands of times been suggested to me, yet God hath helped me over. I have argued thus with myself. That there is a God, I see. If ever this God hath revealed himself, it must be in His word, and this must be it or none. Have I not found that operation by it that no human invention can work upon the

---

[5]   David, the Psalmist and King of Israel. See Psalm 139: 23–4.

[6]   Psalm 119:8.

[7]   Manna was the food sent by God to the Hebrews when they were wandering in the desert. The saints are promised "hidden manna," or spiritual food in Revelation 2:17.

[8]   A stone monument commemorating a victory over the Philistines (1 Samuel 7:12).

soul, hath not judgments befallen divers who have scorned and contemned it, hath it not been preserved through all ages maugre[9] all the heathen tyrants and all of the enemies who have opposed it? Is there any story but that which shows the beginnings of times, and how the world came to be as we see? Do we not know the prophecies in it fulfilled which could not have been so long foretold by any but God Himself?

When I have got over this block, then have I another put in my way, that admit this be the true God whom we worship, and that be his word, yet why may not the Popish religion be the right? They have the same God, the same Christ, the same word. They only enterpret it one way, we another.

This hath sometimes stuck with me, and more it would, but the vain fooleries that are in their religion together with their lying miracles and cruel persecutions of the saints, which admit were they as they term them, yet not so to be dealt withal.

The consideration of these things and many the like would soon turn me to my own religion again.

But some new troubles I have had since the world has been filled with blasphemy and sectaries[10], and some who have been accounted sincere Christians have been carried away with them, that sometimes I have said, "Is there faith upon the earth?" and I have not known what to think; but then I have remembered the works of Christ that so it must be, and if it were possible, the very elect should be deceived. "Behold," saith our Saviour, "I have told you before." That hath stayed my heart, and I can now say, "Return, O my Soul, to thy rest, upon this rock Christ Jesus will I build my faith, and if I perish, I perish;" but I know all the Powers of Hell shall never prevail against it. I know whom I have trusted, and whom I have believed, and that He is able to keep that I have committed to His charge.

Now to the King, immortal, eternal and invisible, the only wise God, be honour, and glory for ever and ever, Amen.

This was written in much sickness and weakness, and is very weakly and imperfectly done, but if you can pick any benefit out of it, it is the mark which I aimed at.

1867

The New England Primer (1683?)

Puritan culture was quintessentially a literate culture. From its inception, the Protestant Reformation embraced Martin Luther's notion of "the priesthood of all believers" – that everyone, high or low, male or female, young or old, was expected to work out his or her salvation individually. Ministers and teachers would act as intermediaries, but a crucial feature of Protestant devotion was private meditation and soul-searching, a large component of which comprised reading the word of God. The Puritans who came to the New World carried with them a need for widespread literacy, especially in a vernacular language, the prevention of which they regarded as the work of Satan or demonic, Latin-spewing papists. As early as 1647, the General Court of the Massachusetts Bay Colony made literacy the responsibility of local townships, hoping to reverse, as they said, "one cheife piect of ye ould deluder, Satan, to keepe men from the knowledge of ye Scriptures, as in former times by keeping them

---

9 In spite of.
10 Members of religious sects; from the Puritan perspective, heretics.

in an unknown tongue . . ." They were also vitally concerned with the transmission of their hard-won values, "that learning may not be buried in ye grave of our fathers in ye church and commonwealth." Sheer reading ability without "proper" understanding could result in a plethora of beliefs that would undermine social solidarity and cultural stability. Such a centrifugal tendency was the inevitable result of most dissenting movements, and was already much in evidence in the early New England colonies, where individual churches drafted their own covenants for members, and every minister penned his own catechism for teaching his congregation. To combat these democratizing and individualist tendencies, the *New England Primer* came into being.

"Primers," or books of primary instruction, containing the Ten Commandments, the Lord's Prayer, some Psalms and other articles of Christian belief, date back to the invention of printing. Eventually, they tied instruction in the alphabet to the learning of basic religious precepts. In New England, the *Primer*, along with a Bible and *The Bay Psalme Book* (1640), were the books most commonly owned. Between 1680 and 1830, an estimated six to eight million copies of the *Primer* were printed, some under regional titles or, after 1776, under national titles like *The American Primer* or *The Columbian Primer*, all of which had less success than the original.

Despite its popularity, however, both the author and the date of the first appearance of the *New England Primer* are still a mystery. The first mention of the ubiquitous hornbook is in the Stationer's Register of London in October 1683, but the oldest extant copy, from which the following selections come, was printed in Boston in 1727. Some historians attribute its authorship to Benjamin Harris, a London bookseller and ardent Protestant with a penchant for scribbling verse who set up shop in Boston in 1686. In London, Harris had printed the *Protestant Tutor*, a precursor of the *New England Primer* that contained its essential features: an Alphabet, the Syllabarium, the Alphabet of Lessons, the Lord's Prayer, Creed, Ten Commandments, the poem and picture of the martyred John Rogers, and the names of the Books of the Bible. The *New England Primer* also included a Catechism, which was either a simplified version of the Westminster Assembly's "Shorter Catechism," a series of questions and answers about Protestant doctrine,

or an even shorter version by the esteemed Boston minister, John Cotton, entitled "Spiritual Milk for American Babes," which first appeared separately in 1641. A final component was "A Dialogue between Christ, Youth, and the Devil," a poetical treatment of the temptation of a young man and his ultimate fall.

It is fair to say that the Puritan ideals embodied in the *Primer* shaped the early northern colonies, molding children from the earliest ages, as well as servants, apprentices, and Native American converts learning to read English, into an orderly, pious conformity that embodied the values of its predecessors. It taught first and foremost the "equality" of sin: "In *Adam's* Fall, We Sinned all," as the first rhyme of the picture alphabet famously intoned. But comfort immediately appeared, and it was, not surprisingly, offered by a religiously inflected literacy: "Thy Life to Mend, This *Book* Attend." This sentiment is reinforced by the most famous part of the *Primer*, the poem by John Rogers, who was the first and best known of the Protestant martyrs of Queen Mary's reign. Illustrating the poem is a woodcut of the martyr burning at the stake, "His Wife, with nine small Children, and one at her Breast," looking dolefully on. Dying "with wonderful Patience," Rogers rehearses the tenets of his Protestant faith for his children, "That you may read and understand, and keep it in your mind." He exhorts them to "Lay up [God's] Laws within your heart, and print them in your thought."

Acquisition, apprehension, inculcation, and transmission of the basic truths and values as the Puritans saw them were goals the *Primer* was designed to meet. Nor was this a static vehicle of cultural conditioning. The contents of the *Primer* changed with the times, including Watts' Songs for Children in the revivalist period and political material in the revolutionary period. Around 1790, the content underwent a marked secularization, and soon the religious aspects of the *Primer* were dropped. Although an edition was printed as late as 1886, the schoolbook that shaped the nation's beginnings had gone, some would say thankfully, out of style.

PRIMARY WORK

The New England Primer, 1683? (facsimile reprint of the earliest known edition (1727) 1897, 1962).
The New England Primer Enlarged, 1687.

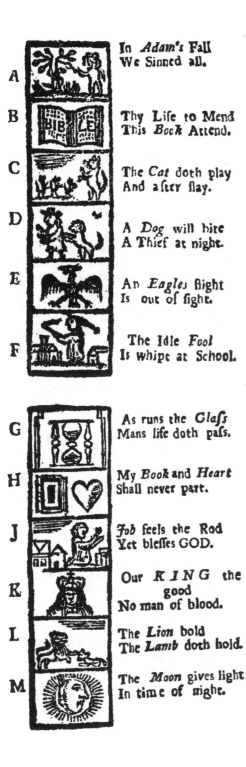

A — In *Adam's* Fall
We Sinned all.

B — Thy Life to Mend
This *Book* Attend.

C — The *Cat* doth play
And after flay.

D — A *Dog* will bite
A Thief at night.

E — An *Eagles* flight
Is out of fight.

F — The Idle *Fool*
Is whipt at School.

G — As runs the *Glafs*
Mans life doth pafs.

H — My *Book* and *Heart*
Shall never part.

J — *Job* feels the Rod
Yet bleffes GOD.

K — Our *KING* the good
No man of blood.

L — The *Lion* bold
The *Lamb* doth hold.

M — The *Moon* gives light
In time of night.

N — *Nightingales* fing
In Time of Spring.

O — The *Royal Oak*
it was the Tree
That fav'd His
Royal Majeftie.

P — *Peter* denies
His Lord and cries.

Q — Queen *Efther* comes
in Royal State
To Save the JEWS
from difmal Fate

R — *Rachol* doth mourn
For her firft born.

S — *Samuel* anoints
Whom God appoints

T — *Time* cuts down all
Both great and fmall.

U — *Uriah's* beauteous Wife
Made *David* feek his
Life.

W — *Whales* in the Sea
God's Voice obey.

X — *Xerxes* the great did
die,
And fo muft you & I.

Y — *Youth* forward flips
Death fooneft nips.

Z — *Zacheus* he
Did climb the Tree
His Lord to fee.

Now the Child being entred in his Letters and Spelling, let him learn these and such like Sentences by Heart, whereby he will be both instructed in his Duty, and encouraged in his Learning.

The Dutiful Child's Promises,

I Will fear GOD, and honour the KING.
I will honour my Father & Mother.
I will Obey my Superiours.
I will Submit to my Elders.
I will Love my Friends.
I will hate no Man.
I will forgive my Enemies, and pray to God for them.
I will as much as in me lies keep all God's Holy Commandments.

I will learn my Catechism.
I will keep the Lord's Day Holy.
I will Reverence God's Sanctuary,
For our GOD is a consuming Fire.

An Alphabet of Lessons for Youth.

A Wise Son makes a glad Father, but a foolish Son is the heaviness of his Mother.

B Etter is a little with the fear of the Lord, than great treasure and trouble therewith.

C Ome unto CHRIST all ye that labour and are heavy laden, and He will give you rest.

D O not the abominable thing which I hate, saith the Lord.

E Xcept a Man be born again, he cannot see the Kingdom of God.

F Oolishness is bound up in the heart of a Child, but the rod of Correction shall drive it far from him.

G Rieve not the Holy Spirit.

H Oliness becomes God's House for ever.

I T is good for me to draw near unto God.

K Eep thy Heart with all Diligence, for out of it are the issues of Life.

L Iars shall have their part in the lake which burns with fire and brimstone.

M Any are the Afflictions of the Righteous, but the Lord delivers them out of them all.

N OW is the accepted time, now is the day of Salvation.

O Ut of the abundance of the heart the mouth speaketh.

P Ray to thy Father which is in secret, and thy Father which sees in secret, shall reward thee openly.

Q Uit you like Men, be strong, stand fast in the Faith.

R Emember thy Creator in the days of thy Youth.

S Alvation belongeth to the Lord.

T Rust in God at all times ye people, pour out your hearts before him.

U Pon the wicked God shall rain an horrible Tempest.

W O to the wicked, it shall be ill with him, for the reward of his hands shall be given him.

E X Hort one another daily while is is called to day, lest any of you be hardened through the deceitfulness of Sin.

Y Oung Men ye have overcome the wicked one.

Z Eal hath consumed me, because thy enemies have forgotten the words of God.   *Choice Sentences.*

1. Praying will make thee leave sinning, or sinning will make thee leave praying.

2. Our Weakness and Inabilities break not the bond of our Duties.

3. What we are afraid to speak before Men, we should be afraid to think before God.

MR. *John Rogers*, Minifter of the Gofpel in *London*, was the firft Martyr in Q. *Mary's* Reign, and was burnt at *Smithfield, Febru:any* the fourteenth, 1554. His Wife, with nine fmall Children, and one

at her Breaft, following him to the Stake, with which forrowful fight he was not in the leaft daunted, but with wonderful Patience died couragioufly for the Gofpel of Jefus Chrift.

Some few Days before his Death, he writ the following Exhortation to his Children.

Give ear my Children to my words,
 whom God hath dearly bought,
Lay up his Laws within your heart,
 and print them in your thought,
I leave you here a little Book,
 for you to look upon;
That you may fee your Fathers face,
 when he is dead and gone.
Who for the hope of heavenly things,
 while he did here remain,
Gave over all his golden Years.
 to Prifon and to Pain.
Where I among my Iron Bands,
 inclofed in the dark,

Not many days before my Death.
 I did compofe this Work.
And for Example to your Youth,
 to whom I wifh all good;
I fend you here God's perfect Truth,
 and feel it with my Blood.
To you my Heirs of earthly Things,
 which I do leave behind,
That you may read and underftand,
 and keep it in your mind.
That as you have been Heirs of that
 which once fhall wear away,
You alfo may poffefs that part,
 which never fhall decay.
Keep always GOD before your eyes
 with all your whole intent;
Commit no Sin in any wife,
 keep his Commandement.
Abhor that arrant Whore of Rome,
 and all her Blafphemies;
And drink not of her cursed Cup,
 obey not her decrees.
Give honour to your Mother dear,
 remember well her pain;

And recompenfe her in her Age
 with the like love again.
Be always ready for her help,
 and let her not decay;
Remember well your Father all
 that fhould have been your ftay.
Give of your Portion to the Poor,
 as Riches do arife;
And from the needy naked Soul
 turn not away your eyes.
For he that doth not hear the cry
 of thofe that ftand in need,
Shall cry himfelf and not be heard,
 when he does hope to fpeed.
If GOD hath given you increafe
 and bleffed well your ftore,
Remember you are put in truft,
 and fhould relieve the poor.
Beware of feul and filthy Lufts,
 let fuch things have no place,
Keep clean your Veffels in the Lord,
 that he may you embrace.
Ye are the Temples of the Lord,
 for you are dearly bought.

And they that do defile the fame
shall surely come to nought.
Be never Proud by any means,
build not thy house too high,
But always have before your eyes,
that you are born to die.
Defraud not him that hired is,
your labour to sustain;
And pay him still without delay,
his wages for his pain.
And as you would another Man
against you should proceed,
Do you the same to them again.
if they do stand in need.
Impart your Fortion to the Poor,
in Money and in Meat,
And send the feeble fainting Soul
of that which you do eat.
Ask Counsel always of the wise,
give ear unto the end,
And ne'r refuse the sweet rebuke
of him that is thy Friend.
Be always thankful to the Lord,
with Prayer and with Praise,

Begging of him to bless your work,
and to direct your ways.
Seek first I say the living GOD,
and always him adore;
And then be sure that he will bless
your basket and your store.
And I beseech Almighty GOD,
replenish you with Grace,
That I may meet you in the Heav'ns,
and see you face to face.
And tho' the Fire my Body burns,
contrary to my kind;
That I cannot enjoy your love,
according to my mind.
Yet I do hope that when the Heav'ns,
shall vanish like a scrowl,
I shall see you in perfect shape,
in Body and in Soul,
And that I may enjoy your love,
and you enjoy the Land
I do beseech the living LORD
to hold you in his hand.
Though here my Body be adjudg'd
in flaming Fire to fry,

My Soul I trust will straight ascend,
to live with GOD on high.
What though this Carcase smart a while,
what though this Life decay,
My Soul I trust will be with GOD,
and live with him for aye.
I know I am a Sinner born,
from the Original;
And that I do deserve to die,
by my Fore-Fathers fall.
But by our Saviour's precious Blood,
which on the Cross was spilt,
Who freely offer'd up his Life,
to save our Souls from Guilt,
I hope Redemption I shall have,
and all that in him trust;
When I shall see him face to face,
and live among the Just.
Why then should I fear Deaths grim look,
since Christ for me did die?
For King and Cæsar, Rich and Poor,
the force of Death, must trie.
When I am chained to the Stake,
and Faggots girt me round,

Then pray the Lord my Soul in Heav'n
may be with Glory crown'd.
Come welcome Death, the end of fears,
I am prepar'd to die;
Those earthly Flames will send my Soul,
up to the Lord on high.
Farewel my Children to the World,
where you must yet remain;
The Lord of Host be your defence
till we do meet again.
Farewel my true and loving Wife,
my Children and my Friends,
I hope in Heaven to see you all,
when all things have their ends
If you go on to serve the Lord,
as you have now begun,
You shall walk safely all your days,
until your life be done.
GOD grant you so to end your days,
as he shall think it best,
That I may meet you in the Heav'ns,
where I do hope to rest.

FURTHER READING

Paul Leicester Ford (ed) *The New-England Primer: A History of its Origins and Development* (New York: Dodd, Mead and Company; 1897, rpt. 1962).

George Livermore, *The Origin, History, and Character of the New England Primer* (New York: C.F. Heartman, 1915).

David Watters, "'I Spake as a Child': Authority, Metaphor and The New-England Primer," *Early American Literature*, Winter, 20, 3 (1985–6) pp. 193–213.

Elisa New, "'Both Great and Small': Adult Proportion and Divine Scale in Edward Taylor's 'Preface' and The New-England Primer," *Early American Literature*, 28, 2 (1993) pp. 120–32.

Benjamin Church (1639–1717)

Benjamin Church's compelling account of his role in the Puritans' second major conflict with the New England Native Americans, Metacom's (or King Philip's) war, created the prototype for the hero of the American frontier myth. His father Robert, who probably came over from England with John Winthrop's fleet in 1630 and settled in Plymouth, fought in the Pequot War (1636–7). Like his father, Church was trained as a carpenter. He married Alice Southworth, whose father was a person of standing in Plymouth and a Proprietor of the company authorized to settle the land at Sakonnet, in what is now southern Rhode Island. Church joined this company, received two lots and built his home on the neck which, he remarks, "was full of Indians," and founded the town of Little Compton. In the years after the war, he played an energetic role in establishing plantations, building churches and schools, and participating in the governments of several towns in the area as constable, deputy, juryman, magistrate, selectman, assessor, and moderator. He also took a commission as a major in the first four Eastern Expeditions against the French and Indians in Nova Scotia and as a colonel in the fifth expedition of 1704. After this last campaign, and under somewhat of a cloud, he retired to Little Compton where, in order to set the record straight, he dictated his memoirs of his earlier military successes to his son Thomas, which were published in Boston in 1716.

The tragic seventeen-month long conflict in which Church played such a crucial role essentially broke the power of Native American resistance to English domination in New England. At the outbreak of violence, in June 1675, there were between 36,000 and 45,000 white settlers in about 110 small plantations in New England and about 20,000 Native Americans. There were also an estimated 4,000 "praying Indians," converts to Christianity living together in "praying towns." Although there had been peace since the end of the Pequot War in 1637 during which both sides made efforts to live together, the growing white population continued to encroach on Indian lands, making the seasonally nomadic Native lifeways impossible. Puritan missionaries continued to fight for and win converts. Massasoit, chief of the Wampanoags, had maintained friendly relations with Plymouth colony from their arrival in 1621 to his death in 1661. However, the Wampanoags were one of the so-called "free" tribes who pledged their allegiance to the English crown, rather than to any colony, and thereby retained the right to dispose of their land as they chose. Needing more land for their expanding settlements, Plymouth tried to compel Wamsutta, eldest son of Massasoit, to grant them sole rights to purchase Wampanoag land. When he died of a fever in their custody, Plymouth authorities hauled in his younger brother and successor, Metacom, renamed Philip.

Although Metacom agreed to their demands, further encroachment during the 1660s – including the area around the Mount Hope peninsula where Church settled – strained Indian tolerance. In 1667 and 1671, Plymouth accused Metacom of plotting against the colonists with other tribes and humiliated him with ever larger fines. When three of Metacom's braves were captured, tried, and executed by the colonists on June 8, 1675 on suspicion that they killed John Sassamon, a converted Indian minister and former secretary to Metacom who had betrayed his plans for resistance to the Plymouth government, the issue of sovereignty came to a head. Wampanoags and their allies began attacking English settlements, and by autumn, the bloodiest conflict in American history began,

which the colonists named, somewhat mislead-
ingly, "King Philip's War."

Church does not analyze cause and effect or give
a general account of the war. Rather, with a crusty
self-reliance, deflationary humor, and penchant for
joking that all come to characterize the frontier
hero, he highlights dramatic incidents in which
he played the leading role. He grows impatient
with the uninformed tactics of the United Colonies, whose leaders initially reject his strategy for
defeating Metacom. When they finally commission him to train a small band of white rangers
and allow him to enlist friendly Indians from whom
he learns how to meet other Indians in battle, they
pay him and his men a pittance. Although Church
often invokes divine providence as his shield and
protection, he has an uneasy relation with Puritan
orthodoxy. Unlike the "official" *apologias* by
William Hubbard and Increase Mather, which were
rushed into print to justify the destructive war,
Church's account was written from notes and recollections almost forty years after the events. In
this later historical moment, his unorthodox representation of the war gained a widespread audience.

The official chroniclers, and later on, Cotton
Mather who lionized Church as a Puritan hero, saw
the war first as the punishment of a God angry
with his backsliding chosen people, and later as a
didactic moral fable. By contrast, Church experienced the war first hand in the field where his prag-
matism and humor, rather than state policy and
self-righteousness, were often the wisest course.
Even his original title, "Entertaining Passages Relating to Philip's War" suggests excitement and
amusement, not edification. Unlike many of the
soldiers who fought in the war, he chose to live in
the wilderness among Native Americans whom he
regarded not as a group to be proselytized or
demonized, but as individual friends with whom
he was intimate – and valiant enemies whom he
respected. This almost unique attitude led to his
military accomplishments, but as happens in many
of the later frontier stories, especially Cooper's
Leatherstocking Tales, this very success helped to
destroy the Native culture he embraced. Because
he parleyed honestly with the squaw-sachem
Awashonks (whom some commentators claim was

his mistress), her warriors pledged their loyalty to
him and to Plymouth. He prepared the campaign
and ambush that defeated Metacom, and ordered
his grisly execution in the field. Although the destruction of this "wild beast king" was the climax
for writers like Hubbard and Mather, Church
downplays it. The climax of his account is his own
brilliant outwitting of Metacom's wily captain,
Annawon, who rewards Church with the prize of
Metacom's regalia. This dramatic scene not only
captures the dignity and pathos of the Wampanoag
defeat, but enacts the metaphorical transfer of
Metacom's power to the white man who outdid
him. Ironically, this symbolic inheritance of Native power insures the destruction of the land
and peoples that turned the restless settler into
an "American" hero. Although Church often acts
independently of either white or Native morality,
his exploits helped to firmly entrench Puritan
dominance in the region. In a further irony, like
Mary Rowlandson's contemporary narrative describing her captivity during Philip's War,
Church's "diary," which had been out of print since
1716, was reissued in the 1770s as inspiration for
a new generation of colonists to raise arms, not
against the "redskins," but against the "redcoats."

PRIMARY WORK

Entertaining Passages Relating to Philip's *War which Began
in the Month of* June, *1675. As Also of Expeditions More
lately made Against the Common Enemy and* Indian *Rebels,
in the Eastern Parts of* New-England: *with Some Account
of the Divine Providence towards Benj. Church Esqr;* by T.
C., 1716.

FURTHER READING

D. E. Leach, *Flintlock and Tomahawk* (New York:
Macmillan, 1958).

Richard Slotkin, *So Dreadfull a Judgement: Puritan Re-
sponses to King Philip's War* (Hanover: University of
New England Press, 1978).

Russell Bourne, *The Red King's Rebellion: Racial Politics
in New England, 1675–78* (New York: Atheneum,
1990).

Jill Lepore, *The Name of War: King Philip's War and the
Origins of American Identity* (New York: Knopf, 1998).

FROM *ENTERTAINING PASSAGES RELATING TO PHILIP'S WAR*[1]

In the year 1674 Mr Benjamin Church of Duxbury, being providentially at Plymouth in the time of the Court, fell into acquaintance with Captain John Almy, of Rhode Island. Captain Almy with great importunity, invited him to ride with him and view that part of Plymouth Colony that lay next to Rhode Island known then by their Indian names of Pocasset and Sogkonate[2]. . . .

The next spring advancing, while Mr Church was diligently settling his new farm, . . . the rumor of a war between the English and the natives gave check to his projects. People began to be very jealous of the Indians, and indeed they had no small reason to suspect that they had formed a design of war upon the English. Mr Church had it daily suggested to him that the Indians were plotting a bloody design, that Philip, the great Mount-hope sachem[3] was leader therein; and so it proved: he was sending his messengers to all the neighboring sachems to engage them in confederacy with him in the war. . . .

The Great Swamp Fight

And now strong suspicion began to arise of the Narraganset Indians, that they were ill-affected and designed mischief . . . The next winter they began their hostilities upon the English. The United Colonies then agreed to send an army to suppress them, Governor Winslow to command the army.[4] . . . Their next move was to a swamp which the Indians had fortified with a fort.[5] Mr Church rode in the General's guard when the bloody engagement began; but being impatient of being out of the heat of the action, importunately begged leave of the General that he might run down to the assistance of his friends. The General yielded to his request provided he could rally some hands to go with him. Thirty men immediately drew out and followed him. They entered the swamp and passed over the log that was the passage into the fort, where they saw many men and several valiant captains lie slain. Mr Church, spying Captain Gardner of Salem amidst the wigwams in the east end of the fort, made toward him, but on a sudden, while they were looking each other in the face, Captain Gardner settled down. Mr Church stepped to him and, seeing the blood run down his cheek, lifted up his cap, and called him by his name. He looked up in his face, but spoke not a word, being mortally shot through the head. And, observing his wound, Mr Church found the ball entered his head on the side that was next the upland where the English entered the swamp. Upon which, he dispatched information to the General that the best and forwardest of his army that hazarded their lives to enter the fort, upon the muzzle of the enemy's guns, were shot in their backs and killed by them that lay behind. . . .

---

[1]   The text, with slight modification, is from *Diary of King Philip's War, 1675–76 by Colonel Benjamin Church*, Alan and Mary Simpson, eds (Chester, Connecticut: Pequot Press, 1975).

[2]   Another spelling of Sekonit or Sakonnet.

[3]   Metacom was the younger son of Asuhmequn, renamed Massasoit, chief sachem of the Wampanoags. They dubbed him "King Philip" for what they considered his proud ways and tyrannical rule, and named the war after him, although many other powerful New England tribes were involved. Wampanoag territory extended from the middle of

Narragansett Bay to Plymouth, Cape Cod and Martha's Vineyard, with ancestral seats in the Mount Hope area north of Sekonit around Mount Hope Bay, the eastern branch of Narragansett Bay.

[4]   The United Colonies were a loose confederation of Massachusetts, Connecticut, and Plymouth. Josiah Winslow (1629–80), son of the first governor of Plymouth, Edward Winslow. Over a thousand men were recruited for the war.

[5]   The fort was a stockade of logs, reinforced by dense hedge, enclosing five or six acres of upland in the middle of the Great Swamp, and entered by narrow passages across a log.

Reunion with Awashonks[6]

. . . [Church] then ordered Jack[7] to go tell Awashonks that he designed to go up with her in the evening and to lodge in her camp that night. Then, taking some of the Indians with him, he went back to the river to take care of Mr Howland[8]. Mr Church, being a mind to try what metal he was made of, imparted his notion to the Indians that were with him and gave them directions how to act their parts. When he came pretty near the place, he and his Englishmen pretendedly fled, firing on their retreat towards the Indians that pursued them, and they firing as fast after them. Mr Howland, being upon his guard, hearing the guns, and by and by seeing the motion both of the English and Indians, concluded his friends were distressed, was soon on the full career on horseback to meet them, until he, perceiving their laughing, mistrusted the truth. As soon as Mr Church had given him the news, they hasted away to Awashonks.

Upon their arrival, they were immediately conducted to a shelter, open on one side, whither Awashonks and her chiefs soon came and paid their respects. And the multitudes gave shouts as made the heavens to ring. It being now about sunsetting, or near the dusk of the evening, the Netops[9] came running from all quarters laden with the tops of dry pines and the like combustible matter, making a huge pile thereof near Mr Church's shelter, on the open side thereof. But by this time supper was brought in, in three dishes; viz., a curious young bass in one dish, eels and flat fish in a second, and shell fish in a third, but neither bread nor salt to be seen at table.

But by that time supper was over, the mighty pile of pine knots and tops was fired, and all the Indians great and small gathered in a ring around it. Awashonks with the oldest of her people, men and women mixed, kneeling down, made the first ring next the fire, and all the lusty stout men standing up made the next; and then all the rabble in a confused crew surrounded on the outside. Then the chief Captain stepped in between the rings and the fire, with a spear in one hand and a hatchet in the other, danced round the fire, and began to fight with it, making mention of all the several nations and companies of Indians in the country that were enemies to the English. And, at naming of every particular tribe of Indians, he would draw out and fight a new fire-brand, and at his finishing his fight with each particular fire-brand, would bow to him and thank him. And, when he had named all the several nations and tribes, and fought them all, he stuck down his spear and hatchet, and came out; and another stepped in and acted over the same dance, with more fury, if possible, than the first. And, when about half-a-dozen of their chiefs had thus acted their parts, the Captain of the Guard stepped up to Mr Church and told him they were making soldiers for him, and what they had been doing was all one swearing of them, and, having in that manner engaged all the lusty stout men. Awashonks and her chiefs came to Mr Church and told him that now they were all engaged to fight for the English, and he might call forth all, or any of them at any time as he saw occasion to fight the enemy. And presented him with a very fine firelock.

Mr Church accepts their offer, drew out a number of them, and set out next morning before day for Plymouth, where they arrived safe the same day.

---

[6] In June 1676, the United Colonies adopted Church's strategy for fighting the Narragansetts, which was to muster a large army and use friendly Indians as soldiers, and he returned to Sekonit to muster men. While there, he arranged a meeting with Awashonks, a squaw-sachem of the Wampanoags, who, because of his long absence, had allied with Metacom.

[7] Jack Havens, an Indian allied with the colonists who acted as interpreter for Church.

[8] Jabez Howland, another resident of Sekonit and Church's trusted lieutenant.

[9] Algonkian word for "friends." Settlers used it as a greeting and so it came to mean "Indian."

Tactics of Indian Warfare

He soon went out again, and this stroke he drove many weeks. And, when he took any number of prisoners, he would pick out some that he took a fancy to, and would tell them, he took a particular fancy to them and had chose them for himself to make soldiers of; and, if any would behave themselves well, he would do well by them and they should be his men and not sold out of the country. If he perceived they looked surly, and his Indian soldiers called them "treacherous dogs," as some of them would sometimes do, all the notice he would take of it would only be to clap them on the back and tell them, "Come, come, you look wild and surly, and mutter, but that signifies nothing. These, my best soldiers were a little while ago as wild and surly as you are now. By that time you have been but one day along with me, you'll love me too, and be as brisk as any of them."

And it proved so. For there was none of them but, after they had been a little while with him, and seen his behavior, and how cheerful and successful his men were, would be as ready to pilot him to any place where the Indians dwelt or haunted (though their own fathers or nearest relations should be among them), or to fight for him, as any of his own men.

Captain Church was in two particulars much advantaged by the great English army that was now abroad. One was, that they drove the enemy down to that part of the country, viz., to the eastward of Taunton River, by which means his business was nearer home. The other was that whenever he fell on with a push upon any body of the enemy (were they never so many), they fled, expecting the great army. And his manner of marching through the woods was such, as if he were discovered, they appeared to be more than they were. For he always marched at a wide distance, one from another, partly for their safety; and this was an Indian custom, to march thin and scatter. Captain Church enquired of some of the Indians that were become his soldiers, how they got such advantage often of the English in their marches through the woods. They told him that the Indians gained great advantage of the English by two things: the Indians always took care in their marches and fights not to come too thick together. But the English always kept in a heap together; that it was as easy to hit them as to hit an house. The other was, that, if any time they discovered a company of English soldiers in the woods, they knew that there was all, for the English never scattered, but the Indians always divided and scattered. . . .

Philip's Forces Routed Near Bridgewater

Captain Church pursuing, sent Mr Isaac Howland[10], with a party on one side of the swamp, while himself, with the rest, ran on the other side, agreeing to run on each side until they met on the further end, placing some men in secure stands at that end of the swamp where Philip entered, concluding that if they headed him and beat him back, that he would take back in his own track. . . . Many, both men, women, and children of the enemy were imprisoned at this time; while Philip, Tispaquin, Totoson, etc., concluded that the English would pursue them upon their tracks, so were waylaying their tracks at the first end of the swamp, hoping to gain a shot upon Captain Church . . .

But Philip, having waited all this while in vain, now moves on after the rest of his company to see what was become of them. And, by this time, Captain Church was got into the swamp ready to meet him; and, as it happened, made the first discovery, clapped behind a tree until

---

[10]   Younger brother of Jabez Howland and one of the first settlers of Middleborough.

Philip's company came pretty near, and then fired upon them, killed many of them; and a close skirmish followed. Upon this, Philip, having grounds sufficient to suspect the event of his company that went before them, fled back upon his own track and, coming to the place where the ambush lay, they fired on each other, and one Lucas, of Plymouth, not being so careful as he might have been about his stand, was killed by the Indians. . . .

Captain Church drove his prisoners that night into Bridgewater Pound, and set his Indian soldiers to guard them. They, being well treated with victuals and drink, they had a merry night; and the prisoners laughed as loud as the soldiers, not being so treated a long time before.

Some of the Indians now said to Captain Church, "Sir, you have now made Philip ready to die, for you have made him as poor and miserable as he used to make the English, for you have now killed or taken all his relations." That they believed he would now soon have his head, and that this bout had almost broke his heart. . . .

Philip Killed

Then Captain Church offered Captain Golding that he should have the honor (if he would please accept of it) to beat up Philip's headquarters. He accepted the offer and had his alloted number drawn out to him, and the pilot. Captain Church's instructions to him were to be very careful in his approach to the enemy, and be sure not to show himself until by daylight they might see and discern their own men from the enemy. Told him also that his custom in the like cases was to creep with his company on their bellies, until they came as near as they could; and that as soon as the enemy discovered them, they would cry out; and that was the word for his men to fire and fall on. Directed him, when the enemy should start and take into the swamp, they should pursue with speed, every man shouting and making what noise they could; for he would give orders to his ambuscade to fire on any that should come silently.

Captain Church, knowing it was Philip's custom to be foremost in flight, went down to the swamp and gave Captain William of Situate the command of the right wing of the ambush, and placed an Englishman and an Indian together behind such shelters of trees, that he could find and took care to place them at such distance as none might pass undiscovered between them; charged them to be careful of themselves and of hurting their friends; and to fire at any that should come silently through the swamp.

But it being somewhat further through the swamp than he was aware of, he wanted men to make up his ambuscade. Having placed what men he had, he took Major Sanford by the hand, said, "Sir, I have so placed them that 'tis scarce possible Philip should escape them."

The same moment a shot whistled over their heads, and then the noise of a gun towards Philip's camp. Captain Church at first thought it might be some gun fired by accident, but, before he could speak, a whole volley followed, which was earlier than he expected. One of Philip's gang going forth to ease himself, when he had done, looked round him, and Captain Golding thought the Indian looked right at him (though probably 'twas but his conceit), so fired at him, and, upon his firing, the whole company that were with him fired upon the enemy's shelter before the Indians had time to rise from their sleep, and so overshot them. But their shelter was open on that side next the swamp, built so on purpose for the convenience of flight on occasion. They were soon in the swamp, and Philip the foremost, who, starting at the first gun, threw his petunk[11] and powder horn over his head, catched up his gun, and ran as fast as he could scamper, without any more clothes than his small breeches and stockings, and

---

[11]   Pouch in which Indians carried their corn meal.

ran directly upon two of Captain Church's ambush. They let him come fair within shot, and the Englishman's[12] gun missing fire, he bid the Indian fire away. And he did so to purpose, sent one musket bullet through his heart, and another not above two inches from it. He fell upon his face in the mud and water, with his gun under him.

By this time, the enemy perceived they were waylaid on the east side of the swamp, tacked short about. One of the enemy who seemed to be a great surly old fellow, hallooed with a loud voice and often called out, "Iootash! Iootash![13]"

Captain Church called to his Indian, Peter[14], and asked him, who that was that called so? He answered, it was old Annawon, Philip's great captain, calling on his soldiers to stand to it and fight stoutly.

Now the enemy, finding that place of the swamp which was not ambushed, many of them made their escape in the English tracks. The man that had shot down Philip ran with all speed to Captain Church and informed him of his exploit, who commanded him to be silent about it and let no man more know it until they had drove the swamp clean. But, when they had drove the swamp through and found the enemy had escaped, or at least the most of them, and the sun now up, and so the dew gone, that they could not so easily track them, the whole company met together at the place where the enemies' night shelter was. And then Captain Church gave them the news of Philip's death upon which the whole army gave three loud huzzahs.

Captain Church ordered his body to be pulled out of the mire on to the upland, so some of Captain Church's Indians took hold of him by his stockings, and some, by his small breeches (being otherwise naked), and drew him through the mud unto the upland. And a doleful, great, naked, dirty beast he looked like.

Captain Church then said that, forasmuch as he had caused many an Englishman's body to lie unburied and rot above ground, that not one of his bones should be buried. And, calling his old Indian executioner bid him behead and quarter him.[15]

Accordingly, he came with his hatchet and stood over him, but, before he struck, he made a small speech, directing it to Philip, and said, he had been a very great man, and had made many a man afraid of him, but so big as he was, he would now chop his ass for him. And so went to work and did as he was ordered.

Philip, having one very remarkable hand, being much scarred, occasioned by the splitting of a pistol in it formerly, Captain Church gave the head and that hand to Alderman, the Indian who shot him, to show to such gentlemen as would bestow gratuities upon him. And accordingly, he got many a penny by it.

This being on the last day of the week,[16] the Captain with his company returned to the Island, tarried there until Tuesday; and then went off and ranged through all the woods to Plymouth, and received their premium, which was thirty shillings per head for all the enemies which they had killed or taken, instead of all wages. And Philip's head went at the same price.

---

[12] He has been identified as Caleb Cook, grandson of *Mayflower* Pilgrim Francis Cook. According to his family's tradition, he traded his gun for the Indian's gun that shot Metacom, of which the lock is in the Massachusetts Historical Society and the barrel is in the Pilgrim Society in Plymouth.

[13] "Fight, fight!"

[14] Possibly Peter, son of Awashonks.

[15] According to English law, this was the punishment for treason, the crime the colonists believed Metacom had committed, and which Church was authorized to administer in the field. In 1660, Parliament ordered the same sentence to be carried out on the already dead and buried bodies of Oliver Cromwell and two other regicides when King Charles II was restored to the throne. Metacom's head was taken to Plymouth and placed on a pole where it remained for a generation. Cotton Mather recounts how many years later he "took off the jaw from the Blasphemous exposed Skull of that Leviathan," a powerful image of silencing. The quartered parts of his body were hung on four trees.

[16] August 12, 1676.

Methinks it's scanty reward and poor encouragement; though it was better than what had been some time before. For this march they received four shillings and sixpence a man, which was all the reward they had, except the honor of killing Philip. This was in the latter end of August, 1676.

The Capture of Annawon

... The Captain was now in great straight of mind what to do next. He had a mind to give Annawon a visit, now knew where to find him,[17] but his company was very small, but half-a-dozen men beside himself, and was under a necessity to send somebody back to acquaint his lieutenant and company with his proceedings. However, he asked his small company that were with him, whether they would willingly go with him and give Annawon a visit? They told him, they were always ready to obey his commands. But withal told him, that they knew this Captain Annawon was a great soldier, that he had been a valiant captain under Asuhmequin, Philip's father; and that he had been Philip's chieftain all this war, a very subtle man and of great resolution, and had often said that he would never be taken alive by the English. And, moreover, they knew that the men that were with him were resolute fellows, some of Philip's chief soldiers, and therefore feared whether it was practicable to make an attempt upon him with so small a handful of assistants as now were with him. Told him further, that it would be a pity that, after all the great things he had done, he should throw away his life at last.

Upon which he replied, that he doubted not Annawon was a subtle and valiant man, that he had a long time but in vain sought for him, and never till now could find his quarters; and he was very loath to miss of the opportunity and doubted not but that if they would cheerfully go with him, the same Almighty Providence that had hitherto protected and befriended them would do so still.

Upon this, with one consent, they said they would go.

Captain Church then turned to one Cook[18], of Plymouth (the only Englishman then with him), and asked him, what he thought if it? Who replied, "Sir, I am never afraid of going anywhere when you are with me." ...

When it began to grow dark, the old man stood up again. Captain Church asked him if he would take a gun and fight for him? He bowed very low and prayed him not to impose such a thing on him, as to fight against Captain Annawon, his old friend. "But," says he, "I will go along with you, and be helpful to you, and will lay hands on any man that shall offer hurt to you." ...[19]

Now, Captain Church had told Captain Annawon's company, as he had ordered his Indians to tell the others, that their lives should all be spared, excepting Captain Annawon's, and it was not in his power to promise him his life, but he must carry him to his masters at Plymouth, and he would entreat them for his life.

Now, when Captain Church found not only his own men, but all the Indians fast asleep, Annawon only excepted, whom he perceived was as broad awake as himself; and so they lay looking one upon the other perhaps an hour. Captain Church said nothing to him, for he could not speak Indian, and thought Annawon could not speak English. At length, Annawon raised

---

[17] Church captured an old man, a member of Metacom's council, who agreed to pilot them to Annawon's stronghold in the swamp.

[18] Caleb Cook, who had missed being the killer of Metacom.

[19] The small group crept up on Annawon's company in the shadow of the old man and his daughter carrying baskets as if they were full of provisions, muffled by the noise of an old squaw pounding corn meal in a mortar.

himself up, cast off his blanket, and with no more clothes than his small breeches, walked a little way back from the company. Captain Church thought no other but that he had occasion to ease himself, and so walked to some distance rather than offend him with the stink. But, by and by, he was gone out of sight and hearing; and then Captain Church began to suspect some ill-design in him, and got all the guns close to him, and crowded himself close under young Annawon, that if he should anywhere get a gun, he should not make a shot at him without endangering his son. Lying very still awhile, waiting for the event, at length he heard some-body coming the same way that Annawon went. The moon now shining bright, he saw him at a distance coming with something in his hands, and, coming up to Captain Church, he fell upon his knees before him and offered him what he had brought. And, speaking in plain English, said,

"Great Captain, you have killed Philip and conquered his country, for I believe that I and my company are the last that war against the English, so suppose the war is ended by your means; and therefore these things belong unto you."

Philip's Regalia

Then, opening his pack, he pulled out Philip's belt, curiously wrought with wompom, being nine inches broad, wrought with black and white wompom in various figures and flowers, and pictures of many birds and beasts. This, when hung upon Captain Church's shoulders, it reached his ankles. And another belt of wompom he presented him with, wrought after the former manner, which Philip was wont to put upon his head. It had two flags on the back part which hung down on his back, and another small belt with a star upon the end of it, which he used to hang on his breast. And they were all edged with red hair, which Annawon said they got in the Muh-hog's[20] country. Then he pulled out two horns of glazed powder and a red cloth blanket. He told Captain Church, these were Philip's royalties which he was wont to adorn himself with when he sat in state. That he thought himself happy that he had an oppor-tunity to present them, to Captain Church, who had won them.[21] Spent the remainder of the night in discourse, and gave an account of what mighty success he had formerly in wars against many nations of Indians, when served Asuhmequin, Philip's father. . . .

Accordingly[22], Captain Church, accompanied with several gentlemen and others went out and took divers[23] parties of Indians. And in one of which parties there was a certain old man whom Captain Church seemed to take particular notice of and, asking him where he belonged, who told him, to Swanzey; the Captain asked his name, who replied his name was Conscience.

"Conscience," said the Captain (smiling), "then the war is over, for that was what they were searching for, it being much wanted." And then returned the said Conscience to his post again at Swanzey, to a certain person the said Indian desired to be sold to, and returned home.

1716

---

[20] Mohawk's.

[21] Church brought the regalia to Governor Winslow who sent them to King Charles II, calling them in the accompa-nying letter, "these few Indian rarities, being the best of our spoyles, and the best of the ornaments and treasure of sachem Philip the grand Rebell . . ." They were later lost.

[22] To a commission from Governor Winslow dated Janu-ary 1677 "to scour the woods of some of the lurking en-emy."

[23] Several.

Edward Taylor (1642?–1729)

Like the "American" poetic tradition he is thought by some to begin, Edward Taylor was beset by belatedness. Born in Sketchley, Leicestershire, England, around 1642 at the outbreak of civil war between King Charles I and the Puritans in Parliament, he was too young to participate in the victories of the New Model Army or the establishment of the Puritan Commonwealth under Oliver Cromwell in 1649. Growing up in the heated atmosphere of non-conformity, however, forged his Puritan character and convictions. The son of a yeoman farmer, Taylor attended Cambridge University for several years and probably taught school for a time. But after the collapse of the Commonwealth and the Restoration of the monarchy under Charles II in 1660, Taylor was barred from clerical training and other means of livelihood for refusing to subscribe to the Act of Uniformity of 1662, which required acknowledging the king as the head of the national church. He chose to leave England and in 1668 arrived in Boston, where he was welcomed by important men of the community. Already in his late twenties, he spent the next three years as an upperclassman at Harvard College where he held the responsible position of butler, collecting payment for food and drink, and shared a room with Samuel Sewall who became a lifelong friend. But he had missed the heady days of God's chosen people establishing their city upon a hill. The founders' energy and sense of mission had been diminished by death, sectarian struggle, and the sheer expansion of the colony.

In an elegy for the minister John Allen, who along with several other influential patriarchs died during his time at Harvard, Taylor wondered anxiously, "Shall none/ Be left behinde to tell's the Quondam Glory/ Of this Plantation?" Recapturing some of the Puritan errand's "Quondam Glory" may have been what motivated Taylor in 1671 to accept the call as minister to the small settlement of Westfield on the Bay colony's westernmost frontier. In this rural town where he lived for almost sixty years, facing all the hardships of a pioneering community including Indian attacks, floods, and sectarian challenges from more progressive neighbors, Taylor could himself be a founding father and relive that heroic saga. In 1679, after many delays, the Westfield church was established and

shaped almost wholly according to Taylor's orthodox Puritan vision. Solomon Stoddard, grandfather of Jonathan Edwards and the most famous of the ministers in attendance (who would later become Taylor's bitter antagonist in a dispute over the Lord's Supper), offered the right hand of fellowship. No other church officers were elected until 1692. Not only did Taylor perform the numerous tasks of minister, leading the community as its eminently learned teacher, strict disciplinarian, and pious spiritual guide, writing treatises, keeping up with events in Boston through correspondence, and defending his beliefs in public debates, but he was also chief physician to the town, a frontier farmer (his appointment came with fifteen acres), and family man. Taylor married Elizabeth Fitch, daughter of a minister, in 1674, who bore him eight children, five of whom did not survive infancy, before her own death in 1689. In 1692 he married Ruth Wyllys, from a prominent Hartford family, who bore him six children.

Taylor's energetic public life and ministerial zeal, however, gave no hint of his extensive poetic activity, which he carried on in relative secret throughout his adult life. Schooled in the ancient languages and literatures, in rhetoric, logic, mathematics, and divinity, Taylor read widely and even copied whole manuscripts out by hand from books lent to him by friends. His earliest poetic attempts were formulaic funeral elegies on Harvard worthies, but after he moved to Westfield, his poetry become more varied and intense. In 1674 he began his first group of poetic paraphrases of the Psalms, transcribing a second group in the early 1680s. During the period 1674–83, he also composed a series of "occasional" verse, lyrical meditations on natural observations which were shown to reveal a spiritual truth. The most moving of this group is Taylor's wrenching experience of loss, "Upon Wedlock, and Death of Children," a masculine counterpart to Anne Bradstreet's poems on her marriage and the early deaths of her grandchildren. It is not surprising that Taylor had a copy of the 1678 edition of Bradstreet's poems in his library. But Taylor's spiritual ambitions for poetry as a means to defend religious orthodoxy were much grander, and in the late 1670s, he wrote his first major poem, *Gods Determinations touching his Elect; and the Elects*

Combat in their Conversion, and Coming up to God in Christ together with the Comfortable Effects thereof. Comprised of thirty-five poems of varying meter and points of view, *Gods Determinations* begins with the creation and fall ("The Preface"), charts the struggles of the Elect saints to overcome Satan's accusations and "sophestries" with the help of Christ's "succour," and finally celebrates the ecstatic enjoyment of "church fellowship," the communal worship of justified, regenerate souls. Although modern tastes prefer Taylor's shorter lyrics, *Gods Determinations* is part of an august religious and Puritan tradition of narratives of spiritual warfare (such as the work of Milton and Bunyan, and Michael Wigglesworth's *Day of Doom*) in which the mighty sweep of providential history forms a dramatic background for the spiritual strivings of the human soul.

Taylor's lifelong opus and arguably colonial New England's greatest poetic achievement are two series of lyrics entitled *Preparatory Meditations before my Approach to the Lord's Supper,* comprising two hundred and seventeen poems composed over a forty-three year period beginning in 1682. Taylor followed the policy of his conservative predecessors who maintained that the sacrament of the Lord's Supper was not a ritual meant to convert Christians, but was the highest ordinance of the church reserved to full members who had proven themselves, to the satisfaction of the congregation, to be regenerate souls. As "the nearest harbor of divine access," the sacrament celebrated the promised marriage of Christ and the elect soul glimpsed in that ritual but only fully consummated in the afterlife. Saving grace was necessary because, whereas in Catholicism, priests transformed the bread and wine into the "real" body and blood of Christ collectively for communicants, in Protestantism, individual believers achieved, through grace, a sacramental frame of mind in which to make a worthy "spiritual reception" of the earthly elements. Preparation for receiving the sacrament consisted of examining the soul for signs of grace – a state of active self-abandonment and utter passivity before God's will. To achieve this paradoxical state, Puritan divines recommended the ancient tradition of meditation which drew on the three faculties of the soul: Memory provided scriptural doctrines which Judgement weighed and considered, thus stimulating the affections of hope and desire to activate the Will.

Taylor's poems illustrate the "holy kind of violence" necessary to purge the sinful, doubting, stubborn, contaminated self. Influenced by the English metaphysical poets like John Donne and George Herbert, but giving their witty, polished style a rough, earthy, and sometimes grotesque treatment, Taylor confronted this dilemma: How can I write myself into self-effacement? And once abjected, how can I possibly fulfill my religious/poetic obligation which is to sing God's praises? Nothing less than his eternal life, so it seemed to Taylor, depended upon the answer to these literary questions. According to the *Preparatory Meditations,* the answer lay in the saint's transformation from the active writer or singer of praises, to the passive instrument of God's activity – the trajectory of most of the Meditations. In unvarying verse form and imagery that is often violent, discordant, visually illogical, and highly erotic, Taylor struggles to arouse his spiritual desire to become the true bride: to be broken and remade by Christ. The gendered imagery is crucial here, for the Puritans regarded "the feminine" as inherently passive, but also considered it a position which could be – and in terms of orthodox Puritan doctrines of salvation, had to be – occupied by men. It is not surprising that almost a third of the Meditations from the second series take scriptural texts from The Song of Solomon, the biblical book read by the Puritans as the ultimate allegory of the soul's betrothal to God.

The significance of the sacrament for Taylor depended on its exclusivity, which was seriously challenged by the liberalizing doctrines of Solomon Stoddard, his neighbor in Northampton. Stoddard hastened the dissolution of Puritan orthodoxy by opening church membership and admitting communicants to the sacrament without evidence of conversion. Despite a bitter debate in print between the two learned men, a year before Taylor's death, his successor guided the Westfield congregation into an adoption of Stoddard's practices. But as Taylor reveals in his final two poems, "A Valediction to all the World Preparatory for Death" and "A Fig for thee Oh! Death," he had already begun to take his leave of earthly concerns. Although he sometimes shared his poetry with friends and possibly with his congregation, only a few stanzas were published during his lifetime. Nevertheless, he composed successive drafts, revised extensively, and carefully transcribed finished poems into a leatherbound manuscript entitled "Poetical Works," which came to over 400 pages. Still unpublished is Taylor's "A Metrical History of Christianity," which is 430 manuscript pages – over 20,000 lines! In 1937, Thomas Johnson discovered the manuscript of "Poetical Works" which had been left in the Yale University Library by Ezra Stiles, Taylor's grandson and former president of Yale, and published a small sampling of poetry. It proved to be a discovery that laid bare the lyric heart of the Puritan imagination.

PRIMARY WORKS

The Poetical Works of Edward Taylor, ed. Thomas H. Johnson, 1939.

The Poems of Edward Taylor, ed. Donald E. Stanford, 1960, abridged ed. 1963, rpt. 1989.

Edward Taylor's Christographia, ed. Norman Grabo, 1962.

A Transcript of Edward Taylor's Metrical History of Christianity, ed. Donald E. Stanford, 1962, rpt. 1977.

The Diary of Edward Taylor, ed. Francis Murphy, 1964.

Edward Taylor's Treatise Concerning the Lord's Supper, ed. Norman S. Grabo, 1965.

The Unpublished Writings of Edward Taylor: vol. 1, *Edward Taylor's "Church Records" and Related Sermons*; vol. 2, *Edward Taylor vs. Solomon Stoddard: The Nature of the*

Lord's Supper; vol. 3, *Edward Taylor's Minor Poetry*, eds Thomas M. and Virginia L. Davis, 1981.

Harmony of the Gospels, 4 vols, eds Thomas M. and Virginia L. Davis, 1983.

Upon the Types of the Old Testament, 2 vols, ed. Charles W. Mignon, 1989.

FURTHER READING

Norman S. Grabo, *Edward Taylor* (Boston: Twayne, 1961, revised 1988).

Early American Literature, special Taylor issue, 4, Winter 1969–70.

Karl Keller, *The Example of Edward Taylor* (Amherst: University of Massachusetts Press, 1975).

Karen E. Rowe, *Saint and Singer: Edward Taylor's Typology and the Poetics of Meditation* (Cambridge: Cambridge University Press, 1986).

Thomas M. Davis, *A Reading of Edward Taylor* (Newark: University of Delaware Press, 1992).

Jeffrey A. Hammond, *Edward Taylor: Fifty Years of Scholarship and Criticism* (Columbia, SC: Camden House, 1993).

Michael Shuldiner (ed.) *The Tayloring Shop: Essays in Honor of Thomas M. and Virginia L. Davis* (Newark: University of Delaware Press, 1997).

FROM *GODS DETERMINATIONS*[1]

The Preface

Infinity, when all things it beheld
In Nothing, and of Nothing all did build,
Upon what Base was fixt the Lath, wherein
He turn'd this Globe, and riggalld[2] it so trim?
Who blew the Bellows of his Furnace Vast?
Or held the Mould wherein the world was Cast?
Who laid its Corner Stone? Or whose Command?[3]
Where stand the Pillars upon which it stands?
Who Lac'de and Fillitted[4] the earth so fine,
With Rivers like green Ribbons Smaragdine[5]?
Who made the Sea's its Selvedge[6], and it locks

---

[1]   Taylor's sequence of thirty-five poems in a debate format exploring the soul's progress from the creation, fall, redemption through Christ, temptation by Satan, joy of church fellowship, and finally, resurrection in heaven. The full title is *Gods Determinations touching his Elect; and the Elects Combat in their Conversion, and Coming up to God in Christ together with the Comfortable Effects thereof*. It was completed around 1680, and transcribed in Taylor's book manuscript between 1681 and 1682. The text is from Donald Stanford (ed.) *Poems* (New

Haven: Yale University Press, 1960).

[2]   To make a ring-shaped mark or groove in wood or stone.

[3]   An echo of Job 38:4–8.

[4]   Trimmed in an ornamental manner, by punching holes and passing a ribbon through.

[5]   Bright emerald green, from smaragd, a precious bright green stone.

[6]   The finished border of woven fabric that prevents unraveling.

Like a Quilt Ball within a Silver Box?[7]
Who Spread its Canopy? Or Curtains Spun?
Who in this Bowling Alley bowld the Sun?
Who made it always when it rises set
To go at once both down, and up to get?
Who th'Curtain rods made for this Tapistry?
Who hung the twinckling Lanthorns in the Sky?
Who? who did this? or who is he? Why, know
Its Onely Might Almighty this did doe.
His hand hath made this noble worke which Stands
His Glorious Handywork not made by hands.
Who spake all things from nothing; and with ease
Can speake all things to nothing, if he please.
Whose Little finger at his pleasure Can
Out mete[8] ten thousand worlds with halfe a Span:
Whose Might Almighty can by half a looks
Root up the rocks and rock the hills by th'roots.
Can take this mighty World up in his hande,
And shake it like a Squitchen[9] or a Wand.
Whose single Frown will make the Heavens shake
Like as an aspen leafe the Winde makes quake.
Oh! what a might is this Whose single frown
Doth shake the world as it would shake it down?[10]
Which All from Nothing fet[11], from Nothing, All:
Hath All on Nothing set, lets Nothing fall.
Gave All to nothing Man indeed, whereby
Through nothing man all might him Glorify.
In Nothing then imbosst the brightest Gem
More pretious than all pretiousness in them.
But Nothing man did throw down all by Sin:
And darkened that lightsom Gem in him.
    That now his Brightest Diamond is grown
    Darker by far than any Coalpit Stone.

*c.*1680   1939

The Souls Groan to Christ for Succour

Good Lord, behold this Dreadfull Enemy
    Who makes me tremble with his fierce assaults,
I dare not trust, yet feare to give the ly,
    For in my soul, my soul finds many faults.
    And though I justify myselfe to's face:
    I do Condemn myselfe before thy Grace.

---

7 Elaborately decorated and treasured pincushions were kept in ornate boxes.
8 To measure out.
9 Switch made of a young sapling.
10 England experienced several large earthquakes in 1661, in 1668 (several weeks before Taylor's departure), in 1678, and in 1680. Such natural occurrences were interpreted as providential signs of God's power and judgment.
11 Fetch or summon by force.

He strives to mount my sins, and them advance
    Above thy Merits, Pardons, or Good Will
Thy Grace to lessen, and thy Wrath t'inhance
    As if thou couldst not pay the sinners bill.
    He Chiefly injures thy rich Grace, I finde
    Though I confess my heart to sin inclin'de.

Those Graces which thy Grace enwrought in mee,
    He makes as nothing but a pack of Sins.
He maketh Grace no grace, but Crueltie,
    Is Graces Honey Comb, a Comb of Stings?
    This makes me ready leave thy Grace and run.
    Which if I do, I finde I am undone.

I know he is thy Cur, therefore I bee
    Perplexed lest I from thy Pasture stray.
He bayghs, and barks so veh'mently at mee.
    Come rate[12] this Cur, Lord, breake his teeth I pray.
    Remember me I humbly pray thee first.
    Then halter up this Cur that is so Curst.

*c.*1680   1939

The Joy of Church Fellowship rightly attended[13]

In Heaven soaring up, I dropt an Eare
    On Earth: and oh! sweet Melody:
And listening, found it was the Saints who were
    Encoacht for Heaven that sang for Joy.
    For in Christs Coach they sweetly sing;
    As they to Glory ride therein.

Oh! joyous hearts! Enfir'de with holy Flame!
    Is speech thus tassled with praise?
Will not your inward fire of Joy contain;
    That it in open flames doth blaze?
    For in Christs Coach Saints sweetly sing
    As they to Glory ride therein.

And if a string do slip, by Chance, they soon
    Do screw it up again:[14] whereby
They set it in a more melodious Tune
    And a Diviner Harmony.
    For in Christs Coach they sweetly sing
    As they to Glory ride therein.

---

12   Berate; to scold or rebuke.
13   The last poem of the sequence, in which Taylor describes the spiritual fellowship of the "visible saints" as a coach in which they will eventually ride up to heaven.

14   The strings on a musical instrument which are adjusted by tightening or loosening pegs, and thus "tuning" it. It is a figure for the internal regulation or "harmony" of the congregation and each individual saint within it.

In all their Acts, publick, and private, nay
   And secret too, they praise impart.
But in their Acts Divine and Worship, they
   With Hymns do offer up their Heart.
   Thus in Christs Coach they sweetly sing
   As they to Glory ride therein.

Some few not in; and some whose Time, and Place
   Block up this Coaches way do goe
As Travellers afoot, and so do trace
   The Road that gives them right thereto
   While in this Coach these sweetly sing
   As they to Glory ride therein.

*c.*1680   1939

From "Poetical Works"[1]

4. Huswifery[2]

Make mee, O Lord, thy Spining Wheele compleat.
   Thy Holy Words my Distaff make for meet
Make mine Affections thy Swift Flyers neate
   And make my Soule thy holy Spoole to bee.
   My Conversation make to be thy Reele
   And reele the yarn there on Spun of thy Wheele.[3]

Make me thy Loome then, knit therein this Twine:
   And make thy Holy Spirit, Lord, winde quills[4]:
Then weave the Web thyselfe. The yarn is fine.
   Thine Ordinances make my Fulling Mills[5].
   Then dy the same in Heavenly Colours Choice,
   All pinkt[6] with Varnisht Flowers of Paradise.

Then cloath therewith mine Understanding, Will,
   Affections, Judgment, Conscience, Memory
My Words & Actions, that their Shine may fill
   My wayes with glory and thee glorify.

---

[1]   In the manuscript of "Poetical Works," a group of eight short numbered poems, probably copied in the early 1680s, on "occurrants occasioning what follows." The texts are from *Edward Taylor's Minor Poetry*, eds Thomas and Virginia Davis (Boston: Twayne, 1981).

[2]   Housekeeping: specifically the spinning of flax and weaving of linen by which women provided clothes for their households. Taylor makes this an elaborate metaphor for the production of grace in the soul, symbolized by the "holy robes of glory" worn by the regenerate Christian.

[3]   In this stanza Taylor allegorizes the parts of a spinning wheel. The "distaff" holds the raw wool or flax; the "flyers" regulate the speed of the wheel; the "spool" twists the yarn; the "reel" winds up the finished thread.

[4]   To wind thread or yarn on quills or bobbins, spindles or spools.

[5]   Places where cloth is beaten with wooden mallets and cleaned with fuller's earth or soap.

[6]   To finish a raw edge of cloth by cutting it in a decorative pattern.

Then mine apparell shall display before yee
That I am Cloathd in Holy robes for glory.

c.1682–3   1937

6. Upon Wedlock and Death of Children[7]

A Curious Knot[8] God made in Paradise,
    And drew it out inamled neatly Fresh.
It was the True-Love Knot, more Sweet than spice
    And set with all the flowers of Graces Dress.
    Its Weddens Knot, that ne're can be unti'de
    No Alexanders Sword[9] can it divide

The Slips[10] here planted, gay & glorious grow;
    Unless and hellish breath do sindge their Plumes.
Here Primrose, Cowslips, Roses, Lilies blow[11],
    With Violets & Pinkes that voide perfumes.
    Whose beatious leaves ore lai'd with Hony Dew.
    And Chanting birds Cherp out sweet Musick true.

When in this Knot I planted was, my Stock
    Soon knotted, & a manly flower out brake.[12]
And after it my branch again did knot
    Brought out another Flower its Sweet breathd mate.[13]
    One knot gave one tother the tothers place.
    Whence Checkling[14] Smiles fought in each others face.

But oh! a glorious hand from glory came
    Guarded with Angells, soon did Crop this flower
Which almost tore the root up of the same[15]
    At that unlookt for, Dolesom, darksome houre.
    In pray're to Christ perfum'de[16] it did ascend,
    And Angells bright did it to heaven tend.

7   Taylor married Elizabeth Fitch in 1674 and had eight children with her, five of whom died in infancy. In a letter of condolence written 14 August 1686, Taylor sent stanzas 5 and 7 from this poem to his long-time friend, Samuel Sewall, on the occasion of his son's death. This letter was published at the end of Cotton Mather's *Right Thoughts in Sad Hours, Representing the Comforts and the Duties of Good Men under all their Afflictions; And Particularly, That one, the Untimely Death of Children* (London, 1689), constituting the only publication of Taylor's poetry.
8   A flower garden, but figuratively the bond of Adam and Eve as husband and wife which prefigures the union between God and the soul.
9   Alexander the Great (356–323 BC) was the King of Macedonia, known for his military exploits. The Phrygians chose Gordius, a peasant, for their king, who consecrated his wagon to Jupiter and tied it to a tree so artfully that the ends could

not be found. Rumor spread that the man who could untie this knot would be king of Asia, and when it was shown to Alexander, he cut it with his sword, saying, "It is thus we loose our knots."
10   Plant cuttings used for propagation or grafting.
11   Bloom.
12   Taylor's first son, Samuel, born August 27, 1675, grew to maturity.
13   Elizabeth, born December 27, 1676 and died on December 25, 1677 (see following stanza).
14   Chuckling.
15   The death of the child severely affected its parents.
16   In the Old Testament, incense was offered to God as a form of prayer and praise, but Taylor is also extending the flower metaphor. In the next stanza, "perfum'd" means "inspired."

But pausing on't, this Sweet perfum'd my thought,
 Christ would in Glory have a Flowre, Choice, Prime,
And having Choice, chose this my branch forth brought;
 Lord take it. I thanke thee, thou takst ought of mine,
  It is my pledge in glory, part of mee
  Is now in it, Lord, glorifi'de with thee.

But praying ore my branch, my branch did Sprout
 And bore another manly flower, & gay[17]
And after that another, Sweet brake out,[18]
 The which the former hand soon got away.
  But oh! the tortures, Vomit, Screechings, groans,
  And Six weeks Fever would pierce hearts like Stones.

Griefe o're doth flow: & nature fault would finde
 Were not thy Will, my Spell Charm, Joy, & Gem:
That as I said, I say, take, Lord, they're thine.
 I piecemeale pass to Glory bright in them.
  I joy, may I sweet Flowers for Glory breed,
  Whether thou getst them green, or lets them Seed.

c. 1682   1937

FROM *PREPARATORY MEDITATIONS*[1]

Prologue

Lord, Can a Crumb of Dust the Earth outweigh,
 Outmatch all mountains, nay the Chrystall Sky?
Imbosom in't designs that shall Display
 And trace into the Boundless Deity?
 Yea hand a Pen whose moysture cloth guild ore
 Eternall Glory with a glorious glore[2].

If it its Pen had of an Angels Quill[3],
 And Sharpend on a Pretious Stone ground tite,
And dipt in Liquid Gold, and mov'de by Skill
 In Christall leaves should golden Letters write
 It would but blot and blur yea jag, and jar
 Unless thou mak'st the Pen, and Scribener.

---

[17] James, born on October 12, 1678, grew to maturity.

[18] Abigail, born August 6, 1681, and died August 22, 1682.

PREPARATORY MEDITATIONS

[1] The complete title is *Preparatory Meditations before my Approach to the Lords Supper. Chiefly upon the Doctrin preached upon the Day of administration.* Taylor composed two series of these meditations at irregular intervals between 1682 and 1725, and transcribed all 217 poems into his manuscript book. The text is from *The Poems of Edward Taylor*, ed. Donald Stanford (New Haven: Yale University Press, 1960).

[2] Glory (Scottish).

[3] Pen made from the feather of a goose by slitting and pointing the lower tip; here from an angel's wing.

I am this Crumb of Dust which is design'd
To make my Pen unto thy Praise alone,
And my dull Phancy[4] *I would gladly grinde*
Unto an Edge on Zions Pretious Stone[5].
And Write in Liquid Gold upon thy Name
My Letters till thy glory forth doth flame.

Let not th'attempts breake down my Dust I pray
Nor laugh thou them to scorn but pardon give.
Inspire this Crumb of Dust till it display
Thy Glory through't: and then thy dust shall live.
Its failings then thou'lt overlook I trust,
They being Slips slipt from thy Crumb of Dust.

Thy Crumb of Dust breaths two words from its breast,
That thou wilt guide its pen to write aright
To Prove thou art, and that thou art the best
And shew thy Properties to shine most bright.
And then thy Works will shine as flowers on Stems
Or as in Jewellary Shops, do jems.

*c.*1683   1939

First Series

Meditation 8: John 6.51. I Am the Living Bread.

I kening[6] through Astronomy Divine
   The Worlds bright Battlement, wherein I spy
A Golden Path my Pensill cannot line,
   From that bright Throne unto my Threshold ly.
   And while my puzzled thoughts about it pore
   I finde the Bread of Life in't at my dore.

When that this Bird of Paradise put in
   This Wicker Cage (my Corps) to tweedle praise
Had peckt the Fruite forbad: and so did fling
   Away its Food; and lost its golden dayes;
   It fell into Celestiall Famine sore:
   And never could attain a morsell more.[7]

---

4   Fancy, or imagination; the power of conception or representation in art. Puritans were wary of this mental capacity because it could be delusive unless governed by the Will or Reason.

5   The precious stones that adorn the heavenly city, the New Jerusalem or Zion. See Revelation 21:11, 19–21.

6   To catch sight of or discover by sight, here through the science of "divine astronomy."

7   Like the caged "bird of Paradise," the soul is imprisoned in the body. Here Taylor recapitulates the Fall and eviction from Eden as the breaking of the initial Covenant of Works that God established with Adam and Eve which left the soul with no source of spiritual sustenance.

Alas! alas! Poore Bird, what wilt thou doe?
    The Creatures field no food for Souls e're gave.
And if thou knock at Angells dores they show
    An Empty Barrell: they no soul bread have.
    Alas! Poore Bird, the Worlds White Loafe is done.
    And cannot yield thee here the smallest Crumb.

In this sad state, Gods Tender Bowells[8] run
    Out streams of Grace: And he to end all strife
The Purest Wheate in Heaven, his deare-dear Son
    Grinds, and kneads up into this Bread of Life.
    Which Bread of Life from Heaven down came and stands
    Disht on thy Table up by Angells Hands.

Did God mould up this Bread in Heaven, and bake,
    Which from his Table came, and to thine goeth?
Doth he bespeake thee thus, This Soule Bread take.
    Come Eate thy fill of this thy Gods White Loafe?[9]
    Its Food too fine for Angells, yet come, take
    And Eate thy fill. Its Heavens Sugar Cake.

What Grace is this knead in this Loafe? This thing
    Souls are but petty things it to admire.
Yee Angells, help: This fill would to the brim
    Heav'ns whelm'd-down Chrystall meele Bowle,[10] yea and higher.
    This Bread of Life dropt in thy mouth, doth Cry.
    Eate, Eate me, Soul, and thou shalt never dy.

8 June 1684   1937

Meditation 40: 1 John 2.2. He is a Propitiation for our Sin.

Still I complain; I am complaining still.
    Oh! woe is me! Was ever Heart like mine?[11]
A Sty of Filth, a Trough of Washing-Swill
    A Dunghill Pit, a Puddle of mere Slime.
    A Nest of Vipers, Hive of Hornets Stings.
    A Bag of Poyson, Civit-Box[12] of Sins.

---

8 Intestines or the interior of the body, seat of tenderness and pity.

9 This echoes God's commandment to the Israelites in the desert to collect the manna, or heavenly bread, which He provided for them (see Exodus 13:16), and Christ's miracle of feeding five thousand people with a few loaves of barley bread and fishes (see John 6:1–14). Both are linked with the Passover meal, which prefigures the Last Supper, at which Christ instituted the ritual of the Lord's Supper (see Luke 22:19).

10 A bowl turned upside down. The pun on "Chrystall" and "Christ all," along with the allusions to bread-making (meele), suggest that the grace "kneaded" up by God in the

sacrifice of his son and offered to believers in the sacrament of the Supper as bread (body) and wine (blood) would fill the Heavens with radiant light, nourish the soul, and bring it everlasting life, thus allowing the poet to "ken" paradise through his faith which he cannot discern through mere science.

11 This phrase, which becomes the refrain of the Meditation, is probably an echo of the refrain in George Herbert's poem, "The Sacrifice:" "Was ever grief like mine?"

12 Used in making perfumes, containing fluid from the scent glands of various cat-like mammals of the family Viverridae, of Africa and Asia, having a musky odor.

Was ever Heart like mine? So bad? black? Vile?
  Is any Divell blacker? Or can Hell
Produce its match? It is the very Soile
  Where Satan reads his Charms, and sets his Spell.
  His Bowling Ally, where he sheeres his fleece
  At Nine Pins, Nine Holes, Morrice, Fox and Geese.[13]

His Palace Garden where his courtiers walke.
  His Jewells Cabbinet. Here his Caball[14]
Do sham it, and truss up their Privie talk
  In Fardells[15] of Consults and bundles all.
  His shambles[16], and his Butchers stale's herein.
  It is the Fuddling[17] Schoole of every sin.

Was ever Heart like mine? Pride, Passion, fell.
  Ath'ism, Blasphemy, pot, pipe it, dance
Play Barlybreaks[18], and at last Couple in Hell.
  At Cudgells, Kit-Cat[19], Cards and Dice here prance.
  At Noddy, Ruff-and-trumpt, Jing, Post-and-Pare,
  Put, One-and-thirty, and such other ware.[20]

Grace shuffled is away: Patience oft sticks
  Too soon, or draws itselfe out, and's out Put.
Faith's over trumpt, and oft doth lose her tricks.
  Repentance's Chalkt up Noddy, and out shut.
  They Post, and Pare off Grace thus, and its shine.
  Alas! alas! was ever Heart like mine?

Sometimes methinks the serpents head I mall:[21]
  Now all is still: my spirits do recreute[22].
But ere my Harpe can tune sweet praise, they fall
  On me afresh, and tare me at my Root.
  They bite like Badgers now nay worse, although
  I tooke them toothless sculls, rot long agoe.

---

[13] Nine pins is skittles, a bowling game played with nine pins. Nine holes was a boys' game played with a ball and nine round holes in the ground or on a board. Morrice or Nine Men's Morris, was a game like checkers or chess which could be played on a table or board, but was also played in a field. Fox and geese was a boys' game played with marbles or pegs.

[14] A conspiratorial group of plotters or intriguers.

[15] Fardells are bundles, especially burdens or loads of sin.

[16] A place for slaughtering animals, abbatoir.

[17] Befuddling, bewildering, misleading.

[18] A game played by six people, three of each sex, formed into couples. One couple stands in "hell," a plot of ground between two other plots, and tries to catch the other couples as they pass through.

[19] Kit-cat was a boy's game like baseball on a smaller scale.

[20] Noddy was a card game like cribbage. Ruff-and-trumpt: Ruff was a card game, and trumping at cards was a feature of popular card games like whist. Jing or jinks or jink game was a card game derived from another called Spoil-five. Post-and-pare was a card game played with three cards each, in which the players bet on their own hands. Put was also a card game. One-and-thirty was a card game resembling vingt-un.

[21] A reference to God's prophecy after the fall that He would put "enmity" between the serpent and the offspring of women; that she would "strike its head" in punishment, but also as a way of putting temptation behind her.

[22] To refresh, reinvigorate or renew.

My Reason now's more than my sense, I feele
  I have more Sight than Sense. Which seems to bee
A Rod of Sun beams t'whip mee for my Steele.
   My Spirits spiritless, and dull in mee
   For my dead prayerless Prayers: the Spirits winde
   Scarce blows my mill about. I little grinde.

Was ever Heart like mine? My Lord, declare.
  I know not what to do: What shall I doe?
I wonder, split I don't upon Despare.
   Its grace's wonder that I wrack not so.
   I faintly shun't: although I see this Case
   Would say, my sin is greater than thy grace.

Hope's Day-peep dawns hence through this chinch. Christs name
  Propitiation is for sins. Lord, take
It so for mine. Thus quench thy burning flame
   In that clear stream that from his side forth brake.
   I can no Comfort take while thus I see
   Hells cursed Imps thus jetting strut in mee.

Lord take thy sword: these Anakims[23] destroy:
  Then soake my soule in Zions Bucking tub[24]
With Holy Soap, and Nitre[25], and rich Lye.
   From all Defilement me cleanse, wash and rub.
   Then wrince, and wring mee out till th'water fall
   As pure as in the Well: not foule at all.

And let thy Sun, shine on my Head out cleare.
  And bathe my Heart within its radient beams:
Thy Christ make my Propitiation Deare.
   Thy Praise shall from my Heart breake forth in streams.
   This reeching Vertue of Christs blood will quench
   Thy Wrath, slay Sin and in thy Love mee bench.[26]

12 February 1690   1943

Second Series

Meditation 43: Rom. 9.5. *God blessed forever*

When, Lord, I seeke to shew thy praises, then
  Thy shining Majesty doth stund my minde,

---

23 Anglicized plural of the Hebrew word "anakim" (singular "anak"): an Old Testament race of giants of southern Canaan, who were virtually annihilated by the Israelites; see Joshua 11:21.
24 A tub used for bucking, steeping or boiling yarn, cloth or clothes in a lye of wood ashes or other cleansing substance.
25 Salpetre or natron, a crystal used medicinally.
26 To seat him firmly in Christ's love.

Encramps my tongue and tongue ties fast my Pen,
    That all my doings, do not what's designd.
    My Speeche's Organs are so trancifide[27]
    My words stand startld, can't thy praises stride.

Nay Speeches Bloomery can't from the Ore
    Of Reasons mine, melt words for to define
Thy Deity, nor t'deck the reechs that sore
    From Loves rich Vales, sweeter than hony rhimes.
    Words though the finest twine of reason, are
    Too Course a web for Deity to ware.

Words Mentall are syllabicated thoughts:
    Words Orall but thoughts Whiffld in the Winde
Words Writ, are incky, Goose quill-slabbred draughts,[28]
    Although the fairest blossoms of the minde.
    Then can such glasses cleare enough descry
    My Love to thee, or thy rich Deity?

Words are befould, Thoughts filthy fumes that smoake,
    From Smutty Huts, like Will-a-Wisps that rise
From Quaugmires, run ore bogs where frogs do Croake,
    Lead all astray led by them by the eyes.
    My muddy Words so dark thy Deity,
    And cloude the Sun-Shine, and its Shining Sky.

Yet spare mee, Lord, to use this hurden ware[29].
    I have no finer Stuff to use, and I
Will use it now my Creed but to declare
    And not thy Glorious Selfe to beautify.
    Thou art all-God: all Godhead then is thine
    Although the manhood there unto doth joyne.

Thou art all Godhead bright, although there bee
    Something beside the Godhead in thee bright.
Thou art all Infinite although in thee
    There is a nature pure, not infinite.
    Thou art Almighty, though thy Humane tent
    Of Humane frailty upon earth did sent.

He needs must be the Deity most High,
    To whom all properties essensiall to
The Godhead do belong Essentially
    And not to others: nor from Godhead go

---

[27] Entranced, stupefied.

[28] Sloppy drafts or sketches.

[29] Coarse fabric made from flax or hemp.

And thou art thus, my Lord, to Godhead joynd.
We finde thee thus in Holy Writ definde.

Thou art Eternall; Infinite thou art;
  Omnipotent, Omniscient, Evrywhere,
All Holy, Just, Good, Gracious, True, in heart,
  Immortal, though with mortall nature here.
  Religious worship hence belongs to thee
From men and angells: all, of each degree.

Be thou my God, and make mee thine Elect
  To kiss thy feet, and worship give to thee:
Accept of mee, and make mee thee accept.
  So I'st be safe, and thou shalt served bee.
  I'le bring thee praise, buskt up[30] in Songs perfum'de,
  When thou with grace my Soule hast sweetly tun'de.

26 October 1701   1954

Samuel Sewall (1652–1730)

Although Samuel Sewall was a well-known public figure in provincial Boston, since the publication of his extensive diary in the late 1870s, historians have been fascinated by the revelations of his private life. Rather soon after the death of his beloved wife of forty-two years, Sewall embarked on a series of frustrating courtships which he recorded in often hilarious detail. These have been treated as welcomed levity in the usually doleful and self-righteous drama of the Puritan errand. Sewall's diary, which covers fifty-five years, also records the profound changes that were taking place in colonial and Puritan culture at the turn of the century that betokened even larger changes to come. Born in England, Sewall was nine years old when he and his mother joined his father, Henry Sewall, a Puritan minister turned businessman, in New England where he had gone to manage the considerable estates he had inherited from his father. They settled in Newbury, Massachusetts, north of Boston, a rich and wild landscape whose beauty Sewall would later extol in a pamphlet entitled *Phænomena quædam Apocalyptica* as the site of the Puritans' New Jerusalem. A studious boy, Sewall was placed un-

der the instruction of the town's minister and matriculated with the class of 1671 at Harvard College, where in his senior year he became "chum and bedfellow" of the minister and poet Edward Taylor of Westfield. Like Taylor, Sewall held to the orthodox ways of the Puritan founders, and bristled against innovation, sectarianism, or dilution of the "visible Church." He loved books and throughout his life read widely in theology, with a special interest in biblical prophecies. But he was also outgoing and immensely social. While seven of his eleven fellow graduates became preachers, Sewall's marriage in 1676 to Hannah Hull determined the direction of his career.

Hannah was the daughter of John Hull, Master of the Mint and one of the wealthiest men in the colony. When "Father Hull" died in 1684, Sewall inherited a considerable estate and became a successful merchant. His affluence allowed him to pursue his learned hobbies as well as a distinguished career of public service. From 1681 to 1684, he managed the colony's printing press, and from 1684 to 1686, he was a member of the governor's Council. In 1688, he assisted Increase Mather in

---

[30]   Dressed up or decked out.

renegotiating the new charter for the colony in England, and served as a member of the new General Court for thirty-three years (1692–1725). Appointed Justice of the Superior Court in 1692, he served as Chief Justice of Massachusetts from 1718 to 1728. Called upon to moderate public meetings, serve as magistrate, perform marriages, and execute wills, Sewall traveled throughout the colony, dined with all its important citizens, and was familiar with its intricate social fabric.

Sewall began his diary on December 3, 1673 and continued until December 25, 1728. Unlike John Winthrop's *Journal* a generation earlier, Sewall's extensive account of his daily activities gives us insight into the private as well as public life of a busy and very worldly Puritan believer. Never missing an opportunity to "improve" natural events to reveal God's will, Sewall discovered a pious moral in large and small incidents alike: from the hailstorm that seemed to target the houses of ministers, to the breaking of his chamberpot or the feeding of his chickens. Yet, Sewall was not an unthinking believer, and his reading of signs led him to some unexpected illuminations. Appointed to the Court of Oyer and Terminer that judged the Salem witchcraft trials in 1692 in which nineteen people who steadfastly protested their innocence were executed, Sewall finally came to understand the deaths of two of his children and other family losses (he fathered fourteen children, but only six lived beyond childhood) as God's judgment for his role in that tragedy. On a fast day in January 1695, the distinguished jurist gave his minister, Samuel Willard, a statement of contrition to be read out in church. He was the only one of the judges to make such a public apology.

Sewall's understanding of the Bible and Christian ethics also led him to take a principled stand against slavery in opposition to the Body of Liberties, a document drafted by the Puritan founders in 1641 which allowed slavery in the colonies. By 1700, the year Sewall published *The Selling of Joseph*, not only was slavery deeply entrenched and growing (by 1720 there were around 2,000 slaves in Massachusetts), but Puritan merchants were reaping enormous profits from the trade. As early as 1673, Sewall's diary records his discomfort with slavery and the treatment of Negro servants, and well into the eighteenth century he recounts his horror at having "Indians and Negros being Rated with Horses and Hogs" and prevented from marrying or punished severely for mixed marriages. His conscience was finally pricked at the appearance of a petition to the General Court to free a slave and his wife who had been treated unfairly. This was most likely a slave named Adam, whose owner John Saffin, a part-time slave trader and poet, had reneged on a promise to free him after a certain amount of service. Enraged by Sewall's pamphlet which indirectly indicted him, Saffin wrote a reply in 1701 entitled *A Brief and Candid Answer to a late Printed Sheet, Entitled the Selling of Joseph*. The debate and the controversy that ensued provoked the influential Boston minister Cotton Mather to publish *The Negro Christianized* in 1706, a pamphlet that argued for the conversion of black slaves. Despite the controversy, and the "frowns and hard words" Sewall received for his efforts, in 1703 with his help Adam was finally released. Sewall, however, does not argue for racial equality; rather, he cites the words of a revered English Puritan, William Ames, who declared that "liberty in the natural account is the very next thing to life itself, yea by many is preferred before it," a sentiment that will form the foundation of a particularly "American" ideal.

PRIMARY WORKS

Phænomena quædam Apocalyptica ad aspectum novi orbis configurata. Or, Some few lines towards a description of the new heaven as it makes to those who stand upon the new earth, 1697.

The Selling of Joseph: A Memorial, 1700, ed. Sidney Kaplan, 1969.

A memorial relating to the Kennebeck Indians, 1721.

The Diary of Samuel Sewall, ed. M. Halsey Thomas, 2 vols, 1973.

FURTHER READING

Ola Winslow, *Samuel Sewall of Boston* (New York: Macmillan, 1964).

L. W. Towner, "The Sewall-Saffin Dialogue on Slavery," *William and Mary Quarterly*, 21 (1964) pp. 40–52.

David D. Hall, "The Mental World of Samuel Sewall," *Proceedings of the Massachusetts Historical Society*, 92 (1980) pp. 21–44.

Lawrence Rosenwald, "Sewall's Diary and the Margins of Puritan Literature," *American Literature*, October, 58, 3 (1986) pp. 325–41.

David Lovejoy, "Between Hell and Plum Island: Samuel Sewall and the Legacy of the Witches 1692–97," *New England Quarterly*, September, 70, 3 (1997) pp. 355–67.

FROM *PHÆNOMENA QUÆDAM APOCALYPTICA AD ASPECTUM NOVI ORBIS CONFIGURATA. OR, SOME FEW LINES TOWARDS A DESCRIPTION OF THE NEW HEAVEN AS IT MAKES TO THOSE WHO STAND UPON THE NEW EARTH*[1]

Not to begin to be, and so not to be limited by the concernments of time and place, is the prerogative of God alone. But as it is the privilege of creatures that God has given them a beginning, so to deny their actions or them the respect they bear to place and successive duration is, under a pretense of promotion, to take away their very being. Yet notwithstanding, some things have had this to glory of: that they have been time out of mind, and their continuance refuses to be measured by the memory of man. Whereas New England and Boston of the Massachusetts have this to make mention of – that they can tell their age, and account it their honor to have their birth and parentage kept in everlasting remembrance. And in very deed, the families and churches which first ventured to follow Christ through the Atlantic Ocean into a strange land full of wild men were so religious, their end so holy, their self-denial in pursuing of it so extraordinary, that I can't but hope that the plantation has thereby gained a very strong crasis[2]; and that it will be very long lasting. . . .

As long as Plum Island[3] shall faithfully keep the commanded post, notwithstanding all the hectoring words and hard blows of the proud and boisterous ocean; as long as any salmon or sturgeon shall swim in the streams of the Merrimack; or any perch or pickerel in Crane Pond; as long as the sea-fowl shall know the time of their coming and not neglect seasonably to visit the places of their acquaintance; as long as any cattle shall be fed with the grass growing in the meadows, which do humbly bow down themselves before Turkey Hills, and shall from thence pleasantly look down upon the River Parker, and the fruitful marshes lying beneath; as long as any free and harmless doves shall find a white oak or other tree within the township, to perch, or feed, or build a careless nest upon, and shall voluntarily present themselves to perform the office of gleaners after barley harvest; as long as nature shall not grow old and dote[4], but shall constantly remember to give the rows of Indian corn their education, by pairs; So long shall Christians be born there; and being first made meet, shall from thence be translated, to be made partakers of the inheritance of the saints in light.

1697

THE SELLING OF JOSEPH, A MEMORIAL[1]

Forasmuch as Liberty *is in real value next unto Life*[2]*: None ought to part with it themselves, or deprive others of it, but upon most mature Consideration.*

[1] "Phenomena concerning the Apocalypse as it appears to those standing upon the New Earth" (Latin). This was a pamphlet Sewall published in 1697 detailing his belief, supported by evidence he gathered from scripture and recent history, that the prophecy foretold in the Book of Revelation was being fulfilled in America. Thus, he argued, America and even New England may "be the seat of the New Jerusalem." This text is from the 3rd edition (Boston, 1727).

[2] Physical constitution.

[3] A beach close to Newbury, Massachusetts, where Sewall grew up.

[4] Senile.

JOSEPH

[1] One of the first anti-slavery tracts to be published in America. The text, slightly modernized, is the one published by Green and Allen, Boston, June 24, 1700.

[2] Sewall's translation of the passage, "quia Libertas ex naturali æstimatione proxime accedit ad vitam ipsam," from

The Numerousness of Slaves at this day in the Province, and the Uneasiness of them under their Slavery, hath put many upon thinking whether the Foundation of it be firmly and well laid; so as to sustain the Vast Weight that is build upon it. It is most certain that all Men, as they are the Sons of *Adam*, are Coheirs; and have equal Right unto Liberty, and all other outward Comforts of Life. *God hath given the Earth* [with all its Commodities] *unto the Sons of Adam, Psal. 115. 16. And hath made of One Blood, all Nations of Men, for to dwell on all the face of the Earth, and hath determined the Times before appointed, and the bounds of their habitation: That they should seek the Lord. Forasmuch then as we are the Offspring of GOD &c. Act 17. 26, 27, 29.* Now although the Title given by the last ADAM, doth infinitely better Mens Estates, respecting GOD and themselves; and grants them a most beneficial and inviolable Lease under the Broad Seal of Heaven, who were before only Tenants at Will: Yet through the Indulgence of GOD to our First Parents after the Fall, the outward Estate of all and every of their Children, remains the same, as to one another. So that Originally, and Naturally, there is no such thing as Slavery. *Joseph* was rightfully no more a Slave to his Brethren, than they were to him: and they had no more Authority to *Sell* him, than they had to *Slay* him. And if *they* had nothing to do to Sell him; the *Ishmaelites* bargaining with them, and paying down Twenty pieces of Silver could not make a Title. Neither could *Potiphar* have any better Interest in him than the *Ishmaelites* had. Gen. 37. 20, 27, 28.[3] For he that shall in this case plead *Alteration of Property*, seems to have forfeited a great part of his own claim to Humanity. There is no proportion between Twenty Pieces of Silver, and LIBERTY. The Commodity it self is the Claimer. If *Arabian* Gold be imported in any quantities, most are afraid to meddle with it, though they might have it at easy rates; lest if it should have been wrongfully taken from the Owners, it should kindle a fire to the Consumption of their whole Estate. 'Tis pity there should be more Caution used in buying a Horse, or a little lifeless dust; than there is in purchasing Men and Women: Whenas they are the Offspring of GOD, and their Liberty is,

> . . . *Auro pretiosior Omni*[4]

And seeing GOD hath said, *He that Stealeth a Man and Selleth him, or if he be found in his hand, he shall surely be put to Death. Exod. 21. 16.* This Law being of Everlasting Equity, wherein Man Stealing is ranked amongst the most atrocious of Capital Crimes: What louder Cry can there be made of that Celebrated Warning,

> *Caveat Emptor!*[5]

And all things considered, it would conduce more to the Welfare of the Province, to have White Servants for a Term of Years, than to have Slaves for Life. Few can endure to hear of a Negro's being made free; and indeed they can seldom use their freedom well; yet their continual aspiring after their forbidden Liberty, renders them Unwilling Servants. And there is such a disparity in their Conditions, Colour & Hair, that they can never embody with us, and

---

William Ames' *De conscientia, et eius iure, vel casibus* (London, 1623), with which he also ends this tract. Dr Williams Ames (1576–1633) was a revered English Puritan who fled to Holland in 1610, but died before he could emigrate to New England.

[3] Joseph, the youngest and favorite son of Jacob, incurred the wrath of his brothers who conspired together to slay him, cast him into a pit and say a wild animal devoured him. To avoid having his blood on their hands, however, they decided to sell him to Ishmaelite merchants for twenty pieces of gold. He was brought into Egypt and sold to Potiphar, an officer of Pharaoh.

[4] "More precious than all gold" (Latin).

[5] "Let the buyer beware" (Latin).

grow up into orderly Families, to the Peopling of the Land: but still remain in our Body Politick as a kind of extravasat Blood[6]. As many Negro men as there are among us, so many empty places there are in our Train Bands, and the places taken up of Men that might make Husbands for our Daughters. And the Sons and Daughters of *New England* would become more like *Jacob*, and *Rachel*, if this Slavery were thrust quite out of doors. Moreover it is too well known what temptations Masters are under, to connive at the Fornication of their Slaves; lest they should be obliged to find them Wives, or pay their Fines. It seems to be practically pleaded that they might be Lawless; 'tis thought much of, that the Law should have Satisfaction for their Thefts, and other Immoralities; by which means, *Holiness to the Lord*, is more rarely engraven upon this sort of Servitude. It is likewise most lamentable to think, how in taking Negros out of *Africa*, and Selling of them here, That which GOD has joyned together men do boldly rent asunder; Men from their Country, Husbands from their Wives, Parents from their Children. How horrible is the Uncleanness, Mortality, if not Murder, that the Ships are guilty of that bring great Crouds of these miserable Men, and Women. Methinks, when we are bemoaning the barbarous Usage of our Friends and Kinsfolk in *Africa*: it might not be unseasonable to enquire whether we are not culpable in forcing the *Africans* to become Slaves amongst our selves. And it may be a question whether all the Benefit received by *Negro* Slaves, will balance the Accompt of Cash laid out upon them; and for the Redemption of our own enslaved Friends out of *Africa*. Besides all the Persons and Estates that have perished there.

Obj. 1. *These Blackamores are of the Posterity of Cham, and therefore are under the Curse of Slavery.* Gen. 9. 25, 26, 27.[7]

Answ. Of all Offices, one would not begg this; *viz.* Uncall'd for, to be an Executioner of the Vindictive Wrath of God; the extent and duration of which is to us uncertain. If this ever was a Commission; How do we know but that it is long since out of Date? Many have found it to their Cost, that a Prophetical Denunciation of Judgment against a Person or People, would not warrant them to inflict that evil. If it would, *Hazael* might justify himself in all he did against his Master, and the *Israelites*, from 2 Kings 8. 10, 12.[8]

But it is possible that by cursory reading, this Text may have been mistaken. For *Canaan* is the Person Cursed three times over, without the mentioning of *Cham*. Good Expositors suppose the Curse entaild on him, and that this Prophesie was accomplished in the Extirpation of the Canaanites, and in the Servitude of the *Gibeonites*. *Vide Pareum.*[9] Whereas the Blackmores are not descended of *Canaan*, but of *Cush*. Psal. 68. 31. *Princes shall come out of Egypt* [Mizraim], *Ethiopia* [Cush] *shall soon stretch out her hands unto God.* Under which Names, all *Africa* may be comprehended; and their Promised Conversion ought to be prayed for. *Jer.* 13. 23. *Can the Ethiopian change his skin?* This shows that Black Men are the Posterity of *Cush*: Who time out of mind have been distinguished by their Colour. And for want of the true, *Ovid* assigns a fabulous cause of it.

---

[6] Blood forced out of its customary vessels.

[7] The biblical passage frequently cited as a divine sanction for slavery. Ham, Noah's youngest son, saw his father asleep and naked in his tent. When he told his older brothers, they covered their father. Upon awakening, Noah said of his youngest son, who would became the father of the Canaanites: "Cursed be Canaan; lowest of slaves shall he be unto his brethren. And he said, Blessed be the Lord God of Shem; and Canaan shall be his servant. God shall enlarge Japheth, and he shall dwell in the tents of Shem; and Canaan shall be his servant."

[8] Hazael, a servant to King Ben-hadad of Aram, was sent to inquire of Elisha, a holy man of God, whether the king would recover from his illness. Elisha foresaw the king's death at the hands of Hazael, who succeeded him, and who persecuted the people of Israel.

[9] "See Pareus" (Latin). David Pareus (1548–1622), a famous Protestant theologian from Heidelberg, whose biblical commentaries Sewall frequently cited.

> *Sanguine tum credunt in corpora sunma vocato*
> *Æthiopum populus nigrum traxisse colorem.*
> Metamorph. lib. 2.[10]

Obj. 2. *The* Nigers *are brought out of a Pagan Country, into places where the Gospel is Preached.*

Answ. Evil must not be done, that good may come of it. The extraordinary and comprehensive Benefit accruing to the Church of God, and to Joseph personally, did not rectify his brethrens Sale of him.

Obj. 3. *The* Africans *have Wars one with another: Our Ships bring lawful Captives taken in those Wars.*

Answ. For ought is known, their Wars are much such as were between *Jacob's* Sons and their Brother *Joseph.* If they be between Town and Town; Provincial, or National: Every War is upon one side Unjust. An Unlawful War can't make lawful Captives. And by Receiving, we are in danger to promote, and partake in their Barbarous Cruelties. I am sure, if some Gentlemen should go down to the *Brewsters* to take the Air, and Fish: And a stronger party from Hull should Surprise them, and Sell them for Slaves to a Ship outward bound: they would think themselves unjustly dealt with; both by Sellers and Buyers. And yet 'tis to be feared, we have no other kind of Title to our *Nigers. Therefore all things whatsoever ye would that men should do to you, do ye even so to them: For this is the Law and the Prophets.* Matt. 7. 12.

Obj. 4. Abraham *had Servants bought with his Money, and born in his House.*

Answ. Until the Circumstances of *Abraham's* purchase be recorded, no Argument can be drawn from it. In the mean time, Charity obliges us to conclude, that He knew it was lawful and good.

It is Observable that the *Israelites* were strictly forbidden the buying, or selling one another for Slaves. *Levit.* 25. 39. 46.[11] *Jer.* 34. 8. . .22.[12] And GOD gaged His Blessing in lieu of any

---

[10]   Ovid (43 BC–AD 17?), the Roman poet, tells the story of Phaeton, son of Helios, in his *Metamorphoses*, Book 2. Phaeton got permission to drive Helios' sun-chariot for one day, but was nearly overthrown and almost set the world on fire. Ovid says, "It was then, as men think, that the peoples of Ethiopia became black-skinned, since the blood was drawn to the surface of their bodies by the heat."

[11]   Leviticus 25:39: "And if thy brother that dwelleth by thee be waxen poor, and be sold unto thee; thou shalt not compel him to serve as a bondservant;" 46, "And ye shall take them as an inheritance for your children after you, to inherit them for a possession; they shall be your bondmen for ever: but over your brethren the children of Israel, ye shall not rule one over another with rigor."

[12]   Jeremiah 34:8–22: "This is the word that came unto Jeremiah from the Lord, after that the king Zedekiah had made a covenant with all the people which were at Jerusalem, to proclaim liberty unto them; That every man should let his manservant, and every man his maidservant, being an Hebrew or an Hebrewess, go free; that none should serve himself of them, to wit, of a Jew his brother. Now when all princes, and all the people, which had entered into the covenant, heard that every one should let his manservant, and every one his maidservant, go free, that none should serve themselves of them any more, then they obeyed, and let them

go. But afterward they turned, and caused the servants and the handmaids, whom they had let go free, to return, and brought them into subjection for servants and for handmaids. Therefore the word of the Lord came to Jeremiah from the Lord, saying, Thus saith the Lord, the God of Israel: I made a covenant with your fathers in the day that I brought them forth out of the land of Egypt, out of the house of bondmen, saying, At the end of seven years let ye go every man his brother an Hebrew, which hath been sold unto thee; and when he hath served thee six years, thou shalt let him go free from thee: but your fathers hearkened not unto me, neither inclined their ear. And ye were now turned, and had done right in my sight, in proclaiming liberty, every man to his neighbor; and ye had made a covenant before me in the house which is called by my name, and caused every man his servant, and every man his handmaid, who he had set at liberty at their pleasure, to return and brought them into subjection, to be unto you for servants and for handmaids. Therefore saith the Lord: Ye have not hearkened unto me, in proclaiming liberty, every one to his brother, and every man to his neighbor: behold, I proclaim a liberty for you, saith the Lord, to the sword, to the pestilence, and to the famine: and I will make you to be removed into all the kingdoms of the earth. And I will give the men that have transgressed my covenant, which have not per-loss they might conceipt they suffered thereby. Deut. 15. 18.[13] And since the partition Wall is broken down, inordinate Self love should likewise be demolished. GOD expects that Christians should be of a more Ingenuous and benign frame of spirit. Christians should carry it to all the World, as the *Israelites* were to carry it one towards another. And for men obstinately to persist in holding their Neighbours and Brethren under the Rigor of perpetual Bondage, seems to be no proper way of gaining Assurance that God has given them Spiritual Freedom. Our Blessed Saviour has altered the Measures of the ancient Love-Song, and set it to a most excellent New Tune, which all ought to be ambitious of learning. *Matt.* 5 43, 44.[14] *Job* 13. 34.[15] These *Ethiopians*, as black as they are; seeing they are the Sons and Daughters of the First *Adam,* the Brethren and Sisters of the Last ADAM, and the Offspring of GOD; They ought to be treated with a Respect agreeable.

Servitus perfecta voluntaria, inter Christianum & Christianum, ex parte servi patientis sæpe est licita, quia est necessaria: sed ex parte dominti agentis, & procurando & exercendo vix potest esse licita: quia non convenit regulæ illi generali: Quæcunque volueritis ut faxiant vobis homines, ita & vos facite eis. Matt. 7. 12.

Perfecta servitus pœnæ, non potest jure locum habere, nisi ex delicto gravi quod ultimum supplicium aliquo modo meretur: quia Libertas ex naturali æstimatione proxime accedit ad vitam ipsam, & eidem a multis præferri solet.

Ames. Cas. Consc. Lib. 5. Cap. 23. Thes. 2, 3.[16]

1700

Cotton Mather (1663–1728)

Although Cotton Mather's public involvement in the sensational Salem witchcraft trials made him look like the stereotypical Puritan – narrow, superstitious, and self-righteous, his career and writ-

---

formed the words of the covenant which they had made before me, when they cut the calf in twain, and passed between the parts thereof, The princes of Judah, and the princes of Jerusalem, the eunuchs, and the priests, and all the people of the land, which passed between the parts of the calf; I will even give them into the hand of their enemies, and into the hand of them that seek their life: and their dead bodies shall be for meat unto the fowls of the heaven, and to the beasts of the earth. And Zedekiah king of Judah and his princes will I give into the hand of their enemies, and into the hand of them that seek their life, and into the hand of the king of Babylon's army, which are gone up from you. Behold I will command, saith the Lord, and cause them to return to this city; and burn it with fire: and I will make the cities of Judah a desolation without an inhabitant."

[13] In describing the laws the Hebrews must follow once settled in the Promised Land, Moses gave the rule about freeing Hebrew slaves after six years of labor reiterated in Jeremiah 34:8, and added, "the Lord thy God shall bless thee in all that thou doest."

[14] In Matthew 5:43–44, Jesus teaches, "Ye have heard that it hath been said, Thou shalt love they neighbor, and hate thine enemy. But I say unto you, Love your enemies, bless them that curse you, do good to them that hate you, and pray for them which despitefully use you, and persecute you."

[15] In Job 13:34, Jesus says, "A new commandment I give unto you, That ye love one another, as I have loved you, that ye also love one another."

[16] This is the complete passage from Ames' *De conscientia*, cited in translation at the beginning of the tract. It is from a translated edition entitled *Conscience with the Power and Cares thereof* (London 1643), Book 5, Chapter 23, Theses 2, 3: "2.2 Perfect servitude, so it be voluntary, is on the patients part often lawfull betweene Christian and Christian, because indeed it is necessary: but on the Masters part who is the agent, in procuring and exercising the authority, it is scarce lawfull; in respect it thwarts the generall Canon, *What would you have men doe unto you, even so doe unto them;* Matth. 17.12. 3.3, Perfect servitude, by way of punishment, can have no place by right, unlesse for some hainous offence, which might deserve the severest punishment, to wit, death: because our liberty in the naturall account, is the very next thing to life it selfe, yea by many is preferred before it."

ing prove him to be brilliant, scientific, and quite human. His very name bespeaks a formidable genealogy: he was the grandson of John Cotton, the preeminent minister of Boston's First Church, and Richard Mather, first minister of Dorchester; the son of Increase Mather, the respected minister of Boston's North Church and President of Harvard College. Expecting him to carry on the clerical calling of the family, his father educated him at home and sent him to Harvard at the age of eleven. Although he excelled academically, he was not popular with the other students and suffered from a bad stutter. While Mather had dreams of outdoing his father, he also dreamed of being a physician, but laid aside his personal predilections and was installed as his father's assistant in the Second Church of Boston at the young age of twenty-two. A year later he married the first of two wives who bore him a total of fifteen children.

Thereafter, father and son worked closely together as spiritual and community leaders of orthodox Puritan opinion. Cotton minded the congregation while his father journeyed to England in 1688 to protest the presence of Royal Governor Andros, who had been appointed by King James II, a Catholic, to govern the predominantly Puritan colony since the invalidation of its original charter in 1684. When James was weakened by his attempt to reverse the Reformation in Old England and was finally replaced by William of Orange, husband of James' Protestant daughter Mary, the former power elite in New England moved against Governor Andros in a bloodless "revolution" led by Cotton Mather and Simon Bradstreet, the poet's husband and last of the old governors. Meanwhile, in London, Increase Mather deftly lobbied all parties and in 1691 negotiated a new royal charter for Massachusetts, also influencing the appointment of the new colonial governor and council.

Ironically, it was changes brought about by the new charter that reduced the Mathers' influence on the public life of the colony they so cherished. Massachusetts was growing, and secular interests were challenging the old, pre-capitalist ideals of business and belief. The tragic events at Salem, in which nineteen people were executed for refusing to confess to charges of witchcraft leveled by their neighbors and a group of young women (all confessors went free), shook the colony and played very badly in Europe and England. Although Increase Mather in 1693 published the tract Cases of Conscience, which counseled judicious theological skepticism of the

methods used at the trials and thus helped to end the persecutions, Cotton Mather never signed the preface as did many Boston ministers. Then, the new charter, by establishing liberty of conscience (for everyone but Catholics!), technically removed the Congregational Church from its powerful position, ending the dream of a Puritan commonwealth, and encouraging what orthodox Puritans had always feared most: the spread of toleration. While Cotton pressed for an alliance between Congregationalists and Presbyterians against other "innovators" and interlopers, more liberal Protestants took power. One consequence was the ousting of Increase from the presidency of Harvard. When Cotton was not asked to be his successor, both looked towards Yale in Connecticut to carry on the old faith. Cotton refused Yale's offer of the presidency, and began to turn away from institutional commitments and political battles. This withdrawal inward characterized the latter part of his life, which was also fraught with personal losses and disappointments. The deaths of his first two wives were compounded by the insanity of his third wife, and his favorite son, named after his father, proved to be embarrassingly wild and ungovernable. Although he remained an important figure in the religious culture of eastern Massachusetts, Mather never equaled his father's diplomatic and worldly influence and only outlived him by five years.

But while the son failed to match his father in outward achievements, he more than outdid him in literary production. Cotton Mather's tumultuous spiritual life, and his rigorous regimen of devotion which included six to seven hours of worship daily, fueled his literary labors. He produced over four hundred publications and, at his death, left a considerable body of unpublished work, including the manuscript of Biblia Americana, a compendious commentary attempting to reconcile scripture and scientific truth, which he considered his masterpiece. Although his interest in science began in his early years and culminated in his election to the Royal Society in 1712, his support of smallpox inoculations, and many important scientific works, such as The Christian Philosopher (1720), Mather is better known for the shameful pseudo-science of his accounts of witchcraft in New England. Mather had become somewhat of an expert in witchcraft in the 1680s, and so was asked by the court of Oyer and Terminer, authorized by Governor William Phipps, to record the interrogations of the accused in Salem before they came to trial. In his framing commentary, Cotton argues that the fearsome presence of Satan in Salem not only confirmed the existence of the supernatural realm, but should goad increasingly secularized New Englanders into a lively remembrance of the original Puritan mission. Mather's account of Hannah Dustan's captivity during King Williams' War portrays another strong Puritan goodwife's triumph over the local version of Satan, the Native American who, in this narrative is Catholic as well as unaccountably pious.

Perhaps sensing the passing of the old order, in the 1690s Mather began writing his encyclopedic history of New England, *Magnalia Christi Americana*, which not only rehearses the events and mission of the plantation of God's chosen people in the New World, but offers revealing biographies of its leading men shaped to fit the mold of Puritan piety and zeal. Mather argues for "christianizing" but not freeing Negro slaves in his sermon of 1721, which stands in stark contrast to the antislavery arguments of an old family friend and prominent jurist, Samuel Sewall, described elsewhere in this volume. While Mather's religious zeal and scientific interests presage the writing of Jonathan Edwards and his reformist spirit inspired men like Benjamin Franklin, Mather's baroque and heavily ornamented style of writing is distinctive. Not merely a show of erudition or classical learning, Mather's proliferating allusions and playful turns of phrase, though out of style at the time he wrote, anchored him and his subjects to worlds of learning and sacred history that were still present and vivifying to the preeminent son of the Puritan experiment in New England.

PRIMARY WORKS

The Wonders of the Invisible World, 1692.
Magnalia Christi Americana; or, The Ecclesiastical History of New England from its First Planting, in the Year 1620, unto the Year of Our Lord, 1698, 1702.
The Negro Christianized. An Essay to Excite and Assist the Good Work, The Instruction of Negro-Servants in Christianity, 1706.
The Christian Philosopher, 1720.
Diary of Cotton Mather 1681–1724.
Agricola, c. 1725.
Manductio ad Ministerium, 1726.

FURTHER READING

Robert Middlekauf, *The Mathers: Three Generations of Puritan Intellectuals, 1596–1728* (New York: Oxford, 1971).
Sacvan Bercovitch, *The Puritan Origins of the American Self* (New Haven: Yale University Press, 1975).
John Demos, *Entertaining Satan: Witchcraft and the Culture of early New England* (New York: Oxford University Press, 1982).
Mitchell Breitwieser, *Cotton Mather and Benjamin Franklin: The Price of Representative Personality* (Cambridge: Cambridge University Press, 1984).
Kenneth Silverman, *The Life and Times of Cotton Mather* (New York: Harper & Row, 1984).
Christopher Felker, *Reinventing Cotton Mather in the American Renaissance* (Boston: Northeastern University Press, 1994).

FROM *DECENNIUM LUCTUOSUM* [THE CAPTIVITY OF HANNAH DUSTAN][1]

Article XXV: A Notable Exploit; wherein Dux Foemina Facti[2]

On March 15, 1697, the Salvages made a descent upon the Skirts of Haverhill, Murdering and Captivating about Thirty-Nine Persons, Burning about Half a Dozen Houses. In this Broil,

---

[1]   "Sorrowful Decade" (Latin), the title of Mather's account of New England's Indian warfare during the Anglo-French imperial conflict known as King William's War (1689–97). Hannah Dustan's story was the most notable captivity after the narrative of Mary Rowlandson's captivity in Metacom's War, published in 1682. They are linked by the fact that one of Dustan's captors had lived in the Rowlandson household. Mather first told Dustan's story in an appendix to *Humiliations Followed with Deliverances* (1697), and later re-worked it into *Decennium Luctuosum*, published in Boston, 1699. He then incorporated it into his *Magnalia Christi Americana*, Book VII. It was retold in the nineteenth century by John Greenleaf Whittier, Henry Thoreau and Nathaniel Hawthorne. The text, with modifications, is from *Decennium Luctuosum*, 1699.

[2]   "The leader is a woman" (Latin), from Virgil's *Aeneid* I: 364. This motto was put on medals commemorating Queen Elizabeth's victory over the Spanish Armada in 1588.

one Hannah Dustan, having lain in about a Week[3], attended with her Nurse, Mary Neff, a Widow[4], a Body of Terrible Indians drew near unto the House, where she lay, with Designs to carry on their Bloody Devastations. Her Husband[5] hastened from his Employments abroad, unto the Relief of his Distressed Family; and first bidding Seven of his Eight children (which were from Two to Seventeen years of Age) to get away as fast as they could, unto some Garrison in the Town, he went in, to inform his Wife of the horrible Distress come upon them. E'er she could get up, the fierce Indians were got so near, that utterly despairing to do her any Service, he ran out after his Children; Resolving that on the Horse which he had with him, he would Ride away with That which he should in this Extremity find his Affections to pitch most upon, and leave the Rest unto the care of the Divine Providence. He overtook his Children about Forty Rod from his Door; but then, such was the Agony of his Parental Affections, that he found it impossible for him to Distinguish any one of them from the rest; wherefore he took up a Courageous Resolution to Live and dy with them all. A party of Indians came up with him; and now, though they Fired at him, and he Fired at them, yet he manfully kept at the Reer of his Little Army of Unarmed Children, while they Marched off, with the pace of a Child of Five years old; until, by the Singular Providence of God, he arrived safe with them all, unto a place of Safety, about a Mile or two from his House. But his House must the mean Time have more dismal Tragedies acted at it. The Nurse trying to Escape, with the New-born Infant, fell into the Hands of the Formidable Salvages; and those furious Tawnies coming into the House, bid poor Dustan to Rise Immediately. Full of Astonishment, she did so; and sitting down in the Chimney with an Heart full of most fearful Expectation, she saw the Raging Dragons rifle all that they could carry away, and set the House on Fire. About Nineteen or Twenty Indians now led these away, with about Half a Score other English Captives; but e'er they had gone many Steps, they dash'd out the Brains of the Infant against a Tree; and several of the other Captives, as they began to Tire in the sad Journey, were soon sent unto their Long Home; the Salvages would presently bury their Hatchets in their Brains, and leave their Carcases on the Ground for Birds and Beasts to feed upon. However, Dustan (with her Nurse), notwithstanding her present Condition, Travelled that Night, about a Dozen Miles, and then kept up with their New Masters in a long Travel of an Hundred and Fifty Miles, more or less, within a few Days Ensuing, without any sensible Damage, in their Health, from the Hardships of their Travel, their lodging, their Diet, and their many other Difficulties.

These Two poor Women were now in the Hands of those, whose Tender Mercies are Cruelties; but in the Good God, who hath all Hearts in His own Hands, heard the Sighs of these Prisoners, and gave them to find unexpected Favour from the Master, who laid claim unto them. That Indian Family consisted of Twelve Persons; Two Stout men, Three Women, and Seven Children; and for the Shame of many an English Family, that has the Character of Prayerless upon it, I must now Publish what these poor Women assure me: 'Tis this; In Obedience to the Instructions which the French have given them, they would have Prayers in their Family, no less than Thrice Every Day; in the Morning, at Noon, and in the Evening; nor would they ordinarily let their Children Eat or Sleep, without first saying their Prayers. Indeed these Idolaters were like the rest of their whiter Brethren, Persecutors; and would not endure, that these poor Women should Retire to their English Prayers, if they could hinder them. Nevertheless, the poor Women had nothing but fervent Prayers, to make their Lives

---

3   After having given birth.

4   Neff was about fifty years old and a local midwife. Her husband had been killed in the Indian wars in Maine.

5   Thomas Dustan, also spelled Dustin or Dustun, was a farmer and bricklayer.

Comfortable, or Tolerable; and by being daily sent out, upon Business, they had Opportunities together and asunder, to do like another Hannah, in Pouring out their Souls before the Lord:[6] Nor did their praying Friends among ourselves, forbear to Pour out Supplications for them. Now, they could not observe it without some wonder, that their Indian Master, sometimes when he saw them Dejected, would say unto them, "What need you Trouble your self? If your God will have you delivered, you shall be so!" And it seems, that our God would have it so to be. This Indian Family was now travelling with these Two Captive Women, (and an English Youth, taken from Worcester, a year and a half before[7],) unto a Rendezvous of Salvages, which they call, a Town, some where beyond Penacook[8]; and they still told these poor Women, that when they came to this Town, they must be Stript, and Scourg'd and run the Gantlet through the whole Army of Indians. They said, this was the Fashion, when the Captives first came to a Town; and they derided some of the Fainthearted English, which they said, fainted and swoon'd away under the Torments of this Discipline.[9] But on April 30, While they were yet, it may be about an Hundred and Fifty Miles from the Indian Town, a little before Break of Day, when the whole Crew was in a Dead Sleep; (Reader, see if it prove not So!) one of these Women took up a Resolution, to imitate the Action of Jael upon Sisera[10]; and being where she had not her own Life secured by any Law unto her, she thought she was not Forbidden by any Law to take away the Life of the Murderers, by whom her Child had been butchered. She heartened the Nurse, and the Youth, to assist her in this Enterprize; and all furnishing themselves with Hatchets for the purpose, they struck such Home Blows, upon the Heads of their Sleeping Oppressors, that e'er they could any of them Struggle into any Effectual Resistance, at the Feet of these poor Prisoners, they bow'd, they fell, they lay down: at their feet they bowed, they fell; where they bowed, there they fell down Dead.[11] Only one Squaw escaped sorely wounded from them, in the Dark; and one Boy, whom they Reserved Asleep, intending to bring him away with them, suddenly wak'd, and skuttled away from this Desolation. But cutting off the Scalps of the Ten Wretches, they came off, and Received Fifty Pounds from the General Assembly of the Province, as a Recompence of their Action; besides which they Received many presents of Congratulation from their more private Friends; but none gave 'em a greater Tast of Bounty than Colonel Nicholson, the Governor of Maryland, who hearing of their Action, sent 'em a very generous Token of his Favour.

1697

1699

---

[6] Hannah, wife of Elkanah, prayed fervently to God for a child, and became the mother of Samuel, a judge, prophet, and leader in early Israel. See 1 Samuel: 1–2.

[7] Samuel Lenorson or Leonardson, who had been captured near Lake Quinsigamond in Worcester, Massachusetts.

[8] Near present-day Concord, New Hampshire.

[9] Running captives through a gauntlet to determine their character was a frequent practice among northeastern Indians and was often the prelude to adoption into a tribe.

[10] Sisera was the captain of the army of Jabin, a king of Canaan who held the Israelites in bondage. They rebelled under the leadership of Deborah. After Sisera's great army was defeated, he fled and came to the tent of Jael, wife of Heber the Kenite, who at first gave him refuge, but after he was asleep, killed him by driving a nail through his temple, and so helped liberate the Israelis. See Judges 4.

[11] See Judges 5:27.

FROM *MAGNALIA CHRISTI AMERICANA*[1]

From *A General Introduction*

Dicam hoc propter utilitatem eorum qui Lecturi sunt hoc opus.

Theodoret[2]

1. I WRITE the *Wonders* of the CHRISTIAN RELIGION, flying from the Depravations of *Europe*, to the *American Strand*. And, assisted by the Holy Author of that *Religion*, I do, with all Conscience of *Truth*, required therein by Him, who is the *Truth* itself, Report the *Wonderful Displays* of His Infinite Power, Wisdom, Goodness, and Faithfulness, wherewith His Divine Providence hath *Irradiated* an *Indian Wilderness*.

I Relate the *Considerable Matters*, that produced and attended the First Settlement of COLONIES, which have been Renowned for the Degree of REFORMATION, Professed and Attained by *Evangelical Churches*, erected in those *Ends of the Earth*: And a *Field* being thus prepared, I proceed unto a Relation of the *Considerable Matters* which have been acted thereupon. . . .

3. It is the History of these PROTESTANTS, that is here attempted; PROTESTANTS that highly honoured and affected *The Church of* ENGLAND, and humbly Petition to be a *Part* of it: But by the Mistake of a few powerful *Brethren*, driven to seek a place for the Exercise of the *Protestant Religion*, according to the Light of their Consciences, in the Desarts of *America*. And in this Attempt I have proposed, not only to preserve and secure the Interest of *Religion*, in the Churches of that little country NEW-ENGLAND, so far as the Lord Jesus Christ may please to Bless it for that End, but also to offer unto the Churches of the *Reformation*, abroad in the World, some small *Memorials*, that may be serviceable unto the Designs of *Reformation*, whereto, I believe, they are quickly to be awakened . . . When the Blessed Martyr *Constantine* was carried with other Martyrs, in a *Dung-Cart*, unto the place of Execution, he pleasantly said, *Well, yet we are a precious Odour to God in Christ*. Tho' the *Reformed Churches* in the *American Regions*, have, by very Injurious Representations of their Brethren (all which they desire to Forget and Forgive!) been many times thrown into a *Dung-Cart*; yet, as they have been a *precious Odour to God in Christ*, so, I hope, they will be a *precious Odour* unto *His People*; and not only *Precious*, but *Useful* also, when the *History* of them shall come to be considered. A *Reformation of the Church* is coming on, and I cannot but thereunto say, with the dying *Cyrus* to his Children in *Xenophon*[3] . . . *Learn from the things that have been done already, for this is the best way of Learning*. The Reader hath here an Account of *The Things that have been done already*. *Bernard* upon the Clause in the *Canticles*, [*O thou fairest among Women*] has this ingenious Gloss, *Pulchram, non omnimodo quidem, sed pulchram inter mulieres cam dicit, videliciet cum Distinctione, quatenus et ex hoc amplius reprimatur, & sciat quid desit sibi*.[4] Thus, I do not say, That the Churches of *New-England* are the most

---

[1]   The title translated is "A History of Christ's Wonderful Works in America" (Latin). The *Magnalia* contains seven books covering the history of the New England colonies. First published in London, 1702, these selections, with slight modification, are from *Magnalia Christi Americana, Books I and II*, eds Kenneth Murdock with Elizabeth Miller (Cambridge, Massachusetts: Belknap Press, 1977).

[2]   "This I say for the good of those who shall read the book." Printed in the original text in Greek and Latin, this passage is from Theodoret (393?–457), a Greek bishop and church historian.

[3]   Xenophon (430?–355?BC), a Greek author whose book *Anabasis* records the accomplishments of Cyrus the Younger, a prince of Persia.

[4]   "He says that she is fair, not in a universal sense, but fair among women, plainly with a distinction, to which extent his praise is qualified and she may know what she lacks" (Latin); from the commentaries upon Canticles, another name for The Song of Solomon, I:8, by Bernard of Clairvaux (1090–1153), a French Cicercian abbot and noted preacher. The Puritans understood the Bride of Canticles to be a figure for the Spouse of Christ or the Church.

Regular that can be; yet I do say, and am sure, That they are very like unto those that were in the *First Ages* of Christianity. And if I assert, That in the *Reformation* of the Church, the State of it in those *First Ages*, is to be not a little considered, the Great *Peter Ramus*[5], among others, has emboldened me . . . In short, The *First Age* was the *Golden Age*: To return unto *That*, will make a Man a *Protestant*, and I may add, a *Puritan*. 'Tis possible, That our Lord Jesus Christ carried some Thousands of *Reformers* into the Retirements of an *American Desert*, on purpose, that, with an opportunity granted unto many of his Faithful Servants, to enjoy the precious *Liberty* of their *Ministry*, tho' in the midst of many *Temptations* all their days, he might there, *To* them first, and then *By* them, give a *Specimen* of many Good Things, which He would have His Churches elsewhere aspire and arise unto: And *This* being done, He knows whether there be not *All done*, that *New-England* was planted for; and whether the Plantations may not, soon after this, *Come to Nothing*. Upon that Expression in the Sacred Scripture, *Cast the unprofitable Servant into Outer Darkness*,[6] it hath been imagined by some, That the *Regiones Exteræ* of America, are the *Tenebræ Exteriores*,[7] which the *Unprofitable* are there condemned unto. No doubt, the Authors of those Ecclesiastical Impositions and Severities, which drove the English Christians into the *Dark Regions* of America, esteemed those *Christians* to be very *unprofitable* sort of Creatures. But behold, *ye European* Churches, There are *Golden Candlesticks* [more than *twice Seven times Seven!*][8] in the midst of this *Outer Darkness*: Unto the *upright* Children of *Abraham*, here hath arisen *Light in Darkness*. And let us humbly speak it, it shall be *Profitable* for you to consider the *Light*, which from the midst of this *Outer Darkness*, is not to be Darted over unto the other side of the *Atlantick Ocean*. But we must therewithal ask your Prayers, that these *Golden Candlesticks* may not *quickly* be *Removed out of their place!*

4. But whether *New-England* may *Live* any where else or no, it must *Live* in our *History*! . .

FROM *THE NEGRO CHRISTIANIZED*[1]

It is a *Golden Sentence*, that has been sometimes quoted from *Chrysostom*; That *for a man to know the Art of Alms, is more than for a man to be Crowned with the Diamond of Kings: But to Convert one Soul unto God, is more than to pour out Ten Thousand Talents into the Baskets of the Poor.*[2] Truly, to Raise a *Soul*, from a dark State of Ignorance and Wickedness, to the Knowledge of GOD, and the Belief of CHRIST and the practice of our Holy and Lovely Religion; 'Tis the noblest Work, that ever was undertaken among the Children of men. An Opportunity to Endeavour

---

[5]   Pierre de la Ramée (1515–70), also known by his latinized name, was a French philosopher and educational reformer who converted to Protestantism and died in the St Bartholomew's Day massacre in 1570. His logical method was adopted by English Protestants and became the standard procedure of New England ministers in reasoning and sermonizing. Mather refers to the famous statement Ramus made to the Cardinal of Lorrain in 1561 when he publicly announced his conversion to Protestantism: "Among the many favours with which you have enriched me, this I shall keep in remembrance . . . that of the fifteen centuries since Christ, the first is truly golden and that the rest, the further they are removed the more they are wretched and degenerate; therefore when I had free choice, I preferred the golden age."

[6]   Matthew 25:30.

[7]   Outer regions of America are the Outer shadows or darkness (Latin).

[8]   See Revelation 1:12–13, 20. In his vision, John of Patmos sees seven golden lampstands which Christ explains stand for the seven early churches of Ephesus, Smyrna, Pergamum, Thyatira, Sardis, Philadelphia, and Laodicea.

THE NEGRO

[1]   First published in Boston, 1706.

[2]   John Chrysostom (347?–407), a famous Christian scholar, argues in his *Homilies on First Corinthians*, Homily III, that "although thou give countless treasure unto the poor, thou wilt do no such work as he who converteth one soul."

the CONVERSION of a Soul, from a Life of *Sin*, which is indeed a woeful *Death*, to Fear God, and Love CHRIST, and by a Religious Life to Escape the Paths of the Destroyer; it cannot but be Acceptable to all that have themselves had in themselves Experience of such a *Conversion*. And such an Opportunity there is in your Hands, O all you that have any **Negroes** in your Houses; an Opportunity to try, Whether you may not be the Happy *Instruments*, of Converting, the *Blackest* Instances of *Blindness* and *Baseness*, into admirable *Candidates* of Eternal Blessedness. Let not this Opportunity be Lost; if you have any concern for *Souls*, your Own or Others; but, make a Trial Whether by your Means, the most *Bruitish* of Creatures upon Earth may not come to be disposed, in some Degree, like the *Angels* of Heaven; and the *Vassals* of Satan, become the *Children* of God. Suppose these Wretched Negroes, to be the Offspring of *Cham*[3] (which yet is not so very certain,) yet let us make a Trial, Whether the CHRIST who *dwelt in the Tents of Shem*, have not some of His Chosen among them; Let us make a Trial, Whether they that have been Scorched and Blacken'd By the Sun of *Africa*, may not come to have their Minds Healed by the more Benign *Beams* of the *Sun* of *Righteousness*.

It is come to pass by the *Providence* of God, without which there comes nothing to pass, that Poor **Negroes** are cast under your Government and Protection. You take them into your *Families*, you look on them as part of your *Possessions*, and you Expect from their Service, a Support, and perhaps an Increase, of your other *Possessions*. How agreeable would it be, if a Religious Master or Mistress thus attended, would now think with themselves! Who can tell but that this Poor Creature may Belong to the Election of God! *Who can tell, but that God may have sent this Poor Creature into my Hands, that so One of the Elect may by my means be Called; & by my Instruction be made Wise unto Salvation! The glorious God will put an unspeakable Glory Upon me, if it may be so!* The Considerations that would move you, To Teach your *Negroes* the *Truths* of the Glorious Gospel, as far as you can, and bring them, if it may be, to Live according to those *Truths*, a *Sober*, and a *Righteous*, and a *Godly* Life; They are *Innumerable*; And, if you would after a *Reasonable* manner consider, the Pleas which we have to make on the behalf of *God*, and of the *Souls* which He has made, one would wonder that they should not be *Irresistible*. *Show* your selves Men, and let *Rational Arguments* have their Force upon you, to make you treat, not as *Bruits* but as *Men*, those *Rational Creatures* whom God has made your *Servants*.

For,

First; The Great GOD *Commands* it, and *Requires* it of you; to do what you can that *Your Servants*, may also be *His*. It was an Admonition once given; Eph. 5.9.[4] *Masters, Know that your Master is in Heaven*. You will confess, That the God of Heaven is your *Master*. If your *Negroes* do not comply with your *Commands*, into what Anger, what Language, Perhaps into a misbecoming *Fury*, are you transported? But you are now to attend unto the *Commands* of your more Absolute *Master*; and they are His *Commands* concerning your *Negroes* too. What can be more Expressive; than those words of the Christian Law? Col. 4.1. *Masters, give unto your Servants, that which is Just & Equal, knowing that ye also have a Master in Heaven*. Of what *Servants* is this Injunction to be understood? Verily, of *Slaves*. For *Servants* were generally such, at the time of Writing the New Testament. Wherefore, *Masters*, As it is *Just & Equal*, that your *Servants* be not *Over-wrought*, and that while they *Work* for you, you should *Feed* them, and *Cloath* them, and afford convenient *Rest* unto them, and make their Lives comfortable; So it is *Just* and

---

[3]   In Genesis 9:22–27, Ham (or Cham), Noah's son, saw his father naked as he slept, and alerted his two brothers, who covered up their father. When Noah awoke, he cursed Ham, the ancestor of the Canaanite people, condemning him to be a "servant of servants," and blessed Shem. Africans were thought to be descendants of Ham; thus, this passage was cited by supporters of slavery as biblical sanction.

[4]   It is Ephesians 6:9.

Equal, that you should Acquaint them, as far as you can, with the way to Salvation by JESUS CHRIST. You deny your *Master in Heaven*, if you do nothing to bring your *Servants* unto the Knowledge and Service of that glorious *Master*. One Table of the *Ten Commandments*, has this for the Sum of it; *Thou shalt Love thy Neighbour as thy self*: Man, Thy *Negro* is thy *Neighbour*. T'were an Ignorance, unworthy of a *Man*, to imagine otherwise. Yea, if thou canst grant, *That God hath made of one Blood, all Nations of men*, he is thy *Brother* too. Now canst thou *Love* thy *Negro*, and be willing to see him ly under the Rage of Sin, and the Wrath of God? Canst thou *Love* him, and yet refuse to do any thing, that his miserable Soul may be rescued from Eternal miseries? Oh! Let thy *Love* to that Poor *Soul*, appear in thy concern, to make it, if thou canst, as happy as thy own! We are Commanded, Gal. 6.10. *As we have opportunity let us Do Good unto all men, especially unto them, who are of the Houshold of Faith.* Certainly, we have *Opportunity*, to *Do Good* unto our *Servants*, who are of our *own Houshold*; certainly, we may do something to *make them Good*, and bring them to be of the *Houshold of Faith*. In a word, All the Commandments in the Bible, which bespeak our *Charity* to the *Souls* of others, and our *Endeavour* that the *Souls* of others may be delivered from the Snares of Death; every one of these do oblige us, to do what we can, for the *Souls* of our *Negroes*. They are more nearly *Related* unto us, than many others are; we are more fully *capable* to do for them, than for many others. . . .

Yea, the pious *Masters*, that have instituted their *Servants* in Christian Piety, will even in this Life have a sensible *Recompence*. The more Serviceable, and Obedient and obliging Behaviour of their *Servants* unto them, will be a sensible & a notable *Recompence*. Be assured, Syrs; Your *Servants* will be the *Better Servants*, for being made *Christian Servants*. To *Christianize* them aright, will be to fill them with all *Goodness*. *Christianity* is nothing but the very Mass of Universal *Goodness*. Were your *Servants* well tinged with the Spirit of *Christianity*, it would render them exceeding *Dutiful* unto their *Masters*; exceeding *Patient* under their *Masters*, exceeding faithful in their Business, and afraid of speaking or doing any thing that may justly displease you. It has been observed, that those *Masters* who have used their *Negroes* with most of *Humanity* in allowing them all the Comforts of Life, that are necessary and *Convenient* for them, (Who have remembered, that by the Law of God, even an *Ass* was to be relieved, When *Sinking under his Burden*,[5] and an *Ox* might not be *Muzzled* when *Treading out the Corn*;[6] and that if a *Just man will regard the Life of his Beast*, he will much more allow the comforts of life to and not hide himself *from his own Flesh*:) have been better *Serv'd*, had more work done for them, and better done, than those *Inhumane Masters*, who have used their *Negroes* worse than their *Horses*. And those *Masters* doubtless, who use their *Negroes* with most of *Christianity*, and use most pains to inform them in, and conform them to, Christianity, will find themselves no losers by it. *Onesimus* was doubtless a *Slave*[7]: but this poor *Slave*, on whose behalf a great Apostle of God was more than a little concerned; yea, one Book in our Bible was Written on his behalf! When he was *Christianized*, it was presently said unto his *Master*, Philem. 11. *In time past he was unprofitable to thee, but now he will be profitable.* But many *Masters* whose *Negroes* have greatly vexed them, with miscarriages, may do well to examine, Whether Heaven be not chastising of them for their failing in their Duty about their *Negroes*. Had they done more, to make their *Negroes* the knowing and willing *Servants* of God, it may be, God would have made their *Negroes* better *Servants* to them. Syrs, you may Read your *Sin* in the *Punishment*.

---

[5] One of the laws Moses sets out for the children of Israel: "If thou seest the ass of him that hateth thee lying under his burden and wouldst forebear to help him, thou shalt surely help with him" (Exodus 23:5).

[6] Deuteronomy 25:4. Paul, in 1 Corinthians 9:9 and 1 Timothy 5:18, refers to the Mosaic protection of oxen.

[7] Onesimus, a name meaning "useful" or "profitable," was a slave boy and companion to Paul in prison. In his Epistle to Philemon, Paul asks forgiveness for this boy whom he has converted.

And now, what *Objection* can any Man Living have, to refund the force of these *Considerations*? Produce the *cause*, O Impiety, *Bring forth thy strong reasons*, and let all men see what Idle and silly cavils, are thy best *Reasons* against this Work of God.

It has been cavilled, by some, that it is questionable Whether the *Negroes* have *Rational Souls*, or no. But let that *Bruitish* insinuation be never Whispered any more. Certainly, their *Discourse*, will abundantly prove, that they have *Reason*. *Reason* showes it self in the *Design* which they daily act upon. The vast improvement that *Education* has made upon *some* of them, argues that there is a *Reasonable Soul* in *all* of them. An old Roman, and Pagan, would call upon the Owner of such Servants, *Homines tamen esse memento*.[8] They are Men, and not Beasts that you have bought, and they must be used accordingly. 'Tis true; They are *Barbarous*. But so were our own *Ancestors*. The *Britons* were in many things as *Barbarous*, but a little before our Saviours Nativity, as the *Negroes* are at this day if there be any Credit in *Caesars Commentaries*. *Christianity* will be the best cure for this *Barbarity*. Their *Complexion* sometimes is made an Argument, why nothing should be done for them. A *Gay* sort of argument! As if the great God went by the *Complexion* of Men, in His Favours to them! As if none but *Whites* might hope to be Favoured and Accepted with God! Whereas it is well known, That the *Whites*, are the least part of Mankind. The biggest part of Mankind, perhaps, are *Copper-Coloured*; a sort of *Tawnies*. And our *English* that inhabit some Climates, do seem growing apace to be not much unlike unto them. As if, because a people, from the long force of the *African Sun & Soil* upon them, (improved perhaps, to further Degrees by maternal imaginations, and other accidents,) are come at length to have the small *Fibres* of their *Veins*, and the Blood in them, a little more Interspersed thro their Skin than other People, this must render them less valuable to Heaven than the rest of Mankind? Away with such Trifles. The God who *looks on the Heart*, is not moved by the colour of the *Skin*; is not more propitious to one *Colour* than another. Say rather, with the Apostle; Acts 10.34, 35. *Of a truth I perceive, that God is no respecter of persons, but in every Nation, he that feareth Him and worketh Righteousness, is accepted with Him*. Indeed their *Stupidity* is a *Discouragement*. It may seem, unto as little purpose, to *Teach*, as to *wash an Æthiopian*. But the greater their *Stupidity*, the greater must be our *Application*. If we can't learn them so much as we *Would*, let us learn them as much as we *Can*. A little divine *Light* and *Grace* infused into them, will be of great account. And the more *Difficult* it is, to fetch such *forlorn things* up out of the perdition whereinto they are fallen, the more *Laudable* is the undertaking: There will be the more of a *Triumph*, if we prosper in the undertaking. Let us encourage our selves from that word, Mat. 3.9 *God is able of these Stones, to raise up Children unto Abraham*.

Well; But if the *Negroes* are *Christianized*, they will be *Baptized*; and their *Baptism* will presently entitle them to their *Freedom*, so our *Money* is thrown away.

Man, If this were true; that a *Slave* bought with thy *Money*, were by thy means brought unto the *Things that accompany Salvation*, and thou shouldest from this time have no more Service from him, yet thy *Money* were not thrown away. That Man's *Money will perish with him*, yet he had rather the *Souls* in his *Family* should *Perish* than that he should lose a little *Money*. And suppose it were so, that *Baptism* gave a legal Title to *Freedom*.[9] Is there no guarding against this Inconvenience? You may by sufficient *Indentures*, keep off the things, which you reckon so Inconvenient. But it is all a Mistake. There is no such thing. What *Law* is it, that Sets the *Baptized Slave* at *Liberty*? Not the *Law of Christianity*: that allows of *Slavery*; Only it wonderfully Dulcifies, and Mollifies, and Moderates the Circumstances of it. *Christianity* directs a

---

8   "But remember that they are men" (Latin).

9   The belief that baptism conferred freedom was popularized by works such as Morgan Godwin's *The Negro's & Indi-* *ans Advocate* (1680). The court decision in the Yorke-Talbot case in 1729 confirmed Mather's assertion.

Slave, upon his embracing the *Law of the Redeemer*, to satisfy himself, *That he is the Lords Free-man*, tho' he continues a *Slave*. It supposes, (Col. 3.11.) That there are *Bond* as well as *Free*, among those that have been *Renewed in the Knowledge and Image of Jesus Christ.* Will the *Canon-law* do it? No; The *Canons* of Numberless *Councils*, mention, the *Slaves* of *Christians*, without any contradiction. Will the *Civil Law* do it? No: Tell, if you can, any part of *Christendom*, wherein *Slaves* are not frequently to be met withal. But is not *Freedom* to be claim'd for a *Baptised Slave*, by the *English* Constitution? The English *Laws*, about *Villains*[10], or, *Slaves*, will not say so; for by those *Laws*, they may be granted *for Life*, like a *Lease*, and passed over with a *Mannor*, like other *Goods or Chattels*. And by those *Laws*, the Lords may sieze the Bodies of their *Slaves* even while a Writt, *De libertate probanda*,[11] is depending. These English *Laws* were made when the *Lords* & the *Slaves*, were both of them *Christians*; and they stand still unrepealed. If there are not now such *Slaves* in *England* as formerly, it is from the *Lords*, more than from the *Laws*. The *Baptised* then are not thereby entitled unto their *Liberty*. Howbeit, if they have arrived unto such a measure of *Christianity*, that *some are forbid Water for the Baptising of them*, it is fit, that they should enjoy those *comfortable circumstances* with us, which are due to them, not only as the *Children of Adam*, but also as our *Brethren*, on the same level with us in the expectations of a blessed Immortality, thro' the *Second Adam*[12]. Whatever Slaughter the Assertion may make among the pretensions which are made unto *Christianity*, yet while the *sixteenth* Chapter of *Matthew* is in the Bible,[13] it must be asserted; the *Christian*, who cannot so far Deny *himself*: can be no *Disciple* of the Lord JESUS CHRIST. But, O Christian, thy *Slave* will not Serve thee one jot the worse for that *Self denial*. . . .

1706

---

[10] Villain was the term for a feudal serf. In the case of *Chamberline* v. *Marley* (1696–7), the concept of villeinage was used to argue that English law supported the absolute ownership of people and property.

[11] "Proving freedom" (Latin).

[12] Christ.

[13] In Matthew 16:24 Jesus tells his followers, "If any man will come after me, let him deny himself, and take up his cross, and follow me."

Middle Atlantic:
New Netherland

Jacob Steendam (1616–?)

Born in Amsterdam, Jacob Steendam was in the service of the East India Company for fifteen years. In 1649 and 1650 he published in Holland a collection of poems called *Den Distelvink* (the Thistle-finch or Goldfinch), consisting of love songs and emblems, nuptial and triumphant odes, and spiritual songs. Shortly thereafter, he embarked for New Amsterdam; on arrival, he purchased a house and land and set himself up as a merchant, presenting a petition to the authorities to be allowed to import slaves and other articles from West Africa. In "The Complaint of New Amsterdam", published in 1659, New Amsterdam is personified as a beautiful young woman, daughter of Amsterdam, born in wartime but abandoned by her sponsors (the East India Company). The poem goes on to describe the encroachments of English settlers (un-flatteringly dubbed "the Swine") and the prosperity of the colony despite its neglect at the hands of the Dutch.

PRIMARY WORK

Henry C. Murphy (ed. and trans.) *Anthology of New Netherland, or Translations from the Early Dutch Poets of New York, with Memoirs of their Lives* (Originally published in 1865 by The Bradford Club, Port Washington; New York: Ira J. Friedman, Inc., 1969).

FURTHER READING

J. Franklin Jameson (ed.) *Narratives of New Netherland, 1609–1664* (New York: C. Scribner's Sons, 1909).
Mary Ferris, "A Note about Jacob Steendam," *De Halve Maen* (New York), 90, 3 (1976) p. 14.

"THE COMPLAINT OF NEW AMSTERDAM"

I'm a grandchild of the Gods
Who on th'Amstel[1] have abodes;
Whence their orders forth are sent
Swift for aid and punishment.

I, of Amsterdam, was born,
Early of her breasts forlorn;
From her care so quickly weaned
Oft have I my fate bemoaned.

---

[1]   A river in western Holland.

From my youth up left alone
Naught save hardship have I known;
Dangers have beset my way
From the first I saw the day.
    Think you that a cause for marvel?
This will then the thread unravel,
And the circumstances trace,
Which upon my birth took place.
    Would you ask for my descent?
Long the time was it I spent
In the loins of warlike Mars[2].
    'T seems my mother, seized with fears,
    Prematurely brought me forth.
But I now am very loth[3]
To inform how this befel;
Though 'twas thus, I know full well.
    Bacchus[4], too, – it is no dream,–
First beheld the daylight's beam
From the thigh of Jupiter[5].
But my reasons go too far.
    My own matter must I say,
And not loiter by the way,
E'en though Bacchus
Oft has proven
Friend to me in my misfortune.
    Now the mid-wife who received me,
Was Bellona[6]; in suspense, she
Long did sit in trembling fear,
For the travail was severe.
    From the moment I was born,
Indian neighbors made me mourn.
They pursued me night and day,
While my mother kept away.
    But my sponsors[7] did supply
Better my necessity;
They sustained my feeble life;
They procured a bounteous wife
    As my nurse, who did not spare
To my lips her paps[8] to bare.
This was Ceres[9]; freely she

Rendered what has nurtured me.
    Her most dearly will I prize;
She has made my horns to rise;
Trained my growth through tender years,
'Midst my burdens and my cares.
    True, both simple 'twas and scant,
What I had to feed my want.
Oft 'twas nought except Supawn[10]
And the flesh of buck or fawn.
    When I thus began to grow
No more care did they bestow.
Yet my breasts are full and neat,
And my hips are firmly set.
    Neptune[11] shows me his good will;
Mer'cry[12], quick, exerts his skill
Me t'adorn with silk and gold;
Whence I'm sought by suitors bold.
    Stricken by my cheek's fresh bloom,
By my beauteous youthful form,
They attempt to seize the treasure
To enjoy their wanton pleasure.
    They, my orchards too, would plunder.
Truly 'tis a special wonder,
That a maid, with such a portion,
Does not suffer more misfortune:
    For, I venture to proclaim,
No one can a maiden name,
Who with richer land is blessed
Than th'estate by me possessed.
    See! Two streams my garden bind,
From the East and North they wind,–
Rivers pouring in the sea,
Rich in fish, beyond degree.[13]
    Milk and butter; fruits to eat
No one can enumerate;
Ev'ry vegetable known;
Grain the best that e'er was grown.
    All the blessings man e'er knew,
Here does our Great Giver strew,
(And a climate ne'er more pure)

2   God of war.
3   Reluctant.
4   God of wine.
5   Jupiter visited Semele, mother of Bacchus, in all his godly might. As a result, the pregnant Semele was reduced to ashes, but the unborn child was saved from the flames and placed within Jupiter's thigh, where he remained until he was born.
6   Roman goddess of war.
7   The Dutch West India Company.
8   Breasts.
9   Goddess of corn and harvests.
10   Boiled corn meal.
11   God of the sea.
12   The god Mercury was the patron of travelers and merchants.
13   Probably the Hudson and East Rivers.

But for me, – yet immature,
   Fraught with danger; for the Swine[14]
Trample down these crops of mine;
Up-root, too, my choicest land;
Still and dumb, the while, I stand,
   In the hope, my mother's arm
Will protect me from the harm.
She can succor my distress.
Now my wish, my sole request,–
   Is for men to till my land;

So I'll not in silence stand.
I have lab'rors[15] almost none;
Let my household large become;
   I'll my mother's kitchen furnish
With my knicknacks, with my surplus;
With tobacco, furs and grain;
So that Prussia she'll disdain.

JACOB STEENDAM
Noch vaster[16]

1659

Henricus Selyns (1636–1701)

Born in Holland, Henricus Selyns was for many years a minister in the church at Brueukelen (later Brooklyn), a small congregation of twenty-seven persons, in the colony of New Amsterdam. His poem "Bridal Torch" is a curious blend of the literary genres of the epithalamion or poem celebrating a marriage, (in this case, celebrating the wedding of the rector of the Latin School in New Amsterdam) and the narrative of an Indian massacre. Using metaphors from classic mythology and from the Old Testament, it reflects the deep impact made on the colonists by the Indian massacre of Dutch settlers which took place in 1663, with references to the natural phenomena (earthquakes,

meteorites, and so forth) which Selyns viewed as omens of this calamity.

After the end of Dutch rule, Selyns went back to Holland, but returned to New Amsterdam in 1682. There he served for many years as the minister of the Dutch Reformed Church, and died in 1701 in what had by then become New York.

PRIMARY WORK

Henry C. Murphy (ed. and trans.) *Anthology of New Netherland, or Translations from the Early Dutch Poets of New York, with Memoirs of their Lives* (Originally published in 1865 by The Bradford Club, Port Washington; New York: Ira J. Friedman, Inc., 1969).

"BRIDAL TORCH"

For Rev. Aegidius Luyck, Rector of the Latin School at New Amsterdam, and Judith Van Isendoorn, Lighted shortly after the Esopus Murder[1] Committed at Wiltwyck, in New Netherland, by the Indians, in the year 1663.

   How soon the flame of war the flame of love destroys!
   For Mars[2] comes wickedly, the innocent to injure;

---

[14] Presumably, the English.
[15] Laborers.
[16] A whimsical play on Steendam's own name. Steendam means "stone dam", while "Noch vaster" signifies "still firmer."

SELYNS
[1] A massacre of Dutch settlers. Esopus, later called Wiltwyck, was the name given to a settlement made by the Dutch in 1652 on the west bank of the Hudson River.
[2] God of war.

Nor does it Cupid[3] please, who peace and love enjoys,
And starts, at sight of arms, to hide himself from danger.
He sees the treachery, unlooked for, but designed,
And says: "Can this be right, so stealthily to come in?
They show a friendly smile, but cloak a hostile mind;
'Tis well to fear for Absalom's and Joab's cunning."[4]
His words are yet still warm, and does he not behold,
Alas! house after house, with Indian monsters posted?
Child upon child burnt up? and man on man lain cold?
Barn upon barn consumed? and pregnant women roasted?
They flee, each where he can. "From Wiltwyck is my home,
I go," so speaks the wight[5], "in woods and hills t'abide in."
He bow and arrow seeks; but they had both become
The Indian's ready spoil, who here and there were hiding.
When he is robb'd of these, his weapons are all gone.
And had he not betimes unto his wings betaken,
They sure had killed or wounded him, or captive borne
For Indian chiefs to serve, or Indian forts to work in.
But quickly sat he on the mountains of Katskil,[6]
And thus his woe bewailed: "Domestic joys ne'er bless you,
Till Hymen[7] tends my loves, and wedlock serves my will.
And cursed by you those thoughts, whence wantonness[8] doth issue;
Uncleanness, drunkenness and base and sordid pride,–
The land's three crying sins, – this ruin have effected,
And driven happiness and peace your land aside.
For gross debauchery, such punishment's inflicted;
Whose warnings often giv'n did little heed command.
"Remember," he continued, "the earth how it was shaken[9],
How fires fell from the sky, and small-pox scourged the land;
And then seek for those lives, whose lives have now been taken.
Insensibly all trade and pleasure go to naught,
And daily wickedness produces daily evil.
What wind was that?" he asked; "it is with sorrow fraught,
And with repentant sighs; so 't all at last be paid will."
With these and like complaints the rogue his time did spend,
And then flew back again, to town and hamlet hieing[10].
But where he flew nor bow nor arrow had to bend;
And his vocation so with difficulty plying.
It happened him by chance he soon his arrow found;
Dropped in the way it lies, just where the Indians lost it.
He hesitates not long, but has it sharply ground.

---

3 God of love.
4 In the Old Testament, Absalom, son of David, was banished but was restored to favor through the good offices of his cousin Joab. Absalom later revolted against David and was killed by Joab, who found him caught by the hair in an oak tree.
5 Creature, human being.

6 The Catskills, a mountain range in upstate New York.
7 The god of marriage.
8 Lust, licentiousness.
9 A reference to the 1664 earthquake which affected New England and Canada.
10 Going.

And this, it seems, his passion and displeasure soothed;
Although the former is the latter quite unlike.
Who is by love enthralled? Who is he whom love stifles?
Whate'er love be, it puts no sods upon the dyke,
Its strength is feeble, and its arrows are mere trifles.
If this the reason be, that fewer married are,
And more do journeys make, is worthy of reflection,
Unless it be, on their account, who boldly dare,
And wrongly too, the right of property to weaken;
Who force on force employ and thirst for Christian blood,—
(when patience would have served), nor have Christ's flock in keeping.
Although the harmless rogue nor service does, nor good,
'Tis best to leave the savage children sleeping.
Whoever bides his time, he spends no time, what else he spends.
Why is it then too late, to wait the fitting hour?
Since that is wisely fixed to suit the country's ends,
The law of higher law, the strength of higher power.
But Cupid's true design does not this point concern.
At last, our sufferings and punishment diminish;
The captives, now and then, as from the grave return;
The savage monster's slain; his wife and children vanish;
His maize is all destroyed; his fort burnt to the ground;
His guns for booty ta'en; his seewan[11] fills our coffers.
They fly into the woods, wand'ring the land around;
The fugitives not found, no chance for glory offers.
Oft through interpreters, for terms the Indians sue;
The port of peace to gain they earnestly endeavor.
When Cupid hears of this, he comes with great ado
And asks, "Who has my bow?" and wails, "Where is my quiver?"
"What villainy is this, ye scoundrels," cries the wight[12],
"Have I committed aught[13], that you should thus reward me?
Unless it be, my shafts do amorous pains excite?
I shoot you only in the measure you regard me."
They gave his weapons back, but made him no reply,
Seeking to hush his wrath by thus his arms restoring.
He quickly seizes them, and draws his bow on high,
As if he wished to pierce some special mark above him.
The fort, New Amsterdam, is now by all possessed;
While Judith stands beneath, Luyck looks from the embrasure,
And ere they see or think, he shoots Luyck in the breast.
Nor does one shaft suffice his cov'nant-making pleasure.
"Where did he shoot? Where was 't he shot?" inquire the folks.
Luyck speaks not, for he feels something his heart is boring.
As all look up at Luyck, so Judith upward looks.
He shoots a second time and pierces Isendooren.

---

[11]   Corn.

[12]   Creature.

[13]   Anything.

This great commotion makes and causes, far and wide,
Re-echoings of joy. While speaks he not, the cry
Resounds throughout the land: "Joy to the groom and bride,
Joy to the married pair, and joy eternally."
"Blessings a thousand fold, attend them both," they shout,
"In body and in soul, here and hereafter flowing.
Joy fill the house within: no sorrow lurk without:
Who gives us happiness, the same on them bestowing."
Now we, who from this rogue, do neither child of Mars[14],
Nor Venus[15] understand, nor yet the ways of mortals,
Save what to wedlock leads and from uncleanness bars,
Wish them the best increase, and joy within their portals.
May this new married pair, peace and salvation know:
The budding hopes of Luyck and worth of Isendooren,
Develope more and more, and thus with time so grow,
They at the dying hour, the port of heaven may moor in.

1865

---

[14]   God of war.   [15]   Goddess of love.

Middle Atlantic:
Pennsylvania

Francis Daniel Pastorius (1651–1720?)

Born in Franconia (Germany) in 1651, Francis Daniel Pastorius studied law at the universites of Strasbourg, Basel, and Jena. He was a widely read man, with interests in agriculture, science, history, and theology. When the city of Frankfurt became a center of the Pietist movement, which advocated the reform of the Lutheran church, Pastorius was drawn into their circle, and when William Penn (who had visited Frankfurt in 1677) exhorted the Pietists and Mennonites of Germany to emigrate to the New World to take part in his "holy experiment," Pastorius set sail for America in 1683 as agent for a Frankfurt group which had bought 15,000 acres of land. There, he founded Germantown, where he served as justice of the peace, schoolmaster, and scrivener. His letters offer a vivid picture of daily life in Germantown, of its inhabitants, and of the Native peoples in the surrounding areas.

PRIMARY WORK

Circumstantial Geographical Description of Pennsylvania, by Francis Daniel Pastorius, 1700, in Narratives of Early Pennsylvania, West New Jersey and Delaware, 1630–1707, ed. Albert Cook Meyers, trans. Gertrude Kimball (New York: Barnes & Noble, 1912).

FURTHER READING

Albert Faust, Bernhardt, *Francis Daniel Pastorius and the 250th Anniversary of the Founding of Germantown* (Philadelphia: Carl Schurz Memorial Foundation, 1934).
Christoph Schweitzer, "Excursus: German Baroque Literature in Colonial America," *German Baroque Literature: The European Perspective*, ed. Hoffmeister, Gerhart (New York: Ungar, 1983) pp. 178–93.

FROM "POSITIVE INFORMATION FROM AMERICA, CONCERNING THE COUNTRY OF PENNSYLVANIA, FROM A GERMAN WHO HAS MIGRATED THITHER. DATED PENNSYLVANIA, MARCH 7, 1684"

Philadelphia daily increases in houses and inhabitants and presently a house of correction will be built in order that those who are not willing to live in a Philadelphian manner may be disciplined, for some such are to be found, to whom fittingly applies what our dear friend (Van de Walle) mentions in his letter, that we have here more distress from the spoiled christians than from the Indians. Furthermore here and there other towns are laid out; for the Society[1] is beginning to build about an hour and a half from here[2] one bearing the name of Franckfurt, where they have erected a mill and a glass factory. Not far from there, namely two hours from here, lies our Germantown, where already forty-two people are living in twelve dwellings. They are mostly linen weavers and not any too skilled in agriculture. These good people laid out all their substance upon the journey, so that if William Penn[3] had not advanced provisions to them, they must have become servants to others. The way from here to Germantown they have now, by frequent going to and fro, trodden out into good shape. Of that town I can say no more at present than that it lies on black fruitful soil and is half surrounded with pleasant streams like a natural defense. The chief street therein is sixty feet wide and the cross street forty. Every family has a house lot of three acres.

As to the inhabitants, I cannot better classify them than into the native and the engrafted[4]. For if I were to call the former savages and the latter Christians, I should do great injustice to many of both varieties. Of the latter sort, I have already mentioned above, that the incoming ships are not altogether to be compared with Noah's Ark. The Lutheran preacher, who ought as a *statua Mercurialis*[5] to show the Swedes the way to heaven, is, to say it in one word, a drunkard. Also there are coiners of false money and other vicious persons here whom nevertheless, it may be hoped, the wind of God's vengeance will in his own time drive away like chaff. On the other hand there is no lack of pious, God-fearing people, and I can with truth affirm that I have nowhere in Europe seen the notice posted up, as here in our Philadelphia, that such an one has found this or that, and that the loser may call for it at his house; often, however, the converse, Lost this or that; he who returns it again shall receive a reward, etc.

Of these new engrafted strangers I will for the present say no more than that among them some High Germans are to be found who have lived already twenty years in this land and consequently are, so to speak, naturalized, namely, Silesians, Brandenburgers, Holsteiners[6], Swiss, etc., also a Nuremberg man called Jan Jaquet; but will briefly give my account of those who are erroneously called savages. . . . They have coal-black hair, while the Swedish children born here have hair snow-white. I was once dining with William Penn, where one of their kings sat at table with us. William Penn, who can speak their language fairly fluently, said to him that I was a German, etc. He came accordingly on the third of October, and on the twelfth of December another king and queen came to my house. Also many common persons over-run[7] me very often, to whom however I almost always show my love with a piece of bread and a drink of beer, whereby an answering affection is awakened in them and they commonly call me "Teutschmann[8]," also "Carissimo" (that is, brother). Their language is manly and in my opinion is little inferior to the Italian in gravity, etc. As to their manner and nature, one must so to speak subdistinguish them into those who have associated for some time with the so-called Christians and those who are just beginning to come forth out of their burrows. For the former are crafty and deceitful, which they owe to the above-mentioned nominal Christians. *Semper enim aliquid haeret.*[9] Such a one lately pledged me his strap as security that he would

---

[1] The Free Society of Traders.
[2] From Philadelphia.
[3] William Penn (1644–1718), noted Quaker, founder of Pennsylvania.
[4] Transplanted.
[5] Literally, "statue of Mercury," the god and guide of travelers.

[6] Silesia, Brandenburg, and Holstein were all part of the Germanic Confederation.
[7] Visit.
[8] Literally, German man.
[9] "For always something adheres."

bring me a turkey, but in its place he brought an eagle and wished to persuade me that it was a turkey. When however I showed him that I had seen many eagles he acknowledged to a Swede who stood by that he had done it out of deception, in the belief that because we had lately come into the land I should not know such birds so accurately. Another at my fireside tested the brandy thus: he stuck his finger into it and then put the latter into the fire to see whether water had been mingled with the liquor. Those of the second class, on the contrary, are of a reasonable spirit, injure nobody, and we have nothing whatever to fear from them. One thing lately struck deeply into my heart when I pondered the sincere admonition of our Savior, that we His disciples should take no thought for the morrow, because thus do the Gentiles. Ah, thought I to myself, how entirely has all been now perverted! When we Christians are not provided for a month and more how displeased are we, while these heathen in so wonderful a spirit of resignation refer their sustenance to God. Just at that time I saw four of them eating together. The earth was at once their table and their bench. A pumpkin, cooked in plain water, without butter or spice, was all their food. Their spoons were mussel-shells, with which they supped the warm water. Their plates were oak leaves, which they had no need to clean after the meal, nor, when they needed others, to give themselves much trouble about them. Now, dear friend, let us not hesitate to learn contentment from these people, that they may not hereafter shame us before the judgment-seat of Jesus Christ.

  1684

LETTER OF FRANCIS DANIEL PASTORIUS FROM PENNSYLVANIA TO TOBIAS SCHUMBERGIUS[1], HIS FORMER TEACHER

World of grieving, your deceiving glories bid I now adieu;
All your cheating joys, and fleeting, turn me with contempt from you.
Though you render bright with splendour the appearance of today,
Day revolves, your charm dissolves, and sinks, like salt in ice, away.
Rulers regal, striking legal terrors into human hearts,
Now are lying low and sighing, smitten through with hellish darts.
Old and hoary[2] Popes, whose glory cardinals proclaim, and bow
Lowly bending without ending – lords of Rome, where are ye now?
Where the learning of discerning Doctors full of scholars' pride?
Where the hearty friend of party, blindly fighting for his side?
Where the famous chiefs, who shame us with the glory of their deeds,
Whom the savage zeal to ravage ever on to warfare leads?
All the mighty are but flighty, spectral forms, and shadows vain;
All the glory transitory, honours brief and joys inane.
All are banished, all have banished, naught but names remain behind,
Illustrations, adumbrations, of the fate of human kind.
Gone is Cato[3], gone is Plato[4], Cyrus[5], Croesus[6], Socrates[7],

---

[1] Tobias Schumberg, rector of the Latin school at Windsheim.

[2] White-haired.

[3] Marcus Porcius Cato (234–140 BC), Roman statesman.

[4] Noted Greek philosopher (427–347 BC).

[5] King of Persia, founder of the Persian empire (*d.* 528 BC).

[6] A wealthy king of Lydia in the sixth century BC.

[7] Socrates (469–399 BC), Athenian philosopher.

Periander[8], Alexander[9], Xerxes[10], and Hippocrates[11],
Maximinus[12], Contintinus[13], Gyges[14], Anaxagoras[15],
Epicurus[16], Palinurus[17], Demonax[18], Pythagoras[19],
Caesar[20] glorious, the victorious, laying many chieftains low;
Nor could glowing speech or flowing Ovid[21] save or Cicero[22].
Needless is it to revisit with our censure those who've gone
Through those portals. Hear, ye mortals, the conclusion I have drawn.
They that now are throned in power, they shall also pass away,
As there passes from our glasses[23] imaged form or figure gay.
Where Death's grievous hand shall leave us all beneath the churchyard stone,
Pains infernal, life eternal, we shall reap as we have sown.
Hence, adoring and imploring, Jesu's mercy loud I call,
That his leading and his pleading bring me to that heavenly hall
Of the trinal[24] God, where final joy awaits the blessed all.

1693

---

[8]   A tyrant of Corinth, who ruled in the sixth century BC.

[9]   Alexander the Great (356–323 BC), King of Macedon, conqueror of many lands.

[10]   Xerxes, King of Persia (519?–465 BC).

[11]   Hippocrates (460–357 BC), Greek physician, known as the Father of Medicine.

[12]   Caius Julius Maximinus (173–238 AD), Roman emperor.

[13]   A Roman statesman.

[14]   King of Lydia (716–678 BC)

[15]   Anaxagoras (500–428 BC), Greek philosopher, known as the father of modern science.

[16]   Epicurus (341–270 BC), Greek philosopher.

[17]   A character in Virgil's Aeneid.

[18]   A celebrated philosopher of Crete.

[19]   A Greek philosopher of the fifth century BC.

[20]   A Roman emperor of the Augustan line.

[21]   Ovid (43 BC–AD 17), Roman poet.

[22]   Marcus Tullus Cicero (106–43 BC), Roman orator.

[23]   Mirrors.

[24]   Three-formed.

Native American Views

The impact of European colonization on the Native peoples of what is now the United States was nothing short of calamitous. Entire tribes were decimated, not only as a result of direct violence but also because of new diseases brought by Europeans, such as smallpox, yellow fever, and measles, as well as from the exploitative working conditions imposed on the Native peoples by their colonial masters. The fabric of Native society was changed forever, and the imposition of European religious ideology, coinciding with the demise of elders, storytellers, healers, and clan relatives challenged Native spiritual traditions and symbolic systems, while Native economies became increasingly dependent on trade with Europeans. Despite the fact that many of the Eastern tribes were sedentary farmers, the European settlers' appetite for land led them to dismiss these peoples as rootless nomads in order to justify their encroachments upon Indian lands.

The following selections demonstrate the rhetorical eloquence, political skill, and negotiating capacity of Native American leaders faced with the disintegration of their cultures. Powhatan, in his speech to Captain John Smith, voices his perplexity at the aggressive attitudes and ingratitude of the settlers of Jamestown, who had been saved from starvation by the Natives, and questions their apparent need to obtain by force what they could obtain by merely exercising good will. The Narragansett Act of Submission provides further evidence of Native American political savvy. In it, in view of their decreasing population, the territorial encroachment of settlers, and the annihilation of many tribes by disease and warfare, the Narragansetts adopt the intelligent strategy of placing themselves directly under the protection of King Charles I rather than submitting to the Puritan authorities in New England, in a radical assertion of their own status (and thus their equality with the Puritans) as subjects of the king. The excerpt from the document (originally written in the Massachusett language) of the Gay Head Indians objecting to the sale of tribal lands to the Governor of New York provides testimony to Native beliefs about the nature of landholding and the obligations of leadership, and demonstrates the primacy of collective concerns over individual profit. Finally, the oration of the Onandaga leader Garangula (Grande Guele or Big Throat in French), delivered to the Governor of New France, Joseph Antoine Lefebre de La Barre, who had hoped that he could bluff the Iroquois into making substantial concessions, is a demonstration of Native statesmanship, with its tone of elegant disdain and its awareness of the possibilities (and the limits) of political and military power.

PRIMARY WORK

Colin Calloway (ed.) *The World Turned Upside Down: Indian Voices from Early America* (Boston: Bedford Books, 1994).

FURTHER READING

Andrew Knaut, *The Pueblo Revolt of 1680: Conquest and Resistance in Seventeenth-Century New Mexico* (Norman:

University of Oklahoma Press, 1995).

Kathleen J. Bragdon, *Native People of Southern New England, 1500–1650* (Norman: University of Oklahoma Press, 1996).

José Antonio Brandao, *Your Fyre Shall burn No More: Iroquois Policy towards New France and its Native Allies*

to 1701 (Lincoln, Nebraska: University of Nebraska Press, 1997).

Carroll Riley, *The Kachina and the Cross: Indians and Spaniards in the early Southwest* (Salt Lake City: University of Utah Press, 1999).

Powhatan, *Speech to Captain John Smith*

(in "Proceedings of the English Colony in Virginia")

Captain Smith, you may understand that I having seen the death of all my people thrice[1], and not any one living of these three generations but myself, I know the difference of Peace and War better than any in my country. But now I am old and ere long must die, my brethren, namely Opitchapam, Opechancanough, and Kakataugh,[2] my two sisters, and their two daughters, are distinctly each other's successors. I wish their experience no less than mine, and your love to them no less than mine to you. But this bruit[3] from Nandsamund, that you are come to destroy my Country, so much frightens all my people as they dare not visit you. What will it avail you to take that by force that you may quickly have by love, or to destroy them that provide you food. What can you get by war, when we can hide our provision and fly to the woods? Whereby you must famish[4] by wronging us your friends. And why are you jealous of our loves[5] seeing us unarmed, and are still willing to feed you with that that you cannot get but by our labours? Do you think I am so simple not to know it is better to eat good meat, lie well, and sleep quietly with my women and children, laugh and be merry with you, have copper, hatchets, or what I want being your friend, than be forced to flee from all, to lie cold in the woods, feed upon acorns, roots, and such trash, and be so hunted by you that I can neither rest, eat nor sleep, but my tired men must watch, and if a twig but break, everyone cries, "There comes Captain Smith:" then I must flee I know not whither, and thus with miserable fear, end my miserable life, leaving my pleasures to such youths as you, which through your rash unadvisedness[6] may quickly as miserably end, for want of what which you never know where to find. Let this therefore assure you of our love, and every year our friendly trade shall furnish you with corn, and now also, if you would come in friendly manner to see us, and not thus with your guns and swords as to invade your foes.

1609   1612

---

[1]   Probably a reference to three epidemics.

[2]   Rulers of the populous chiefdom of Pamunkey, near the mouth of the Pamunkey River. Opechancanough was taken prisoner by Smith and led the later wars of resistance against the English in Virginia.

[3]   Rumour.

[4]   Starve.

[5]   Uneasy about our allegiance.

[6]   Recklessness.

Narragansett Indians, *Act of Submission*

(from *Records of the Colony of Rhode Island*)

The Act and Deed of the voluntary and free submission of the chief Sachem, and the rest of the Princes, with the whole people of the Narragansetts, to the Government and Protection of that Honourable state of Old England, set down here, verbatim.

Know all men, colonies, peoples, and nations, to whom the fame hereof shall come; that we, the chief Sachems, Princes or Governors of the Narragansetts (in that part of America now called New England), together with the joint and unanimous consent of all our people and subjects, inhabitants thereof, do upon serious consideration, mature and deliberate advice and counsel, great and weighty grounds and measures moving us thereunto, whereof one most effectual to us, is, that noble fame we have heard of that Great and Mighty Prince, Charles[1], King of Great Britain, in that honourable and princely care he has of all his servants, and true and loyal subjects, the consideration whereof moves and bends our hearts with one consent, freely, voluntarily, and most humbly to submit, subject, and give over ourselves, peoples, lands, rights, inheritances, and possessions whatsoever, in ourselves and our heirs successively for ever, unto the protection, care and government of that worthy and royal Prince, Charles, King of Great Britain and Ireland, his heirs and successors forever, to be ruled and governed according to the ancient and honourable laws and customs, established in that so renowned realm and kingdom of Old England; we do, therefore, by these presents, confess and most willingly and submissively acknowledge ourselves to be the humble, loving and obedient servants and subjects of his Majesty; to be ruled, ordered, and disposed of, in ourselves and ours, according to his princely wisdom, counsel and laws of that honourable state of Old England; *upon condition of His Majesties royal protection*, and righting us of what wrong is, or may be done unto us, according to his honourable laws and customs, exercised amongst his subjects, in their preservation and safety, and in the defeating and overthrow of his, and their enemies; not that we find ourselves necessitated hereunto, in respect of our relation, or occasion we have, or may have, with any of the natives in these parts, knowing ourselves sufficient defence, and able to judge in any matter or cause in that respect; but have just cause of jealousy and suspicion of some of His Majesty's pretended subjects. Therefore our desire is, to have our matters and causes heard and tried according to his just and equal laws, in that way and order His Highness shall please to appoint: *Nor can we yield over ourselves unto any, that are subjects themselves in any case*; having ourselves been the chief Sachems[2] or Princes successively, of the country, time out of mind; and for our present and lawful enacting hereof, being so far remote from His Majesty, we have, by joint consent, made choice of four of his loyal and loving subjects, our trusty and well-beloved friends, Samuel Gorton[3], John Wickes, Randall Houlden and John Warner, whom we have deputed, and made our lawful Attorneys or Commissioners, not only for the acting and performing of this our Deed, on behalf of His Highness, but also for the safe custody, careful conveyance and declaration hereof unto his grace: being done upon the lands of the Narragansetts, at a Court or General Assembly called and assembled together, of purpose, for the public enacting, and manifestation hereof.

---

[1]   King Charles I, executed in 1649 in Great Britain during the English Civil War.

[2]   Leaders, rulers.

[3]   Samuel Gorton was a religious radical frequently at odds with the Puritan authorities. He and his associates had settled on Narragansett land with Miantonomi's permission.

And, for the further confirmation and establishing of this our Act and Deed, we, the abovesaid Sachems or Princes, subscribed our names and set our seals hereunto, as so many testimonies of our faith and truth, our love and loyalty to that dread Sovereign, and that according to the Englishmen's account. Dated the nineteenth day of April, one thousand six hundred and forty-four.

Pessicus, his mark, Chief Sachem, and successor of that late deceased Miantonomy.

The mark of that ancient Canonicus, Protector of that late deceased Miantonomy, during the time of his nonnage.[4]

The mark of Mixan, son and heir of that abovesaid Canonicus.

Witnessed by two of the chief counsellors to Sachem Pessicus.

Indians:

Awashoosse, his mark

Tomanick, his mark

Sealed and delivered, in the presence of these persons:

English: Christopher Helme, Robert Potter, Richard Carder.

1644   1856

Mittark, *Agreement of Gay Head Indians Not to Sell Land to the English*

I am Muttak, sachem[1] of Gay Head and Nashaquitsa as far as Wanemessit. Know this all people. I, Muttak, and my chief men and my children and my people, these are our lands. Forever we own them, and our posterity forever shall own them. I, Muttak, and we the chief men, and with our children and all our (common) people (present), have agreed that no one (shall) sell land. But if anyone larcenously[2] sells land, you shall take (back) your land, because it is forever your possession. But if anyone does not keep this agreement, he shall fall (and) have nothing more of this land at Gay Head and Nashaquitsa at all forever. I Muttak and we the chief men and our posterity say: And it shall be so forever. I Ummuttak say this, and my chief men: if any of these sons of mine protects my sachemship, he shall forever be a sachem. But if any of my sons does not protect my sachemship and sells it, he shall fall forever. And we chief men say this, and our sachem: if any of these sons of ours protects our chieftainship, he shall forever be a chief man. But if any of our sons does not protect our chieftainship and sells it, he shall fall forever. I Ummutak, sachem, say this and my chief men; this is our agreement. We say it before God. It shall be so forever. I Ummutak, this is my hand, on the date September 11, 1681 . . .

1681

---

4   The Narragansett sachems Pessicus and Canonicus were, respectively, brother and uncle of Miantonomi.

MITTARK

1   Chief, ruler.

2   I.e. sells the land illegally and thus commits theft.

Garangula, *Speech to New France's Governor La Barre*

Yonnondio[1], I honour you, and the warriors that are with me all likewise honour you. Your interpreter has finished your speech; I now begin mine. My words make haste to reach your ears. Hearken to them.

Yonnondio, you must have believed when you left Quebec that the Sun had burnt up all the forests which render our country unaccessible to the French, or that the lakes had so far overflown their banks, that they had surrounded our castles, and that it was impossible for us to get out of them. Yes, Yonnondio, surely you must have thought so, and the curiosity of seeing so great a country burnt up, or under water, has brought you so far. Now you are undeceived, since that I and my Warriors are come to assure you that the Senecas, Cayugas, Onondagas, Oneidas and Mohawks[2] are all alive. I thank you, in their name, for bringing back into their country the calumet[3] which your predecessor received from their hands. It was happy for you that you left under ground that murdering hatchet which has been so often dyed in the blood of the French. Hear, Yonnondio, I do not sleep, I have my eyes open, and the sun which enlightens me discovers to me a great Captain at the head of a company of soldiers, who speaks as if he were dreaming. He says that he only came to the lake to smoke on the great calumet with the Onondagas. But Garangula says that he sees the contrary, that it was to knock them on the head, if sickness had not weakened the arms of the French.

I see Yonnondio raving in a camp of sick men, whose lives the Great Spirit has saved, by inflicting this sickness on them. Hear, Yonnondio, our women had taken their clubs, our children and old men had carried their bows and arrows into the heart of your camp, if our warriors had not disarmed them and retained them when your messenger, Ohquesse, appeared in our castle. It is done, and I have said it.

Hear, Yonnondio, we plundered none of the French, but those that carried guns, powder and ball[4] to the Twihtwies and Chictaghicks[5], because those arms might have cost us our lives. Herein we follow the example of the Jesuits, who stave[6] all the barrels of rum brought to our castle, lest the drunken Indians knock them on the head. Our warriors have not beavers enough to pay for all those arms that they have taken, and our old men are not afraid of war. *This Belt preserves my Words.*

We carried the English into our Lakes, to traffic there with the Utawawas and Quatoghies, as the Adirondacks[7] brought the French into our castles, to carry on a trade which the English say is theirs. We are born free, we neither depend on Yonnondio nor Corlaer[8].

We may go where we please, and carry with us whom we please, and buy and sell what we please. If your Allies be your slaves, use them as such. Command them to receive no other but your people. *This Belt preserves my Words.*

We knocked the Twihtwies and Chictaghiks on the head, because they had cut down the Trees of Peace[9] which were the limits of our country. They have hunted beavers on our lands; they have acted contrary to the custom of all Indian, for they left none of the beavers alive, they killed both male and female. They brought the Satanas[10] into their country, to take part with

---

[1]   Or Onontio, governor.

[2]   Designated by the Europeans as the Five Civilized Tribes.

[3]   The ceremonial peace pipe.

[4]   Bullets.

[5]   The Miami and Illinois Indians.

[6]   Broke open.

[7]   The Ottawa, Huron and Algonquin Indians.

[8]   *Corlaer* was the Iroquois title for the Governor of New York.

[9]   A metaphor for bringing war into Iroquois country.

[10]   The Shawnees.

them, and armed them after they had concerted ill designs against us. We have done less than either the English or French, that have usurped the lands of so many Indian Nations, and chased them from their own country. *This Belt preserves my Words.*

Hear, Yonnondio, what I say is the voice of all the Five Nations. Hear what they answer. Open your ears to what they speak. The Senecas, Cayugas, Onondagas, Oneidas and Mohawks say that when they buried the hatchet at Cardarckui[11] (in the presence of your predecessor) in the middle of the Fort, they planted the Tree of Peace, in the same place, to be there carefully preserved, that in place of a retreat for soldiers, that Fort might be a rendezvous[12] of merchants; that in place of arms and munitions of war, beavers and merchandise should only enter there.

Hear, Yonnondio, take care for the future, that so great a number of soldiers as appear here do not choke the Tree of Peace planted in so small a fort. It will be a great loss, if after it had so easily taken root, you should stop its growth and prevent its covering your country and ours with its branches. I assure you, in the name of the Five Nations, that our warriors shall dance to the calumet of peace under its leaves, and shall remain quiet on their mats, and shall never dig up the hatchet until their brethren, Yonnondio or Corlaer shall either jointly or separately endeavour to attack the country which the Great Spirit has given to our Ancestors. *This Belt preserves my Words, and this other, the authority which the Five Nations have given me.*

1684

THE COMING OF THE SPANISH AND THE PUEBLO REVOLT: A HOPI PERSPECTIVE

Pueblo perspectives on the coming of European colonizers, and on the Pueblo Revolt of 1680 that drove the Spaniards out of northern Mexico for over a decade, differ markedly from the Spanish versions of these events. (See Don Antonio de Otermín's "Letter on the Pueblo Revolt" earlier in Part 2.) The following excerpt was transcribed from Hopi oral accounts by Edmund Nequatewa (1880?–1969), of the Sun Forehead Clan, and member of the powerful One Horned Fraternity, a society allowed to tell all clan stories belonging to the clans of their village. His account describes not only the ideological rigidity of the Spanish missionaries, with their heavy-handed attempts to eradicate Hopi spiritual traditions and rituals, but also their exploitation of the Native peoples. As well, this account details the careful planning underlying the Pueblo Revolt, and reveals that the Hopi, far from being passive victims, were prepared to resort to violent resistance when necessary.

PRIMARY WORK

Edmund Nequatewa, *Truth of a Hopi: Stories relating to the Origin, Myths and Clan Histories of the Hopi* (Flagstaff: Northland Publishing, 1936, 1967).

FURTHER READING

Joe Sando, *The Pueblo Indians* (San Francisco: The Indian Historian Press, 1976).

How the Spaniards Came to Shung-opovi, How They Built a Mission and How the Hopis Destroyed the Mission.

. . . When the Spaniards came, the Hopi thought that they were the ones they were looking for – their white brother, the Bahana, their savior. The Spaniards visited Shung-opovi several

---

[11] Fort Frontenac.   [12] Meeting-place.

times before the missions were established. The people of Michongnovi welcomed them so the priest who was with the white men built the first Hopi mission at Michongnovi. The people of Shung-opovi were at first afraid of the priest, but later they decided he was really the Bahana, the savior, and let him build a mission at Shung-opovi.

Well, about this time the Strap Clan were ruling at Shung-opovi, and they were the ones who gave permission to establish the mission. The Spaniards, whom they called Castilla[1], told the people they had much more power than all their chiefs and a whole lot more power than the witches. The people were very much afraid of them, particularly if they had much more power than the witches. They were so scared that they could do nothing but allow themselves to be made slaves. Whatever they wanted done must be done. Any man in power who was in this position the Hopi called a *Tota-achi*, which means a grouchy person who will not do anything himself, like a child. They couldn't refuse, or they would be slashed to death or punished in some way. There were two Tota-achi.

The missionary did not like the ceremonies. He did not like the Kachinas[2] and he destroyed the altars and the customs. He called it idol worship and burned up all the ceremonial things in the plaza.

When the priests started to build the mission, the men were sent away over near the San Francisco peaks to get the pine or spruce beams. These beams were cut and put into shape roughly and were then left till the next year when they had dried out. Beams of that size were hard to carry and the first few times they tried to carry these beams on their backs, twenty to thirty men walking side by side under the beam. But this was rather hard in rough places and one end had to swing around. So finally they figured out a way of carrying the beam in between them. They lined up two by two with the beam between the lines. In doing this, some of the Hopi were given authority by the missionary to look after these men and to see if they all did their duty. If any man gave out on the way he was simply left to die. There was great suffering. Some died for lack of food and water, while others developed scabs and sores on their bodies.

It took a good many years for them to get enough beams to Shung-opovi to build the mission. When this mission was finally built, all the people in the village had to come there to worship, and those who did not come were punished severely. In that way their own religion was altogether wiped out, because they were not allowed to worship in their own way. All this trouble was a heavy burden on them and they thought it was on account of this that they were having a heavy drought at this time. They thought their gods had given them up because they weren't worshipping the way they should.

Now during this time the men would go out pretending they were going on a hunting trip and they would go to some hiding place, to make their prayer offerings. So today, a good many of these places are still to be found where they left their little stone bowls in which they ground their copper ore to paint the prayer sticks. These places are called Puwa-kiki, cave places. If these men were caught they were severely punished.

Now this man, Tota-achi (the priest) was going from bad to worse. He was not doing the people any good and he was always figuring what he could do to harm them. So he thought out how the water from different springs or rivers would taste and he was always sending some man to these springs to get water for him to drink, but it was noticed that he always chose the men who had pretty wives. He tried to send them far away so that they would be gone two or three days, so it was not very long until they began to see what he was doing. The men were

---

[1]   I.e. Castile.
[2]   Kachinas are deified ancestral spirits believed among the Hopi to visit the pueblos at intervals. As well, the term is used to designate masked kachina impersonators who dance in traditional ceremonies.

even sent to the Little Colorado River to get water for him, or to Moencopi. Finally, when a man was sent out he'd go out into the rocks and hide, and when the night came he would come home. Then the priest, thinking the man was away, would come to visit his wife, but instead the man would be there. Many men were punished for this.

All this time the priest, who had great power, wanted all the young girls to be brought to him when they were about thirteen or fourteen years old. They had to live with the priest. He told the people they would become better women if they lived with him for about three years. Now one of these girls told what the Tota-achi was doing and a brother of the girl heard of this, and he asked his sister about it, and he was very angry. This brother went to the mission and wanted to kill the priest that very day, but the priest scared him and he did nothing. So the Shung-opovi people sent this boy, who was a good runner, to Awatovi to see if they were doing the same thing over there, which they were. So that was how they got all the evidence against the priest.

Then the chief at Awatovi sent word by this boy that all the priests would be killed on the fourth day after the full moon. They had no calendar and that was the best way they had of setting the date. In order to make sure that everyone would rise up and do this thing on the fourth day the boy was given a cotton string with knots in it and each day he was to untie one of these knots until they were all out and that would be the day for the attack.[3]

Things were getting worse and worse so the chief of Shung-opovi went over to Michongnovi and the two chiefs discussed their troubles. "He is not the savior and it is your duty to kill him," said the chief of Shung-opovi. The chief of Michongnovi replied, "If I end his life, my own life is ended."

Now the priest would not let the people manufacture prayer offerings, so they had to make them among the rocks in the cliffs out of sight, so again one day the chief of Shung-opovi went to Michongnovi with tobacco and materials to make prayer offering. He was joined by the chief of Michongnovi and the two went a mile north to a cave. For four days they lived there heartbroken in the cave. Then the chief of Michongnovi took the prayer offerings and climbed to the top of the Corn Rock and deposited them in the shrine, for according to the ancient agreement with the Michongnovi people it was their duty to do away with the enemy.

He then, with some of his best men, went to Shung-opovi, but he carried no weapons. He placed his men at every door of the priest's house. Then he knocked on the door and walked in. He asked the priest to come out but the priest was suspicious and would not come out. The chief asked the priest four times and each time the priest refused. Finally, the priest said, "I think you are up to something."

The chief said, "I have come to kill you." "You can't kill me," cried the priest, "you have no power to kill me. If you do I will come to life and wipe out your whole tribe."

The chief returned, "If you have this power, then blow me out into the air; my gods have more power than you have. My gods have put a heart into me to enter your home. I have no weapons. You have your weapons handy, hanging on the wall. My gods have prevented you from getting your weapons."

The old priest made a rush and grabbed his sword from the wall. The chief of Michongnovi yelled and the doors were broken open. The priest cut down the chief and fought right and left but was soon overpowered, and his sword taken from him.

They tied his hands behind his back. Out of the big beams outside they made a tripod. They hung him on the beams, kindled a fire and burned him.

1937

---

3 I.e. the Hopi phase of the Pueblo uprising.

Part Three:
The Eighteenth Century

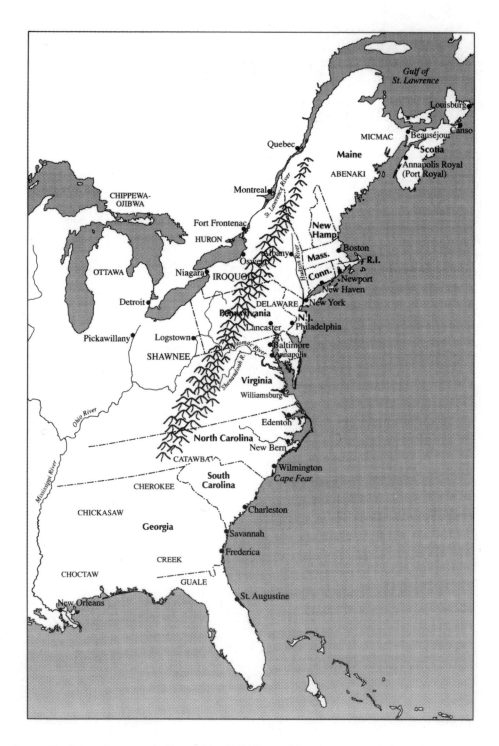

Eastern North America, 1715–60. From Richard Middleton, *Colonial America*, 2nd edn (Oxford: Blackwell Publishers, 1997). (With permission of the author.)

Introduction

Colonization and creolization continued throughout North America during the first half of the eighteenth century. The logical outcomes of these processes – large demographic shifts displacing the Native American population, and a growing sense of settlers' identity with their land of birth or adoption and difference from their European roots – caused major changes and upheavals in the second half of the century, when Anglo-American culture came to dominate the continent. While the seventeenth century ended in a temporary peace between French and English colonists, hostilities were renewed when war broke out in Europe again in 1702. England attempted to consolidate its colonial holdings and negotiate with the powerful Iroquois confederacy, but failed. Meanwhile, the French built a series of forts along the upper Mississippi to exclude the English from the western fur trade, and began expanding into Louisiana. French Jesuit missionaries made many converts among the northern tribes. But events in Europe once again determined the fate of the New World. The European war, called the War of the Spanish Succession, ended with the Treaty of Utrecht in 1713. Under its terms, Spain lost its European possessions, and turned its attention to renewing colonizing efforts in the Americas, and the French ceded Newfoundland and Nova Scotia to the English, securing the frontiers of Maine. Most Native tribes along the eastern seaboard had been subdued or pushed west off their ancestral lands, clearing the way for increased European settlement. With this peace, a period of rapid growth began during which many of the colonies in North America expanded into provincial centers with paper money, banks, printing presses, newspapers, and institutions of higher learning.

Immigration boomed, especially among groups of Scotch-Irish, German, Dutch, French Protestants, and European Jews, who settled in the middle and southern colonies and the West Indies, establishing businesses, farms and plantations. The Spanish continued to settle in Florida, California and the Southwest, where Franciscan priests set up chains of missions to proselytize among the indigenous populations. Thousands of African slaves were brought in to the middle and southern colonies and the West Indies to work the plantations and produce staple products that were shipped back to Europe, enriching the mother countries. New England became a largely mercantile economy, benefitting enormously from the slave trade but also continually affected by conflicts among the European powers. Since life in the colonies was much healthier than in Europe, the population soared, and the standard of living rose for most white people who owned property or businesses. Women, however, whether in urban or rural settings, were still restricted by the predominant patriarchal family structure, conventional gender roles, and beliefs in female inferiority, physically, mentally, and morally. In addition, by mid-century, there was a growing population of urban poor, and a growing population of freed blacks who were denied civil rights and opportunities. Individual Native Americans could reap some educational benefits upon conversion to Christianity, but tribes faced the take-over and buy-out of their lands from the juggernaut of white expansion.

The surge in immigration, and the economic growth it spurred, were accompanied by an influx of crucial ideas into the New World, particularly the intellectual revolution occurring in Europe known as the Enlightenment. Many thinkers contributed to this movement, shaking off the last vestiges of medieval authoritarianism and dogma, and elevating the rational capacity of humans to observe the world, discover its natural laws, and shape its social and political institutions. Most formative were the discoveries of Sir Isaac Newton (1642–1727), whose *Principia Mathematica* or *Mathematical Principles of Natural Philosophy* (1687) described the universe as a complicated mechanism governed by natural laws which could be discerned and understood by ordinary people. The Deity of this universe no longer intervened inscrutably in the lives of humans, as Puritans like Cotton Mather believed, but operated within natural laws, and was revealed by the magnificent order of the physical world. Newton's discoveries led to an explosion in scientific research, especially among educated amateurs and naturalists, nourished by the foundation of the Royal Society in 1662. The bright light of reason was turned on all the former "mysteries," weakening human faith in revealed religion and in the divine right of priests, kings, and hierarchical rule in all spheres of life. In philosophy, John Locke (1632–1704) argued that rather than having some kind of innate knowledge of good and evil, people were born as *tabula rasa* or blank slates upon which sensation and experience in and of the world inscribed knowledge and selfhood. Thus, people were not predestined to salvation or damnation, but could be taught to be virtuous – or evil – by the social and cultural institutions which shaped them. If neither wealth nor inherited position were divinely ordained, they could be overthrown or abolished. When Locke declared "life, liberty, and the pursuit of happiness" the goals of human existence, he laid the foundation for the republican and democratic movements that stormed through Europe and radically shaped American political thought, if not reality.

While neither Newton or Locke saw their ideas in conflict with traditional Christianity, other thinkers drew from them a benevolent, distant God to replace the wrathful Jehovah of Calvinism. Religion among intellectuals and the upper classes became Deism, a secular faith without church or priest and validated not by divine revelation, but by scientific observation and logic. Still other thinkers, principally Jonathan Edwards (1703–58), a minister, theologian, and philosopher in Northampton, Massachusetts, used Newtonian science and Lockean empiricism to infuse Calvinism with a new energy. Nature became the very book of God in whose beauty was written a grand, glorious, intelligible message of grace. With his prodigious intellect, Edwards succeeded in presenting the most intractable Puritan doctrines – of election and predestination – as supremely reasonable and, in terms that imply sensory experience, "sweet" and "delightful." In his preaching, the inflexible Puritan morphology of conversion became a subtle psychology of individual surrender to the sovereignty of God. He stressed not a blind faith in or merely intellectual understanding of doctrine but a personal experience of what he famously called "the religious affections." Edwards' enlightened theology helped to produce the waves of religious revivals that swept the eastern seaboard in the 1730s and 1740s. People from all classes and walks of life, especially the non-elite, found a common belief in this time of growing dispersal and rapid expansion. The charismatic preaching of English methodists like George Whitefield, who visited the middle colonies and New

England in the 1740s at the height of the Great Awakening, drew large crowds and waves of conversions. Barred from pulpits and university halls, Whitefield and his ilk often preached in open fields which, like his emphasis on individual experience over traditional authority, reinforced the democratic implications of this religious movement.

At the same time, relations among the imperial powers in Europe were coming to a head. Burgeoning expansion of the Anglo-American colonies caused the next inevitable conflict, which began with Spain in the Caribbean over the treatment of British commerce after the Treaty of Utrecht. In 1740, the British attacked Spanish-held ports and beseiged St Augustine on the Florida mainland for a month. Although forced to retreat, they were more successful in defending Georgia from the Spanish counterattack. For this operation, Britain asked the colonists to help in their defense, and four battalions were raised from eleven colonies. It was the first time the colonists were collectively called "Americans." Meanwhile, in Europe, France joined Spain in the war against Britain. "King George's War," 1739–48, took a particularly heavy toll on New England, which was harshly taxed and bitterly disappointed by the treaty, in which British negotiators returned Louisburg, an important fishing port on the northernmost tip of Nova Scotia, to the French for other colonial concessions. Indian attacks on the western frontier in Pennsylvania and the encroachment of the French in the Ohio River valley, to maintain links between New France and Louisiana, made it clear that the scale of warfare had changed dramatically. The Anglo-Americans would need increased aid from Britain in order to stop the French. That effort produced the French and Indian War (1754–63), the American phase of the more complex Seven Years War in Europe (1756–63), during which British forces retook the fort at Louisburg, and captured Quebec and Montreal. The Treaty of Paris (1763) that concluded the conflict gave Britain all of France's North American holdings as well as Spanish Florida, in exchange for which Spain acquired the Louisiana Territory and New Orleans from France. The powerful confederacy of Indian tribes allied to France were forced to submit to the British. Unhappy under British rule, an alliance of tribes living in the northwest territories (western Pennsylvania and Michigan) led by Pontiac rose up and attacked settlers, but the power of the confederacy had been essentially broken. Although Britain would have preferred to get France's lucrative sugar plantations in the West Indies, its acquisition of Canada sealed British dominance in North America, but also, ironically, sowed the seeds of the conflict that would spark the colonists' bid for independence in the next decade.

The war left Britain with enormous debts and a depleted treasury which they tried to fill by taxing their colonies, many of whose inhabitants were not of English derivation. First there was the Sugar Act of 1764 and the Stamp Act of 1765, which sparked riots and elicited from indignant colonists a "Declaration of Rights and Grievances." Colonists wanted greater freedom to engage in commerce that was monopolized by Britain. They saw the quartering of British troops in the colonies as a potentially repressive, rather than defensive, force. In addition, many fiercely opposed the appointment of an Anglican bishop for North America, for which the Church of England had been campaigning, and feared that the corruption of the British government threatened colonial liberty. Although the Stamp Act was repealed, in 1767 Parliament passed the Revenue or Townshend Acts, which generated revenue by taxing trade. The colonists, whose assemblies were now communicating among themselves, responded with economic boycotts and non-importation of taxed goods like paper, paint, sugar, linen. In March 1770, an angry crowd in Boston confronted a military detachment, which fired on them, killing five people, including the slave Crispus Attucks. "The Boston Massacre," as it became known, brought thousands of working people out of the countryside ready to take up arms. In April 1770, Parliament removed the Townshend duties on all goods, except tea, and in December 1773 Boston patriots dressed as Indians, dumped tea from British ships into Boston Harbor. Parliament responded to "the Boston Tea Party," by making an example of Massachusetts and passing what became known as the "Intolerable Acts," closing the port of Boston, revoking Massachusetts' 1691 charter and suspending its assembly, and appointing Thomas Gage, commander-in-chief in North America, governor. At the same time, Parliament expanded the province of Quebec to include the French-speaking western territories, a move that overturned other colonies' rights to the land. In September 1774, the first Continental Congress was held in Philadelphia, advocating boycott, to which Parliament responded with the Coercive Acts, restricting colonial trade to Britain and Ireland. In April 1775, British troops advancing from Boston to capture a cache of arms at Concord were met by a band of Massachusetts minutemen at Lexington, and the first battle of the war ended in an American victory.

There would be many battles and defeats before the war for Independence concluded with the British surrender in 1781 and the signing of the Treaty of Versailles in 1783. A post-war depression and the failure of the Articles of Confederation to unite the colonies elicited calls for a stronger central government, and in 1787, a group of delegates drafted a Constitution that based its authority in the will of the "people," and their elected representatives. Despite regional differences and a bitter debate over the definition of "the people," which finally excluded women, Native Americans, and counted African-American slaves as three-fifths of a person, the Constitution was ratified and George Washington, revered commander of the Continental Army, was elected the first president of the newly organized United States. The post-revolutionary period was a time of consolidation, as an extremely diverse continental population attempted to come to terms with a freshly minted federal government and a still undefined national identity. Many people migrated to the west and south, and states began to fund public elementary education to create a literate and informed electorate. Women benefitted somewhat from the need for an informed public by filling the role of "Republican mothers," instilling civic virtue in sons and republican values in the daughters who would take their places. Many people, especially free blacks like organizer Prince Hall and minister Lemuel Haynes, perceived the contradiction between the rhetoric of revolutionary liberty and the practice of slavery. Vermont was the first state to abolish slavery in 1777, and many northern states followed, but with Ely Whitney's invention of the cotton gin in 1793, southern colonies became even more dependent upon slave labor to produce the staple crops that enriched their booming economies. Although the Constitution made the importation of slaves illegal after twenty years, the national trade in human beings and the practice of slavery continued, and would become a dominant issue of national politics in the next century.

During the eighteenth century, North American culture was transformed from a largely communal and oral culture to an extensively literate and more individualized one. At the beginning of the century, the colonies had one newspaper; by 1800 there were over two hundred. Magazines, most quite ephemeral, sprung up in urban centers, an indication of a growing readership increasingly interested in specifically "American" themes and subjects. Later British American colonial writers reflect not only the growing diversity of provincial life, but its increasing secularization. The spiritual autobiographies and journals of the Puritans give way to personal narratives that often focus on the writer's place in a rapidly changing world. Even the personal narratives of religious figures like Jonathan Edwards and the Quaker John Woolman evince a growing awareness of moral and ethical issues. Travel narratives become increasingly popular, as even women, like the formidable Sarah Kemble Knight, can undertake arduous journeys that allow them to observe a wide range of colonial life. Similar trends appear in the Spanish colonial literature from this period. Alonso Carrió de la Vandera's picaresque travelogue satirizes the ostentation of the colonial elites, and Rafael de Landívar captures the pastoral landscape of Mexico in neo-classical terms that link it to a timeless, noble world. These writers express an emerging national identity that, under the leadership of patriots such as José Martí and Simón Bolívar, result in independence for countries like Chile, Peru and Argentina in the first decades of the nineteenth century, and Mexico in 1821. The emergence of Canadian identity can be traced in the texts of colonial Francophone writers. Baron Lahontan uses his descriptions of the Native peoples of Canada to distance himself from certain facets of French culture, while Pierre François-Xavier de Charlevoix describes the bustling towns of Quebec and New Orleans. Women writers such as Marie-Andrée Duplessis de Sainte-Hélène and Elisabeth Begon portray a world not only of war, but of balls and gaiety. In addition, military men such as Jean-Bernard Bossu and Louis Antoine de Bougainville write of wrestling with alligators and of the difficulties in maintaining morale among their troops.

Predominant themes in the second half of the century are the struggle for freedom and independence, the definition of a national identity and the expression of racial, ethnic, gender, and sectional differences within that overarching vision. The cause of liberty and revolution elicited heightened prose and poetry from writers such Tom Paine, Thomas Jefferson, John Adams, Phillis Wheatley, and Philip Freneau, and poignant private reflections from Abigail Adams. The electrifying effect of revolutionary discourse, and the spectacle of colonists throwing off the bands of imperial monarchical rule and setting up a republican government sent shock waves through the world. In 1789, the French people rose in revolution against the *ancien regime*, and in 1791 Toussaint L'Ouverture led and justified a rebellion among slaves in the French colony of St Domingue, later to become the independent nation of Haiti. Jefferson strove to defend the Americas as a whole from European claims of their degeneracy in comparison to the old world. This argument involved much more than biology; in pointing out the logical inconsistencies in Count Buffon's arguments, and giving evidence from Virginia of the potential of the New World to equal and outstrip the old, Jefferson was defending the social and political experiments he played a large part setting into motion.

In writing their own life narratives, many writers contributed to the evolving, multifaceted notion of a specifically "American" character. Benjamin Franklin's influential autobiography has become the classic story of the self-made man moving within the newly egalitarian society of the New World, shaping himself as a virtuous being and channeling his energies into improving the common lot. Hector St John de Crèvecoeur expressed the Americanness of white immigrants who had made the wilderness their home and freedom from corrupting European fetters their creed. These canonized texts have to be read alongside the narratives of growing up as a Native American by Samson Occom, or being kidnapped and enslaved in Virginia and the West Indies by Olaudah Equiano. For other writers of color, like Phillis Wheatley, we must read between the lines to discern the full critique of dominant culture's attitude towards racial difference. White women also laid claim to the rhetoric of equality and natural rights, campaigning, like Judith Sargent Murray, for increased educational opportunities. All of these are eloquent testimony to the contradiction – and failure – of American revolutionary rhetoric, which promised equality to all, but bestowed it on only on the privileged few, and the resulting narrowness and exclusivity of the national identity called "American."

Later Colonial Writers of the Americas

Sarah Kemble Knight (1666–1727)

The journey and the journal were conventional modes of experience and expression in colonial New England. While Sarah Kemble Knight continued this tradition, she also reshaped the genre and pointed it in new, fruitful directions. Knight was a fairly independent and unusually hearty woman for her time. Born in Boston the year Michael Wigglesworth wrote his stinging jeremiad, "God's Controversy with New England," Knight kept a shop on Moon Street and also taught handwriting to local children. At twenty-two, she married Richard Knight, a shipmaster who acted as an agent in London for an American company, and had one child, Elizabeth, born on May 8, 1689. Not only did she maintain her shop after her marriage, but she shouldered much of the work related to her husband's business even before his death, around 1706. She was also a successful entrepreneur. As a widow, Knight followed her daughter who, upon marriage to John Livingston, moved to New London, Connecticut. She remained actively engaged in business and real estate, and when she died in 1727, left her daughter a considerable estate of over £1800.

Part of Knight's income came from copying legal documents, and the knowledge she gained from this may have motivated her to undertake the arduous journey to New Haven she recorded in her *Journal*, to help settle the estate of Caleb Trowbridge, whose widow was probably her sister. The route she took was established, but by no means easy. Yet Knight moved almost as a free agent – she was entirely dependent on guides – through a landscape of rural and urban New England, spending about two weeks on the road and a long sojourn of several months in New York City visiting family. With a practiced eye, she observes the foibles and characters of inhabitants along the entire spectrum of early colonial society: from black slaves and Indians, indigent whites, backwoods bumpkins, to class-conscious innkeepers, affluent New York goodwives, and the uppercrust of the ruling elite.

Consciousness of her own place in hierarchical colonial society as a middling, educated, business woman renders her commentary intelligent, satirical, and, above all, humorous – the last quality we would expect from the pen of a Puritan woman. In Knight's treatment, the venerable metaphor of travel as spiritual journey becomes a boisterous satire – as some have suggested, in the tradition of the picaresque, a genre of literature chronicling the life and adventures of an engaging rogue. Although no rogue, Knight is a supremely engaging figure, comfortable with a wide range of literary discourse, from country slang and jokes in Latin, to piquant observations and neo-classical satiric and poetic conventions. Several types and levels of humor operate in her work, foreshadowing the rich vein of American comic writing which this authentically native voice anticipated. The *Journal* remained in manuscript for over a century, until Theodore Dwight published it in 1825, in part as a demonstration of the existence and value of particularly "American" works, "unfashionable as they still are."

PRIMARY WORKS

The Journal of Madam Knight, and Rev Mr Buckingham, from the Original Manuscripts, written in 1704 and 1710 (New York: Wilder and Campbell, 1825).

FURTHER READING

John Seelye, *Prophetic Waters: the River in Early American Life and Literature* (New York: Oxford University Press, 1977).

Sargent Bush, Jr, "Introduction," *The Journal of Madam Knight, Journeys in New Worlds, Early American Women's Narratives*, ed. William L. Andrews (Madison: University of Wisconsin Press, 1990) pp. 63–83.

Julia Stern, "To Relish and to Spew: Disgust as Cultural Critique in *The Journal of Madam Knight*," *Legacy: A Journal of American Women Writers*, 14 (1997) pp. 1–12.

FROM *THE JOURNAL OF MADAME KNIGHT*[1]

Monday, Octb'r the second, 1704. – About three o'clock afternoon, I begun my journey from Boston to New-Haven; being about two hundred mile. My Kinsman, Capt. Robert Luist, waited on me as farr as Dedham, where I was to meet the Western post. . . .

In about an how'r, or something more, after we left the Swamp, wee come to Billingses, where I was to Lodg.[2] My Guide dismounted and very Complaisantly help't me down and shewd the door, signing to me with his hand to go in; wch I Gladly did – but had not gone many steps into the room, ere I was Interrogated by a young Lady I understood afterwards was the Eldest daughter of the family, with these, or words to this purpose, (viz.) Law for mee – what in the world brings You here at this time a night? – I never see a woman on the Rode so Dreadfull late, in all the days of my versall[3] life. Who are You? Where are You going? I'm scar'd out of my wits – with much now of the same Kind. I stood aghast, Prepareing to reply, when in comes my Guide – to him Madam turn'd, Roreing out: Lawfull heart, John, is it You? – how de do! Where in the world are you going with this woman? Who is she? John made no Ansr but sat down in the corner, fumbled out his black Junk[4], and saluted that instead of Debb; she then turned agen to me and fell anew into her silly questions, without asking me to sitt down.

I told her shee treated me very Rudely, and I did not think it my duty to answer her unmannerly Questions. But to get ridd of them, I told her I come there to have the post's company with me to-morrow on my Journey, &c. Miss star'd awhile, drew a chair, bid me sitt, And then run up stairs and putts on two or three Rings, (or else I had not seen them before,) and returning, sett herself just before me, showing the way to Reding[5], that I might see her ornaments, perhaps to gain the more respect. But her Granam's new Rung sow[6], had it appeared, would [have] affected me as much. I paid honest John with money and dram according to contract, and Dismist him, and prayed Miss to shew me where I must Lodg. Shee conducted

---

[1]   Knight's journal was first published from what the editor described as a nearly complete manuscript, except that the first sheet was torn away, causing two breaks early in the narrative. The text, with slight modifications, is from *The Journal of Madam Knight, and Rev Mr Buckingham, from the Original Manuscripts, written in 1704 and 1710* (New York: Wilder and Campbell, 1825).

[2]   Billings's Inn at old Dorchester, now Sharon, Massachu-setts, also frequented by Knight's contemporary, Samuel Sewall.

[3]   Whole, entire; abbreviation of "universal."

[4]   A reference to pieces of old rope, and thus a comment on the poor quality of John's tobacco.

[5]   Gesturing with her hands.

[6]   A female pig with a ring in its nose to prevent it from rooting.

me to a parlour in a little back Lento, wch was almost fill'd with the bedsted, wch was so high that I was forced to climb on a chair to gitt up to the wretched bed that lay on it; on wch having Stretcht my tired Limbs, and lay'd my head on a Sad-coloured pillow, I began to think on the transactions of the past day.

Tuesday, October the third, about 8 in the morning. I with the Post proceeded forward without observing anything remarkable . . .

The Rode here was very even and the day pleasant, it being now near Sunsett. But the Post told mee we had near 14 miles to Ride to the next Stage, (where we were to Lodg.). I askt him of the rest of the Rode, foreseeing wee must travail in the night. He told mee there was a bad River we were to Ride thro', which was so very fierce a hors could sometimes hardly stem it: But it was but narrow, and wee should soon be over. I cannot express The concern of mind this relation sett me in: no thoughts but those of the dangero's River could entertain my Imagination, and they were as formidable as various, still Tormenting me with blackest Ideas of my approaching fate – Sometimes seeing myself drowning, otherwhiles drowned, and at the best like a holy Sister Just come out of a Spiritual Bath in dripping Garments.[7]

Now was the Glorious Luminary, his swift Coursers arrived at his Stage, leaving poor me the rest of this part of the lower world in darkness, with which *wee* were soon Surrounded. The only Glimmering we now had was from the spangled Skies, whose Imperfect Reflections rendered every Object formidable. Each lifeless Trunk, with its shatter'd Limbs, appear'd an Armed Enymie; and every little stump like a Ravenous devourer. Nor could I so much as discern my Guide, when at any distance, which added to the terror.

Thus, absolutely lost in Thought, and dying with the very thoughts of drowning, I come up wth the post, who I did not see till even with his Hors: he told mee he stopt for mee; and we Rode on Very deliberately a few paces, when we entred a Thickett of Trees and Shrubs, and I perceived by the Hors's going, we were on the descent of a Hill, w^ch, as wee came neerer the bottom, 'twas totaly dark wth the Trees that surrounded it. But I knew by the Going of the Hors wee had entred the water, which my Guide told mee was the hazzrdos River he had told me off; and hee, riding up close to my side, Bid me not fear – we should be over Imediatly. I now ralyed all the Courage I was mistriss of, Knowing that I must either Venture my fate of drowning, or be left like the Children in the wood.[8] So, as the Post bid me, I gave Reins to my Nagg; and sitting as stedy as just before in the Cannoo, in a few minutes got safe to the other side, which hee told mee was the Narragansett country.[9]

Here we found great difficulty in Travailing, the way being very narrow, and on each side the Trees and bushes gave us very unpleasant welcomes wth their Branches and bow's, wch wee could not avoid, it being so exceeding dark. My Guide, as before so now, putt on harder than I, wth my weary bones, could follow; so left mee and the way beehind him. Now Returned my distressed apprehensions of the place where I was: the dolesome woods, my Company next to none, Going I knew not whither, and encompassed wth Terrifying darkness; The least of which was enough to startle a more Masculine courage. Added to which the Reflections, as in the afternoon of the day that my Call[10] was very questionable, wch till then I had not so prudently as I ought considered. Now, coming to the foot of a hill, I found great difficulty in ascending;

7   Allusion to baptism by immersion, a practice of the Baptists of Rhode Island.
8   Title of a late sixteenth century English ballad about two young orphans whose uncle left them in the woods to die.

9   Territory in southwestern Rhode Island originally occupied by the powerful Narragansett tribe.
10   As in spiritual calling or vocation, which in Calvinist doctrine, leads believers to salvation.

But being got to the Top, was there amply recompensed with the friendly Appearance of the Kind Conductress of the night, Just then Advancing above the Horisontall Line. The Raptures wch the Sight of that fair Planett produced in mee, caus'd mee, for the Moment, to forgett my present wearyness and past toils; and Inspired me for most of the remaining way with very divirting tho'ts, some of which, with the other Occurances of the day, I reserved to note down when I should come to my Stage. My thoughts on the sight of the moon were to this purpose:

> Fair Cynthia,[11] all the Homage that I may
> Unto a Creature, unto thee I pay;
> In Lonesome woods to meet so kind a guide
> To Mee's more worth than all the world beside.
> Some Joy I felt just now, when safe got or'e
> Yon Surly River to this Rugged shore,
> Deeming Rough welcomes from these clownish Trees,
> Better than Lodgings wth Nereidees.[12]
> Yet swelling fears surprise; all dark appears –
> Nothing but Light can disipate those fears.
> My fainting vitals can't lend strength to say,
> But softly whisper, O I wish 'twere day
> The murmer hardly warm'd the Ambient air,
> E're thy Bright Aspect rescues from dispair:
> Makes the old Hagg her sable mantle loose,
> And a Bright Joy do's through my Soul diffuse.
> The Boistero's Trees now Lend a Passage Free,
> And pleasent prospects thou giv'st light to see.

From hence wee kept on, with more ease than before: the way being smooth and even, the night warm and serene, and the Tall and thick Trees at a distance, especially whenn the moon glar'd light through the branches, fill'd my Imagination wth the pleasent delusion of a Sumpteous citty, fill'd wth famous Buildings and churches, wth their spiring steeples, Balconies, Galleries and I know not what: Granduers wch I had heard of, and wch the stories of foreign countries had given me the Idea of.

> Here stood a Lofty church – there is a steeple,
> And there the Grand Parade – O see the people!
> That Famouse Castle there, were I but nigh,
> To see the mote and Bridg and walls so high –
> They'r very fine! sais my deluded eye.

Being thus agreably entertain'd without a thou't of any thing but thoughts themselves, I on a suden was Rous'd from these pleasing Imaginations, by the Post's sounding his horn, which assured mee hee was arrived at the Stage, where we were to Lodg: and that musick was then most musickall and agreeable to mee.

Being come to Mr Havens',[13] I was very civilly Received, and courteously entertained, in a clean comfortable House; and the Good woman was very active in helping off my Riding

---

[11]   Name for the moon personified as a goddess.
[12]   Nereids were sea nymphs of classical mythology.
[13]   Havens' Tavern at Kingstown, Rhode Island.

clothes, and then ask't what I would eat. I told her I had some Chocolett, if shee would prepare it; which with the help of some Milk, and a little clean brass Kettle, she soon effected to my satisfaction. I then betook me to my Apartment, wch was a little Room parted from the Kitchen by a single bord partition; where, after I had noted the Occurrances of the past day, I went to bed, which, tho' pretty hard, Yet neet and handsome. But I could get no sleep, because of the Clamor of some of the Town tope-ers in next Room, Who were entred into a strong debate concerning the Signifycation of the name of their Country, (viz.) *Narragansett*. One said it was named so by the Indians, because there grew a Brier there, of a prodigious Highth and bigness, the like hardly ever known, called by the Indians Narragansett; And quotes an Indian of so Barberous a name for his Author, that I could not write it. His Antago-nist Replyed no – It was from a Spring it had its name, wch hee well knew where it was, which was extreem cold in summer, and as Hott as could be imagined in the winter, which was much resorted too by the natives, and by them called Narragansett, (Hott and Cold,) and that was the originall of their places name – with a thousand Impertinances not worth notice, wch He utter'd with such a Roreing voice and Thundering blows with the fist of wickedness on the Table, that it peirced my very head. I heartily fretted, and wish't 'um tongue tyed; but wth as little succes as a freind of mine once, who was (as shee said) kept a whole night awake, on a Jorny, by a country Left.[14] and a Sergent, Insigne and a Deacon, contriving how to bring a triangle into a Square. They kept calling for 'tother Gill[15], wch while they were swallowing, was some Intermission; But presently, like Oyle to fire, encreased the flame. I set my Candle on a Chest by the bed side, and setting up, fell to my old way of composing my Resentments, in the following manner:

> I ask thy Aid, O Potent Rum!
> To Charm these wrangling Topers Dum.
> Thou hast their Giddy Brains possest –
> The man confounded wth the Beast –
> And I, poor I, can get no rest.
> Intoxicate them with thy fumes:
> O still their Tongues till morning comes!

And I know not but my wishes took effect; for the dispute soon ended wth 'tother Dram; and so Good night!

Wednesday, Octob^r 4th. About four in the morning, we set out for Kingston (for so was the Town called) with a french Docter in our company. Hee and the Post put on very furiously, so that I could not keep up with them, only as now and then they'd stop till they see mee. This Rode was poorly furnished wth accommodations for Travellers, so that we were forced to ride 22 miles by the post's account, but neerer thirty by mine, before wee could bait[16] so much as our Horses, wch I exceedingly complained of. But the post encourag'd mee, by saying wee should be well accommodated anon at mr. Devills, a few miles further. But I questioned whether we ought to go to the Devil to be helpt out of affliction. However, like the rest of Deluded souls that post to the Infernal denn, Wee made all possible speed to this Devil's Habitation; where alliting, in full assurance of good accommodation, wee were going in. But meeting his two daughters, as I suposed twins, they so neerly resembled each other, both in

---

[14] Abbreviation for leftenant, now spelled lieutenant.

[15] Vessel for drinking holding a quarter pint.

[16] To stop and feed and water horse, refresh passengers.

features and habit, and look't as old as the Divel himselfe, and quite as Ugly, We desired entertainm't, but could hardly get a word out of 'um, till with our Importunity, telling them our necesity, &c. they call'd the old Sophister[17], who was as sparing of his words as his daughters had bin, and no, or none, was the reply's hee made us to our demands. Hee differed only in this from the old fellow[18] in to'ther Country: hee let us depart. However, I thought it proper to warn poor Travailers to endeavour to Avoid falling into circumstances like ours, wch at our next Stage I sat down and did as followeth:

> May all that dread the cruel feind of night
> Keep on, and not at this curs't Mansion light.
> 'Tis Hell; 'tis Hell! and Devills here do dwell:
> Here dwells the Devill – surely this's Hell.
> Nothing but Wants: a drop to cool yo'r Tongue
> Cant be procur'd these cruel Feinds among.
> Plenty of horrid Grins and looks sevear,
> Hunger and thirst, But pitty's bannish'd here–
> The Right hand keep, if Hell on Earth you fear!

Thus leaving this habitation of cruelty, we went forward; and arriving at an Ordinary about two mile further, found tollerable accommodation. But our Hostes, being a pretty full mouth'd old creature, entertain'd our fellow travailer, the french Docter, wth Inumirable complaints of her bodily infirmities; and whisperd to him so lou'd, that all the House had as full a hearing as hee: which was very divirting to the company, (of which there was a great many,) as one might see by their sneering. But poor weary I slipt out to enter my mind in my Jornal, and left my Great Landly with her Talkative Guests to themselves.

From hence we proceeded (about ten forenoon) through the Narragansett country, pretty Leisurely; and about one afternoon come to Paukataug River, wch was about two hundred paces over, and now very high, and no way over to to'ther side but this. I darid not venture to Ride thro, my courage at best in such cases but small, And now at the Lowest Ebb, by reason of my weary, very weary, hungry and uneasy Circumstances. So takeing leave of my company, tho' wth no little Reluctance, that I could not proceed wth them on my Jorny, Stop at a little cottage Just by the River, to wait the Waters falling, wch the old man that lived there said would be in a little time, and he would conduct me safe over. This little Hutt was one of the wretchedest I ever saw a habitation for human creatures. It was suported with shores[19] enclosed with Clapbords, laid on Lengthways, and so much asunder, that the Light come throu' every where; the doore tyed on wth a cord in the place of hinges; The floor the bear earth; no windows but such as the thin covering afforded, nor any furniture but a Bedd wth a glass Bottle hanging at the head on't; an earthan cupp, a small pewter Bason, A Bord wth sticks to stand on, instead of a table, and a block or two in the corner instead of chairs. The family were the old man, his wife and two Children; all and every part being the picture of poverty. Notwithstanding both the Hutt and its Inhabitance were very clean and tydee: to the crossing the Old Proverb, that bare walls make giddy[20] hows-wifes.

I Blest myselfe that I was not one of this misserable crew; and the Impressions their wretchedness formed in me caused mee on the very Spott to say:

---

[17] Someone who argues with plausible but fallacious arguments, as Satan was said to do.
[18] The devil.
[19] Posts to support the building.
[20] Inattentive.

Tho' Ill at ease, A stranger and alone,
All my fatigu's shall not extort a grone.
These Indigents have hunger wth their ease;
Their best is wors behalfe then my disease.
Their Misirable hutt wch Heat and Cold
Alternately without Repulse do hold;
Their Lodgings thyn and hard, their Indian fare,
The mean Apparel which the wretches wear,
And their ten thousand ills wch can't be told,
Makes nature er'e 'tis midle age'd look old.
When I reflect, my late fatigues do seem
Only a notion or forgotten Dreem. . . .

Saturday, Oct. 7th, we sett out early in the Morning, and being something unaquainted wth the way, having ask't it of some wee mett, they told us wee must Ride a mile or two and turne down a Lane on the Right hand; and by their Direction wee Rode on but not Yet comeing to the turning, we mett a Young fellow and ask't him how farr it was to the Lane which turn'd down towards Guilford. Hee said wee must Ride a little further, and turn down by the Corner of uncle Sams Lott. My Guide vented his Spleen at the Lubber; and we soon after came into the Rhode, and keeping still on, without any thing further Remarkabell, about two a clock afternoon we arrived at New Haven, where I was received with all Posible Respects and civility. Here I discharged Mr Wheeler with a reward to his satisfaction, and took some time to rest after so long and toilsome a Journey; and Inform'd myselfe of the manners and customs of the place, and at the same time employed myselfe in the afair I went there upon.

They are Govern'd by the same Laws as wee in Boston, (or little differing,) thr'out this whole Colony of Connecticot, And much the same way of Church Government, and many of them good, Sociable people, and I hope Religious too: but a little too much Independant in their principalls, and, as I have been told, were formerly in their Zeal very Riggid in their Administrations towards such as their Lawes made Offenders, even to a harmless Kiss or Innocent merriment among Young people. Whipping being a frequent and counted an easy Punishment, about wch as other Crimes, the Judges were absolute in their Sentences. They told mee a pleasant story about a pair of Justices in those parts, wch I may not omit the relation of.

A negro Slave belonging to a man in the Town, stole a hogs head from his master, and gave or sold it to an Indian, native of the place. The Indian sold it in the neighbourhood, and so the theft was found out. Thereupon the Heathen was Seized, and carried to the Justices House to be Examined. But his worship (it seems) was gone into the feild, with a Brother in office, to gather in his Pompions[21]. Whither the malefactor is hurried, And Complaint made, and satisfaction in the name of Justice demanded. Their Worships cann't proceed in form without a Bench: whereupon they Order one to be Imediately erected, which, for want of fitter materials, they made with pompions – which being finished, down setts their Worships, and the Malefactor call'd, and by the Senior Justice Interrogated after the following manner. You Indian why did You steal from this man? You sho'dn't do so – it's a Grandy wicked thing to steal. Hol't Hol't cryes Justice Junr Brother, You speak negro to him. I'le ask him. You sirrah, why did You steal this man's Hoggshead? Hoggshead? (replys the Indian,) me no stomany. No? says his Worship; and pulling off his hatt, Patted his own head with his hand, sais, Tatapa – You, Tatapa – you; all one this. Hoggshead all one this. Hah! says Netop, now me stomany

---

[21]   Pumpkins.

that.[22] Whereupon the Company fell into a great fitt of Laughter, even to Roreing. Silence is comanded, but to no effect: for they continued perfectly Shouting. Nay, sais his worship, in an angry tone, if it be so, *take mee off the Bench.*

Their Diversions in this part of the Country are on Lecture days and Training days mostly: on the former there is Riding from town to town.

And on training dayes The Youth divert themselves by Shooting at the Target, as they call it, (but it very much resembles a pillory,) where hee that hitts neerest the white has some yards of Red Ribbin presented him, wch being tied to his hattband, the two ends streeming down his back, he is Led away in Triumph, wth great applause, as the winners of the Olympiack Games. They generally marry very young: the males oftener as I am told under twentie than above; they generally make public wedings, and have a way something singular (as they say) in some of them, viz. Just before Joyning hands the Bridegroom quitts the place, who is soon followed by the Bridesmen, and as it were, dragg'd back to duty – being the reverse to the former practice among us, to steal m' Pride[23].

There are great plenty of Oysters all along by the sea side, as farr as I Rode in the Collony, and those very good. And they Generally lived very well and comfortably in their famelies. But too Indulgent (especially the farmers) to their slaves: sufering too great familiarity from them, permitting th^m to sit at Table and eat with them, (as they say to save time,) and into the dish goes the black hoof as freely as the white hand. They told me that there was a farmer lived nere the Town where I lodgd who had some difference wth his slave, concerning something the master had promised him and did not punctualy perform; wch caused some hard words between them; But at length they put the matter to Arbitration and Bound themselves to stand to the award of such as they named – wch done, the Arbitrators Having heard the Allegations of both parties, Order the master to pay 40^s [shillings] to black face, and acknowledge his fault. And so the matter ended: the poor master very honestly standing to the award.

There are every where in the Towns as I passed, a Number of Indians the Natives of the Country, and are the most salvage of all the salvages of that kind that I had ever Seen: little or no care taken (as I heard upon enquiry) to make them otherwise. They have in some places Landes of their owne, and Govern'd by Law's of their own making; – they marry many wives and at pleasure put them away, and on the least dislike or fickle humour, on either side, *saying stand away* to one another is a sufficient Divorce. And indeed those uncomely *Stand aways* are too much in Vougue among the English in this (Indulgent Colony) as their Records plentifully prove; and that on very trivial matters, of which some have been told me, but are not proper to be Related by a Female pen, tho some of that foolish sex have had too large a share in the story.

If the natives committ any crime on their own precincts among themselves, the English takes no Cognezens of. But if on the English ground, they are punishable by our Laws. They mourn for their Dead by blacking their faces, and cutting their hair, after an Awkerd and frightfull manner; But can't bear You should mention the names of their dead Relations to them: they trade most for Rum, for wch they^d hazzard their very lives; and the English fit them Generally as well, by seasoning it plentifully with water.

They give the title of merchant to every trader; who Rate their Goods according to the time

---

[22] Tatapa means the same as, equal to, a phrase the judge uses to compare the Indian's head to the stolen hogshead, which is either a large barrel or cask or the head of a slaughtered pig. But in pointing to his own head to clarify his meaning, the Judge becomes the butt of the laughter. Netop is Algonquian for friend or brother, or more generally, an Indian. Stomany, from the context, means to understand.

[23] "Steal Mistress Pride," was the term for a wedding ritual popular in early rural New England in which the bride was taken to the local tavern where she was redeemed by the purchase of a dinner for the "captors."

and spetia[24] they pay in: viz. Pay, mony, Pay as mony, and trusting. *Pay* is Grain, Pork, Beef, &c. at the prices sett by the General Court that Year; *mony* is pieces of Eight, Ryalls, or Boston or Bay shillings (as they call them,) or Good hard money, as sometimes silver coin is termed by them; also Wampom, viz. Indian beads w[ch] serves for change. *Pay as mony* is provisions, as afores[d] one Third cheaper then as the Assembly or Gene[l] Court sets it; and *Trust* as they and the merchant agree for time.

Now, when the buyer comes to ask for a comodity, sometimes before the merchant answers that he has it, he sais, is *Your pay redy?* Perhaps the Chap Reply's Yes: what do You pay in? say's the merchant. The buyer having answered, then the price is set; as suppose he wants a sixpenny knife, in pay it is 12d[25] – in pay as money eight pence, and hard money its own price, viz. 6d. It seems a very Intricate way of trade and what Lex Mercatoriats[26] had not thought of:

Being at a merchants house, in comes a tall country fellow, wth his alfogeos[27] full of Tobacco; for they seldom Loose their Cudd, but keep Chewing and Spitting as long as they'r eyes are open, – he advanc't to the midle of the Room, makes an Awkward Nodd, and spitting a Large deal of Aromatick Tincture, he gave a scrape with his shovel like shoo, leaving a small shovel full of dirt on the floor, made a full stop, Hugging his own pretty Body with his hands under his arms, Stood staring rown'd him, like a Catt let out of a Baskett. At last, like the creature Balaam Rode on[28], he opened his mouth and said: have You any Ribinen for Hatbands to sell I pray? The Questions and Answers about the pay being past, the Ribin is bro't and opened. Bumpkin Simpers, cryes its confounded Gay I vow; and beckning to the door, in comes Jone Tawdry, dropping about 50 curtsees, and stands by him: hee shows her the Ribin. *Law, You*, sais shee, *its right Gent*, do You, take it, *tis dreadfull pretty*. Then she enquires, *have You any hood silk I pray?* W[ch] being brought and bought, Have You any *thred silk to sew it* wth says shee, w[ch] being accomodated wth they Departed. They Generaly stand after they come in a great while speachless, and sometimes dont say a word till they are askt what they want, which I Impute to the Awe they stand in of the merchants, who they are constantly almost Indebted too; and must take what they bring without Liberty to choose for themselves; but they serve them as well, making the merchants stay long enough for their pay.

We may Observe here the great necessity and bennifitt both of Education and Conversation; for these people have as Large a portion of mother witt, and sometimes a Larger, than those who have bin brought up in Citties; But for want of emprovements, Render themselves almost Ridiculos, as above. I should be glad if they would leave such follies, and am sure all that Love Clean Houses (at least) would be glad on't too.

They are generaly very plain in their dress, throuout all the Colony, as I saw, and follow one another in their modes; that You may know where they belong, especially the women, meet them where you will.

Their Cheif Red Letter day is St. Election, w[ch] is annualy Observed according to Charter, to choose their Govenr: a blessing they can never be thankfull enough for, as they will find, if ever it be their hard fortune to loose it. The present Govenor in Conecticott is the Hon'ble John Winthrop Esq.[29] A Gentleman of an Ancient and Honourable Family, whose Father was Govenor here sometime before, and his Grand father had bin Govr of the Massachusetts. This gentleman is a very curteous and afable person, much Given to Hospitality, and has by his

---

[24]   Kind, as in type of payment (Latin).

[25]   "d" signified pence, from the Roman "denarius" and French "denier," which, like the English penny, was made of copper.

[26]   Mercantile law (Latin).

[27]   An approximation of *alforjas*, Spanish for "saddlebags," and used to refer to cheeks.

[28]   An ass (see Numbers 22:20).

[29]   Fitz-John Winthrop (1639–1707), grandson of John Winthrop.

Good services Gain'd the affections of the people as much as any who had bin before him in that post.

[Knight sojourned in New York City for a time and then made the return trip]
Wee were now in the colony of the Massachusetts . . . and the next day being March 3d wee got safe home to Boston, where I found my aged and tender mother and my Dear and only Child in good health with open arms redy to receive me, and my Kind relations and friends flocking in to welcome mee and hear the story of my transactions and travails I having this day bin five months from home and now I cannot fully express my Joy and Satisfaction. But desire sincearly to adore my Great Benefactor for thus graciously carying forth and returning in safety his unworthy handmaid.

1704   1825

Louis Armand de Lom d'Arce, Baron de Lahontan (1666–1715)

Born into a family of impecunious aristocrats, Louis Armand de Lom d'Arce, Baron of Lahontan, set out for Quebec in 1683 and remained there as a military officer for the next ten years. After a series of disputes with Brouillan, the Governor of Newfoundland, he departed abruptly for France. In order to avoid arrest as a deserter, he wandered between Denmark and the Low Countries. After a period in the court of Hanover, where he became a friend of the philosopher Leibnitz, he died in 1715.

Lahontan's account of his travels, *New Voyages to North America*, was first published in 1703 as a desperate resort of a bankrupt fugitive. By all accounts, the book was a best-seller, with ten editions between 1704 and 1741. Written mostly in the form of letters to someone described as an "old relation" to whom Lahontan had promised letters in exchange for financial assistance, it was translated into English (under the patronage of the Duke of Devonshire), German, Dutch, and Italian. Its success is easy to understand, with its lively and occasionally apocryphal accounts of adventures at sea, its portraits of the colonial society of New France and of the culture of Native Canadian groups, its recounting of Native traditional stories and its racy (and often misogynist) descriptions of marriage and courtship not only among the French settlers but also among Canadian Indians.

PRIMARY WORK

New Voyages to North America, containing an Account of the Several Nations of that vast Continent; their Customs, Commerce, and Way of Navigation upon the Lakes and Rivers; the Several Attempts of the English and French to dispossess one another; with the Reasons of the Miscarriage of the former; and the various Adventures between the French, and the Iroquois Confederates of England, from 1683 to 1694, in Two Volumes, anon. trans. (London: Printed for H. Bonwick, 1703).

FURTHER READING

Charles Scruggs, "La Hontan: Precursor of the Enlightenment and the Myth of the Noble Savage," *The Language Quarterly*, Spring–Summer 19, 3–4 (1981) pp. 23–5, 31.

Christoph Wolfart, "Lahontan's Bestseller," *Historiographia Linguistica: International Journal for the History of the Language Sciences/Revue Internationale pour l'Histoire* 16, 1–2 (1989) pp. 1–24.

Nancy Nahra, "The Secular Continent of Baron de Lahontan," *Historical Reflections/Reflexions Historiques*, Fall, 18, 3 (1992) pp. 59–75.

Frontispiece to Lahontan's *New Voyages to North America*, vol. II (from the English edition of 1703). The legend, from the Latin, is "He tramples on laws and royal authority."

NEW VOYAGES TO NORTH AMERICA . . .

From *Volume I*

From *Preface*

Having flattered myself with the vain hopes of retrieving the King of France's favor, before the declaration of this War[1]; I was so far from thinking to put these letters, and memoirs, to the press, that I designed to have committed them to the flames, if that Monarch had done me the honors of reinstating me in my former places, with the good leave of Messieurs de Ponchartrain[2]. It was with that view that I neglected to put them in such a dress as might now be wished for, for the satisfaction of the reader that gives himself the trouble to peruse them.

Between the fifteenth and sixteenth year of my age I went to Canada, and there took care to keep up a constant correspondence by Letters with an old relation, who had required of me a narrative of the occurrences of that country, upon the account of the yearly assistance he gave me. It is these very letters that make the greatest part of the first Volume. They contain an account of all that passed between the English, the French, the Iroquois, and the other savage nations from the year 1683, to 1694. Together with a great many curious remarks that may be of use to those who have any knowledge of the English or French colonies.

The whole is written with a great deal of fidelity, for I represent things just as they are. I neither flatter nor spare any person whatsoever; I attribute to the Iroquois the glory they have purchased on several occasions, though at the same time I hate that rascally people, as much as horns and law-suits.[3] Notwithstanding the veneration I have for the clergy, I impute to them all the mischief the Iroquois have done to the French colonies, in the course of a War that had never been undertaken, if it had not been for the counsels of these pious Church-men.[4]

The reader is desired to take notice that the towns of New York are known to the French by their old names only, and for that reason I was obliged to make use of the same in my letters as well as my maps. They give the name of New York to all that country that reaches from the source of the river to the mouth, that is, to the island, upon which there stands a city called in the time of the Dutch Manathe[5], and now by the English, New York. In like manner the plantation of Albany, that lies towards the head of the river, is called by the French Orange.

Farther: I would not have the reader to take it amiss, that the thoughts of the savages are set forth in an European dress. The occasion of that choice proceeded from the relation I corresponded with; for that honest gentleman ridiculed the metaphorical harangue of the Grangula[6]; and entreated me not to make a literal translation of a language that was so stuffed with fictions and savage hyperboles. It is for this reason that all the discourses and arguments of those nations are here accommodated to the European style and way of speaking; for having complied with my friend's request, I contented myself in keeping only a copy of the letters I wrote to him, during my pilgrimage in the country of these naked philosophers.

It will not be improper to acquaint the reader by the bye, that those who know my faults, do as little justice to these people, as they do to me, in alleging I am a savage myself, and that that

---

[1] The War of the Spanish Succession (1703–13).

[2] Louis Phelypeaux, Count of Ponchartrain, and his son Jérome were powerful ministers in the French court in the last years of Louis XIV's reign.

[3] Horns were the traditional attribute of the cuckolded husband.

[4] The French and Indian War.

[5] Now Manhattan.

[6] The Latinized form of La Grande Guele (Big Mouth), the name given by the French to Otréouaté, an Iroquois chieftain known for his rhetorical ability.

makes me speak so favorably of my fellow-savages. These observers do me a great deal of honor, as long as they do not explain themselves so as to make me directly of the same character with that which is tacked to the word Savage by the Europeans in their way of thinking: for in saying only that I am of the same temper with the savages, they give me without design[7] the character of the most honest man in the world. It is an uncontested truth, that the nations which are not debauched by the neighborhood of the Europeans are strangers to the measures of *Meum* and *Tuum*[8], and to all laws, judges and priests. This cannot be called into question, since all travelers who have visited those countries vouch for its truth; and a great many of different professions have given the world repeated assurances that it is so. Now this being granted, we ought not to scruple[9] to believe that these are wise and reasonable people. I take a man who must be quite blind who does not see that the property of goods (I do not speak of the engrossing[10] of women) is the only source of all the disorders that perplex the European societies. Upon that consideration it will be easy to perceive that I have not spoken widely in describing that wisdom and acuteness which shines through the words and actions of these poor Americans. If all the world had access to the books of voyages that are found in some well-stocked libraries, they would find in above a hundred descriptions of Canada an infinity of discourses and arguments offered by the savages, which are incredibly stronger and more nervous[11] than those I have inserted in my Memoirs . . .

> From *Letter I: Dated at the Port of Quebec, Nov. 8, 1683. Containing a description of the passage from France to Canada; with some remarks upon the coasts, channels, &c. and the variations of the needle*[12]

Sir,

I am surprised to find that a voyage to the New World is so formidable to those who are obliged to undertake it; for I solemnly protest that it is far from being what the world commonly takes it for. It is true, the passage is in some measure long; but then the hopes of viewing an unknown country, atones for the tediousness of the voyage.

. . . We discerned the Cape[13] about noon; and in order to confirm the discovery, stood in upon it with all sails aloft. At last, being assured that it was the promontory we looked for, an universal joy was spread throughout the ship, and the fate of the wretches that we had thrown overboard was quite forgot. Then the sailors set about the christening of those who had never made the voyage before, and indeed they had done it sooner, if it had not been for the death of our abovementioned companions. This christening I speak of is an impertinent ceremony practiced by seafaring men, whose humors are as strange and extravagant as the element itself on which they foolishly trust themselves.[14] By virtue of a custom of old standing, they profane the Sacrament of baptism in an unaccountable manner. Upon that occasion, the old sailors being blackened all over, and disguised with rags and ropes, force the greener sort that have never passed some certain degrees of latitude before, to fall down on their knees, and to swear upon a book of sea charts, that upon all occasions they will practice upon others the same ceremony that is then made use of towards them. After the administration of this ridiculous oath, they throw fifty buckets full of water upon their head, belly and thighs, and indeed all

---

7   I.e. without meaning to do so.

8   In Latin, mine and yours, i.e. the concept of private property.

9   Hesitate.

10   Impregnating.

11   Gripping.

12   Compass.

13   Cape Race, in southeastern Newfoundland.

14   I.e. the sea.

over their body, without any regard to times of seasons. This piece of folly is chiefly practiced under the Equator, under the Tropics, under the Polar Circles, upon the bank of Newfoundland, and in the Straits of Gibraltar, the Sund, and the Dardanelles. As for persons of note or character, they are exempted from the ceremony, at the expense of five or six bottles of brandy for the ship's crew.

Three or four days after the performance of this solemnity, we discovered Cape Ray[15], and so made up to St Lawrence Bay, in the mouth of which we were becalmed for a little while; and during that calm, we had a clearer and pleasanter day than any we had seen in the passage. It looked as if that day had been vouchsafed us by way of recompense for the rains, fogs, and high winds, that we encountered by the way. There we saw an engagement between a whale and a sword-fish, at the distance of a gunshot from our frigate. We were perfectly charmed when we saw the sword-fish jump out of the water in order to dart its spear into the body of the whale, when obliged to take breath. This entertaining show lasted at least two hours, sometimes to the starboard, sometimes to the larboard of the ship[16]. The sailors, among whom superstition prevails as much as among the Egyptians, took this for a presage of some mighty storm; but the prophecy ended in two or three days of contrary winds, during which time we traversed between the island of Newfoundland and that of Cape Breton . . .

. . . We have received advice, that the Governor has marked out quarters for our troops in some villages or cantons adjacent to this city; so that I am obliged to prepare to go ashore, and therefore must make an end of this letter. I cannot as yet give you any account of the country, excepting that it is already mortally cold. As to the river, I mean to give you a more ample description of it, when I come to know it better. We are informed that M. de la Salle[17] is just returned from his travels, which he undertook upon the discovery of a great river that falls into the Gulf of Mexico, and that he embarks tomorrow for France. He is perfectly well acquainted with Canada, and for that reason you ought to visit him, if you go to Paris this Winter.

I am, Sir,
Yours, &c.

Letter II: Dated at the Canton of Beauprè, May 2, 1684. Containing a description of the plantations of Canada, and the manner in which they were first formed. As also an account of the transportation of whores from France to that country; together with a view of its climate and soil

Sir,

As soon as we landed last year, Mr De la Barre lodged our three companies in some cantons or quarters in the neighborhood of Quebec. The planters call these places *cotes*, which in France signifies no more than the seacoast; though in this country where the names of Town and Village are unknown, that word is made use of to express a seignory[18] or manor, the houses of which lie at the distance of two or three hundred paces one from another, and are seated on the brink of the River of St Lawrence. In earnest, Sir, the boors[19] of those manors live with more ease and convenience than an infinity of the gentlemen in France. I am out indeed in calling them boors, for that name is as little known here as in Spain; whether it be that they pay no

---

[15]   Located in southwest Newfoundland.

[16]   To the right and left of the ship.

[17]   René Robert Cavelier, Sieur de la Salle (1643–87), French explorer and traveler.

[18]   The territory or jurisdiction of a seigneur or lord. Feu-

dalism was established in New France by an act of Richelieu in 1627.

[19]   Cultivators of the soil; alternatively, coarse ill-bred rustics.

taxes, and enjoy the liberty of hunting and fishing; or that the easiness of their life, puts them upon a level with the nobility. The poorest of them have four arpents[20] of ground in front, and thirty or forty in depth. The whole country being a continued forrest of lofty trees, the stumps of which must be grubbed up before they can make use of a plough. It is true, this is a troublesome and chargeable task at first; but in a short time after they make up their losses, for when the virgin ground is capable of receiving seed, it yields an increase to the rate of a hundredfold. Corn is there sown in May, and reaped about the middle of September. Instead of threshing the sheaves in the field, they convey them to barns, where they lie till the coldest season of the winter, at which time the grain is more easily disengaged from the ear. In this country they likewise sow peas, which are much esteemed in France. All sorts of grain are very cheap here, as well as butcher's meat and fowl. The price of wood is almost nothing, in comparison with the charge of its carriage, which after all is [also] very inconsiderable.

Most of the inhabitants are a free sort of people that removed hither from France, and brought with them but little money to set up withal. The rest are those who were soldiers about thirty or forty years ago, at which time the regiment of Carignan was broken[21], and they exchanged a military post for the trade of agriculture. Neither the one nor the other paid anything for the grounds they possess, no more than the officers of these troops, who marked out to themselves certain portions of unmanured and woody lands; for this vast continent is nothing else than one continued forest. The Governors General allowed the officers three or four leagues of ground in front, with as much depth as they pleased; and at the same time the officers gave the soldiers as much ground as they pleased upon the condition of a crown per arpent, by way of fief[22].

After a reform of these troops, several ships were sent hither from France, with a cargo of women of an ordinary reputation, under the direction of some old stale nuns, who ranged them in three classes. The vestal virgins were heaped up (if I may so speak) one above another, in three different apartments, where the bridegrooms singled out their brides just as a butcher does a ewe from amongst a flock of sheep. In these three seraglios, there was such variety and change of diet, as could satisfy the most whimsical appetites; for here was some big some little, some fair some brown, some fat and some meagre. In fine, there was such accommodation that everyone might be fitted to his mind. And indeed the market had such a run, that in fifteen days time they were all disposed of. I am told that the fattest went off best, upon the apprehension that these being less active, would keep truer to their engagements, and hold out better against the nipping cold of the winter. But after all, a great many of the He-Adventurers found themselves mistaken in their measures. However, let that be as it will, it affords a very curious remark; that in some parts of the world to which the vicious European women are transported, the mob[23] of those countries does seriously believe that their sins are so defaced[24] by the ridiculous christening I took notice of before, and they are looked upon ever after as ladies of virtue, of honor, and of an untarnished conduct of life. The sparks[25] that wanted to be married made their addresses to the abovementioned governesses, to whom they were obliged to give an account of their goods and estates, before they were allowed to make their choice in the three seraglios[26]. After their choice was determined, the marriage was concluded upon the spot, in the presence of a priest, and a public notary; and the next day the Governor-General bestowed upon the married couple a bull, a cow, a hog, a sow, a cock, a hen, two barrels of salt

---

20 An archaic French measure of land, equivalent to 0.85 acre.

21 I.e. dissolved.

22 Fee.

23 Common people.

24 Effaced or removed.

25 Young men.

26 Harems.

meat, and eleven crowns, together with a certain coat of arms called by the Greeks *kerata*[27]. The officers, having a nicer taste than the soldiers, made their application to the daughters of the ancient gentlemen of the country, of those of the richer sort of inhabitants; for you know that Canada has been possessed by the French above a hundred years.

In this country everyone lives in a good and a well furnished house; and most of the houses are of wood, and two stories high. Their chimneys are large, by reason of the prodigious fires they make to guard themselves from the cold, which is there beyond all measure, from the month of December to that of April. During that space of time, the river is always frozen over, notwithstanding the flowing and ebbing of the sea; and the snow upon the ground is three or four foot deep, which is very strange in a country that lies in the latitude of forty-seven degrees and some odd minutes. Most people impute the extraordinary snow to the number of mountains with which this vast continent is replenished. Whatever is in that matter, I must take notice of one thing, that seems very strange, namely, that the summer days are much longer here than in Paris. The weather is then so clear and serene, that in three weeks time you shall not see a cloud on the horizon. I hope to go to Quebec with the first opportunity, for I have orders to be in readiness to embark within fifteen days for Montreal, which is the city of this country that lies farthest up toward the head of the river.

I am, Sir,

Yours, &c.

From *Volume II*

A Discourse of the Habit, Houses, Complexion and Temperament of the Savages of North America

. . . I have read some histories of Canada, which were written at several times by the monks[28], and must own that they have given some plain and exact descriptions of such countries as they knew; but at the same time they are widely mistaken in their accounts of the manners and customs of the savages. The Recollets[29] brand the savages for stupid, gross and rustic persons, incapable of thought or reflection. But the Jesuits give them other sort of language[30], for they entitle them to good sense, to a tenacious memory, and to a quick apprehension seasoned with a solid judgement. The former allege that it is to no purpose to preach the Gospel to a sort of people that have less knowledge than the brutes. On the other hand the latter (I mean the Jesuits) give it out, that these savages take pleasure in hearing the word of God, and readily apprehend the meaning of the Scriptures.[31] In the meantime, it is no difficult matter to point to the reasons that influence the one and the other to such allegations; the mystery is easily unraveled by those who know that these two orders cannot set their horses together in Canada.[32]

I have seen so many impertinent accounts of this country, and those written by authors that passed for saints, that I now begin to believe that all History is one continued series of Pyrrhonism[33]. Had I been unacquainted with the language of the savages, I might have credited all that was said of them; but the opportunity I had of conversing with that people served

---

[27] Horns, the symbol of the cuckold.

[28] Probably the *Jesuit Relations*, forty volumes of which were published in Paris between 1632 and 1673.

[29] A missionary religious order.

[30] I.e. describe them in different terms.

[31] I.e. the Jesuits credit the Indians with good sense.

[32] Lahontan is implying that the differences in the attitude of the two rival orders toward the Native peoples of Canada was derived from the varying success of their respective missions.

[33] Pyrrho, a Greek Sceptic philosopher of the third century BC.

to undeceive me, and gave me to understand, that the Recollets and the Jesuits content themselves with glancing at things without taking notice of the (almost) invincible aversion of the savages to the truths of Christianity. Both the one and the other had good reason to be cautious of touching upon that string. In the meantime suffer me to acquaint you, that upon this head I only speak of the savages of Canada, excluding those that live beyond the River of Mississippi, of whose manners and customs I could not acquire a perfect scheme, by reason that I was unacquainted with their languages, not to mention that I had not time to make any long stay in their country. In the Journal of my voyage upon the long River, I acquainted you that they are a very polite people, which you will likewise infer from the circumstances in that discourse.

Those who represented the savages to be as rough as bears, never had the opportunity of seeing them; for they have neither beard nor hair in any part of their body, not so much as under their arm-pits. This is true of both sexes, if I may credit those who ought to know better than I. Generally they are proper well-made persons, and fitter companions to American than to European women. The Iroquois are of a larger stature, and withal more valiant and cunning than the other nations; but at the same time they are neither so nimble nor so dexterous at the exercises of war of hunting, which they never go about but in great numbers. The Illinois, the Oumamis[34], and the Outagamins[35], with some other adjacent nations, are of an indifferent size, and run like greyhounds, if the comparison be allowable. The Ottawa, and most of the other savages to the northward (excepting the Sauteurs[36] and the Clistinos[37]) are cowardly, ugly, and ungainly fellows; but the Hurons are a brave, active and daring people, resembling the Iroquois in their stature and countenance.

All the savages are of a sanguine constitution, inclining to an olive color, and generally speaking they have good faces and proper persons. It is a great rarity to find any among them that are lame, hunchbacked, one-eyed, blind, or dumb. Their eyes are large and black as well as their hair; their teeth are white like ivory, and the breath that springs from their mouth in expiration is as pure as the air that they suck in in inspiration, notwithstanding they eat no bread; which shows that we are mistaken in Europe, in fancying that the eating of meat without bread makes one's breath stink. They are neither so strong nor so vigorous as most of the French are in raising of weights with their arms, or carrying of burdens on their backs; but to make amends for that, they are indefatigable and inured to hardships, insomuch that the inconveniences of cold or heat have no impression upon them; their whole time being spent in the way of exercise, whether in running up and down at hunting and fishing, or in dancing and playing at foot-ball, or such games as require the motion of the legs.

. . . The savages are very healthy, and unacquainted with an infinity of diseases that plague the Europeans, such as palsy[38], dropsy[39], gout, phtisick[40], asthma, gravel[41], and the stone[42]. But at the same time they are liable to the smallpox, and to pleurisies[43]. If a man dies at the age of sixty years, they think he dies young, for they commonly live to eighty or a hundred; nay, I met with two that were turned of a hundred several years[44]. But there are some of them that do not live so long, because they voluntarily shorten thier lives by poisoning themselves, as I shall show you elsewhere. In this point they seem to join issue with Zeno[45] and the Stoics,

34 Miami.
35 Fox.
36 The Ojibwa or Anishinabe.
37 Cree.
38 Paralysis of the limbs.
39 Abnormal retention of fluids.
40 Tuberculosis.
41 Gallstones.
42 Kidney stones.
43 Diseases of the lungs.
44 I.e. were several years older than 100.
45 A Greek philosopher (270?–342? BC) of the Stoic school.

who vindicate self-murder; and from thence I conclude, that the Americans[46] are as great fools as these great philosphers.

From *A Short View of the Humors and Customs of the Savages*

The savages are utter strangers to distinctions of property, for what belongs to one is equally another's. If any one of them be in danger at the Beaver Hunting, the rest fly to his assistance without being so much as asked. If his fusee[47] bursts, they are ready to offer him their own. If any of his children be killed or taken by the enemy, he is preferently furnished with as many slaves as he has occasion for. Money is in use with none of them but those that are Christians, who live in the suburbs of the towns. The others will not touch or so much as look upon silver, but give it the odious name of the French Serpent. They will tell you that among us the people murder, plunder, defame, and betray one another for money, that the husbands make merchandise of their wives, and the mothers of their daughters, for the lucre of that metal. They think it unaccountable that one man should have more than another, and that the rich should have more respect than the poor. In short, they say, the name of savages which we bestow upon them would fit ourselves better, since there is nothing in our actions that bears an appearance of wisdom. Such as have been in France were continually teasing us with the faults and disorders they observed in our towns, as being occasioned by money. It is in vain to remonstrate to them how useful the distinction of property is for the support of a society: they make a jest of what is to be said on that head. In fine, they neither quarrel nor fight nor slander one another. They scoff at arts and sciences, and laugh at the difference of degrees which is observed with us. They brand us for slaves, and call us miserable souls whose life is not worth having, alleging that we degrade ourselves in subjecting ourselves to one man who possesses the whole power, and is bound by no law but his own will; that we have continual jars[48] among ourselves; that our children rebel against their parents; that we imprison one another, and publicly promote our own destruction. Besides, they value themselves above anything that you can imagine, and this is the reason they always give for it: That one is as much Master as another, and since men are all made of the same clay there should be no distinction or superiority among them. They pretend that their contented way of living far surpasses our riches; that all our sciences are not so valuable as the art of leading a peaceful calm life; that a man is not a man with us any farther than riches will make him; but among them the true qualifications of a man are to run well, to hunt, to bend the bow and manage the fuzee[49], to work a canoe, to understand war, to know forests, to subsist upon a little, to build cottages, to fell trees, and to be able to travel a hundred leagues in a wood without any guide or other provision than his bow and arrows. They say we are great cheats in selling them bad wares four times dearer than they are worth, by way of exchange for their beaver skins; that our fuzees are continually bursting and laming them, after they have paid sufficient prices for them. I wish I had time to recount the innumerable absurdities they are guilty of relating to our customs, but to be particular upon that head would be a work of ten or twelve days. . . .

. . . They pay an infinite deference to old age. The son that laughs at his father's advice shall tremble before his grandfather. In a word, they take the ancient men for oracles, and follow their counsel accordingly. If a man tells his son it is time he should marry, or go to the war, or the hunting, or shooting, he shall answer carelessly, "That's valiant, I thought so." But if his grandfather tell him so, the answer is, "That's good. It shall be done." If by chance they kill a

---

46   Native Americans.
47   Probably a mistranslation of *fusil* or musket.

48   Conflicts.
49   Musket.

partridge, a goose, or a duck, or catch any delicate fish, they never fail to present it to their oldest relations.

The savages are wholly free from care. They do nothing but eat, drink, sleep, and ramble about in the night when they are at their villages. Having no set hours for meals, they eat when they are hungry, and commonly do it in a large company, feasting here and there by turns. The women and girls do the same among themselves, and do not admit any men into their company at that time . . . It is not to be denied but the savages are a very sensible people, and are perfectly well acquainted with the interest of their nations. They are great moralists, especially when they criticize on the manners of the Europeans, and are mightily upon their guard in our company, unless it be with such as they are intimately acquainted with. In other matters they are incredulous and obstinate to the last degree, and are not able to distinguish between a chimerical supposition and an undoubted truth, or between a fair and a false consequence . . .

From *An Account of the Amours and Marriages of the Savages*

I could recount a thousand curious things relating to the courtship and the way of marrying among the savages; but the relation of so many particulars would be too tedious, for which reason I shall only confine myself to what is most essential on that subject.

It may be justly said that the men are as cold and indifferent as the girls are passionate and warm. The former love nothing but war and hunting, and their utmost ambition reaches no farther. When they are at home and have nothing to do, they run with the match, that is, they are nightwalkers. The young men do not marry until they are thirty years of age, for they pretend that the enjoyment of women does so enervate[50] them that they have not the same measure of strength to undergo great fatigues, and that their hams[51] are too weak for long marches or quick pursuits. In pursuance of this thought, it is alleged that those who have married, or strolled in the nights too often, are taken by the Iroquois, by reason of the weakness of their limbs, and the decay of their vigor. But after all, we must not imagine that they live chaste until that age; for they pretend that excessive continence occasions vapors, disorders of the kidneys, and a suppression of urine, so that it is necessary for their health to have a run once a week.

If the savages were capable of being subjected to the Empire of Love, they must needs have an extraordinary command of themselves to disguise the just jealousy they might have of their mistresses, and at the same time to carry it fair with their rivals. I know the humor of the savages better than a great many French people that have lived among them all their lifetime, for I studied their customs so narrowly and exactly that all their conduct of life is as perfectly well known to me, as if I had been among them all my lifetime. And it is this exact knowledge that prompts me to say that they are altogether strangers to that blind duty which we call love. They content themselves with a tender friendship that is not liable to all the extravagancies that the passion of love raises in such breasts as harbor it. In a word, they live with such tranquility that one may call their love simple goodwill, and their discretion upon that head is unimaginable. Their friendship is firm, but free of transport, for they are very careful in preserving the liberty and freedom of their heart, which they look upon as the most valuable treasure upon earth. From whence I conclude that they are not altogether so savage as we are.

. . . Some young women will not hear of a husband through a principle of debauchery. That sort of women are called *Ickoue ne Kioussa*, i.e. Hunting Women, for they commonly accom-

---

50   Weaken.   51   Buttocks.

pany the huntsmen in their diversions. To justify their conduct, they allege that they find themselves to be of too indifferent a temper to brook the conjugal yoke, to be too careless for the bringing up of children, and too impatient to bear the passing of the whole winter in the village. Thus it is that they cover and disguise their lewdness. Their parents or relations dare not censure their vicious conduct; on the contrary, they seem to approve of it, in declaring, as I said before, that their daughters have the command of their own bodies and may dispose of their persons as they think fit, they being at liberty to do what they please. In short, the children of these common women are accounted a lawful issue, and entitled to all the privileges of other children, abating for[52] one thing, namely, that the noted warriors or counselors will not accept them for their sons in law, and that they cannot enter into alliance with certain ancient families, though at the same time these families are not possessed of any peculiar right or pre-eminence. The Jesuits do their utmost to prevent the lewd practices of these whores by preaching to their parents that their indulgence is very disagreeable to the Great Spirit, that they must answer before God for not confining their children to the measures of continence and chastity, and that a fire is kindled in the other world to torment them for ever unless they take more care to correct vice.

To such remonstrances the men reply, "That's admirable," and the women usually tell the good fathers[53] in a deriding way that if their threats be well grounded, the mountains of the other world must consist of the ashes of souls.

1703

William Byrd II (1674–1744)

Considered the most "cultivated" of colonial writers, William Byrd II published almost nothing in his lifetime, confessing in a satirical self-portrait that his "amorous" nature blunted the edge of his literary ambition. But there is evidence, from the secret diaries he assiduously kept in code which recorded everything from his breakfasts to his peccadillos, his copious notebooks, crammed commonplace books and vast correspondence, that Byrd was an inveterate, even compulsive, writer. Heir to a large estate in Virginia begun by his great-grandfather and enlarged by succeeding generations, Byrd received a classical education in England and a taste for learning and study that stayed with him all his life. Because his father expected him to take over his large tobacco plantation, lucrative trade with the Indians as well as his public offices in the colonial Virginia government, the young Byrd remained in London to learn about business, eventually entering the Middle Temple and being duly admitted to the bar. There he moved in the high-

est social circles, frequenting the theater, making friends with contemporary writers like William Congreve and William Wycherley, and men of science like Sir Robert Southwell, president of the Royal Society, who helped the young Byrd get elected to that august body at the age of twenty-two.

When he inherited his father's estate in 1705, Byrd took up his place in Virginia public life with relish, marrying a wealthy woman, becoming the receiver-general of the colony and a member of the House of Burgesses where he served for his entire life. He returned to London in 1715, representing the House against the machinations of the governor, Alexander Spotswood, a conflict that generated his long feud with James Blair. After his wife died of smallpox in 1716, he plunged again into London's social whirl, but remarried and in 1726 returned permanently to Virginia. There, he replaced his father's wooden mansion at Westover with a grand brick structure and amassed a huge library,

---

[52]   Except for.

[53]   I.e. the Jesuits.

rivaled only by Cotton Mather's in Boston. He continued to serve the colony's interests, which dovetailed nicely with his own, and made several expeditions to the frontier, including the one commissioned by Virginia in 1728 to settle its vexed and long-standing dispute with North Carolina concerning their shared boundary. This expedition, which lasted sixteen weeks, with a six month hiatus from April to September, and covered six hundred miles over swampy and mountainous terrain, generated Byrd's most famous works, *The Histories of the Dividing Line*. Always greedy for land, he bought large tracts on the frontier, including the land given to the North Carolinian commissioners as payment for their service in establishing the dividing line. The cities of Richmond and Petersburg, which he helped found, were carved out of his properties.

Byrd was a man of two worlds and epitomized the colonial gentleman and Enlightenment dilettante. In his London years, he wrote light verse, comic satires, and occasional pieces which circulated among friends. When he settled permanently in Virginia, he began to focus on American subjects with an interest in natural history, but he always had a sophisticated audience of privileged English readers in mind. *The Histories*, his most ambitious works, were clearly meant for specific – and different – coteries, and express his own understanding of the necessity of fixing social and cultural divisions and distinctions: between the Virginians and North Carolinians, which is also the crucial distinction between industry and idleness; between the commissioners and their "men;" a distinction of rank and class; between lecherous men and vulnerable females, a "natural" difference; and between white settlers and native Americans, a complex distinction embedded in a deeply entrenched colonialist discourse. The most obvious division is between *The History of the Dividing Line*, which Byrd was supposedly preparing for publication, and *The Secret History*, written before the more "official" work and serving as its source. *The Secret History*, which first appeared in 1929, is shorter, racier and more explicit in its humorous characterizations of the commissioners, the conflicts among them, and Byrd's mock-heroic role in what he reveals to be a rowdy, bawdy adventure. *The History*, longer and more expansive, first appeared in 1841, but circulated widely among people like Thomas Jefferson, who had copies of both *Histories* in his possession. *The History* has an easy, gossipy style, ornamented with classical allusions and piquant perceptions, and characterized by paragraphs that often build to an engaging observation or comic turn. Each version develops a distinct tone meant for different audiences, but they can also be read comparatively to reveal a fascinating processes of colonial self-representation.

PRIMARY WORKS

The Prose Works of William Byrd of Westover, ed. Louis B. Wright (Cambridge: Belknap Press, 1966).

The London Diary, 1717–1721, and Other Writings, eds Louis B. Wright and Marion Tinling, 1958.

Another Secret Diary of William Byrd of Westover, 1739–1741, with Letters and Literary Exercises, 1696–1726, ed. Maude H. Woodfin, 1942.

The Correspondence of the Three William Byrds, ed. Marion Tinling, 1977.

FURTHER READING

Donald Siebert, Jr, "William Byrd's Histories of the Line: The Fashioning of a Hero," *American Literature*, 47 (1976) pp. 535–51.

Robert Bain, "William Byrd of Westover," *The History of Southern Literature*, eds Rubin, Jackson, Rayburn, Simpson, Young (Baton Rouge: Louisiana State University Press, 1985) pp. 48–56.

Kenneth Lockridge, *The Diary, and Life, of William Byrd II of Virginia, 1674–1744* (Chapel Hill: University of North Carolina Press, 1987).

Dana Nelson, "Economies of Morality and Power: Reading 'Race' in Two Colonial Texts," *A Mixed Race: Ethnicity in Early America*, ed. Frank Shuffleton (New York: Oxford University Press: 1993) pp. 19–38.

FROM *THE SECRET HISTORY OF THE LINE*[1]

The Governor and Council of Virginia in the year 1727 received an express order from His Majesty to appoint commissioners who, in conjunction with others to be named by the government of North Carolina, should run the line betwixt the two colonies. . . .

March 5. At break of day we turned out, properly speaking, and blest our landlord's eyes with half a pistole[2]. About seven we embarked and . . . about two we were joined by Judge Jumble and Plausible, two of the Carolina commissioners; the other two, Shoebrush and Puzzlecause[3], lagged behind, which was the more unlucky because we could enter on no business for want of the Carolina commission which these gentlemen had in their keeping. Jumble was brother to the late Dean of York, and if His Honor had not formerly been a pirate himself, he seemed intimately acquainted with many of them. Plausible had been bred in Christ's Hospital and had a tongue as smooth as the Commissary, and was altogether as well qualified to be of the Society of Jesus. These worthy gentlemen were attended by Boötes[4] as their surveyor, a young man of much industry but no experience.

We had now nothing to do but to reconnoiter the place. The high land ended in a bluff point, from which a spit of sand extended itself to the southeast about half a mile. The inlet lies between this spit and another on the south side, leaving a shoal passage for the sea not above a mile over. On the east are shoals that run out two or three miles, over which the breakers rise mountains high with a terrible noise. I often cast a longing eye toward England and sighed. . . .

March 9. . . . One of our piraguas[5] set the surveyors and five men over North River. They landed in a miry marsh, which led to a very deep pocosin[6]. . . .

While they were struggling with these difficulties, we commissioners went in state in the other piragua Northwest River and rowed up as high as Mr Merchant's. He lives near half a mile from the river, having a causeway leading through a filthy swamp to his plantation. I encamped in his pasture with the men, though the other commissioners indulged themselves so far as to lie in the house. But it seems they broke the rules of hospitality by several gross freedoms they offered to take with our landlord's sister. She was indeed a pretty girl, and therefore it was prudent to send her out of harm's way. I was the more concerned at this unhandsome behavior because the people were extremely civil to us and deserved a better treatment.

March 11. We ordered the surveyors early to their business . . . In the meanwhile, Shoebrush and I took a walk into the woods and called at a cottage where a dark angel surprised us with her charms. Her complexion was a deep copper, so that her fine shape and regular features made her appear like a statue *en bronze* done by a masterly hand. Shoebrush was smitten at the

---

[1] The text, with slight modification, is from *The Prose Works of William Byrd of Westover*, ed. Louis B. Wright (Cambridge: Belknap Press, 1966).

[2] From *pistolet*, a Spanish gold coin, referring to any foreign coin.

[3] Byrd gave satirical names to all the commissioners and surveyors. Judge Jumble: Christopher Gale, Chief Justice and Collector of Customs; Plausible: Edward Moseley (*d.*1749), influential political leader of North Carolina; Shoebrush: John Lovick, deputy of the Proprietors and later

Surveyor General; Puzzlecause: William Little, a native of Massachusetts and Harvard graduate, later Attorney General of North Carolina. His name for himself was "Steddy."

[4] Samuel Swan (1704–72), nephew of Edward Moseley and member of the North Carolina Assembly. Boötes, the northern constellation called the Wagoner, contains the bright star Arcturus.

[5] A large canoe made of the trunk of a tree, or a flat bottom sailing barge.

[6] A swamp (Algonquian).

first glance and examined all her neat proportions with a critical exactness. She struggled just enough to make her admirer more eager, so that if I had not been there, he would have been in danger of carrying his joke a little too far.

March 14. . . . After a march of two miles through a very bad way, the men sweating under their burdens, we arrived at the edge of the Dismal[7], where the surveyors had left off the night before. . . . The reeds, which grew about twelve feet high, were so thick and so interlaced with bamboo briers that our pioneers were forced to open a passage. The ground, if I may properly call it so, was so spongy that the prints of our feet were instantly filled with water. Amongst the reeds here and there stood a white cedar, commonly mistaken for juniper. Of this sort was the soil for about half a mile together, after which we came to a piece of high land about one hundred yards in breadth.

March 15. . . . About eleven we set off and called at an ordinary[8] eight miles off, not far from the great bridge. Then we proceeded eight miles farther to honest Timothy Ives's, who supplied us with everything that was necessary. He had a tall, straight daughter of a yielding, sandy complexion, who having the curiosity to see the tent, Puzzlecause gallanted her thither, and might have made her free of it had not we come seasonably to save the damsel's chastity. Here both our cookery and bedding were more cleanly than ordinary. The parson lay with Puzzlecause in the tent to keep him honest or, peradventure, to partake of his diversion if he should be otherwise.

March 19. We dispatched men to the north and south, to fire guns on the edge of the Dismal by way of signal, but could gain no intelligence of our people. . .

My landlord's daughter, Rachel, offered her service to wash my linen and regaled me with a mess of hominy, tossed up with rank butter and glyster sugar[9]. This I was forced to eat to show that nothing from so fair a hand could be disagreeable. She was a smart lass, and, when I desired the parson to make a memorandum of his christenings that we might keep an account of the good we did, she asked me very pertly who was to keep an account of the evil? I told her she should be my secretary for that if she would go along with me. Mr Pugh and Mr O'Shield helped to fill up our house, so that my landlady told us in her cups that now we must lie three in a bed.

March 25. . . . Our landlord had not the good fortune to please Firebrand[10] with our dinner, but, surely, when people do their best, a reasonable man would be satisfied. But he endeavored to mend his entertainment by making hot love to honest Ruth, who would by no means be charmed either with his persuasion or his person. While the master was employed in making love to one sister, the man made his passion known to the other; only he was more boisterous and employed force when he could not succeed by fair means. Though one of the men rescued the poor girl from this violent lover but was so much his friend as to keep the shameful secret from those whose duty it would have been to punish such violations of hospitality, . . .

April 4. Here we called a council of war whether we should proceed any farther this season, and we carried it by a majority of votes to run the line only about two miles beyond this place. . . .

---

7 The Great Dismal Swamp, named by Byrd, is a vast marshy region on the Coastal Plain of southeastern Virginia and northeastern North Carolina. At the time it was about 40 miles long and covered about 2,000 square miles, but has been drained to less than half that area now.

8 Tavern.

9 A possible misreading of "caster sugar."

10 Richard Fitzwilliam, a Collector of Customs in Virginia, later appointed Surveyor General of all Duties and Importations for the Carolinas, Maryland, Virginia, Pennsylvania, Bahama Islands, and Jamaica.

April 7. . . . Thither we went [to Nottoway Town], having given notice by a runner that we were coming, that the Indians might be at home to entertain us. Our landlord showed us the way, and the scouts had no sooner spied us but they gave notice of our approach to the whole town by perpetual whoops and cries, which to a stranger sound very dismal. This called their great men to the fort, where we alighted and were conducted to the best cabins. All the furniture of those apartments was hurdles[11] covered with clean mats. The young men had painted themselves in a hideous manner, not for beauty but terror, and in that equipage entertained us with some of their war dances. The ladies had put on all their ornaments to charm us, but the whole winter's dirt was so crusted on their skins that it required a strong appetite to accost them. Whatever we were, our men were not quite so nice but were hunting after them all night. But though Meanwell[12] might perhaps want inclination to these sad-colored ladies, yet curiosity made him try the difference between them and other women, to the disobligation of his ruffles, which betrayed what he had been doing.

Instead of being entertained by these Indians, we entertained them with bacon and rum, which they accepted of very kindly, the ladies as well as the men. They offered us no bedfellows, according to the good Indian fashion, which we had reason to take unkindly. Only the Queen of Weyanoke told Steddy[13] that her daughter had been at his service if she had not been too young.

Some Indian men were lurking all night about our cabin, with the felonious intent to pilfer what they could lay their hands upon, and their dogs slunk into us in the night and eat up what remained of our provisions.

April 8. When we were dressed, Meanwell and I visited most of the princesses at their own apartments, but the smoke was so great there, the fire being made in the middle of the cabins, that we were not able to see their charms. Prince James's princess sent my wife a fine basket of her own making, with the expectation of receiving from her some present of ten times its value. An Indian present, like those made to princes, is only a liberality put out to interest and a bribe placed to the greatest advantage.

I could discern by some of our gentlemen's linen, discolored by the soil of the Indian ladies, that they had been convincing themselves in the point of their having no fur.

About ten we marched out of the town, some of the Indians giving us a volley of small arms at our departure. We drank our chocolate at one Jones's, about four miles from the town, and then proceeded over Blackwater Bridge to Colonel Henry Harrison's where we were very handsomely entertained and congratulated one another upon our return into Christendom.

[The expedition is resumed the following fall.]

November 16. . . . While the horses were marching round, Meanwell and I made a visit to Cornelius Keith, who lived rather in a pen than a house with his wife and six children. I never beheld such a scene of poverty in this happy part of the world. The hovel they lay in had no roof to cover those wretches from the injuries of the weather, but when it rained or was colder than ordinary the whole family took refuge in a fodder stack. The poor man had raised a kind of a house, but for want of nails it remained uncovered. I gave him a note on Major Mumford for nails for that purpose and so made a whole family happy at a very small expense. The man can read and write very well and by way of trade can make and set up quernstones[14], and yet is poorer than any Highland Scot or bogtrotting Irishman.

---

11   A framework made from branches.
12   William Dandridge, business partner of Governor Spotswood, and later a member of the Council.
13   Byrd's name for himself.
14   Grinding stones used in milling.

November 22. . . . We arrived at Coggins Point about four, where my servants attended with boats in order to transport us to Westover[15].

1728   1929

FROM *THE HISTORY OF THE DIVIDING LINE*[1]

Before I enter upon the journal of the line between Virginia and North Carolina, it will be necessary to clear the way to it by showing how the other British colonies on the main have, one after another, been carved out of Virginia by grants from His Majesty's royal predecessors. All that part of the northern American continent now under the dominion of the King of Great Britain and stretching quite as far as the Cape of Florida went at first under the general name of Virginia.

The only distinction in those early days was that all the coast to the southward of Chesapeake Bay was called South Virginia and all to the northward of it North Virginia.

The first settlement of this fine country was owing to that great ornament of the British nation, Sir Walter Raleigh[2] who obtained a grant thereof from Queen Elizabeth, of ever-glorious memory, by letters patent[3] dated March 25, 1584. . . .

From Kecoughtan[4] they extended themselves as far as Jamestown, where, like true Englishmen, they built a church that cost no more than fifty pounds and a tavern that cost five hundred.

They had now made peace with the Indians, but there was one thing wanting to make that peace lasting. The natives could by no means persuade themselves that the English were heartily their friends so long as they disdained to intermarry with them. And, in earnest, had the English consulted their own security and the good of the colony, had they intended either to civilize or convert these gentiles, they would have brought their stomachs to embrace this prudent alliance.

The Indians are generally tall and well proportioned, which may make full amends for the darkness of their complexions. Add to this that they are healthy and strong, with constitutions untainted by lewdness and not enfeebled by luxury. Besides, morals and all considered, I cannot think the Indians were much greater heathens than the first adventurers, who, had they been good Christians, would have had the charity to take this only method of converting the natives to Christianity. For, after all that can be said, a sprightly lover is the most prevailing missionary that can be sent amongst these or any other infidels.[5]

Besides, the poor Indians would have had less reason to complain that the English took away their land if they had received it by way of a portion with their daughters. Had such affinities been contracted in the beginning, how much bloodshed had been prevented and how populous would the country have been, and, consequently, how considerable! Nor would the shade of the skin have been any reproach at this day, for if a Moor may be washed white in three generations, surely an Indian might have been blanched in two.

---

[15]   Byrd's large family estate.

THE HISTORY

[1]   The text, with slight modification, is from *The Prose Works of William Byrd of Westover*, ed. Louis B. Wright (Cambridge: Belknap Press, 1966).

[2]   Sir Walter Ralegh (1552?–1618), a military and naval commander who organized many early explorations of the New World.

[3]   Public letters of authorization signed by a sovereign.

[4]   An Indian village, now Hampton, Virginia.

[5]   Robert Beverley, Byrd's brother-in-law and contemporary, makes a similar argument in his *History and Present State of Virginia* (1705).

The French, for their parts, have not been so squeamish in Canada, who upon trial find abundance of attraction in the Indians. Their late grand monarch thought it not below even the dignity of a Frenchman to become one flesh with this people and therefore ordered 100 livres for any of his subjects, man or woman, that would intermarry with a native.

By this piece of policy we find the French interest very much strengthened amongst the savages and their religion, such as it is, propagated just as far as their love. And I heartily wish this well-concerted scheme don't hereafter give the French an advantage over His Majesty's good subjects on the northern continent of America.

About the same time New England was pared off from Virginia by letters patent bearing date April 10, 1608. . . .

But about the year 1620 a large swarm of dissenters[6] fled thither from the severities of their stepmother, the church. These saints[7], conceiving the same aversion to the copper complexion of the natives with that of the first adventurers to Virginia, would on no terms contract alliances with them, afraid, perhaps, like the Jews of old, lest they might be drawn into idolatry by those strange women.

Whatever disgusted them I can't say, but this false delicacy, creating in the Indians a jealousy that the English were ill affected toward them, was the cause that many of them were cut off and the rest exposed to various distresses. . .

March 11. . . . We had encamped so early that we found time in the evening to walk near half a mile into the woods. There we came upon a family of mulattoes that called themselves free, though by the shyness of the master of the house, who took care to keep least in sight, their freedom seemed a little doubtful. It is certain many slaves shelter themselves in this obscure part of the world, nor will any of their righteous neighbors discover them. On the contrary, they find their account in settling such fugitives on some out-of-the way corner of their land to raise stocks for a mean and inconsiderable share, well knowing their condition makes it necessary for them to submit to any terms. Nor were these worthy borderers content to shelter runaway slaves, but debtors and criminals have often met with the like indulgence. But if the government of North Carolina have encouraged this unneighborly policy in order to increase their people, it is no more than what ancient Rome did before them, which was made a city of refuge for all debtors and fugitives and from that wretched beginning grew up in time to be mistress of great part of the world. And, considering how Fortune delights in bringing great things out of small, who knows but Carolina may, one time or other, come to be the seat of some other great empire?

March 14. . . . In the meantime the three commissioners returned out of the Dismal the same way they went in and, having joined their brethren, proceeded that night as far as Mr Wilson's. This worthy person lives within sight of the Dismal, in the skirts whereof his stocks range and maintain themselves all the winter, and yet he knew as little of it as he did of *Terra Australis Incognita*[8]. He told us a Canterbury tale of a North Briton whose curiosity spurred him a long way into this great desert, as he called it, near twenty years ago, but he, having no compass nor seeing the sun for several days together, wandered about till he was almost famished; but at last he bethought himself of a secret his countrymen make use of to pilot themselves in a dark day. He took a fat louse out of his collar and exposed it to the open day on a piece of white paper, which he brought along with him for his journal. The poor insect, having no eyelids, turned himself about till he found the darkest part of the heavens and so made the

---

[6]   Protestants who had separated from the Church of England and were living in Leyden, Holland. Their story is told by William Bradford, in Part 2 of this volume.

[7]   A term for the members of "purified" Puritan congregations.

[8]   Unknown southern region (Latin).

best of his way toward the North. By this direction he steered himself safe out and gave such a frightful account of the monsters he saw and the distresses he underwent that no mortal since has been hardy enough to go upon the like dangerous discovery.

March 25. . . . Surely there is no place in the world where the inhabitants live with less labor than in North Carolina. It approaches nearer to the description of Lubberland[9] than any other, by the great felicity of the climate, the easiness of raising provisions, and the slothfulness of the people. Indian corn is of so great increase that a little pains will subsist a very large family with bread, and then they may have meat without any pains at all, by the help of the low grounds and the great variety of mast that grows on the high land. The men, for their parts, just like the Indians, impose all the work upon the poor women. They make their wives rise out of their beds early in the morning, at the same time that they lie and snore till the sun has risen one-third of his course and dispersed all the unwholesome damps. Then, after stretching and yawning for half an hour, they light their pipes, and, under the protection of a cloud of smoke, venture out into the open air; though if it happen to be ever so little cold they quickly return shivering into the chimney corner. When the weather is mild, they stand leaning with both their arms upon the cornfield fence and gravely consider whether they had best go and take a small heat at the hoe but generally find reasons to put it off till another time. Thus they loiter away their lives, like Solomon's sluggard[10], with their arms across, and at the winding up of the year scarcely have bread to eat. To speak the truth, 'tis a thorough aversion to labor that makes people file off to North Carolina, where plenty and a warm sun confirm them in their disposition to laziness for their whole lives.

April 6. Thus we finished our spring campaign, and having taken leave of our Carolina friends and agreed to meet them again the tenth of September following . . .

April 7. . . . In the morning we dispatched a runner to the Nottoway town to let the Indians know we intended them a visit that evening, and our honest landlord was so kind as to be our pilot thither, being about four miles from his house. . . .

The whole number of people belonging to the Nottoway town, if you include women and children, amount to about two hundred. These are the only Indians of any consequence now remaining within the limits of Virginia. The rest are either removed or dwindled to a very inconsiderable number, either by destroying one another or else by the smallpox and other diseases. Though nothing has been so fatal to them as their ungovernable passion for rum, with which, I am sorry to say it, they have been but too liberally supplied by the English that live near them.

And here I must lament the bad success Mr Boyle's[11] charity has hitherto had toward converting any of these poor heathens to Christianity. Many children of our neighboring Indians have been brought up in the College of William and Mary. They have been taught to read and write and been carefully instructed in the principles of the Christian religion till they came to be men. Yet after they returned home, instead of civilizing and converting the rest, they have immediately relapsed into infidelity and barbarism themselves.

And some of them, too, have made the worst use of the knowledge they acquired among the English by employing it against their benefactors. Besides, as they unhappily forget all the good they learn and remember the ill, they are apt to be more vicious and disorderly than the rest of their countrymen. . . .

---

9   Seventeenth-century name for "Cockaigne," an imaginary land of extreme luxury and ease described in a thirteenth-century French fabliau.

10   See Proverbs 6:–11.

11   Robert Boyle (1627–91) was a natural philosopher and chemist and governor of the Corporation for the Spread of the Gospel in New England (1661–89). The College of William and Mary used a bequest from him to build Brafferton Hall in 1723 to house and educate Indians.

April 8. We rested on our clean mats very comfortably, though alone, and the next morning went to the toilet of some of the Indian ladies, where, what with the charms of their persons and the smoke of their apartments, we were almost blinded. They offered to give us silk-grass baskets of their own making, which we modestly refused, knowing that an Indian present, like that of a nun, is a liberality put out to interest and a bribe placed to the greatest advantage. Our chaplain observed with concern that the ruffles of some of our fellow travelers were a little discolored with puccoon[12], wherewith the good man had been told those ladies used to improve their invisible charms.

About ten o'clock we march[ed] out of town in good order, and the war captains saluted us with a volley of small arms. From thence we proceeded over Blackwater Bridge to Colonel Henry Harrison's, where we congratulated each other upon our return into Christendom.

Thus ended our progress for this season . . .

October [31.] . . . In the evening we pitched our tent near Miry Creek, though an uncomfortable place to lodge in, purely for the advantage of the canes. Our hunters killed a large doe and two bears, which made all other misfortunes easy. Certainly no Tartar ever loved horseflesh or Hottentot[13] guts and garbage better than woodsmen do bear. The truth of it is, it may be proper food perhaps for such as work or ride it off, but, with our chaplain's leave, who loved it much, I think it not a very proper diet for saints, because 'tis apt to make them a little too rampant. And, now, for the good of mankind and for the better peopling an infant colony, which has no want but that of inhabitants, I will venture to publish a secret of importance which our Indian disclosed to me. I asked him the reason why few or none of his countrywomen were barren. To which curious question be answered, with a broad grin upon his face, they had an infallible secret for that. Upon my being importunate to know what the secret might be, he informed me that if any Indian woman did not prove with child at a decent time after marriage, the husband, to save his reputation with the women, forthwith entered into a bear diet for six weeks, which in that time makes him so vigorous that he grows exceedingly impertinent to his poor wife, and 'tis great odds but he makes her a mother in nine months. And thus much I am able to say besides for the reputation of the bear diet, that all the married men of our company were joyful fathers within forty weeks after they got home, and most of the single men had children sworn to them within the same time, our chaplain always excepted, who, with much ado, made a shift to cast out that importunate kind of devil by dint of fasting and prayer.

November 12. . . . These Indians [the Tuscarora] have a very odd tradition amongst them that many years ago their nation was grown so dishonest that no man could keep any of his goods or so much as his loving wife to himself; that, however, their god, being unwilling to root them out for their crimes, did them the honor to send a messenger from Heaven to instruct them and set them a perfect example of integrity and kind behavior toward one another. But this holy person, with all his eloquence and sanctity of life, was able to make very little reformation amongst them. Some few old men did listen a little to his wholesome advice, but all the young fellows were quite incorrigible. They not only neglected his precepts but derided and evilly entreated his person. At last, taking upon him to reprove some young rakes of the Conechta clan very sharply for their impiety, they were so provoked at the freedom of his rebukes that they tied him to a tree and shot him with arrows through the heart. But their god took instant vengeance on all who had a hand in that monstrous act by lightning from Heaven,

---

12   Red dye from local plants.

13   Tartar: an inhabitant of Tartary, region of Central Asia.

Hottentot: the Khoikhoin people or "pygmies" of southwestern Africa.

and has ever since visited their nation with a continued train of calamities; nor will he ever leave off punishing and wasting their people till he shall have blotted every living soul of them out of the world.

1728–30   1841

Pierre François-Xavier de Charlevoix
(1682–1761)

At the end of the seventeenth century, the French traveler Dièreville complained of the difference he had encountered between the New France he had observed at first hand and the descriptions of it he had found in books, particularly that of Baron Lahontan. Years later, Father Pierre François-Xavier de Charlevoix, a Jesuit priest sent to Canada in 1705, would echo this criticism, deploring the runaway success of Lahontan's *New Voyages to North America* and characterizing it as "a monstrous hodgepodge of fables." He was particularly outraged by Lahontan's anti-clericalism and what he saw as the book's libertine tendencies. In 1719, Charlevoix was officially asked to study the question of the boundaries of Acadia, then a source of conflict between the French and the English. Shortly thereafter, from 1720 to 1723, he carried out at the orders of the King an extensive journey into the interior of the American continent to gather information about the Western Sea.

After returning to France, Charlevoix dedicated himself to writing his own account of his experiences in New France. His *Journal of a Voyage to North America*, first published in 1744, is notable for its descriptions of colonial Quebec and New Orleans, as well as for its detailed discussions of the rituals and social structure of Native groups (particularly the Natchez) of the lower Mississippi Valley.

PRIMARY WORK

Journal of a Voyage to North America, undertaken by the Order of the French King, containing the geographical description and natural history of that country, particularly Canada, together with an Account of the Customs, Characters, Religion, Manners and Traditions of the original Inhabitants, in a Series of Letters to the Duchess of Lesdiguières, anon. trans. (London: R. & J. Dodsley, 1761).

FURTHER READING

Christian Marouby, "From Early Anthropology to the Literature of the Savage: The Naturalization of the Primitive," *Studies in Eighteenth-Century Culture*, 14 (1985) pp. 289–98.

JOURNAL OF A VOYAGE TO NORTH AMERICA, UNDERTAKEN BY THE ORDER OF THE FRENCH KING

From *Letter III: Description of Quebec; character of its inhabitants, and the manner of living in the French colony*

Quebec, 28 October, 1720

Madam,

I am now going to write you some particulars concerning Quebec; all the descriptions I have hitherto seen of it are so faulty, that I imagined I should do you a pleasure in drawing you a true portrait of this capital of New France. It is truly worthy of being known, were it only for the singularity of its situation; there being no other city besides this in the known world that can boast of a fresh water harbor a hundred and twenty leagues from the sea, and that capable of containing a hundred ships of the line. It certainly stands on the most navigable river in the universe.

. . . When Samuel Champlain[1] founded this city in 1608, the tide usually rose to the foot of the rock. Since that time the river has retired by little and little, and has at last left dry a large piece of ground, on which the lower town has since been built, and which is now sufficiently elevated above the water's edge, to secure its inhabitants against the inundations of the river. The first thing you meet with on landing is a pretty large square, and of an irregular form, having in front a row of well-built houses, the back part of which leans against the rock, so that they have no great depth. These form a street of a considerable length, occupying the right and left as far as the two ways which lead to the upper town. The square is bounded towards the left by a small church, and towards the right by two rows of houses placed in a parallel direction. There is also another street on the other side between the church and the harbor, and at the turning of the river under Cape Diamond, there is likewise another pretty long flight of houses on the bank of a creek called the Bay of Mothers. This quarter may be reckoned properly enough a sort of suburbs to the lower town.

Between this suburb and the great street, you go up to the higher town by so steep an ascent, that it has been found necessary to cut it into steps. Thus it is impossible to ascend it except on foot. But in going from the square toward the right a way has been made, the declivity of which is much more gentle, which is lined with houses. At the place where these two ways meet begins that part of the upper town which faces the river, there being another lower town on the side towards the little river St Charles. The first building worth of notice you meet with on your right hand in the former of those sides, is the bishop's palace; the left being entirely occupied with private houses. When you are got about twenty paces farther, you find yourself between two tolerably large squares; that toward the left is the place of arms, fronting which, is the fort or citadel, where the governor-general resides; on the opposite side stands the convent of the Recollects, the other sides of the square being lined with handsome houses.

. . . The cathedral would make but an indifferent parish church in one of the smallest towns in France; judge then whether it deserves to be the seat of the sole bishopric in all the French empire in America, which is much more extensive than that of the Romans ever was. No architecture, the choir, the great altar, and chapels, have all the air of a country church. What is most passable in it, is a very high tower, solidly built, and which, at a distance, has no bad effect. The seminary which adjoins to this church is a large square, the buildings of which are not yet finished, what is already completed is well executed, and has all the conveniences necessary in this country. This house is now rebuilding for the third time, it was burnt down to the ground in 1703, and in the month of October, in the year 1705, when it was near completely rebuilt, it was again almost entirely consumed by the flames. From the garden you discover the whole of the road and the river St Charles, as far as the eye can reach.

. . . After having informed you of what relates to the exterior of our capital, I must now say a word or two with respect to its principal inhabitants; This is its best side, and if by considering only its houses, we might reduce it to the rank of our smallest cities in France, yet the quality of those who inhabit it, will sufficiently vindicate us in bestowing upon it the title of a capital.

---

[1]   Samuel de Champlain (1570–1635), founder of Quebec.

I have already said, that they reckon no more than seven thousand souls at Quebec; yet you find in it a small number of the best company, where nothing is wanting that can possibly contribute to form an agreeable society. A governor-general, with an état-major[2], a noblesse[3], officers, and troops, an intendant[4], with a superior council, and subaltern jurisdictions, a commissary of the marine, a grand provost, and surveyor of the highways, with a grand master of the waters and forests, whose jurisdiction is the most extensive in the world; rich merchants, or such as live as if they were so; a bishop and numerous seminary; the Recollects and Jesuits, three communities of women well educated, assemblies, full as brilliant as anywhere, at the lady Governor's, and lady Intendants'[5]. Enough, in my opinion, to enable all sorts of persons whatever to pass their time very agreeably.

They accordingly do so, every one contributing all in his power to make life agreeable and cheerful. They play at cards, or go abroad on parties of pleasure in the summertime in caleshes[6] or canoes, in winter, in sledges upon the snow, or on skates upon the ice. Hunting is a great exercise amongst them, and there are a number of gentlemen who have no other way of providing handsomely for their subsistence. The current news consists of a very few articles, and those of Europe arrive all at once, though they supply matter of discourse for great part of the year. They reason like politicians on what is past, and form conjectures on what is likely to happen; the sciences and fine arts have also their part, so that the conversation never flags for want of matter. The Canadians, that is to say, the Creoles of Canada draw in with their native breath an air of freedom, which renders them very agreeable in the commerce of life, and no where in the world is our language spoken in greater purity. There is not even the smallest foreign accent remarked in their pronunciation.

You meet with no rich men in this country, and it is really great pity, every one endeavoring to put as good a face on it as possible, and nobody scarce thinking of laying up wealth. They make good cheer, provided they are also able to be at the expense of fine clothes; if not, they retrench in the article of the table to be able to appear well-dressed. And indeed, we must allow, that dress becomes our Creolians extremely well. They are all here of very advantageous stature, and both sexes have the finest complexion in the world; a gay and sprightly behavior, with great sweetness and politeness of manners are common to all of them; and the least rusticity, either in language or behavior, is utterly unknown even in the remotest and most distant parts.

The case is very different, as I am informed, with respect to our English neighbors, and to judge of the two colonies by the way of life, behavior, and speech of the inhabitants, nobody would hesitate to say that ours were the most flourishing. In New England and the other provinces of the continent of America subject to the British empire, there prevails an opulence which they are utterly at a loss how to use; and in New France, a poverty hid by an air of being in easy circumstances, which seems not at all studied. Trade, and the cultivation of their plantations, strengthen the first, whereas the second is supported by the industry of its inhabitants, and the taste of the nation diffuses over it something infinitely pleasing. The English planter amasses wealth, and never makes any superfluous expense; the French inhabitant again enjoys what he has acquired, and often makes a parade of what he is not possessed of. That labors for his polarity; this again leaves his offspring involved in the same necessities he was in himself at his first setting out, and to extricate themselves as they can. The English Americans are averse to war, because they have a great deal to lose; they take no care to manage the

---

[2]   Military council.
[3]   Nobility.
[4]   Provincial administrator.

[5]   I.e. the wives of the Governor and the Intendants.
[6]   A two-wheeled carriage.

Indians from a belief that they stand in no need of them. The French youth, for very different reasons, abominate the thoughts of peace, and live well with the natives, whose esteem they easily gain in time of war, and their friendship at all times. I might carry the parallel a great way further, but I am obliged to conclude; the King's ship is just going to set sail, and the merchantmen are making ready to follow her, so that, perhaps, in three days' time, there will not be so much as a single vessel of any sort in the road . . .

From *Letter XXX: Voyage from the Akansas*[7] *to the Natchez. Description of the country. Of the river of the Yasous.*[8] *Of the Customs, Manners, and Religion of the Natchez.*

(At the Natchez, 25 December, 1721)

. . . The entrance into the river of the Yasous lies North-West and South-East, and is about an Arpent[9] in breadth. Its waters are of a reddish color, and are said to affect those who drink them with the bloody flux. The air is, besides, extremely unwholesome.

. . . There are a great many alligators in this river, and I have seen two of them from twelve to fifteen feet in length. They are never heard but in the night-time, and their cry so much resembles the bellowing of bulls, that people are frequently deceived by it. Our people, notwithstanding, bathe in this river as freely as in the Seine. On my testifying my surprise at this, I was told, that they had nothing to fear; that indeed, when in the water, they were constantly surrounded by these animals, but that none of them came near them, and seemed only to watch them, in order to fall upon them, the moment they were going to leave the river; that then, in order to drive them away, they made a splashing in the water with a stick, which they took care to be provided with, that they had sufficient time to secure themselves.

. . . The grant of the Maloins is well situated, and nothing is wanting to make it turn out to advantage but Negroes, or hired servants. I should rather choose to employ the latter, because, the time of their service being expired, they become inhabitants, and increase the number of the king's natural subjects; whereas the former always continue aliens: and who can be certain but that, by being multiplied in our colonies, they may not one day become our most formidable enemies! Can we depend upon slaves who are only attached to us by fear, and who never can have the pleasure of calling the place in which they are born by the endearing name of their native country?

. . .The grand chief of the Natchez bears the name of Sun, and, as among the Hurons, the son of his nearest female relations always succeeds him. This person has the quality of woman-chief, and great honors are paid her, though she seldom meddles in affairs of government. She has, as well as the chief himself, the power of life and death, and it is a usual thing for them to order their guards, whom they call *Allouez*, to dispatch anyone who has the misfortune to be obnoxious to either. "Go rid me of this dog," say they, and they are instantly obeyed. Their subjects, and even the chiefs of their villages, never come into their presence without saluting them thrice, and raising a cry, or rather a sort of howling. They do the same thing when they withdraw, and always retire going backwards. When they meet them they are obliged to stop, range themselves in order on the road, and howl in the manner above mentioned till they are past. They are likeways obliged to carry them the best of their harvest, and of the product of their hunting and fishing. In fine, no one, not even their nearest relations, and those who

---

[7] Arkansas.
[8] The Yazoos.

[9] An Old French measure of land, equivalent to 0.85 acre.

compose their nobility, when they have the honor to eat with them, have a right to drink out of the same cup, or put their hands in the same dish.

. . . When the grand chief, or the woman chief, die, all the Allouez are obliged to follow them to the other world, nor are they the only persons who have this honor: for it is certainly reckoned one, and as such, greatly sought after. The death of a chief has been sometimes known to cost the lives of above a hundred persons, and I have been told there are few Natchez of any considerable note who die without being attended to the country of souls, by some of their relations, friends, or servants. It appears from the different relations I have seen of these horrible ceremonies that there is much variation in them. Here follows an account of the obsequies of a woman chief, which I had from a traveler who was an eye-witness of it, and on whose sincerity I have good reason to depend.

The husband of this woman not being noble, that is to say, of the family of the Sun, his eldest son, according to custom, strangled him. Afterwards, everything was taken out of the cabin, and a sort of triumphant car[10] was erected of it, on which they placed the body of the deceased and that of her husband. Immediately after, twelve little children, whom their parents had strangled, by order of the eldest son of the woman chief, who succeeded to her dignity, were laid around the carcasses. This done, they erected in the public square fourteen scaffolds adorned with branches of trees and stuffs, on which were painted various figures. These scaffolds were designed for an equal number of persons, who were to attend the woman-chief to the other world. Their relations flood round them, looking upon the permission given them to sacrifice themselves in this manner, as the greatest honor that could be done to their families. They are sometimes ten years in soliciting this favor beforehand, and those who obtain it, are obliged to spin the cord themselves with which they are to be strangled.

They appeared on the scaffold dressed in their richest habits, each having a large shell in his right hand. Their nearest relation stood on the same hand, having a battle-axe in his left, and the cord which is to do the execution under his left arm. From time to time he sings the death-cry, at which the fourteen victims come down from the scaffolds, and dance all together in the square before the temple and the cabin of the woman-chief. This and the following days great respect is paid them, each has five domestics to attend him, and their faces are painted red. Some add, that during the eight days preceding their death, they wear a red ribbon on their leg, and that all that time every one is solicitous to regale them. Be this as it will, at the time I am now speaking of, the fathers and mothers of the strangled children took them in their arms, and disposed themselves on each side of the cabin, the fourteen destined to die placed themselves in the same manner, and were followed by the friends and relations of the deceased, who had all their hair cut off, which is their way of mourning: all this time they made the air resound with such frightful cries, that one would have thought all the devils in hell had broken loose, in order to come to howl in this place; this was followed with dances and songs; those who were to die danced, and the relations of the woman-chief sang.

At last the procession began. The fathers and mothers carrying their dead children appeared first, walking two and two, and went immediately before the litter, in which was the corpse of the woman-chief, carried on the shoulders of four men. The rest followed in the same order. At every ten paces the children were thrown upon the ground, those who carried the litter trampling upon them, so that when the procession arrived at the temple, their little bodies were quite torn to pieces.

While they were interring the corpse of the woman-chief in the temple, the fourteen per-

---

10   Carriage or platform, made from the timber of the cabin.

sons destined to die were undressed and seated on the ground before the gate, having each two Indians about him, one seated on his knees, and the other holding his hands behind him. The cords were passed round their necks, their heads were covered with the skin of a roe-buck, and after being made to drink a glass of water, the relations of the woman-chief, who sung all the time, drew the cords at each end till they were strangled. After which all the carcasses were thrown together into a ditch and covered with earth.

When the grand chief dies, his nurse, if still alive, must die likewise. But it has often happened that the French, not being able to prevent this barbarity, have obtained leave to baptize the children who were to be strangled, and thus have prevented their accompanying those in whose honor they were strangled, to their pretended paradise.

I know no nation on the continent, where the sex is more disorderly than in this. They are even forced by the grand chief and his subalterns to prostitute themselves to all comers, and a woman is not the less esteemed for being public. Though polygamy is permitted and the number of wives which a man may have is unlimited, yet every one for the most part contents himself with one, whom he may divorce at pleasure; but this, however, is a liberty never used by any but the chiefs. The women are tolerably well-looked[11] for savages, and neat enough in their dress, and everything belonging to them. The daughters of a noble family are allowed to marry none but private men, but they have a right to turn away their husbands, when they think proper, and marry another, provided there is no alliance between them.

If their husbands are unfaithful to them, they may cause them to be put to death, but are not subject to the same law themselves: on the contrary, they may entertain as many gallants as they please, without the husband's daring to take it amiss, this being a privilege attached to the blood of the sun[12]. He stands in a respectful posture, in the presence of his wife, never eats with her, salutes her in the same manner as the rest of her domestics, and all the privilege which this burdensome alliance procures him, is an exemption from travel and some authority over his wife's servants.

From *Letter XXXI: Description of the Capital of Louisiana*

New Orleans, 10 January, 1722

Madam,

I am now at last arrived at this famous city of *Nouvelle Orleans*, New Orleans. Those who have given it this name, must have imagined Orleans was of the feminine gender[13]. But of what consequence is this? Custom, which is superior to all the laws of grammar, has fixed it so.

This is the first city which one of the greatest rivers in the world has seen erected on its banks. If the eight hundred fine houses and the five parishes which our Mercury bestowed upon it two years ago, are at present reduced to a hundred barracks, placed in no very good order; to a large warehouse built of timber; to two or three houses which would be no ornament to a village in France; to one half of a sorry warehouse, formerly set aside for divine service, and was scarce appropriated for that purpose, when it was removed to a tent: what pleasure, on the other hand, must it give to see this future capital of an immense and beautiful country increasing insensibly, and to be able, not with a sigh like Virgil's hero, when speaking of his native country consumed by the flames, *et campus ubi Trojae fuit*[14], but full of the best grounded hopes to say, that this wild

---

[11]   Good-looking.

[12]   I.e. of the chief.

[13]   If Orleans had been gendered masculine, it would have been *Nouveau Orleans*.

[14]   "And the field where Troy was:" from Virgil's *Aeneid* 3:11.

and desert place, at present almost entirely covered over with canes and trees, shall one day, and perhaps that day is not very far off, become the capital of a large and rich colony.

Your Grace will, perhaps, ask me upon what these hopes are founded? They are founded on the situation of this city on the banks of a navigable river, at the distance of thirty-three leagues from the sea, from which a vessel may come up in twenty-four hours; on the fertility of its soil; on the mildness and wholesomeness of the climate, in 30 degrees north latitude; on the industry of the inhabitants; on its neighborhood[15] to Mexico, the Havana, the finest islands of America, and lastly, to the English colonies. Can there be anything more requisite to render a city flourishing? Rome and Paris had not such considerable beginnings, were not built under such happy auspices, and their founders met not with those advantages on the Seine and Tiber, which we have found on the Mississippi, in comparison of which, these two rivers are no more than brooks.

. . . On the fifth day of the new year we said mass; about three leagues from the habitation of Madam de Mezières, in a grant belong to M. Diron d'Artaguette, inspector-general of the troops of Louisiana. We had here a monstrous large tortoise brought us; and we were told that these animals had just broke through a large bar or iron; if the fact is true, and to believe it I should have seen it, the spittle of these animals must be a strong dissolvent: I should not indeed choose to trust my leg in their throat. What is certain is, that the creature I saw was large enough to satisfy ten men of the strongest appetites. We stayed the whole day in this grant, which is no farther advanced than the rest, and is called *le Baton Rouge*[16], or the red-staff plantation.

The next day we advanced eleven leagues, and encamped a little below the Bayagoulas, which we left upon our right, after having visited the ruins of an ancient village, which I have already mentioned. This was very well peopled about twenty years ago; but the smallpox destroyed part of the inhabitants, and the rest have dispersed in such a manner, that no accounts have been heard of them for several years, and it is doubted if so much as one single family of them is now remaining. Its situation was very magnificent, and the Messrs. Paris have now a grant here, which they planted with white mulberries[17], and have already raised very fine silk. They have likewise begun to cultivate tobacco and indigo with success. If the proprietors of the grants were everywhere as industrious, they would soon be reimbursed their expenses.

From *Letter XXXII: Reflections on the Grants*

26 January 1722

. . . I have met with none who have been on the spot who have spoken disadvantageously of Louisiana, but three sorts of persons whose testimony can be of no great weight. The first are the sailors, who, from the road at the island of Dauphine, have been able to see nothing but that island covered with a barren sand, and the coast of Biloxi still more sandy, and have suffered themselves to be persuaded, that the entrance of the Mississippi is impracticable to vessels above a certain bulk; and that the country is uninhabitable for fifty leagues up the river. They would have been of a very different opinion, had they had penetration enough[18] to distrust those persons who spoke in this manner, and to discover the motives which made them do so.

---

[15]   Proximity.
[16]   Later the capital of Louisiana.

[17]   Mulberries were used to feed silkworms.
[18]   I.e. had they been intelligent enough.

The second are wretches, who being banished from France for their crimes or ill-behavior, true or supposed, or who, in order to shun the pursuits of their creditors, lifted themselves among the troops, or hired themselves to the plantations. Both of them, looking on this country as a place of banishment only, were consequently shocked with everything: they have no tie to bind them, nor any concern for the progress of a colony of which they are involuntary members, and give themselves very little trouble about the advantages it is capable of procuring to the state.

The third are such, who having seen nothing but misery in a country for which excessive sums have been disbursed, attribute to it, without reflection, what ought solely to be laid to the incapacity or negligence of those who were charged with the settling it. You are, besides, not unacquainted with the reasons for publishing that Louisiana contained in its bosom immense treasures; and that its value to us was very near equal to the famous mines of St Barbe, and others still richer, from which we flattered ourselves we should be able to drive the possessors with ease: and because these ridiculous tales found credit with fools, instead of imputing the mistake to themselves, into which their foolish credulity had engaged them, they discharged their ill humor upon this country, in which they found no one article that had been promised them.

1761

Marie-Andrée Duplessis de Sainte-Hélène (1687–1760)

Born in Paris, Marie-Andrée Duplessis de Sainte Hélène arrived in Canada at the age of fifteen, where in 1707 she took the veil. From 1718 to 1721, at the suggestion of Mother Jeanne-Françoise Juchereau de la Ferté, the venerable superior of her order who inspired the project and provided source material, the young nun wrote the *Annales de l'Hotel-Dieu de Québec*. In it, she describes the installation of the nuns in New France, their acquisition of several properties, the foundation of their Hospital, the epidemics which flooded it with patients, the arrival of ships, the struggle against the Iroquois, and conflicts with the English. After 1732, Sister Duplessis became Superior of her religious order.

PRIMARY WORK

Translated by Susan Castillo from *Anthologie da la Littérature Québécoise, Vol. I (1534–1760) Écrits de la Nouvelle France*, ed. Léopold LeBlanc (Montreal: La Presse, 1978).

FROM *THE ANNALS OF THE HOTEL-DIEU, QUEBEC*

The Image of Hell

The hand of God weighed heavily on this country, and redoubled the blows with which He wishes to chastise it. This, at least, was what we feared, for in the year of 1711, the English, constant in their undertaking, were on the verge of becoming masters of Canada. They had raised a powerful army which came towards us, commanded by Neglesson[1]. They lacked noth-

---

[1]   Sir Francis Nicholson (1660–1728).

ing, not cannons, foodstuffs, munitions; they were joined by several savage nations whom they had covered with gifts and who were to accompany them and give them considerable support. The large warships which they had been awaiting for a long time from Old England had reached Baston[2], bringing hardened soldiers as reinforcements. They had, in short, done their utmost to equip an adequate fleet.

. . . Not long thereafter, we heard that the English army which was approaching by land had slowed down, that their forts and munitions had been burned. We did not know the reasons for this defeat, but as it was advantageous to us, it gave us hope. Troops and the militia were brought down from Montreal to succor Quebec, leaving only old men, in the certainty that there were no more enemies to fear there. They all arrived gaily, even showing their impatience to go and fight; during the day, they fortified the city, and spent the night in diversions, dancing and laughing, so much so that they prevented the citizens of Quebec from getting any sleep. A young Englishman, a very honest man called Pigeon, who had been taken prisoner by a small party of savages near Acadia, witnessed this joy, and could not hide his astonishment. He told the officers of this country that he admired the warlike inclinations of the Canadians, whom he saw dancing and leaping about while waiting for the enemy, and that in England it was necessary to beat the inhabitants to make them take up arms; that when they did so, they did so very badly, but added that here even the women showed courage and that they were Amazons.

Time was passing by without our hearing of the fleet. The winds seemed to be favorable to it, but it did not advance at all. Many people were tempted to believe that everything that had been said of this navy was only a dream. Nonetheless on 15 October, it was reported in Quebec at dawn that two large vessels had been sighted fifteen leagues from here, that they had attempted to land and that the inhabitants had shot at them. This revived all the alarms, and until eight o'clock in the morning no one doubted that this was the vanguard of the fleet. It was the last day of a novena to Our Lady of Pity at the Cathedral, which was well attended, and on leaving Mass, it was a pleasant surprise to see passengers from France, who assured us that they had encountered nothing disagreeable on the river; that indeed the local inhabitants had shot at their ship and they had been unable to land; that they judged that they had been taken for enemies; that the King's ship, the Héros, was nearby; that it was commanded by Monsieur de Beaumont, brother of Monsieur de Beauharnois, from then on Commander General of Canada; that it was richly loaded and very well armed, and that if we were awaiting the English, they would aid us in defeating them.

The joy and gratitude that this event inspired in us are hard to express. It was hard to understand how this vessel could have escaped from enemy hands; it seemed miraculous and indeed it was, as was recognized when the outcome of this matter was known.

1718–21   1978

Elisabeth Begon (1696–1755)

Marie-Elisabeth Rocher de la Morandière was born in Montreal in 1696. In 1718, she married the naval ensign Claude-Michel Begon, who later left her a widow. In her letters to her widowed son-in-law, she describes the daily life of her household, which consisted of her father, her granddaughter, a niece

---

²   Boston.

she had raised (Tilly) and an older woman, to whom she refers as Mater; a constant visitor as well was the Governor General, Barrin de La Galissonnière, a distant relative.

Madame Begon's letters to her son-in-law, with whom she clearly was in love (and who died in Louisiana), offer a vivid description of day-to-day life in colonial Montreal in the eighteenth century.

PRIMARY WORK

Translated by Susan Castillo from excerpts from the *Correspondance de Madame Begon, 1748–1753*, in *Anthologie de la Littérature Québécoise, Vol. 1, Écrits de la*

Nouvelle France, ed. Léopold LeBlanc (Montreal: La Press, 1978).

FURTHER READING

Catherine Rubinger, "Love, or Family Love, in New France: A New Reading of the Letters of Madame Begon," *Man and Nature: Proceedings of the Canadian Society for Eighteenth-Century Studies* (Edmonton: Academic Printing & Pub., 1992) pp. 187–99.

Catherine Rubinger, "The Influence of Women in Eighteenth-Century New France," *Femmes Savantes et Femmes d'Esprit: Women Intellectuals of the French Eighteenth Century*, eds Roland Bonnel and Catherine Rubinger (New York: Peter Lang, 1994) pp. 419–43.

FROM *THE CORRESPONDENCE OF MADAME BEGON, 1748–1753*

November 12, 1748

At the moment, my dear son, now that I have managed to catch up on difficult correspondence, I will be able, with the same satisfaction that dealing with you has always given me, to write every day, and to repeat to you a hundred times that it is my only remaining consolation. You know, dear son, how hard your absence is for me to endure. If your leaving caused me pain, imagine my feelings now, alone for three-fourths of the day with my dear granddaughter.

I wrote to you that Mater and Tilly have been in Quebec with M. de Tilly on 15 July. They only returned a few days ago, enthusiastic about the pleasures of Quebec where the military commander makes everyone dance. Their black clothing prevented them from attending all these fêtes, but they ate very well there and have seen this glittering atmosphere that gives an air to fashionable conversations. Madame Lanaudière is the belle of the ball there, nothing can compare with her.

. . . Our general[1] is always the same, and I believe he regards it all pityingly. It is said that he sends reports to Court such as they have never yet had. I think the country would lose a great deal if it lost him.

Farewell, dear son, until tomorrow. I wish you perfect health, and would like very much to have news of you.

The 13th.

I was telling you yesterday, dear son, that I would have liked to have news of you. You can easily imagine that this is because it is the only thing that can take away the pain of your absence; but this is what must be endured until the end of May. What a long time, and how many castles I shall build on what you tell me, dear son; how I wish you would tire of Mississippi. I would praise the Lord, if I were persuaded that it was to your advantage, for I declare that I feel aversion for this country. I cannot think of your going there without feeling a pain of which I am not mistress, and I hope that Providence will provide and will not crush me completely, and will reunite me with a son who is my entire consolation.

---

[1] Barrin de la Galissonière, the Governor General.

I must speak to you a bit of the latest news of our country. M. Picquet has left to go visit a place near Fort Frontenac, in order to make a settlement there to plant the Faith among the Five Nations. You know the devotion of these peoples and can imagine success better than anyone else. M. de Longueuil does not seem happy, and it is not difficult to disentangle the reasons. He is counting hard on the government here. I do not know if he will succeed, for he has saved nothing. He acts accordingly, and says so so loudly that everyone is laughing at him.

Farewell. Perhaps this is enough for you, for for me, I would wish to do nothing else but tell you that I am there.

The 17th.

We had a foot of snow last night, dear son, and that has made me grumble all morning long. How fortunate you are to be in a country free of such cold spells. I tremble in advance, at the mere thought of nine months of snow. But that will not matter if I go away next autumn. What would I do in Canada, if M. de La Galissonnière goes away? That would be the last straw. You know how people think in this country. Those who are friends of those in power or who are connected to them in some way are courted, but when this is not the case, I know what happens. That would make me take my leave with great satisfaction, especially because I would be nearer to you, dear son, you who are my only remaining consolation.

The 18th.

The idea some of our fellow citizens seem to have that the General pays me a great deal of attention and that he can refuse me nothing causes them to come visit me often. But I am no fool, and I have told the Marquis that his marked attentions to me often obliged me to see people whom I do not like at all, and who beg me to ask him difficult questions. But I know how to do so. How pitiful, dear son, these people are! . . .

The 19th.

. . . M. de Longueil, commandant of this town, would do better if he gave enough to eat to those who arrive; but he even complains to those from whom he could expect a favor. If he is not Governor of Montreal next year, I wonder if he will destroy himself, for he is counting heavily on it.

The 27th.

What can I tell you, dear son? I know nothing: that I love you? That isn't new to you. That your absence pains me? You must know it. That I am almost always ill? My age is a contributing factor. What can I tell you? That I see every day faces which bore me, and which I know come to see me because they want to court the General. You know me and you can be sure that I feel under no obligation to them . . .

9 February 1749

The ladies and girls have a lovely ball this evening given by the Quartermaster and, as his house is too small, he has taken over the entire floor of M. Varin's house and has removed all the furniture and has had rattan chairs and everything else necessary for the ball taken there. All the officers' wives and daughters have been asked: imagine how many people there will be. Mater is going, the only one from our house. Tilly was invited, but she is ill. Tomorrow I shall give you more news of this fête, which will only begin at eight in the evening.

Farewell, dear son, love your mother.

The 10th.

Good morning, dear son. I think the entire town is still asleep except for me, for the ball only came to an end at half past six this morning. Mater came back in a dreadful mood, and found nowhere to sleep here, for there is only a bed in my bedroom. Imagine what she looked like: sleeping in the chair, her *derrière* in the air, snoring as I have never heard her snore. With each person who came in or out, she woke up with a start and said, "How happy I would be if I were like those who are in their own house!" Finally she got up and sat in an armchair, her head between her legs. M. Picquet, who carted her along for part of the matinée, teased her mercilessly and preached at her. Indeed, at her age she can do without this sort of assembly. I think it is this that is tormenting her at present, for she is not so stupid as not to be aware that people are laughing at her. Still, when one is made to be in polite society, one must, whatever it costs. M. Picquet, despite his preaching, did not persuade her of this.

The 14th.

How lucky, dear son, for those who dance, that they had some days to rest, for I believe that if not they would have died: they left the ball at 6 o'clock this morning. I am sure that many of them do not observe Easter, and especially those who will go to the play that will be staged in the three days before the start of Lent. All the women and girls in town were invited, even Mme. du Vivier who danced until early in the morning. De Muy told me after dinner that from now on he did not wish for his wife and daughter to go, and that it was not right to spend the nights dancing while the Holy Sacrament is on display. I do not know how successful he will be.

People say that M. Bigot spends the evenings of these balls contemplating his folded hands. He dances two or three minuets, if that. You portrayed him well to me; he is admirably tranquil. Mme. Thiery is the belle of the ball, and Mme. Lavaltrie and the Ramesay girls.

The 15th.

. . . What are you doing, dear son, and where are you? This is what I do not know, nor shall I know any time soon, which gives me great pain. Adieu.

1748–53   1978

Richard Lewis (1700?–1734)

Although celebrated and widely published in his time, Richard Lewis has been all but forgotten as a writer. Emigrating from Wales as a young man in 1718, Lewis settled in Maryland and became a schoolmaster and member of the Assembly. He began contributing poetry to the *Maryland Gazette*, and was the most frequently reprinted colonial poet of the early eighteenth century. Using English forms of classical models like the pastoral, Lewis put the American landscape, now a mixture of the wild and tame, into verse for an increasingly discriminating colonial audience eager for *belle lettres* that would affirm its sophistication. "A Journey from Patapsko to Annapolis" not only celebrates local flora and fauna, but finds it superior to the English landscape of the Augustan poets and the idyllic world of classical masters like Virgil and Claudian. That Lewis was read by his English contemporaries is clear from the drubbing he received at the hands of master satirist Alexander Pope, who in his witty masterpiece, *The Dunciad*, laughs at Lewis' local imagery, particularly his rhapsodic description of the hummingbird, indigenous to the Americas. In its self-consciousness and philosophical allegorizing, Lewis' poem signals the end of seventeenth century pietism and the beginning of a struggle to build a republic of letters.

PRIMARY WORKS

"Food for Criticks," 1730.

"A Journey from Patapsko to Annapolis, April 4, 1730," 1732.

FURTHER READING

J. A. Leo Lemay, "Richard Lewis and Augustan American Poetry," *PMLA: Publications of the Modern Language Association of America*, 83 (1968) pp. 80–101.

Christopher Johnson, "A Spiritual Pilgrimage Through a Deistic Universe: Richard Lewis's 'A Journey from Patapsko to Annapolis, April 4, 1730'," *Early American Literature*, 27, 2 (1992) pp. 117–27.

A JOURNEY FROM PATAPSKO TO ANNAPOLIS, APRIL 4, 1730[1]

Me vero primum dulces ante omnia Musae,
Quarum sacra fero ingenti perculsus amore,
Accipiant; Coelique vias & Sydera *monstrent;*
          . . .
Sin has ne possim Naturae accedere partes
Frigidus obstiterit circum praecordia Sanguis,
Rura *mihi, &* rigui *placeant in Vallibus*
          Amnes,
Flumina *amen,* Sylvasque *inglorius.*
                    VIRG. *Geor.* 2[2]

At length the *wintry* Horrors disappear,
And *April* views with Smiles the infant
          Year;
The grateful Earth from frosty Chains
          unbound,
Pours out its *vernal* Treasures all around,
Her Face bedeckt with Grass, with Buds the
          Trees are crown'd.
In this soft Season, 'ere the Dawn of Day,
I mount my Horse, and lonely take my
          Way,
From woody Hills that shade *Patapsko's*
          Head,

(In whose deep Vales he makes his stony
          Bed,
From whence he rushes with resistless
          Force,
Tho' huge rough Rocks retard his rapid
          Course,)
Down to *Annapolis,* on that smooth Stream,
Which took from fair *Anne-Arundel* its
          Name.[3]
And now the *Star* that ushers in the Day,[4]
Begins to pale her ineffectual Ray.
The *Moon,* with blunted Horns, now shines
          less bright,
Her fading Face eclips'd with growing
          Light;
The fleecy Clouds with streaky Lustre glow,
And Day quits Heav'n to view the Earth
          below.
Oe'r yon tall *Pines* the *Sun* shews half his
          Face,
And fires their floating Foliage with his
          Rays;
Now sheds aslant on Earth his lightsome
          Beams,

---

[1]   The Patapsko River empties into Chesapeake Bay at present-day Baltimore, which was first named for the river. The text, with slight modification, is from *The Weekly Register*, London, January 1, 1732. Notes from that edition are indicated.

[2]   "Ye sacred Muses! with whose beauty fired, My soul is ravished, and my brain inspired – Whose priest I am, whose holy fillets wear – . . . Give me the ways of wandering stars to know, The depths of heaven above, and earth below: . . . But, if my heavy blood restrain the flight Of my free soul, aspiring to the height Of nature, and unclouded fields of

light – My next desire is, void of care and strife, To lead a soft, secure, inglorious life – " (Virgil, *Georgics*, 2:475–77, 483–87, trans. John Dryden, 1697, the translation Lewis refers to later in the poem.)

[3]   Anne Arundell was the wife of Cecilius Calvert, eldest son of the first Baron of Baltimore, who founded the colony of Maryland as a refuge for English Roman Catholics. The county of Anne-Arundel in central Maryland and the capital of Maryland, Annapolis, are named after her.

[4]   "Venus" (1732 ed.).

That trembling shine in many-colour'd
    Streams:
Slow-rising from the Marsh, the Mist
    recedes,
The Trees, emerging, rear their dewy Heads;
Their dewy Heads the *Sun* with Pleasure
    views,
And brightens into Pearls the pendent
    Dews.
    The *Beasts* uprising, quit their leafy Beds,
And to the cheerful *Sun* erect their Heads;
All joyful rise, except the filthy *Swine*,
On obscene Litter stretch'd they snore
    supine:
In vain the Day awakes, Sleep seals their
    Eyes,
Till Hunger breaks the Bond and bids them
    rise.
Mean while the *Sun* with more exalted Ray,
From cloudless Skies distributes riper Day;
Thro' sylvan Scenes my Journey I pursue,
Ten thousand Beauties rising to my View;
Which kindle in my Breast poetic Flame,
And bid me my CREATOR'S praise
    proclaim;
Tho' my low Verse ill-suits the noble
    Theme.
    Here various Flourets grace the teeming
    Plains,
Adorn'd by Nature's Hand with beauteous
    Stains;
First-born of *Spring*, here the *Pacone* appears,
Whose golden Root a silver Blossom rears.
In spreading Tufts, see there the *Crowfoot*
    blue,
On whose green Leaves still shines a globous
    Dew;
Behold the *Cinque-foil*, with its dazling Dye
Of flaming Yellow, wounds the tender Eye:[5]
But there, enclos'd the grassy *Wheat* is seen,
To heal the aching Sight with cheerful
    Green.
    Safe in yon cottage dwells the *Monarch-*
    Swain,

His *Subject-Flocks*, close-grazing, hide the
    Plain;
For him they live; – and die t'uphold his
    Reign.
Viands unbought his well-till'd Lands
    afford,
And smiling *Plenty* waits upon his Board;
Health shines with sprightly Beams around
    his Head,
And *Sleep*, with downy Wings, o'er-shades
    his Bed;
His *Sons* robust his daily Labours share,
Patient of Toil, Companions of his Care:
And all their Toils with sweet Success are
    crown'd.
In graceful Ranks there *Trees* adorn the
    Ground,
The *Peach*, the *Plum*, the *Apple*, here are
    found;
Delicious Fruits! Which from their Kernels
    rise,
So fruitful is the Soil – so mild the Skies.
The lowly *Quince* yon sloping Hill o'er-
    shades.
Here lofty *Cherry-Trees* erect their Heads;
High in the Air each spiry Summer waves,
Whose Blooms thick-springing yield no
    Space for Leaves;
Evolving Odours fill the ambient Air,
The *Birds* delighted to the Grove repair:
On ev'ry Tree behold a tuneful Throng,
The vocal Vallies echo to their Song.
    But what is *He*[6], who perch'd above the
    rest,
Pours out such various Musick from his
    Breast!
His Breast, whose Plumes a cheerful White
    display,
His quiv'ring Wings are dress'd in sober
    Grey.
Sure, all the *Muses*, this their Bird inspire!
And *He*, alone, is equal to the Choir
Of warbling Songsters who around him
    play,

---

5   Pacone or tumeric root has a greenish-white flower in
spring. Crowfoot thrives in winter and has a white flower.
Cinquefoil, genus *potentilla*, has a bright yellow flower.

6   The Mock Bird (1732 ed.).

While, Echo like, *He* answers ev'ry Lay.
The chirping *Lark* now sings with sprightly
     Note,
Responsive to her Strain *He* shapes his
     Throat:
Now the poor widow'd *Turtle* wails her
     Mate,
While in soft Sounds *He* cooes to mourn his
     Fate.
Oh, sweet Musician, thou dost far excel
The soothing Song of pleasing *Philomel*[7]!
Sweet is her Song, but in few Notes
     confin'd;
But thine, thou *Mimic* of the feath'ry Kind,
Runs thro' all Notes! – *Thou* only know'st
     them *All*,
At once the *Copy*, – *and th'Original*.
     My *Ear* thus charm'd, mine *Eye* with
          Pleasure sees,
Hov'ring about the Flow'rs, th'industrious
     Bees.
Like them in Size, the *Humming-Bird* I view,
Like them, *He* sucks his Food, the Honey-
     Dew,
With nimble Tongue, and Beak of jetty
     Hue.
He takes with rapid Whirl his noisy Flight,
His gemmy Plumage strikes the Gazer's
     Sight;
And as he moves his ever-flutt'ring Wings,
Ten thousand Colours he around him flings.
Now I behold the Em'rald's vivid Green,
Now scarlet, now a purple Die is seen;
In brightest Blue, his Breast *He* now arrays,
Then strait his Plumes emit a golden Blaze.
Thus whirring round he flies, and varying
     still,
He mocks the *Poet's* and the *Painter's* Skill;
Who may forever strive with fruitless Pains,
To catch and fix those beauteous changeful
     Stains;
While Scarlet now, and now the Purple
     shines,

And Gold, to Blue its transient Gloss
     resigns.
Each quits, and quickly each resumes its
     Place,
And ever-varying dies each other chase.
Smallest of Birds, what Beauties shine in
     thee!
A living *Rainbow* on thy Breast I see.
     Oh had that *Bard*[8] in whose heart-
          pleasing Lines,
The *Phoenix* in a Blaze of Glory shines,
Beheld those Wonders which are shewn in
     Thee,
That *bird* had lost his Immortality!
Thou in His Verse hadst stretch'd thy
     flutt'ring Wing
Above all other Birds, – their beauteous
     King.
     But now th'enclos'd Plantation I forsake
And onwards thro' the Woods my Journey
     take;
The level Road, the longsome Way
     beguiles,
A blooming Wilderness around me smiles;
Here hardy *Oak*, there fragment *Hick'ry*
     grows,
Their bursting Buds the tender Leaves
     disclose;
The tender Leaves in downy Robes appear,
Trembling, they seem to move with
     cautious Fear,
Yet new to Life, and Strangers to the Air.
Here stately *Pines* unite their whisp'ring
     Heads,
And with a solemn Gloom embrown the
     Glades.
See there a green *Savane* opens wide,
Thro' which smooth Streams in wanton
     Mazes glide;
Thick-branching Shrubs o'er-hang the silver
     Streams,
Which scarcely deign t'admit the solar
     Beams.

---

7   The nightingale, "lover of song" (Latin).
8   "Claudian" (1732 edn). Claudius Claudianus (370?–404?
BC) was the last important poet of the classical tradition in

Latin, who wrote mythological epics popular in the Middle
Ages.

While with Delight on this soft Scene I
    gaze,
The *Cattle* upward look, and cease to graze,
But into covert run thro' various Ways.
And now the Clouds in black Assemblage
    rise,
And dreary Darkness overspreads the Skies,
Thro' which the Sun strives to transmit his
    Beams,
"But sheds his sickly light in straggling
    Streams."9
Hush'd is the Musick of the wood-land
    Choir,
Fore-knowing of the Storm, the Birds retire
For Shelter, and forsake the shrubby Plains,
And dumb Horror thro' the Forest reigns;
In that lone House which opens wide its
    Door,
Safe may I tarry till the Storm is o'er.
    Hark how the *Thunder* rolls with solemn
    Sound!
And see the forceful *Lightning* dart a
    Wound,
On yon toll Oak! – Behold its Top laid bare!
Its Body rent, and scatter'd thro' the Air
The Splinters fly! – Now – now the *Winds*
    arise,
From different Quarters of the lowring
    Skies;
Forth-issuing fierce, the *West* and *South*
    engage,
The waving Forest bends beneath their
    Rage:
But where the winding Valley checks their
    Course,
They roar and ravage with redoubled Force;
With circling Sweep in dreadful
    Whirlwinds move
And from its Roots tear up the gloomy
    Grove,
Down-rushing fall the Trees, and beat the
    Ground,
In Fragments flue the shatter'd Limbs
    around;

Tremble the Under-woods, the Vales
    resound.
    Follows, with patt'ring Noise, the icy
    Hail,
And *Rain*, fast falling, floods the lowly Vale.
Again the *Thunders* roll, the *Lightnings* fly,
And as they first disturb'd, now clear the
    Sky;
For lo, the *Gust* decreases by Degrees,
The dying *Winds* but sob amidst the Trees;
With pleasing Softness falls the silver Rain,
Thro' which at first faint-gleaming o'er the
    Plain,
The Orb of Light scarce darts a watry Ray
To gild the Drops that fall from ev'ry Spray;
But soon the dusky Vapours are dispell'd,
And thro' the Mist that late his Face
    conceal'd,
Bursts the broad *Sun*, triumphant in a Blaze
Too keen for Sight – Yon Cloud refracts his
    Rays,
The mingling Beams compose th' *ethereal*
    Bow,
How sweet, how soft, its melting Colours
    glow!
Gaily they shine, by heav'nly Pencils laid,
Yet vanish swift, – How soon does *Beauty*
    fade!
    The *Storm* is past, my Journey I renew,
And a new Scene of Pleasure greets my
    View:
Wash'd by the copious Rain the gummy
    Pine,
Does cheerful, with unsully'd Verdure shine;
The *Dogwood* Flow'rs assume a snowy white,
The *Maple* blushing gratifies the Sight:
No verdant leaves the lovely *Red-Bud* grace,
Cornation blossoms now supply their Place.
The *Sassafras* unfolds its fragrant Bloom,
The *Vine* affords an exquisite Perfume;
These grateful Scents wide-wafting thro' the
    Air
The smelling Sense with balmy Odours
    cheer.

---

9   An allusion to Dryden's translation of Virgil's *Georgics*,
Bk. I:550–51: "Or if thro' mists he shoots his sullen beams,/
Frugal of light, in loose and straggling streams."

And now the *Birds*, sweet singing, stretch
   their Throats,
And in one Choir unite their various Notes,
Nor yet unpleasing is the *Turtle's* Voice,
Tho' he complains while other Birds rejoice.
   These vernal Joys, all restless Thoughts
     controul,
And gently-soothing calm the troubled
     Soul.
   While such Delights my Senses entertain,
I scarce perceive that I have left the *Plain*;
'Till now the Summit of a *Mount* I gain:
Low at whose sandy Base the *River* glides,
Slow-rolling near their Height his languid
   Tides;
Shade above Shade, the Trees in rising
   Ranks,
Cloath with eternal Green his steepy Banks:
The Flood, well pleas'd, reflects their
   verdant Gleam
From the smooth Mirror of his limpid
   Stream.
   But see the *Hawk*, who with acute
     Survey,
Towring in Air predestinates his Prey
Amid the Floods! – Down dropping from on
   high,
He strikes the *Fish*, and bears him thro' the
   Sky.
The Stream disturb'd, no longer shews the
   Scene
That lately stain'd its silver Waves with
   green;
In spreading Circles roll the troubled
   Floods,
And to the Shores bear off the pictur'd
   Woods.
   Now looking round I view the out-
     stretch'd *Land*,
O'er which the Sight exerts a wide
   Command;
The fertile Vallies, and the naked Hills,
The Cattle feeding near the chrystal Rills;
The Lawns wide-op'ning to the sunny Ray,
And mazy Thickets that exclude the Day.

A-while the Eye is pleas'd these Scenes to
   trace,
Then hurrying o'er the intermediate Space,
Far distant Mountains drest in Blue appear,
And all their Woods are lost in empty Air.
   The *Sun* near setting now arrays his Head
In milder Beams and lengthens ev'ry Shade.
The rising Clouds usurping on the Day
A bright Variety of Dies display;
About the wide Horizon swift they fly,
"And chase a Change of Colours round the
   Sky":[10]
And now I view but half the *flaming*
   Sphere,
Now one faint Glimmer shoots along the
   Air,
And all his golden Glories disappear.
   Onwards the *Ev'ning* moves in Habit
     grey,
And for her Sister *Night* prepares the Way.
The plumy People seek their secret Nests,
To Rest repair the ruminating Beasts.
Now deep'ning Shades confess th' Approach
   of Night,
Imperfect Images elude the Sight:
From earthly Objects I remove mine Eye,
And view with Look erect the vaulted Sky;
Where dimly-shining now the Stars appear,
At first thin-scatt'ring thro' the misty Air;
Till Night confirm'd, her jetty Throne
   ascends,
On her the *Moon* in clouded State attends,
But soon unveil'd her lovely Face is seen,
And *Stars* unnumber'd wait around their
   Queen;
Rang'd by their MAKER'S Hand in just
   Array,
They march majestic thro' th'ethereal Way.
   Are these bright Luminaries hung on
     high
Only to please with twinkling Rays our
   Eye?
Or may we rather count each *Star* a *Sun*,
Round *which full peopled Worlds* their
   Courses run?

---

[10] An allusion to James Thomson's description of Summer in his poem, *The Seasons* (1726–30): "See, how at once the bright effulgent sun,/ Rising direct, swift chases from the sky/ The short-lived Twilight . . ." (ll. 635–37).

Orb above Orb harmoniously they steer
Their various voyages thro' Seas of Air.
   Snatch me some *Angel* to those high
      Abodes,
The Seats perhaps of *Saints* and *Demigods!*
Where such as bravely scorn'd the galling
      Yoke
Of *vulgar Error*, and her Fetters broke;
Where *Patriots* who fix the publick Good,
In Fields of Battle sacrific'd their Blood;
Where *pious Priests* who Charity proclaim'd,
And *Poets* whom a *virtuous Muse* enflam'd;
Philosophers who strove to mend our Hearts,
And such as polish'd Life with *useful Arts*,
Obtain a Place; when by the Hand of Death
Touch'd, they retire from this poor Speck of
      Earth;
Their *Spirits* freed from bodily Alloy
Perceive a Fore-taste of that endless Joy,
Which from Eternity hath been prepar'd,
To crown their labours with a vast Reward.
While to these Orbs my wand'ring
      Thoughts aspire,
A falling *Meteor* shoots his lambent Fire;
Thrown from the heav'nly Space he seeks
   the Earth,
From whence he first deriv'd his humble
   Birth.
   The *Mind* advis'd by this instructive
      Sight,
Descending sudden from th'aerial Height,
Obliges me to view a different Scene,
Of more importance to myself, tho' mean.
These distant Objects I no more pursue,
But turning inward my reflective View
My working Fancy helps me to survey,
In the just Picture of this *April day*,
My life o'er past, – a Course of thirty *Years*
Blest with few Joys, perplex'd with
      num'rous Cares.
   In the dim Twilight of our *Infancy*,
Scarce can the Eye surrounding Objects see;
Then thoughtless *Childhood* leads us pleas'd
   and gay,
In Life's fair Morning thro' a flow'ry Way:
The *Youth* in Schools inquisitive of Good,
Science pursues thro' *Learning's* mazy Wood;
Whose lofty Trees, he, to his Grief

perceives,
Are often bare of *Fruit*, and only fill'd with
   Leaves:
Thro' lonely Wilds his tedious Journey lies,
At last a brighter Prospect cheers his Eyes;
Now the gay Fields of *Poetry* he views,
And joyous listens to the *tuneful Muse*;
Now *History* affords him vast Delight,
And opens lovely Landscapes to his Sight:
But ah too soon this Scene of Pleasure flies!
And o'er his Head tempestous Troubles rise.
He hears the Thunders roll, he feels the
      Rains,
Before a friendly Shelter he obtains;
And thence beholds with Grief the furious
      Storm
The *noon-tide* Beauties of his *Life* deform:
He views the *painted Bow* in distant Skies;
Hence, in his Heart some Gleams of
      Comfort rise;
He hopes the *Gust* has almost spent its
      Force,
And that he safely may pursue his Course.
   Thus far *my Life* does with the *Day* agree,
Oh may its coming Stage from Storms be
   free!
While passing thro' the World's most
      private Way,
With Pleasure I my MAKER'S Works
      survey;
Within my Heart let *Peace* a Dwelling find,
Let my *Goodwill* extend to *all Mankind*:
Freed from *Necessity*, and blest with *Health*;
Give me *Content*, let others toil for *Wealth*:
In *busy* Scenes of Life let me exert
A *careful Hand*, and wear an *honest Heart*;
And suffer me my *leisure* Hours to spend,
With chosen *Books*, or a well-natur'd *Friend*.
Thus journeying on, as I advance in Age
May I look back with Pleasure on my Stage;
And as the setting *Sun* withdrew his Light
To rise on other Worlds serene and bright,
Cheerful may I resign my vital Breath,
Nor anxious tremble at th' Approach of
      Death;
Which shall (I hope) but strip me of *my*
      Clay,
And to a better World my Soul convey.

Thus musing, I my silent Moments
spend,
Till to the *River's* margin I descend,
From whence I may discern my *Journey's*
end:
Annapolis adorns its further Shore,
To which the *Boat* attends to bear me o'er.
And now the moving *Boat* the Flood
divides,
While the *Stars* "tremble on the floating
Tides;"[11]
Pleas'd with the Sight, again I raise mine
Eye
To the Bright Glories of the azure Sky;
And while these Works of God's creative
Hand,
The *Moon* and *Stars*, that move at his
Command,
Obedient thro' their circling Course on
high,
Employ my Sight, – struck with amaze I
cry,
ALMIGHTY LORD! whom Heav'n and
Earth proclaim,
The *Author* of their universal Frame,
Wilt thou vouchsafe to view the *Son of Man*,
Thy Creature, who but *Yesterday* began,
Thro' animated Clay to draw his Breath,
To-morrow doom'd a Prey to ruthless Death!
TREMENDOUS GOD! May I not justly
fear,
That I, unworthy Object of thy Care,
Into this World from thy bright Presence
tost,
Am in th'Immensity of *Nature* lost!
And that my Notions of the *World above*,
Are but Creations of my own *Self-love*;
To feed my coward Heart, afraid to die,
With *fancied* Feasts of *Immortality*!
These thoughts, which thy amazing
Works suggest,

Oh glorious FATHER, rack my troubled
Breast.
Yet, GRACIOUS GOD, reflecting that
my Frame
From *Thee* deriv'd in animating Flame,
And that what e'er I am, however mean,
By thy Command I enter'd on this Scene
Of Life, – thy wretched *Creature of a Day*,
Condemn'd to travel thro' a tiresome Way;
Upon whose Banks (perhaps to cheer my
Toil)
I see thin Verdures rise, and *Daisies* smile:
Poor Comforts these, my Pains t'alleviate!
While on my Head tempestuous Troubles
beat.
And must I, when I quit this earthly Scene,
Sink total into *Death*, and never rise again?
No sure, – These *Thoughts* which in my
Bosom roll
Must issue from a *never-dying Soul*;
These active *Thoughts* that penetrate the Sky,
Excursive into dark Futurity;
Which hope eternal Happiness to gain,
Could never be bestow'd on *Man* in vain.
To *Thee*, OH FATHER, fill'd with fervent
Zeal,
And sunk in humble Silence I appeal;
Take me, my great CREATOR to *Thy Care*,
And gracious listen to my ardent Prayer!
SUPREME OF BEINGS, omnipresent
Power!
My great Preserver from my natal Hour,
Fountain of Wisdom, boundless Deity,
OMNISCIENT GOD, my Wants are
known to THEE,
With Mercy look on mine Infirmity!
Whatever State thou shalt for me ordain,
Whether my Lot in Life be *Joy* or *Pain*;
Patient let me sustain thy wise Decree,
And learn to *know myself* and *honour Thee*.

1732

---

[11]   An allusion to Alexander Pope's mock-epic *Rape of the
Lock* (1714): "The sun-beams trembling on the floating
tydes" (Canto II: 48).

Jonathan Edwards (1703–1758)

Popularly known as the frenzy-inducing preacher of the Great Awakening, Jonathan Edwards was the last great Puritan thinker who attempted to reconcile a religious worldview dominated by belief in Scripture with the eighteenth-century Enlightenment world of empiricism and reason. Edwards was born in the newly established settlement of East Windsor, Connecticut, son of Timothy Edwards, a Harvard educated Congregational minister, and grandson, on his mother's side, of the eminent Puritan minister and theologian, Solomon Stoddard. As the only son of eleven children, and a precocious child, Edwards was rigorously trained by his father and sent in 1716 to Yale College, which had been established by Cotton Mather to correct the liberal leanings of the younger Harvard faculty. At Yale, a major gift of books to the library introduced Edwards to recent writers in science and philosophy such as Sir Isaac Newton and John Locke. Newton's work on optics and Locke's empirical philosophy would exert important influence on Edwards' later work.

After his graduation in 1720, and two years of postgraduate study, Edwards briefly served as pastor of a Presbyterian church in New York City, but returned to New Haven to finish his masters in theology, and became a tutor at the College in 1724. During this period, Edwards began to make extensive notes on everything from plants and animals, to physics and optics, as well as religious ideas, moral issues and cultural mores, organizing them into notebooks on different topics which became the repository for the ideas that would flower in his sermons and treatises. One of these notebooks, entitled *Images of Divine Things* contained 212 entries that illustrate Edwards' application of typology, a Medieval method of biblical hermeneutics in which persons and events in the Old Testament functioned as types or forerunners of their fulfillments or antitypes in the New Testament. Edwards' innovation, later taken up by Emerson and the New England Transcendentalists, was to extend typology beyond Scripture to his minute observations of nature and human nature, so that the whole material world becomes an unending analogy of divine presence.

In 1726, Edwards settled down in Northampton to assist his aging grandfather and then, at Stoddard's death in 1729, to take over as minister of the large and influential congregation. He married Sarah Pierpont, the daughter of a New Haven minister he had met at college and had a large family of eleven surviving children. In 1734, he delivered a series of sermons that produced a number of dramatic conversions in the Northampton congregation. The letter Edwards wrote about it, expanded and published under the title, *A Faithful Narrative of the Surprising Work of God* in 1737, brought him international notice. This revival anticipated the more extensive "Great Awakening" that would sweep the eastern seaboard in 1739–40. Edwards used his classic revivalist sermon, *Sinners in the Hands of an Angry God*, with its vivid imagery and relentless argument, as an instrument to "awaken" local congregations to a lively sense of their imminent danger from unrepentant sin. Although it is Edwards' most famous sermon, it is only one of the more than 1200 sermons he wrote and preached in his lifetime, most of them unpublished, until the large-scale project begun by general editor Perry Miller in 1957 to edit all of Edwards' extant works.

The legacy of the Great Awakening was a mixed one for Edwards. In 1748, after many years of reluctant adherence to his grandfather Stoddard's liberal policies of admitting applicants to full church membership who had not made a profession of faith, Edwards finally refused to comply. In 1750, the Northampton congregation recommended the dismissal of their internationally renowned minister. Edwards remained in Northampton, rejecting all offers of ministerial posts until 1751, when he became the administrator for a Congregational mission to the Mahican and Mohawk Indians in Stockbridge, Massachusetts. The position gave Edwards more time for reflection, and in the last four years of his life, he produced the major treatises upon which his reputation as a philosopher rests. In 1757, Edwards reluctantly agreed to accept the presidency of the College of New Jersey, now Princeton. In order to guard against a smallpox epidemic in the area, Edwards agreed to be inoculated, but died from the infected serum three months later. He was only fifty-five years old.

Edwards' impressive intellectual achievements have somewhat obscured the personal aspects of his thinking. A striking example is his "Apostrophe to Sarah Pierpont," which he supposedly composed as an undergraduate when he was twenty and she thirteen. In this short piece, Edwards casts the young woman as an exemplum of piety that even he strove to emulate. Edwards' ceaseless interest in the psychological processes of the self spurred him to write his own "Personal Narrative" of religious conversion. Composed sometime between the Northampton revival and the Great Awakening, this self-analysis departs from the strict "morphology of conversion" or set sequence of experiences prescribed by earlier Puritan divines, conforming rather to the key elements of conversion Edwards described in *Religious Affections*, namely a thorough, willing and joyous submission to God's will and divine sovereignty. The precarious synthesis Edwards was able to forge between Calvinist determinism and Enlightenment empiricism could not last. Only when the English Romantics of the next century swept away the scaffolding of rationalism could the New England Transcendentalists recapture Edwards' ecstatic, nearly mystical vision of the divine in nature.

PRIMARY WORKS

A Faithful Narrative of the Surprising Work of God in the Conversions of Many Hundred Souls . . . , 1737.
A Treatise Concerning the Religious Affections, 1746.
Freedom of the Will, 1754.
The Great Christian Doctrine of Original Sin, 1758.
Concerning the End for Which God Created the World and The Nature of True Virtue, 1765.
The Works of President Edwards, ed. Sereno Dwight, 1829–30.
The Works of Jonathan Edwards, gen. ed. Perry Miller, 17 vols, 1957–.

FURTHER READING

Perry Miller, Jonathan Edwards (New York: Sloan, 1949; rpt. Amherst: University of Massachusetts Press, 1981).
Nathan Hatch and Harry Stout (eds) Jonathan Edwards and the American Experience (New York: Oxford University Press, 1988).
Joseph Conforti, Jonathan Edwards, Religious Tradition and American Culture (Chapel Hill: University of North Carolina Press, 1995).
Christopher Grasso, "Images and Shadows of Jonathan Edwards," American Literary History, Winter, 8, 4 (1996) pp. 683–98.

FROM *IMAGES OF DIVINE THINGS*[1]

7. That the things of the world are ordered [and] designed to shadow forth spiritual things, appears by the Apostle's[2] arguing spiritual things from them. I Cor. 15:36, "Thou fool, that which thou sowest is not quickened, except it die." If the sowing of seed and its springing were not designedly ordered to have an agreeableness to the resurrection[3], there could be no sort of argument in that which the Apostle alleges; either to argue the resurrection itself or the manner of it, either its certainty, or probability, or possibility. See how the Apostle's argument is thus founded (Heb. 9:16–17) about the validity of a testament.

8. Again, it is apparent and allowed that there is a great and remarkable analogy in God's works. There is a wonderful resemblance in the effects which God produces, and consentaneity[4] in his manner of working in one thing and another, throughout all nature. It is very observable in the visible world. Therefore 'tis allowed that God does purposely make and order one thing to be in an agreeableness and harmony with another. And if so, why should not we suppose

---

[1]   Composed in 1728, the 212 entries in this notebook develop Edwards' theory of typology, a method of biblical interpretation which understood events and persons in the Old Testament as types or forerunners of their fulfillment or anti-types in the New Testament. By applying this way of reading to nature, history and human experience, Edwards anticipates the "Transcendentalists" of the nineteenth century. The text, with slight modification, is from *The Works of Jonathan Edwards*, vol. 11, *Typological Writings*, eds Wallace Anderson and Mason Lowance, Jr, with David Watters (New Haven: Yale University Press, 1993).

[2]   Paul.

[3]   Of Christ.

[4]   Agreeableness, accord.

that he makes the inferior in imitation of the superior, the material of the spiritual, on purpose to have a resemblance and shadow of them? We see that even in the material world God makes one part of it strangely to agree with another; and why is it not reasonable to suppose he makes the whole as a shadow of the spiritual world? . . .

63. In the manner in which birds and squirrels that are charmed by serpents go into their mouths and are destroyed by them, is a lively representation of the manner in which sinners under the gospel are very often charmed and destroyed by the devil. The animal that is charmed by the serpents seems to be in a great exercise and fear, screams and makes ado, but yet don't flee ways. It comes nearer to the serpent, and then seems to have its distress increased and goes a little back again, but then comes still nearer than ever, and then appears as if greatly affrighted and runs or flies back again a little way, but yet don't flee quite away, and soon comes a little nearer and a little nearer with seeming fear and stress that drives 'em a little back between whiles, until at length they come so [near] that the serpent can lay hold of them: and so they become their prey.

Just thus, ofentimes sinners under the gospel are bewitched by their lusts. They have considerable fears of destruction and remorse of conscience that makes 'em hang back, and they have a great deal of exercise between while, and some partial reformations, but yet they don't flee away. They won't wholly forsake their beloved lusts, but return to 'em again; and so whatever warnings they have, and whatever checks of conscience that may exercise 'em and make [them] go back a little and stand off for a while, yet they will keep their beloved sin in sight, and won't utterly break off from it and forsake [it], but will return to it again and again, and go a little further and a little further, until Satan remedilessly makes a prey of them. But if anyone comes and kills the serpent, the animal immediately escapes. So the way in which poor souls are delivered from the snare of the devil is by Christ's coming and bruising the serpent's head.

118. IMAGES OF DIVINE THINGS. It is with many of these things as it was with the sacrifices of old. They are often repeated, whereas the antitype is continual and never comes to pass by once. Thus sleep is an image of death that is repeated every night. So the morning is the image of the resurrections. So the spring of the year is the image of the resurrection, which is repeated every year. And so of many other things that might be mentioned. They are repeated to show two things: viz. That the thing shadowed is not yet fulfilled; and second, to signify the great importance of the antitype, that we need to be so renewedly and continually put in mind of it.

156. The Book of Scripture is the interpreter of the book of nature two ways: viz. By declaring to us those spiritual mysteries that are indeed signified or typified in the constitutions of the natural world; and secondly, in actually making application of the signs and types in the book of nature as representations of those spiritual mysteries in many instances.

1728   1948

"APOSTROPHE TO SARAH PIERPONT"[1]

They say there is a young lady in [New Haven] who is beloved of that almighty Being, who made and rules the world, and that there are certain seasons in which this great Being, in some

[1]   Written in about 1723 when Sarah was thirteen years old and Edwards was twenty. They married in 1727. The text, with slight modification, is from *The Works of Jonathan*   *Edwards*, vol. 16, *Letters and Personal Writings*, ed. George Claghorn (New Haven: Yale University Press, 1998).

way or other invisible, comes to her and fills her mind with exceeding sweet delight, and that she hardly cares for anything, except to meditate on him – that she expects after a while to be received up where he is, to be raised up out of the world and caught up into heaven; being assured that he loves her too well to let her remain at a distance from him always. There she is to dwell with him, and to be ravished with his love and delight forever. Therefore, if you present all the world before her, with the richest of its treasures, she disregards it and cares not for it, and is unmindful of any pain or affliction. She has a strange sweetness in her mind, and singular purity in her affections; is most just and conscientious in all her actions; and you could not persuade her to do anything wrong or sinful, if you would give her all the world, lest she should offend this great Being. She is of a wonderful sweetness, calmness and universal benevolence of mind; especially after those seasons in which this great God has manifested himself to her mind. She will sometimes go about from place to place, singing sweetly; and seems to be always full of joy and pleasure; and no one knows for what. She loves to be alone, and to wander in the fields and on the mountains, and seems to have someone invisible always conversing with her.

1723   1829–30

PERSONAL NARRATIVE[1]

I had a variety of concerns and exercises[2] about my soul from my childhood; but had two more remarkable seasons of awakening, before I met with that change, by which I was brought to those new dispositions, and that new sense of things, that I have since had. The first time was when I was a boy, some years before I went to college, at a time of remarkable awakening in my father's congregation. I was then very much affected for many months, and concerned about the things of religion, and my soul's salvation; and was abundant in duties. I used to pray five times a day in secret, and to spend much time in religious talk with other boys; and used to meet with them to pray together. I experienced I know not what kind of delight in religion. My mind was much engaged in it, and had much self-righteous pleasure; and it was my delight to abound in religious duties. I, with some of my schoolmates joined together, and built a booth in a swamp, in a very secret and retired place, for a place of prayer. And besides, I had particular secret places of my own in the woods, where I used to retire by myself; and used to be from time to time much affected. My affections seemed to be lively and easily moved, and I seemed to be in my element, when engaged in religious duties. And I am ready to think, many are deceived with such affections, and such a kind of delight, as I then had in religion, and mistake it for grace.

But in process of time, my convictions and affections wore off; and I entirely lost all those affections and delights, and left off secret prayer, at least as to any constant performance of it; and returned like a dog to his vomit, and went on in ways of sin.[3]

Indeed, I was at some times very uneasy, especially towards the latter part of the time of my

---

[1] From an internal reference, the composition of *Personal Narrative* can be dated after 1739. It was published after Edwards' death by his friend Samuel Hopkins, who found it among his papers, with the title "An Account of His Conversion, Experiences, and Religious Exercises," in *The Life and Character of the Late Rev. Mr. Jonathan Edwards* (1765).

The text, with slight modification, is from *The Works of Jonathan Edwards*, vol. 16, *Letters and Personal Writings*, ed. George Claghorn (New Haven: Yale University Press, 1980).

[2] Agitations.

[3] "As a dog returneth to his vomit, so a fool returneth to his folly" (Proverbs 26:11).

being at college. Till it pleased God, in my last year at college, at a time when I was in the midst of many uneasy thoughts about the state of my soul, to seize me with a pleurisy; in which he brought me nigh to the grave, and shook me over the pit of hell.

But yet, it was not long after my recovery, before I fell again into my old ways of sin. But God would not suffer me to go on with any quietness; but I had great and violent inward struggles: till after many conflicts with wicked inclinations, and repeated resolutions, and bonds that I laid myself under by a kind of vows to God, I was brought wholly to break off all former wicked ways, and all ways of known outward sin; and to apply myself to seek my salvation, and practice the duties of religion: but without that kind of affection and delight, that I had formerly experienced. My concern now wrought more by inward struggles and conflicts, and self-reflections. I made seeking my salvation the main business of my life. But yet it seems to me, I sought after a miserable manner: which has made me sometimes since to question, whether ever it issued in that which was saving; being ready to doubt, whether such miserable seeking was ever succeeded. But yet I was brought to seek salvation, in a manner that I never was before. I felt a spirit to part with all things in the world, for an interest in Christ. My concern continued and prevailed, with many exercising things and inward struggles; but yet it never seemed to be proper to express my concern that I had, by the name of terror.

From my childhood up, my mind had been wont to be full of objections against the doctrine of God's sovereignty, in choosing whom he would to eternal life, and rejecting whom he pleased; leaving them eternally to perish, and be everlastingly tormented in hell. It used to appear like a horrible doctrine to me. But I remember the time very well, when I seemed to be convinced, and fully satisfied, as to this sovereignty of God, and his justice in thus eternally disposing of men, according to his sovereign pleasure. But never could give an account, how, or by what means, I was thus convinced; not in the least imagining, in the time of it, nor a long time after, that there was any extraordinary influence of God's Spirit in it: but only that now I saw further, and my reason apprehended the justice and reasonableness of it. However, my mind rested in it; and it put an end to all those cavils and objections, that I had till then abode with me, all the preceding part of my life. And there has been a wonderful alteration in my mind, with respect to the doctrine of God's sovereignty, from that day to this; so that I scarce ever have found so much as the rising of an objection against God's sovereignty, in the most absolute sense, in showing mercy on whom he will show mercy, and hardening and eternally damning whom he will.[4] God's absolute sovereignty, and justice, with respect to salvation and damnation, is what my mind seems to rest assured of, as much as of anything that I see with my eyes; at least it is so at times. But I have oftentimes since that first conviction, had quite another kind of sense of God's sovereignty, than I had then. I have often since, not only had a conviction, but a *delightful* conviction. The doctrine of God's sovereignty has very often appeared, an exceeding pleasant, bright and sweet doctrine to me: and absolute sovereignty is what I love to ascribe to God. But my first conviction was not with this.

The first that I remember that ever I found anything of that sort of inward, sweet delight in God and divine things, that I have lived much in since, was on reading those words, I Tim. 1:17: "Now unto the King eternal, immortal, invisible, the only wise God, be honor and glory forever and ever, Amen." As I read the words, there came into my soul, and was as it were diffused through it, a sense of the glory of the Divine Being; a new sense, quite different from anything I ever experienced before. Never any words of Scripture seemed to me as these words did. I thought with myself, how excellent a Being that was; and how happy I should be, if I might enjoy that God, and be wrapped up to God in heaven, and be as it were swallowed up in

4   Romans 9:18.

him. I kept saying, and as it were singing over these words of Scripture to myself; and went to prayer, to pray to God that I might enjoy him; and prayed in a manner quite different from what I used to do; with a new sort of affection. But it never came into my thought, that there was anything spiritual, or of a saving nature in this.

From about that time, I began to have a new kind of apprehensions and ideas of Christ, and the work of redemption, and the glorious way of salvation by him. I had an inward, sweet sense of these things, that at times came into my heart; and my soul was led away in pleasant views and contemplations of them. And my mind was greatly engaged, to spend my time in reading and meditating on Christ; and the beauty and excellency of his person, and the lovely way of salvation, by free grace in him. I found no books so delightful to me, as those that treated of these subjects. Those words, Cant. 2:1, used to be abundantly with me: "I am the rose of Sharon, the lily of the valleys." The words seemed to me, sweetly to represent, the loveliness and beauty of Jesus Christ. And the whole Book of Canticles[5] used to be pleasant to me; and I used to be much in reading it, about that time. And found, from time to time, an inward sweetness, that used, as it were, to carry me away in my contemplations; in what I know not how to express otherwise, than by a calm, sweet abstraction of soul from all the concerns of this world; and a kind of vision, or fixed ideas and imaginations, of being alone in the mountains, or some solitary wilderness, far from all mankind, sweetly conversing with Christ, and wrapped and swallowed up in God. The sense I had of divine things, would often of a sudden as it were, kindle up a sweet burning in my heart; an ardor of my soul, that I know not how to express.

Not long after I first began to experience these things, I gave an account to my father, of some things that had passed in my mind. I was pretty much affected by the discourse we had together. And when the discourse was ended, I walked abroad alone, in a solitary place in my father's pasture, for contemplation. And as I was walking there, and looked up on the sky and clouds; there came into my mind, a sweet sense of the glorious majesty and grace of God, that I know not how to express. I seemed to see them both in a sweet conjunction: majesty and meekness joined together: it was a sweet and gentle, and holy majesty; and also a majestic meekness; an awful sweetness; a high, and great, and holy gentleness.

After this my sense of divine things gradually increased, and became more and more lively, and had more of that inward sweetness. The appearance of everything was altered: there seemed to be, as it were, a calm, sweet cast, or appearance of divine glory, in almost everything. God's excellency, his wisdom, his purity and love, seemed to appear in everything; in the sun, moon and stars; in the clouds, and blue sky; in the grass, flowers, trees; in the water, and all nature; which used greatly to fix my mind. I often used to sit and view the moon, for a long time; and so in the daytime, spent much time in viewing the clouds and sky, to behold the sweet glory of God in these things: in the meantime, singing forth with a low voice, my contemplations of the Creator and Redeemer. And scarce anything, among all the works of nature, was so sweet to me as thunder and lightning. Formerly, nothing had been so terrible to me. I used to be a person uncommonly terrified with thunder: and it used to strike me with terror, when I saw a thunderstorm rising. But now, on the contrary, it rejoiced me. I felt God at the first appearance of a thunderstorm. And used to take the opportunity at such times, to fix myself to view the clouds, and see the lightnings play, and hear the majestic and awful voice of God's thunder: which oftentimes was exceeding entertaining, leading me to sweet contemplations of my great and glorious God. And while I viewed, used to spend my time, as it always seemed natural to me, to sing or chant forth my meditations; to speak my thoughts in soliloquies, and speak with a singing voice.

5   Another name for the Song of Solomon.

I felt then a great satisfaction as to my good estate[6]. But that did not content me. I had vehement longings of soul after God and Christ, and after more holiness; wherewith my heart seemed to be full, and ready to break: which often brought to my mind, the words of the Psalmist, Ps. 119:28, "My soul breaketh for the longing it hath." I often felt a mourning and lamenting in my heart, that I had not turned to God sooner, that I might have had more time to grow in grace. My mind was greatly fixed on divine things; I was almost perpetually in the contemplation of them. Spent most of my time in thinking of divine things, year after year. And used to spend abundance of my time, in walking alone in the woods, and solitary places, for meditation, soliloquy and prayer, and converse with God. And it was always my manner, at such times, to sing forth my contemplations. And was almost constantly in ejaculatory prayer, wherever I was. Prayer seemed to be natural to me; as the breath, by which the inward burnings of my heart had vent.

The delights which I now felt in things of religion, were of an exceeding different kind, from those forementioned, that I had when I was a boy. They were totally of another kind; and what I then had no more notion or idea of, than one born blind has of pleasant and beautiful colors. They were of a more inward, pure, soul-animating and refreshing nature. Those former delights, never reached the heart; and did not arise from any sight of the divine excellency of the things of God; or any taste of the soul-satisfying, and life-giving good, there is in them.

My sense of divine things seemed gradually to increase, till I went to preach at New York; which was about a year and a half after they began.[7] While I was there, I felt them, very sensibly, in a much higher degree, than I had done before. My longings after God and holiness, were much increased. Pure and humble, holy and heavenly Christianity, appeared exceeding amiable to me. I felt in me a burning desire to be in everything a complete Christian; and conformed to the blessed image of Christ: and that I might live in all things, according to the pure, sweet and blessed rules of the gospel. I had an eager thirsting after progress in these things. My longings after it, put me upon pursuing and pressing after them. It was my continual strife day and night, and constant inquiry, how I should be more holy, and live more holily, and more becoming a child of God, and disciple of Christ. I sought an increase of grace and holiness, and that I might live an holy life, with vastly more earnestness, than ever I sought grace, before I had it. I used to be continually examining myself, and studying and contriving for likely ways and means, how I should live holily, with far greater diligence and earnestness, than ever I pursued anything in my life: but with too great a dependence on my own strength; which afterwards proved a great damage to me. My experience had not then taught me, as it has done since, my extreme feebleness and impotence, every manner of way; and the innumerable and bottomless depths of secret corruption and deceit, that there was in my heart. However, I went on with my eager pursuit after more holiness; and sweet conformity to Christ. . . .

Holiness, as I then wrote down some of my contemplations on it, appeared to me to be of a sweet, pleasant, charming, serene, calm nature. It seemed to me, it brought an inexpressible purity, brightness, peacefulness and ravishment to the soul: and that it made the soul like a field or garden of God, with all manner of pleasant flowers; that is all pleasant, delightful and undisturbed; enjoying a sweet calm, and the gently vivifying beams of the sun. The soul of a true Christian, as I then wrote my meditations, appeared like such a little white flower, as we see in the spring of the year; low and humble on the ground, opening its bosom, to receive the

---

6   Spiritual state.
7   Edwards assisted at a Presbyterian Church in New York
from August 1722 to April 1723.

pleasant beams of the sun's glory; rejoicing as it were, in a calm rapture; diffusing around a sweet fragrancy; standing peacefully and lovingly, in the midst of other flowers round about; all in like manner opening their bosoms, to drink in the light of the sun.

There was no part of creature-holiness, that I then, and at other times, had so great a sense of the loveliness of, as humility, brokenness of heart and poverty of spirit: and there was nothing that I had such a spirit to long for. My heart as it were panted after this, to lie low before God, and in the dust; that I might be nothing, and that God might be all; that I might become as a little child[8].

While I was there at New York, I sometimes was much affected with reflections on my past life, considering how late it was, before I began to be truly religious; and how wickedly I had lived till then: and once so as to weep abundantly, and for a considerable time together.

On January 12, 1722–23, I made a solemn dedication of myself to God, and wrote it down; giving up myself, and all that I had to God; to be for the future in no respect my own; to act as one that had no right to himself, in any respect. And solemnly vowed to take God for my whole portion and felicity; looking on nothing else as any part of my happiness, nor acting as if it were: and his law for the constant rule of my obedience: engaging to fight with all my might, against the world, the flesh and the devil, to the end of my life. But have reason to be infinitely humbled, when I consider, how much I have failed of answering my obligation.

I had then abundance of sweet religious conversation in the family where I lived, with Mr John Smith, and his pious mother. My heart was knit in affection to those, in whom were appearances of true piety; and I could bear the thoughts of no other companions, but such as were holy, and the disciples of the blessed Jesus.

I had great longings for the advancement of Christ's kingdom in the world. My secret prayer used to be in great part taken up in praying for it. If I heard the least hint of any thing that happened in any part of the world, that appeared to me, in some respect or other, to have a favorable aspect on the interest of Christ's kingdom, my soul eagerly catched at it; and it would much animate and refresh me. I used to be earnest to read public newsletters, mainly for that end; to see if I could not find some news favorable to the interest of religion in the world. . . .

I have loved the doctrines of the gospel: they have been to my soul like green pastures. The gospel has seemed to me to be the richest treasure; the treasure that I have most desired, and longed that it might dwell richly in me. The way of salvation by Christ, has appeared in a general way, glorious and excellent, and most pleasant and beautiful. It has often seemed to me, that it would in a great measure spoil heaven, to receive it in any other way. That text has often been affecting and delightful to me, Isaiah 32:2, "A man shall be an hiding place from the wind, and a covert from the tempest; as rivers of water in a dry place, as the shadow of a great rock in a weary land."

It has often appeared sweet to me, to be united to Christ; to have him for my head, and to be a member of his body: and also to have Christ for my teacher and prophet. I very often think with sweetness and longings and pantings of soul, of being a little child, taking hold of Christ, to be led by him through the wilderness of this world. That text, Matt. 18, at the beginning, has often been sweet to me: "Except ye be converted, and become as little children, ye shall not enter into the kingdom of heaven." I love to think of coming to Christ, to receive salvation of him, poor in spirit, and quite empty of self; humbly exalting him alone; cut entirely off from

---

8   "Verily I say unto you, Whosoever shall not receive the kingdom of God as a little child, he shall not enter therein" (Mark 10:15).

my own root, and to grow into, and out of Christ: to have God in Christ to be all in all; and to live by faith on the Son of God, a life of humble, unfeigned confidence in him. That Scripture has often been sweet to me, Ps. 115:1, "Not unto us, O Lord, not unto us, but unto thy name give glory, for thy mercy, and for thy truth's sake." And those words of Christ, Luke 10:21, "In that hour Jesus rejoiced in spirit, and said, I thank thee, O Father, Lord of heaven and earth, that thou hast hid these things from the wise and prudent, and hast revealed them unto babes: even so, Father; for so it seemed good in thy sight." That sovereignty of God that Christ rejoiced in, seemed to me to be worthy to be rejoiced in; and that rejoicing of Christ, seemed to me to show the excellency of Christ, and the Spirit that he was of.

Sometimes only mentioning a single word, causes my heart to burn within me: or only seeing the name of Christ, or the name of some attribute of God. And God has appeared glorious to me, on account of the Trinity. It has made me have exalting thoughts of God, that he subsists in three persons; Father, Son, and Holy Ghost. . . .

Once, as I rid out into the woods for my health, anno 1737; and having lit from my horse in a retired place, as my manner commonly has been, to walk for divine contemplation and prayer; I had a view, that for me was extraordinary, of the glory of the Son of God; as mediator between God and man; and his wonderful, great, full, pure and sweet grace and love, and meek and gentle condescension. This grace, that appeared to me so calm and sweet, appeared great above the heavens. The person of Christ appeared ineffably excellent, with an excellency great enough to swallow up all thought and conception. Which continued, as near as I can judge, about an hour; which kept me, the bigger part of the time, in a flood of tears, and weeping aloud. I felt withal, an ardency of soul to be, what I know not otherwise how to express, than to be emptied and annihilated; to lie in the dust, and to be full of Christ alone; to love him with a holy and pure love; to trust in him; to live upon him; to serve and follow him, and to be totally wrapped up in the fullness of Christ; and to be perfectly sanctified and made pure, with a divine and heavenly purity. I have several other times, and views very much of the same nature, and that have had the same effects. . . .

I have often since I lived in this town[9], had very affecting views of my own sinfulness and vileness; very frequently so as to hold me in a kind of loud weeping, sometimes for a considerable time together: so that I have often been forced to shut myself up. I have had a vastly greater sense of my own wickedness, and the badness of my heart, since my conversion, than ever I had before. It has often appeared to me, that if God should mark iniquity against me, I should appear the very worst of all mankind; of all that have been since the beginning of the world to this time: and that I should have by far the lowest place in hell. When others that have come to talk with me about their soul concerns, have expressed the sense they have had of their own wickedness, by saying that it seemed to them, that they were as bad as the devil himself; I thought their expressions seemed exceeding faint and feeble, to represent my wickedness. I thought I should wonder, that they should content themselves with such expressions as these, if I had any reason to imagine, that their sin bore any proportion to mine. It seemed to me, I should wonder at myself, if I should express my wickedness in such feeble terms as they did.

My wickedness, as I am in myself, has long appeared to me perfectly ineffable, and infinitely swallowing up all thought and imagination; like an infinite deluge, or infinite mountains over my head. I know not how to express better, what my sins appear to me to be, than by heaping infinite upon infinite, and multiplying infinite by infinite. I go about very often, for

---

[9] Northampton, Massachusetts, the town in the Connecticut Valley where Edwards moved in 1726 to assist his aging grandfather, Solomon Stoddard, and the center of several spiritual awakenings.

this many years, with these expressions in my mind, and in my mouth, "Infinite upon Infinite. Infinite upon Infinite!" When I look into my heart, and take a view of my wickedness, it looks like an abyss infinitely deeper than hell. And it appears to me, that were it not for free grace, exalted and raised up to the infinite height of all the fullness and glory of the great Jehovah, and the arm of his power and grace stretched forth, in all the majesty of his power, and in all the glory of his sovereignty; I should appear sunk down in my sins infinitely below hell itself, far beyond sight of everything, but the piercing eye of God's grace, that can pierce even down to such a depth, and to the bottom of such an abyss.

And yet, I be not in the least inclined to think, that I have a greater conviction of sin than ordinary. It seems to me, my conviction of sin is exceeding small, and faint. It appears to me enough to amaze me, that I have no more sense of my sin. I know certainly, that I have very little sense of my sinfulness. That my sins appear to me so great, don't seem to me to be, because I have so much more conviction of sin than other Christians, but because I am so much worse, and have so much more wickedness to be convinced of. When I have had these turns of weeping and crying for my sins, I thought I knew in the time of it, that my repentance was nothing to my sin.

I have greatly longed of late, for a broken heart, and to lie low before God. And when I ask for humility of God, I can't bear the thoughts of being no more humble, than other Christians. It seems to me, that though their degrees of humility may be suitable for them; yet it would be a vile self-exaltation in me, not to be the lowest in humility of all mankind. Others speak of their longing to be humbled to the dust. Though that may be a proper expression for them, I always think for myself, that I ought to be humbled down below hell. 'Tis an expression that it has long been natural for me to use in prayer to God. I ought to lie infinitely low before God.

It is affecting to me to think, how ignorant I was, when I was a young Christian, of the bottomless, infinite depths of wickedness, pride, hypocrisy and deceit left in my heart.

I have vastly a greater sense, of my universal, exceeding dependence on God's grace and strength, and mere good pleasure, of late, than I used formerly to have; and have experienced more of an abhorrence of my own righteousness. The thought of any comfort or joy, arising in me, on any consideration, or reflection on my own amiableness, or any of my performances or experiences, or any goodness of heart or life, is nauseous and detestable to me. And yet I am greatly afflicted with a proud and self-righteous spirit; much more sensibly, than I used to be formerly. I see that serpent rising and putting forth its head, continually, everywhere, all around me.

Though it seems to me, that in some respects I was a far better Christian, for two or three years after my first conversion, than I am now; and lived in a more constant delight and pleasure: yet of late years, I have had a more full and constant sense of the absolute sovereignty of God, and a delight in that sovereignty; and have had more of a sense of the glory of Christ, as a mediator, as revealed in the gospel. On one Saturday night in particular, had a particular discovery of the excellency of the gospel of Christ, above all other doctrines; so that I could not but say to myself; "This is my chosen light, my chosen doctrine:" and of Christ, "This is my chosen prophet." It appeared to me to be sweet beyond all expression, to follow Christ, and to be taught and enlightened and instructed by him; to learn of him, and live to him.

Another Saturday night, January 1738–39, had such a sense, how sweet and blessed a thing it was, to walk in the way of duty, to do that which was right and meet to be done, and agreeable to the holy mind of God; that it caused me to break forth into a kind of a loud weeping, which held me some time; so that I was forced to shut myself up, and fasten the doors. I could not but as it were cry out, "How happy are they which do that which is right in the sight of God! They are blessed indeed, they are the happy ones!" I had at the same time, a very affecting sense, how meet and suitable it was that God should govern the world, and order all things according to his own pleasure; and I rejoiced in it, that God reigned, and that his will was done.

c. 1739–40   1765

Elizabeth Ashbridge (1713–1755)

The little we know about Elizabeth Ashbridge comes from her autobiography and what can be inferred from records of the Society of Friends after she was received into their ministry in 1738. But since her autobiography exists only in copies by other hands, it may not be an accurate record of her self-representation. The story Ashbridge tells is remarkable and remarkably melodramatic. Born into a well-off English Anglican family with a devoted mother, she was disowned by her father after she eloped at fourteen and became a widow five months later. Growing up "Wild & Airy" with relatives in Ireland, one of whom was a Quaker she found "disagreeable," Ashbridge wanted to go to America, and at nineteen was duped into three years of indentured servitude to a cruel master to pay for her passage. Rejecting a career on the stage, she instead married a man named Sullivan she "had no Value for," and entered a period of domestic captivity, being incessantly uprooted and suffering physical abuse. The one constant Ashbridge depicted in her short life was her longing to find a religious belief and a religious community that would sustain her.

On a visit to relatives in Pennsylvania, she met Quakers who changed her world. Then began the long, painful progress towards her private declaration of the inviolability of her conscience despite marital duty and physical violence, and the concomitant public acknowledgment of her commitment to the thoroughly reviled Quaker faith. Her account leaves off just at the point where it would have become most interesting: after she received notification of her husband's death in 1742, freeing her to make choices according to her conscience and principles. We know she chose to marry the Quaker, Aaron Ashbridge, in 1746, and went to live with him in Goshen, north of Philadelphia. We know that she became one of the most highly respected members of the Society of Friends in the Philadelphia area. We also know that she began to

feel drawn to evangelize in Britain, and that in 1753, she became a Public Friend, authorized by her local Society, the Goshen Meeting, to travel and preach. Finally, we know from letters and testimonials by others that her conversation and ministry were "very acceptable" to the London Quakers and to other people she met in her travels, and that she died in that effort. Ashbridge gave her life in the service of her hard-won beliefs. When put in the historical context of the spread of Quakerism, her story tells us a good deal about mid-eighteenth century gender conventions, and about the perennial struggles faced by determined women to find a voice within a male-dominated religious culture.

By the time Ashbridge was born, Quakerism had taken firm hold in England and Ireland, spreading in the New World to the colonies of Pennsylvania and East and West Jersey. George Fox, the sect's founder, began gathering followers in the 1640s, establishing the Society of Friends in 1652, the year of his great vision on Pendle Hill. His writings, and those of his wife, Margaret Fell Fox, lay out the doctrines of a mystical and egalitarian Christianity. Taking the central tenet of Luther's Reformation, "the priesthood of all believers," to its logical conclusion, they argued that each person contained an inward spirit or Inner Light, which is the presence of the divine. This light, they claimed, was promised to all, not just the elect, and did not require an official ministry to express or nurture. Furthermore, they argued that the inequality of the sexes was a product of the Fall, and could be healed by those who dwelled in and spoke from this Inner Light.

As might be expected, Quakers suffered vicious persecution by New England Puritans. By 1661, four Quakers had been executed in Boston and many more were tortured and exiled. The most famous was Mary Dyer, who many years before had been a friend of Anne Hutchinson, the central player in the Antinomian Controversy of 1636–7 that had nearly torn the fledgling colony apart. Like Hutchinson, Quakers, especially women, represented a serious threat not only to institutional authority and religious hierarchy, but to the male monopoly on power and on public speech. Although Ashbridge was such a creation of her times that she pitied the first Quaker woman preacher she heard in Boston "for her Ignorance (as I thought)," it becomes clear that her central concern was the rejection of male-dominated, hypocritical and empty religious practices. In Quaker meetings, and in her transformation into a Public Friend, she found an unmediated, intuitive, individual revelation that finally allowed her to throw off her dependence on all man-made ties. Her evangelism made her speaking one with her living.

Although completed much earlier and circulated among Friends, Ashbridge's autobiography was not published until 1774, the same year John Woolman's now classic Quaker autobiography appeared. Ashbridge's work remains obscure, but letters indicate that in 1757 Woolman asked Aaron Ashbridge to send him a copy of Elizabeth's "journal," two years after Woolman began his own. It is likely, but not clear, that these two writers met. Finally, it is important to recognize the profound influence Quakerism had, not only within the colonies, afflicted during the mid-eighteenth century by rampant materialism and individualism, but in the creation of a literature of progressive politics and morality, most notably the work of Emerson and Whitman, and in the formation of a morally inflected strand of US feminism.

PRIMARY WORK

Some Account of the Fore Part of the Life of Elizabeth Ashbridge, who died in Truth's service at the house of Robert Lecky at Kilnock in the Country of Carlow Ireland; the 16th of the 5th mo. 1755. Written by her own Hand many years ago, 1774.

FURTHER READING

Margaret Hope Bacon, *The Quiet Rebels: The Story of the Quakers in America* (New York: Basic Books, 1969).

Daniel B. Shea, "Elizabeth Ashbridge and the Voice Within," *Journeys in New Worlds: Early American Women's Narratives*, ed. William L. Andrews (Madison: University of Wisconsin Press, 1990) pp. 119–46.

Cristine Levenduski, *Peculiar Power: A Quaker Woman Preacher in Eighteenth Century America* (Washington, DC: Smithsonian, 1996).

William Scheick, "Logonomic Conflict in Hanson's Captivity Narrative and Ashbridge's Autobiography," *Eighteenth Century: Theory and Interpretation*, Spring, 37, 1 (1996) pp. 3–21.

FROM *SOME ACCOUNT OF THE FORE PART OF THE LIFE OF ELIZABETH ASHBRIDGE . . .* [1]

{The end of Ashbridge's indenture}

So when I had Served near three years, I bought off the remainder of my Time & then took to my Needle, by which I could maintain my Self handsomely: but, alas, I was not Sufficiently Punished; I had got released from one cruel Servitude and then not Contented got into another, and this for Life. A few months after, I married a young man that fell in Love with me for my Dancing, a Poor Motive for a man to Choose a Wife, or a Woman a Husband. But for my Part I fell in Love with nothing I saw in him and it seems unaccountable that I who had refused several, both in this Country & Ireland, at Last married a man I had no Value for.

In a few Days after we were Married he took me from [New] York. Being a Schoolmaster he had hired in the Country to keep school; he led me to New England and there settled in a place called Westerly in Rhode Island Government. With regard to Religion he was much like my Self, without any, and when in Drink would use the worst of Oaths. I do not mention this to

---

[1]   The text, with slight modification, is from "Some Account of the Fore Part of the Life of Elizabeth Ashbridge," ed. Daniel B. Shea, *Journeys in New Worlds: Early American* *Women's Narratives*, ed. William L. Andrews (Madison: University of Wisconsin Press, 1990).

Expose my husband; but to Shew the Effect it had on me, for I now saw my Self ruined as I thought, being joined to a man I had no Love for & that was a Pattern of no good to me; then I began to think what a Couple we were, like two joining hands and going to destruction, & there upon Concluded if I was not forsaken of heaven to alter my Course of Life. But to Set my Affections upon the Divine being & not Love my husband seemed Impossible: therefore I Daily Desired with Tears that my Affections might be in a right manner set upon my husband, and can say in a little time my Love was Sincere to him.

I now resolved to do my Duty to God; & Expecting I must come to the knowledge of it by the Scriptures I took to reading them with a Resolution to follow their Directions, but the more I read the more uneasy I grew, especially about Baptism; for altho' I had reason to believe I had been Sprinkled in my Infancy, because at the age of Thirteen I Passed under the Bishop's hands for Confirmation (as twas Called) yet I could not find any Precedent for that Practice & lighting on that place where it is said, "he that believes & is Baptized" &C.[2], here I observed Belief went before Baptism, which I was not Capable of when Sprinkled: hence grew much Dissatisfied, & Living in a Neighborhood that were mostly Seventh day Baptists[3], I Conversed much with them. At Length thinking it my Real Duty, I was In the Winter time Baptised by one of their Teachers, but Did not joyn Strictly with them, tho' I began to think the Seventh Day was the true Sabbath, & for some time kept it. My husband Did not Oppose me, for he saw I grew more Affectionate to him. I did not Leave off Singing & Dancing so, but that I could divert him when he'd ask me. But I did not find that Satisfaction in what I had done as I Expected.

Soon after this my husband and I concluded to go for England & for that End went to Boston & there found a Ship bound for Liverpool. We agreed for our Passage & Expected to Sail in two Weeks:– but my time was not to go yet, for there Came a Gentleman who hired the ship to Carry him & his Attendance to Philadelphia & to take no other Passengers; & there being no other Ship near Sailing we for that time gave it out. We stayed Several weeks in Boston, & I still continued Dissatisfied as to Religion; tho' I had reformed my Conduct so as to be accounted by those that knew me a sober Woman yet was not Content, for Even then I expected to find the Sweets of Such a Change, & though several thought me Religious, I did not think so my Self, but what to Do to be so was an utter Stranger. I used to Converse with People of all societies as Opportunity offer'd and like many others had got a Pretty Deal of Head Knowledge, & Several Societies thought me of their Opinions severally; But I joined Strictly with none, resolving never to leave Searching till I had found the truth: this was in the Twenty Second year of my age.

While we were in Boston I one Day went into the Quaker meeting not Expecting to find what I wanted, but out of Curiosity. At this Meeting there was a Woman friend spoke, at which I was a Little surprised, for tho' I had heard of Women's preaching I had never heard one before. I looked on her with Pity for her Ignorance (as I thought) & Contempt of her Practise, saying to my self, "I am sure you are a fool, for if ever I should turn Quaker, which will never be, I would not be a preacher." – In these and such like thoughts, I sat while She was Speaking; after she had done there Stood up a man, which I could better Bear. He spoke well & I thought raised sound Doctrine from good Joshua's resolution (Viz) "as for me and my house we will serve the Lord," &C.[4] After he had sat silent a while he went to prayer, which

---

[2]   "He who believes and is baptized shall be saved, but he who does not believe shall be condemned" (Mark 16:16).

[3]   Also known as "Dunkers," from their ritual of baptism by immersion or "dunking." They came over in the 1730s

and 40s and settled in Pennsylvania, and eventually joined the Moravian religious community.

[4]   Joshua 24:15.

was something so awful & Affecting as drew tears from my Eyes yet a Stranger to the Cause.

Soon after this we Left Boston, & my husband being Given to ramble, which was very Disagreeable to me, but I must submit, we Came to Rhode Island by Water, from thence to the East End of Long Island, where we hired to keep School. This Place was mostly Settled with Presbyterians. I soon got Acquainted with some of the most Religious of them, for tho' I was poor yet was favored with Reception amongst People of the Best Credit, & had frequent Discourses with them, but the more I was acquainted, the worse I liked their Opinions, so Remained Dissatisfy'd; . . .

My Husband soon hired further up the Island where we were nearer a Church of England to which I used to go, for tho' I Disliked some of their ways, yet I liked them best; but now a fresh Exercise fell upon me, and of such a Sort as I had never heard of any being in the like, & while under it I thought my self alone. – I was in the Second month sitting by a fire in Company with Several, my Husband also present; there arose a Thunder Gust, & with the Noise that struck my Ear, a voice attended, even as the Sound of a mighty Trumpet, piercing thro' me with these words, "O! Eternity, Eternity, the Endless term of Long Eternity:" at which I was Exceedingly Surprised, sitting speechless as in a trance, and in a moment saw my Self in such a state as made me Despair of ever being in a happy one. I seemed to see a Long Roll wrote in Black Characters, at sight whereof I heard a Voice say to me, "this is thy Sins;" I then saw Sin to be Exceeding Sinful, but this was not all, for Immediately followed another Saying, "and the Blood of Christ is not Sufficient to wash them out; this is shewn thee that thou mays't Confess thy Damnation is just & not in order that they should be forgiven."

All this while I sat Speechless; at Last I got up trembling, & threw my self on a Bed: the Company thought my Indisposition proceeded only from a fright at the Thunder, but Alas, it was of another kind, and from that time for several months I was in the utmost Despair, and if any time I would endeavor to hope or lay hold of any Gracious promise, the old Accuser would Come in, telling me, it was now too Late, I had withstood the day of Mercy till it was over, & that I should add to my Sins by praying for Pardon & provoke Divine Vengeance to make a Monument of Wrath of me. I was like one already in torment; my Sleep Departed from me, I Eat little, I became extremely melancholy, and took no delight in any thing. Had all the world been mine & the Glory of it, I would now have Gladly a given it for one glimpse of hope; My husband was Shock'd, to See me so changed, I that once Could divert him with a Song (in which he greatly delighted), nay after I grew Religious as to the outward, could now Do it no longer. My Singing now was turned into mourning & my Dancing into Lamentations: My Nights and Days were one Continual Scene of Sorrows: I let none know my Desperate Condition – My husband used all means in his power to divert my Melancholy, but in vain, the wound was too Deep to be healed with any thing short of the true Balm of Gilead[5]. I Durst not go much alone for fear of Evil Spirits, but when I did my husband would not Suffer it, & if I took the Bible, he would take it from me saying, "how you are altered, you used to be agreeable Company but now I have no Comfort of you." I endeavored to bear all with Patience, expecting soon to bear more than man could inflict upon me.

At Length I went to the Priest to see if he Could relieve me, but he was a Stranger to my Case: he advised me to take the Sacrament & use some innocent diversions, and lent me a Book of prayers, which he said was fit for my Condition, but all was in Vain. As to the Sacrament, I thought my Self in a State very unfit to receive it worthily, and could not use the Prayers, for I then thought if Ever my Prayers would be acceptable, I should be enabled to pray without

---

[5] Literally, an ointment, but figuratively, a spiritual anointing suggesting conversion. See Jeremiah 46:11: "Go up to Gilead and take balm, O virgin daughter of Egypt! In vain you have used many medicines; there is no healing for you."

form. Diversions were burdensome, for as I said above, my husband used all means tending that way to no Purpose, yet he with some others once persuaded me to go to the Raising of a building (where such Company were Collected) in Expectation of Alleviating my grief, but contrariwise it proved a means of adding to my Sorrow: for in the mean time there came an officer to summon a jury to Inquire concerning the Body of a man that had hanged himself which as soon as I understood seemed to be attended with a Voice saying, "thou shall be the next Monument of such Wrath, for thou art not worthy to Die a natural Death," and for Two Months was Daily tempted to destroy myself and some times so strong that I could hardly resist, thro' fear of that sort when I went alone, I used to throw off my apron & garters, & if I had a knife cast it from me Crying, "Lord keep me from taking that Life thou gave, and which thou Would have made happy if I had on my Part joined with the Offers of Thy Grace, and had regarded the Convictions attending me from my youth: the fault is my own, thou O Lord art clear;" & yet so great was my Agony that I desired Death that I might know the worst of my Torments, of which I had so sharp a foretaste. All this while I Could not shed a Tear; my heart was as hard as a Stone & my life Miserable, but God that's full of Mercy and Long forbearance, in his own good time delivered my Soul out of this Thralldom. . . .

I now began to think of my Relations in Pennsylvania whom I had not yet seen; and having a great Desire that way, Got Leave of my Husband to go & also a Certificate from the Priest on Long Island in order that if I made any stay, I might be receiv'd as a Member wherever I came . . .

Hence I came to Trenton [New Jersey] Ferry, where I met with no small Mortification upon hearing that my Relations were Quakers, & what was the worst of all my Aunt a Preacher. I was Sorry to hear it, for I was Exceedingly prejudiced against these People & have often wondered with what face they Could Call them Selves Christians. I Repented my Coming and had a mind to have turned back. At Last I Concluded to go & see them since I was so far on my journey, but Expected little Comfort from my Visit. But see how God brings unforeseen things to Pass, for by my going there I was brought to my Knowledge of his Truth – I went from Trenton to Philadelphia by Water, thence to my Uncle's on Horseback, where I met with very kind reception; for tho' my Uncle was dead and my Aunt married again, yet both her husband and She received me in a very kind manner.

I had not been there three Hours before I met with a Shock, & my opinion began to alter with respect to these People. – For seeing a Book lying on the Table (& being much for reading) I took it up: My Aunt Observing said, "Cousin that is a Quakers' Book," for Perceiving I was not a Quaker, I suppose she thought I would not like it: I made her no answer but revolving in my mind, "what can these People write about, for I have heard that they Deny the Scriptures & have no other bible but George Fox's Journal[6], & Deny all the holy Ordinances?" So resolved to read, but had not read two Pages before my very heart burned within me and Tears Issued from my Eyes, which I was Afraid would be seen; therefore with the Book . . . walked into the garden, sat Down, and the piece being Small, read it through before I went in; but Some Times was forced to Stop to Vent my Tears, my heart as it were uttering these involuntary Expressions; "my God must I (if ever I come to the true knowledge of thy Truth) be of this man's Opinion, who has sought thee as I have done & join with these People that a few hours ago I preferred the Papists before? O thou, the God of my Salvation & of my life, who hast in an abundant manner manifested thy Long Suffering & tender Mercy, Redeeming me as from the Lowest Hell, a Monument of thy grace: Lord, my soul beseecheth thee to Direct

---

[6]   George Fox (1624–91), English founder of the Society of Friends. His *Journal*, published in 1694, recounted the persecutions he suffered for his beliefs and served as a model for Quakers and other religious non-conformists.

me in the right way & keep me from Error, and then According to thy Covenant, I'll think nothing too near to Part with for thy names Sake. If these things be so, Oh! happy People thus beloved of God."

After I came a little to my Self again I washed my face least any in the House should perceive I had been weeping. But this night got but Little Sleep, for the old Enemy began to Suggest that I was one of those that wavered & was not Steadfast in the faith, advancing several Texts of Scripture against me & them, as, in the Latter Days there should be those that would deceive the very Elect[7]: & these were they, & that I was in danger of being deluded. Here the Subtle Serpent transformed himself so hiddenly that I verily believed this to be a timely Caution from a good Angel – so resolved to beware of the Deceiver, & for Some weeks Did not touch any of their Books . . .

In a few weeks there was an afternoon's Meeting held at my Uncle's to which came that Servant of the Lord William Hammans who was made then Instrumental to the Convincing me of the truth more Perfectly, & helping me over Some great Doubts: tho' I believe no one did ever sit in Greater opposition than I did when he first stood up; but I was soon brought Down for he preached the Gospel with such Power I was forced to give up & Confess it was the truth. As soon as meeting Ended I Endeavored to get alone, for I was not fit to be seen, I being So broken; yet afterward the Restless adversary assaulted me again, on this wise. In the morning before this meeting, I had been Disputing with my Uncle about Baptism, which was the subject this good Man Dwelt upon, which was handled so Clearly as to answer all my Scruples beyond all objection: yet the Crooked Serpent alleged that the Sermon that I had heard did not proceed from divine Revelation but that my Uncle and Aunt had acquainted the friend of me; which being Strongly Suggested, I fell to Accusing them with it, of which they both cleared themselves saying they had not seen him Since my Coming into these Parts until he came into the meeting. I then Concluded he was a messenger sent of God to me, & with fervent Cryes Desired I might be Directed a right and now Laid aside all Prejudice & set my heart open to receive the truth in the Love of it. And the Lord in his own good time revealed to my Soul not only the Beauty there is in truth, & how those should shine that continue faithful to it, but also the Emptiness of all shadows, which in the day were Glorious, but now he the Son of Glory was come to put an end to them all, & to Establish Everlasting Righteousness in the room thereof, which is a work in the Soul. He likewise let me see that all I had gone through was to prepare me for this Day & that the time was near that he would require me to go forth & declare to others what he the God of Mercy had done for my Soul; at which I was surprised and begged to be excused for fear I should bring dishonor to the truth, and cause his Holy name to be Evil spoken of.

All the while, I never Let any know the Condition I was in, nor did I appear like a Friend, & fear'd a Discovery. I now began to think of returning to my husband but found a restraint to stay where I was. I then Hired to keep School & hearing of a place for him, wrote desiring him to come to me, but Let him know nothing how it was with me. I loved to go to meetings, but did not like to be seen to go on week days, and therefore to shun it used to go from my school through the woods, but notwithstanding all my care the Neighbors that were not friends began to revile me, calling me Quaker, saying they supposed I intended to be a fool and turn Preacher; I then receiv'd the same censure that I (a little above a year before) had Passed on one of the handmaids of the Lord at Boston, & so weak was I, alas! I could not bear the reproach, &

---

[7]   "For false Christs and false prophets will arise, and will show great signs and wonders, so as to lead astray if possible, even the elect" (Matthew 24:24).

in order to Change their Opinions got into greater Excess in Apparel than I had freedom to Wear for some time before I came Acquainted with Friends.[8]

In this Condition I continued till my Husband came, & then began the Tryal of my Faith. Before he reached me he heard I was turned Quaker, at which he stampt, saying, "I'd rather heard She had been dead as well as I Love her, for if so, all my comfort is gone." He then came to me & had not seen me before for four Months. I got up & met him saying, "My Dear, I am glad to see thee," at which he flew in a Passion of anger & said, "the Divel thee thee, don't thee me."[9] I used all the mild means I could to pacify him, & at Length got him fit to go & Speak to my Relations, but he was Alarmed, and as soon as we got alone said, "so I see your Quaker relations have made you one." I told him they had not, which was true, nor had I ever told him how it was with me: but he would have it that I was one, & therefore would not let me stay among them; & having found a place to his mind, hired and came Directly back to fetch me hence, & in one afternoon walked near thirty Miles to keep me from Meeting, the next Day being first Day[10]; & on the Morrow took me to the Afforesaid Place & hired Lodgings at a churchman's house; who was one of the Wardens, & a bitter Enemy to Friends & used to Do all he could to irritate my Husband against them, & would tell me abundance of Ridiculous Stuff; but my Judgment was too Clearly convinced to believe it.

I still did not appear like a Friend, but they all believed I was one. When my Husband and he Used to be making their Diversion & reviling, I used to sit in silence, but now and then an involuntary sigh would break from me: at which he would tell my husband: "there, did not I tell you that your wife was a Quaker; & She will be a preacher." Upon which My Husband once in a Great rage came up to me, & Shaking his hand over me, said, "you had better be hanged in that Day." I then, Peter like[11], in a panic denied my being a Quaker, at which great horror seized upon me, which Continued near three Months: so that I again feared that by Denying the Lord that Bought me, the heavens were Shut against me; for great Darkness Surrounded, & I was again plunged into Despair. I used to Walk much alone in the Wood, where no Eye saw nor Ear heard, & there Lament my miserable Condition, & have often gone from Morning till Night and have not broke my Fast.

Thus I was brought so Low that my Life was a burden to me; the Devil seem'd to Vaunt that tho' the Sins of my youth were forgiven, yet now he was sure of Me, for that I had Committed the unpardonable Sin & Hell inevitable would be my portion, & my Torment would be greater than if I had hanged my Self at first. . .

{They remove to Freehold, New Jersey}

Here According to my Desire we Settled; my husband got one School & I the Other, & took a Room at a Friend's house a Mile from Each School and Eight Miles from the Meeting House: – before next first day we were got to our new Settlement: & now Concluded to Let my husband to see I was determined to joyn with Friends. When first day Came I directed my Self to him in this manner, "My Dear, art thou willing to let me go to a Meeting?," at which he flew into a rage, saying, "No you can't." I then Drew up my resolution & told him as a Dutyful Wife ought, So I was ready to obey all his Lawfull Commands, but where they Imposed upon

---

[8] The Society of Friends adopted a simple form of dress, usually in gray, that stood in stark contrast especially to the colorful and complicated women's fashions of the times and was, thus, easily recognized.

[9] Quakers used the familiar forms of address, *thee* and *thou*, to indicate an equality among all people.

[10] Quakers referred to the days of the week and the months of the year by numbers to avoid the conventional names which refer to pagan deities and mythological figures.

[11] Like the Apostle Peter, who denied Christ three times.

my Conscience, I no longer Durst: For I had already done it too Long, & wronged my Self by it, & tho' he was near & I loved him as a Wife ought, yet God was nearer than all the World to me, & had made me sensible this was the way I ought to go, the which I Assured him was no Small Cross to my own will, yet had Given up My Heart, & hoped that he that Called for it would Enable me the residue of my Life to keep it steadily devoted to him, whatever I Suffered for it, adding I hoped not to make him any the worse Wife for it. But all I could Say was in vain; he was Inflexible & Would not Consent.

I had now put my hand to the Plough, & resolved not to Look back, so went without Leave; but Expected to be immediately followed and forced back, but he did not: I went to one of the neighbors and got a Girl to Show me the way, then went on rejoicing & Praising God in my heart, who had thus far given me Power and another Opportunity to Confess to his Truth. Thus for some time I had to go Eight Miles on foot to Meetings, which I never thought hard; My Husband soon bought a Horse, but would not Let me ride him, neither when my Shoes were worn out would he Let me have a new Pair, thinking by that means to keep me from going to Meetings, but this did not hinder me, for I have taken Strings & tyed round to keep them on.

He finding no hard Usage could alter my resolution, neither threatening to beat me, nor doing it, for he several times Struck me with sore Blows, which I Endeavored to bear with Patience, believing the time would Come when he would see I was in the right (which he Accordingly Did), he once came up to me & took out his pen knife saying, "if you offer to go to Meeting tomorrow, with this knife I'll cripple you, for you shall not be a Quaker." I made him no Answer, but when Morning came, set out as Usual & he was not Suffered to hurt me. In Despair of recovering me himself, he now flew to the Priest for help and told him I had been a very Religious Woman in the way of the Church of England, was a member of it, and had a good Certificate from Long Island, but now was bewitched and turn'd Quaker, which almost broke his heart. He therefore Desired as he was one who had the Care of souls, he would Come and pay me a Visit and use his Endeavors to reclaim me & hoped by the Blessing of God it would be done. The Priest Consented to Come, the time was Set, which was to be that Day two Weeks, for he said he could not come Sooner. My Husband Came home extremely pleased, and told me of it, at which I smiled saying, "I hope to be enabled to give him a reason for the hope that is in me," at the same time believing the Priest would never Trouble me (nor ever did).

Before his Appointed time came it was required of me in a more Publick manner to Confess to the world what I was and to give up in Prayer in a Meeting, the sight of which & the power that attended it made me Tremble, & I could not hold my Self still. I now again desired Death & would have freely given up my Natural Life a Ransom; & what made it harder to me I was not yet taken under the care of Friends, & what kept me from requesting it was for fear I might be overcome & bring a Scandal on the Society. I begged to be Excused till I was joined to Friends & then I would give up freely, to which I receiv'd this Answer, as tho' I had heard a Distinct Voice: "I am a Covenant keeping God, and the word that I spoke to thee when I found thee In Distress, even that I would never leave thee nor forsake thee if thou would be obedient to what I should make known to thee, I will Assuredly make good: but if thou refuse, my Spirit shall not always strive; fear not, I will make way for thee through all thy difficulties, which shall be many for my names Sake, but be thou faithful & I will give thee a Crown of Life." I being then Sure it was God that Spoke said, "thy will O God, be done, I am in thy hand; do with me according to thy Word," & gave up. But after it was over the Enemy came in like a flood, telling me I had done what I ought not, & Should now bring Dishonor to this People. This gave me a Little Shock, but it did not at this time Last Long.

This Day as Usual I had gone on foot. My husband (as he afterwards told me) lying on the Bed at home, these Words ran thro' him, "Lord where shall I fly to shun thee &C.,"[12] upon which he arose and seeing it Rain got his horse and Came to fetch me; and Coming just as the Meeting broke up, I got on horseback as quick as possible, least he Should hear what had happened. Nevertheless he heard of it, and as soon as we were got into the woods he began, saying, "What do you mean thus to make my Life unhappy? What, could you not be a Quaker without turning fool after this manner?" I Answered in Tears saying, "my Dear, look on me with Pity, if thou hast any. Can'st thou think, that I in the Bloom of my Days, would bear all that thou knowest of & a great deal more that thou knowest not of if I did not believe it to be my Duty?" This took hold of him, & taking my hand he said, "Well, I'll E'en give you up, for I see it don't avail to Strive. If it be of God I can't over throw it, & if it be of yourself it will soon fall." I saw tears stand in his Eyes, at which my heart was overcome with joy, & I would not have Changed Conditions with a Queen.

I already began to reap the fruits of my Obedience, but my Tryal Ended not here, the time being up that the Priest was to come; but no Priest Appeared. My Husband went to fetch him, but he would not come, saying he was busy; which, so Displeased my husband, that he'd never go to hear him more, & for Some time went to no place of Worship. – Now the Unwearied adversary found out another Scheme, and with it wrought so Strong that I thought all I had gone through but a little to this: It came upon me in such an unexpected manner, in hearing a Woman relate a book she had read in which it was Asserted that Christ was not the son of God. As soon as She had Spoke these words, if a man had spoke I could not have more distinctly heard these words, "no more he is, it's all a fancy & the Contrivance of men," & an horror of Great Darkness fell upon me, which Continued for three weeks.

The Exercise I was under I am not Able to Express, neither durst I let any know how it was with me. I again sought Desolate Places where I might make my moan, & have Lain whole nights, & don't know that my Eyes were Shut to Sleep. I again thought my self alone, but would not let go my Faith in him, often saying in my heart, "I'll believe till I Die," & kept a hope that he that had Delivered me out of the Paw of the Bear & out of the jaws of the Devouring Lion, would in his own time Deliver me out of his temptation also; which he in Mercy Did, and let me see that this was for my good, in order to Prepare me for future Service which he had for me to Do & that it was Necessary his Ministers should be dipt into all States, that thereby they might be able to Speak to all Conditions, for which my Soul was thankful to him, the God of Mercies, who had at Several times redeemed me from great distress, & I found the truth of his Words, that all things should work together for good to those that Loved and feared him, which I did with my whole heart & hope ever shall while I have a being. This happened just after my first appearance, & Friends had not been to talk with me, nor did they know well what to do till I had appeared again, which was not for some time, when the Monthly Meeting appointed four Friends to give me a Visit, which I was Glad of; and gave them such Satisfaction, that they left me well Satisfy'd. I then joined with Friends.

My Husband still went to no place of Worship. One day he said, "I'd go to Meeting, only I am afraid I shall hear you Clack, which I cannot bear." I used no persuasions, yet when Meeting time Came, he got the horse, took me behind him & went to Meeting: but for several months if he saw me offer to rise, he would go out, till once I got up before he was aware & then (as he afterwards said) he was ashamed to go, and from that time never did, nor hindered me from going to Meetings. And tho' he (poor man) did not take up the Cross, yet his judgment was Convinced: & sometimes in a flood of tears would say, "My Dear, I have seen the

---

12 Psalm 139:7.

Beauty there is in the Truth, & that thou art in the Right, and I Pray God Preserve thee in it. But as for me the Cross is too heavy, I cannot Bear it." I told him, I hoped he that had given me strength Would also favor him: "O!" said he, "I can't bear the Reproach thou Doest, to be Called turncoat & to become a Laughing Stock to the World; but I'll no Longer hinder thee," which I looked on as a great favor, that my way was thus far made easy, and a little hope remained that my Prayers would be heard on his account.

In this Place he had got linked in with some, that he was afraid would make game of him, which Indeed they already Did, asking him when he Designed to Commence Preacher, for that they saw he intended to turn Quaker, & seemed to Love his Wife better since she did than before (we were now got to a little house by our Selves which though Mean, and little to put in it, our Bed no better than Chaff, yet I was truly Content & did not Envy the Rich their Riches; the only Desire I had now was my own preservation, & to be Bless'd with the Reformation of my husband). These men used to Come to our house & there Provoke my husband to Sit up and Drink, some times till near day, while I have been sorrowing in a Stable. As I once sat in this Condition I heard my husband say to his Company, "I can't bear any Longer to Afflict my Poor Wife in this manner, for whatever you may think of her, I do believe she is a good Woman," upon which he came to me and said, "Come in, my Dear; God has Given thee a Deal of Patience. I'll put an End to this Practice;" and so he did, for this was the Last time they sat up at Night.

My Husband now thought that if he was in any Place where it was not known that he'd been so bitter against Friends, he Could do better than here. But I was much against his Moving; fearing it would tend to his hurt, having been for some months much Altered for the Better, & would often in a broken and Affectionate Manner condemn his bad Usage to me: I told him I hoped it had been for my Good, even to the Better Establishing me in the Truth, & therefore would not have him to be Afflicted about it, & According to the Measure of Grace received did what I could both by Example & Advice for his good: and my advice was for him to fight thro' here, fearing he would Grow Weaker and the Enemy Gain advantage over him, if he thus fled: but All I could say did not prevail against his Moving; & hearing of a place at Bordentown [New Jersey] went there, but that did not suit; he then Moved to Mount Holly [New Jersey] & there we Settled. He got a good School & So Did I.

Here we might have Done very well; we soon got our house Prettily furnished for Poor folks; I now began to think I wanted but one thing to complete my Happiness, Viz. the Reformation of my husband, which Alas! I had too much reason to Doubt; for it fell out according to my Fears, & he grew worse here, & took much to Drinking, so that it Seemed as if my Life was to be a Continual scene of Sorrows & most Earnestly I Pray'd to Almighty God to Endue me with Patience to bear my Afflictions & submit to his Providence, which I can say in Truth I did without murmuring or ever uttering an unsavory expression to the Best of my Knowledge; except once, my husband Coming home a little in drink (in which frame he was very fractious) & finding me at Work by a Candle, came to me, put it out & fetching me a box on the Ear said, "you don't Earn your light;" on which unkind Usage (for he had not struck me for Two Years so it went hard with me) I utter'd these Rash Expressions, "thou art a Vile Man," & was a little angry, but soon recovered & was Sorry for it; he struck me again, which I received without so much as a word in return, & that likewise Displeased him: so he went on in a Distracted like manner uttering Several Expressions that bespoke Despair, as that he now believed that he was predestined to damnation, & he did not care how soon God would Strike him Dead, & the like. I durst say but Little; at Length in the Bitterness of my Soul, I Broke out in these Words, "Lord look Down on mine Afflictions and deliver me by some means or Other." I was answered, I Should Soon be, & so I was, but in such a manner, as I Verily thought It would have killed me – in a little time he went to Burlington where he got in Drink, & Enlisted him Self to go a Common soldier to Cuba anno 1740.

I had drank many bitter Cups – but this Seemed to Exceed them all for indeed my very Senses Seemed Shaken; I now a Thousand times blamed my Self for making Such an unadvised request, fearing I had Displeased God in it, & tho' he had Granted it, it was in Displeasure, & Suffered to be in this manner to Punish me; Tho' I can truly say I never Desired his Death, no more than my own, nay not so much. I have since had cause to believe his mind was benefited by the Undertaking, (which hope makes up for all I have Suffered from him) being Informed he did in the army what he Could not Do at home (Viz) Suffered for the Testimony of Truth. When they Came to prepare for an Engagement he refused to fight; for which he was whipt and brought before the General, who asked him why he Enlisted if he would not fight; "I did it," said he, "in a drunken frolic, when the Divel had the Better of me, but my judgment is convinced that I ought not, neither will I whatever I Suffer; I have but one Life, & you may take that if you Please, but I'll never take up Arms."[13] – They used him with much Cruelty to make him yield but Could not, by means whereof he was So Disabled that the General sent him to the Hospital at Chelsea[14], where in Nine Months time he Died & I hope made a Good End, for which I prayed both night & Day, till I heard of his Death.

Thus I thought it my duty to say what I could in his Favor, as I have been obliged to say so much of his hard usage to me, all which I hope Did me Good, & altho' he was so bad, yet had Several Good Properties, & I never thought him the Worst of Men. He was one I Lov'd & had he let Religion have its Perfect work, I should have thought my Self Happy in the Lowest State of Life; & I've Cause to bless God, who Enabled me in the Station of a Wife to Do my Duty & now a Widow to Submit to his Will, always believing everything he does to be right. May he in all Stations of Life so Preserve me by the arm of Divine Power, that I may never forget his tender mercies to me, the Remembrance whereof doth often Bow my Soul, in Humility before his Throne, saying, "Lord, what was I; that thou should have reveal'd to me the Knowledge of thy Truth, & do so much for me, who Deserved thy Displeasure rather, But in me hast thou shewn thy Long Suffering & tender Mercy; may thou O God be Glorified and I abased for it is thy own Works that praise thee, and of a Truth to the humble Soul thou Makest every bitter thing Sweet. – The End.–

after 1742   1774

Alonso Carrió de la Vandera (1715?–?)

The authorship of *El Lazarillo: A Guide for Inexperienced Travelers*, one of the most fascinating travel books of eighteenth century South America, has been the subject of debate for many years. Published clandestinely in Lima in 1775–6, it was falsely dated 1773. The book is purportedly the narrative of an Indian, Calixto Bustamante Carlos Inca, nicknamed Concolorcorvo (Crow-Colored), relating the travels of the Spanish postal commissioner Alonso Carrió de la Vandera from Uruguay to Perú and describing the customs of people met along the way. Recent scholarship, however, has established that the book was authored by Carrió de la Vandera himself, and that for some reason

---

[13] Quakers were also pacifists, and Sullivan's refusal to fight is his expression, finally, of Quaker principles, for which he also suffers abuse and death.

[14] In present day London, England.

he did not wish for his identity to be divulged.

Carrió's text, with its vivid descriptions of colonial Perú, follows many of the conventions of the Spanish picaresque novel, including its themes of marginality and anticlericalism. The work is dedicated to the people it describes: the travelers, guided by *lazarillos* or rogues, and "lazy persons of sedentary exercise," mostly Europeans. Though Carrió's portrayals of Indians are for the most part negative in tone (and at times disturbingly racist), he is no less scathing about Spaniards, whom he characterizes as effete and extravagant. In the dialogues between the Inspector (Carrió himself) and the Inca Calixto Bustamante Carlos Inca, the reader can observe the emergence of a Creole identity, with all its ambiguities and contradictions.

PRIMARY WORK

Concolorcorvo, *El Lazarillo: A Guide for Inexperienced Travelers between Buenos Aires and Lima, 1773*, trans. Walter D. Kline (Bloomington: Indiana University Press, 1965).

FURTHER READING

Mariselle Melendez, "The Reevaluation of the Image of the Mestizo in El lazarillo de ciegos caminantes," *Indiana Journal of Hispanic Literatures*, Spring, 2, 2 (1994) pp. 171–84.

Mariselle Melendez, "Sexuality and Hybridity in El lazarillo de ciegos caminantes," *Latin American Literary Review*, Jan–June, 24, 47 (1996) pp. 41–57.

Ruth Hill, "Transatlantic Rebuke of Rationalism: Subtext and Sources in El lazarillo de ciegos caminantes," *Dieciocho: Hispanic Enlightenment*, Fall, 21, 2 (1998) pp. 167–79.

EL LAZARILLO: A GUIDE FOR INEXPERIENCED TRAVELERS . . .

Prologue and Dedication to Those Treated Herein

Just as weighty writers, such as Mr Lead, and even those of a lighter vein, e.g., Mr Cork, direct their lengthy prologues to wise, prudent, and pious men, perhaps to be exonerated from their criticism, I, inasmuch as I am a fish between two waters, that is, neither as ponderous as the first group nor of as little weight as the second, direct mine to people who are commonly called rowdies or querulous sorts, whether they use the sword, carbine, or pistol, or are adept with the boles, horn cup, and lasso. I speak, finally, to the tired, thirsty, and dusty travelers, detaining them a short time,

> By way of epitaph
> On their sepulchre,
> Pantheon or cenotaph.

Although my principal purpose is to address travelers, I shall not refrain from speaking occasionally to the lazy persons of sedentary exercise, and particularly to those from across the sea, wherefore I beg the men from those shores to overlook all those matters in the kingdom which may be better omitted because of their notoriety.

It is well known here that we half breeds respect the Spaniards as sons of the Sun, and thus I have not the courage (although I am descended from royal blood in a line as straight as a rainbow) to threaten my readers with the lack of respect customarily shown by the more contemptible writers; therefore, when the title *señor* or *caballero* does not serve the purpose, I put a V[1] so that everyone might accord himself the treatment which he deserves or which his fantasy dictates.

---

[1]   The initial letter of Vuesamerced, Vuecencia (Your Grace, Your Excellency) and other possible titles.

. . . I am a pure Indian, except for my mother's deceits, for which I am not responsible. Two of my cousins, princesses of royal birth, preserve their virginity, to their regret, in a convent in Cuzco where our king maintains them. I find myself ambitious to obtain the job of beadle[2] in Cuzco's Cathedral, in order to enjoy ecclesiastical immunity, and in securing that appointment, my authorship of this travelogue will be useful because, though God and my conscience compel me to acknowledge that I had the help of others in writing it, people who in their leisure moments whispered in my ear, and was aided by a certain monk of San Juan de Dios who supplied the Latin tags, I am largely responsible for padding out in paraphrase what the Inspector Don Alonso Carrió told me in fewer words. Imitating his style, I mixed in some amusing bits in order to entertain the traveler for whom I particularly wrote. I'll see to it that the substance of my trip be reduced to a hundred octave pages. Into less than a quarter of that amount did the Inspector compress the essential part, as can be seen in the rough draft that is still in my possession, but that sort of brief account does not instruct the public that has not seen those vast countries and therefore cannot understand what may be found there. I keep close to the truth. The great cosmographer, Dr Cosme Bueno[3], at the end of his annual report, gave a general idea of the kingdom, dealing individually with each bishopric. This is a work truly useful and necessary to help provide a complete history of this vast viceregency.

If the time and erudition wasted by the great Pedro de Peralta in his *Lima Founded* and *Spain Vindicated*[4] had been devoted to composing a civil and natural history of Peru, I do not doubt that he would have acquired more fame, besides giving luster and splendor to the whole monarchy, but most men are inclined to prefer events in a far-away country, while completely overlooking what is happening in their own country. I am not implying that Peralta y Barnuevo did not know the history of this kingdom; I only condemn his choice from what I heard mentioned by wise men.

Arriving one afternoon at the countryhouse of a Tucuman gentleman, with the Inspector and the rest of his company, we noticed that the host talked in a very odd manner and asked strange questions. On his table were four very tattered books with worn bindings. One was about the trip to China made by Fernan Mendez Pinto[5]; one was "The Theatre of the Gods," and the third was a short history of Charlemagne and his Twelve Peers of France. The fourth was Perez de Hita's "Civil Wars of Granada."[6] The Inspector, who was the one leafing through these books and who had read them with great pleasure during his youth, praised his host's library, then asked him if he had read other books. The good gentleman replied that he knew them by heart but in order not to forget their contents, he read them daily because one ought to read only a few books and pick out the best. Observing the extravagance of this good man, the Inspector asked him if he knew the name of the present King of Spain and the Indies; to which the gentleman answered that his name was Charles III, as he well knew because he had heard him mentioned in the Governor's proclamation. He added that he had also heard that he was a fine gentleman, of cape and sword.

"And the name of this fine gentleman's father," the Inspector continued. "What was his name?"

To this the gentleman answered promptly that naturally everybody knew that. The Inspector, remembering the response of a wise Frenchman, persisted in inquiring about the name,

---

[2] An official whose duty it is to keep order in church.

[3] Cosme Bueno was an eighteenth-century Peruvian scientist who served as royal cosmographer from 1757 to 1798.

[4] Pedro de Peralta, Peruvian scientist, historian and poet, author of *Lima fundada* (1732), a Baroque epic poem about the founding of Lima, and *Historia de España vindicada* (1730).

[5] Probably a Spanish translation of *Peregrinação*, by the Portuguese writer Fernão Mendes Pinto.

[6] A sixteenth-century work dealing with the fall of Granada and the war against the Moors.

and the gentleman answered at once that it was Charles II, actually his great grandfather. He could furnish no details of his own country beyond seven or eight leagues round about, and what he did tell was so imperfect and distorted that it seemed the delirium of dream of a man half asleep.

I was going to continue my Prologue but about this time the Inspector said he wanted to read it. He told me it was plenty long for the book, and if I made it much longer, people would say this about it:

> "The architect is a fool or boor
> Whose building's eclipsed by the size of the door."

Or a proverb that says about the same thing:

> "A house in the mountains, the work of a nut,
> With a fancy facade and behind it, a hut."

"I don't believe, don Alonso," said I, "that my Prologue deserves such a censure because there will be a great big house." To which he replied in Latin: "Not all that is great is good, but all that is good is great."

I did not pass judgment on his Latin because the Inspector only wanted me to know that he was quoting a sentence from Tacitus[7], with which I close, putting my finger in my mouth, my pen in my inkwell, and my inkwell in the corner of my room until another trip makes its appearance, unless before then I make my final farewell to my readers.

From *Chapter XVIII: The Indolence of the Indians. The Opinion of the Author. The Name Concolorcorvo*

I had importuned the Inspector to suggest a solution to the several charges which Spaniards make reciprocally against each other about oppressing the Indians, taking away their possessions, and using them more harshly than if they were slaves. "Come now, Señor Inca. How many questions like that do you expect to ask me?" "More than two hundred," I replied. "Then go to the jail," he answered, "where there are plenty of idle birds of all kinds; there you will find a great variety of opinions, and you may accept those you deem best." "There is no idleness in jail," I answered, "because they need the time to scratch themselves and to kill their lice." "You are wrong," he told me, "because most of them eat lice, these loathsome animals, put them into a small tubular container, and when some man or woman passes near the bars and does not give them alms, they blow two hundred lice on his back, and in less than a minute they are scattered from his neck over his entire body, causing unbearable ravage, because these starving creatures are going from a sterile pasture to one of abundance. But, to shorten the discussion, I should like to hear your candid opinion about these tyrannies and extortions. Speak now as a Spaniard, but do not forget the general skepticism of the Indians."

"In good time, Señor Don Alonso, but explain to me the meaning of skepticism." "This word," he said, "means universal doubt in all matters. The Indians doubt everything. I shall illustrate with two very different examples; the first illustrates what little faith they have, and

---

7   A Roman historian of the first century AD.

the second, their scanty talent and excess of malice. Ask an Indian, instructed in the faith, if Jesus Christ is really present in the Sacred Host, and he replies, 'He probably is.' If he is asked whether a thousand sheep have been stolen from him, even though he has never had any sheep, he answers, 'They probably were.' Reconcile these two standards for me, Señor Concolorcorvo, and answer the first question I put to you." "I confess, sir," I said, "that the Indians in general have nothing worthy of being coveted by the Spaniards, because their entire wealth, speaking of the most prosperous ones, amounts to a yoke of oxen, a plow, a small hut in which they keep their meager harvest of corn and potatoes, along with all their furniture, which is scarcely worth 4 pesos, with some of them maintaining the mules provided by the *corregidor* to aid in transporting their belongings. The ordinary and lazy Indians, who occupy the larger part of the provinces, do not have one-fourth of these scanty possessions which are derived from application and work. Their house is reduced to a straw-covered hovel, called *ycho*, with a door which is entered with difficulty on all fours; their furniture corresponds, but if it were thrown into the street, it would just be picked up by another Indian servant in greater state of wretchedness. Therefore, I say that the Spaniards of this century . . ." "And all centuries," added the Inspector. ". . . had no need, and I believe they never will have, to rob the Indians, since the latter, in general, think of nothing but their leisure and drunken orgies, which are followed by other brutal acts. I affirm that my countrymen are not the ones robbed, but rather they are the robbers of the Spaniards."

"Your critique is very fine," said the inspector, "but it pointed out to me that, in the time of the native monarchs and caciques, the Indians were in worse condition, because those princes and leaders kept them reduced to an oppressive servitude since they worked their land, with the strength of their arms, for their scarce food supplies, and never knew any meat other than that of the llama, vicuña and alpaca, from the wool of which they wove their clothes. The Spaniards only did away with, or at least decreased, the abominable acts among these wretched people, and introduced the profitable use of cattle, horses, mules and sheep, iron tools for working the fields and mines, nets and hooks for taking advantage of the products and gifts from the rivers and sea, as well as an endless number of other artifices and tools for working with less discomfort."

"With what nation," I asked, "would you compare the Indians, considering the configuration of the face, the color, and their customs?" "With themselves," replied the inspector. "I have traversed almost all of New Spain and this entire kingdom of Peru, and I have found no other difference than what one finds between hens' eggs. Anyone who has seen one Indian may consider he has seen them all; only in the paintings of your Inca ancestors, and even in you and others saying they are descended from the royal Inca house, have I observed more divergence; your faces resemble those of the Moors in the nose and mouth, although the latter have an ashen color, while you have that of a crow's wing." "Perhaps for that reason I was given the name Concolorcorvo."

From *Chapter XXVI: A Brief Comparison of the Cities of Lima and Cuzco. Characteristic Aspects. The Residents of Lima and Mexico. The Dress of the Lima Women. Reasons for their Vitality. Singular Features, Wedding Beds, Cradles, and Household Furnishings*

I attempted to write a description of Lima, but the inspector told me it was an undertaking which many intellectual giants had been unable to accomplish, and that it would be ludicrous for a pygmy to undertake it. "But, Señor inspector, is it possible that I should end such a detailed itinerary without saying anything about Lima?" "Yes, Señor Inca, because this is not a matter for you, but rather for me, since my commission ends here. Señor Don Jorge Juan," he added, "Don Antonio de Ulloa, and the greatest cosmographer in the kingdom, Doctor Don Cosme Bueno, described the singular aspects of this city with the quill from a swan, and you cannot add anything of importance with your goose quill." "Nevertheless," I replied, "please tell me what difference there is between this city and that in which I was born." "I suppose, Señor Inca," he answered, "that you are devoted to Cuzco, your homeland, and you want me to say that it surpasses Lima in all aspects, but you are mistaken because, leaving aside its location and its common lands, you must have observed that the King maintains a viceroy in splendor in this great capital with an assignation from the King which is equivalent to all the income from the family estates in Cuzco. It has, as well, three military units financed by the Crown: a well equipped and well paid cavalry, an infantry, and halberdiers[8] – who serve not only for ostentation and splendor, but also for the personal security and peace among the large population – to which is added a complete Audiencia[9], courts of higher accounting and of the Royal Inquisition, a university, a theater for plays, and public parks near the city, which are not found in Cuzco or in any other city in the kingdom.

"Lima supports 250 carriages and more than a thousand calashes[10], which are different from the former only in that they have two wheels, are pulled by a mule, and are more subject to being upset. There is nothing of this in your great city. In the matter of clothing, one is as foolish as the other, the only difference being in the matter of tastes, size of families and commerce, in which Lima greatly surpasses Cuzco. In this city there are many titles of marquis and count, and an even greater number of gentlemen belonging to the orders of Santiago and Calatrava, who, with the exception of one or two, have sufficient income to maintain themselves with splendor, to which are added many first sons and gentlemen who support themselves with their farms and other respectable businesses, giving luster to the city. I have no doubt that in the city of your birth, as in the others of this vast viceroyalty, there are illustrious families, but the total of all of them does not match that of this city, where little notice is given to the conquistadors, for although there was no lack of noble families among them, such families increased as the conquest became firmly established.

"With the selection of men for the tribunals and other honorable positions, there came to this capital from Spain many second sons of illustrious families, some already married and others who acquired the state here, and even many of those who were destined for the interior provinces came to establish themselves here in the capital, as has happened in the courts all over the world. Many subjects who came from Spain for the sole purpose of seeking a fortune kept their nobility concealed until they acquired their fortune and could maintain their luster in such an expensive place where luxury is too well established. In Cuzco and the other cities in the sierra and part of the valleys, the only costly items are dress and the household furnishings which maintain their splendor for centuries. The most important lady in Cuzco has five or six maid servants, serving her well, on whose clothing she scarcely spends as much as is spent here on one Negro servant of average account. In this city, without considering the farms, there are 1½ million pesos squandered, because generally speaking, there is not a slave who saves his master as much money as is spent on him. Their infirmities, genuine or feigned, are not only expensive to the masters because of the medicine, physician, or surgeon, but also due to their absence and lack of service. Every Negro child born in one of these houses costs the

8   Royal bodyguards, carrying a pike.   10   A low-wheeled carriage with a folding top.
9   Municipal government.

master over 700 pesos before he reaches an age when he may be put into service. This evil situation has no remedy as long as they are products of legitimate marriages, but it could be remedied in part by reducing the male servants to a smaller number, as is happening everywhere in the world.

"The multitude of servants adds to the confusion of the household, invites anxiety, obstructs service, and causes the children of the family to become lazy so that they can scarcely dress themselves at the age of 12, besides other difficulties which I shall pass over. This present situation, along with the expensive clothing which is provided from the cradle onward, due to the overindulgence of some mothers, are two bleeding sores which are noticeably draining the wealth."

"I have no doubt, Señor Concolorcorvo, that you, since you have seen only the exteriors and roofs, or I should say flat roofs, of the houses, probably think that the one in which I live is the best in the city, since it has the coat of arms above the main door and three or four rooms of considerable size. This house, in its present state, should be considered as one of the fourth class houses, that is, there are many others which are three times better. The residents of Lima do not fancy the adorning of the doorways with embossments and large coats of arms which add beauty in the large cities. The tile roofs here are useless, due to the lack of rain, which may be considered a serious lack for clearing their skies and cleaning their streets, for although a number of ditches cross the streets, pure water does not flow in them; since they are of little depth and the water is scarce, they hold only excrement and urine, which are prejudicial to health and ruinous to the buildings as is publicly known to all. The great palace of the viceroy, viewed from the facade, appears to be a town hall such as those in the two Castiles[11], but its interior shows the grandeur of the person inhabiting it. The same is true of other houses belonging to distinguished people, as you will see in time.

"The nobility of Lima is not debatable, unless it can be in the rest of the world as well, because every year we are seeing Creoles inherit some of the oldest seigniories[12] and primogenitures of Spain. I do not give examples so as not to offend those families on which I have no definite information and because it is not my intention to offer a defense for them. The present viceroy, His Excellency Señor Don Manuel de Amat y Junient, greatly enhanced the city with parks and other public works of advantage to the State. I cannot make mention of them all, for it would be necessary to write a large, bulky volume and to have another pen, but no one can deny that his genius and ingenuity are, and have been, superior to that of all viceroys in matters of culture and good taste.

"The people of talent of Lima seem to be outstanding in all the kingdom. This stems from their having an earlier and more permanent cultivation of the mind. A child from this city expresses himself well at the age of four, while highlanders can scarcely express themselves in Castilian at eight, making many solecisms, which comes from the fact that they are studying two languages at once: Castilian and their native tongue, which is the most common at home among the nurses, maids, and mothers; and thus, when they go to the Spanish school, which is usually taught by an ignorant man, instead of 'Give me a glass of cold water,' they say, 'A glass of cold water give me' (which corresponds to *Uno chiri apamuy*), considered gross and stupid by ignorant persons. The Biscayans[13] (I speak of the common ones) use the same word order and, for this reason, understand Quechua much better.

"I protest to you, Señor Inca, that for 40 years I have been observing the peculiarities of the

---

[11]   Castile was and is divided into two regions, Castilla la Vieja and Castilla la Nueva (Old and New Castile).

[12]   The territory or jurisdiction of a lord.

[13]   Settlers from the province of Vizcaya in the Basque country, hence speakers of the Basque language.

talented Creoles in both Americas, and comparing them in general, I find them no different from the peninsulars[14]. The comparison which has been made up to the present between the Creoles from Lima and those from Spain who take up residence here is unjust. Here the white youth is rare who does not devote himself to learning from an early age, while rare is the one who comes from Spain with even the slightest superficial knowledge, except for those publicly employed for letters. It is notorious that the outstanding are not always selected, because in addition to the fact that they, trusting in their merits, can always find positions in Spain, they do not wish to risk their lives in a long sea voyage and change of climate, or in having no patrons with whom to locate satisfactorily here. If the stage were changed, that is, if all vocations were made available in Lima, one would clearly see that proportionately there were as many learned men as on the peninsula and that any city in Spain comparable to this one would be matched in creative talent, good judgment and literary production, without considering the several giants in this area, so rare that one scarcely finds two in one century – like the great Peralta, the Lima son so well-known in all of Europe, who was praised so highly by the most beautiful and critical pen Galicia has produced in this century.[15]

"In keeping with this, I am going to satisfy the Peruvians and the other Creoles from the Mexican empire, whence sprang the common opinion concerning the weakening or short duration of mental soundness necessary for continuing learning after 40 or 50 years of age. Mexico City is the antipode of Lima. The air of the latter is extremely damp while that of Mexico is dry and thin. The soil of Lima, by nature, begs to be dry, and if any damage is experienced, it is from the dampness brought by the ditches interwoven among the streets and houses. To find water in Lima it is necessary to dig down 200 *varas*[16]. In Mexico water is found at less than 1 *vara*, but the effect of the air is such that lower rooms are protected from dampness by a flooring less than 1 palm high. Products are kept in the storehouses for many years without noticing moisture, and sugar, which becomes damp in Lima in storerooms on the upper floors, dries out so much on the ground floor in Mexico that it becomes like flint. Metals keep their luster for many years, while in Lima they lose it in a short time; and so it is with other things which happen due to the humidity or dryness of the air. The atmosphere of Mexico City is impregnated with salt, because all its environs are filled with this substance. There is a kind of salt, with the appearance of brown soil, called *taquesquite*, which the natives say spoils and rots the teeth, covering them with a black tartar; and thus it is rare to find a set of teeth which preserves its white luster. Almost all Mexicans of both sexes experience this destruction from a very early age, which is complicated by continuous catarrh. Convulsions are so common that rarely did I enter a church of some congregation without seeing a man or woman suffering from them, falling on the floor as if he were struck by epilepsy, accompanied by twisting the throat and mouth until the latter kissed the ear. The first aid offered by bystanders is to wrap the victim in their capes, which are capable of suffocating a strong man, but this temporary remedy has been seen and proved effective.

"Syphilis is as common as the catarrh, but it is easily cured. *Matlasague*[17], which is an intestinal fever, causes great destruction, especially among the Indians. Pneumonia is very dangerous and to be feared, but especially bad is the evacuation from both orifices of the body at the same time, which the Mexicans, with great propriety, call *miserere*; in conclusion, Mexico City is probably the most sickly place among all the cities in the world. The Europeans, and even the Creoles born and reared to a robust age in the interior provinces, do not suffer, or

---

[14]   I.e. from the natives of the Iberian peninsula.

[15]   The critic Father Benito Feijoo (1676–1764), Spanish Enlightenment thinker and essayist.

[16]   One *vara* is the equivalent of 2.8 feet.

[17]   Probably dysentery.

rather, they resist, the malignant influences of the place for a long time.

"Without a change of clothes, the Mexicans are as distinguishable from the Peruvians as women are from men. In general they are of a very delicate complexion. Rarely is one found with a complete set of teeth at 15, and almost everyone wears a white handkerchief covering his mouth from ear to ear, some to protect themselves from the air, others to cover their inkwell mouths, as they say with propriety among themselves, and even the most polished ladies are not exempt from this misery; but since this imperfection is so common, these ladies are as sought after by their own men and by foreigners as all other women in the world, because they are as neat and discreet as the ladies from Lima, although the latter surpass them in manner of speaking and in the bloom of the complexion, which springs from their keeping their teeth until old age, and from the mildness of the air and climate which is conducive to keeping the skin more smooth and pliant. The ladies from Lima prefer the color of jasmine to that of roses on their faces, and thus they use less vermilion than any other women in the world.

"The Mexican ladies can shine in the four corners of the earth, as soon as they relinquish their natural teeth in favor of a good supply of ivory ones, which are now in use, to make their speech more smooth and sonorous in order to compete with the ladies of Lima, scoffing at their *tequesquite,* and aided by their reddish color, long hair, airy gait, and other charms. If Mexico boasts of having a mill in every house, the ladies of Lima match it with their fulling-mills[18], which serve the same purposes, except that cocoa cannot be ground in them. If there is one syringe in every house in Mexico (I am not speaking of the poor ones), here there are two in every house of average decency and probity, and in addition, each one has an apothecary bag for the succor of sudden illnesses. There may be some truth in the story of the sedate and serious José Ruiz de la Camara, who was acquainted with an old Mexican woman who knew nine effective remedies for curing hemorrhoids, but here the most untalented woman knows more remedies for all kinds of illnesses than Hippocrates and Galen[19] together. The women of Lima and Mexico acquire this knowledge out of necessity, since they live in morbifical[20] places."

"It seems to me," I replied to the inspector, "that the ladies of Lima contract many infirmities due to the little protection afforded their feet and the dampness they receive through them."

"You are mistaken, Señor Concolorcorvo," the inspector answered. "The Indian women and other common people go barefooted, as do poor people in many other parts of the world, and they do not contract illness as a result. The young ladies are not of a different nature. They are raised with this fragile footwear, and from a very early age they wear dresses above the ankle, resembling imperial curtains, and they wrap themselves up in the same fashion as those accustomed to a capitular[21] cloak or a collegiate cassock. However, their shoes have two bad features, or I should say, three. The first is that they give an extraordinary shape to their feet, for which they can be pardoned since it is the native style. The second is the costliness of these shoes, due to their short duration and their exquisite embroidery, and the third is the dust which they pick up, gaining entry through the huge hallways, balconies, and windows which open from them for the exhalation of vapors of their prisoners!

"The Mexican women dress and wear shoes in the style of Europe, as I have been told, for in my time they used clothing of a mestizo fashion which from the waist up imitated somewhat the dress of the Indian women, with the *guipil* and the *quisquemel, tobagillas* (blouses in the summer and shawls in the winter) which correspond here to the printed cottons newly discov-

---

[18] A mill used to shrink woolen cloth.

[19] Hippocrates and Galen were distinguished Greek physicians of Classical antiquity.

[20] Places whose climate or location are not favorable to health.

[21] Ecclesiastical.

ered among the young ladies (loose garments in the summer and mantillas of frizzed baize in the winter). To make a worthy comparison between the ladies of Lima and Mexico it would be necessary to compose a lengthy discourse, but I cannot pass over one particular quality of the Mexicans. They make better use of a few servants. They speak to them very little and very slowly, and in gatherings: *Loquantur arcana per digitos*[23]; they are the most clever pantomimists in the world, but I have noticed that their gestures do not follow any general rule, because I have observed that some servants who returned to service in a house confessed that they still did not understand the signs of their mistress because they varied from those used before."

"I am amazed," I said to the inspector, "at the ability and skill of the Mexican ladies who succeed in expressing themselves and being understood by means of gestures. I confess that from the time I was born I have never heard that word but now, according to what you have said, I understand that this word indicates those movements of the hand and face with which newborn babies and deaf mutes express themselves, which is understood by those who deal with them; it is a pity that the ladies of Lima do not introduce this language into their houses, in order to relieve themselves of so much shouting." "The women of Lima, Señor Inca, are as skilled as the Mexicans, and, generally speaking, as able as all the others in the world, but these ladies are served by the most base people in the human race, particularly with reference to the men. The men servants in the rest of the world study the best method of serving, but here the greatest skill is devoted to studying how to serve little and badly. The most prudent and long-suffering lady becomes impatient three or four times every day, in spite of having been reared from the cradle among these people, who, besides being gross by nature, are debased by the forced servitude; this evil is almost irremediable unless steps are taken to deny the many aids given to the Spanish and mestizo women through displaced charity. I know very well that people of good judgment will be of my opinion, and with a little reflection, the dandies would adopt my way of thinking and would not maintain a sizeable number of hypocrites and idlers without any qualifications other than that of having a white face. My digression is becoming prolix and it is time to return to our discourse.

"Mexican youth is so devoted to learning from an early age that it greatly surpasses that of Lima. As soon as they learn to write poorly and to translate Latin even worse, they are put in the many schools which exist so they may practice the science of *ergo*. All the collegians in Mexico attend the university in the morning and afternoon, and it is a pleasure to see these collegians, walking in two rows in the streets, some arguing while others are reviewing their lessons. In the university the little fellows are invited to resume their syllogisms. There is no entertainment in the colleges other than studying and debating, and even in the doorways of the assessor's office and in the barbershop, one hears nothing but *concede majorem, nego minorem, distingo consequens*, and *contra ita argumentor*,[24] with all the other jargon used by dialecticians, so that there is not a section in the whole of that great city where one does not hear this noise, despite that made by the many carriages, and hawkers of almanacs, novenas and other printed matter, as well as those who sell sweets and other dainty tidbits.

"With this continual studying, cases of rheumatism and catarrh increase, being more common among people who devote themselves to studying and nocturnal meditation, and for this reason the most industrious subjects find it impossible to continue these rigorous tasks after 50 years of age, much less to write articles of importance. They themselves have made this known, and are doing it now, saying that their minds are fleeting. Anyone would believe it to see their pale and lean appearance and the mouth void of teeth and molars; therefore they

---

[23]   They speak their secrets with their hands.

[24]   I concede the major premise, deny the minor premise, and distinguish the consequence; I argue against it.

only produce works which need little incubation, like a sermon or the description of a festival, along with some witty poems and pictures which enliven their imagination. This, Señor Inca, has been the reason for attributing to the Spanish Americans a weakening of mental faculties which does not exist even in the Mexican Creoles of lazy and valetudinary[25] life. I communicated with many of the latter in Mexico, and I found them of sound judgment and witty in their conversations; at the same time I observed that this great city had many lawyers and doctors working continuously, the greater part of them being Creoles from that city. Lawyers at least have to search through books, peruse records, dictate petitions, and prepare defences in the royal tribunal. For all this they must exhaust their reasoning just as the doctors, who are the most studious men, or at least they should be, since these men command the gallows and the scalpel. From all this it may be deduced that a considerable portion of the Creoles of Mexico preserve sufficient vigor and strength of brain for study and deep cogitation."

"If this is true, Señor Don Alonso," I replied, "then what was the basis for the opinion that Spanish Americans lost their soundness of faculties at the age of 50 or 60?" "The same," he replied, "as that held by Quevedo[26] in writing the following verses:

> A desire since childhood I have stressed,
> And before, if that could be,
> A doctor without gloves to see,
> A lawyer who sans beard was blessed,
> A poet that was neatly dressed,
> A Creole giving money at his will,
> And I say this not for sake of ill.

"This is not true," said the inspector, "because in America, contrary to the satire against Creoles, they are not only generous, but wasteful. It is a fact that the natives of Peru are the most frugal in all the Americas, and even so they have squandered large fortunes in a short time, not only in their own country, but also in Spain and other parts of Europe, as is well known.

"No one is ignorant of the results of the generosities of youth. Men of good judgment who support themselves in an honorable fashion, are considered the world over as greedy men who labor to lay up riches. Usually, Señor Inca, these are not the avaricious men of whom the Scriptures speak, but rather men of great benefit to the State. It is they who restore the maidens, succor widows and the poor with debts, and support the hospitals. The generous people, so celebrated in the world, are nothing more than those who squander what the world produces, and usually the fruits of someone else's toil. Their entire generosity amounts to enlarging their retinue and languishing in vain pursuits, leaving their family and descendants a patrimony of wind.

"But, to return to our subject, I would like to ask: What harm is done the Spanish Americans by saying that just as their mental faculties excel, so they weaken at 60 years of age, or 50, as some have said? Señor Feijoo[27] denies that mental soundness excels, but he concedes that its application does, which is the same thing. He affirms that many Creoles graduate as doctors in both branches of law at the age of 20. Before graduating, it is natural for them to have been teachers in the sciences which they studied, as is common in America, without being professors. It is natural that for the remaining 30 years they should be engaged in public instruction

---

[25]   I.e. the life of an invalid.

[26]   Francisco Gómes de Quevedo y Villegas (1580–1645), Spanish poet and satirist.

[27]   Father Benito Feijoo (1676–1764), Spanish Enlightenment thinker.

and a continuation of their studies. If European Spaniards (and I say the same about other countries) begin their major study at the age of 20, when the Americans are already graduated, or capable of graduating as doctors, it is natural that because of their slower study they cannot be graduated until the age of 35, speaking of those of average talent, and they cannot serve the world of letters more than 25 years, while the Creoles may serve 30, because after 70 years of age, there are few who devote themselves to public instruction, either because it causes them great annoyance or because they are occupied in the secular or ecclesiastical ministry. If Americans know as much at the age of 50 as Europeans do at 70, and are as useful because of their teaching and writing, they should be more applauded, just as that worker who produces in one day a statue of a perfection equal to that of another who executes it in two. It is a fact that there are countries in which the strength of the brain is preserved longer than in others, and in this matter there is a great difference between Lima and Mexico. In Mexico the lightness and dryness of the air, and other influences, dull the brain and cause insomnia. The opposite is true in Lima, because its heavy and damp air strengthens the brain and induces sleep, thus leaving mental powers nimble for pursuing the tasks of cogitation. The Mexicans cannot but weaken themselves greatly with their frequent baths in hot water.

"Do you have any other questions, Señor Inca?" "I should like to ask first," I said to him, "if you consider shameful the dress of the women of Lima, and the rest of this kingdom of Peru." "You are one of those poor devils," he said to me, "of which there are so many in this kingdom and in other parts of the world. The native dress of common usage is not shameful. The portraits of the great Catholic princesses give us an idea of the customs of the countries. These great ladies are the models of honesty, and yet they bare their arms to the elbow and their neck and bosom so far as to show the beginning of that place from which comes our first nourishment. The high fit of the waist is allowed on the dresses which they call 'courtly', because for ordinary days, when they have no need to display costly necklaces on their bosoms, they use kerchiefs of the finest chiffon, which cover the low neckline. This same style is observed, although more rigorously, by persons of grandeur and is imitated by the honorable common people. Those who go to extremes in this formality are considered indecent and shameful, and are censured by people of good judgment. From the waist down the European ladies are covered to the ankles, and only public dancers bare their calves to show the adroitness of their movements, but they take precaution to wear stockings of plain black satin so as not to shock the public.

"The ladies of Lima and the others living between Piura and Potosi – and the same is true of the common people, except the Indian and newly-recruited Negro women – follow a style contrary to that of Europeans, Mexicans, and the ladies of Buenos Aires; that is, whereas the latter display the greatest luster from the neck to the bosom, with adornments on their arms and wrists, the ladies from Lima conceal this splendor with a veil, not at all transparent, when it is hot, and in cold weather they cover themselves with a double muffler, which in reality is very extravagant. All their splendor is based on the lower parts, from their garter to the soles of their feet. Nothing certain is known about the origin of this dress, but I believe they were trying to imitate paintings made of angels. The more formal and decent ladies of this region show half their ankle. The bizarre or showy women use a tier of crimped cloth, baring the lower calf, while those whom the public considers shameful (and with sufficient reason, for they are that) raise their underskirts to the knee in the fashion of the imperial drape. These women treat ladies of good judgment as old-fashioned, and the young ones who imitate them, as fools. These are much lauded by the people of little judgment, and the aforementioned ladies are applauded by persons of honor and talent, and especially by men and women of virtue.

. . . Do you have any more questions, Señor Crab[28], because I am getting annoyed." "Oh, yes, Señor; I would like to know if you have seen anything singular in this city which distinguishes it from the rest you have seen in the dominions of our Monarch." "A rare offer! I suppose," he said, "that you, Señor Crab, do not wish to hear bagatelles, but things of great significance." " No, Señor." "Well then consider these two aspects: the first is the grandeur of the wedding beds and the second the cradles and furnishings for the newly born infants in opulent homes. The first are almost *ad pompom*, and the second *ad usum*.[29]" "What comprises these sumptuous beds, cradles, and furnishings?" To this he replied, "The bed clothes are the most exquisite woven in the best mills in Europe. Draperies at the head and foot are made of scarlet damask no less, decorated with the finest golden braid and fringes made in Milan. The bedspreads, adorned in the same fashion, are of the richest silk stub woven in Lyons, France. The sheets and pillows are the finest linen made in Cambray, adorned with the widest and most delicate laces and inlays woven in Flanders, to which is added a large cloth, similarly decorated and so transparent that through it one may perceive the splendor of the pillows, which on the upper part, have scarcely one span of Dutch batiste. The cradle and furnishings of the child are of the same stuff, without mentioning the jewels for adorning the infant, who is usually bedecked with brilliant stones, which I consider a single expense because they also serve for the other children, except those which are filched by the nurses and servants. So Creoles from houses of average opulence can boast of having been reared in better diapers than the princes of Europe and even those around the Great Turk with all his seraglio[30]."

c. 1775

John Woolman (1720–1772)

The tradition of Quaker journals dates back to the sect's founder, George Fox, whose journal was prescribed reading for followers of the faith since the late seventeenth century. Of the many first person accounts by Quakers written in the eighteenth century, John Woolman's journal is the most widely read and influential. It was used in the nineteenth century in the struggle for the abolition of slavery, and inspired Emerson and Whitman. In the twentieth century, several generations of pacifists and fighters for social justice have been renewed by Woolman's account of a life lived "speaking truth to power." Woolman was born in Burlington County, New Jersey, near Philadelphia, into a large, middle class family deeply rooted in the Quaker colony they helped to settle. His father was a farmer and fruit grower with associations to many businessmen in Philadelphia. The fourth of thirteen

children, Woolman had the customary formal education in the local village school up to age fourteen, but was encouraged by his parents to develop a life-long practice of self-education. Woolman's adolescence was fraught with intense inner conflict between a natural high spiritedness and a strong religious vocation. His religious calling won out, and at age twenty-one, he left his father's farm to tend a retail store and learn tailoring in Mount Holly, a few miles away. Eventually opening his own shop, he prospered, and in 1749 married Sarah Ellis, a long time acquaintance. But like many Quakers, he believed that humans were first and foremost spiritual beings, and that a Christian's highest responsibility was to bring the inner life of spirit and the outer life of action into balance. In 1756, Woolman gave up his successful retail business and supported his family through his tai-

---

[28]   The inspector is undoubtedly suggesting here that Concolorcorvo, in his persistent questions, is like the crab whose claw seldom frees its prey once it has been grasped.

[29]   The former are made for show, the latter for use.
[30]   Harem.

loring work, supplemented by surveying, writing legal documents, schoolteaching and fruit-growing. It was also in this year that he began his celebrated journal.

Throughout his childhood, Woolman and his family attended "meeting" on Sunday, the Quaker form of religious worship. According to the customs of the Society of Friends, founded by George Fox in 1652, people gathered together in a simple meeting house, men and boys sitting on one side, and women and girls on the other. Silence reigned as the congregants waited for an inward motion prompting them to speak, which Quakers believed was the expression of the "inner light" in each person. There was no official Quaker ministry, but if people spoke frequently at meeting in particularly edifying ways, they were acknowledged as preachers, certified by their local meeting, and authorized to visit other local meetings or travel to far-flung Quaker communities to preach and evangelize. At twenty-three, Woolman made the first of thirty missionary journeys he would undertake during his life, ranging all through the colonies from New England to the Carolinas. It was on these trips that Woolman saw first hand the effects of slave holding, the scramble for wealth and luxury, and the use of war to determine the outcome of conflicts. These three interlocking social concerns form the core issues on which Woolman took principled stands in his very effective ministry and in his influential writing.

Quakers were, from their beginnings, committed to equality, between the sexes and among people of all classes and colors, and shunned gestures of deference, like removing one's hat indoors, or using titles of address (both of which got them into trouble in courtrooms, where they frequently appeared to answer charges). The logical extension of this commitment for Woolman was an early commitment to the abolition of slavery. Like George Fox, who in 1656 confronted Oliver Cromwell, Woolman preferred to engage people directly, as he did those who asked him to draw up wills and bills of sale for the transfer of slaves. For thirty years, he visited with prominent Quakers who owned slaves, and insisted upon paying any slaves whose labor provided his room or board. He refused to use dyes or sugar because they were produced by slave labor. His most effective efforts in the cause of abolition were his two essays, *Some Considerations on the Keeping of Negroes*. These essays prompted the Philadelphia Yearly Meeting to pro-

hibit slave owning in 1776, and many other meetings followed suit.

One of Woolman's arguments against slavery was the inequality it promoted, which stemmed in part from the use of the labor of others in the unchecked pursuit and accumulation of wealth. Quakers had always extolled voluntary simplicity in all aspects of life, but Woolman perceived the domino effect of materialism and how it eroded common morality: wives wanting fancy dress urged their fishermen husbands to take risks; indigent white frontiersman driven off plantations by inordinate rents sold rum to Native Americans. Furthermore, Woolman understood the relation between economic inequality and war. In his *Journal*, Woolman recounted his struggle with the dilemma of pacifism in the face of patriotic calls to fight for and contribute taxes to the security of the colonies and British interests in North America during the French and Indian war. Not to pay taxes, Woolman reasoned coolly, "was exceeding disagreeable, but to do a thing contrary to my conscience appeared yet more dreadful." His dangerous mission to the Wyalusing Indians on the Pennsylvania frontier, on the brink of Pontiac's war with the colonies, shows his commitment to peace as well as his recognition of the interlocking nature of inequality, materialism and war.

PRIMARY WORKS

Some Considerations on the Keeping of Negroes, 1754.
Considerations on Keeping Negroes, Part Second, 1762.
Journal, 1774.
The Works of John Woolman, 1774: rpt. ed. William Beardsley, 1970.
A Word of Remembrance and Caution to the Rich {A Plea for the Poor], 1793.
The Journal and Major Essays of John Woolman, ed. Phillips Moulton, 1971.

FURTHER READING

Edwin Cady, *John Woolman* (New York: Washington Square, 1965).

Paul Rosenblatt, *John Woolman* (New York: Twayne, 1969).

Phillips Moulton, "The Influence of the Writings of John Woolman," *Quaker History: Bulletin of the Friends Historical Association*, 60, 1 (1970) pp. 3–13.

Margaret Stewart, "John Woolman's 'Kindness beyond Expression': Collective Identity vs. Individualism and White Supremacy," *Early American Literature*, 26, 3 (1991) pp. 251–75.

FROM *THE JOURNAL OF JOHN WOOLMAN*[1]

1720–1742

I have often felt a motion of love to leave some hints in writing of my experience of the goodness of God, and now, in the thirty-sixth year of my age, I begin this work. I was born in Northampton, in Burlington County in West Jersey, AD 1720, and before I was seven years old I began to be acquainted with the operations of divine love. Through the care of my parents, I was taught to read near as soon as I was capable of it and as I went from school one Seventh Day[2], I remember, while my companions went to play by the way, I went forward out of sight; and sitting down, I read the twenty-second chapter of the Revelations: "He showed me a river of water, clear as crystal, proceeding out of the throne of God and the Lamb, etc." And in reading it my mind was drawn to seek after that pure habitation which I then believed God had prepared for his servants. The place where I sat and the sweetness that attended my mind remains fresh in my memory.

This and the like gracious visitations[3] had that effect upon me, that when boys used ill language it troubled me, and through the continued mercies of God I was preserved from it. The pious instructions of my parents were often fresh in my mind when I happened amongst wicked children, and was of use to me. My parents, having a large family of children, used frequently on First Days after meeting[4] to put us to read in the Holy Scriptures or some religious books, one after another, the rest sitting by without much conversation, which I have since often thought was a good practice. From what I had read and heard, I believed there had been in past ages people who walked in uprightness before God in a degree exceeding any that I knew, or heard of, now living; and the apprehension of there being less steadiness and firmness amongst people in this age than in past ages often troubled me while I was a child. . . .

Another thing remarkable in my childhood was that once, going to a neighbor's house, I saw on the way a robin sitting on her nest; and as I came near she went off, but having young ones, flew about and with many cries expressed her concern for them. I stood and threw stones at her, till one striking her, she fell down dead. At first I was pleased with the exploit, but after a few minutes was seized with horror, as having in a sportive way killed an innocent creature while she was careful for her young. I beheld her lying dead and thought those young ones for which she was so careful must now perish for want of their dam to nourish them; and after some painful considerations on the subject, I climbed up the tree, took all the young birds and killed them, supposing that better than to leave them to pine away and die miserably, and believed in this case that Scripture proverb was fulfilled, "The tender mercies of the wicked are cruel."[5] I then went on my errand, but for some hours could think of little else but the cruelties I had committed, and was much troubled.

Thus he whose tender mercies are over all his works hath placed a principle in the human mind which incites to exercise goodness toward every living creature; and this being singly

---

[1]   Begun in 1656, Woolman's journal was published in 1774. The text, with slight modifications, is from *The Journal and Major Essays of John Woolman*, ed. Phillips Moulton (New York: Oxford University Press, 1971).

[2]   Saturday. In Woolman's day, Quakers used numbers for the days of the weeks and months of the year in order to avoid references to pagan deities.

[3]   By the spirit or presence of God.

[4]   On Sundays, after Quaker worship which consisted of "meeting," or gathering of Friends for common prayer and spontaneous preaching by members moved by the spirit to speak.

[5]   Proverbs 12:10.

attended to, people become tender-hearted and sympathizing, but being frequently and totally rejected, the mind shuts itself up in a contrary disposition.

About the twelfth year of my age, my father being abroad, my mother reproved me for some misconduct, to which I made an undutiful reply; and the next First Day as I was with my father returning from meeting, he told me he understood I had behaved amiss to my mother and advised me to be more careful in future. I knew myself blameable, and in shame and confusion remained silent. Being thus awakened to a sense of my wickedness, I felt remorse in my mind, and getting home I retired and prayed to the Lord to forgive me, and do not remember that I ever after that spoke unhandsomely to either of my parents, however foolish in other things.

Having attained the age of sixteen years, I began to love wanton company, and though I was preserved from profane language or scandalous conduct, still I perceived a plant in me which produced much wild grapes. Yet my merciful Father forsook me not utterly, but at times through his grace I was brought seriously to consider my ways, and the sight of my backsliding affected me with sorrow. But for want of rightly attending to the reproofs of instruction, vanity was added to vanity, and repentance to repentance; upon the whole my mind was more and more alienated from the Truth[6], and I hastened toward destruction. While I meditate on the gulf toward which I traveled and reflect on my youthful disobedience, for these things I weep; mine eye runneth down with water.

Advancing in age the number of my acquaintance increased, and thereby my way grew more difficult. Though I had heretofore found comfort in reading the Holy Scriptures and thinking on heavenly things, I was now estranged therefrom. I knew I was going from the flock of Christ and had no resolution to return; hence serious reflections were uneasy to me and youthful vanities and diversions my greatest pleasure. Running in this road I found many like myself, and we associated in that which is reverse to true friendship.

But in this swift race it pleased God to visit me with sickness, so that I doubted of recovering. And then did darkness, horror, and amazement with full force seize me, even when my pain and distress of body was very great. I thought it would have been better for me never to have had a being than to see the day which I now saw. I was filled with confusion, and in great affliction both of mind and body I lay and bewailed myself. I had not confidence to lift up my cries to God, whom I had thus offended, but in a deep sense of my great folly I was humbled before him, and at length that Word which is as a fire and a hammer broke and dissolved my rebellious heart. And then my cries were put up in contrition, and in the multitude of his mercies I found inward relief, and felt a close engagement that if he was pleased to restore my health, I might walk humbly before him.

After my recovery this exercise[7] remained with me a considerable time; but by degrees giving way to youthful vanities, they gained strength, and getting with wanton young people I lost ground. The Lord had been very gracious and spoke peace to me in the time of my distress, and I now most ungratefully turned again to folly, on which account at times I felt sharp reproof but did not get low enough to cry for help. I was not so hardy as to commit things scandalous, but to exceed in vanity and promote mirth was my chief study. Still I retained a love and esteem for pious people, and their company brought an awe upon me.

My dear parents several times admonished me in the fear of the Lord, and their admonition entered into my heart and had a good effect for a season, but not getting deep enough to pray rightly, the tempter when he came found entrance. I remember once, having spent a part of

---

[6]   What Woolman regards as ultimate spiritual reality or   [7]   Inner turmoil of a spiritual nature.
divinity.

the day in wantonness, as I went to bed at night there lay in a window near my bed a Bible, which I opened, and first cast my eye on the text, "We lie down in our shame, and our confusion covers us."[8] This I knew to be my case, and meeting with so unexpected a reproof, I was somewhat affected with it and went to bed under remorse of conscience, which I soon cast off again.

Thus time passed on; my heart was replenished with mirth and wantonness, while pleasing scenes of vanity were presented to my imagination till I attained the age of eighteen years, near which time I felt the judgments of God in my soul like a consuming fire, and looking over my past life the prospect was moving. I was often sad and longed to be delivered from those vanities; then again my heart was strongly inclined to them, and there was in me a sore conflict. At times I turned to folly, and then again sorrow and confusion took hold of me. In a while I resolved totally to leave off some of my vanities, but there was a secret reserve in my heart of the more refined part of them, and I was not low enough to find true peace. Thus for some months I had great trouble, there remaining in me an unsubjected will which rendered my labours fruitless, till at length through the merciful continuance of heavenly visitations I was made to bow down in spirit before the Lord.

I remember one evening I had spent some time in reading a pious author, and walking out alone I humbly prayed to the Lord for his help, that I might be delivered from all those vanities which so ensnared me. Thus being brought low, he helped me; and as I learned to bear the cross I felt refreshment to come from his presence; but not keeping in that strength which gave victory, I lost ground again, the sense of which greatly affected me; and I sought deserts and lonely places and there with tears did confess my sins to God and humbly craved help of him. And I may say with reverence he was near to me in my troubles, and in those times of humiliation opened my ear to discipline.

I was now led to look seriously at the means by which I was drawn from the pure Truth, and learned this: that if I would live in the life which the faithful servants of God lived in, I must not go into company as heretofore in my own will, but all the cravings of sense must be governed by a divine principle. In times of sorrow and abasement these instructions were sealed upon me, and I felt the power of Christ prevail over selfish desires, so that I was preserved in a good degree of steadiness. And being young and believing at that time that a single life was best for me, I was strengthened to keep from such company as had often been a snare to me.

I kept steady to meetings, spent First Days after noon chiefly in reading the Scriptures and other good books, and was early convinced in my mind that true religion consisted in an inward life, wherein the heart doth love and reverence God the Creator and learn to exercise true justice and goodness, not only toward all men but also toward the brute creatures; that as the mind was moved on an inward principle to love God as an invisible, incomprehensible being, on the same principle it was moved to love him in all his manifestations in the visible world; that as by his breath the flame of life was kindled in all animal and sensitive creatures, to say we love God as unseen and at the same time exercise cruelty toward the least creature moving by his life, or by life derived from him, was a contradiction in itself.

I found no narrowness respecting sects and opinions, but believed that sincere, upright-hearted people in every Society[9] who truly loved God were accepted of him.

As I lived under the cross and simply followed the openings of Truth[10], my mind from day

---

[8] Jeremiah 3:25.

[9] A religious sect or denomination, but often refers to the Society of Friends, the official name of the Quakers.

[10] Revelations and guidance from God.

to day was more enlightened; my former acquaintance was left to judge of me as they would, for I found it safest for me to live in private and keep these things sealed up in my own breast.

While I silently ponder on that change wrought in me, I find no language equal to it nor any means to convey to another a clear idea of it. I looked upon the works of God in this visible creation and an awfulness covered me; my heart was tender and often contrite, and a universal love to my fellow creatures increased in me. This will be understood by such who have trodden in the same path. Some glances of real beauty may be seen in their faces who dwell in true meekness. There is a harmony in the sound of that voice to which divine love gives utterance, and some appearance of right order in their temper and conduct whose passions are fully regulated. Yet all these do not fully show forth that inward life to such who have not felt it, but this white stone and new name is known rightly to such only who have it.[11]

Now though I had been thus strengthened to bear the cross, I still found myself in great danger, having many weaknesses attending me and strong temptations to wrestle with, in the feeling whereof I frequently withdrew into private places and often with tears besought the Lord to help me, whose gracious ear was open to my cry.

All this time I lived with my parents and wrought on the plantation, and having had schooling pretty well for a planter, I used to improve in winter evenings and other leisure times. And being now in the twenty-first year of my age, a man in much business shopkeeping and baking asked me if I would hire with him to tend shop and keep books. I acquainted my father with the proposal, and after some deliberation it was agreed for me to go.

At home I had lived retired, and now having a prospect of being much in the way of company, I felt frequent and fervent cries in my heart to God, the Father of Mercies, that he would preserve me from all taint and corruption, that in this more public employ I might serve him, my gracious Redeemer, in that humility and self-denial with which I had been in a small degree exercised in a very private life.

The man who employed me furnished a shop in Mount Holly, about five miles from my father's house and six from his own, and there I lived alone and tended his shop. Shortly after my settlement here I was visited by several young people, my former acquaintance, who knew not but vanities would be as agreeable to me now as ever; and at these times I cried to the Lord in secret for wisdom and strength, for I felt myself encompassed with difficulties and had fresh occasion to bewail the follies of time past in contracting a familiarity with a libertine people. And as I had now left my father's house outwardly, I found my Heavenly Father to be merciful to me beyond what I can express.

By day I was much amongst people and had many trials to go through, but in evenings I was mostly alone and may with thankfulness acknowledge that in those times the spirit of supplication was often poured upon me, under which I was frequently exercised and felt my strength renewed. . . .

After a while my former acquaintance gave over expecting me as one of their company, and I began to be known to some whose conversation was helpful to me. And now, as I had experienced the love of God through Jesus Christ to redeem me from many pollutions and to be a succor to me through a sea of conflicts, with which no person was fully acquainted, and as my heart was often enlarged in this heavenly principle, I felt a tender compassion for the youth who remained entangled in snares like those which had entangled me. From one month to another this love and tenderness increased, and my mind was more strongly engaged for the good of my fellow creatures.

---

[11] See Revelation 2:17: "To him that overcometh will I give to eat of the hidden manna, and will I give him a white stone, and in the stone a new name written, which no man knoweth saving he that receiveth it."

I went to meetings in an awful frame of mind and endeavored to be inwardly acquainted with the language of the True Shepherd. And one day being under a strong exercise of spirit, I stood up and said some words in a meeting, but not keeping close to the divine opening, I said more than was required of me; and being soon sensible of my error, I was afflicted in mind some weeks without any light or comfort, even to that degree that I could take satisfaction in nothing. I remembered God and was troubled, and in the depth of my distress he had pity upon me and sent the Comforter. I then felt forgiveness for my offense, and my mind became calm and quiet, being truly thankful to my gracious Redeemer for his mercies. And after this, feeling the spring of divine love opened and a concern to speak, I said a few words in a meeting, in which I found peace. This I believe was about six weeks from the first time, and as I was thus humbled and disciplined under the cross, my understanding became more strengthened to distinguish the language of the pure Spirit which inwardly moves upon the heart and taught [me] to wait in silence sometimes many weeks together, until I felt that rise which prepares the creature to stand like a trumpet through which the Lord speaks to his flock.

From an inward purifying, and steadfast abiding under it, springs a lively operative desire for the good of others. All faithful people are not called to the public ministry, but whoever are, are called to minister of that which they have tasted and handled spiritually. The outward modes of worship are various, but wherever men are true ministers of Jesus Christ it is from the operation of his spirit upon their hearts, first purifying them and thus giving them a feeling sense of the conditions of others. This truth was early fixed in my mind, and I was taught to watch the pure opening and to take heed lest while I was standing to speak, my own will should get uppermost and cause me to utter words from worldly wisdom and depart from the channel of the true gospel ministry.

In the management of my outward affairs I may say with thankfulness I found Truth to be my support, and I was respected in my master's family, who came to live in Mount Holly within two year after my going there.

About the twenty-third year of my age, I had many fresh and heavenly openings in respect to the care and providence of the Almighty over his creatures in general, and over man as the most noble amongst those which are visible. And being clearly convinced in my judgment that to place my whole trust in God was best for me, I felt renewed engagements that in all things I might act on an inward principle of virtue and pursue worldly business no further than as Truth opened my way therein. . . .

My employer, having a Negro woman, sold her and directed me to write a bill of sale, the man being waiting who bought her. The thing was sudden, and though the thoughts of writing an instrument of slavery for one of my fellow creatures felt uneasy[12], yet I remembered I was hired by the year, that it was my master who directed me to do it, and that it was an elderly man, a member of our Society, who bought her; so through weakness I gave way and wrote it, but at the executing it, I was so afflicted in my mind that I said before my master and the Friend that I believed slavekeeping to be a practice inconsistent with the Christian religion. This in some degree abated my uneasiness, yet as often as I reflected seriously upon it I thought I should have been clearer if I had desired to be excused from it as a thing against my conscience, for such it was. And some time after this a young man of our Society spake to me to write an instrument of slavery, he having lately taken a Negro into his house. I told him I was not easy to write it, for though many kept slaves in our Society, as in others, I still believed the practice was not right, and desired to be excused from writing [it]. I spoke to him in good

---

12 That is, uneasy in his conscience.

will, and he told me that keeping slaves was not altogether agreeable to his mind, but that the slave being a gift made to his wife, he had accepted of her.

1743–1748

Two things were remarkable to me in this journey[13]. First, in regard to my entertainment: When I eat, drank, and lodged free-cost with people who lived in ease on the hard labor of their slaves, I felt uneasy; and as my mind was inward to the Lord, I found, from place to place, this uneasiness return upon me at times through the whole visit. Where the masters bore a good share of the burden and lived frugal, so that their servants were well provided for and their labor moderate, I felt more easy; but where they lived in a costly way and laid heavy burdens on their slaves, my exercise was often great, and I frequently had conversation with them in private concerning it. Secondly, this trade of importing them from their native country being much encouraged amongst them and the white people and their children so generally living without much labor was frequently the subject of my serious thoughts. And I saw in these southern provinces so many vices and corruptions increased by this trade and this way of life that it appeared to me as a dark gloominess hanging over the land; and though now many willingly run into it, yet in future the consequence will be grievous to posterity! I express it as it hath appeared to me, not at once nor twice, but as a matter fixed on my mind.

1761–1763

11th [month], 176[2. . . . Having many years felt love in my heart toward the natives of this land who dwell far back in the wilderness, whose ancestors were the owners and possessors of the land where we dwell, and who for a very small consideration assigned their inheritance to us, and being at Philadelphia in the 8th month, 1761, on a visit to some Friends who had slaves, I fell in company with some of those natives who lived on the east branch of the river Susquehanna at an Indian town called Wyalusing, about two hundred miles from Philadelphia. And in conversation with them by an interpreter, as also by observations on their countenance and conduct, I believed some of them were measurably acquainted with that divine power which subjects the rough and forward will of the creature; and at times I felt inward drawings toward a visit to that place . . .

. . . on the 9th day, 6th month, . . . we met with an Indian trader lately come from Wyoming, and in conversation with him I perceived that many white people do often sell rum to the Indians, which I believe is a great evil. First, they being thereby deprived of the use of their reason and their spirits violently agitated, quarrels often arise which ends in mischief, and the bitterness and resentments occasioned hereby are frequently of long continuance. Again, their skins and furs, gotten through much fatigue and hard travels in hunting, with which they intended to buy clothing, these when they begin to be intoxicated they often sell at a low rate for more rum; and afterward when they suffer for want of the necessaries of life, [they] are angry with those who for the sake of gain took the advantage of them. Of this their chiefs have often complained at their treaties with the English.

Where cunning people pass counterfeits and impose that on others which is only good for nothing, it is considered as a wickedness, but to sell that to people which we know does them harm and which often works their ruin, for the sake of gain, manifests a hardened and

---

[13]   Through Maryland, Virginia, and Carolina.

corrupt heart and is an evil which demands the care of all true lovers of virtue to suppress. And while my mind this evening was thus employed, I also remembered that the people on the frontier, among whom this evil is too common, are often poor people, who venture to the outside of a colony that they may live more independent on such who are wealthy, who often set high rents on their land, being renewedly confirmed in a belief that if all our inhabitants lived according to sound wisdom, laboring to promote universal love and righteousness, and ceased from every inordinate desire after wealth and from all customs which are tinctured with luxury, the way would be easy for our inhabitants, though much more numerous than at present, to live comfortably on honest employments, without having that temptation they are often under of being drawn into schemes to make settlements on lands which have not been purchased of the Indians, or of applying to that wicked practice of selling rum to them. . . .

13th day, 6th month. The sun appearing, we set forward, and as I rode over the barren hills my meditations were on the alterations of the circumstances of the natives of this land since the coming in of the English. The lands near the sea are conveniently situated for fishing. The lands near the rivers, where the tides flow, and some above, are in many places fertile and not mountainous, while the running of the tides makes passing up and down easy with any kind of traffic. Those natives have in some places, for trifling considerations, sold their inheritance so favorably situated, and in other places been driven back by superior force, so that in many places, as their way of clothing themselves is now altered from what it was and they far remote from us, [they] have to pass over mountains, swamps, and barren deserts, where travelling is very troublesome, in bringing their skins and furs to trade with us.

By the extending of English settlements and partly by English hunters, those wild beasts they chiefly depend on for a subsistence are not so plenty as they were, and people too often, for the sake of gain, open a door for them to waste their skins and furs in purchasing a liquor which tends to the ruin of them and their families.

My own will and desires being now very much broken and my heart with much earnestness turned to the Lord, to whom alone I looked for help in the dangers before me, I had a prospect of the English along the coast for upward of nine hundred miles where I have traveled. And the favorable situation of the English and the difficulties attending the natives in many places, and the Negroes, were open before me. And a weighty and heavenly care came over my mind, and love filled my heart toward all mankind, in which I felt a strong engagement that we might be obedient to the Lord while in tender mercies he is yet calling to us, and so attend to pure universal righteousness as to give no just cause of offense to the Gentiles, who do not profess Christianity, whether the blacks from Africa or the native inhabitants of this continent. And here I was led into a close, laborious inquiry whether I, as an individual, kept clear from all things which tended to stir up or were connected with wars, either in this land or Africa, and my heart was deeply concerned that in future I might in all things keep steadily to the pure Truth and live and walk in the plainness and simplicity of a sincere follower of Christ. . . .

18th day, 6th month. . . . So near evening I was at their meeting, where the pure gospel love was felt, to the tendering some of our hearts. And the interpreters, endeavoring to acquaint the people with what I said, in short sentences, found some difficulty, as none of them were quite perfect in the English and Delaware tongue. So they helped one another and we labored along, divine love attending. And afterwards feeling my mind covered with the spirit of prayer, I told the interpreters that I found it in my heart to pray to God and believed if I prayed right he would hear me, and expressed my willingness for them to omit interpreting; so our meeting ended with a degree of divine love. And before the people went out I observed Papunehang[14] (the man who had been zealous in laboring for a reformation in that town, being then very tender) spoke to one of the interpreters, and I was afterward told that he said in substance as follows: "I love to feel where words come from."

1756–72   1774

Jean-Bernard Bossu (1720–1792)

Jean-Bernard Bossu was born in a village south-west of Dijon in 1720. His career as an officer in the French Navy took him on three different occasions to the French colony of Louisiana. The account of his first two journeys (1751–7 and 1757–62), to the Mississippi Valley and to what now is Alabama, was published in Paris in 1768 with the title *Nouveaux Voyages aux Indes occidentales; Contenant une Rélation des differens Peuples qui habitent les environs du grand Fleuve Saint-Louis, appellé vulgairement le Missisipi; leur Religion; leur gouvernement; leurs moeurs, leurs guerres et leur commerce*, and was translated into English in 1771. The following excerpts offer a vision of colonial New Orleans and its inhabitants, Bossu's description of his struggle with a hungry alligator, and advice on how to remain healthy in the climate of the New World.

PRIMARY WORK

Jean-Bernard Bossu, *Travels in the Interior of North America, 1751–1762*, trans. and ed. Seymour Feiler (Norman: University of Oklahoma Press, 1962).

FURTHER READING

Jeanne Carriat, "Autour des Nouveaux Voyages aux Indes occidentales de Jean-Bernard Bossu: Travaux du Centre d'Etude de la Lit. Fr. du XVIIe et XVIIIe siecles," *L'Annee 1768 a travers la presse traitée par l'ordinateur*, eds Paul Jansen and Jean Varloot (Paris: CNRS, 1981) pp. 215–30.

Samuel Dickinson, ed. and trans., *New Travels in North America: 1770–1771* by Jean-Bernard Bossu (Natchitoches, La.: Northwestern State University Press, 1982).

TRAVELS IN THE INTERIOR OF NORTH AMERICA, 1751–1762

From *Letter II*

To the Marquis de d'Estrade.
Sir:
. . . We expect to leave for the Illinois post August 20; Monsieur de Macarty, who will go with us, has been named commander by the Court. My visit to the different nations during this long trip will enable me to give you a detailed description of the beautiful Mississippi and of the people who inhabit its shores.

In the meantime, I shall describe the capital of Louisiana, but I do not think that it is necessary to speak of the city at length, since you are doubtless familiar with most of the maps and articles published on it. I simply want to call to your attention that New Orleans with its well-laid-out streets, is bigger and more heavily populated today than formerly. There are four

---

[14]   Papunehang (1705?–75), chief of the Delaware Indians, their representative, and their spiritual leader before and after his conversion to Christianity.

types of inhabitants: Europeans, Indians, Africans or Negroes, and half bloods, born of Europeans and savages native to the country.

Those born of French fathers and French, or European, mothers are called Creoles. They are generally very brave, tall, and well built and have a natural inclination toward the arts and sciences. Since these studies cannot be pursued very well because of the shortage of good teachers, rich and well-intentioned fathers send their children to France, the best school for all things.

As for the fair sex, whose only duty is to please, they are already born with that advantage here and do not have to go to Europe to acquire it artificially.

New Orleans and Mobile are the only cities where there is no *patois*[1]; the French spoken here is good.

Negroes are brought over from Africa to clear the land, which is excellent for growing indigo, tobacco, rice, corn, and sugar cane; there are sugar plantations which are already doing very well. This country offers a delightful life to the merchants, artisans, and foreigners who inhabit it because of its healthful climate, its fertile soil, and its beautiful site. The city is situated on the banks of the Mississippi, one of the biggest rivers in the world, which flows through eight hundred leagues of explored country. Its pure and delicious waters flow forty leagues among numerous plantations, which offer a delightful scene on both banks of the river, where there is a great deal of hunting, fishing, and other pleasures of life.

The Capuchins were the first monks to go to New Orleans as missionaries in 1723. The superior of these good monks, who are concerned solely with their religious work, is vicar of the parish. The Jesuits settled in Louisiana two years later, and these shrewd politicians managed to exploit the richest plantation in the colony, obtained through their intrigues. The Ursulines[2] were sent over at about the same time. These pious women, whose zeal is certainly to be commended, educate young ladies; they also take orphans into their school, for each of whom they receive fifty crowns from the King. These same nuns were in charge of the military hospital . . .

From *Letter XVII*

. . . on August 22, 1759, I left Mobile with three boats manned by soldiers and Mobile Indians, who volunteered to help this Frenchman on his trip in exchange for a few trinkets. We took off from Mobile and, after having gone fifteen leagues, arrived at the juncture of the Alabama and the Tombigbee rivers. On August 27, we started up the Tombigbee to reach the fort. Since the weather was good, I chose a campsite on the edge of the river. Out of their abundant catch, the Indians gave me a catfish, a species which can attain a length of four feet and which the natives usually dry. Because of the fine weather, I did not bother to pitch my tent but simply chose an isolated spot on a grass-covered height overlooking the river. Finding this a good place to rest, I spread out the bearskin I had taken on the island we had pretended was mine. I wrapped myself in my tent and covered my face against the evening dampness, which is dangerous in this season. This little precaution almost cost me my life, as you will see.

I carefully placed the fish near my feet so no one could steal it, but something worse happened. I had already been sleeping deeply and peacefully for an hour, with no fear of the local Indians, who are our friends and allies, when I suddenly felt something of extraordinary strength dragging me off. I awoke with a start, thinking that someone was playing a trick on me. I had

---

[1] Local dialect.   [2] An order of teaching nuns.

never before been so frightened, and I think that I had good cause to be this time. I thought the Devil was dragging me off. I shouted for help. My men answered that I was having a nightmare. You can imagine my amazement when, fully awake, I saw a twenty-foot-long alligator! I was frightened by his size as well as by the disgusting smell of musk exuded by these animals. Attracted by the catfish in the bottom of my tent canvas, the alligator had come out of the river in the dead of night. These amphibians are extremely voracious. This one threw himself hungrily on my fish, and, carrying its prey into the river, dragged me off, too, by a corner of the tent in which I was wrapped. I had just the time to untangle myself on the very edge of the precipice and was fortunate enough to get off with only a good scare. I was able to save the bearskin, which never leaves me. As simple as this event seems, it is considered a miracle by those who believe in the supernatural.

The Acolapissas and the Washas, small tribes which live north of New Orleans, wrestle alligators in the water. This is how they do it. Armed with a piece of hardwood or an iron bar pointed at both ends, which he holds in the center, an Indian swims out with his weapon in front of him. The alligator approaches with his jaws wide open to snap off and eat the swimmer's arm. The Indian jams the piece of wood into the mouth of the alligator, who, in biting down, pierces both his jaws and so locks them that he can neither open nor close his mouth. The Indian then drags the animal out of the water. These people engage in the sport quite often, as do the Negroes of Guinea and Senegal.

1768

Louis Antoine de Bougainville (1729–1811)

Though his early education was in law, Louis Antoine de Bougainville went on to become a distinguished mathematician (with two books on integral calculus) and soldier. During the Seven Years War, he went to Canada as aide to General Louis Joseph de Montcalm, commanding troops at the siege of Quebec in 1759. He later led a scientific expedition to the South Seas, from which he brought back the flower (bougainvillea) which bears his name.

PRIMARY WORK

Louis Antoine de Bougainville, *Adventure in the Wilder-*

ness: The American Journals of Louis Antoine de Bougainville, 1756–1760, ed. and trans. Edward P. Hamilton (Norman: University of Oklahoma Press, 1964).

FURTHER READING

Beatrice Waggaman, "Law and the Imaginary: Bougainville's Voyage around the World, diss.," *Dissertation Abstracts International*, Nov., 46, 5 (1985) p. 1297A.

Mary Kimbrough, "The Relative Obscurity of Bougainville's Voyage," *Studies on Voltaire and the Eighteenth Century*, 305 (1992) pp. 1600–2.

FROM *ADVENTURE IN THE WILDERNESS*

11 July, 1756: At noon there arrived at Montreal M. Marin, a colony officer who spent the winter at the post at Stinking Bay[1], and who led five hundred Indians to Presque Isle, the

---

[1] Now Green Bay, Wisconsin.

rendezvous assigned for all the Indians from the Far West[2]. All have decamped, having heard it said that there was smallpox at all our forts. The Indians fear nothing so much as this disease; in fact it treats them cruelly when they are attacked by it, either because of lack of proper care, or because of a susceptibility in their blood. Only the Indians of the Menominee tribe, or the Wild Oats people, to the number of about forty, have, according to their expression, closed their eyes and risked death to come with M. Marin, first to join M. de Villiers, with whom they were in the attack on the English *bateaux*[3], and afterwards to go downriver to Montreal. Wild oats are a kind of grain resembling oats, which are used just like rice and which are a very healthful form of nourishment. This plant forms the totem of this nation. The Menominees are always strongly attached to the French. They came in five great birchbark canoes with six scalps and several prisoners. Arrived opposite to Montreal, the canoes were placed in several lines, they lay to for some time, the Indians saluted with a discharge of guns and loud cries to which three cannon shot replied. Afterwards they came ashore and went up to the Chateau in double file, the prisoners in the middle carrying wands decorated with feathers. These prisoners were not maltreated, as is customary upon entering into cities and villages. Entered into M. de Vaudreuil's[4] presence, the prisoners sat down on the ground in a circle, and the Indian chief, with action and force that surprised me, made a short enough speech, the gist of which was that the Menominees were different from the other tribes which held back part of their captures, and that they always brought back to their father all the meat they had taken. Then they danced around the captives to the sound of a sort of tambourine placed in the middle. Extraordinary spectacle, more suited to terrify than to please; curious, however, to the eye of a philosopher who seeks to study man in conditions nearest to nature. These men were naked save for a piece of cloth in front and behind, the face and body painted, feathers on their heads, symbol and signal of war, tomahawk and spear in their hand. In general these are brawny men, large and of good appearance; almost all are very fat. One could not have better hearing than those people. All the movements of their body mark the cadence with great exactness. This dance is (like) the pyrrhic (dance)[5] of the Greeks. The dance ended, they were given meat and wine. The prisoners were sent off to jail with a detachment to prevent the Algonquins and the Iroquois of the Sault[6] who were at Montreal from knocking them on the head, these Indians being in mourning for the men they had lost.

30 July . . . In the morning an Indian council to [try to] hold the thirty Menominees. Pork, wine, tobacco, vermilion, and eighteen strings of wampum, to a value of forty pistoles[7], since yesterday. They will end up by leaving after all. In the afternoon they sang the war song and have qualified this ceremony by praying to the Master of Life. They asked for a dog, because they dreamed that one would bring them good luck in war. A child of six danced without a breechclout because they do not give one until a child is ten. After the defeat of the barges[8], his parents gave him an Englishman to kill to stop him crying. Three days ago they took an Englishwoman prisoner. Her reception was to be turned over to the Indian women, who treated her humanely enough, only giving her a shower of blows with sticks.

8 October: Rainy day, the work interrupted. These works go very slowly, the soldiers, corrupted by the great amount of money[9], by the example of the Indians and Canadians,

---

[2] In the original text, *pays d'en haut*. A more accurate translation might be "from the Northern country."

[3] Ships.

[4] Rigaud de Vaudreuil (1703–79), brother of the governor of Canada.

[5] Danced around a fire.

[6] Sault St Louis, a Jesuit mission.

[7] A French coin.

[8] Perhaps a reference to the battle with the English general Bradstreet.

[9] French soldiers received extra pay for working on the fort.

breathing an air permeated with independence, work indolently. The engineer[10] is almost never at the works. It is not to his interest that the fort should be completed quickly. He has the exclusive privilege of selling wine (it sells for 55 sous a bottle), and all the money of the workmen, and even the pay of the soldiers, goes to the canteen. Moreover he has built this fort of horizontal timbers in a country where stone, limestone and sand are found in abundance, where in getting the stone to face (the walls), the ditch is made at the same time, where there is doubtless wood, but men are lacking to cut it, square it, haul it, where there are neither wagons nor horses. It is an odd thing, this engineer gives the workers certificates which have the value of money, without anyone controlling their issue, and all of these certificates come back to him.

. . . The Indians go hunting every day, proof that the English Indians have gone back to their villages. When these Indians believe themselves safe from attack there certainly is no danger to fear. Those who remain here get drunk and, since they have lost all their spirit, everything is permitted them.

The troops work with ardor. There is at the Falls a sawmill which under the direction of M. de L(otbinière) never was got in shape to make planks, they had even decided to abandon it. M. de la P(ause) was put in charge of the mill, and he got it in shape to get out 150 planks in twenty-four hours. It cost the King [blank space in the original text] crowns and yet could not run; five hundred francs and one of our officers has accomplished what this great sum and the Vauban of Canada could not achieve. Unfortunately it is to the interest of this Vauban that the work should drag out. The canteen must have its business. Wine here is six livres a quart; I note this difference in price, it is the thermometer of peculation[11] in this country.

The Potawatomi old men who remained here yesterday made medicine to learn the news of their brothers. The hut shook, the medicine men sweated drops of blood, and at last the devil came and told them that their brothers would return shortly with scalps and prisoners. A medicine man in the medicine house is just like the priestess of Delphi on her tripod or Canidie[12] evoking the shades.

Eight Indians and as many Canadians left this evening from the portage camp in two canoes to go and make a strike at Fort George.

13 October: This morning the battalion of Languedoc was reviewed. It has 353 men, having only nine companies and a tenth one of provisional grenadiers drawn from the other nine. Four companies are in England (as prisoners).[13]

The weather, which has been very fine up to the present, appears to be setting in to snow and cold. The east, north, and northeast winds are the ones that bring rain and fog in this country. It is the contrary in France and this difference comes from the situation of this country with respect to the sea.

Eleven Iroquois who left here three days ago to go and reconnoiter the end of the bay returned today. They reported that they had found only trails still quite fresh. Say what you will, the wisest thing to do is to put no trust in the reports of Indians and halfbreeds.

Just the same, this talent they have of finding tracks in the woods and of following them without losing them, a talent one cannot dismiss in doubt without refusing to accept the evidence, can be regarded as a perfection of the instinct. They see in the tracks the number that have passed, whether they are Indians or Europeans, if the tracks are fresh or old, if they are of healthy or of sick people, dragging feet or hurrying ones, marks of sticks used as supports. It is

---

[10]   Michael Chartier de Lotbiniere, a young officer, relative of Governor Vaudreuil.

[11]   Speculation.

[12]   A sorceress of Naples, invoked by Horace.

[13]   They were captured in 1755 by the British Navy.

rarely that they are deceived or mistaken. They follow their prey for one hundred, two hundred, six hundred leagues with a constancy and a sureness which never loses courage or leads them astray. As regards their sense of direction in the woods, it is of a complete sureness. If they have left a place where they put their canoes, whatever distance they may have gone, whatever turns they may have made, crossing rivers, mountains, they come directly back to the place where their canoes were left. Observation of the sun, the inclination of trees and of leaves that they look at, a long practice, and finally an instinct superior to all reasons, these are their guides, and these guides never lead them astray.

14 October: Indian council indicated for tomorrow to decide about a score who came here to go and make a strike.

The soldiers have too much money. A soldier of Languedoc yesterday lost one hundred *louis*[14]. This country is dangerous for discipline. Pray God that it alone suffers from it.[15]

19 October: Money changing goes on here just as in la Rue Quincampoix[16]. M. de L(otbinière)'s certificates are in poor repute. A man who has silver or gold changes it for colony paper notes at 12 per cent profit. Then he changes for those of Lobitotiere's, sometimes at a quarter, a third, or even a half of their value in profit. He sends these to Montreal and the treasurer gives colony notes in exchange at no other cost than four deniers for the livre[17]. The colony notes come back to camp and the circuit starts again. It is a shuttle which produces great profits. M. de L. makes no difficulty in taking up the notes, he even, they say, has exchange agents to take them back.

28–30 September, 1757: The ship the *Liberté*, carrying complete clothing for 3200 men and 60 recruits, entered the harbor today. At first it, as well as several others, had a cargo of wheat and salt pork. The order came to unload in order to take on another cargo. It is the result of some intrigue among the subordinate ministers. We suffer from its effects. The cause is unknown to us; we can only suspect it.

They are giving out bills of exchange for the notes. They are in three maturities[18] as usual. The only change is that only a quarter is payable the first year, the rest by halves in the two following.

The epidemics continue to make great ravages. The first battalion of Berry left the city. It is established in winter quarters in the parishes of Beaupré, Beauport, etc. The soldiers will be fed by the inhabitants, whom the King pays for this purpose.

1–10 October: News from Montreal. Misery commences to make itself felt. The harvest is of the very worst in this government[19], which usually is the granary of Canada.

12 December, 1757–1 March, 1758: (a summary): On the ninth they started to issue horse meat to the troops. The women of Montreal went and threw it at M. de Vaudreuil's feet. He yielded and consequently, the soldiers at La Marine regiment the next day at pay assembly refused to take any. It was necessary to have recourse to the Chevalier de Levis, whose voice quieted the unrest. They will not boast of his having this duty[20], the more so since all unrest is contagious in a country where one breathes independence.

The party of Indians commanded by Sieur de Langis took ninety scalps and three prisoners at Fort Lydius. They learned nothing. An English detachment has again come to Carillon; their expedition ended in killing some oxen. There was at this fort the start of a mutiny which

---

[14]   A unit of French currency.

[15]   I.e. that only the colony suffers and not the mother country.

[16]   A Paris street where many financial institutions were located.

[17]   Both deniers and livres are units of currency. Normally, there were ten deniers in one livre.

[18]   I.e. they come due at three different dates.

[19]   I.e. this region.

[20]   I.e. the Chevalier de Levis is not to be envied.

the excellent conduct of Sieur de Hebecourt quelled. One of the most mutinous had the pox. They had him given a triple dose of mercury to put him out of the way of doing any harm.

4 October 1758: . . . In the last ten years the country has changed its condition. Before that time one was happy there because with little one still had in abundance all things necessary for life; one did not wish to be rich, one did not even have the idea of wealth; no one was poor. . . . The amount of money increases in the colony and, consequently, the price of commodities.

The earlier simplicity blushes at first because it finds itself vying with a most affected superfluity; luxury comes in and with it corruption of customs, of feelings, avarice, greed, the spirit of graft. The way to pay court is to seem to want to make a fortune. Delicacy as to means is publicly mocked, treated as folly. The example of the leader produces the usual result, that is to say, many imitators. Everybody wants to trade; conditions are all confused; trade, wiped out by exclusive privileges and by the all-powerful (holders of) the privileges, groans, complains, but its powerless voice, stifled, cannot make itself heard. It is necessary to submit to a law which is going to destroy it.

To what cannot man accustom himself? Force of habit extends even to enduring grief. Extortion has raised its mask, it no longer knows limits. Enterprises increase, multiply; a single society eats up all the interior commerce, the exterior also, all the substance of the country that it devours. It plays with the lives of men.

The inhabitants, worn out by excessive work, consume in pure loss to themselves, their strength, their time, their youth. Agriculture languishes, the population decreases, war comes, and it is the Grand Society[21] which through outrages useful to its interest alone furnishes the ambitious English with the pretext of lighting the torch. An exhausted colony cannot sustain the fatigue and the expense. The speculators do not tire at all. The peril of Canada which becomes that of the state, makes no change in their method; this dried-up land can no longer furnish anything for their greed. Well! It is the wealth of the state itself they wish. All is put underway to rob the King; means which one cannot give names to, because up to now, no one has thought of them. At last, unheard of thing, this Society, a law to itself, is the true Commissary General, itself it sets the prices. They traffic with our subsistence, with our life. Is there no remedy for this evil which is so extreme? And is it necessary that one man alone should exhaust the finances of France, abuse our dangers and our misery, and compromise the glory of the nation?

Rafael Landívar (1731–1793)

Born into a wealthy family in Guatemala, Rafael Landívar entered the priesthood in 1755. He went on to teach rhetoric and philosophy in the local Jesuit college and later became its director. When the Jesuits were banished from the dominions of Spain in 1767 on the order of King Charles III, Landívar went into exile in Bologna, where he died in 1793.

It was in Bologna that Landívar composed his poem *Rusticatio Mexicana*. Originally written in Latin hexameters and clearly taking inspiration from Virgil's pastoral poetry, *Rusticatio Mexicana* offers the reader a lyrical description of the floating gardens of Mexico, the beauties of New World nature, and the diversions of the people.

---

[21]   The consortium of investors responsible for colonizing New France.

PRIMARY WORK

Rafael Landívar, *Rusticatio Mexicana*, trans. G. W. Regenos (New Orleans: Middle America Research Institute, 1948).

FURTHER READING

John Browning, "Rafael Landívar's Rusticatio Mexicana: Natural History and Political Subversion," *Ideologies*

and Literature: Journal of Hispanic and Lusophone Discourse Analysis, Spring 1, 3 (1985) pp. 9–30.

Graciela Nemes, "Rafael Landivar and Poetic Echoes of the Enlightenment," *The Ibero-American Enlightenment*, ed. A. Owen Aldridge (Urbana: University of Illinois Press, 1971) pp. 298–308.

Antony Higgins, *Constructing the Criollo Archive: Subjects of Knowledge in the Bibliotheca Mexicana and the Rusticatio Mexicana* (West Lafayette: Purdue University Press, 2000).

RUSTICATIO MEXICANA

From *The Lakes of Mexico*

At the outset the Mexicans established in the middle of a marsh a city to become finally after many years the seat of a mighty empire. But with such pride this illustrious people erected majestic temples to the gods, and palaces for the kings, and castles and homes, and they grew so rapidly that the king, to whom they had long been subject and to whom they had paid tribute, was beset with grave misgivings. He was, of course, pained to see this people and city growing. He therefore ruthlessly bade these unfortunate people pay another kind of tribute, more burdensome and beyond their means. They must bring to him over the calm waters sweet-scented gardens rich in fruits and covered with green vegetation. And if the men should declare that these demands could not then be met, he was ready to exterminate both the city and the people. They all groaned and filled the sacred temples of the gods with their lamentations. With dishevelled hair the crowds ran about wildly. Yet all things were overcome by the ready ingenuity of the people.

Relying on their wit and alertness of mind, the citizens set themselves to the task, and leaving behind their homes and the waters they go deep into the dark forest and into places far away in search of thick-leafed groves of broom trees for mats. Each one is assigned his task, each one his special duties. Some quickly tear the branches from the pliant stem, some load the boats, while others move the cargo along with their oars. They briskly carry on the work, and cheerfully perform these difficult tasks. Now when the workmen have piled high the branches and prepared everything with due deliberation, they come together and weave from these boughs light carpets which resemble long mats. They spread them out near the city walls, and they place them when woven on the open waters, leaving many paths here and there over the deep. But in order that angry winds not cast hither and thither the results of their labors or the receding sea carry them away with its swiftly moving waters, they take precautions by fastening the wicker mats by rope to posts of knotty oak driven into the bottom of the lake.

When the Mexicans find that their work has met with success, they turn their prows eagerly to the shore. They then return to the gay fields, and scattering themselves out over the plowed land dig up rich soil for the seeds. Not so busily do throngs of bees throughout the blossoming countryside gather nectar when in the great forest they are building new hives and supplying their swarms with honey. Next the men load their boats with the soil which they have collected and they beat the restless waters with many a stroke of the oar. And when they have come to the carpets extending out over the waters, they spread over them the dirt which has been gathered and consign the moist seeds to the fertile soil. One man scatters grains of wheat over the floating fields, another finds pleasure in sowing fertile vegetable seeds, and there are not wanting those for whom the flower once sacred to pagan Venus[1] blushes, the glory of spring, the lovely queen of the garden. And when the people see the green field in the midst of the billows, all are exceedingly happy and, pushing with their oars the floating field across the blue waters, they render the exacting gift to the cruel tyrant. But with foresight they reserve for themselves other gardens on the lake of Flora[2], and by cultivating them assiduously, preserve them as an undying memorial of their labor.

But if a thief should strip the well-tilled garden, or a violent storm damage the ripened harvest, the ingenious husbandman[3] moves his little floating field over the waters to another place and avoids these grievous losses. So the people have as many fields smiling with flowers as there are mats seen floating quietly over the waters.

The adjoining shore is envious of this wealth and splendor of the floating land and tries to rival it by adorning itself with green elms, cherry, fruitful pear, ruddy apple, laurel, pine, cedar and stately oaks, and gracing its meadows with perennial spring.

Moreover, it hides so many birds in its shady wood that the re-echoing forest resounds with soft melody. There the winged companies bedecked in many colors joyously make their way on bright-colored wings through the clear sky, filling the air with music and causing the shore to ring with their sweet songs. Sweetly sings the sparrow, bedecked with a wide rose-colored crest, his neck draped with reddish down. There also frolics the *centzontlus*[4], prince of birds, noted for the remarkable range of his songs and surpassed by no others in the quality of his voice, a bird unknown to the Old World. It simulates the voice of men, of birds, and of dogs, and even strains of music sung to the accompaniment of the lyre. At one time he sings in rhythm, now he imitates a rapacious kite[5], again he mocks a cat, or repeats the call of a blaring bugle; he merrily barks, he frets, he chirps. When confined to a cage he amuses himself by flitting about and singing and continues his melodies day and night without sleeping. Not with such soft plaintive strains does sad Philomela[6] lament her misfortune while concealed beneath the deep shadow of the woodland she fills the poplars with her tremulous notes, as the *cenzontlus* enlivens the shores with his charming mockery.

Such is the music, such are the waters, and such the lovely shores to which in early spring the gallant young men come in their little boats at the time when yellow flowers are blooming in profusion on the floating fields and spring crowns the meadows with bright roses. Each one embarks on a light double-oared skiff, lightening his spirits with gentle strains of music, to which in the distance Echo indistinctly replies; and the forest, struck by the sweet melodies, resounds. Then they draw up their swift boats for hard-fought contests and churn the soft waters with the beating of the oars until victory decks a vessel with green laurel. Then both losers and winner alike cut oblique paths around the floating gardens and travel along the winding shores, pushing their boats through the flowers. As once upon a time in proud Crete noble Theseus[7] skillfully escaped from the secret windings of the labyrinth, groping his way along the bewildering turns of the treacherous maze, so these young men of the city trace with the oar uncertain pathways across the swaying gardens.

---

[1] Myrtle.

[2] The Roman goddess of flowers, gardens and Spring.

[3] Farmer.

[4] Probably the mockingbird. The term is derived from the earlier form *cenzontlatolis*, meaning "countless voices."

[5] A type of bird.

[6] The nightingale.

[7] Theseus, King of Athens, reputedly found his way out of the labyrinth by leaving a thread in his wake.

From *Processing of Silver and Gold*

. . . Now that I have with much toil worked the mines, I shall forthwith crush the stones which have been carried to the rich estates and diligently try to bring forth precious quantities of silver and gold from the avaricious rocks and fill the whole world with the riches obtained.

You, O Fortune, who look with serene eyes upon the sorrowing, and are pleased to bring prompt relief to the wretched, behold my body weary with the tremendous task and regard the pains long spent on so great an endeavor. Faithfully reserve for me the wealth which once you promised and propitiously wrest from the crushed rock its treasures, and so long as the earth yields its precious stones, so long as grass grows in the fields, you will see my offerings hanging in your shrines.

Some distance from the mine are flourishing estates, known for their spacious grounds, fresh waters, wide colonnades, storehouses, and magnificent buildings. In these a lively fire heats large furnaces, and a heavy mill and an iron-supported machine grind the bones of the mountain filled with shining metals. To this place sturdy mules convey the rough ore from the mountain, and the men immediately set about to split it apart with heavy sledges and grind it, when thus broken, into fine pieces.

Now to crush these sharp pieces again and again, a large machine is set up equipped with heavy iron pounders and shining brass. This is kept in motion by mules flying briskly around, or by a heavy waterfall. Young boys standing on each side steadily shovel the ore under the pounders that the revolving machine may quickly break the sharp stones by its repeated blows and overcome their strong resistance. The process is continued until the stones have been crushed into fine sand, and light dust flies from the rock. This is caught in boxes placed alongside the massive pounders and securely fastened to the machine. A very thin gauze of finely woven bronze wire securely covers them.

This is hazardous work and frequently endangers the lives of the boys, cutting short their wretched existence by an untimely death. For the dust, having unlocked the cavities of the nose, penetrates the top of the brain and passes down into the lower part of the chest, breaking down into the lower part of the chest, breaking off the thread of life in its bloom following the third lustrum[8]. The boys must therefore be paid good wages for daring thus to risk their lives.

If at any time pieces of rock should escape the strokes of the iron and stubbornly resist the crushers, they are driven between the stones of a mill and bruised until they are reduced to fine particles under the weight of the heavy rock and rise up in a gust of wind like fine dust.

When these particles of pulverized rock have floated about in the air for a considerable time, they suddenly alight on the level surface of the spacious grounds where they are formed by the men into piles and moistened with water. From the moist powder mud is formed and then sprinkled with an abundance of salt. When the following has lighted the earth with the lamp of Phoebus[9], the men treat the thick mud which they have saturated with salt, and at a definite time they add more salt.

Then an expert in the industry seeks to discover all the diseases of the mixture, for it often suffers grievous disorders, to find out whether the illness is causing the patient excruciating chills, or whether high fever is consuming it. Hence he dissolves the salty mixture in a bowl of quicksilver. Then after adding water he carefully examines the vessel, moving it in every direction and shifting the mud from side to side. After that, if the metal, when pressed by the finger, settles in the vessel and begins to assume a cold leadlike appearance, it is evident that

---

[8]   I.e. after the age of fifteen.   [9]   The Sun.

the mud is suffering with a cold. But if it should become milky and cause the water to turn white, this is an indication that the mud is ill and being consumed with high fever. For these diseases, however, medicine affords a prompt relief.

If a cold should happen to irritate the metallic mud, a physician skilled in Apollo's art[10] administers warm relief. Crushed rocks of copper he lays for a long time in strong brine and afterwards heats the mixture over raging flames until he sees it giving up pus-like matter and rendering the water turbid in its decomposition. Then he spreads the trembling patient under the bright sun, sprinkles the copper upon it, and thus repels the disease.[11]

. . . In the meantime there is suspended from a high beam a closely woven linen bag having the shape of a cone and made in such a way as to retain the silver but discharge the quicksilver[12]. This bag is filled with the deposit taken from the basin, and because of its texture tenaciously holds the pure silver but discharges most of the mercury. The men place this in trays and store it away in the house.

When the men have taken the bags from the lofty beam and lowered them to the ground, at last they draw the silver out of the avaricious[13] bosoms, glad to take into their hands the ductile[14] substance and then to amuse themselves by modeling various objects. As a happy group of young children enjoys playing with wax and fashioning simple figures to suit the fancy, now molding in the hand a calf, now making a little vase or a small box, and now again a steep mountain, in like manner the simple folk play in the easily worked silver. Each one, indeed, makes heavy plates or forms little round balls from the soft substance.

. . . The melted silver, agitated in the red-hot furnace by the heat of the blazing fire, shakes the round walls with its waves and boils furiously. As the sea, when its waters are agitated by a strong wind, now opens up its waters into valleys, now lashes the stars, and now shakes the curving shores with terrific blows, in like manner the molten silver seethes among the flames. But when the impurities have disappeared from the hot furnace, and ravishing Vulcan[15] has boiled down the silver with his consuming fire, immediately the whole surface sinks to the very bottom, becoming still and calm. At once, the bellows are put aside, the fire is removed, and the men take the sheet of silver out of the black furnace.

Gold, on the other hand, does not weary the boys with such distressing toil, gold, a child of Phoebus[16] and similar to Phoebus, surpassing all other metals in splendor. Mighty fortune allows it to inhabit palaces and to be enthroned on the august head of kings. More than all other things gold captivates the heart of mortals, for it more quickly enriches its possessor and frees him from toil. Scarcely indeed has the machine, bristling with metal pounders, and the massive mill crushed the rocks until the men throw mercury over the dust and run it through the heavy rollers of the mill. The mill gladly receives into its deep bosom this rich stream of precious earth. The men then take it out and wash it in water, after which they squeeze it through bags and purify it in a crucible. Just as when armed men while marching along attack a man of noble birth, immediately cut off every avenue of escape, and torment the besieged man, wantonly striking him again and again and threatening death, but he, unable to resist the weapons of the crowd, wisely tries to escape such danger by promptly submitting his neck to the insolent band, so it is that the golden metal, descended from Phoebus, yields with bended head to the merciless thief.

Sometimes, too, the men will refine the sparkling gold in double furnaces, arranged in

---

[10]   Medicine.
[11]   I.e. cures the cold.
[12]   Mercury.
[13]   Miserly.

[14]   Malleable.
[15]   God of fire, patron of metal-workers.
[16]   The Sun.

proper manner, to increase the master's profits and reduce the cost.

When these operations have been completed through the persistent efforts of the men, an inspector, sent by the king of Spain, examines the extracted silver and gold. He rolls the small pellets into a single plate, and from this he snips off with his stout pincers a small piece which he keeps for himself as a fitting reward for his trouble. This he tests in the fire, and he determines how much gold the greedy silver has appropriated and concealed within its own mass. Then in the same manner he tests with fire the value of the gold and duly sets aside a fifth part for the crown[17]. As soon as the pieces of gold and silver have been stamped, the overseer carefully hides them in a safe place.

From *Birds*

. . . The world knows nothing more remarkable than the tiny humming bird, bereft of the gift of sweet song, but renowned for the brilliant plumage which covers its small frame. Its body is diminutive, perhaps no larger than the thumb, but protected by mother nature with a beak, sharp and almost as long as the bird's entire body. It has green plumage of golden brightness interspersed with the various colors of the sun. It surpasses in flight the speed of the west wind and creates a dull humming sound with its whirring wings. Moreover, if it should wish to draw dewy nectar from a fragrant flower to nourish its body, for it refuses to feed on any other food, on fluttering wings it holds itself suspended in midair while it draws out the nectarine liquor through its slender mouth. So fast, indeed, does it beat its delicate wings that they elude the watchful eye by their rapid motion, and you might suppose the bird to be suspended in the air by a thread. Now if winter should descend on the forest from the north, and the shifting winds become colder with the coming of the rainy season, on light wing the humming bird swiftly abandons our chilly country and flower gardens, and hiding away for a long time in the dark shadows of the mountain like cunning Procne[18], indulges in peaceful slumber until Aries makes the days equal to the starlit nights[19], and the return of spring restores to the meadows their former glory.

From *Sports*

. . . Straightway shall I myself turn to the cocks ready for gallant battles, nor is it right that I should fail to disclose fights which reveal an unheard-of form of wild insanity. Scarcely is the crested fowl strutting fiercely along with arched neck, maintaining an air of haughty disdain and eager to assail his mates with unceasing battles, when an insane passion for sport and a barbarous desire for pleasure causes him to be taken from the poultry-yard and placed in a small cage. His foot is tied fast with a rope and he is carefully kept for fights. The bird at first frets and makes long laments, frantically trying to free himself from his new fetters. Soon, however, he becomes accustomed to his food and pleasant surroundings and struts majestically around in the coop, frequently saluting in song both the moon and the sun. A reddish comb rises on his crested head, his wattles[20] too are red, and a tuft of feathers streams over his neck. His waving tail spreads out in ruffled plumage, gracefully arching his head and leaving uncov-

---

[17] The so-called *quinta real* (royal fifth) was customarily set aside for the Crown.

[18] The nightingale.

[19] In the period from 21 March to 20 April.

[20] Fleshy folds of skin on the throat.

ered the hornlike spurs by which he defends himself. But the unscrupulous men who delight in driving these fierce birds into bitter conflict cut off their weapons and their comb and wattles, leaving only a small portion of the left spur, to which the gamester attaches a tiny little blade, fastening it tightly to the leg with a small cord. And when the eagerly awaited day appointed for the fights arrives, each man brings into the bloody fray his brightly armed gamecock growling and flinging out threats.

There is always a small area of level ground, previously dedicated to the dreadful fury of Mars[21], splotched with the blood of recent slaughter and surrounded with many wooden benches which provide seats for the spectators as they loudly cheer the victors and vie with one another in heavy betting.

When the bustling crowd has filled these benches, at once a pair of fighters, equipped with deadly spurs, is set down in the middle of the arena. The ferocious hearts of the cock are immediately fired with anger, their cheeks turn red, fire comes into their eyes, and with ruffled feathers and necks bent low they advance swiftly to battle. Yet not too fast may the bird of Mars[22] dare to commit himself to the perils of war or to challenge his foe to armed conflict, but first he must watch the movements of his enemy and explore every avenue of approach. Then with a sudden leap he flings himself into the air toward his opponent, beating breast with breast, and with iron-tipped spur he fiercely thrusts him back, interlocking foot with foot and spur with spur, nor does he ever dismiss the violent passion from his heart until he has his victim lying prostrate on the yellow sand. Feathers fly and entrails flow from the lacerated stomach; and the brave warrior pours out a warm stream of blood upon the wide field as he succumbs to an evil fate. The winner exults amid the cheers of the large gathering, he shakes his golden breast, and lustily sings of his glorious triumph. As bulls that wildly run over all the plain sometimes interlock horns and slash one another with many a wound and continue to deal blow after blow and to weary the foe until a hard won victory comes to the one with invincible horns, so the cock, protected by his shining spur, struggles desperately to win the victory. If, however, the dastardly winner should become frightened while his foe is writhing in the agony of death and raising his fluffy feathers from off his forehead turn away in flight, at once the infamous and cowardly victor is deserted, and the laurels, the victor's prize, are placed instead upon the brow of the dead.

Then the people stage one deadly fight after another until Phoebus[23] touches the middle of the heavens and night veils the sky in dark shadows.

1781

---

[21]   God of war.   [23]   The Sun.
[22]   The fighting cock.

Contested Visions:
Revolution and Nation

Benjamin Franklin (1706–1790)

The French adored him and considered him on a par with such *philosophes* as Voltaire and Rousseau. The English vilified him as the "inventor and first planner" of colonial resistance. He was the only patriot to have signed the four founding documents of the republic: the Declaration of Independence, the treaty of alliance with France, the peace treaty ending the war with England, and the Constitution. At his death, the esteem in which his fellow Americans held him rivaled that of George Washington. His *Autobiography* is the only bestseller from the eighteenth century that remains a perennial favorite at home and abroad, and has come to define the "American" self and quintessentially American values.

Franklin was born in Boston, the tenth and youngest son in a family of fifteen children. His parents were staunch Congregationalists with frugal New England values. His father, Josiah, was a tallow chandler who emigrated from England in 1683 to escape religious persecution, and sent his son to Boston Grammar School in preparation for entering the ministry. Financial need curtailed his study after only two years, but because Franklin disliked his father's trade, he was apprenticed at twelve to his brother James, a printer. This suited Franklin's precocious nature and encouraged his love of reading and books. Early in his life, he abandoned his parents' narrow faith for a mode of free-thinking he would develop into a unique version

of deistic belief. He improved his writing skills by imitating the style of contemporary English essayists James Addison and Richard Steele, which he came across in an issue of the *Spectator*. His first major publication came in 1722 with a series of fourteen essays written in the persona of widow "Silence Dogood," which Franklin submitted anonymously to his brother James' irreverent newspaper, the *New-England Courant*. Although only sixteen, Franklin had mastered a popular style that allowed him to satirize staid Boston society, dour Puritan religion, and ingrown local politics. Frequently in trouble with authorities who censored his paper, James defied their orders, and spent time in prison and in hiding in order to avoid arrest, leaving the operation of the *Courant* to his young sibling. But Franklin chafed under James' harsh treatment, and in 1723, he broke his indentures and secretly left for Philadelphia where he hoped to find work in the printing trade.

The story of the next thirty-five years of Franklin's life in Philadelphia has become the stuff of legend – how he walked into town at seventeen with two puffy rolls under his arms, his clothes stuffed into his pockets and little else, and parlayed his printing and personal skills into a highly lucrative trade that allowed him to retire from business at forty-two in order to spend his time divided between scientific experimentation, invention, and "doing good" for the public. At twenty-four, after hard work and shrewd investments, Franklin owned his own printing shop, and was the editor and publisher of the highly successful newspaper, the *Pennsylvania Gazette*. He married Deborah Read, the daughter of his first landlady, with whom he had three children. He already had two children out of wedlock, and at his marriage, he took William into his household who would later become the governor of New Jersey and a loyalist during the Revolution. Franklin's business brought him into contact with the major figures in Pennsylvania politics, and his philanthropic projects – establishing

BENJAMIN FRANKLIN.

Né à Bofton, dans la nouvelle Angleterre le 17 Janvier 1706

"Benjamin Franklin in 1777," by Augustus de Saint-Aubin, after a drawing by N. C. Cochin. (By permission of the Philadelphia Museum of Art, the Mrs John D. Rockefeller Collection.) The Ledgend, in French, reads, "Born in Boston in New England, on 17 January 1706." This engraving depicts Franklin as the French liked to imagine him, as the wily New World man complete with fur hat and homespun clothes.

the first circulating libraries and fire companies, an academy that would become the University of Pennsylvania, a charity hospital, and the American Philosophical Society – gave him a high public profile. His small club, the Junto, which began as a means of self-improvement for a handful of friends, became a highly influential instrument for shaping public attitudes and policies. He invented a more efficient wood-burning stove, bifocal glasses, and the lightning rod, and made significant contributions to the study of natural science, especially electricity, which brought him international repute.

Many of Franklin's projects were jump-started by his finely tuned writing which appeared as pamphlets or newspaper essays. As a printer and publisher, he was perfectly positioned to disseminate his own ideas for projects, which he often attributed to an anonymous "we" or fictitious, persona. His philanthropic pamphlets developed the voice of the altruistically minded citizen and, above all, the reasonable man. In 1733, he brought out the first *Almanack* under the editorship of the fictitious Richard Saunders, or "Poor Richard." Chock full of proverbial wisdom, pungent wit and country humor borrowed from many sources and adapted to a readership Franklin knew well, it became the most popular almanac in the colonies.

In 1757, his success in local politics prompted Pennsylvania to appoint him its agent in ongoing disputes with England, and his success in this led other colonies to follow suit. During his two decades as colonial agent in the mother country, Franklin published acidic satires on the folly of colonial rule. Returning to Philadelphia in May, 1775, he was chosen as a representative to the second Continental Congress and helped to draft the Declaration of Independence. In October 1776, Franklin was appointed the colonies' representative to France, America's major ally during the Revolution. There, the seventy year old Franklin charmed the sophisticated French at court and in the influential literary salons by wearing a frontiersman's fur hat, simple, homespun clothing, and carrying a stout stick made of apple wood. At the same time as he deliberately cultivated a rustic "American" image to reinforce the naturalness of the American cause, he also proved himself intelligent, witty, and wonderfully diplomatic. During this period, he wrote and printed on a small press he set up at his residence in Passy the charming short pieces called "bagatelles." The lightness of

his touch in these flirtatious *jeu d'esprit* is heightened by comparison to the savage satire of contemporaneous essays like "The Sale of the Hessians," written in response to the British deployment of Hessian mercenaries in the colonies. In declining health, Franklin returned to Philadelphia in 1785, where he was named a delegate to the Constitutional Congress, and spent considerable energy trying to heal the conflicts between the states in order to insure the ratification of the Constitution.

Franklin's most sustained effort is his *Autobiography*. He began composing it on a retreat to the English countryside in 1771, and addressed it to his son William. Encouraged by Quaker friends, a group with a long tradition of reading and writing edifying "journals," and others who felt his life was "representative" and "instructive," Franklin worked on the *Autobiography* at three other times – in 1784 in Passy, and in 1788 and 1789 in Philadelphia – eighteen years in all. He revised parts of it extensively, achieving a deliberately colloquial tone, but it remained unfinished at his death the following year. Although Franklin was inspired by Cotton Mather's *Bonifacius, an Essay . . . To Do Good* (1710) and the archetypal biographies of eminent Puritans in *Magnalia Christi Americana* (1702), his *Autobiography* contradicts the conventional religious conversion narrative by putting "Providence" on a par with reason and nature, putting Jesus on a par with Socrates in the controversial "Art of Virtue" section of Part Two, excerpted below, and demonstrating one's ability to correct the "errata" or mistakes one made in life out of "necessity."

The *Autobiography* has been hailed – and derided – as the classic articulation of the "American Dream," the first "rags to riches" story. But it is also, more complexly, the story of an individual's rise from obscurity to power and prominence, in a radically new, democratically organized, supposedly enlightened society, that allegorizes America's similar trajectory in the world. Although suffused with optimism about the possibilities for individual as well as national success held out by the virtues of industry, frugality, moderation, self-improvement, and common sense, the *Autobiography* is not without its dark moments, its exposure of wishful self-deception, the pitfalls of vanity, and the manipulative quality of consolidating, consensus-loving narrative and rhetorical strategies at a crucial moment in the formation of the new republic.

PRIMARY WORKS

The Writings of Benjamin Franklin, ed. Albert Henry Smyth, 10 vols, 1905–1907.

The Papers of Benjamin Franklin, eds Leonard W. Labaree et. al., 34 vols, 1959 –.

The Autobiography of Benjamin Franklin: A Genetic Text, eds J. A. Leo Lemay and P. M. Zall, 1981.

Benjamin Franklin's Autobiography, eds J. A Leo Lemay and P. M. Zall, 1986.

Benjamin Franklin, ed. J. A. Leo Lemay, 1987.

FURTHER READING

James Sappenfield, *A Sweet Instruction: Franklin's Journalism as a Literary Apprenticeship* (Carbondale: South Illinois University Press, 1973).

J. A. Leo Lemay, ed., *The Oldest Revolutionary: Essays on Benjamin Franklin* (Philadelphia: University of Pennsylvania Press, 1976).

Douglas Anderson, *The Radical Enlightenments of Benjamin Franklin* (Baltimore: Johns Hopkins University Press, 1997).

Walter Kerry, *Benjamin Franklin and his Gods* (Urbana, University of Illinois Press, 1999).

EPITAPH[1]

The Body of
B. Franklin,
Printer;
Like the Cover of an old Book,
Its Contents torn out,
And stript of its Lettering and Gilding,
Lies here, Food for Worms.
But the Work shall not be wholly lost:
For it will, as he believ'd, appear once more,
In a new & more perfect Edition,
Corrected and amended
By the Author.
He was born Jan. 6, 1706
Died—17–

1728

FROM *THE AUTOBIOGRAPHY*[2] [PART TWO][3]

Continuation of the Account of my Life.
Begun at Passy 1784

It is some time since I receiv'd the above Letters, but I have been too busy till now to think of complying with the Request they contain. It might too be much better done if I were at home among my Papers, which would aid my Memory, & help to ascertain Dates. But my Return

---

[1] The text, with slight modification, is from *Benjamin Franklin: Writings*, ed. J. A. Leo Lemay (New York: Library of America, 1987).

[2] The text, with slight modification, is from *The Autobiography of Benjamin Franklin: A Genetic Text*, eds J. A. Leo Lemay and P. M. Zall (Knoxville: University of Tennessee Press, 1981).

[3] Franklin composed the second part of his autobiography at the Hôtel de Valentenois in Passy, a suburb of Paris, while he was the American representative to the Peace Treaty with Britain at the end of the Revolutionary war.

being uncertain, and having just now a little Leisure, I will endeavour to recollect & write what I can; If I live to get home, it may there be corrected and improv'd.

Not having any Copy here of what is already written, I know not whether an Account is given of the means I used to establish the Philadelphia publick Library, which from a small Beginning is now become so considerable, though I remember to have come down to near the Time of that Transaction, 1730. I will therefore begin here, with an Account of it, which may be struck out if found to have been already given.–

At the time I establish'd my self in Pensylvania, there was not a good Bookseller's Shop in any of the Colonies to the Southward of Boston. In New-York & Philadelphia the Printers were indeed Stationers, they sold only Paper, &c. Almanacks, Ballads, and a few common School Books. Those who lov'd Reading were oblig'd to send for their Books from England. – The Members of the Junto had each a few.[4] We had left the Alehouse where we first met, and hired a Room to hold our Club in. I propos'd that we should all of us bring our Books to that Room, where they would not only be ready to consult in our Conferences, but become a common Benefit, each of us being at Liberty to borrow such as he wish'd to read at home. This was accordingly done, and for some time contented us. Finding the Advantage of this little Collection, I propos'd to tender the Benefit from Books more common by commencing a Public Subscription Library. I drew a Sketch of the Plan and Rules that would be necessary, and got a skilful Conveyancer Mr Charles Brockden[5] to put the whole in Form of Articles of Agreement to be subscribed, by which each Subscriber engag'd to pay a certain Sum down for the first Purchase of Books and an annual Contribution for encreasing them. – So few were the Readers at that time in Philadelphia, and the Majority of us so poor, that I was not able with great Industry to find more than Fifty Persons, mostly Young Tradesmen, willing to pay down for this purpose Forty shillings each, & Ten Shillings per Annum. On this little Fund we began. The Books were imported. The Library was open one Day in the Week for lending them to the Subscribers, on their Promisory Notes to pay Double the Value if not duly returned. The Institution soon manifested its Utility, was imitated by other Towns and in other Provinces, the Librarys were augmented by Donations, Reading became fashionable, and our People having no publick Amusements to divert their Attention from Study became better acquainted with Books, and in a few Years were observ'd by Strangers to be better instructed & more intelligent than People of the same Rank generally are in other Countries.–

When we were about to sign the above-mentioned Articles, which were to be binding on us, our Heirs, &c for fifty Years, Mr Brockden, the Scrivener, said to us, "You are young Men, but it is scarce probable that any of you will live to see the Expiration of the Term fix'd in this Instrument." A Number of us, however, are yet living: But the Instrument was after a few Years rendred null by a Charter that incorporated & gave Perpetuity to the Company.

The Objections, & Reluctances I met with in Soliciting the Subscriptions, made me soon feel the Impropriety of presenting one's self as the Proposer of any useful Project that might be suppos'd to raise one's Reputation in the smallest degree above that of one's Neighbours, when one has need of their Assistance to accomplish that Project. I therefore put my self as much as I could out of sight, and stated it as a Scheme of *a Number of Friends*, who had requested me to go about and propose it to Such as they thought Lovers of Reading. In this way my Affair went on more smoothly, and I ever after practis'd it on such Occasions; and from my frequent Successes, can heartily reccomend it. The present little Sacrifice of your Vanity will afterwards be amply repaid. If it remains a while uncertain to whom the Merit belongs, some

---

4   The "Junto" was a small club of Franklin's "most ingenious" friends, formed for "mutual Improvement," which met for almost forty years.

5   Charles Brockden (1683–1769), Philadelphia's leading drafter of legal documents.

one more vain than yourself will be encourag'd to claim it, and then even Envy will be dispos'd to do you justice, by plucking those assum'd Feathers, & restoring them to their right Owner.

This Library afforded me the Means of Improvement by constant Study, for which I set apart an Hour or two each Day; and thus repair'd in some Degree the Loss of the Learned Education my Father once intended for me. Reading was the only Amusement I allow'd my self. I spent no time in Taverns, Games, or Frolicks of any kind. And my Industry in my Business continu'd as indefatigable as it was necessary. I was in debt, for my Printing-house, I had a young Family coming on to be educated,[6] and I had to contend with for Business two Printers who were establish'd in the Place before me. My Circumstances however grew daily easier: my original Habits of Frugality continuing. And My Father having among his Instructions to me when a Boy, frequently repeated a Proverb of Solomon, *"Seest thou a Man diligent in his Calling, he shall stand before Kings, he shall not stand before mean Men."*[7] I from thence consider'd Industry as a Means of obtaining Wealth and Distinction, which encourag'd me; tho' I did not think that I should ever literally stand before Kings, which however has since happened. – for I have stood before five, & even had the honour of sitting down with one, the King of Denmark, to Dinner.[8]

We have an English Proverb that says,

> He that would thrive
> Must ask his Wife;

it was lucky for me that I had one as much dispos'd to Industry & Frugality as my self. She assisted me chearfully in my Business, folding & stitching Pamphlets, tending Shop, purchasing old Linen Rags for the Paper-makers, &c &c. We kept no idle Servants, our Table was plain & simple, our Furniture of the cheapest. For instance my Breakfast was a long time Bread & Milk, (no Tea,) and I ate it out of a twopenny earthen Porringer with a Pewter Spoon. But mark how Luxury will enter Families, and make a Progress, in Spite of Principle. Being Call'd one Morning to Breakfast, I found it in a China Bowl with a Spoon of Silver. They had been bought for me without my Knowledge by my Wife, and had cost her the enormous Sum of three and twenty Shillings, for which she had no other Excuse or Apology to make, but that she thought *her* Husband deserv'd a Silver Spoon & China Bowl as well as any of his Neighbours. This was the first Appearance of Plate & China in our House, which afterwards in a Course of Years as our Wealth increas'd, augmented gradually to several Hundred Pounds in Value.

I had been religiously educated as a Presbyterian; and tho' some of the Dogmas of that Persuasion, such as the Eternal Decrees of God, Election, Reprobation,[9] &c. appear'd to me unintelligible, others doubtful, & I early absented myself from the Public Assemblies of the Sect, Sunday being my Studying-Day, I never was without some religious Principles; I never doubted, for instance, the Existance of the Deity, that he made the World, & govern'd it by his Providence; that the most acceptable Service of God was the doing Good to Man; that our Souls are immortal; and that all Crime will be punished & Virtue rewarded either here or hereafter; these I esteem'd the Essentials of every Religion, and being to be found in all the Religions we had in our Country I respected them all, tho' with different degrees of Respect as

---

[6] Franklin had three children: William, born *c.*1731, Francis, born in 1732, and Sarah, born in 1743.

[7] Proverbs 22:29.

[8] Louis XV and Louis XVI of France, George II and George III of England, and Charles VI of Denmark.

[9] Election: God's predetermination, before birth, who will be saved and who damned. Reprobation: punishment.

I found them more or less mix'd with other Articles which without any Tendency to inspire, promote or confirm Morality, serv'd principally to divide us & make us unfriendly to one another. – This Respect to all, with an Opinion that the worst had some good Effects, induc'd me to avoid all Discourse that might tend to lessen the good Opinion another might have of his own Religion; and as our Province increas'd in People and new Places of worship were continually wanted, & generally erected by voluntary Contribution, my Mite for such purpose, whatever might be the Sect, was never refused.–

Tho' I seldom attended any Public Worship, I had still an Opinion of its Propriety, and of its Utility when rightly conducted, and I regularly paid my annual Subscription for the Support of the only Presbyterian Minister or Meeting we had in Philadelphia. He us'd to visit me sometimes as a Friend, and admonish me to attend his Administrations, and I was now and then prevail'd on to do so, once for five Sundays successively. Had he been, *in my Opinion*, a good Preacher perhaps I might have continued, notwithstanding the occasion I had for the Sunday's Leisure in my Course of Study: But his Discourses were chiefly either polemic, Arguments, or Explications of the peculiar Doctrines of our Sect, and were all to me very dry, uninteresting and unedifying, since not a single moral Principle was inculcated or enforc'd, their Aim seeming to be rather to make us Presbyterians than good Citizens. At length he took for his Text that Verse of the 4th Chapter of Philippians, *Finally, Brethren, Whatsoever Things are true, honest, just, pure, lovely, or of good report, if there be any virtue, or any praise, think on these Things*;[10] & I imagin'd in a Sermon on such a Text, we could not miss of having some Morality: But he confin'd himself to five Points only as meant by the Apostle, viz. 1. Keeping holy the Sabbath Day. 2. Being diligent in Reading the Holy Scriptures. 3. Attending duly the Publick Worship. 4. Partaking of the Sacrament. 5. Paying a due Respect to God's Ministers. – These might be all good Things, but as they were not the kind of good Things that I expected from that Text, I despaired of ever meeting with them from any other, was disgusted, and attended his Preaching no more. – I had some Years before compos'd a little Liturgy or Form of Prayer for my own private Use, viz. in 1728 entitled, *Articles of Belief & Acts of Religion*.[11] I return'd to the Use of this, and went no more to the public Assemblies. – My Conduct might be blameable, but I leave it without attempting farther to excuse it, my present purpose being to relate Facts, and not to make Apologies for them.–

It was about this time that I conceivd the bold and arduous Project of arriving at moral Perfection. I wish'd to live without committing any Fault at any time; I would conquer all that either Natural Inclination, Custom, or Company might lead me into. As I knew, or thought I knew, what was right and wrong, I did not see why I might not *always* do the one and avoid the other. But I soon found I had undertaken a Task of more Difficulty than I had imagined: While my Care was employ'd in guarding against one Fault, I was often surpriz'd by another. Habit took the Advantage of Inattention. Inclination was sometimes too strong for Reason. I councluded at length, that the mere speculative Conviction that it was our Interest to be compleatly virtuous, was not sufficient to prevent our Slipping, and that the contrary Habits must be broken and good Ones acquired and established, before we can have any Dependance on a steady uniform Rectitude of Conduct. For this purpose I therefore contriv'd the following Method.

In the various Enumerations of the moral Virtues I had met with in my Reading, I found the Catalogue more or less numerous, as different Writers included more or fewer Ideas under

---

[10]   Philippians 4:8.
[11]   Only the first part of this survives, and includes a statement of "First Principles," with expressions of "Adoration,"

"Petition," and "Thanks." The "Adoration" section includes singing John Milton's "Hymn to the Creator."

the same Name. Temperance, for Example, was by some confin'd to Eating & Drinking, while by others it was extended to mean the moderating every other Pleasure, Appetite, Inclination or Passion, bodily or mental, even to our Avarice & Ambition. I proposd to myself, for the sake of Clearness, to use rather more Names with fewer Ideas annex'd to each, than a few Names with more Ideas; and I included under Thirteen Names of Virtues all that at that time occurr'd to me as necessary or desirable, and annex'd to each a short Precept, which fully express'd the Extent I gave to its Meaning.–

These Names of Virtues with their Precepts were

1. TEMPERANCE.
   Eat not to Dulness.
   Drink not to Elevation.
2. SILENCE.
   Speak not but what may benefit others or your self. Avoid trifling Conversation.
3. ORDER.
   Let all your Things have their Places. Let each Part of your Business have its Time.
4. RESOLUTION.
   Resolve to perform what you ought. Perform without fail what you resolve.
5. FRUGALITY.
   Make no Expence but to do good to others or yourself: i.e. Waste nothing.
6. INDUSTRY.
   Lose no Time. – Be always employ'd in something useful. – Cut off all unnecessary Actions.–
7. SINCERITY.
   Use no hurtful Deceit.
   Think innocently and justly; and, if you speak; speak accordingly.
8. JUSTICE.
   Wrong none, by doing injuries or omitting the Benefits that are your Duty.
9. MODERATION.
   Avoid Extreams. Forbear resenting Injuries so much as you think they deserve.
10. CLEANLINESS
    Tolerate no Uncleanness in Body, Cloaths or Habitation.
11. TRANQUILITY
    Be not disturbed at Trifles, or at Accidents common or unavoidable.
12. CHASTITY.
    Rarely use Venery but for Health or Offspring; Never to Dulness, Weakness, or the Injury of your own or another's Peace or Reputation.–
13. HUMILITY.
    Imitate Jesus and Socrates.–

My intention being to acquire the *Habitude* of all these Virtues, I Judg'd it would be well not to distract my Attention by attempting the whole at once, but to fix it on one of them at a time, and when I should be Master of that, then to proceed to another, and so on till I should have gone thro' the thirteen. And as the previous Acquisition of some might facilitate the Acquisition of certain others, I arrang'd them with that View as they stand above. *Temperance* first, as it tends to procure that Coolness & Clearness of Head, which is so necessary where constant Vigilance was to be kept up, and Guard maintained, against the unremitting Attraction of ancient Habits, and the Force of perpetual Temptations. This being acquir'd & establish'd,

Silence would be more easy, and my Desire being to gain Knowledge at the same time that I improv'd in Virtue, and considering that in Conversation it was obtain'd rather by the Use of the Ears than of the Tongue, & therefore wishing to break a Habit I was getting into of Prattling, Punning & Joking, which only made me acceptable to trifling Company, I gave *Silence* the second Place. This, and the next, *Order*, I expected would allow me more Time for attending to my Project and my Studies; RESOLUTION once become habitual, would keep me firm in my Endeavours to obtain all the subsequent Virtues; *Frugality & Industry*, by freeing me from my remaining Debt, & producing Affluence & Independance would make more easy the Practice of *Sincerity* and *Justice*, &c. &c.. Conceiving then that agreeable to the Advice of Pythagoras in his Golden Verses[12], daily Examination would be necessary, I contriv'd the following Method for conducting that Examination.

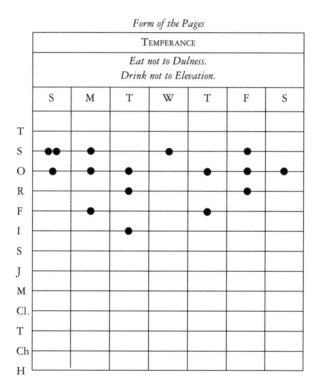

Form of the Pages

TEMPERANCE						
Eat not to Dulness. *Drink not to Elevation.*						
S	M	T	W	T	F	S

(rows: T, S, O, R, F, I, S, J, M, Cl., T, Ch, H)

[12] Pythagoras (*b.* 580? BC), Greek philosopher and mathematician. Franklin's note here gives a translation of the "Golden Verses:" "Let not the stealing God of Sleep surprize,/ Nor creep in Slumbers on the weary Eyes,/ Ere ev'ry Action of the former Day,/ Strictly thou dost, and *righteously* survey./ With Rev'rence at thy own Tribunal stand,/ And answer justly to thy own Demand. /Where have I been? In what have I transgrest?/ What Good or Ill has this Day's Life exprest?/ Where have I fail'd in what I ought to do?/ In what to GOD, to Man, or to myself I owe?/ Inquire severe whate'er from first to last,/ From Morning's Dawn till Ev'nings Gloom has past./ If Evil were thy Deeds, repenting mourn,/ And let thy Soul with strong Remorse be torn:/ If Good, the Good with Peace of Mind repay,/ And to thy secret Self with Pleasure say,/ Rejoice, my Heart, for all went well to Day."

I made a little Book in which I allotted a Page for each of the Virtues. I rul'd each Page with red Ink so as to have seven Columns, one for each Day of the Week, marking each Column with a Letter for the Day. I cross'd these Columns with thirteen red Lines, marking the Beginning of each Line with the first Letter of one of the Virtues, on which Line & in its proper Column I might mark by a little black Spot every Fault I found upon Examination, to have been committed respecting that Virtue upon that Day.

I determined to give a Week's strict Attention to each of the Virtues successively. Thus in the first Week my great Guard was to avoid every the least Offence against Temperance, leaving the other Virtues to their ordinary Chance, only marking every Evening the Faults of the Day. Thus if in the first Week I could keep my first Line marked T clear of Spots, I suppos'd the Habit at Virtue so much strengthen'd and its opposite weaken'd, that I might venture extending my Attention to include the next, and for the following Week keep both Lines clear of Spots. Proceeding thus to the last, I could go thro' a Course compleat in Thirteen Weeks, and four Courses in a Year. – And like him who having a Garden to weed, does not attempt to eradicate all the bad Herbs at once, which would exceed his Reach and his Strength, but works on one of the Beds at a time, & having accomplish'd the first proceeds to a second; so I should have, (I hoped) the encouraging Pleasure of seeing on my Pages the Progress I made in Virtue, by clearing successively my Lines of their Spots, till in the End by a Number of Courses, I should be happy in viewing a clean Book after a thirteen Weeks daily Examination.

This my little Book had for its Motto these Lines from *Addison's Cato*;[13]

> *Here will I hold: If there is a Pow'r above us,*
> *(And that there is, all Nature cries aloud*
> *Thro' all her Works) he must delight in Virtue,*
> *And that which he delights in must be happy.*

Another from *Cicero*.[14]

> *O Vitæ Philasophia Dux! O Virtutum indigatrix, expultrixque vitiorum! Unus dies bene, &*
> *ex preceptis tuis actus, peccanti immortalitati est anteponendus.*

Another from the Proverbs of Solomon speaking of Wisdom or Virtue;

> Length of Days is in her right hand, and in her Left Hand Riches and Honours; Her Ways are Ways of Pleasantness, and all her Paths are Peace.   III, 16, 17.

And conceiving God to be the Fountain of Wisdom, I thought it right and necessary to solicit his Assistance for obtaining it; to this End I form'd the following little Prayer, which was prefix'd to my Tables of Examination; for daily Use.

> *O Powerful Goodness! bountiful Father! merciful Guide! Increase in me that Wisdom which*
> *discovers my truest Interests; Strengthen my Resolutions to perform what that Wisdom dictates.*
> *Accept my kind Offices to thy other Children, as the only Return in my Power for thy continual*
> *Favors to me.*

---

[13]   Joseph Addison, *Cato, a Tragedy* (1713). Act V, 1, 15–18. Franklin also used these lines as an epigraph for his *Articles of Belief and Acts of Religion*.
[14]   Cicero, *Tusculan Disputations*, Act V, 2, 5, with several lines omitted after *vitiorum*: "Oh philosophy, guide of life! Oh searcher out of virtues and expeller of vices! . . . One day lived well and according to thy precepts is to be preferred to an eternity of sin" (Latin).

I us'd also sometimes a little Prayer which I took from *Thomson's* Poems[15]. viz

> *Father of Light and Life, thou Good supreme,*
> *O teach me what is good, teach me thy self!*
> *Save me from Folly, Vanity and Vice,*
> *From every low Pursuit, and fill my Soul*
> *With Knowledge, conscious Peace, & Virtue pure,*
> *Sacred, substantial, neverfading Bliss!*

The Precept of *Order* requiring that *every Part of my Business should have its allotted Time*, one Page in my little Book contain'd the following Scheme of Employment for the Twenty-four Hours of a natural Day,

The Morning Question, What Good shall I do this Day?	5 6 7	Rise, wash, and address *Powerful Goodness*; contrive Day's Business and take the Resolution of the Day; prosecute the present Study: and breakfast? –
	8 9 10 11	Work.
	12 1	Read, or overlook my Accounts, and dine.
	2 3 4 5	Work.
Evening Question, What Good have I done today?	6 7 8 9	Put Things in their Places, Supper, Musick, or Diversion, or Conversation, Examination of the Day.
	10 11 12 1 2 3 4	Sleep. –

<hr>

[15] James Thomson (1700–1748), *The Seasons*, "Winter" (1726), lines 218–23.

I enter'd upon the Execution of this Plan for Self Examination, and continu'd it with occasional Intermissions for some time. I was surpriz'd to find myself so much fuller of Faults than I had imagined, but I had the Satisfaction of seeing them diminish. To avoid the Trouble of renewing now & then my little Book, which by scraping out the Marks on the Paper of old Faults to make room for new Ones in a new Course, became full of Holes: I transferr'd my Tables & Precepts to the Ivory Leaves of a Memorandum Book, on which the Lines were drawn with red Ink that made a durable Stain, and on those Lines I mark'd my Faults with a black Lead Pencil, which Marks I could easily wipe out with a wet Sponge. After a while I went thro' one Course only in a Year, and afterwards only one in several Years; till at length I omitted them entirely, being employ'd in Voyages & Business abroad with a Multiplicity of Affairs, that interfered. But I always carried my little Book with me. My Scheme of ORDER, gave me the most Trouble, and I found, that tho' it might be practicable where a Man's Business was such as to leave him the Disposition of his Time, that of a Journey-man Printer for instance, it was not possible to be exactly observ'd by a Master, who must mix with the World, and often receive People of Business at their own Hours. – *Order* too, with regard to Places for Things, Papers, &c. I found extreamly difficult to acquire. I had not been early accustomed to it, & having an exceeding good Memory, I was not so sensible of the Inconvenience attending Want of Method. This Article therefore cost me so much painful Attention & my Faults in it vex'd me so much, and I made so little Progress in Amendment, & had such frequent Relapses, that I was almost ready to give up the Attempt, and content my self with a faulty Character in that respect. Like the Man who in buying an Ax of a Smith my Neighbour, desired to have the whole of its Surface as bright as the Edge; the Smith consented to grind it bright for him if he would turn the Wheel. He turn'd while the Smith press'd the broad Face of the Ax hard & heavily on the Stone, which made the Turning of it very fatiguing. The Man came every now & then from the Wheel to see how the Work went on; and at length would take his Ax as it was without further Grinding. No, says the Smith, Turn on, turn on; we shall have it bright by and by; as yet 'tis only speckled. Yes, says the Man; but – *I think I like a speckled Ax best.* – And I believe this may have been the Case with many who having for want of some such Means as I employ'd found the Difficulty of obtaining good, & breaking bad Habits, in other Points of Vice & Virtue, have given up the Struggle, & concluded that *a speckled Ax was best.* For something that pretended to be Reason was every now and then suggesting to me, that such extream Nicety as I exacted of my self might be a kind of Foppery in Morals, which if it were known would make me ridiculous; that a perfect Character might be attended with the Inconvenience of being envied and hated; and that a benevolent Man should allow a few Faults in himself, to keep his Friends in Countenance. In Truth I found myself incorrigible with respect to *Order*; and now I am grown old, and my Memory bad, I feel very sensibly the want of it. But on the whole, tho' I never arrived at the Perfection I had been so ambitious of obtaining, but fell far short of it, yet I was by the Endeavour made a better and a happier Man than I otherwise should have been, if I had not attempted it; As those who aim at perfect Writing by imitating the engraved Copies, tho' they never reach the wish'd for Excellence of those Copies, their Hand is mended by the Endeavour, and is tolerable while it continues fair & legible.–

And it may be well my Posterity should be informed, that to this little Artifice, with the Blessing of God, their Ancestor ow'd the constant Felicity of his Life down to his 79th Year in which this is written. What Reverses may attend the Remainder is in the Hand of Providence: But if they arrive the Reflection on past Happiness enjoy'd ought to help his Bearing them with more Resignation. To *Temperance* he ascribes his long-continu'd Health, & what is still left to him of a good Constitution. To *Industry* and *Frugality* the early Easiness of his Circumstances, & Acquisition of his Fortune, with all that Knowledge which enabled him to be an useful Citizen, and obtain'd for him some Degree of Reputation among the Learned. To *Sincerity & Justice* the Confidence of his Country, and the honourable Employs it conferr'd upon him. And to the joint Influence of the whole Mass of the Virtues, even in their imperfect State he was able to acquire them, all that Evenness of Temper, & that Chearfulness in Conversation which makes his Company still sought for, & agreable even to his younger Acquaintance. I hope therefore that some of my Descendants may follow the Example & reap the Benefit.—

It will be remark'd that, tho' my Scheme was not wholly without Religion there was in it no Mark of any of the distinguishing Tenets of any particular Sect. – I had purposely avoided them; for being fully persuaded of the Utility and Excellency of my Method, and that it might be serviceable to People in all Religions, and intending some time or other to publish it, I would not have any thing in it that should prejudice any one of any Sect against it. – I purposed writing a little Comment on each Virtue, in which I would have shown the Advantages of possessing it, & the Mischiefs attending its opposite Vice; and I should have called my Book the ART *of Virtue*, because it would have shown the *Means & Manner* of obtaining Virtue; which would have distinguish'd it from the mere Exhortation to be good, that does not instruct & indicate the Means; but is like the Apostle's Man of verbal Charity, who only, without showing to the Naked & the Hungry how or where they might get Cloaths or Victuals, exhorted them to be fed & clothed. *James* II, 15, 16.[16]—

But it so happened that my Intention of writing & publishing this Comment was never fulfilled. I did indeed, from time to time put down short Hints of the Sentiments, Reasonings, &c. to be made use of in it; some of which I have still by me: But the necessary close Attention to private Business in the earlier part of Life, and public Business since, have occasioned my postponing it. For it being connected in my Mind with a *great and extensive Project* that required the whole Man to execute, and which an unforeseen Succession of Employs prevented my attending to, it has hitherto remain'd unfinish'd.

In this Piece it was my Design to explain and embrace this Doctrine, that vicious Actions are not hurtful because they are forbidden, but forbidden because they are hurtful, the Nature of Man alone consider'd: That it was therefore every ones Interest to be virtuous, who wish'd to be happy even in this World. And I should from this Circumstance, there being always in the World a Number of rich Merchants, Nobility, States and Princes, who have need of honest Instruments for the Management of their Affairs, and such being so rare, have endeavoured to convince young Persons, that no Qualities were so likely to make a poor Man's Fortune as those of Probity & Integrity.

My List of Virtues contain'd at first but twelve: But a Quaker Friend having kindly inform'd me that I was generally thought proud; that my Pride show'd itself frequently in Conversation; that I was not content with being in the right when discussing any Point, but was overbearing & rather insolent; of which he convinc'd me by mentioning several Instances; – I determined endeavouring to cure myself if I could of this Vice or Folly among the rest, and I added *Humility* to my List, giving an extensive Meaning to the Word. – I cannot boast of much Success in acquiring the *Reality* of this Virtue; but I had a good deal with regard to the *Appearance* of it. – I made it a Rule to forbear all direct Contradiction to the Sentiments of others, and all positive Assertion of my own. I even forbid myself agreable to the old Laws of our Junto, the Use of every Word or Expression in the Language that imported[17] a fix'd Opinion; such as *certainly, undoubtedly,* &c. and I adopted instead of them, *I conceive, I apprehend,*

---

[16] "If a brother or sister be naked, and destitute of daily food, and One of you say unto them, depart in peace, be ye warmed and filled: notwithstanding ye give them not those things which are needful to the body; what doth it profit?"

[17] Suggested.

or *I imagine* a thing to be so or so, or it so appears to me at present. – When another asserted something that I thought an Error, I deny'd my self the Pleasure of contradicting him abruptly, and of showing immediately some Absurdity in his Proposition; and in answering I began by observing that in certain Cases or Circumstances his Opinion would be right, but that in the present case there *appear'd* or *seem'd* to me some Difference, &c. I soon found the Advantage of this Change in my Manners. The Conversations I engag'd in went on more pleasantly. The modest way in which I propos'd my Opinions, procur'd them a readier Reception and less Contradiction; I had less Mortification when I was found to be in the wrong, and I more easily prevail'd with others to give up their Mistakes & join with me when I happen'd to be in the right. And this Mode, which I at first put on, with some violence to natural Inclination, became at length so easy & so habitual to me, that perhaps for these Fifty Years past no one has ever heard a dogmatical Expression escape me. And to this Habit (after my Character of Integrity) I think it principally owing, that I had early so much Weight with my Fellow Citizens, when I proposed new Institutions, or Alterations in the old; and so much Influence in public Councils when I became a Member. For I was but a bad Speaker, never eloquent, subject to much Hesitation in my choice of Words, hardly correct in Language, and yet I generally carried my Points.–

In reality there is perhaps no one of our natural Passions so hard to subdue as *Pride*. Disguise it, struggle with it, beat it down, stifle it, mortify it as much as one pleases, it is still alive, and will every now and then peep out and show itself. You will see it perhaps often in this History. For even if I could conceive that I had compleatly overcome it, I should probably be proud of my Humility.–

Thus far written at Passy 1784.

1784   1868

Samson Occom (1727–1792)

The first major Indian writer in North America, Occom was born at Mohegan, a small Indian settlement in New England. He was a precocious child, and after his conversion at the age of sixteen, his mother arranged for him to attend school under the Congregational minister Eleazar Wheelock, who ran a free school for whites and Indians in Lebanon, Connecticut. Occom attended school for four years, and distinguished himself. But poor health and failing eyesight prevented further study, and he accepted a call to become schoolmaster and minister to the small remnant of the Montauk tribe living on Long Island. In 1759 he was ordained by the Long Island Presbytery. He was selected to tour England between 1764 and 1765, where he delivered some three hundred sermons in an effort to obtain funds for Wheelock's

Indian Charity School, which was moved in 1770 to Hanover, New Hampshire, later to become Dartmouth College. Occom was angered by reports of the shrinking enrollment of Indians at the school, and became less willing to follow Wheelock's directions. This, and Occom's growing commitment to Native issues, caused a break between the two.

Along with his son-in-law, Joseph Johnson, Occom formulated a plan to found Brothertown, an independent community of converted Indians on land offered by the Oneida tribe in western New York. In 1784, Occom traveled around New England raising funds for the resettlement of converted Indians at Brothertown and other villages in the region. In 1789, he and his family moved there, and he spent the last years of his life trying to insure permanent settlements for New England

Indians against land claims and plots by white speculators to lease the land for a fraction of its worth. But after the War of 1812, the expansion of white settlements forced the Brothertown Indians out, and they eventually resettled in the Green Bay area of Wisconsin.

Occom's major work is *A Sermon at the Execution of Moses Paul*, a converted Mohegan. Thrown out of a tavern in Bethany for drunkennes, Paul took revenge by waiting outside and killing the first person to emerge, who happened to be Moses Cook, a leading citizen of Waterbury, Connecticut. Occom's emotional polemic against the evils of drinking electrified the large crowd at the execution, and his sermon went through at least nineteen editions after its initial publication in 1772. Occom was reputed to have been a fine singer, and author of a collection of spiritual hymns published in 1774, as well as a brief history of the Montauk published posthumously in 1809, and a short memoir of his life. This narrative provides insight into constrained representations of the racialized self in the late eighteenth century.

PRIMARY WORKS

A Sermon Preached by Samon Occom, Minister of the Gospel, and Missionary to the Indians; at the Execution of Moses Paul an Indian, 1772.
Collection of Hymns and Spiritual Songs, 1774.

FURTHER READING

Henry Bowden, *American Indians and Christian Missions: Studies in Cultural Conflict* (Chicago: University of Chicago Press, 1981).
David Murray, *Forked Tongues: Speech, Writing, and Representation in North American Indian Texts* (Bloomington: University of Indiana Press, 1991).
Dana Nelson, "'(I Speak like a Fool but I am Constrained)': Samson Occom's Short Narrative and Economies of the Racial Self," *Early Native American Writing: New Critical Essays*, ed. Helen Jaskowski (New York: Cambridge University Press, 1996) pp. 42–65.
Bernd Peyer, *The Tutor'd Mind: Indian Missionary Writers in Ant-bellum America* (Amherst: University of Massachusetts Press, 1997).

A SHORT NARRATIVE OF MY LIFE[1]

From my Birth till I received the Christian Religion

I was Born a Heathen and Brought up In Heathenism, till I was between 16 & 17 years of age, at a Place Calld Mohegan, in New London, Connecticut, in New England. My Parents Livd a wandering life, for did all the Indians at Mohegan, they Chiefly Depended upon Hunting, Fishing, & Fowling for their Living and had no Connection with the English, excepting to Traffic with them in their small Trifles; and they Strictly maintained and followed their Heathenish Ways, Customs & Religion, though there was Some Preaching among them. Once a Fortnight, in ye Summer Season, a Minister from New London used to come up, and the Indians to attend; not that they regarded the Christian Religion, but they had Blankets given to them every Fall of the Year and for these things they would attend and there was a Sort of School kept, when I was quite young, but I believe there never was one that ever Learnt to read any thing, – and when I was about 10 Years of age there was a man who went about among the Indian Wigwams, and wherever he Could find the Indian Children, would make them read; but the Children Used to take Care to keep out of his way; – and he used to Catch me Some times and make me Say over my Letters; and I believe I learnt Some of them. But this was Soon over too; and all this Time there was not one amongst us, that made a Profession of Christianity – Neither did we Cultivate our Land, nor kept any Sort of Creatures except Dogs, which we used in Hunting; and we Dwelt in Wigwams.

---

[1] This unpublished autobiographical sketch was written September 17, 1768. The original, along with other unpublished writings by Occom, is among the Wheelock Papers at the Dartmouth College Library.

These are a Sort of Tents, Covered with Matts, made of Flags. And to this Time we were unaquainted with the English Tongue in general though there were a few, who understood a little of it.

From the Time of our Reformation till I left Mr Wheelocks

When I was 16 years of age, we heard a Strange Rumor among the English, that there were Extraordinary Ministers Preaching from Place to Place and a Strange Concern among the White People. This was in the Spring of the Year. But we Saw nothing of these things, till Some Time in the Summer, when Some Ministers began to visit us and Preach the Word of God; and the Common People all Came frequently and exhorted us to the things of God, which it pleased the Lord, as I humbly hope, to Bless and accompany with Divine Influence to the Conviction and Saving Conversion of a Number of us; amongst whom I was one that was Imprest with the things we had heard. These Preachers did not only come to us, but we frequently went to their meetings and Churches. After I was awakened & converted, I went to all the meetings, I could come at; & Continued under Trouble of Mind about 6 months; at which time I began to Learn the English Letters; got me a Primer, and used to go to my English Neighbours frequently for Assistance in Reading, but went to no School. And when I was 17 years of age, I had, as I trust, a Discovery of the way of Salvation through Jesus Christ, and was enabl'd to put my trust in him alone for Life & Salvation. From this Time the Distress and Burden of my mind was removed, and I found Serenity and Pleasure of Soul, in Serving God. By this time I just began to Read in the New Testament without Spelling, – and I had a Stronger Desire Still to Learn to read the Word of God, and at the Same Time had an uncommon Pity and Compassion to my Poor Brethren According to the Flesh. I used to wish I was capable of Instructing my poor Kindred. I used to think, if I Could once Learn to Read I would Instruct the poor Children in Reading, – and used frequently to talk with our Indians Concerning Religion. This continued till I was in my 19th year: by this Time I Could Read a little in the Bible. At this Time my Poor Mother was going to Lebanon, and having had Some Knowledge of Mr Wheelock[2] and hearing he had a Number of English youth under his Tuition, I had a great Inclination to go to him and be with him a week or a Fortnight, and Desired my Mother to Ask Mr Wheelock whether he would take me a little while to Instruct me in Reading. Mother did so; and when She Came Back, She Said Mr Wheelock wanted to See me as Soon as possible. So I went up, thinking I Should be back again in a few Days; when I got up there, he received me With kindness and Compassion and in Stead of Staying a Forthnight or 3 Weeks, I Spent 4 Years with him. – After I had been with him Some Time, he began to acquaint his Friends of my being with him, and of his Intentions of Educating me, and my Circumstances. And the good People began to give Some Assistance to Mr Wheelock, and gave me Some old and Some New Clothes. Then he represented the Case to the Honorable Commissioners at Boston, who were Commission'd by the Honorable Society in London for Propagating the gospel among the Indians in New England and parts adjacent, and they allowed him 60 £ in old Tender, which was about 6 £ Sterling, and they Continu'd it 2 or 3 years, I can't tell exactly. – While I was at Mr Wheelock's,

---

[2] Eleazar Wheelock (1711–79), a graduate of Yale College and Congregational minister in Lebanon, Connecticut, who was a popular preacher during the Great Awakening. When the free school he founded to educate both Indians and whites failed, the governor of New Hampshire offered him a township of land where he and about thirty students established the town of Hanover in 1770. The school he founded there was named Dartmouth College after the second Earl of Dartmouth.

I was very weakly and my Health much impaired, and at the End of 4 Years, I over Strained my Eyes to such a Degree, I Could not persue my Studies any Longer; and out of these 4 years I Lost Just about one year; – And was obliged to quit my Studies.

From the Time I left Mr Wheelock till I went to Europe

As soon as I left Mr Wheelock, I endeavored to find Some Employ among the Indians; went to Nahantuck, thinking they may want a School Master, but they had one; then went to Narraganset, and they were Indifferent about a School, and went back to Mohegan, and heard a number of our Indians were going to Montauk, on Long Island, and I went with them, and the Indians there were very desirous to have me keep a School amongst them, and I Consented, and went back a while to Mohegan and Some time in November I went on the Island, I think it is 17 years ago last November. I agreed to keep School with them Half a Year, and left it with them to give me what they Pleased; and they took turns to Provide Food for me. I had near 30 Scholars this winter; I had an evening School too for those that could not attend the Day School – and began to Carry on their meetings, they had a Minister, one Mr Horton, the Scotch Society's Missionary; but he Spent, I think two thirds of his Time at Sheenecock, 30 Miles from Montauk.[3] We met together 3 times for Divine Worship every Sabbath and once on every Wednesday evening. I (used) to read the Scriptures to them and used to expound upon Some particular Passages in my own Tongue. Visited the Sick and attended their Burials. – When the half year expired, they Desired me to Continue with them, which I complied with, for another half year, when I had fulfilled that, they were urgent to have me Stay Longer, So I continued amongst them till I was Married[4], which was about 2 years after I went there. And Continued to Instruct them in the Same manner as I did before. After I was married a while, I found there was need of a Support more than I needed while I was Single, – and made my Case Known to Mr Buell and to Mr Wheelock, and also the Needy Circumstances and the Desires of these Indians of my Continuing amongst them, and the Commissioners were so good as to grant £ 15 a year Sterling – And I kept on in my Service as usual, yea I had additional Service; I kept School as I did before and Carried on the Religious Meetings as often as ever, and attended the Sick and their Funerals, and did what Writings they wanted, and often Sat as a Judge to reconcile and Decide their Matters Between them, and had visitors of Indians from all Quarters; and, as our Custom is, we freely Entertain all Visitors. And was fetched often from my Tribe and from others to see into their Affairs Both Religious, Temporal, – Besides my Domestic Concerns. And it Pleased the Lord to Increase my Family fast – and Soon after I was Married, Mr Horton left these Indians and the Shenecock & after this I was (alone) and then I had the whole care of these Indians at Montauk, and visited the Shenecock Indians often. Used to set out Saturdays towards Night and come back again Mondays. I have been obliged to Set out from Home after Sun Set, and Ride 30 Miles in the Night, to Preach to these Indians. And Some Indians at Shenecock Sent their Children to my School at Montauk, I kept one of them Some Time, and had a Young Man a half year from Mohegan, a Lad from Nahantuck, who was with me almost a year; and had little or nothing for keeping them.

My Method in the School was, as Soon as the Children got together, and took their proper Seats, I Prayed with them, then began to hear them. I generally began (after some of them

---

[3] Azariah Horton organized churches among the Shinnecock, Montauk, and Poosepatuck Indians, all small remnant bands living on Long Island.

[4] In 1751 Occom married Mary Fowler, daughter of an influential Montauk family. They raised twelve children.

Could Spell and Read,) With those that were yet in their Alphabets, So around, as they were properly Seated till I got through and I obliged them to Study their Books, and to help one another. When they could not make out a hard word they Brought it to me – and I usually heard them, in the Summer Season 8 Times a Day 4 in the morning, and in ye after Noon. – In the Winter Season 6 Times a Day, As Soon as they could Spell, they were obliged to Spell when ever they wanted to go out. I concluded with Prayer; I generally heard my Evening Scholars 3 Times Round, And as they go out the School, every one, that Can Spell, is obliged to Spell a Word, and to go out Leisurely one after another. I Catechised 3 or 4 Times a Week according to the Assembly's Shout or Catechism, and many Times Proposed Questions of my own, and in my own Tongue. I found Difficulty with Some Children, who were Some what Dull, most of these can soon learn to Say over their Letters, they Distinguish the Sounds by the Ear, but their Eyes can't Distinguish the Letters, and the way I took to cure them was by making an Alphabet on Small bits of paper, and glued them on Small Chips of Cedar after this manner A B & C. I put these on Letters in order on a Bench then point to one Letter and bid a Child to take notice of it, and then I order the Child to fetch me the Letter from the Bench; if he Brings the Letter, it is well, if not he must go again and again till he brings ye right Letter. When they can bring any Letters this way, then I just Jumble them together, and bid them to set them in Alphabetical order, and it is a Pleasure to them; and they soon Learn their Letters this way.[5] – I frequently Discussed or Exhorted my Scholars, in Religious matters. – My Method in our Religious Meetings was this; Sabbath Morning we Assemble together about 10 o'C and begin with Singing; we generally Sung Dr Watt's Psalms or Hymns. I distinctly read the Psalm or Hymn first, and then gave the meaning of it to them, after that Sing, then Pray, and Sing again after Prayer. Then proceed to Read from Suitable portion of Scripture, and so Just give the plain Sense of it in Familiar Discourse and apply it to them. So continued with Prayer and Singing. In the after Noon and Evening we Proceed in the Same Manner, and so in Wednesday Evening. Some Time after Mr Horton left these Indians, there was a remarkable revival of religion among these Indians and many were hopefully converted to the Saving knowledge of God in Jesus. It is to be observed before Mr Horton left these Indians they had Some Prejudices infused in their minds, by Some Enthusiastical Exhorters from New England, against Mr Horton, and many of them had left him; by this means he was Discouraged, and was disposed from these Indians. And being acquainted with the Enthusiasts in New England & the make and the Disposition of the Indians I took a mild way to reclaim them. I opposed them not openly but let them go on in their way, and whenever I had an opportunity, I would read Such pages of the Scriptures, and I thought would confound their Notions, and I would come to them with all Authority, Saying, "these Saith the Lord"; and by this means, the Lord was pleased to Bless my poor Endeavours, and they were reclaimed, and Brought to hear almost any of the ministers. – I am now to give an Account of my Circumstances and manner of Living. I Dwelt in a Wigwam, a Small Hut with Small Poles and Covered with Matts made of Flags, and I was obligd to remove twice a Year, about 2 miles Distance, by reason of the Scarcity of wood, for in one Neck of Land they Planted their Corn, and in another, they had their wood, and I was obligd to have my Corn carted and my Hay also, – and I got my Ground Plow'd every year, which Cost me about 12 shillings an acre; and I kept a Cow and a Horse, for which I paid 21 shillings every year York currency[6], and went 18 miles to Mill for every Dust of meal we

---

[5] This anticipates the methods of Friedrich Froebel, famous nineteenth-century German educator and reformer, who founded kindergarten and conducted similar experiments in 1837.

[6] New York currency; a York shilling was worth 12½ cents.

used in my family. I Hired or Joined with my Neighbours to go to Mill, with a Horse or ox Cart, or on Horse Back, and Some time went myself. My Family Increasing fast, and my Visitors also. I was obligd to contrive every way to Support my Family; I took all opportunities, to get Some thing to feed my Family Daily. I Planted my own Corn, Potatoes, and Beans; I used to be out hoeing my Corn Some times before Sun Rise and after my School is Dismist, and by this means I was able to raise my own Pork, for I was allowed to keep 5 Swine. Some mornings & Evenings I would be out with my Hook and Line to Catch fish, and in the Fall of Year and in the Spring, I used my gun, and fed my Family with Fowls. I Could more than pay for my Powder & Shot with Feathers[7]. At other Times I Bound old Books for Easthampton People, made wooden Spoons and Ladles, Stocked Guns, & worked on Cedar to make Pails, (Piggins)[8], and Churns & C. Besides all these Difficulties I met with advers Providence, I bought a Mare, had it but a little while, and she fell into the Quick Sand and Died, After a while Bought another, I kept her about half year, and she was gone, and I never have heard of nor Seen her from that Day to this; it was Supposed Some Rogue Stole her. I got another and Died with a Distemper, and last of all I Bought a Young Mare, and kept her till She had one Colt, and She broke her Leg and Died, and Presently after the Colt Died also. In the whole I Lost 5 Horse Kind; all these Losses helped to pull me down; and by this Time I got greatly in Debt, and acquainted my Circumstances to Some of my Friends, and they Represented my Case to the Commissioners of Boston, and Interceded with them for me, and they were pleased to vote 15 £ for my Help, and Soon after Sent a Letter to my good Friend at New London, acquainting him that they had Superseded their Vote; and my Friends were so good as to represent my Needy Circumstances Still to them, and they were so good at Last, as to Vote £ 15 and Sent it, for which I am very thankful; and the Revd Mr Buell[9] was so kind as to write in my behalf to the gentlemen of Boston; and he told me they were much Displeased with him, and heard also once again that they blamed me for being Extravagant; I Can't Conceive how these gentlemen would have me Live. I am ready to (forgive) their Ignorance, and I would wish they had Changed Circumstances with me but one month, that they may know, by experience what my Case really was; but I am now fully convinced, that it was not Ignorance, For I believe it can be proved to the world that these Same Gentlemen gave a young Missionary a Single man, one Hundred Pounds for one year, and fifty Pounds for an Interpreter, and thirty Pounds for an Introducer; so it Cost them one Hundred & Eighty Pounds in one Single Year, and they Sent too where there was no Need of a Missionary.

Now you See what difference they made between me and other missionaries; they gave me 180 Pounds for 12 years Service, which they gave for one years Services in another Mission. — In my Service (I speak like a fool, but I am Constrained) I was my own Interpreter. I was both a School master and Minister to the Indians, yea I was their Ear, Eye & Hand, as Well as Mouth. I leave it with the World, as wicked as it is, to Judge, whether I ought not to have had half as much, they gave a young man Just mentioned which would have been but £ 50 a year; and if they ought to have given me that, I am not under obligations to them, I owe them nothing at all; what can be the Reason that they used me after this manner? I can't think of any thing, but this as a Poor Indian Boy Said, Who was Bound out to an English Family, and he used to Drive Plow for a young man, and he whipt and Beat him allmost every Day, and the young man found fault with him, and Complained of him to his master and the poor Boy was

---

[7] Feathers were a popular ornament among white settlers and Europeans, and so important for exchange.

[8] A small wooden pail with a stave for a handle.

[9] Samuel Buell, Congregational minister who knew Occom in Connecticut and had a very high opinion of his abilities.

Called to answer for himself before his master, and he was asked, what it was he did, that he was So Complained of and beat almost every Day. He Said, he did not know, but he Supposed it was because he could not drive any better; but says he, I Drive as well as I know how; and at other Times he Beats me, because he is of a mind to beat me; but says he believes he Beats me for the most of the Time "because I am an Indian".

So I am ready to Say, they have used me thus, because I Can't Influence the Indians so well as other missionaries; but I can assure them I have endeavoured to teach them as well as I know how; – but I must Say, "I believe it is because I am a poor Indian". I Can't help that God has made me So; I did not make my self so.–

1768   1982, 1990

Lucy Terry (Prince) (1730–1821)

Brought from Africa to Rhode Island as a young child, Luce Bijah as she was called was purchased by Ebenezer Wells of Deerfield. In the frontier settlement, she gained a reputation as a storyteller, and in 1756 married Abijah Prince, a free black and an entrepreneur who eventually purchased his wife's freedom. In 1764, the couple moved to Vermont where they lived for the rest of their lives, raising six children, one of whom Terry tried unsuccessfully to enroll in Williams College. She did, however, successfully argue part of a case the couple brought against a neighbor who tried to encroach on their land which went to the United States Supreme Court. "Bars Fight," an account of an Indian attack on the frontier settlement during the skirmishes that characterized the ongoing conflict between the French and the British for dominance in North America, is the only poem of Terry's that survives. It was handed down orally in the Deerfield community for a hundred years until it was recorded by historian Josiah Holland in 1855. Its date of composition, 1746, makes Terry the first Black American poet.

FURTHER READING

Carolivia Herron, "Early African American Poetry," *The Columbia History of American Poetry*, eds Jay Parini and Brett Millier (New York: Columbia University Press, 1993) pp. 16–32.

"BARS FIGHT"[1]

August, 'twas the twenty-fifth,
Seventeen hundred forty-six;
The Indians did in ambush lay,
 Some very valiant men to slay,
The names of whom I'll not leave out.
 Samuel Allen like a hero fout,
And though he was so brave and bold,
His face no more shall we behold.

Eleazer Hawks was killed outright,
Before he had time to fight, –
Before he did the Indians see,
Was shot and killed immediately.
Oliver Amsden he was slain,
Which caused his friends much grief and
 pain.
Simeon Amsden they found dead,

---

[1] "Bars" is a colonial term for meadow. The text is from Josiah Holland, *History of Western Massachusetts*, vol. 2 (Springfield, Massachusetts: S. Bowles and Co., 1855).

Not many rods distant from his head.
Adonijah Gillett, we do hear,
Did lose his life which was so dear.
John Sadler fled across the water,
And thus escaped the dreadful slaughter.
Eunice Allen see the Indians coming,
And hopes to save herself by running,

And had not her petticoats stopped her,
The awful creatures had not catched her,
Nor tommy hawked her on her head,
And left her on the ground for dead.
Young Samuel Allen, Oh lackaday!
Was taken and carried to Canada.
1746   1885

Abigail Smith Adams (1744–1818) John Adams (1735–1826)

They met when Abigail was fifteen and John twenty-three. She was the daughter of a well-to-do Congregational minister from Weymouth who had a small library and encouraged a lively, literate social atmosphere. He was the son of a farmer and graduate from Harvard, who had taught school and studied law in Worcester, and was returning to his native Braintree, now Quincy, Massachusetts, to set up a law practice. They married in 1764 and their remarkable partnership lasted for the next fifty-four years, through a tumultuous period in the nation's history. Although John had the distinguished national and international career, and Abigail managed their family and farmstead, as a couple and through over 300 letters they exchanged during John's long absences, they are associated with the events leading up to the American Revolution and the founding of the Republic.

Abigail had no formal education, an omission she regretted bitterly. To escape the narrowness of their lives, she and her sisters wrote letters for entertainment and self-improvement, choosing pen names for themselves. Early letters between Abigail and John were signed Diana and Lysander, but later Abigail chose the pen name Portia, for the virtuous Roman matron and learned woman jurist of Shakespeare's *The Merchant of Venice*. From the beginning, her letters indicate a keen intelligence and strong desire for experience of the world, people, and events, which she had to gain vicariously through the extensive correspondence she kept up for most of her life. Although she urged her husband in a letter of March 31, 1776 "to remember the Ladies" in the formation of the new republic, reminding him of his own maxim that "all Men

would be tyrants if they could," and promising to foment female "Rebellion" if he failed, she successfully fulfilled her role as manager of their domestic sphere. Eventually, she accepted and even "gloried" in her sacrifice of John's presence, just as John gloried in his sacrifices for the new nation.

John Adams was ambitious but also self-doubting, and believed that it was Abigail who would "form me to that happy Temper, that can reconcile a quick Discernment with a perfect Candour." To support his growing family, they moved to Boston in 1768, where John's early opposition to British tyranny and defense of Boston radicals won him election as a delegate to what became known as the first Continental Congress in Philadelphia in 1774. He departed Braintree on August 10, and for the next quarter of a century, was an important and sometimes controversial public figure. He spent almost ten years abroad, in France, England, and the Netherlands, promoting American interests for Congress. Returning in 1783, he was elected vice president for two terms (1788 and 1792), and president in 1796.

John Adams was a prolific writer, penning numerous private letters, diary entries, letters to the press, formal reports and essays propounding his views on the formation and maintenance of republican and federal government. He was an indefatigable supporter of colonial resistance under the pen name Novanglus. His letters to Abigail combine the worldly and the intimate. Although he deflected her well-aimed petition to include women in the new republic with the defensive response that women really "wear the pants," other letters, like his reply to Andrew Sullivan, suggest that he considered her ideas seriously, but recognized their radical, and thus, dangerously unsettling, import.

The long public life of the Adamses, and the Federalist regime, ended on the morning of Thomas Jefferson's inauguration as president in 1800. Disappointed at losing the election and exasperated with a press and public that he felt insufficiently acknowledged his contributions, John returned to Braintree and to the private life Abigail so longed for. During this long retirement, Benjamin Rush, a distinguished Philadelphia physician, and mutual friend of Adams and Jefferson, took it upon himself to reconcile the two estranged friends whom he had come to regard as the personification of the ideals of the American Republic. After much effort on Rush's part, in 1812, Adams wrote Jefferson the first letter of a long and brilliant exchange which continued until July 4, 1826, the day both of them died. Covering everything from natural science, ancient and recent history, religion, and, of course, political theory, these letters reveal Adams' passionate, obstinate nature

and conservative position, and Jefferson's compassionate and unswerving idealism.

PRIMARY WORKS

The Adams-Jefferson Letters, ed. Lester J. Cappon, 2 vols, 1959.
Diary and Autobiography of John Adams, ed. L. H. Butterfield, 4 vols, 1961.
The Book of Abigail and John: Selected Letters of the Adams Family 1762–1784, eds L. H. Butterfield, Marc Friedlaender, and Mary-Jo Kline (Cambridge: Harvard University Press, 1975).
Papers of John Adams, ed. Robert Taylor, 10 vols, 1977–.

FURTHER READING

Merrill Peterson, *Adams and Jefferson: A Revolutionary Dialogue* (New York: Oxford University Press, 1978).
Joseph Ellis, *Passionate Sage: John Adams and America's Original Intentions* (New York: Norton, 1993).
Rosemary Keller, *Patriotism and the Female Sex: Abigail Adams and the American Revolution* (New York: Carlson Publishers, 1994).
Edith Gelles, *First Thoughts: Life and Letters of Abigail Adams* (New York: Twayne Publishers, 1998).

FROM LETTERS OF ABIGAIL AND JOHN ADAMS[1]

Abigail Adams to John Adams

Braintree, March 31, 1776

I have sometimes been ready to think that the passion for Liberty cannot be Equelly Strong in the Breasts of those who have been accustomed to deprive their fellow Creatures of theirs. Of this I am certain that it is not founded upon that generous and christian principal of doing to others as we would that others do unto us. . . .

. . . – I long to hear that you have declared an independancy – and by the way in the new Code of Laws which I suppose it will be necessary for you to make I desire you would Remember the Ladies, and be more generous and favourable to them than your ancestors. Do not put such unlimited power into the hands of the Husbands. Remember all Men would be tyrants if they could. If perticuliar care and attention is not paid to the Ladies we are determined to foment a Rebelion, and will not hold ourselves bound by any Laws in which we have no voice or Representation.

That your Sex are Naturally Tyrannical is a Truth so thoroughly established as to admit of no dispute, but such of you as wish to be happy willingly give up the harsh title of Master for the more tender and endearing one of Friend. Why then, not put it out of the power of the vicious and the Lawless to use us with cruelty and indignity with impunity. Men of Sense in

---

[1]   Letters between Abigail and John Adams are from *The Book of Abigail and John: Selected Letters of the Adams Family,* 1762–1784. The original spelling has been retained; clarifications are in square brackets.

all Ages abhor those customs which treat us only as the vassals of your Sex. Regard us then as Beings placed by providence under your protection and in immitation of the Supreem Being make use of that power only for our happiness.

1776   1848

John Adams to Abigail Adams

Ap. 14. 1776

You justly complain of my short Letters, but the critical State of Things and the Multiplicity of Avocations must plead my Excuse. You ask where the Fleet is. The inclosed Papers will inform you. You ask what Sort of Defence Virginia can make. I believe they will make an able Defence. Their Militia and minute Men have been some time employed in training them selves, and they have Nine Battallions of regulars as they call them, maintained among them, under good Officers, at the Continental Expence. They have set up a Number of Manufactories of Fire Arms, which are busily employed. They are tolerably supplied with Powder, and are successfull and assiduous, in making Salt Petre. Their neighbouring Sister or rather Daughter Colony of North Carolina, which is a warlike Colony, and has several Battallions at the Continental Expence, as well as a pretty good Militia, are ready to assist them, and they are in very good Spirits, and determined to make a brave Resistance. – The Gentry are very rich, and the common People very poor. This Inequality of Property, gives an Aristocratical Turn to all their Proceedings, and occasions a strong Aversion in their Patricians, to Common Sense. But the Spirit of these Barons, is coming down, and it must submit. . . .

As to Declarations of Independency, be patient. Read our Privateering Laws, and our Commercial Laws. What signifies a Word.

As to your extraordinary Code of Laws, I cannot but laugh. We have been told that our Struggle has loosened the bands of Government every where. That Children and Apprentices were disobedient – that schools and Colledges were grown turbulent – that Indians slighted their Guardians and Negroes grew insolent to their Masters. But your Letter was the first Intimation that another Tribe more numerous and powerfull than all the rest were grown discontented. – This is rather too coarse a Compliment but you are so saucy, I wont blot it out.

Depend upon it, We know better than to repeal our Masculine systems. Altho they are in full Force, you know they are little more than Theory. We dare not exert our Power in its full Latitude. We are obliged to go fair, and softly, and in Practice you know We are the subjects. We have only the Name of Masters, and rather than give up this, which would compleatly subject Us to the Despotism of, the Peticoat, I hope General Washington, and all our brave Heroes would fight. I am sure every good Politician would plot, as long as he would against Despotism, Empire, Monarchy, Aristocracy, Oligarchy, or Ochlocracy[2]. – A fine story indeed. I begin to think the Ministry as deep as they are wicked. After stirring up Tories, Landjobbers, Trimmers, Bigots, Canadians, Indians, Negroes, Hanoverians, Hessians, Russians, Irish Roman Catholicks, Scotch Renegadoes, at last they have stimulated the [ ] to demand new Priviledges and threaten to rebell.

1776   1975

[2]   Mob-rule; rule by the lowest of people.

John Adams to James Sullivan[3]

Philadelphia, 26 May, 1776.

. . . . It is certain, in Theory, that the only moral Foundation of Government is, the Consent of the People. But to what an Extent Shall We carry this Principle? Shall We Say that every Individual of the Community, old and young, male and female, as well as rich and poor, must consent, expressly, to every Act of Legislation? No, you will Say. This is impossible. How, then, does the Right arise in the Majority to govern the Minority, against their will? Whence arises the Right of the Men to govern the Women, without their Consent? Whence the Right of the old to bind the Young, without theirs?

But let us first Suppose that the whole Community, of every Age, Rank, Sex, and Condition, has a Right to vote. This Community is assembled – A Motion is made, and carried by a Majority of one Voice. The Minority will not agree to this. Whence arises the Right of the Majority to govern, and the Obligation of the Minority to obey? From Necessity, you will Say, because there can be no other Rule. But why exclude Women? You will Say, because their Delicacy renders them unfit for Practice and Experience in the great Businesses of Life, and the hardy Enterprizes of War, as well as the arduous Cares of State. Besides, their attention is So much engaged with the necessary Nurture of their Children, that Nature has made them fittest for domestic Cares. And Children have not Judgment or Will of their own. True. But will not these Reasons apply to others? Is it not equally true, that Men in general, in every Society, who are wholly destitute of Property, are also too little acquainted with public Affairs to form a Right Judgment, and too dependent upon other Men to have a Will of their own? If this is a Fact, if you give to every Man who has no Property, a Vote, will you not make a fine encouraging Provision for Corruption, by your fundamental Law? Such is the Frailty of the human Heart, that very few Men who have no Property, have any Judgment of their own. They talk and vote as they are directed by Some Man of property, who has attached their Minds to his Interest. . . .

Your idea that those Laws which affect the lives and personal Liberty of all, or which inflict corporal Punishment, affect those who are not qualified to vote, as well as those who are, is just. But so they do Women, as well as Men; Children, as well as Adults. What Reason should there be for excluding a Man of Twenty years Eleven months and twenty-seven days old, from a Vote, when you admit one who is twenty-one? The Reason is, you must fix upon Some Period in Life, when the Understanding and Will of men in general, is fit to be trusted by the Public. Will not the Same Reason justify the State in fixing upon Some certain Quantity of Property, as a Qualification?

The Same Reasoning which will induce you to admit all Men who have no Property, to vote, with those who have, for those Laws which affect the Person, will prove that you ought to admit Women and Children; for, generally Speaking, Women and Children have as good Judgments, and as independent Minds, as those men who are wholly destitute of Property; these last being to all Intents and Purposes as much dependent upon others, who will please to feed, clothe, and employ them, as Women are upon their Husbands or Children on their Parents. . . .

Depend upon it, Sir, it is dangerous to open So fruitful a Source of Controversy and Alterca-

---

[3] This letter is from *Papers of John Adams*, ed. Robert J. Taylor, 10 vols (Cambridge: Harvard University Press, 1979) vol. 4. James Sullivan (1744–1808), a Massachusetts lawyer who traveled the Eastern Court Circuit in Maine with Adams in 1774, was a member of the Massachusetts House and appointed to superior court. His letter to Adams does not mention women specifically, but Abigail had brought up the issue of women's rights several times in her letters.

tion as could be opened by attempting to alter the Qualifications of Voters; there will be no End of it. New Claims will arise, Women will demand a Vote, Lads from 12 to 21 will think their Rights not enough attended to, and every Man who has not a Farthing, will demand an equal Voice with any other, in all Acts of state. It tends to confound and destroy all Distinctions, and prostrate all Ranks to one common Levell. I am &c.

1776   1850

John Adams to Abigail Adams

Philadelphia, July 3, 1776

. . . Yesterday the greatest Question was decided, which ever was debated in America, and a greater perhaps, never was or will be decided among Men. A Resolution was passed without one dissenting Colony "that these united Colonies, are, and of right ought to be free and independent States, and as such, they have, and of Right ought to have full Power to make War, conclude Peace, establish Commerce, and to do all the other Acts and Things, which other States may rightfully do." You will see in a few days a Declaration setting forth the Causes, which have impell'd Us to this mighty Revolution, and the Reasons which will justify it, in the Sight of God and Man. A Plan of Confederation will be taken up in a few days.

When I look back to the Year 1761, and recollect the Argument concerning Writs of Assistance, in the Superiour Court, which I have hitherto considered as the Commencement of the Controversy, between Great Britain and America,[4] and run through the whole Period from that Time to this, and recollect the series of political Events, the Chain of Causes and Effects, I am surprized at the Suddenness, as well as Greatness of this Revolution. Britain has been fill'd with Folly, and America with Wisdom, at least this is my judgment. – Time must determine. It is the Will of Heaven, that the two Countries should be sundered forever. It may be the Will of Heaven that America shall suffer Calamities still more wasting and Distresses yet more dreadfull. If this is to be the Case, it will have this good Effect, at least: it will inspire Us with many Virtues, which We have not, and correct many Errors, Follies, and Vices, which threaten to disturb, dishonour, and destroy Us. – The Furnace of Affliction produces Refinement, in States as well as Individuals. And the new Governments we are assuming, in every Part, will require a Purification from our Vices, and an Augmentation of our Virtues or they will be no Blessings. The People will have unbounded Power. And the People are extreamly addicted to Corruption and Venality, as well as the Great. – I am not without Apprehensions from this Quarter. But I must submit all my Hopes and Fears, to an overruling Providence, in which, unfashionable as the Faith may be, I firmly believe.

Abigail Adams to John Adams

June 30 [1778]

Dearest of Friends

. . . Now I know you are safe[5] I wish myself with you. Whenever you entertain such a wish recollect that I would have willingly hazarded all dangers to have been your companion, but as that was not permitted you must console me in your absence by a Recital of all your adventures, tho methinks I would not have them in all respects too similar to those related of your

---

4   Writs of assistance were general search warrants and posed a threat to civil liberty.

5   Adams journeyed to France to join Franklin in the negotiations for support during the American Revolution.

venerable Colleigue, Whose Mentor like appearance,[6] age and philosiphy must certainly lead the polite scientifick Ladies of France to suppose they are embraceing the God of Wisdom, in a Humane Form,[7] but I who own that I never yet wish'd an Angle whom I loved a Man,[8] shall be full as content if those divine Honours are omitted. The whole Heart of my Friend is in the Bosom of his partner, more than half a score of years has so riveted [it] there that the fabrick which contains it must crumble into Dust e'er the particles an be seperated. I can hear of the Brilliant accomplishment[s] of any of my Sex with pleasure and rejoice in that Liberality of Sentiment which acknowledges them. At the same time I regret the trifling narrow contracted Education of the Females of my own country. I have entertained a superiour opinion of the accomplishments of the French Ladies ever since I read the Letters of Dr Sherbear[9], who professes that he had rather take the opinion of an accomplished Lady in matters of polite writing than the first wits of Itally and should think himself safer with her approbation than of a long List of Literati, and he give[s] this reason for it that Women have in general more delicate Sensations than Men, what touches them is for the most part true in Nature, whereas men warpt by Education, judge amiss from previous prejudice and refering all things to the model of the ancients, condemn that by comparison where no true Similitud ought to be expected.

But in this country you need not be told how much female Education is neglected, nor how fashionable it has been to ridicule Female learning, tho I acknowled[ge] it my happiness to be connected with a person of a more generous mind and liberal Sentiments. I cannot forbear transcribing a few Generous Sentiments which I lately met with upon this Subject. If women says the writer are to be esteemed our Enemies, methinks it is an Ignoble Cowardice thus to disarm them and not allow them the same weapons we use ourselves, but if they deserve the title of our Friends tis an inhumane Tyranny to debar them of priviliges of ingenious Education which would also render their Friendship so much the more delightfull to themselves and us. Nature is seldom observed to be niggardly of her choisest Gifts to the Sex, their Senses are generally as quick as ours, their Reason as nervious[10], their judgment as mature and solid. Add but to these natural perfections the advantages of acquired learning what polite and charming creatures would they prove whilst their external Beauty does the office of a Crystal to the Lamp not shrowding but discloseing their Brighter intellects. Nor need we fear to loose our Empire over them by thus improveing their native abilities since where there is most Learning, Sence and knowledge there is always observed to be the most modesty and Rectitude of manners.

1778   1875

---

[6] Mentor was an Ithacan noble whose identity the goddess Athena assumed as the guide and advisor of the young Telemachus, son of Odysseus; thus, any experienced and trusted counselor.

[7] Abigail refers here to Benjamin Franklin, the senior member of the Commission, whose "dissipated" lifestyle John had described to his wife in earlier letters. Although in his seventies, Franklin slept late, spent his days with entertaining hordes of French visitors, always dined out, and spent his evenings at plays, literary or scientific salons, in the company of many young, accomplished ladies. "This Course of Life," Adams wrote, "contributed to his Pleasure and I believe to his health and Longevity. . . . I had so much respect

and compassion for his Age, that I should have been happy to have done all the Business or rather all the Drudgery, if I could have been favoured with a few moments in a day to receive his Advice concerning the manner in which it ought to be done."

[8] Alexander Pope (1688–1744), *Epistle from Eloise to Abelard* (1717), ll 69–70: "Back thro' the paths of pleasing sense I ran,/ Nor wish'd an Angel whom I love'd a Man."

[9] John Shebbeare (1709–88), notorious English satirist and author of a series of "Letters to the people of England," (1755), which both John and Abigail had read.

[10] Vigorous, strong.

Abigail Adams to John Adams

April 10th, 1782

My dearest Friend

The restoration of my dearest Friend from so dangerous a Sickness, demands all my gratitude
. . . Hope is my best Friend and kindest comforter; she assures me that the pure unabated
affection, which neither time or absence can allay or abate, shall e'er long be crowned with the
completion of its fondest wishes, in the safe return of the beloved object; the age of romance
has long ago past, but the affection of almost Infant years has matured and strengthend untill
it has become a vital principle, nor has the world any thing to bestow which could in the
smallest degree compensate for the loss. Desire and Sorrow were denounced upon our Sex; as a
punishment for the transgression of Eve. I have sometimes thought that we are formed to
experience more exquisite Sensations than is the Lot of your Sex. More tender and susceptable
by Nature of those impression[s] which create happiness or misiry, we Suffer and enjoy in a
higher degree. I never wonderd at the philosopher who thanked the Gods that he was created
a Man rather than a Woman.

I cannot say, but that I was dissapointed when I found that your return to your native land
was a still distant Idea. I think your Situation cannot be so dissagreable as I feared it was, yet
that dreadfull climate is my terror.[11] – You mortify me indeed when you talk of sending
Charles to Colledge, who it is not probable will be fit under three or four years. Surely my dear
Friend fleeting as time is I cannot reconcile myself to the Idea of living in this cruel State of
Seperation for [4?] or even three years to come. Eight years have already past, since you could
call yourself an Inhabitant of this State. I shall assume the Signature of Penelope, for my dear
Ulysses has already been a wanderer from me near half the term of years that, that Hero was
encountering Neptune, Calipso, the Circes and Syrens[12]. In the poetical Language of Penelope
I shall address you

> "Oh! haste to me! A Little longer Stay
> Will ev'ry grace, each fancy'd charm decay:
> Increasing cares, and times resistless rage
> Will waste my bloom, and wither it to age."

You will ask me I suppose what is become of my patriotick virtue? It is that which most
ardently calls for your return. I greatly fear that the climate in which you now reside will prove
fatal to your Life, whilst your Life and usefullness might be many years of Service to your
Country in a more Healthy climate. If the Essentials of her political system are safe, as I would
fain hope they are, yet the impositions and injuries, to which she is hourly liable, and daily
suffering, call for the exertions of her wisest and ablest citizens. You know by many years

---

[11]   In 1781, Adams was dispatched as minister plenipo-
tentiary to the Netherlands, to negotiate a treaty of amity
and commerce, and set up residence in Amsterdam.

[12]   In Homer's Odyssey, all of these figures tried to prevent Odysseus from returning home to Ithaca and his wife
Penelope. Neptune, the Roman god of the sea (in Greek,
Poseidon), could change shape at will and opposed Odysseus'
passage. Calypso, nymph of the mythical island of Ogygia,
entertained Odysseus for seven years but could not overcome his longing for home even by a promise of immortal-

ity. Odysseus visited the isle of Circe, a sorceress and daughter
of Helios, who turned all his men into swine. Protected by
an herb from Hermes, he resisted her spell and saved his
men, but stayed with her a year before resuming his journey. The Sirens were half bird and half women, who lured
sailors to their deaths by the sweetness of their song. On
Circe's advice, Odysseus stopped up his crew's ears with wax,
but had himself tied to the mast so he could hear their song
but not steer the ship out of its course.

experience what it is to struggle with difficulties – with wickedness in high places – from thence you are led to covet a private Station as the post of Honour, but should such an Idea generally prevail, who would be left to stem the torrent?

Should we at this day possess those invaluable Blessings transmitted us by our venerable Ancestors, if they had not inforced by their example, what they taught by their precepts?

> "While pride, oppression and injustice reign
> the World will still demand her Catos[13] presence."

Why should I indulge an Idea, that whilst the active powers of my Friend remain, they will not be devoted to the Service of his country?

Can I believe that the Man who fears neither poverty or dangers, who sees not charms sufficient either in Riches, power or places to tempt him in the least to swerve from the purest Sentiments of Honour and Delicacy; will retire, unnoticed, Fameless to a Rustick cottage there by dint of Labour to earn his Bread. I need not much examination of my Heart to say I would not willingly consent to it.[14]

Have not Cincinnatus and Regulus[15] been handed down to posterity, with immortal honour?

Without fortune it is more than probably we shall end our days, but let the well earned Fame of having Sacrificed those prospects, from a principal of universal Benevolence and good will to Man, descend as an inheritance to our ofspring. The Luxery of Foreign Nations may possibly infect them but they have not before them an example of it, so far as respects their domestick life. They are not Bred up with an Idea of possessing Hereditary riches or Grandeur. Retired from the Capital, they see little of the extravagance or disipation, which prevails there, and at the close of the day, in lieu of the Card table, some usefull Book employs their leisure hours. These habits early fixed, and daily inculcated, will I hope render them usefull and ornamental Members of Society. – But we cannot see into futurity.

1782   1875

FROM *THE ADAMS–JEFFERSON LETTERS*[1]

John Adams to Thomas Jefferson

Quincy, Sept. 2, 1813

. . . Now, my Friend, who are the ἄριστοι ["aristocrats"]? Philosophy may Answer "The Wise and Good." But the World, Mankind, have by their practice always answered, "the rich,

---

[13] Marcus Porcius Cato (95–46 BC), known as Cato the Younger, a leader of the Optimates, the conservative senatorial aristocracy who tried to preserve the Roman Republic against power seekers like Julius Caesar.

[14] However, in July 1782, Abigail bought 1620 acres of land in Vermont, part of her dream of a retreat from public controversies for her and John, which he resisted.

[15] Lucius Quinctius Cincinnatus (*d.*519? BC), legendary Roman statesman who gained fame for his selfless devotion to the republic in times of crisis and for giving up the reins of power when the crisis was over. Marcus Atilius Regulus

(*fl.* third century BC), Roman general and statesman whose career, greatly embellished by legend, the Romans considered a model of heroic endurance.

ADAMS–JEFFERSON

[1] All texts, with slight modification, are from *The Adams–Jefferson Letters: The Complete Correspondence Between Thomas Jefferson and Abigail and John Adams*, ed. Lester Cappon, 2 vols (Chapel Hill: University of North Carolina Press, 1959) vol. 2.

the beautiful and well born." And Philosophers themselves in marrying their Children prefer the rich the handsome and the well descended to the wise and good.

What chance have Talents and Virtues in competition, with Wealth and Birth? and Beauty? Haud facile emergunt, quorum Virtutibus obstant [i.e., obstat] Res Angusta Domi.

> One truth is clear, by all the World confess'd
> Slow rises worth, by Poverty oppress'd.[2]

The five Pillars of Aristocracy, are Beauty, Wealth, Birth, Genius and Virtues. Any one of the three first, can at any time over bear any one or both of the two last.

Let me ask again, what a Wave of publick Opinion, in favour of Birth has been spread over the Globe, by Abraham, by Hercules, by Mahomet, by Guelphs, Ghibellines, Bourbons, and a miserable Scottish Chief Steuart?[3] By Zingis[4] by, by, by, a million others? And what a Wave will be spread by Napoleon and by Washington? Their remotest Cousins will be sought and will be proud, and will avail themselves of their descent. Call this Principle, Prejudice, Folly, Ignorance, Baseness, Slavery, Stupidity, Adulation, Superstition or what you will. I will not contradict you. But the Fact, in natural, moral, political and domestic History I cannot deny or dispute or question.

And is this great Fact in the natural History of Man? This unalterable Principle of Morals, Philosophy, Policy domestic felicity, and dayly Experience from the Creation; to be overlooked, forgotten neglected, or hypocritically waived out of Sight; by a Legislator? By a professed Writer upon civil Government, and upon Constitutions of civil Government?

Thus far I had written, when your favour of Aug. 22 was laid on my table, from the Post Office. I can only say at present that I can pursue this idle Speculation no farther, at least till I have replied to this fresh proof of your friendship and Confidence. Mrs. A. joins in cordial Thanks, with

John Adams

You may laugh at the introduction of Beauty, among the Pillars of Aristocracy. But Madame Barry[5] says Le veritable Royauté est la B[e]autee ["true royalty is beauty"], and there is not a more certain Truth. Beauty, Grace, Figure, Attitude, Movement, have in innumerable Instances prevailed over Wealth, Birth, Talents Virtues and every thing else, in Men of the highest rank, greatest Power, and sometimes, the most exalted Genius, greatest Fame, and highest Merit.

1813   1850

---

[2] Juvenal (60?–140?), satirist of Roman vices under the empire; from *Satires*, 3: 164–165.

[3] Stuart, the royal house of Scotland from 1371; in 1603, James VI of Scotland became King James I of England. Despite much skirmishing among contenders, the Stuarts remained on the throne until 1714, except for the interruption of the Commonwealth, 1649–1660. "The Bourbons:" Henry IV's heirs, kings of France uninterruptedly from 1610 to 1792. During a thirteenth-century clash between Pope Innocent IV and the Holy Roman Emperor Frederick II in Italy, "the Guelphs" were the pro-papal party and "the Ghibellines" were the pro-imperial party. "Mahomet:" the prophet of the Islam religion; Muslim rulers all claim to be

"sons of Mahomet." "Hercules:" hero of Greek and Roman mythology, whose enormous strength won him immortality as a god. "Abraham:" patriarch of the ancient Hebrews from whom all Jews are descended.

[4] Zangi or Zengi (1084–1186), Iraqi ruler who founded the Zangid dynasty and led the first important counterattacks against the crusader kingdoms in the Middle East.

[5] Marie-Jeanne Bécu, comtess du Barry (1743–93), illegitimate daughter of lower-class parents and a shop assistant, whose beauty captivated many noble lovers. She was the last mistress of the French king Louis XV from 1768–74, and was condemned during the Revolution and guillotined in 1793.

Thomas Jefferson to John Adams

Monticello Oct. 28, [18]13.

. . . For I agree with you that there is a natural aristocracy among men. The grounds of this are virtue and talents. Formerly bodily powers gave place among the aristoi. But since the invention of gunpowder has armed the weak as well as the strong with missile death, bodily strength, like beauty, good humor, politeness and other accomplishments, has become but an auxiliary ground of distinction. There is also an artificial aristocracy founded on wealth and birth, without either virtue or talents; for with these it would belong to the first class. The natural aristocracy I consider as the most precious gift of nature for the instruction, the trusts, and government of society. And indeed it would have been inconsistent in creation to have formed man for the social state, and not to have provided virtue and wisdom enough to manage the concerns of the society. May we not even say that that form of government is the best which provides the most effectually for a pure selection of these natural aristoi into the offices of government? The artificial aristocracy is a mischievous ingredient in government, and provision should be made to prevent it's ascendancy. On the question, What is the best provision, you and I differ; but we differ as rational friends, using the free exercise of our own reason, and mutually indulging it's errors. *You* think it best to put the pseudo-aristoi into a separate chamber of legislation where they may be hindered from doing mischief by their coordinate branches, and where also they may be a protections to wealth against the Agrarian and plundering enterprises of the majority of the people. I think that to give them power in order to prevent them from doing mischief, is arming them for it, and increasing instead of remedying the evil. For if the coordinate branches can arrest their action, so may they that of the coordinates. Mischief may be done negatively as well as positively. Of this a cabal in the Senate of the U. S. has furnished many proofs. Nor do I believe them necessary to protect the wealthy; because enough of these will find their way into every branch of the legislation to protect themselves. From 15. To 20. Legislatures of our own, in action for 30. Years past, have proved that no fears of an equalization of property are to be apprehended from them.

I think the best remedy is exactly that provided by all our constitutions, to leave to the citizens the free election and separation of the aristoi from the pseudo-aristoi, of the wheat from the chaff. In general they will elect the real good and wise. In some instances, wealth may corrupt, and birth blind them; but not in sufficient degree to endanger the society. . . .

But even in Europe a change has sensibly taken place in the mind of Man. Science had liberated the ideas of those who read and reflect, and the American example had kindled feelings of right in the people. An insurrection has consequently begun, of science, talents and courage against rank and birth, which have fallen into contempt. It has failed in it's first effort, because the mobs of the cities, the instrument used for it's accomplishment, debased by ignorance, poverty and vice, could not be restrained to rational action. But the world will recover from the panic of this first catastrophe. Science is progressive, and talents and enterprize on the alert. Resort may be had to the people of the country, a more governable power from their principles and subordination; and rank, and birth, and tinsel-aristocracy will finally shrink into insignificance, even there. This however we have no right to meddle with. . . .

Th: Jefferson

1813   1963

Adams to Jefferson

Quincy, November 15, [18]13

Dear Sir

I cannot appease my melancholly commiseration for our Armies in this furious snow storm in any way so well as by studying your Letter of Oct. 28.

We are now explicitly agreed, in one important point, vizt. That "there is a natural Aristocracy among men; the grounds of which are Virtue and Talents."

You very justly indulge a little merriment upon this solemn subject of Aristocracy. I often laugh at it too, for there is nothing in this laughable world more ridiculous than the management of it by almost all the nations of the Earth. But while We smile, Mankind have reason to say to Us, as the froggs said to the Boys, What is Sport to you is Wounds and death to Us. When I consider the weakness, the folly, the Pride, the Vanity, the Selfishness, the Artifice, the low craft and meaning cunning, the want of Principle, the Avarice, the unbounded Ambition, the unfeeling Cruelty of a majority of those (in all Nations) who are allowed an aristocratical influence; and on the other hand, the Stupidity with which the more numerous multitude, not only become their Dupes, but even love to be Taken in by their Tricks: I feel a stronger disposition to weep at their destiny, than to laugh at their Folly.

But tho' We have agreed in one point, in Words, it is not yet certain that We are perfectly agreed in Sense. Fashion has introduced an indeterminate Use of the Word "Talents." Education, Wealth, Strength, Beauty, Stature, Birth, Marriage, graceful Attitudes and Motions, Gait, Air, Complexion, Physiognomy, are Talents, as well as Genius and Science and learning. Any one of these Talents, that in fact commands or influences true Votes in Society, gives to the Man who possesses it, the Character of an Aristocrat, in my Sense of the Word.

Pick up, the first 100 men you meet, and make a Republick. Every Man will have an equal Vote. But when deliberations and discussions are opened it will be found that 25, by their Talents, Virtues being equal, will be able to carry 50 Votes. Every one of these 25, is an Aristocrat, in my Sense of the Word; whether he obtains his one Vote in Addition to his own, by his Birth Fortune, Figure, Eloquence, Science, learning, Craft Cunning, or even his Character for good fellowship and a bon vivant.

. . . I will select a single Example: for female Aristocrats are nearly as formidable in Society as male.

A daughter of a green Grocer, walks the Streets in London dayly with a baskett of Cabbage, Sprouts, Dandlions and Spinage on her head. She is observed by the Painters to have a beautiful Face, an elegant figure, a graceful Step and a debonair. They hire her to Sitt. She complies, and is painted by forty Artists in a Circle around her. The scientific Sir William Hamilton outbids the Painters, sends her to Schools for a genteel Education and Marries her. This Lady not only causes the Tryumphs of the Nile of Copinhagen and Trafalgar, but seperates Naples from France and finally banishes the King and Queen from Sicilly.[6] Such is the Aristocracy of the natural Talent of Beauty. Millions of Examples might be quoted from History sacred and profane, from Eve, Hannah, Deborah Susanna Abigail, Judith, Ruth, down to Hellen Madame

---

[6]   Adams outlines the career of Emma, Lady Hamilton (originally Amy Lyon, daughter of a blacksmith, 1761–1815), wife of Sir William Hamilton, archaeologist and British envoy to Naples, and lover of Admiral, Lord Nelson. Her beauty made her the frequent subject of the painter George Romney. She was the diplomatic intermediary between her husband and her close friend Queen Maria Carolina of Naples. It was said that her influence in Naples facilitated Nelson's victory over the French in the Battle of the Nile in 1798, and propelled Nelson's other triumphs in the battle of Copenhagen (1801) and Trafalgar (1805), in which he died.

de Maintenon and Mrs Fitzherbert.[7] For mercy's sake do not compell me to look to our chaste States and Territories, to find Women; one of whom lett go, would, in the Words of Holopherne's Guards "deceive the whole Earth. . . . "

Your distinction between natural and artificial Aristocracy does not appear to me well founded. Birth and Wealth are conferred on some Men, as imperiously by Nature, as Genius, Strength or Beauty. The Heir is honours and Riches, and power has often no more merit in procuring these Advantages, than he has in obtaining an handsome face or an elegant figure. When Aristocracies, are established by human Laws and honour Wealth and Power are made hereditary by municipal Laws and political Institutions, then I acknowledge artificial Aristocracy to commence: but this never commences, till Corruption in Elections becomes dominant and uncontroulable. But this artificial Aristocracy can never last. The everlasting Envys, Jealousies, Rivalries and quarrells among them, their cruel rapacities upon the poor ignorant People their followers, compell these to sett up Caesar, a Demagogue to be a Monarch and Master, pour mettre chacun a sa place ["to put each one in his place"]. Here you have the origin of all artificial Aristocracy, which is the origin of all Monarchy. And both artificial Aristocracy, and Monarchy, and civil, military, political and hierarchical Despotism, have all grown out of the natural Aristocracy of "Virtues and Talents." We, to be sure, are far remote from this. Many hundred years must roll away before We shall be corrupted. Our pure, virtuous, public spirited federative Republick will last for ever, govern the Globe and introduce the perfection of Man, his perfectability being already proved by Price Priestly, Condorcet Rousseau Diderot and Godwin. . . .[8]

Your distinction between the aristoi and pseudo aristoi, will not help the matter. I would trust one as soon as the other with unlimited Power. The Law wisely refuses an Oath as a witness in his own cause to the Saint as well as to the Sinner.

You suppose a difference of Opinion between You and me, on the Subject of Aristocracy. I can find none. I dislike and detest hereditary honours, Offices Emoluments established by Law. So do you. I am for ex[c]luding legal hereditary distinctions from the U.S. as long as

---

[7] All influential women. Maria Fitzherbert (1756–1837), because of her Roman Catholicism, was secretly married to the Prince of Wales, the future George IV of Great Britain. "Madame de Maintenon:" Françoise d'Aubigné, marquise de Maintenon (1635–1719), second wife and influential, untitled queen of King Louis XIV of France. "Hellen:" Helen, wife of Menelaus, who was kidnapped by Paris and over whom the Trojan war was fought. "Ruth:" Moabite daughter-in-law of Naomi, who insisted upon returning to Israel with her mother-in-law when they were both widowed, and married Boaz, bearing a child for Naomi, who was the grandfather of King David. "Judith:" Jewish heroine who disguised herself as a prostitute and entered the enemy camp to behead Holofernes, general of the Assyrian king Nebuchadnezzar. When she held up his head, her countrymen rushed upon the invading army and defeated it. "Abigail:" wife of King David who called herself "the handmaid of David." "Susanna:" Young woman, from the Old Testament Apocrypha, accused by some Jewish elders, who had unsuccessfully tried to compromise her, of adultery, was proven innocent by the prophet Daniel. "Deborah:" A Hebrew prophet and judge of Israel who led troops against Sisera and sang a famous song of triumph (see Judges 5).

"Hannah:" Old Testament wife of Elkenah and mother of the prophet Samuel. "Eve:" first woman, companion of Adam, who was tempted by the serpent to eat of the Tree of Knowledge.

[8] William Godwin (1756–1836), English social philosopher, political journalist, and religious dissenter who advanced atheism, anarchism, and personal freedom. "Diderot:" Denis Diderot (1713–84), French writer and philosopher who, from 1745 to 1772, served as chief editor of the *Encyclopédie*, principal work of the Enlightenment. "Rousseau:" Jean Jacques Rousseau (1712–78), Swiss-born French philosopher and political theorist who argued for natural innocence and an egalitarian form of government in *The Social Contract* (1762). "Condorcet:" Marie-Jean-Antoine-Nicolas de Caritat, marquis de Condorcet (1743–94), French Enlightenment philosopher who formulated the idea of the indefinite perfectibility of humankind. "Priestly:" Joseph Priestley (1733–1804), English clergyman, political theorist, and physical scientist whose work contributed to advances in liberal political and religious thought and in experimental science. "Price:" Reverend Richard Price (1723–91), British dissenter and moral philosopher, ardent supporter of the American and French revolutions.

possible. So are you. I only say that Mankind have not yet discovered any remedy against irresistable Corruption in Elections to Offices of great Power and Profit, but making them hereditary. . . .

John Adams

1813   1963

J. Hector St John de Crèvecoeur (1735–1813)

Born to an affluent family from Normandy, J. Hector St John de Crèvecoeur emigrated to New France at the age of twenty-four. There he served as a mapmaker with a French regiment in the St Lawrence Valley during the French and Indian War. When the war ended in 1759, the young cartographer settled in the then British colony of New York, becoming a naturalized citizen in 1765. His profession took him to many parts of colonial North America, including the Appalachians, the Mississippi Valley, and the Great Lakes. In 1769 he married Mehetable Tippet, the daughter of a wealthy Tory, purchased a farm he called Pine Hill, and settled down to what he would later recall as an idyllic existence. This came to a dramatic end with the outbreak of the American Revolution. Crèvecoeur tried valiantly to avoid taking sides, but finally was forced to attempt an escape to France, leaving his family in the care of friends. In New York, however, he was captured, imprisoned, and released in 1780 to go into exile.

In 1782, his *Letters from an American Farmer* was published in London, and Crèvecoeur went to Paris, where he made an impression on the glittering intellectual salons of the time. He was appointed French Consul in New York in 1783 and returned to the New World, only to find his wife dead and his beloved Pine Hill burned to the ground; he was, however, able to discover the whereabouts of his children. He later retired to the French countryside, where he died in 1813.

Crèvecoeur's *Letters from an American Farmer* is, without a doubt, one of the texts that have most strongly influenced European perceptions of the United States. In it, he articulates the concept of America as a vast melting-pot into which immigrants from diverse countries are poured and national differences are veiled or erased altogether.

For Crèvecoeur, Americanness is reserved to only Europeans and descendants of Europeans, who as a result of their transplantation to the New World and of their distance from the rigid class structures of Europe are able to prosper. He is not blind, however, to some of the ways in which his optimistic vision is contradicted by the reality of American experience: in his Letter IX, he observes at first hand the horrors of slavery. Finally, in Letter XII, Crèvecoeur evokes the drama not only of his own family caught up in the violence of armed conflict, but also of his own divided loyalties.

PRIMARY WORKS

Letters from an American Farmer, 1782, 1783.
Lettres d'un Cultivateur Américain, 1784.
Voyage dans la Haute Pennsylvanie et dans l'état de New York, 1801.
Sketches of Eighteenth Century America, eds Henir Bourdin, Ralph Gabriel, and Stanley Williams, 1925.
More Letters of the American Farmer: an Edition of the Essays in English left Unpublished by Crèvecoeur, ed. Dennis Moore, 1995.

FURTHER READING

Thomas Philbrick, *St John de Crèvecoeur* (New York: Twayne, 1970).
Gay Wilson and Roger Asselineu, *St John de Crèvecoeur: The Life of An American Farmer* (New York: Viking Press, 1987).
Elizabeth Cook, *Epistolary Bodies: Gender and Genre in the Eighteenth-Century Republic of Letters* (Stanford: Stanford University Press, 1996).
Nancy Ruttenberg, *Democratic Personality: Popular Voice and the Trial of American Authorship* (Stanford: Stanford University Press, 1998).

LETTERS FROM AN AMERICAN FARMER[1]

From *Letter III: What is an American?*

I wish I could be acquainted with the feelings and thoughts which must agitate the heart and present themselves to the mind of an enlightened Englishman when he first lands on this continent. He must greatly rejoice that he lived at a time to see this fair country discovered and settled; he must necessarily feel a share of national pride when he views the chain of settlements which embellish these extended shores. When he says to himself, "This is the work of my countrymen, who, when convulsed by factions[2], afflicted by a variety of miseries and wants, restless and impatient, took refuge here. They brought along with them their national genius[3], to which they principally owe what liberty they enjoy and what substance they possess." Here he sees the industry of his native country displayed in a new manner and traces in their works the embryos of all the arts, sciences, and ingenuity which flourish in Europe. Here he beholds fair cities, substantial villages, extensive fields, an immense country filled with decent houses, good roads, orchards, meadows, and bridges where an hundred years ago all was wild, woody, and uncultivated! What a train of pleasing ideas this fair spectacle must suggest; it is a prospect which must inspire a good citizen with the most heart-felt pleasure. The difficulty consists in the manner of viewing so extensive a scene. He is arrived on a new continent; a modern society offers itself to his contemplation, different from what he had hitherto seen. It is not composed, as in Europe, of great lords who possess everything and of a herd of people who have nothing. Here are no aristocratical families, no courts, no kings, no bishops, no ecclesiastical dominion, no invisible power giving to a few a very visible one, no great manufactures employing thousands, no great refinements of luxury. The rich and the poor are not so far removed from each other as they are in Europe. Some few towns excepted, we are all tillers of the earth, from Nova Scotia to West Florida. We are a people of cultivators scattered over an immense territory, communicating with each other by means of good roads and navigable rivers, united by the silken bands of mild government, all respecting the laws without dreading their power, because they are equitable. We are all animated with the spirit of an industry which is unfettered and unrestrained, because each person works for himself. If he travels through our rural districts, he views not the hostile castle and the haughty mansion, contrasted with the clay-built hut and miserable cabin, where cattle and men help to keep each other warm and dwell in meanness, smoke, and indigence[4]. A pleasing uniformity of decent competence appears throughout our habitations. The meanest of our log-houses is a dry and comfortable habitation. Lawyer or merchant are the fairest titles our towns afford; that of a farmer is the only appellation of the rural inhabitants of our country. It must take some time ere he can reconcile himself to our dictionary, which is but short in words of dignity and names of honour. There, on a Sunday, he sees a congregation of respectable farmers and their wives, all clad in neat homespun, well mounted, or riding in their own humble waggons. There is not among them an esquire, saving the unlettered magistrate. There he sees a parson as simple as his flock, a farmer who does not riot[5] on the labour of others. We have no princes for whom we toil, starve, and bleed; we are the most perfect society now existing in the world.

---

[1]   The text, with slight modification, is from the London edition of 1783 which incorporated corrections made by the author to the original 1782 edition.

[2]   Disputes.

[3]   Specific traits of national character.

[4]   Poverty.

[5]   Indulge himself.

Here man is free as he ought to be, nor is this pleasing equality so transitory as many others are. Many ages will not see the shores of our great lakes replenished with inland nations, nor the unknown bounds of North America entirely peopled. Who can tell how far it extends? Who can tell the millions of men whom it will feed and contain? For no European foot has as yet travelled half the extent of this mighty continent!

The next wish of this traveller will be to know whence came all these people. They are a mixture of English, Scotch, Irish, French, Dutch, Germans, and Swedes. From this promiscuous breed, that race now called Americans have arisen. The eastern provinces[6] must indeed be excepted as being the unmixed descendants of Englishmen. I have heard many wish that they had been more intermixed also; for my part, I am no wisher and think it much better as it has happened. They exhibit a most conspicuous figure in this great and variegated[7] picture; they too enter for a great share in the pleasing perspective displayed in these thirteen provinces. I know it is fashionable to reflect on them, but I respect them for what they have done; for the accuracy and wisdom with which they have settled their territory; for the decency of their manners; for their early love of letters; their ancient college[8], the first in this hemisphere; for their industry, which to me who am but a farmer is the criterion of everything. There never was a people, situated as they are, who with so ungrateful a soil have done more in so short a time. Do you think that the monarchical ingredients which are more prevalent in other governments have purged them from all foul stains? Their histories assert the contrary.

In this great American asylum[9], the poor of Europe have by some means met together, and in consequence of various causes; to what purpose should they ask one another what countrymen they are? Alas, two thirds of them had no country. Can a wretch who wanders about, who works and starves, whose life is a continual scene of sore affliction or pinching penury – can that man call England or any other kingdom his country? A country that had no bread for him, whose fields procured him no harvest, who met with nothing but the frowns of the rich, the severity of the laws, with jails and punishments, who owned not a single foot of the extensive surface of this planet? No! Urged by a variety of motives, here they came. Everything has tended to regenerate them: new laws, a new mode of living, a new social system; here they are become men: in Europe they were as so many useless plants, wanting vegetative mould and refreshing showers; they withered, and were mowed down by want, hunger, and war; but now, by the power of transplantation, like all other plants they have taken root and flourished! Formerly they were not numbered in any civil lists[10] of their country, except in those of the poor; here they rank as citizens. By what invisible power hath this surprising metamorphosis been performed? By that of the laws and that of their industry. The laws, the indulgent laws, protect them as they arrive, stamping on them the symbol of adoption; they receive ample rewards for their labours; these accumulated rewards procure them lands; those lands confer on them the title of freemen, and to that title every benefit is affixed which men can possibly require. This is the great operation daily performed by our laws. Whence proceed these laws? From our government. Whence that government? It is derived from the original genius and strong desire of the people ratified and confirmed by the crown. This is the great chain which links us all, this is the picture which every province exhibits, Nova Scotia excepted. There the crown has done all[11]; either there were no people who had genius or it was not much attended to; the consequence is that the province is very thinly inhabited indeed;

---

6   New England.
7   Many-colored.
8   Harvard, founded in 1636.
9   Refuge.

10   I.e. were not employees of the central government.
11   A reference to the French Acadians' banishment from Nova Scotia.

the power of the crown in conjunction with the musketos has prevented men from settling there. Yet some parts of it flourished once, and it contained a mild, harmless set of people. But for the fault of a few leaders, the whole was banished. The greatest political error the crown ever committed in America was to cut off men from a country which wanted nothing but men!

What attachment can a poor European emigrant have for a country where he had nothing? The knowledge of the language, the love of a few kindred as poor as himself, were the only cords that tied him; his country is now that which gives him his land, bread, protection, and consequence; *Ubi panis ibi patria*[12] is the motto of all emigrants. What, then, is the American, this new man? He is either an European or the descendant of an European; hence that strange mixture of blood, which you will find in no other country. I could point out to you a family whose grandfather was an Englishman, whose wife was Dutch, whose son married a French woman, and whose present four sons have now four wives of different nations. *He* is an American, who, leaving behind him all his ancient prejudices and manners, receives new ones from the new mode of life he has embraced, the new government he obeys, and the new rank he holds. He becomes an American by being received in the broad lap of our great Alma Mater[13]. Here individuals of all nations are melted into a new race of men, whose labours and posterity will one day cause great changes in the world. Americans are the western pilgrims who are carrying along with them that great mass of arts, sciences, vigour, and industry which began long since in the East; they will finish the great circle. The Americans were once scattered all over Europe; here they are incorporated into one of the finest systems of population which has ever appeared, and which will hereafter become distinct by the power of the different climates they inhabit. The American ought therefore to love this country much better than that wherein either he or his forefathers were born. Here the rewards of his industry follow with equal steps the progress of his labour; his labour is founded on the basis of nature, self-interest; can it want a stronger allurement? Wives and children, who before in vain demanded of him a morsel of bread, now, fat and frolicsome, gladly help their father to clear those fields whence exuberant crops are to arise to feed and to clothe them all, without any part being claimed, either by a despotic prince, a rich abbot, or a mighty lord. Here religion demands but little of him: a small voluntary salary to the minister and gratitude to God; can he refuse these? The American is a new man, who acts upon new principles; he must therefore entertain new ideas and form new opinions. From involuntary idleness, servile dependence, penury, and useless labour, he has passed to toils of a very different nature, rewarded by ample subsistence. This is an American.

. . . Now we arrive near the great woods, near the last inhabited districts[14]; there men seem to be placed still farther beyond the reach of government, which in some measure leaves them to themselves. How can it pervade every corner, as they were driven there by misfortunes, necessity of beginnings, desire of acquiring large tracks of land, idleness, frequent want of economy[15], ancient debts; the reunion of such people does not afford a very pleasing spectacle. When discord, want of unity and friendship, when either drunkenness or idleness prevail in such remote districts, contention, inactivity, and wretchedness must ensue. There are not the same remedies to these evils as in a long-established community. The few magistrates they have are in general little better than the rest; they are often in a perfect state of war; that of man against man, sometimes decided by blows, sometimes by means of the law; that of man

---

[12] Loosely translated, "one's country is where there is bread."

[13] In this context, Motherland.

[14] The land west of the original 13 colonies and east of the Mississippi River.

[15] Extravagance.

against every wild inhabitant of these venerable woods, of which they are come to dispossess them. There men appear to be no better than carnivorous animals of a superior rank, living on the flesh of wild animals when they can catch them, and when they are not able, they subsist on grain. He who would wish to see America in its proper light and have a true idea of its feeble beginnings and barbarous rudiments must visit our extended line of frontiers, where the last settlers dwell and where he may see the first labours of settlement, the mode of clearing the earth, in all their different appearances, where men are wholly left dependent on their native tempers and on the spur of uncertain industry, which often fails when not sanctified by the efficacy of law and check of shame, many families exhibit the most hideous parts of our society. They are a kind of forlorn hope, preceding by ten or twelve years the most respectable army of veterans which come after them. In that space, prosperity will polish some, vice and the law will drive off the rest, who, uniting again with others like themselves, will recede still farther, making room for more industrious people, who will finish their improvements, convert the log-house into a convenient habitation, and rejoicing that the first heavy labors are finished, will change in a few years that hitherto barbarous country into a fine, fertile, well-regulated district. Such is our progress; such is the march of the Europeans toward the interior parts of this continent . . .

. . . Europe contains hardly any other distinctions but lords and tenants; this fair country alone is settled by freeholders, the possessors of the soil they cultivate, members of the government they obey, and the framers of their own laws, by means of their representatives. This is a thought which you have taught me to cherish; our distance from Europe, far from diminishing, rather adds to our usefulness and consequence as men and subjects. Had our forefathers remained there, they would only have crowded it and perhaps prolonged those convulsions which had shaken it so long. Every industrious European who transports himself here may be compared to a sprout growing at the foot of a great tree; it enjoys and draws but a little portion of sap; wrench it from the parent roots, transplant it, and it will become a tree bearing fruit also. Colonists are therefore entitled to the consideration due to the most useful subjects; a hundred families barely existing in some parts of Scotland will here in six years cause an annual exportation of 10,000 bushels of wheat, 100 bushels being but a common quantity for an industrious family to sell if they cultivate good land. It is here, then, that the idle may be employed, the useless become useful, and the poor become rich; but by riches I do not mean gold and silver – we have but little of those metals; I mean a better sort of wealth – cleared lands, cattle, good houses, good clothes, and an increase of people to enjoy them.

. . . An European, when he first arrives, seems limited in his intentions, as well as in his views; but he very suddenly alters his scale; two hundred miles formerly appeared a very great distance, it is now but a trifle; he no sooner breathes our air than he forms schemes and embarks in designs he never would have thought of in his own country. There the plenitude of society confines many useful ideas and often, extinguishes the most laudable schemes, which here ripen into maturity. Thus Europeans become Americans.

But how is this accomplished in that crowd of low, indigent people who flock here every year from all parts of Europe? I will tell you; they no sooner arrive than they immediately feel the good effects of that plenty of provisions we possess: they fare on our best food, and are kindly entertained; their talents, character, and peculiar industry are immediately inquired into; they find countrymen everywhere disseminated, let them come from whatever part of Europe. Let me select one as an epitome of the rest: he is hired, he goes to work, and works moderately; instead of being employed by a haughty person, he finds himself with his equal, placed at the substantial table of the farmer, or else at an inferior one as good; his wages are high, his bed is not like that bed of sorrow on which he used to lie; if he behaves with propriety, and is faithful, he is caressed, and becomes as it were a member of the family. He begins to feel the effects of a sort of resurrection; hitherto he had not lived, but simply vegetated; he now feels himself a man because he is treated as such; the laws of his own country had overlooked him in his insignificancy; the laws of this cover him with their mantle. Judge what an alteration there must arise in the mind and the thoughts of this man. He begins to forget his former servitude and dependence; his heart involuntarily swells and glows; this first swell inspires him with those new thoughts which constitute an American. What love can he entertain for a country where his existence was a burthen to him; if he is a generous, good man, the love of this new adoptive parent will sink deep into his heart. He looks around and sees many a prosperous person who but a few years before was as poor as himself. This encourages him much; he begins to form some little scheme, the first, alas, he ever formed in his life. If he is wise, he thus spends two or three years, in which time he acquires knowledge, the use of tools, the modes of working the lands, felling trees, etc. This prepares the foundation of a good name, the most useful acquisition he can make. He is encouraged, he has gained friends; he is advised and directed; he feels bold, he purchases some land; he gives all the money he has brought over, as well as what he has earned, and trusts to the God of harvests for the discharge of the rest. His good name procures him credit. He is now possessed of the deed, conveying to him and his posterity the fee simple and absolute property of two hundred acres of land, situated on such a river. What an epocha[16] in this man's life! He is become a freeholder, from perhaps a German boor[17]. He is now an American, a Pennsylvanian, an English subject. He is naturalised; his name is enrolled with those of the other citizens of the province. Instead of being a vagrant, he has a place of residence; he is called the inhabitant of such a county, or of such a district, and for the first time in his life counts for something, for hitherto he had been a cypher[18]. I only repeat what I have heard many say, and no wonder their hearts should glow and be agitated with a multitude of feelings, not easy to describe. From nothing to start into being; from a servant to the rank of a master; from being the slave of some despotic prince, to become a free man, invested with lands to which every municipal blessing is annexed! What a change indeed! It is in consequence of that change that he becomes an American. This great metamorphosis has a double effect: it extinguishes all his European prejudices, he forgets that mechanism of subordination, that servility of disposition which poverty had taught him; and sometimes he is apt to forget it too much, often passing from one extreme to the other. If he is a good man, he forms schemes of future prosperity, he proposes to educate his children better than he has been educated himself; he thinks of future modes of conduct, feels an ardour to labour he never felt before. Pride steps in and leads him to everything that the laws do not forbid; he respects them; with a heart-felt gratitude he looks toward the east, toward that insular government from whose wisdom all his new felicity is derived and under whose wings and protection he now lives. These reflections constitute him the good man and the good subject. Ye poor Europeans – ye who sweat great; ye who are obliged and work for the great; ye who are obliged to give so many many sheaves to the church, so many to your lords, so many to your government, and have hardly any left for yourselves; ye who are held in less estimation than favourite hunters or useless lap-dogs; ye who only breathe the air of nature because it cannot be withholden from you – it is here that ye can conceive the possibility of those feelings I have been describing; it is here the laws of naturalisation invite every one to partake of our great labours and felicity, to till unrented, untaxed lands! Many, corrupted beyond the power of amendment, have brought with them all their vices, and disregarding the

---

[16]   Moment.

[17]   Peasant.

[18]   I.e. a nonentity, without influence.

advantages held to them, have gone on in their former career of iniquity until they have been overtaken and punished by our laws. It is not every emigrant who succeeds; no, it is only the sober, the honest, and industrious. Happy those to whom this transition has served as a powerful, spur to labour, to prosperity, and to the good establishment of children, born in the days of their poverty and who had no other portion to expect but the rags of their parents had it not been for their happy emigration. Others, again, have been led astray by this enchanting scene; their new pride, instead of leading them to the fields, has kept them in idleness; the idea of possessing lands is all that satisfied them – though surrounded with fertility, they have mouldered away, their time in inactivity, misinformed husbandry, and ineffectual endeavours.

. . . After a foreigner from any part of Europe is arrived and become a citizen, let him devoutly listen to the voice of our great parent, which says to him, "Welcome to my shores, distressed European; bless the hour in which thou didst see my verdant fields, my fair navigable rivers, and my green mountains! If thou wilt work, I have bread for thee; if thou wilt be honest, sober, and industrious, I have greater rewards to confer on thee – ease and independence. I will give thee fields to feed and clothe thee, a comfortable fireside to sit by and tell thy children by what means thou hast prospered, and a decent bed to repose on. I shall endow thee beside with the immunities of a freeman. If thou wilt carefully educate thy children, teach them gratitude to God and reverence to that government, that philanthropic government, which has collected here so many men and made them happy, I will also provide for thy progeny; and to every good man this ought to be the most holy, the most powerful, the most earnest wish he can possibly form, as well as the most consolatory prospect when he dies. Go thou and work and till; thou shalt prosper, provided thou be just grateful, and industrious."

From *Letter IX: Description of Charles Town; Thoughts on Slavery; On Physical Evil; A Melancholy Scene*

Charles Town[19] is, in the north, what Lima is in the south; both are capitals of the richest provinces of their respective hemispheres; you may therefore conjecture that both cities must exhibit the appearances necessarily resulting from riches. Peru abounding in gold, Lima is filled with inhabitants who enjoy all those gradations of pleasure, refinement, and luxury which proceed from wealth. Carolina produces commodities more valuable perhaps than gold because they are gained by greater industry; it exhibits also on our northern stage a display of riches and luxury inferior indeed to the former, but far superior to what are to be seen in our northern towns. Its situation is admirable, being built at the confluence of two large rivers, which receive in their course a great number of inferior streams, all navigable in the spring for flat boats. Here the produce of this extensive territory concenters[20]; here therefore is the seat of the most valuable exportation; their wharfs, their docks, their magazines[21], are extremely convenient to facilitate this great commercial business. The inhabitants are the gayest in America; it is called the centre of our *beau monde*[22] and is always filled with the richest planters in the province, who resort hither in quest of health and pleasure.

The round of pleasure and the expenses of those citizens' tables are much superior to what you would imagine; indeed, the growth of this town and province has been astonishingly rapid . . . The heat of the climate, which is sometimes very great in the interior parts of the country, is always temperate in Charles Town, though sometimes when they have no sea breezes,

---

[19]   Charleston, South Carolina.
[20]   Is concentrated.

[21]   Warehouses.
[22]   Society.

the sun is too powerful. The climate renders excesses of all kinds very dangerous, particularly those of the table; and yet, insensible or fearless of danger, they live on and enjoy a short and a merry life. The rays of their sun seem to urge them irresistibly, to dissipation and pleasure: on the contrary, the women, from being abstemious[23], reach to a longer period of life and seldom die without having had several husbands. An European at his first arrival must be greatly surprised when he sees the elegance of their houses, their sumptuous furniture, as well as the magnificence of their tables. Can he imagine himself in a country the establishment of which is so recent?

The three principal classes of inhabitants are lawyers, planters, and merchants; this is the province which has afforded to the first the richest spoils, for nothing can exceed their wealth, their power, and their influence. They have reached the *ne plus ultra*[24] of worldly felicity; no plantation is secured, no title is good, no will is valid, but what they dictate, regulate, and approve.

. . . While all is joy, festivity, and happiness in Charles Town, would you imagine that scenes of misery overspread in the country? Their ears by habit are become deaf, their hearts are hardened; they neither see, hear, nor feel for the woes of their poor slaves, from whose painful labours all their wealth proceeds. Here the horrors of slavery, the hardship of incessant toils, are unseen; and no one thinks with compassion of those showers of sweat and of tears which from the bodies of Africans daily drop and moisten the ground they till. The cracks of the whip urging these miserable beings to excessive labour are far too distant from the gay capital to be heard. The chosen race eat, drink, and live happy, while the unfortunate one grubs up the ground, raises indigo, or husks the rice, exposed to a sun full as scorching as their native one, without the support of good food, without the cordials of any cheering liquor. This great contrast has often afforded me subjects of the most afflicting meditations. On the one side, behold a people enjoying all that life affords most bewitching and pleasurable, without labour, without fatigue, hardly subjected to the trouble of wishing. With gold, dug from Peruvian mountains, they order vessels to the coasts of Guinea; by virtue of that gold, wars, murders, and devastations are committed in some harmless, peaceable African neighbourhood where dwelt innocent people who even knew not but that all men were black. The daughter torn from her weeping mother, the child from the wretched parents, the wife from the loving husband; whole families swept away and brought through storms and tempests to this rich metropolis! There, arranged like horses at a fair, they are branded like cattle and then driven to toil, to starve, and to languish for a few years on the different plantations of these citizens. And for whom must they work? For persons they know not, and who have no other power over them than that of violence, no other right than what this accursed metal has given them! Strange order of things! Oh, Nature, where art thou? Are not these blacks thy children as well as we? On the other side, nothing is to be seen but the most diffusive misery and wretchedness, unrelieved even in thought or wish! Day after day they drudge on without any prospect of ever reaping for themselves; they are obliged to devote their lives, their limbs, their will, and every vital exertion to swell the wealth of masters who look not upon them with half the kindness and affection with which they consider their dogs and horses. Kindness and affection are not the portion of those who till the earth, who carry burthens, who convert the logs into useful boards. This reward, simple and natural as one would conceive it, would border on humanity; and planters must have none of it!

If Negroes are permitted to become fathers, this fatal indulgence only tends to increase their misery; the poor companions of their scanty pleasures are likewise the companions of

---

[23]   Sparing in the enjoyment of appetites.   [24]   The highest point.

their labors; and when at some critical seasons they could wish to see them relieved, with tears in their eyes they behold them perhaps doubly oppressed, obliged to bear the burden of Nature – a fatal present – as well as that of unabated tasks. How many have I seen cursing the irresistible propensity and regretting that by having tasted of those harmless joys they had become the authors of double misery to their wives. Like their masters, they are not permitted to partake of those ineffable sensations with which Nature inspires the hearts of fathers and mothers; they must repel them all and become callous and passive. This unnatural state often occasions the most acute, the most pungent of their afflictions; they have no time, like us, tenderly to rear their helpless offspring, to nurse them on their knees, to enjoy the delight of being parents. Their paternal fondness is embittered by considering that if their children live, they must live to be slaves like themselves; no time is allowed them to exercise their pious office; the mothers must fasten them on their backs and, with this double load, follow their husbands in the fields, where they too often hear no other sound than that of the voice or whip of the taskmaster and the cries of their infants, broiling in the sun. These unfortunate creatures cry and weep like their parents, without a possibility of relief; the very instinct of the brute, so laudable, so irresistible, runs counter here to their master's interest; and to that god, all the laws of Nature must give way. Thus planters get rich; so raw, so inexperienced am I in this mode of life that were I to be possessed of a plantation, and my slaves treated as in general they are here, never could I rest in peace; my sleep would be perpetually disturbed by a retrospect of the frauds committed in Africa in order to entrap them, frauds surpassing in enormity everything which a common mind can possibly conceive. I should be thinking of the barbarous treatment they meet with on shipboard, of their anguish, of the despair necessarily inspired by their situation, when torn from their friends and relations, when delivered into the hands of a people differently coloured, whom they cannot understand, carried in a strange machine over an ever agitated element, which they had never seen before, and finally delivered over to the severities of the whippers and the excessive labors of the field. Can it be possible that the force of custom should ever make me deaf to all these reflections and as insensible to the injustice of that trade and to their miseries as the rich inhabitants of this town seem to be?

. . . But is it really true, as I have heard it asserted here, that those blacks are incapable of feeling the spurs of emulation and the cheerful sound of encouragement? By no means; there are a thousand proofs existing of their gratitude and fidelity: those hearts in which such noble dispositions can grow are then like ours; they are susceptible of every generous sentiment, of every useful motive of action; they are capable of receiving lights, of imbibing ideas that would greatly alleviate the weight of their miseries. But what methods have in general been made use of to obtain so desirable an end? None; the day in which they arrive and are sold is the first of their labours, labours which from that hour admit of no respite; for though indulged by law with relaxation on Sundays, they are obliged to employ that time which is intended for rest to till their little plantations. What can be expected from wretches in such circumstances? Forced from their native country, cruelly treated when on board, and not less so on the plantations to which they are driven, is there anything in this treatment but what must kindle all the passions, sow the seeds of inveterate resentment, and nourish a wish of perpetual revenge?

. . . Everywhere one part of the human species is taught the art of shedding the blood of the other, of setting fire to their dwellings, of leveling the works of their industry: half of the existence of nations regularly employed in destroying other nations. What little political felicity is to be met with here and there has cost oceans of blood to purchase, as if good was never to be the portion of unhappy man. Republics, kingdoms, monarchies, founded either on fraud or successful violence, increase by pursuing the steps of the same policy until they are destroyed in their turn, either by the influence of their own crimes or by more successful but equally criminal enemies.

. . . The following scene will, I hope, account for these melancholy reflections and apologise for the gloomy thoughts with which I have filled this letter: my mind is, and always has been, oppressed since I became a witness to it. I was not long since invited to dine with a planter who lived three miles from – , where he then resided. In order to avoid the heat of the sun, I resolved to go on foot, sheltered in a small path leading through a pleasant wood. I was leisurely travelling along, attentively examining some peculiar plants which I had collected, when all at once I felt the air strongly agitated, though the day was perfectly calm and sultry. I immediately cast my eyes toward the cleared ground, from which I was but a small distance, in order to see whether it was not occasioned by a sudden shower, when at that instant a sound resembling a deep rough voice, uttered, as I thought, a few inarticulate monosyllables. Alarmed and surprised, I precipitately looked all round, when I perceived at about six rods distance something resembling a cage, suspended to the limbs of a tree, all the branches of which appeared covered with large birds of prey, fluttering about and anxiously endeavouring to perch on the cage. Actuated by an involuntary motion of my hands more than by any design of my mind, I fired at them; they all flew to a short distance, with a most hideous noise, when, horrid to think and painful to repeat, I perceived a Negro, suspended in the cage and left there to expire! I shudder when I recollect that the birds had already picked out his eyes; his cheek-bones were bare; his arms had been attacked in several places; and his body seemed covered with a multitude of wounds. From the edges of the hollow sockets and from the lacerations with which he was disfigured, the blood slowly dropped and tinged the ground beneath. No sooner were the birds flown than swarms of insects covered the whole body of this unfortunate wretch, eager to feed on his mangled flesh and to drink his blood. I found myself suddenly arrested by the power of affright and terror; my nerves were convulsed; I trembled; I stood motionless, involuntarily contemplating the fate of this Negro in all its dismal latitude. The living spectre, though deprived of his eyes, could still distinctly hear, and in his uncouth dialect begged me to give him some water, to allay his thirst. Humanity herself would have recoiled back with horror; she would have balanced whether to lessen such reliefless distress or mercifully with one blow to end this dreadful scene of agonizing torture! Had I had a ball in my gun, I certainly should have dispatched him, but finding myself unable to perform so kind an office, I sought, though trembling, to relieve him as well as I could. A shell ready fixed to a pole, which had been used by some Negroes, presented itself to me; filled it with water, and with trembling hands I guided it to the quivering lips of the wretched sufferer. Urged by the irresistible power of thirst, he endeavoured to meet it, as he instinctively guessed its approach by the noise it made in passing through the bars of the cage. "Tanky you, white man; tanky you; puta some poison and give me." "How long have you been hanging there?" I asked him. "Two days, and me no die; the birds, the birds; aaah me!" Oppressed with the reflections which this shocking spectacle afforded me, I mustered strength enough to walk away and soon reached the house at which I intended to dine. There I heard that the reason for this slave's being thus punished was on account of his having killed the overseer of the plantation. They told me that the laws of self-preservation rendered such executions necessary, and supported the doctrine of slavery with the arguments generally made use of to justify the practice, with the repetition of which I shall not trouble you at present. Adieu.

From *Letter XII: Distresses of a Frontier Man*

. . . I am divided between the respect I feel for the ancient connexion and the fear of innovations, with the consequence of which I am not well acquainted, as they are embraced by my own countrymen. I am conscious that I was happy before this unfortunate revolution. I feel that I am no longer so; therefore I regret the change. This is the only mode of reasoning adapted to persons in my situation. If I attach myself to the mother country, which is 3,000 miles from me, I become what is called an enemy to my own region; if I follow the rest of my countrymen, I become opposed to our ancient masters: both extremes appear equally dangerous to a person of so little weight and consequence as I am, whose energy and example are of no avail. As to the argument on which the dispute is founded, I know little about it. Much has been said and written on both sides, but who has a judgement capacious and clear enough to decide? The great moving principles which actuate both parties are much hid from vulgar eyes, like mine; nothing but the plausible and the probable are offered to our contemplation. The innocent class are always the victims of the few; they are in all countries and at all times the inferior agents on which the popular phantom is erected; they clamour and must toil and bleed, and are always sure of meeting with oppression and rebuke. It is for the sake of the great leaders on both sides that so much blood must be spilt; that of the people is counted as nothing.

. . . Great Source of wisdom! Inspire me with light sufficient to guide my benighted steps out of this intricate maze! Shall I discard all my ancient principles, shall I renounce that name, that nation which I held once so respectable? I feel the powerful attraction; the sentiments they inspired, grew with my earliest knowledge and were grafted upon the first rudiments of my education. On the other hand, shall I arm myself against that country where I first drew breath, against the playmates of my youth, my bosom friends, my acquaintance? The idea makes me shudder! Must I be called a parricide, a traitor, a villain, lose the esteem of all those whom I love to preserve my own, be shunned like a rattlesnake, or be pointed at like a bear? I have neither heroism nor magnanimity enough to make so great a sacrifice. Here I am tied, I am fastened by numerous strings, nor do I repine at the pressure they cause; ignorant as I am, I can pervade the utmost extent of the calamities which have already overtaken our poor afflicted country.

Our fate, the fate of thousands, is, then, necessarily involved in the dark wheel of fortune. Why, then, so many useless reasonings; we are the sport of fate. Farewell education, principles, love of our country, farewell; all are become useless to the generality of us: he who governs himself according to what he calls his principles may be punished either by one party or the other for those very principles. He who proceeds, without principle, as chance, timidity, or self-preservation directs, will not perhaps fare better, but he will be less blamed. What are *we* in the great scale of events, we poor defenceless frontier inhabitants? What is it to the gazing world whether we breathe or whether we die? Whatever virtue, whatever merit and disinterestedness we may exhibit in our secluded retreats, of what avail? We are like the pismires[25] destroyed by the plough, whose destruction prevents not the future crop. Self-preservation, therefore, the rule of Nature, seems to be the best rule of conduct; what good can we do by vain resistance, by useless efforts?

1782, 1783

---

[25] Ants.

Prince Hall (1735?–1807)

Although his life before the American Revolution remains shadowy, after the Revolution, Prince Hall became the most prominent black citizen in Boston, founding the world's first lodge of black Freemasonry, and inaugurating a long history of Black benevolent societies that pressed for political, social and economic improvement for freed black people and the emancipation of slaves. The black population in New England, both freed and enslaved, soared during the mid-eighteenth century. Their presence – and inequitable treatment – indicted the very principles upon which the Revolution was fought, and inspired five unsuccessful petitions by Boston's black citizens to the General Court in 1773 and 1774 to abolish slavery, a fight that Prince Hall continued.

Born around 1735, Hall's parents and birthplace remain unknown. His name first appears in the 1740s as the slave of William Hall of Boston, a leather dresser, who taught Hall the trade. In 1756, Hall fathered a son, Primus, and who went on to fight in the Revolution. In 1762, Hall joined the Congregational Church on School Street "in full communion," and married Sarah Ritchie, a slave. In the Spring of 1770, his master freed him, and Hall made his living as a leather dresser, retailer of small goods and caterer, with a small house and leather workshop at the sign of the Golden Fleece. He also probably fought in the Revolution (at least six black Prince Halls of Massachusetts are listed in the rolls of the army and navy).

This is important, because in 1775, Hall and fourteen other free black men accepted an offer to become members of an army lodge of Masons attached to a British regiment stationed in Boston. Such a structure for black solidarity raised concerns among patriots. Abigail Adams, for example, wrote to her husband John of a "conspiracy of negroes" who had submitted a "petition to the [British] Governor, telling him that they would fight for him provided he would arm them, and engage to liberate them if he conquered." When the British left in 1776, African Lodge No. 1, as it was called, had permission to meet, but did not get a charter until 1787, when it was renumbered as Lodge 459, with Prince Hall as Master. A similar challenge faced the Lodge during Shays' Rebellion in 1786–7. Although the freed blacks of

Boston had more sympathy for the debt-ridden veterans and farmers rebelling in western Massachusetts, Hall decided that masonry "enjoins upon us to be peaceable subjects to the civil powers where we reside," and he wrote offering Governor Bowdoin 700 troops to help quell the insurrection. This offer, though sorely needed, was rejected ostensibly because white officers might not want to serve with blacks, but the fear of a "conspiracy" of armed black men lingered. Despite these obstacles, Hall's organizational skills not only secured the existence of Lodge No. 459 (later No. 370), but inspired a proliferation of black Freemasonry which he brought together in an association of black Masonic Grand Lodges that today remains a thriving, international fraternal society with many thousands of members.

A strategic organizer, Hall was also a tireless writer in the cause of abolition and the improvement of black communal life. He wrote letters to the Masonic officials in London, to Boston newspapers, and to his black counterparts in Providence and Philadelphia, which also had African Union Societies. In Boston, its membership overlapped with the Masonic Lodge. His most important work was a series of petitions to the General Court which he wrote on behalf of his Lodge and free blacks in Boston: in 1777 for the abolition of slavery; in 1787, along with seventy-three other prominent black citizens, for financial and other assistance for the resettlement of blacks in Africa, which was accepted by the Assembly but quickly buried in committee; again in 1787, to protest the lack of public education for black citizens who paid taxes; and in 1788, to protest the kidnapping of three free black Bostonians into slavery. Although the three men were safely returned, and the General Court closed Massachusetts ports to slave trading from Africa, it also ruled that blacks who could not produce a certificate of citizenship would be jailed and whipped. In 1792 and again in 1797, Hall, now Grandmaster, delivered the "charge" to his Lodge on the traditional feast of St John, printed below. His concerns about continued discrimination echo the charge delivered in 1789 by Reverend John Marrant, the first Black minister ordained in the Anglican church, appointed by Hall as the chaplain for his African Lodge. Although Hall hails the slave revolt in Saint-Domingue that will end with the creation of independent Haiti in 1804, and demands equality of opportunity for Boston's blacks, he also sounds the ground notes of black middle-class accommodation to US society: faith in God, loyalty to civil institutions, public respectability, and universal benevolence.

PRIMARY WORKS

A CHARGE, Delivered to the Brethren of the AFRICAN LODGE on the 25th of June, 1792, At the Hall of Brother William Smith, in Charlestown. By the Right Worshipful Master PRINCE HALL. Printed at the Request of the Lodge. Printed and sold at the Bible and Heart, Cornhill, Boston.

A CHARGE Delivered to the AFRICAN LODGE June 24, 1797, at Metonomy. By the Right Worshipful PRINCE HALL. Published by the Desire of the Members of Said Lodge. 1797.

FURTHER READING

William Muraskin, Middle Class Blacks in a White Society: Prince Hall's Freemasonry in America (Berkeley: University of California Press, 1975).

Charles H. Wesley, Prince Hall: Life and Legacy (Washington: United Supreme Council, Southern Jurisdiction, 1977).

Sidney Kaplan, "Prince Hall: Organizer," The Black Presence in the Era of the American Revolution 1770–1800, 1973, rev. ed. (Amherst: University of Massachusetts Press, 1989).

Maurice Wallace, "'Are We Men?': Prince Hall, Martin Delany, and the Masculine Ideal in Black Freemasonry, 1775–1865," American Literary History Fall, 9, 3 (1997) pp. 396–424.

A CHARGE DELIVERD TO THE AFRICAN LODGE JUNE 24, 1797, AT METONOMY. BY THE RIGHT WORSHIPFUL PRINCE HALL. PUBLISHED BY THE DESIRE OF THE MEMBERS OF SAID LODGE. 1797.[1]

Beloved Brethren of the African Lodge,
'Tis now five years since I deliver'd a Charge to you on some parts and points of Masonry. As one branch or superstructure on the foundation; when I endeavoured to shew you the duty of a Mason to a Mason, and charity or love to all mankind, as the mark and image of the great God, and the Father of the human race.[2]

I shall now attempt to shew you that it is our duty to sympathise with our fellow men under their troubles, the families of our brethren who are gone: we hope to the Grand Lodge above, here to return no more. But the cheerfulness that you have ever had to relieve them, and ease their burdens, under their sorrows, will never be forgotten by them; and in this manner you will never be weary in doing good.

But my brethren, although we are to begin here, we must not end here; for only look around you and you will see and hear of numbers of our fellow men crying out with holy Job, Have pity on me, O my friends, for the hand of the Lord hath touched me. And this is not to be

---

[1]   The text, with slight modification, is from Dorothy Porter, *Early Negro Writing 1760–1837* (Boston: Beacon Press, 1971).

[2]   Hall delivered this charge on June 25, 1792. It can also be found in Porter's *Early Negro Writing 1760–1837*.

confined to parties or colours; not to towns or states; not to a kingdom, but to the kingdoms of the whole earth, over whom Christ the king is head and grand master.

Among these numerous sons and daughters of distress, I shall begin with our friends and brethren; and first, let us see them dragg'd from their native country by the iron hand of tyranny and oppression, from their dear friends and connections, with weeping eyes and aching hearts, to a strange land and strange people, whose tender mercies are cruel; and there to bear the iron yoke of slavery and cruelty til death as a friend shall relieve them. And must not the unhappy condition of these our fellow men draw forth our hearty prayer and wishes for their deliverance from these merchants and traders, whose characters you have in the xviii chap. of the Revelations 11, 12, & 13 verses[3], and who knows but these same sort of traders may in a short time, in the like manner, bewail the loss of the African traffick, to their shame and confusion: and if I mistake not, it now begins to dawn in some of the West-India islands[4]; which puts me in mind of a nation (that I have somewhere read of) called Ethiopeans, that cannot change their skin: But God can and will change their conditions, and their hearts too; and let Boston and the world know, that He hath no respect of persons; and that that bulwark of envy, pride, scorn; and contempt, which is so visible to be seen in some and felt, shall fall, to rise no more.

When we hear of the bloody wars which are now in the world, and thousands of our fellow men slain; fathers and mothers bewailing the loss of their sons; wives for the loss of their husbands; towns and cities burnt and destroy'd; what must be the heart-felt sorrow and distress of these poor and unhappy people! Though we cannot help them, the distance being so great, yet we may sympathize with them in their troubles, and mingle a tear of sorrow with them, and do as we are exhorted to – weep with those that weep.

Thus my brethren we see what a chequered world we live in. Sometimes happy in having our wives and children like olive-branches about our tables; receiving the bounties of our great Benefactor. The next year, or month, or week we may be deprived of some of them, and we go mourning about the streets, so in societies; we are this day to celebrate this Feast of St John's, and the next week we might be called upon to attend a funeral of some one here, as we have experienced since our last in this Lodge. So in the common affairs of life we sometimes enjoy health and prosperity; at another time sickness and adversity, crosses and disappointments.

So in states and kingdoms; sometimes in tranquility, then wars and tumults: rich today, and poor tomorrow; which shews that there is not an independent mortal on earth, but dependent one upon the other, from the king to the beggar.

The great law-giver, Moses, who instructed by his father-in-law, Jethro, an Ethiopean, how to regulate his courts of justice and what sort of men to choose for the different offices; hear now my words, said he, I will give you counsel, and God shall be with you; be thou for the people to Godward, that though mayest bring the causes unto God, and thou shall teach them ordinances and laws, and shall shew the way wherein they must walk, and the work that they must do: moreover thou shall provide out of all the people, able men, such as fear God, men of truth, hating covetousness, and places such over them, to be rulers of thousands, of hundreds and of tens.

So Moses hearkened to the voice of his father-in-law, and did all that he said. Exodus xviii. 22–24.

This is the first and grandest lecture that Moses ever received from the mouth of man; for

---

[3] "And the merchants of the earth shall weep and mourn over her [great city of Babylon]; for no man buyeth their merchandise any more" (Revelation 18:11).

[4] In 1791, slaves in the French colony of Saint-Domingue revolted, and on January 1, 1801, the whole island was declared independent. The war with France had laid waste the country and destroyed the economy.

Jethro understood geometry as well as laws, *that* a Mason may plainly see: so a little captive servant maid by whose advice Nomen, the great general of Syria's army, was healed of his leprosy; and by a servant his proud spirit was brought down: 2 Kings v. 3–14.[5] The feelings of this little captive for this great man, her captor, was so great, that she forgot her state of captivity and felt for the distress of her enemy. Would to God (said she to her mistress) my lord were with the prophets in Samaria, he should be healed of his leprosy: So after he went to the prophet, his proud host was so haughty that he not only disdained the prophet's direction, but derided the good old prophet; and had it not been for his servant he would have gone to his grave with a double leprosy, the outward and the inward, in the heart, which is the worst of leprosies; a black heart is worse than a white leprosy.

How unlike was this great general's behaviour to that of as grand a character, and as well beloved by his prince as he was; I mean Obadiah, to like a prophet. See for this 1st Kings xviii. From 7 to the 16th.

And as Obadiah was in the way, behold, Elijah met him, and he knew him, and fell on his face, and said, Art not thou, my Lord, Elijah, and he told him, Yea, go and tell thy Lord, behold Elijah is here: and so on to the 16th verse. Thus we see that great and good men have, and always will have, a respect for ministers and servants of God. Another instance of this is in Acts viii. 27 to 31, of the European Eunuch, a man of great authority, to Philip, the apostle: here is mutual love and friendship between them. This minister of Jesus Christ did not think himself too good to receive the hand, and ride in a chariot with a black man in the face of day; neither did this great monarch (for so he was) think it beneath him to take a poor servant of the Lord by the hand, and invite him into his carriage, though but with a staff, one coat, and no money in his pocket. So our Grand Master, Solomon, was not asham'd to take the Queen of Sheba by the hand, and lead her into his court, at the hour of high twelve, and there converse with her on points of masonry (for if ever there was a female mason in the world she was one) and other curious matters; and gratified her, by shewing her all his riches and curious pieces of architecture in the temple, and in his house: After some time staying with her, he loaded her with much rich presents: he gave her the right hand of affection and parted in love.[6]

I hope that no one will dare openly (tho' in fact the behaviour of some implies as much) to say, as our Lord said on another occasion, Behold a greater than Solomon is here.[7] But yet let them consider that our Grand Master Solomon did not divide the living child, whatever he might do with the dead one, neither did he pretend to make a law to forbid the parties from having free intercourse with one another without the fear of censure, or be turned out of the synagogue.

Now my brethren, as we see and experience that all things here are frail and changeable and nothing here to be depended upon: Let us seek those things which are above, which are sure, and stedfast, and unchangeable, and at the same time let us pray to Almighty God, while we remain in the tabernacle, that he would give us the grace of patience and strength to bear up under all our troubles, which at this day God knows we have our share. Patience I say, for were we not possess'd of a great measure of it you could not bear up under the daily insults you meet with in the streets of Boston; much more on public days of recreation, how are you shamefully abus'd, and that at such a degree that you may truly be said to carry your lives in your hands, and the arrows of death are flying about your heads; helpless old women have their clothes torn

5   The Syrian general is Naaman, the captive maid is from Israel, the prophet in Samaria is Elisha.

6   See 1 Kings 10: 1–13.

7   "The queen of the south shall rise up in the judgment with this generation, and shall condemn it: for she came from the uttermost parts of the earth to hear the wisdom of Solomon; and, behold, a greater than Solomon is here" (Matthew 12:42; also Luke 11:31).

off their backs, even to the exposing of their nakedness; and by whom are these disgraceful and abusive actions committed, not by the men born and bred in Boston, for they are better bred; but by a mob or horde of shameless, low-lived, envious, spiteful persons, some of them not long since, servants in gentlemen's kitchens, scouring knives, tending horses, and driving chaise. 'Twas said by a gentleman who saw that filthy behaviour in the common, that in all the places he had been in, he never saw so cruel behaviour in all his life, and that a slave in the West-Indies, on Sunday or holidays enjoys himself and friends without any molestation. Not only this man, but many in town who hath seen their behaviour to you, and that without any provocation – twenty or thirty cowards fall upon one man – have wonder'd at the patience of the Blacks: 'tis not for want of courage in you, for they know that they dare not face you man for man, but in a mob, which we despise, and had rather suffer wrong than to do wrong, to the disturbance of the community and the disgrace of our reputation: for every good citizen doth honour to the laws of the State where he resides.

My brethren, let us not be cast down under these and many other abuses we at present labour under: for the darkest is before the break of day. My brethren, let us remember what a dark day it was with our African brethren six years ago, in the French West-Indies.[8] Nothing but the snap of the whip was heard from morning to evening; hanging, broken on the wheel, burning, and all manner of tortures inflicted on those unhappy people for nothing else but to gratify their masters pride, wantonness, and cruelty: but blessed be God, the scene is changed; they now confess that God hath no respect of persons, and therefore receive them as their friends, and treat them as brothers. Thus doth Ethiopia begin to stretch forth her hand, from a sink of slavery to freedom and equality.

Although you are deprived of the means of education, yet you are not deprived of the means of meditation; by which I mean thinking, hearing and weighing matters, men, and things in your own mind, and making that judgment of them as you think reasonable to satisfy your minds and give an answer to those who may ask you a question. This nature hath furnished you with, without letter learning; and some have made great progress therein, some of those I have heard repeat psalms and hymns, and a great part of a sermon, only by hearing it read or preached and why not in other things in nature: how many of this class of our brethren that follow the seas can foretell a storm some days before it comes; whether it will be a heavy or light, a long or short one; foretell a hurricane, whether it will be destructive or moderate, without any other means than observation and consideration.

So in the observation of the heavenly bodies, this same class without a telescope or other apparatus have through a smoak'd glass observed the eclipse of the sun: One being ask'd what he saw through his smoaked glass, said, Saw, saw, de clipsey, or de clipseys. And what do you think of it? – Stop, dere be two. Right, and what do they look like? – Look like, why if I tell you, they look like two ships sailing one bigger than tother; so they sail by one another, and make no noise. As simple as the answers are they have a meaning, and shew that God can out of the mouth of babes and Africans shew forth his glory; let us then love and adore him as the God who defends us and supports us and will support us under our pressures, let them be ever so heavy and pressing. Let us by the blessing of God, in whatsoever state we are, or may be in, to be content; for clouds and darkness are about him; but justice and truth is his habitation; who hath said, Vengeance is mine and I will repay it[9], therefore let us kiss the rod and be still, and see the works of the Lord.

---

8   Allusion to the bloody slave revolt begun in the French colony of Saint-Domingue on August 24, 1791, which abol-ished slavery in 1795 and which, in 1804, produced the independent nation of Haiti.

9   Romans 12:19.

Another thing I would warn you against, is the slavish fear of man, which bringest a snare, saith Solomon.[10] This passion of fear, like pride and envy, hath slain its thousands. – What but this makes so many perjure themselves; for fear of offending them at home they are a little depending on for some trifles: A man that is under a panic of fear, is afraid to be alone; you cannot hear of a robbery or house broke open or set on fire but he hath an accomplice with him, who must share the spoil with him; whereas if he was truly bold, and void of fear, he would keep the whole plunder to himself: so when either of them is detected and not the other, he may be call'd to oath to keep it secret, but through fear, (and that passion is so strong) he will not confess, till the fatal cord is put on his neck; then death will deliver him from the fear of man, and he will confess the truth when it will not be of any good to himself or the community: nor is this passion of fear only to be found in this class of men, but among the great.

What was the reason that our African kings and princes have plunged themselves and their peaceable kingdoms into bloody wars, to the destroying of towns and kingdoms, but the fear of the report of a great gun or the glittering of arms and swords, which struck these kings near the seaports with such a panic of fear, as not only to destroy the peace and happiness of their inland brethren, but plung'd millions of their fellow countrymen into slavery and cruel bondage.

So in other countries; see Felix trembling on his throne.[11] How many Emperors and kings have left their kingdoms and best friends at the sight of a handful of men in arms: how many have we seen that have left their estates and their friends and ran over to the stronger side as they thought; all through the fear of men, who is but a worm, and hath no more power to hurt his fellow worm, without the permission of God, than a real worm.

Thus we see, my brethren, what a miserable condition it is to be under the slavish fear of men; it is of such a destructive nature to mankind, that the scriptures every where from Genesis to the Revelations warns us against it; and even our blessed Saviour himself forbids us from this slavish fear of man, in his sermon on the mount; and the only way to avoid it is to be in the fear of God: let a man consider the greatness of his power, as the maker and upholder of all things here below, and that in Him we live, and move, and have our being, the giver of the mercies we enjoy here from day to day, and that our lives are in his hands, and that he made the heavens, the sun, moon and stars to move in their various orders; let us thus view the greatness of God, and then turn our eyes on mortal man, a worm, a shade, a wafer, and see whether he is an object of fear or not; on the contrary, you will think him in his best estate to be but vanity, feeble and a dependent mortal, and stands in need of your help, and cannot do without your assistance, in some way or other; and yet some of these poor mortals will try to make you believe they are Gods, but worship them not. My brethren, let us pay all due respect to all whom God hath put in places of honor over us: do justly and be faithful to them that hire you, and treat them with that respect they may deserve; but worship no man. Worship God, this much is your duty as christians and as masons.

We see then how becoming and necessary it is to have a fellow feeling for our distres'd brethren of the human race, in their troubles, both spiritual and temporal – How refreshing it is to a sick man, to see his sympathising friends around his bed, ready to administer all the relief in their power; although they can't relieve his bodily pain yet they may ease his mind by good instructions and cheer his heart by their company.

How doth it cheer up the heart of a man when his house is on fire, to see a number of friends coming to his relief; he is so transported that he almost forgets his loss and his danger, and fills him with love and gratitude; and their joys and sorrows are mutual.

---

10   Proverbs 29:25.
11   The governor of Cæsarea who kept the apostle Paul in   custody when a band of Jews conspired to kill him. See Acts 23:24 ff.

So a man wreck'd at sea, how must it revive his drooping heart to see a ship bearing down for his relief.

How doth it rejoice the heart of a stranger in a strange land to see the people cheerful and pleasant and are ready to help him.

How did it, think you, cheer the heart of those our poor unhappy African brethren, to see a ship commissioned from God, and from a nation that without flattery faith, that all men are free and are brethren; I say to see them in an instant deliver such a number from their cruel bolts and galling chains, and to be fed like men and treated like brethren. Where is the man that has the least spark of humanity, that will not rejoice with them; and bless a righteous God who knows how and when to relieve the oppressed, as we see he did in the deliverance of the captives among the Algerines;[12] how sudden were they delivered by the sympathising members of the Congress of the United States, who now enjoy the free air of peace and liberty, to their great joy and surprise, to them and their friends. Here we see the hand of God in various ways bringing about his own glory for the good of mankind, by the mutual help of their fellow men; which ought to teach us in all our straits, be they what they may, to put our trust in Him, firmly believing that he is able and will deliver us and defend us against all our enemies; and that no weapon form'd against us shall prosper; only let us be steady and uniform in our walks, speech and behaviour; always doing to all men as we wish and desire they would do to us in the like cases and circumstances.

Live and act as Masons, that you may die as Masons; let those despisers see, altho' many of us cannot read, yet by our searches and researches into men and things, we have supplied that defect; and if they will let us we shall call ourselves a charter'd lodge of just and lawful Masons; be always ready to give an answer to those that ask you a question; give the right hand of affection and fellowship to whom it justly belongs; let their colour and complexion be what it will, let their nation be what it may, for they are your brethren, and it is your indispensable duty so to do; let them as Masons deny this, and we & the world know what to think of them be they ever so grand: for we know this was Solomon's creed, Solomon's creed did I say, it is the decree of the Almighty, and all Masons have learnt it: 'tis plain market language, and plain and true facts need no apologies.

I shall now conclude with an old poem which I found among some papers:[13]

> Let blind admirers handsome faces praise,
> And graceful features to great honour raise,
> The glories of the red and white express,
> I know no beauty but in holiness;
> If God of beauty be the uncreate
> Perfect idea, in this lower state,
> The greatest beauties of an human mould
> Who most resemble Him we justly hold;
> Whom we resemble not in flesh and blood,
> But being pure and holy, just and good:
> May such a beauty fall but to my share,
> For curious shape or face I'll never care.

1797

---

[12]   In the summer of 1796, Joel Barlow, the poet, helped to free the eighty-eight remaining sailors taken captive by Algeria during the crisis of 1787 with Britain. The ransom, authorized by Congress, was around a million dollars, roughly one-sixth of the federal budget.

[13]   John Rawlet (1642–86), "True Beauty" in *Poetick Miscellanies of Mr John Rawlet* (London, 1687).

Thomas Paine (1737–1809)

Tom Paine spent only thirteen years in America, but became the leading polemicist of the American Revolution. His early life in England prepared him to be a revolutionary. He was born in Thetford, Norfolk, to a Quaker father and Anglican mother. He attended the local grammar school and apprenticed to his father's trade of staymaker. Intelligent and restless, he went to sea for a short time, but returned, and in 1759, opened his own staymaking business and married his first wife, Mary Lambert, a servant, who died less than a year later. In 1762, Paine became a government tax collector, but lost his position in 1765 for false reporting. He then taught at a London academy, was reinstated as a tax collector, and tried unsuccessfully to organize the excisemen to petition Parliament for increased salaries. In London, Paine attended meetings of radical underground political groups, as well as scientific lectures, where he absorbed the Newtonian physics that, through its elevation of reason, opened the world of thought to everyone, and made the equality of "men" an important new idea of political life. Through his friendship with the mathematician George Lewis Scott, Paine met Benjamin Franklin, who would be helpful to him later on. After another failed marriage and failed business endeavor in Lewes, Sussex, in 1774, Paine decided to try his luck in the American colonies.

On Franklin's recommendation, Paine arrived in Philadelphia and became the editor of the *Pennsylvania Magazine*. His most important contribution was the anonymously published pamphlet, *Common Sense* (1776), which urged immediate separation from Britain and sought in simple language to justify rebellion and the establishment of a republican form of representative government. The impact of this pamphlet was electrifying; at least twenty-five editions were published in 1776, and it was circulated widely, read to the illiterate and furiously discussed on all levels of colonial society. Soon revealed as its author, and charged with treason by the British, Paine did not advance new arguments in his pamphlet; most of this territory had been well plowed by the more conservative revolutionary writers like John Adams, Alexander Hamilton, and James Madison. But Paine presented the familiar reasons for revolution in secular terms and vivid, accessible language. He shared

with the more radical revolutionaries, like Franklin and Thomas Jefferson, a philosophy of natural rights that could not logically justify privilege, wealth and political power accorded to people by birth. Although Paine joined the Continental Army when war broke out, he really fought the war with words. In December 1776, just after General Washington was retreating from his defeat in New York, across New Jersey into Pennsylvania, Paine published the first of sixteen papers entitled *The American Crisis*, which he continued to bring out until the end of the war in 1783. These were gripping pieces aimed at keeping the rebels fighting. The first and most famous one so affected General Washington that he ordered it read to his men on Christmas Eve, 1776, just before the bedraggled troops crossed the Delaware above Trenton, where they surprised and defeated the Hessian mercenaries in the pay of Britain.

Paine's effective rhetoric earned him a controversial paid position as Secretary to the Congress' Committee on Foreign Affairs, which allowed him to continue to write. But politics in the post-Revolutionary era were complex, and though Paine was allied with the Federalists in their bid for a strong centralized government, he grew impatient with the process, and his incendiary personality marginalized him. In 1787, he returned to England and Europe to gain support for a single span iron bridge he designed, with no success. When the prominent political theorist, Edmund Burke, who had initially supported the American colonies, wrote *Reflections on the Revolution in France*, denouncing republicanism and praising the wisdom of a hereditary monarchy, Paine responded with *The Rights of Man, Parts 1 and 2*. Paine's response cannot compare with the polish and erudition of Burke's writing, but his valiant attempt signaled his irrevocable break with Federalist ideas. Furthermore, in his extraordinary response, Paine described what we recognize today as the outline of a welfare state and suggested the possibilities of redistributive economic justice, ideas he enlarged in *Agrarian Justice* (1797), his last major work.

His arguments in *The Rights of Man* earned him an indictment for sedition, and in 1792, Paine fled England for Paris, where his radical ideas earned him the position of "citizen" and an elected seat in the French Convention, the revolutionary assembly. Not able to speak French put him at a great disadvantage, and when he condemned as barbaric the execution of King Louis XVI, he was accused of supporting royalty and thrown into Luxembourg Prison. After ten anxious months, James Madison, the American Ambassador, procured his release. During this period, Paine wrote and published *The Age of Reason*, a copy of which was smuggled back to America by the poet Joel Barlow. Intended as an expression of the premises of Enlightenment Deism, an unorthodox belief in natural religion supported widely by colonial leaders like Franklin, Washington and Jefferson, Paine's bitter attacks on Christianity and its biblical basis were ridiculed and reviled in England and America. Readers in America especially, during the 1790s, had grown quite conservative in matters of religion. In addition, political opponents used distortions of Paine's ideas to damage Jefferson, who was forced to trim his religious critique and break with Paine. On his return to America in 1802, Paine was vilified as an atheist and a threat to democracy. Ostracized and poor, he lived out the rest of his life in New Rochelle, New York. Denied burial in the local

Quaker graveyard, he was buried on this farm, but in 1819, William Cobbett, a supporter who wanted to give Paine a proper burial in England, exhumed the remains, which were somehow lost after Cobbett's death.

PRIMARY WORKS

The Writings of Thomas Paine, ed. Moncure D. Conway, 4 vols, 1894–1896.
The Complete Writings of Thomas Paine, ed. Philip S. Foner, 2 vols, 1945.

FURTHER READING

Eric Foner, *Tom Paine and Revolutionary America* (New York: Oxford University Press, 1976).
A. Owen Aldridge, *Thomas Paine's American Ideology* (Newark: University of Delaware Press, 1984).
Edward Hutchinson and William Scheick, *Paine, Scripture and Authority: The Age of Reason as Religious and Political Idea* (Bethlehem, PA: Lehigh University Press, 1994).
John Keane, *Tom Paine: A Political Life* (Boston: Little Brown, 1995).

FROM *COMMON SENSE*[1]

Man knows no Master save creating HEAVEN,
Or those whom Choice and common Good ordain.
THOMSON[2]

Introduction

Perhaps the sentiments contained in the following pages, are not *yet* sufficiently fashionable to procure them general favor; a long habit of not thinking a thing *wrong*, gives it a superficial appearance of being *right*, and raises at first a formidable outcry in defence of custom. But the tumult soon subsides. Time makes more converts than reason.

As a long and violent abuse of power, is generally the Means of calling the right of it in

---

[1] First published on January 10, 1776, an expanded edition, prepared by Paine, was published a month later, and sold almost half a million copies. The full title was *Common Sense: Addressed to the Inhabitants of America, on the following Interesting Subjects: I. Of the Origin and Design of Government, with Concise Remarks on the English Constitution. II. Of Monarchy and Hereditary Succession. III. Thoughts on the Present State of American Affairs. IV. Of the Present Ability of America, with*

Some Miscellaneous Reflections. The text, with slight modifications, is from the expanded edition of 1776, reprinted in *The Complete Writings of Thomas Paine*, ed. Philip S. Foner, 2 vols, 1945.

[2] James Thomson (1700–1748), Scottish born English poet and a forerunner of Romanticism, from *Liberty: A Poem* (1736), part IV, lines 636–7.

question (and in Matters too which might never have been thought of, had not the Sufferers been aggravated into the inquiry) and as the King of England hath undertaken in his *own Right*, to support the Parliament in what he calls *Theirs*, and as the good people of this country are grievously oppressed by the combination, they have an undoubted privilege to inquire into the pretensions of both, and equally to reject the usurpation of either.

In the following sheets, the author hath studiously avoided every thing which is personal among ourselves. Compliments as well as censure to individuals make no part thereof. The wise, and the worthy, need not the triumph of a pamphlet; and those whose sentiments are injudicious, or unfriendly, will cease of themselves unless too much pains are bestowed upon their conversion.

The cause of America is in a great measure the cause of all mankind. Many circumstances hath, and will arise, which are not local, but universal, and through which the principles of all Lovers of Mankind are affected, and in the Event of which, their Affections are interested. The laying a Country desolate with Fire and Sword, declaring War against the natural rights of all Mankind, and extirpating the Defenders thereof from the Face of the Earth, is the Concern of every Man to whom Nature hath given the Power of feeling; of which Class, regardless of Party Censure, is the

AUTHOR

From *III: Thoughts on the Present State of American Affairs*

In the following pages I offer nothing more than simple facts, plain arguments, and common sense; and have no other preliminaries to settle with the reader, than that he will divest himself of prejudice and prepossession, and suffer his reason and his feelings to determine for themselves; that he will put *on*, or rather that he will not put *off*, the true character of a man, and generously enlarge his views beyond the present day.

Volumes have been written on the subject of the struggle between England and America. Men of all ranks have embarked in the controversy, from different motives, and with various designs; but all have been ineffectual, and the period of debate is closed. Arms, as the last resource, decide the contest; the appeal was the choice of the king, and the continent hath accepted the challenge.

It hath been reported of the late Mr Pelham[3] (who tho' an able minister was not without his faults) that on his being attacked in the house of commons, on the score, that his measures were only of a temporary kind, replied *"they will last my time."* Should a thought so fatal and unmanly possess the Colonies in the present contest, the name of ancestors will be remembered by future generations with detestation.

The sun never shined on a cause of greater worth. 'Tis not the affair of a city, a country, a province, or a kingdom, but of a continent – of at least one eighth part of the habitable globe. 'Tis not the concern of a day, a year, or all age; posterity are virtually involved in the contest, and will be more or less affected, even to the end of time, by the proceedings now. Now is the seed time of continental union, faith and honor. The least fracture now will be like a name engraved with the point of a pin on the tender rind of a young oak; the wound will enlarge with the tree, and posterity read it in full grown characters.

By referring the matter from argument to arms, a new æra for politics is struck; a new

3 Henry Pelham (1696–1754), first lord of the treasury or
prime minister of Britain, 1743–54.

method of thinking hath arisen. All plans, proposals, &c. prior to the nineteenth of April, *i.e.* to the commencement of hostilities[4], are like the almanacks of the last year; which, though proper then, are superceded and useless now. Whatever was advanced by the advocates on either side of the question then, terminated in one and the same point, viz. a union with Great-Britain; the only difference between the parties was the method of effecting it; the one proposing force, the other friendship; but it hath so far happened that the first hath failed, and the second hath withdrawn her influence.

As much hath been said of the advantages of reconciliation, which, like all agreeable dream, hath passed away and left us as we were, it is but right, that we should examine the contrary side of the argument, and inquire into some of the many material injuries which these colonies sustain, and always will sustain, by being connected with, and dependant on Great-Britain. To examine that connexion and dependance, on the principles of nature and common sense, to see what we have to trust to, if separated, and what we are to expect, if dependant.

I have heard it asserted by some, that as America hath flourished under her former connexion with Great-Britain, that the same connexion is necessary towards her future happiness, and will always have the same effect. Nothing can be more fallacious than this kind of argument. We may as well assert that because a child has thrived upon milk, that it is never to have meat, or that the first twenty years of our lives is to become a precedent for the next twenty. But even this is admitting more than is true, for I answer roundly, that America would have flourished as much, and probably much more, had no European power had any thing to do with her. The commerce, by which she hath enriched herself are the necessaries of life, and will always have a market while eating is the custom of Europe.

But she has protected us, say some. That she hath engrossed[5] us is true, and defended the continent at our expence as well as her own is admitted, and she would have defended Turkey from the same motive, viz. the sake of trade and dominion.

Alas, we have been long led away by ancient prejudices, and made large sacrifices to superstition. We have boasted the protection of Great-Britain, without considering, that her motive was *interest* not *attachment*; that she did not protect us from *our enemies* on *our account*, but from *her enemies* on *her own account*, from those who had no quarrel with us on any *other account*, and who will always be our enemies on the *same account*. Let Britain wave her pretensions to the continent, or the continent throw off the dependance, and we should be at peace with France and Spain were they at war with Britain. The miseries of Hanover last war[6] ought to warn us against connexions.

It hath lately been asserted in parliament, that the colonies have no relation to each other but through the parent country, *i.e.* that Pennsylvania and the Jerseys[7], and so on for the rest, are sister colonies by the way of England; this is certainly a very round-about way of proving relationship, but it is the nearest and only true way of proving enemyship, if I may so call it. France and Spain never were, nor perhaps ever will be our enemies as *Americans*, but as our being the *subjects of Great-Britain*.

But Britain is the parent country, say some. Then the more shame upon her conduct. Even brutes do not devour their young, nor savages make war upon their families; wherefore the assertion, if true, turns to her reproach; but it happens not to be true, or only partly so, and the

---

4   The Battle of Lexington, which took place on April 19, 1775, when the "Minutemen" of Lexington, Massachusetts, defended their stores of ammunition against British soldiers.
5   Dominated.
6   The Seven Years' War (1756–63), in America called "The

French and Indian War," which originally involved Prussia and Austria, but eventually involved all the major European powers. King George III of Great Britain was descended from the Prussian House of Hanover.

7   The colony was divided into East and West until 1702.

phrase *parent* or *mother country* hath been jesuitically[8] adopted by the king and his parasites, with a low papistical design of gaining an unfair bias on the credulous weakness of our minds. Europe, and not England, is the parent country of America. This new world hath been the asylum for the persecuted lovers of civil and religious liberty from *every part* of Europe. Hither have they fled, not from the tender embraces of the mother, but from the cruelty of the monster; and it is so far true of England, that the same tyranny which drove the first emigrants from home, pursues their descendants still.

In this extensive quarter of the globe, we forget the narrow limits of three hundred and sixty miles (the extent of England) and carry our friendship on a larger scale; we claim brotherhood with every European christian, and triumph in the generosity of the sentiment.

It is pleasant to observe by what regular gradations we surmount the force of local prejudice, as we enlarge our acquaintance with the world. A man born in any town in England divided into parishes, will naturally associate most with his fellow parishioners (because their interests in many cases will be common) and distinguish him by the name of *neighbor*; if he meet him but a few miles from home, he drops the narrow idea of a street, and salutes him by the name of *townsman*; if he travel out of the county, and meet him in any other, he forgets the minor divisions of street and town, and calls him *countryman*, i.e. *county-man*; but if in their foreign excursions they should associate in France or any other part of *Europe*, their local remembrance would be enlarged into that of *Englishmen*. And by a just parity of reasoning, all Europeans meeting in America, or any other quarter of the globe, are *countrymen*; for England, Holland, Germany, or Sweden, when compared with the whole, stand in the same places on the larger scale, which the divisions of street, town, and county do on the smaller ones; distinctions too limited for continental minds. Not one third of the inhabitants, even of this province[9] are of English descent. Wherefore I reprobate the phrase of parent or mother country applied to England only, as being false, selfish, narrow and ungenerous.

But admitting, that we were all of English descent, what does it amount to? Nothing. Britain, being now an open enemy, extinguishes every other name and title: And to say that reconciliation is our duty, is truly farcical. The first king of England, of the present line (William the Conqueror) was a Frenchman, and half the Peers of England are descendants from the same country; wherefore, by the same method of reasoning, England ought to be governed by France.

Much hath been said of the united strength of Britain and the colonies, that in conjunction they might bid defiance to the world. But this is mere presumption; the fate of war is uncertain, neither do the expressions mean any thing; for this continent would never suffer itself to be drained of inhabitants, to support the British arms in either Asia, Africa, or Europe.

Besides, what have we to do with setting the world at defiance? Our plan is commerce, and that, well attended to, will secure us the peace and friendship of all Europe; because, it is the interest of all Europe to have America a *free port*. Her trade will always be a protection, and her barrenness of gold and silver secure her from invaders.

I challenge the warmest advocate for reconciliation, to shew, a single advantage that this continent can reap, by being connected with Great Britain. I repeat the challenge, not a single advantage is derived. Our corn will fetch its price in any market in Europe, and our imported goods must be paid for buy them where we will.

But the injuries and disadvantages we sustain by that connexion, are without number; and our duty to mankind at large, as well as to ourselves, instruct us to renounce the alliance: Because, any submission to, or dependance on Great-Britain, tends directly to involve this

---

[8] Cunningly and deceitfully, like Jesuits, a Catholic order.   [9] Pennsylvania.

continent in European wars and quarrels; and sets it at variance with nations, who would otherwise seek our friendship, and against whom, we have neither anger nor complaint. As Europe is our market for trade, we ought to form no partial connection with any part of it. It is the true interest of America to steer clear of European contentions, which she never can do, while by her dependance on Britain, she is made the make-weight in the scale of British politics.

Europe is too thickly planted with kingdoms to be long at peace, and whenever a war breaks out between England and any foreign power, the trade of America goes to ruin, *because of her connexion with Britain*. The next war may not turn out like the last[10], and should it not, the advocates for reconciliation now will be wishing for separation then, because, neutrality in that case, would be a safer convoy than a man of war. Every thing that is right or natural pleads for separation. The blood of the slain, the weeping voice of nature cries, 'TIS TIME TO PART. Even the distance at which the Almighty hath placed England and America, is a strong and natural proof, that the authority of the one, over the other, was never the design of Heaven. The time likewise at which the continent was discovered, adds weight to the argument, and the manner in which it was peopled increases the force of it. The reformation was preceded by the discovery of America, as if the Almighty graciously meant to open a sanctuary to the persecuted in future years, when home should afford neither friendship nor safety.

The authority of Great-Britain over this continent, is a form of government, which sooner or later must have an end: And a Serious mind can draw no true pleasure by looking forward, under the painful and positive conviction, that what he calls "the present constitution" is merely temporary. As parents, we can have no joy, knowing that *this government* is not sufficiently lasting to ensure any thing which we may bequeath to posterity: And by a plain method of argument, as we are running the next generation into debt, we ought to do the work of it, otherwise we use them meanly and pitifully. In order to discover the line of our duty rightly, we should take our children in our hand, and fix our station a few years farther into life; that eminence will present a prospect, which a few present fears and prejudices conceal from our sight.

Though I would carefully avoid giving unnecessary offence, yet I am inclined to believe, that all those who espouse the doctrine of reconciliation, may be included within the following descriptions. Interested men, who are not to be trusted; weak men, who *cannot* see; prejudiced men, who *will not* see; and a certain set of moderate men, who think better of the European world than it deserves; and this last class, by an ill-judged deliberation, will be the cause of more calamities to this continent, than all the other three.

It is the good fortune of many to live distant from the scene of sorrow; the evil is not sufficiently brought to *their* doors to make *them* feel the precariousness with which all American property is possessed. But let our imaginations transport us for a few moments to Boston[11], that seat of wretchedness will teach us wisdom, and instruct us for ever to renounce a power in whom we can have no trust. The inhabitants of that unfortunate city, who but a few months ago were in ease and affluence, have now, no other alternative than to stay and starve, or turn out to beg. Endangered by the fire of their friends if they continue within the city, and plundered by the soldiery if they leave it. In their present condition they are prisoners without the hope of redemption, and in a general attack for their relief, they would be exposed to the fury of both armies.

10   The Seven Years' War, which concluded with the Treaty of Paris in 1763, in which Britain gained Canada from France.
11   Boston was occupied by the British since June 1774, and under siege by the Americans from April 1775 until their evacuation on March 17, 1776.

Men of passive tempers took somewhat lightly over the offences of Britain, and, still hoping for the best, are apt to call out, "*Come, come, we shall be friends again, for all this.*" But examine the passions and feelings of mankind, bring the doctrine of reconciliation to the touchstone of nature, and then tell me, whether you can hereafter love, honor, and faithfully serve the power that hath carried fire and sword into your land? If you cannot do all these, then are you only deceiving yourselves, and by your delay bringing ruin upon posterity. Your future connexion with Britain, whom you can neither love nor honor, will be forced and unnatural, and being formed only on the plan of present convenience, will in a little time fall into a relapse more wretched than the first. But if you say, you can still pass the violations over, then I ask, Hath your house been burnt? Hath your property been destroyed before your face? Are your wife and children destitute of a bed to lie on, or bread to live on? Have you lost a parent or a child by their hands, and yourself the ruined and wretched survivor? If you have not, then are you not a judge of those who have. But if you have, and still can shake hands with the murderers, then are you unworthy the name of husband, father, friend, or lover, and whatever may be your rank or title in life, you have the heart of a coward, and the spirit of a sycophant.

This is not inflaming or exaggerating matters, but trying them by those feelings and affections which nature justifies, and without which, we should be incapable of discharging the social duties of life, or enjoying the felicities of it. I mean not to exhibit horror for the purpose of provoking revenge, but to awaken us from fatal and unmanly slumbers, that we may pursue determinately some fixed object. It is not in the power of Britain or of Europe to conquer America, if she do not conquer herself by *delay* and *timidity*. The present winter is worth an age if rightly employed, but if lost or neglected, the whole continent will partake of the misfortune; and there is no punishment which that man will not deserve, be he who, or what, or where he will, that may be the means of sacrificing a season so precious and useful.

It is repugnant to reason, to the universal order of things to all examples from former ages, to suppose, that this continent can longer remain subject to any external power. The most sanguine in Britain does not think so. The utmost stretch of human wisdom cannot, at this time, compass a plan short of separation, which can promise the continent even a year's security. Reconciliation is *now* a falacious dream. Nature hath deserted the connexion, and Art cannot supply her place. For, as Milton wisely expresses, "never can true reconcilement grow where wounds of deadly hate have pierced so deep."[12]

Every quiet method for peace hath been ineffectual. Our prayers have been rejected with disdain; and only tended to convince us, that nothing flatters vanity, or confirms obstinacy in Kings more than repeated petitioning – and nothing hath contributed more than that very measure to make the Kings of Europe absolute: Witness Denmark and Sweden. Wherefore, since nothing but blows will do, for God's sake, let us come to a final separation, and not leave the next generation to be cutting throats, under the violated unmeaning names of parent and child.

To say, they will never attempt it again is idle and visionary, we thought so at the repeal of the stamp-act[13], yet a year or two undeceived us; as well may we suppose that nations, which have been once defeated, will never renew the quarrel.

As to government matters, it is not in the power of Britain to do this continent justice: The business of it will soon be too weighty, and intricate, to be managed with any tolerable degree

---

[12] John Milton (1608–74), English poet, Puritan, and republican, from *Paradise Lost* (1667), Book 4, lines 98–9.
[13] Parliament repealed the Stamp Act in March 1766 after widespread protest in the colonies, but in 1767 reasserted its right to tax the colonies by enacting import duties on glass, lead, paint, paper, and tea (called the Townshend Acts).

of convenience, by a power, so distant from us, and so very ignorant of us; for if they cannot conquer us, they cannot govern us. To be always running three or four thousand miles with a tale or a petition, waiting four or five months for an answer, which when obtained requires five or six more to explain it in, will in a few years be looked upon as folly and childishness – There was a time when it was proper, and there is a proper time for it to cease.

Small islands not capable of protecting themselves, are the proper objects for kingdoms to take under their care; but there is something very absurd, in supposing a continent to be perpetually governed by an island. In no instance hath nature made the satellite larger than its primary planet, and as England and America, with respect to each other, reverses the common order of nature, it is evident they belong to different systems: England to Europe, America to itself.

I am not induced by motives of pride, party, or resentment to espouse the doctrine of separation and independance; I am clearly, positively, and conscientiously persuaded that it is the true interest of this continent to be so; that every thing short of *that* is mere patchwork, that it can afford no lasting felicity, – that it is leaving the sword to our children, and shrinking back at a time, when, a little more, a little farther, would have rendered this continent the glory of the earth.

As Britain hath not manifested the least inclination towards a compromise, we may be assured that no terms can be obtained worthy the acceptance of the continent, or any ways equal to the expence of blood and treasure we have been already put to. . . .

A government of our own is our natural right: And when a man seriously reflects on the precariousness of human affairs, he will become convinced, that it is infinitely wiser and safer, to form a constitution of our own in a cool deliberate manner, while we have it in our power, than to trust such an interesting event to time and chance. If we omit it now, some Massanello[14] may hereafter arise, who laying hold of popular disquietudes, may collect together the desperate and the discontented, and by assuming to themselves the powers of government, may sweep away the liberties of the continent like a deluge. Should the government of America return again into the hands of Britain, the tottering situation of things, will be a temptation for some desperate adventurer to try his fortune; and in such a case, what relief can Britain give? Ere she could hear the news, the fatal business might be done; and ourselves suffering like the wretched Britons under the oppression of the Conqueror. Ye that oppose independance now, ye know not what ye do; ye are opening a door to eternal tyranny, by keeping vacant the seat of government. There are thousands, and tens of thousands, who would think it glorious to expel from the continent, that barbarous and hellish power, which hath stirred up the Indians and Negroes to destroy us, the cruelty hath a double guilt, it is dealing brutally by us, and treacherously by them.

To talk of friendship with those in whom our reason forbids us to have faith, and our affections wounded through a thousand pores instruct us to detest, is madness and folly. Every day wears out the little remains of kindred between us and them, and can there be any reason to hope, that as the relationship expires, the affection will increase, or that we shall agree better, when we have ten times more and greater concerns to quarrel over than ever?

Ye that tell us of harmony and reconciliation, can ye restore to us the time that is past? Can ye give to prostitution its former innocence? Neither can ye reconcile Britain and America. The last cord now is broken, the people of England are presenting addresses against us. There

---

[14] "Thomas Anello, otherwise Massanello, a fisherman of Naples, who after spiriting up his countrymen in the public market place, against the oppression of the Spaniard, to whom the place was then subject, prompted them to revolt, and in the space of a day became king" [Paine's note].

are injuries which nature cannot forgive; she would cease to be nature if she did. As well can the lover forgive the ravisher of his mistress, as the continent forgive the murders of Britain. The Almighty hath implanted in us these unextinguishable feelings for good and wise purposes. They are the guardians of his image in our hearts. They distinguish us from the herd of common animals. The social compact would dissolve, and justice be extirpated from the earth, or have only a casual existence were we callous to the touches of affection. The robber, and the murderer, would often escape unpunished, did not the injuries which our tempers sustain, provoke us into justice.

O ye that love mankind! Ye that dare oppose, not only the tyranny, but the tyrant, stand forth! Every spot of the old world is overrun with oppression. Freedom hath been hunted round the globe. Asia, and Africa, have long expelled her. – Europe regards her like a stranger, and England hath given her warning to depart. O! receive the fugitive, and prepare in time an asylum for mankind.

1776

Thomas Jefferson (1743–1826)

Despite his distinguished achievements in public life, Thomas Jefferson seems to embody the contradictions upon which the United State was founded. He is the author of the initiating document of the new nation that declared life synonymous with liberty and expressed the fundamental principle "that all men are created equal," yet he could not, in his own practices, live up to those democratic ideals. He was an aristocrat and an agrarian, who feared the emergence of an urban, industrial proletariat. He was a patriot deeply committed to freedom, yet he owned slaves and fathered slaves. He argued for the abolition of slavery, but feared miscegenation and supported repatriation of freed slaves to Africa. He recognized the eloquence and complexity of Native American culture, but as president pursued a patronizing policy of "drubbing" and then "bribing them to peace."

Jefferson was born at Shadwell, his family's farm in what was rural Virginia, the son of Jane Randolph, from a prominent Virginia family, and Peter Jefferson, a local magistrate and surveyor. His father died when he was fourteen, and in 1760 Jefferson went to study at William and Mary College in Williamsburg. In this thriving town, he was fortunate to come under the mentorship of three men who strongly influenced his life: Doctor William Small, a Scottish immigrant who taught mathematics and introduced Jefferson to Scottish Enlightenment thought; George Wythe, a self-

educated man who became a distinguished Virginia lawyer, US judge, and law teacher; and Frances Fauquier, lieutenant governor of Virginia at the time, and a member of the Royal Society. After joining the bar, Jefferson was elected to the Virginia House of Burgesses. Outspoken in his conviction that England had no authority over the American colonies, Jefferson was selected as a delegate to the Second Continental congress, and appointed, along with Benjamin Franklin, John Adams, Roger Sherman, and Robert Livingston, to draft a declaration declaring independence. The draft they produced was largely Jefferson's effort, but differs in important ways from the version that was finally adopted, unanimously, by the thirteen colonies. As he makes clear in the versions copied into his *Autobiography*, Jefferson criticized the English more harshly and also wanted to include a strong statement against slavery. He was elected governor of Virginia in 1779 and 1780, but resigned under a cloud after the legislature, which had retreated to Charlottesville, was nearly captured by the invading British army.

Jefferson retired to Monticello, a lovely home he designed and built on an estate he had increased from his father's modest holdings. There, he completed his only book, *Notes on the State of Virginia* (1787), in response to a request about information on the state. It is a work that reflects Jefferson's wide range of interests in natural history, geography, geology, Native American culture and anthropology, social history and politics, as well as his concerns with the formation of post-revolutionary American society. He used the text as an occasion to refute the theories of the most famous naturalist of the time, Count de Buffon, who argued that all species of animals and plants, including humans, in the New World, were inferior by comparison with the Old World. To counter Buffon was not merely to make a biological point, but to justify the entire American experiment of social and political republicanism which Jefferson helped to originate.

In describing Virginia, Jefferson articulated his agrarian and democratic ideals: that the "people" – by which he meant white men – had a right to a portion of land which would support them and their families, and that given education and freedom of and from religious beliefs, they were fully capable of resisting tyranny and electing representatives. Alongside this idealism and his support of abolitionism, Jefferson gave voice to more problematic attitudes about racial differences in his meditations on slavery and its effects in Queries XIV and XVIII. In 1784, he was called out of retirement to become minister to France, and with Benjamin Franklin negotiated the Treaty of Paris that ended the war. He was appointed by George Washington as the first secretary of state. In 1796, he ran for president and was defeated by John Adams, but in 1800, he defeated Adams and served two terms. Retiring again to Monticello in 1809, he continued his voluminous correspondence, his agricultural experiments, his collecting of art and

books, and his reading. Jefferson remarked that he wanted to be remembered for three things: authoring the Declaration of Independence, adopting the Virginia Statute for Religious Freedom (1786), and founding the University of Virginia. He has left a complex legacy.

PRIMARY WORKS

The Writings of Thomas Jefferson, 10 vols, ed. Paul Leicester Ford, New York, 1892–9.

The Writings of Thomas Jefferson, 20 vols, eds Andrew Lipscomb and Albert Bergh, Washington, DC, 1903–4.

The *Papers of Thomas Jefferson,* 27 vols, eds Julian P. Boyd, Charles Cullen *et al.*, Princeton, 1950–97.

Notes on the State of Virginia, ed. William Peden, Chapel Hill, 1954.

Thomas Jefferson: Writings, ed. Merrill D. Peterson, Library of America, 1984.

FURTHER READING

Dumas Malone, *Jefferson and his Times,* 6 vols (Boston: Little Brown, 1948–81).

Merrill D. Peterson, *Thomas Jefferson and the New Nation: A Biography* (New York: Oxford University Press, 1970).

John Chester Miller, *The Wolf by the Ears: Thomas Jefferson and Slavery* (New York: Free Press, 1977).

Peter Onuf (ed.) *Jeffersonian Legacies* (Charlottesville: University Press of Virginia, 1993).

Anthony Wallace, *Jefferson and the Indians: The Tragic Fate of the First Americans* (Cambridge: Harvard University Press, 1999).

FROM *AUTOBIOGRAPHY 1743–1790* [DECLARATION OF INDEPENDENCE][1]

. . . Congress proceeded the same day [July 1st] to consider the declaration of Independence which had been reported & lain on the table the Friday preceding, and on Monday referred to a commee[2] of the whole. The pusillanimous idea that we had friends in England worth keeping terms with, still haunted the minds of many. For this reason those passages which conveyed censures on the people of England were struck out, lest they should give them offence. The clause too, reprobating the enslaving the inhabitants of Africa, was struck out in complaisance to South Carolina and Georgia, who had never attempted to restrain the importation of slaves, and who on the contrary still wished to continue it. Our northern brethren also I

---

[1]   Jefferson never prepared his *Autobiography* for publication and so it retains his abbreviations, filled out in square brackets, where necessary. The text, with slight modification, is from *Thomas Jefferson: Writings,* ed. Merrill D. Peterson (New York: Library of America, 1984).

[2]   Jefferson's abbreviation for "committee."

believe felt a little tender under those censures; for tho' their people have very few slaves themselves yet they had been pretty considerable carriers of them to others. The debates having taken up the greater parts of the 2d, 3d, 4th days of July were, in the evening of the last, closed the declaration was reported by the commee, agreed to by the house and signed by every member present except Mr Dickinson[3]. As the sentiments of men are known not only by what they receive, but what they reject also, I will state the form of the declaration as originally reported. The parts struck out by Congress shall be distinguished by a black line drawn under them; & those inserted by them shall be placed in the margin or in a concurrent column.

A Declaration by the Representatives of the United States of America, in General Congress Assembled.

When in the course of human events it becomes necessary for one people to dissolve the political bands which have connected them with another, and to assume among the powers of the earth the separate & equal station to which the laws of nature and of nature's God entitle them, a decent respect to the opinions of mankind requires that they should declare the causes which impel them to the separation.

We hold these truths to be self-evident: that all men are created equal; that they are endowed by their creator with <u>inherent and</u> inalienable rights; that
among these are life, liberty, & the pursuit of happiness: that to secure these rights, governments are instituted among men, deriving their just powers from the consent of the governed; that whenever any form of government becomes destructive of these ends, it is the right of the people to alter or abolish it, & to institute new government, laying it's foundation on such principles, & organizing it's powers in such form, as to them shall seem most likely to effect their safety & happiness. Prudence indeed will dictate that governments long established should not be changed for light & transient causes; and accordingly all experience hath shown that mankind are more disposed to suffer while evils are sufferable, than to right themselves by abolishing the forms to which they are accustomed. But when a long train of abuses & usurpations <u>begun at a distinguished period and</u> pursuing invariably the same object, evinces a design to reduce them under absolute despotism, it is their right, it is their duty to throw off such government, & to provide new guards

certain

---

[3]   John Dickinson (1732–1808), Philadelphia lawyer, patriot leader, and author of *Letters from a Farmer in Pennsylvania* (1767–68) which turned opinion against the Townshend Acts that harshly taxed imports. Dickinson did not sign the Declaration of Independence, hoping for reconciliation with England.

for their future security. Such has been the patient sufferance of these colonies; & such is now the necessity which constrains them to <u>expunge</u> their former [alter] systems of government. The history of the present king of Great Britain[4] is a history of <u>unremitting</u> injuries [repeated] & usurpations,<u> among which appears no solitary fact</u> [all having] <u>to contradict the uniform tenor of the rest but all have</u> in direct object the establishment of an absolute tyranny over these states. To prove this let facts be submitted to a candid world <u>for the truth of which we pledge a faith yet unsullied by falsehood</u>.

He has refused his assent to laws the most wholesome & necessary for the public good.

He has forbidden his governors to pass laws of immediate & pressing importance, unless suspended in their operation till his assent should be obtained; & when so suspended, he has utterly neglected to attend to them.

He has refused to pass other laws for the accommodation of large districts of people, unless those people would relinquish the right of representation in the legislature, a right inestimable to them, & formidable to tyrants only.

He has called together legislative bodies at places unusual, uncomfortable, and distant from the depository of their public records, for the sole purpose of fatiguing them into compliance with his measures.

He has dissolved representative houses repeatedly <u>&</u> <u>continually</u> for opposing with manly firmness his invasions on the rights of the people.

He has refused for a long time after such dissolutions to cause others to be elected, whereby the legislative powers, incapable of annihilation, have returned to the people at large for their exercise, the state remaining in the meantime exposed to all the dangers of invasion from without & convulsions within.

He has endeavored to prevent the population of these states; for that purpose obstructing the laws for naturalization of foreigners, refusing to pass others to encourage their migrations hither, & raising the conditions of new appropriations of lands.

He has <u>suffered</u> the administration of justice <u>totally</u> [obstructed] <u>to cease in some of these states</u> refusing his assent to [by] laws for establishing judiciary powers.

He has made <u>our</u> judges dependent on his will alone, for the tenure of their offices, & the amount & paiment of their salaries.

---

4   King George III (1738–1820).

He has erected a multitude of new offices <u>by a self assumed power</u> and sent hither swarms of new officers to harass our people and eat out their substance.

He has kept among us in times of peace standing armies <u>and ships of war</u> without the consent of our legislatures.

He has affected to render the military independent of, & superior to the civil power.

He has combined with others[5] to subject us to a jurisdiction foreign to our constitutions & unacknowledged by our laws, giving his assent to their acts of pretended legislation for quartering large bodies of armed troops among us; for protecting them by a mock-trial from punishment for any murders which they should commit on the inhabitants of these states; for cutting off our trade with all parts of the world; for imposing taxes on us without our consent; for depriving us [ ] of the benefits of trial by jury; for transport-   in many cases
ing us beyond seas to be tried for pretended offences; for abolishing the free system of English laws in a neighboring province[6], establishing therein an arbitrary government, and enlarging it's boundaries, so as to render it at once an example and fit instrument for introducing the same absolute rule into these <u>states</u>; for   colonies
taking away our charters, abolishing our most valuable laws, and altering fundamentally the forms of our governments; for suspending our own legislatures, & declaring themselves invested with power to legislate for us in all cases whatsoever.

He has abdicated government here <u>withdrawing his governors, and declaring us out of his allegiance & protection.</u>   by declaring us out of his protection, and
waging war against us.

He has plundered our seas, ravaged our coasts, burnt our towns, & destroyed the lives of our people.

He is at this time transporting large armies of foreign mercenaries[7] to compleat the works of death, desolation & tyranny already begun with circumstances of cruelty and perfidy [ ] unworthy the head of a civilized   scarcely paralleled in the most barbarous
nation.   ages, & totally

He has constrained our fellow citizens taken captive on the high seas to bear arms against their country, to become the executioners of their friends & brethren, or to fall themselves by their hands.

---

5   The British Parliament.

6   The Quebec Act of 1774, considered one of the "intolerable acts," which recognized the Roman Catholic religion in Quebec and extended the borders of the province to the Ohio River, restoring French civil law and thus angering the New England colonies.

7   Hessian soldiers hired by England to fight against the colonies.

He has [*excited domestic insurrection among us, & has*] endeavored to bring on the inhabitants of our frontiers the merciless Indian savages, whose known rule of warfare is an undistinguished destruction of ages and sexes, & conditions <u>of existence.</u>

<u>He has waged cruel war against human nature itself, violating it's most sacred rights of life and liberty in the persons of a distant people who never offended him, captivating & carrying them into slavery in another hemisphere, or to incur miserable death in their transportation thither. This piratical warfare, the opprobium of INFIDEL powers, is the warfare of the CHRISTIAN king of Great Britain. Determined to keep open a market where MEN should be bought & sold, he has prostituted his negative for suppressing every legislative attempt to prohibit or to restrain this execrable commerce. And that this assemblage of horrors might want no fact of distinguished die, he is now exciting those very people to rise in arms among us, and to purchase that liberty of which he has deprived them, by murdering the people on whom he also obtruded them: thus paying off former crimes committed against the LIBERTIES of one people with crimes which he urges them to commit against the LIVES of another.</u>

In every stage of these oppressions we have petitioned for redress in the most humble terms: our repeated petitions have been answered only by repeated injuries.

A prince whose character is thus marked by every act which may define a tyrant is unfit to be the ruler of a [*free*] people <u>who mean to be free. Future ages will scarcely believe that the hardiness of one man adventured, within the short compass of twelve years only, to lay a foundation so broad & so undisguised for tyranny over a people fostered & fixed in principles of freedom.</u>

Nor have we been wanting in attentions to our British brethren. We have warned them from time to time of attempts by their legislature to extend <u>a</u> [*an unwarrantable*] jurisdiction over <u>these our states</u> [*us*]. We have reminded them of the circumstances of our emigration & settlement here, <u>no one of which could warrant so strange a pretension: that these were effected at the expense of our own blood & treasure, unassisted by the wealth or the strength of Great Britain: that in constituting indeed our several forms of government, we had adopted one common king, thereby laying a foundation for perpetual league & amity with them: but that submission to their parliament was no part of our constitution, nor ever in idea, if history may be credited: and,</u> we [*have*] appealed to their native justice and magnanimity [*and we have conjured them by*] <u>as well as to</u> the ties of our common kindred to disavow these usurpations which <u>were likely to</u> interrupt our connection and correspondence.

They too have been deaf to the voice of justice & consanguinity, <u>and when occasions have been given them, by the regular course of their laws, of removing from their councils the disturbers of our harmony, they have, by their free election, re-established them in power. At this very time too they are permitting their chief magistrate to send over not only soldiers of our common blood, but Scotch & foreign mercenaries to invade & destroy us. These facts have given the last stab to agonizing affection, and manly spirit bids us to renounce forever these unfeeling brethren. We must endeavor to forget our former love for them, and hold them as we hold the rest of mankind, enemies in war, in peace friends. We might have been a free and a great people together; but a communication of grandeur & of freedom it seems is below their dignity. Be it so, since they will have it. The road to happiness & to glory is open to us too. We will tread it apart from them, and</u> acquiesce in the necessity which denounces our eternal separation [ ].

We therefore the representatives of the United States of America in General Congress assembled do in the name & by authority of the good people of <u>these states reject & renounce all allegiance & subjection to the kings of Great Britain & all others who may hereafter claim by, through or under them: we utterly dissolve all political connection which may heretofore have subsisted between us & the people or parliament of Great Britain: & finally we do assert & declare these colonies to be free & independent states</u>, & that as free & independent states, they have full power to levy war, conclude peace, contract alliances, establish commerce, & to do all other acts & things which independent states may of right do.

And for the support of this declaration we mutually pledge to each other our lives, our fortunes, & our sacred honor.

would inevitably

We must therefore

and hold them as we hold the rest of mankind, enemies in war, in peace friends.

We therefore the representatives of the United States of America in General Congress assembled, appealing to the supreme judge of the world for the rectitude of our intentions, do in the name, & by the authority of the good people of these colonies, solemnly publish & declare that these united colonies are of right ought to be free & independent states; that they are absolved from all allegiance to the British crown, and that all political connection between them & the state of Great Britain is, & ought to be, totally dissolved; & that as free & independent states they have full power to levy war, conclude peace, contract alliances, establish commerce & to do all other acts & things which independent states may of right do.

And for the support of this declaration, with a firm reliance on the protection of divine providence we mutually pledge to each other our lives, our fortunes, & our sacred honor.

The Declaration thus signed on the 4th, on paper was engrossed[8] on parchment, & signed again on the 2d. of August.

1821

1829

---

[8]   Written in a legal hand.

NOTES ON THE STATE OF VIRGINIA[1]

From *Query VI: Productions mineral, vegetable and animal*

. . . The opinion advanced by the Count de Buffon[2] is 1. That the animals common both to the old and new world are smaller in the latter. 2. That those peculiar to the new are on a smaller scale. 3. That those which have been domesticated in both have degenerated in American. And 4. That on the whole it exhibits fewer species. . . .

Hitherto I have considered this hypothesis as applied to brute animals only, and not in its extension to the man of America, whether aboriginal or transplanted. It is the opinion of Mons. de Buffon that the former furnishes no exception to it. . . .

. . . To judge of the truth of this, to form a just estimate of their[3] genius and mental powers, more facts are wanting, and great allowance to be made for those circumstances of their situation which call for a display of particular talents only. This done, we shall probably find that they are formed in mind as well as in body, on the same module with the[4] "Homo sapiens Europaes." The principles of their society forbidding all compulsion, they are to be led to duty and to enterprize by personal influence and persuasion. Hence eloquence in council, bravery and address in war, become the foundations of all consequence with them. To these acquirements all their faculties are directed. Of their bravery and address in war we have multiplied proofs, because we have been the subjects on which they were exercised. Of their eminence in oratory we have fewer examples, because it is displayed chiefly in their own councils. Some, however, we have of very superior luster. I may challenge the whole orations of Demosthenes and Cicero,[5] and of any more eminent orator, if Europe has furnished more eminent, to produce a single passage, superior to the speech of Logan, a Mingo chief, to Lord Dunmore, when governor of this state.[6] And, as a testimony of their talents in this line, I beg leave to introduce it, first stating the incidents necessary for understanding it. In the spring of the year 1774, a robbery and murder were committed on an inhabitant of the frontiers of Virginia, by two Indians of the Shawanee tribe. The neighboring whites, according to their custom, undertook to punish this outrage in a summary way. Col. Cresap[7], a man infamous for the many murders he had

[1]   The text is from the edition supervised by Jefferson, after the threat of an unauthorized French translation, and published by John Stockdale in London, 1787, which is reprinted in *Thomas Jefferson: Writings*, ed. Merrill D. Peterson (New York: Library of America, 1984).

[2]   Georges Louis Leclerc, Comte de Buffon (1707–88), noted French naturalist who argued that North American species were degenerate in his *Histoire naturelle, generale et particuliere* (*Natural History* 1769).

[3]   Native Americans.

[4]   "Linn. Syst, Definition of a Man" (Jefferson's note). Definition according to Linnaean nomenclature, which categorized all plants and animals into genus and species, under Latin names.

[5]   The two most famous classical orators: Demosthenes (384–322 BC), an Athenian statesman and orator, known for his simplicity and directness; Marcus Tullius Cicero (106–43 BC), noted Roman orator, statesman and writer.

[6]   "Mingo:" one of the Iroquois tribes. John Murray, earl

of Dunmore (1732–1809), colonial governor of Virginia from 1771 to 1775.

[7]   Michael Cresap (1742–75), a frontiersman and soldier from Maryland. When his role in this incident and the accuracy of the account were questioned, Jefferson investigated further, and in the *Appendix to the Notes on Virginia Relative to the Murder of Logan's Family* to the edition published in Philadelphia in 1800, he asked that in future editions the passage between "In the spring of the year 1774 . . ." and ". . . distinguished as a friend of the whites" be changed to: "In the spring of the year 1774, a robbery was committed by some Indians on certain land-adventurers on the river Ohio. The whites in that quarter, according to their custom, undertook to punish this outrage in a summary way. Captain Michael Cresap, and a certain Daniel Great-house, leading on these parties, surprized, at different times, travelling and hunting parties of the Indians, having their women and children with them, and murdered many. Among these were unfortunately the family of Logan, a chief celebrated in peace and war, and long distinguished as the friend of the whites."

committed on those much-injured people, collected a party, and proceeded down the Kanhaway in quest of vengeance. Unfortunately a canoe of women and children, with one man only, was seen coming from the opposite shore, unarmed, and unsuspecting an hostile attack from the whites. Cresap and his party concealed themselves on the bank of the river, and the moment the canoe reached the shore, singled out their objects, and, at one fire, killed every person in it. This happened to be the family of Logan, who had long been distinguished as a friend of the whites. This unworthy return provoked his vengeance. He accordingly signalized himself in the war which ensued. In the autumn of the same year, a decisive battle was fought at the mouth of the Great Kanhaway, between the collected forces of the Shawanees, Mingoes, and Delawares, and a detachment of the Virginia militia. The Indians were defeated, and sued for peace. Logan however disdained to be seen among the suppliants. But, lest the sincerity of a treaty should be distrusted, from which so distinguished a chief absented himself, he sent by a messenger the following speech to be delivered to Lord Dunmore.

'I appeal to any white man to say, if ever he entered Logan's cabin hungry, and he gave him not meat; if ever he came cold and naked, and he clothed him not. During the course of the last long and bloody war, Logan remained idle in his cabin, an advocate for peace. Such was my love for the whites, that my countrymen pointed as they passed, and said, 'Logan is the friend of white men.' I had even thought to have lived with you, but for the injuries of one man. Col. Cresap, the last spring, in cold blood, and unprovoked, murdered all the relations of Logan, not sparing even my women and children. There runs not a drop of my blood in the veins of any living creature. This called on me for revenge. I have sought it: I have killed many: I have fully glutted my vengeance. For my country, I rejoice at the beams of peace. But do not harbor a thought that mine is the joy of fear. Logan never felt fear. He will not turn on his heel to save his life. Who is there to mourn for Logan? – Not one."

Before we condemn the Indians of this continent as wanting genius, we must consider that letters have not yet been introduced among them. Were we to compare them in their present state with the Europeans North of the Alps, when the Roman arms and arts first crossed those mountains, the comparison would be unequal, because, at that time, those parts of Europe were swarming with numbers; because numbers produce emulation, and multiply the chances of improvement, and one improvement begets another. Yet I may safely ask, How many good poets, how many able mathematicians, how many great inventors in arts or sciences, had Europe North of the Alps then produced? And it was sixteen centuries after this before a Newton[8] could be formed. I do not mean to deny, that there are varieties in the race of man, distinguished by their powers both of body and mind. I believe there are, as I see to be the case in the races of other animals. I only mean to suggest a doubt, whether the bulk and faculties of animals depend on the side of the Atlantic on which their food happens to grow, or which furnishes the elements of which they are compounded?

From *Query XIV: Laws*

. . . Since the establishment of our new government, this order of things is but little changed. . . .

Many of the laws which were in force during the monarchy being relative merely to that form of government, or inculcating principles inconsistent with republicanism, the first assembly which met after the establishment of the commonwealth appointed a committee to

---

[8]   Sir Isaac Newton (1642–1727), English mathematician and natural philosopher whose theories about light and grav- ity, in popular form, transformed the way most people regarded the world.

revise the whole code, to reduce it into proper form and volume, and report it to the assembly. This work has been executed by three gentlemen, and reported; but probably will not be taken up till a restoration of peace shall leave to the legislature leisure to go through such a work.[9]

The plan of the revisal was this. The common law of England, by which is meant, that part of the English law which was anterior to the date of the oldest statutes extant, is made the basis of the work. It was thought dangerous to attempt to reduce it to a text: it was therefore left to be collected from the usual monuments of it. Necessary alterations in that, and so much of the whole body of the British statutes, and of acts of assembly, as were thought proper to be retained, were digested into 126 new acts, in which simplicity of stile was aimed at, as far as was safe. The following are the most remarkable alterations proposed:

To change the rules of descent, so as that the lands of any person dying intestate shall be divisible equally among all his children, or other representatives, in equal degree.

To make slaves distributable among the next of kin, as other moveables.

To have all public expences, whether of the general treasury, or of a parish or county, (as for time maintenance of the poor, building bridges, court-houses, &c.) supplied by assessments on the citizens, in proportion to their property.

To hire undertakers for keeping the public roads in repair, and indemnify individuals through whose lands new roads shall be opened.

To define with precision time rules whereby aliens should become citizens, and citizens make themselves aliens.

To establish religious freedom on the broadest bottom.

To emancipate all slaves born after passing the act. The bill reported by the revisors does not itself contain this proposition; but an amendment containing it was prepared, to be offered to the legislature whenever the bill should be taken up, and further directing, that they should continue with their parents to a certain age, then be brought up, at the public expence, to tillage, arts or sciences, according to their geniusses, till the females should be eighteen, and the males twenty-one years of age, when they should be colonized to such place as the circumstances of the time should render most proper, sending them out with arms, implements of household and of the handicraft arts, feeds, pairs of the useful domestic animals, &c. to declare them a free and independant people, and extend to them our alliance and protection, till they shall have acquired strength; and to send vessels at the same time to other parts of the world for an equal number of white inhabitants; to induce whom to migrate hither, proper encouragements were to be proposed. It will probably be asked, Why not retain and incorporate the blacks into the state, and thus save the expence of supplying, by importation of white settlers, the vacancies they will leave? Deep rooted prejudices entertained by the whites; ten thousand recollections, by the blacks, of the injuries they have sustained; new provocations; the real distinctions which nature has made; and many other circumstances, will divide us into parties, and produce convulsions which will probably never end but in the extermination of the one or the other race. – To these objections, which are political, may be added others, which are physical and moral. The first difference which strikes us is that of color. Whether the black of the negro resides in the reticular membrane between the skin and scarf-skin, or in the scarf-skin itself, whether it proceeds from the color of the blood, the color of the bile, or from that of some other secretion, the difference is fixed in nature, and is as real as if its seat and cause were better known to us. And is this difference of no importance? Is it not the foundation of a greater or less share of beauty in the two races? Are not the fine mixtures of red and white, the

---

[9]   Jefferson was one of three members of the Committee of
Revisors.

expressions of every passion by greater or less suffusions of color in the one, preferable to that eternal monotony, which reigns in the countenances, that immoveable veil of black which covers all the emotions of the other race? Add to these, flowing hair, a more elegant symmetry of form, their own judgment in favor of the whites, declared by their preference of them, as uniformly as is the preference of the Oranootan for the black women over those of his own species. The circumstance of superior beauty, is thought worthy attention in the propagation of our horses, dogs, and other domestic animals; why not in that of man? Besides those of color, figure, and hair, there are other physical distinctions proving a difference of race. They have less hair on the face and body. They secrete less by the kidnies, and more by the glands of the skin, which gives them a very strong and disagreeable odor. This greater degree of transpiration renders them more tolerant of heat, and less so of cold, than the whites. Perhaps too a difference of structure in the pulmonary apparatus, which a late ingenious experimentalist[10] has discovered to be the principal regulator of animal heat, may have disabled them from extricating, in the act of inspiration, so much of that fluid from the outer air, or obliged them in expiration, to part with more of it. They seem to require less sleep. A black, after hard labor through the day, will be induced by the slightest amusements to sit up till midnight, or later, though knowing he must be out with the first dawn of the morning. They are at least as brave, and more adventuresome. But this may perhaps proceed from a want of fore-thought, which prevents their seeing a danger till it be present. When present, they do not go through it with more coolness or steadiness than the whites. They are more ardent after their female: but love seems with them to be more an eager desire, than a tender delicate mixture of sentiment and sensation. Their griefs are transient. Those numberless afflictions, which render it doubtful whether heaven has given life to us in mercy or in wrath, are less felt, and sooner forgotten with them. In general, their existence appears to participate more of sensation than reflection. To this must be ascribed their disposition to sleep when abstracted from their diversions, and unemployed in labor. An animal whose body is at rest, and who does not reflect, must be disposed to sleep of course. Comparing them by their faculties of memory, reason, and imagination, it appears to me, that in memory they are equal to the whites; in reason much inferior, as I think one could scarcely be found capable of tracing and comprehending the investigations of Euclid[11]; and that in imagination they are dull, tasteless, and anomalous. It would be unfair to follow them to Africa for this investigation. We will consider them here, on the same stage with the whites, and where the facts are not apocryphal on which a judgment is to be formed. It will be right to make great allowances for the difference of condition, of education, of conversation, of the sphere in which they move. Many millions of them have been brought to, and born in America. Most of them indeed have been confined to tillage, to their own homes, and their own society: yet many have been so situated, that they might have availed themselves of the conversation of their masters; many have been brought up to the handicraft arts, and from that circumstance have always been associated with the whites. Some have been liberally educated, and all have lived in countries where the arts and sciences are cultivated to a considerable degree, and have had before their eyes samples of the best works from abroad. The Indians, with no advantages of this kind, will often carve figures on their pipes not destitute of design and merit. They will crayon out an animal, a plant, or a country, so as to prove the existence of a germ in their minds which only wants cultivation. They astonish you with strokes of the most sublime oratory; such as prove their reason and sentiment strong, their imagination glowing and elevated. But never yet could I find that a black had uttered a thought

---

10   "Crawford" (Jefferson's note).

11   Euclid (*fl.* 300 BC), a Greek mathematician whose

Elements in thirteen books became the basis of all geometry.

above the level of plain narration; never see even an elementary trait of painting or sculpture. In music they are more generally gifted than the whites with accurate ears for tune and time, and they have been found capable of imagining a small catch.[12] Whether they will be equal to the composition of a more extensive run of melody, or of complicated harmony, is yet to be proved. Misery is often the parent of the most affecting touches in poetry. – Among the blacks is misery enough, God knows, but no poetry. Love is the peculiar œstrum[13] of the poet. Their love is ardent, but it kindles the senses only, not the imagination. Religion indeed has produced a Phyllis Whately; but it could not produce a poet. The compositions published under her name are below the dignity of criticism. The heroes of the Dunciad are to her, as Hercules to the author of that poem.[14] Ignatius Sancho[15] has approached nearer to merit in composition; yet his letters do more honor to the heart than the head. They breathe the purest effusions of friendship and general philanthropy, and shew how great a degree of the latter may be compounded with strong religious zeal. He is often happy in the turn of his compliments, and his stile is easy and familiar, except when he affects a Shandean[16] fabrication of words. But his imagination is wild and extravagant, escapes incessantly from every restraint of reason and taste, and, in the course of its vagaries, leaves a tract of thought as incoherent and eccentric, as is the course of a meteor through the sky. His subjects should often have led him to a process of sober reasoning: yet we find him always substituting sentiment for demonstration. Upon the whole, though we admit him to the first place among those of his own color who have presented themselves to the public judgment, yet when we compare him with the writers of the race among whom he lived, and particularly with the epistolary class, in which he has taken his own stand, we are compelled to enroll him at the bottom of the column. This criticism supposes the letters published under his name to be genuine, and to have received amendment from no other hand; points which would be of easy investigation. The improvement of the blacks in body and mind, in the first instance of their mixture with the whites, has been observed by every one, and proves that their inferiority is not the effect merely of their condition of life. We know that among the Romans, about the Augustan age especially, the condition of their slaves was much more deplorable than that of the blacks on the continent of America. The two sexes were confined in Separate apartments, because to raise a child cost the master more than to buy one. Cato, for a very restricted indulgence to his slaves in this particular,[17] took from them a certain price. But in this country the slaves multiply as fast as the

---

[12] "The instrument proper to them is the Banjar, which they brought hither from Africa, and which is the original of the guitar, its chords being precisely the four lower chords of the guitar" (Jefferson's note). Catch: a short musical composition, usually for three voices, which sing the same melody, but the second singer starts after the first singer finishes the first line and so on; a round.

[13] Stimulant, motivator, from œstrus, a parasitical flea infesting fish, but also referring to the "estrus" or hormonally driven mating season of animals.

[14] *The Dunciad* (1728; final version 1748), a brilliant satire on dullness in heroic couplets by English poet, Alexander Pope (1688–1744), whose heroes are poetasters, publishers and pedants. Phillis Wheatley (1753–84), a slave and poet in Boston, imitated Pope's popular style; see selections from her poetry in this anthology.

[15] Ignatius Sancho (1729–80), brought as a slave from Guinea to England and supported by the Duke of Montagu

and his family. He wrote 159 letters, including several to author Laurence Sterne, which were published posthumously in London, 1782.

[16] As in the novel, *The Life and Opinions of Tristram Shandy, Gentleman* (1759–67), by English writer Laurence Sterne (1713–68), who was a friend and correspondent of Sancho's. The novel is known for its many typographical peculiarities and neologisms.

[17] Τους δουλους εταξεν ὡρισμενου νομισματος ταις θεραπαινισιν. – Plutarch. Cato" (Jefferson's note). "He permitted the male slaves to consort with the bondwomen for a fixed price" (Greek), from Plutarch (46?–120?), Greek biographer and author of *Parallel Lives*, which contrasts Greek and Roman subjects. Marcus Porcius Cato, the Elder (234–149 BC) was a Roman statesman who struggled against enemies of the state abroad, especially Carthage, and moral laxity at home. His agricultural treatise *De Re Rustica*, cited by Jefferson below, is his only extant work.

free inhabitants. Their situation and manners place the commerce between the two sexes almost without restraint, – The same Cato, on a principle of oeconomy, always sold his sick and superannuated slaves. He gives it as a standing precept to a master visiting his farm, to sell his old oxen, old waggons, old tools, old and diseased servants, and every thing else become useless. "Vendat boves vetulos, plaustrum vetnus, ferramenta vetera, servum senem, servum morbosum, & si quid aliud supersit vendat." Cato de re rustica. c. 2. The American slaves cannot enumerate this among the injuries and insults they receive. It was the common practice to expose in the island of Æsculapius, in the Tyber[18], diseased slaves, whose cure was like to become tedious. The Emperor Claudius[19], by an edict, gave freedom to such of them as should recover, and first declared, that if any person chose to kill rather than to expose them, it should be deemed homicide. The exposing them is a crime of which no instance has existed with us; and were it to be followed by death, it would be punished capitally. We are told of a certain Vedius Pollio, who, in the presence of Augustus[20], would have given a slave as food to his fish, for having broken a glass. With the Romans, the regular method of taking the evidence of their slaves was under torture. Here it has been thought better never to resort to their evidence. When a master was murdered, all his slaves, in the same house, or within hearing, were condemned to death. Here punishment falls on the guilty only, and as precise proof is required against him as against a freeman. Yet notwithstanding these and other discouraging circumstances among the Romans, their slaves were often their rarest artists. They excelled too in science, insomuch as to be usually employed as tutors to their master's children. Epictetus, Terence, and Phaedrus[21], were slaves. But they were of the race of whites. It is not their condition then, but nature, which has produced the distinction. Whether further observation will or will not verify the conjecture, that nature has been less bountiful to them in the endowments of the head, I believe that in those of the heart she will be found to have done them justice. That disposition to theft with which they have been branded, must be ascribed to their situation, and not to any depravity of the moral sense. The man, in whose favor no laws of property exist, probably feels himself less bound to respect those made in favor of others. When arguing for ourselves, we lay it down as a fundamental, that laws, to be just, must give a reciprocation of right: that, without this, they are mere arbitrary rules of conduct, founded in force, and not in conscience: and it is a problem which I give to the master to solve, whether the religious precepts against the violation of property were not framed for him as well as his slave? And whether the slave may not as justifiably take a little from one, who has taken all from him, as he may slay one who would slay him? That a change in the relations in which a man is placed should change his ideas of moral right and wrong, is neither new, nor peculiar to the color of the blacks. Homer tells us it was so 2600 years ago.

Ἥμισυ γάζ τ' ἀρετῆς ἀποαίνυται εὐρυθπα Ζεὺς
Ἀνέρος, ευτ' ἄν μιν κατὰ δουλιον ἧμαζ ἕλησιν.
Od 17.323.

---

[18] Tyber: river running through Rome. "The Island of Æsculapius:" an island in the Tiber about 1,100 feet long and less than 330 feet at its widest, and a place of healing since the Temple of Æsculapius was erected after the plague of 291 BC.

[19] Claudius I (10 BC–AD 54), emperor of Rome from AD 41 to AD 54.

[20] Augustus (originally Caius Octavius, 63 BC–AD 14), the great-nephew of Julius Ceasar and first emperor of Rome.

In his marginal notes, Jefferson cites "Suet. Claud. 25," a reference to the Roman biographer and antiquarian Gaius Suetonius Tranquillus (69–122?), and his *De vita Caesarum* (*Lives of the Caesars*), full of gossip and scandal relating to the lives of the first eleven emperors.

[21] Phaedrus (15 BC–AD 50), a slave by birth, freed and educated in the household of the emperor Augustus, he was the first writer to Latinize whole books of fables, then circulating under the name of Aesop. Terence (195–159? BC), the

>   Jove fix'd it certain, that whatever day
>   Makes man a slave, takes half his worth away.

But the slaves of which Homer speaks were whites. Notwithstanding these considerations which must weaken their respect for the laws of property, we find among them numerous instances of the most rigid integrity, and as many as among their better instructed masters, of benevolence, gratitude, and unshaken fidelity. – The opinion, that they are inferior in the faculties of reason and imagination, must be hazarded with great diffidence. To justify a general conclusion, requires many observations, even where the subject may be submitted to the Anatomical knife, to Optical glasses, to analysis by fire, or by solvents. How much more then where it is a faculty, not a substance, we are examining; where it eludes the research of all the senses; where the conditions of its existence are various and variously combined; where the effects of those which are present or absent bid defiance to calculation; let me add too, as a circumstance of great tenderness, where our conclusion would degrade a whole race of men from the rank in the scale of beings which their Creator may perhaps have given them. To our reproach it must be said, that though for a century and a half we have had under our eyes the races of black and of red men, they have never yet been viewed by us as subjects of natural history. I advance it therefore as a suspicion only, that the blacks, whether originally a distinct race, or made distinct by time and circumstances are inferior to the whites in the endowments both of body and mind. It is not against experience to suppose, that different species of the same genus, or varieties of the same species, may possess different qualifications. Will not a lover of natural history then, one who views the gradations in all the races of animals with the eye of philosophy, excuse an effort to keep those in the department of man as distinct as nature has formed them? This unfortunate difference of color, and perhaps of faculty, is a powerful obstacle to the emancipation of these people. Many of their advocates, while they wish to vindicate the liberty of human nature, are anxious also to preserve its dignity and beauty. Some of these, embarrassed by the question "What further is to be done with them?" join themselves in opposition with those who are actuated by sordid avarice only. Among the Romans emancipation required but one effort. The slave, when made free, might mix with, without staining the blood of his master. But with us a second is necessary, unknown to history. When freed, he is to be removed beyond the reach of mixture. . . .

From *Query XVIII: Manners*

The particular customs and manners that may happen to be received in that state?

It is difficult to determine on the standard by which the manners of a nation may be tried, whether *catholic*, or *particular*. It is more difficult for a native to bring to that standard the manners of his own nation, familiarized to him by habit. There must doubtless be an unhappy influence on the manners of our people produced by the existence of slavery among us. The whole commerce between master and slave is a perpetual exercise of the most boisterous passions, the most unremitting despotism on the one part, and degrading submissions on the other. Our children see this, and learn to imitate it; for man is an imitative animal. This

---

slave of a Roman senator who educated and freed him; he then became a leading Roman comic dramatist and wrote six plays that are the basis for the modern comedy of man-   ners. Epictetus (55–135?), enslaved as a boy, he was eventually freed and became a philosopher associated with the Stoics, remembered for the religious tone of his teachings.

quality is the germ of all education in him. From his cradle to his grave he is learning to do what he sees others do. If a parent could find no motive either in his philanthropy or his self-love, for restraining the intemperance of passion towards his slave, it should always be a sufficient one that his child is present. But generally it is not sufficient. The parent storms, the child looks on, catches the lineaments of wrath, puts on the same airs in the circle of smaller slaves, gives a loose to his worst of passions, and thus nursed, educated, and daily exercised in tyranny, cannot but be stamped by it with odious peculiarities. The man must be a prodigy who can retain his manners and morals undepraved by such circumstances. And with what execration should the statesman be loaded, who permitting one half the citizens thus to trample on the rights of the other, transforms those into despots, and these into enemies, destroys the morals of the one part, and the amor patriæ[22] of the other. For if a slave can have a country in this world, it must be any other in preference to that in which he is born to live and labor for another: in which he must lock up the faculties of his nature, contribute as far as depends on his individual endeavors to the evanishment of the human race, or entail his own miserable condition on the endless generations proceeding from him. With the morals of the people, their industry also is destroyed. For in a warm climate, no man will labor for himself who can make another labor for him. This is so true, that of the proprietors of slaves a very small proportion indeed are ever seen to labor. And can the liberties of a nation be thought secure when we have removed their only firm basis, a conviction in the minds of the people that these liberties are of the gift of God? That they are not to be violated but with his wrath? Indeed I tremble for my country when I reflect that God is just: that his justice cannot sleep for ever: that considering numbers, nature and natural means only, a revolution of the wheel of fortune, an exchange of situation, is among possible events: that it may become probable by supernatural interference! The Almighty has no attribute which can take side with us in such a contest. – But it is impossible to be temperate and to pursue this subject through the various considerations of policy, of morals, of history natural and civil. We must be contented to hope they will force their way into every one's mind. I think a change already perceptible, since the origin of the present revolution. The spirit of the master is abating, that of the slave rising from the dust, his condition mollifying, the way I hope preparing, under the auspices of heaven, for a total emancipation, and that this is disposed, in the order of events, to be with the consent of the masters, rather than by their extirpation.

1780–81   1787

Toussaint L'Ouverture (1744?–1803)

Born a slave in 1744, Toussaint L'Ouverture led history's most successful slave rebellion on the Caribbean island of Saint Domingue and later shaped the revolution that would create Haiti, the first black nation in the Western hemisphere. At the time of the French Revolution, St Domingue was possibly the richest colony in the world, with plantations producing coffee, sugar, indigo, tobacco and cotton. Under the mercantilist system instituted by the French minister Colbert in the seventeenth century, the colony was required to ship all these products to France, and to purchase all imports from the mother country as well. St Domingue society consisted of several castes, within which there existed complex stratifications due to origin and color: the *grands blancs* of the planter aristoc-

22   "Love of home or native land" (Latin).

racy, the *petits blancs,* a nascent (and largely racist) bourgeoisie in direct competition with the Negroes, the *affranchis* (free people of color), consisting of free blacks or mixed bloods who despite the discrimination they experienced at the hands of the ruling classes were one of the pillars of the existing system, and finally nearly half a million slaves. With the Revolution in France, demands for greater political and economic independence for St Domingue mushroomed into a movement to give the full rights of citizenship to people of color and subsequently led to the proclamation of Negro emancipation. After the success of his revolt, Toussaint L'Ouverture followed a policy of moderation and reconciliation, with the goal of creating a multiracial society ruled by a benevolent despot, based on the plantation system, with loose ties to Republican France. Nonetheless, after a period of growing disaffection among blacks due to what they perceived as Toussaint's penchant for intrigue and inclination to grant favors to the whites, he was defeated and subsequently deported to France, where he died in prison.

PRIMARY WORK

George F. Tyson, *Toussaint L'Ouverture* (Englewood Cliffs: Prentice-Hall, 1973).

FURTHER READING

C.L.R. James, *The Black Jacobins: Toussaint L'Ouverture and the San Domingo Revolution* (New York: Vintage, 1989).

PROCLAMATIONS AND LETTERS

The following two revolutionary proclamations took place in response to the degree issued in August 1793 by Leger Sonthonax, the French Civil Commissioner of Saint Domingue, proclaiming the emancipation of the slaves. As Toussaint explicitly states, freedom was something to be gained by the blacks themselves, not something to be conceded by whites.

Proclamation of 25 August 1793

Having been the first to champion your cause, it is my duty to continue to labor for it. I cannot permit another to rob me of the initiative. Since I have begun, I will know how to conclude. Join me and you will enjoy the rights of freemen sooner than any other way. Neither whites nor mulattoes have formulated my plans; it is to the Supreme Being alone that I owe my inspiration. We have begun, we have carried on, we will know how to reach the goal.

Proclamation of 29 August 1793

Brothers and Friends:
I am Toussaint L'Ouverture. My name is perhaps known to you. I have undertaken to avenge you. I want liberty and equality to reign throughout St Domingue[1]. I am working towards that end. Come and join me, brothers, and combat by our side for the same cause.

Letter to General Laveaux[2], 18 May 1794

In the following excerpt, Toussaint sets forth his reasons for allying himself with the French rather than with the Spanish or English.

---

[1]   The western third of the island of Hispaniola, later the independent nation of Haiti.

[2]   The Governor of St Domingue.

It is true, General, that I had been deceived by the enemies of the Republic; but what man can pride himself on avoiding all the traps of wickedness? In truth, I fell into their snares, but not without knowing the reason. You must recall the advances I had made to you before the disasters at Le Cap[3], in which I stated that my only goal was to unite us in the struggle against the enemies of France.

Unhappily for everyone, the means of reconciliation that I proposed – *the recognition of the liberty of the blacks and a general amnesty* – were rejected. My heart bled, and I shed tears over the unfortunate fate of my country, perceiving the misfortunes that must follow. I wasn't mistaken: fatal experience proved the reality of my predictions. Meanwhile, the Spanish offered their protection to me and to all those who would fight for the cause of the kings, and having always fought in order to have liberty I accepted their offers, seeing myself abandoned by my brothers the French. But a later experience opened my eyes to these perfidious protectors, and having understood their villainous deceit, I saw clearly that they intended to make us slaughter one another in order to diminish our numbers so as to overwhelm the survivors and reenslave them. No, they will never attain their infamous objective, and we will avenge ourselves in our turn upon these contemptible beings. Therefore, let us unite forever and, forgetting the past, occupy ourselves hereafter only with exterminating our enemies and avenging ourselves, in particular, upon our perfidious neighbors.

From *Letter to the Minister of Marine, 13 April 1799*

The following excerpt, often referred to as Toussaint's political testament, lays out his negotiating strategy and analyzes the early phases of the revolutionary movement.

The first successes obtained in Europe by the partisans of liberty over the agents of despotism were not slow to ignite the sacred fire of patriotism in the souls of all Frenchmen in St Domingue. At that time, men's hopes turned to France, whose first steps toward her regeneration promised them a happier future; . . . they wanted to escape from their arbitrary government, but they did not intend the revolution to destroy either the prejudice that debased the men of color or the slavery of the blacks, whom they held in dependency by the strongest law. In their opinion, the benefits of the French regeneration were only for them. They proved it by their obstinate refusal to allow the people of color to enjoy their political rights and the slaves to enjoy the liberty that they claimed. Thus, while the whites were erecting another form of government upon the rubble of despotism, the men of color and the blacks united themselves in order to claim their political existence; the resistance of the former having become stronger, it was necessary for the latter to rise up in order to obtain [political recognition] by force of arms. The whites, fearing that this legitimate resistance would bring general liberty to St Domingue, sought to separate the men of color from the cause of the blacks in accordance with Machiavelli's principle of divide and rule.[4] Renouncing their claims over the men of color, they accepted the April Decree [1792].[5] As they had anticipated, the men of color, many of whom were slaveholders, had only been using the blacks to gain their own political demands. Fearing the enfranchisement of the blacks, the men of color deserted their comrades in arms,

---

[3] The town of Le Cap was destroyed as the result of the suppression of a revolt by the *petits blancs* by an army of slaves and free men of color.

[4] Niccolò Mahiavelli (1469–1527), Florentine statesman and political philosopher who set out his practical and some-

times cynical ideas about monarchic rule in *Il Principe* (*The Prince*, 1512).

[5] The decree of the French Assembly giving full citizenship to people of color.

their companions in misfortune, and aligned themselves with the whites to subdue them.

Treacherously abandoned, the blacks fought for some time against the reunited whites and the men of color; but, pressed on all sides, losing hope, they accepted the offers of the Spanish king, who, having at that time declared war on France, offered freedom to those blacks of St Domingue who would join his armies. Indeed, the silence of pre-Republican France on the long-standing claims for their natural rights made by the most interested, the noblest, the most useful portion of the population of St Domingue . . . extinguished all glimmer of hope in the hearts of the black slaves and forced them, in spite of themselves, to throw themselves into the arms of a protective power that offered the only benefit for which they would fight. More unfortunate than guilty, they turned their arms against their fatherland . . . .

Such were the crimes of these blacks, which have earned them to this day the insulting titles of brigands, insurgents, rebels under the orders of Jean François[6]. At that time I was one of the leaders of these auxiliary troops, and I can say without fear of contradiction that I owed my elevation in these circumstances only to the confidence that I had inspired in my brothers by the virtues for which I am still honored today.

Meanwhile, the Spanish, benefiting from the internal divisions to which the French part of St Domingue had fallen prey and aided by the courage that gave to these same blacks the hope of imminent freedom, seized almost all of the North and a large part of the West. Le Cap, surrounded by them on all sides and besieged by land and sea, was experiencing all the horrors of the cruelest famine. . . . The Republic that had just been proclaimed in St Domingue was recognized only in the territory from Le Cap to Port-de-Paix, and the guilty excesses of its agents were not calculated to gain it adherents. But, following their departure for France, they [the Civil Commissioners] left the reins of power in the hands of General Laveaux, who lost no time endearing himself by a wise and paternal administration. It was sometime after this period that, having received the order to attack Le Cap and convinced by my information about the distressing state to which this city was reduced, of its powerlessness to resist the torrent that must engulf it, I went over to the Republic with the blacks under my command.

Letters to the Directory

As the Revolution in France drifted steadily to the right, conservative forces in the Assembly began to call for the restoration of order in the colonies. Vienot Vaublanc was the leader of a reactionary faction which deplored the situation in St Domingue in violently racist speeches. Toussaint, fearing the impact on French public opinion of Vienot Vaublanc's speeches, sent several letters to the Directory, the group of five men which ruled France after the fall of Robespierre.

From *Letter to the Directory, 28 October 1797*

Citizen Directors,

At the moment when I thought I had just rendered eminent service to the Republic and to my fellow citizens, when I had just proven my recognition of the justice of the French people toward us, when I believed myself worthy of the confidence that the Government had placed in me and which I will never cease to merit, a speech was made in the *Corps Legislatif* during the meeting of 22 May 1797 by Vienot Vaublanc . . . and, while going through it, I had the sorrow of seeing my intentions slandered on every page and the political existence of my brothers threatened.

---

[6]   A revolutionary leader, who later betrayed Toussaint.

A similar speech from the mouth of a man whose fortune had been momentarily wiped out by the revolution in St Domingue would not surprise me, the loser has the right to complain up to a certain point, but what must profoundly affect me is that the *Corps Legislatif* could have approved and sanctioned such declamations, which are so unsuitable to the restoration of our tranquility; which, instead of spurring the field-negroes to work, can only arouse them by allowing them to believe that the representatives of the French people were their enemies.

In order to justify myself in your eyes and in the eyes of my fellow citizens, whose esteem I so eagerly desire, I am going to apply myself to refuting the assertions of citizen Vaublanc . . . and . . . prove that the enemies of our liberty have only been motivated in this event by a spirit of personal vengeance and that the public interest and respect for the Constitution have been continually trampled under foot by them. . . .

> *Second Assertion:* "Everyone is agreed in portraying the Colony in the most shocking state of disorder and groaning under the military government. And what a military government! In whose hands is it confined? In that of ignorant and gross negroes, incapable of distinguishing between unrestrained license and austere liberty." . . .

This shocking disorder in which the Commission found St Domingue was not the consequence of the liberty given to the blacks but the result of the uprising of thirty Ventôse[7], for, prior to this period, order and harmony reigned in all Republican territory as far as the absence of laws would allow. All citizens blindly obeyed the orders of General Laveaux; his will was the national will for them, and they submitted to him as a man invested with the authority emanating from the generous nation that had shattered their chains.

If, upon the arrival of the Commission, St Domingue groaned under a military government, this power was not in the hands of the blacks; they were subordinate to it, and they only executed the orders of General Laveaux. These were the blacks who, when France was threatened with the loss of this Colony, employed their arms and their weapons to conserve it, to reconquer the greatest part of its territory that treason had handed over to the Spanish and English. . . . These were the blacks who, with the good citizens of the other two colors, flew to the rescue of General Laveaux in the Villate Affair and who, by repressing the audacious rebels who wished to destroy the national representation, restored it to its rightful depository.

Such was the conduct of those blacks in whose hands citizen Vienot Vaublanc said the military government of St Domingue found itself, such are those negroes he accuses of being ignorant, and gross; undoubtedly they are, because without education there can only be ignorance and grossness. But must one impute to them the crime of this educational deficiency or, more correctly, accuse those who prevented them by the most atrocious punishments from obtaining it? And are only civilized people capable of distinguishing between good and evil, of having notions of charity and justice? The men of St Domingue have been deprived of an education; but even so, they no longer remain in a state of nature, and because they haven't arrived at the degree of perfection that education bestows, they do not merit being classed apart from the rest of mankind, being confused with animals. . . .

Undoubtedly, one can reproach the inhabitants of St Domingue, including the blacks, for many faults, even terrible crimes. But even in France, where the limits of sociability are clearly drawn, doesn't one see its inhabitants, in the struggle between despotism and liberty, going to

---

[7] Ventose, in the revolutionary calendar, was the Wind
Month (19 February to 20 March).

all the excesses for which the blacks are reproached by their enemies? The fury of the two parties has been equal in St Domingue; and if the excesses of the blacks in these critical moments haven't exceeded those committed in Europe, must not an impartial judge pronounce in favor of the former? Since it is our enemies themselves who present us as ignorant and gross, aren't we more excusable than those who, unlike us, were not deprived of the advantages of education and civilization? Surrounded by fierce enemies, oft cruel masters; without any other support than the charitable intentions of the friends of freedom in France, of whose existence we were hardly aware; driven to excessive errors by opposing parties who were rapidly destroying each other; knowing, at first, only the laws of the Mother-Country that favored the pretensions of our enemies and, since our liberty, receiving only the semiyearly or yearly instructions of our government, and no assistance, but almost always slanders or diatribes from our old oppressors – how can we not be pardoned some moments of ill-conduct, some gross faults, of which we were the first victims? Why, above all, reflect upon unreproachable men, upon the vast majority of the blacks, the faults of the lesser part, who, in time, had been reclaimed by the attentions of the majority to order and respect for the superior authorities?

> *Fourth Assertion:* "I believed upon my arrival here [in St Domingue]," continues General Rochambeau[8], "that I was going to find the laws of liberty and equality established in a positive manner; but I was grievously mistaken; there is liberty in this land only for the commanders of Africans and men of color, who treat the rest of their fellows like beasts of burden. The whites are everywhere vexed and humiliated."

If General Rochambeau had reflected philosophically on the course of events, especially those of the human spirit, he would not find it so astonishing that the laws of liberty and equality were not precisely established in an American country whose connection with the Mother Country had been neglected for so long; he would have felt that at a time when Europeans daily perjured themselves by handing over their quarters to the enemies of their country, prudence dictated that Government entrust its defense to the men of color and blacks whose interests were intimately linked to the triumph of the Republic; he would have felt that the military government then ruling the colony, by giving great power to the district commanders, could have led them astray in the labyrinths of uncertainty resulting from the absence of laws; he would have recalled that Martinique, defended by Europeans, fell prey to the English, whereas, St Domingue, defended by the blacks and men of color whom Rochambeau accuses, remained constantly, faithful to France. More accurately, if he had made the slightest, effort to familiarize himself impartially with the law before his pronouncement, he wouldn't have generalized on the intentions of the blacks in respect to some anti-republican whites; he wouldn't have been so certain that they were all vexed and humiliated. I shall not call upon those among the whites who remained faithful to the principles of the Constitution by respecting them regardless of men's color . . . : it was natural for the blacks to pay them the tribute of their gratitude; but it is to those who, openly declaring themselves the enemies of the principles of the Constitution, fought against them and whom a change of mind, more or less sincere, has brought back amongst us and reconciled with the country; it is these people whom I call upon to report the truth, to tell whether they weren't welcomed and protected and if, when they professed republican sentiments, they experienced the least vexation. When the proprietors of St Domingue, when the Europeans who go there, instead of becoming the echoes of citizen

8   Count Jean-Baptiste Rochambeau (1725–1807), a conservative general.

Vaublanc by seeking to spread doubt about the liberty of the black people, show the intention of respecting this liberty, they will see growing in the hearts of these men the love and attachment that they have never ceased to hold for the whites in general and their former masters in particular, despite all of those who have tried to reestablish slavery and restore the rule of tyranny in St Domingue.

> *Fifth Assertion:* "I believe," continues General Rochambeau, "it will be difficult to reestablish order amongst the squanderers because by proscribing the Africans they will push them to revolt when they want to reduce their influence and credit; I am not even afraid to predict that after having armed them it will one day be necessary to fight to make them return to work."

The prediction of General Rochambeau will undoubtedly be fulfilled should he reappear at the head of an army in order to return the blacks to slavery, because they will be forced to defend the liberty that the Constitution guarantees; but that this army may be necessary to force them to return to their rustic work is already flatly contradicted by what they have done in agriculture for the past year. . . . I will not be contradicted when I assert that agriculture prospers in St Domingue beyond even the hopes of this colony's truest friends, that the zeal of the field-negroes is also as satisfactory as can be desired, and that the results of their rustic work are surprising when one reflects that in the middle of a war they were frequently obliged to take up arms in our own defense and that of our freedom, which we hold dearer than life; and, if he finds among them some men who are so stupid as not to feel the need for work, their chiefs have enough control to make them understand that without work there is no freedom. France must be just toward her colonial children, and soon her commerce and inhabitants will no longer miss the riches they will extract from their greatest prosperity; but, should the projects of citizen Vaublanc have some influence upon the French government, it is reminded that in the heart of Jamaica – the Blue Mountains – there exists a small number of men [the Maroons][9] so jealous of their liberty as to have forced the pride and power of the English to respect, to this very day, their natural rights, which the French Constitution guaranteed to us. . . .

> *Eighth Assertion:* "A little after their arrival, the Agents had the impudence to welcome the negroes who had fought under the rebel chief Jean François, who had burned the plain and destroyed the greatest part of the colony. . . . These negroes had everywhere abandoned agriculture; their current cry is that this country belongs to them, that they don't want to see a single white man there. At the same time that they are swearing a fierce hatred of the whites, that is to say, the only true Frenchmen, they are fighting a civil war among themselves."

I swear to God, that in order to better the cause of the blacks, I disavow the excesses to which some of them were carried; subterfuge is far from me, I will speak the truth, even against myself. I confess that the reproaches made here against the rebel band of Jean François are justly merited. I haven't waited until today to deplore his blindness; but it was the delirium of some individuals and not of all the blacks, and must one confuse, under the same appellation of brigands, those who persisted in a guilty conduct with those who fought them and made them return to their duty? If, because some blacks have committed some cruelties, it can be

---

9   A guerrilla group of escaped slaves.

deduced that all blacks are cruel, then it would be right to accuse of barbarity the European French and all the nations of the world. But the French Senate will not participate in such an injustice; it knows how to repulse the passions agitated by the enemies of liberty; it will not confuse one unbridled, undisciplined rebel band with men who since the rule of liberty in St Domingue have given unquestionable proofs of loyalty to the Republic, have shed their blood for it, have assured its triumph, and who, by acts of goodness and humanity, by their return to order and to work, by their attachment to France, have redeemed a part of the errors to which their enemies had driven them and their ignorance had led them.

If it were true that the blacks were so wrong to think that the properties on St Domingue belonged to them, why wouldn't they make themselves masters by driving off men of other colors, whom they could easily master by their numerical superiority? If they had sworn a fierce hatred against the whites, how is it that at this moment the white population of Le Cap equals that of the blacks and men of color? How is it that more than half of the sugar planters of the Le Cap plain are white? If union and fraternity didn't reign among men of all classes, would whites, reds, and blacks be seen living in perfect equality? Without the union of all classes would European soldiers, along with blacks, be seen pursuing the same careers as their fellow citizens in Europe? Would one see them so lively in combat and often only to obtain the same triumphs as their noble rivals?

And then citizen Vaublanc proceeded to apply himself to inflaming the passions of the men of St Domingue, to reviving barbarous prejudices, by proclaiming that the whites in St Domingue are the only true Frenchmen! Does he include under this appellation the traitors paid by the English, those who following odious treachery introduced this perfidious nation into the territory of freedom? In this case, we retain the honor of not meriting this honorable name; but if the friends of freedom classify under this respectable denomination men submitting heart and soul to the French Constitution, to its beneficial laws, men who cherish the French friends of our country, we swear that we have, and will always have, the right to be called French citizens.

> *Ninth Assertion:* "Alternately tyrants and victims, they outrage the sweetest natural sentiments, they renounce the kindest affections and sell their own children to the English, an infamous traffic which dishonors both buyer and seller in the eyes of humanity."

I acknowledge with a shudder that the charge made against the black rebels in the mountains of Grand-Rivière, who are fighting under the English flag and are led by French *émigrés*, of having sold some blacks is unfortunately too well founded; but has this charge ever been made against the blacks loyal to the Republic? And haven't these miserable rebels been driven to these infamous acts by the whites, . . . partisans of the system citizen Vaublanc seems to want to restore to the colony? Against these misguided men, simultaneously guilty and victims, citizen Vaublanc pours all the odium merited by actions so criminal as to be equally reproved by the laws of nature and the social order; but why, at the same time, doesn't he apply himself to tarnishing the monsters who have taught these crimes to the blacks and who have all been, by a barbarous guild on the coast of Africa, wrenching the son from his mother, the brother from his sister, the father from his son? Why does he only accuse those who, kept in ignorance by unjust laws that he undoubtedly wishes to see revived, were at first unable to recognize their rights and duties to the point of becoming the instruments of their own misfortune, while glossing over the outrages committed in cold blood by civilized men like himself, who were therefore even more atrocious since they committed evil knowingly, allowing the lure of gold to suppress the cry of their conscience? Will the crimes of powerful men always be glorified? And will the error of weak men always be a source of oppression for them and their posterity? No! . . . I appeal to the justice of the French Nation. . . .

> *Thirteenth Assertion:* "It is impossible to ignore that the existence of the Europeans in the colony is extremely precarious. In the South, in the mountains of the East, when the blacks are in revolt it is always against their European managers. Since our arrival, a great number have perished in this manner, and we have the misfortune to see that we are without, means to suppress them."

An unanswerable proof, that these partial revolts were only the effect of the perfidious machinations of the enemies of St Domingue's prosperity is that they were always suppressed by the authority of the law, is that by executing those who were its leaders, the sword of justice stopped their propagation. . . . But even supposing that the evils brought about by these movements should be the work of some villainous blacks, must those who did not participate in them and trembled with horror at the news of these disasters also be accused? This, however, is the injustice repeatedly done to black people; for the crime committed by some individuals, people feel free to condemn us all. Instantly forgotten are our past services, our future services, our fidelity and gratitude to France. And what would citizen Vaublanc say if, because the French Revolution produced some Marats[10], Robespierres[11], Carriers[12], Sonthonax[13], etc. etc. etc., the traitors who handed over Toulon to the English; because it produced the bloody scenes of the Vendée[14], the September massacres[15], the slaughter of a great part of the most virtuous members, of the National Convention, the most sincere friends of the Republic and Liberty, in France and the colonies; if, because some *émigré* troops took up arms against their country, which they had previously sold to the foreign powers, a voice arose from St Domingue and cried to the French people:

> You have committed inexcusable crimes because you shunned those more informed and civilized than you. The discussions of the legislative bodies, their laws which were rapidly transmitted to you, the enlightened magistrates charged with executing them, were before your eyes, at your side; you have ignored their voice, you have trampled upon your most sacred duties, you have reviled the Fatherland. Men unworthy of liberty, you were only made for slavery; restore the kings and their iron scepture; only those who opposed revolution were right, only they had good intentions; and the ancien régime that you had the barbarity to destroy was a government much too kind and just for you.

Far be it from me to want to excuse the crimes of the revolution in St Domingue by comparing them to even greater crimes, but citizen Vaublanc, while threatening us in the *Corps Legislatif*, didn't bother to justify the crimes that have afflicted us and which could only be attributed to

---

[10] Jean Paul Marat (1743–93), French revolutionary politician responsible for the September Massacres in Paris.
[11] Maximilien Isidore de Robespierre (1758–94), radical Revolutionary politician and orator who launched the Reign of Terror.
[12] Jean-Baptiste Carrier (1756–94), radical politician later tried for mass murder and guillotined.
[13] Leger-Felicite Sonthonax, a radical French commissioner

who made Toussaint Governor-General. Toussaint was repelled by his proposals to exterminate the Europeans.
[14] A 1793 peasant revolt against the Revolution, provoked mainly by moves against the Roman Catholic Church.
[15] The indiscriminate slaughter of several thousand people carried out by an anti-royalist Paris mob in September 1792.

a small number. . . . However, this former proprietor of slaves couldn't ignore what slavery was like; perhaps he had witnessed the cruelties exercised upon the miserable blacks, victims of their capricious masters, some of whom were kind but the greatest number of whom were true tyrants. And what would Vaublanc say if, having only the same natural rights as us, he was in his turn reduced to slavery? Would he endure without complaint the insults, the miseries, the tortures, the whippings? And if he had the good fortune to recover his liberty, would he listen without shuddering to the howls of those who wished to tear it from him? . . . Certainly not; in the same way he so indecently accuses the black people of the excesses of a few of their members, we would unjustly accuse the entirety of France of the excesses of a small number of partisans of the old system. Less enlightened than citizen Vaublanc, we know, nevertheless, that whatever their color, only one distinction must exist between men, that of good and evil. When blacks, men of color, and whites are under the same laws, they must be equally protected and they must be equally repressed when they deviate from them. Such is my opinion; such are my desires.

Olaudah Equiano (1745–1797)

Although he was taken first to Barbados and then to work on a Virginia plantation after being kidnapped from his African village, Olaudah Equiano cannot rightly be called an African-American. When he finally purchased his freedom with the money he made by investing three pence of his own, and trading for his Quaker master Robert King as well as himself, he left Philadelphia and never returned. He adopted England as his home, married an Englishwoman, Susanna Cullen, in 1792, with whom he had two daughters, and fought there for the abolition of slavery. Still, his widely read autobiography is regarded as the first great African-American slave narrative, whose effective use of popular literary traditions set the pattern for that genre. In that text, Equiano styled himself "the African," and it is this perspective – as an unwilling participant in the triangular trade between Africa, England and the New World whose racial identity was forced upon him – that Equiano provides an invaluable glimpse into the Atlantic world of the eighteenth century.

Kidnapped when he was eleven from the African home he describes as ordered, idyllic and perfectly civilized, Equiano details the barbaric horrors of the slave ship – in which he and millions of Africans endured the Middle passage to the Americas. On the Virginia plantation, he was shocked to see a woman slave wearing an "iron muzzle" that "locked her mouth . . . fast." He was quickly bought by Lt Michael Henry Pascal, with whom he served in the British navy during the Seven Years' War between France and England. It was Pascal who forced on Equiano the name *Gustavus Vassa*, after a Swedish nobleman who had led a successful revolt against Danish rule in the sixteenth century and was the hero of a popular English play at the time. In 1763, Equiano was taken to the British colony of Montserrat in the West Indies and sold to Robert King, a merchant whose trade also including slaves. During this time, Equiano observed the inhumanity of slavery in the West Indies. Having gained some literacy from friendly passengers, and accounting skills from King, Equiano managed to earn the forty pounds with which he bought his freedom on July 10, 1766. Intending to settle in England, Equiano continued to travel around the world on exploratory expeditions to the Arctic and Central America. Back in England, he furthered his education and his commitment to Christianity, and dedicated himself to the cause of abolition. In 1783, he exposed the notorious case of the ship *Zong*, whose owners had thrown 132 shackled slaves overboard, and later made insurance claims for the loss. In 1787, he supported a scheme to repatriate impoverished blacks to Sierre Leone, which ended in failure. He wrote letters to newspapers and met with abolitionist leaders, but his most valuable contribution to the cause was his autobiography.

First published in London in 1789, and in New York in 1791, Equiano's narrative became an international bestseller, with eight English editions as well as Dutch, Russian and French editions. It was reprinted several times in England and America in the nineteenth century, to help abolitionists restate the case against slavery. More than a political tool, Equiano's story set the pattern for the African-American slave narrative and other abolitionist writing. The text strategically weaves together a variety of literary types – the spiritual autobiography perfected by many Protestant writers, especially John Bunyan, whose *Pilgrim's Progress* was the most popular book in England in the eighteenth century; the picaresque novel of adventure; the ever-popular travel account; and important elements of the sentimental novel. Defined by a heartless, inhumane system, Equiano redefined himself by mastering the essential tools of the master – economics and language.

PRIMARY WORK

The Interesting Narrative of the Life of Olaudah Equiano, or Gustavus Vassa, the African, Written by Himself, 1789.

FURTHER READING

Angelo Costanzo, *Surprizing Narrative: Oldaudah Equiano and the Beginning of Black Autobiography* (New York: Greenwood Press, 1987).

Susan Marren, "Between Slavery and Freedom: The Transgressive Self in Olaudah Equiano's Autobiography," *PMLA: Publications of the Modern Language Association of America*, January, 108, 1 (1993) pp. 94–105.

James Walvin, *An African's Life: The Life and Times of Olaudah Equiano, 1745–1797* (London: Cassell, 1998).

FROM *THE INTERESTING NARRATIVE OF THE LIFE OF OLAUDAH EQUIANO, OR GUSTAVUS VASSA, THE AFRICAN, WRITTEN BY HIMSELF*[1]

From Chapter 2 {The Slave Ship}

. . . The first object which saluted my eyes when I arrived on the coast was the sea, and a slave ship which was then riding at anchor and waiting for its cargo. These filled me with astonishment, which was soon converted into terror when I was carried on board. I was immediately handled and tossed up to see if I were sound by some of the crew, and I was now persuaded that I had gotten into a world of bad spirits and that they were going to kill me. Their complexions too differing so much from ours, their long hair and the language they spoke (which was very different from any I had ever heard) united to confirm me in this belief. Indeed such were the horrors of my views and fears at the moment that, if ten thousand worlds had been my own, I would have freely parted with them all to have exchanged my condition with that of the meanest slave in my own country. When I looked round the ship too and saw a large furnace of copper boiling and a multitude of black people of every description chained together, every one of their countenances expressing dejection and sorrow, I no longer doubted of my fate; and quite overpowered with horror and anguish, I fell motionless on the deck and fainted. When I recovered a little I found some black people about me, who I believed were some of those who had brought me on board and had been receiving their pay; they talked to me in order to cheer me, but all in vain. I asked them if we were not to be eaten by those white men with horrible looks, red faces, and loose hair. They told me I was not, and one of the crew brought me a small portion of spirituous liquor in a wine glass, but being afraid of him I would not take it out of his hand. One of the blacks therefore took it from him and gave it to me, and I took a little down my palate, which instead of reviving me, as they thought it would, threw me into the

[1]   The text, with slight modification, is from the first American printing, *The Interesting Narrative of the Life of* *Olaudah Equiano, or Gustavus Vassa, the African* (New York, 1791).

greatest consternation at the strange feeling it produced, having never tasted such any liquor before. Soon after this the blacks who brought me on board went off, and left me abandoned to despair.

I now saw myself deprived of all chance of returning to my native country or even the least glimpse of hope of gaining the shore, which I now considered as friendly; and I even wished for my former slavery[2] in preference to my present situation, which was filled with horrors of every kind, still heightened by my ignorance of what I was to undergo. I was not long suffered to indulge my grief; I was soon put down under the decks, and there I received such a salutation in my nostrils as I had never experienced in my life: so that with the loathsomeness of the stench and crying together, I became so sick and low that I was not able to eat, nor had I the least desire to taste anything. I now wished for the last friend, death, to relieve me; but soon, to my grief, two of the white men offered me eatables, and on my refusing to eat, one of them held me fast by the hands and laid me across I think the windlass[3], and tied my feet while the other flogged me severely. I had never experienced anything of this kind before, and although, not being used to the water, I naturally feared that element the first time I saw it, yet nevertheless could I have got over the nettings I would have jumped over the side, but I could not; and besides, the crew used to watch us very closely who were not chained down to the decks, lest we should leap into the water: and I have seen some of these poor African prisoners most severely cut for attempting to do so, and hourly whipped for not eating. This indeed was often the case with myself.

In a little time after, amongst the poor chained men I found some of my own nation, which in a small degree gave ease to my mind. I inquired of these what was to be done with us; they gave me to understand we were to be carried to these white people's country to work for them. I then was a little revived, and thought if it were no worse than working, my situation was not so desperate: but still I feared I should be put to death, the white people looked and acted, as I thought, in so savage a manner; for I had never seen among my people such instances of brutal cruelty, and this not only shown towards us blacks but also to some of the whites themselves. One white man in particular I saw, when we were permitted to be on deck, flogged so unmercifully with a large rope near the foremast that he died in consequence of it; and they tossed him over the side as they would have done a brute. This made me fear these people the more, and I expected nothing less than to be treated in the same manner. I could not help expressing my fears and apprehensions to some of my countrymen: I asked them if these people had no country but lived in this hollow place (the ship): they told me they did not, but came from a distant one. "Then," said I, "how comes it in all our country we never heard of them?" They told me because they lived so very far off. I then asked where were their women? had they any like themselves? I was told they had: "and why," said I, "do we not see them?" They answered, because they were left behind. I asked how the vessel could go? They told me they could not tell, but that there were cloths put upon the masts by the help of the ropes I saw, and then the vessel went on; and the white men had some spell or magic they put in the water when they liked in order to stop the vessel. I was exceedingly amazed at this account and really thought they were spirits. I therefore wished much to be from amongst them for I expected they would sacrifice me: but my wishes were vain, for we were so quartered that it was impossible for any of us to make our escape.

---

[2]   Equiano was kidnapped from his village of Essaka in the inland kingdom of Benin, now Nigeria, and enslaved by several Africans, before being brought to the West coast for shipment to America.

[3]   A large winch used to hoist in rope or chains.

While we stayed on the coast I was mostly on deck, and one day, to my great astonishment, I saw one of these vessels coming in with the sails up. As soon as the whites saw it they gave a great shout, at which we were amazed; and the more so as the vessel appeared larger by approaching nearer. At last she came to an anchor in my sight, and when the anchor was let go I and my countrymen who saw it were lost in astonishment to observe the vessel stop, and were now convinced it was done by magic. Soon after this the other ship got her boats out, and they came on board of us, and the people of both ships seemed very glad to see each other. Several of the strangers also shook hands with us black people, and made motions with their hands, signifying I suppose we were to go to their country; but we did not understand them.

At last, when the ship we were in had got in all her cargo, they made ready with many fearful noises, and we were all put under deck so that we could not see how they managed the vessel. But this disappointment was the last of my sorrow. The stench of the hold while we were on the coast was so intolerably loathsome that it was dangerous to remain there for any time, and some of us had been permitted to stay on the deck for the fresh air; but now that the whole ship's cargo were confined together it became absolutely pestilential. The closeness of the place and the heat of the climate, added to the number in the ship, which was so crowded that each had scarcely room to turn himself, almost suffocated us. This produced copious perspirations, so that the air soon became unfit for respiration from a variety of loathsome smells, and brought on a sickness among the slaves, of which many died, thus falling victims to the improvident avarice, as I may call it, of their purchasers. This wretched situation was again aggravated by the galling of the chains, now become insupportable, and the filth of the necessary tubs[4], into which the children often fell and were almost suffocated. The shrieks of the women and the groans of the dying rendered the whole scene of horror almost inconceivable. Happily perhaps for myself I was soon reduced so low here that it was thought necessary to keep me almost always on deck, and from my extreme youth I was not put in fetters. In this situation I expected every hour to share the fate of my companions, some of whom were almost daily brought upon deck at the point of death, which I began to hope would soon put an end to my miseries. Often did I think many of the inhabitants of the deep much more happy than myself. I envied them the freedom they enjoyed, and as often wished I could change my condition for theirs. Every circumstance I met with served only to render my state more painful, and heighten my apprehensions and my opinion of the cruelty of the whites.

One day they had taken a number of fishes, and when they had killed and satisfied themselves with as many as they thought fit, to our astonishment who were on the deck, rather than give any of them to us to eat as we expected, they tossed the remaining fish into the sea again, although we begged and prayed for some as well as we could, but in vain; and some of my countrymen, being pressed by hunger, took an opportunity when they thought no one saw them of trying to get a little privately; but they were discovered, and the attempt procured them some very severe floggings.

One day, when we had a smooth sea and moderate wind, two of my wearied countrymen who were chained together (I was near them at the time), preferring death to such a life of misery, somehow made through the nettings and jumped into the sea: immediately another quite dejected fellow, who on account of his illness was suffered to be out of irons, also followed their example; and I believe many more would very soon have done the same if they had not been prevented by the ship's crew, who were instantly alarmed. Those of us that were the most active were in a moment put down under the deck, and there was such a noise and confusion amongst the people of the ship as I never heard before, to stop her and get the boat

---

4 Latrines.

out to go after the slaves. However two of the wretches were drowned, but they got the other and afterwards flogged him unmercifully for thus attempting to prefer death to slavery. In this manner we continued to undergo more hardships than I can now relate, hardships which are inseparable from this accursed trade. Many a time we were near suffocation from the want of fresh air, which we were often without for whole days together. This and the stench of the necessary tubs carried off many.

During our passage I first saw flying fishes, which surprised me very much: they used frequently to fly across the ship and many of them fell on the deck. I also now first saw the use of the quadrant; I had often with astonishment seen the mariners make observations with it, and I could not think what it meant. They at last took notice of my surprise, and one of them, willing to increase it as well as to gratify my curiosity, made me one day look through it. The clouds appeared to me to be land, which disappeared as they passed along. This heightened my wonder, and I was now more persuaded than ever that I was in another world and that everything about me was magic.

At last we came in sight of the island of Barbados, at which the whites on board gave a great shout and made many signs of joy to us. We did not know what to think of this, but as the vessel drew nearer we plainly saw the harbor and other ships of different kinds and sizes, and we soon anchored amongst them off Bridgetown. Many merchants and planters now came on board, though it was in the evening. They put us in separate parcels and examined us attentively. They also made us jump, and pointed to the land, signifying we were to go there. We thought by this we should be eaten by these ugly men, as they appeared to us; and when soon after we were all put down under the deck again, there was much dread and trembling among us, and nothing but bitter cries to be heard all the night from these apprehensions, insomuch that at last the white people got some old slaves from the land to pacify us. They told us we were not to be eaten but to work, and were soon to go on land where we should see many of our country people. This report eased us much; and sure enough soon after we were landed there came to us Africans of all languages.

We were conducted immediately to the merchant's yard, where we were all pent up together like so many sheep in a fold without regard to sex or age. As every object was new to me everything I saw filled me with surprise. What struck me first was that the houses were built with stories, and in every other respect different from those in Africa: but I was still more astonished on seeing people on horseback. I did not know what this could mean, and indeed I thought these people were full of nothing but magical arts. While I was in this astonishment one of my fellow prisoners spoke to a countryman of his about the horses, who said they were the same kind they had in their country. I understood them though they were from a distant part of Africa, and I thought it odd I had not seen any horses there; but afterwards when I came to converse with different Africans I found they had many horses amongst them, and much larger than those I then saw.

We were not many days in the merchant's custody before we were sold after their usual manner, which is this: On a signal given, (as the beat of a drum) the buyers rush at once into the yard where the slaves are confined, and make choice of that parcel they like best. The noise and clamor with which this is attended and the eagerness visible in the countenances of the buyers serve not a little to increase the apprehensions of the terrified Africans, who may well be supposed to consider them as the ministers of that destruction to which they think themselves devoted. In this manner, without scruple, are relations and friends separated, most of them never to see each other again.

I remember in the vessel in which I was brought over, in the men's apartment there were several brothers who, in the sale, were sold in different lots; and it was very moving on this occasion to see and hear their cries at parting. O, ye nominal Christians![5] might not an African ask you, Learned you this from your God who says unto you, Do unto all men as you would men should do unto you? Is it not enough that we are torn from our country and friends to toil for your luxury and lust of gain? Must every tender feeling be likewise sacrificed to your avarice? Are the dearest friends and relations, now rendered more dear by their separation from their kindred, still to be parted from each other and thus prevented from cheering the gloom of slavery with the small comfort of being together and mingling their sufferings and sorrows? Why are parents to lose their children, brothers their sisters, or husbands their wives? Surely this is a new refinement in cruelty which, while it has no advantage to atone for it, thus aggravates distress and adds fresh horrors even to the wretchedness of slavery.

From *Chapter Five*[6]

The small account in which the life of a negro is held in the West Indies is so universally known that it might seem impertinent to quote the following extract, if some people had not been hardy enough of late to assert that negroes are on the same footing in that respect as Europeans. By the 329th Act, page 125, of the Assembly of Barbadoes; it is enacted "That if any negro, or other slave, under punishment by his master, or his order; for running away, or any other crime or misdemeanor towards his said master, unfortunately shall suffer in life or member, no person whatsoever shall be liable to a fine, but if any man shall out of *wantonness, or only of bloody-mindedness, or cruel intention, wilfully kill a negro, or other slave, of his own, he shall pay into the public treasury fifteen pounds sterling.*" And it is the same in most, if not all, of the West India islands. Is not this one of the many acts of the islands which call loudly for redress? And do not the assembly which enacted it deserve the appellation of savages and brutes rather than of Christians and men? It is an act at once unmerciful, unjust, and unwise, which for cruelty would disgrace an assembly of those who are called barbarians, and for its injustice and *insanity* would shock the morality and common sense of a Samoyed or a Hottentot[7].

Shocking as this and many more acts of the bloody West India code at first view appear, how is the iniquity of it heightened when we consider to whom it may be extended! Mr James Tobin, a zealous laborer in the vineyard of slavery,[8] gives an account of a French planter of his acquaintance in the island of Martinique who showed him many mulattoes working in the fields like beasts of burden, and he told Mr Tobin these were all the produce of his own loins! And I myself have known similar instances. Pray, reader, are these sons and daughters of the French planter less his children by being begotten on a black woman? And what must be the virtue of those legislators and the feelings of those fathers, who estimate the lives of their sons, however begotten, at no more than fifteen pounds, though they should be murdered, as the acts says, *out of wantonness and bloody-mindedness!* But is not the slave trade entirely at war with the heart of man? And surely that which is begun by breaking down the barriers of virtue involves in its continuance destruction to every principle, and buries all sentiments in ruin!

I have often seen slaves, particularly those who were meager, in different islands, put into scales and weighed, and then sold from three pence to six pence or nine pence a pound. My master, however, whose humanity was shocked at this mode, used to sell such by the lump.

---

[5]   Christians in name only.

[6]   In early 1763, Equiano was forced onto a ship bound for the island of Montserrat in the West Indies by his master, and was sold by the captain to a Quaker merchant, Robert King, who treated him kindly. While there, however, he observed many horrors.

[7]   Samoyeds are Mongolians who inhabit Siberia; Hottentots inhabit southern Africa. Both were regarded by Europeans as barbaric.

[8]   James Tobin was an English merchant and plantation owner in Nevis from 1775 to 1783, who wrote three pamphlets defending slavery.

And at or after a sale it was not uncommon to see negroes taken from their wives, wives taken from their husbands, and children from their parents, and sent off to other islands, and wherever else their merciless lords chose; and probably never more during life to see each other! Oftentimes my heart bled at these partings, when the friends of the departed have been at the waterside, and with sighs and tears have kept their eyes fixed on the vessel till it went out of sight.

A poor Creole negro I knew well, who, after having been often thus transported from island to island, at last resided in Montserrat. This man used to tell me many melancholy tales of himself. Generally, after he had done working for his master, he used to employ his few leisure moments to go a-fishing. When he had any fish his master would frequently take them from him without paying him, and at other times some other white people would serve him in the same manner. One day he said to me, very movingly, "Sometimes when a white man take away my fish I go to my master, and he get me my right; and when my master by strength take away my fishes, what me must do? I can't go to anybody to be righted; then," said the poor man, looking up above, "I must look up to God Mighty in the top for right". This artless tale moved me much and I could not help feeling the just causes Moses had in redressing his brother against the Egyptian.[9] I exhorted the man to look up still to the God on the top since there was no redress below. Though I little thought then that I myself should more than once experience such imposition and read the same exhortation hereafter in my own transactions in the islands, and that even this poor man and I should some time after suffer together in the same manner, as shall be related hereafter.

Nor was such usage as this confined to particular places or individuals, for in all the different islands in which I have been (and I have visited no less than fifteen) the treatment of the slaves was nearly the same; so nearly indeed, that the history of an island or even a plantation, with a few such exceptions as I have mentioned, might serve for a history of the whole. Such a tendency has the slave trade to debauch men's minds and harden them to every feeling of humanity! For I will not suppose that the dealers in slaves are born worse than other men — No, it is the fatality of this mistaken avarice that it corrupts the milk of human kindness and turns it into gall. And had the pursuits of those men been different, they might have been as generous, as tender-hearted and just, as they are unfeeling, rapacious and cruel. Surely this traffic cannot be good, which spreads like a pestilence and taints what it touches! which violates that first natural right of mankind, equality and independency, and gives one man a dominion over his fellows which God could never intend! For it raises the owner to a state as far above man as it depresses the slave below it, and with all the presumption of human pride, sets a distinction between them, immeasurable in extent and endless in duration! Yet how mistaken is the avarice even of the planters! Are slaves more useful by being thus humbled to the condition of brutes; than they would be if suffered to enjoy the privileges of men? The freedom which diffuses health and prosperity throughout Britain answers you — No. When you make men slaves you deprive them of half their virtue, you set them in your own conduct an example of fraud, rapine, and cruelty, and compel them to live with you in a state of war, and yet you complain that they are not honest or faithful! You stupefy them with stripes and think it necessary to keep them in a state of ignorance, and yet you assert that they are incapable of learning, that their minds are such a barren soil or moor that culture would be lost on them, and that they come from a climate where nature, though prodigal of her bounties in a degree unknown to yourselves, has left man alone scant and unfinished and incapable of enjoying the treasures she had poured out for him! — An assertion at once impious and absurd. Why

9   See Exodus 2:11–12.

do you use those instruments of torture? Are they fit to be applied by one rational being to another? And are ye not struck with shame and mortification to see the partakers of your nature reduced so low? But above all, are there no dangers attending this mode of treatment? Are you not hourly in dread of an insurrection? Nor would it be surprising: for when

> ' – No peace is given
> To us enslav'd, but custody severe;
> And stripes and arbitrary punishment
> Inflicted – what peace can we return?
> But to our power, hostility and hate;
> Untam'd reluctance, and revenge, though slow.
> Yet ever plotting how the conqueror least
> May reap his conquest, and may least rejoice
> In doing what we most in suffering feel.[10]

But by changing your conduct and treating your slaves as men every cause of fear would be banished. They would be faithful, honest, intelligent and vigorous; and peace, prosperity, and happiness would attend you.

From *Chapter 12*

... I hope to have the satisfaction of seeing the renovation of liberty and justice resting on the British government, to vindicate the honor of our common nature. These are concerns which do not perhaps belong to any particular office: but, to speak more seriously to every man of sentiment, actions like these are the just and sure foundation of future fame; a reversion, though remote, is coveted by some noble minds as a substantial good. It is upon these grounds that I hope and expect the attention of gentlemen in power. These are designs consonant to the elevation of their rank and the dignity of their stations: they are ends suitable to the nature of a free and generous government; and, connected with views of empire and dominion, suited to the benevolence and solid merit of the legislature. It is a pursuit of substantial greatness. – May the time come – at least the speculation to me is pleasing – when the sable people shall gratefully commemorate the auspicious era of extensive freedom. Then shall those persons[11] particularly be named with praise and honor, who generously proposed and stood forth in the cause of humanity, liberty, and good policy; and brought to the ear of the legislature designs worthy of royal patronage and adoption. May Heaven make the British senators the dispersers of light, liberty, and science, to the uttermost parts of the earth: then will be glory to God on the highest, on earth peace, and good-will to men: – Glory, honor, peace, etc. to every soul of man that worketh good, to the Britons first, (because to them the Gospel is preached) and also to the nations. "Those that honor their Maker have mercy on the poor." "It is righteousness exalteth a nation; but sin is a reproach to any people; destruction shall be to the workers of

[10]   John Milton (1608–74), *Paradise Lost.* 2:332–4, Beelzebub's speech to the rebelling angels opposing surrender and peace. Line 332 actually reads, "for what peace will be giv'n ... "

[11]   "Granville Sharp, Esq, the Rev Thomas Clarkson, the Rev James Ramsay, our approved friends, men of virtue, are an honor to their country, ornamental to human nature, happy in themselves, and benefactors to mankind!" (Equiano's note). Ramsay (1733–89), born in Scotland, was a doctor and sailor who became a priest on Nevis and St Kitts, and wrote *An Essay on the Treatment and Conversion of African Slaves in the British Sugar Colonies* (1784). His plans to educate slaves on those islands infuriated the planters. James Tobin viciously attacked him in his pro-slavery pamphlet *Cursory Remarks upon the Reverend Mr Ramsay's Essay* (1785), and he died under the strain of such abuse at the beginning of Parliament's debate on slavery in 1789.

iniquity, and the wicked shall fall by their own wickedness."[12] May the blessings of the Lord be upon the heads of all those who commiserated the cases of the oppressed negroes, and the fear of God prolong their days; and may their expectations be filled with gladness! "The liberal devise liberal things, and by liberal things shall stand," Isaiah xxxii. 8. They can say with pious Job, "Did not I weep for him that was in trouble? was not my soul grieved for the poor?" Job xxx. 25. . . .

I have only therefore to request the reader's indulgence and conclude. I am far from the vanity of thinking there is any merit in this narrative: I hope censure will be suspended when it is considered that it was written by one who was as unwilling as unable to adorn the plainness of truth by the coloring of imagination. My life and fortune have been extremely checkered and my adventures various. Even those I have related are considerably abridged. If any incident in this little work should appear uninteresting and trifling to most readers, I can only say as my excuse, for mentioning it that almost every event of my life made an impression on my mind and influenced my conduct. I early accustomed myself to look for the hand of God in the minutest occurrence and to learn from it a lesson of morality and religion, and in this light every circumstance I have related was to me of importance. After all, what makes any event important, unless by its observation we become better and wiser, and learn "to do justly, to love mercy, and walk humbly before God"?[13] To those who are possessed of this spirit there is scarcely any book of incident so trifling that does not afford some profit, while to others the experience of ages seems of no use; and even to pour out to them the treasures of wisdom is throwing the jewels of instruction away.

1789   1791

Judith Sargent Murray (1751–1820)

At the height of her popularity and powers in the last decades of the eighteenth century, Judith Sargent Murray was the most intellectually gifted and widely recognized woman writer of her time. In many ways, her life illustrated her unwavering belief in the untapped capacities of women, and her commitment to improving those capacities as a necessary step in the creation of true republican citizenship. She was the oldest child of Judith Saunders and Captain Winthrop Sargent, a prominent merchant family of Gloucester, Massachusetts. Because as a child she showed remarkable intellectual abilities, her parents allowed her to study with her younger brother, Winthrop, Jr, who was being prepared by a local clergyman for Harvard. They studied the classical languages and literatures, mathematics, and astronomy. And though her brother shared his college lessons with her on his school breaks, Murray always regretted her lack of formal education, which led to her life-long advocacy of self-improvement and better educational instruction for girls. At eighteen, she married a wealthy Gloucester sea captain and trader, John Stevens. The marriage, which was not a happy one, lasted for seventeen years, during which time Murray began her writing career and drafted some of her most influential essays. Two years after her husband's death in 1786, she married John Murray, a close friend of the Sargent family and a Universalist minister. They shared a belief in this liberal branch of Protestant Christianity, as well as intellectual interests, and their marriage proved to be an egalitarian one. In 1793, they moved to Boston where Murray had a much wider intellectual world that fed her blossoming career as a writer. When John Murray died in 1815, she went to live with her only daughter, Julia, who had married a wealthy plantation owner in Natchez, Mississippi.

---

[12] Proverbs 14:31, 14:34.   [13] Micah 6:8.

Murray began writing poetry, but the essay became her favorite form, and when the events of the Revolution turned her attention to issues of liberty and human rights, she began publishing in magazines under the pen name Constantia. "Desultory Thoughts upon the Utility of Encouraging a Degree of Self-Complacency, Especially in Female Bosoms," was her first published essay, and it expressed the ideas that would resound throughout her writing: that lack of education and opportunity, not inherent weakness or inability, cause female "inferiority" and social subordination. She intensified this argument in her most influential essay, "On the Equality of the Sexes." Two years later, she read Mary Wollstonecraft's controversial *A Vindication of the Rights of Women*, which appeared in 1792 and confirmed Murray's own ideas.

In the years between 1792 and 1794 Murray published two concurrent series of essays. One, *The Repository*, explored social and religious issues. The other, *The Gleaner*, used a male speaker, Mr Vigillius, and discussed a wide range of topics in contemporary politics and history. Within these essays was a short novel, *The Story of Margaretta*, which developed a new female heroine whose education prompted her to be virtuous, and whose virtue was rewarded with an egalitarian marriage. Murray's point was that when women, like men, can improve and exercise their minds, they will be less vulnerable to the passions, better able to judge literature and life for themselves, and thus, better spouses and citizens of the new republic. Convinced

of the power of art to shape social and cultural values, Murray wrote two plays in the 1790s, *The Medium, or Virtue Triumphant*, and *The Traveller Returned*, that, like Royall Tyler's *The Contrast* (1790), infused energy into the pursuit of national forms of art. Although Murray's feminism envisioned women within what today we regard as the limited category of "Republican Motherhood," her complex vision of reform inspired the next generation of feminists at Seneca Falls, who also called upon Revolutionary rhetoric to make good its promise of liberty and justice for all.

Primary Works

The Gleaner, originally appeared in the *Massachusetts Magazine*, 1792–1794, published as *The Gleaner; A Miscellaneous Production*, 3 vols, 1798.
The Repository, Massachusetts Magazine, 1792–4.
The Medium, or Virtue Triumphant, 1795.
The Traveller Returned, 1796.
Selected Writings of Judith Sargent Murray, ed. Sharon Harris, 1995.

Further Reading

Nina Baym (ed.) "Introduction," *The Gleaner* (Schnectady: Union College Press, 1992).
Kristin Wilcox, "The Scribblings of a Plain Man and the Temerity of a Woman: Gender and Genre in Judith Sargent Murray's The Gleaner," *Early American Literature*, 30, 2 (1995) pp. 121–44.
Sheila Skemp, *Judith Sargent Murray: A Brief Biography with Documents* (Boston: Bedford, 1998).

"Desultory Thoughts upon the Utility of Encouraging a Degree of Self-Complacency, Especially in Female Bosoms"[1]

> Self-estimation, kept within due bounds,
> However oddly the assertion sounds,
> May, of the fairest efforts be the root,
> May yield the embow'ring shade – the mellow fruit;
> May stimulate to most exalted deeds,
> Direct the soul where blooming honor leads;
> May give her there, to act a noble part,
> To virtuous pleasures yield the willing heart.

---

[1]   This essay originally appeared in *The Gentleman and Lady's Town and Country Magazine: or, Repository of Instruction and Entertainment*, 6 (October 1784).

Self-estimation will debasement shun,
And, in the path of wisdom, joy to run;
An unbecoming act in fears to do,
And still, its exaltation keeps in view.
"To rev'rence self," a Bard long since directed,
And, on each moral truth he well reflected;
But, lost to conscious worth, to decent pride,
Compass nor helm there is, our course to guide:
Nor may we anchor cast, for rudely tost
In an unfathomd sea, each motive's lost,
Wildly amid contending waves we're beat,
And rocks and quick sands, shoals and depths we meet;
'Till, dash'd in pieces, or, till found'ring, we
One common wreck of all our prospects see!
   Nor, do we mourn, for we were lost to fame,
And never hap'd to reach a tow'ring name;
Ne'er taught to "rev'rence self," or to aspire,
Our bosoms never caught ambition's fire;
An indolence of virtue still prevail'd,
Nor the sweet gale of praise was e'er inhal'd;
Rous'd by a new stimulus, no kindling glow.
No soothing emulations gentle flow,
We judg'd that nature, not to us inclin'd,
In narrow bounds our progress had confin'd,
And, that our forms, to say the very best,
Only, not frightful, were by all confest.

I think, to teach young minds to aspire, ought to be the ground work of education: many a laudable achievement is lost, from a persuasion that our efforts are unequal to the arduous attainment. Ambition is a noble principle, which properly directed, may be productive of the most valuable consequences. It is amazing to what heights the mind by exertion may tow'r: I would, therefore, have my pupils believe, that every thing in the compass of mortality, was placed within their grasp, and that, the avidity of application, the intenseness of study, were only requisite to endow them with every external grace, and mental accomplishment. Thus I should impel them to progress on, if I could not lead them to the heights I would wish them to attain. It is too common with parents to expatiate in their hearing, upon all the foibles of their children, and to let their virtues pass, in appearance, unregarded: this they do, least they should, (were they to commend) swell their little hearts to pride, and implant in their tender minds, undue conceptions of their own importance. Those, for example, who have the care of a beautiful female, they assiduously guard every avenue, they arrest the stream of due admiration, and endeavor to divest her of all idea of the bounties of nature: what is the consequence? She grows up, and of course mixes with those who are less interested: strangers will be sincere; she encounters the tongue of the flatterer, he will exaggerate, she finds herself possessed of accomplishments which have been studiously concealed from her, she throws the reins upon the neck of fancy, and gives every encomiast[2] full credit for his most extravagant eulogy. Her natural connexions, her home is rendered disagreeable, and she hastes to the scenes, whence

2   A praiser, eulogizer, flatterer.

arise the sweet perfume of adulation, and when she can obtain the regard due to a merit, which she supposes altogether uncommon. Those who have made her acquainted with the dear secret, she considers as her best friends; and it is more than probable, that she will soon fall a sacrifice to some worthless character, whose interest may lead him to the most hyperbolical lengths in the round of flattery. Now, I should be solicitous that my daughter should possess for me the fondest love, as well as that respect which gives birth to duty; in order to promote this wish of my soul, from my lips she should be accustomed to hear the most pleasing truths, and, as in the course of my instructions, I should doubtless find myself but too often impelled to wound the delicacy of youthful sensibility. I would therefore, be careful to avail myself of this exuberating balance: I would, from the early dawn of reason, address her as a rational being; hence, I apprehend, the most valuable consequences would result: in some such language as this, she might from time to time be accosted. A pleasing form is undoubtedly advantageous, nature, my dear, hath furnished you with an agreeable person, your glass, was I to be silent, would inform you that you are pretty, your appearance will sufficiently recommend you to a stranger, the flatterer will give a more than mortal finishing to every feature; but, it must be your part, my sweet girl, to render yourself worthy respect from higher motives: you must learn "to reverence yourself," that is, your intellectual existence; you must join my efforts, in endeavoring to adorn your mind, for, it is from the proper furnishing of that, you will become indeed a valuable person, you will, as I said, give birth to the most favorable impressions at first sight: but, how mortifying should this be all, if, upon a more extensive knowledge you should be discovered to possess no one mental charm, to be fit only at best, to be hung up as a pleasing picture among the paintings of some spacious hall. The flatterer, indeed, will still pursue you, but it will be from interested views, and he will smile at your undoing! Now, then, my best Love, is the time for you to lay in such a fund of useful knowledge, as shall continue, and augment every kind sentiment in regard to you, as shall set you above the snares of the artful betrayer.

Thus, that sweet form, shall serve but as a polished casket, which will contain a most beautiful gem, highly finished, and calculated for advantage, as well as ornament. Was she, I say, habituated thus to reflect, she would be taught to aspire; she would learn to estimate every accomplishment, according to its proper value; and, when the voice of adulation should assail her ear, as she had early been initiated into its true meaning, and from youth been accustomed to the language of praise; her attention would not be captivated, the Siren's song[3] would not borrow the aid of novelty, her young mind would not be enervated or intoxicated, by a delicious surprise, she would possess her soul in serenity, and by that means, rise superior to the deep-laid schemes which, too, commonly, encompass the steps of beauty.

Neither should those to whom nature had been parsimonious, be tortured by me with degrading comparisons; every advantage I would expatiate upon, and there are few who possess not some personal charms; I would teach them to gloss over their imperfections, inasmuch as, I do think, an agreeable form, a very necessary introduction to society, and of course it behoves us to render our appearance as pleasing as possible: I would, I must repeat, by all means guard them against a low estimation of self, I would leave no charm undiscovered or unmarked, for the penetrating eye of the pretended admirer, to make unto himself a merit by holding up to her view; thus, I would destroy the weapons of flattery, or render them useless, by leaving not the least room for their operation.

A young lady, growing up with the idea, that she possesses few, or no personal attractions,

---

[3] In Greek mythology, a monster, half woman, half bird, who lured sailors to death by the sweetness of their song; thus, any distraction that draws one away from the correct path.

and that her mental abilities are of an inferior kind, imbibing at the same time, a most melancholly idea of a female, descending down the vale of life in an unprotected state; taught also to regard her character ridiculously contemptible, will, too probably, throw herself away upon the first who approaches her with tenders of love, however indifferent may be her chance for happiness, least if she omits the present day of grace, she may never be so happy as to meet a second offer, and must then inevitably be stigmatized with that dreaded title, an Old Maid, must rank with a class whom she has been accustomed to regard as burthens upon society, and objects whom she might with impunity turn into ridicule! Certainly love, friendship and esteem, ought to take place of marriage, but, the woman thus circumstanced, will seldom regard these previous requisites to felicity, if she can but insure the honors, which she, in idea, associates with a matrimonial connection – to prevent which great evil, I would early impress under proper regulations, a reverence of self; I would endeavor to rear to worth, and a consciousness thereof: I would be solicitous to inspire the glow of virtue, with that elevation of soul, that dignity, which is ever attendant upon self-approbation, arising from the genuine source of innate rectitude. I must be excused for thus insisting upon my hypothesis, as I am, from observation, persuaded, that many have suffered materially all their life long, from a depression of soul, early inculcated, in compliance to a false maxim, which hath supposed pride would thereby be eradicated. I know there is a contrary extreme, and I would, in almost all cases, prefer the happy medium. However, if these fugitive hints may induce some abler pen to improve thereon, the exemplification will give pleasure to the heart of
CONSTANTIA.
October 22, 1784.

Philip Freneau (1752–1832)

Philip Morin Freneau, son of a Huguenot tradesman, was born in New York. He later attended the College of Nassau (Princeton), where he joined the American Whig Society. There, he honed his skills as a poet and polemicist, writing satirical verse and prose against the other undergraduate club, the Cliosophical Society. His poem "The Rising Glory of America", written in collaboration with his fellow students James Madison and Hugh Henry Breckenridge, and read at the Princeton commencement exercises in 1771, describes the Spanish discoverers and conquests, speculates about the origins of the Indians, characterizes North American expansion as essentially benevolent and Arcadian in nature, and lists the colonists' grievances against Britain. Given the embryonic character of the American literary market, he was unable to support himself as a writer on graduating and worked in a variety of occupations, as a schoolteacher, farmer, and newspaper editor among others. Nonetheless he continued to write and publish poetry, and gained notoriety for his vitriolic satires of British officials. As might be expected, he was forced to leave New York for the West Indies, where he remained for two years and witnessed the horrors of slavery first hand. Joining the revolutionary forces as a blockade runner, he was captured in 1780 and held prisoner by the British. Unchastened by the experience, he later participated in the *Freeman's Journal* and continued to write poetic invective denouncing British tyranny, earning himself the title of "The Poet of the Revolution".

PRIMARY WORKS

The Poems of Philip Freneau, Poet of the American Revolution, 3 vols, ed. Fred Lewis Pattee, 1902.
Poems of Freneau, ed. Harry Hayden Clark, 1929.
Letters on Various Interesting and Important Subjects, fac., ed. Harry Hayden Clark, 1943.
The Last Poems of Philip Freneau, ed. Lewis Leary, 1945.
Prose, ed. Philip Marsh, 1955.

The *Newspaper Verse of Philip Freneau*, ed. Judith Hiltner, 1986.

FURTHER READING

Lewis Leary, *That Rascal Freneau: A Study in Literary Failure* (New Brunswick: Rutgers University Press, 1941).

Mary Bowden, *Philip Freneau* (Boston: Twayne, 1976).
Philip Marsh, *The Works of Philip Freneau: A Critical Study* (Metuchen, NJ: Scarecrow Press, 1968).
Eric Wertheimer, "Commencement Ceremonies: History and Identity in 'The Rising Glory of America,' 1771 and 1786," *Early American Literature*, 29, 1 (1994) pp. 35–58.

"THE RISING GLORY OF AMERICA"[1]

Being part of a Dialogue pronounced on a public occasion[2]

ARGUMENT. The subject proposed – The discovery of America by Columbus – A philosophical enquiry into the origin of the savages of America – The first planters from Europe – Causes of their migration to America – The difficulties they encountered from the jealousy of the natives – Agriculture descanted on – Commerce and navigation – Science – Future prospects of British usurpation, tyranny, and devastation on this side of the Atlantic – The more comfortable one of Independence, Liberty and Peace – Conclusion.

Acasto
Now shall the adventurous muse attempt a
  theme
More new, more noble, and more flush of
  fame
Than all that went before–
Now through the veil of ancient days renew
The period famed when first Columbus
  touched
These shores so long unknown – though
  various toils,
Famine, and death, the hero forced his way,
Through oceans pregnant with perpetual
  storms,
And climates hostile to adventurous man.
But why, to prompt your tears, should we
  resume,
The tale of Cortez[3], furious chief, ordained
With Indian blood to dye the sands, and
  choak[4]
Famed Mexico, thy streams with dead? or
  why

Once more revive the tale so oft rehearsed
Of Atalbilipa[5], by the thirst of gold,
(Too conquering motive in the human
  breast.)
Deprived of life, which not Peru's rich ore
Nor Mexico's vast mines could then re-
  deem?
Better these northern realms demand our
  song,
Designed by nature for the rural reign,
For agriculture's toil. – No blood we shed
For metals buried in a rocky waste.–
Cursed be that ore, which brutal makes our
  race
And prompts mankind to shed their
  kindred blood.

Eugenio
–But whence arose
That vagrant race who love the shady vale
And choose the forest for their dark abode?–
For long has this perplext the sages' skill

---

[1] The texts are from *Poems of Freneau*, ed. Harry Hayden Clark (New York: Hafner Publishing Co., 1929).
[2] This poem was read at the commencement exercises of the College of New Jersey (now Princeton University).

[3] Hernán Cortés (1485–1547), the Spanish conqueror of Mexico.
[4] Choke.
[5] Atahuallpa, thirteenth and last emperor of the Incas, held for ransom and executed by Pizarro.

To investigate. – Tradition lends no aid
To unveil this secret to the human eye,
When first these various nations, north and
    south,
Possest these shores, or from what countries
    came,–
Whether they sprang from some primaeval[6]
    head
In their own lands, like Adam in the east,–
Yet this the sacred oracles deny,
And reason, too, reclaims against the
    thought:
For when the general deluge drowned the
    world
Where could their tribes have found
    security,
Where find their fate, but in the ghastly
    deep?–
Unless, as others dream, some chosen few
High on the Andes, wrapt in endless snow,
Where winter in his wildest fury reigns,
And subtile aether[7] scarce our life main-
    tains.
But here philosophers oppose the scheme:
This earth, they say, nor hills nor mountains
    knew
Ere yet the universal flood prevailed:
But when the mighty waters rose aloft,
Roused by the winds, they shook their solid
    base,
And, in convulsions, tore the deluged world,
'Till by the winds assuaged, again they fell,
And all their ragged bed exposed to view.
Perhaps far wandering toward the northern
    pole
The streights[8] of Zembla[9], and the frozen
    zone,
And where the eastern Greenland almost
    joins
America's north point, the hardy tribes
Of banished Jews, Siberians, Tartars[10] wild

Came over icy mountains, or on floats,
First reached these coasts, hid from the
    world beside.–
And yet another argument more strange,
Reserved for men of deeper thought, and
    late,
Presents itself to view. – In Peleg's days[11]
(So says the Hebrew seer's unerring pen)
This mighty mass of earth, this solid globe,
Was cleft in twain, – "divided" east and
    west,
While then perhaps the deep Atlantic
    roll'd,–
Through the vast chasm, and laved[12] the
    solid world;
And traces indisputable remain
Of this primaeval land now sunk and lost.–
The islands rising in our eastern main
Are but small fragments of this continent,
Whose two extremities were Newfoundland
And St Helena[13]. – One far in the north,
Where shivering seamen view with strange
    surprise
The guiding pole-star glittering o'er their
    heads;
The other near the southern tropic rears
Its head above the waves – Bermuda's isles,
Cape Verd[14], Canary[15], Britain, and the
    Azores,
With fam'd Hibernia[16], are but broken
    parts
Of some prodigious waste, which once
    sustain'd
Nations and tribes, of vanished memory,
Forests and towns, and beasts of every class,
Where navies now explore their briny[17]
    way.

Leander
Your sophistry[18], Eugenio, makes me smile
The roving mind of man delights to dwell

6   Ancient.
7   Rarefied or thin air.
8   Straits.
9   An archipelago in the Berents Sea.
10   People from west central Russia.
11   Cf. Genesis 10:5.
12   Washed.

13   An island in the South Atlantic.
14   The Cape Verde archipelago.
15   The Canary Islands.
16   Ireland.
17   Salty.
18   Subtly deceptive reasoning.

On hidden things, merely because they're
hid:
He thinks his knowledge far beyond all
limit,
And boldly fathoms Nature's darkest
haunts;—
But for uncertainties, your broken isles,
Your northern Tartars[19], and your wander-
ing Jews,
(The flimsy cobwebs of a sophist's brain)
Hear what the voice of history proclaims—
The Carthagenians[20], ere the Roman yoke
Broke their proud spirits, and enslaved them
too,
For navigation were renowned as much
As haughty Tyre[21] with all her hundred
fleets,
Full many a league their venturous seamen
sailed
Through streight Gibraltar[22], down the
western shore
Of Africa, to the Canary Isles:
By them called Fortunate so Flaccus[23] sings.
Because eternal spring there clothes the
fields
And fruits delicious bloom throughout the
year.—
From voyaging here, this inference I draw,
Perhaps some barque[24] with all her numer-
ous crew
Falling to leeward[25] of her destined port,
Caught by the eastern Trade, was hurried on
Before the unceasing blast to Indian isles,
Brazil, La Plata[26], or the coasts more south—
There stranded, and unable to return,
Forever from their native skies estranged
Doubtless they made these virgin climes
their own,
And in the course of long revolving years
A numerous progeny from these arose,
And spread throughout the coasts — those

whom we call
Brazilians, Mexicans, Peruvians rich,
The tribes of Chili[27], Patagona[28], and those
Who till the shores of Amazon's long
stream.—
When first the power of Europe here
attained,
Vast empires, kingdoms, cities, palaces
And polished nations stock'd the fertile
land.
Who has not heard of Cusco[29], Lima[30], and
the town of Mexico — huge cities form'd
From Indian architecture; ere the arms
Of haughty Spain disturb'd the peaceful
soil.—
But here, amid this northern dark domain
No towns were seen to rise. – No arts were
here;
The tribes unskill'd to raise the lofty maste,
Or force the daring prow thro' adverse
waves,
Gazed on the pregnant soil, and craved
alone
Life from the unaided genius of the
ground,—
This indicates they were a different race;
From whom descended, 'tis not ours to say—
That power, no doubt, who furnish'd trees,
and plants,
And animals to this vast continent,
Spoke into being man among the rest,—
But what a change is here! – what arts arise!
What towns and capitals! How commerce
waves
Her gaudy flags, where silence reign'd
before.

Acasto
Speak, learned Eugenio, for I've heard you
tell

---

[19]   Russians.
[20]   Carthage, a great city of antiquity, located on the north coast of Africa.
[21]   A major Phoenician seaport.
[22]   The Strait of Gibraltar.
[23]   Gaius Valerius Flaccus (*fl.* first century AD), author of the epic *Argonautica*.

[24]   Ship.
[25]   Facing the direction in which the wind is blowing.
[26]   A city in Argentina.
[27]   Chile.
[28]   A semi-arid plateau in southern Argentina.
[29]   Cuzco, former capital of the Incan empire.
[30]   The capital city of Peru.

The dismal story, and the cause that
brought
The first adventurers to these western
shores!
The glorious cause that urged our fathers
first
To visit climes unknown, and wilder woods
Than e'er Tartarian[31] or Norwegian saw,
And with fair culture to adorn a soil
That never felt industrious swain before.

Eugenio
All this long story to rehearse, would tire;
Besides, the sun towards the west retreats,
Nor can the noblest theme retard his speed,
Nor loftiest verse – not that which sang the
fall
Of Troy divine, and fierce Achilles'[32] ire.
Yet hear a part: By persecution wronged,
And sacerdotal rage, our fathers came
From Europe's hostile shores to these
abodes,
Here to enjoy a liberty in *faith*,
Secure from tyranny and base controul.
For this they left their country and their
friends,
And plough'd the Atlantic wave in quest of
peace;
And found new shores, and sylvan[33] settle-
ments,
And men, alike unknowing and unknown.
Hence, by the care of each adventurous *chief*
New governments (their wealth unenvied
yet)
Were form'd on liberty and virtue's plan.
These searching out uncultivated tracts
Conceived new plans of towns, and capitals,
And spacious provinces – Why should I
name
Thee, Penn[34], the Solon[35] of our western
lands;

Sagacious[36] legislator, whom the world
Admires, long dead: an infant colony,
Nursed by thy care, now rises o'er the rest
Like that tall pyramid in Egypt's waste
Oe'r all the neighbouring piles, they also
great.
Why should I name those heroes so well
known,
Who peopled all the rest of Canada
To Georgia's farthest coasts, West Florida,
Or Apalchian[37] mountains? – Yet what
streams
Of blood were shed! what Indian hosts were
slain
Before the days of peace were quite restored!

Leander
Yes, while they overturn'd the rugged soil
And swept the forests from the shaded plain
'Midst dangers, foes, and death, fierce
Indian tribes
With vengeful malice arm'd, and black
design,
Oft murdered, or dispersed, these colonies–
Encouraged, too, by Gallia's[38] hostile sons,
A warlike race, who late their arms
display'd,
At Quebec, Montreal, and farthest coasts
Of Labrador, or Cape Breton, where now
The British standard awes the subject host.
Here, those brave chiefs, who, lavish of their
blood,
Fought in Britannia's cause, in battle fell!–
What heart but mourns the untimely fate of
Wolfe[39],
Who, dying, conquered! – or what breast
but beats
To share a fate like his, and die like him!

Acasto
But why alone commemorate the dead,

---

[31]   Russian.
[32]   The legendary hero of the Trojan War.
[33]   Settlements in the forest.
[34]   William Penn (1644–1718), Quaker leader, founder of
Pennsylvania and advocate of religious freedom.
[35]   Solon (630?–560? BC), Athenian statesman and legislator.

[36]   Wise.
[37]   Appalachian.
[38]   France's; a reference to the French and Indian war (1754–
63).
[39]   James Wolfe (1727–59), commander of the British army
at the capture of Quebec from the French in 1759.

And pass those glorious heroes by, who yet
Breathe the same air, and see the light with
    us?–
The dead, Leander, are but empty names,
And they who fall today the same to us
As they who fell ten centuries ago!–
Lost are they all that shined on earth before;
Rome's boldest champions in the dust are
    laid,
Ajax[40] and great Achilles[41] are no more,
And Philip's warlike son[42], an empty
    shade!–
A Washington[43] among our sons of fame
Will rise conspicuous as the morning star
Among the inferior lights–
To distant wilds Virginia sent him forth–
With her brave sons he gallantly opposed
The bold invaders of his country's rights[44],
Where wild Ohio[45] pours the mazy[46] flood,
And mighty meadows skirt his subject
    streams.–
But now delighting in his elm tree's shade,
Where deep Potowmac[47] laves[48] the en-
    chanting shore,
He prunes the tender vine, or bids the soil
Luxuriant harvests to the sun displayed.–
Behold a different scene – not thus em-
    ployed
Were Cortez, and Pizarro[49], pride of Spain,
Whom blood and murder only satisfied,
And all to glut their avarice and ambition!–

Eugenio
Such is the curse, Acasto, where the soul
Humane is wanting – but we boast no feats
Of cruelty like Europe's murdering breed–
Our milder epithet is merciful,

And each American, true hearted, learns
To conquer, and to spare; for coward souls
Alone seek vengeance on a vanquished foe.
Gold, fatal gold, was the alluring bait
To Spain's rapacious tribes – hence rose the
    wars
From Chili[50] to the Caribbean sea,
And Montezuma's[51] Mexican domains:
More blest are we, with whose unenvied soil
Nature decreed no mingling gold to shine,
No flaming diamond, precious emerald,
No blushing sapphire, ruby, chrysolite,
Or jasper red – more noble riches flow
From agriculture, and the industrious swain,
Who tills the fertile vale, or mountain's
    brow
Content to lead a safe, a humble life,
Among his native hills, romantic shades
Such as the muse of Greece of old did feign,
Allured the Olympian gods from chrystal
    skies,
Envying such lovely scenes to mortal man.

Leander
Long has the rural life been justly fam'd,
And bards[52] of old their pleasing pictures
    drew
Of flowery meads[53], and groves, and gliding
    streams:
Hence, old Arcadia[54] – wood-nymphs,
    satyrs, fauns;
And hence Elysium[55], fancied heaven
    below!–
Fair agriculture, not unworthy kings,
Once exercised the royal hand, or those
Whose virtues raised them to the rank of
    gods.

40   A legendary Greek hero.
41   A hero of the Trojan War.
42   Alexander the Great (356–323 BC).
43   George Washington (1732–99), first President of the
United States.
44   A reference to Washingon's participation in the French
and Indian War.
45   The Ohio River.
46   Wandering.
47   The Potomac River.
48   Bathes.

49   Francisco Pizarro (1475?–1541), the Spanish conqueror
of Peru.
50   Chile.
51   Montezuma (1470?–1520), Aztec emperor of Mexico,
dethroned by Cortés.
52   Poets.
53   Meadows, fields.
54   A district in the Peloponnesus, represented in Classical
poetry as rural and idyllic.
55   Paradise.

See Laertes[56] in his shepherd weeds
Far from his pompous throne and court
   august,
Digging the grateful soil, where round him
   rise,
Sons of the earth, the tall aspiring oaks,
Or orchards, boasting of more fertile
   boughs,
Laden with apples red, sweet scented peach,
Pear, cherry, apricot, or spungy plum;
While through the glebe[57] the industrious
   oxen draw
The earth-inverting plough. – Those
   Romans too
Febricius and Camillus[58], loved a life
Of neat simplicity and rustic bliss,
And from the noisy Forum hastening far,
From busy camps, and sycophants[59], and
   crowns,
'Midst woods and fields spent the remains of
   life
Where full enjoyment still awaits the wise.
How grateful, to behold the harvests rise
And mighty crops adorn the extended
   plains!–
Fair plenty smiles throughout, while lowing
   herds
Stalk o'er the shrubby hill or grassy mead,
Or at some shallow river slake their thirst.–
The inclosure[60], now, succeeds the shep-
   herd's care,
Yet milk-white flocks adorn the well
   stock'd farm,
And court the attention of the industrious
   swain[61]–
Their fleece rewards him well, and when the
   winds
Blow with a keener blast, and from the
   north
Pour mingled tempests through a sunless
   sky
(Ice, sleet, and rattling hail) secure he sits

Warm in his cottage, fearless of the storm,
Enjoying now the toils of milder moons,
Yet hoping for the spring. – such are the
   joys,
And such the toils of those whom heaven
   hath bless'd
With souls enamoured of a country life.

Acasto

Such are the visions of the rustic reign–
But this alone, the fountain of support,
Would scarce employ the varying mind of
   man;
Each seeks employ, and each a different way:
Strip Commerce of her sail, and men once
   more
Would be converted into savages–
No nation e'er grew social and refined
'Till Commerce first had wing'd the adven-
   turous prow
Or sent the slow-paced caravan, afar,
To waft their produce to some other clime,
And bring the wished exchange – thus
   came, of old,
Golconda's golden ore, and thus the wealth
Of Ophir[62], to the wisest of mankind.

Eugenio

Great is the praise of Commerce, and the
   men
Deserve our praise, who spread the un-
   daunted sail,
And traverse every sea – their dangers great,
Death still to combat in the unfeeling gale,
And every billow but a gaping grave:–
There, skies and waters, wearying on the
   eye,
For weeks and months no other prospect
   yield
But barren wastes, unfathomed depths,
   where not
The blissful haunt of human form is seen

---

[56]   King of Ithaca, father of Ulysses.
[57]   Field.
[58]   Semi-mythical Roman heroes, mentioned in Plutarch's
Lives.
[59]   Flatterers.

[60]   Fenced field.
[61]   Rural youth.
[62]   An area of Saudi Arabia, from which according to Old
Testament tradition King Solomon obtained gold and precious stones in large quantities.

To cheer the unsocial horrors of the way—
Yet all these bold designs to Science owe
Their rise and glory – Hail, fair Science! Thou
Transplanted from the eastern skies, dost bloom
In these blest regions – Greece and Rome no more
Detain the Muses on Citheron's brow,
Or old Olympus[63], crowned with waving woods,
Or Haemus'[64] top, where once was heard the harp,
Sweet Orpheus' harp, that gained his cause below,
And pierced the souls of Orcus[65] and his bride;
That hushed to silence by its voice divine
Thy melancholy waters, and the gales
O Hebrus[66]! That o'er they sad surface blow.—
No more the maids round Alpheus'[67] waters stray,
Where he with Arethusa's[68] stream doth mix,
Or where swift Tiber[69] disembogues his waves
Into the Italian sea, so long unsung;
Hither they wing their way, the last, the best
Of countries, where the arts shall rise and grow,
And arms shall have their day – even now we boast
A Franklin[70], prince of all philosophy,
A genius piercing as the electric fire,
Bright as the lightning's flash, explained so well
By him, the rival of Britannia's sage![71]
This is the land of every joyous sound,

Of liberty and life, sweet liberty!
Without whose aid the noblest genius fails,
And Science irretrievably must die.

Leander
But come, Eugenio, since we know the past—
What hinders to pervade with searching eye
The mystic scenes of dark futurity!
Say, shall we ask what empires yet must rise,
What kingdoms, powers and states, where now are seen
Mere dreary wastes, and awful solitude,
Where Melancholy sits, with eye forlorn
And time anticipates, when we shall spread
Dominion from the north, and south, and west,
Far from the Atlantic to Pacific shores,
And people half the convex of the main!—
A glorious theme! – but how shall mortals dare
To pierce the dark events of future years
And scenes unravel, only known to fate?

Acasto
This might we do, if warmed by that bright coal
Snatch'd from the altar of cherubic fire
Which touched Isaiah's[72] lips – or if the spirit
Of Jeremy and Amos[73], prophets old,
Might swell the heaving breast – I see, I see
Freedom's established reign; cities, and men,
Numerous as sands upon the ocean shore,
And empires rising where the sun descends!—
The Ohio soon shall glide by many a town
Of note; and where the Mississippi stream,

---

[63] The ridge of Citheron, often mentioned in Classical poetry, and Mount Olympus, home of the gods.
[64] A mountain range in northern Greece.
[65] One of the names of Pluto, god of infernal regions.
[66] A river in Greece.
[67] A river of Arcadia.
[68] A nymph, pursued by the river god Altheus and transformed into a fountain.

[69] The river which flows through Rome.
[70] Benjamin Franklin (1706–90), American patriot and statesman, known for his experiments with lightning.
[71] Sir Isaac Newton.
[72] The first great Hebrew prophet.
[73] Jeremiah and Amos, both Hebrew prophets mentioned in the Old Testament.

By forests shaded, now runs weeping on,
Nations shall grow, and states not less in
    fame
Than Greece and Rome of old! – we too
    shall boast
Our Scipio's[74], Solon's[75], Cato's[76], sages,
    chiefs
That in the lap of time yet dormant lie,
Waiting the joyous hour of life and light–
O snatch me hence, ye muses, to those days
When, through the veil of dark antiquity,
A race shall hear of us as things remote,
That blossomed in the morn of days –
    Indeed,
How could I weep that we exist so soon,
Just in the dawning of these mighty times,
Whose scenes are painting for eternity!
Dissentions that shall swell the trump of
    fame,
And ruin hovering o'er all monarchy!

Eugenio
Nor shall these angry tumults here subside
Nor murder cease[77], through all these
    provinces,
Till foreign crowns have vanished from their
    view
And dazzle here no more – no more presume
To awe the spirit of fair Liberty–
Vengeance must cut the thread – and
    Britain, sure
Will curse her fatal obstinacy for it!
Bent on the ruin of this injured country
She will not listen to our humble prayers,
Though offered with submission:
Like vagabonds and objects of destruction,
Like those whom all mankind are sworn to
    hate,
She casts us off from her protection,
And will invite the nations round about,
Russians and Germans, slaves and savages,
To come and have a share in our perdition–

O cruel race, O unrelenting Britain,
Who bloody beasts will hire to cut our
    throats
Who war will wage with prattling inno-
    cence,
And basely murder unoffending women!–
Will stab their prisoners when they cry for
    quarter,
Will burn our towns, and from his lodging
    turn
The poor inhabitant to sleep in tempests!–
These will be wrongs, indeed, and all
    sufficient
To kindle up our souls to deeds of horrors,
And give to every arm the nerves of
    Sampson[78]
These are the men that fill the world with
    ruin,
And every region mourns their greedy
    sway,–
Not only for ambition–
But what are this world's goods, that they
    for them
Should exercise perpetual butchery?
What are these mighty riches we possess,
That they should send so far to plunder
    them?–
Already have we felt their potent arm–
And ever since that inauspicious day,
When first Sir Francis Bernard[79]
His ruffians planted at the council door,
And made the assembly room a home for
    vagrants,
And soldiers, rank and file – e'er since that
    day
This wretched land, that drinks its chil-
    dren's gore,
Has been a scene a scene of tumult and
    confusion!
Are there not evils in the world enough?
Are we so happy that they envy us?
Have we not toiled to satisfy their harpies[80],

---

74   Publius Cornelius Scipio (237–183 BC), Roman general.
75   Solon (638–558 BC), Athenian statesman.
76   Cato (234–140 BC), Roman statesman.
77   An allusion to the Boston Massacre, which took place
on 5 March 1770.

78   A hero of the Old Testament, known for his strength.
See Judges 17,
79   The colonial Governor of New Jersey and Massachusetts.
80   Rapacious persons, plunderers.

Kings' deputies, that are insatiable;
Whose practice is to incense the royal mind
And make us despicable in his view?–
Have we not all the evils to contend with
That, in this life, mankind are subject to,
Pain, sickness, poverty, and natural death–
But into every wound that nature gave
They will a dagger plunge, and make them
    mortal!

Leander
Enough, enough! – such dismal scenes you
    paint,
I almost shudder at the recollection–
What! Are they dogs that they would
    mangle us?–
Are these the men that come with base
    design
To rob the hive, and kill the industrious
    bee!–
To brighter skies I turn my ravished view,
And fairer prospects from the future draw–
Here independent power shall hold her
    sway,
And public virtue warm the patriot breast:
No traces shall remain of tyranny,
And laws, a pattern to the world beside
Be here enacted first.–

Acasto
And when a train of rolling years are past,
(So sung the exiled seer in Patmos isle)
A new Jerusalem, sent down from heaven,
Shall grace our happy earth, – perhaps this
    land,
Whose ample bosom shall receive, though
    late
Myriads of saints, with their immortal king,
To live and reign on earth a thousand years,
Thence called *Millennium*. Paradise anew

Shall flourish, by no second Adam lost,
No dangerous tree with deadly fruit shall
    grow,
No tempting serpent to allure the soul
From native innocence. A Canaan[81] here,
Another *Canaan* shall excel the old,
And from a fairer Pisgah's[82] top be seen.
No thistle here, nor thorn, nor briar shall
    spring,
Earth's curse before: the lion and the lamb
In mutual friendship linked, shall browse
    the shrub,
And timours[83] deer with softened tygers
    stray
O'er mead[84], or lofty hill, or grassy plain;
Another Jordan's stream shall glide along,
And Siloah's[85] brook in circling eddies flow:
Groves shall adorn their verdant banks, on
    which
The happy people, free from toils and death,
Shall find secure repose. No fierce disease,
No fevers, slow consumption, ghastly
    plague,
(Fate's ancient ministers) again proclaim
Perpetual war with man: fair fruits shall
    bloom,
Fair to the eye, and sweeter to the taste;
Nature's loud storms be hushed, and seas no
    more
Rage hostile to mankind – and, worse than
    all,
The fiercer passions of the human breast
Shall kindle up to deeds of death no more
But all subside in universal peace.–
–Such days the world,
And such AMERICA at last shall have
When ages, yet to come, have run their
    round,
And future years of bliss alone remain.

1775

---

[81] The Promised Land of the Israelites.
[82] The mountain from which Moses beheld the Promised Land.
[83] Timid.
[84] Meadow.
[85] Shiloah, a Jewish sanctuary north of Bethel.

"A POLITICAL LITANY"

Libera Nos, Domine. – Deliver us, o Lord, not only from British Dependence, but also

From a junto[1] that labour with absolute power,
Whose schemes disappointed have made them look sour,
From the lords of the council, who fight against freedom,
Who still follow on where delusion shall lead them.

From the group at St James's[2], who slight our petitions,
And fools that are waiting for further submissions–
From a nation whose manners are rough and severe,
From scoundrels and rascals, – do keep us all clear.

From pirates sent out by command of the king
To murder and plunder, but never to swing;
From Wallace and Greaves, and Vipers and Roses[3],
Who if heaven pleases, we'll give bloody noses.

From the valiant Dunmore[4], with his crew of banditti,
Who plunder Virginians at Williamsburg city,
From hot-headed Montague[5], mighty to swear,
The little fat man, with his pretty white hair.

From bishops in Britain, who butchers are grown,
From slaves that would die for a smile from the throne,
From assemblies that vote against Congress proceedings,
(Who now see the fruit of their stupid misleadings.)

From Tyron[6] the mighty, who flies from our city,
And swelled with importance disdains the committee[7]:
(But since he is pleased to proclaim us his foes,
what the devil care we where the devil he goes.)

From the caitiff[8], Lord North[9], who would bind us in chains,
From a royal king Log[10], with his tooth-full of brains,
Who dreams, and is certain (when taking a nap)
He has conquered our lands, as they lay on his map.

---

[1] A political elite.
[2] I.e. the court of George III.
[3] Captains and ships in the British Navy, then employed on the American coast (Freneau's note).
[4] John Murray Dunmore (1732–1809), British colonial Governor of Virginia, whose troops seized the colony's gunpowder in April, 1775.
[5] John Montagu (1719–95), Admiral of the British Navy.

[6] William Tyron (1725–88), Tory governor of New York, who fled the city at the beginning of the Revolution.
[7] The Committee of Safety, the patriot organization directing the revolutionary effort in New York.
[8] Coward.
[9] Frederick North (1732–92), Prime Minister of Britain.
[10] An allusion to George III. In one of Aesop's fables, when a group of frogs demand a king, they receive a log instead.

From a kingdom that bullies, and hectors, and swears,
We send up to heaven our wishes and prayers
That we, disunited, may freemen be still,
And Britain go on – to be damned if she will.

1775

"GEORGE THE THIRD'S SOLILOQUY"

What mean these dreams, and hideous
    forms that rise
Night after night, tormenting to my eyes–
No real foes these horrid shapes can be,
But thrice as much they vex and torture me.
How cursed is he – how doubly cursed am
    I–
Who lives in pain, and yet who dares not
    die;
To him no joy this world of nature brings,
In vain the wild rose blooms, the daisy
    springs.
Is this a prelude to some new disgrace,
Some baleful omen to my name and race!–
It may be so – ere mighty Caesar[1] died
Presaging Nature felt his doom, and sighed;
A bellowing voice through midnight groves
    was heard,
And threatening ghosts at dusk of eve
    appeared–
Ere[2] Brutus[3] fell, to adverse fates a prey,
His evil genius met him on the way,
And so may mine! but who would yield so
    soon
A prize some luckier hour may make my
    own?
Shame seize my crown ere such a deed be
    mine–
No – to the last my squadrons shall com-
    bine,
And slay my foes, while foes remain to slay,
Or heaven shall grant me one successful day.
Is there a robber close in Newgate[4] hemmed,

Is there a cut-throat, fettered[5] and con-
    demned?
Haste, loyal slaves, to George's standard
    come,
Attend his lectures when you hear the
    drum;
Your chains I break – for better days
    prepare,
Come out, my friends, from prison and from
    care,
Far to the west I plan your desperate sway,
There 'tis no sin to ravage, burn and slay.
There, without fear, your bloody aims
    pursue,
And shew mankind what English thieves
    can do.
That day, when first I mounted to the
    throne,
I swore to let all foreign foes alone.
Through love of peace to terms did I
    advance,
And made, they say, a shameful league with
    France.
But different scenes rise horrid to my view,
I charged my hosts to plunder and subdue–
At first, indeed, I though short wars to wage
And sent some jail-birds to be led by Gage[6],
For 'twas but right, that those we marked
    for slaves
Should be reduced by cowards, fools and
    knaves;
Awhile directed by his feeble hand,
Whose troops were kicked and pelted

---

[1] Julius Caesar (100–44 BC), Emperor of Rome, slain by
an assassin on the Ides of March.
[2] Before.
[3] The assassin of Julius Caesar.

[4] A notorious London prison.
[5] Chained.
[6] Thomas Gage (1721–87), British commander at Bun-
ker Hill.

through the land,
Or starved in Boston, cursed the unlucky
    hour
They left their dungeons for that fatal shore.
France aids them now, a desperate game I
    play,
And hostile Spain will to the same, they say;
My armies vanquished, and my heroes fled,
My people murmuring, and my commerce
    dead,
My shattered navy pelted, bruised, and
    clubbed
By Dutchmen bullied, and by Frenchmen
    drubbed,
My name abhorred, my nation in disgrace,
How should I act in such a mournful case!
My hopes and joys are vanished with my
    coin,
My ruined army, and my lost Burgoyne![7]
What shall I do – confess my labours vain,
Or whet my tusks, and to the charge again!
But where's my force – my choicest troops
    are fled,
If I were owned the boldest of mankind,
And hell with all her flames inspired my
    mind,
Could I at once with Spain and France
    contend,
And fight the rebels on the world's green
    end?–
The pangs of parting I can ne'er endure

Yet part we must, and part to meet no
    more?
Oh! Blast this Congress[8], blast each upstart
    State
On whose commands ten thousand captains
    wait;
From various climes that dire Assembly
    came,
True to their trust, as hostile to my fame,
'Tis these, ah these, have ruined half my
    sway,
Disgraced my arms, and led my slaves
    astray–
Cursed be the hour, when I these wars
    begun:
The fiends of darkness then possessed my
    mind,
And powers unfriendly to the human kind.
To wasting grief, and sullen rage a prey,
To Scotland's utmost verge I'll take my way,
And while the billows rage, as fiercely
    weep–
Ye highland lads, my rugged fate bemoan,
Assist me with one sympathizing groan,
For late I find the nations are my foes,
I must submit, and that with bloody nose,
Or, like our James[9], fly basely from the
    state,
Or share, what still is worse – old
    Charles's[10] fate.

                                              1779

"TO SIR TOBY"[1]

A Sugar Planter in the interior parts of Jamaica, near the City of San Jago de la Vega, (Spanish
Town), 1784.

"The motions of his spirit are black as night,
And his affections dark as Erebus."
SHAKESPEARE[2]

---

7   John Burgoyne (1723–92), the British general who surrendered to Gates at Saratoga in 1777.
8   The First Continental Congress (1774), at which delegates advised the people to arm, and proposed to cut off
trade with Britain.
9   James II of England, forced to flee into exile.

10   Charles I, executed by Puritan forces.

SIR TOBY
1   In some versions titled "The Island Field Negro."
2   An allusion to "The Merchant of Venice," V, i, 79.

If there exists a hell – the case is clear–
Sir Toby's slaves enjoy that portion here;
Here are no blazing brimstone lakes – 'tis true;
But kindled Rum too often burns as blue;
In which some fiend, whom nature must detest,
Steeps Toby's brand, and marks poor Cudjoe's breast.[3]

Here whips on whips excite perpetual fears,
And mingled howlings vibrate on my ears;
Here nature's plagues abound, to fret and tease,
Snakes, scorpions, despots, lizards, centipedes–
No arts, no care escapes the busy lash;
All have their dues – and all are paid in cash–
The eternal driver keeps a steady eye
On a black herd, who would his vengeance fly.
But chained, imprisoned, on a burning soil,
For the mean avarice of a tyrant, toil!
The lengthy cart-whip guards this monster's reign–
And cracks, like pistols, from the fields of cane.

Ye powers! who formed these wretched tribes, relate
What they had done, to merit such a fate!
Why were they brought from Eboe's[4] sultry waste,
To see that plenty which they must not taste–
Food, which they cannot buy, and dare not steal;
Yams and potatoes – many a scanty meal!–

One, with a gibbet[5] wakes his Negro's fears,
One to the windmill nails him by the ears;
One keeps his slave in darkened dens, unfed,
One puts the wretch in pickle ere he's dead:
This, from a tree suspends him by the thumbs,
That, from his table grudges even the crumbs!

O'er yond' rough hills a tribe of females go,
Each with her gourd, her infant, and her hoe;
Scorched by a sun that has no mercy here,
Driven by a devil, whom men call overseer–
In chains, twelve wretches to their labors haste;
Twice twelve I saw, with iron collars graced!–

Are such the fruits that spring from vast domains?
Is wealth, thus got, Sir Toby, worth your pains!–
Who would your wealth on terms, like these, possess,
Where all we see is pregnant with distress–
Angola's[6] natives scourged by ruffian hands,

---

3 "This passage has a reference to the West India custom (sanctioned by law) of branding a newly imported slave on the breast, with a red-hot iron, as evidence of the purchaser's property." (Freneau's note.)

4 "A small Negro kingdom near the river Senegal." (Freneau's note.)

5 Gallows.

6 Angola, the former Portuguese colony, from which slaves were exported.

And toil's hard product shipp'd to foreign lands.
    Talk not of blossoms, and your endless spring;
What joy, what smile, can scenes of misery bring?–
Though Nature, here, has every blessing spread,
Poor is the labourer – and how meanly fed!–
    Here Stygian paintings light and shade renew,
Pictures of hell, that Virgil's pencil drew:[7]
Here, surly Charons[8] make their annual trip,
And ghosts arrive in every Guinea ship[9],
To find what beasts these western isles afford,
Plutonian scourges, and despotic lords:–
    Here, they, of stuff determined to be free,
Must climb the rude cliffs of the Liguanee[10];
Beyond the clouds, in skulking haste repair,
And hardly safe from brother traitors[11] there.

1792

Lemuel Haynes (1753–1833)

Lemuel Haynes, an important but relatively unknown writer, presents a fascinating paradox. Although he was of mixed race, he identified as an "African," and though he was never a slave, he felt keenly the oppression of African slaves in America. He lived and worked in a predominantly white world, and though he wrote an extraordinary essay on the evils of slavery, he did not join with other blacks in the African benevolent societies that were flourishing in cities of the eastern seaboard, but ministered to white people for all of his life. Out of these experiences of "doubleness," however, he made a significant contribution to the national conversation about freedom and the meaning of "true republicanism."

Born to a white mother and black father in West Hartford, Connecticut, Haynes was abandoned by his parents and raised as an indentured servant in the supportive foster home of Protestant evangelical, David Rose of Granville. There, he learned to farm, received basic schooling and was immersed

in the Bible and religious literature. He was allowed to follow his intellectual curiosity, borrowing books to read after work and composing poetry. When his indenture ended, he enlisted as a Minuteman, marched at Lexington and served with the Continental Army. Many freed blacks did the same, but Haynes translated his Revolutionary zeal, tempered by his Calvinst theology, into an extraordinary essay he titled "Liberty Further Extended," in which he argued for the extension of the premises of the Revolution to black slaves. Haynes combined the theory of "natural rights" elaborated in Jefferson's Declaration of Independence with the philosophy of human will detailed by Jonathan Edwards, and the intensity of the evangelical revivalist preachers, but it would take the rest of the nation almost a century, and a bloody civil war, to realize his vision of emancipation.

After the war, Haynes continued to work on the Rose family farm and study. He was licensed to preach by local ministers, and preached in Granville

---

7   An allusion to the description of Hell in Virgil's *Aeneid*.
8   Charon was the boatman who ferried the souls of the damned over the river Styx into the underworld.
9   Slave ship.
10   A mountain range in Jamaica.

11   "Alluding to the *Independent* Negroes in the blue mountains, who for a stipulated reward, deliver up every fugitive that falls into their hands to the English Government." (Freneau's note.)

for five years before being ordained by the conservative New Light Association of Ministers in Litchfield County, a group that, like many others in the northeast, was resisting the innovations of liberal theologians. He received a proposal of marriage from Elizabeth Babbit, a white woman, which he accepted; they had ten children and a long life together. He preached in Torrington, Vermont on the frontier until he received a call from the West Parish of Rutland, Vermont, where he stayed from 1778 to 1818. Although he moved successfully in the white world, and was respected for his learning, piety, and preaching skills, consciousness of his "difference" never left him. About his dismissal he said that "he lived with the people in Rutland thirty years, and they were so sagacious that at the end of that time they found out that he was a *nigger*, and so turned him away." He went to preach in Manchester, Vermont for several years, and spent the last decade of his life ministering in upstate New York.

"Liberty Further Extended" remained unpublished until its discovery in 1983. Although he wrote patriotic political addresses, Haynes was known primarily as a preacher with a prodigious memory for Scripture and wrote over 5,500 sermons at Rutland, 400 of them funeral sermons. His most famous sermon, "Universal Salvation," was a short, satiric rebuttal to the liberal Universalists about why Calvinist preachers, who believed in predestination, needed to call their congregations to repentance. It was reprinted throughout the northeast in over seventy editions until 1865. Haynes' thinking illustrates the extent to which evangelical Protestantism played a crucial role in the development and extension of radical democratic ideas of freedom and justice for writers of color in the Revolutionary and post-Revolutionary eras.

PRIMARY WORK

Black Preacher to White America: The Collected Writings of Lemuel Haynes, 1774–1833, ed. Richard Newman, 1990.

FURTHER READING

Timothy Mather Cooley, *Sketches of the Life and Character of the Rev. Lemuel Haynes, A.M., for Many Years Pastor of a Church in Rutland, Vt., and late in Granville, New-York* (New York: Harper, 1837).

Richard Newman, *Lemuel Haynes: a Bio-bibliography* (New York: Lambeth Press, 1984).

Rita Roberts, "Patriotism and Political Criticism: The Evolution of Political Consciousness in the Mind of a Black Revolutionary Soldier," *Eighteenth-Century Studies*, Summer, 27, 4 (1994) pp. 569–88.

"LIBERTY FURTHER EXTENDED"[1]

We hold these truths to be self-Evident, that all men are created Equal, that they are Endowed By their Creator with Ceartain unalienable rights, that among these are Life, Liberty, and the pursuit of happyness.

Congress

The Preface. As *Tyrony* had its Origin from the infernal regions: so it is the Deuty, and honner of Every son of freedom to repel her first motions. But while we are Engaged in the important struggle, it cannot Be tho't impertinent for us to turn one Eye into our own Breast, for a little moment, and See, whether thro' some inadvertency, or a self-contracted Spirit, we Do not find the monster Lurking in our own Bosom; that now while we are inspir'd with so noble a Spirit

---

[1]   The full title of the essay in manuscript is "Liberty Further Extended: Or Free Thoughts on the Illegality of Slavekeeping; Wherein those arguments that Are used in its vindication Are plainly confuted. Together with an humble Address to such as are Concerned in the practise. By Lemuel Haynes." It was found at Harvard and first printed in 1983. The text, with the original spelling, structure and punctuation, is from *Black Preacher to White America: The Collected Writings of Lemuel Haynes, 1774–1833*, ed. Richard Newman, (New York: Carlson Publishing, 1990).

and Becoming Zeal, we may Be Disposed to tear her from us. If the following would produce such an Effect the auther should rejoice.

It is Evident, by ocular demonstration, that man by his Depravety, hath procured many Courupt habits which are detrimental to society; And altho' there is a way pre[s]crib'd Whereby man may be re-instated into the favour of god, yet these courupt habits are Not Extirpated, nor can the subject of renovation Bost of perfection, 'till he Leaps into a state of immortal Existance. yet it hath pleas'd the majesty of Heaven to Exhibet his will to men, and Endow them With an intulect Which is susceptible of speculation; yet, as I observ'd before, man, in consequence of the fall is Liable to digrations. But to proceed,

Liberty, & freedom, is an innate principle, which is unmovebly placed in the human Species; and to see a man aspire after it, is not Enigmatical, seeing he acts no ways incompatible with his own Nature; consequently, he that would infring upon a mans Liberty may reasonably Expect to meet with oposision, seeing the Defendant cannot Comply to Non-resistance, unless he Counter-acts the very Laws of nature.

Liberty is a Jewel which was handed Down to man from the cabinet of heaven, and is Coaeval with his Existance. And as it proceed from the Supreme Legislature of the univers, so it is he which hath a sole right to take away; therefore, he that would take away a mans Liberty assumes a prerogative that Belongs to another, and acts out of his own domain.

One man may bost a superorety above another in point of Natural previledg; yet if he can produse no convincive arguments in vindication of this preheminence his hypothesis is to Be Suspected. To affirm, that an Englishman has a right to his Liberty, is a truth which has Been so clearly Evinced, Especially of Late, that to spend time in illustrating this, would be But Superfluous tautology. But I query, whether Liberty is so contracted a principle as to be Confin'd to any nation under Heaven; nay, I think it not hyperbolical to affirm, that Even an affrican, has Equally as good a right to his Liberty in common with Englishmen.

I know that those that are concerned in the Slave-trade, Do pretend to Bring arguments in vindication of their practise; yet if we give them a candid Examination, we shall find them (Even those of the most cogent kind) to be Essencially Deficient. We live in a day wherein *Liberty & freedom* is the subject of many millions Concern; and the important Struggle hath alread caused great Effusion of Blood; men seem to manifest the most sanguine resolution not to Let their natural rights go without their Lives go with them; a resolution, one would think Every one that has the Least Love to his country, or futer posterity, would fully confide in, yet while we are so zelous to maintain, and foster our own invaded rights, it cannot be tho't impertinent for us Candidly to reflect on our own conduct, and I doubt not But that we shall find that subsisting in the midst of us, that may with propriety be stiled Opression, nay, much greater opression, than that which Englishmen seem so much to spurn at. I mean an oppression which they, themselves, impose upon others.

It is not my Business to Enquire into Every particular practise, that is practised in this Land, that may come under this Odeus Character; But, what I have in view, is humbly to offer som free thoughts, on the practise of *Slave-keeping*. Opression, is not spoken of, nor ranked in the sacred oracles, among the Least of those sins, that are the procurcing Caus of those signal Judgments, which god is pleasd to bring upon the Children of men. Therefore let us attend. I mean to white [write] with freedom, yet with the greatest Submission.

And the main proposition, which I intend for some Breif illustration is this, Namely, That an *African*, or, in other terms, *that a Negro may Justly Chalenge, and has an undeniable right to his* ["freed(om)" is blotted out] *Liberty: Consequently, the practise of Slave-keeping, which so much abounds in this Land is illicit.*

Every privilege that mankind Enjoy have their Origen from god; and whatever acts are passed in any Earthly Court, which are Derogatory to those Edicts that are passed in the Court of Heaven, the act is *void*. If I have a perticular previledg granted to me by god, and the act is not revoked nor the power that granted the benefit vacated, (as it is imposable but that god should Ever remain immutable) then he that would infringe upon my Benifit, assumes an unreasonable, and tyrannic power.

It hath pleased god to *make of one Blood all nations of men, for to dwell upon the face of the Earth.* Acts 17, 26. And as all are of one Species, so there are the same Laws, and aspiring principles placed in all nations; and the Effect that these Laws will produce, are Similar to Each other. Consequently we may suppose, that what is precious to one man, is precious to another, and what is irksom, or intolarable to one man, is so to another, consider'd in a Law of Nature. Therefore we may reasonably Conclude, that Liberty is Equally as pre[c]ious to a *Black man*, as it is to a *white one*, and Bondage Equally as intollarable to the one as it is to the other: Seeing it Effects the Laws of nature Equally as much in the one as it Does in the other. But, as I observed Before, those privileges that are granted to us By the Divine Being, no one has the Least right to take them from us without our consen[t]; and there is Not the Least precept, or practise, in the Sacred Scriptures, that constitutes a Black man a Slave, any more than a white one.

Shall a mans Couler Be the Decisive Criterion whereby to Judg of his natural right? or Becaus a man is not of the same couler with his Neighbour, shall he Be Deprived of those things that Distuingsheth [Distinguisheth] him from the Beasts of the field?

I would ask, whence is it that an Englishman is so far Distinguished from an Affrican in point of Natural privilege? Did he recieve it in his origenal constitution? or By Some Subsequent grant? Or Does he Bost of some hygher Descent that gives him this pre-heminance? for my part I can find no such revelation. It is a Lamantable consequence of the fall, that mankind, have an insatiable thurst after Superorety one over another: So that however common or prevalent the practise may be, it Does not amount, Even to a Surcomstance, that the practise is warrentable.

God has been pleas'd to distiungs [distinguish] some men from others, as to natural abilitys, But not as to natural *right*, as they came out of his hands.

But sometimes men by their flagitious[2] practise forfeit their Liberty into the hands of men, By Becomcing unfit for society; But have the *affricans* Ever as a Nation, forfited their Liberty in this manner? What Ever individuals have done; yet, I Believe, no such Chaleng can be made upon them, as a Body. As there should be Some rule whereby to govern the conduct of men; so it is the Deuty, and intrest of a community, to form a system of *Law*, that is calculated to promote the commercial intrest of Each other: and so Long as it produses so Blessed an Effect, it should be maintained. But when, instead of contributing to the well Being of the community, it proves banefull to its subjects over whome it Extends, then it is hygh time to call it in question. Should any ask, where shall we find any system of Law whereby to regulate our moral Conduct? I think their is none so Explicit and indeffinite, as that which was given By the Blessed Saviour of the world. *As you would that men should do unto you, do you Even so to them.* One would think, that the mention of the precept, would strike conviction to the heart of these Slavetraders; unless an aviricious Disposision, governs the Laws of humanity.

If we strictly adhear to the rule, we shall not impose anything upon Others, But what we should Be willing should Be imposed upon us were we in their Condision.

. . . "But, say they [Africans], it is observable, that Wherever Christianity comes, there comes with it a Sword, a gun, powder, and Ball." And thus it Brings ignominy upon our holy religion, and mak[e]s the Name of Christians sound Odious in the Ears of the heathen. O Christianity, how art thou Disgraced, how art thou reproached, By the vicious practises of those

---

[2]   Deeply criminal, extremely wicked.

upon whome thou dost smile! Let us go on to consider the great hardships, and sufferings, those Slaves are put to, in order to be transported into these plantations. There are generally many hundred slaves put on board a vessel, and they are Shackkled together, two by two, wors than Crimanals going to the place of Execution; and they are Crouded together as close as posable, and almost naked; and their sufferings are so great, as I have Been Credibly informed, that it often Carries off one third of them on their passage; yea, many have put an End to their own Lives for very anguish; And as some have manifested a Disposition to rise in their Defence, they have Been put to the most Cruel torters, and Deaths as human art could inflict. And O! the Sorrows, the Greif the Distress, and anguish which attends them! and not onely them But their frinds also in their Own Country, when they must forever part with Each Other? What must be the plaintive noats that the tend[er] parents must assume for the Loss of their Exiled *Child*? Or the husband for his Departed wife? and how Do the Crys of their Departed friends Eccho from the watry Deep! Do not I really hear the fond mother Expressing her Sorrows, in accents that mite well peirce the most obdurate heart? "O! my Child, why was thy Destiny hung on so precarious a theread! unhappy fate! O that I were a captive with thee or for thee! [About seventy-five words are crossed out and utterly illegible. The mother's words continue:] Cursed Be the Day wherein I Bare thee, and Let that inauspicious Night be remembered no more. Come, O King of terrors. Dissipate my greif, and send my woes into oblivion."

But I need Not stand painting the Dreery Sene. Let me rather appeal to tender parents, whether this is Exaggarating matters? Let me ask them what would be their Distress. Should one of their Dearest *Children* Be snach'd from them, in a Clendestine manner, and carried to *Africa*, or some other forreign Land, to be under the most abject Slavery for Life, among a strang people? would it not imbitter all your Domestic Comforts? would he not Be Ever upon your mind? nay, Doth not nature Even recoil at the reflection?

And is not their many ready to say, (unless void of natural Effections) that it would not fail to Bring them Down with sorrow to the grave? And surely, this has Been the awfull fate of some of those *Negros* that have been Brought into these plantations; which is not to be wondered at, unless we suppose them to be without natural Effections: which is to rank them Below the very Beasts of the field.

O! what an Emens Deal of Affrican-Blood hath Been Shed by the inhuman Cruelty of Englishmen! that reside in a Christian Land! Both at home, and in their own Country? they being the fomenters of those wars, that is absolutely necessary, in order to carry on this cursed trade; and in their Emigration into these colonys? and By their merciless masters, in some parts at Least? O ye that have made yourselves Drunk with human Blood! altho' you may go with impunity here in this Life, yet God will hear the Crys of that innocent Blood, which crys from the Sea, and from the ground against you, Like the Blood of Abel[3], more pealfull [?] than thunder, *vengence! vengence!* What will you Do in that Day when God shall make inquisision for Blood? he will make you Drink the phials of his indignation which Like a potable Stream shall Be poured out without the Least mixture of mercy; Believe it, Sirs, their shall not a Drop of Blood, which you have Spilt unjustly, Be Lost in forgetfullness. But it Shall Bleed affresh, and testify against you, in the Day when God shall Deal with Sinners.

We know that under the Levitical Oeconomy, *man-stealing* was to Be punished with Death;[4]

---

[3]   Abel, son of Adam and Eve, was killed by his brother Cain because God preferred Abel's offering over Cain's. God says to Cain, "What hast thou done? The voice of thy brother's blood crieth unto me from the ground" (Genesis 4:10).
[4]   The "Levitical Oeconomy" were the laws given by God to Moses in the desert, forming the ancient system of ritual administered by the tribe of Levi. The ban against man-stealing is from Deuteronomy 24:7: "If a man be found stealing any of his brethren of the children of Israel, and maketh merchandise of him, or selleth him; then that thief shall die; and thou shalt put evil away from among you."

so [?] we Esteem those that Steal any of our Earthy Commadety gilty of a very heinous Crime: What then must Be an adiquate punishment to Be inflicted on those that Seal [steal] men?

Men were made for more noble Ends than to be Drove to market, like Sheep and oxen. "Our being Christians, (says one) Does not give us the Least Liberty to trample on heathen, nor Does it give us the Least Superority over them." And not only are they gilty of *man-stealing* that are the immediate actors in this trade, But those in these colonys that Buy them at their hands, are far from Being guiltless: for when they saw the theif they consented with him. if men would forbear to Buy Slaves off the hands of the Slave-merchants, then the trade would of necessaty cease; if I buy a man, whether I am told he was stole, or not, yet I have no right to Enslave him, Because he is a human Being: and the immutable Laws of God, and indefeasible Laws of nature, pronounced him free.

Is it not exceeding strang that mankind should Become such mere vassals to their own carnal avarice as Even to imbrue their hands in inocent Blood? and to Bring such intollerable opressiones upon others, that were they themselves to feel them, perhaps they would Esteem Death preferable – pray consider the miserys of a Slave, Being under the absolute controul of another, subject to continual Embarisments, fatiues, and corections at the will of a master; it is as much impossable for us to bring a man heartely to acquiesce in a passive obedience in this case, as it would be to stop a man's Breath, and yet have it caus no convulsion in nature. those negros amongst us that have Children, they, viz. their *Children* are brought up under a partial Disapline: their white masters haveing but Little, or no Effection for them. So that we may suppose, that the abuses that they recieve from the hands of their masters are often very considerable; their parents Being placed in such a Situation as not being able to perform relative Deutys. Such are those restrictions they are kept under By their task-masters that they are render'd incapable of performing those morral Deutys Either to God or man that are infinitely binding on all the human race; how often are they Seperated from Each other, here in this Land at many hundred miles Distance, Children from parents, and parents from Children, Husbands from wives, and wives from Husbands? those whom God hath Joined together, and pronounced one flesh, man assumes a prerogative to put asunder. What can be more abject than their condission? in short, if I may so speak 'tis a hell upon Earth; and all this for filthy Lucres sake:[5] Be astonished, O ye Heavens, at this! I believe it would Be much Better for these Colonys if their was never a Slave Brought into this Land; theirby our poor are put to great Extremitys, by reason of the plentifullness of Labour, which otherwise would fall into their hands.

I shall now go on to take under Consideration some of those *arguments* which those that are Concern'd in the Slave-trade Do use in vindication of their practise; which arguments, I shall Endevour to Shew, are Lame, and Defective.

The first argument that I shall take notice of is this viz. *that in all probability the Negros are of Canaans posterity, which ware Destined by the almighty to Slavery, theirfore the practise is warrantable.* To which I answer, Whethear the Negros are of Canaans posterity or not, perhaps is not known By any mortal under Heaven. But allowing they were actually of Canaans posterity, yet we have no reason to think that this Curs Lasted any Longer than the comeing of Christ: when that Sun of riteousness arose this wall of partition was Broken Down. Under the *Law*, their were many External Cerimonies that were tipecal of Spiritual things; or which Shadowed forth the purity, & perfection of the Gospel . . .

---

[5] Several of the apostles exhorted their followers against the pursuit of "filthy lucre" or material wealth. See 1 Timothy 3:3, 3:8; Peter 5:2.

But now our glorious hygh preist hath visably appear'd in the flesh, and hath Establish'd a more glorious Oeconomy. . . . it is plain Beyond all Doubt, that at the comeing of Christ, this curse that was upon *Canaan*, was taken off; and I think there is not the Least force in this argument than there would Be to argue that an imperfect Contexture of *parts*, or Base *Birth*, Should Deprive any from Gospel previleges; or Bring up any of those antiquated Ceremonies from oblivion, and reduse them into practise.

But you will say that Slave-keeping was practised Even under the Gospel, for we find *Paul*, and the other apostles Exhorting *Servants to be obedient to their masters*. To which I reply, that it mite be they were Speaking to Servants in *minority* in General; But Doubtless it was practised in the Days of the Apostles from what *St Paul* Says, *1. Corin. 7 21. art thou called, being a servant? care not for it; but if thou mayest Be made free, use it rather*. So that the Apostle seems to recomend freedom if attainable, q.d. "if it is thy unhappy Lot to be a slave, yet if thou art Spiritually free Let the former appear so minute a thing when compared with the Latter that it is comparitively unworthy of notice; yet Since freedom is so Exclent a jewel, which none have a right to Extirpate, and if there is any hope of attaining it, use all Lawfull measures for that purpose." So that however Extant or preval[e]nt it mite Be in that or this age; yet it does not in the Least reverse the unchangeable Laws of God, or of nature; or make that Become Lawfull which is in itself unlawfull; neither is it Strange, if we consider the moral Depravity of mans nature, thro'out all ages of the world, that mankind should Deviate from the unering rules of Heaven. But again, another argument which some use to maintain their intollerable opression upon others is this, viz., *that those Negros that are Brought into these plantations are Generally prisoners, taken in their wars, and would otherwise fall a sacrifice to the resentment of their own people*. But this argument, I think, is plainly confuted By the forecited account which Mr *Boasman* gives, as well as many others. Again, some say they *Came honestly By their Slaves, Becaus they Bought them of their parents*, (that is, those that Brought them from Africa) *and rewarded them wellfor them*. But without Doubt this is, for the most part fals; But allowing they Did actually Buy them of their parents, yet I query, whether parents have any right to sel their Children for Slaves: if parents have a right to Be free, then it follows that their Children have Equally as good a right to their freedom, Even *Hereditary*. So, (to use the words of a Learned writer) "one has no Body to Blame But himself, in case he shall find himself Deprived of a man whome he tho't By Buying for a price he had made his own; for he Dealt in a trade which was illicit, and was prohibited by the most obvious Dictates of Humanity. for these resons Every one of those unfortunate men who are pretended to be Slaves, has a right to Be Declared free, for he never Lost his Liberty; he could not Lose it; his prince had no power to Dispose of him. of cours the Sale was *ipso Jure*[6] void."

But I shall take notice of one argument more which these Slave-traders use, and it is this, viz. *that those Negros that are Emigrated into these colonies are brought out of a Land of Darkness under the meridian Light of the Gospel; and so it is a great Blessing instead of a Curs*. But I would ask, who is this that Darkneth counsel By words with out knoledg? Let us attend to the great appostle Speaking to us in *Rom. 3.8.* where he reproves some slanderers who told it as a maxim preached By the apostles that they said *Let us Do Evil that Good may come, whose Damnation* the inspired penman pronounces with an Emphasis *to Be Just*. And again *Chap.* 6 vers 1. where By way of interagation he asks, *Shall we continue in Sin that grace may abound?* The answer is obvious, *God forbid*. But that those Slavemerchants that trade upon the coasts of Africa do not aim at the Spiritual good of their Slaves, is Evident By their Behaviour towards them; if they had their Spiritual good at heart, we should Expect that those Slave-merchants that trade upon their

---

[6]   "By the operation of the law itself" (Latin).

coasts, would, insted of Causing quarrelings, and Blood-Shed among them, which is repugnant to Christianity, and below the Character of humanity, Be Sollicitous to Demean Exampleary
among them, that By their wholesom conduct, those heathen mite be Enduced to Entertain
hygh, and admiring tho'ts of our holy religion. Those Slaves in these Colonies are generally
kept under the greatest ignorance, and Blindness, and they are scersly Ever told by their white
masters whether there is a Supreme Being that governs the univers; or wheather there is any
reward, or punishments Beyond the grave. Nay such are those restrictions that they are kept
under that they Scersly know that they have a right to Be free, or if they Do they are not
allowed to Speak in their defence; Such is their abject condission, that that *genius* that is
peculiar to the human race, cannot have that Cultivation that the polite world is favour'd
with, and therefore they are stiled the ignorant part of the world; whereas were they under the
Same advantages to git knoledge with them, perhaps their progress in arts would not be
inferior.

But should we give ourselves the trouble to Enquire into the grand motive that indulges
men to concearn themselves in a trade So vile and abandon, we Shall find it to Be this, Namely,
to Stimulate their Carnal avarice, and to maintain men in pride, Luxury, and idleness, and how
much it hath Subserv'd to this vile purpose I Leave the Candid publick to Judge: I speak it
with reverence yet I think all must give in that it hath such a tendency.

But altho god is of Long patience, yet it does not Last always, nay, he has *whet* his *glittering
Sword, and his hand hath already taken hold on Judgement*;[7] for who knows how far that the unjust
Oppression which hath abounded in this Land, may be the procuring cause of this very Judge-
ment that now impends, which so much portends *Slavery?*

For this is God's way of working, Often he brings the Same Judgements, or Evils upon men,
as they unriteously Bring upon others. As is plain from *Judges* 1 and on. . . .

Again *Rev. 16.6 for they have Shed the Blood of Saints and prophets, and thou hast given them Blood
to Drink, for they are worthy.* And *chap.* 18.6. *Reward her Even as She rewarded you.* I say this is
often God's way of Dealing, by retaliating Back upon men the Same Evils that they unjustly
Bring upon others. I Don't Say that we have reason to think that *Oppression* is the alone caus of
this Judgement that God is pleas'd to Bring upon this Land, Nay, But we have the greatest
reason to think that this is not one of the Least. And whatever some may think that I am
instigated By a fals zeal; and all that I have Said upon the Subject is mere Novelty: yet I am not
afraid to appeal to the consience of any rational and honnest man, as to the truth of what I have
just hinted at; and if any will not confide in what I have humbly offer'd, I am persuaded it
must be such Short-Sited persons whose Contracted Eyes never penetrate thro' the narrow
confines of Self, and are mere Vassals to filthy Lucre.

But I Cannot persuade myself to make a period to this Small *Treatise*, without humbly
addressing myself, more perticularly, unto all such as are Concearn'd in the practise of *Slave-
keeping*.

Sirs, Should I persue the Dictates of nature, resulting from a sense of my own inability, I
should be far from attempting to form this address: Nevertheless, I think that a mere Superficial reflection upon the merits of the Cause, may Serve as an ample apology, for this humble
attempt. Therefore hopeing you will take it well at my hands, I persume, (tho' with the greatest Submission) to Crave your attention, while I offer you a few words.

Perhaps you will think the preceeding pages unworthy of Speculation: well, Let that be as it
will; I would Sollicit you Seriously to reflect on your conduct, wheather you are not gilty of
unjust Oppression. Can you wash your hands, and say, I am Clean from this Sin? Perhaps you

---

7 Deuteronomy 32:4.

will Dare to Say it Before men; But Dare you Say it Before the tremendous tribunal of that God Before Whome we must all, in a few precarious moments appear? then whatever fair glosses we may have put upon our Conduct, that god whose Eyes pervade the utmost Extent of human tho't, and Surveys with one intuitive view, the affairs of men; he will Examin into the matter himself, and will set Every thing upon its own Basis; and impartiallity Shall Be Seen flourishing throughout that Sollemn assembly. Alas! Shall men hazard their precious Souls for a little of the transetory things of time. O *Sirs!* Let that pity, and compassion, which is peculiar to mankind, Especially to Englishmen, no Longer Lie Dormant in your Breast: Let it run free thro' Disinterested Benevolence. then how would these iron yoaks Spontaneously fall from the gauled Necks of the oppress'd! And that Disparity, in point of Natural previlege, which is the Bane of Society, would Be Cast upon the utmost coasts of Oblivion. If this was the impulsive Exercise that animated all your actions, your Conscience's wold Be the onely Standard unto which I need appeal. think it nor uncharitable, nor Censorious to say, that whenever we Erect our Battery, so as it is Like to prove a Detriment to the intrest of any, we Loos their attention. or, if we Don't Entirely Loos that, yet if true Christian candour is wanting we cannot Be in a Suitable frame for Speculation: So that the good Effect that these Otherwise mite have, will prove abortive. If I could once persuade you to reflect upon the matter with a Single, and an impartial Eye, I am almost assured that no more need to be Said upon the Subject: But whether I shall Be so happy as to persuade you to Cherish such an Exercise I know not: yet I think it is very obvious from what I have humbly offer'd, that so far forth as you have Been Concerned in the *Slave-trade*, so far it is that you have assumed an oppressive, and tyrannic power. Therefore is it not hygh time to undo these heavy Burdens, and Let the Oppressed go free? And while you manifest such a noble and magnanimous Spirit, to maintain inviobly your own Natural rights, and militate so much against Despotism, as it hath respect unto yourselves, you do not assume the Same usurpations, and are no Less tyrannic. Pray let there be a congruity amidst you Conduct, Least you fall amongst that Class the inspir'd pen-man Speaks of. *Rom.* 2.21 and on. *thou therefore which teacheth another, teachest thou not thy Self? thou that preachest a man Should not Steal, Dost thou Steal? thou that sayest, a man Should not Commit adultery, Dost thou Commit adultery? thou that abhoreth idols, Dost thou Commit Sacrilege? thou that makest thy Bost of the Law, through Breaking the Law Dishonnerest thou God?* While you thus Sway your tyrant Scepter over others, you have nothing to Expect But to Share in the Bitter pill. 'Twas an Exelent note that I Lately read in a modern peice, and it was this. "O when shall America be consistantly Engaged in the Cause of Liberty!" If you have any Love to yourselves, or any Love to this Land, if you have any Love to your fellow-men, Break these intollerable yoaks, and Let their names Be remembered no more, Least they Be retorted on your own necks, and you Sink under them; for god will not hold you guiltless.

Sirs, the important Caus in which you are Engag'd in is of a[n] Exelent nature, 'tis ornamental to your Characters, and will, undoubtedly, immortalize your names thro' the Latest posterity. And it is pleasing to Behold that patriottick Zeal which fire's your Breast; But it is Strange that you Should want the Least Stimulation to further Expressions of so noble a Spirit. Some gentlemen have Determined to Contend in a Consistant manner: they have *Let the oppressed go free*, and I cannot think it is for the want of such a generous princaple in you, But thro' some inadvertancy that [end of extant manuscript].

1776?   1983, 1990

Phillis Wheatley (1753–1784)

Phillis Wheatley was born in 1753 somewhere in Africa. At the age of eight she was taken from her family by slave traders, transported to the New World, and sold in Boston in 1761 to a wealthy tailor, John Wheatley, as a servant to his twin children Nathaniel and Mary, who were approximately a decade older. By most accounts, she was treated kindly, and Mary, on observing Phillis attempting to write letters on a wall, began to teach her how to write. The young slave proved to have a brilliant mind and a thirst for knowledge; within sixteen months, she had learned to read and write, and in 1767 her first published poem appeared in the Newport *Mercury*. In 1770, her *Elegiac Poem on the Death of George Whitefield* was published in America and went through several reprintings, with an English edition in 1771. On traveling to England two years later with Nathaniel, Phillis Wheatley caused a sensation; she was introduced to London aristocrats, abolitionist philanthropists, and diplomats.

The reception of her work, however, was mixed at best. One critic, John Langhorne, remarked, "The poems written by this young negro bear no endemial marks of solar fire or spirit. They are merely imitative; and indeed, most of those people have a turn for imitation, though they have little or none for invention." An anonymous critic writing in the *Critical Review* declared, "The negroes of Africa are generally treated as a dull, ignorant, and ignoble race of men, fit only to be slaves, and incapable of any considerable attainments in the liberal arts and sciences. A poet or poetess amongst them, of any tolerable genius, would be a prodigy in literature. Phillis Wheatley, the author of these poems, is this literary phenomenon." He adds, however, that ". . . The whole is indeed extraordinary, considered as the production of a young negro who was, but a few years since, an illiterate barbarian."

In our day, Wheatley has been the object of considerable critical scrutiny. Marginalized in her own time due to her race and gender, pilloried by contemporary critics who see her as a traitor to her race because of her Classical allusions and recourse to European forms of versification, Wheatley offers a fascinating glimpse at the ways in which an intelligent woman managed to negotiate an intellectual identity for herself in the midst of a culture which viewed her as a commodity to be bought and sold, both before and after the American Revolution

Phillis Wheatley was freed after the death of her "owners" in 1774. She married John Peters, another freed slave, who was an ambitious, literate shopkeeper in Boston, later jailed for debt. They had three children, all of whom died in infancy. Although Wheatley was supposedly at work on a second volume of poems, it never came to fruition. Wheatley died in poverty in 1784.

PRIMARY WORKS

Poems on Various Subjects, Religious and Moral, 1773.

Memoir and Poems of Phillis Wheatley, A Native African and Slave, 1834.

Letters of Phillis Wheatley, the Negro Slave of Boston, ed. Charles Deane, 1864.

Phillis Wheatley, Poems and Letters. First Collected Edition, ed. Charles F. Heartman, 1915.

The Poems of Phillis Wheatley, ed. Julian Mason, 1966.

The Collected Works of Phillis Wheatley, ed. John C. Shields, 1988.

FURTHER READING

William H. Robinson, ed., *Critical Essays on Phillis Wheatley* (New York: Garland Publishers, 1982).

William Robinson, *Phillis Wheatley and her Writings* (New York: Garland Publishers, 1984).

June Jordan, "The Difficult Miracle of Black Poetry in America, or Something like a Sonnet for Phillis Wheatley," *Massachusetts Review*, 27, 2 (1986) pp. 252–62.

John C. Shields, "Phillis Wheately's Subversion of Classical Styles," *Style*, 27, 2 (1993) pp. 252–70.

Kristin Wilcox, "The Body into Print: The Marketing of Phillis Wheatley," *American Literature*, 71, 1 (1999) pp. 1–29.

Frontispiece, *Poems on Various Subjects, Religious and Moral, by Phillis Wheatley, London, 1773*, the only known portrait of the writer, commissioned by the Countess of Huntingdon, Wheatley's patron. (By permission of the Photograhs and Print Division, Schomburg Center for Research in Black Culture, The New York Public Library, Astor, Lenox and Tilden Foundations.)

FROM *POEMS ON VARIOUS SUBJECTS, RELIGIOUS AND MORAL*[1]

"To Mæcenas"[2]

Mæcenas, you, beneath the myrtle shade,
Read o'er what poets sung, and shepherds play'd.
What felt those poets but you feel the same?
Does not your soul possess the sacred flame?
Their noble strains your equal genius shares
In softer language, and diviner airs.

While *Homer*[3] paints lo! circumfus'd[4] in air,
Celestial Gods in mortal forms appear;
Swift as they move hear each recess rebound,
Heav'n quakes, earth trembles, and the shores resound.
Great Sire of verse, before my mortal eyes,
The lightnings blaze across the vaulted skies,
And, as the thunder shakes the heav'nly plains,
A deep-felt horror thrills through all my veins.
When gentler strains demand thy graceful song,
The length'ning line moves languishing along.
When great *Patroclus* courts *Achilles'*[5] aid,
The grateful tribute of my tears is paid;
Prone on the shore he feels the pangs of love,
And stern *Pelides*[6] tend'rest passions move.

Great *Maro's*[7] strain in heav'nly numbers flows,
The *Nine*[8] inspire, and all the bosom glows.
O could I rival thine and *Virgil's*[9] page,
Or claim the *Muses* with the *Mantuan* Sage;
Soon the same beauties should my mind adorn
And the same ardors in my soul should burn:
Then should my song in bolder notes arise,
And all my numbers pleasingly surprize;
But here I sit, and mourn a grov'ling mind,
That fain would mount, and ride upon the wind.

---

[1] The texts, with slight modification, are from *The Collected Works of Phillis Wheatley*, ed. John C. Shields (New York: Oxford University Press, 1988).

[2] The Roman Gaius Cilnius Mæcenas, liberal patron of the arts, and especially Latin poets Horace and Virgil. Critics agree that Wheatley was addressing a living person, probably a contemporary poet, but do not agree on the identity.

[3] Greek poet of the *Iliad* and *Odyssey*.

[4] Surrounded.

[5] Greek heroes during the Trojan war, and inseparable friends. Wheatley is alluding to the scene in which Patroclus begs Achilles to let him wear Achilles' armor and go to the aid of the Greeks. See *The Iliad*, translated by Alexander Pope, Book 16, ll. 3–8.

[6] An epithet for Achilles, identifying him as the son of Peleus, king of Phthia.

[7] Publius Vergilius Maro, or the poet Virgil, who was born near Mantua.

[8] The Nine Muses.

[9] Roman epic poet, author of the *Aeneid*.

Not you, my friend, these plaintive strains become,
Not you, whose bosom is the *Muses* home;
When they from tow'ring *Helicon*[10] retire,
They fan in you the bright immortal fire,
But I less happy, cannot raise the song,
The fault'ring music dies upon my tongue.

The happier *Terence*[11] all the choir inspir'd,
His soul replenish'd, and his bosom fir'd;
But say ye *Muses,* why this partial grace,
To one alone of *Afric's* sable race;
From age to age transmitting thus his name
With the first glory in the rolls of fame?

Thy virtues, great Mæcenas! shall be sung
In praise of him, from whom those virtues sprung;
While blooming wreaths around thy temples spread,
I'll snatch a laurel from thine honour'd head,
While you indulgent smile upon the deed.

As long as *Thames* in streams majestic flows,
Or *Naiads*[12] in their oozy beds repose,
While Phœbus[13] reigns above the starry train,
While bright *Aurora*[14] purples o'er the main,
So long, great Sir, the muse thy praise shall sing,
So long thy praise shall make *Parnassus*[15] ring:
Then grant, *Mæcenas,* thy paternal rays,
Hear me propitious, and defend my lays[16].

1773

"To the University of Cambridge, in New England"[1]

While an intrinsic ardor prompts to write,
The muses promise to assist my pen;
'Twas not long since I left my native shore,
The land of errors, and Egyptian gloom:
Father of mercy, 'twas thy gracious hand
Brought me in safety from those dark abodes.

[10] A mountain range in Greece, reputed to be the home of Apollo and the Muses.
[11] A Roman comic poet (198–159 BC), an African by birth and at first a slave, but freed by his achievements in writing.
[12] Mythological nymphs said to preside over lakes, rivers and brooks.
[13] The sun.

[14] Goddess of the dawn.
[15] The mountain sacred to Apollo and the Muses.
[16] Ballad or narrative poem.

TO THE UNIVERSITY OF CAMBRIDGE
[1] Harvard University, where during this period the students had a reputation for boisterousness.

Students, to you 'tis giv'n to scan the heights
Above, to traverse the ethereal[2] space,
And mark the systems of revolving worlds.
Still more, ye sons of science, ye receive
The blissful news by messengers from heav'n,
How Jesus' blood for your redemption flows.
See him with hands out-stretch upon the cross;
Immense compassion in his bosom glows;
He hears revilers, nor resents their scorn:
What matchless mercy in the Son of God!
When the whole human race by sin has fall'n,
He deign'd to die that they might rise again,
And share with him in the sublimest skies,
Life without death, and glory without end.

Improve your privileges while they stay,
Ye pupils, and each hour redeem, that bears
Or good or bad report of you to heav'n.
Let sin, that baneful evil to the soul,
By you be shunn'd, nor once remit your guard;
Suppress the deadly serpent in its egg.
Ye blooming plants of human race divine,
An Ethiop[3] tells you 'tis your greatest foe;
Its transient sweetness turns to endless pain,
And in immense perdition sinks the soul.

1767   1773

"On Being Brought from Africa to America"[1]

'Twas mercy brought me from my pagan land,
Taught my benighted soul to understand
That there's a God, that there's a Savior too:
Once I redemption neither sought nor knew.
Some view our sable race with scornful eye,
"Their color is a diabolic dye."
Remember, Christians, Negroes, black as Cain[2],
May be refin'd, and join th' angelic train.

1773

---

[2]   Heavenly, celestial.
[3]   In this context, a person of African origin.

BROUGHT FROM AFRICA
[1]   In a letter to her publisher, Wheatley's owner, John Wheatley, states: "Phillis was brought from Africa to America in the year 1761, between 7 and 8 years of age. Without any assistance from school education, and by only what she was taught in the family, she, in sixteen months from her arrival, attained the English language (to which she was an utter stranger before), to such a degree as to read any, the most difficult parts of the sacred writings, to the great astonishment of all who heard her."
[2]   According to Biblical tradition, it was Ham (and not Cain) who was cursed with blackness.

"On the Death of the Rev. Mr. George Whitefield"[1]

Hail, happy saint, on thine immortal throne,
Possest of glory, life, and bliss unknown;
We hear no more the music of thy tongue,
Thy wonted auditories[2] cease to throng.
Thy sermons in unequall'd accents flow'd,
And ev'ry bosom with devotion glow'd;
Thou didst in strains of eloquence refin'd
Inflame the heart, and captivate the mind.
Unhappy we the setting sun deplore,
So glorious once, but ah! it shines no more.

    Behold the prophet in his tow'ring flight!
He leaves the earth for heav'n's unmeasur'd height,
And worlds unknown receive him from our sight.
There *Whitefield* wings with rapid course his way,
And sails to *Zion* through vast seas of day.
Thy pray'rs, great saint, and thine incessant cries
Have pierc'd the bosom of thy native skies.
Thou moon hast seen, and all the stars of light,
How he has wrestled with his God by night.
He pray'd that grace in ev'ry heart might dwell,
He long'd to see *America* excel;
He charg'd its youth that ev'ry grace divine
Should with full luster in their conduct shine;
That Savior, which his soul did first receive,
The greatest gift that ev'n a God can give,
He freely offer'd to the num'rous throng,
That on his lips with list'ning pleasure hung.

    "Take him, ye wretched, for your only good,
"Take him[,] ye starving sinners, for your food;
"Ye thirsty, come to this life-giving stream,
"Ye preachers, take him for your joyful theme;
"Take him[,] my dear *Americans*," he said,
"Be your complaints on his kind bosom laid:
"Take him, ye *Africans*, he longs for you,
"*Impartial Savior* is his title due:
"Wash'd in the fountain of redeeming blood,
"You shall be son, and kings, and priests to God."

---

[1]   George Whitefield (1714–70), personal chaplain to the Countess of Huntingdon and popular Christian evangelist known in colonial America as "the Great Awakener" for his indefatigable and charismatic preaching. He made seven trips to America and died there in Newburyport, Massachusetts, after preaching in Boston. He may have stayed briefly with the Wheatleys. This poem was widely reprinted, and first brought Wheatley to the attention of the Countess, who later became her patron, and allowed Wheatley to dedicate her volume of poems to her.

[2]   Audiences, congregations.

Great Countess[3], we *Americans* revere
Thy name, and mingle in thy grief sincere;
New England deeply feels, the *Orphans* mourn,
Their more than father will no more return.

But, though arrested by the hand of death,
Whitefield no more exerts his lab'ring breath,
Yet let us view him in th'eternal skies,
Let every heart to this bright vision rise;
While the tomb safe retains its sacred trust,
Till life divine re-animates his dust.

1770, 1771, 1773

"To the Right Honorable William, Earl of Dartmouth, His Majesty's Principal Secretary of State for North America, &c"[1]

Hail, happy day, when, smiling like the morn,
Fair *Freedom* rose *New-England* to adorn:
The northern clime beneath her genial ray,
Dartmouth, congratulates thy blissful sway:
Elate with hope her race no longer mourns,
Each soul expands, each grateful bosom burns,
While in thine hand with pleasure we behold
The silken reins, and *Freedom's* charms unfold.
Long lost to realms beneath the northern skies

She shines supreme, while hated *faction* dies
Soon as appear'd the *Goddess* long desir'd,
Sick at the view, she languish'd and expir'd;
Thus from the splendors of the morning light
The owl in sadness seeks the caves of night.

No more, America, in mournful strain
Of wrongs, and grievance unredress'd complain,
No longer shalt thou dread the iron chain,
Which wanton *Tyranny* with lawless hand
Had made, with it meant t' enslave the land.

Should you, my lord, while you peruse my song,
Wonder from whence my love of *Freedom* sprung,
Whence flow these wishes for the common good,

---

3   Selina Hastings, Countess of Huntingdon (1707–91), religious activist who used her wealth to support English Methodism and Christian revivalism, with whom the Wheatleys were in correspondence.

Secretary of State for the Colonies, 1772–5, sympathetic to the Methodist movement and a friend of the Countess of Huntingdon, to whom Wheatley dedicated the 1773 volume. Wheatley saw his appointment as helpful to the colonies' desire for less restrictions from England.

TO THE EARL OF DARTMOUTH
1   William Legge, second Earl of Dartmouth (1731–1801),

By feeling hearts alone best understood,
I, young in life, by seeming cruel fate
Was snatch'd from *Afric's* fancy'd[2] happy seat:
What pangs excruciating must molest,
What sorrows labor in my parent's breast?
Steel'd was that soul and by no misery mov'd
That from a father seiz'd his babe belov'd
Such, such my case. And can I then but pray
Others may never feel tyrannic sway?

    For favors past, great Sir, our thanks are due,
And thee we ask thy favors to renew,
Since in thy pow'r, as in thy will before.
To soothe the griefs, which thou did'st once deplore.
May heav'nly grace the sacred sanction give
To all thy works, and thou for ever live
Not only on the wings of fleeting *Fame*
Though praise immortal crowns the patriot's name,
But to conduct to heav'ns refulgent[3] fane[4],
May fiery coursers[5] sweep th' ethereal[6] plain,
And bear thee upwards to that blest abode,
Where, like the prophet, thou shalt find thy God.

1773

A Farewell to AMERICA. To Mrs S. W.[1]

I.

Adieu, *New England*'s smiling meads,
    Adieu, the flow'ry plain:
I leave thine op'ning charms, O spring,
    And tempt the roaring main.

II.

In vain for me the flow'rets rise,
    And Boast their gaudy pride,
While here beneath the northern skies
    I mourn for *health* deny'd.

III.

Celestial maid of rosy hue,
    O let me feel thy reign!
I languish till thy face I view,
    Thy vanish'd joys regain.

IV.

Susannah mourns, nor can I bear
    To see thy crystal show'r,
Or mark the tender falling tear
    At sad departure's hour;

---

[2] Imagined, recalled.
[3] Sparkling.
[4] Sanctuary.
[5] Horses.
[6] Heavenly.

A FAREWELL
[1] Susanna Wheatley, Wheatley's mistress. Wheatley was journeying to England to promote her poetry and, ostensibly, for her health. The last two stanzas, however, hint that Wheatley might have been "tempted" there by Lord Mansfield's recent decision in the Somerset case of 1772, which offered the possibility of asylum to all blacks shipped out of England against their will. Wheatley does return to Boston, and is freed by her owners in 1774.

V.

Not unregarding can I see
   Her soul with grief opprest:
But let no sighs, no groans for me,
   Steal from her pensive breast.

VI.

In vain the feather'd warblers sing,
   In vain the garden blooms,
And on the bosom of the spring
   Breathes out her sweet perfumes,

VII.

While for *Britannia's* distant shore
   We sweep the liquid plain,
And with astonish'd eyes explore
   The wide-extended main.

VIII.

Lo! *Health* appears! celestial dame!
   Complacent and serene,
With *Hebe's* mantle o'er her Frame,[2]
   With soul-delighting mein.

IX.

To mark the vale where *London* lies
   With misty vapours crown'd,
Which cloud *Aurora's* thousand dyes,
   And veil her charms around,

X.

Why, *Phœbus*, moves they car so slow?
   So slow thy rising ray?
Give us the famous town to view,
   Thou glorious king of day!

XI.

For thee, *Britannia*, I resign
   New-England's smiling fields;
To view again her charms divine,
   What joy the prospect yields!

XII.

But thou! Temptation hence away,
   With all they fatal train
Nor once seduce my soul away,
   By thine enchanting strain.

XIII.

Thrice happy they, whose heav'nly shield
   Secures their souls from harms,
And fell *Temptation* on the field
   Of all its pow'r disarms!

Boston, May 7, 1773.   1773

LETTER TO SAMSON OCCOM[1]

Reverend and honoured Sir,
"I have this day received your obliging kind epistle, and am greatly satisfied with your reasons respecting the negroes, and think highly reasonable what you offer in vindication of their natural rights: Those that invade them cannot be insensible that the divine light is chasing away the thick darkness which broods over the land of Africa; and the chaos which has reigned so long, is converting into beautiful order, and reveals more and more clearly the glorious dispensation of civil and religious liberty, which are so inseparably united, that there is little or no enjoyment of one without the other: Otherwise, perhaps, the Israelites had been less solicitous for their freedom from Egyptian slavery; I do not say they would have been

---

[2] Hebe was the Greek goddess of eternal youth, but in some ancient traditions she was also identified as freeing people from bondage.

TO OCCOM
[1] Samson Occom (1723–92), converted Mohegan Indian minister, and long-time friend of Wheatley's. This widely reprinted letter first appeared in the *Connecticut Gazette*.

contented without it, by no means; for in every human breast God has implanted a principle, which we call love of freedom; it is impatient of oppression, and pants for deliverance; and by the leave of our modern Egyptians[2] I will assert, that the same principle lives in us. God grant deliverance in his own way and time, and get him honour upon all those whose avarice impels them to countenance and help forward the calamities of their fellow creatures. This I desire not for their hurt, but to convince them of the strange absurdity of their conduct, whose words and actions are so diametrically opposite. How well the cry for liberty, and the reverse disposition for the exercise of oppressive power over others agree – I humbly think it does not require the penetration of a philosopher to determine."

February 11, 1774

EXTANT POEM NOT INCLUDED IN *POEMS*[1]

"America"

New England first a wilderness was found,
Till for a continent 'twas destin'd round;
From field to field the savage monsters run
E'r yet Brittania had her work begun.
Thy power, O Liberty, makes strong the weak,
And (wond'rous instinct) Ethiopians speak
Sometimes by simile, a victory's won.
A certain lady had an only son;
He grew up daily, virtuous as he grew.
Fearing his strength which she undoubted knew,
She laid some taxes on her darling son,
And would have laid another act there on.
"Amend your manners, I'll the task remove,"
Was said with seeming sympathy and love.
By many scourges she his goodness tried
Until at length the best of infants cried;
He wept, Brittania turn'd a senseless ear.
At last awaken'd by maternal fear
"Why weeps Americus[2], why weeps my child?"
Thus spake Brittania, thus benign and mild.
"My dear mama," said he, "shall I repeat—
Then prostrate fell, at her maternal feet.
"What ails the rebel?" great Brittania cried.
"Indeed," said he, "you have no cause to chide
"You see each day my fluent tears, my food,
"Without regard, what no more English blood?
"Was length of time drove from our English veins

---

[2]   That is, slave-owners.

AMERICA
[1]   The text, with slight modification, is from *The Collected*

Works of Phillis Wheatley, ed. John C. Shields (New York: Oxford University Press, 1988).
[2]   America.

"The kindred he to Great Brittania deigns?"
'Tis thus with thee, O Brittain, keeping down
New English force, thou fear'st his tyranny and thou didst frown.
He weeps afresh to feel this iron chain;
Turn, O Brittania, claim thy child again,
Riech o Love, drive by thy powerful charms
Indolence slumbering in forgetful arms.
See Agenoria[3] diligent employs
Her sons, and thus with rapture she replies,
"Arise my sons, with one consent arise,"
Lest distant continents with vult'ring eyes
Should charge America with negligence;
They praise industry but no pride commence
To raise their own profusion, O Brittain see,
By this New England will increase like thee.

1768

Charles Brockden Brown (1771–1810)

Charles Brockden Brown is often regarded as America's first novelist of importance, and while that title can be disputed (Susanna Rowson certainly lays as much if not more claim to the honor), he is certainly a significant novelist who attempted to support himself by his writing. His failure tells us much about the prevailing attitude towards imaginative literature in the early republican period. Brown was born into an affluent Quaker family in Philadelphia, studied at the renowned Friends' Latin school and, on his parents' urging, began to study law at sixteen. Despite his family's disapproval, Brown decided to move to New York City where he met budding intellectuals and writers who supported his desire to write. He read widely in the classics and the European intellectuals of the day. The political writing of William Godwin and feminist work of Mary Wollstonecraft, in particular, helped shape his ideas and sparked a remarkably productive period. In one year, between 1798 and 1799, he published all or parts of four novels: *Wieland*, *Ormond*, *Edgar Huntly*, and the first part of *Arthur Mervyn*, as well as the first two parts of the dialogue *Alcuin*. In 1801, two other novels appeared: *Clara Howard* and *Jane Talbot*. Because

he was unable to support himself by writing fiction, he turned to journalism and founded the short-lived *Monthly Magazine and American Review*. His next venture, *The Literary Magazine and American Register*, founded in 1803, lasted for three years, after which he began *The American Register, or General Repository of History, Politics, and Science*, a semi-annual journal that signaled his move away from imaginative literature to politics and history. He died a few years later of tuberculosis, only thirty-nine years old.

Brown described himself as a "story-teller moralist," saw the fiction writer as a "purveyor of truths," and emphasized the didactic purpose of his imaginative writing. Even so, his remarkable narratives, which turn on unexpected transformations and explore psychological states as well as moral questions, deftly undermine the epistemological certainty of "fact," sense perceptions, and human rationality. He reconceptualized the novel in terms considered specifically "American," away from the sentimental and seduction plots of the English novel which, in the eyes of early republican culture, discredited the genre as "feminine." In soliciting a cultivated readership, he rejected

---

[3]   "Agenoria:" Etruscan goddess of action, courage, and industry.

the prevailing attitudes about gender that associated women with the passions and exiled them from
the public, civic sphere. Although his first four
novels are named for male characters, *Wieland* has
a female narrator and protagonist, and *Ormond* is
the story of Constantia Dudley's quest for economic
independence. *Alcuin* fits this pattern, for although
it is narrated by its titular male speaker, it is largely
a dialogue between the eccentric Alcuin and Mrs
Carter, a feisty republican matron, who argues eloquently for the social injustice of women's subordination in education, politics, and marriage.
Brown eventually wrote four parts to the dialogue,
one of which details the narrator's fantastic journey to a world where the sexes are absolutely equal
– a vision that tests the limits of Mrs Carter's liberal feminism, and complicates the polemic of the
piece with fictional techniques that are the hallmark of Brown's style.

PRIMARY WORKS

The Novels of Charles Brockden Brown, 7 vols, 1827, 1887.
The Novels and Related Works of Charles Brockden Brown,
   Bicentennial edition, 1977–1987.

FURTHER READING

Norman S. Grabo, *The Coincidental Art of Charles Brockden
   Brown* (Chapel Hill: University of North Carolina
   Press, 1981).
Robert Arner, "Historical Essay," *Alcuin, A Dialogue*, *The
   Novels and Related Works of Charles Brockden Brown*,
   vol. 6 (Kent State University Press, 1987).
Donald Ringe, *Charles Brockden Brown*, rev. ed. (Boston:
   Twayne, 1991).
Steven Watts, *The Romance of Real Life: Charles Brockden
   Brown and the Origins of American Culture* (Baltimore:
   Johns Hopkins University Press, 1994).

FROM *ALCUIN* PART I[1]

I called last evening on Mrs Carter. I had no previous acquaintance with her. Her brother is a
man of letters, who, nevertheless finds little leisure from the engagements of a toilsome profession. He scarcely spends an evening at home, yet takes care to invite, specially and generally
to his house, everyone who enjoys the reputation of learning and probity. His sister became,
on the death of her husband, his house-keeper. She was always at home. . . .

[Mrs Carter:] What think you of female education? Mine has been frivolous. I can make a
pie, and cut out a gown. To this only I am indebted to my teachers. If I have added any thing
to these valuable attainments, it is through my own efforts, and not by the assistance or encouragement of others.

And ought it not to be so? What can render men wise but their own efforts? Does curiosity
derive no encouragement from the possession of the power and materials? You are taught to
read and to write. Quills, paper, and books are at hand. Instruments and machines are forthcoming to those who can purchase them. If you be insensible to the pleasures and benefits of
knowledge, and are therefore ignorant and trifling, truly, it is not for want of assistance and
encouragement.

I shall find no difficulty (said the lady) to admit that the system is not such as to condemn
all women, without exception, to stupidity. As it is, we have only to lament that a sentence so
unjust is executed on by far the greater number. But you forget how seldom those who are
most fortunately situated, are permitted to cater for themselves. Their conduct in this case, as
in all others, is subject to the controul of others who are guided by established prejudices, and
are careful to remember that we are women. They think a being of this sex is to be instructed
in a manner different from those of another. Schools, and colleges, and public instructors are

[1]   The first two parts of *Alcuin*, entitled "The Rights of
Women," were serialized in Philadelphia in the *Weekly
Magazine*, March 17, 1798. The text, with slight modification, is from *The Novels and Related Works of Charles Brockden
Brown*, Bicentennial edition, vol. 6 (Kent State University
Press, 1987).

provided in all the abstruse sciences and learned languages; but whatever may be their advantages, are not women totally excluded from them?

It would be prudent (said I), in the first place, to ascertain the amount of those advantages, before we indulge ourselves in lamenting the loss of them. Let us consider whether a public education be not unfavorable to moral and intellectual improvement; or, at least, whether it be preferable to the domestic method. Whether most knowledge be obtained by listening to hired professors, or by reading books. Whether the abstruse sciences be best studied in a closet or a college. Whether the ancient tongues be worth learning. Whether, since languages are of no use but as avenues to knowledge, our native tongue, especially in its present state of refinement, be not the best. Before we lament the exclusion of women from colleges, all these points must be settled; unless they shall be precluded by reflecting that places of public education, which are colleges in all respects but the name, are, perhaps, as numerous for females as for males.

They differ (said the lady) from colleges in this, that a very different plan of instruction is followed. I know of no female school where Latin is taught, or geometry, or chymistry.

Yet, Madam, there are female geometricians, and chymists, and scholars, not a few. Were I desirous that my son or daughter should become either of these, I should not deem the assistance of a college indispensible. Suppose an anatomist should open his school to pupils of both sexes, and solicit equally their attendance, would you comply with the invitation?

No, because that pursuit has no attractions for me. But if I had a friend whose curiosity was directed to it, why should I dissuade her from it?

Perhaps (said I) you are but little acquainted with the real circumstances of such a scene. If your disdain of prejudices should prompt you to adventure one visit, I question whether you would find any inclination to repeat it.

Perhaps not (said she); but that mode of instruction in all the experimental sciences is not, perhaps, the best. A numerous company can derive little benefit from a dissection in their presence. A closer and more deliberate inspection than the circumstances of a large company will allow, seems requisite. But the assembly need not be a mixed one. Objections on the score of delicacy, though they are more specious than sound, and owe their force more to our weakness than our wisdom, would be removed by making the whole company, professor and pupils, female. But this would be obviating an imaginary evil at the price of a real one. Nothing has been more injurious than the separation of the sexes. They associate in childhood without restraint, but the period quickly arrives when they are obliged to take different paths. Ideas, maxims, and pursuits, wholly opposite, engross their attention. Different systems of morality, different languages, or, at least, the same words with a different set of meanings, are adopted. All intercourse between them is fettered and embarrassed. On one side, all is reserve and artifice; on the other, adulation and affected humility. The same end must be compassed by opposite means. The man must affect a disproportionable ardor; while the woman must counterfeit indifference or aversion. Her tongue has no office, but to belie the sentiments of her heart, and the dictates of her understanding.

By marriage she loses all right to separate property. The will of her husband is the criterion of all her duties. All merit is comprised in unlimited obedience. She must not expostulate or rebel. In all contests with him, she must hope to prevail by blandishments and tears; not by appeals to justice, and addresses to reason. She will be most applauded when she smiles with most perseverance on her oppressor, and when, with the undistinguishing attachment of a dog, no caprice or cruelty shall be able to estrange her affection.

Surely, Madam, this picture is exaggerated. You derive it from some other source than your own experience, or even your own observation.

No, I believe the picture to be generally exact. No doubt there are exceptions. I believe myself to be one. I think myself exempt from the grosser defects of women, but by no means free from the influence of a mistaken education. But why should you think the picture exaggerated? Man is the strongest. This is the reason why, in the earliest stage of society, the females are slaves. The tendency of rational improvement is to equalize conditions: to abolish all distinctions but those that are founded on truth and reason: to limit the reign of brute force and uncontrolable accidents. Women have unquestionably benefited by the progress that has hitherto taken place. If I look abroad, I may see reason to congratulate myself on being born in this age and country. Women that are no where totally exempt from servitude, no where admitted to their true rank in society, may yet be subject to different degrees or kinds of servitude. Perhaps there is no country in the world where the yoke is lighter than here; but this persuasion, though in one view it may afford us consolation, ought not to blind us to our true condition, or weaken our efforts to remove the evils that still oppress us. It is manifest that we are hardly and unjustly treated. The natives of the most distant regions do not less resemble each other, than the male and female of the same tribe, in consequence of the different discipline to which they are subject. Now this is palpably absurd. Men and women are partakers of the same nature. They are rational beings, and, as such, the same principles of truth and equity must be applicable to both.

To this I replied, certainly Madam; but it is obvious to enquire to which of the sexes the distinction is most favorable. In some respects different paths are allotted to them, but I am apt to suspect that of the woman to be strewed with fewest thorns; to be beset with fewest asperities; and to lead, if not absolutely in conformity to truth and equity, yet with fewest deviations from it. There are evils incident to your condition as women. As human beings, we all lie under considerable disadvantages; but it is of an unequal lot that you complain. The institutions of society have injuriously and capriciously distinguished you. True it is, laws, which have commonly been male births, have treated you unjustly; but it has been with that species of injustice that has given birth to nobles and kings. They have distinguished you by irrational and undeserved indulgences. They have exempted you from a thousand toils and cares. Their tenderness has secluded you from tumult and noise: your persons are sacred from profane violences; your eyes from ghastly spectacles; your ears from a thousand discords by which ours are incessantly invaded. Yours are the peacefullest recesses of the mansion. Your hours glide along in sportive chat, in harmless recreation, or voluptuous indolence; or in labors so light, as scarcely to be termed encroachments on the reign of contemplation. Your industry delights in the graceful and minute: it enlarges the empire of the senses, and improves the flexibility of the fibers. The art of the needle, by the luster of its hues and the delicacy of its touches, is able to mimic all the forms of nature, and portray all the images of fancy: and the needle but prepares the hand for doing wonders on the harp, for conjuring up the "piano" to melt, and the "forte" to astound us.

This (cried the lady) is a very partial description. It can apply only to the opulent, and but to few of them. Meanwhile how shall we estimate the hardships of the lower class. You have only pronounced a panegyric on indolence and luxury. Eminent virtue and true happiness are not to be found in this element.

True (returned I). I have only attempted to justify the male sex from the charge of cruelty. Ease and luxury are pernicious. Kings and nobles, the rich and the idle, enjoy no genuine content. Their lot is hard enough; but still it is better than brutal ignorance and unintermitted toil; than nakedness and hunger. There must be one condition of society that approaches nearer than any other to the standard of rectitude and happiness. For this, it is our duty to search; and, having found it, endeavor to reduce every other condition to this desirable mean.

It is useful, meanwhile, to ascertain the relative importance of different conditions; and since deplorable evils are annexed to every state, to discover in what respects, and in what degree, one is more or less eligible than another. Half of the community are females. Let the whole community be divided into classes; and let us enquire whether the wives, and daughters, and single women of each class, be not placed in a more favorable situation than the husbands, sons, and single men of the same class. Our answer will surely be in the affirmative.

There is (said the lady) but one important question relative to this subject. Are women as high in the scale of social felicity and usefulness as they may and ought to be?

To this (said I) there can be but one answer: No. At present they are only higher on that scale than the men. You will observe, Madam, I speak only of that state of society which we enjoy. If you had excluded sex from the question, I must have made the same answer. Human beings, it is to be hoped, are destined to a better condition on this stage, or some other, than is now allotted them.

1798

Bibliography

James Axtell, *After Columbus: Essays in the Ethnohistory of North America* (New York: Oxford University Press, 1989).

Bernard Bailyn, *The Ideological Origins of the American Revolution* (Cambridge: Harvard University Press, 1992).

Patricia Bonomi, *Under the Cope of Heaven: Religion, Society and Politics in Colonial America* (New York: Oxford University Press, 1986).

C. R. Boxer, *The Portuguese Seaborne Empire, 1415–1825* (Manchester: Carcanet, 1991).

David Cressy, *Coming Over: Migration and Communication Between England and New England in the Seventeenth Century* (Cambridge: Cambridge University Press, 1987).

Cathy Davidson, *Revolution and the Word: The Rise of the Novel in America* (New York: Oxford University Press, 1986).

J. H. Elliott, *The Old World and the New, 1492–1650* (Cambridge: Cambridge University Press, 1970).

Jean Franco, *Plotting Women: Gender and Representation in Mexico* (New York: Columbia University Press, 1989).

Wayne Franklin, *Discoverers, Explorers, Settlers: The Diligent Writers of Early America* (Chicago: University of Chicago Press, 1979).

Philip Greven, *The Protestant Temperament: Patterns of Child-Rearing, Religious Experience and the Self in early America* (New York: Knopf, 1977).

Lewis Hanke, *Aristotle and the American Indians: A Study in Race Prejudice in the Modern World* (London: Hollis and Carter, 1959).

Peter Hulme, *Colonial Encounters: Europe and the Native Caribbean, 1492–1797* (London, New York: Methuen, 1986).

Francis Jennings, *The Invasion of America: Indians, Colonialism and the Cant of Conquest* (Chapel Hill: University of North Carolina Press, 1975).

Winthrop Jordan, *White Over Black: American Attitudes towards the Negro, 1550–1812* (Chapel Hill: University of North Carolina, 1968).

Linda Kerber, *Women of the Republic: Intellect and Ideology in Revolutionary America* (Chapel Hill: University of North Carolina Press, 1980).

Philip Kopper, *The Smithsonian Book of North American Indians: Before the Coming of the Europeans* (Washington, DC: Smithsonian Books, 1986).

Gesa Mackenthun, *Metaphors of Dispossession: American Beginnings and the Translation of Empire, 1492–1637* (Norman: University of Oklahoma Press, 1997).

Edmundo O'Gorman, *The Invention of America: An Inquiry into the Historical Nature of the New World and the Meaning of its History* (Westport, Connecticut: Greenwood Press, 1972).

Anthony Pagden, *European Encounters with the New World* (New Haven: Yale University Press, 1993).

Mary Louise Pratt, *Imperial Eyes: Travel Writing and Transculturation* (London: Routledge, 1992).

Bernard Sheehan, *Seeds of Extinction: Jeffersonian Philanthropy and the American Indian* (Chapel Hill: University of North Carolina Press, 1973).

David Shields, *Civil Tongues and Polite Letters in British America* (Chapel Hill: University of North Carolina Press, 1997).

Frank Shuffleton (ed.) *A Mixed Race: Ethnicity in Early America* (New York: Oxford University Press, 1993).

William Spengemann, *A New World of Words: Redefining Early American Literature* (New Haven: Yale University Press, 1994).

Steve Stern, *Peru's Indian Peoples and the Challenge of Spanish Conquest* (Madison: University of Wisconsin Press, 1993).

Tzvetan Todorov, *The Conquest of America*, trans. Richard Howard (New York: Harper & Row, 1987).

Laurel Thatcher Ulrich, *Goodwives* (New York: Knopf, 1982).

Index